More Than Just a

Internet Resources

Step 1 Connect to OK Math Online macmillanmh.com

Step 2 Connect to online resources by using QuickPass codes. You can connect directly to the chapter you want.

OK9831c1

Enter this code with the appropriate chapter number.

For Students

Connect to the student edition ***eBook*** that contains all of the following online assets. You don't need to take your textbook home every night.

- Personal Tutor
- Extra Examples
- Self-Check Quizzes
- Multilingual eGlossary
- Concepts in Motion
- Chapter Test Practice
- Test Practice
- Math Adventures with Dot and Ray
- Math Tool Chest
- Math Songs

For Teachers

Connect to professional development content at macmillanmh.com and the ***eBook Advance Tracker*** at AdvanceTracker.com

For Parents

Connect to macmillanmh.com for access to the ***eBook*** and all the resources for students and teachers that are listed above.

Macmillan McGraw-Hill

Oklahoma Math Connects

5

Authors

Altieri • Balka • Day • Gonsalves • Grace • Krulik
Malloy • Molix-Bailey • Moseley • Mowry • Myren
Price • Reynosa • Santa Cruz • Silbey • Vielhaber

Macmillan/McGraw-Hill

About the Cover

Developing fluency with fractions, decimals, and polyhedral solids are featured topics in Fifth grade. The mathematical symbols shown on the mountain goat's snowboard will help students gain momentum as they carve their way through higher levels of math. Have students locate parallel and intersecting lines on the ski lift, and use at least one of the symbols on the snowboard to describe the ski lift chairs.

The McGraw·Hill Companies

Macmillan/McGraw-Hill

Send all inquiries to:
Macmillan/McGraw-Hill
8787 Orion Place
Columbus, OH 43240-4027

ISBN: 978-0-02-100983-1
MHID: 0-02-100983-X

Oklahoma Math Connects, Grade 5

Printed in the United States of America.

1 2 3 4 5 6 7 8 9 10 027/055 18 17 16 15 14 13 12 11 10 09

Contents in Brief

Authors

Mary Behr Altieri
Putnam/Northern Westchester BOCES
Yorktown Heights, New York

Don S. Balka
Professor Emeritus
Saint Mary's College
Notre Dame, Indiana

Roger Day, Ph.D.
Mathematics Department Chair
Pontiac Township High School
Pontiac, Illinois

Philip D. Gonsalves
Mathematics Coordinator
Alameda County Office of Education and California State University East Bay
Hayward, California

Ellen C. Grace
Consultant
Albuquerque, New Mexico

Stephen Krulik
Professor Emeritus Mathematics Education
Temple University
Cherry Hill, New Jersey

Carol E. Malloy, Ph.D.
Associate Professor of Mathematics Education
University of North Carolina at Chapel Hill
Chapel Hill, North Carolina

Rhonda J. Molix-Bailey
Mathematics Consultant
Mathematics by Design
Desoto, Texas

Lois Gordon Moseley
Staff Developer
NUMBERS: Mathematics Professional Development
Houston, Texas

Brian Mowry
Independent Math Educational Consultant/Part-Time Pre-K Instructional Specialist
Austin Independent School District
Austin, Texas

Authors

Christina L. Myren
Consultant Teacher
Conejo Valley Unified School District
Thousand Oaks, California

Jack Price
Professor Emeritus
California State Polytechnic University
Pomona, California

Mary Esther Reynosa
Instructional Specialist for Elementary Mathematics
Northside Independent School District
San Antonio, Texas

Rafaela M. Santa Cruz
SDSU/CGU Doctoral Program in Education
San Diego State University
San Diego, California

Robyn Silbey
Math Content Coach
Montgomery County Public Schools
Gaithersburg, Maryland

Kathleen Vielhaber
Mathematics Consultant
St. Louis, Missouri

Contributing Authors

Donna J. Long
Mathematics Consultant
Indianapolis, Indiana

FOLDABLES **Dinah Zike**
Educational Consultant
Dinah-Might Activities, Inc.
San Antonio, Texas

Welcome to

Oklahoma Math Connects

GRADE 5

Master Oklahoma's Priority Academic Student Skills in 3 Easy Steps

1 Practice the Standards throughout the Lessons

- The lessons address Oklahoma's Priority Academic Skills (PASS) for Mathematics.
- Your textbook also contains more lessons for Oklahoma. Look for the *Focus on Oklahoma* section after the Table of Contents.
- Lessons contain test practice questions that are aligned to Oklahoma's Priority Academic Student Skills. These questions are like those found on the OCCT and they will provide you with ongoing opportunities to sharpen your test-taking skills.

Honeybee

2 Practice the Standards throughout the Chapter

Every chapter contains two full pages of Test Practice. The Test Practice gives you a chance to put your math skills to use.

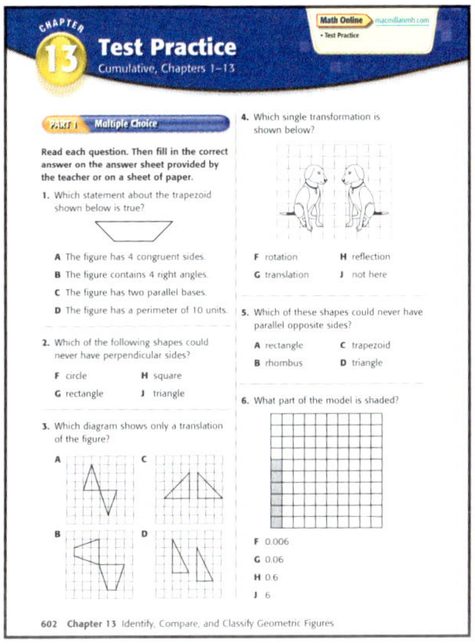
CHAPTER 13 Test Practice
Cumulative, Chapters 1–13

PART 1 Multiple Choice

Read each question. Then fill in the correct answer on the answer sheet provided by the teacher or on a sheet of paper.

1. Which statement about the trapezoid shown below is true?

A The figure has 4 congruent sides.
B The figure contains 4 right angles.
C The figure has two parallel bases.
D The figure has a perimeter of 10 units.

2. Which of the following shapes could never have perpendicular sides?

F circle H square
G rectangle J triangle

3. Which diagram shows only a translation of the figure?

4. Which single transformation is shown below?

F rotation H reflection
G translation J not here

5. Which of these shapes could never have parallel opposite sides?

A rectangle C trapezoid
B rhombus D triangle

6. What part of the model is shaded?

F 0.006
G 0.06
H 0.6
J 6

602 Chapter 13 Identify, Compare, and Classify Geometric Figures

3 Practice the Standards Before the Test

If you've followed steps 1 and 2, you should be more than ready for the OCCT test. But just in case you want to make sure, use the *Get Ready for the OCCT* section at the end of your book to practice questions that are organized by strand. Lesson references are included for you should you need a little refresher.

Oklahoma Reviewers

Each Oklahoma Reviewer gave feedback and suggestions for improving the effectiveness of the PreK-8 *Oklahoma Math Connects* program.

Kristi Adams
Mathematics Teacher
Owasso 6th Grade Center
Owasso, OK

Tom Dill
Math Teacher
Robert S. Kerr Elementary
Tulsa, OK

Lahonda Gardella
Mathematics Teacher
Monroney Middle School
Midwest City, OK

Robert Hanna
Mathematics Teacher
Monroney Middle School
Midwest City, OK

Joe Mercier
Secondary Math Curriculum Specialist
Tulsa Public Schools
Tulsa, OK

Teresa R. McCain
Kindergarten Teacher
Bixby North Elementary
Bixby, OK

Cathy O'Dell
Mathematics Teacher
Union High School
Tulsa, OK

Linda Scott
Mathematics Teacher
Brink Junior High School
Oklahoma City, OK

Tonya Williams
Mathematics Teacher
Edison Middle School
Tulsa, OK

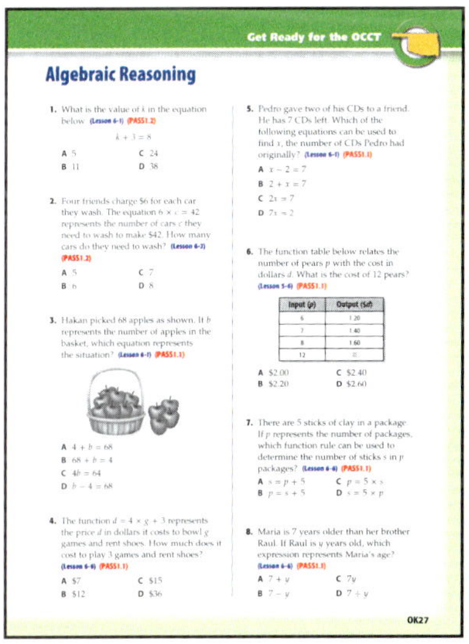
Get Ready for the OCCT

Algebraic Reasoning

OK27

Start Smart

OK PASS

H.O.T. Problems

WRITING IN MATH 3, 5, 7, 9, 11, 13

Chapter 1 Use Place Value

CHAPTER 2 Add and Subtract Whole Numbers and Decimals

Chapter 3 Multiply Whole Numbers

Contents

CHAPTER 4 Divide Whole Numbers

CHAPTER 5 Use Algebraic Expressions

CHAPTER 6 Use Equations and Function Tables

CHAPTER 7 Display and Interpret Data

Chapter 8 Develop Fraction Concepts

CHAPTER 9 Use Factors and Multiples

Chapter 10 Add and Subtract Fractions

CHAPTER 11 Use Measures in the Customary System

Chapter 12 Use Measures in the Metric System

CHAPTER 13 Identify, Compare, and Classify Geometric Figures

Chapter 14 Measure Perimeter, Area, and Volume

Chapter 15 Use Probability to Make Predictions

Looking Ahead

OK PASS Problem-Solving Projects

H.O.T. Problems

Higher Order Thinking LA5, LA9, LA13, LA17, LA21, LA25

Writing in Math LA5, LA9, LA13, LA17, LA21, LA25

Student Handbook

Built-In Workbook

Reference

FOCUS ON

Oklahoma

GRADE 5

Contents

OK PASS

OK 1 Circle Graphs

MAIN IDEA

I will draw conclusions from circle graphs and construct circle graphs.

OK PASS

5.1.a Compare and translate displays of data and justify the selection of the type of table of graph (e.g., charts, tables, bar graphs, pictographs, line graphs, **circle graphs,** Venn diagrams). *Also addresses 5.1.b, 5M1.2, 5M5.2.*

New Vocabulary

circle graph

OK Math Online

macmillanmh.com

GET READY to Learn

A group of 200 fifth graders were surveyed about which type of transportation they use most often to get to school. The results are shown in the table.

Transportation Survey Results

Type of Transportation	Number of Students
Bike	10
Carpool	10
Walk	50
School Bus	130

The results of the survey are shown below in the circle graph. A **circle graph** is used to compare data that are parts of a whole.

Circle Graphs

Key Concept

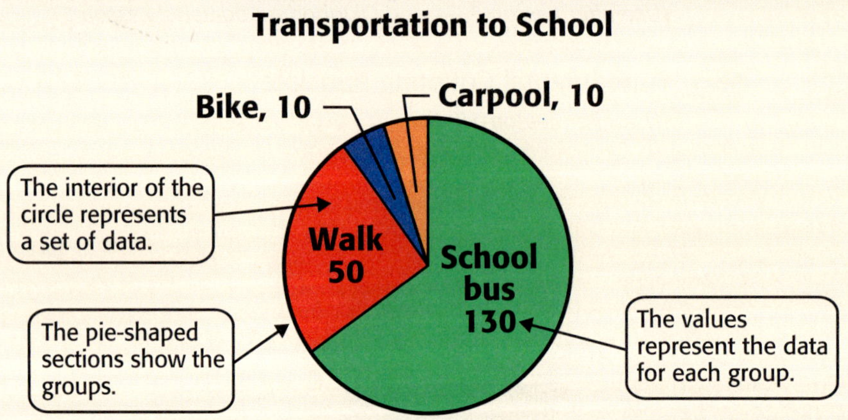

You can use circle graphs to draw conclusions.

Real-World EXAMPLES Draw Conclusions

SURVEYS Refer to circle graph above.

1. **Which type of transportation do students use most often?**
   The "school bus" section of the circle is largest section. So, most of the students take the school bus to school.

2. **Which section of the circle graph represents the type of transportation that the least number of students use?**
   The "bike" and "carpool" sections are the smallest sections. So, the least amount of students bike or carpool to school.

You can organize real-world data to construct a circle graph.

Real-World EXAMPLE Construct a Circle Graph

3 POPCORN Hiroshi surveyed 100 students in his school to see which flavor of popcorn they like best. The table at the right shows the results of the survey. Construct a circle graph that displays the survey results.

Popcorn Flavor	Number of Responses
Butter	43
Caramel	22
Cheddar	23
Plain	12

- A little less than half of the students chose butter. So, shade a little less than half of the circle and label it "Butter."
- A little less than a quarter of the students each chose caramel and cheddar. So, shade a little less than a quarter of the circle for the sections "Caramel" and "Cheddar."
- Shade the rest of the circle a fourth color and label it "Plain."
- Give the graph a title.

Popcorn Flavor

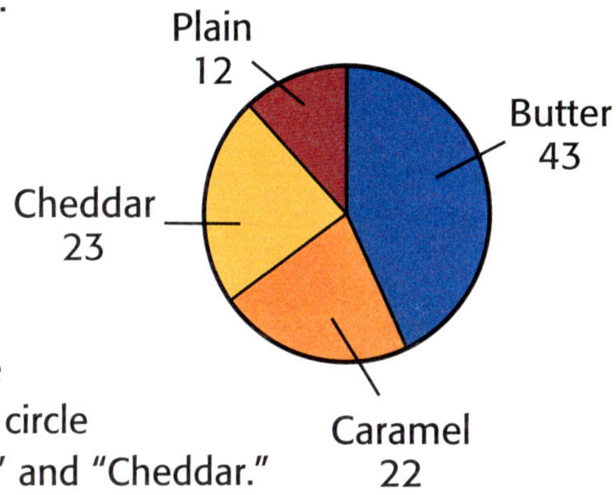

CHECK What You Know

SUMMER PLANS One hundred students were asked about their summer plans. The circle graph shows the survey results. Example 1 (p. OK2)

Summer Plans

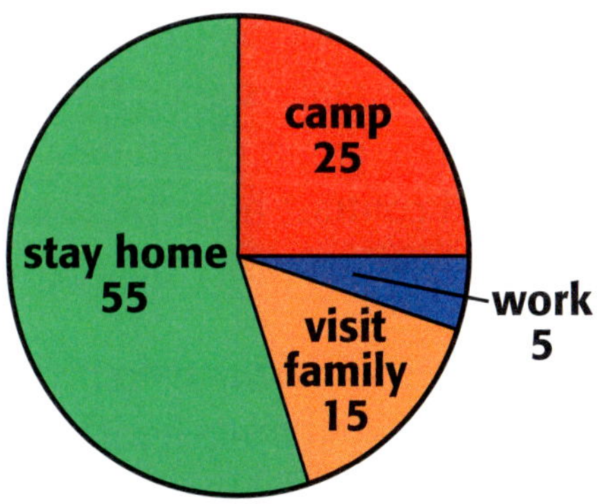

1. What are most of the students planning to do for the summer?

2. How many more students plan on going to camp than visit family?

3. **MOVIES** The table shows the responses of 100 students surveyed about their pet peeves at the movies. Construct a circle graph of the data. Then write a few sentences describing some conclusions you can make about the data. Example 2 (p. OK3)

Pet Peeve	Number of Responses
bad manners	49
preshow commercials	24
overpriced food	15
babies/noisy children	12

4. Talk About It Explain when you would use a circle graph.

Practice and Problem Solving

Write a few sentences describing some conclusions you can make about the data in each circle graph shown below. Example 1 (p. OK2)

5. **Number of Pets**

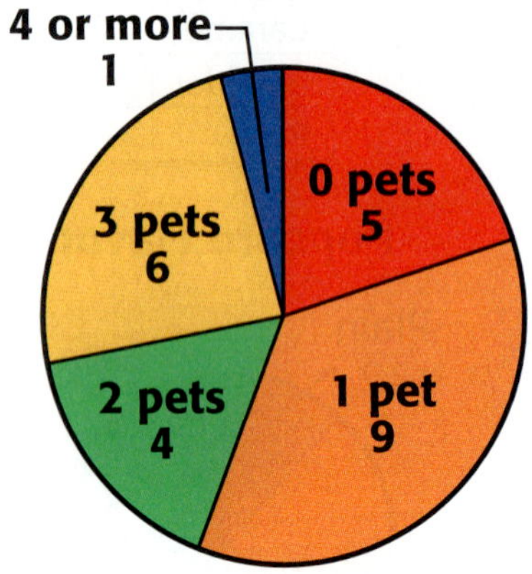

6. **Car Colors**

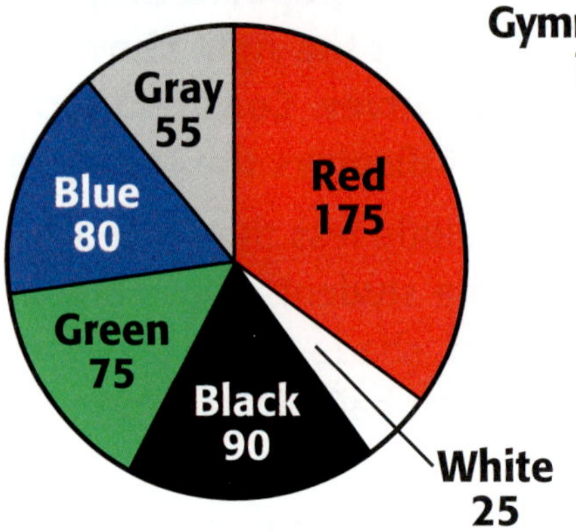

7. **Class Enrollment**

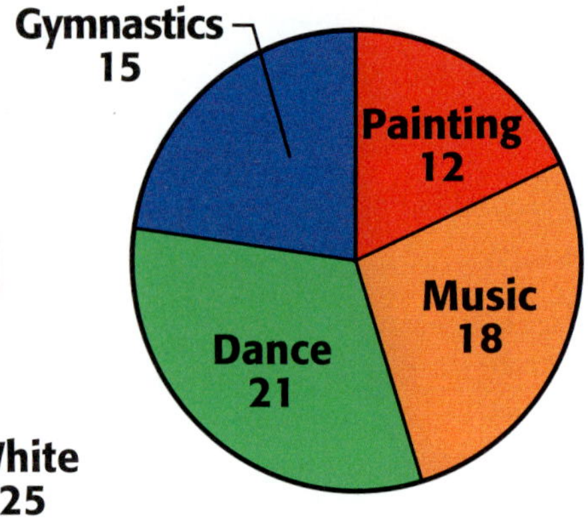

8. Jasmine counted the number of coins in her piggy bank. The table shows the results. Construct a circle graph of the data. Then write a few sentences describing some conclusions you can make about the data. Example 2 (p. OK3)

Coin	Number
Dime	44
Nickel	27
Penny	12
Quarter	17

9. One hundred students voted in an election for class president. Eighteen students voted for Anita, 22 voted for Guido, 26 voted for Mei-Ling, and 34 voted for Tyrone. Construct a circle graph of the data. Then write a few sentences describing some conclusions you can make about the data.

10. The bar graph shows the results of a recent poll of 100 students about which type of radio station they prefer. Construct a circle graph of the data. Then compare and contrast how the bar graph and circle graph display the data.

Radio Station Preferences

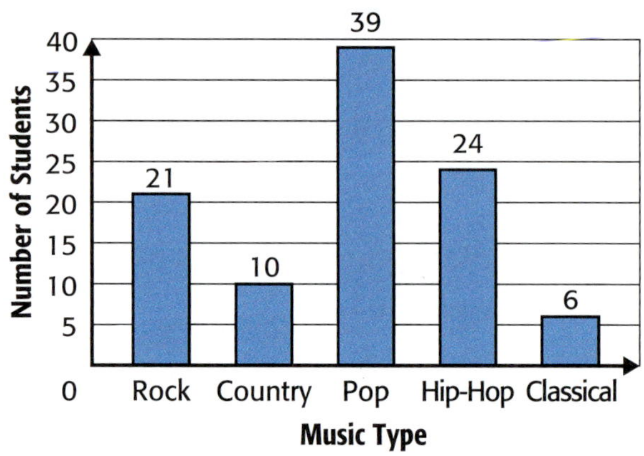

11. Mrs. Thorne wants to display the number of canned goods her class brought in each day this week for the canned food drive. Which type of display should Mrs. Thorne use to show the number of cans her class collected each day? Justify your selection.

12. Would it be more appropriate to use a circle graph to display favorite types of sports or tracked sales of frozen yogurt? Explain your reasoning.

H.O.T. Problems

13. COLLECT THE DATA Collect some data that can be displayed using a circle graph. Record the data in a table. Then write a few sentences describing some conclusions you can make about the data.

14. REASONING Nate surveyed 100 colleges about their average price for admission to a college basketball game. He found that 18 schools charged \$25–\$29, 12 charged \$20–\$24, 37 charged \$15–\$19, and 33 charged \$10–\$14. Display this data in circle graph and another type of statistical display. Which display best represents the data? Explain.

15. WRITING IN ►MATH Write a few sentences explaining to a friend how to construct a circle graph from the data in the table at the right.

Favorite Sport	Number of Responses
Baseball	11
Basketball	11
Football	78

OCCT Practice

PASS5.1.a, PASS5.1.b

16. The circle graph shows the results of survey about favorite types of after-school activities. Which table best represents the information shown in the circle graph?

Favorite After-School Activities

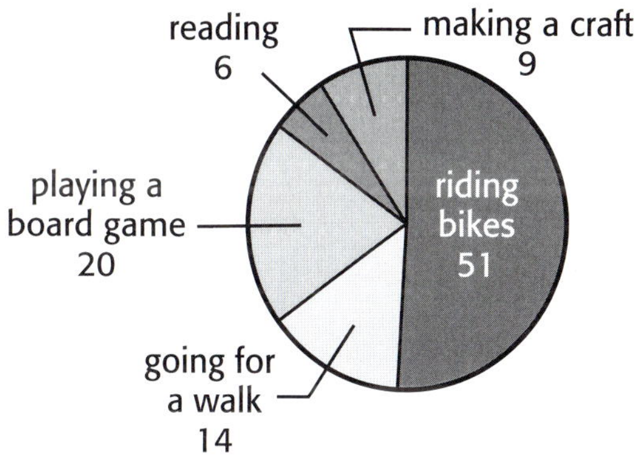

A

Activity	Number of Responses
going for a walk	14
making a craft	9
playing a board game	20
reading	6
riding bikes	51

B

Activity	Number of Responses
going for a walk	10
making a craft	5
playing a board game	20
reading	5
riding bikes	50

C

Activity	Number of Responses
going for a walk	14
making a craft	6
playing a board game	20
reading	9
riding bikes	51

D

Activity	Number of Responses
going for a walk	14
making a craft	9
playing a board game	20
reading	6
riding bikes	40

OK 2 Venn Diagrams

GET READY to Learn

Hands-On Mini Lab

SURVEYS Nicholas asked 20 of his classmates what they use when taking notes: a pencil or a pen. The results are shown in the table at the right.

Taking Notes	
Writing Tool	Number of Students
Pencil	18
Pen	15
Neither	2

1. Display the information in a bar graph.

2. Display the information in a circle graph.

3. If Nicholas surveyed 20 classmates, why do the numbers in the second column have a sum of 18 + 15 + 2 or 35?

4. Does either graph tell you how many people use both pencil and pen?

MAIN IDEA

I will use Venn diagrams to solve problems.

OK PASS

5.1.a Compare and translate displays of data and justify the selection of the type of table or graph (e.g., charts, **tables, bar graphs,** pictographs, line graphs, circle graphs, **Venn diagrams).** *Also addresses 5M1.1, 5M1.5, 5M5.1, 5M5.2.*

New Vocabulary

Venn diagram

OK Math Online

macmillanmh.com

A **Venn diagram** is an arrangement of overlapping circles used to show how two or more sets of data are related. The data presented in the table above is displayed in the Venn diagram below.

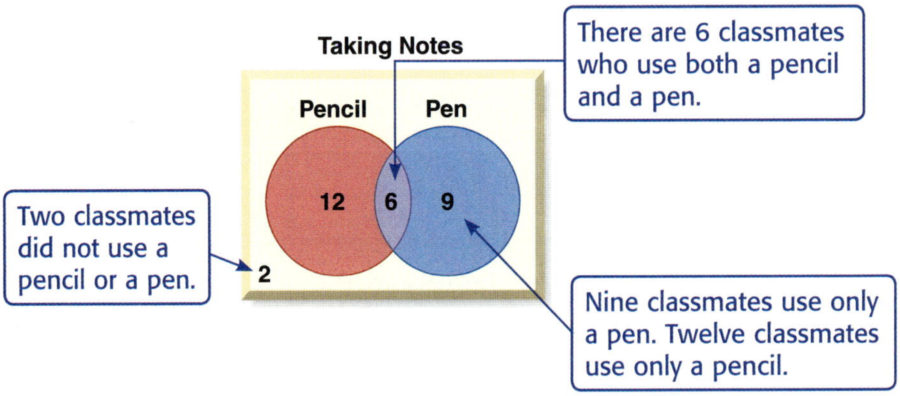

A Venn diagram uses two overlapping circles to show two attributes, like the diagram above. To show three attributes, you can use a Venn diagram with three overlapping circles, like the one shown on the next page.

The Venn diagram below shows the following information.

- 10 students participate in the Drama Club only, 8 in Band only, and 12 in the Spanish Club only.
- 4 students participate in both the Drama Club and Band, but not in the Spanish Club.
- 3 students participate in both the Drama Club and the Spanish Club, but not in Band.
- 7 students participate in both the Spanish Club and Band, but not the Drama Club.
- 5 students participate in all three clubs.
- 6 students do not participate in any of the three clubs.

Extracurricular Activities

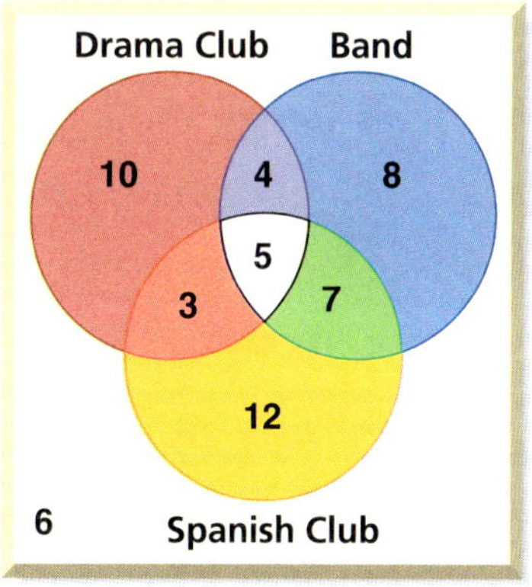

You can use Venn diagrams to explore and solve problems.

EXAMPLES Use a Venn Diagram

COMMUNICATION Refer to the Venn diagram at the right which shows the results of a survey of students.

Communication Use

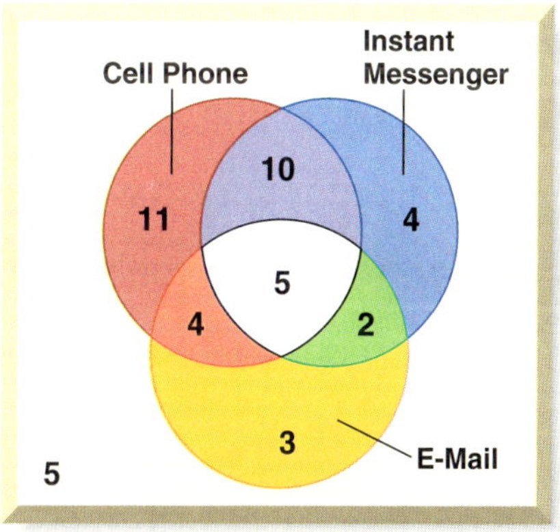

1 How many students communicate by instant messenger and E-mail?

The region where the circle labeled *Instant Messenger* and the circle labeled *E-mail* overlap contains 2 + 5, or 7 students.

2 How many students communicate by cell phone or E-mail?

The regions where the circles labeled *Cell Phone* and *E-mail* overlap contain 11 + 10 + 5 + 4 + 2 + 3, or 35 students.

3 How many students use E-mail but not instant messenger?

Add the number of students in the circle labeled *E-mail* that do not overlap with the circle labeled *Instant Messenger.*

4 + 3 = 7 — Do not count the 5 or the 2 because those students also communicate by instant messenger.

So, 7 students use E-mail but not instant messenger.

4 How many total students were surveyed?

Add the number of students in each region. So, 11 + 10 + 4 + 4 + 5 + 2 + 3 + 5, or 44 students were surveyed.

CHECK What You Know

SPORTS For Exercises 1–6, refer to the Venn diagram at the right which shows the number of students who play baseball, volleyball, and tennis at Washington Middle School. Example 1 (p. OK7)

Sports

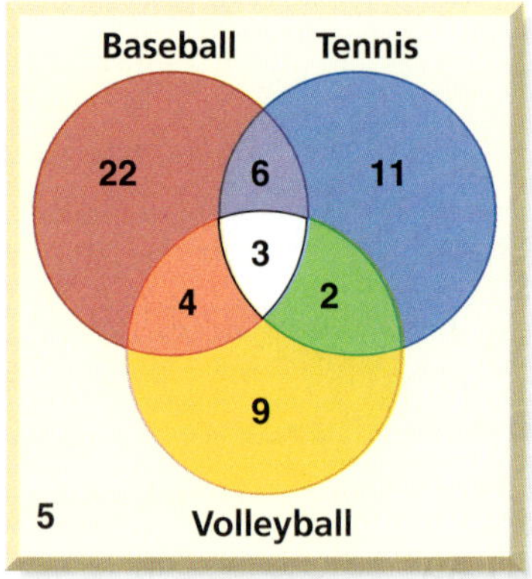

1. How many students play baseball?
2. How many students only play volleyball?
3. How many students play tennis or baseball, but not volleyball?
4. How many students play both volleyball and tennis?
5. How many students play all three sports?
6. How many students play none of the three sports?

Practice and Problem Solving

ZOOS For Exercises 7–12, refer to the Venn diagram at the right which shows the number of zoos in a region that have pandas, tigers, and giraffes. Example 1 (p. OK7)

Zoo Animals

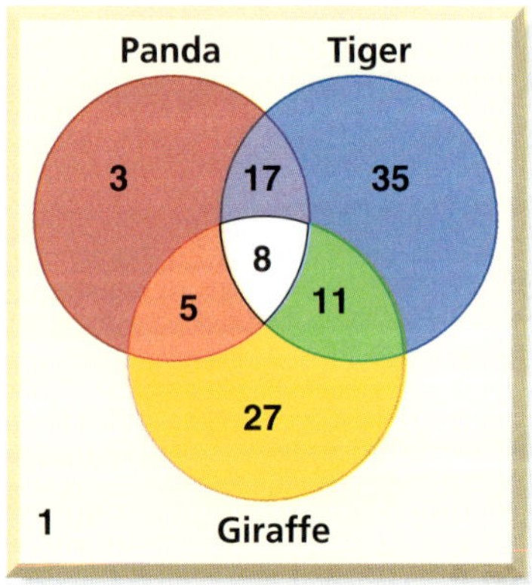

7. How many zoos have a panda?
8. How many zoos only have giraffes?
9. How many zoos have both pandas and giraffes, but not tigers?
10. How many zoos have both tigers and pandas?
11. How many zoos have all three animals?
12. How many zoos have none of the three animals?
13. **MUSIC** Which display is most appropriate to determine the number of students who like only country music? Justify your response.

8th Grade Music Preference

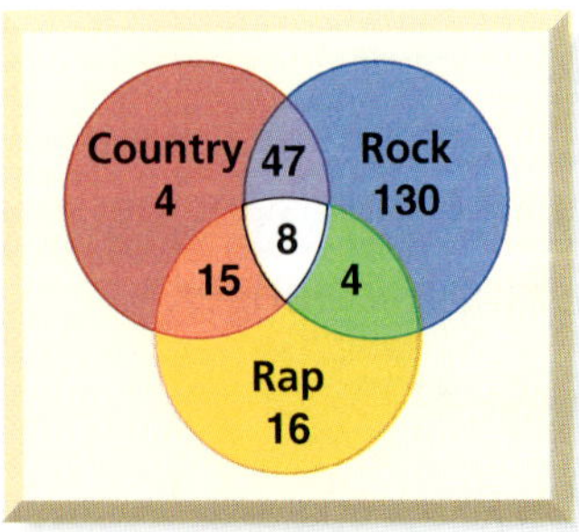

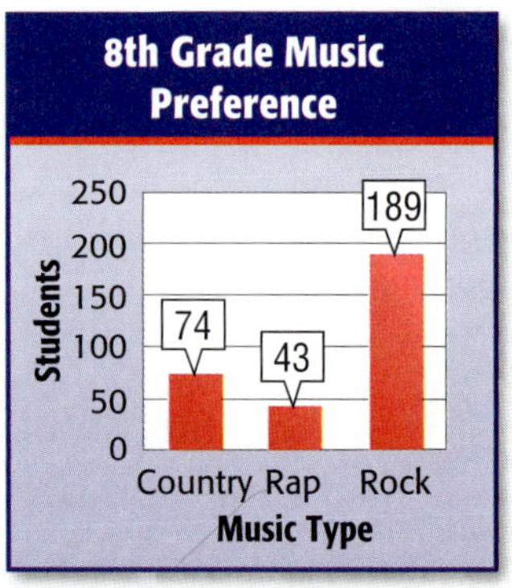

14. **MUSIC** Kristy asked 43 people which format they like to listen to music, MP3 or CD. Of those surveyed, 20 said CD and 38 said MP3. However, 15 people said both CD and MP3. Use a Venn diagram to find how many classmates prefer MP3 format only.

H.O.T. Problems

15. **REASONING** Pedro asked 64 students at Midland Middle School which subjects they like in school: science, math, or social studies. The Venn diagram at the right shows the results of the survey. Use the information below to find the missing numbers in the Venn diagram.

- Thirty students like science.
- Forty-five students like math and social studies.
- Ten students like history but do not like science or math.

Students' Favorite Subject

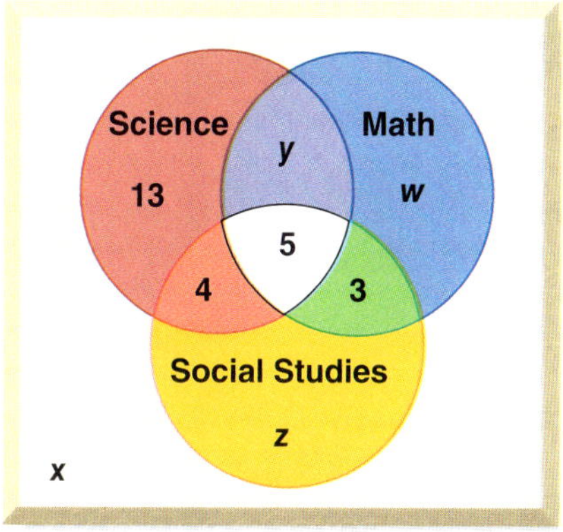

16. **WRITING IN MATH** Draw a Venn diagram to show the relationship between the characteristics of cats and dogs. Then describe your Venn diagram.

OCCT Practice PASS5.1.a

17. David surveyed 24 of his classmates who have at least one brother or sister. The table shows his results. Which Venn diagram matches this information?

Sibling	Number of Classmates
Brother	14
Sister	16

A

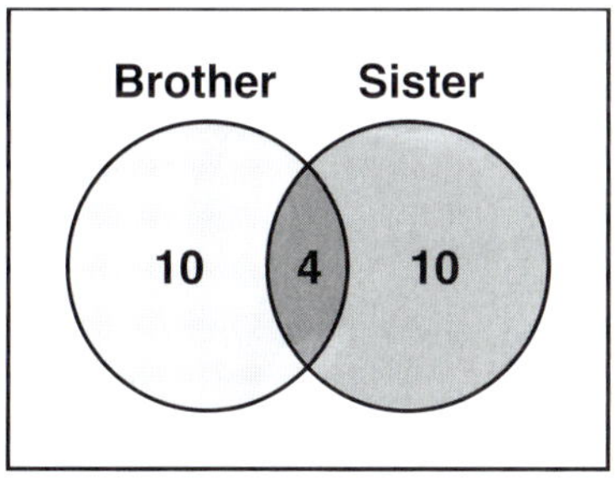

B

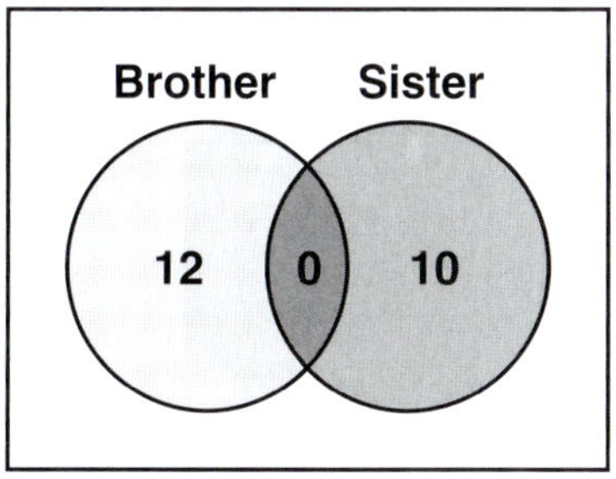

C

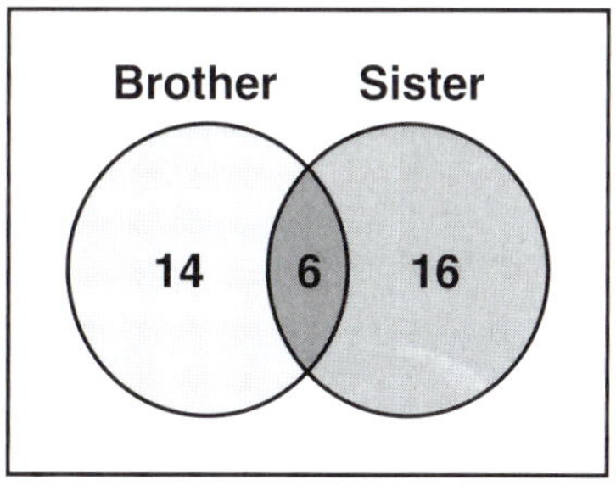

D

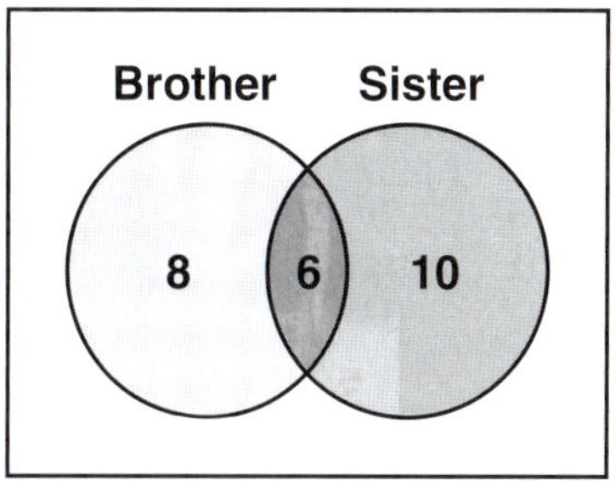

OK 3 Compare and Order Fractions and Decimals

MAIN IDEA

I will compare and order fractions and decimals.

OK PASS

2.1.b Represent with models the connection between fractions and decimals, compare and order fractions and decimals, and be able to convert from one representation to the other to solve problems. (e.g., use 10 × 10 grids, base 10 blocks).

OK Math Online

macmillanmh.com

GET READY to Learn

The models at the right represent the fractions $\frac{4}{5}$ and $\frac{9}{10}$. By lining up the models, you can see that $\frac{9}{10} > \frac{4}{5}$.

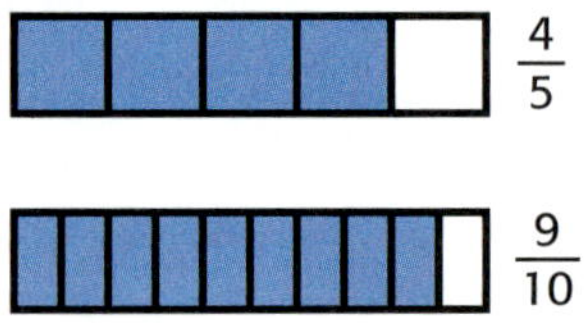

Recall that you learned to compare two fractions using the symbols <, =, and > in Lesson 9-9. In this lesson, you will extend this concept to compare fractions and decimals.

EXAMPLE Compare Fractions and Decimals

1 **Compare the numbers $\frac{2}{3}$ and 0.6.**

One Way: **Use models.**

The models at the right represent $\frac{2}{3}$ and 0.6. By lining up the models, you can see that $\frac{2}{3}$ is greater than 0.6.

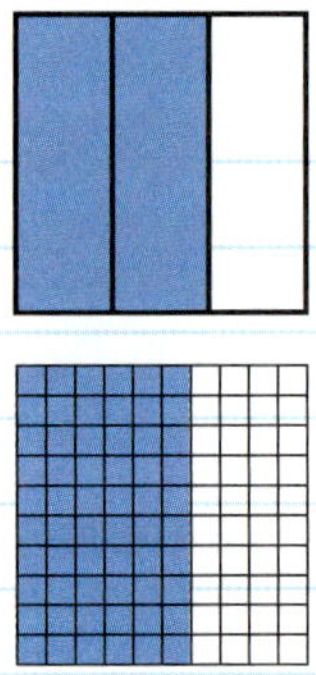

Another Way: **Use a number line.**

Draw a number line separated into thirds. Graph the point $\frac{2}{3}$.

Draw another number line under the first one that counts by tenths. Graph 0.6.

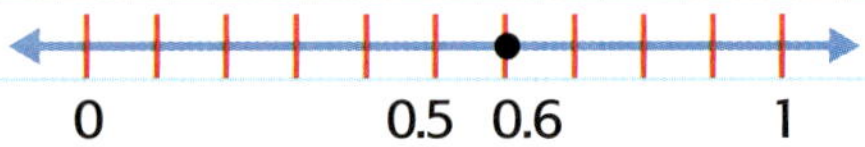

Using either method, you can see that $\frac{2}{3} > 0.6$.

You can also compare numbers by writing both numbers in the same form.

Real-World EXAMPLE

2 **TAXES In a recent survey, 0.4 of the people said that they will use their tax refund to pay bills and $\frac{6}{25}$ said they will spend it on entertainment. Will more people pay bills or spend their refund on entertainment?**

You need to compare the decimal 0.4 to the fraction $\frac{6}{25}$. To compare a decimal and a fraction, you can write both numbers as fractions, or you can write both numbers as decimals.

One Way: Write both numbers as fractions.

To write 0.4 as a fraction, write 0.4 as a fraction with a denominator of 10.

$0.4 = \frac{4}{10}$ The last digit 4 is in the tenths place.

Simplify the fraction.

$\frac{4}{10} = \frac{2}{5}$ Divide the numerator and denominator by the GCF, 2.

Compare both numbers as fractions.

$\frac{2}{5} > \frac{6}{25}$ $\frac{2}{5} = \frac{10}{25}$ and $\frac{10}{25} > \frac{6}{25}$.

Another Way: Write both numbers as decimals.

First write $\frac{6}{25}$ as a fraction with a denominator of 100.

$$\frac{6}{25} = \frac{6 \times 4}{25 \times 4} = \frac{24}{100}$$

Write the fraction $\frac{24}{100}$ as a decimal.

$\frac{24}{100} = 0.24$ 24 hundredths = 0.24

Compare both numbers as decimals.

$0.4 > 0.24$ The tenths digit 4 is greater than the tenths digit 2.

So, more people will use their tax refund to pay bills than spend it on entertainment.

Remember

Sometimes, it is helpful to leave a fraction unsimplified. $\frac{40}{100}$ can easily be written as a percent if you do not simplify the fraction first.

You can also order fractions and decimals. Again, it is helpful to write all the numbers in one form.

EXAMPLE **Order Fractions and Decimals**

3 **Order 0.3, $\frac{3}{100}$, $\frac{7}{20}$, and 0.33 from least to greatest.**

Write all the numbers in one form, such as decimals.

The numbers 0.3 and 0.33 are already written as decimals.

Step 1 Write $\frac{3}{100}$ as a decimal.

$\frac{3}{100} = 0.03$ *three hundredths* = 0.03

Step 2 Write $\frac{7}{20}$ as a decimal.

$\frac{7}{20} = \frac{35}{100}$ (×5) Write an equivalent fraction with a denominator of 100.

$= 0.35$ *thirty-five hundredths* = 0.35

Step 3 From least to greatest, the decimals are 0.03, 0.3, 0.33, and 0.35. So, from least to greatest, the numbers are $\frac{3}{100}$, 0.3, 0.33, and $\frac{7}{20}$.

CHECK What You Know

Replace each ● with <, >, or = to make a true sentence.
See Examples 1, 2 (pp. OK10–OK11)

1. $\frac{3}{4}$ ● 0.7 **2.** 0.4 ● $\frac{2}{5}$ **3.** 0.08 ● $\frac{3}{25}$ **4.** $1\frac{1}{2}$ ● 1.55

5. Gary surveyed his fifth grade class to see who will attend camp during the summer vacation. Of the students in his class, 17% will attend an overnight summer camp, $\frac{11}{50}$ will attend a day camp, and 0.59 will not attend any kind of summer camp. Which group of students is the greatest?

Order each set of numbers from least to greatest. See Example 3 (p. OK12)

6. $\frac{17}{25}$, 0.6, 0.062, $\frac{13}{20}$ **7.** 0.2, $\frac{1}{4}$, 0.02, $\frac{3}{20}$

8. Talk About It Refer to Example 1. Which method do you prefer to use to compare two rational numbers? Justify your response.

Practice and Problem Solving

Replace each ● with $<$, $>$, or $=$ to make a true sentence.
See Examples 1, 2 (pp. OK10–OK11)

9. $\frac{2}{3}$ ● 0.6
10. 0.8 ● $\frac{39}{50}$
11. 0.01 ● $\frac{1}{10}$
12. $\frac{3}{5}$ ● 0.6
13. $\frac{5}{8}$ ● 0.58
14. 0.37 ● $\frac{37}{100}$
15. 2.05 ● $2\frac{1}{5}$
16. $3\frac{3}{4}$ ● 3.75

17. At Jefferson Elementary School, $\frac{57}{100}$ of the fifth-grade students spend at least 30 minutes a day on math homework. Of the fourth-grade students, 0.5 spend this same amount. In which grade do a greater percent of students spend at least 30 minutes a day on math homework?

18. At Jeremy's school, $\frac{3}{16}$ of the students are in the band, 0.31 of students play at least one sport, and 0.13 are in the drama club. Of these three, which activity is most popular among students at Jeremy's school?

Order each set of numbers from least to greatest. See Example 3 (p. OK12)

19. 0.99, $\frac{9}{10}$, 0.09, $\frac{19}{20}$
20. $\frac{3}{4}$, 0.8, 0.08, $\frac{7}{10}$
21. $\frac{1}{20}$, 0.07, 0.09, $\frac{2}{25}$
22. 0.84, 0.88, $\frac{41}{50}$, $\frac{4}{5}$

H.O.T. Problems

23. OPEN ENDED Write four numbers in order from least to greatest. Use a combination of fractions and decimals.

24. CHALLENGE Refer to the fraction model at the right. Write two different decimals, one that is greater than the fraction represented by the model, and one that is less.

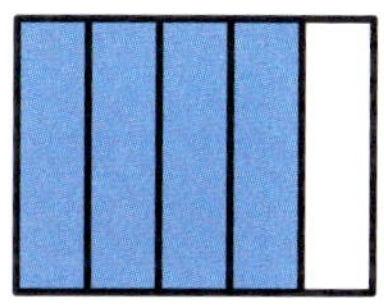

25. CHALLENGE Order $5\frac{3}{8}$, 5.15, $5\frac{3}{10}$, and 5.28 from least to greatest.

26. WRITING IN MATH Write and solve a word problem about a real-world situation in which you would compare fractions and decimals.

OCCT Practice PASS2.1.b

27. Which one of the following statements is true?

A $0.85 < \frac{9}{10}$
B $\frac{2}{3} > 0.75$
C $0.4 = \frac{3}{5}$
D $\frac{1}{2} < 0.55$

28. Which of the following rational numbers is less than 0.48?

F 0.62
G $\frac{3}{5}$
H 0.48
J $\frac{7}{20}$

OK 4 Angle Measurements

MAIN IDEA

I will estimate and compare angle measures.

OK PASS

4.1.a Compare, estimate, and determine the **measurement of angles.** *Also addresses 3.2.*

New Vocabulary

straight angle

OK Math Online

macmillanmh.com

GET READY to Learn

Hands-On Mini Lab

To estimate the measure of an angle, you can use angles that measure 45°, 90°, and 180°.

Make benchmark angles of 45°, 90°, and 180° using paper plates.

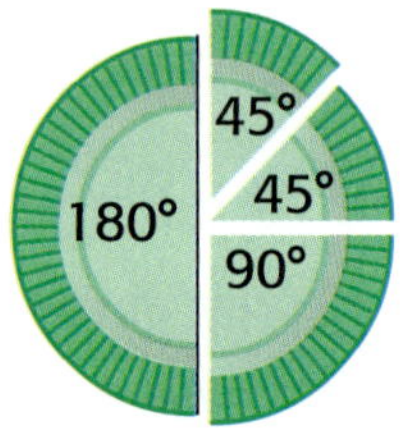

Step 1 Fold a paper plate in half to find the center of the plate.

Step 2 Cut and label wedges as shown.

Use your wedges to determine an estimated size of the angle shown at the right.

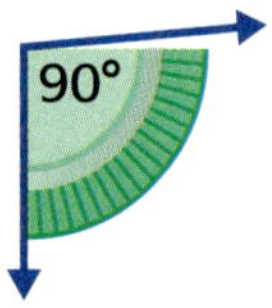

Since the 90°-plate wedge is close to the size of the angle, the angle is about 90°.

To estimate the measure of an angle, compare it to an angle whose measure you know. From the Hands-On Mini Lab, you know the benchmark angles of 45°, 90°, and 180°. Recall from Explore 13-3 that angles can be identified as *right, acute,* or *obtuse.* A *straight angle* is another classification of angles.

Classifications of Angles

Key Concept

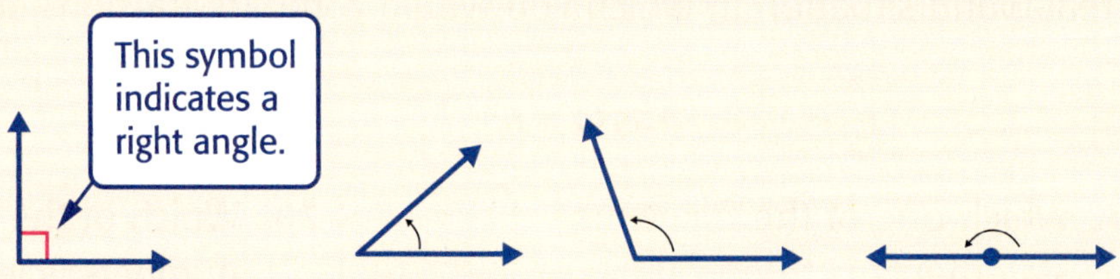

right angle	acute angle	obtuse angle	straight angle
exactly 90°	less than 90°	between 90° and 180°	exactly 180°

EXAMPLE Estimate Angle Measures

1 Estimate the measure of the angle.

The angle appears to be a little less than 90°. So, a reasonable estimate is about 80°.

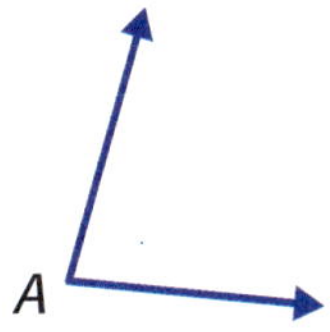

An angle can be named by its vertex. Angle *A* is shown above. You can also use benchmark angles to compare angle measures. You can always use a protractor to compare your estimates to the actual measurements.

EXAMPLE Estimate Angle Measures

2 Compare the measure of angle *B* to angle *C* shown at the right.

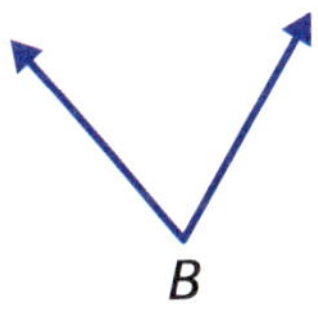

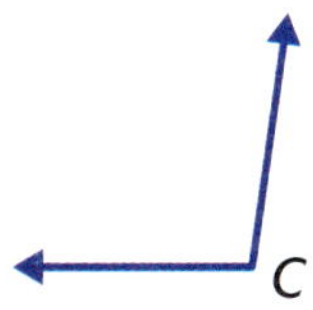

Angle *C* appears to be an obtuse angle. Angle *B* appears to be an acute angle. An obtuse angle measures greater than 90°. An acute angle measures less than 90°. So, the measure of angle *C* is greater than the measure of angle *B*.

CHECK What You Know

Estimate the measure of each angle. Example 1 (p. OK15)

1. 

2. 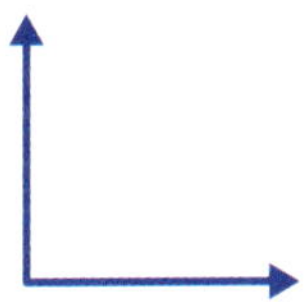

3. 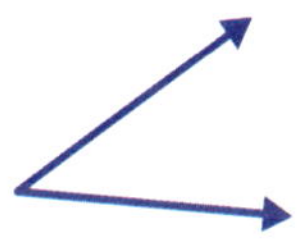

4. 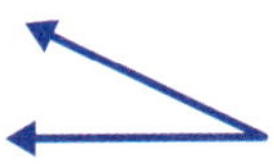

5. 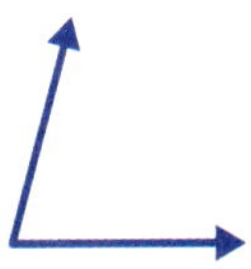

6. 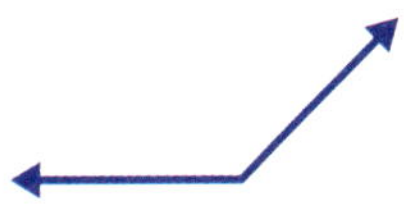

7. Compare the measures of angle *D* and angle *F*. Example 2 (p. OK15)

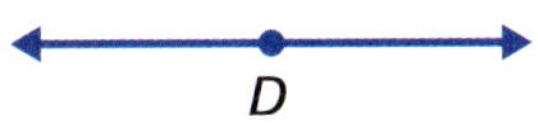

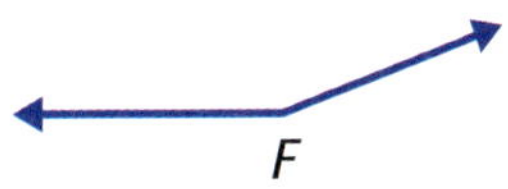

8. **Talk About It** Explain how you would estimate the measure of any given angle.

Practice and Problem Solving

Estimate the measure of the angle. Example 1 (p. OK15)

9. 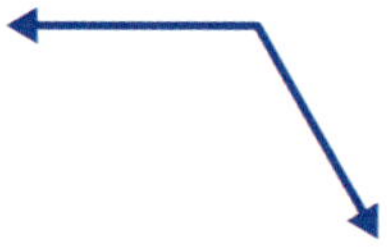

10. 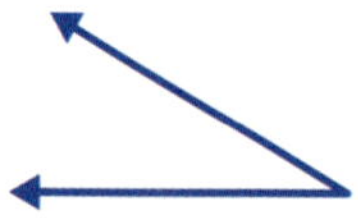

11. 

Compare the measure of each angle. Example 2 (p. OK15)

12. 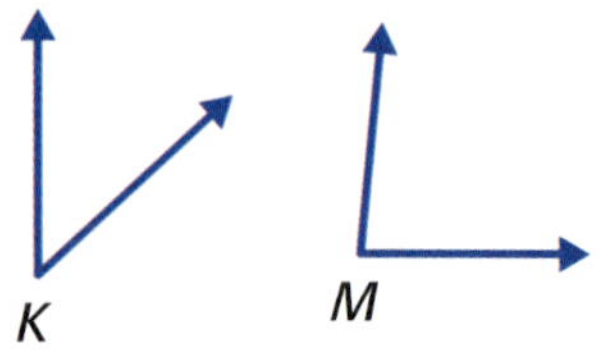

13. 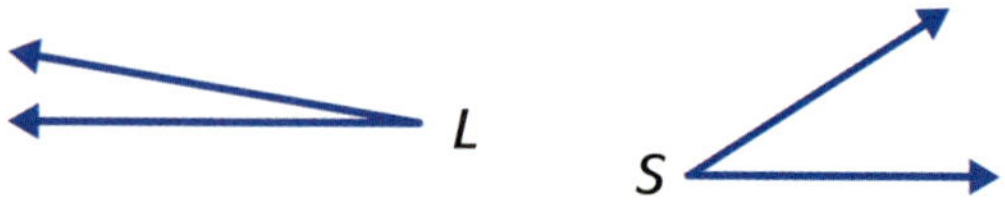

14. Estimate the measure of the angle formed by the hands on the clocks shown. Then compare the measures of each angle.

Estimate the measure of each angle. Then classify each angle as *acute, obtuse, right,* or *straight.*

15. 

16. 

17. 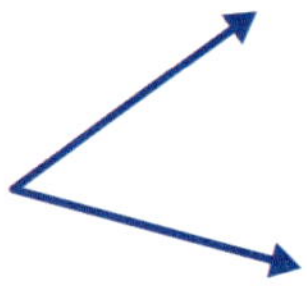

H.O.T. Problems

18. OPEN ENDED Draw a pair of angles for which the statement *The measure of* angle *X* > *The measure of* angle *Y* is true.

19. WRITING IN ►MATH Describe a real-word situation in which drawing a diagram with estimated angle measures would be helpful.

OCCT Practice

PASS3.2, PASS4.1.a

20. Which angle has an approximate measure of 50°?

A 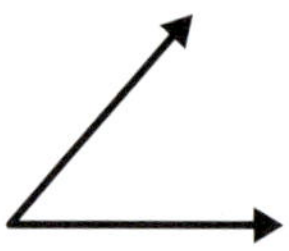

C 

B 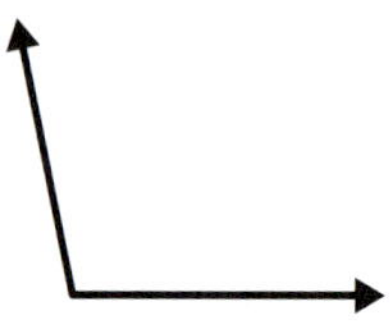

D 

OK 5 Polygons

GET READY to Learn

Compare the figures in Set A to the figures in Set B. What are some similarities and differences between the figures in each set?

Set A **Set B**

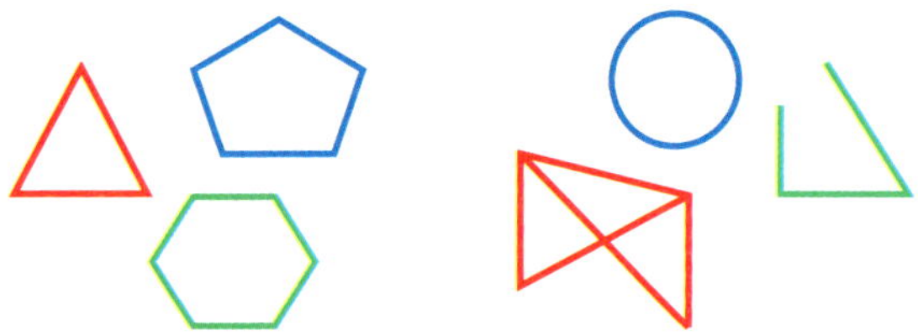

MAIN IDEA

I will identify, classify, and draw polygons.

OK PASS

3.1 Compare and contrast the basic characteristics of circles and **polygons (triangles, quadrilaterals, pentagons, hexagons, heptagons, octagons).**

New Vocabulary

polygon
pentagon
hexagon
heptagon
octagon
nonagon
decagon
regular polygon

OK Math Online

macmillanmh.com

A **polygon** is a closed figure made up of line segments that do not cross each other. Figures that are open or figures that have curved sides are not considered polygons. Figures with line segments that cross each other are not considered polygons.

Polygons **Not Polygons**

You can classify a polygon by the number of its sides. Some common polygons are given in the table below.

Words	pentagon	hexagon	heptagon	octagon	nonagon	decagon
Number of Sides	5	6	7	8	9	10
Models	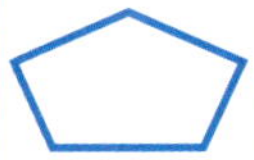					

A **regular polygon** has all sides congruent and all angles congruent. Equilateral triangles and squares are examples of regular polygons.

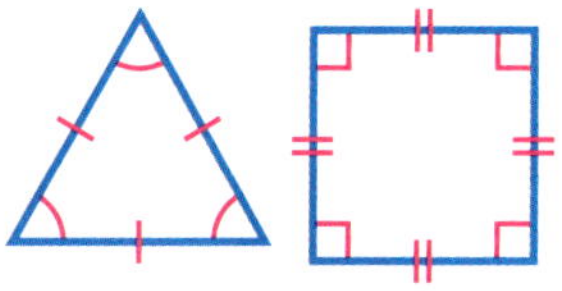

EXAMPLES Compare Polygons

1 Compare the polygons shown below by determining whether each figure is a polygon. If it is, classify the polygon and state whether it is regular. If it is not a polygon, explain why.

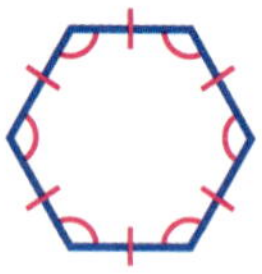

It is a polygon and a regular hexagon.

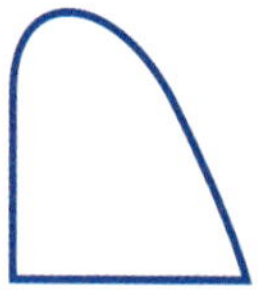

The figure is not a polygon since it has a curved side.

2 Compare and contrast the figures shown at the right.

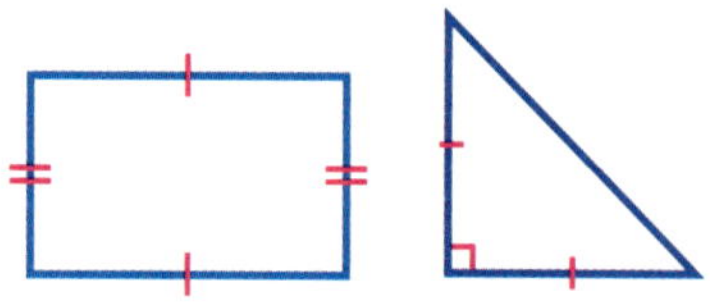

Figure A **Figure B**

Both figures are polygons. Figure A contains four sides and two pairs of congruent sides. It is a rectangle. Figure B has three sides and one pair of congruent sides. It is an isosceles right triangle.

CHECK What You Know

1. Compare the polygons shown below by determining whether each figure is a polygon. If it is, classify the polygon and state whether it is regular. If it is *not* a polygon, explain why. See Example 1 (p. OK18)

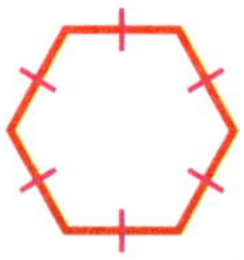

2. Compare and contrast the figures shown below. See Example 2 (p. OK18)

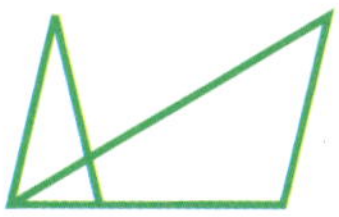

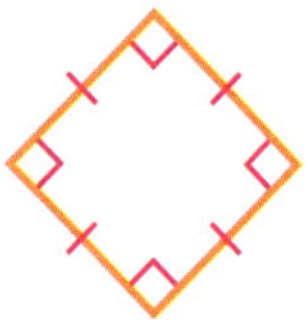

3. Talk About It Explain how you know whether or not a figure is a polygon.

Practice and Problem Solving

Compare the polygons shown by determining whether each figure is a polygon. If it is, classify the polygon and state whether it is regular. If it is *not* a polygon, explain why. See Example 1 (p. OK18)

4. 

5. 

Compare and contrast each figure. See Example 2 (p. OK18)

6.

Figure A

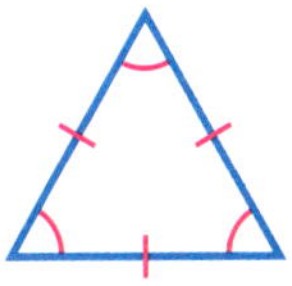

Figure B

7.

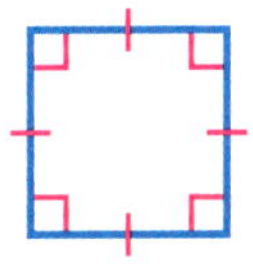

Figure A

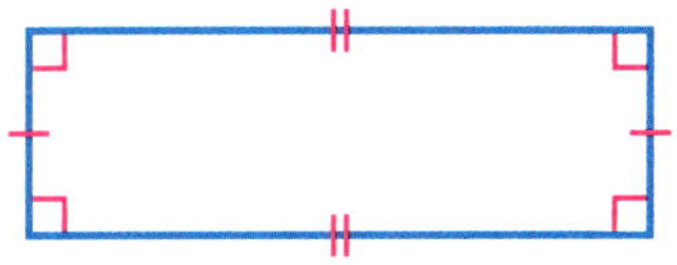

Figure B

H.O.T. Problems

8. **OPEN ENDED** Draw a six-sided polygon and a five-sided polygon. Then write a few sentences comparing the polygons.

9. **CHALLENGE** How many different polygons can be drawn that satisfy the conditions below? Justify your response with an explanation.

a triangle with one obtuse angle and three congruent sides

10. **WRITING IN ▶MATH** Can the circle at the right be classified as a polygon? Explain why or why not.

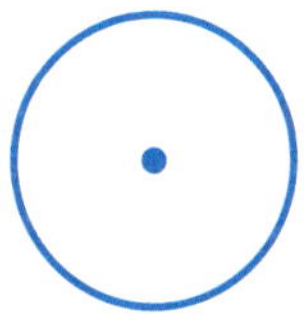

OCCT Practice

PASS3.1

11. All of the following statements are true about polygons except for which one?

A A polygon is classified by the number of sides it has.

B The sides of a polygon cross each other.

C A polygon is formed by three or more line segments.

D The sides of a polygon meet only at its endpoints.

OK 6 Circles

GET READY to Learn

A new dance mat was installed at the local fun center. It is in the shape of a circle and the distance across the circle is 8 feet.

MAIN IDEA

I will describe the characteristics of a circle.

OK PASS

3.1 Compare and contrast the basic characteristics of circles and polygons (triangles, quadrilaterals, pentagons, hexagons, heptagons, octagons).

New Vocabulary

circle
center
diameter
radius

OK Math Online

macmillanmh.com

You have already learned that a polygon is a simple closed figure formed by three or more sides. Recall that a circle is *not* a polygon because it is a curve and does not have three or more sides. A **circle** is the set of all points in a plane that are the same distance from a given point, called the **center**.

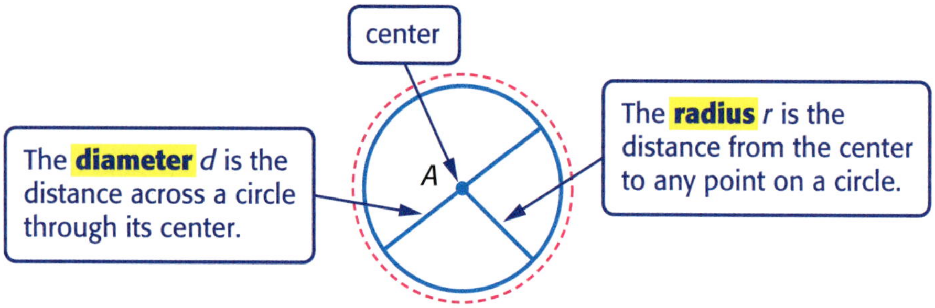

You can identify and describe these characteristics of a circle.

Real-World EXAMPLE

1 BASKETBALL The physical education teacher painted the line shown in red on the basketball court. Identify the part of circle the teacher painted.

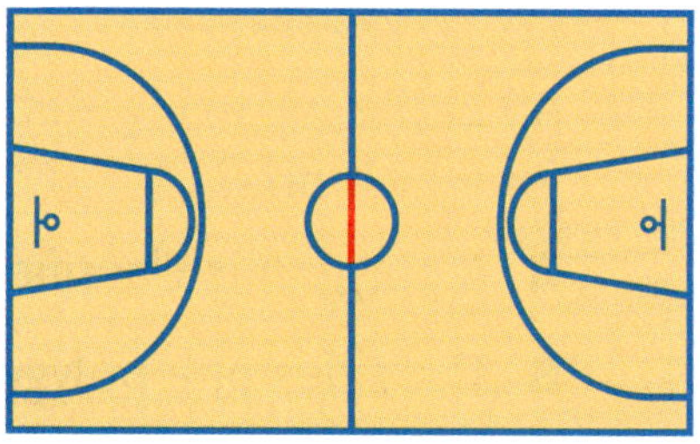

The teacher painted the diameter of the circle.

EXAMPLES Identify and Describe Parts of Circles

Identify and describe the segment shown of each circle.

2 

The segment shown runs from the center of the circle to a point on the circle. This segment is the *radius.*

3 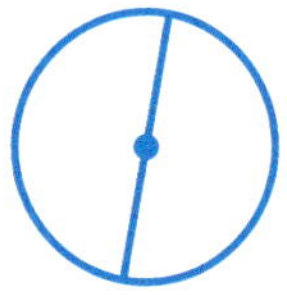

The segment shown runs through the center of the circle and represents the distance across the circle. This segment is the *diameter.*

Circle Relationships

Key Concept

Words	Symbols
The radius r of a circle is half the diameter d.	$r = \frac{1}{2}d$
The diameter d of a circle is 2 times the radius r.	$d = 2r$

EXAMPLE Describe Circle Relationships

4 **Refer to the circle at the right. Write a few sentences describing the relationships between the radius and the diameter.**

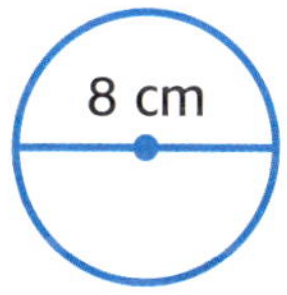

The radius is half the diameter. So, the radius is 4 centimeters.

CHECK What You Know

Identify each of the indicated parts or measures of the circles shown. Write a sentence describing the indicated part or measure. Examples 1–3 (p. OK20–21)

1. 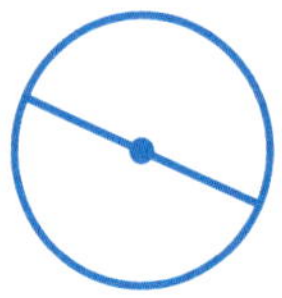

2. 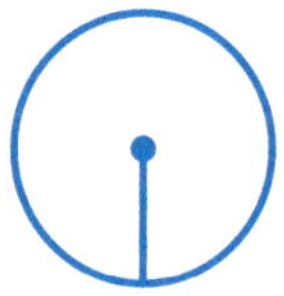

3. 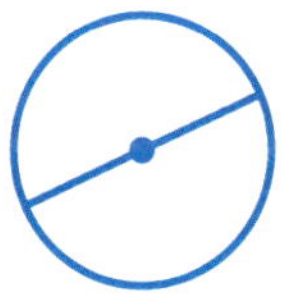

4. **MEASUREMENT** The radius of a circle is 12 inches. Write a few sentences describing the relationship between the radius and diameter. Example 4 (p. OK21)

5. Talk About It Explain how you can find the radius of any circle if you know the measure of the circle's diameter.

Practice and Problem Solving

Identify each of the indicated parts or measures of the circles shown. Write a sentence describing the indicated part or measure. Examples 1–3 (p. OK20–21)

6. 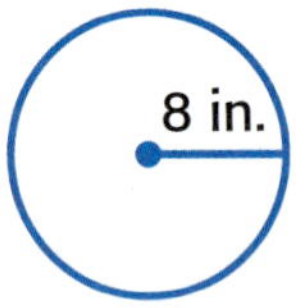

7. 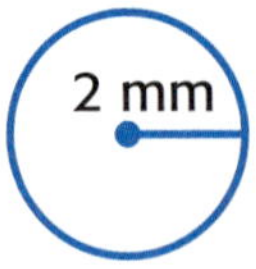

8. 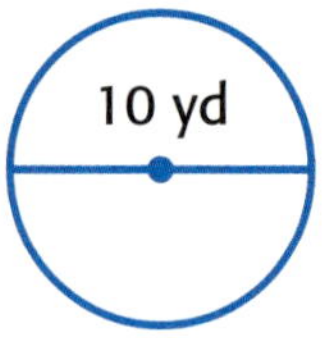

9. **SWIMMING POOLS** Pedro has a circular swimming pool with a radius of 7 feet. Write a few sentences describing the relationship between the radius and diameter. Example 4 (p. OK21)

10. **MEASUREMENT** The diameter of a circle is 6 inches. Write a few sentences describing the relationship between the radius and diameter.

H.O.T. Problems

11. **REASONING** Francesca wants to buy a swimming pool. She needs the outer edge(s) to be equidistant from the center of the pool. Will a rectangular swimming pool fit her needs? Explain.

12. **WRITING IN MATH** Draw a circle with a diameter less than 5 inches. Describe your circle.

OCCT Practice PASS3.1

13. All of the following statements are not true about the diameter of the bicycle wheel below except for which one?

A It is 26.2 inches.

B It is 13.1 inches.

C It is 6.55 inches.

D It is 41.134 inches.

14. Which of the following statements is true regarding the properties of a circle?

A It is a simple closed figure also known as a polygon.

B It is a curved figure with 3 or more sides.

C The diameter of a circle is half of the radius.

D It is not a polygon because it is not comprised of line segments.

OK 7 Fundamental Counting Principle

MAIN IDEA

I will use the fundamental counting principle to determine the number of possible combinations.

OK PASS

5.2.b Use the fundamental counting principle on sets with up to four items to determine the number of possible combinations (e.g. create a tree diagram to see possible combinations). *Also addresses 5M5.1, 5M5.2.*

New Vocabulary

Fundamental Counting Principle

OK Math Online

macmillanmh.com

GET READY to Learn

The Shoe Warehouse sells sandals in different colors and styles.

1. According to the table, how many colors of sandals are available?

2. How many styles are available?

3. Find the product of the two numbers you found in Exercises 1 and 2.

Color	Style
black	platform
brown	slides
tan	wedges
white	
red	

4. Draw a tree diagram to find the number of different color and style combinations. How does the number of outcomes compare to the product you found above?

In the activity above, you discovered that multiplication, instead of a tree diagram, can be used to find the number of possible outcomes in a sample space. This is called the **Fundamental Counting Principle**.

Fundamental Counting Principle — Key Concept

Words If event M has m possible outcomes and event N has n possible outcomes, then event M followed by event N has $m \times n$ possible outcomes.

EXAMPLE Find the Number of Outcomes

1 **Find the total number of outcomes when a coin is tossed and a number cube is rolled.**

coin		number cube		total	
2	·	6	=	12	Fundamental Counting Principle

There are 12 different outcomes.

Check Draw a tree diagram to show the sample space.

The Fundamental Counting Principle can be used to find the number of possible outcomes and solve probability problems in more complex problems, when there are more than two events.

Real-World EXAMPLE

2 JEANS The Jean Shop sells young men's jeans in different sizes, styles, and lengths, as shown in the table. Find the number of jeans available. Then find the probability of selecting a size 32 × 34 (waist × length) slim fit.

The Jeans Shop

Waist Size	Length (in.)	Style
30	30	slim fit
32	32	bootcut
34	34	loose fit
36		
38		

sizes		length		style		total
↓		↓		↓		↓
5	·	**3**	·	**3**	=	**45**

Fundamental Counting Principle

There are 45 different types of jeans to choose from. Out of the 45 possible outcomes, only one is favorable. So, the probability of randomly selecting a 32 × 34 slim fit is $\frac{1}{45}$.

CHECK What You Know

Use the Fundamental Counting Principle to find the total number of outcomes in each situation. Example 1 (p. OK23)

1. tossing a quarter, a dime, and a nickel

2. choosing scrambled, sunny-side up, or poached eggs with bacon or sausage, and milk or orange juice

3. choosing a number on a number cube and picking a marble from the bag at the right

4. CLOTHES Beth has 3 sweaters, 4 blouses, and 6 skirts that coordinate. Find the number of different outfits consisting of a sweater, blouse, and skirt that are possible. Then find the probability of randomly selecting a particular sweater-blouse-skirt outfit. Example 2 (p. OK24)

Practice and Problem Solving

Use the Fundamental Counting Principle to find the total number of outcomes in each situation. Example 1(p. OK23)

Bagels	Cream Cheese
plain	plain
blueberry	chive
cinnamon raisin	sun-dried tomato
garlic	

5. choosing a bagel with one type of cream cheese from the list shown in the table

6. choosing a number from 1 to 20 and a color from 7 colors

7. picking a month of the year and a day of the week

8. choosing from a comedy, horror, or action movie each shown in four theaters

9. choosing iced tea in regular, raspberry, lemon, or peach flavors; sweetened or unsweetened; and in a glass or a plastic container

10. The table shows the cell phone options offered by a company. If a phone with one payment plan and one accessory is given away at random, find the probability that it will be Brand B and have a headset. Explain. Example 2 (p. OK24)

Phone Brands	Payment Plans	Accessories
Brand A	Individual	Leather Case
Brand B	Family	Car Mount
Brand C	Business	Headset
	Government	Travel Charger

H.O.T. Problems

11. **Which One Doesn't Belong?** Identify the choices that do not result in the same number of outcomes as the other two. Explain.

9 drinks, 8 desserts

18 shirts, 4 pants

10 groups, 8 activities

12. **WRITING IN MATH** Explain when you might choose to use the Fundamental Counting Principle to find the number of possible outcomes and when you might choose to use a tree diagram.

OCCT Practice PASS5.2.b

13. Mrs. Lombardo's class had a popcorn party. The students could choose from 3 kinds of popcorn and 3 kinds of drinks. How many different combinations of one popcorn and one drink can a student choose?

A 6 choices

B 8 choices

C 9 choices

D 12 choices

GET READY FOR THE

OCCT

This spring, you will take your Grade 5 OCCT test. OCCT stands for Oklahoma Core Curriculum Tests. You will apply the concepts and skills that you have learned throughout the year in order to answer multiple-choice questions.

Multiple-Choice Items

You will select the correct response from four answer choices. Your teacher will provide you with an answer sheet to fill in your answer choices.

Tips for Success

- Read each problem carefully. Underline key words and think about different ways to solve the problem.
- Watch for key words like **not, least, greatest, first, last,** and **best.**
- Answer questions you are sure about first. If you do not know the answer to a question, skip it and go back to that question later.
- Check your answer to make sure it is reasonable.

How Can I Get Ready?

The OCCT covers the Oklahoma Priority Academic Student Skills (PASS) for Mathematics, Grade 5. The following pages give you practice questions similar to those found on the test. You can use these practice pages in the weeks before the test to determine if you are ready. If you are struggling with any of the items, lesson references are provided so you can go back and review from the pages in your textbook.

Algebraic Reasoning

1. What is the value of k in the equation below **(Lesson 6-1)** **(PASS1.2)**

$$k + 3 = 8$$

A 5 **C** 24
B 11 **D** 38

2. Four friends charge \$6 for each car they wash. The equation $6 \times c = 42$ represents the number of cars c they need to wash to make \$42. How many cars do they need to wash? **(Lesson 6-2)** **(PASS1.2)**

A 5 **C** 7
B 6 **D** 8

3. Hakan picked 68 apples as shown. If b represents the number of apples in the basket, which equation represents the situation? **(Lesson 6-1)** **(PASS1.1)**

A $4 + b = 68$
B $68 + b = 4$
C $4b = 64$
D $b - 4 = 68$

4. The function $d = 4 \times g + 3$ represents the price d in dollars it costs to bowl g games and rent shoes. How much does it cost to play 3 games and rent shoes? **(Lesson 6-6)** **(PASS1.1)**

A \$7 **C** \$15
B \$12 **D** \$36

5. Pedro gave two of his CDs to a friend. He has 7 CDs left. Which of the following equations can be used to find x, the number of CDs Pedro had originally? **(Lesson 6-1)** **(PASS1.1)**

A $x - 2 = 7$
B $2 + x = 7$
C $2x = 7$
D $7x = 2$

6. The function table below relates the number of pears p with the cost in dollars d. What is the cost of 12 pears? **(Lesson 5-6)** **(PASS1.1)**

Input (p)	Output (\$$d$)
6	1.20
7	1.40
8	1.60
12	■

A \$2.00 **C** \$2.40
B \$2.20 **D** \$2.60

7. There are 5 sticks of clay in a package. If p represents the number of packages, which function rule can be used to determine the number of sticks s in p packages? **(Lesson 6-6)** **(PASS1.1)**

A $s = p + 5$ **C** $p = 5 \times s$
B $p = s + 5$ **D** $s = 5 \times p$

8. Maria is 7 years older than her brother Raul. If Raul is y years old, which expression represents Maria's age? **(Lesson 6-6)** **(PASS1.1)**

A $7 + y$ **C** $7y$
B $7 - y$ **D** $7 \div y$

9. James ran twice as many miles as Ty. If Ty ran 4 miles, which equation could be used to find m, the number of miles James ran? **(Lesson 6-2)** **(PASS1.2)**

A $2 \times 4 = m$ **C** $2 \times m = 4$
B $4m = 2$ **D** $m + 2 = 4$

10. Corri made the graph below to show how much she makes mowing lawns. The equation $m = 6h$ describes how much money m she earns mowing lawns.

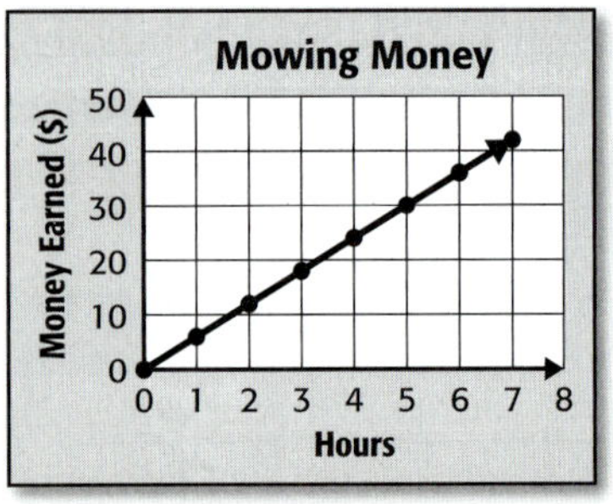

Determine how much money she would earn after mowing lawns for 4 hours. **(Lesson 6-2)** **(PASS1.1)**

A \$18 **C** \$30
B \$24 **D** \$36

11. Which of the following best explains how to mentally and correctly evaluate the following expression using the Associative Property? **(Lesson 2-7)** **(PASS1.3)**

$$23 + (36 + 7)$$

A Add 23 and 36 to get 59. Then add 7 to get 65.
B Add 23 and 7 to get 30. Then add 36 to get 56.
C Add 7 and 36 to get 43. Then add 23 to get 56.
D Add 23 and 7 to get 30. Then add 36 to get 66.

12. Which of the following properties is represented by the following? **(Lesson 3-2)** **(PASS1.3)**

$$3(5 + 1) = 3(5) + 3(1)$$

A Commutative Property of Addition
B Distributive Property
C Associative Property of Addition
D Identity Property

13. Neal caught 4 ground balls at baseball practice yesterday. Today he caught more ground balls. In the two days, he caught a total of 11 ground balls. Which equation could be used to find the number of ground balls he caught today? **(Lesson 6-1)** **(PASS1.1)**

A $x - 4 = 11$
B $4 + x = 11$
C $4x = 11$
D $11x = 4$

14. The price p of a sweater is \$12 more than the price of a pair of jeans at a certain department store. Which expression represents the price of a pair of jeans? **(Lesson 6-6)** **(PASS1.1)**

A $p + 12$ **C** $12p$
B $p - 12$ **D** $p \div 12$

15. Which of the following properties is represented by the following? **(Lesson 3-7)** **(PASS1.3)**

$$62 \cdot 44 = 44 \cdot 62$$

A Commutative Property of Multiplication
B Distributive Property
C Associative Property of Multiplication
D Identity Property

16. After Myron added \$25 to his bank account, his balance was \$132. If m represents the amount he originally had, the equation $25 + m = 132$ represents the situation. How much did he originally have? **(Lesson 6-1)** **(PASS1.2)**

Transaction	Balance (\$)
original	m
added \$25	$25 + m$

A \$97 **C** \$127
B \$107 **D** \$157

17. Which of the following properties is represented by the following? **(Lesson 2-7)** **(PASS1.3)**

$$15 + (9 + 5) = (15 + 5) + 9$$

A Commutative Property of Addition
B Distributive Property
C Associative Property of Addition
D Identity Property

18. The length of a garden is equal to five times its width w. Which expression could represent the length of the garden? **(Lesson 6-6)** **(PASS1.1)**

A $5 + w$ **C** $5w$
B $5 - w$ **D** $5 \div w$

19. A can of tennis balls contains three tennis balls. A physical education teacher needs 24 tennis balls. If c represents the number of cans, the equation $3 \times c = 24$ represents the situation. How many cans of tennis balls are needed? **(Lesson 6-2)** **(PASS1.1)**

A 6 **C** 8
B 7 **D** 9

20. Hans pays 15 cents for every text message that he sends. How much will he have to pay for sending 24 text messages? **(Lesson 6-6)** **(PASS1.1)**

A \$3.60
B \$3.75
C \$3.90
D \$4.05

21. Mei-Ling reads one book every three weeks. Which of the following equations can be used to find x, the number of books she reads in 15 weeks? **(Lesson 6-2)** **(PASS1.1)**

A $x - 3 = 15$
B $3 + x = 15$
C $3x = 15$
D $15x = 3$

22. Which of the following best explains how to mentally and correctly evaluate the following expression using the Distributive Property? **(Lesson 3-2)** **(PASS1.3)**

$$16(2 + 10)$$

A Add 16 and 2 to get 18. Then multiply 16 by 10 to get 160. Finally, add 18 and 160 to get 178.
B Multiply 16 by 2 to get 32. Then multiply 16 by 10 to get 160. Finally, add 32 and 160 to get 182.
C Multiply 16 by 2 to get 32. Then multiply 16 by 10 to get 160. Finally, add 32 and 160 to get 192.
D Multiply 16 by 2 to get 32. Then add 16 and 10 to get 260. Finally, add 32 and 26 to get 58.

23. What is the rule for the pattern shown in the table below? **(Lesson 5-6)** **(PASS1.1)**

Input	Output
1	2
2	5
3	8
4	11

A Multiply by 3. Then subtract 1.
B Multiply by 2. Then add 1.
C Add 1. Then multiply by 2.
D Subtract 1. Then multiply by 2.

24. A case of soda contains 12 cans. Felicia needs 96 cans of soda for a party. If c represents the number of cases, the equation $12 \times c = 96$ represents the situation. How many cases of soda are needed? **(Lesson 6-2)** **(PASS1.2)**

A 6 cases
B 7 cases
C 8 cases
D 9 cases

25. Study the pattern below. What is the rule for the pattern? **(Lesson 9-6)** **(PASS1.1)**

128, 64, 32, 16, 8, 4, 2

A Each number is twice the number before it.
B Each number is two more than the number before it.
C Each number is two less than the number before it.
D Each number is half the number before it.

26. What is the missing number in the pattern below? **(Lesson 9-6)** **(PASS1.1)**

34, 31, 28, 25, 22, ■, 16

A 21
B 19
C 18
D 17

27. Mary Anne scored 31 points in the basketball game. She scored 11 of those points in the first half. If s represents the points she scored in the second half, which equation describes this situation? **(Lesson 6-1)** **(PASS1.1)**

A $11s = 31$
B $s + 11 = 31$
C $s - 11 = 31$
D $s \div 11 = 31$

28. The function table below relates the number of movie tickets m with the cost in dollars d. What is the cost of 7 movie tickets? **(Lesson 5-6)** **(PASS1.1)**

Input (m)	Output ($\$d$)
2	17.00
3	25.50
4	34.00
5	42.50

A \$59.50
B \$51.00
C \$42.50
D \$8.50

Number Sense and Operation

1. Ben has played piano for $4\frac{11}{12}$ years and Alana has played piano for $2\frac{1}{12}$ years. Which of the following is the best estimate for how many more years Ben has played piano than Alana? **(Lesson 10-4)** **(PASS2.2.b)**

A 1 year

B 2 years

C 3 years

D 4 years

2. Alinda wants to run 25 miles each week. The table shows the distances she has run so far this week. How many more miles does she need to run to reach her goal? **(Lesson 2-6)** **(PASS2.1.a)**

Day	Distance (mi)
Monday	3.7
Tuesday	4.8
Wednesday	5.0
Thursday	4.3
Friday	4.1

A 7.6 miles

B 5.6 miles

C 4.1 miles

D 3.1 miles

3. All of the following numbers are factors of 50 except for which one? **(Lesson 9-1)** **(PASS2.1.d)**

A 25

B 10

C 5

D 4

4. The results of a 100-meter dash are listed below. Which shows the correct relationship between the numbers? **(Lesson 1-6)** **(PASS2.1.b)**

Runner	Time (s)
Chapa	18.051
Carlos	18.150

A $18.051 > 18.150$

B $18.051 = 18.150$

C $18.051 < 18.150$

D $18.150 < 18.051$

5. Choose the correct order of the fractions given from least to greatest. **(Lesson 8-5)** **(PASS2.1.b)**

$$\frac{1}{9}, \frac{1}{2}, \frac{1}{3}, \frac{1}{5}, \frac{1}{8}$$

A $\frac{1}{9}, \frac{1}{8}, \frac{1}{5}, \frac{1}{3}, \frac{1}{2}$

B $\frac{1}{2}, \frac{1}{3}, \frac{1}{5}, \frac{1}{8}, \frac{1}{9}$

C $\frac{1}{9}, \frac{1}{2}, \frac{1}{3}, \frac{1}{5}, \frac{1}{8}$

D $\frac{1}{8}, \frac{1}{5}, \frac{1}{3}, \frac{1}{2}, \frac{1}{9}$

6. Grace listed the following fractions on the board. All of the following statements are true concerning the list of fractions except for which one? **(Lesson 9-9)** **(PASS2.1.b)**

$$\frac{1}{2}, \frac{1}{3}, \frac{1}{4}, \frac{1}{5}, \frac{1}{6}$$

A Each denominator is one greater than the one before it.

B Each fraction is less than the one before it.

C All fractions are less than $\frac{1}{7}$.

D The greatest fraction shown is $\frac{1}{2}$.

7. Which set of decimals is listed from greatest to least? **(Lesson 1-7)** **(PASS2.1.b)**

A 4.111, 4.110, 4.104, 4.014
B 4.014, 4.111, 4.104, 4.110
C 4.014, 4.104, 4.110, 4.111
D 4.110, 4.014, 4.111, 4.104

8. Mr. Jackson bought 5 packages of ground beef for the family reunion. The packages weighed 3.2 pounds, 2.45 pounds, 2 pounds, 2.95 pounds, and 1.3 pounds. What is the total amount of ground beef he bought? **(Lesson 2-6)** **(PASS2.2.a)**

A 5.87 pounds
B 9.9 pounds
C 10.65 pounds
D 11.9 pounds

9. A wild animal refuge has 253 elephants. The manager wants to group the elephants in 14 feeding groups of equal size. The equation 253 ÷ 14 = 18 R1 represents this situation. Which statement is true? **(Lesson 4-4)** **(PASS2.2.c)**

A One elephant will be left over.
B There will be 14 elephants in each group.
C Eighteen elephants will be left over.
D Eighteen groups are needed so that no elephants will be left over.

10. Which of the following points would best represent the decimal 1.05? **(Lesson 1-6)** **(PASS2.1.b)**

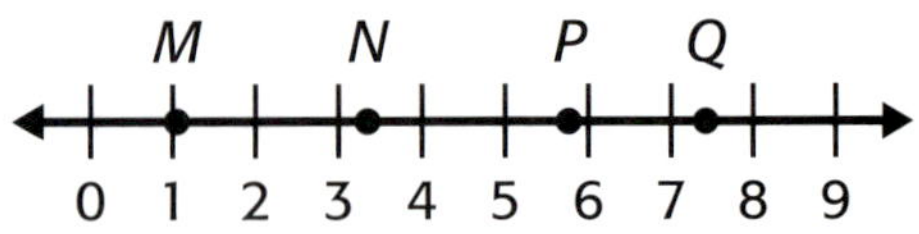

A Point M
B Point N
C Point P
D Point Q

11. Jarvis completed 3 out of his 5 homework assignments. Which fraction is less than $\frac{3}{5}$? **(Lesson 8-5)** **(PASS2.1.b)**

A $\frac{4}{5}$
B $\frac{3}{4}$
C $\frac{5}{8}$
D $\frac{1}{2}$

12. A pet store carries 8 puppies. Of these, 3 are golden retrievers. Which fraction is less than $\frac{3}{8}$? **(Lesson 8-5)** **(PASS2.1.b)**

A $\frac{2}{3}$
B $\frac{3}{5}$
C $\frac{1}{2}$
D $\frac{1}{4}$

13. Teresa ran a 200-meter race in 31.56 seconds. Her friend ran the same race in 34.06 seconds. How much faster was Teresa's time than her friend's? **(Lesson 3-5)** **(PASS2.1.b)**

A 2.5 seconds
B 3 seconds
C 3.04 seconds
D 3.5 seconds

14. Add $\frac{1}{3} + \frac{2}{9}$. Write the sum in simplest form. **(Lesson 10-3)** **(PASS2.2.b)**

A $\frac{5}{9}$

B $\frac{5}{12}$

C $\frac{4}{9}$

D $\frac{1}{4}$

15. The table shows the lengths of three bridges. Which bridge is the longest? **(Lesson 1-6)** **(PASS2.1.b)**

Bridge	Length (ft)
Bridge A	1,641.24
Bridge B	1,614.42
Bridge C	1,614.24
Bridge D	1,624.44

A Bridge A

B Bridge B

C Bridge C

D Bridge D

16. Greta and her friend went hiking and walked $\frac{2}{3}$ of a trail. What fraction of a mile of the trail remains? **(Lesson 10-4)** **(PASS2.2.b)**

A $\frac{1}{4}$

B $\frac{1}{3}$

C $\frac{1}{2}$

D $\frac{2}{3}$

17. Josie noticed that the outside temperature dropped 14 degrees overnight. Which integer best represents this situation? **(Lesson 12-5)** **(PASS2.1.c)**

A 41

B 14

C 0

D -14

18. If Brittany correctly marked 1.009, 0.893, 0.832, and 0.954 on a number line, which number would be closest to zero? **(Lesson 1-7)** **(PASS2.1.b)**

A 1.009

B 0.893

C 0.832

D 0.954

19. Which decimal is read as *seven and sixty-five thousandths?* **(Lesson 1-5)** **(PASS2.1.a)**

A 7.065

B 7.605

C 7.65

D 7,065.0

20. Which number is between 3.214 and 4.076? **(Lesson 1-7)** **(PASS2.1.b)**

A 3.178

B 3.231

C 4.103

D 4.306

21. Savannah wants to find the answer to $\frac{3}{4} - \frac{1}{12}$. What is the first step she should do? **(Lesson 10-4)** **(PASS2.2.b)**

A Change $\frac{3}{4}$ to $\frac{6}{8}$.

B Change $\frac{3}{4}$ to $\frac{9}{12}$.

C Subtract the numerators.

D Subtract the denominators.

22. Which symbol will make a true number sentence when it is placed in the blank? **(Lesson 9-9)** **(PASS2.1.b)**

$$\frac{5}{8} \ \_\_ \ \frac{5}{6}$$

A $<$
B $>$
C $=$
D $\div$

23. Aaron left $\frac{7}{8}$ of a pizza in the refrigerator. On Saturday, he ate $\frac{1}{2}$ of the pizza. What fraction of the entire pizza remained? **(Lesson 10-4)** **(PASS2.2.b)**

A $\frac{7}{8}$ **C** $\frac{1}{2}$
B $\frac{3}{4}$ **D** $\frac{3}{8}$

24. Which digit is in the hundredths place of the number 325.049? **(Lesson 1-5)** **(PASS2.1.a)**

A 9
B 5
C 3
D 4

25. The decimal 14.088 is read as which one of the following? **(Lesson 1-5)** **(PASS2.1.a)**

A fourteen and eighty-eight hundredths
B fourteen and eighty-eight thousandths
C fourteen and eighty-eight ten-thousandths
D fourteen hundred and eighty-eight

26. Which number line shows the graph of 0.5, 0.65, 0.85, and 0.9? **(Lesson 1-7)** **(PASS2.1.b)**

A
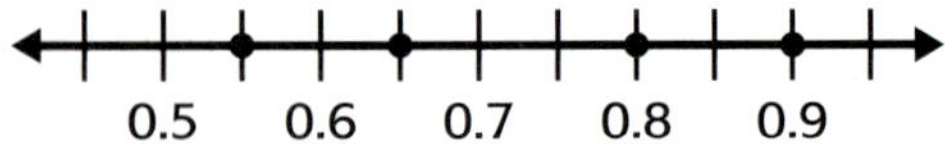

B
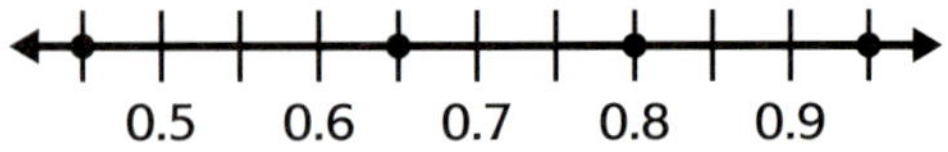

C
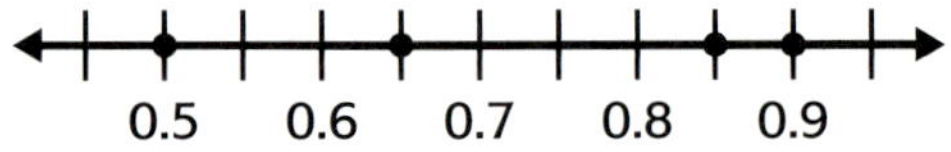

D
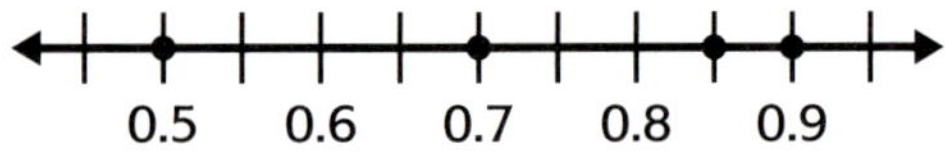

27. The table shows the high temperature yesterday for several cities. Which city had the lowest temperature? **(Lesson 12-5)** **(PASS2.1.c)**

City	Temperature (°F)
Lewis	−1
Neelon	3
Oxley	5
Thompson	−3

A Lewis
B Neelon
C Oxley
D Thompson

28. Louisa planted several types of mint in her garden. Of the garden, $\frac{1}{4}$ is peppermint, $\frac{2}{5}$ is spearmint, and $\frac{1}{6}$ is applemint. What fractional part of the garden are mint plants? **(Lesson 10-3)** **(PASS2.2.b)**

A $\frac{4}{15}$ **C** $\frac{13}{20}$
B $\frac{17}{30}$ **D** $\frac{49}{60}$

29. Which fraction represents the decimal 0.17? (Lesson 8-1) (PASS2.1.b)

A $\frac{17}{10}$ **C** $\frac{1}{7}$

B $\frac{17}{100}$ **D** $\frac{7}{1}$

30. Which digit is in the ten thousands place of the number 2,598,013? (Lesson 1-1) (PASS2.1.a)

A 2
B 5
C 8
D 9

31. The table lists the amount of ribbon the art teacher gave four students to complete their art projects. Which student received the most ribbon? (Lesson 9-9) (PASS2.1.b)

Student	Amount of Ribbon
Evan	$\frac{5}{8}$ inch
Kelsey	0.75 inch
Misu	$\frac{9}{16}$ inch
Taylor	0.5 inch

A Evan
B Kelsey
C Misu
D Taylor

32. Which digit is in the millions place of the number 5,048,732? (Lesson 1-1) (PASS2.1.a)

A 7
B 5
C 4
D 2

33. Which model represents 0.29? (Lesson 1-4) (PASS2.1.b)

A

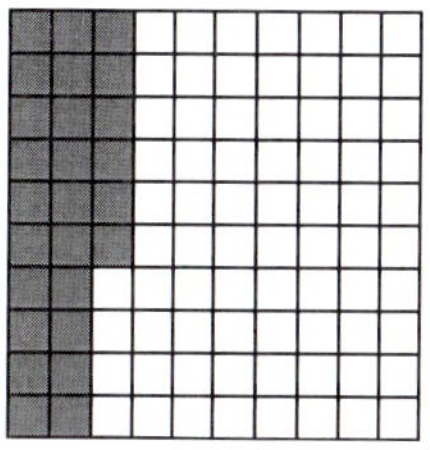

B

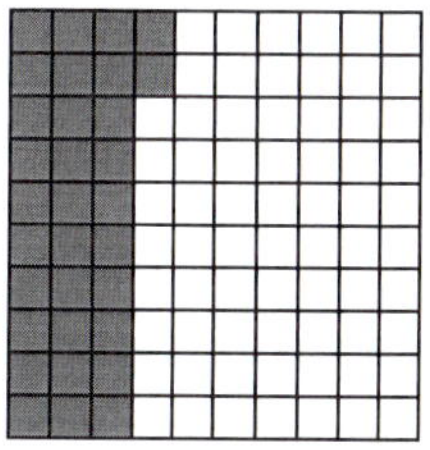

C

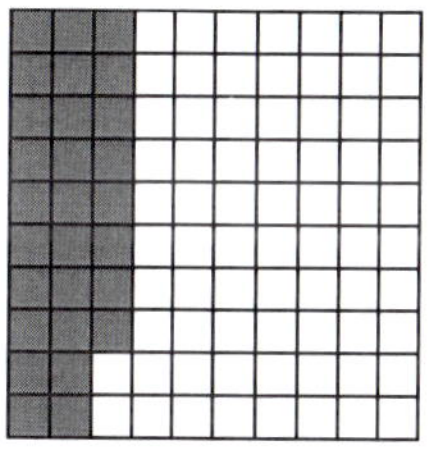

D

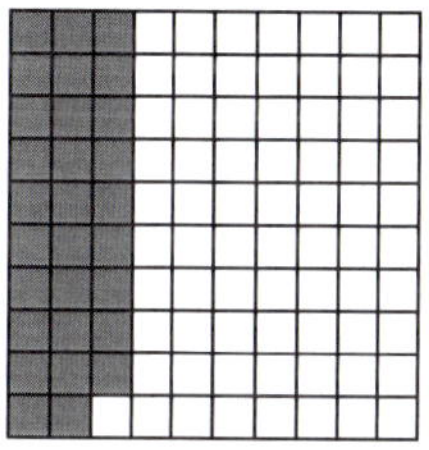

34. The decimal 97.645 is read as which one of the following? (Lesson 1-5) (PASS2.1.a)

A ninety-seven and six hundred forty-five thousandths
B ninety-seven and forty-five thousandths
C ninety-seven hundred and forty-five thousandths
D ninety-seven thousand six hundred forty-five

35. Jordan withdrew \$27 from his savings account. Which of the following integers best represents a withdrawal of \$27? **(Lesson 12-5)** **(PASS2.1.c)**

A −72
B −27
C 27
D 72

36. What decimal is shown in the model below? **(Lesson 1-4)** **(PASS2.1.b)**

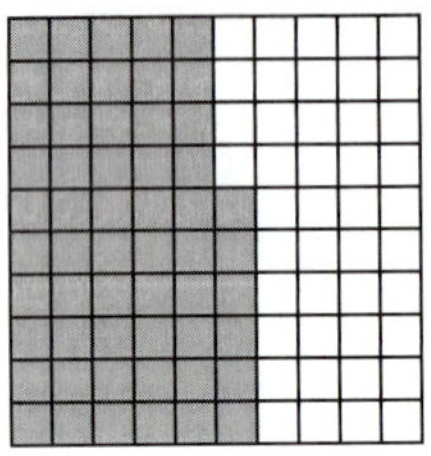

A 0.54
B 0.56
C 0.6
D 0.64

37. All of the following numbers are prime except for which one? **(Lesson 9-2)** **(PASS2.1.d)**

A 5
B 17
C 33
D 41

38. All of the following numbers are multiples of 4 except for which one? **(Lesson 9-7)** **(PASS2.1.d)**

A 12
B 20
C 36
D 46

39. The digit 3 is in which of the following place values of the number 3,112,900? **(Lesson 1-1)** **(PASS2.1.a)**

A millions
B hundred thousands
C ten thousands
D thousands

40. The number 1,000,000 is read as which one of the following? **(Lesson 1-1)** **(PASS2.1.a)**

A one thousand
B one hundred thousand
C one million
D one billion

41. All of the following numbers are composite except for which one? **(Lesson 9-2)** **(PASS2.1.d)**

A 11
B 27
C 35
D 44

42. All of the following numbers are factors of 32 except for which one? **(Lesson 9-1)** **(PASS2.1.d)**

A 12
B 8
C 4
D 2

43. Maggie made 127 cookies for a bake sale. She wants to package them in sets of 5 cookies per bag. Which of the following best represents the number of bags she needs? **(Lesson 4-6)** **(PASS2.2.c)**

A 26 bags with 5 cookies each

B 24 bags with 5 cookies each and 2 bags with 2 cookies each

C 25 bags with 5 cookies each and 1 bag with the remaining 2 cookies

D 23 bags with 5 cookies each and 3 bags with 2 cookies each

44. Refer to the model. Which statement is true concerning the fraction of circles that are shaded? **(Lesson 9-3)** **(PASS2.1.b)**

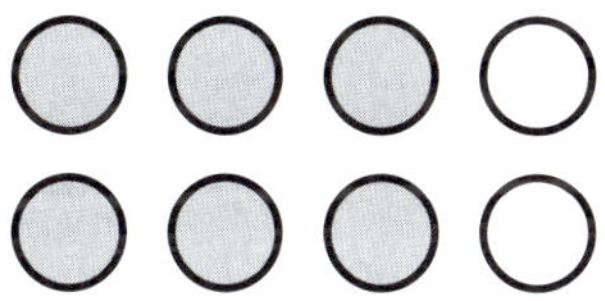

A Three-fourths of the circles are shaded.

B Two-thirds of the circles are shaded.

C One-half of the circles are shaded.

D One-fourth of the circles are shaded.

45. Abigail has 2,408 baseball cards. Which of the following equals 2,408? **(Lesson 1-1)** **(PASS2.1.a)**

A $200 + 40 + 8$

B $2{,}000 + 40 + 8$

C $2{,}000 + 400 + 80$

D $2{,}000 + 400 + 8$

46. Bradley is making a pie. The recipe calls for $3\frac{3}{4}$ cups of flour and $1\frac{1}{8}$ cups of sugar. Which is the best estimate for how much more flour is needed than sugar? **(Lesson 10-6)** **(PASS2.2.b)**

A 4 cups

B 2 cups

C $1\frac{1}{2}$ cups

D 1 cup

47. Divide 486 by 24. **(Lesson 4-4)** **(PASS2.2.c)**

A 20 R 6

B 20 R 4

C 20 R 1

D 20

48. Jared has 250 CDs in his CD collection. He wants to store them on shelves that hold 30 CDs on each shelf. Which of the following best represents the number of shelves he needs? **(Lesson 4-6)** **(PASS2.2.c)**

A 8 shelves with 30 CDs each and 2 shelves with 10 CDs each

B 9 shelves with 30 CDs each and 1 shelf with 20 CDs

C 10 shelves with 30 CDs each

D 8 shelves with 30 CDs each and 1 shelf with 10 CDs

49. A quarter weighs 0.2 ounce. Which of the following correctly compares the weight of a quarter with another number? **(Lesson 1-6)** **(PASS2.1.b)**

A $0.007 > 0.2$

B $0.022 > 0.2$

C $0.200 > 0.2$

D $1.2 < 0.2$

Geometry

1. Which is closest to the measure of the angle shown below? **(Lesson 13-3)** **(PASS3.2)**

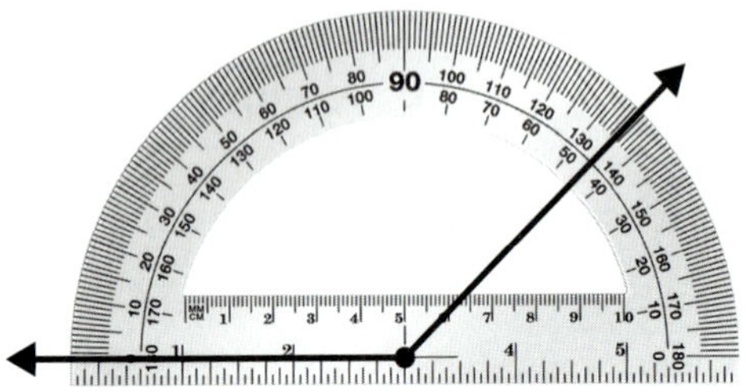

A 45°
B 55°
C 135°
D 145°

2. Classify the triangle below. **(Lesson 13-3)** **(PASS3.1)**

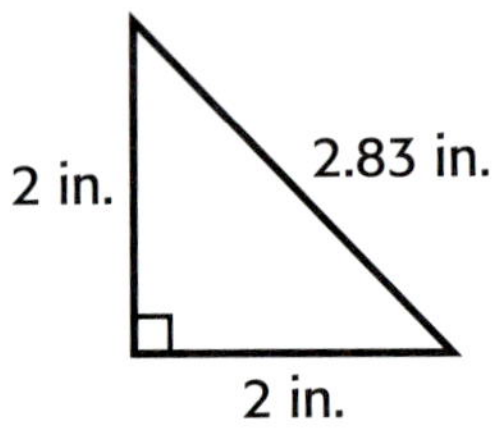

A right obtuse
B right equilateral
C right scalene
D right isosceles

3. Which of the following statements is true concerning a straight angle? **(Lesson OK 4)** **(PASS3.2)**

A A straight angle measures 90°.
B A straight angle measures 100°.
C A straight angle measures 180°.
D A straight angle measures 360°.

4. Which of the following statements classifies the angles in the triangle below? **(Lesson 13-3)** **(PASS3.1)**

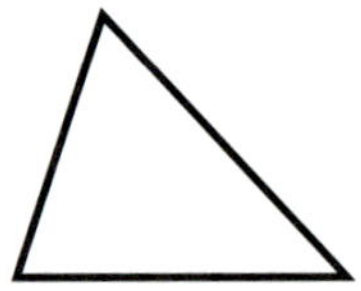

A two acute angles and one obtuse angle
B three acute angles
C one right angle and two acute angles
D two obtuse angles and one right angle

5. Use a protractor to find the measure of the angle shown below. **(Explore 13-3)** **(PASS3.2)**

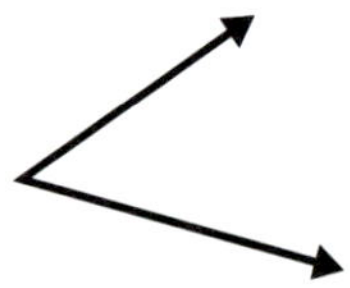

A 45°
B 50°
C 55°
D 60°

6. Kurt made a triangular garden in the corner of his yard as shown below. Classify the triangle. **(Lesson 13-3)** **(PASS3.1)**

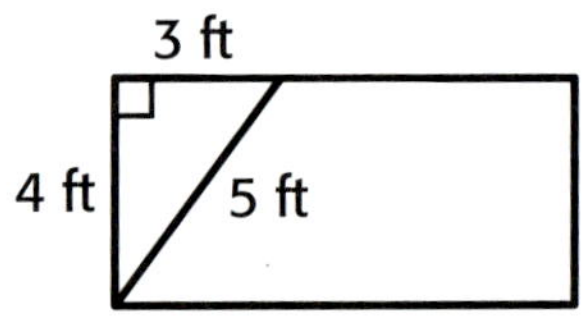

A obtuse scalene
B equilateral
C right isosceles
D right scalene

7. All of the triangles below are right triangles except for which one? **(Lesson 13-3)** **(PASS3.1)**

A 

B 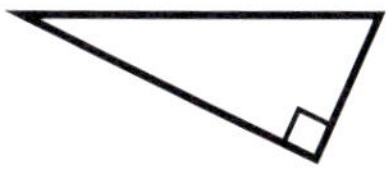

C 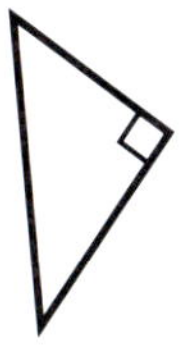

D 

8. Which of the following drawings best represents a quadrilateral with opposite sides parallel and congruent? **(Lesson OK 4)** **(PASS3.1)**

A 

C 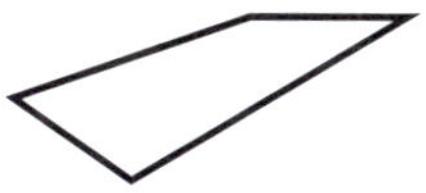

B 

D 

9. Use a protractor to measure and classify the angle shown below. **(Explore 13-3)** **(PASS3.2)**

A 30°; acute
B 70°; acute
C 120°; obtuse
D 150°; obtuse

10. Classify the following triangle in terms of sides and angles. **(Lesson 13-3)** **(PASS3.1)**

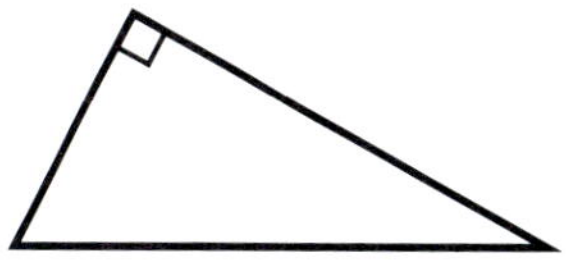

A isosceles right
B equilateral
C equiangular
D scalene right

11. What is the measure of angle *A*? **(Lesson 13-3)** **(PASS3.2)**

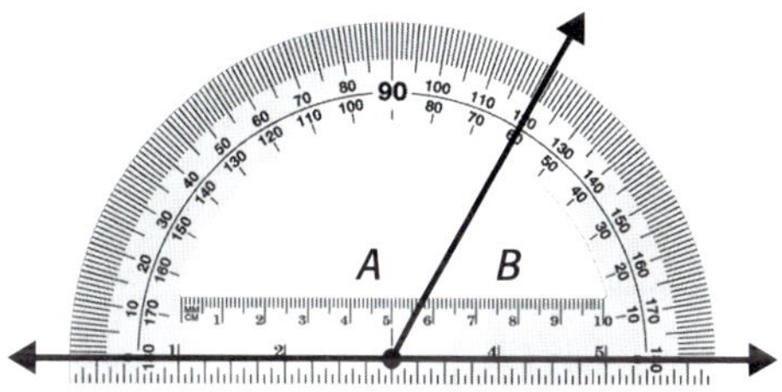

A 60°
B 90°
C 120°
D 180°

12. All of the following figures can be classified as a polygon except for which one? **(Lesson OK 6)** **(PASS3.1)**

A 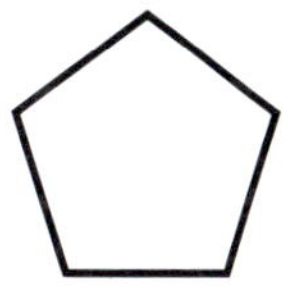

B 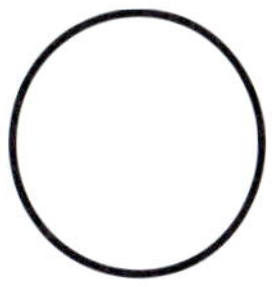

C 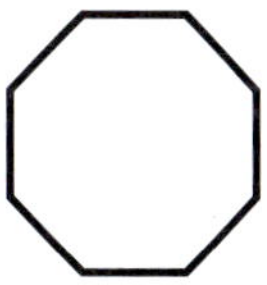

D 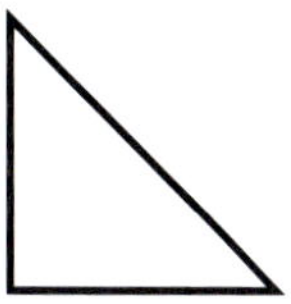

13. All of the following statements are true regarding polygons except for which one? **(Lesson 13-4)** **(PASS3.1)**

A Polygons have three or more sides.

B A circle is an example of a polygon.

C Polygons have straight sides.

D A quadrilateral is an example of a polygon.

14. All of the following figures have at least one right angle except for which one? **(Lesson 13-3)** **(PASS3.1)**

A 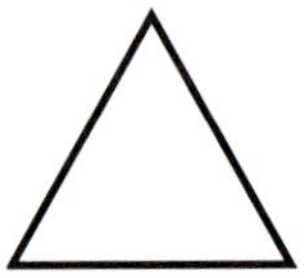

B 

C 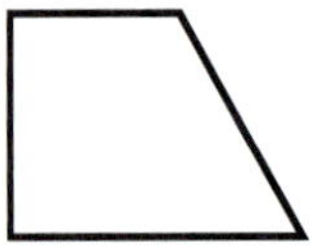

D 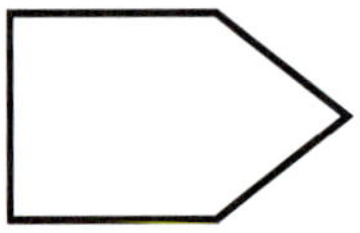

15. All of the following terms can be used to describe the figure below except for which one? **(Lesson 13-4)** **(PASS3.1)**

A quadrilateral

B polygon

C rectangle

D pentagon

16. The diagram shows a map of Wild Horse hiking area. What type of triangle is created by Limestone Ridge, Horseshoe Falls, and Stony Point? **(Lesson 13-3)** **(PASS3.1)**

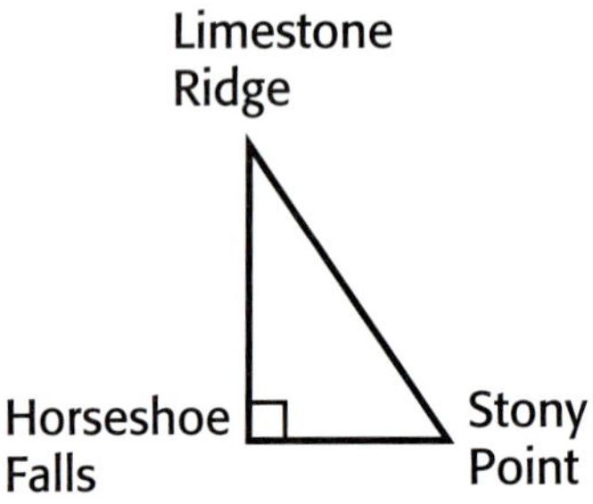

A right triangle

B acute triangle

C equilateral triangle

D isosceles triangle

17. Which of the following polygons contains only obtuse angles? **(Lesson 13-3)** **(PASS3.2)**

A 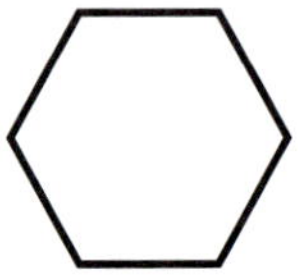

B 

C 

D 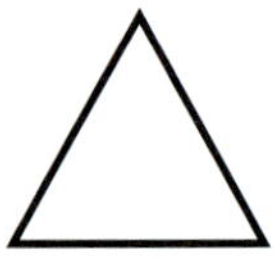

18. Which angle measure is considered an obtuse angle? **(Explore 13-3)** **(PASS3.2)**

A 31°

B 89°

C 90°

D 162°

Measurement

1. What is the area of the rectangle below? **(Lesson 14-3)** **(PASS4.2.b)**

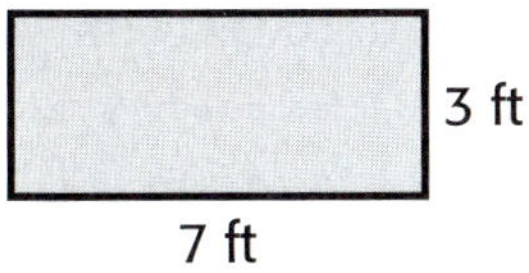

A 21 square feet **C** 14 square feet
B 17 square feet **D** 10 square feet

2. Which of the following shows an angle that measures 80°? **(Lesson 13-3)** **(PASS4.1.a)**

A

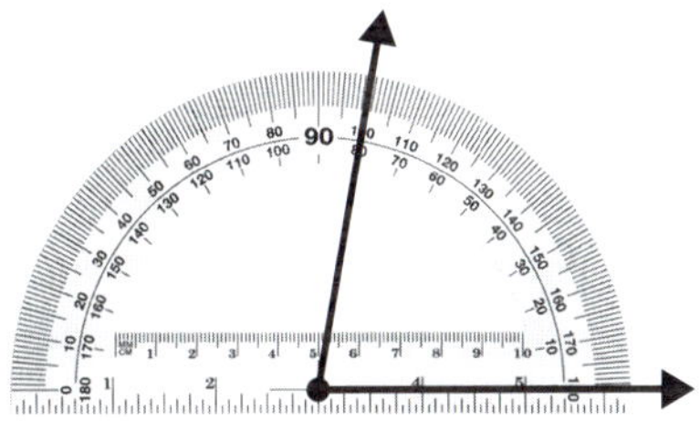

B

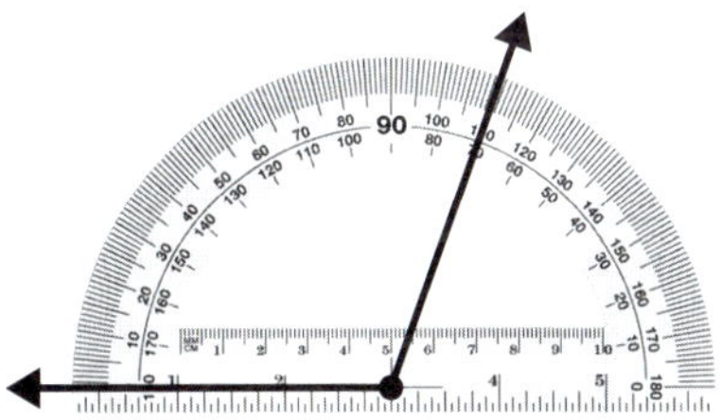

C

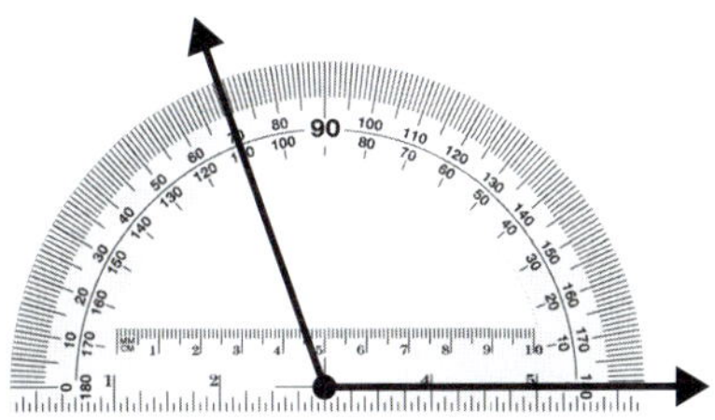

D

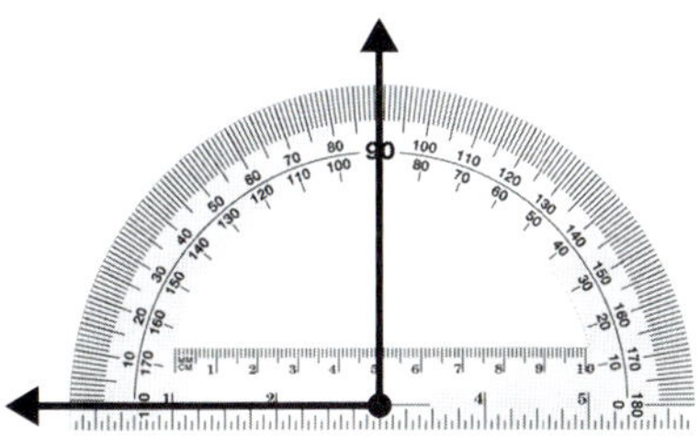

3. Felisa watched a movie that lasted 110 minutes. How many hours and minutes is this? **(Lesson 11-5)** **(PASS4.1.c)**

A 1 hour 50 minutes
B 2 hours 10 minutes
C 2 hours 20 minutes
D 2 hours 30 minutes

4. The table below shows the prices of various sizes of picture frames. What is the total cost of a 3″ by 5″ and an 8″ by 10″ picture frame? **(Lesson 2-6)** **(PASS4.2)**

Size	Price ($)
3″ by 5″	1.99
5″ by 7″	2.59
8″ by 10″	5.79

A \$3.80
B \$4.58
C \$7.78
D \$8.38

5. Find the area of the square below. **(Lesson 14-3)** **(PASS4.2.b)**

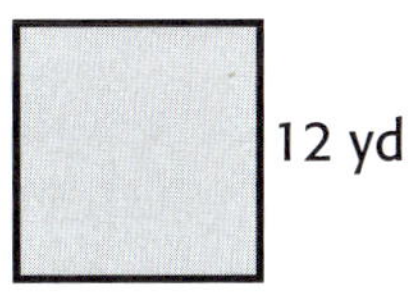

A 256 yd^2
B 144 yd^2
C 48 yd^2
D 24 yd^2

6. Martina bought a new MP3 player for \$79.99. She also downloaded two songs onto her MP3 player. The first song cost \$0.45 and the second song cost \$0.89. What was the total cost of the MP3 player and the two songs? **(Lesson 2-6)** **(PASS4.2)**

A \$85.50
B \$81.33
C \$80.88
D \$80.44

7. Which of the following quadrilaterals has a perimeter of 80 centimeters? **(Lesson 14-1)** **(PASS4.1.b)**

A
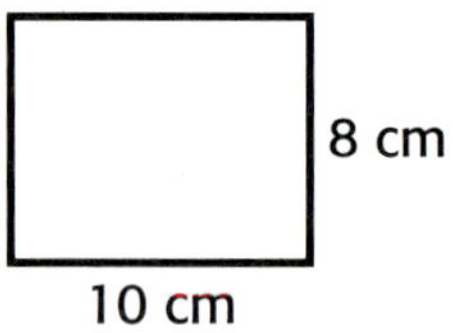

B
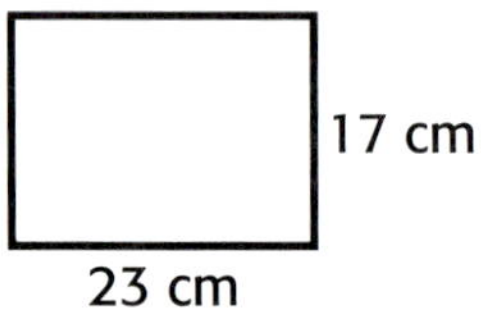

C
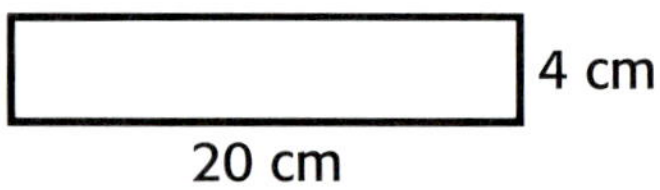

D
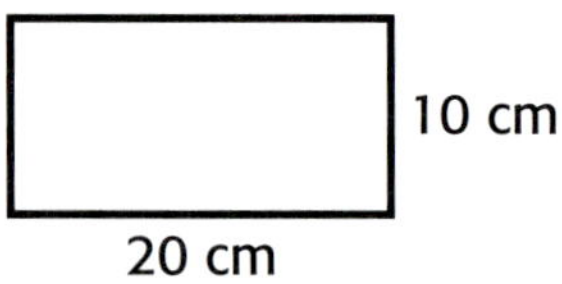

8. All of the following are equivalent to 5 meters except for which one? **(Lesson 12-1)** **(PASS4.1.c)**

A 5,000 millimeters
B 500 centimeters
C 0.05 kilometers
D 0.005 kilometers

9. A square has a side length of 5 inches. A larger square has a side length of 10 inches. How much greater is the area of the larger square than the smaller square? **(Lesson 14-3)** **(PASS4.1.b)**

A 5 in^2 **C** 20 in^2
B 15 in^2 **D** 75 in^2

10. The area of the rectangle shown below is 105 square feet. What is the perimeter of the rectangle? **(Lesson 14-3)** **(PASS4.1.b)**

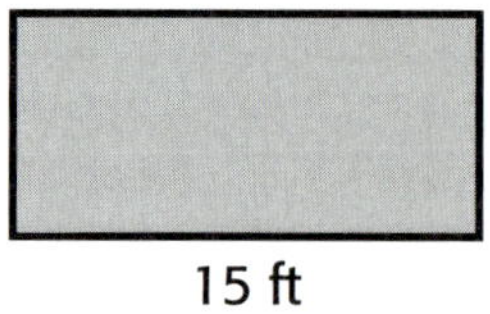

A 7 ft
B 44 ft
C 52 ft
D 210 ft

11. What is the perimeter of the rectangle shown below? **(Lesson 14-1)** **(PASS4.1.b)**

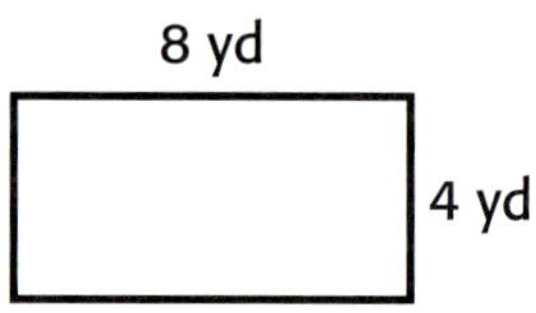

A 64 yd **C** 24 yd
B 32 yd **D** 12 yd

12. There are about 2.54 centimeters in one inch. Which expression gives the apprxoimate number of centimeters in three inches? **(Lesson 2-6)** **(PASS4.1.c)**

A $2.54 + 3 + 2.54$
B $2.54 + 2.54$
C $2.54 + 3$
D $2.54 + 2.54 + 2.54$

13. Which is the area of the soccer field illustrated below? **(Lesson 14-3)** **(PASS4.2.b)**

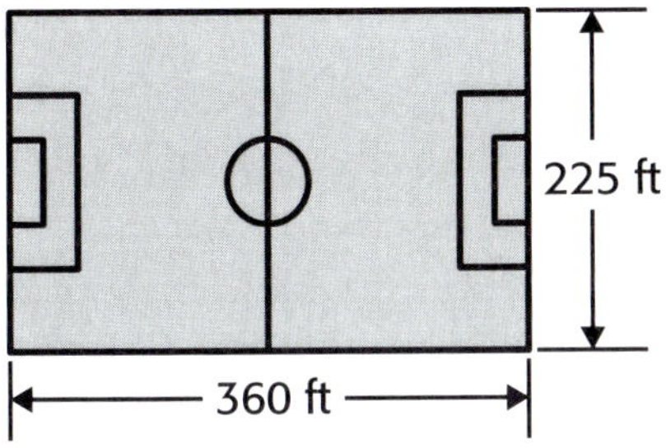

A 1,170 ft
B 8,100 ft^2
C 81,000 ft^2
D 810,000 ft^2

14. What is the area of the rectangle shown below, in square feet? **(Lesson 14-3)** **(PASS4.1.b)**

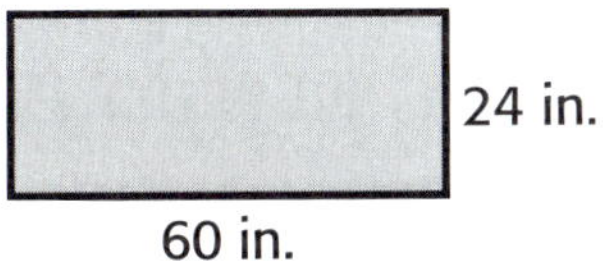

A 1,440 ft^2
B 168 ft^2
C 14 ft^2
D 10 ft^2

15. Which of the following is a reasonable estimate for the height of a ceiling in a bedroom? **(Lesson 12-1)** **(PASS4.1.c)**

A 3 millimeters
B 3 centimeters
C 3 meters
D 3 kilometers

16. The world record for holding breath underwater is 17 minutes 4 seconds. How many total seconds is this? **(Lesson 11-5)** **(PASS4.1.c)**

A 174 seconds
B 257 seconds
C 1,020 seconds
D 1,024 seconds

17. A new skate park is shaped like the rectangle shown below. What is the area of the skate park? **(Lesson 14-3)** **(PASS4.1.b)**

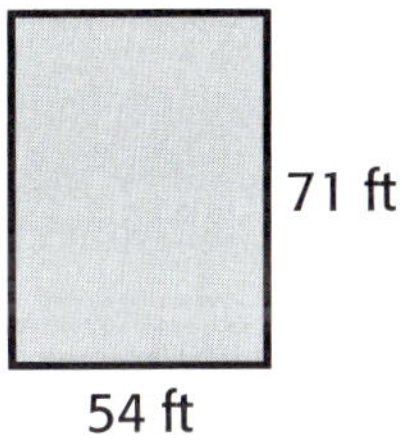

A 125 ft^2
B 250 ft^2
C 1,917 ft^2
D 3,834 ft^2

18. Tickets for the school play cost \$4.65 for students and \$6.75 for adults. Pearl purchased 1 adult ticket and 1 student ticket using a \$20 bill. Which is the best estimate for the amount of change she should receive? **(Lesson 9-7)** **(PASS4.2)**

A about \$4.00
B about \$6.00
C about \$8.00
D about \$10.00

19. An architect's plans for a new house show the thickness of the doors to be used in each room. Which of the following units of length is most appropriate to use to measure the thickness of the doors? **(Lesson 11-1)** **(PASS4.1.c)**

A inch
B foot
C yard
D mile

20. Which of the following measurements is the least? **(Lesson 12-4)** **(PASS4.1.c)**

A 5 liters
B 1,000 milliliters
C 2 liters
D 600,000 milliliters

21. Mr. Mitchell is roasting a turkey. He puts the turkey in the oven at 11:25 A.M. The turkey needs to be in the oven for 3 hours 45 minutes. When will the turkey be ready to take out of the oven? **(Lesson 11-7)** **(PASS4.1.c)**

A 2:05 P.M.
B 2:10 P.M.
C 3:05 P.M.
D 3:10 P.M.

22. Diego needs 3 pens. He can buy one pen for \$1.52 or a package of 3 pens for a total of \$3. How much will he save if he buys a package of 3 pens rather than three individual pens? **(Lesson 2-5)** **(PASS4.2)**

A \$1.52
B \$1.54
C \$1.55
D \$1.56

23. Which of the following units would be most appropriate for finding the perimeter of the rectangle shown below? **(Lesson 12-1)** **(PASS4.2.b)**

A liters
B millimeters
C grams
D kilograms

24. The mass of 6 medium apples is 1 kilogram. Which measurement is equivalent to the mass of the apples? **(Lesson 12-3)** **(PASS4.1.c)**

A 100 grams
B 1,000 grams
C 1,000 centigrams
D 10,000 centigrams

25. All of the following measurements are equivalent except for which one? **(Lesson 12-1)** **(PASS4.1.c)**

A 0.001 kilometers
B 1 meter
C 10 centimeters
D 1,000 millimeters

26. A pony is a small horse that is less than 147 centimeters tall. How high is this in meters? **(Lesson 12-1)** **(PASS4.1.c)**

A 1.47 meters
B 14.7 meters
C 147 meters
D 1,470 meters

27. Christina has a pitcher that holds 1 liter of lemonade. Which measurement is equivalent to 1 liter? **(Lesson 12-4)** **(PASS4.1.c)**

A 10 milliliters
B 100 milliliters
C 1,000 milliliters
D 10,000 milliliters

Data Analysis

1. Emma, Aisha, and Chi-Wei are selling magazine subscriptions. Which of the following information is needed to complete the graph? **(Lesson 7-6)** **(PASS5.1.a)**

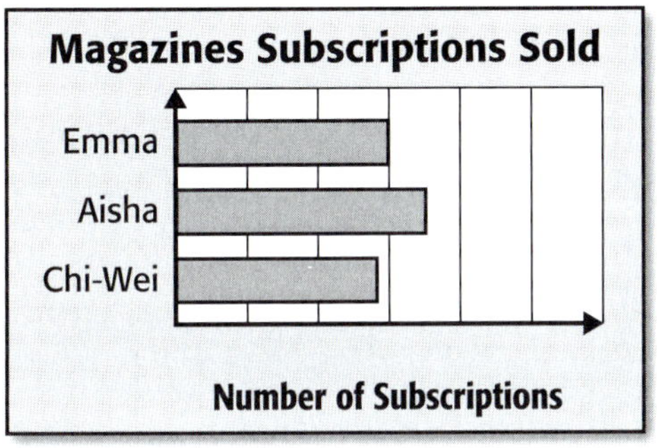

A the scale on the horizontal axis

B the names of the magazines

C the person who sold the least

D the title of the graph

2. The graph shows how far Kimi rode her bike for various lengths of time. At this rate, predict how far she will ride in $3\frac{1}{2}$ hours. **(Lesson 6-5)** **(PASS5.1.a)**

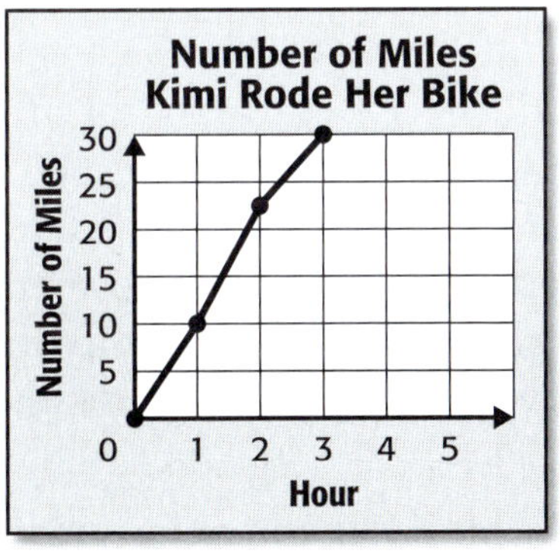

A 25 miles

B 30 miles

C 35 miles

D 45 miles

3. Sam kept track of the number of Calories that he burned per minute while running on the treadmill. How long did it take him to burn 60 Calories? **(Lesson 7-3)** **(PASS5.1.a)**

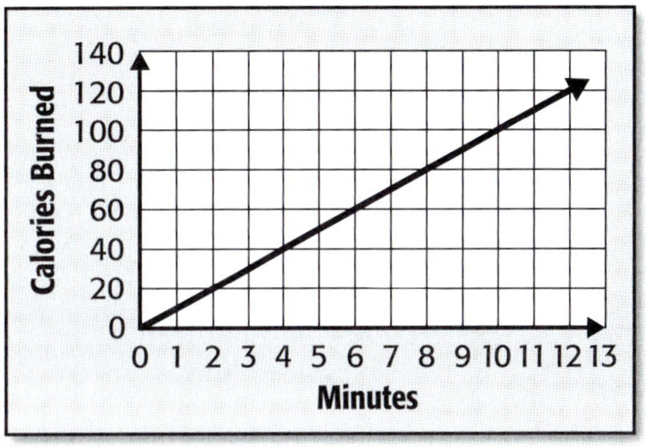

A 4 minutes

B 6 minutes

C 8 minutes

D 10 minutes

4. The graph below shows the average speed of various types of athletes. Which type of athlete has an average speed of about 11 miles per hour? **(Lesson 7-6)** **(PASS5.1.a)**

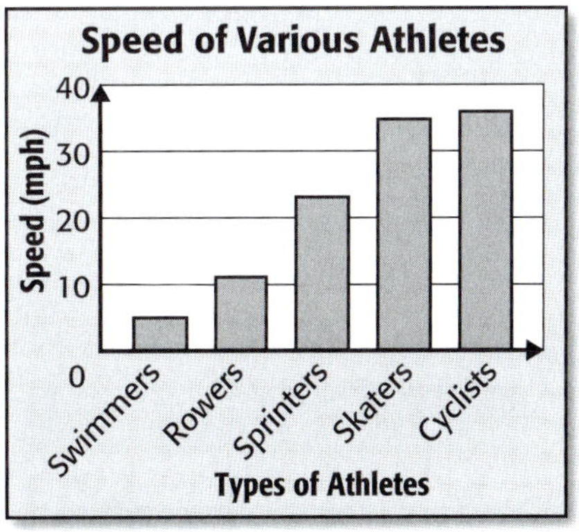

A swimmer

B rower

C sprinter

D skater

5. Which of the following diagrams can be used to find the possible combinations of a red, blue, or yellow shirt and brown or black pants? **(Lesson 15-4)** **(PASS5.2.b)**

A **Shirt** **Pants**

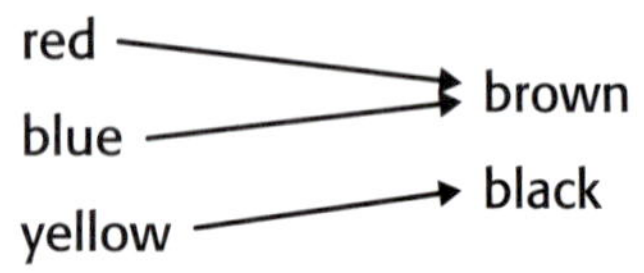

B **Shirt** **Pants**

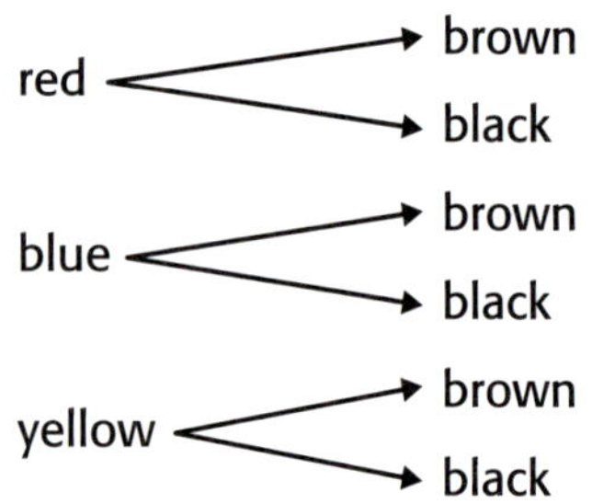

C **Shirt** **Pants**

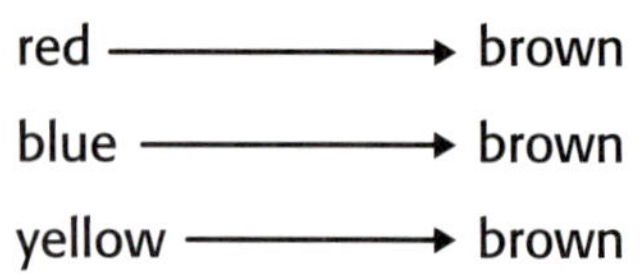

D **Shirt** **Pants**

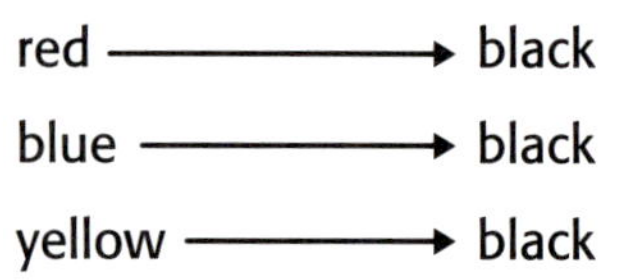

6. The table shows the number of magazine subscriptions sold by each student in Molly's class. Which of the following is the median of the data? **(Lesson 7-1)** **(PASS5.3)**

Number of Subscriptions Sold				
0	2	1	1	5
0	4	3	2	2
3	1	1	0	4

A 1

B 2

C 3

D 5

7. A hat contains 5 red marbles, 2 yellow marbles, and 3 blue marbles. If one marble is randomly selected from the hat, what is the probability that a yellow marble will be selected? **(Lesson 15-2)** **(PASS5.2.a)**

A $\frac{4}{5}$

B $\frac{7}{10}$

C $\frac{2}{5}$

D $\frac{1}{5}$

8. The table shows the number of pets each person has in Myron's class. Which of the following is the range of the data? **(Lesson 7-1)** **(PASS5.3)**

Number of Pets in Myron's Class				
1	3	2	1	4
0	1	0	3	1
0	2	1	0	2

A 1

B 2

C 3

D 4

9. Nico has 10 letter cards that spell the word *ELEMENTARY* when put together. If he picks one card without looking, what is the probability that it will have the letter E on it? **(Lesson 15-2)** **(PASS5.2.a)**

A $\frac{3}{10}$

B $\frac{7}{10}$

C $\frac{3}{5}$

D $\frac{2}{5}$

10. Which data set has a mode of 5? **(Lesson 7-1)** **(PASS5.3)**

A {1, 1, 3, 4, 4, 4, 5}
B {2, 3, 4, 5, 7, 8, 8}
C {3, 3, 3, 3, 5, 5, 5}
D {2, 3, 4, 5, 5, 5, 5}

11. A group of 25 people were surveyed about their income. The median income was $30,000. Which statement describes the group? **(Lesson 7-1)** **(PASS5.3)**

A The average of their incomes is $30,000.
B The most frequent answer was $30,000.
C $30,000 was the middle number when the incomes were arranged from smallest to largest.
D $30,000 was the difference between the highest and the lowest income.

12. The circle graph below shows the portion of Antwon's day that he spends doing various activities. Which activity does Antwon spend the least amount of time doing? **(Lesson OK 1)** **(PASS5.1.a)**

Antwon's Day

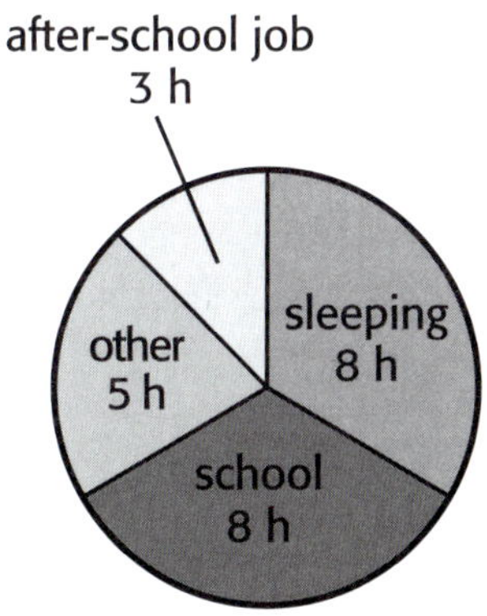

A sleeping
B school
C after-school job
D other

13. Patty has four pairs of pants, seven dress shirts, and three pairs of shoes. Assuming that all outfits can be worn in a fashionable way, how many outfits consisting of a pair of pants, a dress shirt, and a pair of shoes can Patty wear? **(Lesson OK 7)** **(PASS5.3)**

A 84
B 56
C 28
D 14

14. A group of motorists were surveyed about the number of minutes needed to drive to work each day. Their responses were: 10, 20, 35, 90, 40, 25, 30, 45, 15, and 60. What is the range of the data? **(Lesson 7-1)** **(PASS5.3)**

A 10
B 15
C 50
D 80

15. Look at the following menu. How many different combinations of side, sandwich and drink could you choose for lunch? **(Lesson OK 7)** **(PASS5.2)**

The Lunch Spot		
Sides	**Sandwiches**	**Drinks**
veggie chips	hamburger	tea
fries	hot dog	milk
	grilled chicken	water

A 3
B 6
C 9
D 18

To the Student

As you gear up to study mathematics, you are probably wondering, "What will I learn this year?"

- **Number and Operations:** Estimate and find quotients of whole numbers, including quotients of multidigit numbers.
- **Number and Operations:** Add and subtract fractions with unlike denominators.
- **Geometry and Measurement:** Find volume and surface area of three dimensional figures.

Along the way, you'll learn more about problem solving, how to use the tools and language of mathematics, and how to THINK mathematically.

How to Use Your Math Book

Have you ever been in class and not understood all of what was being presented? Or, you understood everything in class, but got stuck on how to solve some of the homework problems? Don't worry. You can find answers in your math book!

- **Read** the **MAIN IDEA** at the beginning of the lesson.
- **Find** the **New Vocabulary** words, **highlighted in yellow**, and read their definitions.
- **Review** the **EXAMPLE** problems, solved step-by-step, to remind you of the day's material.
- **Refer** to the **EXTRA PRACTICE** boxes that show you where you can find extra exercises to practice a concept.
- **Go** to **OK Math Online** where you can find extra examples to coach you through difficult problems.
- **Review** the notes you've taken on your **FOLDABLES**®.
- **Refer** to the **Remember** boxes for information that may help you with your examples and homework practice.

Treasure Hunt

Chapter 1

Let's Get Started

Use the Treasure Hunt below to learn where things are located in each chapter.

1. What is the title of Chapter 1?
2. How can you tell what you'll learn in Lesson 1-1?
3. What is the title of the feature in Lesson 1-1 that tells you how to read a numer on a place-value chart?
4. Suppose you're doing your homework on page 22 and you get stuck on Exercise 13. Where could you find help?
5. List the new vocabulary words that are presented in Lesson 1-1.
6. What is the key concept presented in Lesson 1-4?
7. How many examples are presented in Lesson 1-6?
8. In the margin of Lesson 1-6, there is a Vocabulary Link. What can you learn from that feature?
9. What is the Web address where you could find extra examples?
10. What problem-solving strategy is presented in the Problem-Solving Strategy in Lesson 1-8?
11. What is the Web address that would allow you to take a self-check quiz to be sure you understand the lesson?
12. On what pages will you find the Study Guide and Review for Chapter 1?
13. Suppose you can't figure out how to do Exercise 17 in the Study Guide on page 51. Where could you find help?

Math? Symbols!

Start Smart

Let's Review!

The Capitol Dome

START 1 SMART

Problem Solving

Appalachian Mountains

Black Mountain is the highest point in Kentucky. The peak of Black Mountain is 4,145 feet high. Brush Mountain is another tall mountain in Kentucky. Its height is 3,153 feet.

How much taller is Black Mountain than Brush Mountain?

You can use the four-step problem-solving plan to solve many types of problems. The four steps are Understand, Plan, Solve, and Check.

Did you Know?
Black Mountain is one of the tallest mountains in Appalachia outside the Blue Ridge Mountains region.

Understand

- **Read the problem carefully.**
- **What facts do you know?**
- **What do you need to find?**

You know the heights of Black Mountain and Brush Mountain. You need to find how much taller Black Mountain is than Brush Mountain.

Plan

- **Think about how the facts relate to each other.**
- **Plan a strategy to solve the problem.**

Black Mountain is 4,145 feet tall. Brush Mountain is 3,153 feet tall. To find how much taller Black Mountain is than Brush Mountain, subtract.

Solve

- **Use your plan to solve the problem.**

	3 10 14	
	~~4~~,~~1~~~~4~~5 feet	Black Mountain
−	3,153 feet	Brush Mountain
	992 feet	

Black Mountain is 992 feet taller than Brush Mountain.

Check

- **Look back.**
- **Does your answer make sense?**
- **If not, solve the problem another way.**

You can check the subtraction by using addition.

Brush Mountain		difference		Black Mountain
↓		↓		↓
3,153	+	992	=	4,145

This is the height of Black Mountain. So, the answer is correct.

CHECK What You Know

1. List and describe the steps of the four-step problem-solving plan.

2. WRITING IN ►MATH Use the mountain facts on page 2 to write a real-world problem. Ask a classmate to solve the problem.

START 2 SMART

Number and Operations

New York's Coney Island

The historic Wonder Wheel on Coney Island in New York was built in 1920. It stands 150 feet tall and can hold 144 people.

After riding for five minutes, passengers will have completed about $1\frac{1}{2}$ revolutions along the outer wheel. The model shows the fraction $1\frac{1}{2}$.

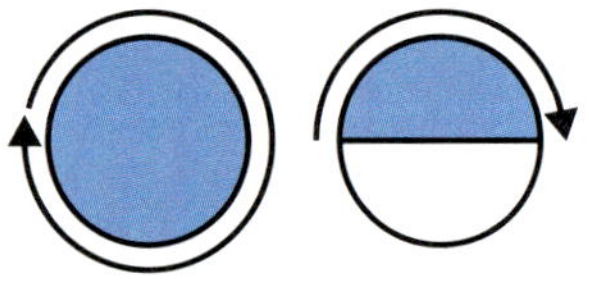

Did you Know

The Wonder Wheel Stands out from other Ferris wheels because it has both an inner and an outer wheel.

CHECK What You Know — Fractions

Draw a model to represent each fraction.

1. $2\frac{3}{4}$

2. $3\frac{2}{3}$

3. $\frac{5}{8}$

4. $1\frac{5}{6}$

5. $\frac{4}{5}$

6. $4\frac{1}{3}$

CHECK What You Know Estimation

The New York Aquarium on Coney Island has 8,000 animals representing 350 species, including walruses. A full-grown walrus can weigh over 1,800 pounds.

For Exercises 7-9, use the table that shows the weights of four different walruses.

Weight of Walruses

walrus	A	B	C	D
weight (lb)	1,279	1,442	1,836	1,112

7. About how much more does walrus C weigh than walrus A?

8. About how much more does walrus B weigh than walrus D?

9. Estimate the combined weight of all of the walruses.

CHECK What You Know Multiplication and Division

The table shows the admission prices to the New York Aquarium on Coney Island.

Admission Prices

Ticket	Price ($)
Adult	12
Senior	8
Student	8

10. On Monday, Jasmine bought 4 adult tickets to the Aquarium. What was the total cost of the tickets?

11. Mrs. Coughlin spent $112 on children's tickets. How many tickets did Mrs. Coughlin purchase?

12. Quan bought children's tickets for himself and 3 friends. How much did Quan spend on tickets?

13. WRITING IN ▸MATH Use the information about admission prices to write a real-world multiplication or division problem.

Start Smart 3 Algebra

Punxsutawney Phil

The people of Punxsutawney, Pennsylvania, celebrate Groundhog Day on February 2. Each year, they gather around to determine whether a groundhog named Phil will see his shadow. According to legend, if Phil sees his shadow, it means there will be six more weeks of winter. How many days are in six weeks? Since there are 7 days in one week, there are 7 × 6, or 42 days in six weeks.

CHECK What You Know — Multiplication and Division

Replace each ■ with a number to make a true number sentence.

1. 132 ÷ ■ = 11

2. 6 × 8 = ■

3. 8 × 7 = ■

4. 120 ÷ ■ = 12

5. 81 ÷ ■ = 9

6. 5 × 4 = ■

7. 12 × 4 = ■

8. 63 ÷ ■ = 7

9. 11 × 10 = ■

CHECK What You Know Patterns

Did you Know?

On average, a groundhog weighs 13 pounds. However, their weight is the heaviest just before winter. This weight gain helps them through hibernation.

In the spring, a female groundhog usually has a litter of about 6 babies.

Number of litters	Number of baby groundhogs
1	6
2	■
3	18
■	24
5	30

10. How many baby groundhogs would be in two litters?

11. How many litters would there be for 24 groundhogs?

CHECK What You Know Multiples of 10 and 100

Replace each ■ with a number to make a true number sentence.

12. 100 × ■ = 600

13. 10 × ■ = 30

14. 9 × 100 = ■

15. 100 × 7 = ■

16. 6 × 10 = ■

17. ■ × 2 = 200

18. WRITING IN MATH Choose a number between 1 and 10. Multiply the number by 10 and 100. Explain how you found your answers.

START SMART 4 Measurement

The Longest Game

In 1984, the Chicago White Sox won Major League Baseball's longest game against the Milwaukee Brewers. The game lasted 8 hours and 6 minutes.

Did you Know?

The final score of Major League Baseball's longest game was Chicago 7 Milwaukee 6. The game lasted 25 innings.

CHECK What You Know — Time

1. An inning of a baseball game begins at 7:45 P.M. and ends at 8:15 P.M. How long was the inning?
2. Joseph and his family drive to the ballpark. They leave their house at 11:30 A.M. and arrive at the stadium 2 hours and 15 minutes later. At what time do Joseph and his family arrive at the stadium?
3. Theresa and her brother went to the concession stand at 1:42 P.M. If they arrived back at their seats at 1:59 P.M., how long were they gone?

CHECK What You Know Temperature

For Exercises 4-7, use the table at the right that shows the temperatures in Chicago on a recent day.

Chicago's Temperature	
Time	**Temperature (°F)**
6:15 A.M.	65
1:30 P.M.	82
9:45 P.M.	73

4. Find the temperature difference between 1:30 P.M. and 6:15 A.M.

5. Between 6:15 A.M. and 10:30 A.M., the temperature rose 8 degrees. What was the temperature at 10:30 A.M.?

6. If the temperature was 68°F at 11:45 P.M., how many degrees did the temperature fall from 9:45 P.M.?

7. WRITING IN MATH Find yesterday's high and low temperatures in your city or town. Then write a real-world problem based on those temperatures. Ask a classmate to solve the problem.

CHECK What You Know Weight

A 2,000-pound bronze statue of Michael Jordan is located outside the home of the Chicago Bulls.

Match the object with the appropriate unit of weight.

8. car — **a.** 1 ounce

9. gorilla — **b.** 2,000 pounds

10. paper clip — **c.** 300 pounds

11. WRITING IN MATH Explain whether you would measure the weight of a basketball in ounces or pounds.

START SMART 5

Geometry

Spectacular Shapes!

The state capital building of South Carolina in Columbia has a large isosceles triangle on the front. An isosceles triangle has at least two sides that are the same length and has one line of symmetry.

Did you Know

The State House in Columbia, South Carolina, weighs more than 70,000 tons.

CHECK What You Know — Symmetry

Write the number of lines of symmetry that each figure has.

1. 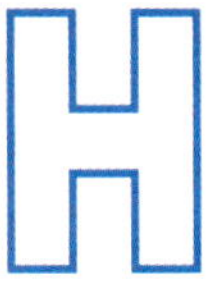

2. 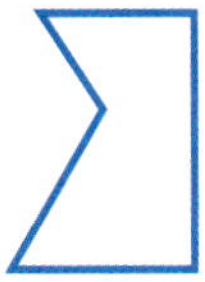

3. 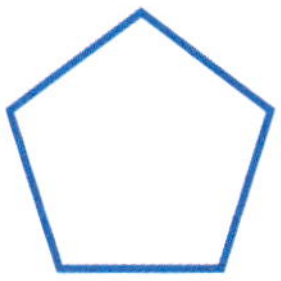

4. 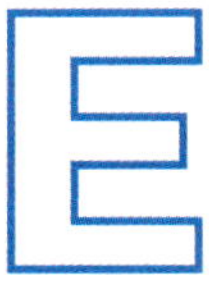

CHECK What You Know Classification

Examples of parallel lines can also be found on the state capital building. Remember that parallel lines are lines that are the same distance apart and never intersect.

Identify each figure and the number of pairs of parallel sides.

5. 

6. 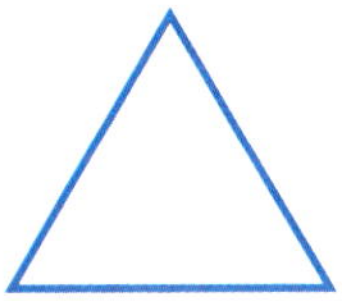

7. 

CHECK What You Know Transformations

The picture below shows a boat's reflection in the ocean.

Tell whether Figure B is a reflection of Figure A.

8. 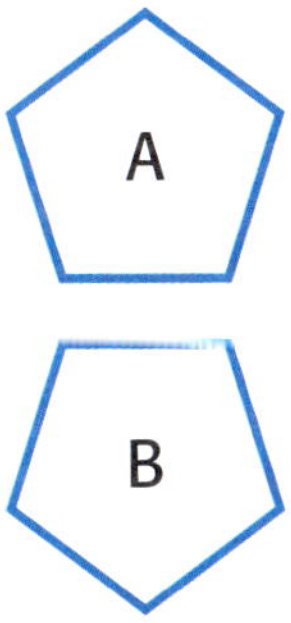

9. 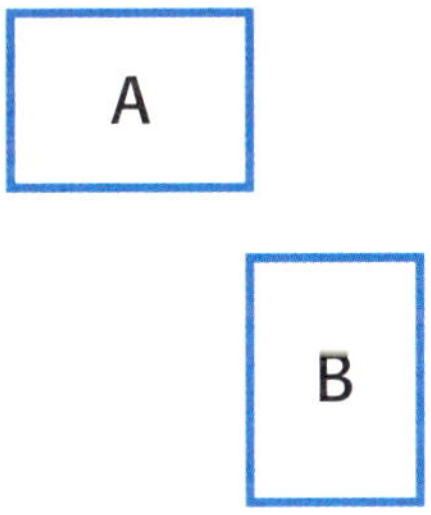

10. 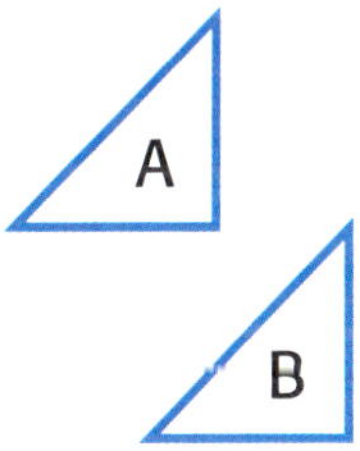

11. **WRITING IN MATH** Decide whether Figure B is a reflection of Figure A. Convince a friend of your answer.

Start Smart 6

Data Analysis

Going to the Beach!

North Carolina is a favorite vacation spot for many Americans. Every year thousands of people flock to the beaches in search of fun and sun.

Did you Know?

North Carolina has over 320 miles of coastline.

CHECK What You Know Outcomes

1. Rita and her family will visit two North Carolina beaches during their vacation. Make a list to show all of the different ways they can visit two beaches.

North Carolina Beaches	
Hatteras	Crystal Coast
Brunswick	Topsail
Nags Head	Ocracoke

2. While at the beach, Rita's family will go fishing, ride jet skis, and parasail. Make a list to show the different orders they can do these activities.

CHECK What You Know Bar Graphs

The North Carolina Museum of Art is located in Raleigh. The museum has a large collection that spans more than 5,000 years in age.

For Exercises 3–5, use the graph at the right. It shows the number of students who went on the fifth grade field trip to the North Carolina Museum of Art.

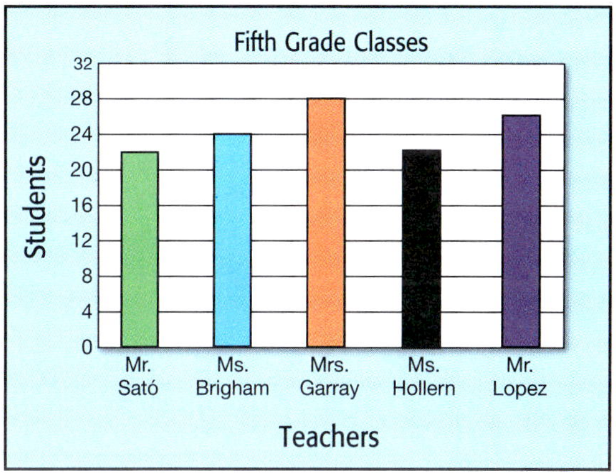

3. Which class had the greatest number of students go on the field trip?

4. Name the two classes that had the same number of students attend the field trip.

5. Which two teachers had a total of 50 students attend the field trip?

6. WRITING IN MATH Explain how to find how many more students from Mrs. Garray's class attended the museum trip than from Mr. Sató's class.

CHAPTER 1

Use Place Value

BIG Idea What is place value?

Place value is the value given to a digit by its position in a number.

Example The total land area of Arizona is 113,635 square miles. The **place-value chart** shows the value of each digit.

Place-Value Chart

hundred thousands	ten thousands	thousands	hundreds	tens	ones
1	1	3	6	3	5

What will I learn in this chapter?

- Use place value to read, write, compare, and order whole numbers.
- Use place value to read, write, compare, and order decimals.
- Solve problems using the *guess and check* strategy.

Key Vocabulary

place value
standard form
expanded form
decimal

Math Online **Student Study Tools at macmillanmh.com**

FOLDABLES® Study Organizer

Make this Foldable to help you organize information about place value. Begin with a sheet of 11″ × 17″ paper.

1. **Fold** the paper in half to make a two column chart.

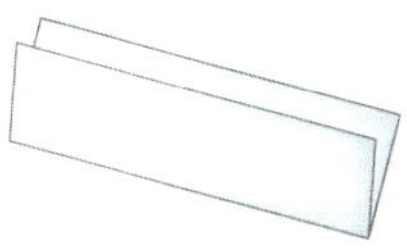

2. **Fold** one side of the paper upwards to create a 3″ tab.

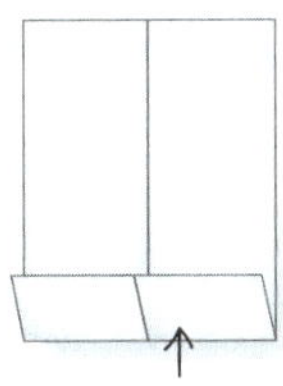

3. **Glue** the outer edges of the 3″ tab to create a pocket.

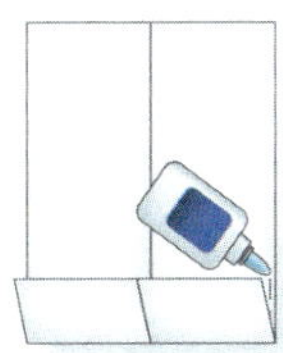

4. **Fold** the top edge down to create a 2″ crease. Unfold to create a heading space for the two column chart.

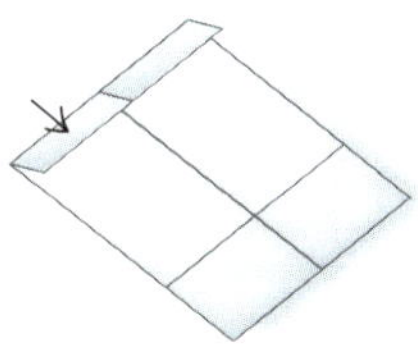

5. **Label** the columns as shown. Use the pockets to store your notes.

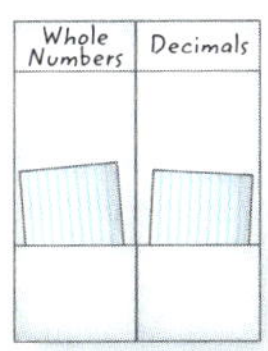

ARE YOU READY for Chapter 1?

You have two ways to check prerequisite skills for this chapter.

Option 2

Math Online Take the Chapter Readiness Quiz at macmillanmh.com.

Option 1

Complete the Quick Check below.

QUICK Check

Write each number in word form. (Prior Grade)

1. 8　　**2.** 15　　**3.** 23

4. 44　　**5.** 160　　**6.** 371

Write the number that represents each point on the number line. (Prior Grade)

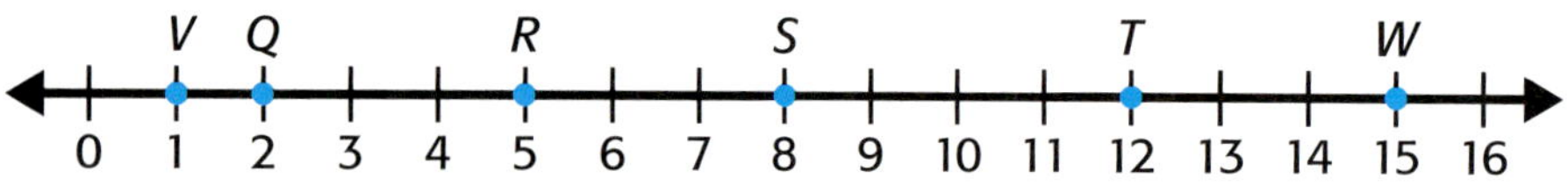

7. *Q*　　**8.** *S*　　**9.** *R*

10. *T*　　**11.** *V*　　**12.** *W*

Write each sentence using the symbols $<$, $>$, or $=$. (Prior Grade)

13. 8 is less than 12.　　**14.** 25 is greater than 10.

15. 136 is equal to 136.　　**16.** 471 is greater than 470.

17. The high temperature yesterday was 64°F. The high temperature today is 70°F. Write *64 is less than 70* using symbols.

1-1 Place Value Through Billions

GET READY to Learn

Parker Ranch in Hawaii spreads across 150,000 acres, making it one of the largest ranches in the United States. There are different ways to represent this number.

You can read it as:

- one hundred fifty thousand

You can write it as:

- 150 thousand
- 100,000 + 50,000

MAIN IDEA

I will read and write whole numbers in standard form, expanded form, word form, and short word form.

New Vocabulary

place-value chart
period
place
place value
value
standard form
expanded form

Math Online

macmillanmh.com

- Extra Examples
- Personal Tutor
- Self-Check Quiz

A **place-value chart**, like the one below, shows the value of the digits in a number. In greater numbers, each group of three digits is separated by commas and is called a **period**.

Thousands Period			Ones Period		
hundreds	tens	ones	hundreds	tens	ones
1	5	0,	0	0	0

A digit and its **place**, or **place value**, name a number. For example, in 150,000, the digit 5 is in the ten thousands place. Its **value** is 5 × 10,000, or 50,000.

EXAMPLE Place Value

1 **Name the place of the underlined digit in <u>3</u>65,200. Then write the value of the digit.**

The digit 3 is in the hundred thousands place. The digit represents 3 × 100,000, or 300,000.

The **standard form** of a number is the usual or common way to write a number using digits. The **expanded form** of a number is a way of writing a number as the sum of the *values* of its digits.

Real-World EXAMPLE — Expanded Form

2 **SPORTS** **The Bristol Motor Speedway in Tennessee has about 147 thousand seats. Write this number in standard form and in expanded form.**

Standard Form: 147,000

Expanded Form:

value of 1 → 100,000   1 is in the hundred thousands place.

value of 4 → 40,000   4 is in the ten thousands place.

value of 7 → 7,000   7 is in the thousands place.

So, in expanded form, 147,000 = 100,000 + 40,000 + 7,000.

EXAMPLE — Word Form

3 **Read and write 1,650,072,900 in word form.**

Billions			Millions			Thousands			Ones		
hundreds	tens	ones	hundreds	tens	ones	hundreds	tens	ones	hundreds	tens	ones
		1,	6	5	0,	0	7	2,	9	0	0

Word Form: one billion, six hundred fifty million, seventy-two thousand, nine hundred

Remember

To read a number, say the number in the period and then the period name.

CHECK What You Know

Name the place of the underlined digit. Then write the value of the digit. See Example 1 (p. 17)

1. <u>6</u>57,230

2. 1<u>5</u>,389,000

3. 4<u>9</u>1,306,200,513

Use place value to write each number in standard form. See Example 2 (p. 18)

4. 12 million, 324 thousand, 500

5. 500,000 + 30,000 + 1,000 + 40 + 6

Write each number in expanded form. Then read and write in word form. See Examples 2, 3 (p. 18)

6. 34,617

7. 205,801,300

8. Weld County, Colorado, has four thousand four square miles. Write this number in standard form.

9. Talk About It Explain the steps you take to write 514,903,365 in word form.

Practice and Problem Solving

EXTRA PRACTICE See page R2.

Name the place of the underlined digit. Then write the value of the digit. See Example 1 (p. 17)

10. 31,567 **11.** 206,943 **12.** 57,926,458

13. 814,210,307,000 **14.** 179,703,341,650 **15.** 41,653,000,241

Use place value to write each number in standard form. See Example 2 (p. 18)

16. 14 million, 286 thousand, 700

17. fifty billion, one hundred million, ninety-five

18. 800,000,000 + 30,000,000 + 2,000,000 + 50,000 + 4,000 + 600 + 70

Write each number in expanded form. Then read and write in word form. See Examples 2, 3 (p. 18)

19. 5,962 **20.** 2,040,391

Read and write each number in word form. See Example 3 (p. 18)

21. 9,200,340 **22.** 107,000,523,094

23. The top animated film of all time earned $436,471,036 in the United States. Write this amount in word form.

24. The U.S. Mint produces about 13 billion coins each year. What is this number in standard form?

Real-World PROBLEM SOLVING

Science The space probe *Cassini* took seven years to travel to Saturn and its largest moon, Titan.

25. How far did the probe travel to Saturn? Write the distance in standard form.

26. How do you read the cost of the mission?

27. Write the speed of the probe as it approached Titan in expanded form.

Facts About the Space Mission	
Distance to Saturn	934 million miles
Distance to Titan	2,200,000,000 miles
Cost of mission	$3,300,000,000
Speed of probe approaching Titan	13,700 miles per hour

Source: CNN

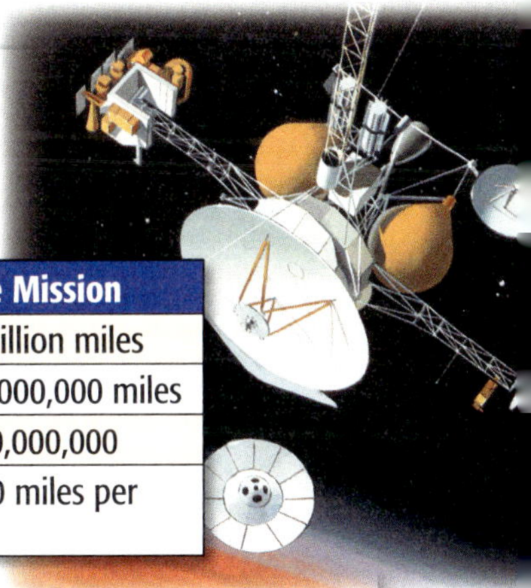

H.O.T. Problems

28. OPEN ENDED Write a number in both standard and expanded form that has 7 in the ten billions place and 5 in the hundred millions place. Then read your number.

29. WRITING IN MATH Explain how place value and periods are useful in reading whole numbers through 999 billion.

1-2 Compare Whole Numbers

MAIN IDEA

I will compare whole numbers.

New Vocabulary

equation
inequality

Math Online

macmillanmh.com

- Extra Examples
- Personal Tutor
- Self-Check Quiz

GET READY to Learn

You can ride the roller coaster if you are 42 inches or taller. So, you will compare your height to 42 inches.

When you compare numbers, they are either equal or *not* equal. If two quantities are equal, they form an **equation**. If two quantities are *not* equal, they form an **inequality**.

Words	Symbol
less than	$<$
greater than	$>$
equal to	$=$

One way to compare numbers is to use a number line.

- Numbers to the right are greater than numbers to the left.
- Numbers to the left are less than numbers to the right.

EXAMPLE Use a Number Line

1 **Replace ● with $<$, $>$, or $=$ to make 214 ● 209 a true sentence.**

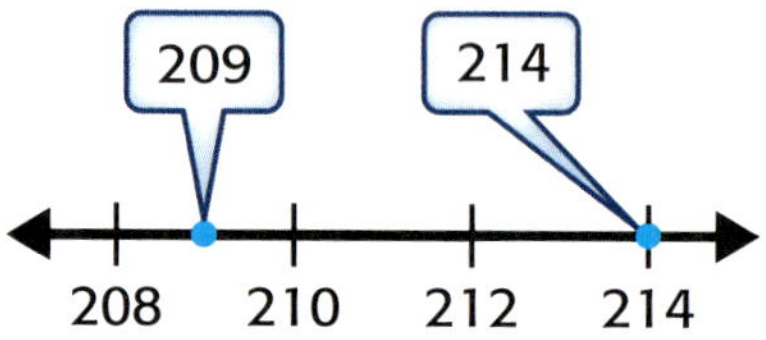

209 is to the left of 214. 214 is to the right of 209.

209 is *less than* 214. ⟵ **Say** ⟶ 214 is *greater than* 209.

$209 < 214$ ⟵ **Write** ⟶ $214 > 209$

So, $214 > 209$.

You can also use place value to compare whole numbers.

Step 1 Line up the digits at the ones place.

Step 2 Starting at the left, find the first position where the digits are different. The number with the greater digit is the greater whole number.

Real-World EXAMPLE — Use Place Value

2 **ROLLER COASTERS** **The Daidarasaurus roller coaster is 7,677 feet long. The Ultimate roller coaster is 7,442 feet long. Which roller coaster is longer?**

Step 1 Write the numbers, lining up the digits in the ones place.

7,677
7,442

Step 2 Compare the digits in each place value, starting from the left.

7,**6**77
7,**4**42

In the thousands place, $7 = 7$.

In the hundreds place, $6 > 4$.

Since $6 > 4$ in the hundreds place, $7{,}677 > 7{,}442$. You can check the reasonableness by using a number line.

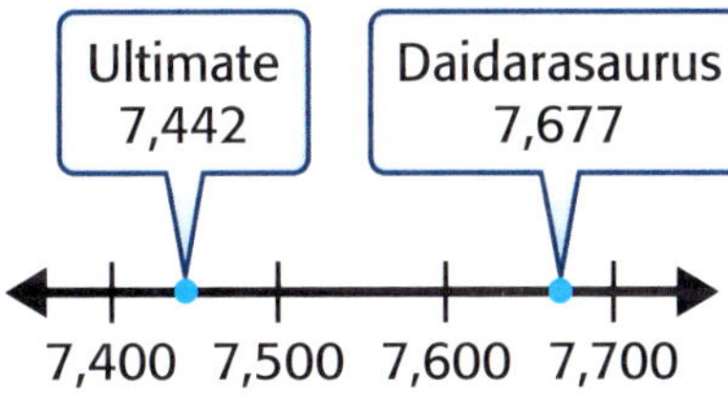

So, the Daidarasaurus roller coaster is longer.

> **Remember**
>
> If the first digit of one number has a greater place value than the first digit of another number, then you can compare without lining up the digits.
>
> For example, $584 > 68$.
>
> hundreds ↲ ↳ tens

CHECK What You Know

Use the number line. Replace each ● with $<$, $>$, or $=$ to make a true sentence.
See Example 1 (p. 20)

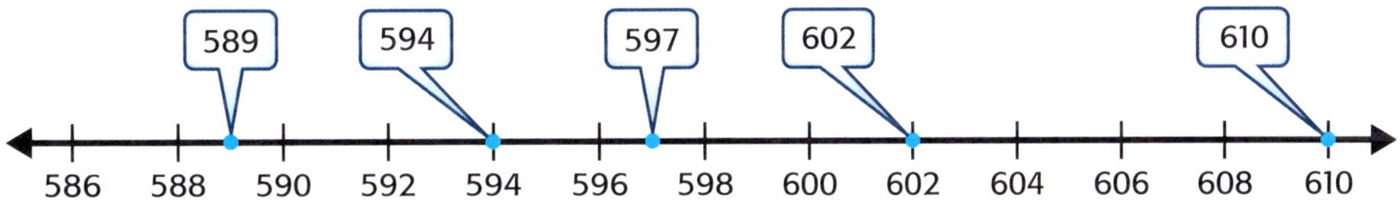

1. 597 ● 589 **2.** 602 ● 610 **3.** 594 ● 594 **4.** 610 ● 589

Replace each ● with $<$, $>$, or $=$ to make a true sentence. See Example 2 (p. 21)

5. 14 ● 9 **6.** 86 ● 79 **7.** 134 ● 1,340

8. 4,260 ● 4,209 **9.** 23,681 ● 24,681 **10.** 5,655,710 ● 5,654,911

11. The Colorado River is 1,450 miles long. The Arkansas River is 1,460 miles long. Which river is longer?

12. **Talk About It** Discuss the steps you would take to compare 81,520 and 81,516.

Practice and Problem Solving

EXTRA PRACTICE See page R2.

Use the number line. Replace each ● with <, >, or = to make a true sentence.
See Example 1 (p. 20)

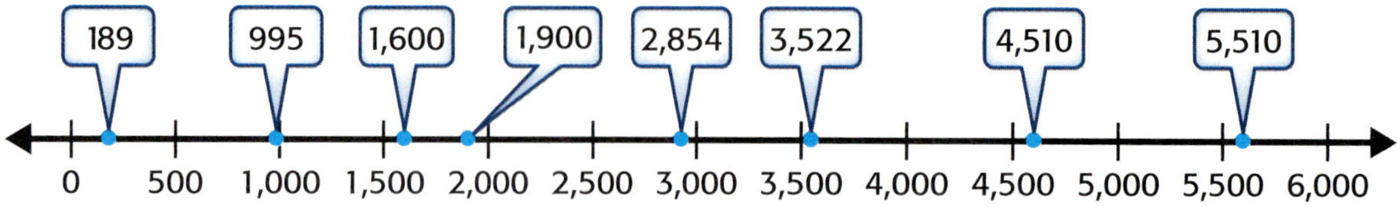

13. 1,600 ● 1,900 **14.** 995 ● 189 **15.** 2,854 ● 4,510 **16.** 3,522 ● 995

17. 189 ● 189 **18.** 5,510 ● 4,510 **19.** 4,618 ● 982 **20.** 189 ● 1,900

Replace each ● with <, >, or = to make a true sentence. See Example 2 (p. 21)

21. 284 ● 290 **22.** 860 ● 780 **23.** 1,076 ● 1,224

24. 3,743 ● 3,842 **25.** 10 ● 1,040 **26.** 2,072 ● 1,955

27. 62,300 ● 62,980 **28.** 4,678 ● 4,678 **29.** 14,092 ● 14,060

30. 364,250 ● 356,350 **31.** 114,208,600 ● 112,300,792

32. 7,655,240,000 ● 7,655,420,000 **33.** 10,856,432,021 ● 10,856,432,020

34. About 213 million songs were downloaded in 2004, and about 320 million were downloaded in 2005. In which year were more songs downloaded?

35. A giant ball of twine in Kansas has a mass of 7,893 kilograms. A giant ball of twine in Minnesota has a mass of 7,802 kilograms. Which ball has the larger mass?

Real-World PROBLEM SOLVING

Social Studies Time lines are used to show the order of events.

Replace each ● with < or > to make a true sentence.

36. 1541 ● 1609

37. 1609 ● 1640

38. 1706 ● 1640

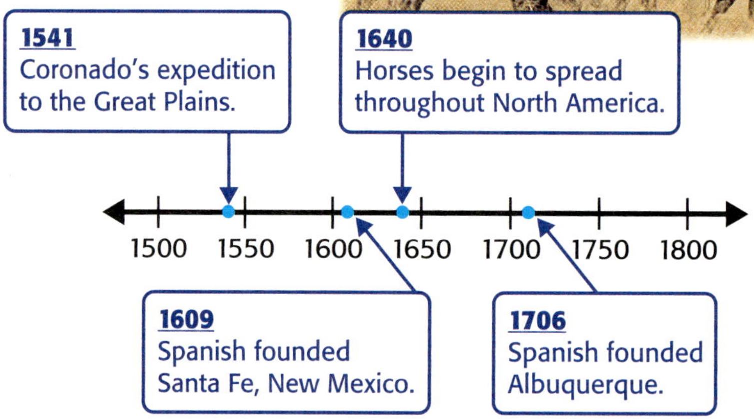

39. In 1750, horses reached the northern part of the Great Plains. Did this happen before or after the Spanish founded Albuquerque? Explain.

H.O.T. Problems

40. **CHALLENGE** Use the digits 4, 7, 1, 9, 3, and 8 one time each to write the greatest and least possible whole numbers in standard form.

41. **OPEN ENDED** Find a missing digit that makes 26,3□4 > 26,351 a true sentence.

42. **NUMBER SENSE** Is the statement x billion > y million *sometimes*, *always*, or *never* true for values of x and y that are greater than zero? Explain.

43. **WRITING IN ▶MATH** Write a word problem about a real-world situation which you solve by comparing whole numbers.

TEST Practice

44. The Pacific Ocean covers about 64,000,000 square miles. How is this number written in words? (Lesson 1-1)

   A Sixty-four thousand

   B Sixty-four million

   C Sixty-four billion

   D Sixty-four trillion

45. Which is a true statement about the dimensions of the box? (Lesson 1-2)

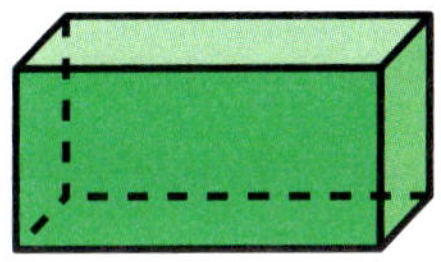

height = 135 cm

width = 74 cm

length = 282 cm

   F The height is greater than the length.

   G The height is greater than the width.

   H The length is less than the height.

   J The width is equal to the height.

Spiral Review

Name the place value of the underlined digit. Then write the number it represents. (Lesson 1-1)

46. 1,268	**47.** 15,809	**48.** 494,268	**49.** 123,475,689

50. The deepest place in the ocean is 35,838 feet below sea level. Read and write this number in word form. (Lesson 1-1)

Use place value to write each number in standard form. (Lesson 1-1)

51. 39 billion, 402 million, 1 thousand, 755

52. six hundred nineteen thousand, twenty-eight

1-3 Problem-Solving Investigation

MAIN IDEA I will use the four-step plan to solve a problem.

P.S.I. TEAM +

TERESA: The table shows the prices, including tax, of the toys sold at Toy Central.

Item	Price
Yo-Yo	$4
Jump rope	$6
Bubbles	$2

I can spend exactly $10 on toys. Which of the following combination of toys can I *not* buy?

- 2 yo-yos and 1 bubbles
- 3 bubbles and 1 yo-yo
- 1 jump rope and 3 bubbles

YOUR MISSION: Determine which combination of toys Teresa cannot buy.

Understand	You know she can spend $10 on toys and the prices of the toys. You need to determine which combination of toys she *cannot* buy.
Plan	You can solve the problem by finding the total cost of each combination of toys.
Solve	2 yo-yos and 1 bubbles: $(2 \times \$4) + (1 \times \$2)$ or $10 ✓ 3 bubbles and 1 yo-yo: $(3 \times \$2) + (1 \times \$4)$ or $10 ✓ 1 jump rope and 3 bubbles: $(1 \times \$6) + (3 \times \$2)$ or $12 So, Teresa *cannot* buy 1 jump rope and 3 bubbles.
Check	Look back at the problem. The combination of 1 jump rope and 3 bubbles costs $12. Since $\$12 > \$10$, the answer makes sense.

Mixed Problem Solving

EXTRA PRACTICE
See page R2.

Use the four-step plan to solve each problem.

PROBLEM-SOLVING SKILLS
- Use the four-step plan.

1. Latvia has 101 movie screens for every one million people. Sweden has 137 movie screens, and the United States has 105 movie screens for every one million people. Which country has the greatest number of movie screens for every one million people?

2. **Measurement** A swimmer set three world records. His times were 53.6 seconds, 24.99 seconds, and 1 minute 55.87 seconds. He swam in the 200-meter, the 50-meter, and the 100-meter backstroke competitions. What were his times for each race? Explain.

3. The cost of one jump rope is shown. If Ofelia has $15, does she have enough money to buy six jump ropes?

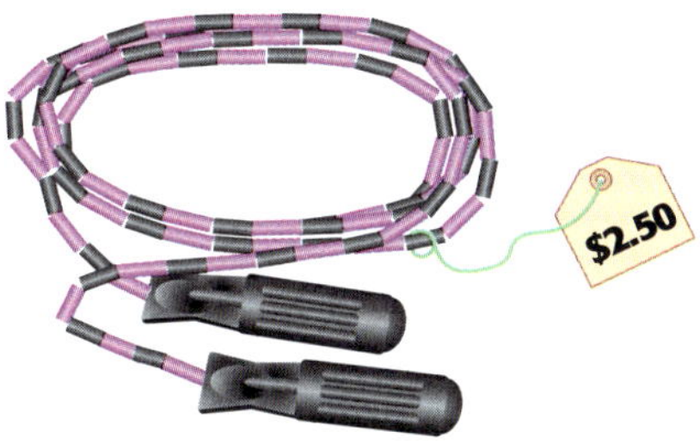

4. Parker cut his pizza into 6 equal slices and ate 3 of them. Tanisha cut her pizza into 8 equal slices and ate 3 of them. If the pizzas were the same size, who ate more? Explain how you know.

5. Shane spent 20 minutes on reading homework. He spent half as many minutes completing his social studies homework. He spent 10 minutes longer on his math homework than his reading homework. How many minutes did he spend on homework?

6. **Measurement** Use the map below. Ty went from his house to school and then to Art's house. Polly went from her house to school and then to Juanita's house. Who traveled farther?

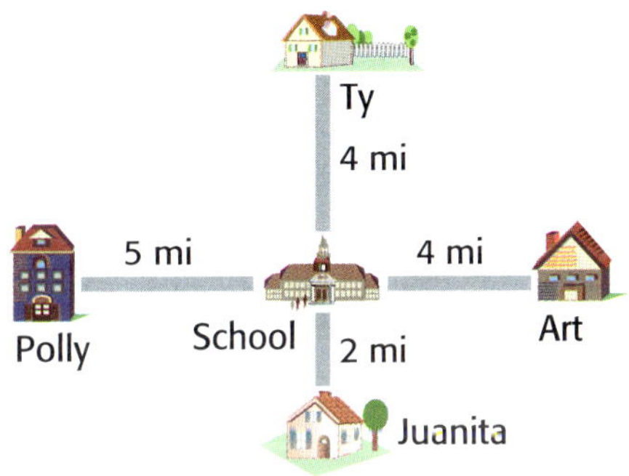

7. Todd has $85 to spend on athletic shoes. The shoes cost $50. If he buys one pair, he gets a second pair for half price. How much money will he have left if he purchases two pairs of the shoes?

8. A relative gives you twice as many dollars as your age on each birthday. You are 11 years old. How much money have you been given over the years by this relative?

9. Twelve students are going on a field trip. Each student pays $6 for a ticket and $3 for lunch. Find the total cost for tickets and lunches.

10. **WRITING IN MATH** Write a problem that you can solve using the four-step plan.

Explore

Math Activity for 1-4

Fractions and Decimals

MAIN IDEA

I will use models to relate decimals to fractions.

New Vocabulary

decimal

decimal point

Fractions and decimals are related. In a place-value chart, the place to the right of the ones place has a value of $\frac{1}{10}$ or one tenth. The next place value has a value of $\frac{1}{100}$ or one hundredth. Numbers that have digits in the tenths place, hundredths place, and beyond are called **decimals**. A **decimal point** is used to separate the ones place from the tenths place.

Fraction	Words	Decimal	Model
$\frac{1}{10}$	one tenth	0.1 (decimal point, tenths place)	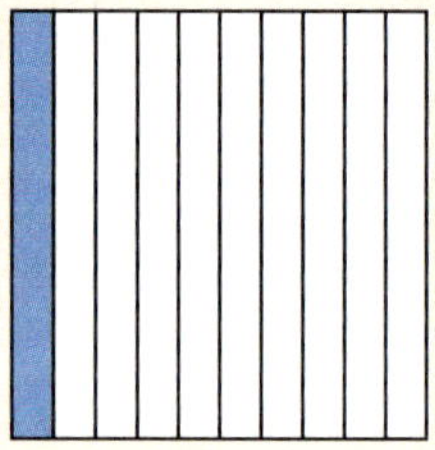

ACTIVITY

1 Use a model to show $\frac{3}{10}$. Then write it in words and as a decimal.

Step 1 Shade 3 rows in a 10 × 10 grid.

Step 2 The model shows three tenths or 0.3.

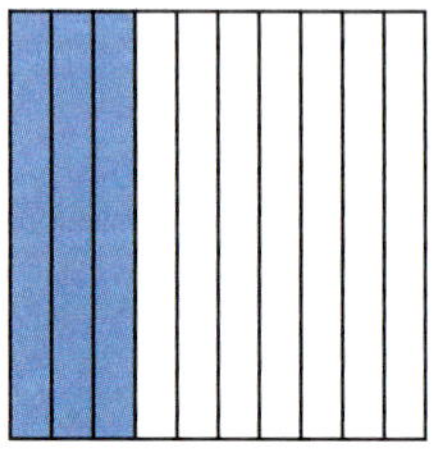

You can use a similar model for $\frac{1}{100}$.

Fraction	Words	Decimal	Model
$\frac{1}{100}$	one hundredth	0.01 (decimal point, hundredths place)	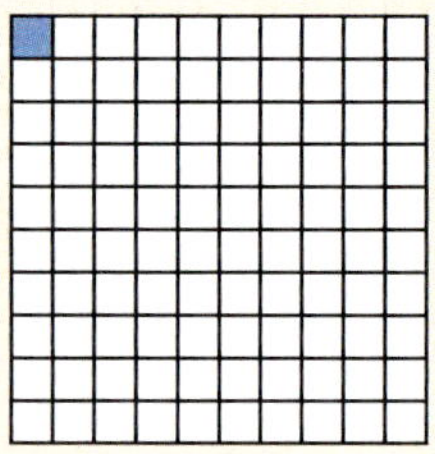

ACTIVITIES

2 **Use a model to show $\frac{9}{100}$. Then write it in words and as a decimal.**

Step 1 Shade 9 of the 100 small squares.

Step 2 The model shows nine hundredths or 0.09.

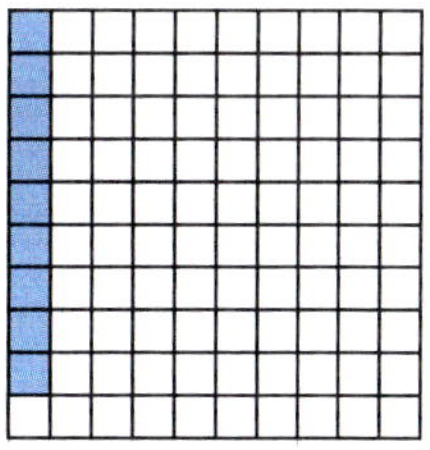

3 **Use a model to show $\frac{34}{100}$. Then write it in words and as a decimal.**

Step 1 Shade 34 of the 100 small squares.

Step 2 The model shows thirty-four hundredths. Notice that there are 3 tenths and 4 hundredths shaded. As a decimal, this is written 0.34.

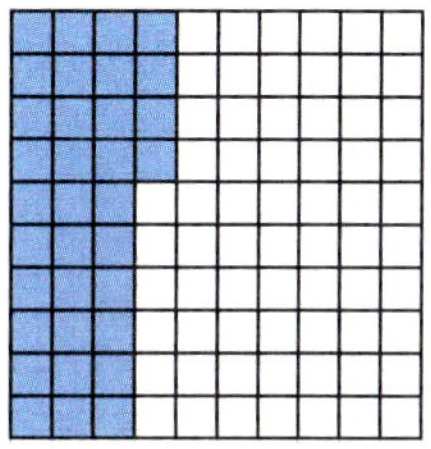

Think About It

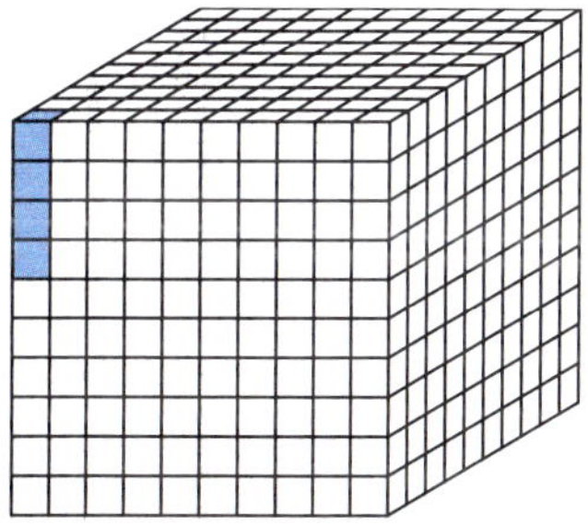

1. The model at the right shows a thousandths cube. What fraction of the model is shaded? Then write as a decimal.
2. Model $\frac{80}{100}$. Then name the fraction as a decimal in two different ways.

CHECK What You Know

Use a model to write each fraction in words and as a decimal.

3. $\frac{7}{10}$ **4.** $\frac{9}{10}$ **5.** $\frac{5}{100}$ **6.** $\frac{63}{100}$

Write the decimal for each model. Write the related fraction.

7.

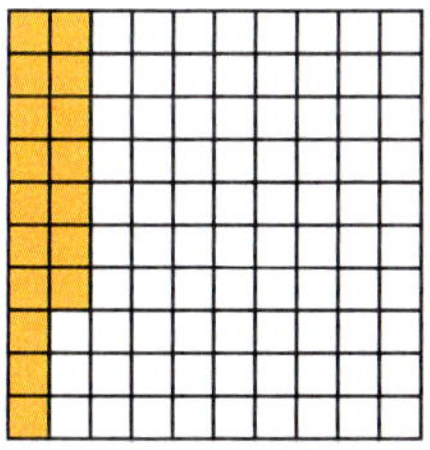

8.

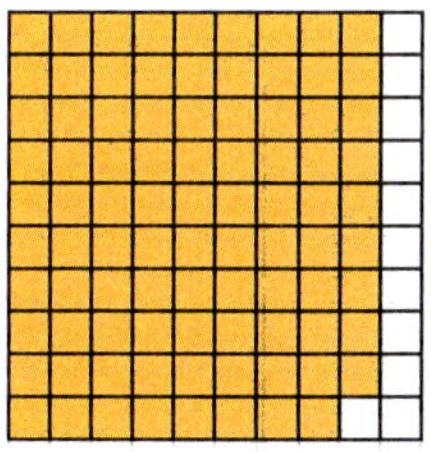

9.

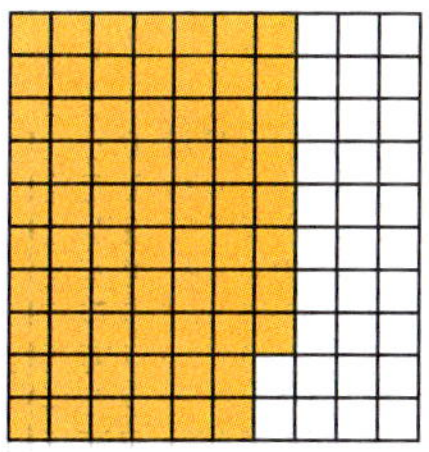

10. WRITING IN MATH Explain why $\frac{45}{100}$ is written as a decimal with a 4 in the tenths place and a 5 in the hundredths place.

1-4 Represent Decimals

MAIN IDEA

I will represent fractions that name tenths, hundredths, and thousandths as decimals.

Math Online

macmillanmh.com

- Extra Examples
- Personal Tutor
- Self-Check Quiz
- Concepts in Motion

GET READY to Learn

Each year, about $\frac{9}{10}$ of the days are sunny in Yuma, Arizona. In Redding, California, about $\frac{88}{100}$ of the days are sunny.

Fractions with denominators of 10, 100, 1,000, and so on can easily be written as decimals.

Fractions to Decimals

Key Concept

Model	Fraction	Decimal
Nine tenths are shaded. 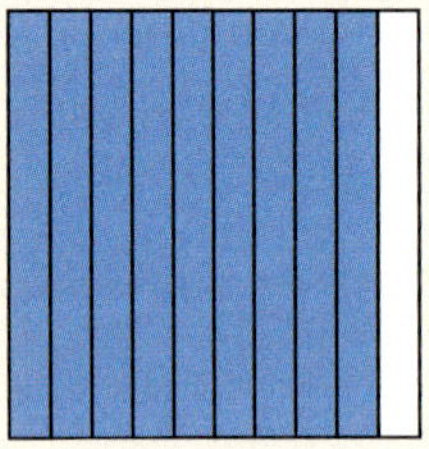	$\frac{9}{10}$	0.9
Eighty-eight hundredths are shaded. 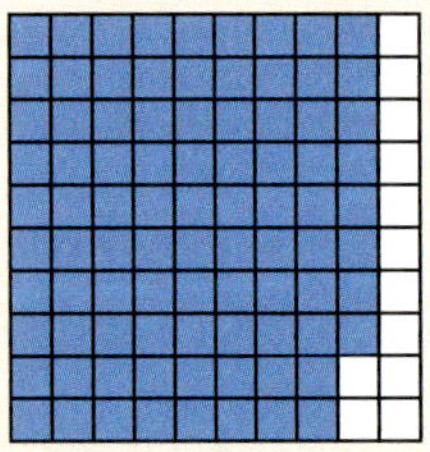	$\frac{88}{100}$	0.88
Sixteen thousandths are shaded. 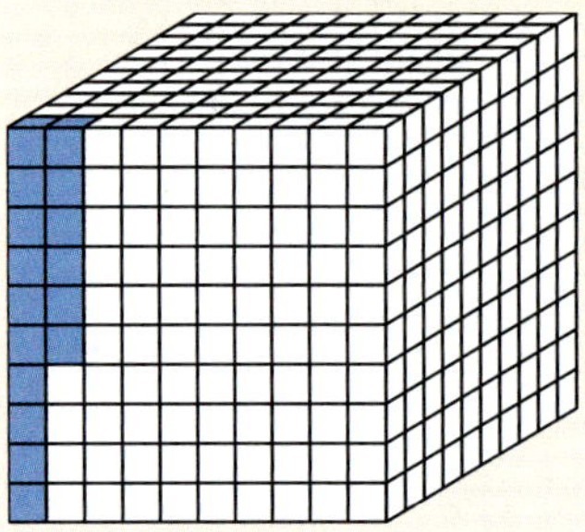	$\frac{16}{1,000}$	0.016

Fractions that name tenths, hundredths, and thousandths have 1 digit, 2 digits, and 3 digits to the right of the decimal point.

EXAMPLE Fractions as Decimals

1 **Write $\frac{35}{100}$ as a decimal.**

$\frac{35}{100}$ is 35 hundredths. Since the fraction names hundredths, there should be two digits to the right of the decimal point.

So, $\frac{35}{100} = 0.35$.

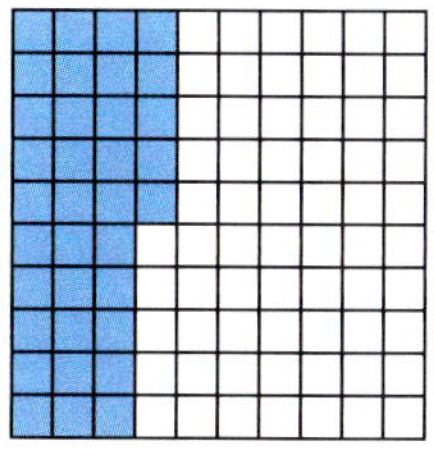

Real-World EXAMPLE Fractions as Decimals

2 **INSECTS** **A bee hummingbird weighs only about $\frac{56}{1,000}$ of an ounce. Represent this fraction as a decimal.**

The fraction names thousandths, so there should be 3 digits to the right of the decimal point.

So, $\frac{56}{1,000} = 0.056$.

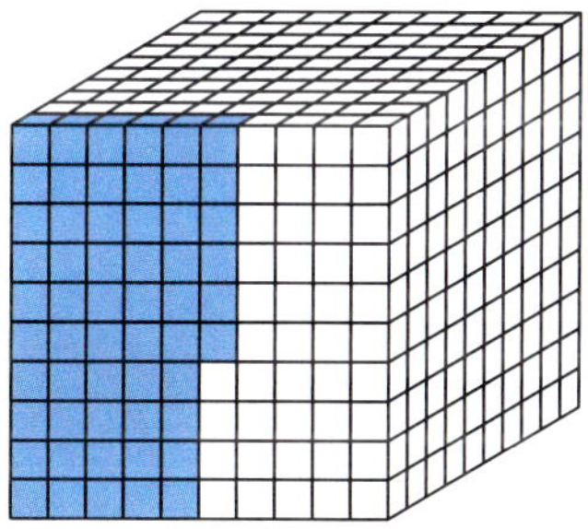

Remember

The decimals 0.056 and 0.560 are not the same. The decimal 0.560 is read *five hundred sixty thousandths.*

CHECK What You Know

Use a model to write each fraction as a decimal. See Examples 1, 2 (p. 29)

1. $\frac{4}{10}$ **2.** $\frac{2}{10}$ **3.** $\frac{58}{100}$ **4.** $\frac{74}{100}$

5. $\frac{6}{100}$ **6.** $\frac{5}{100}$ **7.** $\frac{795}{1,000}$ **8.** $\frac{9}{1,000}$

9. In a class survey, $\frac{60}{100}$ students said that they have a pet. Write this result as a decimal.

10. Talk About It Describe a rule for writing fractions like $\frac{8}{100}$ and $\frac{32}{1,000}$ as decimals.

Practice and Problem Solving

EXTRA PRACTICE See page R3.

Use a model to write each fraction as a decimal. See Examples 1, 2 (p. 29)

11. $\frac{3}{10}$ **12.** $\frac{9}{10}$ **13.** $\frac{86}{100}$ **14.** $\frac{99}{100}$

15. $\frac{107}{1,000}$ **16.** $\frac{387}{1,000}$ **17.** $\frac{51}{1,000}$ **18.** $\frac{80}{1,000}$

19. $\frac{60}{100}$ **20.** $\frac{22}{1,000}$ **21.** $\frac{4}{100}$ **22.** $\frac{1}{1,000}$

23. Mrs. Carroll bought $\frac{8}{10}$ pound of turkey. Write this fraction as a decimal.

24. A runner decreased his time by $\frac{5}{100}$ of a second. Express this decrease as a decimal.

25. About $\frac{7}{10}$ of a person's body weight is water. Write this fraction as a decimal.

26. It rains only 9 hundredths of an inch each year in Ica, Peru. Write this number as a decimal.

Measurement **Write the customary measure for each metric measure as a decimal.**

27. 1 kilometer

28. 1 millimeter

29. 1 gram

30. 1 liter

Metric Measure	Customary Measure
1 kilometer	$\frac{62}{100}$ mile
1 millimeter	$\frac{4}{100}$ inch
1 gram	$\frac{35}{1,000}$ ounce
1 liter	$\frac{908}{1,000}$ quart

H.O.T. Problems

31. **OPEN ENDED** Write a fraction that has a denominator of 100. Then write the fraction as a decimal and draw a model to represent the decimal.

32. **FIND THE ERROR** Ryan and Janelle are writing $\frac{95}{1,000}$ as a decimal. Who is correct? Explain.

Ryan
$\frac{95}{1,000} = 0.095$

Janelle
$\frac{95}{1,000} = 0.950$

33. **WRITING IN ▶MATH** Explain how the word form of a fraction can help you write the fraction as a decimal.

Chapter 1 Mid-Chapter Check

Lessons 1-1 through 1-4

Name the place of the underlined digit. Then write the value of the digit. (Lesson 1-1)

1. $4\underline{2}{,}924{,}603$ **2.** $9\underline{5}3{,}187$

3. **MULTIPLE CHOICE** In which number does 6 have a value of 60,000,000? (Lesson 1-1)

A 1,862,940 **C** 564,103,278

B 16,743,295 **D** 693,751,842

For Exercises 4 and 5, use the graph that shows the size of three Alaskan parks. (Lesson 1-1)

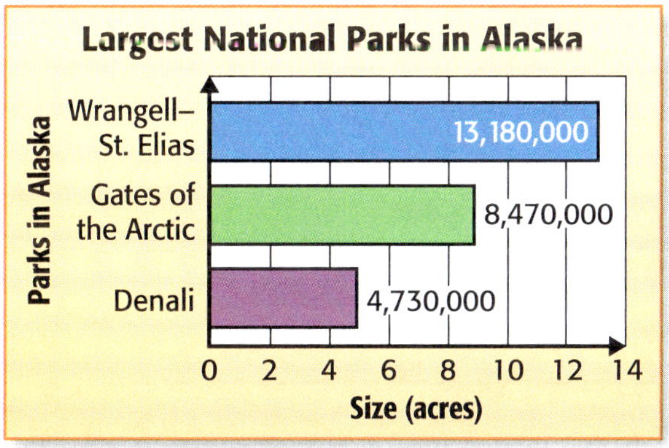

Source: *Scholastic Book of World Records*

4. Write the number of acres of Wrangell–St. Elias in expanded and word form.

5. Write in words how you would read the number of acres in Denali park.

Replace each ● with <, >, or = to make a true sentence. (Lesson 1-2)

6. 84 ● 90 **7.** 542 ● 524

8. 925 ● 1,024 **9.** 6,132 ● 6,231

10. The attendance at Friday's baseball game was 45,673. Sunday's game attendance was 45,761. Which game had a greater attendance? (Lesson 1-2)

11. A fifth grade teacher has 24 students in class. She wants to give each student 3 pencils. If she has 56 pencils, how many more pencils does she need? (Lesson 1-3)

Use a model to write each fraction as a decimal. (Lesson 1-4)

12. $\frac{1}{10}$ **13.** $\frac{85}{100}$

14. $\frac{492}{1{,}000}$ **15.** $\frac{39}{1{,}000}$

16. **MULTIPLE CHOICE** Which decimal represents the shaded part of the figure? (Lesson 1-4)

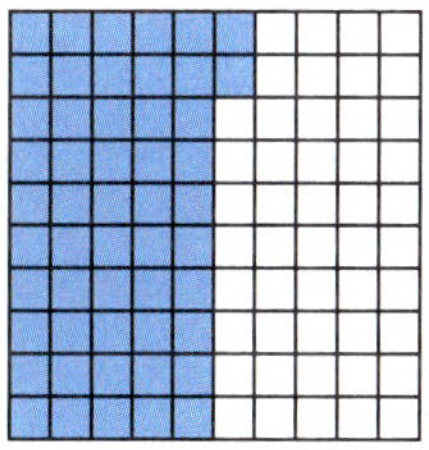

F 0.0052 **H** 0.52

G 0.052 **J** 5.2

17. Write *four hundredths* as a decimal. (Lesson 1-4)

18. **WRITING IN MATH** Describe the difference between 142 thousands and 142 thousandths. Explain how you know. (Lessons 1-2 and 1-4)

1-5 Place Value Through Thousandths

MAIN IDEA

I will read and write decimals in standard form, expanded form, word form, and short word form.

Math Online

macmillanmh.com

- Extra Examples
- Personal Tutor
- Self-Check Quiz

GET READY to Learn

In 2004, Natalie Coughlin of the United States set an Olympic record. She swam the 100-meter backstroke in 59.68 seconds.

You can read the time as:

- fifty-nine and sixty-eight hundredths seconds

You can write the time as:

- 59 and 68 hundredths seconds

You have seen that the place-value chart used for whole numbers can be extended to include decimals like 59.68. The decimal point separates the ones place and the tenths place.

Place-Value Chart

tens	ones	tenths	hundredths	thousandths
5	9 .	6	8	0

The digit 6 is in the tenths place. Its value is 0.6.

The digit 8 is in the hundredths place. Its value is 0.08.

EXAMPLE Place of Digits in Decimals

1 Name the place of the underlined digit in 0.24<u>7</u>. Then write the value of the digit.

The digit 7 is in the thousandths place. The digit represents 0.007.

Just as with whole numbers, you can also write decimals in standard form and expanded form.

EXAMPLE Standard and Expanded Form

2 **Write *five and six hundred fourteen thousandths* in standard form and in expanded form.**

Standard Form: 5.614

Expanded Form:

value of 5 → 5 — 5 is in the ones place.
value of 6 → 0.6 — 6 is in the tenths place.
value of 1 → 0.01 — 1 is in the hundredths place.
value of 4 → 0.004 — 4 is in the thousandths place.

So, in expanded form 5.614 = 5 + 0.6 + 0.01 + 0.004.

To write decimals in word form, use the word *and* for the decimal point and use the place value of the last digit in the number.

Real-World EXAMPLE Decimals in Word Form

3 **Measurement** **Five tree taps produce enough maple sap to make 1 gallon, or about 3.79 liters of syrup. Read and write the number of liters in word form.**

tens	ones	tenths	hundredths	thousandths
	3 .	7	9	

The place value of the last digit, 9, is hundredths.

Word form: three and seventy-nine hundredths

Remember

As with whole numbers, understanding place value can help you read decimals and write them in word form.

Representing Decimals

Concept Summary

Form	Definition	Example
Standard Form	The usual way or commom way of writing a number using digits.	10.49
Expanded Form	A way of writing a number as the sum of the values of its digits to show place value.	10 + 0.4 + 0.09
Word Form	A way of writing a number using words.	Ten and forty-nine hundredths

CHECK What You Know

Name the place of the underlined digit. Then write the value of the digit. See Example 1 (p. 32)

1. 6.14 **2.** 32.095

Write each number in standard form. See Example 2 (p. 33)

3. 5 and 87 hundredths **4.** 20 + 6 + 0.9 + 0.01 + 0.004

Write each number in expanded form. Then read and write in word form. See Examples 2, 3 (p. 33)

5. 19.4 **6.** 35.19 **7.** 1.608 **8.** 2.085

9. A spider can travel one and two tenths miles per hour. Write this as a decimal.

10. Talk About It Discuss how place value is used to read decimals.

Practice and Problem Solving

EXTRA PRACTICE See page R3.

Name the place of the underlined digit. Then write the value of the digit. See Example 1 (p. 32)

11. 63.47 **12.** 9.56 **13.** 4.072 **14.** 81.453

Write each number in standard form. See Example 2 (p. 33)

15. 13 and 9 tenths **16.** fifty and six hundredths

17. 10 + 1 + 0.9 + 0.02 + 0.003 **18.** 7 + 0.1 + 0.005

Write each number in expanded form. Then read and write in word form. See Examples 2, 3 (p. 33)

19. 4.28 **20.** 0.917 **21.** 69.409 **22.** 20.05

23. 13.09 **24.** 0.25 **25.** 92.301 **26.** 2.047

27. An athlete completes a race in 57.505 seconds. Name all the places the digit 5 appears in the number.

28. There was three and five hundredths inches of rain yesterday. Write this number in standard form.

29. A baseball player had a batting average of 0.334 for the season. Write this number in expanded form.

30. The table shows the amount of salt that remains when a cubic foot of water evaporates. Read each number that describes the amount of salt. Then write each number in words.

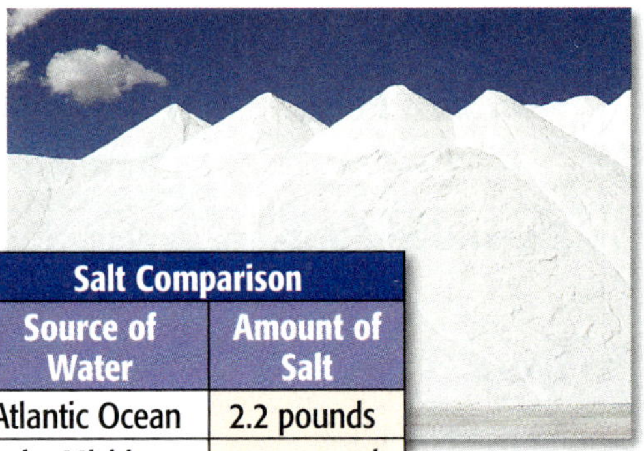

Salt Comparison

Source of Water	Amount of Salt
Atlantic Ocean	2.2 pounds
Lake Michigan	0.01 pound

H.O.T. Problems

31. **OPEN ENDED** Write a number that has 6 in the thousandths place. Then write the number in expanded form and word form.

32. **WHICH ONE DOESN'T BELONG?** Identify the decimal that does not belong with the other three. Explain your reasoning.

five and thirty-nine hundredths	5.39	5 + 0.3 + 0.09	5 and 39 tenths

33. **WRITING IN ▶MATH** Name an advantage of using 0.8 instead of $\frac{8}{10}$.

TEST Practice

34. Which decimal is represented in the model below? **(Lesson 1-5)**

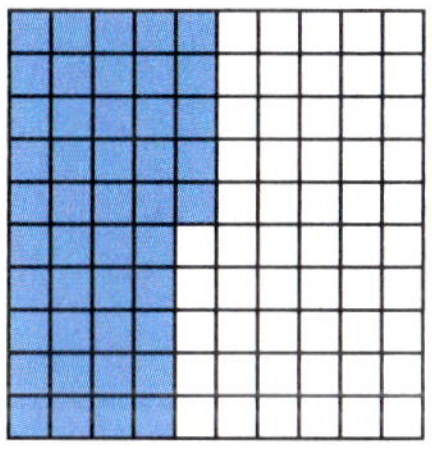

A 45

B 4.5

C 0.45

D 0.045

35. Which decimal represents the total value of 5 nickels, 1 quarter, and 3 dimes when compared to 1 dollar?

F 0.08

G 8.0

H 0.80

J 0.008

Spiral Review

Use a model to write each fraction as a decimal. **(Lesson 1-4)**

36. $\frac{6}{10}$ **37.** $\frac{29}{100}$ **38.** $\frac{541}{1,000}$ **39.** $\frac{7}{100}$

40. The ticket prices for a children's play are shown in the table. Mrs. Rodriguez bought 4 children's tickets, 2 adult tickets, and 1 senior ticket. If she gives the cashier $40, how much change should she receive? **(Lesson 1-3)**

Children	$4.00
Adults	$6.00
Seniors	$3.00

Replace each ● with <, >, or = to make a true sentence. **(Lesson 1-2)**

41. 830 ● 813 **42.** 5,670 ● 590 **43.** 23,904,156 ● 23,904,156

44. About 234 million bushels of apples were produced in the United States in a recent year. Write this number in expanded form. **(Lesson 1-1)**

1-6 Compare Decimals

MAIN IDEA

I will compare decimals.

New Vocabulary

equivalent decimals

Math Online

macmillanmh.com

- Extra Examples
- Personal Tutor
- Self-Check Quiz

GET READY to Learn

Luis downloaded two songs onto his MP3 player. Which song is longer?

Song	Length (min)
1	3.6
2	3.8

Comparing decimals is similar to comparing whole numbers.

Real-World EXAMPLE — Compare Decimals

1 MUSIC Refer to the table above. Which song is longer?

One Way: Use a number line

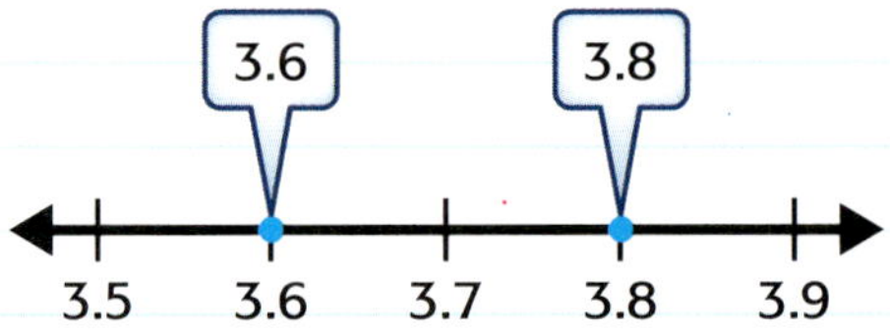

Numbers to the right are greater than numbers to the left. Since 3.8 is to the right of 3.6, $3.8 > 3.6$.

Another Way: Use place value

Step 1	Step 2	Step 3
Line up the decimal points. 3.6 3.8	Compare the digits in the greatest place. 3.6 3.8 The ones digits are the same.	Continue comparing until the digits are different. 3.6 3.8 In the tenths place, $6 < 8$. So, $3.6 < 3.8$.

So, song 2 is longer.

Vocabulary Link
equi-
Everyday use equal

Decimals that have the same value are **equivalent decimals**.

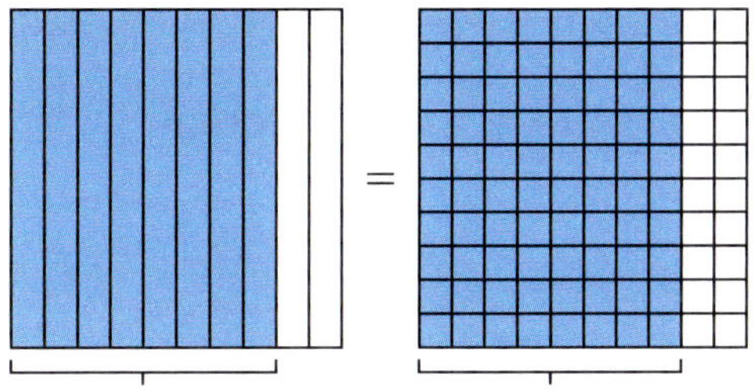

$\frac{8}{10}$ or 0.8 $\quad$ $\frac{80}{100}$ or 0.80

The shaded part of each model is the same. So, 0.8 = 0.80.

The model shows you can *annex*, or place zeros, to the right of a decimal without changing its value.

EXAMPLES Compare Decimals

2 **Replace ● with <, >, or = to make 0.450 ● 0.45 a true sentence.**

0.450 = 0.45**0** Annex a zero. The value does not change.

So, 0.450 = 0.45.

3 **Replace ● with <, >, or = to make 8.69 ● 8.6 a true sentence.**

8.69 → 8.69
8.6 → 8.6**0** Annex a zero to the right of 8.6 so that it has the same number of decimal places as 8.69.

Since 9 > 0 in the hundredths place, 8.69 > 8.6.

CHECK What You Know

Replace each ● with <, >, or = to make a true sentence.
See Examples 1–3 (pp. 36–37)

1. 0.5 ● 0.7	**2.** 0.62 ● 0.26	**3.** 3.7 ● 3.70
4. 4.40 ● 4.44	**5.** 0.003 ● 0.102	**6.** 9.624 ● 9.618
7. 8.001 ● 8.001	**8.** 0.375 ● 0.42	**9.** 6.500 ● 6.5

10. Each year, Wadis Halfa, Sudan, gets about 2.5 millimeters of rain, and Luxar, Egypt, gets about 0.76 millimeter of rain. Which place gets more rain each year?

11. Talk About It Describe how you know if two decimals are equivalent.

Practice and Problem Solving

EXTRA PRACTICE
See page R3.

Replace each ● with <, >, or = to make a true sentence.

See Examples 1–3 (pp. 36–37)

12. 4.4 ● 4.1

13. 0.39 ● 0.37

14. 0.57 ● 0.65

15. 2.15 ● 2.150

16. 0.1 ● 0.006

17. 0.652 ● 0.647

18. 0.09 ● 0.001

19. 7.304 ● 7.30

20. 2.800 ● 2.8

21. 6.57 ● 6.6

22. 0.91 ● 0.90

23. 11.341 ● 11.34

24. 4.972 ● 4.972

25. 124 ● 124.1

26. 3.06 ● 3.814

27. 0.7 ● 0.007

28. 36.504 ● 36.6

29. 5.09 ● 5.10

30. A cat's normal body temperature is 101.5 degrees Fahrenheit. A rabbit's normal body temperature is 103.1 degrees Fahrenheit. Which animal has a lower normal body temperature?

31. **Measurement** Monisha lives 2.16 miles from school and 2.08 miles from the mall. Is Monisha's home closer to school or the mall?

For Exercises 32–34, use the table at the right that shows the cost of posters of famous works of art.

32. Does the poster *Relativity* or the poster *Women and Bird in the Night* cost more?

33. Which poster costs less: *From the Lake, No. 1* or *Waterlillies*?

34. Which poster costs less than *Waterlillies*?

Poster Prices

Poster	Cost ($)
From the Lake, No. 1, Georgia O'Keeffe	16.99
Relativity, M.C. Escher	11.49
Women and Bird in the Night, Joan Miro	18.98
Waterlillies, Claude Monet	15.99

H.O.T. Problems

35. **OPEN ENDED** Write two decimals that are equivalent to 18.7. Tell why.

36. **CHALLENGE** How many times greater is 46 than 0.46? Explain.

37. **WRITING IN MATH** Discuss the similarities and differences between comparing whole numbers and comparing decimals.

TEST Practice

38. Which of the following numbers is greater than 7.02? **(Lesson 1-6)**

A 7.021

B 7.020

C 7.002

D 7.0

39. Which of the following lists three decimalls between 8.6 and 9.2? **(Lesson 1-6)**

F eight and seven tenths, 8.61, 8.5

G eight and seven hundredths, 9.1, 9.0

H eight and eight tenths, 9.21, 9.01

J eight and seventy-five hundredths, 8.80, 9.19

Spiral Review

Use place value to write each number in expanded form. **(Lesson 1-5)**

40. 0.85 **41.** 2.09 **42.** 5.074 **43.** 16.731

44. The model at the right has $\frac{6}{10}$ of its squares shaded. Write the decimal that is represented by the shaded portion. **(Lesson 1-4)**

45. Della wants to score 32 goals this soccer season. So far, she has scored 26 goals and there are 3 games left this season. If she scores the same number of goals in each of the remaining games, how many goals must she score per game to score 32 goals? **(Lesson 1-3)**

Replace each ● with <, >, or = to make a true sentence. **(Lesson 1-2)**

46. 743 ● 842 **47.** 10,361 ● 1,542 **48.** 25,972 ● 52,955

49. The graphic shows the fastest speeds recorded for different activities. Which activity had the fastest speed? **(Lesson 1-2)**

Activity	Speed (miles per hour)
luge	85.38
water skiing	143.08
horse running	43.26

Name the place of the underlined digit. Then write the value of the digit. **(Lesson 1-1)**

50. 4,$\underline{6}$92,013

51. 1$\underline{8}$,925

52. $\underline{2}$7,904,611,000

Fun in the Sun

The Sun is amazing. It is a star that is 4.5 billion years old. At its center, the temperature is 27 million degrees Fahrenheit. That's about 67,000 times hotter than an oven! The Sun is not only incredibly hot, but also very large. If it were hollow, 1,000,000 Earths could fit inside of it. Because the Sun is so big, it has a lot of gravity. This gravity pulls on the 8 planets and keeps them in orbit.

Each planet's orbit is a different shape. Orbital eccentricity describes the shape of a planet's orbit. Scientists use decimals to measure orbital eccentricity. If a planet's orbit is perfectly circular, its orbital eccentricity is 0.0. The more oval-shaped the planet's orbit, the closer the decimal is to 1.0. Because each orbit is different, the planets are not always the same distance from the sun. Scientists describe these distances from the sun as averages.

Planet	Average Distance from Sun (miles)	Orbital Eccentricity
Mercury	35,983,093	0.205
Venus	67,237,910	0.007
Earth	92,955,820	0.017
Mars	141,633,330	0.055
Jupiter	483,682,810	0.094
Saturn	886,526,100	0.057
Uranus	1,783,935,996	0.046
Neptune	2,795,084,800	0.011

Real-World Math

Use the information on page 40 to solve each problem.

1. What planets are more than one billion miles from the Sun?
2. Is Neptune's orbit more circular than Earth's orbit? Explain your reasoning.
3. Which planet's orbit is closest to a circle? Write its orbital eccentricity in word form.
4. Which planet's orbit is closest to an oval? Write its orbital eccentricity in expanded form.
5. Which planet is more than one hundred million miles from the Sun, but less than two hundred million miles from the Sun?
6. The temperature of the Sun at its center is 27 million degrees Fahrenheit. Write this number in standard form.
7. Which 4 planets have orbits that are the most circular? Order these four planets from most circular to least circular.

Did You Know?

If you drove 60 miles per hour, it would take you 176 years to get to the Sun.

1-7 Order Whole Numbers and Decimals

MAIN IDEA

I will order whole numbers and decimals.

Math Online

macmillanmh.com

- Extra Examples
- Personal Tutor
- Self-Check Quiz

GET READY to Learn

The table at the right shows the capacities of National League Football stadiums. You can use place value to order the capacities from greatest to least.

Stadium	Capacity
INVESCO Field Englewood, CO	76,100
Ford Field Detroit, MI	65,000
Qwest Stadium Seattle, WA	67,100

Real-World EXAMPLE — Order Whole Numbers

1 **STADIUMS** **Refer to the table above. Order the capacities of the stadiums from greatest to least.**

One Way: **Use place value**

Step 1 Line up the numbers.	**Step 2** Compare the digits in the greatest place.	**Step 3** Compare the digits in the next place.
76,100	**7**6,100 ← greatest	76,100
65,000	**6**5,000	6**5**,000 ← least
67,100	**6**7,100	6**7**,100

Another Way: **Use a number line**

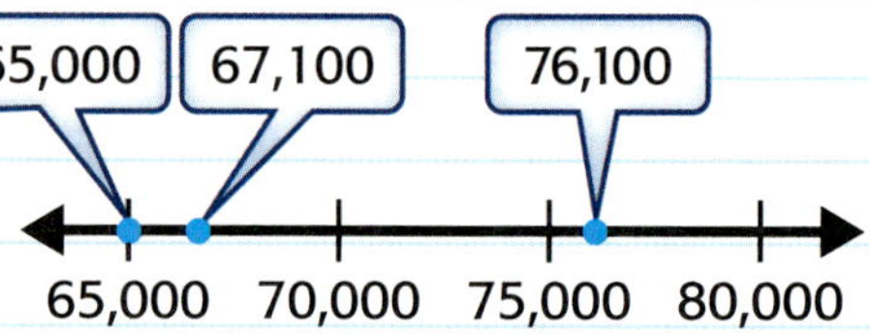

So, the capacities from greatest to least are 76,100, 67,100, and 65,000.

Real-World EXAMPLES

Order Whole Numbers and Decimals

2 **SPORTS** **Ava's scores for three gymnastics events are shown in the table. Order her scores from least to greatest.**

Event	Score
Beam	9.375
Bars	8.950
Floor	9.275

Step 1 Line up the decimal points.	**Step 2** Compare the digits in the greatest place.	**Step 3** Compare the digits in the next place.
9.275	9.275	9.275
8.950	8.950 ← least	8.950
9.375	9.375	9.375 ← greatest

The scores from least to greatest are 8.950, 9.275, and 9.375.

Remember

Annexing zeros is useful when ordering groups of whole numbers and decimals.

3 **MAIL** **Four packages weighing 22.7, 23.84, 22, and 23.9 pounds were mailed. Order the weights from greatest to least.**

Step 1 Line up the decimal points.	**Step 2** Annex zeros so all numbers have the same final place value.	**Step 3** Compare and order using place value.
22.7	22.70	23.90
23.84	23.84	23.84
22	22.00	22.70
23.9	23.90	22.00

The weights from greatest to least are 23.9, 23.84, 22.7, and 22.

CHECK What You Know

Order each set of numbers from least to greatest. See Examples 1–3 (pp. 42–43)

1. Miles traveled: 567, 643, 590, 645
2. Rainfall in inches: 0.76, 0.09, 0.63, 0.24
3. Height of flowers in inches: 8.9, 8.59, 8.705, 8.05
4. Lengths of boxes in centimeters: 52.8, 51, 51.01, 52.47, 51.008
5. The length of insects in centimeters are: 1.35, 0.9, 1.48, and 1.8. Order the sizes of the insects from greatest to least.
6. **Talk About It** Discuss different steps that make ordering numbers easier.

Practice and Problem Solving

EXTRA PRACTICE See page R4.

Order each set of numbers from least to greatest. See Examples 1–3 (pp. 42–43)

7. Ages of teachers: 45, 32, 29, 30

8. Temperatures in °F: 106, 99, 101, 110

9. Baseball game attendances: 7,342, 7,249, 7,300, 7,248

10. Yearly salaries: $32,547, $33,200, $32,830, $32,829

11. Kilometers ran: 4.9, 3.7, 3.4, 4.2

12. Cost of snacks: $2.43, $2.34, $2.05, $2.18, $1.99

13. Masses of bottles in grams: 9.14, 7.99, 9.02, 8.95, 8.91

14. Race times in seconds: 43.789, 67.543, 86.347, 78.432, 34.678

15. Heights of trees in meters: 9.8, 10, 10.2, 9.6, 11

16. Weights of dogs in pounds: 25.4, 26.2, 26, 25.8, 27

17. The table shows the total number of students enrolled in some universities in a recent year. Which university had the greatest number of students enrolled? Which university had the least number of students enrolled?

University Enrollment

University	Number of Students
Michigan State University	44,836
New York University	39,408
Purdue University	40,108
The Ohio State University	50,995
University of South Florida	42,238
University of Washington	39,199

Source: Institute of Education Sciences

18. The following measures are the long jump distances of the top six finishers in the 2004 Summer Olympics. Which distance was greater than 8.32 meters, but less than 8.59 meters?

8.25 m, 8.47 m, 8.59 m,
8.24 m, 8.32 m, 8.31 m

19. The table shows the heights of the tallest indoor waterfalls. Order the heights from greatest to least.

Location	Height (meters)
Hotel Windsor, Michigan	18.3
International Center, Michigan	34.7
Mohegan Sun, Connecticut	26.1
Orchid Hotel, India	21.3
Trump Tower, New York	27.4

Source: *Scholastic Book of World Records*

Data File

The table shows facts about snakes common to different regions of Kentucky.

Snake	Average Adult Body Length (cm)	Average Baby Body Length (cm)
Copperhead	63.5	27.9
Western Cottonmouth	91.25	21.5
Timber Rattlesnake	121.6	29.5
Queen Snake	61	15.2

20. List the average baby body lengths from least to greatest.

21. Write the names of the snakes in order from greatest to least average adult body length.

22. The average length of an adult Eastern Coachwhip snake is 152.4 centimeters. Write a sentence comparing its length to the length of the other snakes listed in the table.

H.O.T. Problems

23. OPEN ENDED Write an ordered list of five numbers whose values are between 50.98 and 51.6. Tell whether your list is from least to greatest or greatest to least.

24. FIND THE ERROR Diego and Abigail are ordering the numbers 0.088, 0.007, 0.4, and 0.19 from least to greatest. Who is correct? Explain.

25. WRITING IN MATH Write a real-world problem that can be solved by finding the least number from: 12.33, 12.2, 11.79, 11.9, and 12.05.

TEST Practice

26. Matt completed his first race in 15.163 seconds. The time of his second race was 15.24 seconds. Which of the following choices correctly shows the relationship between 15.163 and 15.24? (Lesson 1-6)

A $15.163 < 15.24$

B $15.163 > 15.24$

C $15.24 < 15.163$

D $15.24 = 15.163$

27. The table shows the seating capacity of the three largest stadiums in the world. Which is a true statement? (Lesson 1-7)

Stadium	Maximum Seating
Maracaña Municipa (Brazil)	205,000
Rungrado (North Korea)	150,000
Strahov (Czech Republic)	240,000

F The Maracaña Municipa is larger than the Rungrado.

G The Strahov is smaller than the Maracaña Municipa.

H The Maracaña Municipa is the largest stadium.

J The Strahov is the smallest stadium.

Spiral Review

Replace each ● with <, >, or = to make a true sentence. (Lesson 1-6)

28. 46.49 ● 46.5 **29.** 2.79 ● 2.37 **30.** 10.56 ● 10.65

Write each number in word form. (Lesson 1-5)

31. 7.3 **32.** 0.81 **33.** 2.99 **34.** 5.046

35. Mihir has \$29 in his piggy bank. He receives \$35 for his birthday. Does he have enough money to buy a computer game that costs \$68 including tax? (Lesson 1-3)

For Exercises 36–38, use the table. It shows the world's largest freshwater aquariums. (Lesson 1-1)

Largest Freshwater Aquariums	
Aquarium	**Size (sq ft)**
Tennessee Aquarium, Tennessee	130,000
The Freshwater Center, Denmark	91,494
Great Lakes Aquarium, Minnesota	62,382

36. Describe the size of the Tennessee Aquarium in expanded form.

37. How many square feet is The Freshwater Center? Write in expanded form.

38. Describe the size of the Great Lakes Aquarium in word form.

Decimal War

Comparing Decimals

Get Ready!

Players: 2 players

You will need: spinner with digits 0 through 9
paper

Get Set!

- Each player creates ten game sheets like the one shown at the right, one for each of ten rounds.
- Make a spinner as shown.

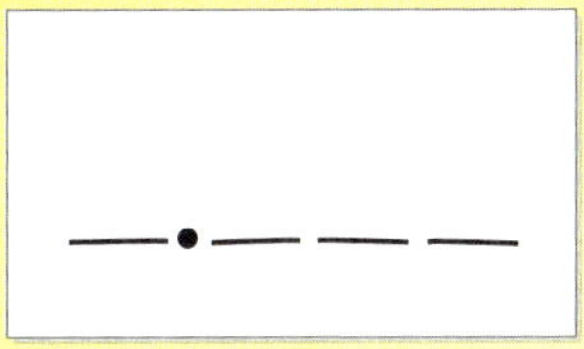

Go!

- One player spins the spinner.
- Each player writes the number in one of the blanks on his or her game sheet.

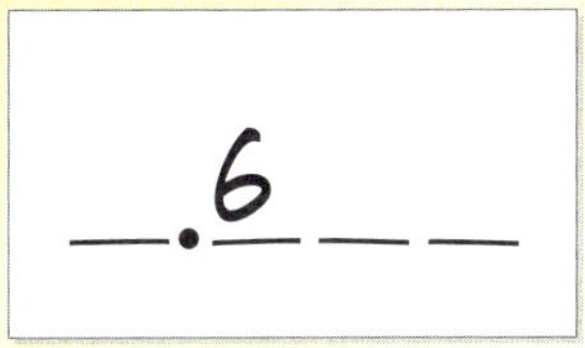

- The other player spins the spinner, and each player writes the number in a blank.
- Play continues until all blanks are filled.
- The person with the greatest decimal scores 1 point. If players have the same decimal, each player scores 1 point.
- Repeat for ten rounds.
- The person with the greatest number of points after ten rounds is the winner.

1-8 Problem-Solving Strategy

MAIN IDEA I will solve problems by using the *guess and check* strategy.

The Bactrian camel has two humps, while the Dromedary camel has just one. Zach counted 19 animals with a total of 27 humps. How many camels of each type are there?

Understand	**What facts do you know?** • Bactrian camels have two humps. • Dromedary camels have one hump. • There are 19 camels with 27 humps. **What do you need to find?** • How many camels of each type are there?
Plan	You can use the *guess and check* strategy to solve the problem. Use combinations of 19 total camels to guess.
Solve	**Guess:** 10 Bactrian camels and 9 Dromedary camels **Check:** $10 \times 2 = 20$ humps — 20 humps + 9 humps = 29 humps $9 \times 1 = 9$ humps — Too high. Try fewer Bactrian camels and more Dromedary camels. **Guess:** 7 Bactrian camels and 12 Dromedary camels **Check:** $7 \times 2 = 14$ humps — 14 humps + 12 humps = 26 humps $12 \times 1 = 12$ humps — Too low. Try more Bactrian camels and less Dromedary camels. **Guess:** 8 Bactrian camels and 11 Dromedary camels **Check:** $8 \times 2 = 16$ humps — 16 humps + 11 humps = 27 humps $11 \times 1 = 11$ humps — ✓ This guess is correct. So, there are 8 Bactrian camels and 11 Dromedary camels.
Check	Look back at the problem. $8 + 11 = 19$ camels and $16 + 11 = 27$ humps. So, the answer is correct.

ANALYZE the Strategy

Refer to the problem on the previous page.

1. Are there any other combinations of each type of camel that Zach could have seen? Explain your reasoning.

2. Suppose you saw 18 camels with a total of 22 humps. How many of each type did you see?

3. Explain how the guess and check method helped you solve this problem.

4. Explain why you should record your guesses and their results in the *solve* step of the problem-solving plan.

PRACTICE the Strategy

EXTRA PRACTICE See page R4.

Solve. Use the *guess and check* strategy.

5. Vanessa sees 14 wheels on a total of 6 bicycles and tricycles. How many bicycles and tricycles are there?

6. Cole spent $66 on rookie cards and Hall of Famer cards. How many of each type of card did he buy?

Baseball Card	Cost
Rookie	4 for $6
Hall of Famer	2 for $9

7. A teacher is having three students take care of 28 goldfish during the summer. He gave some of them to Mary. Then he gave twice as many to Brandon. He gave twice as many to Kaylee as he gave to Brandon. How many fish did each student get?

8. **Measurement** Bike path A is 4 miles long. Bike path B is 7 miles long. If April biked a total of 37 miles, how many times did she bike each path?

9. Stacie counts 26 legs in a barnyard with horses and chickens. If there are 8 animals, how many are horses?

10. Len bought 2 postcards and received $1.35 in change in quarters and dimes. If he got 6 coins back, how many of each coin did he get?

11. The sum of two numbers is 30. Their product is 176. What are the two numbers?

12. A tour director collected $258 for tour packages. Tour package A costs $18 and tour package B costs $22. How many of each tour package were sold?

13. Ticket prices for a science museum are shown in the table. If $162 is collected from a group of 12 people, how many adults and students are in the group?

Customer	Cost
Adult	$18
Student	$12

14. WRITING IN MATH Refer to Exercise 11. How did you use the *guess and check* strategy to find the numbers?

Chapter 1 Study Guide and Review

Math Online macmillanmh.com
- STUDY TO GO
- Vocabulary Review

FOLDABLES® Study Organizer GET READY to Study

Be sure the following Big Ideas are noted in your Foldable.

Key Concepts

Place Value (pp. 17, 32)

- **Place Value** is useful for reading and writing whole numbers and decimals.

  9,000,000,000 → nine billion

  5.38 → five and thirty-eight hundredths

- Whole numbers and decimals can be written in different forms.

  Standard Form: 2,006,000

  Expanded Form: 2,000,000 + 6,000

  Word Form: two million, six thousand

Compare and Order Whole Numbers and Decimals (pp. 20, 36)

- Use a number line or place value to compare and order numbers.

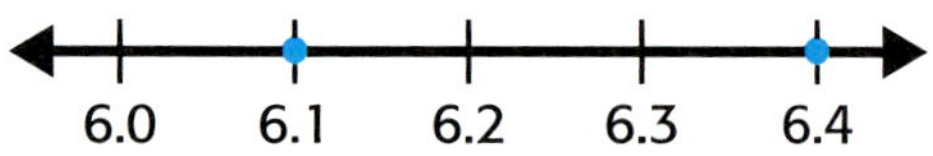

$6.1 < 6.4$

Key Vocabulary

decimal (p. 26)
equation (p. 20)
equivalent decimals (p. 37)
expanded form (p. 17)
inequality (p. 20)
place value (p. 17)
standard form (p. 17)

Vocabulary Check

State whether each sentence is *true* or *false*. If *false*, replace the underlined word or number to make a true sentence.

1. The symbol $>$ means <u>greater than</u>.
2. The number 50.02 written in <u>standard form</u> is 50 + 0.02.
3. The number 7,105 is <u>equal to</u> 7,501.
4. The digit 4 in 24,510,000,000 is in the <u>millions</u> place.
5. A <u>decimal</u> is a number that has at least one digit to the right of the decimal point.
6. Eight and two hundredths written as a decimal is <u>0.802</u>.

Lesson-by-Lesson Review

1-1 Place Value Through Billions (pp. 17–19)

Example 1
Name the place of the underlined digit in 24,900. Then write the value of the digit.

place: ten thousands
value: 20,000

Example 2
Use place value to write the following number in standard form and expanded form.

ten million, twenty thousand, four hundred sixteen

Standard: 10,020,416
Expanded: 10,000,000 + 20,000 + 400 + 10 + 6

Name the place value of the underlined digit. Then write the number it represents.

7. 195,489 **8.** 6,720,341

Use place value to write each number in standard form.

9. 94 billion, 237 million, 108

10. 8,000,000 + 50,000 + 2,000 + 600

Write each number in expanded form. Then read and write in word form.

11. 4,302 **12.** 1,279,018

13. Measurement Montana has an area of 147,165 square miles. Write this number in word form.

1-2 Compare Whole Numbers (pp. 20–23)

Example 3
Replace ● with <, >, or = to make 3,249,800 ● 3,210,756 a true sentence.

Step 1 Line up the digits.

3,249,800
3,210,756

Step 2 Compare each place value, starting at the left.

In the ten thousands place, 4 > 1.

Since 4 > 1 in the ten thousands place, 3,249,800 > 3,210,756.

Replace each ● with <, >, or = to make a true sentence.

14. 98 ● 70

15. 234 ● 1,510

16. 8,960 ● 8,960

17. 814,789,002 ● 814,789,020

18. Is the population of Jacksonville or San Francisco greater?

City	Population
Jacksonville, Florida	777,704
San Francisco, California	744,230

CHAPTER 1

Study Guide and Review

1-3 Problem-Solving Investigation: The Four-Step Plan (pp. 24–25)

Example 4

On Sunday, Li ate 2,072 Calories. On the same day, her brother ate 2,141 Calories. Who ate more Calories on Sunday?

Understand Li ate 2,072 Calories. Her brother ate 2,141 Calories. Find who ate more.

Plan Use place value to determine who ate more Calories on Sunday.

Solve Line up the digits. Compare place value starting at the left. Li's brother ate more Calories.

2,072
2,141

In the hundreds place, 1 > 0.

Check 2,072 < 2,141 ✓

Solve. Use the four-step plan.

19. **Measurement** There are three long tunnels that go under Boston Harbor. The Summer Tunnel is 5,653 feet long. The Callahan Tunnel is 5,070 feet long. The Ted Williams Tunnel is 8,448 feet long. Order the lengths of the tunnels from least to greatest. Which tunnels are shorter than 5,670 feet in length?

20. How much more money is spent on strawberry and grape jelly than the other types of jelly each year?

Yearly Jelly Sales (thousands)	
Strawberry and grape	$371
All others	$285

1-4 Represent Decimals (pp. 28–30)

Example 5

Use a model to write $\frac{41}{1,000}$ as a decimal.

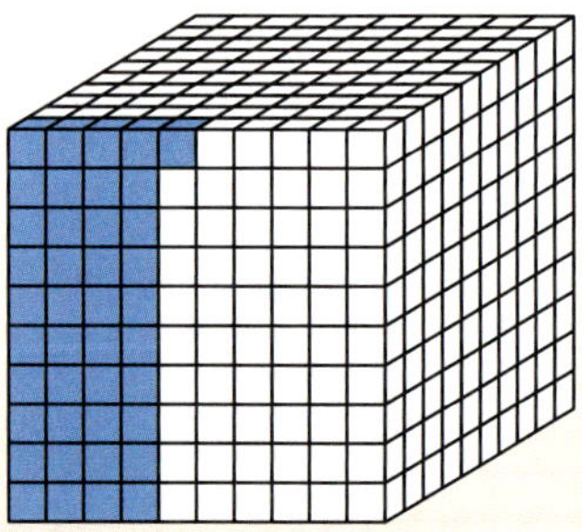

The fraction names thousandths, so there should be 3 digits to the right of the decimal point.

$\frac{41}{1,000} = 0.041$

Use a model to write each fraction as a decimal.

21. $\frac{19}{100}$

22. $\frac{8}{10}$

23. $\frac{644}{1,000}$

24. $\frac{2}{100}$

25. four tenths

26. thirteen thousandths

27. Tommy made six tenths of the free throws he attempted this season. Write the fraction of free throws that he made as a decimal.

1-5 Place Value Through Thousandths (pp. 32–35)

Example 6

Write *eleven and eighty-five hundredths* in standard form.

tens	ones	tenths	hundredths
1	1 .	8	5

Standard Form: 11.85

Example 7

Write 7.394 in expanded form and word form.

Expanded: 7 + 0.3 + 0.09 + 0.004

Word: seven and three hundred ninety-four thousandths

Use place value to write each number in standard form.

28. five and nine tenths

29. 0.7 + 0.01 + 0.002

Write each number in expanded form. Then read and write in word form.

30. 0.53 **31.** 0.068

32. 1.22 **33.** 9.745

34. **Measurement** The winner of an inline skating race finished in 40.375 minutes. Write this time in word form.

1-6 Compare Decimals (pp. 36–39)

Example 8

Replace ● with $<$, $>$, or $=$ to make 5.613 ● 5.619 a true sentence.

Step 1 Line up the decimal points.

5.613
5.619

Step 2 Starting at the left, find the first place the digits are different.

5.61**3**
5.61**9**

In the thousandths place, $3 < 9$.

Since $3 < 9$ in the thousandths place, $5.613 < 5.619$.

Replace each ● with $<$, $>$, or $=$ to make a true sentence.

35. 0.1 ● 0.11 **36.** 0.49 ● 0.71

37. 3.6 ● 3.16 **38.** 9.02 ● 9.020

39. 0.843 ● 0.846 **40.** 4.25 ● 4.025

41. **Measurement** The table shows the speeds of two fish.

Fish	Speed (mi per h)
Bluefin tuna	43.4
Wahoo	48.5

Is the bluefin tuna or the wahoo faster? Tell why.

CHAPTER 1

Study Guide and Review

1-7 Order Whole Numbers and Decimals (pp. 42–46)

Example 9

Order 60.11, 60, and 61.038 from least to greatest.

Step 1	60.11 60 61.038	Line up the decimal points.
Step 2	60.110 60.000 61.038	Annex zeros so all numbers have the same final place value.
Step 3	60.000 60.110 61.038	Compare and order using place value.

The numbers in order from least to greatest are 60, 60.11, and 61.038.

Order each set of numbers from least to greatest.

42. 56, 46, 58, 76

43. 13.84, 13.097, 13, 12.655, 13.6

44. Refer to the table. List these countries from the greatest to least number of bikes per person.

Country	Bikes per Person
China	0.37
Germany	0.88
Japan	0.63
Netherlands	1.10
United States	0.49

Source: *Scholastic Book of World Records*

1-8 Problem-Solving Strategy: Guess and Check (pp. 48–49)

Example 10

Logan buys 10 T-shirts and spends a total of \$96. Long-sleeved shirts cost \$12. Short-sleeved shirts cost \$8. How many of each did he buy?

Use the *guess and check* strategy.

Guess: 5 \$12 shirts, 5 \$8 shirts
Check: $5 \times 12 = 60$, $5 \times 8 = 40$
\$60 + \$40 = \$100 too high

Guess: 4 \$12 shirts, 6 \$8 shirts
Check: $4 \times 12 = 48$, $6 \times 8 = 48$
\$48 + \$48 = \$96 ✓

So, he bought 4 shirts for \$12 each and 6 shirts for \$8 each.

Solve. Use the *guess and check* strategy.

45. The table shows admission costs to an art exhibit.

Customer	Cost
Adult	\$5
Child	\$3

It costs a total of \$37 for 9 people. How many adults and children are in the group?

46. Will ran 120 minutes in the past two days. He ran 20 more minutes the second day than the first day. How many minutes did he run each day?

CHAPTER 1

Chapter Test

Math Online macmillanmh.com
- Chapter Test

Name the place value of the underlined digit. Then write the number it represents.

1. 2$\underline{3}$7,961 **2.** $\underline{8}$04,510,327

3. 6.4$\underline{5}$7 **4.** 0.89$\underline{2}$

5. **MULTIPLE CHOICE** Write 4 million, 76 thousand, 850 in standard form.

A 4,076,085

B 4,076,850

C 4,760,850

D 4,076,850,000

6. A car wash costs $7 for cars and $12 for trucks. If $370 is collected from 40 vehicles, how many cars and trucks were washed? Use the *guess and check* strategy.

Write each number in word form.

7. 18,709 **8.** 3,524,064

9. 23.16 **10.** 5.921

11. **MULTIPLE CHOICE** What part of the model is shaded?

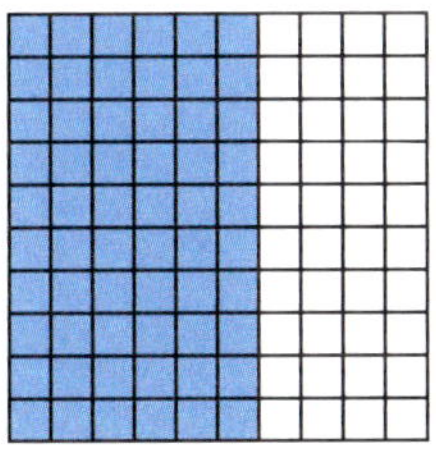

F 0.006 **H** 0.6

G 0.06 **J** 6.0

Write each fraction as a decimal.

12. $\frac{31}{100}$ **13.** $\frac{4}{10}$

14. $\frac{985}{1,000}$ **15.** $\frac{16}{1,000}$

For Exercises 16 and 17, use the table. It shows the length of the largest of each type of whale.

Type of Whale	Length (feet)
Fin whale	90
Sei whale	72
Right whale	60
Blue whale	80

16. Is the sei whale or fin whale longer?

17. Which is smaller: the right whale or the blue whale?

18. China has 4,639 movie theaters. France has 4,365. Which country has more?

Replace each ● with <, >, or = to make a true sentence.

19. 8.9 ● 8.2 **20.** 0.15 ● 0.4

21. 1.251 ● 1.201 **22.** 0.7 ● 0.700

Order each set of numbers from least to greatest.

23. 170, 181, 178, 171

24. 2.587, 2.43, 2.09, 2.23, 2.568

25. **WRITING IN MATH** The table shows tips that a server earned for four days.

Day	Tips ($)
Monday	$40.98
Tuesday	$55.30
Wednesday	$46.20
Thursday	$36.50

On which day(s) did the server earn more than $46? Explain.

CHAPTER 1

Test Practice

Chapter 1

Math Online macmillanmh.com

• Test Practice

TEST Example

The table shows the number of laps Michael swam each day over the past 4 weeks. If the pattern continues, how many laps will he swim each day during the fifth week?

Week	1	2	3	4	5
Laps	10	12	14	16	?

A 16 laps

B 17 laps

C 18 laps

D 20 laps

Read the Test Item

Look for a pattern to find the number of laps during week 5.

Solve the Test Item

Find the increase in laps between each of the first 4 weeks.

Week	1	2	3	4	5
Laps	10	12	14	16	?

+2 +2 +2 +2

The number of laps per day increases by 2 each week. During the fifth week, Michael will swim 16 + 2, or 18 laps per day. The answer is C.

PART 1 Multiple Choice

Read each question. Then fill in the correct answer on the answer sheet provided by your teacher or on a sheet of paper.

1. At a school function, there are 12 parents for every 1 teacher. If there are 72 parents at the function, how many teachers are there?

A 5

B 6

C 7

D 8

2. Start with 168,905.252. Increase the digit in the ten thousands place by 3, and decrease the thousandths digit by 2. What number results?

F 148,905.234

G 171,905.250

H 198,905.232

J 198,905.250

Preparing for Standardized Tests

For test-taking strategies and practice, see pages R42–R55.

3. What fraction is equivalent to the decimal 0.058?

A $\frac{58}{10}$

B $\frac{58}{100}$

C $\frac{58}{1,000}$

D $\frac{58}{10,000}$

---

4. The population of the city where Lydia lives is eight million, six hundred twenty thousand, four hundred one. Which is the standard form of this number?

F 8,602,401

G 8,620,401

H 8,620,410

J 80,620,401

---

5. What portion of the squares is shaded? Express your answer as a decimal and a fraction.

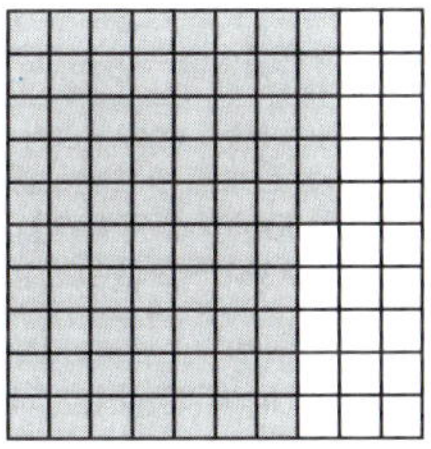

A 0.25, $\frac{25}{100}$

B 0.4, $\frac{40}{100}$

C 0.6, $\frac{60}{100}$

D 0.75, $\frac{75}{100}$

PART 2 Short Response

Record your answers on the sheet provided by your teacher or on a sheet of paper.

6. Write the number of students in the fifth grade in word form.

Grade Sizes	
Grade	Number of Students
5th Grade	237
6th Grade	215

---

7. Eduardo wants to save $770 to buy a new refrigerator. He saves $110 per month. Write a number sentence to show how many months it will take him to save enough money.

PART 3 Extended Response

Record your answers on the answer sheet provided by your teacher or on a sheet of paper. Show your work.

8. Draw a model to represent $\frac{5}{10}$. Then determine if $\frac{5}{10}$ is greater than, less than, or equal to $\frac{1}{2}$. Explain.

---

9. A machinist needs to cut a hole with a diameter of twenty-nine thousandths inch. By mistake, he cuts the hole 0.03 inch. Did he cut the hole too large or too small? Explain.

NEED EXTRA HELP?									
If You Missed Question...	1	2	3	4	5	6	7	8	9
Go to Lesson...	1-3	1-1	1-4	1-1	1-5	1-1	1-8	1-4	1-5

CHAPTER 2 Add and Subtract Whole Numbers and Decimals

BIG Idea How are adding whole numbers and adding decimals the same?

The steps for adding and subtracting whole numbers and decimals are similar. In both cases, you add or subtract digits with the same place value.

Example Chicagoland Speedway's track length is 1.5 miles. Indianapolis Motor Speedway's track length is 2.5 miles. How much longer is the Indianapolis track than the Chicagoland track?

$$\begin{array}{r} 2.5 \\ -\ 1.5 \\ \hline 1.0 \end{array}$$

What will I learn in this chapter?

- Round whole numbers and decimals.
- Estimate sums and differences by rounding.
- Add and subtract whole numbers and decimals.
- Use properties of addition to add whole numbers and decimals mentally.
- Solve problems by using the *work backward* strategy.

Key Vocabulary

round
estimate
compatible numbers
compensation

Math Online **Student Study Tools at macmillanmh.com**

FOLDABLES® Study Organizer

Make this Foldable to help you organize information about whole numbers and decimals. Start with a sheet of 11″ × 17″ paper.

1. **Fold** the short sides toward the middle.

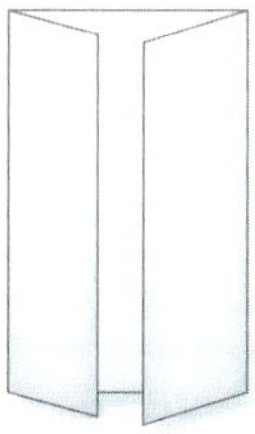

2. **Fold** the top to the bottom. Then open the paper.

3. **Cut** along the second fold to make four tabs.

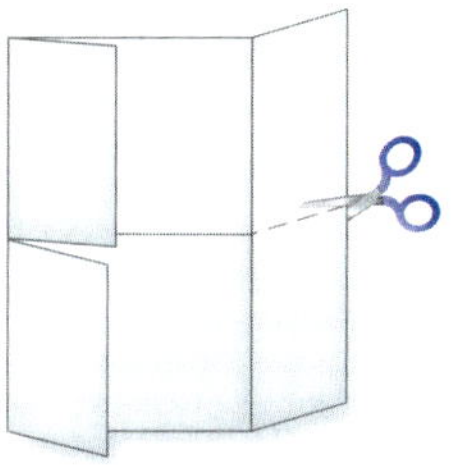

4. **Label** each of the tabs as shown.

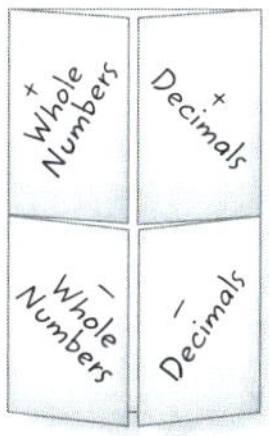

ARE YOU READY for Chapter 2?

You have two ways to check prerequisite skills for this chapter.

Option 2

Math Online Take the Chapter Readiness Quiz at macmillanmh.com.

Option 1

Complete the Quick Check below.

QUICK Check

Name the place-value position of each underlined digit. **(Lessons 1-1 and 1-5)**

1. $\underline{5}2$

2. $13\underline{8}$

3. $4.\underline{3}$

4. $\underline{9}01$

5. $1.2\underline{1}6$

6. $\underline{2},785$

Add. **(Prior Grade)**

7. 7 + 3

8. 2 + 9

9. 60 + 11

10. 52 + 30

11. 7 + 4 + 1

12. 8 + 5 + 1

13. The Pham family has 3 dogs, 1 cat, and 6 fish. The Weber family has 2 dogs, 3 gerbils, and a turtle. How many more pets does the Pham family have than the Weber family?

Complete to correctly rename each number. **(Prior Grade)**

14. 8 tens = 7 tens + __?__ ones

15. 2 hundreds = 1 hundred + __?__ tens

16. 5 hundreds = __?__ hundreds + 10 tens

17. 13 ones = 1 ten + __?__ ones

18. 16 tens = 1 hundred + __?__ tens

2-1 Round Whole Numbers and Decimals

MAIN IDEA

I will round whole numbers and decimals.

New Vocabulary

round

Math Online

macmillanmh.com

- Extra Examples
- Personal Tutor
- Self-Check Quiz

GET READY to Learn

A new species of lobster that measures 5.9 inches long was discovered 7,540 feet deep in the South Pacific Ocean.

Anna described the lobster: "It's about 6 inches long. It was found about 7,500 feet deep in the ocean."

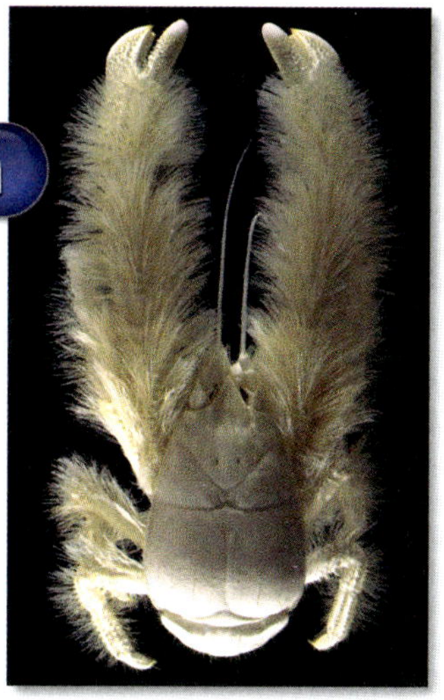

When you **round** a number, you find its approximate value. You can round whole numbers and decimals.

Real-World EXAMPLE — Round Whole Numbers

1 TRAVEL Steve Fossett was the first person to travel 20,626 miles around the world alone in a hot air balloon. Round 20,626 to the nearest thousand. Is it closer to 20,000 or 21,000?

Step 1	Underline the digit in the place to be rounded. In this case, the 0 in the thousands place is to be rounded.	20,626
Step 2	Look at 6, the digit to the right of the underlined digit.	20,**6**26
Step 3	If this digit is 5 or greater, add 1 to the underlined digit. Since 6 > 5, add 1 to the 0.	21,626
Step 4	Replace all digits after the underlined digit with zeros.	21,000

To the nearest thousand, 20,626 rounds to 21,000. The number line shows that 20,626 is closer to 21,000 than to 20,000.

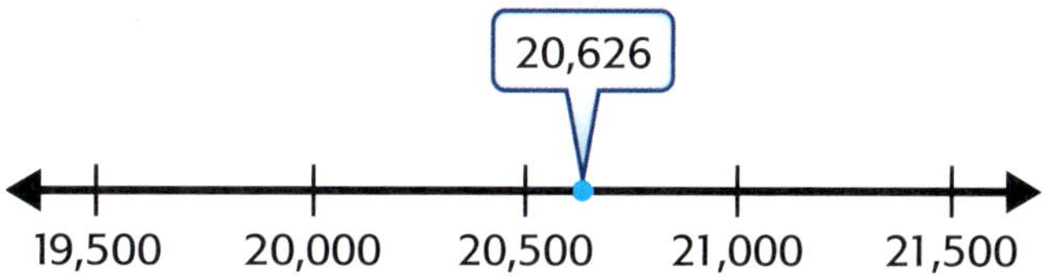

When you round decimals, identify the place being rounded. Determine whether the original number is closer to that place or the next higher place.

Remember

You can use a number line to check if the answer is reasonable.

EXAMPLE Round Decimals

2 **Round 46.73 to the nearest tenth. Is it closer to 46.7 or 46.8?**

Step 1 Underline the digit in the tenths place, 7. 46.73

Step 2 Look at 3, the digit to the right of 7. 46.73

Step 3 If the digit is 4 or less, do not change the underlined digit. Since $3 < 5$, keep the digit 7 the same. 46.73

Step 4 Drop the digit after the underlined digit. 46.7

So, 46.73 rounds to 46.7. On the number line, 46.73 is closer to 46.7 than to 46.8. So, the answer is reasonable.

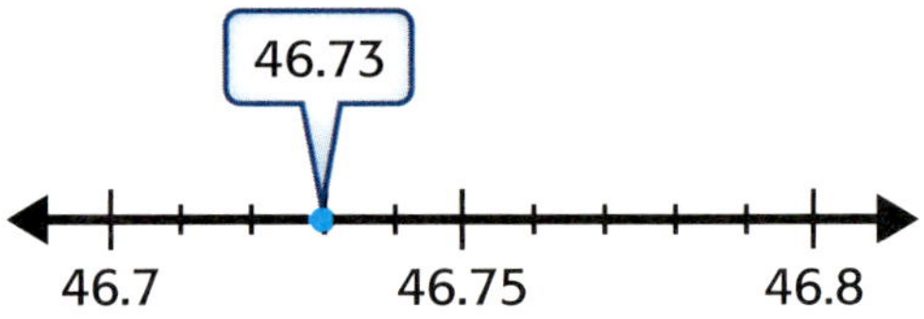

CHECK What You Know

Round each number to the underlined place. See Example 1 (p. 61)

1. 42

2. 8,317

3. 5,729

4. 1,096

Round each decimal to the place indicated. See Example 2 (p. 62)

5. 28.6; ones

6. 4.35; tenths

7. 110.079; hundredths

8. 67.142; ones

9. An ice sheet that covers most of Antarctica is about 1.34 miles thick. To the nearest tenth mile, how thick is the ice?

10. Talk About It Explain how to round 74.685 to the nearest hundredth.

Practice and Problem Solving

EXTRA PRACTICE See page R4.

Round each number to the underlined place. See Example 1 (p. 61)

11. 19

12. 681

13. 735

14. 3,705

15. 106,950

16. 5,750

17. 24,921

18. 692,300

Round each decimal to the place indicated. See Example 2 (p. 62)

19. 6.2; ones

20. 8.17; tenths

21. 0.053; hundredths

22. 19.25; ones

23. 36.81; ones

24. 9.045; tenths

25. 2.526; hundredths

26. 57.009; hundredths

27. A recent Tour de France bike race was 2,274 miles long. How long was the race rounded to the nearest hundred miles?

28. The African bush elephant weighs between 4.4 tons and 7.7 tons. What are its least weight and greatest weight, rounded to the nearest ton?

Real-World PROBLEM SOLVING

Science The table shows what a 95-pound student would weigh on the Sun and on different planets.

Place	Weight (lb)
Jupiter	224.58
Mars	35.815
Sun	2,571.84

Round the weight on the Sun or each planet to the place indicated.

29. Mars; tenths

30. the Sun; thousands

31. Jupiter; tens

32. Jupiter; tenths

H.O.T. Problems

33. **OPEN ENDED** Write two different numbers that when rounded to the nearest tenth will give you 18.3.

34. **NUMBER SENSE** Explain what happens when you round 9,999.999 to any place.

35. **WRITING IN MATH** Describe two real-world situations in which it makes sense to round numbers.

2-2 Estimate Sums and Differences

GET READY to Learn

The table shows the final results of the Skateboard Vert competition in a recent X Games.

Dias scored *about* 10 more points than Hendrix.

Place	Athlete	Points
1	Sandro Dias (Brazil)	88.67
2	Renton Milar (Australia)	80.33
3	Neal Hendrix (U.S.)	79.67

MAIN IDEA

I will estimate sums and differences by rounding and using compatible numbers.

New Vocabulary

estimate

compatible numbers

Math Online

macmillanmh.com

- Extra Examples
- Personal Tutor
- Self-Check Quiz

When you do not need an exact answer or when you want to check whether an answer is reasonable, you can **estimate**. One way to estimate is to use rounding.

EXAMPLE Use Rounding with Whole Numbers

1 Estimate 526 + 193 by rounding.

Round each number to the nearest hundred. Then add.

$$\begin{array}{rcr l} 526 & \rightarrow & 500 & \text{526 is closer to 500 than 600.} \\ +\ 193 & \rightarrow & +\ 200 & \text{193 is closer to 200 than 100.} \\ \hline & & 700 & \end{array}$$

So, 526 + 193 is about 700.

You can also use compatible numbers to estimate sums and differences. **Compatible numbers** are numbers that are easy to add or subtract mentally.

EXAMPLE Use Compatible Numbers

2 Estimate 458 − 340 by using compatible numbers.

Find two numbers that you can easily subtract.

$$\begin{array}{rcr l} 458 & \rightarrow & 450 & \text{458 is close to 450.} \\ -\ 340 & \rightarrow & -\ 350 & \text{340 is close to 350.} \\ \hline & & 100 & \end{array}$$

So, 458 − 340 is about 100.

You can round numbers to any place value that makes estimation easier. If you round numbers to a lesser place value, you are likely to get a more accurate estimate.

Real-World EXAMPLE **Use Rounding with Decimals**

3 **TEMPERATURE** **The average January temperature for Knoxville, Tennessee, is 37.6°F. In Newark, New Jersey, the average is 31.3°F. Estimate the difference in average temperatures.**

One Way	Another Way
Round to the nearest ten. $\begin{array}{r} 37.6 \\ -31.3 \\ \hline \end{array} \rightarrow \begin{array}{r} 40 \\ -30 \\ \hline 10 \end{array}$	Round to the nearest whole number. $\begin{array}{r} 37.6 \\ -31.3 \\ \hline \end{array} \rightarrow \begin{array}{r} 38 \\ -31 \\ \hline 7 \end{array}$

Depending on how the numbers are rounded, the difference in temperatures is about 10°F or about 7°F. The actual difference is 6.3°. So, rounding to the nearest whole number gave the more accurate estimate.

CHECK What You Know

Estimate each sum or difference. Use rounding or compatible numbers. See Examples 1–3 (pp. 64–65)

1. $\begin{array}{r} 28 \\ +13 \\ \hline \end{array}$

2. $\begin{array}{r} 598 \\ -103 \\ \hline \end{array}$

3. $\begin{array}{r} 10.08 \\ +5.6 \\ \hline \end{array}$

4. 104 + 328

5. 2.65 − 0.766

6. 37.58 − 21.25

7. 3,256 + 670

8. 2,521 − 1,247

9. 475.6 − 58.5

10. 751.2 + 82.3

11. The world's largest cherry pie weighed 37,740 pounds. The world's largest apple pie weighed 30,115 pounds. About how much more did the cherry pie weigh?

12. **Talk About It** Tell when it might be appropriate to estimate rather than get the exact answer. Give a real-world example.

Practice and Problem Solving

EXTRA PRACTICE
See page R5.

Estimate each sum or difference. Use rounding or compatible numbers. See Examples 1–3 (pp. 64–65)

13. $\begin{array}{r} 59 \\ -\ 31 \\ \hline \end{array}$

14. $\begin{array}{r} 1,324 \\ +\ 2,064 \\ \hline \end{array}$

15. $\begin{array}{r} 7.6 \\ +\ 1.9 \\ \hline \end{array}$

16. $\begin{array}{r} 824 \\ -\ 637 \\ \hline \end{array}$

17. $\begin{array}{r} 6,820 \\ +\ 195 \\ \hline \end{array}$

18. $\begin{array}{r} 52.85 \\ -\ 9.09 \\ \hline \end{array}$

19. 150.9 + 310.6

20. 19.8 + 9.93

21. 24.86 − 12.49

22. 4.087 − 1.692

23. 3.872 + 12.49

24. 986 − 99

25. 4,201 − 592

26. 791.3 + 38.6

27. 321.75 − 16.65

28. The graphic shows the average speeds of two airplanes in miles per hour. About how much faster is the Foxbat than the Hawkeye? Show your work.

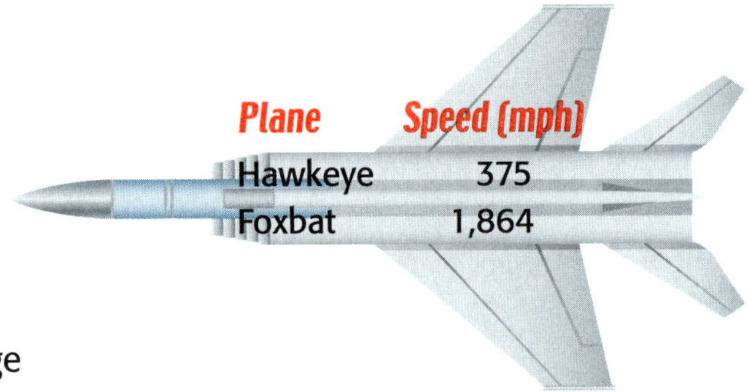

Plane	Speed (mph)
Hawkeye	375
Foxbat	1,864

29. Sophia has $20. She buys a hair band for $3.99, gum for $1.29, and a brush for $6.75. Not including tax, estimate how much change she should receive. Show your work.

H.O.T. Problems

30. **OPEN ENDED** Write a word problem that you can solve by subtracting. Estimate the difference two different ways. Identify which method, if any, gives a more accurate estimate.

31. **FIND THE ERROR** Samuel and Marlina are estimating 529.16 + 110.48 by rounding. Whose estimate is correct? Explain.

Samuel

$$\begin{array}{rcr} 529.16 & \rightarrow & 530 \\ +\ 110.48 & \rightarrow & +\ 100 \\ \hline & & 630 \end{array}$$

Marlina

$$\begin{array}{rcr} 529.16 & \rightarrow & 500 \\ +\ 110.48 & \rightarrow & +\ 100 \\ \hline & & 600 \end{array}$$

32. **WRITING IN ▸MATH** Suppose you round all addends down. Will the estimate be greater than or less than the actual sum? Explain.

TEST Practice

33. The table shows the lengths of four trails at a horseback riding camp. Which is the best estimate for the total length of all the trails? **(Lesson 2-2)**

Trail	A	B	C	D
Length (mi)	2.6	1.8	4.2	3.3

A 8 mi

B 12 mi

C 14 mi

D 15 mi

34. Mr. Jackson bought a plasma television that was on sale for \$1,989. The regular price was \$2,499. Which is the best estimate of the amount of money Mr. Jackson saved by buying the television on sale? **(Lesson 2-1)**

F \$500

G \$1,000

H \$3,000

J \$4,000

Spiral Review

35. The price of a jacket is \$50.49. What is the price of the jacket to the nearest dollar? **(Lesson 2-1)**

36. The Soda Shop sold 12 more milkshakes on Friday than it sold on Thursday. A total of 100 milkshakes were sold. How many were sold on Thursday? Solve. Use the *guess and check* strategy. **(Lesson 1-8)**

37. An ice cube floats in water because it is less dense than water. Density is the measure of mass per unit of volume. List the names of the substances in the table from least to greatest density. **(Lesson 1-7)**

Substance	Density (g/cm^3)
Aluminum	2.7
Cork	0.4
Ice cube	0.9
Water	1.0

Replace each ● with <, >, or = to make a true sentence. (Lesson 1-6)

38. 0.0561 ● 0.15

39. 40.900 ● 40.9

40. 17.22 ● 17.223

Use place value to write each number in standard form. (Lesson 1-5)

41. 13 and 9 tenths

42. 10 + 1 + 0.9 + 0.02 + 0.003

43. Shanti has 85 baseball cards. She buys 12 more cards and sells 19 cards. How many baseball cards does Shanti have now? **(Lesson 1-3)**

2-3 Problem-Solving Strategy

MAIN IDEA I will solve problems by using the *work backward* strategy.

The Nature Club raised $125 to buy and install nesting boxes for birds at a wildlife site. Each box costs $5. It costs $75 to rent a bus so the members can travel to the site. How many boxes can the club buy?

Understand

What facts do you know?

- $125 is available to buy and install the nesting boxes.
- Each box costs $5.
- The bus costs $75.

What do you need to find?

- How many boxes can the club buy?

Plan

You can work backward to find the number of boxes that can be bought. Start with $125, the amount the Nature Club has raised. Then subtract the costs. Recall that subtraction "undoes" addition and that division "undoes" multiplication.

Solve

First, undo the addition of the cost of the bus by subtracting the cost of the bus.

$\$125 - \$75 = \$50$

Then undo the multiplication of the cost of the boxes by dividing by the cost for each box.

$\$50 \div \$5 = 10$

So, ten boxes can be bought.

Check

Look back. Since, $10 \times \$5 = \$50$ and $\$50 + \$75 = \$125$, the answer is correct.

ANALYZE the Strategy

Refer to the problem on the previous page.

1. Explain how using the *work backward* strategy helped you find the number of nesting boxes the club could buy.

2. Suppose the club had $150 to spend. How many boxes could the club buy?

3. What is the best way to check your solution when using the *work backward* strategy?

4. Explain when you would use the *work backward* strategy to solve a problem.

PRACTICE the Strategy

EXTRA PRACTICE
See page R5.

Solve. Use the *work backward* strategy.

5. Students sold raffle tickets to raise money for a field trip. The first 20 tickets sold cost $4 each. To sell more tickets, they lowered the price to $2 each. If they raise $216, how many tickets did they sell in all?

6. Amy collected 15 more cans of food than Peyton. Ling collected 8 more than Amy. Ling collected 72 cans of food. How many cans of food did Peyton collect?

7. Jeanette's sister charges $5 per hour before midnight for babysitting and $8 per hour after midnight. She finished babysitting at 2:00 A.M. and earned $36. At what time did she begin babysitting?

8. Seth bought a movie ticket, popcorn, and a drink. After the movie, he played 4 video games that each cost the same. He spent a total of $19. How much did it cost to play each video game?

Movie Costs

Item	Cost
Popcorn	$4
Drink	$3
Ticket	$8

9. **Measurement** Mandy needs to arrive at softball practice by 5:00 P.M. It takes her 15 minutes to pick up her teammates and then 30 minutes to get to the field. What time must Mandy leave home to be on time for practice?

10. Chet has $4 in change after buying a bike and a helmet. How much money did Chet have originally?

11. Rosa is 3 years older than Omar. Omar is 2 years older than Francesca. Francesca is 8 years younger than Roberto. If Roberto is 21 years old, how old is Rosa?

12. WRITING IN MATH Suppose Molly scored 7 more goals than Papina and Stew scored 2 more than Molly. If Stew scored 15 goals, what operation(s) can you use to find the number of goals Papina scored? Solve then explain your selection(s).

2-4 Add and Subtract Whole Numbers

GET READY to Learn

In a recent year, the two longest-running Broadway plays were *Cats* with 7,485 performances and *The Phantom of the Opera* with 7,829 performances.

The total number of performances is found by adding.

MAIN IDEA

I will add and subtract multi-digit numbers.

Math Online

macmillanmh.com

- Extra Examples
- Personal Tutor
- Self-Check Quiz

Always estimate first. Then add or subtract the digits in each place-value position. Start at the ones place.

EXAMPLES Add or Subtract Whole Numbers

1 **Find 415 + 280.** Estimate 400 + 300 = 700

Step 1 Add the ones.	Step 2 Add the tens.	Step 3 Add the hundreds.
$\begin{array}{r} 415 \\ +\ 280 \\ \hline 5 \end{array}$	$\begin{array}{r} 415 \\ +\ 280 \\ \hline 95 \end{array}$	$\begin{array}{r} 415 \\ +\ 280 \\ \hline 695 \end{array}$

Since 695 is close to the estimate, the answer is reasonable.

2 **Find 3,972 − 741.** Estimate 4,000 − 1,000 = 3,000

Step 1 Subtract the ones.	Step 2 Subtract the tens.	Step 3 Subtract the hundreds and thousands.
$\begin{array}{r} 3{,}972 \\ -\ 741 \\ \hline 1 \end{array}$	$\begin{array}{r} 3{,}972 \\ -\ 741 \\ \hline 31 \end{array}$	$\begin{array}{r} 3{,}972 \\ -\ 741 \\ \hline 3{,}231 \end{array}$

Since 3,231 is close to 3,000, the answer makes sense.

Real-World EXAMPLE **Add with Regrouping**

3 **BROADWAY** **Refer to the beginning of the lesson. How many performances of *Cats* with 7,485 and *Phantom of the Opera* with 7,829 were there?**

Estimate 7,000 + 8,000 = 15,000

Step 1 Add the ones.		**Step 2** Add the tens.		**Step 3** Add the hundreds. Add the thousands.
$\begin{array}{r} ^{1} \\ 7{,}485 \\ +\ 7{,}829 \\ \hline 4 \end{array}$	Rename 14 ones as 1 ten 4 ones.	$\begin{array}{r} ^{1\,1} \\ 7{,}485 \\ +\ 7{,}829 \\ \hline 14 \end{array}$	Rename 11 tens as 1 hundred, 1 ten.	$\begin{array}{r} ^{1\,1\,1} \\ 7{,}485 \\ +\ 7{,}829 \\ \hline 15{,}314 \end{array}$

The total number of performances was 15,314. This answer is close to the estimate. So, the answer is reasonable.

Remember

To add or subtract whole numbers, write the numbers in a column and line up the digits by place value.

EXAMPLE **Subtract with Regrouping**

4 **Find 834 − 561.** **Estimate** 800 − 600 = 200

Step 1 Subtract the ones.	**Step 2** Subtract the tens.		**Step 3** Subtract the hundreds.
$\begin{array}{r} 834 \\ -\ 561 \\ \hline 3 \end{array}$	$\begin{array}{r} ^{7\,13} \\ \not{8}\not{3}4 \\ -\ 561 \\ \hline 73 \end{array}$	3 < 6, so rename 8 hundreds as 7 hundreds, 10 tens. Then, 10 tens + 3 tens = 13 tens.	$\begin{array}{r} ^{7\,13} \\ \not{8}\not{3}4 \\ -\ 561 \\ \hline 273 \end{array}$

Since 273 is close to the estimate, the answer makes sense.

CHECK What You Know

Add or subtract. See Examples 1–4 (pp. 70–71)

1. 20,612 + 1,186 **2.** 611 − 32 **3.** 2,679 + 8,170

4. 4,200 − 1,652 **5.** 7,015 + 4,938 **6.** 67,315 − 28,502

7. The Everest Marathon starts at 17,100 feet above sea level and ends at 11,300 feet above sea level. What is the difference?

8. Talk About It Discuss how place value and regrouping are used when adding and subtracting whole numbers.

Practice and Problem Solving

EXTRA PRACTICE See page R5.

Add or subtract. See Examples 1–4 (pp. 70–71)

9. 407 + 162

10. 2,655 − 41

11. 10,375 + 1,503

12. 2,900 + 1,062

13. 851 − 705

14. 7,319 − 410

15. 739 + 3,824

16. 6,284 − 1,839

17. 4,762 + 594

18. 29,238 + 51,698

19. 215,075 + 6,025

20. 382,500 − 17,986

21. The main section of the Great Wall of China is 2,150 miles long. It also has 2,195 miles of branching walls. What is the total length of the wall? Show your estimate and exact answer.

Data File

New Jersey is a small state, but there are three states that are smaller. Use the table at the right. Show your estimate and your exact answer.

22. How much larger is Connecticut than Rhode Island?

23. What is the total area of Connecticut and Delaware?

24. How much larger is New Jersey than the states of Rhode Island and Delaware combined?

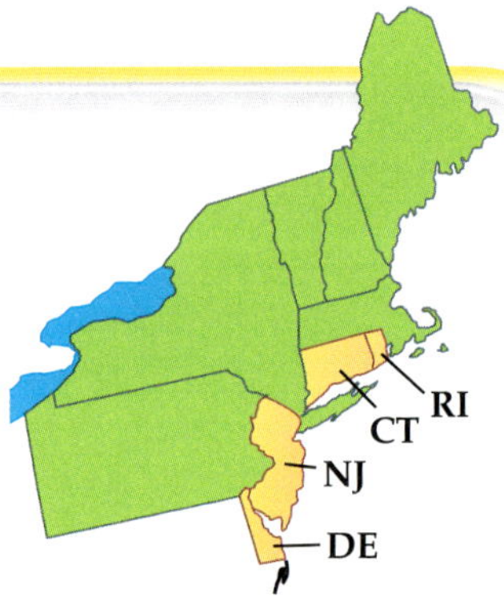

Place	Area (sq mi)
Rhode Island	1,545
Delaware	2,489
Connecticut	5,544
New Jersey	8,722

H.O.T. Problems

25. **OPEN ENDED** Write an addition problem where the estimated sum when rounded to the thousands place is the same as the exact sum.

26. **WHICH ONE DOESN'T BELONG?** Identify the expression that does not belong with the other three. Explain your reasoning.

1,296 − 516	608 + 172	420 + 360	1,049 − 179

27. **CHALLENGE** Arrange the digits 1, 2, 3, 4, 5, and 6 into two whole numbers so that their difference is as close to 1 as possible. Use each digit once.

28. **WRITING IN MATH** Write a real-world problem in which the answer is found by adding 816 and 750. Describe what the sum means.

CHAPTER 2

Mid-Chapter Check

Lessons 2-1 through 2-4

Round each decimal to the place indicated. (Lesson 2-1)

1. 11.8; ones
2. 4.328; tenths
3. 0.016; hundredths
4. **MULTIPLE CHOICE** The population of Irving is 193,649. What is 193,649 rounded to the nearest thousands place? (Lesson 2-1)

   A 200,000 **C** 194,000

   B 190,000 **D** 193,000

5. **Measurement** Estimate the amount of liquid in the sports drink bottle to the nearest ten milliliters. (Lesson 2-1)

Estimate each sum or difference. Use rounding or compatible numbers. (Lesson 2-2)

6. $89 + 62$
7. $15.9 - 12.1$
8. 371 + 1,215
9. 60.3 − 18.55
10. **Measurement** About how much greater is the side of the square than the side of the triangle? Show how you estimated. (Lesson 2-2)

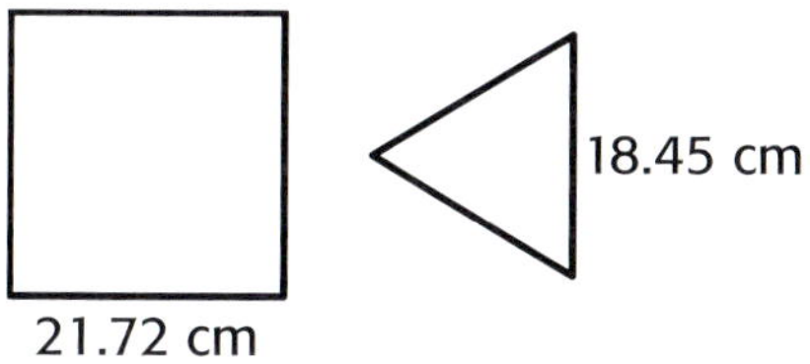

Use the work backward strategy to solve. (Lesson 2-3)

11. The Mitchell Middle School basketball team won 28 more games than they lost. If they won 35 games, how many games did they play?
12. Reuben has $2 in change after buying the sweatshirt and hat shown below. How much money did Reuben have originally?

Add or subtract. (Lesson 2-4)

13. 315 + 120
14. 689 − 71
15. 4,678 − 1,709
16. 25,390 + 82,687
17. **MULTIPLE CHOICE** Algeria, a country in Africa, has an area of 919,590 square miles. The Sahara Desert is located in Algeria. It has an area of 781,651 square miles. How much of Algeria is NOT covered by the Sahara Desert? (Lesson 2-4)

    F 100,000 sq mi **H** 173,939 sq mi

    G 137,939 sq mi **J** 200,000 sq mi

18. **WRITING IN MATH** Explain how you would find the difference of 425 and 214. (Lesson 2-2)

2-5 Problem-Solving Investigation

MAIN IDEA I will learn to determine if a problem needs an estimate or an exact answer.

P.S.I. TEAM +

MANDAR: My family drove to my grandparents' house. We drove 58.6 miles in the first hour, 67.2 miles in the second hour, and 60.5 miles in the third hour. We followed the same route to return home.

YOUR MISSION: Find *about* how far Mandar's family traveled.

Understand	You know that the family drove 58.6 miles, 67.2 miles, and 60.5 miles. You need to find *about* how far Mandar's family traveled altogether.
Plan	Since you only need to find *about* how far they traveled, you can estimate the number of miles traveled each hour. Add the estimated miles. Then double that amount for the trip back home.
Solve	Hour One → 58.6 → 60 Hour Two → 67.2 → 70 Hour Three → + 60.5 → + 60 190 The one-way trip was about 190 miles. The return trip was another 190 miles. Mandar's family traveled about 190 + 190, or 380 miles.
Check	Look back. Since the trip was a total of 6 hours and they drove about 60 miles each hour, find 60 + 60 + 60 + 60 + 60 + 60. Since the sum is 360, 380 miles is reasonable.

Mixed Problem Solving

EXTRA PRACTICE
See page R6.

For each problem, determine whether you need an estimate or an exact answer. Then solve.

PROBLEM-SOLVING SKILLS
- *Use the four-step plan.*
- *Use estimation.*

1. A restaurant can make 95 dinners each night. The restaurant has been sold out for 7 nights in a row. How many dinners were sold during this week?

2. **Measurement** A gardener has 35 feet of fencing to enclose the garden shown. About how much fencing will be left over after the garden is enclosed?

3. A group goes rafting on the Guadalupe River. Each raft carries 12 people. If there are 8 rafts, how many people can go rafting?

4. A family is renting a cabin for $59.95 a day for 5 days. About how much will they pay for the cabin?

5. School raffle tickets cost $3 each. The school's goal is to raise at least $400 from the raffle. If 138 tickets were sold, did the school meet its goal?

6. Students at a high school filled out a survey. The results showed that out of 640 students, 331 speak more than one language. How many students speak only one language?

7. Estella has 9 quarters, 7 dimes, and 5 nickels. Does she have enough money to buy the box of crayons shown?

8. A library wants to buy a new painting that costs $960. So far, the library has collected $375 in donations. About how much more money does the library need to buy the painting?

9. Four friends split the cost of two pizzas. If the total cost of the pizzas was $27.80, about how much will each friend have to pay?

10. On Friday, a museum had 185 visitors. On Saturday there were twice as many visitors as Friday. On Sunday, 50 fewer people visited than Saturday. How many people visited the museum during these three days?

11. **Measurement** The soccer team has a game at 11:00 A.M. The game is 153 miles away. The team leaves at 8:00 A.M. and drives an average of 59 miles each hour. Will the team arrive at the game on time?

12. **WRITING IN MATH** Explain an advantage and a disadvantage of using estimation to solve a problem.

Problem Solving in Social Studies

The Core Facts about Apples

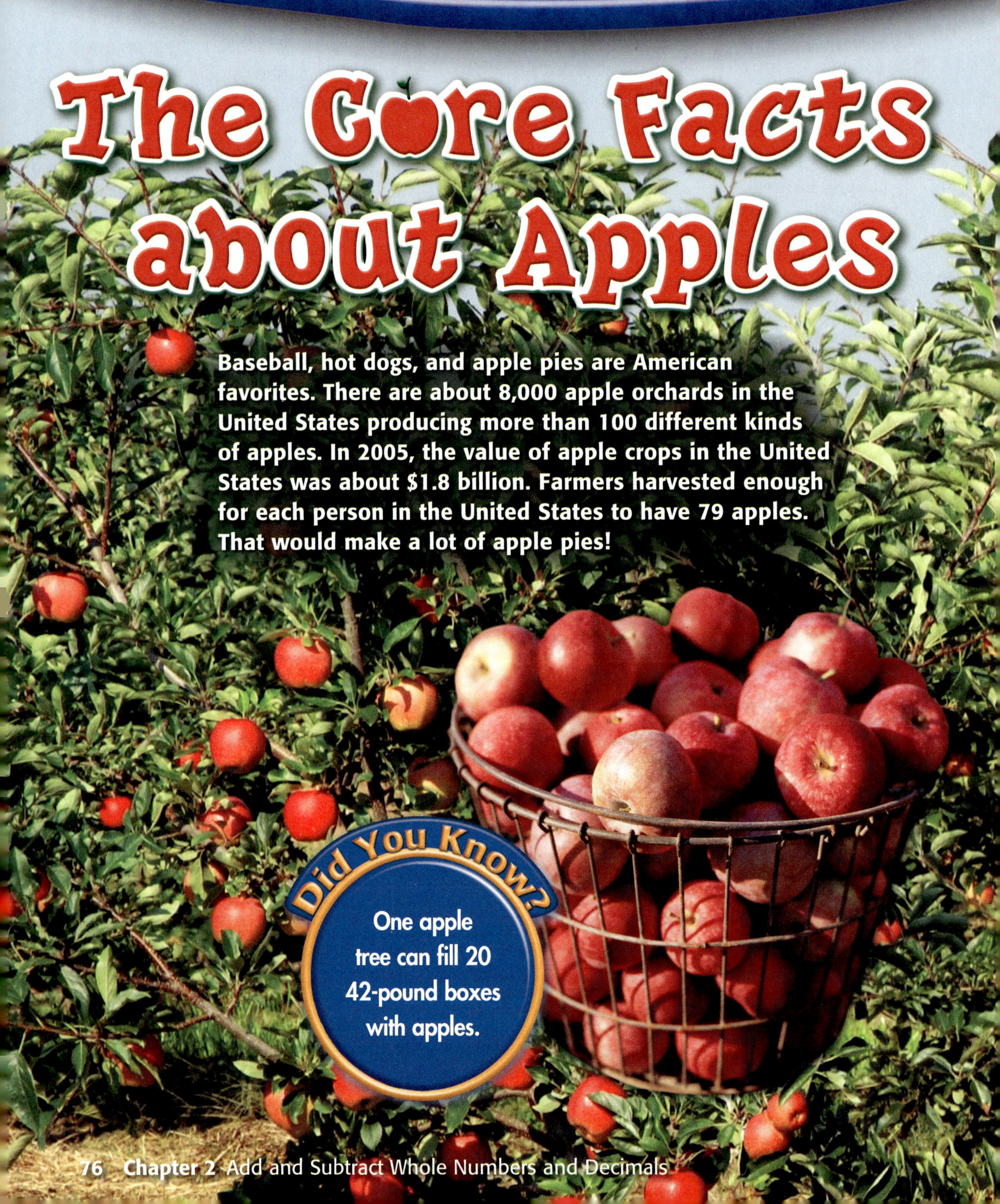

Baseball, hot dogs, and apple pies are American favorites. There are about 8,000 apple orchards in the United States producing more than 100 different kinds of apples. In 2005, the value of apple crops in the United States was about $1.8 billion. Farmers harvested enough for each person in the United States to have 79 apples. That would make a lot of apple pies!

Did You Know?

One apple tree can fill 20 42-pound boxes with apples.

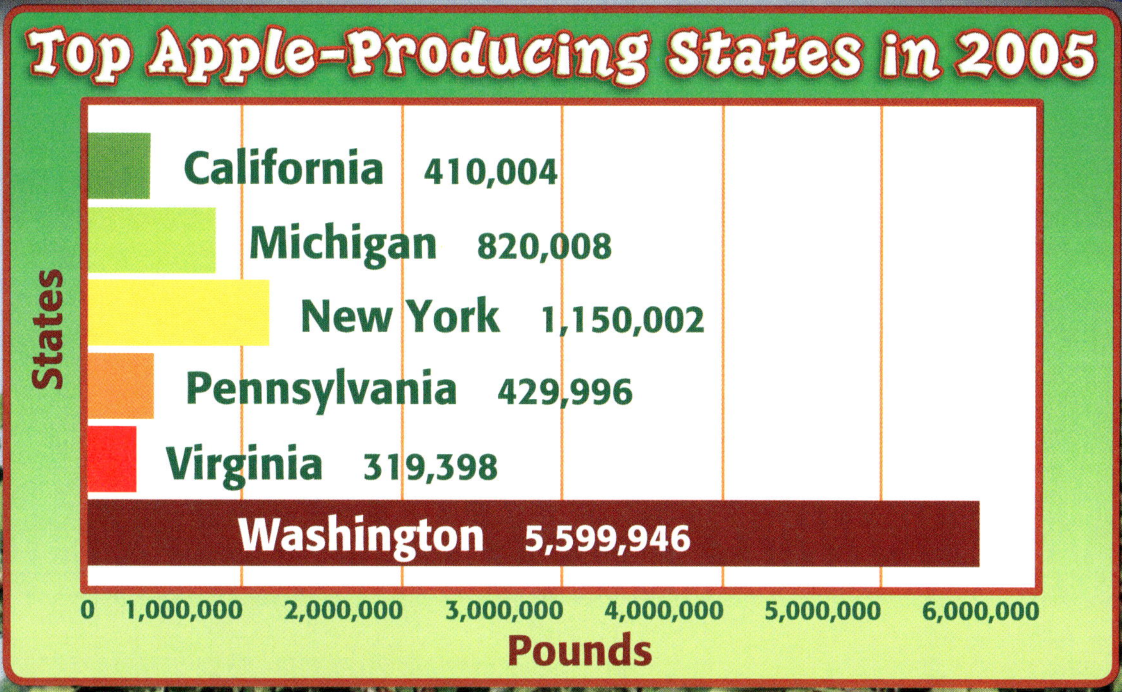

Source: U.S. Apple Association

Real-World Math

Use the information on page 76 and the graph above to solve each problem.

1. Which state produced the least amount of apples? How many pounds of apples did this state produce? Round to the nearest ten thousand.

2. Which state's apple crop was closest to 1 million pounds?

3. In 2001, $1.3 billion worth of apples were grown. How much greater was the apple crop in 2005?

4. What is the difference in apple production between the top two states? Round to the nearest thousand.

5. Use compatible numbers to estimate the total amount of apples produced in Michigan, California, and Pennsylvania.

6. Find the exact sum of the apples produced in Michigan, California, and Pennsylvania. Compare this number to your answer to Exercise 5.

7. Two pounds of apples make one pie. If you want to make 6 pies, how many pounds of apples should you pick?

Explore

Math Activity for 2-6

Add and Subtract Decimals

You can use grid paper to explore adding and subtracting decimals.

MAIN IDEA

I will use models to represent addition and subtraction of decimals.

You Will Need

grid paper
colored pencils

Math Online

macmillanmh.com

• Concepts in Motion

ACTIVITY Use Models to Add Decimals

Find 1.08 + 0.45.

Step 1 **Model 1.08.**

To show 1.08, shade one whole 10-by-10 grid and $\frac{8}{100}$ of a second grid.

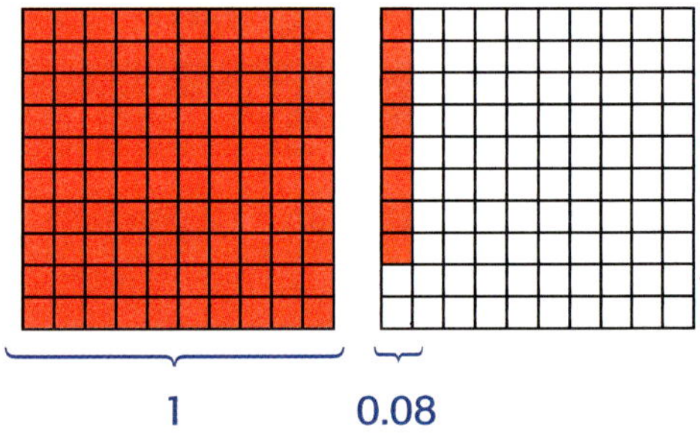

Step 2 **Model 0.45.**

To show 0.45, shade $\frac{45}{100}$ of the second grid using a different color.

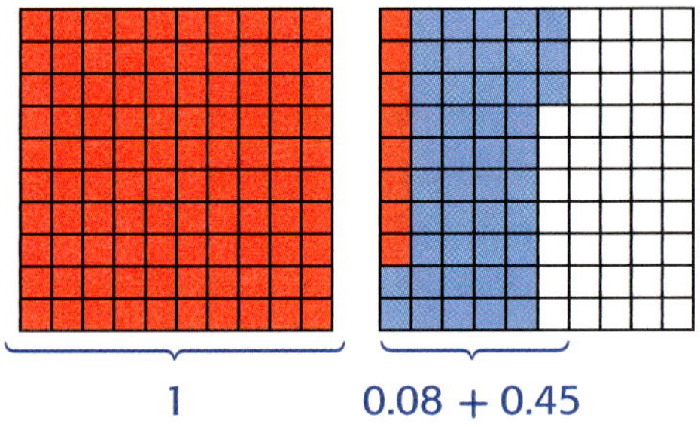

Step 3 **Add the decimals.**

Count the total number of shaded squares. Write the decimal that represents the number of shaded squares. So, 1.08 + 0.45 = 1.53.

ACTIVITY Use Models to Subtract Decimals

Find 2.4 − 1.07.

Step 1 **Model 2.4.**

To show 2.4, shade two whole grids and $\frac{40}{100}$ of a third grid.

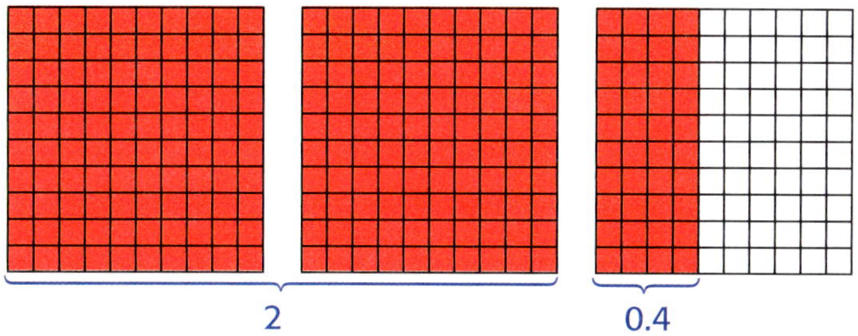

Step 2 **Subtract 1.07.**

To subtract 1.07, cross out 1 whole grid and 7 squares of the third grid. Count the number of squares that remain.

So, 2.4 − 1.07 = 1.33.

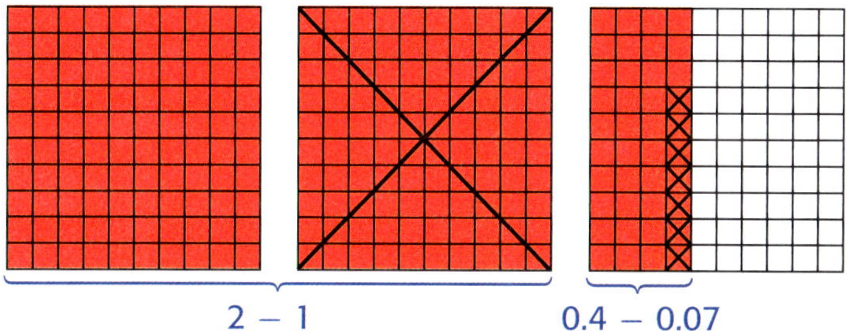

Think About It

1. Explain how using models to find 1.08 + 0.45 is similar to using models to find 108 + 45.

2. Explain how using models to find 2.4 − 1.07 is similar to using models to find 240 − 107.

CHECK What You Know

Add or subtract. Use models.

3. 2.46 + 1.13

4. 2.05 + 1.87

5. 2.91 − 1.8

6. 1.34 − 1.15

7. 0.51 + 0.63

8. 1.74 + 0.36

9. 2.05 − 1.12

10. 2.93 − 2.74

11. WRITING IN ►MATH Explain how to add or subtract decimals without models. Explain where to place the decimal point in the sum or difference.

2-6 Add and Subtract Decimals

MAIN IDEA

I will add and subtract decimals through thousandths.

Math Online

macmillanmh.com

- Extra Examples
- Personal Tutor
- Self-Check Quiz

GET READY to Learn

In Australia, each person eats an average of 44.2 pints of ice cream per year. In the United States, the average is 33.1 pints. How much ice cream is eaten on average by each person in these two countries combined?

Just as with whole numbers, you add digits in the same place-value position. To add decimals, line up the decimal points, add as with whole numbers, and bring the decimal point straight down in the sum.

Real-World EXAMPLE — Add Decimals

1 **ICE CREAM Refer to the information above. Find 44.2 + 33.1 to determine how much ice cream is eaten on average per person in Australia and the United States combined.**

Estimate 44 + 33 = 77

Step 1	**Step 2**	**Step 3**
Line up the decimal points.	Add as with whole numbers.	Bring the decimal point straight down in the sum.
$\begin{array}{r} 44.2 \\ +\ 33.1 \\ \hline \end{array}$	$\begin{array}{r} 44.2 \\ +\ 33.1 \\ \hline 77\ 3 \end{array}$	$\begin{array}{r} 44.2 \\ +\ 33.1 \\ \hline 77.3 \end{array}$

So, 77.3 pints of ice cream are eaten on average per person each year in Australia and the United States combined. This is close to the estimate, so your answer is reasonable.

If the last digits of the numbers in a subtraction problem do not have the same place value, it is helpful to annex zeros before you subtract.

EXAMPLE **Annex Zeros**

2 **Find 19.6 − 4.31.**

Estimate 20 − 4 = 16

Step 1 Line up the decimal points. Annex a zero so that both numbers have the same place value.

$$\begin{array}{r} 19.6\mathbf{0} \\ -\ 4.31 \\ \hline \end{array}$$

Step 2 Subtract as with whole numbers, from right to left. Regroup if necessary.

$$\begin{array}{r} {\scriptstyle 5\,10} \\ 19.\not{6}\not{0} \\ -\ 4.31 \\ \hline 15\ 29 \end{array}$$

Step 3 Bring the decimal point straight down in the difference.

$$\begin{array}{r} 19.60 \\ -\ 4.31 \\ \hline 15.29 \end{array}$$

The difference is 15.29. Since 15.29 is close to the estimate, the answer is reasonable.

Vocabulary Link

Annex

Everyday Use to add something, especially to a building

Math Use to annex a zero means to place a zero to the right of the decimal point without changing the value of the decimal

CHECK What You Know

Add or subtract. See Examples 1–2 (pp. 80–81)

1. $\begin{array}{r} 6.32 \\ +\ 1.46 \\ \hline \end{array}$ **2.** $\begin{array}{r} 0.89 \\ -\ 0.03 \\ \hline \end{array}$ **3.** $\begin{array}{r} 0.54 \\ +\ 7.8 \\ \hline \end{array}$ **4.** $\begin{array}{r} 14.8 \\ -\ 10.26 \\ \hline \end{array}$

5. 25 + 8.46 **6.** 6.57 − 1.2 **7.** 19.21 − 11.03

8. 3.008 + 1.64 **9.** 8.9 − 0.15 **10.** 42.2 + 7.169

11. Paulo bought a hand-held game version of a logic puzzle and batteries from a toy store. Use the table at the right to find the total cost of the two items, not including tax.

Item	Cost ($)
logic puzzle	14.95
batteries	10.39
carrying case	12.73

12. **Talk About It** Explain how annexing zeros might be helpful when adding decimals.

Practice and Problem Solving

EXTRA PRACTICE See page R6.

Add or subtract. See Examples 1–2 (pp. 80–81)

13. 35.08 + 11.9

14. 0.8 − 0.22

15. 9.14 − 2.075

16. 5.603 + 1.22

17. 26.768 + 2.991

18. 12.03 − 0.145

19. An athlete training for the Olympics swims each lap of a four-lap race in the following times: 54.73, 54.56, 54.32, and 54.54 seconds. What is the total time it takes her to swim the four laps?

20. Ethan wants to buy a basketball video game that costs $59.95, including tax. He has $45 in cash and a gift certificate for $15. Is that enough to buy the video game? Explain.

21. Terrance is biking a trail. He bikes 12.6 miles and takes a break. Then he bikes 10.7 miles. If the trail is 35 miles long, how many more miles does Terrance have left to bike?

22. A large bag of sand weighs 48.5 pounds. A small bag of sand weighs 24.6 pounds. Mrs. Waggoner needs 75 pounds. If she buys a large bag and a small bag, how much more sand does she need?

Real-World PROBLEM SOLVING

Music The table shows the frequencies of the lowest and highest notes of some musical instruments. The unit of frequency is called *hertz* (Hz). The difference between these frequencies is called the *pitch range*.

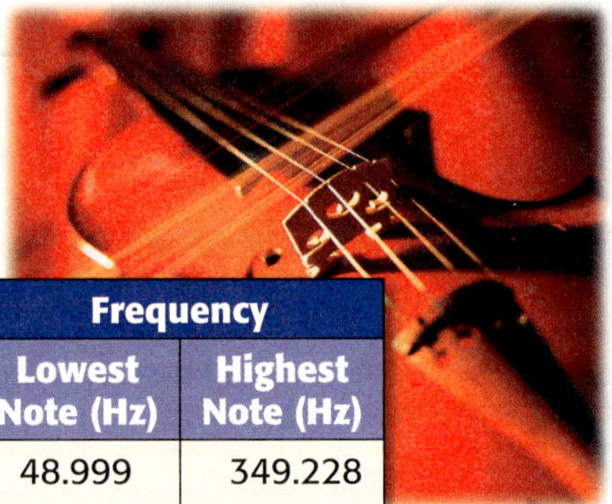

Instrument	Frequency	
	Lowest Note (Hz)	Highest Note (Hz)
bass trombone	48.999	349.228
concert flute	246.942	2,489.02
harp	30.867	2,959.96
violin	195.998	3,951.07

Source: PSB Speakers International

23. What is the pitch range of a bass trombone?

24. What is the pitch range of a harp?

25. Which has a greater pitch range: a concert flute or a violin? Explain.

H.O.T. Problems

26. **OPEN ENDED** Write two different pairs of decimals whose sums are 8.69. One pair should involve regrouping.

27. **NUMBER SENSE** Explain how you know that the sum of 2.4, 3.6, and 5.1 is greater than 10.

28. **WRITING IN MATH** Write a real-world word problem that can be solved by adding or subtracting 34.99 and 5.79. Describe what the solution means.

Game Time

Find the Least Sum

Adding Decimals

Get Ready!

Players: 2 to 4 players

You will need: 10 index cards
paper

Get Set!

- Write a different digit from 0 to 9 on each index card.
- Place the cards in a pile facedown.
- Draw six boxes on a piece a paper with decimal points as shown.

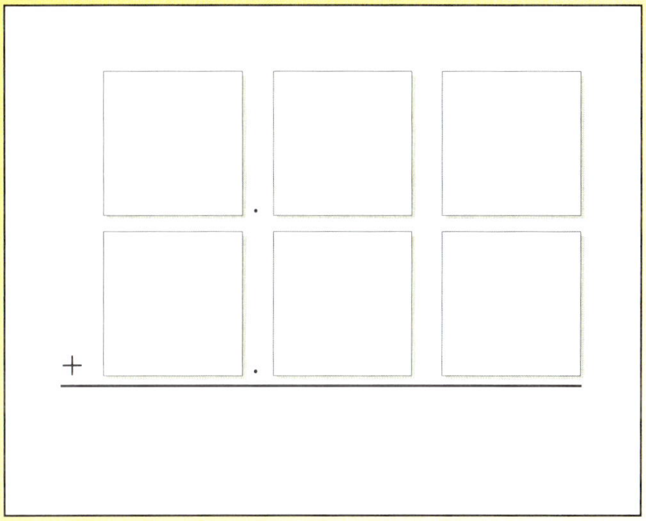

Go!

- Each player takes a turn choosing a card.
- Each time a card is chosen, each player writes the digit from the card on one of the boxes. The goal is to make up the least sum. You may not move digits after you have placed them in a box.
- When all the boxes are full, find the sum of your decimals.
- The player with the least sum is the winner.

Play again!

2-7 Addition Properties

MAIN IDEA

I will use Associative and Commutative Properties to add whole numbers and decimals mentally.

Math Online

macmillanmh.com

- Extra Examples
- Personal Tutor
- Self-Check Quiz

GET READY to Learn

Hannah jogs 2 miles and then walks 1 mile. The next day, she walks 1 mile and then jogs 2 miles. On which day does she go farther?

In the situation above, the order in which Hannah jogged and walked did not change the total distance. This and other properties of addition are given below.

Addition Properties

Key Concept

Commutative Property The order in which numbers are added does not change the sum.

Examples

$7 + 11 = 11 + 7$ $\qquad$ $2.3 + 9.5 = 9.5 + 2.3$

Associative Property The way in which numbers are grouped does not change the sum.

Examples

$(9 + 6) + 4 = 9 + (6 + 4)$ $\qquad$ $1.8 + (0.2 + 5) = (1.8 + 0.2) + 5$

Identity Property The sum of any number and 0 equals the number.

Examples

$14 + 0 = 14$ $\qquad$ $0 + 6.75 = 6.75$

EXAMPLE Name Addition Properties

1 **Identify the addition property used to rewrite the problem below.**

$17 + (3 + 24) = (17 + 3) + 24$

The grouping of the numbers to be added changes. This is the Associative Property of Addition.

You can use properties of addition to simplify adding and to find sums of whole numbers and decimals mentally.

Real-World EXAMPLE **Use Properties to Add Whole Numbers**

2 **ANIMALS Hama recorded the number of birds he saw in the table. Use properties of addition to mentally find the total number of birds he saw.**

BIRDS	NUMBER
Blue Jays	5
Robins	27
Cardinals	15

Since you can easily add 5 and 15, change the order and group those numbers together.

$5 + 27 + 15 = 5 + 15 + 27$	Commutative Property
$= (5 + 15) + 27$	Associative Property
$= 20 + 27$	Add 5 and 15 mentally.
$= 47$	Add 20 and 27 mentally.

Remember

Sums of 10 or a multiple of 10 are compatible numbers. They help you add numbers mentally.

EXAMPLE **Use Properties to Add Decimals**

3 **Use properties of addition to find 0.8 + 5.6 + 0.4 mentally.**

Since $0.6 + 0.4 = 1$, group 5.6 and 0.4 together.

$0.8 + 5.6 + 0.4 = 0.8 + (5.6 + 0.4)$	Associative Property
$= 0.8 + 6.0$	Add 5.6 and 0.4 mentally.
$= 6.8$	Add 0.8 and 6.0 mentally.

You can also form groups of 10 to make adding mentally easier.

EXAMPLE **Partial Sums of 10**

4 **Use properties of addition to find 18 + 26 mentally.**

$18 + 26 = (10 + 8) + (20 + 6)$	$18 = 10 + 8$ and $26 = 20 + 6$
$= 10 + 20 + 8 + 6$	Commutative Property
$= (10 + 20) + (8 + 6)$	Associative Property
$= 30 + 14$	Add inside the parentheses mentally.
$= 44$	Add 30 and 14 mentally.

CHECK What You Know

Identify the addition property used to rewrite each problem. See Example 1 (p. 84)

1. $(11 + 37) + 3 = 11 + (37 + 3)$

2. $0.1 + 8 + 1.9 = 0.1 + 1.9 + 8$

Use properties of addition to find each sum mentally. Show your steps and identify the properties that you used. See Examples 2–4 (p. 85)

3. $9 + 27 + 1$

4. $3.9 + 0.5 + 2.5$

5. $69 + 22$

6. What addition property is shown below?

$$0 + 6.75 = 6.75$$

7. Talk About It Describe how properties of addition help to add numbers mentally.

Practice and Problem Solving

EXTRA PRACTICE See page R6.

Identify the addition property used to rewrite each problem. See Example 1 (p. 84)

8. $20 + 6 = 6 + 20$

9. $19.5 + 0 = 19.5$

10. $49 + (51 + 21) = (49 + 51) + 21$

11. $13 + 11 + 87 = 13 + 87 + 11$

Use properties of addition to find each sum mentally. Show your steps and identify the properties that you used. See Examples 2–4 (p. 85)

12. $15 + 8 + 25$

13. $7.7 + 4.3 + 11$

14. $37 + 26 + 53$

15. $10.9 + 3 + 0.1$

16. $63 + 35$

17. $57 + 48$

Algebra For Exercises 18 and 19, find the value that makes each sentence true.

18. $27 + (37 + 13) = 13 + (27 + \blacksquare)$

19. $(8 + 1.6) + 0.4 = 0.4 + (\blacksquare + 1.6)$

20. The table shows the cost of cheerleading uniforms. Use properties of addition to find the total cost of the uniform mentally. Show your steps and identify the properties that you used.

Cost of Cheerleading Uniforms

Item	Cost
Shoes	$65
Pom poms	$18
T-shirt and shorts	$35

21. In one week, a classroom collected 43, 58, 62, 57, and 42 cans. Find the total number of cans the classroom collected using mental math. Explain how you solved it.

22. Alex spent $2.50 on a snack, $1.24 on gum, $3.76 on a comic book, and $5.50 on lunch. Use mental math to find the total amount that he spent.

H.O.T. Problems

23. OPEN ENDED Write a word problem that can be solved using the Associative Property of Addition. Explain your answer.

24. CHALLENGE Do the Associative and Commutative Properties also work for subtraction? Give examples to support your answer.

25. WRITING IN ▶MATH Jogging 2 miles and then walking 1 mile is the same as walking 1 mile and then jogging 2. This is a *commutative action*. Give another example of a commutative action. Then give an example of an action that is *not* commutative. Explain.

TEST Practice

26. SHORT RESPONSE Fina went to the grocery store and bought eggs for \$1.12, milk for \$2.25, butter for \$0.98, and sugar for \$1.65. If she gave the cashier \$10, how much change in dollars did Fina receive? **(Lesson 2-7)**

27. Round 563.829 to the nearest hundredth. **(Lesson 2-1)**

A 563.81 **C** 563.83

B 563.828 **D** 600

28. Chloe is gluing together two pieces of wood so that their length equals the length of the board below. Which two lengths should she use? **(Lesson 2-6)**

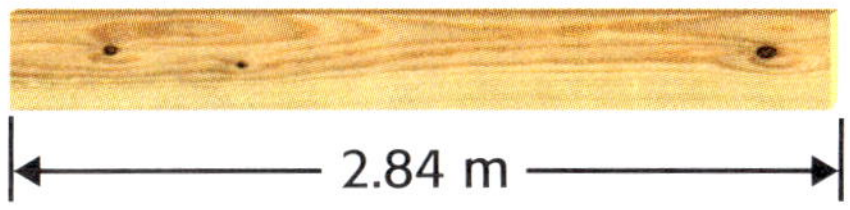

F 1.04 meters and 2.84 meters

G 2.5 meters and 0.3 meter

H 1.8 meters and 1.4 meters

J 1.04 meters and 1.8 meters

Spiral Review

Add or subtract. (Lesson 2-6)

29. 5.08 + 13.7 **30.** 12.01 − 0.23 **31.** 24.8 − 16.095

32. Students at a middle school filled out a survey. The survey showed that out of 1,037 students, 749 are going on a summer vacation. Find how many students are not going on a summer vacation. Is your solution an exact answer or an estimation? Explain. **(Lesson 2-5)**

33. Pablo Picasso's painting, *Self-Portrait,* sold for \$43,500,000. Write the price of the painting in expanded form. **(Lesson 1-1)**

2-8 Add and Subtract Mentally

GET READY to Learn

The table shows the number of dog breeds in two different categories of a dog show.

Category	Number of Breeds
Terrier	28
Toy	23

Which is easier to add:
28 + 23 or 30 + 21?

Are the sums the same?

MAIN IDEA

I will use the compensation strategy to add and subtract whole numbers and decimals mentally.

New Vocabulary

compensation

Math Online

macmillanmh.com

- Extra Examples
- Personal Tutor
- Self-Check Quiz

Sometimes you can use compensation to add mentally. To use **compensation**, add a number to one addend to make the addition easier. Then adjust by subtracting the same number from the other addend.

Real-World EXAMPLE — Add Mentally

1 **DOGS** **Refer to the table above. Use compensation to find 28 + 23, the total number of dog breeds in the two categories.**

$$\begin{array}{ccc} 28 & + & 23 \\ \downarrow +2 & & \downarrow -2 \\ 30 & + & 21 = 51 \end{array}$$

Add 2 to 28. Adjust by subtracting 2 from 23.

The total number of dog breeds in the two categories is 51.

To use compensation to subtract mentally, add or subtract the same amount from both numbers.

EXAMPLE — Subtract Mentally

2 **Use compensation to find 362 − 297.**

$$\begin{array}{ccc} 362 & - & 297 \\ \downarrow +3 & & \downarrow +3 \\ 365 & - & 300 = 65 \end{array}$$

Add 3 to 297. Adjust by adding 3 to 362.

So, 362 − 297 is 65.

EXAMPLES Add or Subtract Decimals Mentally

3 **Use compensation to find 4.6 + 1.5.**

One Way: **Change 4.6 to 5.0.**

4.6	+	1.5		
↓ + 0.4		↓ − 0.4		Add 0.4 to 4.6.
5.0	+	1.1	= 6.1	Adjust by subtracting 0.4 from 1.5.

Another Way: **Change 1.5 to 2.**

4.6	+	1.5		
↓ − 0.5		↓ + 0.5		Add 0.5 to 1.5.
4.1	+	2.0	= 6.1	Adjust by subtracting 0.5 from 4.6.

So, 4.6 + 1.5 = 6.1.

Remember

When adding or subtracting mentally, adjust either number.

Example

160 − 97
↓ ↓
+ 3 + 3
↓ ↓
163 − 100 = 63

4 **Use compensation to find 9.8 − 2.6.**

One Way: **Change 2.6 to 2.0.**

9.8	−	2.6	
↓ − 0.6		↓ − 0.6	
9.2	−	2.0	= 7.2

Another Way: **Change 2.6 to 3.**

9.8	−	2.6	
↓ + 0.4		↓ + 0.4	
10.2	−	3.0	= 7.2

So, 9.8 − 2.6 = 7.2.

CHECK What You Know

Add or subtract mentally. Use compensation. See Examples 1–4 (pp. 88–89)

1. 57 + 36

2. 368 + 197

3. 96 − 35

4. 410 − 318

5. 4.2 + 9.6

6. 8.7 + 3.1

7. 16.5 − 9.3

8. 39.4 − 1.7

9. A burrito costs $4.98 and a soda costs $1.75. Use compensation to find the total cost. Explain the steps you used.

10. Talk About It Discuss the rules for using compensation to add or subtract mentally. When do you add to both numbers and when do you add to one number and subtract from the other number?

Practice and Problem Solving

EXTRA PRACTICE See page R7.

Add or subtract mentally. Use compensation. See Examples 1–4 (pp. 88–89)

11. 98 + 64 **12.** 49 − 33 **13.** 304 − 198 **14.** 397 + 160

15. 188 − 27 **16.** 615 − 220 **17.** 6.7 + 2.4 **18.** 8.2 + 9.9

19. 30.4 − 8.6 **20.** 24.6 + 19.3 **21.** 62.3 − 45.6 **22.** 59.4 + 39.5

23. **Measurement** The height of a wooden pole is 56 inches. A builder attaches a birdhouse to the top of the pole. The height of the birdhouse is 18 inches. Find the total height of the pole and birdhouse.

24. You can burn 336 Calories roller skating and 380 Calories playing basketball per hour. Use mental math to find how many more Calories you can burn per hour playing basketball. Explain the steps you used.

Real-World PROBLEM SOLVING

Science Sound is measured in decibels. The higher the decibel, the louder the sound. The table shows how loud different sounds are.

Sound Source	Decibels
Soft whisper	30
Conversation	60
Rock concert	120
Rocket engine	180
Blue whale	180

25. How much louder is a conversation than a soft whisper?

26. How much louder is a blue whale than a conversation between two people?

H.O.T. Problems

27. **OPEN ENDED** Write a subtraction word problem that can be solved by using compensation. Describe the steps that you used to solve it.

28. **FIND THE ERROR** Megan and Juanita are finding 129 + 67 by using compensation. Who is correct? Explain.

Megan

129 + 67
+1 +1
↓ ↓
130 + 68 = 198

Juanita

129 + 67
+1 −1
↓ ↓
130 + 66 = 196

29. **WRITING IN MATH** Without using paper and pencil, how would you find the sum of 53.7 and 46.55? Explain your steps.

TEST Practice

30. Bailey walked 23 blocks to the library. Then he walked 4 blocks to the post office and then 17 blocks home. How many blocks did he walk in all? (Lesson 2-7)

A 44

B 43

C 40

D 21

31. **SHORT RESPONSE** A video arcade in Fort Lauderdale, Florida, had 844 video arcade games when it opened. Two years later, it had 950 games. How many games did it add in two years? (Lesson 2-7)

32. Which is a true statement about the information in the table? (Lesson 2-6)

Passenger Train	Speed (miles per hour)
MagLev, China	243.0
Nozomi, Japan	162.6
TGV, France	158.0
Acela Express	150.0

F The MagLev is 81 miles per hour faster than the Nozomi.

G The MagLev is 84 miles per hour faster than the TGV.

H The Nozomi is 4.4 miles per hour faster than the TGV.

J The Nozomi is 12.6 miles per hour faster than the Acela Express.

Spiral Review

Use properties of addition to find each sum mentally. Show your steps and identify the properties that you used. (Lesson 2-7)

33. $12 + 65 + 5$ **34.** $39 + 17 + 1$ **35.** $2.6 + 1.3 + 1.7$

Add or subtract. (Lesson 2-6)

36. $0.5 + 1.1$ **37.** $0.95 - 0.62$ **38.** $0.59 + 5.6$ **39.** $28.3 - 10.47$

40. In a recent season, Chad Johnson of the Cincinnati Bengals had 87 receptions. Antonio Gates of the San Diego Chargers had 71 receptions. Estimate how many more receptions Johnson had than Gates. (Lesson 2-2)

41. A cougar has a mass of 102.948 kilograms. Round the mass to the nearest tenth kilogram. (Lesson 2-1)

Order each set of numbers from least to greatest. (Lesson 1-7)

42. 0.557, 0.09, 0.78, 0.67 **43.** 24.3, 24.08, 24.32, 23.98, 24

Study Guide and Review

Math Online macmillanmh.com
- STUDY TO GO
- Vocabulary Review

FOLDABLES® Study Organizer GET READY to Study

Be sure the following Big Ideas are written in your Foldable.

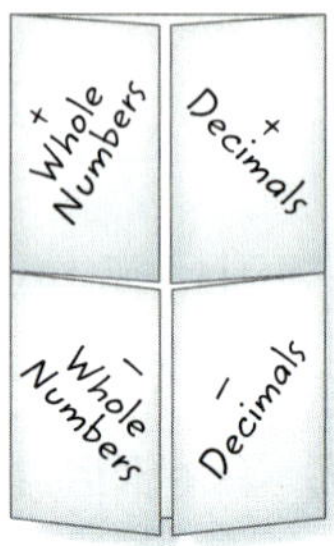

Key Concepts

Estimation

- When you **round** a number, you find its approximate value to a specified place value. (p. 61)

  324 rounded to the nearest ten is 320.
  6.79 rounded to the nearest tenth is 6.8.

- You can use rounding to **estimate** sums and differences. (p. 64)

426	→	400	Round each addend to
+ 385	→	+ 400	the nearest hundred.
		800	The sum is about 800.

- You can also use compatible numbers to estimate sums and differences.

Adding and Subtracting Whole Numbers and Decimals

- To add or subtract numbers, estimate first. Add or subtract digits in each place-value position. (pp. 70, 80)

2,108	36.19
+ 5,643	− 2.07
7,751	34.12

Key Vocabulary

round (p. 61)
estimate (p. 64)
compatible numbers (p. 64)
compensation (p. 88)

Vocabulary Check

Choose the correct term or number to complete each sentence.

1. When you round a number, you find its (approximate, exact) value.
2. Compatible numbers are numbers that (can, cannot) be added or subtracted mentally.
3. The difference between 10.8 and 2.05 is (8.3, 8.75).
4. To find a number that is close to the exact answer, you can (estimate, add).
5. A reasonable estimate for 619 + 285 is (900, 9,000).
6. The (Associative, Commutative) Property states that you can add numbers in any order.
7. You can use (compensation, annexing) to add numbers mentally.

Lesson-by-Lesson Review

2-1 Round Whole Numbers and Decimals (pp. 61–63)

Example 1
Round 4,7̲12 to the underlined digit.

The digit in the place to be rounded is 7. The digit to the right of 7 is 1. Since $1 < 5$, round down.

$4{,}712 \rightarrow 4{,}700$

Example 2
Round 0.8̲65 to the underlined digit.

The digit in the place to be rounded is 8. The digit to the right of 8 is 6. Since $6 > 5$, round up.

$0.865 \rightarrow 0.9$

Round each number to the place indicated.

8. 84; tens

9. 6,755; hundreds

10. 326,023; thousands

11. 0.92; tenths

12. 13.61; ones

13. 75.235; hundredths

14. **Measurement** A person set a world record by eating 14 hard boiled eggs in 14.42 seconds. Round this time to the nearest tenth of a second.

2-2 Estimate Sums and Differences (pp. 64–67)

Example 3
Estimate 945 + 585 using rounding.

Round 945 to 900.
Round 585 to 600.

$$\begin{array}{rcr} 945 & \rightarrow & 900 \\ +\ 585 & \rightarrow & +\ 600 \\ \hline & & 1{,}500 \end{array}$$

The sum is about 1,500.

Estimate each sum or difference. Use rounding or compatible numbers. Show your work.

15. 91 + 14

16. 573 − 429

17. 26.09 − 5.8

18. 3.95 + 11.76

19. 808 − 392

20. 3.162 + 0.624

21. Valeria had $78.51 in her bank at home. She adds $3.67 in change. About how much does she have now? Show your work.

2-3 Problem-Solving Strategy: Work Backward (pp. 68–69)

Example 4

The swim team spent $385 to travel to a swim meet. The bus costs $145, and the hotel costs $30 per person. How many people went on the trip?

Subtract to undo the cost of the bus.

$$\$385 - \$145 = \$240$$

Divide to find the number of people.

$$\$240 \div \$30 = 8$$

So, 8 people went on the trip.

Solve. Use the *work backward* strategy.

22. The science club raised money to clean the beach. They spent $29 on trash bags and $74 on waterproof boots. They still have $47 left. How much did they raise?

23. Mr. Charles cut fresh roses from his garden and gave 10 roses to his neighbor. Then he gave half of what was left to his niece. He kept the remaining 14 roses. How many roses did he cut?

2-4 Add and Subtract Whole Numbers (pp. 70–72)

Example 5

Find 561 + 23.

Estimate 560 + 20 = 580

Add the ones.	Add the tens.	Add the hundreds.
561	561	561
+ 23	+ 23	+ 23
4	84	584

The sum, 584, is close to the estimate.

Example 6

Find 346 − 175.

Estimate 350 − 180 = 170

Subtract the ones and the tens.	Subtract the hundreds.
2 14	2 14
3̸4̸6	3̸4̸6
− 175	− 175
71	171

The difference, 171, is close to 170.

Add or subtract.

24. 78 + 11

25. 435 − 120

26. 3,612 + 546

27. 654 + 13

28. 6,702 − 913

29. Oklahoma and California have the highest American Indian populations, as shown in the table. What is the total American Indian population in those two states?

State	American Indian Population
Oklahoma	252,420
California	242,164

Source: U.S. Census Bureau

2-5 Problem-Solving Investigation: Estimate or an Exact Answer (pp. 74–75)

Example 7

Nina's breakfast cost $2.64. She gave the cashier $5. How much change should Nina receive?

You need to find an exact answer.

Subtract $2.64 from $5.

$$\begin{array}{r} 5.00 \\ -\ 2.64 \\ \hline 2.36 \end{array}$$

Nina's change is $2.36.

For each problem, determine whether you need an estimate or an exact answer. Then solve.

30. A total of 8 fifth-grade teachers donated $15 each to the school's band. How much money did they donate in all?

31. A group of 5 friends are sharing the cost of renting a boat for one day. If the boat costs $144.95, about how much will they each pay for the boat?

32. The local bakery makes 85 pies each day. The bakery has sold all of the pies for 9 days in a row. About how many pies were sold during these 9 days?

2-6 Add and Subtract Decimals (pp. 80–82)

Example 8

Find 8.3 + 10.75.

Estimate 8 + 11 = 19

Line up the decimal points.	Annex a zero.	Add as with whole numbers.
$\begin{array}{r} 8.3 \\ +\ 10.75 \\ \hline \end{array}$	$\begin{array}{r} 8.3\mathbf{0} \\ +\ 10.75 \\ \hline \end{array}$	$\begin{array}{r} 8.30 \\ +\ 10.75 \\ \hline 19.05 \end{array}$

The sum is 19.05. Since this is close to the estimate, the answer is reasonable.

Add or subtract.

33. $\begin{array}{r} 4.8 \\ +\ 5.7 \\ \hline \end{array}$ **34.** $\begin{array}{r} 0.64 \\ -\ 0.52 \\ \hline \end{array}$ **35.** $\begin{array}{r} 8.63 \\ +\ 0.19 \\ \hline \end{array}$

36. 0.625 + 4.8 **37.** 7.013 − 2.21

38. The male human heart weighs an average of 11.1 ounces. This is 1.8 ounces more than the average female's heart. How much does the average female's heart weigh?

39. **Measurement** The Dwarf Goby is the smallest marine fish. Its average length is 0.339 inch for males and 0.35 inch for females. How much longer is the female?

2-7 Addition Properties (pp. 84–87)

Example 9
Identify the addition property used to rewrite the problem below.

$$28 + 5 + 62 = 28 + 62 + 5$$

The order of the numbers changed. This is the Commutative Property.

Example 10
Use properties of addition to find 1.4 + 9.7 + 8.6 mentally.

$1.4 + 9.7 + 8.6$	
$= 1.4 + 8.6 + 9.7$	Commutative Property
$= (1.4 + 8.6) + 9.7$	Associative Property
$= 10 + 9.7$	Add 1.4 and 8.6 mentally.
$= 19.7$	Add 10 and 9.7 mentally.

Identify the addition property used to rewrite each problem.

40. $7 + 65 + 13 = 7 + 13 + 65$

41. $(4 + 0.7) + 0.3 = 4 + (0.7 + 0.3)$

42. $328 + 0 = 328$

Use properties of addition to find each sum mentally. Show your steps and identify the properties that you used.

43. $46 + 4 + 31$

44. $8.7 + 4 + 0.3$

45. Use the Associative Property to group the numbers in the table and find the total amount of money the sports team raised.

Sports Team	Donations ($)
Soccer	3,500
Football	4,250
Tennis	2,750

2-8 Add and Subtract Mentally (pp. 88–91)

Example 11
Find 298 + 511. Use compensation.

298	+	511	
↓ + 2		↓ − 2	
300	+	509	= 809

The sum is 809.

Example 12
Find 3.4 − 1.9. Use compensation.

3.4	−	1.9	
↓ + 0.1		↓ + 0.1	
3.5	−	2.0	= 1.5

The sum is 1.5.

Add or subtract. Use compensation.

46. $27 + 45$

47. $62 - 19$

48. $482 + 329$

49. $932 - 645$

50. $4.92 - 3.74$

51. $12.6 + 7.5$

52. **Measurement** The head and body of a pygmy mouse lemur measures 2.4 inches and its tail measures 5.3 inches. How long is the animal from head to tail?

CHAPTER 2 Chapter Test

Round each number to the place indicated.

1. 785; tens

2. 120,395; thousands

3. 6.93; ones

4. 3.041; tenths

5. **MULTIPLE CHOICE** One megabyte is equal to 1,048,576 bytes. Round this to the nearest thousand.

A 1,050,000 **C** 1,048,600

B 1,049,000 **D** 1,000,000

Estimate each sum or difference. Use rounding or compatible numbers.

6. 653 − 81 **7.** 15,429 + 11,602

8. 9.16 + 2.04 **9.** 73.8 − 59.74

10. **MULTIPLE CHOICE** Which is the best estimate of 46,203 + 84,110?

F 100,000 **H** 130,000

G 120,000 **J** 140,000

11. **Measurement** The table shows the height of mountains. How much taller is Mt. McKinley than Mt. Saint Elias?

Mountain	Height (ft)
Mt. McKinley	20,320
Mt. Saint Elias	18,008

Source: *Time for Kids Almanac*

12. A helicopter flight to and from the rainforest costs $499. Supplies cost $112 for each day. How many days can the scientist study birds in the rainforest if she has a $1,283 budget?

Add or subtract.

13. 4,012 + 853 **14.** 8,871 − 630

15. 3.47 + 1.95 **16.** 260.3 − 71.8

Measurement **For Exercises 17 and 18, use the table that shows the typical lengths of a Rusty Spotted cat.**

Measure	Least Length (in.)	Greatest Length (in.)
body	13.7	18.8
tail	5.9	9.8

17. What is the difference between the greatest and least lengths for the cat's body?

18. How long is a rusty spotted cat if it has the greatest lengths for its body and tail?

Use properties of addition to find each sum mentally.

19. 38 + 19 + 1 **20.** 0.3 + 1.2 + 0.7

21. 75 + 27 + 25 **22.** 1.6 + 33 + 11.4

Add or subtract. Use compensation.

23. 36 + 21 **24.** 14.7 + 8.5

25. **WRITING IN MATH** A speed skater's time in an event was 40.33 seconds. The same skater was 1.08 seconds faster the next time she skated in the event. What was her time in the second race? Explain how you can use compensation to solve.

CHAPTER 2

Test Practice

Cumulative, Chapters 1–2

Math Online macmillanmh.com

• Test Practice

PART 1 Multiple Choice

Read each question. Then fill in the correct answer on the answer sheet provided by your teacher or on a sheet of paper.

1. The times of four runners in a relay race are shown in the table. Estimate the total time of the team.

Runner	1	2	3	4
Time (s)	14.9	15.1	14.8	15.3

A 40 sec

B 45 sec

C 50 sec

D 60 sec

---

2. The cafeteria sells hamburgers for $1.19, bags of chips for $0.49, and drinks for $0.79. Which is the best estimate for the total cost of a hamburger, a bag of chips, and a drink?

F $2.50

G $2.75

H $3.00

J $3.25

---

3. Nathan received $50 for his birthday. He wants to buy the items listed below. All prices include tax. How much will Nathan have left over after paying for these items?

Item	Cost
Video game	$24.89
CD	$11.18
Poster	$7.62

A $5.98

B $6.31

C $7.22

D $8.56

4. Which of the following shows the decimals in order from least to greatest?

F 0.3, 0.28, 0.279, 0.25

G 0.25, 0.28, 0.279, 0.3

H 0.25, 0.279, 0.28, 0.3

J 0.3, 0.25, 0.279, 0.28

---

5. A football team scored 27 points in a game. These points were either 3-point field goals or 7-point touchdowns. How many field goals and touchdowns did the team score?

A 2 field goals and 3 touchdowns

B 2 field goals and 4 touchdowns

C 3 field goals and 2 touchdowns

D 3 field goals and 3 touchdowns

---

6. The population of Springfield is 534,694. How can you write this number in word form?

F five-hundred thirty-four thousand, six-hundred four

G five-hundred thirty-four thousand, six-hundred ninety-four

H five-hundred thirty-four thousand, nine-hundred sixty-four

J five-hundred thirty thousand, six-hundred ninety-four

Preparing for Standardized Tests

For test-taking strategies and practice, see pages R42–R55.

7. Refer to the table that shows the prices of several items. Which is the best estimate for the cost of two notebooks, a pen, and a box of crayons?

Bookstore Prices	
pen	\$0.79
notebook	\$0.49
box of crayons	\$3.69

A \$4.00

B \$4.50

C \$5.00

D \$5.50

8. What is 12.638 rounded to the nearest tenth?

F 10.0

G 12.6

H 12.64

J 13

9. The official weight of a college football is between 14 and 15 ounces. Which of the following weights is NOT between 14 and 15 ounces?

A 14.99 ounces

B 14.12 ounces

C 15.01 ounces

D 14.25 ounces

PART 2 Short Response

Record your answers on the sheet provided by your teacher or on a sheet of paper.

10. Tyree scored 8 points in a basketball game. This was 9 points fewer than Aura scored. Write a number sentence that shows how many points Aura scored.

PART 3 Extended Response

Record your answers on the answer sheet provided by your teacher or on a sheet of paper. Show your work.

11. The table shows the number of hours Lola worked last summer. Show how to estimate the total number of hours she worked in four months.

Month	Hours
May	78.50
June	83.25
July	81.50
August	79.75

12. Explain if an estimate or an exact answer is needed for the problem below.

You need to buy five jerseys that cost \$12 each. How much money will the five jerseys cost?

NEED EXTRA HELP?												
If You Missed Question...	1	2	3	4	5	6	7	8	9	10	11	12
Go to Lesson...	2-2	2-2	2-6	1-6	2-3	1-1	2-2	2-1	1-6	2-7	2-2	2-5

CHAPTER 3

Multiply Whole Numbers

BIG Idea What are products and factors?

When two or more numbers are multiplied, the result is called a **product**. The numbers that are multiplied are **factors** of the product.

Example The price of admission to an aquarium is $18. If 3 people visit the aquarium, the total cost is shown.

$$3 \times \$18 = \$54$$

factors (3 and $18) product ($54)

What will I learn in this chapter?

- Multiply multiples of 10, 100, and 1,000 mentally.
- Estimate products of whole numbers.
- Multiply whole numbers.
- Identify and use properties of multiplication.
- Multiply whole numbers.
- Solve problems by using the *draw a picture* strategy.

Key Vocabulary

Distributive Property

factor

product

Math Online Student Study Tools at macmillanmh.com

TEST Practice

38. A school has 13 classrooms with 28 desks in each room. All the desks in the school are being used by students. How many students are using the desks? **(Lesson 3-6)**

A 41

B 182

C 244

D 364

39. The Stallions basketball team has sold out their last 8 home games. Their gym has 50 rows. Each row has 20 seats. How many people altogether have attended the 8 games? **(Lesson 3-7)**

F 80,000 **H** 800

G 8,000 **J** 80

Spiral Review

Multiply. **(Lesson 3-6)**

40. 12×43 **41.** 80×76 **42.** 304×15 **43.** 61×195

44. A teacher wants to tack three rectangular pictures in a row on a bulletin board. The edges of the pictures can overlap. The teacher wants to put a tack in each corner of each picture. What is the least number of tacks that are needed? **(Lesson 3-5)**

45. Space camp costs $425 for one student. How much would space camp cost for 5 students? **(Lesson 3-4)**

Mr. Armas is ordering some items for his scrapbook store. Use the table to find the cost of each. **(Lesson 3-2)**

Item	Cost
Fancy stickers	$2.00/package
Scrapbook paper	$3.00/package

46. 300 packages of fancy stickers

47. 40 packages of scrapbook paper

Add or subtract. **(Lesson 2-4)**

48. $\begin{array}{r} 27 \\ +\ 41 \\ \hline \end{array}$ **49.** $\begin{array}{r} 309 \\ +\ 521 \\ \hline \end{array}$ **50.** $\begin{array}{r} 1{,}852 \\ -\ 611 \\ \hline \end{array}$ **51.** $\begin{array}{r} 26{,}413 \\ -\ 3{,}750 \\ \hline \end{array}$

Replace each ● with <, >, or = to make a true sentence. **(Lesson 1-7)**

52. 6.7 ● 7.1 **53.** 0.41 ● 0.4 **54.** 8.263 ● 8.253 **55.** 9.50 ● 9.5

The Bone Bank

Did you know you have between 206 and 300 bones in your body? A healthy diet makes them strong, and calcium is an important part of a healthy diet. Adults need only 1,000 milligrams of calcium each day, but fifth graders should eat or drink about 1,200 milligrams. The calcium you eat or drink is deposited in your bones. Therefore, your bones are a "bank" for calcium!

Calcium Counts!

Food	Amount	Calcium
Carrots	1 cup	52 mg
Cheddar cheese	1 ounce	120 mg
Ice cream	1 cup	170 mg
Skim milk	1 cup	300 mg
Wheat bread	1 slice	20 mg
Yogurt	1 cup	490 mg

Did You Know?

Your bones grow until you are 30 years old.

Real-World Math

Use the information on page 130 to solve each problem.

1. If you eat 4 cups of carrots, how much calcium will you deposit in your bone bank? Solve mentally using the Distributive Property.

2. Suppose you eat one cup of yogurt each day for one week. How much calcium will you eat? Solve using the Distributive Property. Show your steps.

3. A man set a world record for drinking about 5 cups of milk in 3.2 seconds! How much calcium did he consume?

4. Suppose you make a grilled cheese sandwich with 4 ounces of cheese and 2 slices of wheat bread. Find the total amount of calcium in your sandwich. Show the steps you used.

5. You have a cup of ice cream every day for 2 weeks. How much calcium will you consume?

3-8 Extending Multiplication

MAIN IDEA

I will multiply to solve problems involving money and greater numbers.

Math Online

macmillanmh.com

- Extra Examples
- Personal Tutor
- Self-Check Quiz

GET READY to Learn

A gel pen at a craft store costs $1.05. Lucinda wants to buy three gel pens, each in a different color. She has $3.50 to spend.

Since Lucinda wants to buy three gel pens, the total cost will be 3 × $1.05. You can estimate the cost using rounding.

Real-World EXAMPLE — Estimate with Money

1 **SHOPPING Refer to the information above. Does Lucinda have enough money to buy three gel pens?**

3 × $1.05
↓ ↓
3 × $1 — Round $1.05 to $1 because $1.05 is closer to $1 than $2.

3 × $1 = $3 — Multiply mentally.

So, 3 × $1.05 is about $3. Since Lucinda has $3.50, she should have enough money to buy three gel pens.

You can also use rounding to estimate products of decimals that do not involve money.

Real-World EXAMPLE — Estimate with Decimals

2 **GASOLINE Mrs. James buys about 15.8 gallons of gas each week for her car. About how many gallons of gas will she buy in 5 weeks?**

Estimate the product of 15.8 and 5.

15.8 × 5
↓ ↓
16 × 5 — Round 15.8 to 16 because 15.8 is closer to 16 than 15.

16 × 5 = 80 — Multiply.

So, 16 × 5 is about 80. Mrs. James buys about 80 gallons of gas in 5 weeks.

Technology can be a useful tool for multiplying greater numbers or for performing many calculations. Always estimate first.

Real-World EXAMPLE Greater Numbers

3 **MEASUREMENT Tasha-Nicole Terani holds the world record for the most number of soccer touches in one minute at 239. If she continues at this rate, how many soccer touches would she have in one day?**

There are 60 minutes in 1 hour and 24 hours in 1 day. Find 60×239 and then multiply the product by 24.

Estimate $239 \times 60 \times 24 \approx 200 \times 60 \times 20$ or 240,000

Use the Calculator feature from your Math Tool Chest™ to find the exact answer.

Enter: 2 3 9
Press: ×
Enter: 6 0
Press: ×
Enter: 2 4
Press: =
Solution: 344160

> **Remember**
> You can find $200 \times 60 \times 20$ mentally by counting zeros in the factors. Write 4 zeros to the right of $2 \times 6 \times 2$ or 24.

Check for Reasonableness
The estimate, 240,000 is less than 344,160. But two of the original numbers were rounded down. So, it is reasonable to expect that the estimate would be less than the exact answer. ✓

Tasha-Nicole would have 344,160 soccer touches in one day.

CHECK What You Know

Estimate each product. See Examples 1–2 (p. 132)

1. $2 \times \$4.10$

2. $5 \times \$12.65$

3. 18.4×10

4. 24.7×3

5. A group of five friends is going to see a movie. If one ticket costs $8.50, estimate the total price of all the tickets.

6. About 325 people have picnics at Kennywood Park each day. The park is open 165 days each year. About how many people have picnics at the park each year?

7. A cantaloupe weighs 1.8 pounds. About how much do 3 cantaloupes weigh?

8. Talk About It Explain how to round 18.9 to the nearest whole number.

Practice and Problem Solving

EXTRA PRACTICE See page R9.

Estimate each product. See Examples 1–2 (p. 132)

9. 4 × $4.62
10. 3 × $23.07
11. $15.50 × 6
12. $16.85 × 9

13. 7.2 × 5
14. 14.5 × 3
15. 8 × 19.7
16. 10 × 26.2

17. **Measurement** Turkey costs $0.89 per pound and weighs 14 pounds. Estimate the total cost.

18. A dragonfly can fly at a speed of 17.8 miles per hour. At that speed, about how far could a dragonfly fly in 5 hours?

19. An average person speaks about 5,000 words each day. There are 365 days in one year. Does the average person speak more than 2,000,000 or less than 2,000,000 words each year? Then use a calculator to find the exact answer.

20. **Measurement** Turtles and tortoises have long life spans. A tortoise can live as long as 150 years. There are 365 days in one year. About how many days could a tortoise live? Then use a calculator to find the exact answer.

Real-World PROBLEM SOLVING

Art *Artsonia* is the world's largest kids' online art museum, where students have their own art gallery online. Friends and family can order items like the ones shown below that display students' artwork.

$15.95

$24.95

$11.95

$5.95

For Exercises 21–24, estimate the cost of each order.

21. 4 keychains

22. 2 plush bears

23. 3 coffee mugs and 2 keychains

24. 5 mouse pads and a plush bear

25. If you have $50, how many coffee mugs can you buy? Use the *guess and check* strategy.

H.O.T. Problems

26. **OPEN ENDED** Write a real-world multiplication problem involving money. Describe the steps that you used to solve the problem.

CHALLENGE **Find the missing digits in each factor.**

27. 3■2 × ■16 = 202,272

28. 2,3■5 × 4■2 = 1,115,830

29. **WRITING IN MATH** Explain why it is important to make an estimate before you use a calculator to multiply.

TEST Practice

30. The speeds of two insects are shown in the table. About how much farther would the hawk moth fly than the hornet in 4 hours? (Lesson 3-8)

Insect	Speed (miles per hour)
Hornet	13.3
Hawk Moth	33.8

A 20 miles

B 40 miles

C 60 miles

D 80 miles

31. The table shows the cost of different types of sandwiches at Don's Deli.

Sandwich Type	Cost
Chicken salad	$3.19
Tuna salad	$2.79
Egg salad	$2.59

Joy bought 2 tuna salad sandwiches and paid with a $10 bill. About how much change should she receive? (Lesson 3-8)

F $7

G $6

H $5

J $4

Spiral Review

Use properties of multiplication to find each product mentally. Show your steps and identify the properties that you used. (Lesson 3-7)

32. 27 × 5 × 2

33. 4 × 30 × 25

34. 20 × 50 × 6

35. Mr. Morales bought 18 boxes of sidewalk chalk. Each box contained 12 pieces of chalk. How many pieces of chalk did Mr. Morales buy? (Lesson 3-6)

Estimate each sum or difference. Show your work. (Lesson 2-2)

36. 306 + 521

37. 6.85 − 1.73

38. 24.11 + 9.5

3-9 Problem-Solving Investigation

MAIN IDEA I will identify extra information or missing information to solve a problem.

P.S.I. TEAM +

LILIA: On Tuesday, I was put in charge of collecting book orders. The cost of each book is $3. There were 7 orders on Wednesday, 5 orders on Thursday, and more orders on Friday and Monday.

YOUR MISSION: Find how many book orders Lilia collected.

Understand	**What facts do you know?** You know the cost of a book. You also know the number of book orders that were collected on Wednesday and Thursday. **What do you need to find?** You need to find the total number of book orders.
Plan	**Is there any information that is not needed?** The cost of a book. **Is there any information that is missing?** You do not know how many book orders were collected on Friday and Monday.
Solve	Since you do not have enough information, the problem cannot be solved.
Check	Read the question again to see if you missed any information. If so, go back and rework the problem. If not, the problem cannot be solved.

Mixed Problem Solving

EXTRA PRACTICE
See page R10.

Solve each problem. If there is extra information, identify it. If there is not enough information, tell what information is needed.

PROBLEM-SOLVING SKILLS
- *Use the four-step plan.*
- *Identify extra or missing information.*

1. Jayden is downloading songs onto his digital music player. The first song is 5 minutes long, the second song is 3 minutes long, and the third song is between the lengths of the first and second and songs. What is the total length of all three songs?

2. Room 220 and Room 222 are having a canned food drive. Refer to the diagram. How many more cans has Room 222 collected than Room 220?

3. Karly is collecting money for a bowl-a-thon. Her goal is to collect $125. So far, she has collected $20 each from three people and $10 each from four people. How much more money does Karly need to collect to have $125?

4. **Measurement** Eli made pancake batter. He has $1\frac{2}{3}$ cup of batter left. How much of the batter did he use?

5. Mrs. Rollins owns a farm. She raises prize chickens. Each chicken has its own cage and eats the same amount of food. Mrs. Rollins bought 100 pounds of chicken food last week. How much food did each chicken eat?

6. Paco studied his spelling words for 4 days. How many words did he study each day if he studied the same amount of words each day?

7. What is the cost of the peaches for a peach pie?

8. **Measurement** Rocco is slicing a loaf of Italian bread to serve with dinner. The cost of the bread was $2.99. He plans to cut the loaf into slices that are 1 inch thick. If the loaf is 18 inches long, how many pieces of bread can be cut from the loaf of bread?

9. **Measurement** The table shows the number of miles the Wong family drove each day on their vacation.

Day	Miles
Day 1	345
Day 2	50
Day 3	89
Day 4	279

How many more miles did they drive on Day 1 than on Day 4?

10. **WRITING IN MATH** Write a problem that has missing information. Explain how to rewrite the problem so that it can be solved.

CHAPTER 3

Study Guide and Review

Math Online macmillanmh.com
- STUDY TO GO
- Vocabulary Review

FOLDABLES Study Organizer GET READY to Study

Be sure the following Big Ideas are written in your Foldable.

Key Concepts

Multiplying Mentally

- You can multiply multiples of 10 mentally by using basic facts and then counting zeros in the factors. (p. 106)

2 zeros → 300; 1 zero → 60

$300 \times 60 = 18{,}000$ ← 3 zeros

Distributive Property

- To multiply a sum by a number, multiply each addend by the number. Then add. (p. 108)

$5 \times (10 + 2) = (5 \times 10) + (5 \times 2)$

Multiplying Whole Numbers

- The steps for multiplying by one- and two-digit numbers are similar. (pp. 116, 122)

$$\begin{array}{r} 14 \\ \times\ 3 \\ \hline 42 \end{array} \qquad \begin{array}{r} 14 \\ \times\ 23 \\ \hline 42 \\ 280 \\ \hline 322 \end{array} \quad \begin{array}{l} \\ \\ 14 \times 3 = 42 \\ 14 \times 20 = 280 \\ \\ \end{array}$$

Key Vocabulary

Distributive Property (p. 108)
factor (p. 103)
product (p. 103)

Vocabulary Check

State whether each sentence is *true* or *false*. If *false*, replace the underlined word or number to make a true sentence.

1. In the sentence $8 \times 2 = 16$, the numbers 8 and 2 are factors of 16.
2. The result when two numbers are multiplied is called a difference.
3. According to the Distributive Property, $2 \times (3 + 1) = (2 \times 3) + (2 \times 1)$.
4. To estimate 38×186, you could find 40×200.
5. When you multiply 80 and 70, the result has 4 zeros.
6. The sentence $2 \times 85 = 85 \times 2$ is an example of the Associative Property.
7. The Identity Property states that a number multiplied by 1 equals the number.

Lesson-by-Lesson Review

3-1 Multiplication Patterns (pp. 103–105)

Example 1
Find 20 × 70 mentally.

The basic fact is 2 × 7 = 14. Now count the zeros in the factors.

1 zero 1 zero
↓ ↓
20 × 70

The product will have 1 + 1 or 2 zeros. Write 2 zeros to the right of 14.

20 × 70 = 1,400

Find each product mentally.

8. 50 × 3
9. 26 × 10
10. 80 × 90
11. 300 × 4
12. 420 × 100
13. 500 × 600

14. A bank cash machine has 600 $20 bills. What is the total value of the $20 bills in the machine?

3-2 The Distributive Property (pp. 108–111)

Example 2
Rewrite 2 × (40 + 1) using the Distributive Property. Then evaluate.

2 × (40 + 1)

= (2 × 40) + (2 × 1)	Distributive Property
= 80 + 2	Find 2 × 40 and 2 × 1.
= 82	Add.

Example 3
Find 3 × 24 mentally.

3 × 24

= 3 × (20 + 4)	Write 24 as 20 + 4.
= (3 × 20) + (3 × 4)	Distributive Property
= 60 + 12	THINK: 3 × 20 = 60 and 3 × 4 = 12
= 72	Add 60 and 12.

Rewrite each expression using the Distributive Property. Then evaluate.

15. 4 × (20 + 6)
16. 3 × (60 + 1)
17. 7 × (10 + 2)
18. 2 × (80 + 1)

Find each product mentally using the Distributive Property. Show the steps that you used.

19. 3 × 17
20. 2 × 28
21. 8 × 31
22. 3 × 65

23. Mia fills 45 pages of her photo album with photos that she took. If she puts 4 photos on each page, how many photos are in the album?

CHAPTER 3

Study Guide and Review

3-3 Estimate Products (pp. 112–115)

Example 4
Estimate 21 × 38.

Round each factor to the nearest ten.

21	→	20	21 is rounded to 20.
× 38	→	× 40	38 is rounded to 40.
		800	

So, 21 × 38 is about 800.

Example 5
Estimate 46 × 107.

Round each factor to its greatest place value.

46	→	50	46 is rounded to 50.
× 107	→	× 100	107 is rounded to 100.
		5,000	

So, 46 × 107 is about 5,000.

Estimate by rounding or compatible numbers. Show your work.

24. 42 × 16

25. 13 × 65

26. 791 × 9

27. 521 × 27

28. 81 × 815

29. 312 × 259

30. Measurement A steamboat tour guide makes the 148-mile trip between Birmingham, Alabama, and Chattanooga, Tennessee, four times. Estimate the total number of miles she travels. Show your work.

3-4 Multiply by One-Digit Numbers (pp. 116–118)

Example 6
Find 7 × 54.

Estimate 7 × 50 = 350

Step 1 Multiply the ones. Regroup.

2
54
× 7
8

Step 2 Multiply the tens. Add the new tens.

2
54
× 7
378

So, 7 × 54 = 378. Since 378 is close to the estimate, the answer is reasonable.

Multiply.

31. 43 × 2

32. 67 × 4

33. 112 × 5

34. 6 × 32

35. 5 × 142

36. 381 × 3

37. A group uses 8 rafts on a white water rafting trip. Each raft carries 14 people. How many people go rafting?

3-5 Problem-Solving Strategy: Draw a Picture (pp. 120–121)

Example 7

Tony's garden is a square 12 feet long. He wants to plant shrubs 4 feet apart around the garden. There will be a shrub in each corner. How many shrubs will he need?

Make a drawing of the garden and the shrubs.

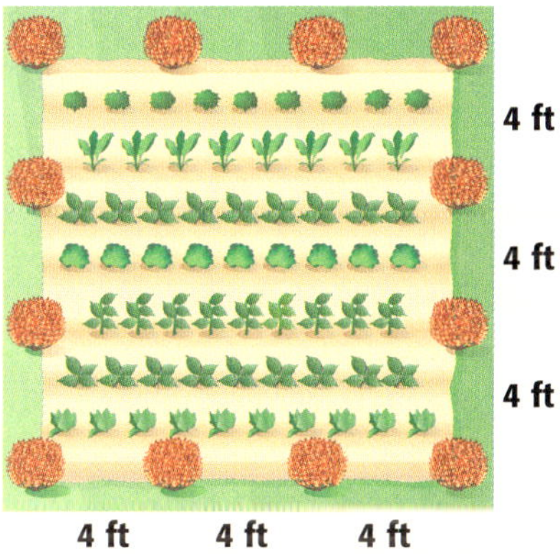

Tony will need 12 shrubs.

Solve by drawing a picture.

38. Cameron's bedroom wall is 13 feet wide. He wants to place two equal-size picture frames side by side along the wall so that the distance between each frame and each edge of the wall is 4 feet. If each picture frame is 2 feet wide, how many feet of space will be between the two frames?

39. A camp is putting a rope fence in a lake to mark the end of the swimming area. The rope is 60 yards long. A buoy is placed at the beginning of the rope. Another buoy is placed every 10 yards. A buoy is placed at the end of the rope. How many buoys are there?

3-6 Multiply by Two-Digit Numbers (pp. 122–124)

Example 8

Find 26 × 34.

Estimate $30 \times 30 = 900$

Step 1 Multiply the ones.

$$\begin{array}{r} \scriptstyle 2 \\ 26 \\ \times\ 34 \\ \hline 104 \end{array}$$

Step 2 Multiply the tens.

$$\begin{array}{r} \scriptstyle 1 \\ 26 \\ \times\ 34 \\ \hline 104 \\ 780 \end{array}$$

Step 3 Add.

$$\begin{array}{r} 26 \\ \times\ 34 \\ \hline 104 \\ 780 \\ \hline 884 \end{array}$$

So, $26 \times 34 = 884$.

Multiply.

40. $\begin{array}{r} 12 \\ \times\ 14 \\ \hline \end{array}$ **41.** $\begin{array}{r} 71 \\ \times\ 23 \\ \hline \end{array}$ **42.** $\begin{array}{r} 108 \\ \times\ 55 \\ \hline \end{array}$

43. 52×130 **44.** 42×312

45. 19×63 **46.** 761×85

47. **Measurement** A Chinese giant salamander weighs about 45 pounds. If 1 pound equals 16 ounces, how many ounces does a Chinese giant salamander weigh?

Chapter 3 Study Guide and Review

3-7 Multiplication Properties (pp. 126–129)

Example 9
Use properties of multiplication to find $(14 \times 2) \times 5$ mentally.

$(14 \times 2) \times 5$
$= 14 \times (2 \times 5)$ Associative Property
$= 14 \times 10$ Find 2×5 mentally.
$= 140$ Find 14×10 mentally.

Use properties of multiplication to find each product mentally. Show your steps and identify the properties that you used.

48. $4 \times 28 \times 25$ **49.** $(19 \times 20) \times 5$

50. **Algebra** What is the value of ■ in the expression below?

$(35 \times 4) \times 5 = 35 \times (■ \times 5)$

3-8 Extending Multiplication (pp. 132–135)

Example 10
Estimate $2 \times \$6.15$.

$2 \times \$6.15$
↓
$2 \times \$6$ Round \$6.15 to \$6.
$2 \times \$6 = \$12$

So, $2 \times \$6.15$ is about \$12.

Estimate.

51. $\$1.20 \times 4$ **52.** 42.4×8

53. A car travels 19.4 miles on one gallon of gas. About how far can it go with 8 gallons of gas?

3-9 Problem-Solving Investigation: Extra or Missing Information (pp. 136–137)

Example 11
Gia studied 75 spelling words over a certain number of days. How many words did she study each day if she studied the same amount of words each day?

You cannot solve this problem because you do not know how many days she studied her spelling words.

Solve the problem. If there is extra information, identify it. If there is not enough information, tell what information is needed.

54. How much higher is Mount Hayes than Mount Olympus?

Mountain	Elevation (ft)
Mount Olympus	2,429
Mount Mitchel	6,684
Mount Hayes	4,216

Chapter Test

Math Online macmillanmh.com
• Chapter Test

Find each product mentally.

1. 400 × 5

2. 60 × 7,000

Find each product mentally using the Distributive Property. Show your work.

3. 4 × 35

4. 3 × 27

5. 5 × 63

6. 2 × 49

7. The sports center is buying new equipment. Use the table to find the cost of 7 kickballs and 5 basketballs.

Ball	Cost
Basketball	$11
Kickball	$14
Soccer ball	$19

Estimate. Show your work.

8. 92×31

9. 410×77

10. **MULTIPLE CHOICE** Each hour, about 88 people visit a particular tourist attraction in Florida. At this rate, about how many people will visit the attraction in four hours?

A 360

B 320

C 270

D 240

Multiply.

11. 46×15

12. 108×21

13. 53×30

14. 179×12

15. **Measurement** The area of a rectangle is the product of its length and width. What is the area of the rectangle below in square centimeters?

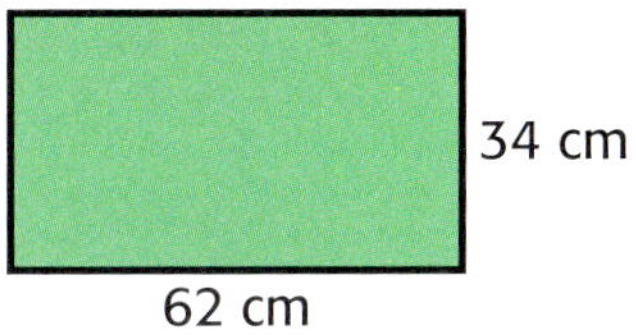

16. Identify the multiplication property that is shown in the sentence below.

$(14 \times 2) \times 50 = 14 \times (2 \times 50)$

17. A technician installed speakers around a square auditorium. She places 10 speakers on each side and one at each corner. How many speakers did she install? Use the *draw a picture* strategy.

18. Estimate 26.3 × 5.

19. **MULTIPLE CHOICE** Bala bought five books priced at $12.79 each. About how much was the total cost, not including tax?

F $45

G $55

H $65

J $75

20. **WRITING IN MATH** The tennis team is selling coupon books. The total sales are $855. How much does each coupon book cost? Explain if there is extra information to solve the problem. If there is not enough information, tell what information is needed. Rewrite the problem and solve.

CHAPTER 3

Test Practice

Math Online macmillanmh.com

• Test Practice

PART 1 Multiple Choice

Read each question. Then fill in the correct answer on the answer sheet provided by your teacher or on a sheet of paper.

1. A souvenir shop has 51 boxes of seashells in stock. Each box contains 9 shells. Which number is the best estimate for the total number of shells?

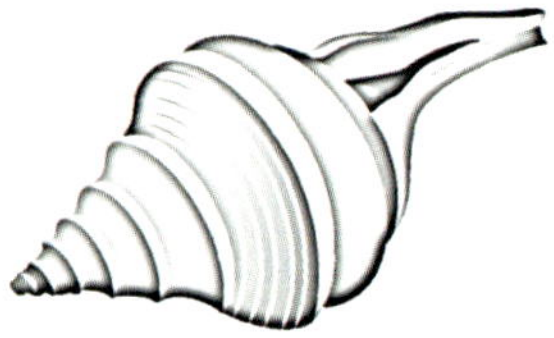

A 380 **C** 420

B 400 **D** 450

---

2. Kenny has 250 stickers in his collection. He has 40 stickers more than Placido and 25 stickers less than Paloma. How many stickers does Paloma have?

F 210 **H** 275

G 225 **J** 290

---

3. How much larger is the area of Colorado than Utah?

State	Area (square miles)
Colorado	104,185 sq mi
Utah	84,876 sq mi

A 16,272 sq mi **C** 22,567 sq mi

B 19,309 sq mi **D** 25,006 sq mi

4. The distance from Earth to the Moon is about 400,000 kilometers. How is this number written in words?

F forty thousand

G four hundred thousand

H four million

J forty million

---

5. Mrs. O'Brien has 28 calculators in her classroom. If each calculator takes 4 batteries, how many batteries are used altogether?

A 112

B 116

C 118

D 124

---

6. The banquet hall has 42 tables with 8 seats each. If 320 seats are occupied, which of the following ways shows how to find the number of empty seats?

F Add 320 to the product of 42 and 8.

G Add 42 to the product of 320 and 8.

H Subtract 320 from the product of 42 and 8.

J Subtract 42 from the product of 320 and 8.

Preparing for Standardized Tests

For test-taking strategies and practice, see pages R42–R55.

7. A car rental company has 29 cars on its lot. Each car has 4 wheels. How many wheels are there altogether at the car rental company lot?

A 84 **C** 116

B 108 **D** 122

8. The price of a stock over the past 4 weeks is shown in the table. If the pattern continues, what will the price be after 5 weeks?

Week	1	2	3	4	5
Price ($)	1.00	1.80	2.60	3.40	?

F $3.80 **H** $4.10

G $4.00 **J** $4.20

9. During the first week of school, Mrs. Mease asked each of her students to bring in three boxes of tissues. If there are 27 students in Mrs. Mease's classroom, how many boxes of tissues will there be?

A 71 **C** 84

B 81 **D** 92

PART 2 Short Response

Record your answers on the sheet provided by your teacher or on a sheet of paper.

10. There are 9 tables in the school cafeteria. Each table can seat 12 people. If every table is full, how many people are seated in the cafeteria at the same time? Draw a diagram to solve.

11. Show how to use the Distributive Property of Multiplication to find $4 \times (9 + 6)$.

PART 3 Extended Response

Record your answers on the answer sheet provided by your teacher or on a sheet of paper. Show your work.

12. A car wash company cleaned a total of 43 cars in one day. The price of each car wash is $14. Estimate how much money the company earned that day.

Is your estimate higher or lower than the actual amount? Explain.

NEED EXTRA HELP?												
If You Missed Question...	1	2	3	4	5	6	7	8	9	10	11	12
Go to Lesson...	2-2	1-3	2-4	1-1	3-4	3-9	3-4	2-6	3-4	3-3	3-2	3-5

CHAPTER 4 Divide Whole Numbers

BIG Idea **What are quotients, dividends, and divisors?**

When one number is divided by another, the result is called a **quotient**. The **dividend** is the number that is divided. The **divisor** is the number used to divide another number.

Example Lions live in social communities called *prides*. The average number of lions in a pride is about 15. Suppose a nature preserve has 300 lions. There are about 300 ÷ 15, or 20 prides.

$$300 \div 15 = 20$$

300 → dividend; 15 → divisor; 20 → quotient

What will I learn in this chapter?

- Divide multiples of 10, 100, and 1,000 mentally.
- Estimate quotients of whole numbers.
- Divide whole numbers.
- Interpret remainders in division problems.
- Solve problems by using the *act it out* strategy.

Key Vocabulary

quotient
dividend
divisor

Math Online Student Study Tools at macmillanmh.com

FOLDABLES® Study Organizer

Make this Foldable to help you organize information about division. Begin with a sheet of 11″ × 17″ paper and six index cards.

1. **Fold** lengthwise about 3″ from the bottom.

2. **Fold** the paper in thirds.

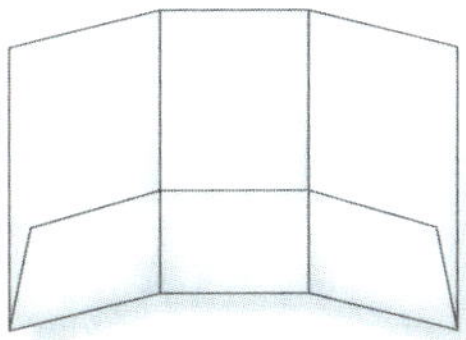

3. **Open** and staple the edges on either side to form three pockets.

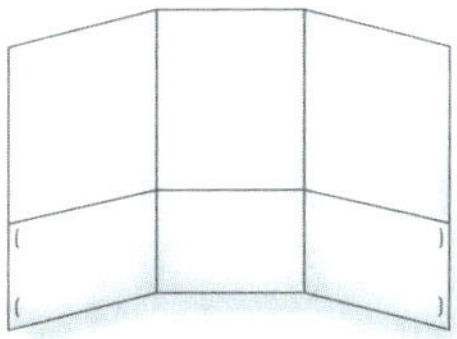

4. **Label** the pockets. Place two index cards in each pocket.

ARE YOU READY for Chapter 4?

You have two ways to check prerequisite skills for this chapter.

Option 2

Math Online Take the Chapter Readiness Quiz at macmillanmh.com.

Option 1

Complete the Quick Check below.

QUICK Check

Divide. (Prior Grade)

1. $8 \div 2$

2. $15 \div 5$

3. $27 \div 3$

4. $28 \div 4$

5. $48 \div 6$

6. $54 \div 9$

7. Three people spend $12 for pizza, $6 for salads, and $6 for drinks at lunch. If they divide the total cost evenly, how much does each person pay?

Write the fact family for each set of numbers. (Prior Grade)

8. 4, 6, 24

9. 2, 5, 10

10. 8, 9, 72

11. 7, 3, 21

12. 6, 5, 30

13. 8, 4, 32

Tell if each number can be divided evenly by 2, 3, 5, 6, or 10. (Prior Grade)

14. 80

15. 90

16. 126

17. 203

18. 765

19. 1,314

20. The 82 members of the fifth grade chorus stand on a stage in rows. Can they stand in 3 equal rows? Explain.

4-1 Division Patterns

MAIN IDEA

I will use basic facts and patterns to divide multiples of 10, 100, and 1,000 mentally.

New Vocabulary

quotient
dividend
divisor

Math Online

macmillanmh.com

- Extra Examples
- Personal Tutor
- Self-Check Quiz

GET READY to Learn

A monarch butterfly can fly 80 miles in one day. To fly 240 miles during migration, it would take 240 ÷ 80, or 3 days.

When one number is divided by another, the result is called a **quotient**. The **dividend** is the number that is divided and the **divisor** is the number used to divide another number.

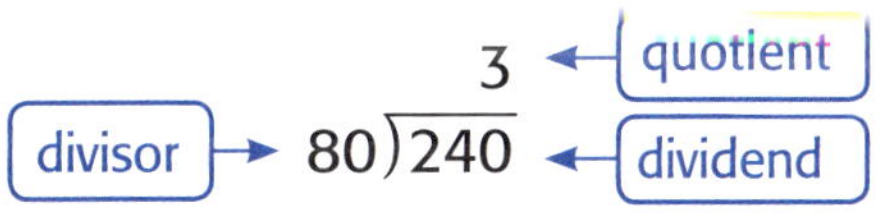

You can use basic facts and patterns to divide by multiples of 10.

24 ÷ 8 = 3	← basic fact →	24 ÷ 8 = 3
240 ÷ 8 = 30		240 ÷ 80 = 3
2,400 ÷ 8 = 300		2,400 ÷ 800 = 3
24,000 ÷ 8 = 3,000		24,000 ÷ 8,000 = 3

EXAMPLE Divide Multiples of 10

1 **Find 600 ÷ 3 mentally.**

Since 600 is a multiple of 10, you can use the basic fact and continue the pattern.

6 ÷ 3 = 2	6 ones divided by 3 equals 2 ones.
60 ÷ 3 = 20	6 tens divided by 3 equals 2 tens.
600 ÷ 3 = 200	6 hundreds divided by 3 equals 2 hundreds.

So, 600 ÷ 3 = 200.

Real-World EXAMPLE — Divide Multiples of 10

2 **MEASUREMENT** **A cow eats 900 pounds of hay over a period of 30 days. How many pounds of hay would the cow eat each day at this rate?**

You need to find 900 ÷ 30.

Remember

In multiplication, count the number of zeros in each factor. Write the zeros to the right of the product of the basic fact.

One Way: **Use fact families.**

3 × 3 = 9	⟷	9 ÷ 3 = 3
30 × 3 = 90	⟷	90 ÷ 30 = 3
30 × 30 = 900	⟷	900 ÷ 30 = 30

Another Way: **Cross out zeros to make division easier.**

90Ø ÷ 3Ø	Cross out the same number of zeros in both the dividend and divisor.
90 ÷ 3 = 30	Divide. THINK: 9 tens ÷ 3 = 3 tens.

So, 900 ÷ 30 = 30.

The cow eats 30 pounds of hay each day.

CHECK What You Know

Divide mentally. See Examples 1–2 (pp. 149–150)

1. 500 ÷ 5

2. 320 ÷ 8

3. 200 ÷ 10

4. 420 ÷ 70

5. 800 ÷ 2

6. 150 ÷ 30

7. 270 ÷ 90

8. 5,600 ÷ 70

9. 2,100 ÷ 30

10. A sailfish grabbed a fishing line and dragged it 300 feet in just 3 seconds. On average, how many feet did the fish drag the line each second?

11. Talk About It Explain how you know that the quotients 48 ÷ 6 and 480 ÷ 60 are equal without doing any computation.

Practice and Problem Solving

EXTRA PRACTICE See page R10.

Divide mentally. See Examples 1–2 (pp. 149–150)

12. 800 ÷ 2 **13.** 900 ÷ 3 **14.** 150 ÷ 5

15. 140 ÷ 7 **16.** 450 ÷ 9 **17.** 280 ÷ 4

18. 180 ÷ 60 **19.** 240 ÷ 30 **20.** 4,200 ÷ 70

21. 1,800 ÷ 30 **22.** 2,000 ÷ 400 **23.** 2,400 ÷ 300

24. A group of 10 people bought tickets to a reptile exhibit and paid a total of $130. What was the price of one ticket?

25. **Measurement** The fastest team in a wheelbarrow race traveled 100 meters in about 20 seconds. On average, how many meters did the team travel each second?

26. **Measurement** Daniela has a 160-ounce bag of potting soil. She puts an equal amount of soil in each pot shown. How much soil will she put in each pot?

27. A video store took in $450 in DVD rentals during one day. If DVDs rent for $9 each, how many DVDs were rented?

H.O.T. Problems

28. **OPEN ENDED** Write a real-world division problem. Identify the dividend, divisor, and quotient.

29. **NUMBER SENSE** Write two different division problems that both have a quotient of 50.

30. **FIND THE ERROR** Alejandro and Megan are finding 5,400 ÷ 90 mentally. Who is correct? Explain.

31. **WRITING IN MATH** Describe how placing zeros at the end of basic division facts helps you divide mentally. Write an example.

4-2 Estimate Quotients

MAIN IDEA

I will estimate quotients using rounding and compatible numbers.

Math Online

macmillanmh.com

- Extra Examples
- Personal Tutor
- Self-Check Quiz

GET READY to Learn

Camp Hickory Hills has 442 registered campers for the summer. If one group leader is needed for every 10 campers, about how many group leaders are needed?

$442 \div 10$

↓ ↓

$400 \div 10 = 40$

So, about 40 group leaders are needed.

To estimate a quotient, you can use compatible numbers, or numbers that are easy to divide mentally. Look for numbers that are part of fact families.

EXAMPLE Find a Compatible Dividend

1 Estimate 156 ÷ 3.

$156 \div 3$

↓ ↓

150 $\div 3$ — Change 156 to 150 because 15 and 3 are compatible numbers.

$150 \div 3 = 50$ — Divide mentally.

So, $156 \div 3$ is about 50.

EXAMPLE Find a Compatible Divisor

2 Estimate 3,200 ÷ 90.

$3{,}200 \div 90$

↓ ↓

$3{,}200 \div$ **80** — Change 90 to 80 because 32 and 8 are compatible numbers.

$3{,}200 \div 80 = 40$ — Divide mentally.

So, $3{,}200 \div 90$ is about 40.

EXAMPLE Use Rounding and Compatible Numbers

3 **Estimate 228 ÷ 43.**

Step 1 Round the divisor to the nearest ten.

$$228 \div 43 \rightarrow 228 \div 40$$

Step 2 Change the dividend to a number that is compatible with 4. Notice it is easy to divide 24 by 4.

$$228 \div 43 \rightarrow 240 \div 40$$

Step 3 Divide mentally.

$$240 \div 40 = 6$$

So, 228 ÷ 43 is about 6.

Real-World EXAMPLE Estimate to Solve Problems

4 **DOGS** **Six dogs equally share a 45-pound bag of dog food each week. About how much does each dog eat each week?**

One Way: Use compatible numbers 45 and 5.	**Another Way:** Use compatible numbers 48 and 6.
45 ÷ 6 ↓ ↓ 45 ÷ 5 = 9	45 ÷ 6 ↓ ↓ 48 ÷ 6 = 8

So, each dog eats about 8 or 9 pounds of dog food each week.

Remember

There are often different ways to estimate quotients.

CHECK What You Know

Estimate. Show your work. See Examples 1–4 (pp. 152–153)

1. 850 ÷ 9

2. 635 ÷ 8

3. 545 ÷ 50

4. 400 ÷ 23

5. 374 ÷ 93

6. 713 ÷ 62

7. 1,200 ÷ 380

8. 624 ÷ 314

9. A box of cereal contains 340 grams. If there are 12 servings, about how many grams are there in one serving? Show how you estimated.

10. Talk About It Explain how you could use compatible numbers to estimate 272 ÷ 4.

Practice and Problem Solving

EXTRA PRACTICE See page R10.

Estimate. Show your work. See Examples 1–4 (pp. 152–153)

11. 397 ÷ 4 **12.** 432 ÷ 7 **13.** 753 ÷ 90 **14.** 253 ÷ 50

15. 554 ÷ 6 **16.** 360 ÷ 7 **17.** 800 ÷ 21 **18.** 150 ÷ 48

19. 300 ÷ 59 **20.** 270 ÷ 32 **21.** 230 ÷ 73 **22.** 244 ÷ 37

23. 680 ÷ 71 **24.** 860 ÷ 318 **25.** 619 ÷ 320 **26.** 786 ÷ 189

Solve. Show your work.

27. A grocery store employee puts 8 bagels in each bag. If she has 385 bagels, about how many bags does she need?

28. **Measurement** Jani drives 232 miles in 4 hours. About how many miles does she drive each hour?

29. There are 598 goldfish divided equally among 23 fish tanks. About how many goldfish are in each tank?

30. **Measurement** Felix has 5 bags of birdseed. Each bag has about 28 ounces of birdseed. If he divides the birdseed equally into 3 containers, about how much birdseed will he put in each container?

31. The table shows how much each fifth grade room earned from a bake sale. The money is going to be given to 6 different charities. If each charity is given an equal amount, about how much will each charity receive? Show how you estimated.

Bake Sale

Room	Earnings($)
110	327
112	425
114	550
116	486

H.O.T. Problems

32. **OPEN ENDED** Write a division problem and show two different ways that you can estimate the quotient using compatible numbers.

33. **NUMBER SENSE** Without calculating, predict whether 23,510 ÷ 615 is greater than or less than 100. Explain your reasoning.

34. **WRITING IN MATH** Write a real-life problem in which you estimate the quotient of two numbers.

TEST Practice

35. Paul took 144 pictures on his vacation using rolls of film like the one shown at the right. Which is the best estimate for the number of rolls of film that he used? (Lesson 4-2)

A less than 5

B between 5 and 7

C between 50 and 70

D more than 70

36. A train traveled 300 miles in 5 hours. How far did the train travel each hour on average? (Lesson 4-1)

F 60 mi

G 150 mi

H 600 mi

J 1,500 mi

37. **SHORT RESPONSE** Mrs. Chong bought 480 bookmarks. If each box contains 60 bookmarks, how many boxes did she buy? (Lesson 4-1)

Spiral Review

Divide mentally. (Lesson 4-1)

38. 400 ÷ 2 **39.** 180 ÷ 3 **40.** 630 ÷ 70 **41.** 2,500 ÷ 500

42. Miss LaHood's class is having a reading challenge. Rafe read 12 books in 7 weeks, Peter read 10 books in 7 weeks, and Misti read 11 books in 7 weeks. How many more books did Rafe read than Peter? Identify any extra or missing information. (Lesson 3-9)

43. The cost of renting a paddleboat at the lake is shown at the right. Estimate how much it will cost to rent the paddle boat for 3 hours. (Lesson 3-8)

Multiply. (Lesson 3-6)

44. 14 × 11 **45.** 38 × 26 **46.** 142 × 51 **47.** 12 × 507

Estimate each sum or difference by rounding. Show your work. (Lesson 2-2)

48. $\begin{array}{r} 58 \\ +\ 61 \\ \hline \end{array}$ **49.** $\begin{array}{r} 327 \\ -\ 106 \\ \hline \end{array}$ **50.** $\begin{array}{r} 19.8 \\ +\ 7.6 \\ \hline \end{array}$ **51.** $\begin{array}{r} 1{,}402 \\ -\ 872 \\ \hline \end{array}$

Explore

Math Activity for 4-3

Use Division Models

MAIN IDEA

I will divide using models.

You will need

base-ten blocks

You can use base-ten blocks to help you divide.

ACTIVITY

1 **At the fair, you need tickets to ride the rides. Three friends share 336 tickets equally. How many tickets will each friend receive?**

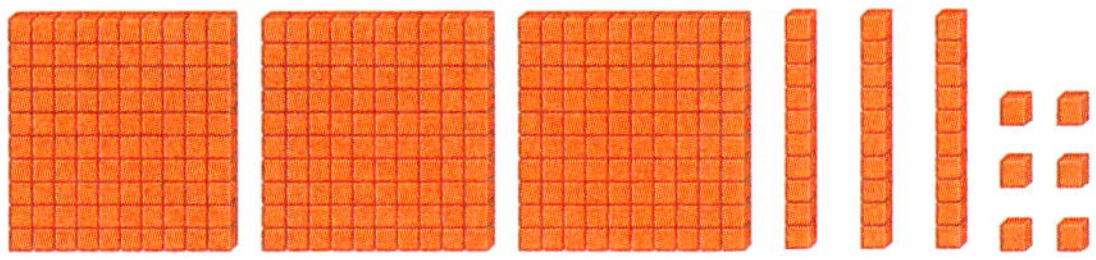

Represent 336 using base-ten blocks.

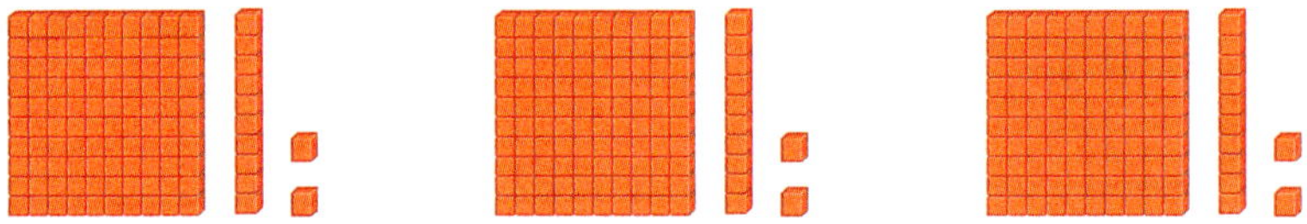

Regroup the base-ten blocks to make 3 equal groups.

When you divide 336 into three groups, there are 112 in each group.

So, $336 \div 3 = 112$.

Use multiplication to check your answer. ✓

$112 \times 3 = 336$.

ACTIVITY

2 **Find 252 ÷ 4.**

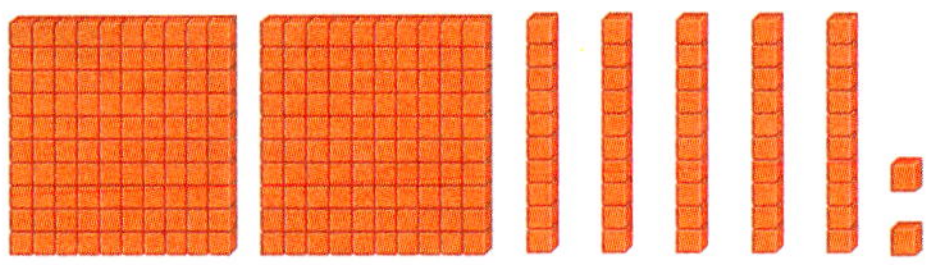

Represent 252 using base-ten blocks.

Regroup the base-ten blocks to make 4 equal groups.

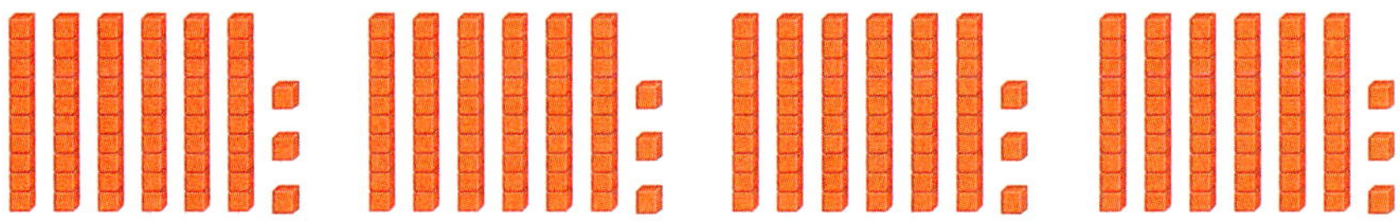

When you divide 252 counters into four groups, there are 63 counters in each group.

So, 252 ÷ 4 = 63.

Use multiplication to check your answer. ✓
63 × 4 = 252.

ACTIVITY Model Remainders

3 Find 136 ÷ 5.

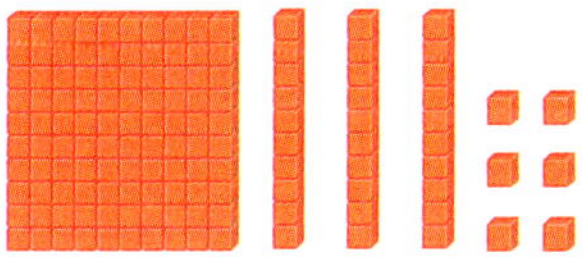

Represent 136 using base-ten blocks

Regroup the base–ten blocks to make 5 equal groups.

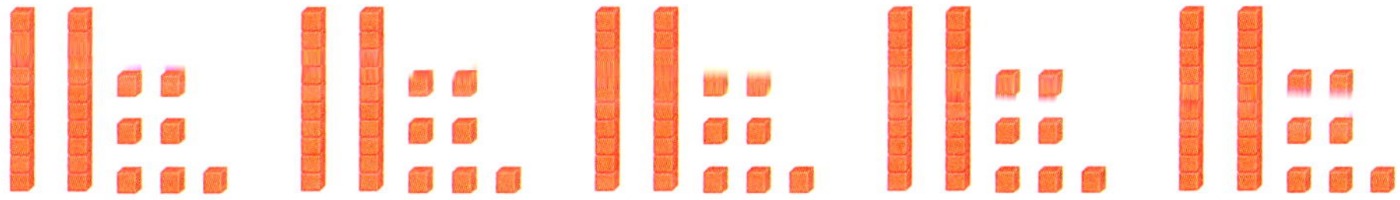

There is one left over.

A *remainder* is the number left after a quotient is found.

When you divide 136 counters into five groups, there are 27 counters in each group with one left over.

So, 136 ÷ 5 = 27 R1.

CHECK What You Know

Use models to find each quotient.

1. 568 ÷ 4 **2.** 104 ÷ 8 **3.** 695 ÷ 5 **4.** 84 ÷ 7

5. 25 ÷ 4 **6.** 19 ÷ 4 **7.** 37 ÷ 8 **8.** 66 ÷ 5

9. WRITING IN ► MATH Write a real-world division problem that can be solved by using base-ten blocks.

4-3 Divide by One-Digit Numbers

MAIN IDEA

I will divide up to a four-digit number by a one-digit number.

New Vocabulary

remainder

Math Online

macmillanmh.com

- Extra Examples
- Personal Tutor
- Self-Check Quiz

GET READY to Learn

Thunder Canyon is a 1,600-foot-long ride at Cedar Point in Sandusky, Ohio. On 8 rafts, it can carry a total of 96 people. How many people can it carry on each raft?

To find the number of people *Thunder Canyon* can carry on each raft, divide 96 by 8. To divide a two-digit number by a one-digit number, first divide the tens.

Real-World EXAMPLE

1 RIDES Refer to the information above. How many people can *Thunder Canyon* carry on each raft?

To solve, divide 96 people into 8 groups. Find 96 ÷ 8.

Estimate 100 ÷ 10 = 10

Step 1

Divide the tens. Can 9 tens be divided among 8? Yes.

```
   1
8)96   Divide: 9 ÷ 8
 - 8   Multiply: 1 × 8
   1   Subtract: 9 − 8
       Compare: 1 < 8
```

Step 2

Bring down the ones. Divide the ones. Can 16 ones be divided among 8? Yes.

```
   12
 8)96
  - 8↓
   16   Divide: 16 ÷ 8
 - 16   Multiply: 2 × 8
    0   Subtract: 16 − 16
        Compare: 0 < 8
```

So, *Thunder Canyon* can carry 12 people on each raft. This is close to the estimate, 10. So, the answer is reasonable.

This same process can be used to divide a three-digit number by a one-digit number. When dividing a three-digit number, the first step is to divide the hundreds.

EXAMPLE Divide by a One-Digit Number

2 **Find $2\overline{)856}$.** **Estimate** $900 \div 2 = 450$

Step 1

Divide the hundreds.

$$\begin{array}{r|l} 4 & \\ 2\overline{)856} & 8 \div 2 \\ -\ 8 & 4 \times 2 \\ \hline 0 & 8 - 8 \\ & 0 < 2 \end{array}$$

Step 2

Bring down the tens.
Divide the tens.

$$\begin{array}{r|l} 42 & \\ 2\overline{)856} & \\ -\ 8\downarrow & \\ \hline 05 & 5 \div 2 \\ -\ 4 & 2 \times 2 \\ \hline 1 & 5 - 4 \\ & 1 < 2 \end{array}$$

Step 3

Bring down the ones.
Divide the ones.

$$\begin{array}{r|l} 428 & \\ 2\overline{)856} & \\ -\ 8\downarrow & \\ \hline 05 & \\ -\ 4\downarrow & \\ \hline 16 & 16 \div 2 \\ -\ 16 & 8 \times 2 \\ \hline 0 & 16 - 16 \\ & 0 < 2 \end{array}$$

The quotient is 428. Compare to the estimate.

If the divisor is not a factor of the dividend, then the answer will include a remainder. A **remainder** is the number left after a quotient is found. It is represented by the capital letter R.

EXAMPLE Division with a Remainder

3 **Find $137 \div 5$.** **Estimate** $150 \div 5 = 30$

Step 1

Divide the hundreds.

$$5\overline{)137}$$

Can 1 hundred be divided among 5? No. So, the first digit will be in the tens place.

Step 2

Divide the tens.

$$\begin{array}{r|l} 2 & \\ 5\overline{)137} & 13 \div 5 \\ -\ 10 & 2 \times 5 \\ \hline 3 & 13 - 10 \\ & 3 < 5 \end{array}$$

Step 3

Bring down the ones.
Divide the ones.

$$\begin{array}{r|l} 27\ \text{R2} & \\ 5\overline{)137} & \\ -\ 10\downarrow & \\ \hline 37 & 37 \div 5 \\ -\ 35 & 7 \times 5 \\ \hline 2 & 37 - 35 \\ & 2 < 5 \end{array}$$

There are no digits left to divide, so 2 is the remainder.

The quotient is 27 R2. Compare to the estimate.

Remember

To check division with a remainder, first multiply the quotient and the divisor. Then add the remainder.

$$\begin{array}{r} 27 \\ \times\ 5 \\ \hline 135 \end{array} \qquad \begin{array}{r} 135 \\ +\ 2 \\ \hline 137\ ✓ \end{array}$$

CHECK What You Know

Divide. See Examples 1–3 (pp. 158–159)

1. $2\overline{)68}$ **2.** $5\overline{)95}$ **3.** $4\overline{)625}$ **4.** $3\overline{)410}$

5. 216 ÷ 3 **6.** 932 ÷ 6 **7.** 2,816 ÷ 5 **8.** 6,982 ÷ 7

9. An adult kangaroo is how many times heavier than a baby kangaroo?

Kangaroo	Weight (lb)
Adult	145
Baby	5

10. Talk About It Does the quotient of 245 and 8 have two or three digits? Explain how you know without solving.

Practice and Problem Solving

EXTRA PRACTICE See page R11.

Divide. See Examples 1–3 (pp. 158–159)

11. $5\overline{)206}$ **12.** $6\overline{)96}$ **13.** $5\overline{)435}$ **14.** $9\overline{)837}$

15. $3\overline{)945}$ **16.** $5\overline{)630}$ **17.** $4\overline{)97}$ **18.** $2\overline{)87}$

19. 210 ÷ 9 **20.** 595 ÷ 4 **21.** 766 ÷ 6 **22.** 267 ÷ 8

23. 428 ÷ 3 **24.** 590 ÷ 8 **25.** 9,350 ÷ 7 **26.** 6,418 ÷ 9

27. A state park has cable cars that travel about 864 yards in 4 minutes. How many yards do the cars travel per minute?

28. Five pre-owned video games cost $185. If all the games cost the same, what is the cost of each game?

29. There were 672 people in the audience at a play. Each ticket cost $3. The audience was seated in 6 sections. If each section had the same number of people in it, how many people were in each section?

30. On Monday, a concession stand manager ordered 985 popcorn bags. If he splits the bags evenly among 5 concession stands, how many popcorn bags will each concession stand receive?

31. Mr. Harris wants to divide his 27 students into equal groups of 4 students each. How many groups of 4 students can he make? How many students will not be in a group of 4?

H.O.T. Problems

32. OPEN ENDED Write a real-world division problem with a divisor of 4 that has no remainder. Then write a real-world division problem with a divisor of 4 that has a remainder.

33. NUMBER SENSE Use the digits 2, 4, and 6 one time each in ■ ■ ÷ ■. Write the division problem with the greatest quotient.

34. WRITING IN ▸MATH Explain how estimation is useful when solving division problems.

TEST Practice

35. Use the table below to make a true statement. (Lesson 4-3)

Weight of Whales	
Mammal	**Weight**
Blue whale	144 tons
Gray whale	36 tons

A blue whale is ________ heavier than a gray whale.

A 3 times **C** 6 times

B 4 times **D** 8 times

36. Lauren poured an equal amount of the solution below in each of 8 test tubes. About how much solution is in each test tube? (Lesson 4-3)

F 30 mL **H** 50 mL

G 40 mL **J** 100 mL

Spiral Review

37. There are 520 baseballs that will be shipped to nine sports stores. Estimate the number of baseballs each store is to receive if they each receive about the same number. (Lesson 4-2)

Divide mentally. (Lesson 4-1)

38. $70 \div 2$ **39.** $400 \div 4$ **40.** $200 \div 5$ **41.** $900 \div 9$

Identify the multiplication property used to rewrite each problem. (Lesson 3-7)

42. $5 \times 100 \times 3 = 5 \times 3 \times 100$ **43.** $(7 \times 5) \times 2 = 7 \times (5 \times 2)$

Estimate. Show your work. (Lesson 3-3)

44. 56×21 **45.** 11×387 **46.** 17×43 **47.** 29×88

4-4 Divide by Two-Digit Numbers

MAIN IDEA

I will divide up to a three-digit number by a two-digit number.

Math Online

macmillanmh.com

- Extra Examples
- Personal Tutor
- Self-Check Quiz

GET READY to Learn

A full sheet cake serves 76 people. To serve 152 people at a party, a bakery needs to make 152 ÷ 76, or 2 sheet cakes.

In this lesson, you will learn how to divide by a two-digit number. This will help you to solve problems like the one above.

Real-World EXAMPLE — Divide by a Two-Digit Number

1 FOOD Refer to the information above. How many sheet cakes are needed to serve 836 people?

Find $76\overline{)836}$.

Estimate 800 ÷ 80 = 10

Step 1

Divide the tens.

```
     1
76)836   Divide: 83 ÷ 76
 - 76    Multiply: 76 × 1
     7   Subtract: 83 − 76
         Compare: 7 < 76
```

Step 2

Divide the ones.

```
    11
76)836
 - 76↓   Bring down the ones.
    76   Divide: 76 ÷ 76
  - 76   Multiply: 1 × 76
     0   Subtract: 76 − 76
         Compare: 0 < 76
```

So, 11 cakes are needed to serve 836 people.

Compare to the estimate, 10. Since 11 is close to 10, the answer is reasonable.

As with division by a one-digit number, it is possible to have a remainder when you divide by a two-digit number.

EXAMPLE Division with a Remainder

2 **Find 751 ÷ 30.** Estimate $750 \div 30 = 25$

Step 1
Divide the tens.

2	
$30\overline{)751}$	$75 \div 30$
-60	2×30
15	$75 - 60$
	$15 < 30$

Step 2
Divide the ones.

25 R1	
$30\overline{)751}$	
$-60\downarrow$	Bring down the ones.
151	$151 \div 30$
-150	5×30
1	$151 - 150$
	$1 < 30$

So, 751 ÷ 30 is 25 R1.

Remember

You can check division with a remainder. Multiply the quotient and the divisor. Then add the remainder.

$$\begin{array}{r} 25 \\ \times\ 30 \\ \hline 750 \end{array} \quad \rightarrow \quad \begin{array}{r} 750 \\ +\ 1 \\ \hline 751 \end{array} \checkmark$$

Real-World EXAMPLE Divide by Two-Digit Numbers

3 **MEASUREMENT** **Mackenzie volunteered 208 hours last year. If she volunteered the same number of hours each week, how many hours did she volunteer each week?**

To solve, find 208 ÷ 52. 1 year = 52 weeks

Estimate $200 \div 50 = 4$

Step 1
Divide the tens.

$52\overline{)208}$

Since 20 tens cannot be divided by 52 ones, move to Step 2.

Step 2
Divide the ones.

4	
$52\overline{)208}$	4×52
-208	$208 - 208$
0	

So, Mackenzie volunteered an average of 4 hours each week.

CHECK What You Know

Divide. See Examples 1–3 (pp. 162–163)

1. $16\overline{)176}$ **2.** $24\overline{)192}$ **3.** 375 ÷ 46 **4.** 289 ÷ 31

5. Mr. Morales buys flags for his store. Each flag costs \$28. How many flags can he buy for \$350?

6. **Talk About It** Explain how estimation is useful when you are dividing by two-digit numbers.

Practice and Problem Solving

EXTRA PRACTICE See page R11.

Divide. See Examples 1–3 (pp. 162–163)

7. $14\overline{)98}$ **8.** $32\overline{)97}$ **9.** $11\overline{)18}$ **10.** $18\overline{)216}$

11. $47\overline{)544}$ **12.** $70\overline{)359}$ **13.** $160 \div 32$ **14.** $901 \div 18$

15. A boat travels 384 miles in 24 hours. What is the average distance the boat travels in 1 hour?

16. Dreanne has 288 pictures. Her album holds 12 pictures on each page. How many pages does she need?

Data File

Oklahoma is one of the top beef producing states. In the first 26 weeks, a calf gains a total of about 320 pounds. In the second 26 weeks, it gains about 370 pounds.

About how many pounds does a calf gain each week for each of the following? Round to the nearest pound.

17. during the first 26 weeks

18. during the second 26 weeks

H.O.T. Problems

19. FIND THE ERROR Aura and Jacob are finding $818 \div 21$. Who is correct? Explain.

Aura

```
     39
21)818
  - 63
    188
  - 188
      0
```

Jacob

```
   38 R20
21)818
  - 63
    188
  - 168
     20
```

20. WRITING IN ▸MATH Describe the similarities and differences when dividing by one-digit numbers and by two-digit numbers.

CHAPTER 4

Mid-Chapter Check

Lessons 4-1 through 4-4

Divide mentally. (Lesson 4-1)

1. 400 ÷ 2
2. 240 ÷ 6
3. 3,500 ÷ 5
4. 420 ÷ 60
5. 4,800 ÷ 800
6. 1,200 ÷ 300

7. **MULTIPLE CHOICE** A total of 180 students went on a field trip. There were 3 buses. If each bus had the same number of students on it, how many students were on each bus? (Lesson 4-1)

A 6

B 36

C 54

D 60

Estimate. Show your work. (Lesson 4-2)

8. 232 ÷ 6
9. 1,765 ÷ 2
10. 5,600 ÷ 71
11. 400 ÷ 54
12. 756 ÷ 170
13. 2,089 ÷ 310

14. **Measurement** The length of a rectangle can be found by dividing the area by the width. Estimate the length of the rectangle below by using compatible numbers and rounding. (Lesson 4-2)

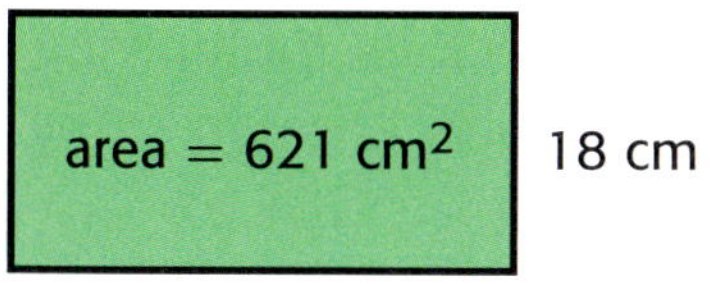

Divide. (Lesson 4-3)

15. 73 ÷ 2
16. 509 ÷ 6
17. 874 ÷ 3
18. 614 ÷ 5

19. **Measurement** The table shows the heights of the three tallest cacti.

Cactus	Height
Saguaro	75 ft
Organ-pipe	48 ft
Opuntia	33 ft

Source: *Scholastic Book of World Records*

Find the height of each cactus in yards. (*Hint:* 1 yard = 3 feet) (Lesson 4-3)

Divide. (Lesson 4-4)

20. 109 ÷ 12
21. 126 ÷ 18
22. 801 ÷ 20
23. 523 ÷ 13

24. **MULTIPLE CHOICE** Suki received $864 for working 12 weeks during the summer. She earned $8 per hour and worked the same number of hours each week. How much did she earn each week? (Lesson 4-4)

F $9

G $72

H $96

J $108

25. **WRITING IN ▸MATH** Can the remainder in a division problem ever equal the divisor? Explain. (Lesson 4-3)

4-5 Problem-Solving Strategy

MAIN IDEA I will solve problems by using the *act it out* strategy.

Annie is using a roll of plastic string to make keychains. The roll of string had 78 inches on it before she started. She has already used 12 inches for one keychain. Is Annie going to have enough plastic string for six more keychains of the same size?

Understand

What facts do you know?

- The roll of string is 78 inches long.
- Each keychain is 12 inches long.
- She has already used 12 inches of string.

What do you need to find?

- Does Annie have enough string to make 6 more keychains?

Plan

Use the *act it out* strategy with a piece of string that is 78 inches long. Mark off the amount used for the first keychain, 12 inches, and continue marking off lengths of 12 inches until there are six more keychains or no more string left.

Solve

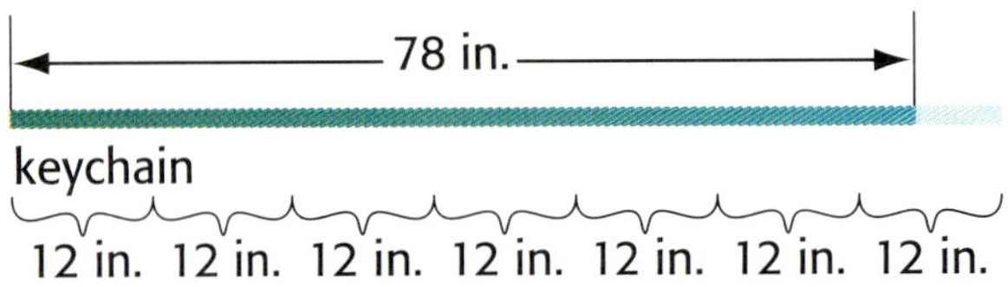

Notice that there is only enough string for 5 more keychains. So, there is not enough plastic string for 6 more keychains.

Check

Look back. Is the answer reasonable? Check by multiplying. Since $12 \times 6 = 72$ and $12 \times 7 = 84$, there is only enough string for 6 keychains in all, not 7.

ANALYZE the Strategy

Refer to the problem on the previous page.

1. If each keychain used 11 inches of string, would the roll of string be long enough for all seven keychains?
2. How does the *act it out* strategy help solve this problem?
3. Explain how the *act it out* strategy is similar to drawing a picture.
4. Give a real-world situation in which you could use the *act it out* strategy.

PRACTICE the Strategy

EXTRA PRACTICE
See page R11.

Solve. Use the *act it out* strategy.

5. Jesse put 15 pennies on his desk. He replaced every third penny with a nickel. Then he replaced every fourth coin with a dime. Finally, he replaced every fifth coin with a quarter. What is the value of the 15 coins that are now on his desk?
6. An aquarium at a pet store has 18 Black Neon Tetra fish in it. A customer buys 12 Black Neon Tetra fish at the same time the store clerk adds 7 more Black Neon Tetra fish to the tank. How many Black Neon Tetra fish are in the aquarium now?
7. A fifth grader takes the change from her pocket and places it on the table. The number of each coin she had in her pocket is shown below.

Coin	Number
Quarter	2
Dime	4
Nickel	3
Penny	5

   How many different combinations of coins can she make with the coins she has to have $0.45?

8. During the summer Ajay wants to read 4 books. In how many different orders can he read the books?

9. Mr. Reyes baked 4 batches of muffins for his class. Each batch had 12 muffins. If Mr. Reyes has 24 students, how many muffins will each student receive?
10. Nolan, Madeline, Marco, Flor, and Julian are entered in a race. Assuming there are not any ties, how many different orders are possible for first and second place?
11. **Measurement** Niko has a roll of wrapping paper that had 40.5 inches on it. He has already used 4.5 inches for one gift. Does he have enough paper to wrap three gifts that require 12 inches of paper each? Explain.
12. **WRITING IN MATH** Explain a disadvantage of using the *act it out* strategy to solve Exercise 10.

Explore

Math Activity for 4-6
Interpret the Remainder

MAIN IDEA

I will interpret the remainder in a division problem.

Math Online

macmillanmh.com

• Concepts in Motion

A *remainder* is the number left after a quotient is found. The following activities show you how to use remainders in different kinds of problems.

ACTIVITY

1 **A group of fifth graders collected 46 cans of food to donate to 3 food banks. If each food bank is to get an equal number of cans, how many cans do they each receive?**

Step 1 Use 46 centimeter cubes to represent the cans of food. Use three paper plates to represent the food banks. Divide the cubes equally among the three plates.

Step 2 Interpret the remainder.

Since each food bank is to get the same number of cans of food, they will each receive 15 cans. There is one can left over.

ACTIVITY

Hands-On Activity

2 **A total of 35 students are going on a field trip to NASA's Johnson Space Center in Houston. If there needs to be an adult for every 8 students, how many adults are needed?**

Use 35 centimeter cubes to represent the students. Use paper plates to represent the adults.

Place 8 cubes on as many plates as possible. Place any leftover cubes on a plate. Interpret the remainder.

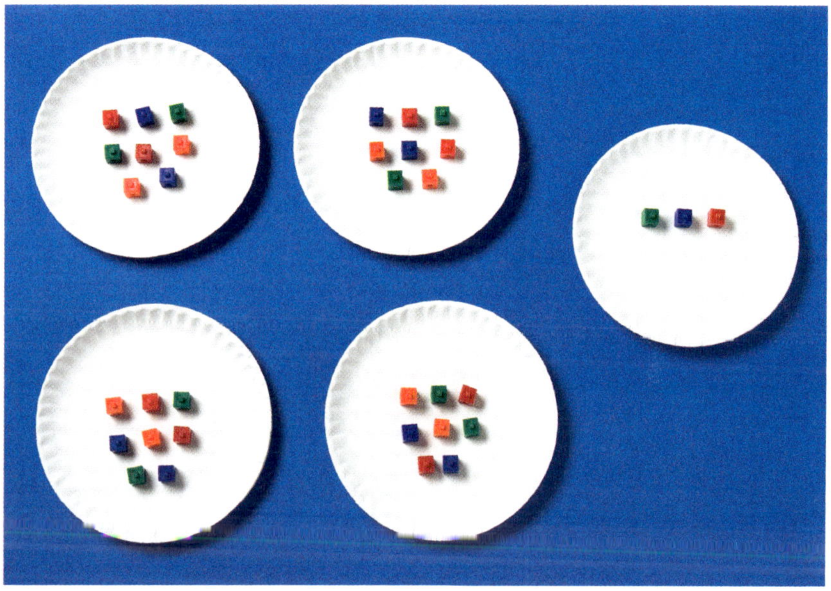

There are 4 groups of 8 students. They will each need an adult. There are 3 students who are not enough for a full group of 8. They will also need an adult.

So, 4 + 1 or 5 adults are needed.

Think About It

1. In Activity 1, the remainder was dropped. Explain why.
2. In Activity 2, the quotient was "rounded up" to 5. Explain why.

CHECK What You Know

State the solution and explain how to interpret the remainder in each division problem.

3. Each picnic table at a park seats 6 people. How many tables will 83 people at a family reunion need?
4. Mrs. Malone has $150 to buy volleyballs for Lincoln Middle School. How many can she buy at $14 each?
5. WRITING IN MATH Suppose 2 friends want to share 5 cookies evenly. Interpret the remainder in two different ways.

4-6 Interpret the Remainder

GET READY to Learn

A state park has 257 evergreens to plant in 9 equal-sized areas. To find the number of evergreens in each area, divide 257 by 9.

MAIN IDEA

I will interpret the remainder in a division problem.

Math Online

macmillanmh.com

- Extra Examples
- Personal Tutor
- Self-Check Quiz

Real-World EXAMPLES — Interpret the Remainder

1 **TREES** **Refer to the information above. How many evergreens are planted in each area? What does the remainder represent?**

Step 1 Divide.

$$\begin{array}{r} 28\text{ R}5 \\ 9\overline{)257} \\ -\ 18 \\ \hline 77 \\ -\ 72 \\ \hline 5 \end{array}$$

Step 2 Interpret the remainder, 5.

The remainder, 5, means there are 5 evergreens left over after 28 are planted in each area.

So, the park plants 28 evergreens in each area and 5 evergreens are left over.

2 **PARTY** **There are 174 guests invited to a dinner. Each table seats 8 guests. How many tables are needed?**

Step 1 Divide.

$$\begin{array}{r} 21\text{ R}6 \\ 8\overline{)174} \\ -\ 16 \\ \hline 14 \\ -\ 8 \\ \hline 6 \end{array}$$

Step 2 Interpret the remainder, 6.

There are 6 guests left over, which is not enough for a full table of 8. But, they also need a table.

So, a total of 21 + 1, or 22 tables are needed.

CHECK What You Know

Solve. Explain how you interpreted the remainder. See Examples 1, 2 (p. 170)

1. A tent is put up with 12 poles. How many tents can be put up with 200 poles?

2. There are 50 students traveling in vans on a field trip. Each van seats 8 students. How many vans are needed?

3. How many scooters shown at the right can a toy store buy for $900?

4. **Talk About It** Discuss the different ways you can interpret the remainder in a division problem.

Practice and Problem Solving

EXTRA PRACTICE See page R12.

Solve. Explain how you interpreted the remainder. See Examples 1, 2 (p. 170)

5. Mrs. Washington made 144 muffins for a bake sale. She puts them into bags of 5 muffins each. How many bags of muffins can she make?

6. Students on the softball team earned $295 from a carwash. How many team jackets shown can they buy?

7. **Measurement** How many 8-foot sections of fencing are needed for 189 feet of fence?

8. Stella has 20 stuffed animals. She wants to store them in plastic bags. She estimates she can fit three stuffed animals in each bag. How many bags will she need?

9. Mrs. Luna is buying scrapbooks for her store. Her budget is $350. How many of the scrapbooks shown can she buy?

10. **Measurement** How many 6-ounce cups can be filled from 4 gallons of juice? (*Hint:* 1 gallon = 128 ounces)

11. **Measurement** Water stations will be placed every 400 meters of a five kilometer race. How many water stations are needed? (*Hint:* 1 kilometer = 1,000 meters)

12. **Measurement** Three yards of fabric will be cut into pieces so that each piece is 8 inches long. How many pieces can be cut? (*Hint:* 1 yard = 36 inches)

Real-World PROBLEM SOLVING

Money Six friends decide to pack and share an extra large submarine sandwich, which is cut into 20 equal size pieces. The cost of the submarine sandwich is $21, not including tax.

13. How much would each friend pay if each one paid the same amount? Explain how you interpreted the remainder.

14. How many pieces would each friend receive if each one receives the same amount? Explain how you interpreted the remainder.

15. Three pieces will fit into one plastic bag. How many plastic bags are needed to pack the 20 pieces? Explain how you interpreted the remainder.

H.O.T. Problems

16. **OPEN ENDED** Write a real-world situation that could be described by the division problem $38 \div 5 = 7$ R3 in which it makes sense to round the quotient up to 8.

17. **CHALLENGE** If the divisor is 30, what is the least three-digit dividend that would give a remainder of 8? Explain.

CHALLENGE For Exercises 18–20, consider each situation. In each case, decide whether you would drop the remainder, round the quotient up, or represent the quotient as a fraction to solve each problem. Explain your reasoning. Then solve each problem.

18. Greg spent $50 on four identical photo frames. How much did he spend on each frame?

19. Two friends share 3 cookies equally. How many cookies did each friend get?

20. **Measurement** A piece of string 50 inches long will be cut into pieces so that each piece is 4 inches long. How many full-length pieces can be cut from the string?

21. **WRITING IN MATH** Write a real-world division problem that can be solved by interpreting the remainder. Does it make sense to round up or down to the next whole number? Explain.

TEST Practice

22. Forty-six students are visiting an art museum. A tour guide is needed for each group of 6 students. How many tour guides are needed? **(Lesson 4-6)**

A 7

B 8

C 40

D 52

23. Ms. Meir wants to divide 135 maps as equally as possible among 4 zoo guides. Which is a true statement? **(Lesson 4-6)**

F All 4 guides will get 34 maps.

G Three guides will get 33 maps and 1 guide will get 34 maps.

H Three guides will get 34 maps and 1 guide will get 33 maps.

J Two guides will get 33 maps and 2 guides will get 34 maps.

Spiral Review

24. Ronada, Tori, Courtney, and Shandra went to see the class play. They sat in the four seats in the tenth row. Ronada was not on either end. Shandra was not in the last seat. Courtney was between Ronada and Tori. In what order did they sit? Use the *act it out* strategy. **(Lesson 4-5)**

25. A class trip costs \$80 for the bus and \$15 admission per student. The whole trip cost \$455. How many students went on the trip? **(Lesson 4-4)**

Find each product mentally. (Lesson 3-1)

26. 4×600 **27.** 30×70 **28.** 10×15 **29.** 80×800

Add or subtract. (Lesson 2-6)

30. $64.2 + 3.9$ **31.** $11.65 + 18.91$ **32.** $7.8 - 4.9$ **33.** $16.2 - 12.8$

34. The library charges \$0.10 for each of the first three days for overdue books. It charges \$0.05 for every day after that. Janelle owed the library \$1.50. How many days overdue was her book? Solve. Use the *work backward* strategy. **(Lesson 2-3)**

35. Measurement Chino is using the ribbon at the right to make spirit ribbons. He also has ribbons that measure 6.4 meters and 6.5 meters. Order the ribbons from least to greatest. **(Lesson 1-7)**

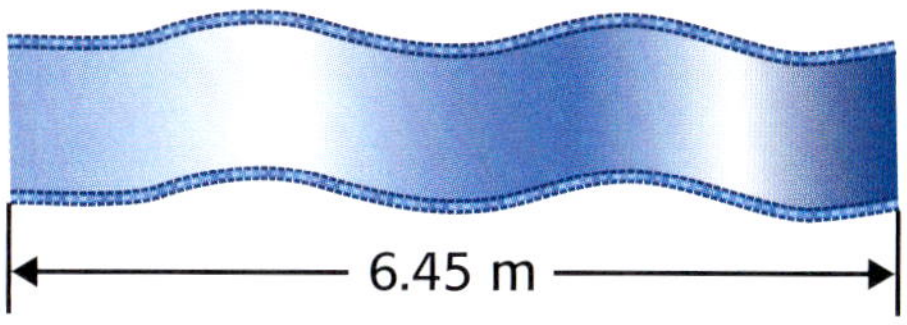

4-7 Extending Division

MAIN IDEA

I will estimate quotients of decimals and greater numbers.

Math Online

macmillanmh.com

- Extra Examples
- Personal Tutor
- Self-Check Quiz

GET READY to Learn

Ms. Glover buys 2 kites for a total of \$15.18. If each kite costs the same, about how much did each kite cost?

To estimate \$15.18 ÷ 2, you can use compatible numbers.

EXAMPLE Divide Money

1 **MONEY Refer to the information above. About how much did each kite cost?**

\$15.18 ÷ 2
↓ ↓
\$16 ÷ 2 — Change \$15.18 to \$16 because 16 and 2 are compatible numbers.

\$16 ÷ 2 = \$8 — Divide mentally.

So, \$15.18 ÷ 2 is about \$8. Each kite costs about \$8.

You can also use compatible numbers to estimate quotients of decimals that do not involve money.

Real-World EXAMPLE Estimate with Decimals

2 **ANIMALS A live sponge is an animal that lives in the ocean. Sponges filter water to get food. One sponge can filter 26.4 liters of water in 4 hours. About how many liters of water can a sponge filter in one hour?**

26.4 ÷ 4
↓ ↓
28 ÷ 4 — Change 26.4 to 28 because 28 and 4 are compatible numbers.

28 ÷ 4 = 7 — Divide mentally.

So, a sponge can filter about 7 liters of water in one hour.

Technology can be a useful tool for dividing greater numbers.

Real-World EXAMPLE Greater Numbers

3 PRESIDENTS Theodore Roosevelt was the twenty-sixth President of the United States. One day, he shook hands with 8,513 people. If he had continued at that rate, in how many days would he have shaken hands with the one-millionth person?

You want to find how many groups of 8,513 are in 1,000,000. So, divide 1,000,000 by 8,513.

Estimate: 1,000,000 ÷ 10,000 = 100

Use the Calculator feature from your Math Tool Chest™ to find the exact answer.

Enter: 1 0 0 0 0 0 0
Press: ÷
Enter: 8 5 1 3
Press: =
Solution: 117.4674028

Check for Reasonableness Compare 117 to the estimate. ✓

When you use a calculator, the remainder is expressed as a decimal. It would take 117 whole days and part of one day to shake 1,000,000 hands. So, President Roosevelt would shake hands with the one-millionth person on day 118.

Remember
Always estimate first and then compare your final answer to the estimate.

CHECK What You Know

Estimate each quotient. See Examples 1, 2 (p. 174)

1. $19.50 ÷ 5

2. $47.25 ÷ 25

3. 16.8 ÷ 4

4. Jake bought 3 drawing pens for $8.07. Each pen costs the same amount. About how much did he spend for 1 pen?

5. Jupiter is about 483,879,000 miles from the Sun. Earth is about 93,000,000 miles from the Sun. About how many times as far from the Sun is Jupiter than Earth? Then use a calculator to find the exact answer rounded to the nearest whole number.

6. Talk About It Describe the steps for estimating dividing money by a whole number.

Practice and Problem Solving

EXTRA PRACTICE See page R12.

Estimate each quotient. See Examples 1, 2 (p. 174)

7. $28.20 ÷ 6 **8.** $7.92 ÷ 6 **9.** 88.3 ÷ 9 **10.** 128.9 ÷ 12

11. It costs $88.50 for 6 adults to see an exhibit on Egyptian mummies. About how much does it cost 1 adult to see the exhibit?

12. **Measurement** There are 74.4 grams of sugar in 3 servings of grapes. About how many grams of sugar are in a single serving?

For Exercises 13 and 14, estimate the quotient. Then use a calculator.

13. A city phone book has 152 pages. There are 46,512 names in the book. How many names are on each page?

14. Population density of a state is found by dividing the number of people by the area of the state. Refer to the table at the right. Which state has the higher population density?

State	Population	Area (square miles)
Texas	23,507,783	295,324
Virginia	7,642,884	42,745

Real-World PROBLEM SOLVING

Measurement The table shows the density of each object. *Density* describes how tightly the particles in an object are packed together. You can find density by dividing an object's mass by its volume.

Substance	Mass (g)	Volume (cm^3)
Aluminum	13.5	5
Gold	56.7	3
Mercury	121.5	9

15. Estimate the density of aluminum.

16. Is the density of gold greater than the density of mercury? Explain.

17. The density of gold is about how many times greater than the density of aluminum?

H.O.T. Problems

18. **OPEN ENDED** Write a division problem involving money. Describe the steps that you used to estimate the quotient.

19. **WRITING IN MATH** If your heart beats 103,698 times in one day, explain how to find the number of times your heart beats per minute.

Mission: Division

Dividing Whole Numbers

Get Ready!

Players: 2, 3, or 4 players

You will need: spinner
index cards

Get Set!

- Each player makes a game sheet like the one shown at the right.
- Make a spinner as shown.

Game Sheet

____ ____ ÷ ____

Go!

- The first person spins the spinner. Each player writes the number in one of the blanks on his or her game sheet. A zero cannot be placed as the divisor.

  The next person spins, and each player writes that number in a blank.

  The next player spins and each player fills in their game sheet. A player loses if he or she cannot use all the numbers.
- All players find their quotients. The player with the greatest quotient earns one point. In case of a tie, those players each earn one point.
- The first person to earn 5 points wins.

Problem Solving in Social Studies

The Statue of Liberty

The Statue of Liberty has become a symbol of freedom since its arrival in the United States. The statue stands on Liberty Island in the New York harbor. It is 151 feet tall and weighs about 448,000 pounds. There are 354 stairs from the bottom of the statue to the crown. What a hike!

When immigrants came to New York between 1886 and 1920, this statue was one of the first things they saw. Today, visitors can travel to the Statue of Liberty by a ferry or a yacht. The yacht, called the *Zephyr*, can hold up to 600 passengers at one time.

Real-World Social Studies

Use the information on pages 178–179 to solve each problem.

1. A total of 459 passengers rode the *Zephyr* to Ellis Island. If the passengers were evenly spread out on each of the ferry's three decks, how many passengers were on each deck?
2. If the *Zephyr* was completely filled, how many people could fit evenly on each deck?
3. How many adult tickets can be purchased with $75? Tell how you interpreted the remainder.
4. How many child tickets can be purchased with $25? Tell how you interpreted the remainder.
5. How many senior tickets can be purchased with $35? Tell how you interpreted the remainder.
6. When school groups visit, one teacher must accompany each group of ten students. How many teachers should accompany a class of 25 students?

Did You Know?

The Statue of Liberty was completed in France. Then it was taken apart and all 350 pieces were shipped to the United States and rebuilt.

Statue of Liberty Ferry Prices ($)

Adult	10
Child (4–12 yr)	4
Senior (+62 yr)	8

Source: The National Park Service

4-8 Problem-Solving Investigation

MAIN IDEA I will choose the best strategy to solve a problem.

P.S.I. TEAM +

JAHIEM: I am helping my mother get ready for a party. I am putting 6 square tables end-to-end to make one large table. One square table can seat one person on each side.

YOUR MISSION: Find the number of people that can sit around the new large table.

Understand

You know that Jahiem is putting 6 square tables end-to-end. A square table can seat one person on each side. Find the number of people that can sit around the new table.

Plan

You could act it out. But it is easier to draw a picture.

Solve

Draw the 6 tables end-to-end. Then count how many seats there are.

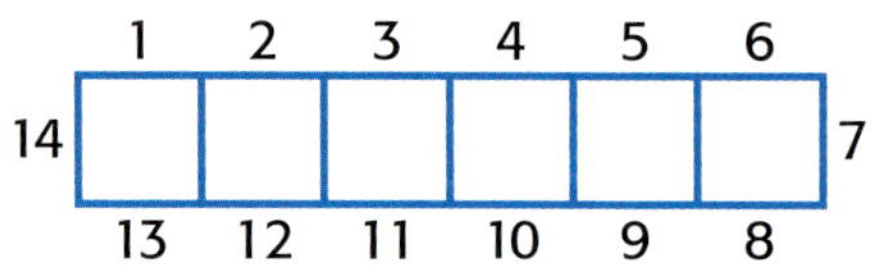

So, Jahiem can seat 14 people around the new table.

Check

Look back. You know that 6 people can sit on one long side. There are two long sides. So, $6 \times 2 = 12$. Then add 2, the number of people that can sit on the ends. So, $12 + 2 = 14$. The answer is correct. ✓

Mixed Problem Solving

EXTRA PRACTICE
See page R12.

Use any strategy shown below to solve each problem.

PROBLEM-SOLVING STRATEGIES
- Draw a picture
- Work backward
- Guess and check
- Act it out

1. On Monday, 56 DVDs were checked out at the library. This is 8 less than twice the amount of books checked out that day. How many books were checked out?

2. **Measurement** Leo takes 20 minutes to walk to practice, 30 minutes to eat dinner, and 15 minutes to warm up. If Leo needs to be ready for hockey practice at 7:15 P.M., what time does he need to leave home?

3. A ride at a theme park lasts $1\frac{1}{2}$ minutes. It takes 2 minutes to prepare the ride for each trip. How many times can the ride be completed in 30 minutes?

4. A cook needs 12 pounds of flour. He wants to spend the least amount of money. How many bags of each type of flour should he buy? What will be the total cost?

5. Kiwi bought flippers and a face mask. The face mask costs $5.96 more than the flippers. The total for the two items, before tax, was $63.94. What was the cost of the flippers?

6. Nicholas bought a camping tent. Each of the four sides of the tent needs two stakes to secure it properly. What is the least number of stakes that are needed?

7. Samantha has four coins worth $0.36. What coins does Samantha have?

8. **Measurement** Mr. Holley is adding 2 feet to the length and width of his garden shown below. Find the distance around his new garden.

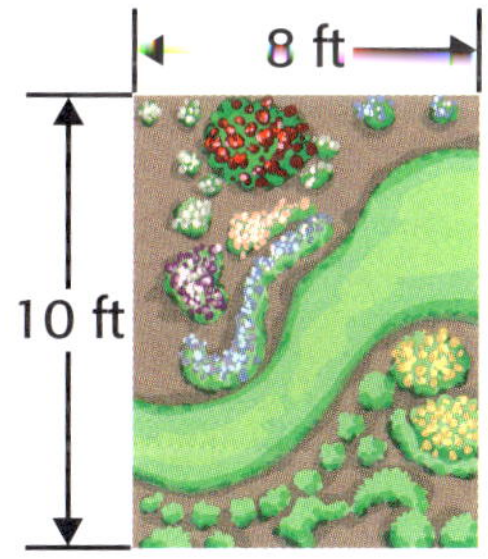

9. The farmer's market sells apples at 2 for $1. How much will 8 apples cost?

10. The fifth grade class is boxing up 85 coloring books to take to the children's hospital. If one box has 15 more books in it than the other box, how many books are in each box?

11. WRITING IN MATH A builder is putting up a fence in a backyard. The yard is 40 feet long and 50 feet wide. How much fencing will the builder need? What strategy would you use to solve this problem? Explain your reasoning and then solve.

CHAPTER 4 Study Guide and Review

Math Online macmillanmh.com

- STUDY TO GO
- Vocabulary Review

FOLDABLES® Study Organizer GET READY to Study

Be sure the following Big Ideas are written in your Foldable.

Key Concepts

Estimating Quotients

- You can use compatible numbers to estimate quotients. (pp. 152–155)

$283 \div 7$

$\downarrow \quad \downarrow$

280 $\div 7$ — 28 and 7 are compatible numbers.

$280 \div 7 = 40$, so $283 \div 7$ is about 40.

Dividing Whole Numbers (pp. 158–164)

$$\begin{array}{r} 32 \\ 2\overline{)64} \\ -6 \\ \hline 04 \\ -4 \\ \hline 0 \end{array}$$

$6 \div 2$

3×2

$4 \div 2$

2×2

Interpret the Remainder (pp. 170–173)

- When interpreting the remainder you can drop the remainder, use only the remainder, or add 1 to the quotient.

Key Vocabulary

dividend (p. 149)

divisor (p. 149)

quotient (p. 149)

remainder (p. 159)

Vocabulary Check

Choose the correct term or number to complete each sentence.

1. When you divide, the answer is called the (dividend, quotient).
2. When you use $450 \div 9$ to estimate $437 \div 9$, you are using (rounding, compatible numbers).
3. The (divisor, remainder) is the number left after a quotient is found.
4. The quotient $1{,}040 \div 5$ is (208, 28).
5. The value of $360 \div 90$ is (4, 40).
6. The best estimate for $6{,}217 \div 186$ is (30, 300).
7. An example of compatible numbers for division is (9 and 45, 9 and 10).

Lesson-by-Lesson Review

4-1 Division Patterns (pp. 149–151)

Example 1
Find 15,000 ÷ 5 mentally.

Step 1 Write the basic fact.
15 ÷ 5 = 3

Step 2 Continue the pattern.
150 ÷ 5 = 30
1,500 ÷ 5 = 300
15,000 ÷ 5 = 3,000

So, 15,000 ÷ 5 = 3,000.

Divide mentally.

8. 420 ÷ 7 **9.** 300 ÷ 3

10. 800 ÷ 20 **11.** 160 ÷ 8

12. 630 ÷ 10 **13.** 400 ÷ 50

14. Mara deposited a total of $240 in her account in the past 6 weeks. If she deposited the same amount each week, what was the amount of each deposit?

15. Jorge's family drove 2,700 miles during their 9-day vacation. If they drove the same distance each day, how many miles did they drive each day?

4-2 Estimate Quotients (pp. 152–155)

Example 2
Estimate 825 ÷ 20.

825 ÷ 20
↓ ↓
800 ÷ 20 Change 825 to 800 because 8 and 2 are compatible.

800 ÷ 20 = 40 Divide mentally.

So, 825 ÷ 20 is about 40.

Example 3
Estimate 356 ÷ 51.

356 ÷ 51
↓ ↓
350 ÷ 50 Change 356 to 350 and 51 to 50 since 35 and 5 are compatible numbers.

350 ÷ 50 = 7 Divide mentally.

So, 356 ÷ 51 is about 7.

Estimate. Show your work.

16. 219 ÷ 2 **17.** 126 ÷ 4

18. 720 ÷ 91 **19.** 182 ÷ 34

20. 800 ÷ 215 **21.** 1,200 ÷ 32

22. 541 ÷ 61 **23.** 4,520 ÷ 52

24. Three plane tickets to New York cost $2,472. If each plane ticket costs the same amount, about how much does one ticket cost? Use compatible numbers to estimate the cost of one ticket.

CHAPTER 4

Study Guide and Review

4-3 Divide by One-Digit Numbers (pp. 158–161)

Example 4

Find 79 ÷ 7.

Estimate $77 \div 7 = 11$

Step 1

Divide the tens.

$$\begin{array}{rl} 1 & \\ 7\overline{)79} & 7 \div 7 \\ -7 & 1 \times 7 \\ \hline 0 & 7 - 7 \end{array}$$

Step 2

Bring down the ones. Divide the ones.

$$\begin{array}{rl} 11 & \\ 7\overline{)79} & \\ -7\downarrow & \\ \hline 09 & 9 \div 7 \\ -7 & 7 \times 1 \\ \hline 2 & 9 - 7 \end{array}$$

So, 79 ÷ 7 = 11 R2. This is close to the estimate, 11, so the answer is reasonable.

Divide.

25. $3\overline{)78}$

26. $2\overline{)146}$

27. 756 ÷ 4

28. 97 ÷ 6

29. 412 ÷ 5

30. 893 ÷ 8

31. A cabinet with four shelves can hold 640 CDs. If the shelves each hold the same number of CDs, how many CDs does each shelf hold?

32. There are 1,250 pieces of mail to be sorted evenly into 5 bags. How many pieces of mail are in each bag?

4-4 Divide by Two-Digit Numbers (pp. 162–164)

Example 5

Find 632 ÷ 89.

Estimate $630 \div 90 = 7$

Step 1

Divide the tens.

$$\begin{array}{rl} 89\overline{)632} & 63 \div 89 \\ & 63 < 89 \end{array}$$

Step 2

Divide the ones.

$$\begin{array}{rl} 7 & \\ 89\overline{)632} & 632 \div 89 \\ -623 & 89 \times 7 \\ \hline 9 & 632 - 623 \\ & 9 < 89 \end{array}$$

So, 632 ÷ 89 = 7 R9. This is close to the estimate, 7, so the answer is reasonable.

Divide.

33. $16\overline{)64}$

34. $20\overline{)451}$

35. 325 ÷ 23

36. 741 ÷ 13

37. 810 ÷ 75

38. 586 ÷ 62

39. A bakery needs 225 pounds of flour. How many 15-pound bags should the bakery buy?

40. At a football camp, 165 players are divided into 15 teams. How many players are on each team?

4-5 Problem-Solving Strategy: Act It Out (pp. 166–167)

Example 6

Measurement **Andre is planting seeds in a rectangular tray 10 inches by 20 inches. How many seeds will fit if each seed needs to be placed 2 inches apart and from the sides?**

Use the *act it out* strategy.

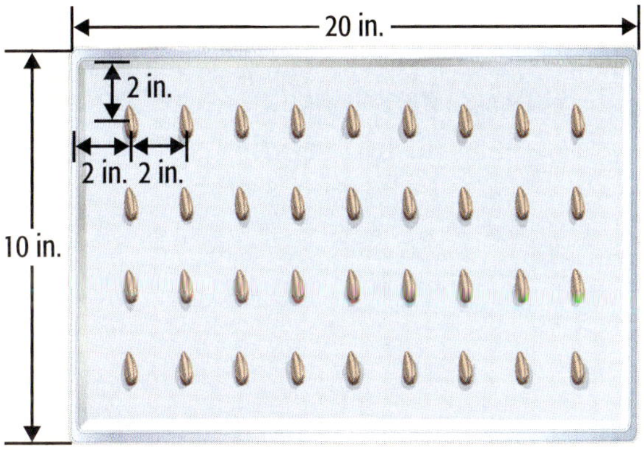

The picture shows that 36 seeds will fit in the tray.

Solve. Use the *act it out* strategy.

41. Ariana has 4 different shirts and 3 pairs of pants. If she wears a different combination of shirt and pants each day, how many days will pass before she must repeat an outfit?

42. At a business meeting, everyone shook hands with everyone else exactly once. There were a total of 15 handshakes. How many people were at the meeting?

43. How many ways are there to represent $0.77 using at least two quarters and only two pennies?

4-6 Interpret the Remainder (pp. 170–173)

Example 7

A florist has 86 roses. She plans to put 5 roses in each box. How many boxes can she fill?

$$\begin{array}{r} 17 \text{ R1} \\ 5\overline{)86} \\ -5 \\ \hline 36 \\ -35 \\ \hline 1 \end{array}$$

She can fill 17 boxes. The remainder 1 means that there is 1 rose left over.

Solve. Explain how you interpreted the remainder.

44. Kyle has 48 oranges. He puts 7 oranges in a bag. How many bags can he fill?

45. A factory received 1,268 sponges. Only 12 sponges fit in each box. How many boxes did the factory receive?

46. A text message has 43 words. If the text message has 8 lines, how many words are on each line?

4-7 Extending Division (pp. 174–176)

Example 8

Kerry bought 4 identical sweatshirts. If he spent \$34 on the sweatshirts, about how much did each sweatshirt cost?

You need to find \$34 ÷ 4.

\$34 ÷ 4
↓
\$36 ÷ 4 — Change \$34 to \$36 because 36 and 4 are compatible numbers.

\$36 ÷ 4 = \$9 — Divide mentally.

So, \$34 ÷ 4 is about \$9. Each sweatshirt costs about \$9.

Check Since \$9 × 4 = \$36, the answer is correct. ✓

Estimate each quotient.

47. \$10.80 ÷ 6 **48.** 23.9 ÷ 5.1

49. A pizza costs \$14.77. If 3 people split the cost evenly, about how much will each person pay?

50. At a state forest, the rangers plant 8,000 seedlings in seedling boxes. Each box holds 164 seeds. About how many boxes are needed to plant all the seedlings?

4-8 Problem-Solving Investigation: Choose a Strategy (pp. 180–181)

Example 9

Measurement **It takes Santos 15 minutes to walk to school, 15 minutes to eat breakfast, and 30 minutes to get ready for school. If he needs to arrive at school at 8:45 A.M., what time does he need to set his alarm clock?**

To find what time Santos should set his alarm clock start at 8:45 and work backward.

8:45 − 15 min. = 8:30
8:30 − 15 min. = 8:15
8:15 − 30 min. = 7:45

So, Santos needs to set his alarm for 7:45 A.M.

Use any strategy to solve each problem.

51. A number multiplied by itself is 256. What is the number?

52. The fifth grade class is planning a field trip. There are 472 students in the fifth grade. If each bus holds 38 people, how many buses will they need for the students?

53. Use the symbols +, −, ×, ÷ to make the following math sentence true. Use each symbol only once.

3 ■ 6 ■ 5 ■ 1 = 22

CHAPTER 4

Chapter Test

Math Online macmillanmh.com
- Chapter Test

Divide mentally.

1. 900 ÷ 100

2. 1,600 ÷ 800

3. 490 ÷ 7

4. 2,400 ÷ 3

5. 300 ÷ 50

6. 3,600 ÷ 90

7. Cedric is saving money to buy a new skateboard that costs $350. If he saves $70 each week, how many weeks will it take him to save enough money to buy the skateboard?

Estimate. Show your work.

8. 588 ÷ 2

9. 276 ÷ 4

10. 455 ÷ 52

11. 800 ÷ 34

12. 3,600 ÷ 84

13. 4,100 ÷ 217

14. **MULTIPLE CHOICE** The table shows the number of deer in a wildlife preserve and the size of the preserve in acres. Which is the best estimate for the number of deer per acre?

Number of Deer	406
Number of Acres	38

A 1

B 10

C 100

D 1,000

Divide. Write answers with remainders.

15. $3\overline{)84}$

16. $4\overline{)156}$

17. $5\overline{)632}$

18. 98 ÷ 7

19. 51 ÷ 20

20. 165 ÷ 12

21. A librarian has 88 new reference books. She puts them on 5 shelves. She puts an equal number of books on each shelf. How many books are left over?

22. **MULTIPLE CHOICE** Ms. Torrez bought a jar of beads that has 525 beads. If she divides the beads equally among 15 bags, how many beads will be in each bag?

F 45

G 35

H 4.5

J 3.5

23. Fifty-two students plan an after-school trip to a museum. There needs to be 1 adult for every 9 students. How many adults are needed? Explain how you interpreted the remainder.

24. A pizza with 10 pieces will be divided among three friends. How many pieces will each friend receive? Explain how you interpreted the remainder.

25. **WRITING IN MATH** A student group visits a butterfly exhibit. They pay $12 for each student, but receive a $34 group discount. The total cost after the discount is $242. How many students were in the group? Explain what strategy you used to solve this problem.

CHAPTER 4

Test Practice

Cumulative, Chapters 1–4

Math Online macmillanmh.com

• Test Practice

PART 1 Multiple Choice

Read each question. Then fill in the correct answer on the answer sheet provided by your teacher or on a sheet of paper.

1. A farmer harvested 868 apples this afternoon. The apples are stored equally in 31 bushels. How many apples are there in each bushel?

A 22
B 24
C 26
D 28

2. A grocery store has 636 eggs on its shelves. The eggs are in cartons of 12 eggs each. How many cartons are there altogether?

F 53
G 56
H 57
J 59

3. There are 276 teachers in attendance at a conference. The teachers are divided into groups of 12. How many groups are there?

A 23
B 25
C 27
D 29

4. So far 480 people have ridden a roller coaster ride at an amusement park. The ride holds a total of 40 people each time it runs. How many times has the roller coaster run?

F 10
G 11
H 12
J 15

5. Mr. Smith has 15 tables in his classroom. Each table has 3 chairs around it. How many chairs are there in the classroom?

A 5
B 36
C 40
D 45

6. Miss Flores drove 360 miles. If she drove 40 miles each hour, how many hours did she drive?

F 4 h
G 6 h
H 8 h
J 9 h

7. Suppose you want to buy 3 dozen cookies for a party. How much will you save off of the regular price with today's special?

A $4.00
B $6.00
C $5.00
D $7.00

Preparing for Standardized Tests
For test-taking strategies and practice, see pages R42–R55.

8. Chris buys a chicken sandwich, a vegetable, and a drink. He pays with $10. How much money will he have left?

Deli Prices	
Chicken Sandwich	$3.75
Cheeseburger	$2.25
Fries	$1.25
Vegetable	$1.25
Drink	$1.35

F $2.95 **H** $3.65
G $3.40 **J** $4.20

9. Which is the best estimate for the product shown below?

7×31.2

A about 280 **C** about 210
B about 250 **D** about 200

10. There are 442 people seated in the school auditorium for an assembly. There are 26 rows in the auditorium, each with the same number of seats. If the auditorium is completely filled, how many seats are there in each row?

F 16 **H** 18
G 17 **J** 19

PART 2 Short Response

Record your answers on the sheet provided by your teacher or on a sheet of paper.

11. Senon has 120 CDs in his collection. The CDs are stored in a book with 8 per page. Write a number sentence to show how many pages of CDs Senon has.

12. Oscar has $47 to buy jerseys for his basketball team. Each jersey costs $6. Oscar figures that he can buy 8 jerseys. Is he correct? Explain.

PART 3 Extended Response

Record your answers on the answer sheet provided by your teacher or on a sheet of paper. Show your work.

13. It takes Javier 720 seconds to run two miles. Explain how to find the number of minutes it takes Javier to run two miles.

14. Explain how 3 friends can share 2 pieces of cake equally. Include a drawing with your explanation.

NEED EXTRA HELP?														
If You Missed Question...	1	2	3	4	5	6	7	8	9	10	11	12	13	14
Go to Lesson...	4-4	4-4	4-4	4-1	4-3	4-1	3-6	2-6	3-8	4-4	4-3	4-6	4-1	4-7

CHAPTER 5 Use Algebraic Expressions

BIG Idea What is an expression?

An **expression** is a combination of variables, numbers, and at least one operation.

operation

variable $x + 9$ number

Example The Shock Wave roller coaster is 116 feet tall. The Flashback roller coaster is *x* feet taller than the Shock Wave. You can use the expression $116 + x$ to find the height of the Flashback.

What will I learn in this chapter?

- Write and evaluate algebraic expressions.
- Illustrate functions using a function machine.
- Complete function tables.
- Solve problems by using the *solve a simpler problem* strategy.

Key Vocabulary

variable
expression
evaluate
function
order of operations

Math Online **Student Study Tools at macmillanmh.com**

FOLDABLES® Study Organizer

Make this Foldable to help you organize information about algebraic expressions. Begin with a sheet of $8\frac{1}{2}'' \times 11''$ paper.

1. **Fold** a 2″ tab along the long side of the paper.

2. **Unfold** the paper and then fold in thirds widthwise.

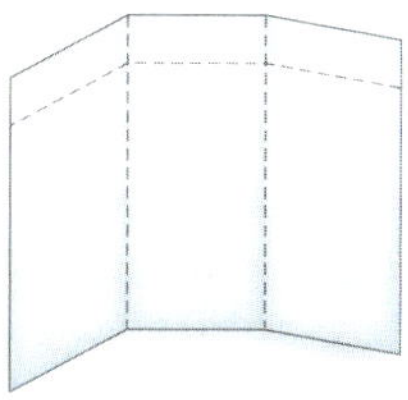

3. **Open** and draw lines along the folds. Label the head of each column as shown. Label the front of the folded table with the chapter title.

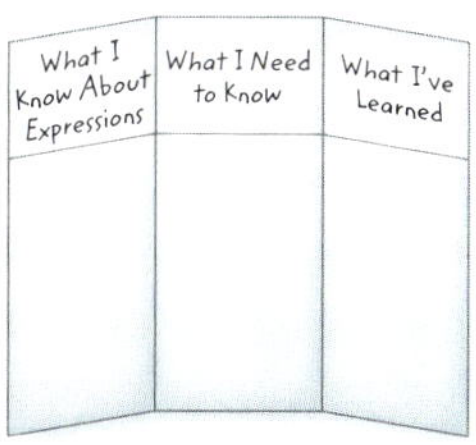

ARE YOU READY for Chapter 5?

You have two ways to check prerequisite skills for this chapter.

Option 2

Math Online Take the Chapter Readiness Quiz at macmillanmh.com.

Option 1

Complete the Quick Check below.

QUICK Check

Add. (Prior grade)

1. $6 + 3$ **2.** $9 + 8$ **3.** $12 + 4$

4. $19 + 2$ **5.** $17 + 18$ **6.** $24 + 35$

7. Fernando has 25 toy cars. If he buys 7 more, how many will he have?

8. **Measurement** Tori uses 2 cups of raisins to make one batch of granola. How many cups of raisins will she use to make 3 batches of granola?

Multiply. (Prior grade)

9. 5×2 **10.** 3×4 **11.** 7×5

12. 11×3 **13.** 15×2 **14.** 20×3

15. Greeting cards cost \$2 each. Find the cost of 6 cards.

16. Sally has 3 boxes of snack bars. She ate one snack bar. There are 7 snack bars left in that box. How many snack bars were in 3 boxes?

Write in word form. Then find the value. (Prior grade)

17. $15 - 6$ **18.** $6 + 4$

19. $10 \div 5$ **20.** 8×3

5-1 Addition Expressions

MAIN IDEA

I will write and evaluate addition expressions.

New Vocabulary

- variable
- expression
- evaluate

Math Online

macmillanmh.com

- Extra Examples
- Personal Tutor
- Self Check Quiz

GET READY to Learn

A bag contains some apples. There are 2 apples outside the bag. The total number of apples is equal to the number of apples in the bag plus 2.

The unknown number of apples can be represented by a variable. A **variable** is a letter or symbol used to represent a number.

The number of apples in the bag is an unknown value. → $x + 2$ ← The number of apples outside the bag is a known value.

An **expression**, like $x + 2$, is a combination of variables, numbers, and at least one operation. When you replace a variable with a number, you can **evaluate**, or find the value of, the expression.

EXAMPLE Evaluate Expressions

1 Evaluate the expression $x + 2$ if $x = 3$.

$x + 2$ Write the expression. Use 1 cup and 2 counters to represent $x + 2$.

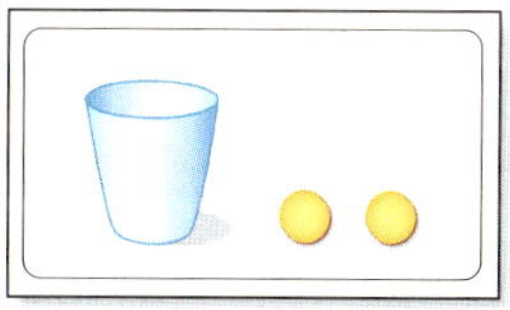

$3 + 2$ Replace x with 3. Place 3 counters in the cup.

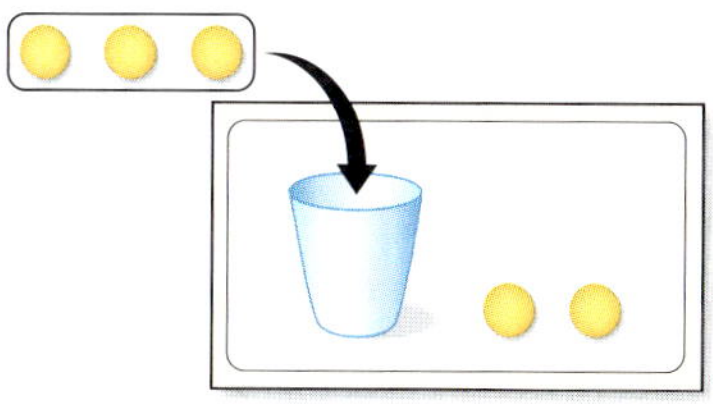

5 Add 3 and 2. There is a total of 5 counters.

Real-World EXAMPLES — Write and Evaluate Expressions

2 **SPORTS** **Steve scored 4 goals. Theresa scored *g* more goals than Steve. Write an expression.**

Words	*g* more goals than Steve
Variable	Let *g* represent how many more goals.
Expression	$4 + g$

Vocabulary Link

Variable

Everyday Use able to change

Math Use a symbol, usually a letter, to represent a number

3 **Refer to Example 2. If $g = 7$, then how many goals did Theresa score?**

$4 + g$ — Write the expression. Use 1 cup and 4 counters to represent $4 + g$.

$4 + 7$ — Replace *g* with 7. Place 7 counters in the cup.

11 — Add 4 and 7. There is a total of 11 counters.

So, Theresa scored 11 goals.

CHECK What You Know

Evaluate each expression if $x = 5$ and $y = 6$. See Example 1 (p. 193)

1. $x + 6$

2. $12 + y$

3. $y + 18$

4. $x + 29$

Write an expression for each real-world situation. Then evaluate it.

See Examples 2, 3 (p. 194)

5. Naomi bought 12 pens. Wu bought *t* more pens than Naomi. If $t = 9$, how many pens did Wu buy?

6. Laura had *y* dollars. Her mom gave her \$15. If $y = 12$, how much money does Laura have?

7. Talk About It Explain how to evaluate the expression $a + 9$ if $a = 11$.

Practice and Problem Solving

EXTRA PRACTICE
See page R13.

Evaluate each expression if $x = 2$ and $y = 9$. See Example 1 (p. 193)

8. $x + 7$	**9.** $5 + y$	**10.** $4 + x$
11. $y + 8$	**12.** $15 + x$	**13.** $y + 12$
14. $23 + x$	**15.** $y + 26$	**16.** $x + 34$

Write an expression for each real-world situation. Then evaluate.
See Examples 2, 3 (pp. 193-194)

17. **Measurement** A tomato plant is t inches tall. In a month, it grows 3 inches taller. If $t = 18$, how tall is the tomato plant?

18. During one season, the Tigers lost 26 more games than they won. If the Tigers won 68 games, how many games did they lose?

19. Carmen went to a water park. She spent \$15 on admission and a certain amount on food. If she spent \$12 on food, how much did Carmen spend in all?

20. Josiah's grade on his last math test was 10 points higher than his first math test. On the first test, he scored p points. If $p = 23$, how many points did he score on the last test?

Data File

Arizona, Georgia, and New Mexico are among the nation's top pecan producers. Most pecan trees are 100 to 140 feet tall.

Write an expression. Then evaluate.

21. A pecan tree was 47 feet tall. In ten years, it grew f feet. If the tree grew 21 feet, what was the new height of the tree?

22. Scott planted 38 pecan trees on Monday. On Tuesday, he planted y trees. If he planted 46 trees on Tuesday, how many pecan trees did he plant in all?

H.O.T. Problems

23. **OPEN ENDED** Write an expression that has a value of 15 if $m = 2$.

24. **WRITING IN MATH** Tell whether the statement below is *sometimes*, *always*, or *never* true. Justify your reasoning.

The expressions $x + 2$ and $y + 2$ represent the same value.

5-2 Problem-Solving Strategy

MAIN IDEA I will solve problems by solving a simpler problem.

Emilio is one of two bakers for Brian's Bakery. Working separately, the two bakers can make a total of 2 cakes in 2 hours. The bakery wants to hire an additional 2 bakers for a large cake order. At this rate, how many cakes can 4 bakers make in 6 hours if they work separately?

Understand

What facts do you know?

- 2 bakers can make 2 cakes in 2 hours.

What do you need to find?

- How many cakes 4 bakers can make in 6 hours.

Plan

You can solve the problem by solving a simpler problem.

Solve

Step 1 Find how long it takes each baker to make 1 cake.

$2 \div 2 = 1$ Each baker makes 1 cake in 2 hours.

Step 2 Find how many cakes each baker can make in 6 hours. Divide by 2 since it takes 2 hours to make one cake.

$6 \div 2 = 3$ Each baker can make 3 cakes in 6 hours.

Step 3 Find how many cakes 4 bakers can make in 6 hours.

$4 \times 3 = 12$

So, 4 bakers can make 12 cakes in 6 hours.

Check

Look back. The number of bakers doubled, so 2×2 or 4 cakes can be made in 2 hours. In 6 hours, the bakers can make 3×4 or 12 cakes. So, the answer is correct. ✓

ANALYZE the Strategy

Refer to the problem on the previous page.

1. Explain why you first found how long it takes each baker to make 1 cake.

2. If the bakers continue making cakes at the same rate, how many cakes can 6 bakers make in 8 hours?

3. Look back at Exercise 2. Check your answer. How do you know it is reasonable? Explain.

4. Explain when you would use the *solve a simpler problem* strategy to solve a problem.

PRACTICE the Strategy

EXTRA PRACTICE See page R13.

Solve. Use the *solve a simpler problem* strategy.

5. **Algebra** Working separately, 3 teenagers can mow 3 lawns in 3 hours. At this rate, how many lawns can 6 teenagers mow in 9 hours?

6. **Measurement** Darby is cutting ribbons for balloons. The roll of ribbon he has is 24 feet long. Each ribbon needs to be 3 feet long. How long will it take Darby to make the cuts if each cut takes 3 seconds?

7. Find the sum of the whole numbers from 1 through 10. Explain your reasoning. Then find the sum of the whole numbers from 1 through 20.

8. Patty wants to buy a new tennis racket. So far, she has saved \$25.00 and \$7.25 from her two babysitting jobs. How much more money does she need to buy the tennis racket shown below?

9. **Measurement** Keith and his friend are going to the movies. The movie starts at 6:45 P.M. and lasts 1 hour and 50 minutes. If Keith's mom will be picking them up at the end of the movie, what time should she pick them up?

10. Charity and her friend each want to buy a piece of pizza, a drink, and an ice cream cone. Charity has \$10 to pay for her and her friend's meal. Does she have enough money? Explain.

Menu

Item	Price
Pizza	\$2.75
Drink	\$0.95
Ice cream cone	\$1.95

11. **Algebra** At the beach, 4 children working separately made 8 sandcastles in an hour. At this rate, how many sandcastles can 12 children make in a $\frac{1}{2}$ hour?

12. **WRITING IN MATH** How is the *solve a simpler problem* strategy similar to the *work backward* strategy?

5-3 Multiplication Expressions

MAIN IDEA

I will write and evaluate multiplication expressions.

Math Online

macmillanmh.com

- Extra Examples
- Personal Tutor
- Self-Check Quiz
- Concepts in Motion

GET READY to Learn

Lola has 2 boxes of crayons. Each box contains the same number of crayons. The total number of crayons is equal to 2 times the number of crayons in each box.

$2n$

The total number of crayons can be represented by the expression $2n$, which means 2 times n.

The number of boxes of crayons is a known value. → $2n$ ← The number of crayons in each box is an unknown value, or variable.

Suppose each box contains 8 crayons. To find the total number of crayons, multiply the number of crayons in each box by 2.

So, each box contains 2×8 or 16 crayons.

EXAMPLE **Evaluate Expressions**

1 Evaluate the expression $2n$ if $n = 5$.

$2n$ Write the expression. Use 2 cups to represent $2n$.

2×5 Replace n with 5. Place 5 counters in each cup.

10 Multiply 2 and 5. There is a total of 10 counters.

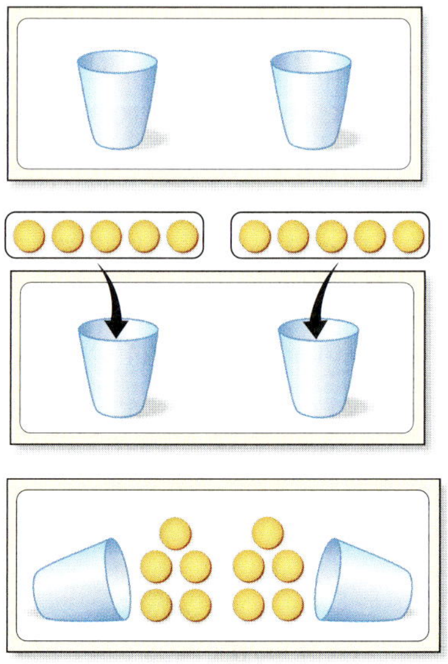

Real-World EXAMPLES

Write and Evaluate Expressions

2 **FOOD** **Ivan made x sandwiches. He used 2 slices of bread for each sandwich he made. Write an expression.**

Words	2 slices of bread for each sandwich
Variable	Let x represent the number of sandwiches.
Expression	$2x$

3 **Refer to Example 2. If $x = 6$, how many slices of bread did Ivan use?**

$2x$ Write the expression. Use 2 cups to represent $2x$.

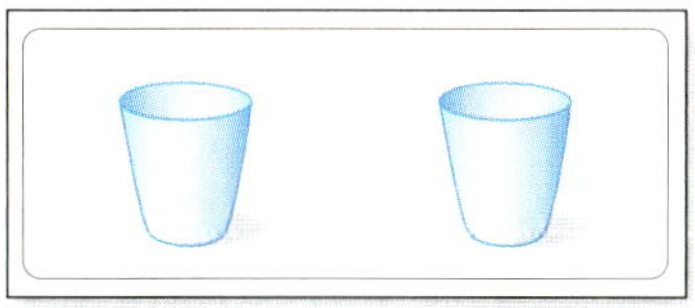

2×6 Replace x with 6. Place 6 counters in each cup.

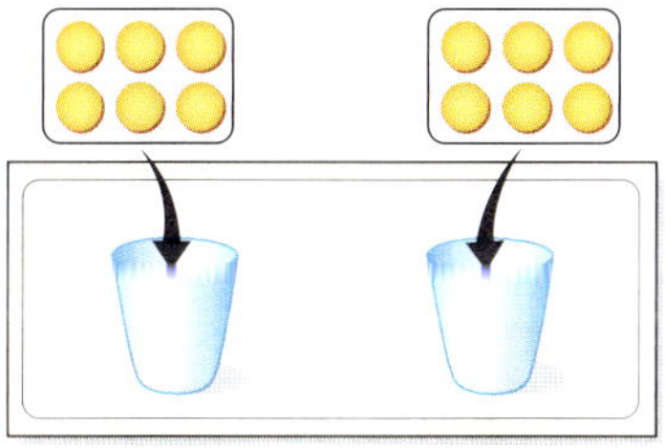

12 Multiply 2 and 6. There is a total of 12 counters.

So, Ivan used 12 slices of bread.

CHECK What You Know

Evaluate each expression if $x = 4$ and $y = 7$. See Example 1 (p. 198)

1. $12y$ **2.** $9x$ **3.** $7y$ **4.** $12x$

Write an expression for each real-world situation. Then evaluate.
See Examples 2, 3 (p. 199)

5. Leon has 4 sheets of stickers. Each sheet contains t stickers. If $t = 8$, how many stickers does Leon have?

6. Jacy bought 5 CDs. Each CD cost c dollars. If $c = 10$, how much did the CDs cost?

7. Talk About It Explain how to evaluate the expression $9b$, if $b = 8$.

Practice and Problem Solving

EXTRA PRACTICE See page R13.

Evaluate each expression if $x = 3$ and $y = 8$. See Example 1 (p. 198)

8. $4x$ **9.** $3y$ **10.** $5x$ **11.** $6y$

12. $9x$ **13.** $8y$ **14.** $12x$ **15.** $11y$

Evaluate each expression if $a = 9$ and $b = 7$. See Example 1 (p. 198)

16. $2a$ **17.** $3b$ **18.** $5b$ **19.** $4a$

20. $8a$ **21.** $9b$ **22.** $11a$ **23.** $12b$

Write an expression for each real-world situation. Then evaluate.
See Examples 2, 3 (p. 199)

24. Cole answered 11 questions correctly on a quiz. Each question was worth q points. If $q = 3$ how many points did Cole earn?

25. Ana mowed ℓ lawns. She earned $10 for every lawn she mowed. If $\ell = 5$, how much money did Ana earn?

26. The home baseball team scored 3 times as many runs as the away team in one season. The table shows how many runs the away team scored. How many runs did the home team score?

Runs Scored

Team	Runs
HOME	?
AWAY	62

27. A roller coaster can hold n passengers. In a half hour, the roller coaster made 6 full runs. The roller coaster can hold 28 passengers. How many passengers rode in the half hour?

H.O.T. Problems

28. **OPEN ENDED** Write a multiplication expression that, when evaluated, has a product of 36. Explain your reasoning.

29. **NUMBER SENSE** Without calculating, predict whether the value of $3n$ is greater than or less than the value of $n + n$ if $n = 8$. Explain.

30. **CHALLENGE** Explain whether the expressions $2n$ and $n + n$ have the same value for any value of n.

31. **WRITING IN MATH** Write a real-world problem that can be represented by a multiplication expression.

TEST Practice

32. Ms. Pena has 28 students in her class. Mrs. Thorne has x more students than Ms. Pena. Which expression could be used to find the total number of students Mrs. Thorne has? **(Lesson 5-1)**

A $28 + x$

B $28 - x$

C $28x$

D $28 \div x$

33. Evaluate the expression $a + b$ if $a = 10$ and $b = 7$. **(Lesson 5-1)**

F 15

G 17

H 19

J 20

34. The table shows how the ticket prices to water parks and plays have increased over the years.

Year	Water Parks	Plays
1990	\$5	\$27
1995	\$10	\$32
2000	\$15	\$37
2005	\$20	\$42

Based on the table, what is the relationship between the ticket prices? **(Lesson 5-3)**

A Water park ticket prices are \$5 more than play ticket prices.

B Water park ticket prices are \$32 less than play ticket prices.

C Play ticket prices are \$22 more than water park ticket prices.

D Play ticket prices are \$22 less than water park ticket prices.

Spiral Review

35. Measurement Mrs. Anderson needs to cut the piece of wood shown at the right into pieces 24 inches long. How many minutes will it take Mrs. Anderson to make the cuts if each cut takes 2 minutes? **(Lesson 5-2)**

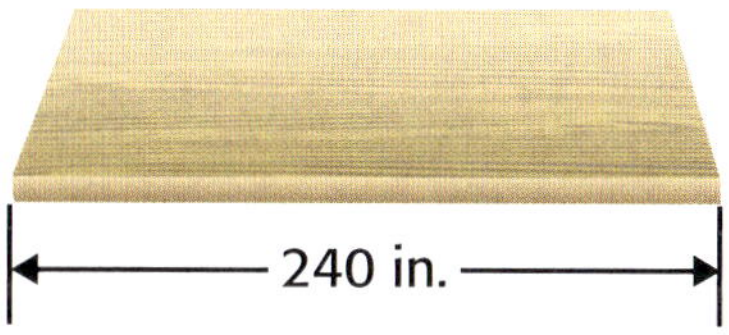

Evaluate each expression if $x = 5$ and $y = 6$. **(Lesson 5-1)**

36. $7 + x$ **37.** $y + 15$ **38.** $y + 23$ **39.** $x + y$

40. Members of the field hockey team washed cars to raise money for new equipment. They charged \$9 for large cars and \$6 for small cars. They raised a total of \$339. If they washed 21 large cars, how many small cars did they wash? **(Lesson 4-8)**

Estimate each sum or difference by rounding. Show your work.
(Lesson 2-2)

41. $2.48 + 6.61$ **42.** $558 - 402$ **43.** $75 + 74$ **44.** $9.42 - 5.75$

5-4 More Algebraic Expressions

MAIN IDEA

I will evaluate algebraic expressions.

Math Online

macmillanmh.com

- Extra Examples
- Personal Tutor
- Self-Check Quiz

GET READY to Learn

The Charlotte Knights are a minor league baseball team in North Carolina. The table shows the ticket prices for a Knights baseball game. The cost of a child's ticket is *d* dollars less than the cost of an adult ticket.

Charlotte Knights Tickets	
Ticket	Cost ($)
Adult	8
Senior	7
Child	?

Real-World EXAMPLE — Write and Evaluate Algebraic Expressions

1 **MONEY** **Refer to the above table. The cost of a child's ticket is *d* dollars less than $8. Write an expression.**

In this case, the words *less than* mean subtraction.

Words	*d* dollars less than 8
Variable	Let *d* represent how many dollars less.
Expression	$8 - d$

Suppose $d = 3$. Find the cost of a child's ticket.

$8 - d$ — Write the expression.

$8 - 3$ — Replace *d* with 3.

5 — Subtract.

So, the cost of a child's ticket is $5.

Real-World EXAMPLE

Write and Evaluate Algebraic Expressions

2 **SCIENCE** **Adam collected half as many insects for science class as Quan. Write an expression.**

In this case, half as many means to divide by 2.

Words	half as many insects as Quan
Variable	Let q represent the number of insects Quan collected
Expression	$q \div 2$

If Quan collected 12 insects, how many did Adam collect?

$q \div 2$ Write the expression.

$12 \div 2$ Replace q with 12.

6 Divide 12 by 2.

So, Adam collected 6 insects.

CHECK What You Know

Write an expression for each phrase. See Examples 1, 2 (pp. 202–203)

1. the sum of 11 and z **2.** p less than 22 **3.** w times 8

Evaluate each expression if $b = 3$ and $c = 4$.

4. $5 + b$ **5.** $c - 3$ **6.** $7c$ **7.** $27 \div b$

Write an expression for each real-world situation. Then evaluate.

8. **Measurement** The length of Kiki's room is 3 feet more than the width w of her room. The width of her room is 9 feet. What is the length of her room?

9. Franklin received $35 for his birthday. Then he bought a movie ticket for $6. How much money does he have now?

10. Curtis wants to buy some DVDs. Each DVD costs $15. If he has $60 to spend, how many DVDs can he buy?

11. **Talk About It** Describe how to evaluate the expression $x \div 5$ if $x = 15$.

Practice and Problem Solving

EXTRA PRACTICE See page R14.

Write an expression for each phrase. See Examples 1, 2 (pp. 202–203)

12. 10 more than *f* **13.** 50 less than *d* **14.** 25 plus *a*

15. 8 times *p* **16.** half of *j* **17.** twice *k*

Evaluate each expression if $r = 5$, $s = 2$, and $t = 8$.

18. $s + 19$ **19.** $34 + t$ **20.** $43 - r$ **21.** $r - s$

22. $4t$ **23.** $5r$ **24.** $18 \div s$ **25.** $25 \div r$

26. $r + t$ **27.** $t - s$ **28.** $12t$ **29.** $t \div s$

Write an expression for each real-world situation. Then evaluate.

30. Norman bought a hot dog and another food item. If the other item he bought was fries, what was the total cost of the food?

31. Tionna received $50 for her birthday. She spent some of the money on a board game that cost $18. How much money does Tionna have left?

32. Yolen had 84 marbles. She divided the marbles equally into a certain number of bags. If each bag had 12 marbles, how many bags did Yolen use?

33. Philip planted 5 rows of sunflower seeds. Each row had *s* seeds. Philip had 7 seeds left over, and each row had 12 seeds. How many sunflower seeds did Philip have?

H.O.T. Problems

34. OPEN ENDED Write two different expressions using *m* and 4, one using multiplication and one using addition. Then evaluate if $m = 6$.

35. WHICH ONE DOESN'T BELONG? Identify the expression that does not belong with the other three. Explain your reasoning.

$36 - a$ if $a = 9$	$19 + b$ if $b = 8$	$9c$ if $c = 3$	$15 + d$ if $d = 9$

36. WRITING IN MATH Explain why the expression *3 less than x* is written as $x - 3$ and not as $3 - x$.

CHAPTER 5

Mid-Chapter Check

Lessons 5-1 through 5-4

1. Aimee has t tickets. Dale has 7 more tickets. Write an expression for the number of tickets Dale has. (Lesson 5-1)

Evaluate each expression if $n = 3$. (Lesson 5-1)

2. $n + 7$
3. $n + 9$
4. $12 + n$
5. $n + 18$

6. Working separately, 5 carpenters can make 10 chairs in 2 days. At this rate, how many chairs can 10 carpenters make in 4 days? Solve. Use the *solve a simpler problem* strategy. (Lesson 5-2)

7. Marcy and her friend can make 8 greeting cards in 32 minutes. How many greeting cards can Marcy and her friend make in 48 minutes? Solve. Use the *solve a simpler problem* strategy. (Lesson 5-2)

Evaluate each expression if $y = 4$. (Lesson 5-3)

8. $3y$
9. $5y$
10. $8y$
11. $11y$

12. **MULTIPLE CHOICE** Alonzo waited x minutes to ride the bumper cars. Pearl waited 3 times as long. Which expression could be used to find the number of minutes Pearl waited? (Lesson 5-3)

    A $3 + x$

    B $3x$

    C $x + 3$

    D $x - 3$

13. Use the table. Mr. Yu bought n new DVDs. If $n = 3$, what was the total cost of the DVDs? (Lesson 5-3)

DVD	Price ($)
New	12
Used	8

14. **MULTIPLE CHOICE** Dario is y years old. His brother Angelo is twice as old as he is. Which expression could be used to find Angelo's age? (Lesson 5-4)

    F $y + 2$

    G $y - 2$

    H $2y$

    J $y \div 2$

Evaluate each expression if $d = 2$ and $f = 6$. (Lesson 5-4)

15. $11 - f$
16. $24 \div d$

Measurement **For Exercises 17 and 18, use the figure below.** (Lesson 5-4)

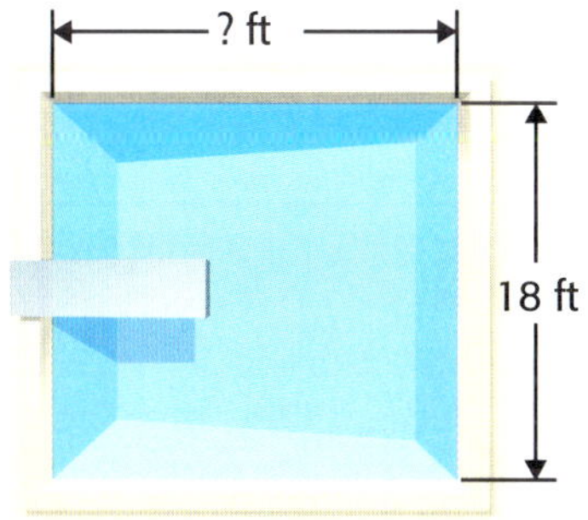

17. Write an expression to show that the length of the swimming pool is x feet more than the width.

18. If $x = 5$, what is the length of the pool?

19. **WRITING IN MATH** Write two different expressions using n and 2, one with division and one with subtraction. Explain how to evaluate them if $n = 6$. (Lesson 5-4)

5-5 Problem-Solving Investigation

MAIN IDEA I will choose the best strategy to solve a problem.

P.S.I. TEAM +

STEPHANIE: I had a lemonade stand. I sold large cups of lemonade for \$0.65 and small cups of lemonade for \$0.40. After one hour, I earned \$6.15. How many of each size did I sell?

YOUR MISSION: Find the number of each size sold.

Understand You know that Stephanie earned \$6.15. She sold large cups for \$0.65 and small cups \$0.40. You need to know how many of each size Stephanie sold.

Plan You need to think about the different combinations of large and small cups she could have sold. So, the *guess and check* strategy is a good choice.

Solve Use a calculator. Since $10 \times \$0.65 = \$6.50$, less than 10 large cups were sold. Let's try 8.

	Large Cup	Earnings	Small Cup	Earnings	Total	
1st guess	8	\$5.20	3	\$1.20	\$6.40	Too much.
2nd guess	6	\$3.90	5	\$2.00	\$5.90	Too little.
3rd guess	7	\$4.55	4	\$1.60	\$6.15	✔

So, Stephanie sold 7 large cups and 4 small cups of lemonade.

Check Look back. Since $7 \times \$0.65 = \$4.55$ and $4 \times \$0.40 = \$1.60$, Stephanie made $\$4.55 + \$1.60$ or \$6.15. So, the answer is correct. ✔

Mixed Problem Solving

EXTRA PRACTICE
See page R14.

Use any strategy shown below to solve each problem.

PROBLEM-SOLVING STRATEGIES
- *Guess and check.*
- *Work backward.*
- *Draw a picture.*
- *Act it out.*
- *Solve a simpler problem.*

1. Jeremy's basketball number is between 30 and 50. The sum of the digits is 4. What is Jeremy's basketball number?

2. **Algebra** Jasmine is making bookmarks. Each day she makes twice as many bookmarks as the day before. On the fifth day she makes 32 bookmarks. How many bookmarks did she make on the first day?

3. **Measurement** A plumber needs to cut the pipe shown below into 2 inch pieces. If one cut takes 3 minutes, how many minutes will it take the plumber to make the cuts?

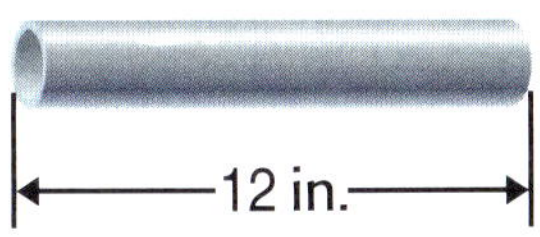

4. Some students are standing in the lunch line. Tammie is fourth. Joy is two places in front of Tammie. Eight places behind Joy is Mike. What place is Mike?

5. **Measurement** A sandbox is made of two squares side by side. Each square is 9 feet by 9 feet. What is the total distance around the sandbox?

6. Rita bought sandwiches for herself and 4 friends. She spent a total of $13.45. How many of each type of sandwich did she buy?

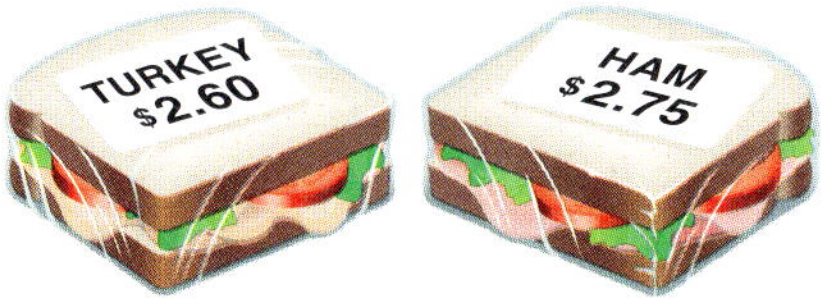

7. **Geometry** Square tables are put together end-to-end to make one long table for a birthday party. A total of 18 people attend the party. How many tables are needed if only one person can sit on each side of the square tables?

8. At the school bake sale, Kenji's mom bought 3 cookies, 1 brownie, and 2 cupcakes. She gave the cashier $2 and received $0.75 in change. Find the cost of each cupcake.

Bake Sale Prices

Item	Price ($)
Cookie	0.15
Brownie	0.20
Cupcake	■

9. An electronics store is selling handheld games at $27 for 3. How much will 5 handheld games cost?

10. WRITING IN MATH Write a real-world problem that you can solve using any problem-solving strategy. What strategy would you use to solve the problem? Explain your reasoning.

Explore

Algebra Activity for 5-6
Function Machines

MAIN IDEA

I will illustrate functions using function machines.

A *function machine* takes a number called the *input* and performs one or more operations on it to produce a new value called the *output*. A *function rule* describes the relationship between each input and output.

ACTIVITY Make a Function Machine

Suppose Marcus is 4 years younger than his sister Lucia. The function rule $n - 4$ can be used to find Marcus' age if you know Lucia's age. Make a function machine for the rule $n - 4$.

Step 1 Cut a sheet of paper in half lengthwise.

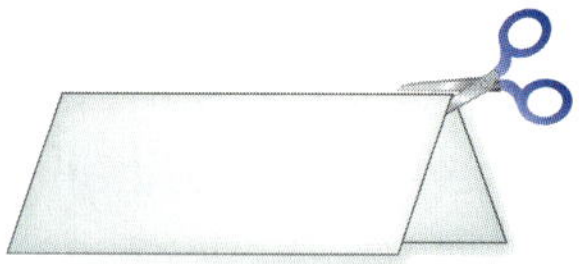

Step 2 Cut four slits into one of the halves. The slits should be at least one inch wide.

Step 3 Cut two narrow strips from the other half of the paper. These strips should be able to slide through the slits you cut on the first half sheet.

Step 4 On one of the narrow strips, write the input numbers 10 through 6 as shown. On the other strip, write the output numbers 6 through 2 as shown.

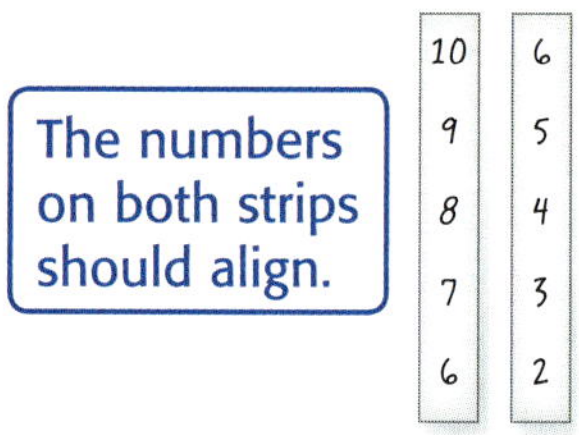

Step 5 Place the strips into the slits as shown. Then tape the ends of the strips together at the top. Write the function rule $n - 4$ as shown.

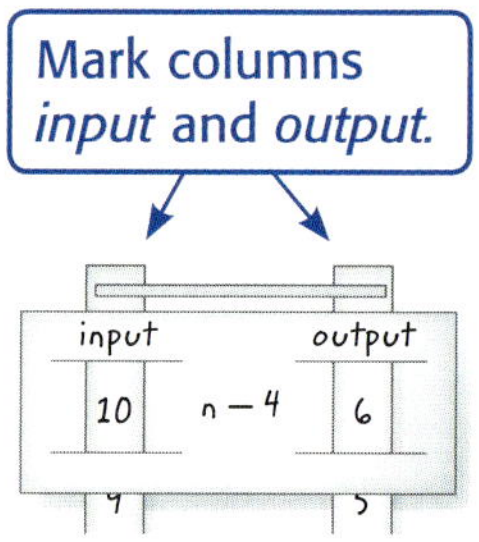

Step 6 Pull the strips up or down so that the input value corresponds to an output value.

Think About It

1. Use the function machine you made to find the output value for each input value. Copy and complete the function table showing the input, output, and function rule.

Lucia's Age Input	Rule: $n - 4$	Marcus' Age Output
10	■	6
9	■	■
8	■	■
7	■	■
6	■	■

2. What patterns do you notice in the function machine?

3. Use the pattern you discovered to predict how old Marcus will be when Lucia is 20 years old.

CHECK What You Know

For Exercises 4–9, write a real-world situation for each expression. Then express the relationship using a function machine. Use the input values 3, 4, 5, and 6 for *n*. Record each input, output, and function rule in a function table.

4. $n + 4$
5. $n - 1$
6. $n + 6$
7. $n - 2$
8. $2n$
9. $3n$

Write the function rule to express the relationship between each set of input and output values. Then write a real-world situation for each function rule.

10.

Input	Rule: ■	Output
28	■	40
29	■	41
30	■	42
31	■	43

11.

Input	Rule: ■	Output
4	■	16
5	■	20
6	■	24
7	■	28

12. Create your own function machine for a real-world situation. Write pairs of inputs and outputs and have a classmate determine the rule.

13. **WRITING IN MATH** Why is using a function machine like finding a pattern? Explain your reasoning.

5-6 Function Tables

MAIN IDEA

I will complete function tables.

New Vocabulary

function
function table
input
output

Math Online

macmillanmh.com

- Extra Examples
- Personal Tutor
- Self-Check Quiz

GET READY to Learn

Did you know giraffes sleep an average of 2 hours per day?

A **function** is a relationship between two variables in which one input quantity is paired with exactly one output quantity. You can use a **function table** to organize input-output values. In the Algebra Activity on page 208, you learned that the **input** is the quantity put into a function. The end amount is the **output**.

Real-World EXAMPLE — Complete a Function Table

1 **ANIMALS** **Refer to the above information. How many hours of sleep will a giraffe get in 5 days? Make a function table.**

In words, the rule is *multiply the number of days by 2*. As an expression, the rule is $2d$.

Multiply the number of days by 2.

Days → Input; Output ← Hours of sleep

Input (d)	$2d$	Output
1	2×1	2
2	2×2	4
3	2×3	6
4	2×4	8
5	2×5	10

In 5 days, a giraffe will sleep about 10 hours.

Real-World EXAMPLE — Find the Function Rule

2 **MEASUREMENT** **A zookeeper feeds each hippopotamus 100 pounds of food a day. Find the function rule. Then make a function table to find how many pounds of food the zoo will need each day for 2, 3, or 4 hippos.**

The output value is 100 times the input value.

Multiply 100 and h.

Number of hippos → Input (h); Pounds of food → Output

Input (h)	$100h$	Output
2	100×2	200
3	100×3	300
4	100×4	400

The zoo will need 200, 300, or 400 pounds of food.

Remember

Since each hippopotamus eats 100 pounds, you should multiply.

CHECK What You Know

Copy and complete each function table for each real-world situation.

See Examples 1, 2 (pp. 210–211)

1. Desmond has 9 more model airplanes than his brother.

Input (x)	$x + 9$	Output
6	■	■
9	■	■
12	■	■

2. Petra walked 6 less blocks than Natalie.

Input (x)	$x - 6$	Output
15	■	■
17	■	■
19	■	■

3. Each comic book costs $4.

Input (x)	$4x$	Output
5	■	■
6	■	■
7	■	■

4. Jared ate half of his pretzels.

Input (x)	$x \div 2$	Output
12	■	■
14	■	■
16	■	■

5. Hiro charges $8 for each dog he washes. Find the function rule. Then make a function table to find how much money he would make if he washes 4, 5, or 6 dogs.

6. **Talk About It** Explain what the function rule $n - 8$ means. Then find the output value if $n = 12$.

Practice and Problem Solving

EXTRA PRACTICE See page R14.

Copy and complete each function table for each real-world situation.
See Example 1 (p. 210)

7. Aidan scored 9 less points than Vince.

Input (x)	$x - 9$	Output
19	■	■
20	■	■
21	■	■

8. Each box weighs 10 pounds.

Input (x)	$10x$	Output
3	■	■
5	■	■
7	■	■

Find the function rule. Then make and complete a function table.
See Example 2 (p. 211)

9. Ginny had a coupon for \$5 off any item at Music Mania. Find the final cost of items that cost \$20, \$25, and \$30.

10. **Measurement** A textbook weighs about 6 pounds. Find the total weight of 5, 7, and 9 textbooks.

11. A certain box can hold 6 muffins. Find the number of boxes you will need if you have 24, 30 and 36 muffins. How many boxes will you need if you have 42 muffins?

12. A shop sells trail mix for \$3.75 per pound. You have a coupon for \$0.75 off each pound of trail mix. Find the cost of 4, 5, and 6 pounds of trail mix. What is the cost of 7 pounds of trail mix?

H.O.T. Problems

13. **OPEN ENDED** Write a function rule involving both addition and multiplication. Choose three input values and find the output values.

14. **FIND THE ERROR** Bly and Sierra are writing a function rule for the expression *5 less than y*. Who is correct? Explain.

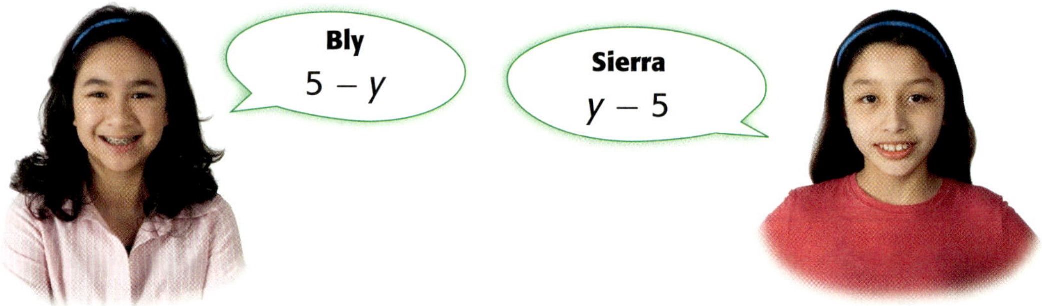

15. **WRITING IN ▶MATH** Write a real-life problem that can be represented by a function table.

TEST Practice

16. Jean is buying stickers. The table shows the price of different numbers of stickers.

Number of Stickers	25	50	75	100	125
Price	\$0.50	\$1.00	\$1.25	\$2.00	\$2.50

What is the relationship between the number of stickers and the price? (Lesson 5-4)

A The price is 25 more than the number of stickers.

B The number of stickers is two times the price.

C The price is two times the number of stickers.

D The number of stickers is 25 less than the price.

17. A milkshake costs \$3. The function rule $3n$ represents the cost of buying any number of milkshakes. Which shows $3n$ in words? (Lesson 5-6)

F n more than 3

G 3 more than n

H 3 times n

J 3 less than n

18. Find the missing value in the function table.

Input (x)	4	5	6	7
Output	32	40	48	■

A 63 **C** 56

B 58 **D** 50

Spiral Review

19. Tickets to the museum cost \$4.50 for adults and \$2.50 for children. The Thorn family spent \$18.50 for tickets. If they bought more adult tickets than children's tickets, how many of each type of ticket did they buy? (Lesson 5-5)

Evaluate each expression if $x = 3$ and $y = 6$. (Lesson 5-4)

20. $18 - x$ **21.** $38 + y$ **22.** $7y$ **23.** $24 \div x$

24. Measurement Mr. Coughlin drove 536 miles in 9 hours. About how many miles does he drive each hour on average? Show your work. (Lesson 4-2)

For Exercises 25 and 26, use the table that shows listeners' favorite types of satellite radio stations. (Lesson 2-4)

Type of Station	Number of Listeners
Music	3,897
Sports	3,160
Entertainment	2,180
News	2,054

25. How many listeners favor either music or news stations?

26. How many more listeners favor sports over entertainment?

Replace each ● with <, >, or = to make a true sentence. (Lesson 1-2)

27. 390 ● 309 **28.** 54 ● 45 **29.** 790 ● 1,669

Extend

Technology Activity for 5-6

Function Tables

MAIN IDEA

I will use technology to create function tables to solve problems.

You can use the Math Tool Chest™ to make function tables.

ACTIVITY Make a Function Table

1 **A bottlenose dolphin must rise to the surface every 6 minutes to breathe. Find the function rule. Then make a function table to find how many times a bottlenose dolphin will surface in 42, 48, and 54 minutes.**

The function rule is $x \div 6$, where x is the number of minutes and y is the number of times that the dolphin will surface.

You can use a function table from the Math Tool Chest™.

- Choose Graphs and click on level two.
- Click on Function Graph.
- Click on the link button in the bottom right-hand corner.
- Click on the formula button. Type the function rule, $x \div 6$.
- Enter the values for x (42, 48, 54) in the x column.
- Look at the values for y to solve the problem.

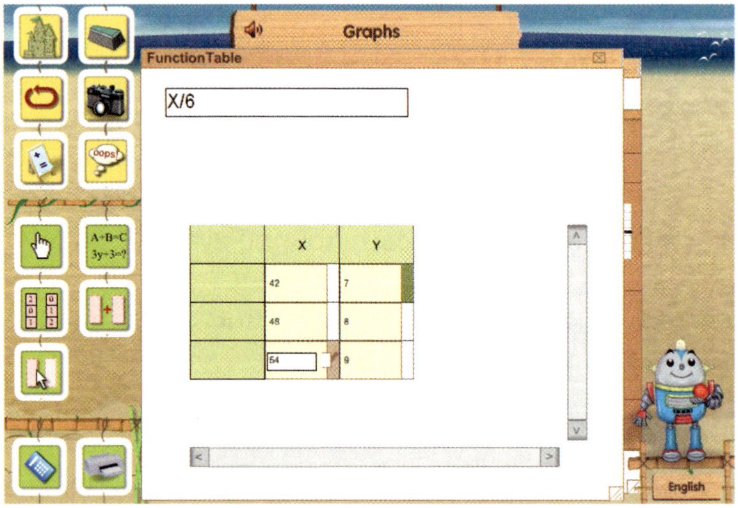

So, a bottlenose dolphin will surface every 7, 8, and 9 minutes.

Tech Link

CHECK What You Know

Find the function rule. Then use the Math Tool Chest™ to make and complete a function table.

1. Ria is 6 years younger than her brother. How old will Ria be when her brother is 12, 17, and 23 years old?

2. The fastest fish is the sailfish. A sailfish can swim 68 miles per hour. How many miles can a sailfish swim in 3, 5, or 7 hours?

3. The width of a flower pot is 4 inches longer than its height. Find the width of the pot if its height is 5, 8, or 12 inches.

4. Each student will receive the same number of pizza rolls. There are 48 pizza rolls. How many rolls will each student receive if there are 6, 12, or 24 students?

5. **WRITING IN ▸MATH** Explain the advantages of using Math Tool Chest™ to make and complete function tables.

For Exercises 6–12, use the function table at the right to solve.

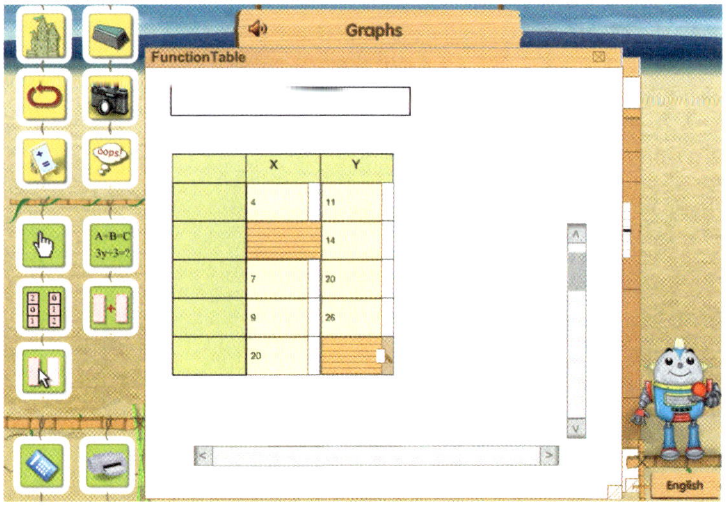

6. Analyze the numbers in the x and y values to find the function rule for the table.

7. If $x = 20$, what is the value of y?

8. If $x = 100$, what is the value of y?

9. If $y = 14$, what is the value of x?

10. If $y = 29$, what is the value of x?

11. An odd number is placed in the x column.What will always be true for the value of y?

12. If an even number is placed in the x column, then what will always be true for the value of y?

13. **WRITING IN ▸MATH** Write a real-world problem that could be solved using a function table.

Problem Solving in Science

UNDERWATER MAPS

Oceans cover $\frac{7}{10}$ of Earth's surface. Just as there are maps of land, there are maps of the ocean's floor. Oceanographers use sonar to measure the depths of different places in the ocean. The average depth of Earth's oceans is 12,200 feet.

Oceanographers send out sound waves from a sonar device on a ship. They measure how long it takes for sound waves to reach the bottom of the ocean and return. They use the fact that sound waves travel through sea water at about 5,000 feet per second. That's about 3,400 miles per hour!

Did You Know?

The deepest part of the ocean floor has been recorded at 36,198 feet. This distance is 7,163 feet greater than the height of Mount Everest, the highest mountain on Earth.

Real-World Math

Use the information from page 216 and the table below to solve each problem. Use a calculator.

1. Make a function table to find the number of feet sound travels through sea water for 1, 2, 3, 4, and 5 seconds.

2. Use your table to estimate how long it will take a sound wave to reach the average depth of Earth's oceans.

3. Suppose your ship sends out a sound wave and it returns to the ship in 8 seconds. About how deep is the ocean where you are?

4. Suppose a thunderstorm is about 1 mile away from where you are standing. About how long will it take before you hear the thunder? (*Hint:* 1 mile = 5,280 feet)

5. **WRITING IN MATH** Explain how to write an expression that gives the number of feet that sound travels through steel for any number of seconds. How would you vary your expression if the sound was traveling through diamond?

Speed of Sound Through Different Media (feet per second)

Medium	Speed
Air (20°C)	1,121
Pure Water	4,882
Sea Water	5,012
Steel	16,000
Diamond	39,240

5-7 Order of Operations

GET READY to Learn

The table shows the number of Calories burned in one minute for two different activities. If you swim for 4 minutes, you will burn 12×4 Calories. If you run for 8 minutes, you will burn 10×8 Calories.

Activity	Calories Burned per Minute
Swimming	12
Running	10

MAIN IDEA

I will use order of operations to evaluate expressions.

New Vocabulary

order of operations

Math Online

macmillanmh.com

- Extra Examples
- Personal Tutor
- Self-Check Quiz

If you do both activities, you need to find the value of the expression $12 \times 4 + 10 \times 8$.

The expression $12 \times 4 + 10 \times 8$ has more than one operation. The **order of operations** tells you which operation to do first, so that everyone finds the same value for the expression.

Order of Operations — Key Concept

1. Perform operations in parentheses.
2. Multiply and divide in order from left to right.
3. Add and subtract in order from left to right.

Real-World EXAMPLE — Evaluate Expressions

1 HEALTH Refer to the information above. How many Calories would you burn doing both activities?

$c = 12 \times 4 + 10 \times 8$

$c = 48 + 80$ Multiply 12 and 4. Multiply 10 and 8.

$c = 128$ Add 48 and 80.

So, you would burn 128 Calories.

Real-World EXAMPLE — Write and Evaluate Expressions

2 **MEASUREMENT** **The table shows the number of minutes Roberto spent playing baseball at camp. Find the total number of minutes he spent playing baseball.**

Baseball Time	
Day	**Time (minutes)**
Monday	60
Tuesday	90
Wednesday	60
Thursday	90
Friday	60

On three days, he played for 60 minutes. On two days, he played for 90 minutes.

$$60 \times 3 + 90 \times 2$$

60: number of minutes; 3: number of days; 90: number of minutes; 2: number of days

Now evaluate.

$m = 60 \times 3 + 90 \times 2$

$m = 180 + 180$ Multiply 60 by 3. Multiply 90 by 2.

$m = 360$ Add 180 and 180.

So, Roberto played 360 minutes of baseball.

Real-World EXAMPLE — Use a Function Table

3 **MONEY** **The cost of renting a popcorn machine is \$8 per hour plus \$30. Find the function rule. Then make a function table to find the cost of renting the popcorn machine for 4, 5, and 6 hours.**

First multiply 8 by the input value. Then, add 30. The function rule is $8x + 30$.

Multiply the input value by 8 and then add 30.

Number of hours → Input (x); Cost → Output

Input (x)	$8x + 30$	Output
4	$(8 \times 4) + 30$	62
5	$(8 \times 5) + 30$	70
6	$(8 \times 6) + 30$	78

Remember

The expression $8x$ means 8 times the value of x.

CHECK What You Know

Find the value of each expression. See Examples 1–3 (pp. 218–219)

1. $12 - 2 \times 5$ **2.** $15 - 3 \times 4$ **3.** $(15 - 3) \times 4$

4. Giselle bought three DVDs that each cost $12. She also had a coupon for $10 off her total purchase. Write an expression to find her final cost. Then evaluate the expression.

5. The table shows the number of minutes Percy read in five days. How many minutes did he read? Write an expression. Then evaluate the expression.

Percy's Reading Time

Day	Time (minutes)
Monday	25
Tuesday	20
Wednesday	25
Thursday	25
Friday	20

6. The cost of shipping books bought on the Internet is $3 plus $1 for each book purchased. Find the function rule. Then make a function table to find the cost of shipping 3, 4, and 5 books.

7. Talk About It Explain why Exercises 2 and 3 have different answers even though the numbers are the same.

Practice and Problem Solving

EXTRA PRACTICE See page R15.

Evaluate each expression. See Examples 1–3 (pp. 218–219)

8. $(15 - 5) \times (3 + 3)$ **9.** $58 - 6 \times 7$ **10.** $32 + 4 \times 8$

11. **Measurement** The total distance around the garden shown below is 2 times the length plus 2 times the width. What is the total distance around the garden?

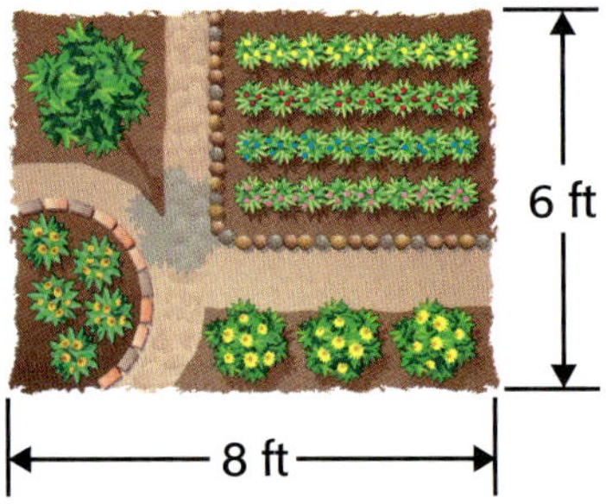

12. Vikram counted the number of cans turned in on Monday morning.

His results are shown. Each  represents 5 cans.

How many cans did Vikram count? Write an expression. Then evaluate the expression.

For Exercises 13 and 14, find the function rule. Then make and complete a function table.

13. **Measurement** A fish tank has 100 gallons of water in it. The water is draining at a rate of 4 gallons per minute. Find how much water is left in the tank after 11, 14, and 17 minutes.

14. Tarie is planning on reading 15 pages of her book each night. She has already read 12 pages. Find the number of pages she has read after 2, 3, and 4 nights. How many pages has she read after 5 nights?

Real-World PROBLEM SOLVING

Algebra Temperature can be measured in degrees Fahrenheit (°F) or in degrees Celsius (°C). When you know a temperature in degrees Fahrenheit, you can find the temperature in degrees Celsius by using the expression $5 \times (F - 32) \div 9$.

15. Find each temperature in degrees Celsius. Copy and complete the table. (*Hint:* If an expression has both multiplication and division, evaluate them in order from left to right.)

Temperature (°F)	$5 \times (F - 32) \div 9$	Temperature (°C)
41	■	■
68	■	■
95	■	■

16. If the temperature of a cup of hot chocolate is 104°F, what is the temperature of the cup of hot chocolate in degrees Celsius?

17. Guess and check to find the temperature in degrees Fahrenheit that would equal 0°C.

H.O.T. Problems

18. **OPEN ENDED** Write an expression using only multiplication and subtraction so that its value is 25.

19. **CHALLENGE** Use each of the numbers 2, 3, 4, and 5 exactly once to write an expression that equals 5.

20. **WRITING IN MATH** Should you ever add or subtract before you multiply in an expression? Explain your reasoning.

TEST Practice

21. Each of Marie's 4 photo albums holds 24 vertical photos and 24 horizontal photos. Which shows one way to find the total number of photos Marie's photo albums can hold? (Lesson 5-7)

A $24 + 24 + 4$

B $24 \times 24 + 4$

C $24 \times 24 \times 4$

D $24 + 24 \times 4$

22. A seating area has 8 rows, with 15 chairs in each row. If 47 seats are occupied, which of the following shows how to find the number of empty chairs? (Lesson 5-6)

F Add 47 to the product of 15 and 8.

G Add 15 to the product of 47 and 8.

H Subtract 47 from the product of 15 and 8.

J Subtract 15 from the product of 47 and 8.

Spiral Review

23. Basketballs cost $18 each. Find a function rule for the cost of *b* balls. Then make a function table to find the cost of 2, 3, and 4 basketballs. What is the cost of 5 basketballs? (Lesson 5-6)

24. Measurement For a concert, Elvio must set up the speakers for a sound system around a square room. Speakers are set up in the corners of the room and 10 yards apart. The room is 60 yards long. How many speakers will Elvio set up? (Lesson 5-5)

Identify the multiplication property used to rewrite each expression. (Lesson 3-7)

25. $25 \times 3 \times 14 = 14 \times 25 \times 3$

26. $4 \times (6 \times 2) = (4 \times 6) \times 2$

27. Measurement The table shows the average weight of leopard seals. What is the difference between the weight of an adult leopard seal and a leopard seal pup? (Lesson 2-4)

Leopard Seal Weight (lb)

Adult	992
Pup	66

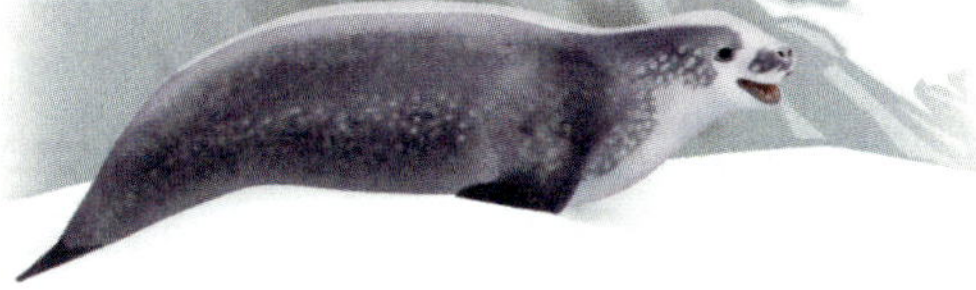

Replace each ● with $<$, $>$, or $=$ to make a true sentence. (Lesson 1-6)

28. 0.41 ● 0.40

29. 3.9 ● 3.7

30. 0.45 ● 0.54

31. 14.3 ● 8.9

Write each fraction as a decimal. (Lesson 1-4)

32. sixty hundredths

33. nine thousandths

34. five tenths

Game Time

Order Matters

Evaluating Expressions

Get Ready!

Players: 2 players

You will need: a number cube
10 index cards

Get Set!

Label the index cards with the expressions as shown.

$2n$	$5n$
$n + 3$	$10n$
$n + 6$	$n + 12$
$2n + 1$	$3n + 2$
$4n + 5$	$20 - 2n$

Go!

- Shuffle the cards. Then spread the cards facedown on the table.
- Player 1 turns over a card and rolls the number cube.
- Player 1 replaces n on his or her card with the number rolled and then evaluates the expression.
- If player 1 correctly evaluates the expression, he or she receives the value of the expression in points. The player can double their points if they correctly provide a real-world example for their expression.
- If player 1 incorrectly evaluates the expression, the card is returned facedown on the table.
- Player 2 takes a turn.
- Continue taking turns until all the cards have been played correctly. Each player adds up their points. The player with the most points wins.

CHAPTER 5

Study Guide and Review

Math Online macmillanmh.com

- STUDY TO GO
- Vocabulary Review

FOLDABLES® Study Organizer GET READY to Study

Be sure the following Big Ideas are written in your Foldable.

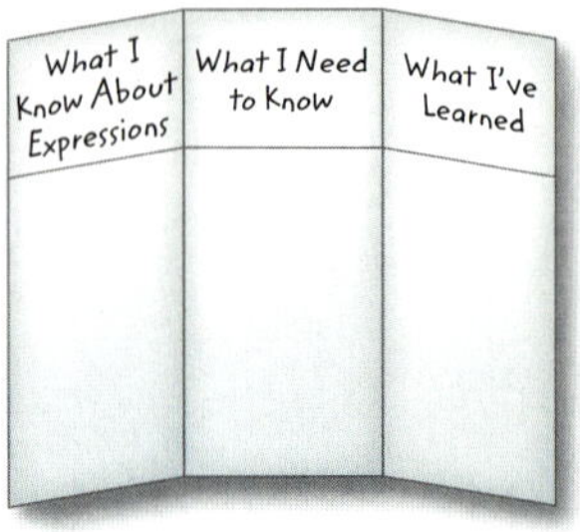

Key Concepts

- A **variable** is a letter or symbol used to represent a number. (p. 193)
- An **expression** is a combination of variables, numbers, and at least one operation. (p. 193)

Evaluating Expressions (p. 193)

- To **evaluate** an expression means to find the value of the expression.

$x + 4$ if $x = 3$

↓

$3 + 4$ or 7

Functions (p. 210)

- A **function** is a relationship between two variables in which one input quantity is paired with one output quantity.

Order of Operations (p. 218)

- The **order of operations** is a set of rules that tell you which operation to do first when evaluating an expression.

Key Vocabulary

evaluate (p. 193)
expression (p. 193)
function (p. 210)
function table (p. 210)
order of operations (p. 218)
variable (p. 193)

Vocabulary Check

State whether each sentence is *true* or *false*. If *false*, replace the underlined word or number to make a true sentence.

1. A function is a relationship in which one input quantity is paired with exactly one output quantity.
2. An expression is a combination of variables, numbers, and at least two operations.
3. A variable represents the known value.
4. A function table can be used to organize input and output values.
5. To evaluate an expression means to find its value.
6. When evaluating $15 - 3 \times 4$, the order of operations tells you to evaluate $15 - 3$ first.

Lesson-by-Lesson Review

5-1 Addition Expressions (pp. 193–195)

Example 1
Evaluate 8 + *a* if *a* = 4.

$8 + a$ Write the expression.

$8 + 4$ Replace *a* with 4.

12 Add 8 and 4.

Evaluate each expression if *x* = 3 and *y* = 6.

7. $y + 6$
8. $4 + x$
9. $18 + x$
10. $y + 14$
11. TJ had *m* marbles. Alvin gave him 7 more marbles. Write an expression to find the total number of marbles. If $m = 45$, how many marbles does TJ have now?

5-2 Problem-Solving Strategy: Solve a Simpler Problem (pp. 196–197)

Example 2
There are 16 teams in a basketball tournament. If a team loses, it is out of the tournament. How many games must be played to determine the winner?

Use the *solve a simpler problem* strategy.

Two teams would play one game.

Team 1, Team 2 → Game 1

Four teams would play three games.

Team 1, Team 2 → Game 1
Team 3, Team 4 → Game 2
Game 1, Game 2 → Game 3

The number of games is equal to the number of teams minus 1. So, 16 − 1 is 15. Fifteen games would be played.

Solve. Use the *solve a simpler problem* strategy.

12. Use the table below. Ms. Villialta needs to buy 3 children's tickets and 1 adult ticket. If she has $20, does she have enough money to buy all the tickets? Explain.

13. **Measurement** Justin and Max working separately can pick a total of 4 baskets of apples in an hour. At this rate, how many baskets of apples can 10 people pick in $\frac{1}{2}$ hour?

Chapter 5 Study Guide and Review

5-3 Multiplication Expressions (pp. 198–201)

Example 3
Evaluate the expression $4w$ if $w = 7$.

$4w$	Write the expression.
4×7	Replace w with 7.
28	Multiply 4 and 7.

Evaluate each expression if $b = 2$ and $c = 5$.

14. $3c$

15. $5b$

16. $12b$

17. $10c$

18. **Measurement** A single brick weighs 4 pounds. Mr. Badilla has b bricks. Write an expression to find the total weight of the bricks. If $b = 9$, find the total weight of the bricks.

5-4 More Algebraic Expressions (pp. 202–204)

Example 4

Measurement The length of the garden is 5 more feet than the width w of a garden. Write an expression.

In this case, the words *more than* mean addition.

w	Start with w.
$w + 5$	Then add 5.

So, $w + 5$ represents 5 *more than the width.*

Then, find the length of the garden if the width is 3 feet.

$w + 5$	Write the expression.
$3 + 5$	Replace w with 3.
8	Add.

The length of the garden is 8 feet.

Write an expression for each phrase.

19. n less than 8

20. multiply 7 by c

21. 12 plus a

22. h divided by 7

Evaluate each expression if $y = 4$ and $z = 8$.

23. $12 - y$

24. $z \div 2$

25. $4y$

26. $23 + z$

27. $8y$

28. $z \div y$

29. Ms. Washer has 42 bottles of water. Each package contains n bottles of water. Write an expression to find the number of packages if each package contains 6 bottles of water. How many packages of water did Ms. Washer buy?

5-5 Problem-Solving Investigation: Choose a Strategy (pp. 206–207)

Example 5

Dee is running for president of student council. Last week she gave half of her buttons away. This week she gave 7 buttons away. There are 16 buttons remaining. How many buttons did Dee have to begin with?

Understand

- 16 buttons are left.
- 7 buttons were given away this week.
- Half of the buttons were given away last week.

Plan To solve this problem, work backward.

Solve Dee gave out 7 buttons. Add 7 to the remaining buttons.

$$16 + 7 = 23$$

There were 23 buttons before Dee handed out any this week. Last week she handed out half of the original amount. So, multiply 23 by 2.

$$23 \times 2 = 46$$

Dee had 46 buttons at the beginning.

Check Look back. Solve it by working forward. First, $46 \div 2 = 23$. Then, $23 - 7 = 16$. The answer is correct.

Use any strategy to solve each problem.

30. At a snack bar, Urick was served before Mirna, but after Mallory. Terrel was the first of the four friends to be served. Which friend was served last?

31. Measurement Softball practice begins at 5:00 P.M. It takes Mandy 15 minutes to get ready and 30 minutes to get to the field. What time must Mandy leave to get to softball practice on time?

32. Macario can buy rolls of film in 18 or 24 exposures. He buys 5 rolls of film and gets 108 exposures. How many rolls of each film did Macario buy?

33. Selena has $150 to spend on skateboarding equipment. Does she have enough money to buy all the equipment listed below? Explain.

Gloves	$14.95
Helmet	$34.50
Skateboard	$84.50
Mouth guard	$9.95

34. Sean is thinking of a number. It has 3 ones. It has twice as many hundreds as ones and 3 times as many tens as ones. It has 2 more thousands than hundreds. What is the number?

5-6 Function Tables (pp. 210–213)

Example 6

Sofia jumped rope for 2 minutes less than her sister. Find the function rule. Then make a function table to find the number of minutes Sofia jumped if her sister jumped for 6, 8, and 10 minutes. How many minutes did Sofia jump if her sister jumped for 10 minutes?

Subtract 2 from each input. The function rule is $x - 2$.

Input (x)	$x - 2$	Output
6	6 − 2	4
8	8 − 2	6
10	10 − 2	8

She jumped for 8 minutes.

35. Dino has 3 more pets than his friend. Copy and complete the table.

Input (x)	$x + 3$	Output
5	■	■
3	■	■
1	■	■

36. Paperback books cost $5 each at Book Smart. Find the function rule. Then make a function table to find the cost of buying 3, 4, and 5 books at Book Smart. What is the cost of 5 books?

5-7 Order of Operations (pp. 218–222)

Example 7

Find the value of $3 \times (4 + 5)$.

$3 \times (4 + 5)$

3×9 Add 4 and 5.

27 Multiply 3 and 9.

So, $3 \times (4 + 5) = 27$.

Find the value of each expression.

37. $(12 + 6) \times 2$

38. $26 - 3 \times 6$

39. Marisol bought 3 pairs of running shorts that cost $15 each from an internet store. Shipping costs an additional $5. Write an expression to find the total cost. Then evaluate the expression.

40. Lonnie has 3 pencils. He buys b boxes of pencils. Each box contains 12 pencils. Use the expression $12b + 3$ to find how many pencils he has if he buys 4 boxes of pencils.

Math Online macmillanmh.com

• Chapter Test

CHAPTER 5 Chapter Test

Evaluate each expression if $x = 7$ and $y = 5$.

1. $x + 7$

2. $12 - y$

3. $21 \div x$

4. $12y$

5. $x + y$

6. xy

7. Della is typing survey questions. She can type 5 words in 10 seconds. At this rate, how many words can she type in 5 minutes? Use the *solve a simpler problem* strategy.

8. Kara made 48 brownies for the bake sale. She packs b brownies in each box. If $b = 12$, write an expression to find how many boxes Kara needs.

Write an expression for each phrase.

9. 4 less than z

10. h times 5

11. **MULTIPLE CHOICE** Mr. Diaz is buying gumballs. The table shows the price of different amounts of gumballs.

Number of Gumballs	20	40	60	80	100
Price	\$2	\$4	\$6	\$8	\$10

What is the relationship between the number of gumballs and the price?

A The price is two times the number of gumballs.

B The price is ten times the number of gumballs.

C The price is half the number of gumballs.

D The number of gumballs is ten times the price.

12. Martin's fish tank has 5 less goldfish than Bill's fish tank. Copy and complete the function table.

Input (x)	$x - 5$	Output
6	■	■
12	■	■
18	■	■

13. Shante can make 4 keychains in an hour. Find a function rule. Then make a function table to find how many keychains Shante can make in 2, 3, and 4 hours. How many keychains can she make in 5 hours?

Find the value of each expression.

14. $5 \times 6 + 2 \times 3$

15. $26 + 7 \times 2$

16. $(4 + z) - 13$ if $z = 28$

17. **MULTIPLE CHOICE** A room has 3 rows of desks. Each row has 8 desks. In addition, there are 4 desks at the back of the room. Which expression could be used to find how many desks there are in all?

F $(8 \times 3) + (8 \times 4)$

G $(3 + 8) + 4$

H $(3 \times 8) + (3 \times 4)$

J $(3 \times 8) + 4$

18. WRITING IN MATH Write an expression whose value is 5 and contains at least two operations.

CHAPTER 5

Test Practice

Cumulative, Chapters 1–5

Math Online macmillanmh.com

• Test Practice

PART 1 Multiple Choice

Read each question. Then fill in the correct answer on the answer sheet provided by your teacher or on a sheet of paper.

1. Mrs. Grey bought 5 boxes of fruit snacks. Each box contains 12 packages of fruit snacks. In addition, she had 4 packages of fruit snacks at home. Which expression could be used to find the total number of fruit snack packages Mrs. Grey has?

A $5 \times 12 + 12 \times 4$

B $4 \times 12 + 5$

C $5 \times 4 + 12$

D $5 \times 12 + 4$

2. Marita is 6 years old. Pablo is 2 years older than Marita. Alita is twice as old as Pablo. Which expression could be used to find Alita's age?

F $2 + (6 \times 2)$

G $2 \times (6 + 2)$

H $6 + (2 \times 2)$

J $6 \times (2 + 2)$

3. The gym teacher bought 8 dodge balls for $32. If each dodge ball costs the same amount, what it the cost of one dodge ball?

A $4

B $6

C $8

D $128

4. There are 120 players at a soccer camp. The players are divided into groups of 15 for warm-ups. How many groups of players are there?

F 6

G 8

H 10

J 15

5. Maryanne has $10 to spend on art supplies. All prices include tax. Which of the following combinations does she NOT have enough money to buy?

Item	Price
Pencils	$4.79
Paper	$5.38
Paintbrush	$2.35
Markers	$4.21
Clay	$2.15

A paper, paintbrush, and clay

B pencils, paintbrush, and clay

C pencils, markers, and clay

D paper and markers

6. The manager of a park keeps track of the number of people who visit the park each day. The table shows part of these records. Which is *not* a way to find the number of people who visit the park each day?

Day	Visitors
3	300
4	400
5	500
6	600
7	700

F Divide 500 by 5.

G Divide 700 by 7.

H Subtract 500 from 600.

J Subtract 500 from 700.

Preparing for Standardized Tests

For test-taking strategies and practice, see pages R42–R55.

7. What is the missing value in the table?

Input	2	4	6	8	10
Ouput	0	■	4	6	8

A 2
B 3
C 5
D 7

8. Tyler tells Nate to choose a number, add 5, and multiply by 8. The answer is 64. Which number did Nate choose?

F 6
G 4
H 3
J 2

9. A store parking lot has 30 rows with 15 spaces in each row. In addition, there are 8 spaces near the front of the store. Which expression can be used to find the total number of parking spaces?

A $(30 \times 15) + 8$
B $(30 \times 15) + (30 \times 8)$
C $(30 + 8) \times 15$
D $(30 + 8) \times (8 + 15)$

10. Evaluate the expression $12x$ if $x = 7$.

F 19
G 52
H 74
J 84

PART 2 Short Response

Record your answers on the answer sheet provided by your teacher or on a sheet of paper.

11. Thomas purchased 60 baseball cards this week and 15 baseball cards last week. If there are 5 cards in each pack, write a number sentence to show how many packs of cards he bought.

12. Name two decimals that are larger than 3.1, but smaller than 3.2.

PART 3 Extended Response

Record your answers on the answer sheet provided by your teacher or on a sheet of paper.

13. Explain the steps to find the value of the expression $150 - (10 \times 7)$. What is the value of the expression?

14. Conner is 8 years younger than Eva. Create a function table to show Eva's age when Conner is 8, 12, and 16 years old. Explain how you can use the function table to find Eva's age when Conner is 30 years old.

NEED EXTRA HELP?														
If You Missed Question...	1	2	3	4	5	6	7	8	9	10	11	12	13	14
Go to Lesson...	5-7	5-7	4-3	4-4	2-6	5-5	5-6	5-5	5-7	5-3	5-7	1-6	5-7	5-6

Chapter 6 Use Equations and Function Tables

BIG Idea What is an equation?

The number sentence $7x = 35$ is an example of an equation. An **equation** is a number sentence that contains an equals sign (=), showing that two expressions are equal.

Example Each day for 7 days, a sea otter ate the same number of pounds of food. The otter ate 35 pounds of food in all.

$$7x = 35$$

7 days → 7

x pounds each day → x

35 pounds in all → 35

What will I learn in this chapter?

- Write and solve equations for problem situations.
- Name and locate points on a coordinate grid.
- Use function tables.
- Solve problems by using the *make a table* strategy.

Key Vocabulary

equation

solve

coordinate grid

ordered pair

graph

Math Online Student Study Tools at macmillanmh.com

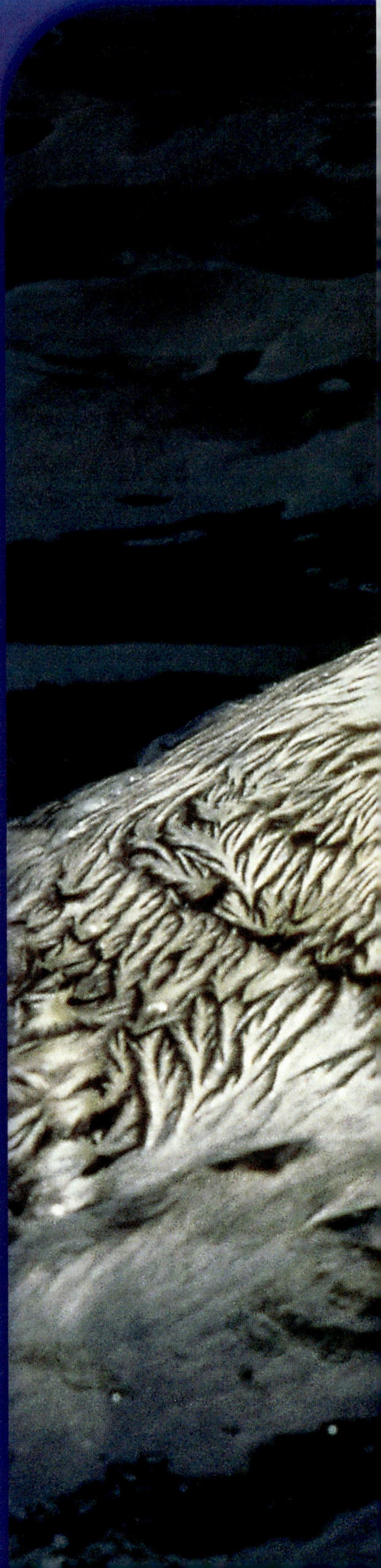

FOLDABLES® **Study Organizer**

Make this Foldable to help you organize information about equations and functions. Begin with a sheet of $8\frac{1}{2}''$ by $11''$ paper.

1. **Fold** the short sides toward the middle.

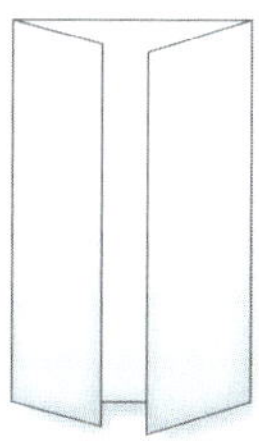

2. **Fold** the top to the bottom.

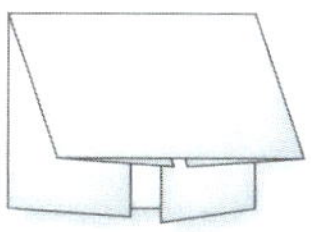

3. **Open.** Cut along the second fold to make four tabs.

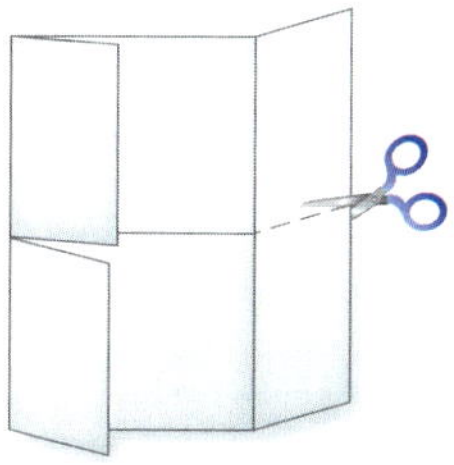

4. **Label** each of the tabs as shown.

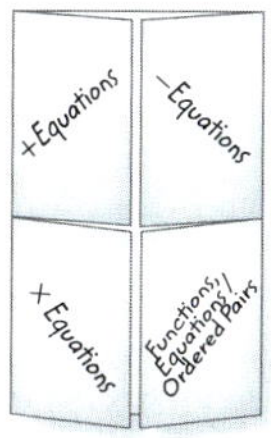

ARE YOU READY for Chapter 6?

You have two ways to check prerequisite skills for this chapter.

Option 2

Math Online Take the Chapter Readiness Quiz at macmillanmh.com.

Option 1

Complete the Quick Check below.

QUICK Check

Find the missing number in each fact family. (Prior Grade)

1. $5 + ■ = 7$

2. $■ + 6 = 9$

3. $■ + 3 = 15$

4. $9 + ■ = 15$

5. $6 + ■ = 14$

6. $■ + 5 = 7$

7. $4 \times ■ = 28$

8. $■ \times 9 = 81$

9. $■ \times 3 = 30$

10. $7 \times ■ = 56$

11. $8 \times ■ = 48$

12. $■ \times 5 = 30$

13. Anderson added 4 more seashells to his collection. Now he has 16 seashells. How many seashells did he have at first?

Write an expression for each situation. (Lessons 5-1 and 5-3)

14. 7 plus *d*

15. 5 less than *t*

16. the sum of 14 and *s*

17. the product of *y* and 7

18. 6 less than *x*

19. *f* increased by 2

20. the product of 8 and *n*

21. the sum of 3 and *z*

22. Hugo has \$4 less than Eloy. If *m* stands for the amount of money Eloy has, write an expression to show how much money Hugo has. If *m* is \$16, how much money does Hugo have?

Explore

Algebra Activity for 6-1
Model Addition Equations

MAIN IDEA

I will write and solve addition equations using models.

You Will Need

algebra mat
cups
counters

New Vocabulary

equation
solve
solution

An **equation** is a number sentence that contains an equals sign, (=), showing that two expressions are equal. To **solve** an equation means to find the value of the variable so the sentence is true. You can use diagrams like cups and counters to represent problem situations.

ACTIVITY

Jack had some goldfish, and then he bought 2 more. Now he has 8 goldfish. Solve the equation $x + 2 = 8$ to find how many goldfish Jack had at first.

Step 1 **Model the equation.**

Place the cup on the left side to show x and two counters to show 2. Place 8 counters on the right side to show 8.

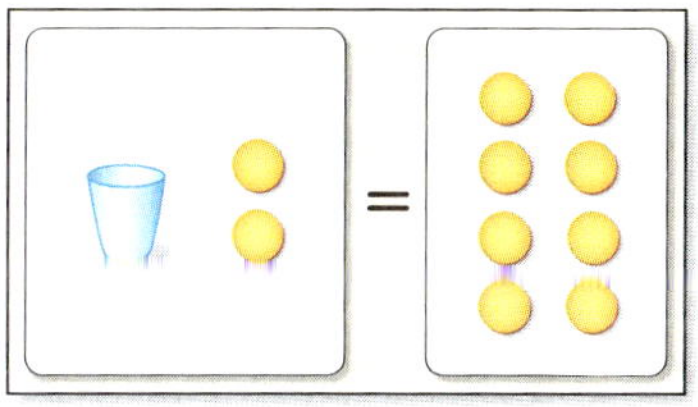

$x + 2 \quad = \quad 8$

Step 2 **Solve the equation.**

THINK How many counters need to be in the cup so there is an equal number of counters on each side of the mat?

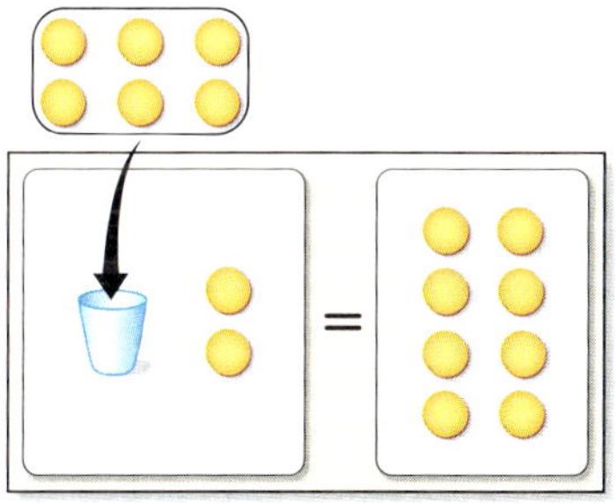

$x = 6$

When you found the number of counters in the cup, you found the solution of the equation. A **solution** is the value of the variable that makes the sentence true.

So, $x = 6$.

Jack had 6 goldfish at first.

Hands-On Activity

Think About It

1. Refer to the opening Activity. What does x represent?
2. How did you know that 6 was the solution to the equation?
3. Describe how you would model $x + 4 = 6$.
4. What is the value of x so that $x + 4 = 6$ is true?

CHECK What You Know

Write an equation for each model. Then solve.

5. 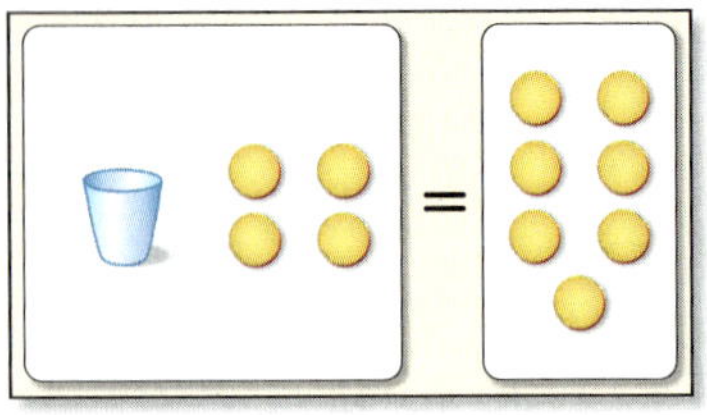

6. 

Solve each equation using cups, counters, and an algebra mat.

7. Calvin added 3 model cars to his collection. Now he has 12 model cars. Use the equation $x + 3 = 12$ to find how many model cars he started with.

8. Mrs. Jones planted 5 rose bushes. Then she planted some more rose bushes. If she planted a total of 11 rose bushes, how many more rose bushes did Mrs. Jones plant? Use the equation $5 + x = 11$.

Write an equation for each problem situation. Then solve each equation using cups, counters, and an algebra mat.

9. Melissa had x dollars in her wallet. Her mother gave her $5 more. Melissa now has $20. How much money did Melissa start with?

10. A bakery sold a total of 14 pies on Wednesday and Thursday. If the bakery sold 6 pies on Wednesday, how many pies did the bakery sell on Thursday?

11. **WRITING IN MATH** Explain why it does not matter on which side of the equals sign the variable is located.

6-1 Addition and Subtraction Equations

MAIN IDEA

I will write and solve addition and subtraction equations.

New Vocabulary

defining the variable

Math Online

macmillanmh.com

- Extra Examples
- Personal Tutor
- Self-Check Quiz

GET READY to Learn

On Monday and Tuesday, Audrey walked a total of 7 blocks. If she walked 3 blocks on Tuesday, how many blocks did she walk on Monday?

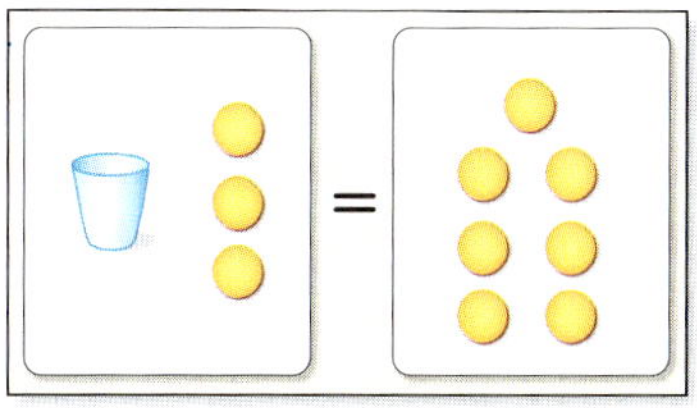

$x + 3 = 7$

The equation $x + 3 = 7$ represents this situation. You can solve this equation using mental math.

EXAMPLE Addition Equations

1 Solve $x + 3 = 7$.

$x + 3 = 7$

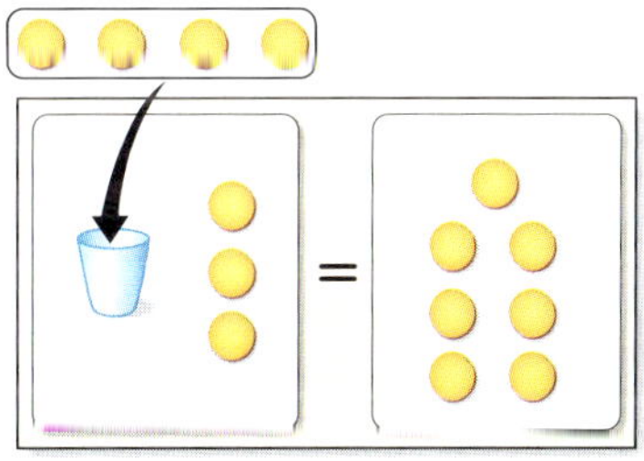

$4 + 3 = 7$ You know that 4 plus 3 is equal to 7.

So, $x = 4$. Audrey walked 4 blocks on Monday.

You can also find solutions using mental math.

EXAMPLE Subtraction Equations

2 Solve $y - 6 = 8$.

$y - 6 = 8$ Write the equation.

THINK What number minus 6 is equal to 8?

$14 - 6 = 8$ You know that 14 minus 6 is 8.

So, $y = 14$. The solution is 14.

Choosing a variable to represent an unknown value is called **defining the variable**.

Real-World EXAMPLE — Write and Solve Equations

3 **FOOD At the school festival, the total cost of a hamburger and a soft drink is \$5. If the drink costs \$2, what is the cost of the hamburger?**

> **Remember**
> You can use the first letter of the word you are defining as a variable. For example: *h* is for the cost of the hamburger.

Words	Cost of hamburger plus cost of a drink is \$5.
Variable	Let h represent the cost of a hamburger.
Equation	$h + 2 = 5$

$h + 2 = 5$ Write the equation.

THINK What number plus 2 is equal to 5?

$3 + 2 = 5$ Replace h with 3 to make the equation true.

So, $h = 3$. The cost of the hamburger is \$3.

To check your solution, replace the variable with 3. Does this make the right side of the equation equal to the left side?

Check $h + 2 = 5$ Write the equation.

$3 + 2 \stackrel{?}{=} 5$ Replace h with 3.

$5 = 5$ ✓ Simplify. The solution is correct.

CHECK What You Know

Solve each equation. Check your solution. See Examples 1, 2 (p. 237)

1. $h + 4 = 8$ **2.** $2 + x = 9$ **3.** $p - 7 = 1$ **4.** $r - 5 = 4$

5. $3 + g = 10$ **6.** $b + 6 = 12$ **7.** $x - 9 = 8$ **8.** $s - 8 = 7$

9. Monya led her softball team in stolen bases. At Wednesday's game, she stole 2 bases giving her a total of 8 stolen bases. Write and solve an equation to find how many stolen bases Monya had before Wednesday's game. See Example 3 (p. 238)

10. Talk About It Explain what it means to solve an equation.

Practice and Problem Solving

EXTRA PRACTICE See page R15.

Solve each equation. Check your solution. See Examples 1, 2 (p. 237)

11. $x + 1 = 5$ **12.** $3 + a = 6$ **13.** $y - 8 = 1$ **14.** $n - 4 = 2$

15. $b - 13 = 1$ **16.** $t - 12 = 4$ **17.** $z + 2 = 11$ **18.** $5 + k = 13$

19. $d - 2 = 18$ **20.** $7 + x = 16$ **21.** $c + 13 = 19$ **22.** $m - 5 = 15$

Write an equation and then solve. Check your solution. See Example 3 (p. 238)

23. A box contained some snack bars. Tyrese ate 4 snack bars. Now there are 8 snack bars left. How many snack bars were there at the beginning?

24. Leroy bought 2 comic books. Now he has 11 comic books in all. How many comic books did Leroy start with?

25. Mrs. Oxley had some glue sticks. She used 8 glue sticks on an art project. Now she has 6 glue sticks left. How many glue sticks did she have at first?

26. In one season, the girl's volleyball team won 16 games. If they played a total of 30 games that season, how many games did they lose?

27. Eugene's team scored 34 points in a game. He scored 12 of the points. How many points did the rest of the team score?

H.O.T. Problems

28. REASONING If $x + 3 = 5$ and $5 = y + 2$, then is it true that $x + 3 = y + 2$? Explain.

29. FIND THE ERROR Daniel and Juliana each solved the equation $a - 5 = 10$. Who is correct? Explain your answer.

Daniel
$a = 5$

Juliana
$a = 15$

30. WRITING IN MATH Explain why the equation $n + 7 = 15$ has the same solution as $15 - n = 7$.

Extend

Algebra Activity for 6-1

Inequalities

MAIN IDEA

Use models to represent and solve simple addition and subtraction inequalities.

Recall that an *inequality* is a mathematical sentence stating that two quantities are *not* equal. The expression $x < 2$ means that the value of x *is less than* 2. To solve an inequality, find the values of the variables so the inequality is true.

ACTIVITIES Solve Inequalities

1 Solve $x < 2$ using a model.

The scale below contains a cup and two positive counters. Note that the left side weighs *less than* the right side. Copy and complete the table.

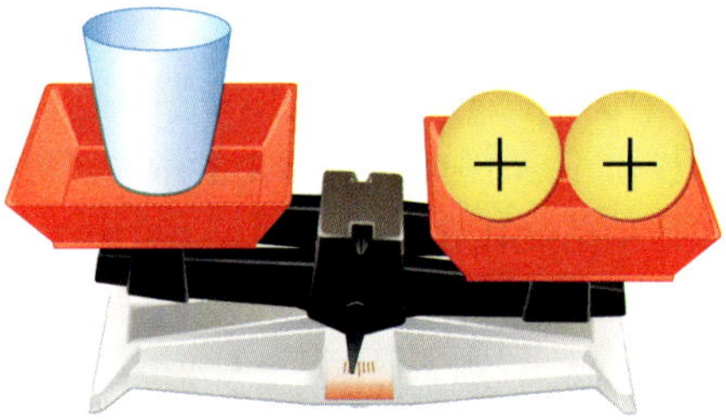

$x < 2$

x	Is $x < 2$?	True or False
0	$0 \overset{?}{<} 2$	true
1	$1 \overset{?}{<} 2$	
2	$2 \overset{?}{<} 2$	
3	$3 \overset{?}{<} 2$	
4	$4 \overset{?}{<} 2$	

So, the solution of $x < 2$ is 0 or 1.

2 Solve $x + 1 < 3$ using a model.

Copy and complete the table.

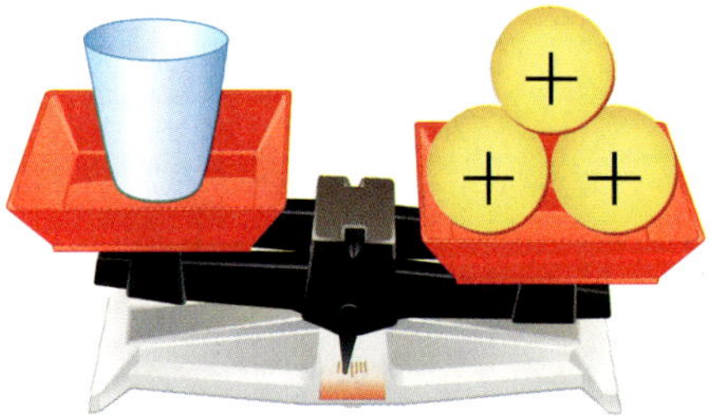

$x + 1 < 3$

x	Is $x+1 < 3$?	True or False
0	$0+1 \overset{?}{<} 3$	true
1	$1+1 \overset{?}{<} 3$	
2	$2+1 \overset{?}{<} 3$	
3	$3+1 \overset{?}{<} 3$	
4	$4+1 \overset{?}{<} 3$	

The solution does not change when one counter is added to each side. Possible values of x include 0 and 1 but do not include 2, 3, or 4. So, the solution of the inequality $x + 1 < 3$ is any number less than 2. This is written $x < 2$.

You can also solve inequalities using models or tables.

Hands-On Activity

Remember

Check your solution by substituting any number greater than 3. For example, substitute 6.

$6 + 2 > 5 = 8 > 5.$

This is true.

ACTIVITY Solve an Addition Inequality

3 Solve $x + 2 > 5$ using mental math.

The model shows one cup and two positive counters on the left side and five positive counters on the right side.

Remove two positive counters from each side of the scale. There are three positive counters remaining on the right scale.

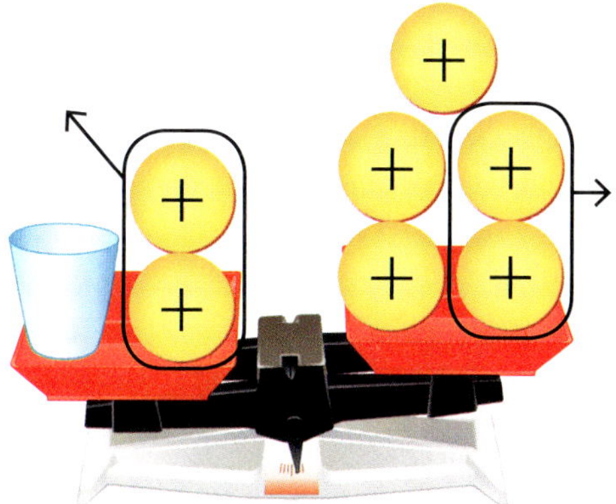

The solution is any number greater than 3. So, $x > 3$.

ACTIVITY Solve a Subtraction Inequality

4 Solve $x - 3 < 7$ using a table.

Check possible values of x. The table suggests that the solution is any number less than 10.

So, $x < 10$.

x	Is $x - 3 \overset{?}{<} 7$?	True or False
8	$8 - 3 \overset{?}{<} 7$	true
9	$9 - 3 \overset{?}{<} 7$	
10	$10 - 3 \overset{?}{<} 7$	
11	$11 - 3 \overset{?}{<} 7$	

Check the solution with other values of x.

CHECK What You Know

Solve each inequality by using a model or mental math.

1. $x + 1 < 6$ **2.** $x - 3 > 1$ **3.** $x + 4 > 8$

4. Write two different inequalities, one involving addition and one involving subtraction, both with the solution $x < 3$.

5. WRITING IN MATH Explain how you could solve the inequality $x + 13 < 18$.

Explore

Algebra Activity for 6-2

Model Multiplication Equations

MAIN IDEA

I will write and solve multiplication equations.

You Will Need

algebra mat
cups
counters

Math Online

macmillanmh.com

- Concepts in Motion

You can use cups and counters to represent problem situations involving multiplication.

ACTIVITY

Two friends split the cost of a pizza evenly. If the cost of the pizza is \$8, how much did each friend spend? Solve the equation $2x = 8$ to find how much each friend spent.

Step 1 **Model the equation.**

Place 2 cups on the left side to show $2x$. Place 8 counters on the right side to show 8.

$2x = 8$

Step 2 **Solve the equation.**

THINK How many counters need to be in each cup so there is an equal number of counters in each cup and an equal number of counters on each side of the mat?

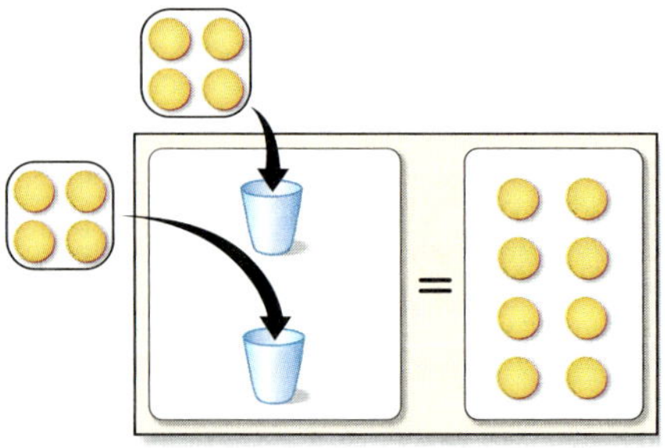

$x = 4$

So, $x = 4$. Each friend paid \$4.

Check $2x = 8$ Write the equation.

$2 \cdot 4 \stackrel{?}{=} 8$ Replace x with 4.

$8 = 8$ ✓ Simplify.

Think About It

1. Describe how you would model $8x = 16$ using cups, counters, and an algebra mat.

2. What is the value of x so that $8x = 16$ is true?

3. Refer to Exercise 2. How would you check your solution?

CHECK What You Know

Write an equation for each model and then solve. Check your solution.

4. 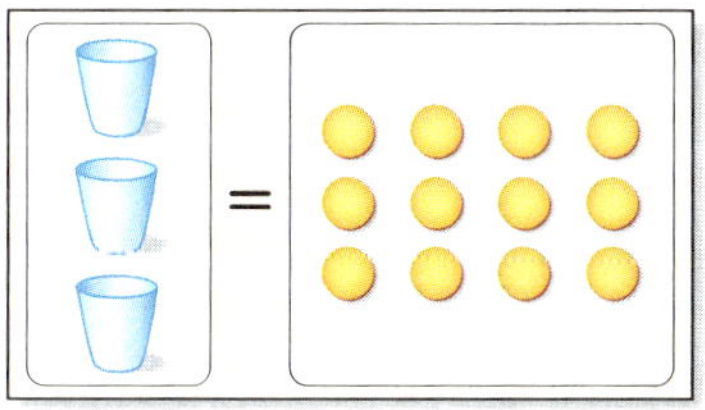

5. 

Solve each equation using cups, counters, and an algebra mat. Check your solution.

6. Jerome bought 3 paperback books from the local bookstore. The total cost of the books was $15. Each book costs the same amount. Use the equation $3c = 15$ to find the cost of one book.

7. Josephina bought 2 boxes of pencils. Each box contained the same amount of pencils. If she had a total of 14 pencils, how many were in one box? Use the equation $2n = 14$.

Write an equation and then solve each equation using cups, counters, and an algebra mat. Check your solution.

8. Mr. Tyznik wants to walk 16 miles in the next 4 days. If he walks the same amount each day, how many miles will he walk each day?

9. Matt and two friends bought tickets to a hockey game. The total cost of the tickets was $24. If each ticket costs the same amount, what was the cost of one ticket?

10. **WRITING IN MATH** Explain why you place an equal number of counters in each cup when you solve a multiplication equation using cups, counters, and an algebra mat.

6-2 Multiplication Equations

MAIN IDEA

I will write and solve multiplication equations.

Math Online

macmillanmh.com

- Extra Examples
- Personal Tutor
- Self-Check Quiz

GET READY to Learn

Carlota bought 2 tickets to the school play for a total of $6. If each ticket costs the same amount, what is the cost of one ticket to the school play?

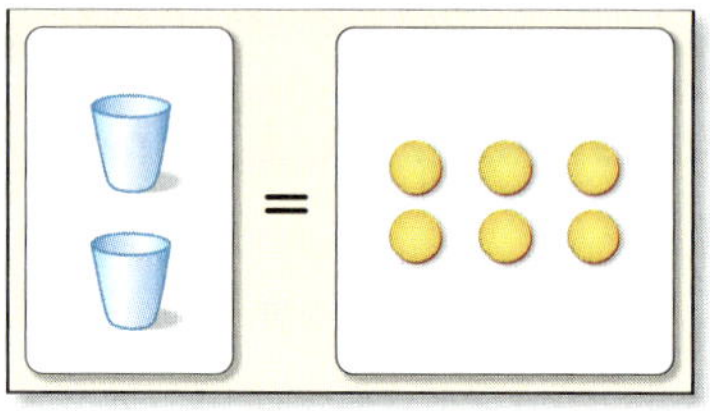

$2t = 6$

To find the cost of one ticket to the school play, solve the multiplication equation $2t = 6$.

EXAMPLES Multiplication Equations

1 Solve $2t = 6$.

$2t = 6$

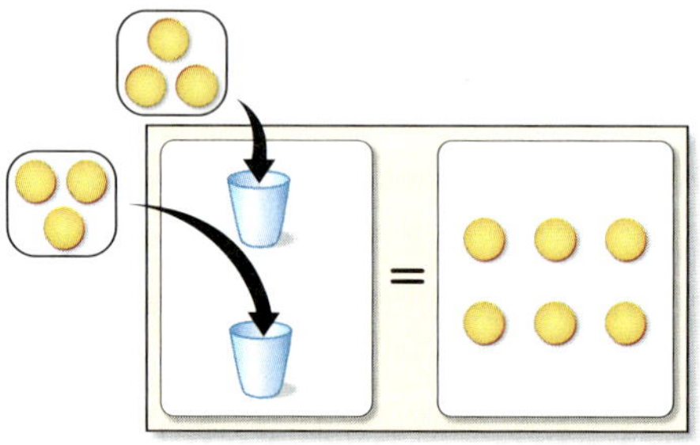

$2 \times 3 = 6$ You know that 2 times 3 is equal to 6.

So, $t = 3$. One ticket to the play costs $3.

2 Solve $20 = 5z$.

$20 = 5z$ Write the equation.

THINK What number times 5 is equal to 20?

$20 = 5 \times 4$ You know that 20 is equal to 5 times 4.

So, $z = 4$.

Real-World EXAMPLE — Write and Solve Equations

3 **FOOTBALL** **In one game, the Carolina Panthers scored 3 times as many points as their opponent. If the Panthers scored 21 points, how many points did their opponent score?**

Words	21 equals 3 times opponent's points.
Variable	Let p represent the opponent's points.
Equation	$21 = 3p$

> **Remember**
> The word *times* means *multiplication*.

$21 = 3p$ Write the equation.

THINK 21 is equal to 3 times what number?

$3 \times 7 = 21$ Replace p with 7.

So, $p = 7$.

The opponent scored 7 points.

To check your solution, replace the variable with 7.

Check: $3p = 21$ Write the equation.

$3 \times 7 \stackrel{?}{=} 21$ Replace p with 7.

$21 = 21$ ✓ Simplify. The solution is correct.

CHECK What You Know

Solve each equation. Check your solution. See Examples 1, 2 (p. 244)

1. $2b = 8$ **2.** $18 = 3t$ **3.** $21 = 7x$ **4.** $6x = 24$

Write an equation and then solve. Check your solution. See Example 3 (p. 244)

5. Irena is twice as old as Yoko. If Irena is 20, how old is Yoko?

6. Five friends earned $30 for doing yard work. If the friends split the money evenly, how much money would each friend receive?

7. To paint a classroom, you need 3 gallons of paint. If you have 27 gallons of paint, how many classrooms can you paint if they are all identical?

8. Talk About It Describe how to find the solution of $8x = 72$.

Practice and Problem Solving

EXTRA PRACTICE See page R15.

Solve each equation. Check your solution. See Examples 1, 2 (p. 244)

9. $4b = 16$ **10.** $18 = 2d$ **11.** $30 = 5h$ **12.** $3z = 27$

13. $7r = 49$ **14.** $8c = 64$ **15.** $55 = 5p$ **16.** $60 = 10g$

17. $33 = 11t$ **18.** $3y = 45$ **19.** $12s = 84$ **20.** $72 = 6x$

Write an equation and then solve. Check your solution. See Example 3 (p. 245)

21. Seven fifth-grade students spent a total of 35 hours cleaning a park. Each student spent an equal amount of time. Find how many hours each student spent cleaning the park.

22. A Girl Scout troop collected 54 cans for the food drive. There are 6 members in the troop, and each member collected the same number of cans. How many cans did each member collect?

For Exercises 23 and 24, use the graphic that shows the number of bottles of water for two different sized boxes.

Box Size	Number of Bottles of Water
Small	32
Large	64

23. Bert and 3 friends evenly divide a large box of water bottles. How many bottles of water does each friend receive?

24. A coach buys one small and one large box of bottled water. She divides the bottles evenly among 8 players. How many bottles will each player receive?

Data File

The Philadelphia Zoo is America's oldest zoo. It opened in 1874. Today, the zoo features over 1,600 animals from around the world.

Philadelphia Zoo Admission Prices

Ticket	Price ($)
Adult	9
Senior (62+)	7
Youth (3–11)	7

Write an equation. Then solve. Check your solution.

25. Mrs. Hawkins bought 1 adult ticket and y youth tickets. If the total cost of the tickets was $37, how many youth tickets did Mrs. Hawkins buy?

26. The Heppner family bought 2 adult tickets, 4 youth tickets, and s senior tickets. The cost of all the tickets was $67. How many senior tickets did the family buy?

H.O.T. Problems

27. OPEN ENDED Write two different multiplication equations that each have a solution of 9.

28. WHICH ONE DOESN'T BELONG? Identify which equation doesn't belong with the other three. Explain your reasoning.

$35 - n = 28$	$21 = 3n$	$n + 49 = 56$	$7n = 63$

29. WRITING IN ►MATH Write a real-world problem that can be solved using a multiplication equation.

TEST Practice

30. Felipa is twice as old as Juan. If Felipa is 12 years old, which equation could be used to find a, Juan's age? (Lesson 6-2)

A $12 \times 2 = a$

B $12a = 2$

C $2 \times a = 12$

D $a + 2 = 12$

31. A full basket contained 27 apples. There are 9 apples left in the basket now. Which equation could be used to find how many apples were taken from the basket? (Lesson 6-1)

F $27 + x = 9$

G $27 - x = 9$

H $27 + 9 = x$

J $x - 9 = 21$

Spiral Review

Algebra **Solve each equation. Check your solution.** (Lesson 6-1)

32. $z + 4 = 20$ **33.** $y - 7 = 9$ **34.** $7 + q = 11$ **35.** $w - 5 = 8$

Algebra **Evaluate each expression.** (Lesson 5-7)

36. $10 - 2 \times 4$ **37.** $10 \times 3 - 2 \times 5$ **38.** $3 + 6 \times 9$

39. The soccer team has $150 to spend on new soccer balls. Soccer balls cost $29 each. How many soccer balls can the team buy? Tell how you interpret the remainder. (Lesson 4-6)

40. The sum of two numbers is 28. Their product is 195. What are the two numbers? Use the *guess and check* strategy to solve. (Lesson 1-8)

Write each fraction as a decimal. (Lesson 1-4)

41. $\frac{7}{10}$ **42.** $\frac{90}{100}$ **43.** $\frac{53}{100}$ **44.** $\frac{23}{1{,}000}$

6-3 Problem-Solving Strategy

MAIN IDEA I will solve problems by making a table.

Julio is saving money to buy a new camping tent. Each week he doubles the amount he saved the previous week. If he saves $1 the first week, how much money will Julio save in 7 weeks?

Understand

What facts do you know?

- Each week he doubles the amount he saved the previous week.
- The first week he saved $1.

What do you need to find?

- How much money he will have saved in 7 weeks.

Plan

You can make a table to solve the problem.

Solve

Draw a table with two rows as shown. In the first row, list each week. Then complete the table by doubling the amount he saved the previous week.

Week	1	2	3	4	5	6	7
Amount Saved	$1	$2	$4	$8	$16	$32	$64

×2 ×2 ×2 ×2 ×2 ×2

Next, add the amount of money he saved each week.
$1 + $2 + $4 + $8 + $16 + $32 + $64 = $127
So, Julio will save $127 in 7 weeks.

Check

Look back. Check to see if the amount saved doubled each week. Use estimation to check for reasonableness. Round each two-digit number to the nearest $10.

$1 + $2 + $4 + $8 + $20 + $30 + $60 = $125 ✓

ANALYZE the Strategy

Refer to the problem on the previous page.

1. Explain why you multiplied each week's savings by 2 to solve the problem.

2. Explain why making a table made this problem easier to solve.

3. Find the amount of money Julio will save in 9 weeks.

4. Suppose Julio tripled the amount of money he saved each week. How many weeks will it take him to save $120?

PRACTICE the Strategy

EXTRA PRACTICE See page R16.

Solve. Use the *make a table* strategy.

5. Algebra Betsy is saving to buy a new sound system. She saves $1 the first week, $3 the second week, $9 the third week, and so on. How much money will she save in 5 weeks?

6. Kendall is planning to buy the laptop shown below. Each month she doubles the amount she saved the previous month. If she saves $20 the first month, in how many months will Kendall have enough money to buy the laptop?

7. Measurement Muna is 3 years old. Her mother is 35 years old. How old will Muna be when her mother is exactly five times as old as she is?

8. Devon bought packages of pencils for $3 each. Each package of pencils contains 12 pencils. If he spent $15 on pencils, how many pencils did he buy?

9. Measurement A recipe for cupcakes calls for 3 cups of flour for every 2 cups of sugar. How many cups of sugar are needed for 18 cups of flour?

10. Mrs. Piant's yearly salary is $42,000 and increases $2,000 per year. Mr. Piant's yearly salary is $37,000 and increases $3,000 per year. In how many years will Mr. and Mrs. Piant make the same salary?

11. Geometry Mr. Ortega is making a model of a staircase he is going to build. Use the picture below to find how many blocks Mr. Ortega will need if the staircase has 12 steps.

12. WRITING IN MATH Write a real-world problem that you can solve using the *make a table* strategy. Explain why making a table is the best strategy to use when solving your problem.

6-4 Geometry: Ordered Pairs

MAIN IDEA

I will name points on a coordinate grid.

New Vocabulary

coordinate grid
origin
ordered pair
***x*-coordinate**
***y*-coordinate**

Math Online

macmillanmh.com

- Extra Examples
- Personal Tutor
- Self-Check Quiz

GET READY to Learn

The map at the right shows Amy's neighborhood. When she walks home from school, she walks right to 3 and up to 5. How could she walk from school to the library? How could she walk to the park?

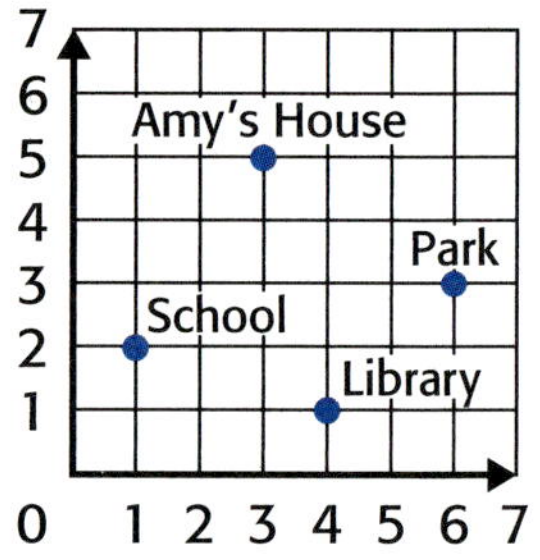

In mathematics, points are located on a coordinate grid.

A **coordinate grid** is formed when two number lines intersect. One number line has numbers along the horizontal axis (across) and the other has numbers along the vertical axis (up). The point where the two axes meet is the **origin**.

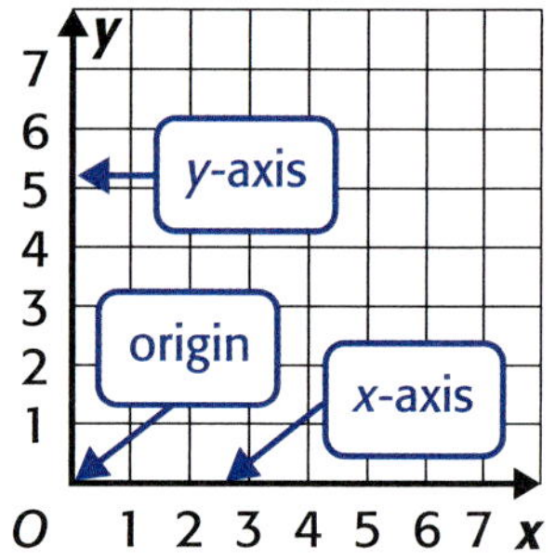

An **ordered pair** is a pair of numbers that is used to name a point on the coordinate grid.

The first number is the ***x*-coordinate** and corresponds to a number on the *x*-axis.

(3, 2)

The second number is the ***y*-coordinate** and corresponds to a number on the *y*-axis.

EXAMPLE Name Points Using Ordered Pairs

1 Name the ordered pair for point *A*.

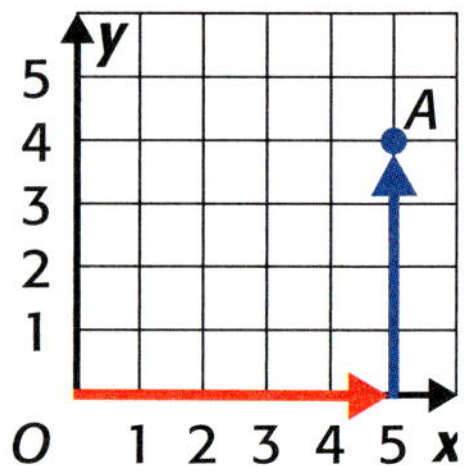

Step 1 Start at the origin (0, 0). Move right along the *x*-axis until you are under point *A*. The *x*-coordinate of the ordered pair is 5.

Step 2 Move up until you reach point *A*. The *y*-coordinate is 4.

So, point *A* is named by the ordered pair (5, 4).

EXAMPLE Name Points Using Ordered Pairs

2 **Name the point for the ordered pair (2, 3).**

Vocabulary Link
Origin
Everyday Use the beginning

Step 1 Start at the origin (0, 0). Move right along the *x*-axis until you reach 2, the *x*-coordinate.

Step 2 Move up until you reach 3, the *y*-coordinate.

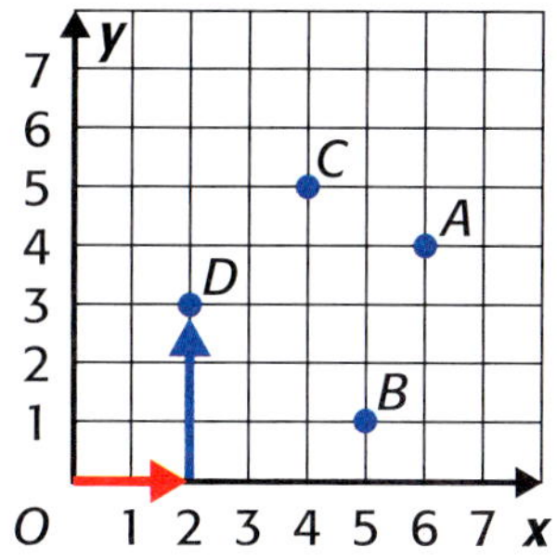

So, point *D* is named by (2, 3).

Real-World EXAMPLE

3 **SCIENCE An archaeologist recorded the location of objects she found at a dig. Use the coordinate grid to name the location of the necklace.**

Step 1 Start at the origin (0, 0). Move right along the *x*-axis until you are under the necklace. The *x*-coordinate is 3.

Step 2 Move up until you reach the necklace. The *y* coordinate is 5.

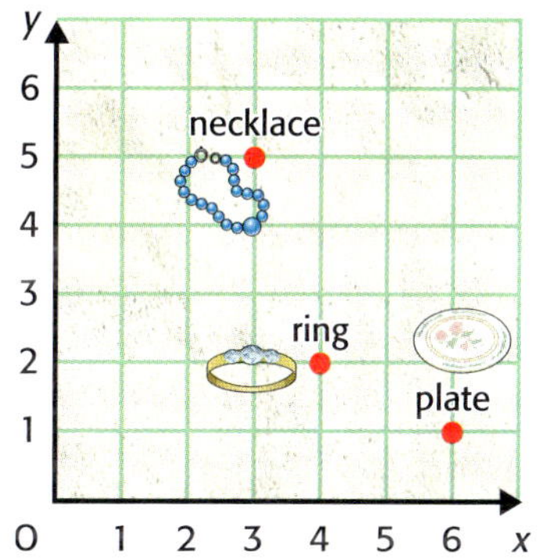

So, the necklace is located at (3, 5).

CHECK What You Know

Locate and name the ordered pair. See Example 1 (p. 250)

1. *A* **2.** *C* **3.** *D*

Locate and name the point. See Example 2 (p. 251)

4. (4, 3) **5.** (1, 6) **6.** (5, 2)

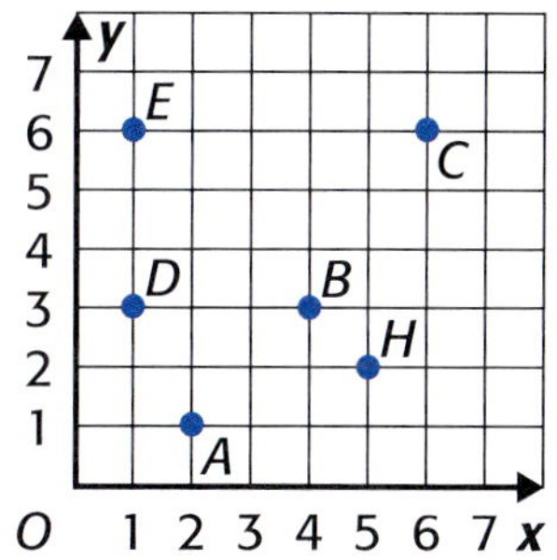

7. Refer to Example 3. Write the ordered pair that names the ring on the grid.

8. Talk About It Are the points at (3, 8) and (8, 3) in the same location? Explain your reasoning.

Practice and Problem Solving

EXTRA PRACTICE
See page R16.

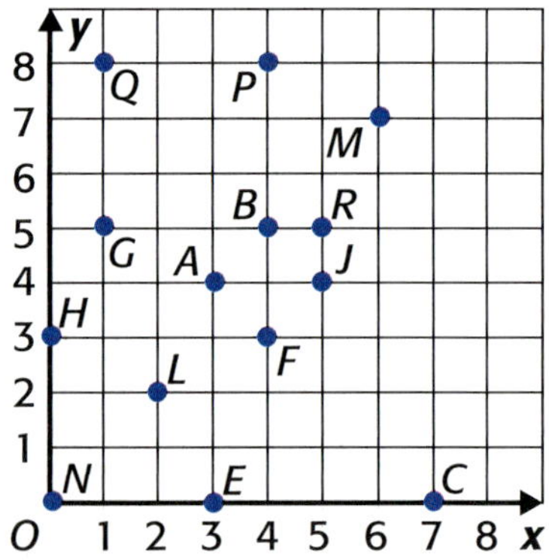

Locate and name the ordered pair. See Example 1 (p. 250)

9. *A* **10.** *J* **11.** *Q*

12. *R* **13.** *E* **14.** *N*

Locate and name the point. See Example 2 (p. 251)

15. (2, 2) **16.** (1, 5) **17.** (4, 8)

18. (0, 3) **19.** (6, 7) **20.** (7, 0)

For Exercises 21–24, use the map of the playground at the right. See Example 3 (p. 251)

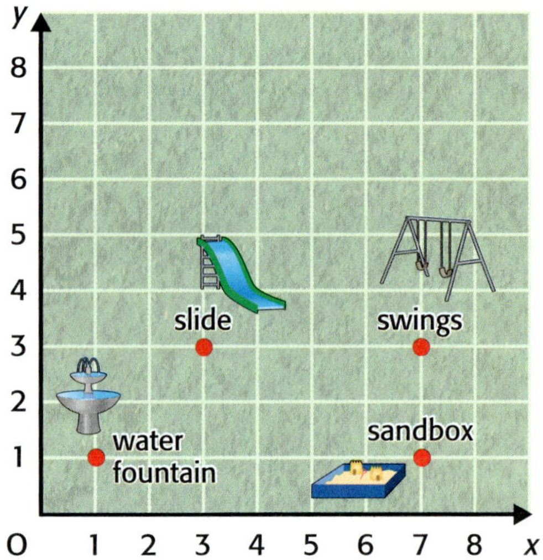

21. What is located at (7, 3)?

22. Write the ordered pair for the sandbox.

23. Suppose the *x*-coordinate of the water fountain was moved to the right 1 unit. What would be the new ordered pair of the water fountain?

24. If the *y*-coordinate of the slide was moved up 2 units, what would be the ordered pair of the slide?

25. Cam identified a point that was 4 units above the origin and 8 units to the right of the origin. What was the ordered pair?

26. Suppose point (6, 5) was moved 3 units to the left and moved 2 units down. Write the new ordered pair.

H.O.T. Problems

27. OPEN ENDED Create a map of a zoo using a coordinate grid. Locate five animals on the map. Include the ordered pairs for the location of the five animals.

28. CHALLENGE Name the ordered pair whose *x*-coordinate and *y*-coordinate are each located on an axis.

29. CHALLENGE Give the coordinates of the point located halfway between (3, 3) and (3, 4).

30. WRITING IN MATH Describe the steps to locate point (7, 4).

CHAPTER 6

Mid-Chapter Check

Lessons 6-1 through 6-4

Solve each equation. Check your solution. (Lesson 6-1)

1. $s + 16 = 30$ **2.** $m - 6 = 51$

3. A bike path is a certain number of miles. Jody has already biked 16 miles and has 9 miles left to bike. How many miles is the bike trail? (Lesson 6-1)

4. MULTIPLE CHOICE Carrie's softball team scored 9 runs. Carrie scored 5 of the runs. Which equation could you use to find how many runs the rest of the team scored? (Lesson 6-1)

A $9 = x + 5$ **C** $9 - x = 14$

B $14 = x + 5$ **D** $x - 5 = 14$

Solve each equation. Check your solution. (Lesson 6-2)

5. $72 = 8y$ **6.** $5g = 40$

7. Measurement It took Mrs. Cook 4 hours to make 60 bookmarks. She made an equal amount of bookmarks each hour. Write and solve an equation to find how many bookmarks she made each hour. (Lesson 6-2)

8. MULTIPLE CHOICE Xavier wants to buy a new video game that costs \$45. He saves \$5 each week. Which equation shows how many weeks it will take until he has enough money for the game? (Lesson 6-2)

F $w = 45 \times 5$ **H** $w = 9 \times 5$

G $45 = w \div 5$ **J** $5w = 45$

9. A gardener is planting flowers in rows. The first row has 28 flowers. Each additional row has 6 fewer flowers than the previous row. If there is a total of 5 rows in the garden, how many flowers will the gardener have to plant? Solve. Use the *make a table* strategy. (Lesson 6-3)

10. Measurement Rakim is training for a bike marathon. He bikes 7.25 miles on the first day. He plans to bike 2.5 more miles each day than he did on the previous day. How many total miles will Rakim have biked after 5 days? Solve. Use the *make a table* strategy. (Lesson 6-3)

For Exercises 11–16, use the map shown.

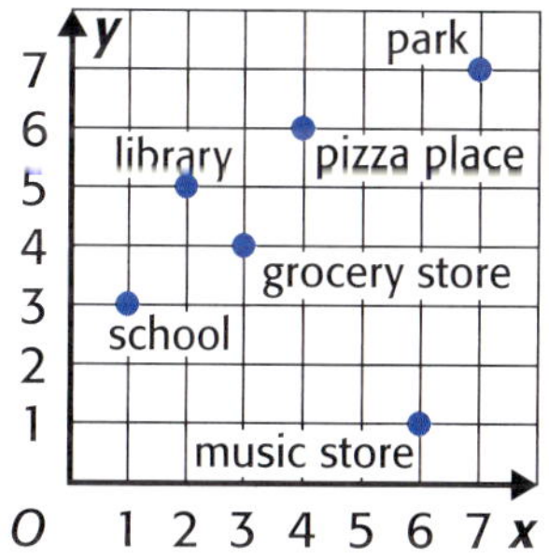

Locate and name the ordered pair for each place on the map. (Lesson 6-4)

11. park **12.** school **13.** library

Locate and name the place on the map for each ordered pair. (Lesson 6-4)

14. (4, 6) **15.** (6, 1) **16.** (3, 4)

17. WRITING IN MATH Explain what it means to *define a variable.*

6-5

Algebra and Geometry: Graph Functions

MAIN IDEA

I will graph points on a coordinate grid.

New Vocabulary

graph

Math Online

macmillanmh.com

- Extra Examples
- Personal Tutor
- Self-Check Quiz

GET READY to Learn

Bailey was making a treasure map for a game he was playing with his friend. From the starting point, he wanted his treasure to be buried 3 places to the right and up 6 units. He marked the spot with an X.

To **graph** a point in mathematics means to place a dot at the point named by an ordered pair.

EXAMPLES Graphing Ordered Pairs

1 **Graph and label point *X*(3, 6) on the coordinate grid.**

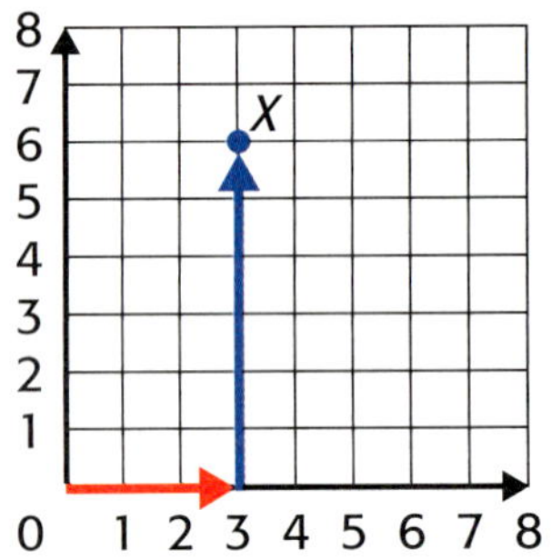

Step 1 Start at the origin (0, 0).

Step 2 Move 3 units to the right on the *x*-axis.

Step 3 Then move up 6 units to locate the point.

Step 4 Draw a dot and label the point *X*.

2 **Graph and label point *M*(2, 4) on the coordinate grid.**

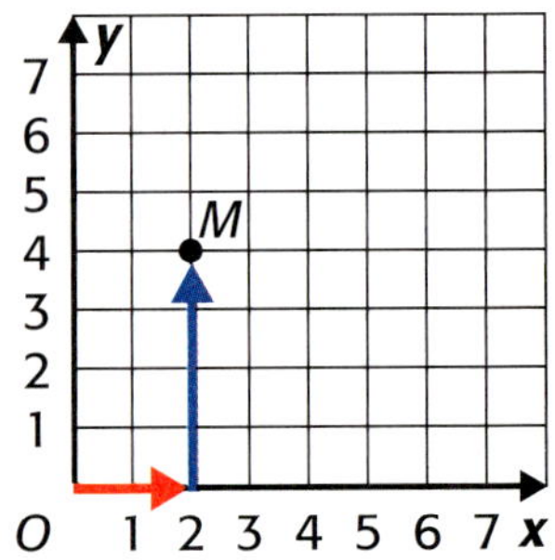

Step 1 Start at the origin (0, 0).

Step 2 Move 2 units to the right on the *x*-axis.

Step 3 Then move up 4 units to locate the point.

Step 4 Draw a dot and label the point *M*.

Review Vocabulary

input the value you put into a function (Lesson 5–6)

output the resulting value of a function (Lesson 5–6)

In Chapter 5, you learned about functions. The input and output values from a function table can be written as ordered pairs.

Real-World EXAMPLE Graphing Functions

3 **BASKETBALL For every shot a basketball player makes from outside the 3-point line, the player scores 3 points. Given the function rule 3*n*, find the total number of points for 1, 2, 3, and 4 of these shots. Make a function table and then graph the ordered pairs.**

The function rule is 3*n*. Multiply the number of 3-point shots made by 3 to find the total points.

3-Point Shots Made (*n*)	Total Points (3*n*)	Ordered Pairs
1	3	(1, 3)
2	6	(2, 6)
3	9	(3, 9)
4	12	(4, 12)

Now graph the ordered pairs.

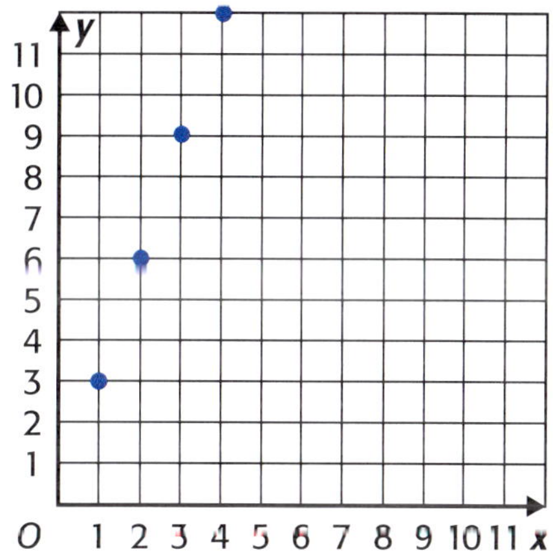

CHECK What You Know

Graph and label each point on a coordinate grid.
See Examples 1, 2 (p. 254)

1. $Z(2, 2)$ **2.** $D(4, 0)$ **3.** $Y(5, 6)$

4. $W(7, 6)$ **5.** $C(0, 4)$ **6.** $B(3, 7)$

7. A bag of birdseed weighs 5 pounds. Given the function rule 5*b*, find the total weight for 0, 1, 2, and 3 bags of birdseed. Make a function table and then graph the ordered pairs. See Example 3 (p. 255)

8. Talk About It Explain how you would graph the point $S(10, 7)$.

Practice and Problem Solving

EXTRA PRACTICE See page R16.

Graph and label each point on a coordinate grid. See Examples 1, 2 (p. 254)

9. $J(1, 1)$ **10.** $K(7, 0)$ **11.** $L(2, 5)$ **12.** $M(0, 6)$

13. $N(4, 1)$ **14.** $P(8, 2)$ **15.** $Q(3, 4)$ **16.** $R(6, 3)$

For Exercises 17–20, make a function table and then graph the ordered pairs on a coordinate grid. See Example 3 (p. 255)

17. Miss Henderson has a coupon for \$2 off any item at Sport Inc. Find the new cost of items if they originally cost \$4, \$6, \$8, and \$10, given the function rule $c - 2$.

18. **Measurement** Amado's book bag weighs 1 pound. Each book that he puts in his book bag weighs 3 pounds. Given the function rule $3n + 1$, find the total weight of the book bag if Amado has 0, 1, 2, and 3 books in his book bag.

19. Reiko works in an electronics store. Every day he earns a flat rate of \$10 plus \$5 per hour. Given the function rule $5h + 10$, find how much Reiko would earn if he worked 2, 3, 4, and 5 hours.

20. Gaspar and Kendra agreed to split the cost of a DVD. Given the function rule $\frac{c}{2}$, find how much each friend would pay if the DVD cost \$8, \$10, \$12, and \$14.

Real-World PROBLEM SOLVING

Science The growth rate of a baby blue whale is one of the fastest in the animal kingdom. The table shows the age in months and length in feet of a baby blue whale.

21. Use the table to write the ordered pairs.

22. Graph the ordered pairs.

23. What is the length of a baby blue whale when it is 2 months old?

24. How old is a baby blue whale that is 37 feet long?

25. Estimate the length of a baby blue whale that is $2\frac{1}{2}$ months old.

Growth of Blue Whale

Age (months)	Length (ft)
0	23
1	27
2	31
3	35
4	39

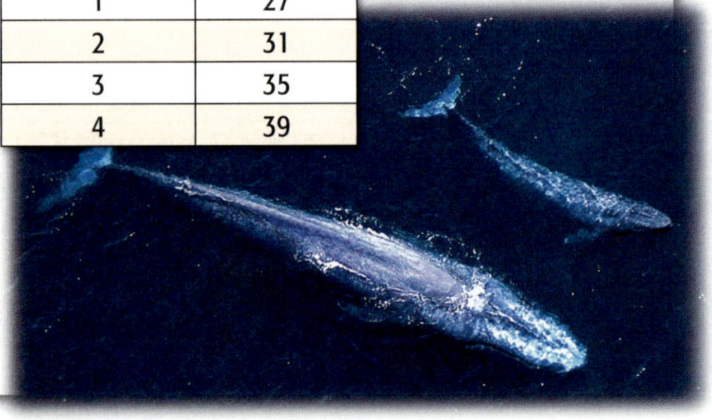

H.O.T. Problems

26. **OPEN ENDED** Write an ordered pair for a point that would be graphed on the *y*-axis.

27. **WRITING IN MATH** Write a real-world problem about a situation that would be represented by the function $15x$.

TEST Practice

28. Ashley made the grid below to show the location of objects in her backyard. Which ordered pair represents the point on the grid labeled tree house? (Lesson 6–4)

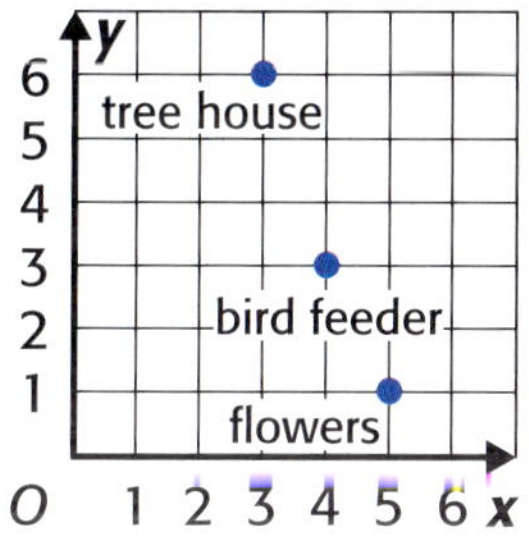

A (5, 1)

B (6, 3)

C (3, 6)

D (4, 3)

29. Which of the following points is located at (4, 0)? (Lesson 6–5)

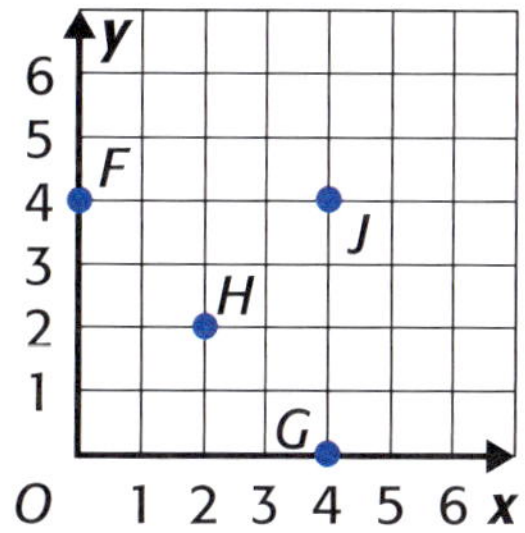

F Point *F*

G Point *G*

H Point *H*

J Point *J*

Spiral Review

Algebra **Solve each equation. Check your solution.** (Lesson 6–4)

30. $3y = 33$

31. $9h = 45$

32. $75 = 5g$

33. $84 = 7w$

34. Jacque is 12 years old. His father is 44 years old. How old will Jacque be when his father is exactly three times as old as he is? Use the *make a table* strategy. (Lesson 6–3)

35. At a bus stop, 7 students got on the bus so that there were a total of 23 students on the bus. Write and solve an equation to find how many students were already on the bus. (Lesson 6–1)

Algebra **Evaluate each expression if $x = 7$ and $y = 8$.** (Lessons 5-1 and 5–3)

36. $6x$

37. $y + x$

38. $y \div 4$

39. $y - x$

Problem Solving in Geography

What's Your Latitude?

Think of your street address. You use this to describe the location of your home. How can you describe this location on Earth? Latitude and longitude are used to describe the position of any place on Earth. They are measured in degrees (°), minutes (′), and seconds (″). For example, San Diego is located at 32°42′55″N, 117°9′23″W. That is 32 degrees, 42 minutes, and 55 seconds north of the equator and 117 degrees, 9 minutes, and 23 seconds west of the Prime Meridian.

Is there a relationship between latitude and temperature? Complete the exercises on page 259 to help you decide.

Did You Know?

The longest latitude line is the equator, whose latitude is zero degrees.

City	Latitude (nearest degree)	High Temperature, 2004 (°F)	Low Temperature, 2004 (°F)
Atlanta, GA	34	95	16
Honolulu, HI	21	92	60
Nashville, TN	36	94	11
New York, NY	41	91	1
San Diego, CA	33	96	41
Seattle, WA	48	96	20

Source: *The World Almanac*

Real-World Math

Use the table above to solve each problem.

1. Which cities had the highest temperature? the lowest temperature?

2. The higher the latitude number is, the farther the location is from the equator. Which city is closest to the equator? Which city is farthest from the equator?

3. Make a table listing the cities from least to greatest latitude. Include latitude and low temperatures. What do you notice about the relationship between latitudes and low temperatures?

4. Write the latitude and the low temperature of each city as an ordered pair. Graph and label the ordered pairs on a coordinate grid.

5. Find the difference between the high and low temperatures for each city. Write the latitude and the temperature difference of each city as an ordered pair.

6. Refer to Exercise 5. Graph and label the ordered pairs on a coordinate grid. Let the x-axis represent the latitude and the y-axis represent the temperature difference. Then describe the graph.

6-6 Functions and Equations

MAIN IDEA

I will find a function rule.

Math Online

macmillanmh.com

- Extra Examples
- Personal Tutor
- Self-Check Quiz

GET READY to Learn

Brady's neighbor pays him \$8 each week to walk her dog. How much money will Brady earn in 5 weeks?

There are two ways to describe the relationship between the number of weeks and money earned.

Real-World EXAMPLE — Describe Relationships

1 **DOGS The amount Brady earns depends on the number of weeks he works. The amount earned is 8 times the number of weeks.**

One Way: Use a function table.

Number of Weeks	1	2	3	4	5
Amount Earned (\$)	8	16	24	32	40

Another Way: Use an equation to represent the function.

Step 1 Define each variable.

Let w = number of weeks

Let m = amount of money earned

Step 2 Write the equation.

$m = 8w$

Step 3 Replace the variable.

$m = 8w$ Write the equation.

$m = 8 \times 5$ Replace w with 5.

$m = 40$ Multiply 8 by 5.

So, Brady earns \$40 in 5 weeks.

Real-World EXAMPLE — Use Functions and Equations

2 **TRANSPORTATION** **The cost of a taxi ride is $3 plus $2 for each mile. What is the total cost of a 7-mile taxi ride?**

Remember

See Lesson 5-6 for a review of function tables.

One Way: **Use a function table.**

Number of Miles	1	2	3	4	5	6	7
Cost ($)	5	7	9	11	13	15	17

Another Way: **Write an equation.**

Step 1 Define each variable.

Let m = number of miles.

Let c = the cost.

Step 2 Write the equation.

$c = 3 + 2m$ The cost equals $3 plus $2 for each mile.

Step 3 Replace the variable.

$c = 3 + 2m$ Write the equation.

$c = 3 + (2 \times 7)$ Replace m with 7.

$c = 3 + 14$ Multiply 2 by 7.

$c = 17$ Add 3 and 14.

So, the cost of a 7-mile taxi ride is $17.

CHECK What You Know

Describe each relationship using a function table or equation.

See Examples 1, 2 (pp. 260–261)

1. The cost c of shipping mittens purchased online is $2 plus $6 for each of p pair of mittens. What is the total cost c of buying 5 pairs?

2. Tia collected $10 for a walk-a-thon and $5 from each of n friends. What is the total amount of donations d she collected from 4 friends?

3. Renee saves $3 a week from her babysitting job. If she saves for 7 weeks, how much money will Renee have?

4. **Talk About It** What information can you find in a function table that is not found in the equation?

Practice and Problem Solving

EXTRA PRACTICE See page R17.

Describe each relationship using a function table or equation. See Example 1, 2 (pp. 260–261)

5. Corrine bought 5 tickets to the skating rink. If she had a coupon for $4 off a total purchase, how much did the tickets cost?

6. Dwayne receives 3 points for every game he wins. He already has 9 points. How many points will he have after winning 7 more games?

7. **Measurement** The width of a garden is equal to one-half of the length. If the length of the garden is 12 feet, what is the width?

8. A three-point shot in basketball counts 3 points. A regular field goal is 2 points. Lina scored 19 points. If she made three 3-point shots, how many 2-point shots did she make?

9. **Measurement** The distance around a sandbox is 4 times the length of one of the sides. If the length of one side is 7 feet, what is the distance around the sandbox?

10. Each box contains 12 mini muffins. Three friends decide to split 4 boxes of mini muffins evenly. How many mini muffins will each friend receive?

11. To rent a bus for a field trip, it costs $50 plus $3 for each person. If a total of 16 students and 4 parents went on the field trip, how much did it cost to rent the bus?

H.O.T. Problems

12. **FIND THE ERROR** Trevor and Toshi translated the phrase *10 is 5 less than a number* into an equation. Who is correct? Explain.

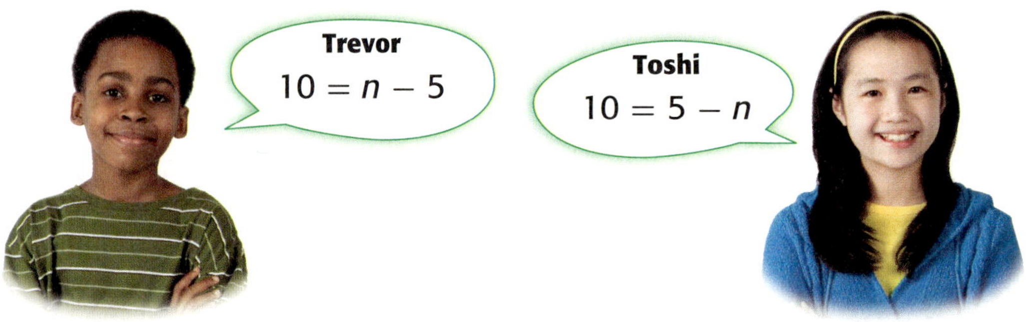

13. **WRITING IN MATH** Which method is easier to use to solve a real-world problem, a function rule or an equation? Explain.

Game Time

Where's My Line?

Naming and Locating Points

Get Ready!

Players: 2 players

You will need: graph paper

Get Set!

- Players should sit so they cannot see each others' papers.
- Each player draws a coordinate grid on graph paper and labels each axis from 0 to 10.
- Then each player draws a straight line on the graph paper. The line should pass through at least three points that are named by ordered pairs of whole numbers.
- Players choose who will go first.

Go!

- Each player begins by naming the ordered pair of one point on his or her line.
- Player 1 calls out a whole number ordered pair. Player 2 calls out "Hit!" if the ordered pair describes a point on his or her line, or "Miss!" if it does not.
- If Player 1 scores a hit, he or she takes another turn. If not, Player 2 takes a turn
- The first player to locate two additional points on the other player's line wins.

Extend

Technology Activity for 6-6

Functions and Equations

You can use Math Tool Chest™ to graph functions.

MAIN IDEA

I will use technology to create function tables and graph ordered pairs.

ACTIVITY Graphing Ordered Pairs

1 **Hector saves \$2 each week. This can be described by $y = 2x$, where x represents the number of weeks and y respresents the amount Hector has saved. Graph this equation.**

First create a function table for $y = 2x$.

Number of weeks (x)	Amount saved (y)
1	2
2	4
3	6
4	8
5	10

Now use the graph feature from the Math Tool Chest™.

- Click on level two. Then choose Coordinate Graph.
- Click on Setup. Choose the graph that goes from 0 to 10 on both axes. Click on Show Ordered Pairs and Connect Points.
- Place the points in your function table on the coordinate grid by clicking the appropriate location.

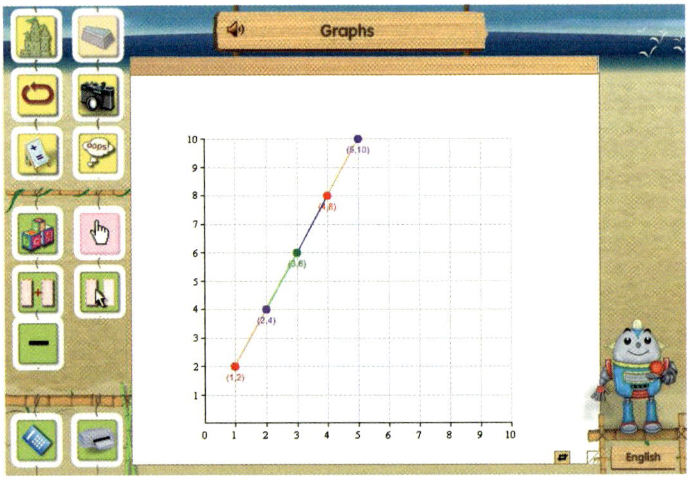

Think About It

1. Suppose Hector decides to save either \$3 each week or \$4 each week. Write an equation for each situation and graph them. How are the graphs the same? How are they different?

ACTIVITY

Tech Link

2 **Misty has already saved \$3 and wants to save \$2 more each week. This can be described by $y = 2x + 3$, where x is the number of weeks and y is the amount that Misty has saved. Graph this equation.**

First create a function table for $y = 2x + 3$. Then use the graph feature from the Math Tool Chest™.

- Click on Setup. Choose a coordinate grid that goes from 0 to 20.
- Place points on the coordinate grid by clicking the appropriate location.

Number of weeks (x)	Amount saved (y)
1	5
2	7
3	9
4	11
5	13
6	15
7	17

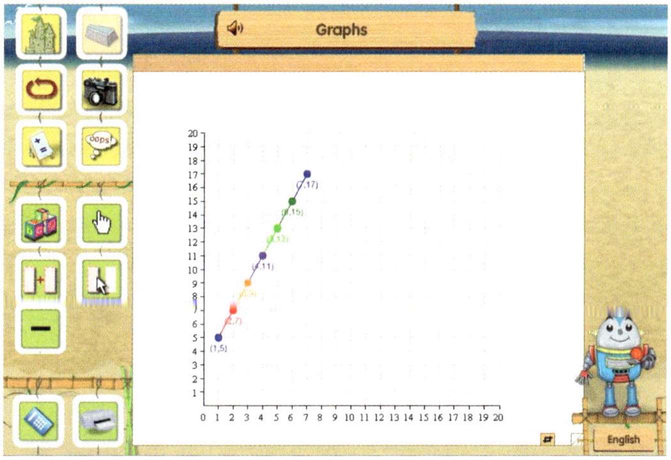

Think About It

2. Suppose Misty had already saved \$10 but still wants to save \$2 more each week. How does this graph differ from the one in Activity 2?

CHECK What You Know

Write an equation, and create a function table. Then graph.

3. Kimbra is paying her sister \$3 a day. If she has already paid \$12, how many days until she will have paid her sister \$21?

4. Josh has to write an 18 page report. He has 6 pages written. He writes 2 more pages per day. How many days will it take him to finish?

5. **WRITING IN ▸MATH** Write your own real-world problem and create a function table. Graph the equation.

6-7 Problem-Solving Investigation

MAIN IDEA I will choose the best strategy to solve a problem.

P.S.I. TEAM +

VICTOR: I bought a small pizza at Pizza Palace. The price of an extra large pizza is equal to 2 times the price of a small pizza plus $3. If the price of an extra large pizza is $17, how much did I pay for the small pizza?

YOUR MISSION: Find the price of a small pizza.

Understand	You know that the price of an extra large pizza is $17. It is equal to 2 times the price of a small pizza plus $3. You need to find the price of a small pizza.
Plan	To solve this problem, you can work backward.
Solve	Since subtraction is the opposite of addition, take the price of the extra large pizza and subtract $3. $\$17 - \$3 = \$14$ Since division is the opposite of multiplication, divide $14 by 2. $\$14 \div 2 = \$7$ The cost of a small pizza is $7.
Check	Look back. Start with the price of a small pizza and multiply by 2. Then add $3. Since $(\$7 \times 2) + \$3 = \$17$, the answer is correct. ✓

Mixed Problem Solving

EXTRA PRACTICE See page R17.

Use any strategy shown below to solve each problem.

PROBLEM-SOLVING STRATEGIES
- Guess and check.
- Work backward.
- Draw a picture.
- Make a table.

1. At a bird sanctuary, Ricky counted 88 birds. Of the birds he counted, 16 were baby birds. If he counted an equal number of adult males and females, how many adult female birds did Ricky count?

2. Mrs. Vallez spent $19.90 on sand toys. How many of each type of sand toy below did Mrs. Vallez buy?

3. Sue has four DVDs and Terry has six DVDs. They put all their DVDs together and sold them for $10 for two. How much money will they earn if they sell all of their DVDs?

4. **Measurement** Jacinda is decorating cookies for a class party. She can decorate five cookies in ten minutes. At this rate, how many cookies can she decorate in an hour?

5. Pia, Evan, and Jonas each prefer a different type of music. They listen to rock, rap, and country. Pia does not like country. Evan does not like country or rap. Which type of music does each person like best?

6. **Algebra** If this pattern continues, how many blocks are in the bottom row of the fifth figure?

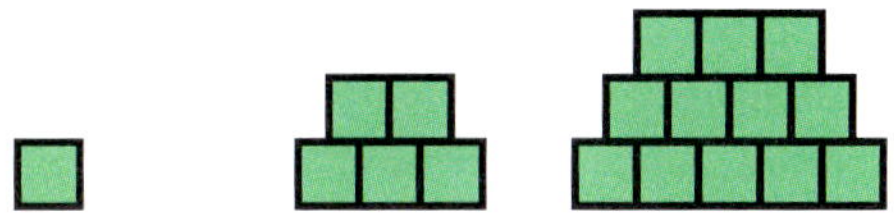

Figure 1 **Figure 2** **Figure 3**

7. The number of new health club members in May was half as many as the number of new members in June. In July, there were 18 more new members than in June. If there were 76 new members in July, how many new members were there altogether during the three months?

8. **Measurement** To make four apple pies you need about two pounds of apples. How many pounds of apples will you need to make 20 apple pies?

9. Mi-Ling sets up tables for visitors at the art museum. Each square table can seat two people on each side. How many people can be seated if 8 square tables are pushed together in a row?

10. **WRITING IN MATH** A number multiplied by itself is 441. What is the number? Is the *guess and check* strategy a reasonable strategy to find the number? Explain.

Math Online macmillanmh.com
- STUDY TO GO
- Vocabulary Review

Chapter 6 Study Guide and Review

FOLDABLES Study Organizer GET READY to Study

Be sure the following Key Vocabulary words and Big Ideas are written in your Foldable.

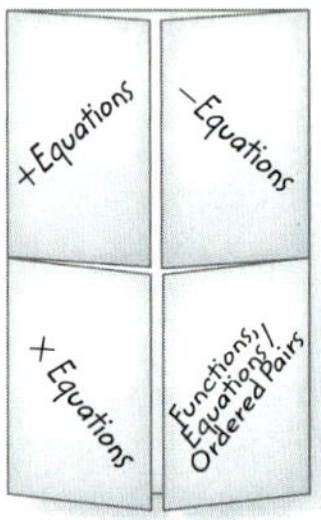

Key Concepts

Solving Equations (p. 235)

- An **equation** is a number sentence that contains an equals sign.
- Check your answer by replacing the variable with your answer to see whether it results in a true sentence.

Ordered Pairs (p. 250)

- A location on a coordinate grid can be described by using an ordered pair.
- An example of an **ordered pair** is (7, 4).

x-coordinate → (7, 4) ← *y*-coordinate

Graph Functions (p. 254)

- To **graph** a point means to place a dot at the point named by the ordered pair.

Functions and Equations (p. 260)

- An equation can represent a function.

Key Vocabulary

coordinate grid (p. 250)
equation (p. 235)
graph (p. 254)
ordered pair (p. 250)
solve (p. 235)

Vocabulary Check

Choose the correct term or number to complete each sentence.

1. An (expression, equation) is a number sentence that contains an equals sign.
2. Points on a coordinate grid are found using (ordered pairs, distance).
3. When you find the value of a variable, you (solve, check) an equation.
4. The ordered pair (0, 0) represents the (coordinate grid, origin).
5. The first number in an ordered pair is the (*x*-coordinate, *y*-coordinate).

Lesson-by-Lesson Review

6-1 Addition and Subtraction Equations (pp. 237–239)

Example 1

Solve $x + 4 = 10$.

$x + 4 = 10$ THINK What number plus 4 is 10?

$6 + 4 = 10$ You know that 6 + 4 is 10.

$x = 6$ The solution is 6.

Check $x + 4 = 10$

$6 + 4 \stackrel{?}{=} 10$

$10 = 10$ ✓

Example 2

Solve $m - 2 = 8$.

$m - 2 = 8$ THINK What number take away 2 is 8?

$10 - 2 = 8$ You know that 10 − 2 is 8.

$m = 10$ The solution is 10.

Solve each equation. Check your solution.

6. $p + 5 = 13$

7. $14 = x - 6$

8. $r - 5 = 3$

9. $22 = 11 + n$

Write an equation and then solve. Check your solution.

10. Jason gave 4 baseball cards to his brother. He now has 16 baseball cards left. How many baseball cards did Jason have at first?

11. Sonia is 10 years old. If the sum of Sonia's and Alberto's ages equals 21, how old is Alberto?

6-2 Multiplication Equations (pp. 241–247)

Example 3

Solve $4s = 32$.

$4s = 32$ THINK 4 times what number is 32?

$4 \times 8 = 32$ You know that 4 times 8 is 32.

$s = 8$ The solution is 8.

Check $4s = 32$

$4 \times 8 \stackrel{?}{=} 32$

$32 = 32$ ✓

Solve each equation. Check your solution.

12. $40 = 10c$

13. $2z = 16$

14. $3k = 27$

15. $56 = 7v$

Write an equation and then solve. Check your solution.

16. Twenty students in Mrs. Lytle's class raised $120 for charity. Each raised the same amount. How much money did each student raise?

17. You have 150 CDs to place in storage boxes. Each box holds 25 CDs. How many boxes will you need? Write and solve an equation.

CHAPTER 6 Study Guide and Review

6-3 Problem-Solving Strategy: Make a Table (pp. 248–249)

Example 4

One marching band formation calls for 9 band members in the front row. Each row in the formation has 3 more band members than the row in front of it. If there are 5 rows, how many band members are there?

Use the *make a table* strategy.

Row	1	2	3	4	5
Members	9	12	15	18	21

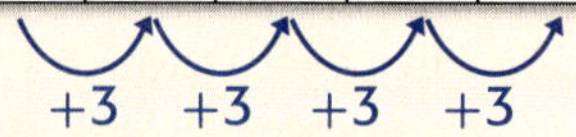

Add the number of band members in each row. $9 + 12 + 15 + 18 + 21 = 75$. So, there are 75 band members.

Solve. Use the *make a table* strategy.

18. Sabrina is saving money for a vacation. She plans to increase her savings by \$3.50 each week until she is saving \$20 each week. If she saves \$2.50 the first week, how many weeks will it take Sabrina until she is saving \$20 each week?

19. Jay is arranging rows of chairs in the gymnasium. In the last row, there are 54 chairs. Each row has 4 fewer chairs than the previous row. If there is a total of 5 rows, how many chairs will Jay have to arrange?

6-4 Geometry: Ordered Pairs (pp. 250–252)

Example 5

Locate and write the ordered pair that names point *T*.

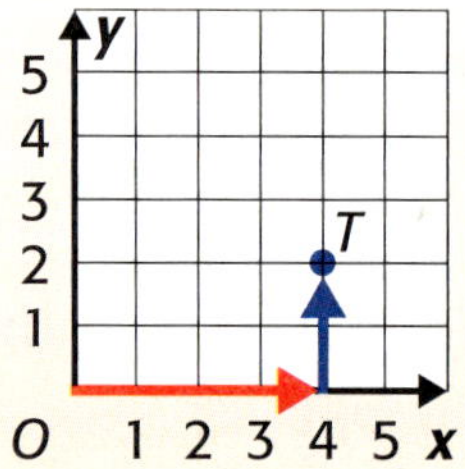

Step 1 Start at the origin (0, 0). Move right along the *x*-axis until you are under point *T*. The *x*-coordinate of the ordered pair is 4.

Step 2 Move up until you reach point *T*. The *y*-coordinate is 2.

So, the point *T* is located at (4, 2).

For Exercises 20–22, use the coordinate grid below.

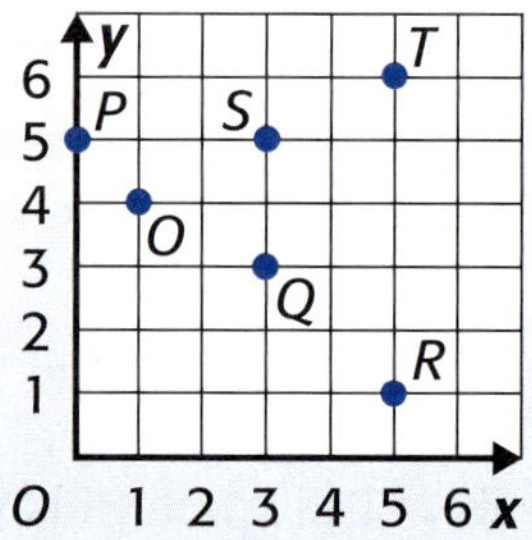

Locate and write the point for each ordered pair.

20. (3, 5) **21.** (5, 6) **22.** (1, 4)

23. Min identified a point that was 5 units above the origin and 2 units to the right of the origin. What was the ordered pair?

6-5 Algebra and Geometry: Graph Functions (pp. 254–257)

Example 6

Graphing Ordered Pairs

Graph and label point *Q*(2, 4).

Step 1 Start at the origin (0, 0).

Step 2 Move 2 units to the right on the *x*-axis.

Step 3 Then move up 4 units to locate the point.

Step 4 Draw a dot and label the point *Q*.

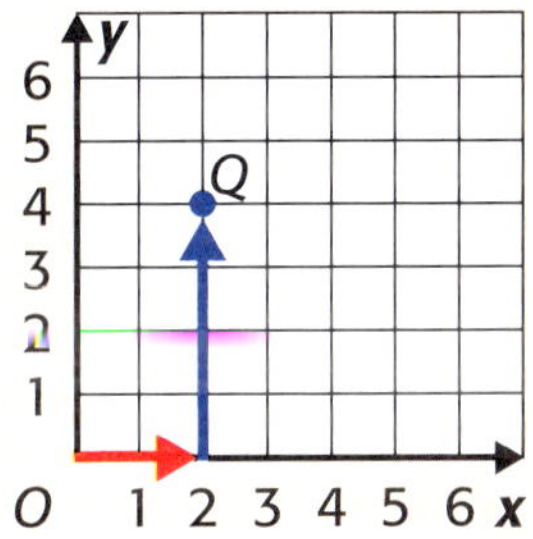

Graph and label each point on a coordinate grid.

24. *A*(4, 1) **25.** *B*(2, 1) **26.** *C*(6, 5)

27. *D*(4, 4) **28.** *E*(2, 7) **29.** *F*(2, 3)

30. A breath mint has 10 calories. Given the function rule 10*x*, find the total number of calories for 1, 2, 3, and 4 breath mints. Make a function table and then graph the ordered pairs.

31. **Measurement** There are 3 feet in one yard. Given the function rule $x \div 3$, find the total number of yards for 3, 6, 9, and 12 feet. Make a function table and then graph the ordered pairs.

6-6 Functions and Equations (pp. 260–262)

Example 7

The cost of renting a canoe is $5 per hour. Find how much it would cost to rent a canoe for 6 hours. Write an equation and then solve.

Step 1 Define each variable.
Let h = number of hours.
Let c = cost.

Step 2 Write the equation.
$c = 5h$

Step 3 Replace the variable.

$c = 5h$	Write the equation.
$c = 5 \times 6$	Replace h with 6.
$c = 30$	Multiply 5 by 6.

The cost is $30.

Describe each relationship using a function table or equation.

32. Yvonne bought a car wash pass that allows her to purchase any number of car washes in advance for $8 per wash. If she bought a pass for 6 washes, how much will it cost?

33. A dog groomer pays her assistant $10 a day plus $5 for each dog she washes. If the assistant washes 12 dogs in one day, how much money will she make?

6-7 Problem-Solving Investigation: Choose a Strategy (pp. 266–267)

Example 8

A gardener wants to enclose his garden that is 15 feet long and 12 feet wide, by placing fence posts every 3 feet including the corners of the garden. Find the number of fence posts the gardener will need to enclose the garden.

Understand
- The garden is 15 feet wide and 12 feet long.
- Set a fence post every 3 feet.
- Posts are to be set at the corners.

Plan Draw a picture.

Solve Draw a 15 by 12 rectangle. Starting from one corner, draw a dot. Continue drawing dots 3 units apart around the rectangle.

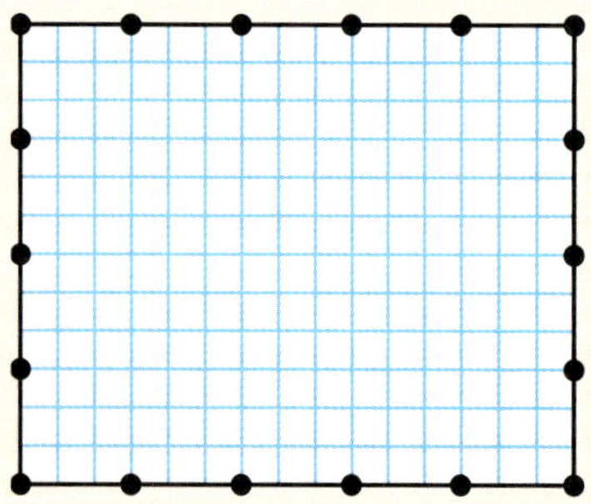

Count the number of dots. The gardener will need 18 posts.

Check Look back.

5 + 4 + 4 + 5 = 18.

The answer is correct. ✓

Use any strategy to solve each problem.

34. Marti can bike 4 miles in 24 minutes. At this rate, how many miles can Marti bike in 120 minutes?

35. The pictures below show the prices of hamburgers and cheeseburgers at a fast food restaurant. Pedro bought a total of 5 burgers for \$4.08. How many of each type of burger did he buy?

36. A soccer coach is enclosing a square practice soccer field. She places a cone every 8 feet including the corners. If each side of the field is 32 feet long, how many cones will the coach need?

37. Elan spent \$8.50 at the school store. He spent \$2.40 on paper, \$0.88 on pencils, and \$2.65 on markers. He spent the rest on a notebook. What was the price of the notebook?

38. Edrick took a bus to visit his grandparents. The bus left at 9:45 A.M. and traveled 325 miles at a rate of 65 miles per hour. What time did the bus arrive?

Chapter Test

Math Online macmillanmh.com
• Chapter Test

Solve each equation. Check your solution.

1. $x + 5 = 8$ **2.** $y - 2 = 11$

3. $6z = 42$ **4.** $9d = 36$

5. $t - 4 = 16$ **6.** $3n = 33$

7. MULTIPLE CHOICE The daily cost of renting a boat is \$50 plus \$6 for each hour. Which equation represents c, the cost in dollars for boating for h hours?

A $c = 50h + 6$ **C** $50 = 6h + c$

B $c = 6h + 50$ **D** $50 = 6c + h$

For Exercises 8–13, use the coordinate grid below.

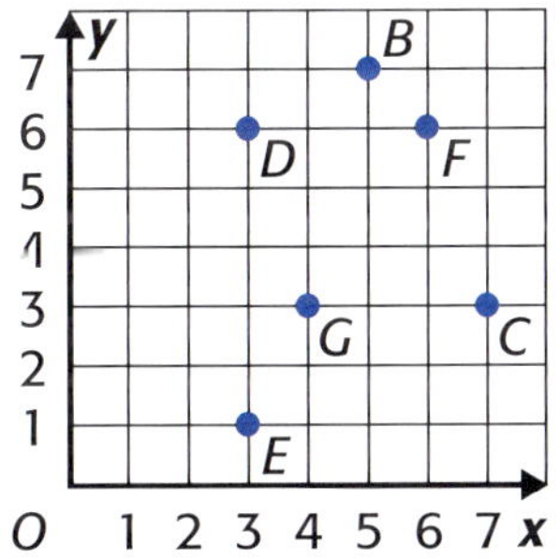

Name the ordered pair for each point.

8. B **9.** C **10.** D

Name the point for each ordered pair.

11. (3, 1) **12.** (4, 3) **13.** (6, 6)

14. A grocery store clerk is stacking soup cans. The bottom row has 21 soup cans. Each additional row has 2 fewer soup cans than the previous row. If there are 8 rows, how many soup cans will the clerk have to stack?

Graph and label each point on a coordinate grid.

15. (2, 7) **16.** (4, 5) **17.** (1, 6)

18. MULTIPLE CHOICE Alyssa made the graph below to show how much she makes babysitting. The equation $m = 5h$ describes how much money m she earns babysitting.

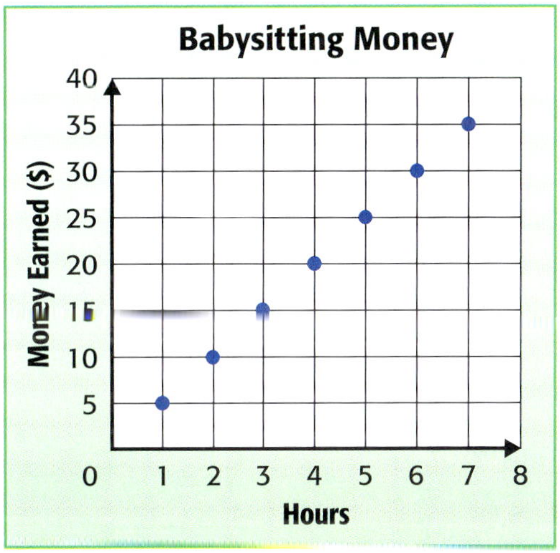

Which ordered pair represents how much money she earns for 4 hours?

F (20, 4) **H** (5, 25)

G (15, 3) **J** (4, 20)

19. The sum of two whole numbers between 20 and 40 is 58. The difference of the two numbers is 12. What are the two numbers? Tell what strategy you used to find the numbers.

20. WRITING IN MATH Explain why the variable x can have any value in $x + 3$, but in $x + 3 = 7$, the variable x can have only one value.

Chapter 6 Test Practice

Cumulative, Chapters 1–6

Math Online macmillanmh.com

• Test Practice

PART 1 Multiple Choice

Read each question. Then fill in the correct answer on the answer sheet provided by your teacher or on a sheet of paper.

1. Which point is located at (2, 4)?

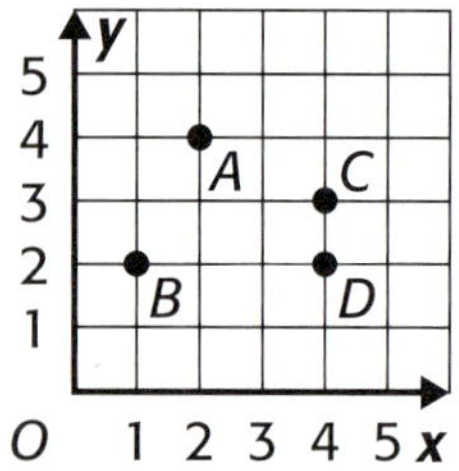

A Point *A** **C** Point *C*

B Point *B* **D** Point *D*

2. Which of the following is greater than 5.023?

F 5.0 **H** 5.022

G 5.02 **J** 5.03

3. Tomas records how much money he has saved. The table shows part of his records. Which is NOT a way to find the amount he saves each week?

Week	Total Saved
2	\$30
3	\$45
4	\$60
5	\$75
6	\$90

A Divide \$60 by 4.

B Divide \$90 by 6.

C Subtract \$45 from \$75.

D Subtract \$60 from \$75.

4. An auditorium has 24 rows with 20 seats in each row. If 305 seats are occupied, which of the following shows a way to find the number of empty seats in the auditorium?

F Subtract 24 from the product of 305 and 20.

G Subtract 305 from the product of 24 and 20.

H Add 305 to the product of 24 and 20.

J Add 24 to the product of 305 and 20.

5. Gregory rode his bike 12 miles around a bicycle track. He wants to find his biking time per mile in minutes. What additional information does he need?

A The number of minutes that he rode.

B The number of feet in 12 miles.

C The number of laps in one mile.

D The number of laps that he rode.

6. There are 640 cans of coffee at a distributon warehouse. The cans will be packed into boxes that hold 40 cans each. How many boxes are needed?

F 12

G 15

H 16

J 18

Preparing for Standardized Tests
For test-taking strategies and practice, see pages R42–R55.

7. Claudio bought 4 cans of green beans priced at \$1.45 each. He used a coupon for \$0.75 off the total cost. Which number sentence can be used to show how much money Claudio needed to buy the beans?

A $(4 + 1.45) - 0.75 = 4.70$

B $(4 \times 1.45) - 0.75 = 5.05$

C $(4 - 1.45) + 0.75 = 3.30$

D $(4 \times 1.45) + 0.75 = 6.55$

---

8. The sum of two numbers is 18. Their product is 72. What are the two numbers?

F 8, 9

G 9, 9

H 6, 12

J 4, 14

---

9. Martin is 12 years old. His father is three times as old as he is. How old will Martin be when his father is 40?

A 15

B 16

C 18

D 20

PART 2 Short Response

Record your answers on the answer sheet provided by your teacher or on a sheet of paper.

10. The numbers below form a pattern. What are the next two numbers in the pattern?

7, 15, 23, 31, 39, ...

---

11. Show how you would use the Distributive Property to evaluate the expression $6 \times (9 + 2)$.

PART 3 Extended Response

Record your answers on the answer sheet provided by your teacher or on a sheet of paper.

12. The graph shows the number of inches of rain during a tropical storm. Create a function table to represent the data. Explain the pattern.

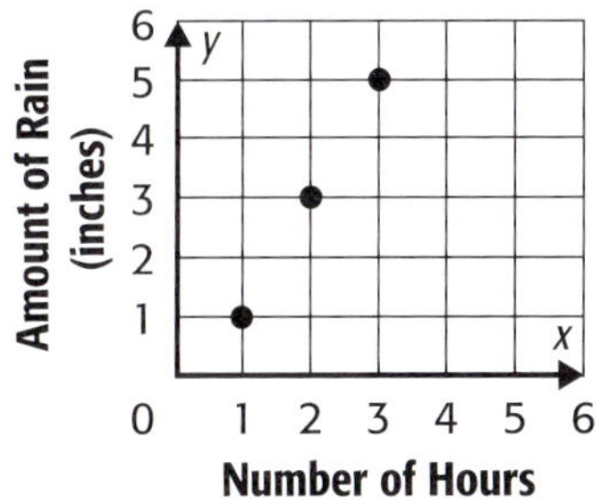

NEED EXTRA HELP?												
If You Missed Question...	1	2	3	4	5	6	7	8	9	10	11	12
Go to Lesson...	6-4	1-6	6-3	6-7	4-3	4-1	5-7	6-7	6-2	6-1	5-7	5-6

CHAPTER 7

Display and Interpret Data

BIG Idea What is data?

Data are pieces of information that are often numerical. There are many ways to organize data.

Example The table below shows data about the world's largest balloon festivals.

The World's Largest Balloon Festivals	
Location	**Number of Balloons**
Albuquerque, New Mexico	1,000
Gallup, New Mexico	200
Greenville, South Carolina	150
Gatineau, Canada	150
Scottsdale, Arizona	150

Source: *Scholastic Book of World Records*

What will I learn in this chapter?

- Find the mean, median, mode, and range of a set of data.
- Make and interpret line plots and frequency tables.
- Make and interpret bar graphs and line graphs.
- Choose and make an appropriate graph for presenting data.
- Solve problems by using the *make a graph* strategy.

Key Vocabulary

line graph
mean
median
mode
range

Math Online **Student Study Tools at macmillanmh.com**

FOLDABLES®
Study Organizer

Make this Foldable to help you organize information about data and graphs. Begin with four sheets of $8\frac{1}{2}'' \times 11''$ graph paper.

1. **Stack** the pages, placing the sheets of paper $\frac{3}{4}$ inch apart.

2. **Roll** up bottom edges so all tabs are the same size.

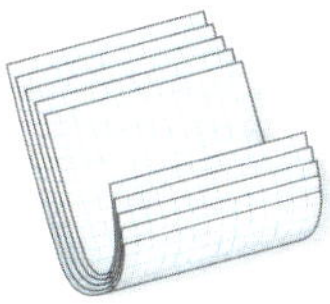

3. **Crease** and staple along the fold.

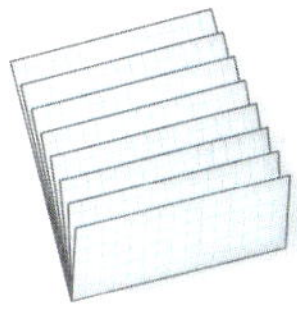

4. **Label** each tab as shown.

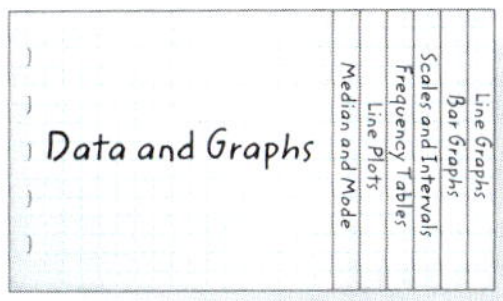

ARE YOU READY for Chapter 7?

You have two ways to check prerequisite skills for this chapter.

Option 2

Math Online Take the Chapter Readiness Quiz at macmillanmh.com.

Option 1

Complete the Quick Check below.

QUICK Check

Order each set of numbers from least to greatest. (Lesson 1-7)

1. 3, 16, 2, 9, 13

2. 18, 11, 22, 19, 14

3. 36, 45, 40, 21, 39, 60

4. 87, 30, 55, 15, 12, 71, 77

5. 1.4, 0.5, 3.2, 1.8, 2.6

6. 3.18, 3.08, 3.2, 3.96, 3.05, 3.68

7. The table shows the costs of disposable cameras. Order the costs from least to greatest. (Lesson 1-7)

Cost of Disposable Cameras			
\$5.99	\$8.50	\$12.95	\$9.95
\$8.95	\$9.05	\$14.99	\$6.75

Subtract. (Lesson 2-4)

8. 24 − 13

9. 36 − 22

10. 32 − 19

11. 65 − 43

12. 80 − 26

13. 112 − 37

14. The original price of a sweater was \$42. It is on sale for \$15 off. Katsu has a coupon for an additional \$10 off. What is the final price of the sweater? (Lesson 2-4)

Write the ordered pair for each point. (Lesson 6-4)

15. *A*

16. *B*

17. *C*

18. *D*

19. *E*

20. *F*

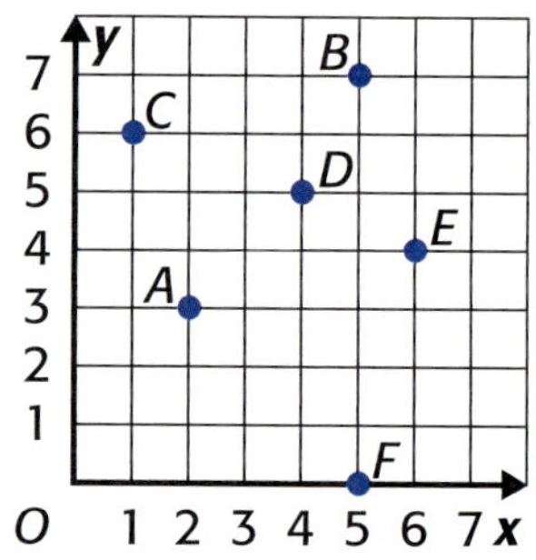

7-1 Mean, Median, and Mode

MAIN IDEA

I will find the mean, median, and mode of a set of data.

New Vocabulary

data
mean
median
mode

Math Online

macmillanmh.com

- Extra Examples
- Personal Tutor
- Self-Check Quiz

GET READY to Learn

The table at the right shows the number of hours some students in Mrs. Parker's class read books in one week.

Hours Reading Books	
Student	**Hours**
Aiden	2
Mark	3
Shyla	1
Krista	2
Malcom	5
Jeff	4
Michelle	4

Data are pieces of information that are often numerical. Mean, median, and mode are three ways to describe data.

- Suppose the total hours reading books was divided equally among all the students, so that each read the same amount of hours. This number is the mean. The **mean** of a set of data is the sum of the data divided by the number of pieces of data.

$$\frac{1 + 2 + 2 + 3 + 4 + 4 + 5}{7} = \frac{21}{7} \text{ or } 3$$

- The **median** of a set of data is the middle number of the ordered data.

1, 2, 2, 3, 4, 4, 5

- The **mode** of a set of data is the number or numbers that occur most often.

1, 2, 2, 3, 4, 4, 5

Real-World EXAMPLE Find the Mean

1 **EXERCISE The table at the right shows the number of hours 12 athletes spend exercising per week. Find the mean of the data.**

Exercise Hours			
9	5	5	7
5	9	4	4
10	6	8	12

Step 1 Find the sum of the data.

$4 + 4 + 5 + 5 + 5 + 6 + 7 + 8 + 9 + 9 + 10 + 12 = 84$

Step 2 Divide by the number of pieces of data.

$84 \div 12 = 7$

So, the mean number of hours students spend exercising per week is 7.

Remember

The mean and median of a set of data do not have to be one of the values in the set.

EXAMPLE Find the Median

2 Find the median of the data. Then describe the data.

12, 5, 5, 6, 9, 10, 4, 5, 4, 7, 8, 9

Step 1 Order the numbers from least to greatest.

4, 4, 5, 5, 5, 6, 7, 8, 9, 9, 10, 12

Step 2 The middle two numbers are 6 and 7. The median is the number halfway between them, 6.5.

So, the median number is 6.5.

Real-World EXAMPLE Find the Mode

3 MOVIES The cost of a movie ticket in different theaters are shown below. Find the mode of the data. Then describe the data.

\$7.00, \$8.00, \$6.00, \$10.50, \$8.50, \$8.00, \$9.75, \$7.50

The ticket price of \$8 occurs twice. The other ticket prices only occur once. So, the mode is \$8.00.

More theaters charge \$8.00 than any other price.

CHECK What You Know

Find the mean, median, and mode of each set of data. See Examples 1–3 (pp. 279–280)

1. cost of lunches: \$5, \$9, \$5, \$6, \$10
2. ages of students: 12, 10, 13, 14, 11, 13, 11
3. inches of rain: 7.3, 8.1, 3, 1, 7.2, 8.1, 7.3
4.

Miniature Golf Scores			
70	72	68	72
83	71	74	76

5.

Cost of Bottled Juice (\$)		
1.20	0.70	0.85
1.10	0.90	1.25

6. Eboni spent 20 minutes on homework on Monday and Tuesday, 35 minutes on Wednesday, 30 minutes on Thursday, and 0 minutes on Friday.
7. Talk About It Describe the steps for finding the median of a set of data.

Practice and Problem Solving

Find the mean, median, and mode of each set of data. See Examples 1–3 (pp. 279–280)

8. bowling scores: 85, 106, 106, 74, 95

9. height of trees in feet: 35, 62, 60, 54, 20

10. length of wire in meters: 0.27, 0.15, 1.19, 0.52, 0.50, 0.20, 0.04

11. number of strikeouts in a softball game: 5, 5, 7, 3, 2, 8, 5

12. letters in spelling words: 9, 8, 7, 7, 9, 7, 6, 7, 10, 9, 7, 6, 9, 8, 11

13.

Height of Students (in.)			
49	52	48	52
63	51	54	56

14.

Number of Pets				
2	1	1	2	3
3	1	0	1	0

15.

Visits to the Amusement Park this Year					
1	4	2	0	2	3
5	2	3	7	1	0

16.

Test Scores			
93	88	85	98
90	96	78	85
92	85	88	90

17. The table shows the number of T-shirts sold each day for three weeks. Find the mean, median, and mode. Then explain which number a manager should use to predict how many T-shirts will be sold each day.

Number of T-shirts Sold						
32	5	5	38	35	40	29
30	31	45	43	36	44	42
39	33	41	50	46	37	34

18. The table shows the number of weeks on *The Billboard Hot 100* chart for each of the top 25 hits. Find the mean, median, and mode.

14	14	13	19	6
11	12	14	25	17
11	3	6	27	19
6	8	9	29	7
11	19	10	16	24

H.O.T. Problems

19. COLLECT THE DATA Use the newspaper to collect a set of real-world data. Use the mean, median, and mode to describe the data.

20. OPEN ENDED Write a set of data that has a median of 14 and a mode of 2.

21. WRITING IN MATH Suppose the median height of the students in your class is 50 inches. What can you conclude about the heights of your classmates? Explain how you know.

7-2 Problem-Solving Investigation

MAIN IDEA I will choose the best strategy to solve a problem.

P.S.I. TEAM +

MAI: I noticed that there were more dogs than cats in the veterinarian's waiting room. The vet said that for about every 3 dogs he sees, he sees 2 cats. If 20 animals were brought in, I wonder how many would be dogs?

YOUR MISSION: Find about how many dogs the vet will see if 20 animals come into the office.

Understand	You know that for every 3 dogs, there are 2 cats. You need to find the number of dogs.
Plan	To solve this problem, you can use red and yellow counters to act out how many dogs and cats the vet will see.
Solve	Use red counters to represent the dogs and yellow counters to represent the cats. Place 3 red counters and 2 yellow counters in a group. Make groups of 5 counters until you have 20 counters.  Add the number of red counters to find about how many dogs the vet will see. $3 + 3 + 3 + 3 = 12$ So, about 12 of the animals will be dogs.
Check	Work backward. Start with 12 red counters and 8 yellow counters. Remove groups of 3 red and 2 yellow counters until none remain.

Mixed Problem Solving

EXTRA PRACTICE
See page R18.

Use any strategy shown below to solve each problem.

PROBLEM-SOLVING STRATEGIES
- Guess and check.
- Act it out.
- Make a table.

1. Zach purchases two books. The total cost is $32. One book costs $8 more than the other. How much does each book cost?

2. Four friends ran a race. Benny finished after Diego and before Alana. Marcia finished after Benny but before Alana. Who won the race?

3. **Measurement** A recipe for banana nut muffins calls for 1 cup bananas and 2 cups of flour. Eboni wants to make more muffins than the recipe yields. In Eboni's batter, there are 6 cups of flour. If she is using the recipe as a guide, how many cups of bananas will she need?

4. The table shows the number of submarine sandwiches sold by members of a hockey club. One number is missing. If the median of the data is 20 and there is more than one mode, find a possible value for the missing number.

Number of Subs Sold

22	18	26	10	11
14	20	18	23	24

5. Mr. Hoy plants 7 more flowers in his garden than his neighbor. If they plant 37 flowers in all, how many flowers does each person plant?

6. Cameron has $40 in his bank account and his brother, Caden, has $35. Caden saves $5 per week and Cameron saves $4 per week. In how many weeks will they both have the same amount in their accounts?

7. **Algebra** A certain type of bacterial cell doubles every 10 minutes. Use the table to determine how many cells there will be after 60 minutes.

Minutes	Number of Cells
0	1
10	2
20	4
30	8
60	■

8. Erica is saving money to buy a new hamster cage. In the first week, she saved $24.80. Each week after the first, she saves $6.50. How much money will Erica have saved in six weeks?

9. Haley is having a birthday party with 7 people. She asks the guests to introduce themselves and shake hands with each of the other guests. How many handshakes will there be?

10. **WRITING IN MATH** What strategy did you use to solve Exercise 9? Explain why your strategy makes sense.

7-3 Line Plots

MAIN IDEA

I will make and interpret line plots.

New Vocabulary

line plot
range
outlier

Math Online

macmillanmh.com

- Extra Examples
- Personal Tutor
- Self-Check Quiz

GET READY to Learn

Students in Mr. Cotter's fifth grade class were asked how many after-school activities they have. Their responses are shown in the table.

Number of After-School Activities

0	2	1	3	3	1
1	1	4	4	0	2
2	1	4	1	3	1
2	3	0	1	2	1

One way to give a picture of the data is to make a line plot. A **line plot** is a graph that uses Xs above a number line to show the number of times values in a set of data occur.

Real-World EXAMPLE Make a Line Plot

1 **ACTIVITIES** **Refer to the table above. Make a line plot of the data. Then describe the data presented in the graph.**

Step 1 Draw and label a number line.

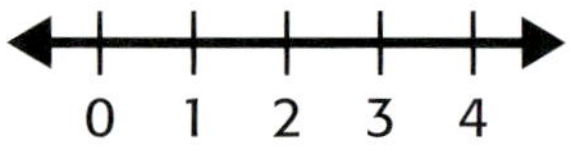

Step 2 Place as many Xs above each number as there are responses for that number.

Step 3 Describe the data.

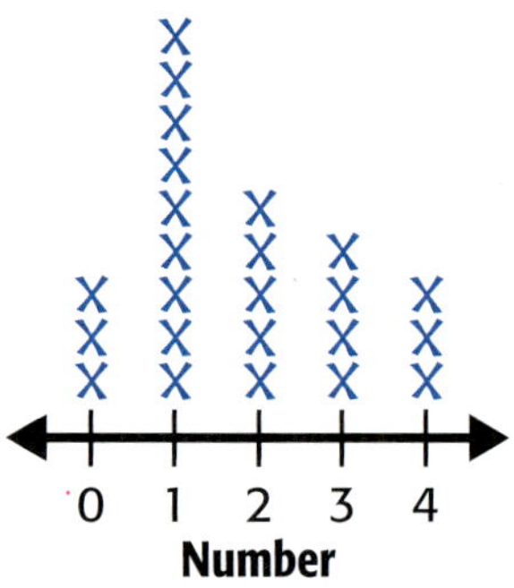

- 24 students responded to the question.
- No one is involved in more than 4 after-school activities.
- Three students are involved in no after-school activities.
- The response given most is 1 after-school activity. This represents the mode.

Vocabulary Link

range

Everyday Use the highest to lowest notes that a person can sing

Math Use the difference between the greatest and least values in a data set

Another way to describe a set of data is to use the range and any outliers.

Range and Outliers

Key Concepts

Words The **range** of a set of data is the difference between the greatest and least values in a data set.

Example **data:** 2, 4, 5, 7, 12 → **range:** 12 – 2 or 10

Words An **outlier** is a data value that is not close to the other values in a data set.

Example **data:** 5, 8, 10, 14, 63 → **outlier:** 63

Real-World EXAMPLES Analyze Line Plots

HATS The line plot shows the prices of cowboy hats.

Prices of Cowboy Hats

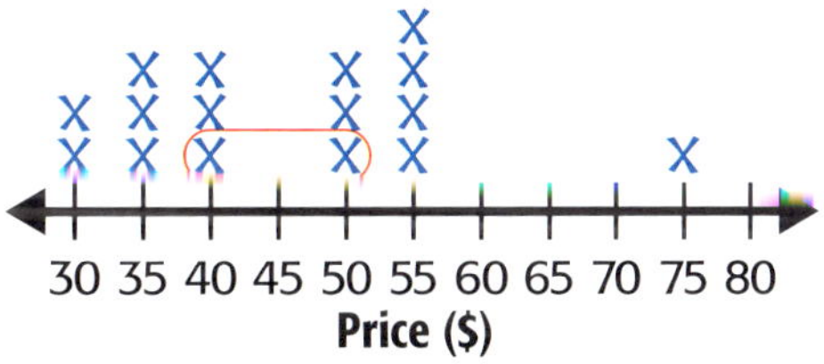

2 Find the median and mode of the data. Then describe the data using them.

There are 16 numbers represented in the line plot. The median is between the 8th and 9th pieces of data.

The two middle numbers, shown on the line plot, are 40 and 50. So, the median is 45. This means that half of the cowboy hats cost more than $45 and half cost less than $45.

The number that appears most often is 55. So, the mode of the data is 55. This means that more cowboy hats cost $55 than any other price.

Remember

You can find the median by counting the Xs on the graph. You do not have to list all of the data values. Cross off a least and a greatest value until you reach the middle.

3 Find the range and any outliers of the data. Then describe the data using them.

range = greatest value – least value
= 75 – 30, or 45

The range of the prices is $45. The price $75 is much higher than the rest of the prices. So, $75 is an outlier.

CHECK What You Know

Draw a line plot for each set of data. Find the median, mode, range, and any outliers of the data shown in the line plot.

See Examples 1–3 (pp. 284–285)

1.

Number of Stories of 15 Tallest Buildings		
101	88	88
110	88	88
80	69	102
78	70	54
85	80	73

2.

Calories in Serving of Peanut Butter			
190	160	210	210
200	188	190	190
188	200	190	210
190	188	200	200

3.

Sum of Two Number Cubes				
10	3	11	5	5
7	5	6	7	6
7	7	12	5	7
9	8	8	8	9
5	9	3	3	11

4. Refer to the line plot in Exercise 3. Write a sentence or two to describe the data.

5. **Talk About It** What are the advantages of representing data in a line plot rather than in a table?

Practice and Problem Solving

EXTRA PRACTICE See page R18.

Draw a line plot for each set of data. Find the median, mode, range, and any outliers of the data shown in the line plot.

See Examples 1–3 (pp. 284–285)

6. Length of summer camps in days: 7, 7, 14, 10, 5, 10, 5, 7, 10, 9, 7, 9, 6, 10, 5, 8, 7, and 8

7. Daily high temperatures in degrees Fahrenheit: 71, 72, 74, 72, 72, 68, 71, 67, 68, 71, 68, 72, 76, 75, 72, 73, 68, 69, 69, 73, 74, 76, 72, and 74

8.

Students' Estimates of Room Length (m)				
10	11	12	12	13
13	13	14	14	14
15	15	15	15	15
16	16	16	17	17
17	17	18	18	25

9.

Number of Songs on MP3 Players				
25	50	40	40	42
50	39	39	42	36
38	42	40	45	38

10.

Hours Spent Watching TV					
3	3	5	2	2	1
2	0	1	1	5	2
0	2	2	3	1	0
2	1	3	2	3	5

11.

Number of Tornadoes				
0	1	1	1	6
0	0	0	0	0
2	1	3	0	0

12. The line plot shows students' number of pets. Find the median, mode, range, or outlier(s). Then write a sentence or two to describe the data set.

Number of Pets

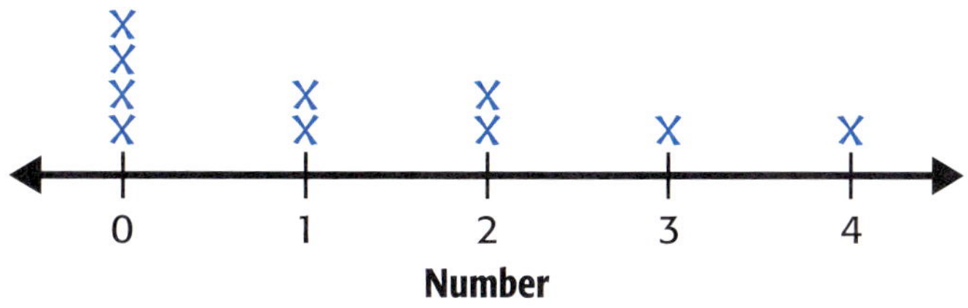

A softball team scored 14, 9, 6, 11, and 9 runs in their last five games. How many runs would the team need to score in the next game so that each statement is true?

13. The range is 10.

14. The mode is 11.

15. The median is $9\frac{1}{2}$.

Real-World PROBLEM SOLVING

Social Studies The table shows the years in which different machines were invented.

16. What is the range of the years of the inventions?

17. Which invention represents the median year?

Year	Machine Invented
1876	Telephone
1885	Bicycle
1927	Television
1933	FM radio
1994	DVDs

Source: *Time for Kids Almanac*

H.O.T. Problems

18. **COLLECT THE DATA** Write a survey question that has a numerical answer. Some examples are "How many CDs do you have?" or "How many feet long is your bedroom?" Ask your friends and family the question. Record the results and organize the data in a line plot. Use the line plot to make conclusions about your data. For example, describe the data using the median, mode, or range.

19. **CHALLENGE** There are several sizes of flying disks in a collection. The range is 8 centimeters. The median is 22 centimeters. The smallest size is 16 centimeters. What is the largest disk in the collection?

20. **WRITING IN MATH** Suppose two sets of data have the same median but different ranges. What can you conclude about the sets?

TEST Practice

21. The table shows the speeds of the world's fastest roller coasters. Which roller coaster in the table represents the median speed? **(Lesson 7-1)**

Roller coaster	Speed (mi per h)
Dodonpa, Japan	107
Kingda Ka, USA	128
Superman the Escape, USA	100
Top Thrill Dragster, USA	120
Tower of Terror, Australia	100

A Dodonpa

B Kingda

C Top Thrill Dragster

D Tower of Terror

22. The line plot shows the number of weekly chores that fifth graders have.

Weekly Chores

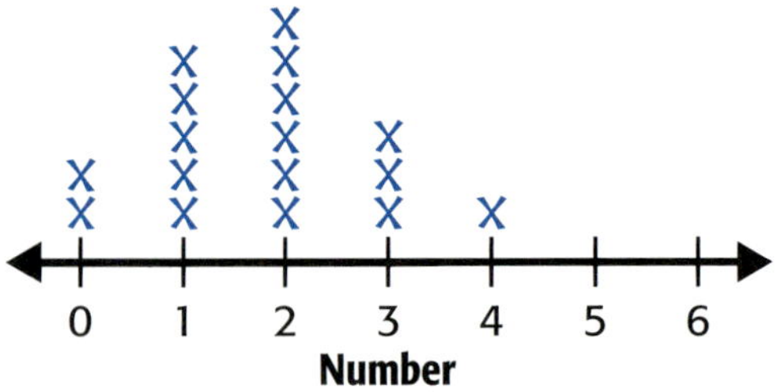

Which represents the range of the data? **(Lesson 7-3)**

F 0

G 2

H 4

J 6

Spiral Review

For Exercises 23 and 24, use the information below. Gia and her three friends went to the movie theater. They each spent $6 on snacks and $8 on a movie ticket. **(Lesson 7-2)**

23. If the total amount the four friends have now is $12, how much money did they have altogether originally?

24. If they each had the same amount of money originally, how much did each friend have?

25. The table shows the number of students who visited the National Wildlife Refuge every day for two weeks. Find the median and mode. **(Lesson 7-1)**

Number of Student Visitors						
68	65	56	62	68	56	56
58	56	63	62	60	65	64

Graph and label each point on a coordinate grid. **(Lesson 6-5)**

26. $J(0, 6)$ **27.** $K(5, 7)$ **28.** $L(4, 0)$ **29.** $M(3, 3)$

Algebra Solve each equation. **(Lesson 6-2)**

30. $4x = 8$ **31.** $6n = 24$ **32.** $15 = 5a$ **33.** $60 = 12r$

7-4 Frequency Tables

MAIN IDEA

I will make and interpret frequency graphs.

New Vocabulary

frequency table

Math Online

macmillanmh.com

- Extra Examples
- Personal Tutor
- Self-Check Quiz

GET READY to Learn

The table shows the number of days that Middletown had thunderstorms each month in a recent year.

Thunderstorm Days			
2	2	1	1
7	5	7	7
6	6	0	0

We can use a **frequency table** to organize data in a table that shows the number of times each data value appears.

Real-World EXAMPLE — Make a Frequency Table

1 THUNDERSTORMS **Refer to the table above. Make a frequency table of the data. Then describe the data.**

Step 1 Make a table with three columns. Label the columns *Number*, *Tally*, and *Frequency* as shown.

Step 2 Use tally marks to record each data value. The last column provides a count, or *frequency*, of the data.

Thunderstorm Days		
Number	Tally	Frequency
0	II	2
1	II	2
2	II	2
3		0
4		0
5	I	1
6	II	2
7	III	3

Step 3 Describe the data.

- The median is $3\frac{1}{2}$. Half of the data are above $3\frac{1}{2}$ and half of the data are below $3\frac{1}{2}$.
- The mode is 7. More months had 7 days of thunderstorms than any other number.
- The range of the data is $7 - 0$ or 7. There are no outliers.

Real-World EXAMPLE — Make and Interpret a Frequency Table

2 **TEXT MESSAGES** **The number of text messages that Sonja sent each day for 25 days is shown. Make a frequency table. Find the, median mode, range, and any outliers. Then describe the data.**

Number of Text Messages				
3	5	2	1	1
4	4	3	3	2
3	1	2	0	4
1	3	2	4	2
3	2	1	3	0

Remember
The first column in the frequency table should always include the least value, the greatest value, and all the values in between.

The least number of text messages is 0, and the greatest number is 5. So, in the first column, write the numbers 0 to 5. Tally the data and add the tallies.

Number of Messages	Tally	Frequency
0	||	2
1	~~||||~~	5
2	~~||||~~ |	6
3	~~||||~~ ||	7
4	||||	4
5	|	1

The median is the 13th number, or 2 messages. Half of the data are above 2 and half are below 2.

The mode is 3 messages, since 3 appears more often than any other number.

The range is 5 − 0, or 5 messages. There are no outliers.

For a frequency table without numbers, you can find the mode of the data, but not the median nor the range.

Real-World EXAMPLE — Non-Numerical Data

3 **PETS** **The table shows the kinds of pets that students have. Make a frequency table of the data. Then describe the mode.**

Pets						
F	D	D	D	C	H	F
D	C	D	D	F	H	C
H	D	C	D	C	C	F

D = dog, C = cat, F = fish, H = hamster

Pet	Tally	Frequency
dog	~~||||~~ |||	8
cat	~~||||~~ |	6
fish	||||	4
hamster	|||	3

Since more students have dogs than any other pet, the mode is dog.

CHECK What You Know

Lamar counted the number of children with each adult who entered a grocery store in one hour. His results are shown at the right. See Examples 1, 2 (pp. 289–290)

Number of Children with Each Adult				
1	2	1	4	0
5	2	2	0	2
0	1	0	5	6
1	2	1	3	4

1. Make a frequency table of the data.

2. Find the median, mode, and range of the data. Identify any outliers. Then describe the data.

The table shows a geography vocabulary list.
See Examples 1, 2 (pp. 289–290)

Vocabulary List		
bay	island	source
hill	dam	range
peninsula	mouth	canal
tributary	ocean	coast
plain	river	valleys
mountain	glacier	

3. Make a frequency table to show the number of letters in each word.

4. Find the median, mode, and range of the data. Identify any outliers in the data. Then describe the data.

5. The table shows the political parties of the 43 United States Presidents as of 2008. What is the mode? What does the mode mean? See Example 3 (p. 290)

Political Party	Frequency
Federalist	2
Democratic-Republican	6
Whig	4
Democrat	13
Republican	18

6. Talk About It Explain how a line plot is similar to a frequency table.

Practice and Problem Solving

EXTRA PRACTICE See page R18.

The table shows the record low May daily temperatures in the city of Lakeview. See Examples 1, 2 (pp. 289–290)

Temperatures (°F)			
42	42	43	43
45	43	46	45
40	44	43	43
43	46	46	46
45	46	46	46

7. Make a frequency table of the data.

8. Find the median, mode, and range of the data. Identify any outliers. Then describe the data.

The table shows the heights of 15 different Collie dogs.
See Examples 1, 2 (pp. 289–290)

Height of Collies (in.)				
24	26	22	22	23
24	25	24	23	23
18	26	25	22	24

9. Make a frequency table of the data.

10. Find the median, mode, and range of the data. Identify any outliers. Then describe the data.

Gerri surveyed her classmates to determine their favorite colors. See Example 3 (p. 290)

Favorite Colors Gerri's Classmates				
K	R	P	G	V
R	V	R	P	P
G	P	G	B	K
B	R	K	G	B
G	B	V	P	R

B: Blue Y: Yellow R: Red G: Green V: Purple P: Pink K: Black

11. Make a frequency table for these data.

12. Describe the mode of the data.

13. Can you determine the median, range, and outliers for these data? Explain.

The table shows the number of each size of T-shirt sold. See Example 3 (p. 290)

T-shirts Sold					
S	S	L	M	S	XL
L	M	M	L	S	M
XL	M	S	L	M	XL
S	L	M	M	L	S
M	S	M	XL	S	M

S = small, M = medium, L = large, XL = extra large

14. Make a frequency table for these data.

15. Describe the mode of the data.

Real-World PROBLEM SOLVING

Science The table shows the top speeds of animals over short distances.

Animal	Speed (miles per hour)	Animal	Speed (miles per hour)
Lion	50	Rabbit	35
Gazelle	50	Cat	30
Wildebeest	50	White-tailed deer	30
Cape hunting dog	45	Grizzly bear	30
Elk	45	Wart hog	30
Ostrich	40	Kangaroo	30
Zebra	40	Elephant	25
Jackal	35	Black mamba snake	20

Source: *Natural History Magazine*

16. Make a frequency table of the speeds.

17. Describe the data. Include the median, mode, and range of the data.

H.O.T. Problems

18. COLLECT THE DATA With a classmate, create a survey about weekend activities. Gather data and make a frequency table to show your results. Report the median, mode, and range of your data. Identify any outliers.

19. WRITING IN MATH Explain how frequency tables help to organize data.

CHAPTER 7 Mid-Chapter Check

Lessons 7-1 through 7-4

Find the mean, median, and mode of each set of data. (Lesson 7-1)

1. daily high temperature in degrees Fahrenheit: 79, 70, 80, 76, 80

2. price of coffee: \$2.99, \$3.50, \$1.21, \$3.50, \$1.50, \$0.99, \$1.50

3. **MULTIPLE CHOICE** The table below shows the miles of shoreline of five different lakes.

Lake	Shoreline (mi)
Camille Creek	320
Trout	233
Clearwater	450
Bay Point	600
Yellow Springs	245

What is the median miles of shoreline? (Lesson 7-1)

A 385 miles **C** 500 miles

B 450 miles **D** 600 miles

4. Mika buys a fishing rod and a hat. His total bill is \$140. The rod is 9 times the cost of the hat. How much does each item cost? (Lesson 7-2)

5. How many more students have one sibling than two? (Lesson 7-4)

Students' Siblings

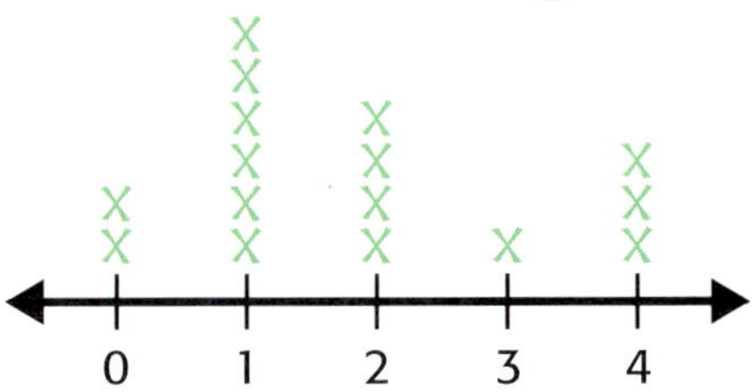

6. Draw a line plot for the data set shown. Then find the median, mode, range, and any outliers. Then describe the data. (Lesson 7-3)

Weight of Apples (oz)					
7	5	5	6	8	7
6	7	8	5	5	5

7. **MULTIPLE CHOICE** Which set of data is shown in the table? (Lesson 7-4)

Price (\$)	Tally	Frequency
15	||	2
16	|	1
17		0
18	|	1
19	|||	3

F \$15, \$15, \$16, \$18, \$19, \$19, \$19

G \$15, \$16, \$17, \$18, \$19, \$19, \$19

H \$15, \$15, \$16, \$16, \$18, \$18, \$19

J \$15, \$16, \$16, \$17, \$18, \$19, \$19

8. **WRITING IN MATH** The table shows the ages of students in a classroom.

Ages of Students						
10	10	11	12	11	11	10
11	10	10	11	11	10	11

Suppose the age of the teacher was added to the data set. Would the median, mode, or range of the data change the most? Explain. (Lesson 7-3)

7-5 Scales and Intervals

MAIN IDEA

I will choose appropriate scales and intervals for frequency tables.

New Vocabulary

scale
interval

Math Online

macmillanmh.com

- Extra Examples
- Personal Tutor
- Self-Check Quiz

GET READY to Learn

There are thirty teams in the NBA. The number of 3-point shots made by each team in the 2006-2007 season have been grouped into six equal intervals. The data are shown at the right.

NBA Teams 3-Point Statistics		
Number Made	**Tally**	**Frequency**
200–299	|	1
300–399	~~||||~~	5
400–499	~~||||~~ ~~||||~~	10
500–599	~~||||~~ ||||	9
600–699	||	2
700–799	|||	3

Source: National Basketball Association

The frequency table has a scale from 200 to 799. The **scale** includes the least and greatest values in the data set. The scale is separated into equal **intervals**. In this case, the interval is 100.

Real-World EXAMPLE — Make a Frequency Table

1 **HATS** **Choose an appropriate scale and interval size for the data shown below. Then make a frequency table.**

Price of Baseball Caps ($)									
18	19	12	24	16	26	16	23	22	25
24	14	18	17	27	22	20	25	20	15

The data are from 12 to 27. Make the scale from 12 to 27 and the interval size 4. The categories are 12–15, 16–19, 20–23, and 24–27.

In the tally column, record the number of caps in each category. Write the total number of tallies in the frequency column.

Price ($)	Tally	Frequency
12–15	|||	3
16–19	~~||||~~ |	6
20–23	~~||||~~	5
24–27	~~||||~~ |	6

Remember

There is only one range for a set of data. However, there are many ways to choose the scale and the interval.

Real-World EXAMPLE — Make a Frequency Table

2 FOOD The table shows concession stand sales for one hour. Make a frequency table of the data. Then write a sentence or two to describe how the data are distributed among the intervals.

Concession Stand Sales ($)			
9.19	6.10	6.40	1.20
3.25	9.80	3.50	8.75
6.40	8.30	1.80	7.00
9.50	3.10	8.80	7.20

The sales range from \$1.20 to \$9.50. You could make the scale from \$0.01 to \$10.00 with an interval size of \$1.99.

Sales ($)	Tally	Frequency
0.01–2.00	||	2
2.01–4.00	|||	3
4.01–6.00		0
6.01–8.00	𝍸	5
8.01–10.00	𝍸 |	6

Most sales were in the \$8.01–\$10.00 interval. No sales were in the \$4.01–\$6.00 interval.

CHECK What You Know

The *United States Specialty Sports Association* (USSSA) ranks sports teams based on tournament wins. The table shows the USSSA points for the top 25 boys 12-and-under baseball teams in a recent season. See Examples 1, 2 (pp. 294–295)

USSSA Points				
850	725	715	695	450
445	425	390	365	340
330	330	320	305	300
300	300	295	280	275
265	260	255	255	245

1. Choose an appropriate scale and interval size for a frequency table that will represent the data. Describe the intervals.

2. Create a frequency table using the scale and interval size you described.

3. Write a sentence or two to describe how the points are distributed among the intervals.

4. Talk About It: Explain how to choose an appropriate scale and interval size when making a frequency table of a set of data.

Practice and Problem Solving

EXTRA PRACTICE
See page R19.

The table shows the millions of cookies sold for the top 15 cookie brands in a recent year. See Examples 1, 2 (pp. 294–295)

Cookie Sales (millions)		
75	50	39
31	29	33
48	56	21
35	20	17
16	14	14

5. Choose an appropriate scale and interval size for a frequency table that will represent the sales. Describe the intervals.

6. Create a frequency table using the scale and interval size you described.

7. Write a sentence or two to describe how the sales information is distributed among the intervals.

Building model rockets is a popular hobby. The table shows the bid prices for a certain model rocket kit at an auction.
See Examples 1, 2 (pp. 294–295)

Bid Prices	
Price ($)	**Number**
30	9
28	1
2	1
21	11
13	15
6	2
9	5
23	4
10	2
16	5

8. Choose an appropriate scale and interval size for a frequency table that will represent the bid prices. Describe the intervals.

9. Create a frequency table using the scale and interval size you described.

10. Write a sentence or two to describe how the bid prices are distributed among the intervals.

The table shows the prices of 11 dog books for children.
See Examples 1, 2 (pp. 294–295)

Title	Price ($)	Title	Price ($)
Pepper's Snow Day	8.99	*Danger at Snow Hill*	4.99
Wind-wild Dog	16.95	*A Puppy for Annie*	15.99
Snowball	3.99	*Helpful Puppy*	5.99
Adam of the Road	6.99	*The Inside Tree*	14.99
Polo: The Runaway Book	16.95	*Sassie: The True Confessions of a Poodle Princess*	15.99
Dogabet	16.95		

11. Choose an appropriate scale and interval size for a frequency table that will represent the list prices of these books. Describe the intervals.

12. Create a frequency table using the scale and interval size you described.

13. Write a sentence or two to describe how the list prices are distributed among the intervals.

The table shows race results to the nearest tenth for the top 25 junior finishers in a recent bicycle race.

See Examples 1, 2 (pp. 294–295)

Time (min)				
37.4	37.8	38.2	39.2	40.9
37.4	37.8	39.2	42.1	37.8
37.4	37.8	39.5	39.5	38.2
37.8	37.8	39.7	39.5	40.2
37.8	37.9	40.1	37.8	37.9

14. Choose an appropriate scale and interval size for a frequency table that will represent the race result times. Describe the intervals.

15. Create a frequency table using the scale and interval size you described.

16. Write a sentence or two to describe how the race result times are distributed among the intervals.

Data File

The Baltimore Blast is a professional indoor soccer team. The table shows the number of shots taken per player.

Baltimore Blast Shots on Goal				
127	103	63	58	57
33	38	41	43	49
31	21	10	9	3
50	51	2	1	1

Source: Baltimore Blast

17. Choose an appropriate scale and interval size for a frequency table that will represent the data. Describe the intervals.

18. Create a frequency table using the scale and interval size you described.

19. Write a sentence or two to describe how the data are distributed among the intervals.

H.O.T. Problems

20. **COLLECT THE DATA** Find a list of real-world data in an almanac. Describe the scale and interval that you would use to make a frequency table of the data. Then make a frequency table.

21. **CHALLENGE** Refer to the frequency table at the beginning of the lesson that shows the number of 3-point shots made by NBA teams. Is it possible to find the median, mode, or range of the data? Explain.

22. **WRITING IN ►MATH** Describe when it is better to use intervals rather than individual values when making a frequency table of data.

TEST Practice

23. The data below describes the average weights of popular breeds of dogs. Which scale and interval would be most appropriate in a frequency table representing the data? (Lesson 7-5)

Average Weights (lb) of Popular Dog Breeds					
70	6	100	20	4	26
30	65	80	70	75	15

A scale: 1–100; interval size: 5

B scale: 1–100; interval size: 10

C scale: 1–50; interval size: 1

D scale: 1–200; interval size: 10

24. Which is a true statement about the data represented by the frequency table below? (Lesson 7-4)

Cost ($)	Tally	Frequency
0–4	卌	5
5–9	卌 I	6
10–14	II	2
15–19	I	1

F None of the values are $0.

H None of the values are $20.

G The greatest number of values is between $0 and $4.

J The greatest value is $19.

Spiral Review

The table shows the number of hours 15 students practiced their musical instruments one week. (Lesson 7-4)

Practice Time (h)				
1	4	4	2	6
3	2	4	5	5
2	5	4	6	1

25. Make a frequency table of the data. Then find the median, mode, range, and any outliers.

For Exercises 26 and 27, use the table that shows the lengths of twelve different lizards. (Lesson 7-3)

Length (cm)			
14	12	14	14
19	18	11	16
30	12	19	15

26. Make a line plot of the data.

27. Find the median, mode, range, and any outliers of the data shown in the line plot.

28. For every $5 that Wesley earns, he saves $3. How much does he save if he earns $25? Use the *make a table* strategy to solve. (Lesson 6-3)

Solve each equation. Check your solution. (Lesson 6-1)

29. $c + 7 = 13$ **30.** $y - 4 = 5$ **31.** $r - 3 = 2$ **32.** $9 + k = 11$

Algebra **Evaluate each expression if $a = 5$ and $b = 8$.** (Lesson 5-3)

33. $2b$ **34.** $4a$ **35.** $9a$ **36.** $7b$

7-6 Bar Graphs

MAIN IDEA

I will make and interpret bar graphs and double bar graphs.

New Vocabulary

bar graph

double bar graph

Math Online

macmillanmh.com

- Extra Examples
- Personal Tutor
- Self-Check Quiz

GET READY to Learn

The table shows students' favorite exhibits at the zoo.

Exhibit	Number of Students
Reptiles	10
Pachyderms	9
Islands of Southeast Asia	8
Herbivores/Carnivores	5
African Forest	15

Another way to organize data is to use a bar graph. A **bar graph** uses bars to display the number of items in each group.

Real-World EXAMPLE — Make and Interpret a Bar Graph

1 ZOO **Make a bar graph of the data in the table above.**

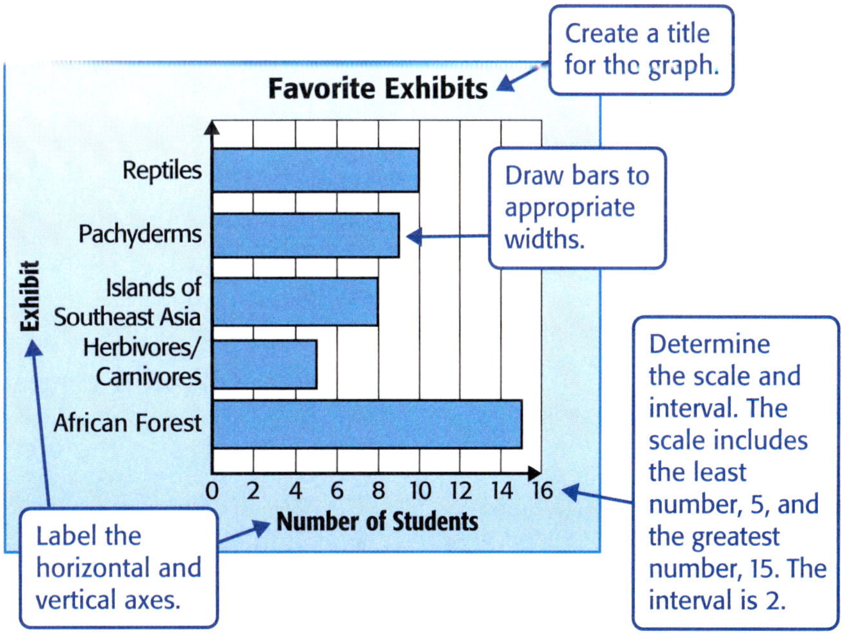

You can see from the graph that more students chose the African Forest exhibit as their favorite exhibit than any other.

A **double bar graph** can be used to display two sets of data dealing with the same subject. You can use a double bar graph to make conclusions about the data.

Real-World EXAMPLE — Make and Interpret a Double Bar Graph

2 MASCOTS The fifth and sixth graders are voting for a new school mascot. The results are shown in the table below.

Mascot	Fifth Grade Votes	Sixth Grade Votes
Cardinals	42	26
Jaguars	21	18
Cougars	33	36
Patriots	12	21
Colts	14	19

Make a double bar graph of the data. Then use the graph to make conclusions about the data.

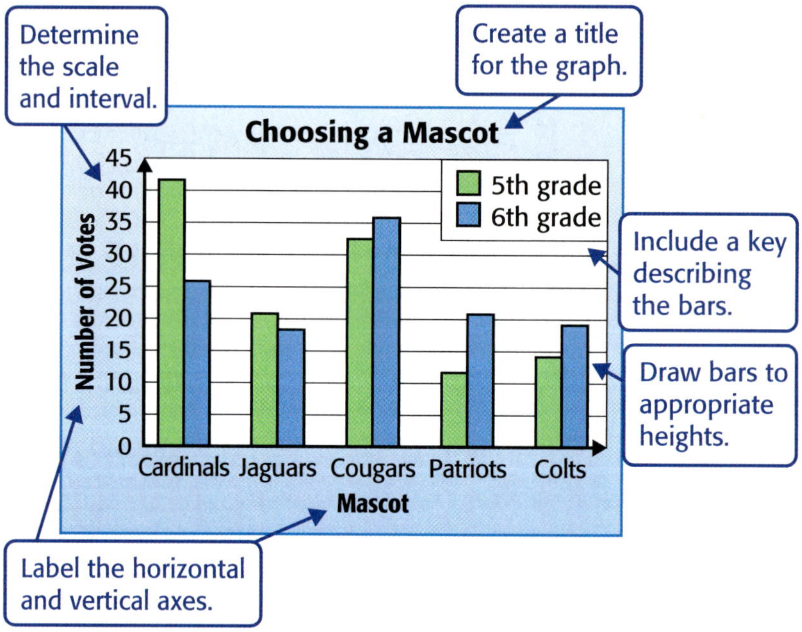

You can make the following conclusions from the graph.

- The mascot that received the greatest number of fifth grade votes was Cardinals.
- The mascot that received the greatest number of sixth grade votes was Cougars.
- The range of fifth grade votes is 42 – 12 or 30. The range of sixth grade votes is 36 – 18 or 18. So, the fifth grade votes were more spread out.

Remember

Always include a key to describe what each bar in a double bar graph represents.

Vocabulary Link

horizontal
Everyday Use flat or level

vertical
Everyday Use up and down

CHECK What You Know

The five longest rivers in the United States are shown in the table. See Examples 1, 2 (pp. 299–300)

U.S. Rivers	
River	**Length (mi)**
Missouri	2,540
Mississippi	2,340
Yukon	1,980
Rio Grande	1,900
St. Lawrence	1,900

1. Make a bar graph of the data. Describe the scale and interval that you used.

2. How much longer is the Missouri than the Yukon?

3. Which river represents the median length? Explain your reasoning.

The 10- and 11-year olds on a soccer team voted on a new name. See Examples 1, 2 (pp. 299–300)

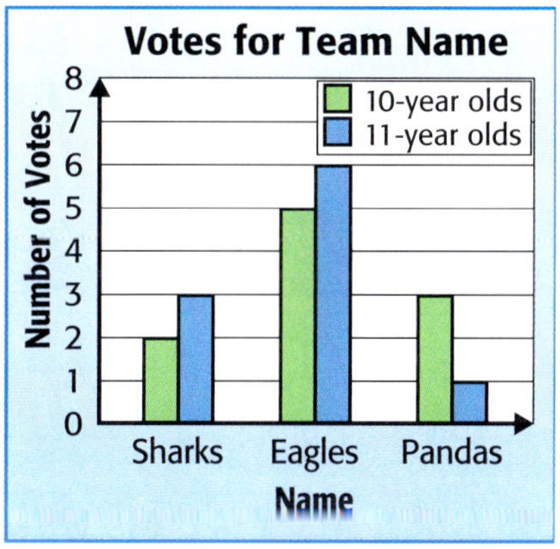

4. Which name received the most votes from 10-year olds?

5. Which name received the most votes from 11-year olds?

6. Which name received the fewest votes overall?

7. How many votes were cast in all?

For Exercises 8 and 9, use the table that shows the number of student absences for one week. See Examples 1, 2 (pp. 299–300)

Student Absences for One Week					
Grade	**Monday**	**Tuesday**	**Wednesday**	**Thursday**	**Friday**
Fourth	7	3	4	6	10
Fifth	5	4	4	5	3

8. Make a bar graph for each of the two data sets.

9. Combine the data sets to create a double bar graph. Then write one or two sentences describing the data in the double bar graph.

10. It is estimated that there were about 100,000 cheetahs in the wild in 1900; about 30,000 in 1950; and about 12,500 in 2006. Make a bar graph to show how the population of the cheetah has declined.

11. **Talk About It** Summarize the steps you take to make a double bar graph.

Practice and Problem Solving

EXTRA PRACTICE
See page R19.

Ice Cream Scoops Sold	
Flavor	**Number**
Chocolate	96
Vanilla	82
Rocky road	43
Strawberry	25
Mint chip	20

For Exercises 12 and 13, use the table that shows the number of scoops of five flavors of ice cream sold one day at Mom's Shoppe. See Examples 1, 2 (pp. 299–300)

12. Make a bar graph of the data. Describe the scale and interval size that you used.

13. Which flavor had the greatest number of scoops?

Stanislaus surveyed students in his school about their favorite snack. For Exercises 14–17, use the graph that shows the results of the survey. See Examples 1, 2 (pp. 299–300)

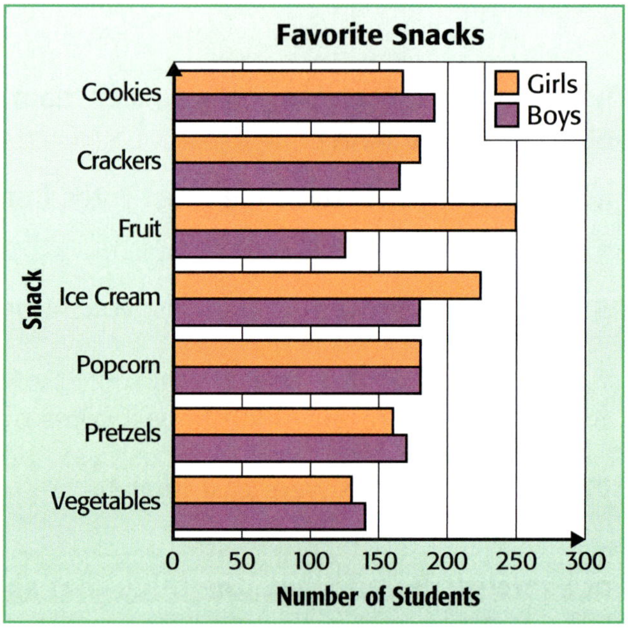

14. Which snack was favored most often by boys?

15. Which snack was favored most often by girls?

16. Which snack had the greatest difference in boys' and girls' favorites?

17. Estimate the range of responses given by the girls.

For Exercises 18–20, use the tables that show the record high daily temperatures in November for two cities.

Record High Daily Temperatures for each day in November (°F)				
Jonesville				
85	85	85	84	81
82	82	82	87	82
81	84	84	80	82
80	85	84	77	81
86	80	82	80	79
81	79	82	84	79
Orchard City				
88	88	87	89	88
89	89	88	88	91
87	89	91	89	90
87	86	85	87	83
83	86	87	87	85
86	85	89	84	82

18. Create a bar graph of the temperatures for each city.

19. Find the median, mode, and range of the temperatures for Jonesville. Then describe the data using them.

20. Combine the bar graphs from Exercise 18 to create a double bar graph. Then write one or two sentences summarizing the data in the double bar graph.

For Exercises 21–23, use the table that shows the ages of first-year teachers for two school districts.

Age of First-Year Teachers (yr)								
District A					District B			
25	23	24	21	24	25	24	22	24
22	22	24	24	23	25	23	23	23
23	22	22	21	26	25	26	23	21
23	23	22	24		26	22		

21. Create a bar graph of the ages of first-year teachers for each district.

22. Find the median, mode, and range of the ages of first-year teachers for District A. Then describe the data using them.

23. Combine the bar graphs from Exercise 21 to create a double bar graph. Then write one or two sentences summarizing the data in the double bar graph.

H.O.T. Problems

24. FIND THE ERROR The graph at the right shows the number of students in the Spanish club in its first three years. Kamila and James are analyzing the data in the graph. Who is correct? Explain.

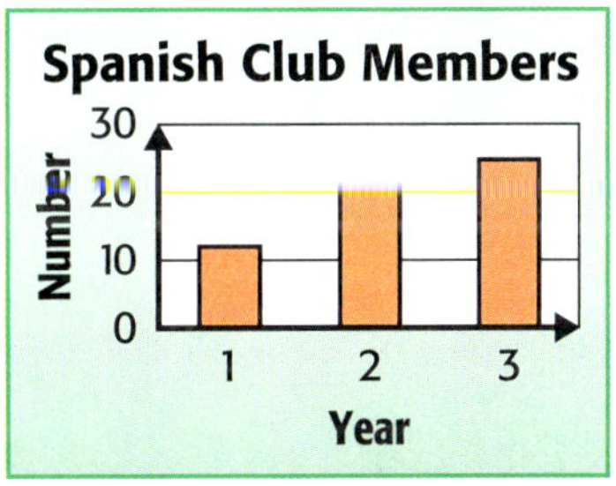

Kamila
The number of members from Year 1 to Year 2 more than doubled.

James
The number of members from Year 1 to Year 3 more than doubled.

25. OPEN ENDED Write a set of four data values. When the data are displayed in a bar graph, two bars have the same height. One of the bars is 10 units taller than the two equal bars.

26. WRITING IN ▸MATH Write a real-world problem that can be represented by using a bar graph. Create a bar graph and write two questions about the graph. Ask another student to use your graph to answer the questions.

Art Work

Artists hold about 290,000 jobs in the United States. Some are cartoonists, sketch artists for law enforcement, or illustrators for medical and scientific publications. Many artists are involved in movie-making and theater productions. Graphic designers and animators help create videos.

About 63% of artists in the United States are self-employed. Some self-employed artists have contracts to work on individual projects for different clients. Fine artists usually sell their work when it is finished, including painters, sculptors, craft artists, and printmakers.

Art Careers Chosen by Students in a Survey

Career	Frequency
Art Museum Director	10
Book Illustrator	14
Cartoonist	16
Computer Graphic Artist	9
Craft Artist	14
Fine Art Restorer	2
Scientific Sketch Artist	12

Average Annual Salary

Profession	Salary ($)
Dancers	27,390
Fashion Designers	60,160
Film and Video Editors	44,540
Fine Artists	43,750
Graphic Designers	41,380
Interior Designers	43,770
Photographers	28,810

Did You Know?

The oldest known paintings are in a cave in France called Grotte Chavet. The paintings were created about 32,000 years ago.

Real-World Math

Use the tables on page 304 to solve each problem.

1. Find the median, mode, range, and any outlier(s) of the salary data.

2. Describe the salary data using the median, mode, and range.

3. Select and make an appropriate display for the data in the frequency table. Justify your selection.

4. Write one or two sentences describing the graph you made in Exercise 3.

5. Find the mode of the data presented in the graph. Explain what the mode represents.

6. Is it possible to find the median and range of the data in the frequency table? Explain.

7-7 Line Graphs

GET READY to Learn

The table shows how the population of Jefferson County has changed from 1930 to 2000.

Year	Population	Year	Population
1930	133,000	1970	245,000
1940	145,000	1980	251,000
1950	195,000	1990	239,000
1960	246,000	2000	252,000

MAIN IDEA

I will make and interpret line graphs and double line graphs.

New Vocabulary

line graph
double line graph

Math Online

macmillanmh.com
- Extra Examples
- Personal Tutor
- Self-Check Quiz

Another way to organize data is to use a line graph. In a **line graph**, plotted points are connected to show changes in data over time.

Real-World EXAMPLE — Make and Interpret a Line Graph

1 **POPULATION** **Refer to the information above. Make a line graph of the data.**

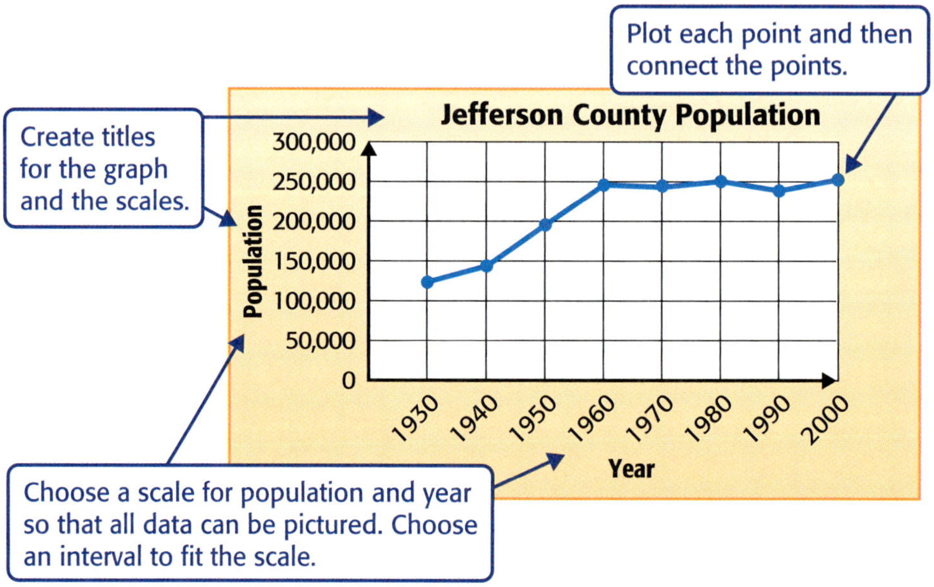

The line graph shows the following information:

- The population increased from 1930 to 1960.
- Since 1960, the population has been stable.

A **double line graph** shows two different data sets, each represented by a line graph. The two line graphs share a common scale.

Real-World EXAMPLE — Make and Interpret a Double Line Graph

2 **TECHNOLOGY** **The table below shows the changes in television viewing and Internet use, not including the use of E-mail, from 2000 to 2006.**

Year	Average Daily Hours	
	Television Viewing	Internet Use
2000	4.1	2.0
2001	4.3	2.1
2002	4.3	2.3
2003	4.4	2.4
2004	4.4	2.6
2005	4.5	2.7
2006	4.6	2.9

Source: Nielsen Media Research, The Harris Poll

Remember

When making a double line graph, make each set of points different, as in Example 2. Another method is to use different colors for the two lines.

Make a double line graph of the data. Then use the graph to describe the changes in television viewing and Internet use from 2000 to 2006.

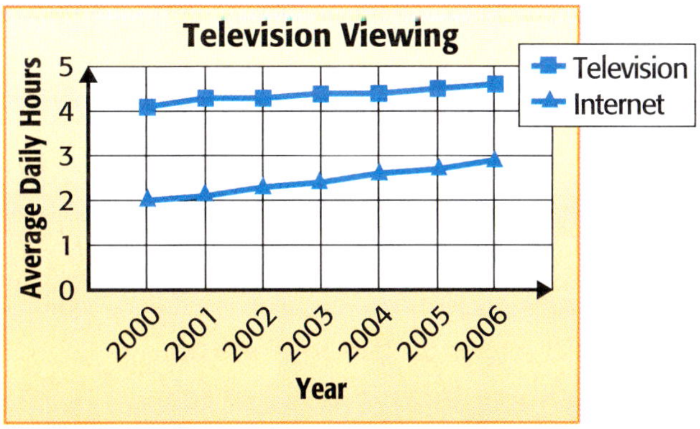

- Both the hours of television viewing and Internet use steadily increased from 2000 to 2006.
- The hours of Internet use appear to be increasing slightly more quickly than the hours of television viewing.
- People still spend more time watching television than using the Internet.

CHECK What You Know

For Exercises 1–4, refer to the line graph at the right. It shows the weight gain of a kitten. See Example 1 (p. 306)

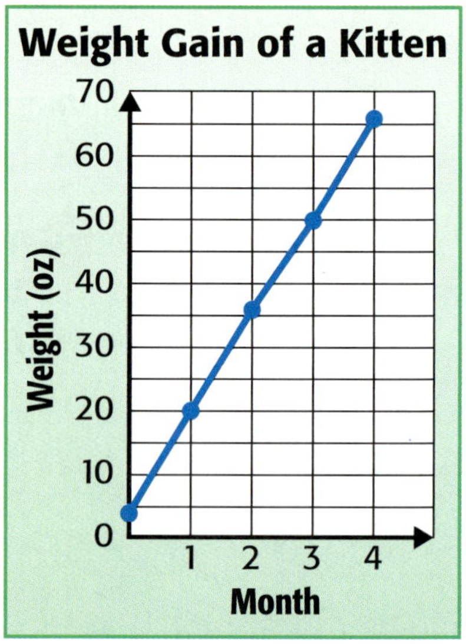

1. What is the scale of the vertical axis?

2. What is the size of each interval on the vertical axis?

3. About how many ounces did the kitten gain per month?

4. Why is a line graph used in this example instead of a bar graph?

The table shows population data for two counties. See Example 2 (p. 307)

Year	County Population	
	County A	County B
1900	1,716	1,641
1910	2,106	2,814
1920	2,064	4,050
1930	2,219	7,691
1940	3,469	10,383
1950	4,252	10,113
1960	7,006	10,975
1970	8,902	9,494
1980	14,260	9,289
1990	17,892	7,976
2000	22,497	7,828

5. Create a double line graph to show the populations from 1900 to 2000.

6. Write a few sentences to describe each county's population change and how the two counties' populations compare over time.

7. Predict each county's population for the 2010 U.S. Census. Explain.

8. Talk About It Explain when you would use a line graph to show data.

Practice and Problem Solving

EXTRA PRACTICE See page R20.

For Exercises 9–11, refer to the line graph at the right that shows total water use for a town. See Example 1 (p. 306)

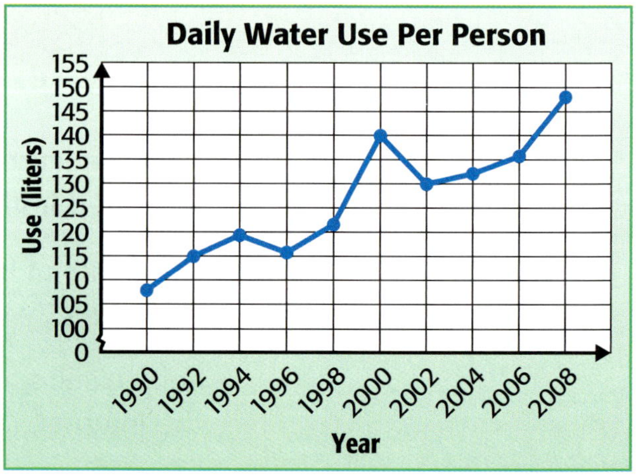

9. What is the scale of each axis?

10. What is the size of each interval on each axis?

11. Describe water use patterns for the town from 1990 to 2008.

The table shows the number of baseball cards that Julian had in his collection. See Example 1 (p. 306)

Year	Total Number of Baseball Cards
2006	35
2007	62
2008	88
2009	110

12. Make a line graph of the data.

13. Write a sentence or two describing the changes from 2006 to 2009.

For Exercises 14–17, refer to the double line graph at the right that shows the number of two different types of first class mail from 1995 to 2005. See Example 2 (p. 307)

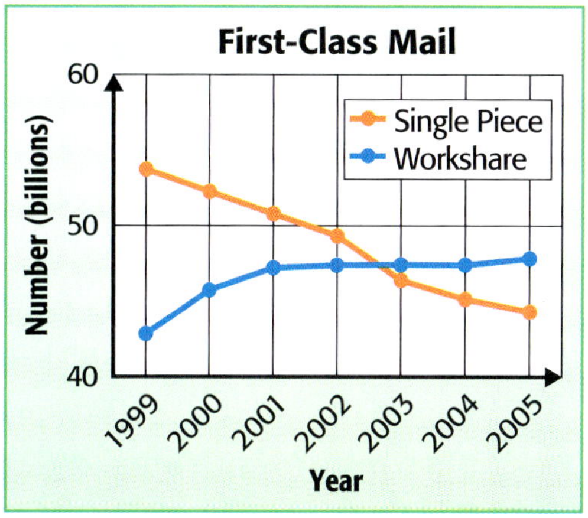

14. What is the scale of each axis?

15. What is the size of each interval on each axis?

16. Describe the patterns the line graphs show about the volume of these two types of first class mail.

17. Predict the volume for single piece first class mail in the year 2010. Explain your reasoning.

For Exercises 18–20, refer to the table at the right. It shows the distance ran by two marathon runners over a one-hour period. See Example 2 (p. 307)

Marathon Running

Time (minutes)	Runner 1 (miles)	Runner 2 (miles)
10	1.8	1.0
20	3.0	1.9
30	4.1	2.7
40	4.7	4.0
50	5.1	4.8
60	5.4	5.7

18. Create a double line graph to show the distance traveled by the two runners in one hour.

19. Write a few sentences describing the distance traveled by each runner.

20. If both runners continued for another hour, predict which runner would be leading the race.

H.O.T. Problems

21. **OPEN ENDED** The line graph at the right has several parts missing. Create a story and a context to go along with the graph. Create axes labels and a title for the graph.

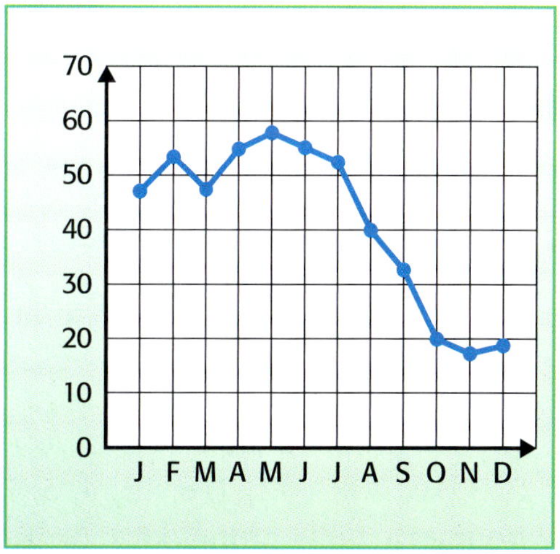

22. **WRITING IN ►MATH** Write a problem that can be solved by making a line graph. Then make the line graph. Solve. Exchange problems and graphs with another person to solve.

TEST Practice

23. Tyson made a graph of the high temperatures for a week. Which statement is true about the graph? (Lesson 7-7)

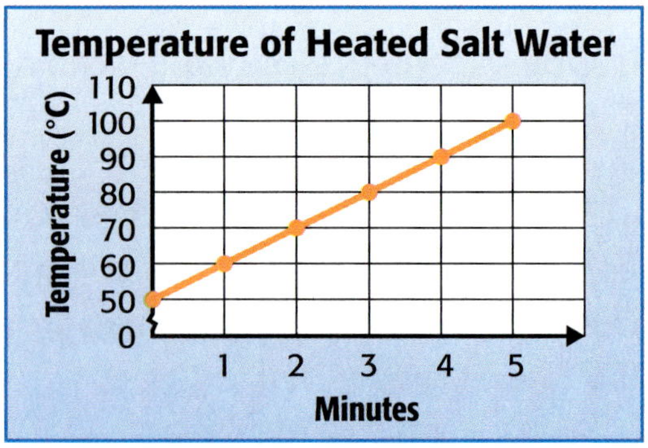

A No temperature was greater than 65°C.

B No temperature was less than 57°C.

C The lowest temperature was at 5 minutes.

D The temperature increased each minute.

---

24. A wildlife refuge is divided into different areas. The graph shows four of the areas and the number of animals in each area. Which table was used to create the graph? (Lesson 7-6)

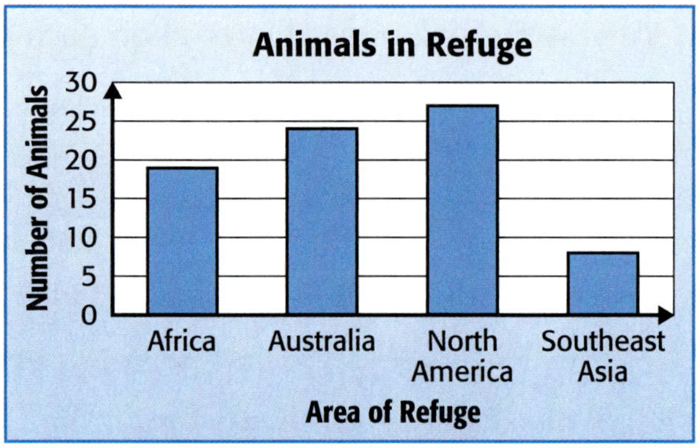

F

Area	Number of Animals
Africa	1
Australia	2
North America	3
Southeast Asia	4

G

Area	Number of Animals
Africa	20
Australia	25
North America	25
Southeast Asia	10

H

Area	Number of Animals
Africa	19
Australia	24
North America	27
Southeast Asia	8

J

Area	Number of Animals
Africa	27
Australia	24
North America	19
Southeast Asia	8

Spiral Review

The table shows students' favorite seasons. (Lesson 7-6)

Season	Number of Votes
Fall	8
Spring	10
Summer	25
Winter	5

25. Make a bar graph of the data.

26. Use the bar graph to write one or two sentences describing the data.

27. The length in minutes of Mrs. Jones' most recent phone calls are: 5, 8, 16, 20, 3, 11, 2, 8, 13, 4, 3, 15, 6, 4, and 17. Create a frequency table of the data. (Lesson 7-5)

Four in a Row

Making a Line Graph

Get Ready!

Players: 2 or more

You will need: 2 number cubes labeled 0–5
paper
grid paper
counters in two different colors

Get Set!

Make a 6 × 6 coordinate grid as shown. Graphs should be big enough for the counters.

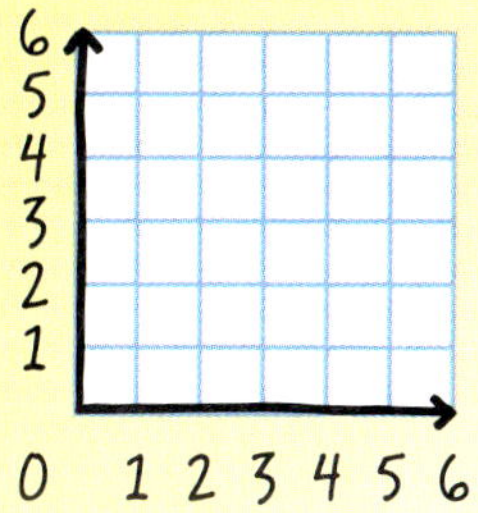

Create a record sheet for each game listing the names of each player.

Go!

- A player tosses the number cubes to make an ordered pair. For example, if the number cubes show 3 and 2, the player could choose to use (3, 2) or (2, 3).

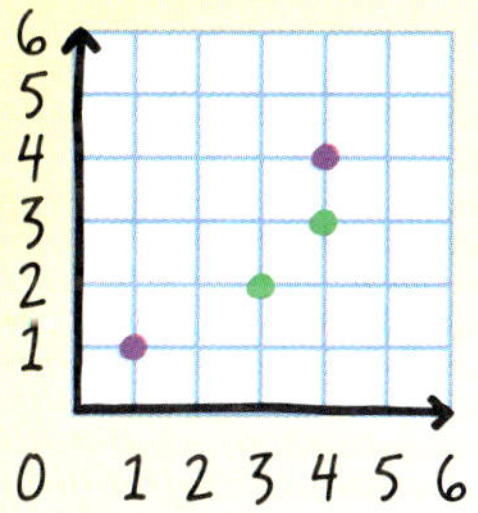

- The player uses a counter to graph the ordered pair on the grid. If both possible ordered pairs are already covered, the player loses a turn. Use different color counters to cover the points.
- Repeat until one player graphs four ordered pairs in a row, column, or diagonal.

7-8 Use an Appropriate Graph

MAIN IDEA

I will select and make an appropriate graph for presenting data.

New Vocabulary

pictograph

Math Online

macmillanmh.com
- Extra Examples
- Personal Tutor
- Self-Check Quiz
- Concepts in Motion

GET READY to Learn

The number of pounds of cans recycled by the fifth grade class are shown in the table.

Recycling Cans	
Week	**Number of Pounds**
1	10
2	14
3	9
4	12

You have learned to represent data using different types of graphs: line plots, bar graphs, double bar graphs, line graphs, and double line graphs. Another type of graph called a **pictograph**, compares data by using picture symbols.

You can use a pictograph to represent the data in the table above.

Step 1 Choose a picture that is related to the data and is easy to draw. For this pictograph, let a can represent the data.

Step 2 Decide how much data each symbol will represent in whole and half symbols. For this situation, you can let one can represent 2 pounds. Then a half-can will represent 1 pound.

Step 3 Draw the pictograph. Include a key showing what each picture symbol represents.

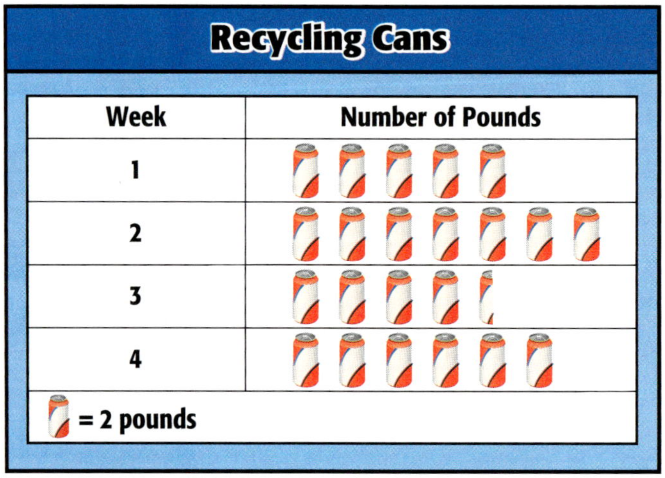

Each type of graph has a different purpose.

Graphs

Concept Summary

A *line plot* shows the frequency of data.

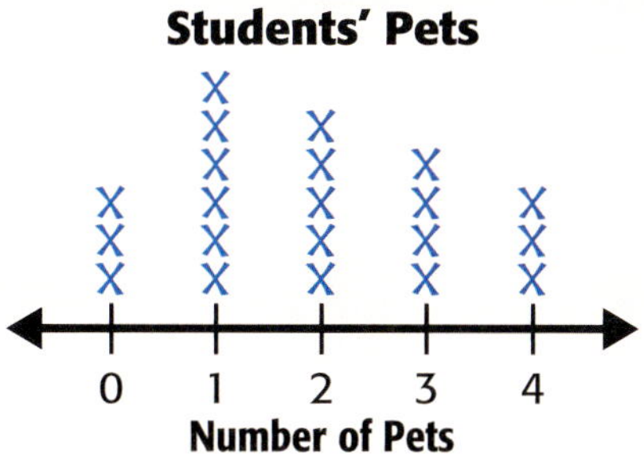

A *bar graph* uses bars to compare data.

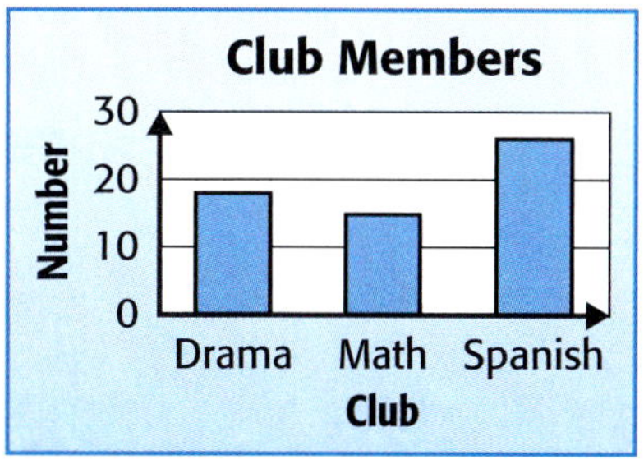

A *line graph* shows changes in data over time.

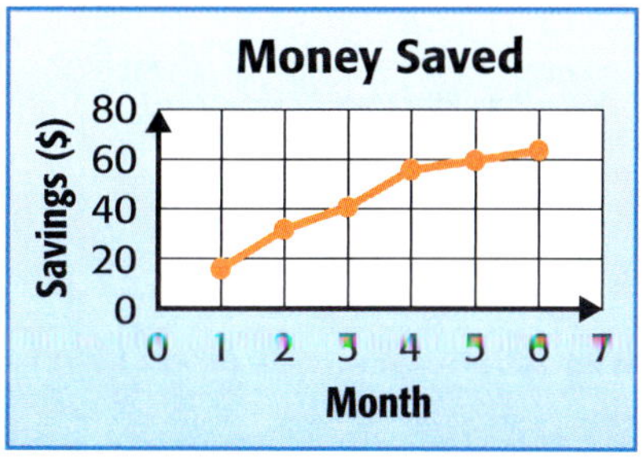

A *pictograph* uses picture symbols to compare data.

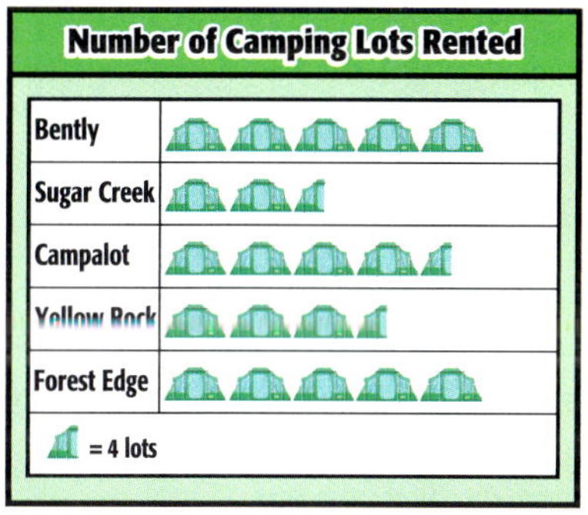

Remember

There is more than one way to graph data correctly. The data in Example 1 could have also been displayed in a bar graph. The bars could represent the number of songs downloaded.

Real-World EXAMPLE Use an Appropriate Graph

1 **MUSIC** **The table shows the number of songs that were downloaded one day by 16 students. Select and make an appropriate graph for presenting the data.**

Downloaded Songs			
3	2	1	1
4	3	4	3
2	2	5	4
3	2	3	3

A line plot could be used to show the frequency of the data.

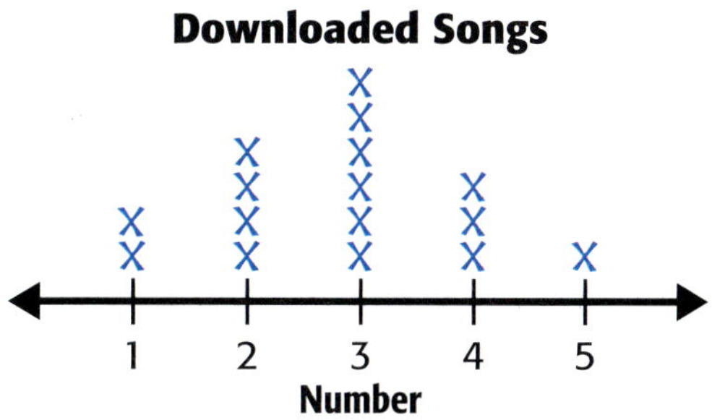

Real-World EXAMPLES

2 **PLANTS** **Carmita was tracking the growth rate of her plant as shown in the table. Select and make an appropriate graph for presenting the data.**

Plant Growth	
Week	Height (in.)
1	1.5
2	2
3	3.5
4	4
5	6

A line graph would be useful to show the changes in the height of the plant throughout the five week period.

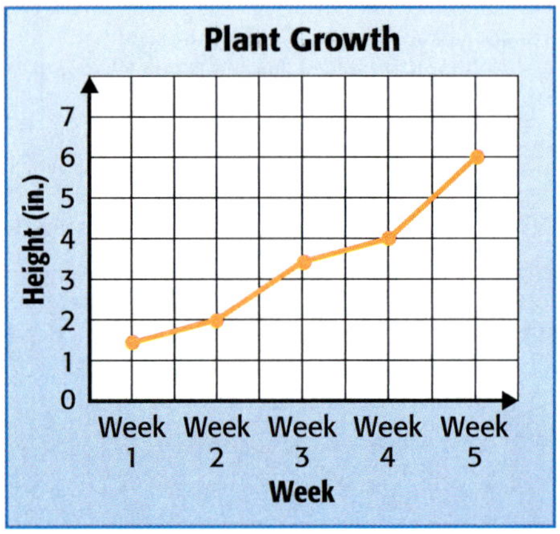

3 **POPULATIONS** **The approximate populations of the five largest United States cities from two different years are shown. Select and make an appropriate graph for presenting the data.**

Population of the Five Largest United States Cities		
City	1990 Census	2000 Census
New York City	7,322,564	8,008,278
Los Angeles	3,485,398	3,694,820
Chicago	2,783,726	2,896,016
Houston	1,630,553	1,953,631
Philadelphia	1,585,577	1,517,550

Remember

When there are two sets of data, use a double bar graph or a double line graph.

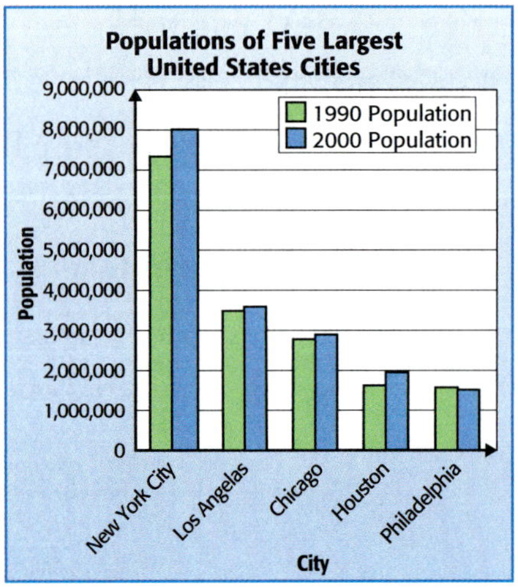

There are two sets of data: the 1990 and 2000 populations. To compare the populations of all five United States cities, use a double bar graph. It allows you to compare both sets of data at a glance.

CHECK What You Know

Which type of graph would you use to display the data in each table? Write *line plot, bar graph, double bar graph, line graph, double line graph*, or *pictograph*. Explain why. Then make the graph. See Examples 1–3 (pp. 313–314)

1.

Tallest Roller Coasters in the World	
Roller Coaster	**Height (ft)**
Kingda Ka	456
Top Thrill Dragster	420
Superman: The Escape	415
Tower of Terror	377
Steel Dragon 2000	318
Millennium Force	310

Source: Coaster Grotto

2.

Car's Acceleration Rate	
Time (sec)	**Speed (mph)**
2	22
4	44
6	60

3.

Smallest Countries	
Country	**Land Area (sq km)**
Vatican City	1
Monaco	2
Nauru	21
Tuvalu	26
San Marino	61

4.

Students' Favorite Movies	
Movie	**Number of Students**
A	30
B	50
C	40
D	20
E	60

5. Talk About It Explain why it is necessary to choose a certain type of graph to represent a set of data. Give an example.

Practice and Problem Solving

EXTRA PRACTICE See page R20.

Which type of graph would you use to display the data in each table? Write *line plot, bar graph, double bar graph, line graph, double line graph*, or *pictograph*. Explain why. Then make the graph.
See Examples 1–3 (pp. 313–314)

6.

Continent	Number of Countries
Africa	53
Asia	44
Europe	46
North America	23
Oceania	14
South America	12
Antarctica	0

7.

Movies Owned by Molly	
Type of Movie	**Number of Movies**
Musical	3
Drama	1
Adventure	2
Comedy	6
Western	2

Which type of graph would you use to display the data in each table? Write *line plot, bar graph, double bar graph, line graph, double line graph*, or *pictograph*. Explain why. Then make the graph.

See Examples 1–3 (pp. 313–314)

8.

Money Earned by the End of Each Hour	
Hour	**Dollars Earned from Video Rentals**
1:00	\$23
2:00	\$45
3:00	\$120
4:00	\$164
5:00	\$210

9.

2005 Touchdowns		
Team	**Number by Running**	**Number by Receiving**
Seattle	29	25
Indianapolis	18	31
New York	17	24
Cincinnati	15	32
San Diego	22	27

Source: National Football League

10.

Number of Text Messages per Day				
8	3	4	10	5
5	7	6	9	8
6	5	4	8	10

11.

Patrick's Growth Rate	
Age (yr)	**Height (in.)**
3	34
6	51
9	53
12	59

12. Malina conducted a survey at her school to determine students' favorite fruits. She recorded her results in the table below. Graph the data to show the results. Explain why you chose the graph that you did.

Fruit	Tally	Number of People
Apples	卌 卌 卌 卌 卌 |	26
Bananas	卌 卌 ||	12
Grapes	卌 卌 卌 卌 |	21
Oranges	卌 卌 卌 |	16
Peaches	卌 |	6
Pineapple	卌	5
Raspberries	||||	4
Strawberries	卌 卌 ||	12

13. Examine the pictograph. If the person who created it was sitting next to you, what question(s) would you ask him or her to help understand the graph?

H.O.T. Problems

14. **COLLECT THE DATA** Take a survey of your class to see what activity they prefer to do on the weekend. Record your results in a table like the one shown below.

Activity	Tally	Frequency
Bicycling		
Skateboarding		
In-line Skating		
Swimming		

Graph the data. Explain what type of graph you used.

15. **CHALLENGE** The two line graphs show the same data about the amount of money in Trong's savings account for a 5-month period. For what purposes might each version of these graphs be useful?

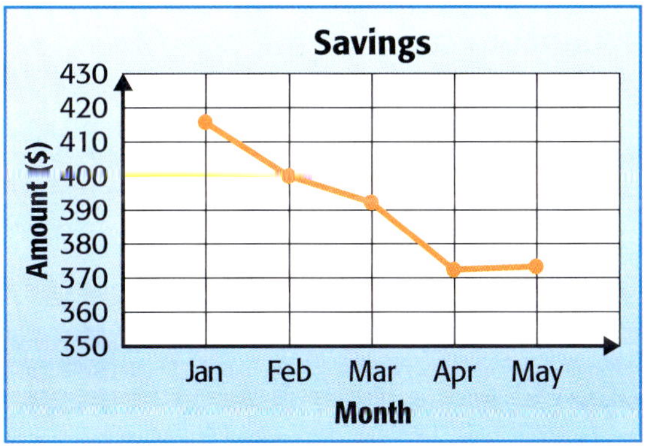

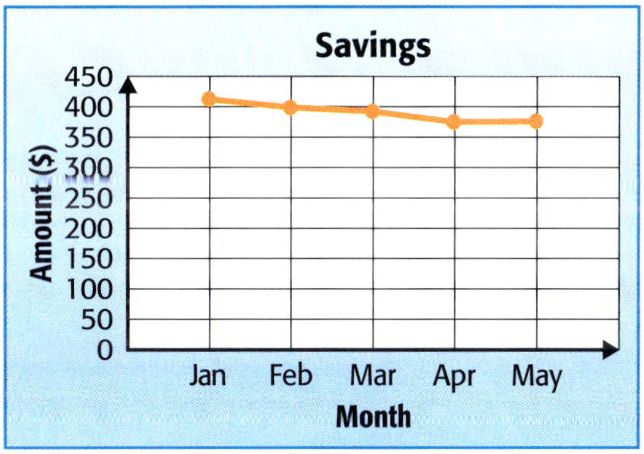

16. **FIND THE ERROR** Four frogs have masses of 91 grams, 95 grams, 105 grams, and 100 grams. Isabella and Eric are choosing which type of graph to use to display the data. Who is correct? Explain.

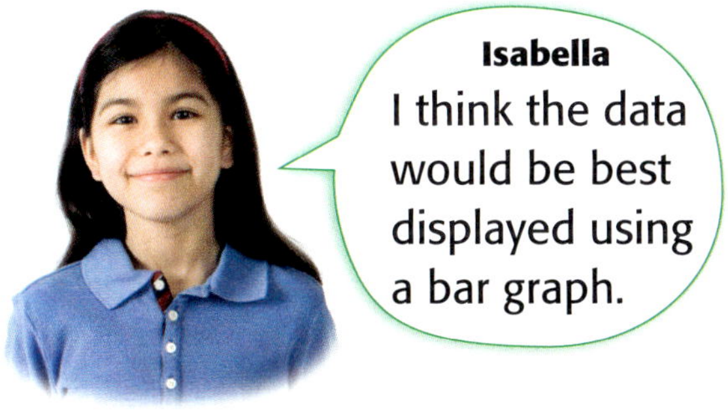

17. **WRITING IN MATH** Describe some of the things you look for in a set of data when you are deciding on the type of graph to use.

Extend

Technology Activity for 7-8

Use an Appropriate Graph

Tech Link

MAIN IDEA

I will use technology to select and create graphs.

You can use Math Tool Chest™ to display data in bar graphs and line graphs.

ACTIVITY Choose an Appropriate Graph

1 **Morgan is writing a paper about why the Boston Celtics are the most successful NBA team in history. She wants to include a graph of the information at the right.**

NBA Championships Won	
Lakers	14
Celtics	16
76ers	3
Bulls	6

A bar graph would be the most appropriate graph to display the data. It would allow Morgan to compare the team's championships.

- Choose Graphs, and click on level two.
- Click on Bar Graph.
- Click on the up arrow next to the ten to increase the y-axis to 20.
- Click on the add bar button to add a fourth bar to the graph.
- Input the correct labels for the x-axis, y-axis, and title.
- Drag each team's bar up to match their total number of championships won.

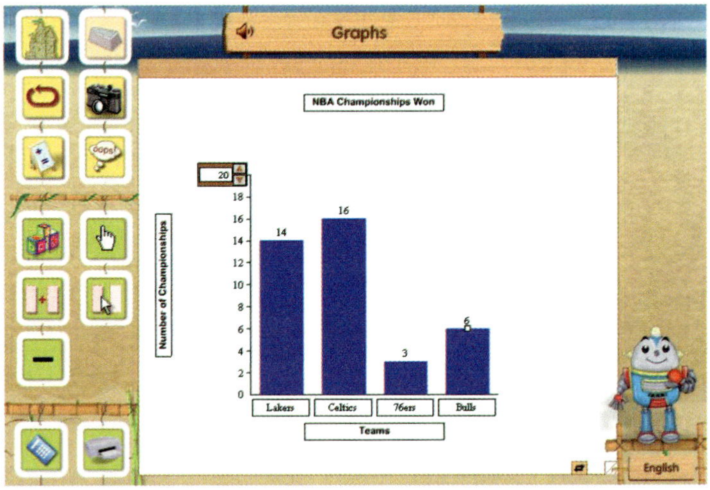

ACTIVITY

Tech Link

2 **Owen started a bike race at 10:00 A.M. and finished at 12:00 P.M. He tracked how far he traveled every 30 minutes. Based on Owen's data, select and make an appropriate graph.**

Biking	
Time	**Distance (mi)**
10:30	8
11:00	8
11:30	6
12:00	5

A line graph would be the most appropriate graph to display Owen's data.

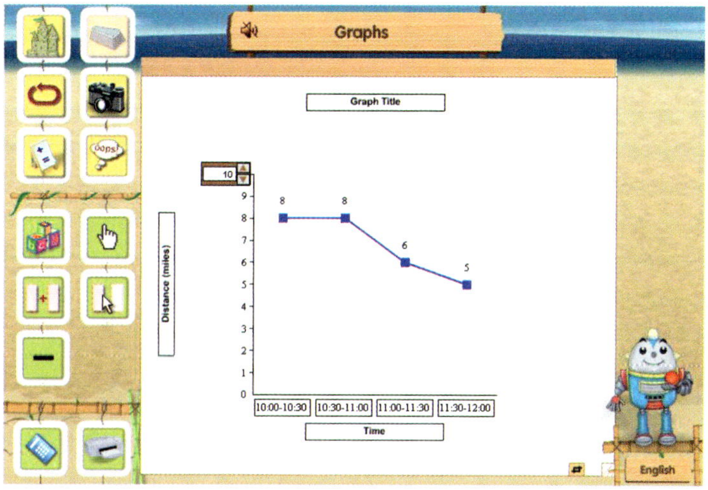

- Choose Graphs, and click level two.
- Click Line Graphs.
- Click the add bar button to add a fourth section.
- Input the labels for the title, times, *x*-axis and *y*-axis.
- Drag the line above each day up to match the number of miles that Owen traveled.

CHECK What You Know

Which type of graph would you use to display the data in each table? Write *bar graph, double bar graph, line graph,* or *double line graph*. Then create the graph using Math Tool Chest™.

1.

Basketball Scoring	
Student	**Points**
Becky	20
Jeff	12
Simeon	15
Pete	8

2.

Puppy's Growth	
Month	**Weight (lb)**
January	8
February	8
March	11
April	10
May	13

3.

Olympic Medals Won	
Type of Medal	**Number of Medals Received**
Bronze	15
Silver	9
Gold	1

4. **COLLECT THE DATA** Collect three different data sets. One set should be appropriate for a line graph, and one for a pictograph. Graph the data.

5. **WRITING IN MATH** Write a sentence or two about each of the graphs you made in Exercise 4. Explain why you chose each type of graph and analyze the data.

7-9 Problem-Solving Strategy

MAIN IDEA I will solve problems by making a graph.

The table shows the number of gallons of lemonade that were needed at the school picnic in recent years. It also shows the temperature the day of the picnic.

Temperature (°F)	Lemonade (gallons)
91	36
80	15
86	22
95	40
87	25

This year, the temperature is expected to be 93°F. About how many gallons of lemonade will be needed?

Understand

What facts do you know?

- You know the temperature and gallons of lemonade.

What do you need to find?

- How much lemonade will be needed if it is 93°F.

Plan

One way to solve the problem is to graph the ordered pairs on a coordinate grid and look for patterns in the data. Making a graph is like drawing a picture of the data.

Solve

Use your plan to solve the problem.

As the temperature increases, the number of gallons of lemonade increases. Place a dot midway between (91, 36) and (95, 40). The graph shows (93, 38). So, about 38 gallons of lemonade should be needed.

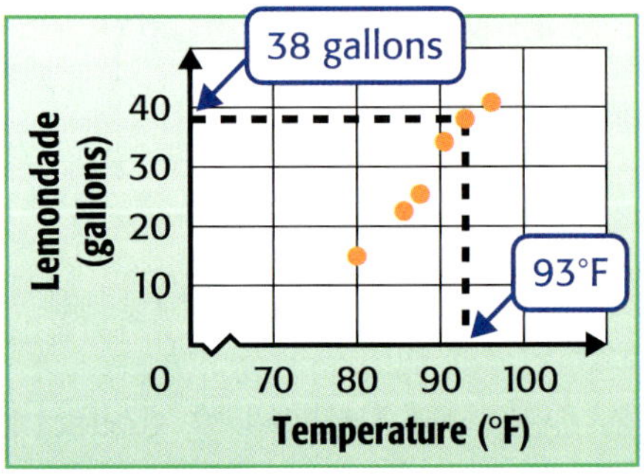

Check

Look back. List the temperatures from least to greatest. When the temperature is between 91°F and 93°F, the gallons of lemonade needed is between 36 and 40. The answer makes sense. ✓

ANALYZE the Strategy

Refer to the problem on the previous page.

1. What are some advantages and disadvantages of showing the data in a graph?

2. What are some advantages and disadvantages of showing the data in a table?

3. Suppose the temperature was expected to be 85°F. How much lemonade would be needed? Explain.

4. One year, the picnic needed 45 gallons of lemonade. Estimate the temperature that day. Explain.

PRACTICE the Strategy

EXTRA PRACTICE See page R21.

Solve by *using a graph.*

5. The table lists the number of wins by the teams in the American Football Conference (AFC) and the National Football Conference (NFC) for a recent season.

Number of Wins	
AFC	12, 10, 7, 6, 13, 8, 8, 4, 12, 8, 8, 6, 14, 9, 9, 2
NFC	10, 9, 8, 5, 13, 8, 6, 3, 10, 8, 7, 4, 9, 8, 7, 5

Graph the data on line plots. Which conference seemed to have the better record? Explain your reasoning using the graph and the term *median*.

6. Company A and Company B make flashlight batteries. Ten batteries from each company were selected and tested to see how many hours they would last. The results are shown below.

Hours of Life from Flashlight Batteries	
Company A	19, 11, 14, 15, 8, 16, 14, 16, 15, 24, 10
Company B	18, 12, 15, 16, 17, 18, 16, 17, 20, 14, 9

Graph the data on line plots. From which company would you purchase batteries? Use the line plots and the term *median* to help explain your reasoning.

For Exercises 7–10, use the table. It gives the number of chirps per minute made by crickets at a given temperature.

Cricket Chirps	
Temperature (°F)	Number
72	136
84	165
68	98
75	110
80	150
94	210
60	84
75	158
92	221
89	178

7. Graph the ordered pairs on a coordinate grid.

8. What appears to happen to the number of chirps as the temperature increases?

9. Suppose the temperature is 65°F. How many times per minute would you expect a cricket to chirp?

10. Suppose you hear a cricket chirp 200 times per minute. About what would you expect the temperature to be?

11. **WRITING IN MATH** Find two different sets of data in the newspaper or from the Internet. Write a real-world problem about the data. Ask a classmate to solve your problem.

CHAPTER 7

Study Guide and Review

Math Online macmillanmh.com

- STUDY TO GO
- Vocabulary Review

FOLDABLES® Study Organizer GET READY to Study

Be sure the following Big Ideas are written in your Foldable.

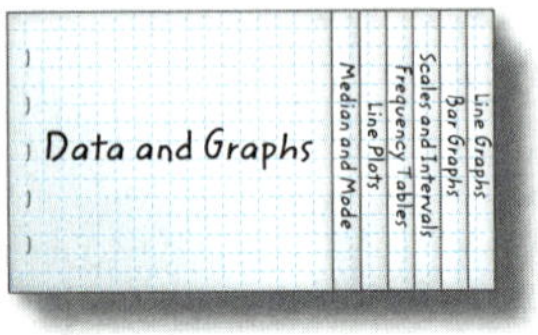

Key Concepts

Mean, Median, and Mode

- The **mean** of a set of data is the sum of the data divided by the number of pieces of data. (p. 279)
- The **median** of a set of data is the middle number of the data that has been written in order. (p. 279)
- The **mode** of a set of data is the number that occurs most often. (p. 280)

Displaying Data

- A **line plot** uses Xs above a number line to show the number of times values in a set of data occur. (p. 284)
- A **frequency table** shows the number of times each data value or each value within an interval appears. (p. 289)
- A **bar graph** uses bars to compare data. (p. 299)
- A **line graph** has plotted points that are connected to show how a quantity changes over time. (p. 306)
- A **pictograph** shows data by using picture symbols. (p. 313)

Key Vocabulary

bar graph (p. 299)
line graph (p. 306)
mean (p. 279)
median (p. 279)
mode (p. 280)
range (p. 285)

Vocabulary Check

Complete. Use a word from the Key Vocabulary list.

1. The middle number in a set of ordered numbers is the __?__.
2. To show the change in temperature over a period of time, use a(n) __?__.
3. The difference between the greatest and least values in a set of data is the __?__.
4. The __?__ in the set of data {4, 6, 2, 3, 3, 5, 7} is 3.
5. A(n) __?__ is a graph that uses bars to compare data.
6. The __?__ of a set of data is the number that occurs most often.

H.O.T. Problems

34. OPEN ENDED Write two improper fractions that would be graphed between points *A* and *B* on the number line.

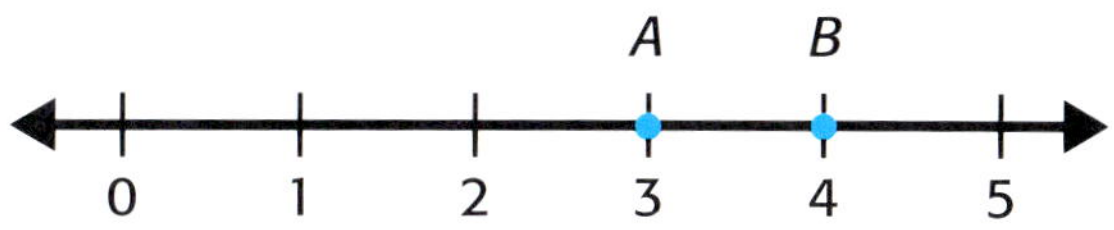

35. FIND THE ERROR Kedar and Ashley are comparing $3\frac{5}{6}$ and $\frac{19}{6}$. Who is correct? Explain.

Kedar

$3\frac{5}{6} = \frac{(3 + 6 + 5)}{6}$

$\frac{14}{6} \bigcirc \frac{19}{6}$

$\frac{14}{6} < \frac{19}{6}$

Ashley

$3\frac{5}{6} = \frac{(3 \times 6) + 5}{6}$

$\frac{23}{6} \bigcirc \frac{19}{6}$

$\frac{23}{6} > \frac{19}{6}$

36. WRITING IN MATH Explain how you can use a number line to compare a fraction and a mixed number.

TEST Practice

37. Which shows the correct relationship between the numbers in the table below? (Lesson 8-5)

Day	Rainfall (in.)
Monday	$\frac{7}{10}$
Tuesday	$1\frac{3}{10}$

A $\frac{7}{10} > 1\frac{3}{10}$

B $\frac{7}{10} = 1\frac{3}{10}$

C $1\frac{3}{10} > \frac{7}{10}$

D $1\frac{3}{10} < \frac{7}{10}$

38. A song is $4\frac{3}{10}$ minutes long. Which is another way of writing $4\frac{3}{10}$? (Lesson 8-4)

F $\frac{7}{10}$

G $\frac{12}{10}$

H $\frac{40}{10}$

J $\frac{43}{10}$

Spiral Review

Write each mixed number as an improper fraction. (Lesson 8-4)

39. $3\frac{1}{5}$ **40.** $1\frac{7}{8}$ **41.** $4\frac{2}{11}$ **42.** $6\frac{5}{9}$

Write each improper fraction as a mixed number. (Lesson 8-2)

43. $\frac{11}{8}$ **44.** $\frac{17}{6}$ **45.** $\frac{37}{5}$ **46.** $\frac{21}{4}$

Problem Solving in Geography

The Great United States

How big is the United States? In total land area, the United States is about three times as large as India and about one and one-third times as large as Australia. However, the United States is only about two-thirds the size of Russia and only accounts for about one-fifteenth of the world's land area.

Source: World Atlas

Did You Know?

About one-fifth of the area of the United States is water.

Real-World Math

Use the information on page 354 to solve each problem.

1. The land size of the United States is about how many times as large as Australia? Write this number as an improper fraction.

2. The land size of Russia is about $2\frac{1}{5}$ times the land size of Australia. Write this mixed number as an improper fraction.

3. The land size of the United States is about $\frac{37}{11}$ times the land size of Argentina. Write this improper fraction as a mixed number

4. Does Russia or Canada account for a greater fraction of the world's land area?

5. Does Brazil or India account for a lesser fraction of the world's land area?

6. Name two countries that account for the same fraction of the world's land area.

8-6 Round Fractions

GET READY to Learn

A poison dart frog is 2 inches long. This is equal to $\frac{2}{12}$ of a foot.

One way to round a fraction is to use a number line.

Real-World EXAMPLE — Round Fractions

1 **ANIMALS** **Refer to the information above. Is the length of a poison dart frog closest to 0 foot, $\frac{1}{2}$ foot, or 1 foot?**

Graph $\frac{2}{12}$ on a number line.

On the number line, $\frac{2}{12}$ is closer to 0 than to $\frac{1}{2}$ or 1. So, the length of a poison dart frog is closest to 0 feet.

MAIN IDEA

I will round fractions to 0, $\frac{1}{2}$, and 1 using a number line.

Math Online

macmillanmh.com
- Extra Examples
- Personal Tutor
- Self-Check Quiz

You can also round fractions mentally.

Rounding Fractions — Key Concept

Round Down

If the numerator is much smaller than the denominator, round the number down to the previous whole number.

Example

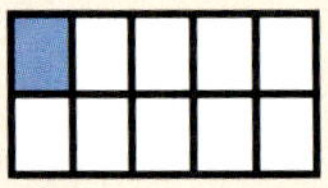

$\frac{1}{10}$ rounds to 0.

Round to $\frac{1}{2}$

If the numerator is about half of the denominator, round the fraction to $\frac{1}{2}$.

Example

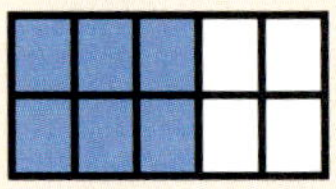

$\frac{6}{10}$ rounds to $\frac{1}{2}$.

Round Up

If the numerator is almost as large as the denominator, round the number up to the next whole number.

Example

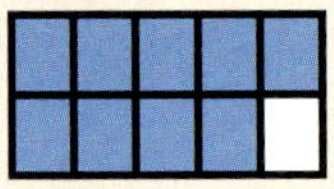

$\frac{9}{10}$ rounds to 1.

EXAMPLES Round Fractions Mentally

Remember

The numerator is the top number in a fraction. The denominator is the bottom number. In the fraction $\frac{4}{9}$, 4 is the numerator and 9 is the denominator.

2 **Round $\frac{4}{9}$ to 0, $\frac{1}{2}$, or 1.**

Since 4 is about half of 9, $\frac{4}{9}$ is closest to $\frac{1}{2}$. You can see from the number line that $\frac{4}{9}$ is closer to $\frac{1}{2}$ than it is to 0 or 1.

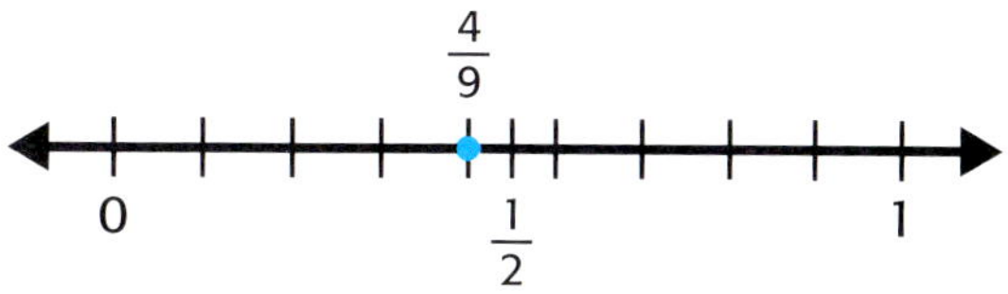

3 **Round $\frac{10}{11}$ to 0, $\frac{1}{2}$, or 1.**

Since 10 is close to 11, $\frac{10}{11}$ is closest to 1.

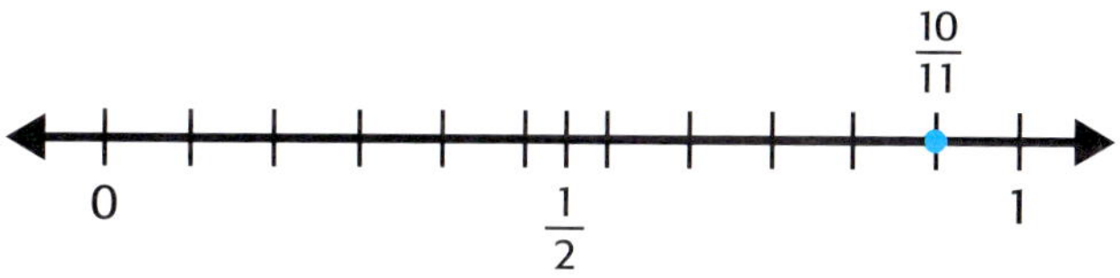

CHECK What You Know

State whether each fraction is closest to 0, $\frac{1}{2}$, or 1.
See Example 1 (p. 356)

1. $\frac{5}{6}$

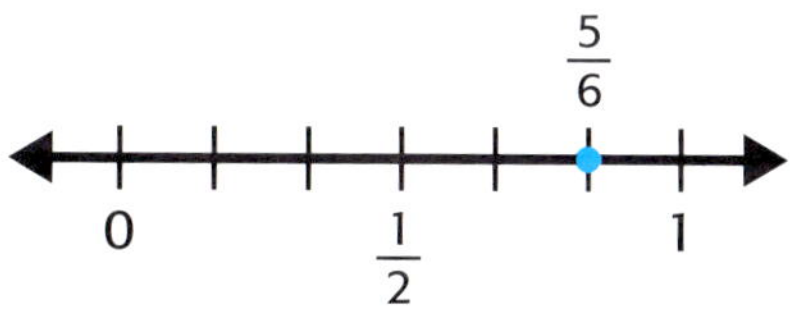

2. $\frac{5}{8}$

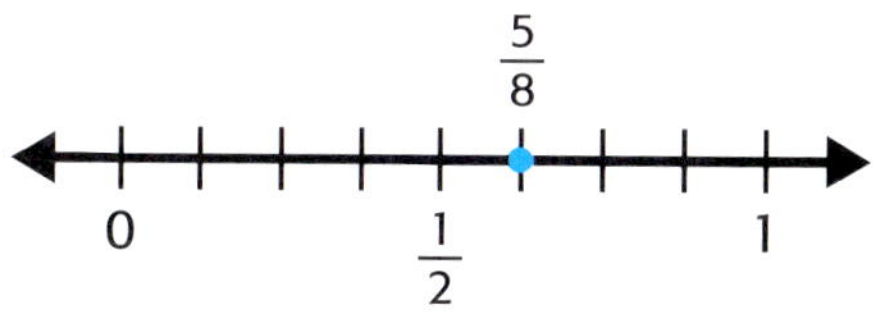

Round each fraction to 0, $\frac{1}{2}$, or 1. See Examples 2, 3 (p. 357)

3. $\frac{1}{8}$ **4.** $\frac{5}{9}$ **5.** $\frac{7}{8}$ **6.** $\frac{3}{7}$

7. $\frac{3}{11}$ **8.** $\frac{4}{5}$ **9.** $\frac{8}{16}$ **10.** $\frac{1}{9}$

11. **Measurement** Round the length of the ribbon to the nearest half inch.

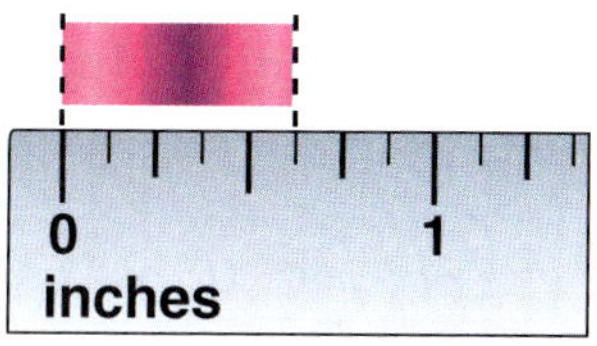

12. Talk About It Tell how to round fractions in your own words.

Practice and Problem Solving

EXTRA PRACTICE See page R23.

State whether each fraction is closest to 0, $\frac{1}{2}$, or 1. See Example 1 (p. 356)

13. $\frac{6}{7}$

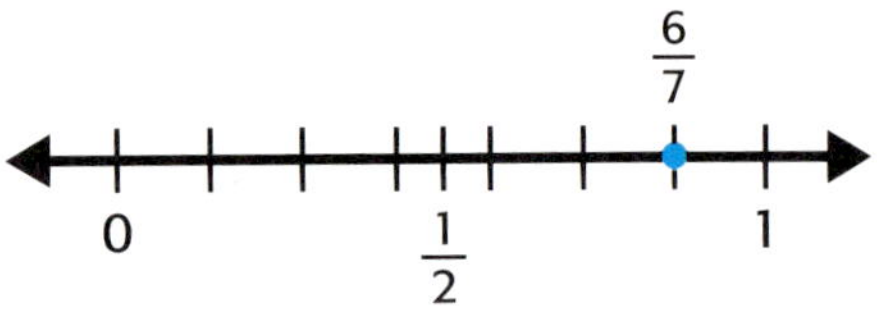

14. $\frac{2}{5}$

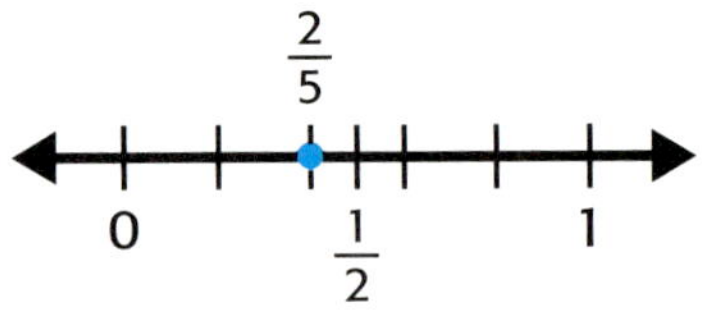

15. $\frac{3}{8}$

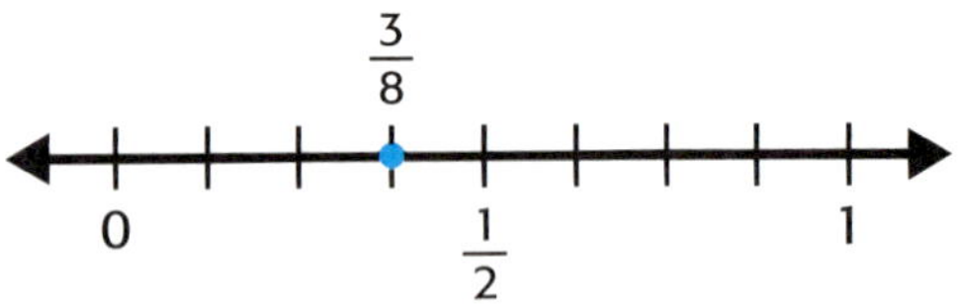

16. $\frac{1}{6}$

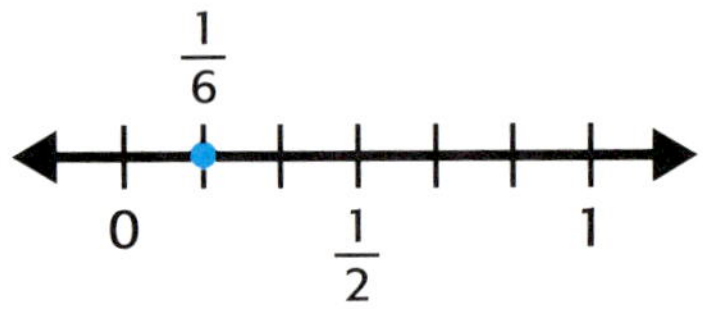

Round each fraction to 0, $\frac{1}{2}$, or 1. See Examples 2–3 (p. 357)

17. $\frac{1}{5}$ **18.** $\frac{1}{14}$ **19.** $\frac{12}{15}$ **20.** $\frac{8}{14}$

21. $\frac{6}{7}$ **22.** $\frac{2}{7}$ **23.** $\frac{6}{11}$ **24.** $\frac{2}{13}$

25. $\frac{9}{17}$ **26.** $\frac{2}{10}$ **27.** $\frac{6}{13}$ **28.** $\frac{14}{16}$

29. Kevin ate $\frac{5}{12}$ of a pizza. Which is a better estimate for the amount of pizza that he ate: about half of the pizza or about all of the pizza?

30. **Measurement** Savannah is using $\frac{15}{16}$ foot squares in a quilt she is making. Are the squares closer to $\frac{1}{2}$ foot or 1 foot long?

31. Peter has read about $\frac{12}{15}$ of his book. Has he read half of his book or almost all of his book?

32. Darius has mowed $\frac{2}{10}$ of his backyard. Which is a better estimate for how much of the lawn he has left to mow: all of the lawn or half of the lawn?

H.O.T. Problems

33. **OPEN ENDED** Write a fraction with a denominator of 15 that you could round to $\frac{1}{2}$.

34. **WHICH ONE DOESN'T BELONG?** Identify the fraction that does not belong with the other three. Explain your reasoning.

$\frac{2}{11}$ $\frac{8}{15}$ $\frac{7}{13}$ $\frac{5}{12}$

35. **CHALLENGE** Write two fractions in which the difference between the numerator and the denominator is 2. One fraction can be rounded to 1 and the other fraction can be rounded to $\frac{1}{2}$.

36. **WRITING IN MATH** Describe two different ways of rounding fractions. When is the best time to use each method?

TEST Practice

37. Samantha shaded $\frac{3}{7}$ of her design.

Which number is the best estimate for the shaded part of her design? (Lesson 8-6)

A 0

B $\frac{1}{7}$

C $\frac{1}{2}$

D 1

38. The table shows the lengths of two different races. Which correctly shows the relationship between the lengths? (Lesson 8-5)

Race	Length
1	$\frac{7}{16}$ mile
2	$\frac{9}{16}$ mile

F $\frac{7}{16} < \frac{9}{16}$

G $\frac{7}{16} > \frac{9}{16}$

H $\frac{9}{16} \geq \frac{7}{16}$

J $\frac{9}{16} = \frac{7}{16}$

Spiral Review

Replace each ● with < or > to make a true statement. (Lesson 8-5)

39. $\frac{9}{4}$ ● $\frac{2}{4}$

40. $\frac{12}{5}$ ● $3\frac{1}{5}$

41. $\frac{13}{9}$ ● $1\frac{2}{9}$

42. Measurement A bike path is $6\frac{3}{4}$ miles long. Write the length of the bike trail as an improper fraction. (Lesson 8-4)

43. Allison surveyed her classmates and found that 17 own a cat and 14 own a dog. Six of those surveyed own both a cat and a dog. How many of her classmates own only a cat? Only a dog? (Lesson 8-3)

The bar graph shows students' favorite colors. (Lesson 7-6)

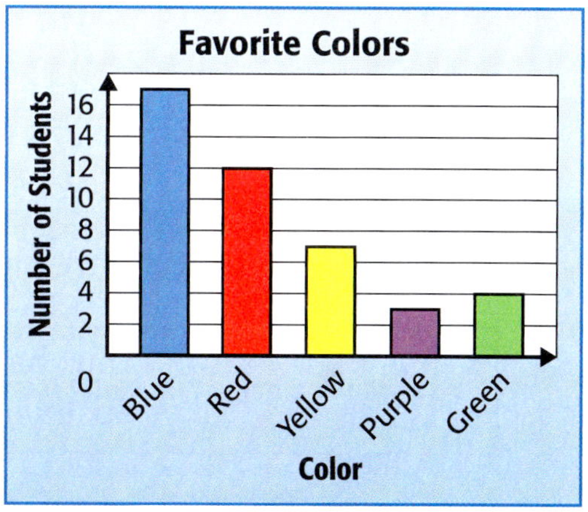

44. What colors were chosen by more than 8 students?

45. How many more students chose yellow as their favorite color than purple?

Algebra Evaluate each expression if $x = 7$. (Lesson 5-7)

46. $5x + 2$

47. $3x - 1$

8-7 Problem-Solving Investigation

MAIN IDEA I will choose the best strategy to solve a problem.

P.S.I. TEAM +

Christian wants to buy a new skateboard. So far, he has saved \$31.26 and \$45.50 from his two lawn mowing jobs. How much more money does he need to buy the skateboard if it costs \$131.99?

YOUR MISSION: Find how much more money Christian needs to buy the skateboard.

Understand	You know that Christian has saved \$31.26 and \$45.50. The skateboard costs \$131.99. You need to know how much more money Christian needs.
Plan	You need to find how much money Christian has now and how much money he still needs. So, breaking the problem down by using the *solve a simpler problem* strategy is a good choice.
Solve	First, find how much money Christian has. \$31.26 + \$45.50 \$76.76 Christian has \$76.76. Then, find how much money he still needs. Subtract \$76.76 from \$131.99. \$131.99 − \$76.76 \$55.23 Christian needs \$55.23.
Check	Look back. \$55.23 + \$31.26 + \$45.50 = \$131.99. So, the answer is correct. ✓

Mixed Problem Solving

EXTRA PRACTICE
See page R23.

Use any strategy shown below to solve each problem.

PROBLEM-SOLVING STRATEGIES

- Guess and check.
- Work backward.
- Make a table.
- Solve a simpler problem.
- Use logical reasoning.

1. **Measurement** A movie starts at 7:10 P.M. and lasts 1 hour and 45 minutes. At what time does the movie end?

2. How many ways can you make change for a $50 bill using only $5, $10, and $20 bills?

3. What two numbers have a sum of 12 and a product of 32?

4. Sports Inc. sells two different sized packages of trading cards. Thomas bought 7 packages of trading cards and spent a total of $16.75. How many of each type of package did he buy?

5. A pipe 10 feet long needs to be cut into pieces 10 inches long. How many minutes will it take if each cut takes two minutes?

6. Gracia has $1.85 in quarters and in dimes only. She has a total of 11 coins. How many of each coin does she have?

7. Joy tells her mother that she scored 4 less than 3 times as many points in Tuesday's game as she scored on Monday. If Joy scored 5 points on Monday, how many points did she score on Tuesday?

8. Rey picks tomatoes. Each day he picks twice as many as the day before. On the fourth day he picks 48 tomatoes. How many does he pick the first day?

9. Mr. Arturo makes two square pans of gelatin. He cuts one pan into 39 more squares than the other pan. How many squares of gelatin does he cut in each pan?

10. Silvia has a paper route. Each week she earns $20 plus $0.10 for each paper she delivers. Last week she earned $32. How many papers did she deliver?

11. The grocery store is having a sale on juice cartons. How much will 10 cartons cost?

12. **WRITING IN MATH** Of the 50 people surveyed at a fitness center, 32 said that they use the treadmills and 24 said that they use the bikes. Six of the people said that they use both. How many people said that they use the bikes, but not the treadmills? What strategy would you use to solve this problem? Explain.

CHAPTER 8

Study Guide and Review

Math Online macmillanmh.com
- STUDY TO GO
- Vocabulary Review

FOLDABLES Study Organizer GET READY to Study

Be sure the following Big Ideas are written in your Foldable.

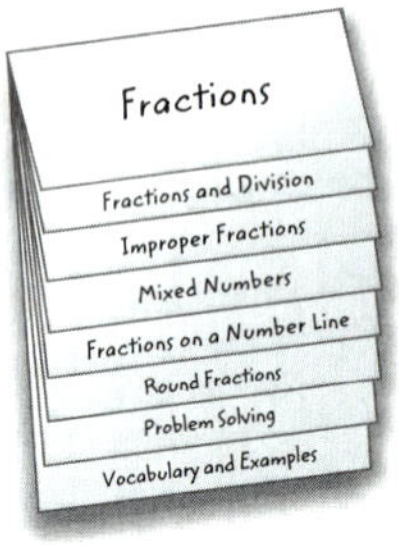

Key Concepts

Improper Fractions and Mixed Numbers

- To write an improper fraction as a mixed number, divide the numerator by the denominator. Write the remainder as a fraction of the divisor. (p. 337)

$$\frac{14}{5} \rightarrow 14 \div 5 = 2\frac{4}{5}$$

- To write a mixed number as an improper fraction, multiply the whole number by the denominator. Then add the numerator. Write the sum over the denominator. (p. 346)

$$6\frac{1}{3} \rightarrow \frac{(6 \times 3) + 1}{3} = \frac{19}{3}$$

Compare Fractions and Mixed Numbers

- Use a number line to compare fractions and mixed numbers. (p. 350)

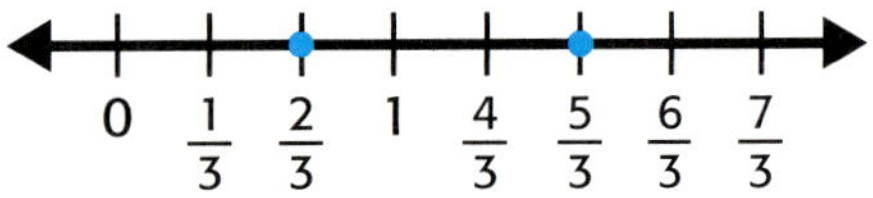

$$\frac{2}{3} < \frac{5}{3}$$

Key Vocabulary

denominator (p. 333)
fraction (p. 333)
improper fraction (p. 337)
mixed number (p. 336)
numerator (p. 333)

Vocabulary Check

State whether each sentence is *true* or *false*. If *false*, replace the underlined word or number to make a true sentence.

1. The top number in a fraction is called the numerator.
2. The number $1\frac{3}{4}$ is an example of an improper fraction.
3. The fraction $\frac{12}{13}$ should be rounded to 1.
4. An improper fraction is a fraction that is greater than or equal to 1.
5. A fraction whose numerator is much smaller than the denominator can be rounded to 0.
6. On a number line, $\frac{8}{7}$ is to the right of $\frac{9}{7}$.
7. The number $\frac{9}{5}$ equals $1\frac{4}{5}$.

Lesson-by-Lesson Review

8-1 Fractions and Division (pp. 333–335)

Example 1

Three people share 2 appetizers. What fraction of an appetizer does each person get?

Words: 2 appetizers divided by 3 people

Symbols: $2 \div 3$

Fraction: $\frac{2}{3}$ ← appetizers, ← people

Each person gets $\frac{2}{3}$ of an appetizer.

Represent each situation using a fraction. Describe what the fraction means.

8. **Measurement** Five gallons of water are used to fill 6 pitchers. How much water did each pitcher use?

9. Three bags of gravel are used to cover the bottom of 4 fish tanks. How much gravel did each fish tank use?

10. Three students share 4 cookies. How many cookies did each person receive?

8-2 Improper Fractions (pp. 338–342)

Example 2

Write $\frac{17}{6}$ as a mixed number.

Find $17 \div 6$. Write the remainder as a fraction.

$$\begin{array}{r} 2 \text{ R5} \\ 6\overline{)17} \\ -12 \\ \hline 5 \end{array} \Rightarrow 2\frac{5}{6}$$

Example 3

Write $\frac{7}{5}$ as a mixed number.

Find $7 \div 5$. Write the remainder as a fraction.

$$\begin{array}{r} 1 \text{ R2} \\ 5\overline{)7} \\ -5 \\ \hline 2 \end{array} \Rightarrow 1\frac{2}{5}$$

Write each improper fraction as a mixed number.

11. $\frac{5}{4}$

12. $\frac{9}{7}$

13. $\frac{16}{8}$

14. $\frac{15}{4}$

15. $\frac{38}{5}$

16. $\frac{26}{11}$

17. Mrs. Vu walked 5 blocks in 2 minutes. Write the number of blocks walked each minute as a mixed number.

18. Adelina cuts 49 inches of ribbon into eight pieces of equal length. How long is each piece? Write the answer with a remainder. Then write as a mixed number. Explain what both numbers mean.

8-3 Problem-Solving Strategy: Use Logical Reasoning (pp. 344–345)

Example 4

Out of a group of fifth graders, 19 like to go to the park and 16 like to go to the zoo. Nine like to go to both places. How many fifth graders like to go to the zoo but not the park?

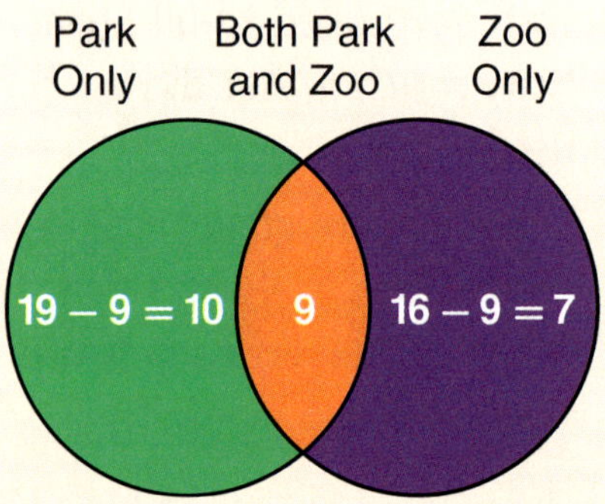

So, 7 fifth graders like the zoo only.

Solve. Use logical reasoning.

19. In Devon's family three people listen to pop music only, and two people listen to both pop and jazz. There are eight people in her family, and everyone listens to music. How many listen to jazz music only?

20. Julio surveyed his friends and found that nine will eat scrambled eggs, five will eat fried eggs, three will not eat eggs at all, and two will eat both scrambled and fried eggs. How many will eat only fried eggs?

8-4 Mixed Numbers (pp. 346–348)

Example 5

Write $5\frac{3}{7}$ as an equivalent improper fraction.

$$5\frac{3}{7} = \frac{(5 \times 7) + 3}{7} = \frac{35 + 3}{7} = \frac{38}{7}$$

Multiply the whole number and denominator. Add the numerator.

Example 6

Write $6\frac{1}{4}$ as an equivalent improper fraction.

$$6\frac{1}{4} = \frac{(6 \times 4) + 1}{4} = \frac{24 + 1}{4} = \frac{25}{4}$$

Multiply the whole number and denominator. Add the numerator.

Write each mixed number as an equivalent improper fraction.

21. $4\frac{1}{7}$ **22.** $9\frac{1}{2}$

23. $1\frac{5}{12}$ **24.** $8\frac{2}{3}$

25. $5\frac{5}{6}$ **26.** $3\frac{4}{9}$

27. A Siberian tiger is $10\frac{1}{4}$ feet long. Write this length as an equivalent improper fraction.

28. A school bus is $18\frac{2}{3}$ feet long. Write this length as an equivalent improper fraction.

8-5 Fractions on a Number Line (pp. 350–353)

Example 7

Replace ● with < or > to make $\frac{5}{4}$ ● $1\frac{3}{4}$ a true statement.

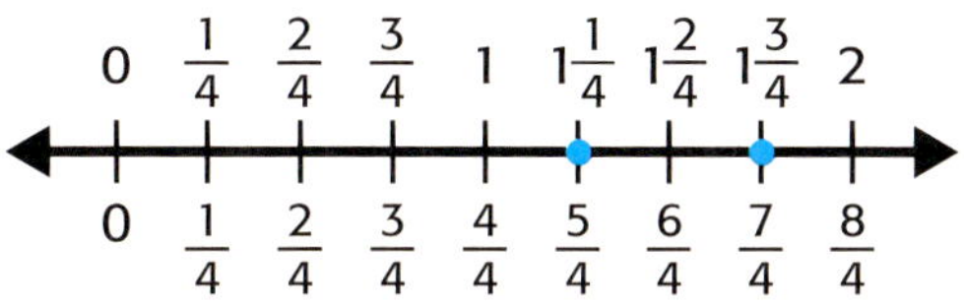

$\frac{5}{4} = 1\frac{1}{4}$. Since $1\frac{3}{4}$ is to the right of $\frac{5}{4}$ on the number line, $\frac{5}{4} < 1\frac{3}{4}$.

Replace each ● with < or > to make a true statement.

29. $\frac{5}{7}$ ● $\frac{3}{7}$

30. $\frac{1}{6}$ ● $\frac{5}{6}$

31. $\frac{6}{8}$ ● $\frac{9}{8}$

32. 2 ● $\frac{10}{3}$

33. $\frac{5}{2}$ ● $1\frac{1}{2}$

34. $3\frac{1}{9}$ ● $3\frac{2}{9}$

35. **Measurement** On Friday, Danielle walked $1\frac{1}{4}$ miles. On Saturday, she walked $\frac{7}{4}$ miles. On which day did she walk farther? Explain.

36. In May, Kina volunteered for $\frac{55}{6}$ hours. In June, she volunteered for $9\frac{5}{6}$ hours. In which month did Kina volunteer more hours? Explain.

8-6 Round Fractions (pp. 356–359)

Example 8

Round $\frac{6}{13}$ to 0, $\frac{1}{2}$, or 1.

Since 6 is about half of 13, $\frac{6}{13}$ is rounded to $\frac{1}{2}$.

Example 9

Round $\frac{2}{18}$ to 0, $\frac{1}{2}$, or 1.

Since 2 is much smaller than 18, $\frac{2}{18}$ is rounded to 0.

Round each fraction to 0, $\frac{1}{2}$, or 1.

37. $\frac{6}{11}$

38. $\frac{16}{17}$

39. $\frac{1}{12}$

40. $\frac{7}{9}$

41. **Measurement** A seedling is $\frac{10}{12}$ inch tall. Round $\frac{10}{12}$ to 0 inch, $\frac{1}{2}$ inch, or 1 inch.

42. Ernesto chewed $\frac{6}{10}$ of a pack of gum. Which is a better estimate for the amount of gum that he chewed: about half of the pack or about all of the pack?

8-7 Problem-Solving Investigation: Choose a Strategy (pp. 360–361)

Example 10

Jarvis and 2 of his friends can shovel snow from 12 driveways in 2 hours. At this rate, how many driveways can Jarvis and his friends shovel in 3 hours?

You can solve the problem by solving a simpler problem.

First, find how many driveways each boy shovels.

$12 \div 3 = 4$ Each boy shovels 4 driveways in 2 hours.

Then, find how many driveways each boy can shovel in 1 hour.

$4 \div 2 = 2$ Each boy shovels 2 driveways in 1 hour.

Then, find how many driveways 3 people can shovel in 1 hour.

$3 \times 2 = 6$ Three boys shovel 6 driveways in 1 hour.

Finally, find how many driveways 3 boys can shovel in 3 hours.

$6 \times 3 = 18$

So, Jarvis and 2 of his friends can shovel 18 driveways in 3 hours.

Use any strategy to solve each problem.

43. **Algebra** Three times some number, plus 3, divided by 2 is equal to 18. Find the number.

44. Find the sum of the first ten even numbers.

45. The admission prices to the local fair are shown. The total cost for 15 people to attend the fair was $148. How many adults and children attended the fair?

Fair Admission Prices	
Ticket	**Price**
Adult	$12
Child	$8

46. **Measurement** Denise has started an exercise program in which she walks daily. She plans to increase the distance that she walks by 0.25 mile each week. If she walks 2.25 miles each day the first week, how many miles will she be walking each day during the fifth week?

47. What two positive integers have a product of 48 and a sum of 14?

48. Kato increases the number of sit-ups he does each week by 8. The first week he did 10 sit-ups. He is now doing 74 sit-ups. How many weeks has he been doing sit-ups?

Math Online macmillanmh.com
• Chapter Test

CHAPTER 8 Chapter Test

Represent each situation using a fraction. Describe what the fraction means.

1. Five people share 3 bags of trail mix. How much trail mix did each person have?

2. Four gallons of water are used to water 3 trees. How much water did each tree use?

3. **MULTIPLE CHOICE** Which fraction is represented by the model below?

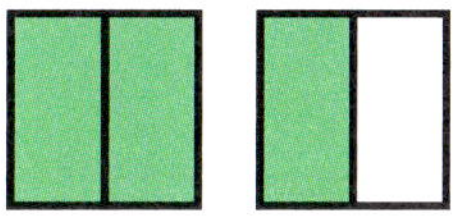

A $\frac{1}{2}$　　**C** $\frac{3}{2}$

B $1\frac{1}{3}$　　**D** $2\frac{1}{2}$

Write each improper fraction as a mixed number.

4. $\frac{20}{3}$　　**5.** $\frac{16}{9}$　　**6.** $\frac{26}{5}$

7. **MULTIPLE CHOICE** A river is $20\frac{1}{3}$ miles long. Which is another way to express this distance?

F $\frac{21}{3}$ mi　　**H** $\frac{61}{3}$ mi

G $\frac{20}{3}$ mi　　**J** $\frac{60}{3}$ mi

8. Martina surveyed her class and found that her classmates had 28 pets with long tails and 36 pets with short ears. Of these pets, 20 have both long tails and short ears. How many pets have long tails but do not have short ears?

Write each mixed number as an improper fraction.

9. $1\frac{3}{7}$　　**10.** $4\frac{1}{10}$　　**11.** $2\frac{5}{9}$

Replace each ● with < or > to make a true statement.

12. $\frac{5}{9}$ ● $\frac{11}{9}$　　**13.** $2\frac{1}{6}$ ● $\frac{8}{6}$

14. **Measurement** Does the bag of peaches or the bag of oranges weigh more? Explain.

Bag	Weight (lb)
Peaches	$2\frac{7}{16}$
Oranges	$\frac{31}{16}$

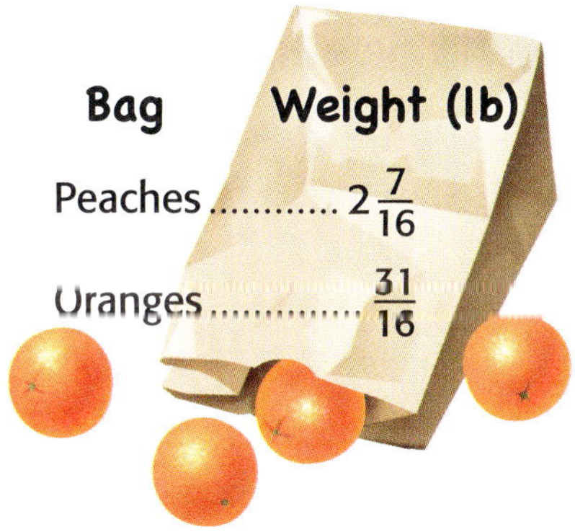

15. **Measurement** The table shows the lengths of two pens. Which is longer?

Pen	Length (in.)
1	$4\frac{5}{8}$
2	$\frac{46}{8}$

Round each fraction to 0, $\frac{1}{2}$, or 1.

16. $\frac{1}{10}$　　**17.** $\frac{4}{7}$　　**18.** $\frac{5}{11}$

19. A number is divided by 2. Next, 6 is subtracted from the quotient. Then 4 is added to the difference. If the result is 18, what is the number?

20. **WRITING IN MATH** How do you know when to round a fraction to 0, $\frac{1}{2}$, or 1?

CHAPTER 8

Test Practice

Cumulative, Chapters 1–8

Math Online macmillanmh.com
• Test Practice

PART 1 Multiple Choice

Read each question. Then fill in the correct answer on the answer sheet provided by your teacher or on a sheet of paper.

1. The table below shows the colors of the cars parked on Jillian's street and the fraction of total number of cars for each color. Which correctly shows the relationship between the fractions?

Cars on Jillian's Street	
Color	**Fraction**
Silver	$\frac{7}{12}$
Black	$\frac{9}{12}$

A $\frac{7}{12} < \frac{9}{12}$

B $\frac{7}{12} > \frac{9}{12}$

C $\frac{9}{12} \leq \frac{7}{12}$

D $\frac{7}{12} \geq \frac{9}{12}$

2. A deep-sea fishing boat spent 126 hours on fishing trips. If the boat made 1 trip per day for 21 days, how long did each trip take?

F 4 h

G 5 h

H 6 h

J 8 h

3. Larry has spent $\frac{9}{16}$ of his birthday money. Which of the following fractions is NOT greater than $\frac{9}{16}$

A $\frac{14}{16}$

B $\frac{12}{16}$

C $\frac{10}{16}$

D $\frac{8}{16}$

4. Benito has 80 books in his room. The books are organized on shelves with 16 books on each shelf. How many shelves does Benito have?

F 5

G 6

H 7

J 8

5. The bar graph shows the results of a survey of 38 fifth graders on their favorite school subject. Which statement about the data shown on the graph is true?

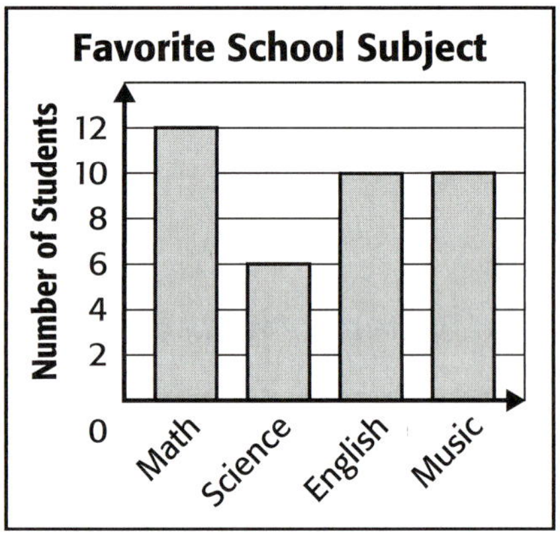

A The range of the data is 20.

B Music was twice as popular as science.

C The same number of students voted for English and math.

D Two more students voted for math than English.

6. What digit is in millions place in the number 7,521,423,201?

F 1

G 2

H 5

J 7

Preparing for Standardized Tests

For test-taking strategies and practice, see pages R42–R55.

7. Ralph recorded the colors of the shirts of the first 36 people that came through the doors at school.

Color	Number
White	18
Black	5
Blue	9
Red	4

Which number represents the fraction of black shirts recorded?

A $\frac{18}{36}$

B $\frac{9}{36}$

C $\frac{5}{36}$

D $\frac{4}{36}$

8. Which is the solution of the equation $x + 4 = 24$?

F 28

G 20

H 8

J 6

9. The table shows the number of text messages Fredricka sent each day for 12 days.

Number of Text Messages			
10	3	8	4
2	5	7	8
0	11	0	6

What graph(s) can be used to display this information?

A bar graph only

B circle graph and bar graph

C pictograph only

D bar graph and line plot

PART 2 Short Response

Record your answers on the answer sheet provided by your teacher or on a sheet of paper.

10. The table shows the number of volunteer hours worked by five students. What is the median number of hours?

Student	1	2	3	4	5
Hours	61	70	65	77	99

11. Nina's cheerleading practice lasted $1\frac{2}{3}$ hours on Friday. Write this mixed number as an improper fraction.

PART 3 Extended Response

Record your answers on the answer sheet provided by your teacher or on a sheet of paper.

12. The lengths of four insects in Tommy's insect collection are $1\frac{1}{6}$ inches, $2\frac{3}{8}$ inches, $1\frac{5}{6}$ inches, and $2\frac{7}{8}$ inches. Draw a model for each insect and order the fractions from least to greatest.

NEED EXTRA HELP?												
If You Missed Question...	1	2	3	4	5	6	7	8	9	10	11	12
Go to Lesson...	8-5	4-4	8-5	4-4	7-6	1-1	8-2	6-1	7-8	7-1	8-4	8-5

CHAPTER 9

Use Factors and Multiples

BIG Idea What are multiples?

A **multiple** of a number is the product of that number and any whole number.

Example It costs $6 for a fifth grade student to enter the Frederik Meijer Gardens and Sculpture Park in Grand Rapids, Michigan. If two fifth grade students enter the park, the cost would be 6×2, or 12. So, 12 is a multiple of 6.

What will I learn in this chapter?

- Identify common factors and common multiples of a set of whole numbers.
- Identify prime and composite numbers.
- Find equivalent fractions and simplify fractions.
- Relate decimals to fractions.
- Compare fractions using a variety of methods, including common denominators.
- Solve problems by using the *look for a pattern* strategy.

Key Vocabulary

common factor
composite number
equivalent fractions
prime number
simplest form

Math Online **Student Study Tools at macmillanmh.com**

FOLDABLES® Study Organizer

Make this Foldable to help you organize information about factors and multiples. Begin with nine sheets of notebook paper.

1. **Fold** 9 sheets of paper in half along the width.

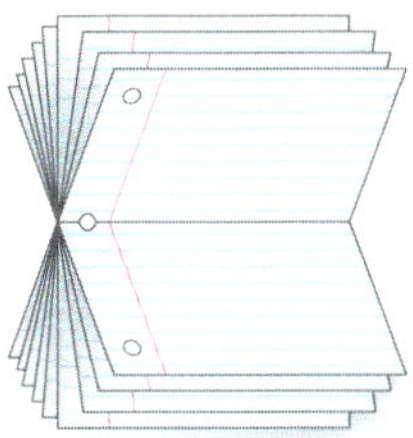

2. **Cut** a 1″ tab along the left edge through one thickness.

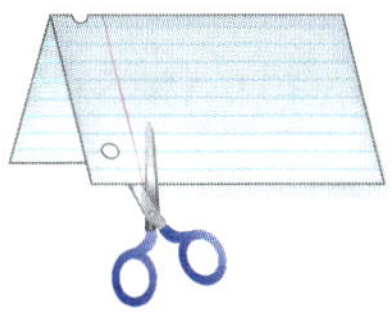

3. **Glue** the 1″ tab down. Write the lesson number and title on the front tab.

4. **Repeat** Steps 2 and 3 for the remaining sheets. Staple them together on the glued tabs to form a booklet.

ARE YOU READY for Chapter 9?

You have two ways to check prerequisite skills for this chapter.

Option 2

Math Online Take the Chapter Readiness Quiz at macmillanmh.com.

Option 1

Complete the Quick Check below.

QUICK Check

Write all of the factors of each number. (Prior Grade)

1. 8 **2.** 11 **3.** 6

4. 15 **5.** 32 **6.** 24

Identify the number of rows and columns in each figure. (Prior Grade)

7. 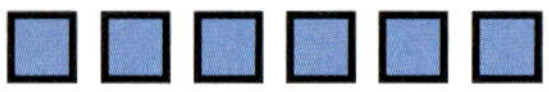

8. 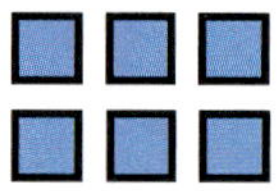

9. 

10. 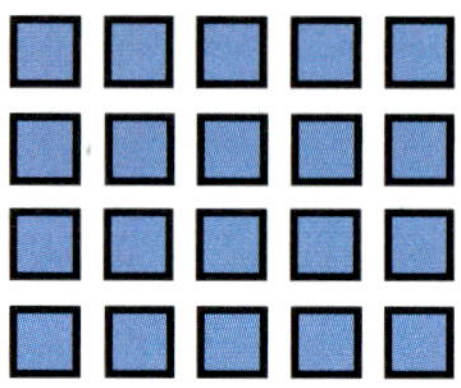

Write each decimal in words. (Lesson 1-4)

11. 0.3 **12.** 0.8 **13.** 0.1

14. 0.45 **15.** 0.06 **16.** 0.04

17. Measurement A rock has a mass of 0.925 kilogram. Write this measure in words.

18. Measurement A bottle of water contains 0.85 pint. Write this amount in words.

9-1 Common Factors

MAIN IDEA

I will identify common factors of a set of whole numbers.

New Vocabulary

common factor

greatest common factor (GCF)

Math Online

macmillanmh.com

- Extra Examples
- Personal Tutor
- Self-Check Quiz

GET READY to Learn

A pet store has 6 dog bones and 18 dog biscuits to give away as samples. They put an equal number of bones and an equal number of biscuits in each sample bag. What is the greatest number of sample bags they can give away?

The factors of 6 and 18 are listed below.

Product	Factors
6	1×6
6	2×3

Product	Factors
18	1×18
18	2×9
18	3×6

factors of 6: **1**, **2**, **3**, **6**

factors of 18: **1**, **2**, **3**, **6**, 9, 18

A **common factor** is a number that is a factor of two or more numbers. So, 1, 2, 3, and 6 are common factors of 6 and 18. Since 6 is the greatest of these common factors, the greatest number of sample bags that can be made is 6.

EXAMPLE Find Common Factors

1 **Find the common factors of 16 and 20.**

Step 1 List all the factors of each number.

$16 = 1 \times 16$ $16 = 2 \times 8$ $16 = 4 \times 4$

factors of 16: 1, 2, 4, 8, 16

$20 = 1 \times 20$ $20 = 2 \times 10$ $20 = 4 \times 5$

factors of 20: 1, 2, 4, 5, 10, 20

Step 2 Find the common factors.

factors of 16: **1**, **2**, **4**, 8, 16

factors of 20: **1**, **2**, **4**, 5, 10, 20

The common factors of 16 and 20 are 1, 2, and 4.

Remember

The number 1 is always a common factor of two or more numbers.

EXAMPLE Numbers with One Common Factor

2 **Find the common factors of 4, 8, and 15.**

factors of 4: **1**, 2, 4
factors of 8: **1**, 2, 4, 8
factors of 15: **1**, 3, 5, 15

The only factor common to all three numbers is 1.

The greatest of the common factors of two or more numbers is called the **greatest common factor (GCF)**.

EXAMPLE Find the Greatest Common Factor

3 **Find the greatest common factor of 10, 15, and 20.**

List all the factors of 10, 15, and 20 to find the common factors.

factors of 10: **1**, 2, **5**, 10
factors of 15: **1**, 3, **5**, 15
factors of 20: **1**, 2, 4, **5**, 10, 20

The common factors are 1 and 5. The greatest of these is 5. So, the greatest common factor, or GCF, of 10, 15, and 20 is 5.

Real-World EXAMPLE Use the Greatest Common Factor

4 **FOOD A chef made 24 baked cheese sticks and 36 egg rolls to arrange on plates. Each plate will have an equal number of cheese sticks and an equal number of egg rolls. What is the greatest number of plates he can arrange?**

First, find the common factors of each number.

factors of 24: **1**, **2**, **3**, **4**, **6**, 8, **12**, 24
factors of 36: **1**, **2**, **3**, **4**, **6**, 9, **12**, 18, 36

common factors of 24 and 36: 1, 2, 3, 4, 6, 12

The chef can arrange 1, 2, 3, 4, 6, or 12 plates with each plate having an equal number of cheese sticks and an equal number of egg rolls. Since 12 is the GCF, the greatest number of plates the chef can arrange is 12.

Check There will be 24 ÷ 12, or 2 cheese sticks and 36 ÷ 12, or 3 egg rolls on each plate. ✓

✓ CHECK What You Know

Find the common factors of each set of numbers. See Examples 1, 2 (pp. 373–374)

1. 9, 12 **2.** 13, 15 **3.** 24, 28, 32 **4.** 10, 30, 50

Find the GCF of each set of numbers. See Examples 3, 4 (p. 374)

5. 8, 14 **6.** 15, 20 **7.** 21, 24, 27 **8.** 30, 48, 60

9. Fourteen boys and 21 girls will be divided into equal groups. Find the greatest number of children that can be in each group if no one is left out.

10. Talk About It Explain the steps for finding the GCF of two numbers. Give an example.

Practice and Problem Solving

EXTRA PRACTICE See page R23.

Find the common factors of each set of numbers. See Examples 1, 2 (pp. 373–374)

11. 5, 20 **12.** 6, 15 **13.** 8, 9 **14.** 14, 25

15. 12, 18, 30 **16.** 27, 36, 45 **17.** 21, 28, 35 **18.** 18, 36, 54

Find the GCF of each set of numbers. See Examples 3, 4 (p. 374)

19. 4, 10 **20.** 15, 18 **21.** 18, 42 **22.** 20, 35

23. 21, 35, 49 **24.** 24, 30, 42 **25.** 12, 18, 26 **26.** 24, 40, 56

27. A grocery store clerk has 16 oranges, 20 apples, and 24 pears. The clerk needs to put an equal number of apples, oranges, and pears into each basket. What is the greatest number of apples that can be in each basket?

28. A gardener has 27 pansies and 36 daisies. If the gardener plants an equal number of each type of flower in each row, what is the greatest number of pansies in each row?

H.O.T. Problems

29. **OPEN ENDED** Write two numbers that have common factors of 1, 3, and 5. Explain how you found the numbers.

30. **NUMBER SENSE** Three numbers have a GCF of 4. The largest number is 12. Explain how to find the other numbers.

31. **WRITING IN ►MATH** Can the GCF of two numbers ever be 1? Explain your answer. Give an example to support it.

Explore

Math Activity for 9-2

Prime and Composite Numbers

MAIN IDEA

I will use models to identify prime and composite numbers.

New Vocabulary

prime

composite

Three bass drums may be stored on shelves in only two different arrangements.

These rectangular arrangements show that the only factors of 3 are 1 and 3.

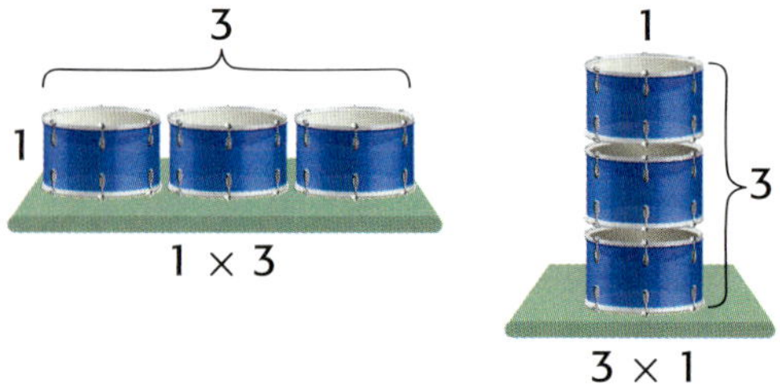

When a number, like 3, has exactly two factors, the number is **prime**.

You can store 4 drums in any of the three ways shown at the right. What are the factors of 4?

When a number, like 4, has more than two factors, the number is **composite**.

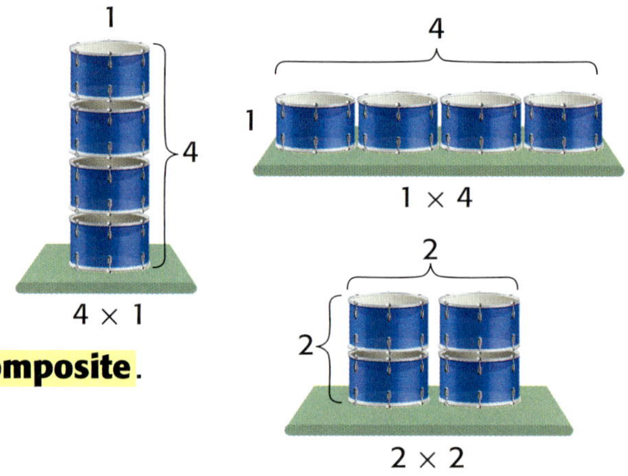

ACTIVITY

1 **Use models to determine whether 6 is *prime* or *composite*.**

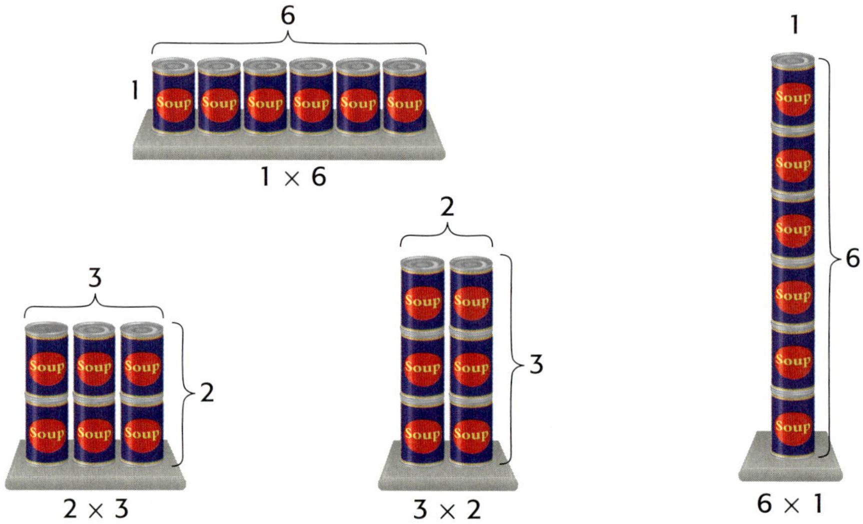

You can arrange the 6 soup cans in four different ways. So, 6 is a composite number.

ACTIVITY

Hands-On Activity

2 **Use models to determine whether 7 is *prime* or *composite*.**

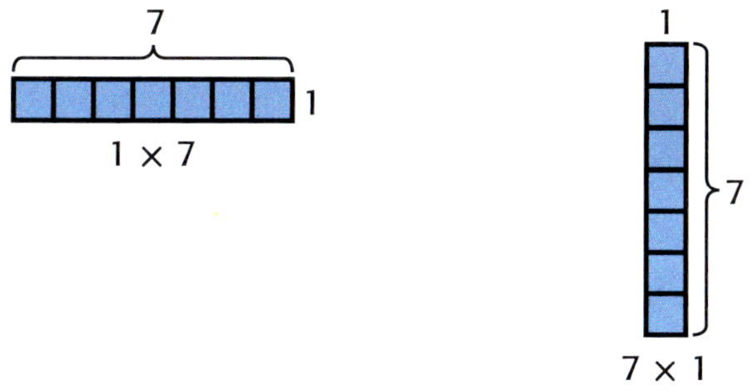

You can arrange the 7 tiles in only 2 ways: 7 × 1 and 1 × 7. So, 7 is a prime number.

Think About It

1. Are all even numbers composite? Use a drawing in your explanation.
2. Are all odd numbers prime? Support your explanation with a drawing.

CHECK What You Know

Use objects or pictures to determine whether each number is *prime* or *composite*. Describe the models that you used.

3. 13	**4.** 10	**5.** 11
6. 8	**7.** 17	**8.** 9

9. Caleb made 12 dinner rolls. He placed the rolls in 3 rows of 4 on a table. In what other ways could he have arranged the rolls in equal rows?
10. Write a number between 20 and 30. Then use objects or pictures to show whether the number is prime or composite.
11. **WRITING IN MATH** Is there a connection between the number of rectangular arrangements that are possible when modeling a number and the number of factors the number has? Explain your reasoning.

9-2 Prime and Composite Numbers

MAIN IDEA

I will identify prime and composite numbers.

New Vocabulary

prime factorization

Math Online

macmillanmh.com

- Extra Examples
- Personal Tutor
- Self-Check Quiz

GET READY to Learn

Stella makes and sells jewelry at craft shows. She has 12 rings that she wants to display in equal rows.

1 row of 12 rings

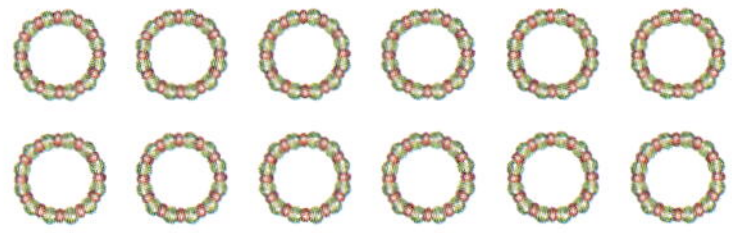

2 rows of 6 rings

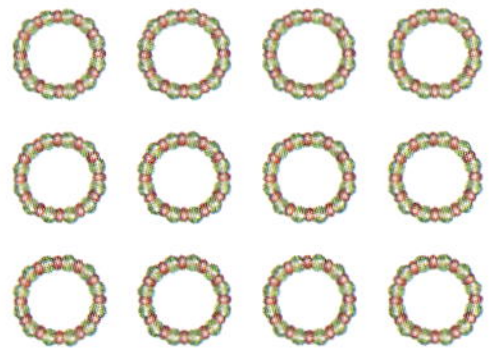

3 rows of 4 rings

In the Math Activity, you learned that a *composite* number has more than two factors. So, 12 is a composite number because its factors are 1, 2, 3, 4, 6, and 12.

The number 5 has only two factors: 1 and 5. So, 5 is a *prime* number.

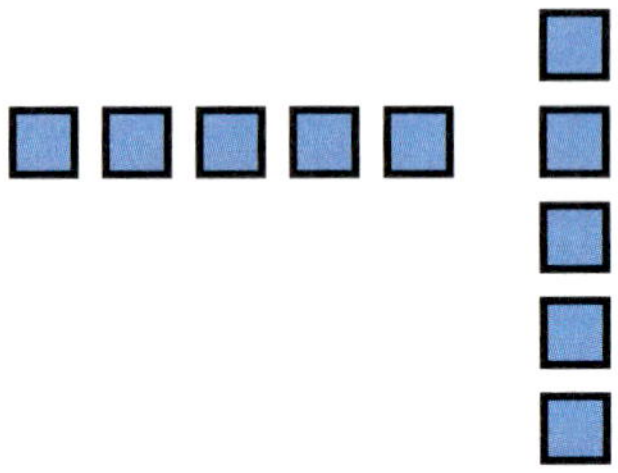

The numbers 1 and 0 are neither prime nor composite.

- 1 has only one factor: 1
- 0 has a never ending number of factors: 0×1, 0×2, 0×3, …

EXAMPLE Use Models

1 **Tell whether the number 10 represented by the model at the right is *prime* or *composite*.**

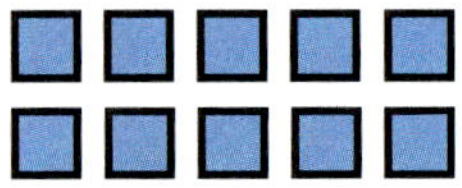

The model shows 2 rows of 5 squares. The squares could also be arranged in 5 rows of 2 squares, 10 rows of 1 square, or 1 row of 10 squares.

So, the number 10 is a composite number because it has more than 2 factors.

Prime and composite numbers can help you solve real-world situations.

Real-World EXAMPLE **Use Factor Pairs**

2 **GEOMETRY** **A banquet hall has 24 square tables that are to be placed together to form a rectangle. Is 24 prime or composite? What does this mean in the problem? What would happen if the banquet hall had only 23 tables?**

factors of 24: 1, 2, 3, 4, 6, 8, 12, 24

Since 24 has more than two factors, it is a composite number. This means that there are more than two ways to arrange the 24 tables. Some of the ways are listed below.

- 1 row of 24 tables
- 3 rows of 8 tables
- 2 rows of 12 tables
- 4 rows of 6 tables

If the banquet hall had only 23 tables, there could be only two possible arrangements, since 23 has only two factors. This is because 23 is a prime number.

- 1 row of 23 tables
- 23 rows of 1 table

Remember

You can use models to identify 24 as prime or composite. Twenty-four counters can be arranged in equal rows in more than two ways. So, 24 is composite.

You can write every composite number as a product of prime numbers. This is called the **prime factorization** of a number. A *factor tree* can be used to find the prime factorization of a number.

EXAMPLE **Find the Prime Factorization of a Number**

3 **Find the prime factorization of 36.**

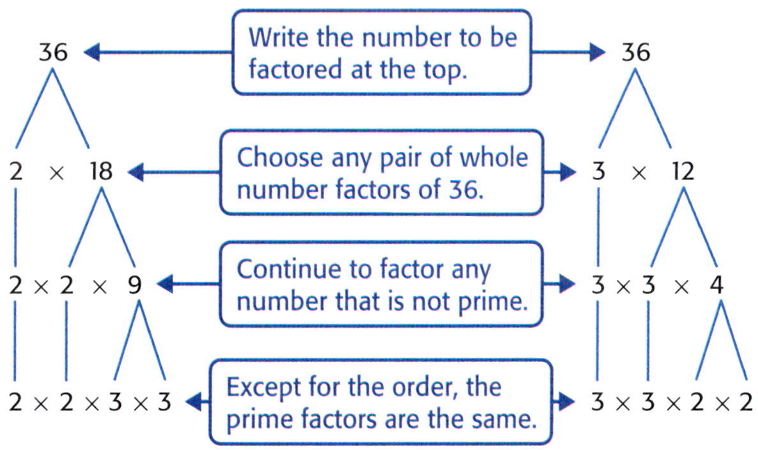

In order, the prime factorization of 36 is 2 × 2 × 3 × 3.

CHECK What You Know

Tell whether the number represented by each model is *prime* or *composite*. See Example 1 (p. 378)

1. 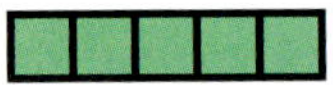

2. 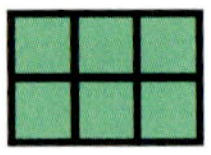

Tell whether each number is *prime* or *composite*. Use objects or models to justify your answer. See Examples 1, 2 (pp. 378–379)

3. 9 **4.** 24 **5.** 17 **6.** 31

Find the prime factorization of each number. See Example 3 (p. 379)

7. 18 **8.** 20 **9.** 24 **10.** 45

11. Is there more than one way for Mark to display 21 model cars if each row has the same number of cars? Explain.

12. Talk About It Is 33 prime or composite? Explain how you know.

Practice and Problem Solving

EXTRA PRACTICE
See page R24.

Tell whether the number represented by each model is *prime* or *composite*. See Example 1 (p. 378)

13. 2 

14. 8 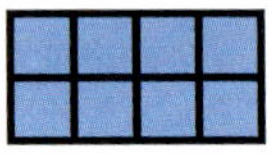

15. 7 

16. 4 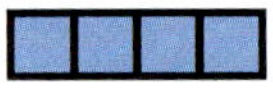

Tell whether each number is *prime* or *composite*. Use objects or models to justify your answer. See Examples 1, 2 (pp. 378–379)

17. 18 **18.** 29 **19.** 15 **20.** 26

21. 13 **22.** 16 **23.** 37 **24.** 53

Find the prime factorization of each number. See Example 3 (p. 379)

25. 16 **26.** 22 **27.** 30 **28.** 42

29. 63 **30.** 70 **31.** 50 **32.** 88

33. A mountain range has 90 mountains that are one mile or more tall. Is 90 a prime or composite number?

34. Alex's birthday is February 29. Is 29 a prime or composite number?

H.O.T. Problems

35. **NUMBER SENSE** Find the least prime number that is greater than 100. Explain.

36. **CHALLENGE** Two prime numbers that have a difference of 2 are called *twin primes*. For example, 5 and 7 are twin primes. Find all pairs of twin primes less than 50.

37. **WRITING IN MATH** Explain how you can use objects or models to tell if a number is prime or composite.

TEST Practice

38. The table shows how many Calories you can burn in 10 minutes for certain activities.

Activity	Number of Calories
Basketball	64
Dancing	35
Hiking	47
Roller skating	57

For which activity is the number of Calories a prime number? (Lesson 9-2)

A basketball

B dancing

C hiking

D roller skating

39. Which group names all the common factors of 27 and 54? (Lesson 9-1)

F 1, 3, 9

G 1, 3, 9, 18

H 1, 3, 9, 27

J 1, 3, 9, 27, 54

40. What is the missing number in the prime factorization of 156?

$$2 \times 2 \times 3 \times \blacksquare$$

A 3

B 5

C 13

D 17

Spiral Review

Find the GCF of each set of numbers. (Lesson 9-1)

41. 6, 15

42. 18, 24

43. 14, 28

44. 10, 25

45. Jackie bought 5 papayas for \$1.99 each and 3 yogurts for \$0.75 each. The cashier gave her \$8 change. What is the least number of coins she could have given the cashier? What would they have been? (Lesson 8-7)

46. The Jackson family went swimming $2\frac{5}{6}$ hours on Saturday and $1\frac{3}{6}$ hours on Sunday. On which day did they spend more time swimming? (Lesson 8-5)

9-3 Equivalent Fractions

MAIN IDEA

I will write a fraction that is equivalent to a given fraction.

New Vocabulary

equivalent fractions

Math Online

macmillanmh.com

- Extra Examples
- Personal Tutor
- Self-Check Quiz

GET READY to Learn

Mrs. Bahn is dividing her garden into thirds. One third of her garden will be used for tomatoes. If her garden is 9 feet wide, she figures that she needs to save a width of 3 feet of the garden for tomatoes. Did she figure correctly?

Equivalent fractions are fractions that have the same value. The fractions $\frac{1}{3}$ and $\frac{3}{9}$ name the same part of the whole. So, they are equivalent fractions. Mrs. Bahn figured correctly.

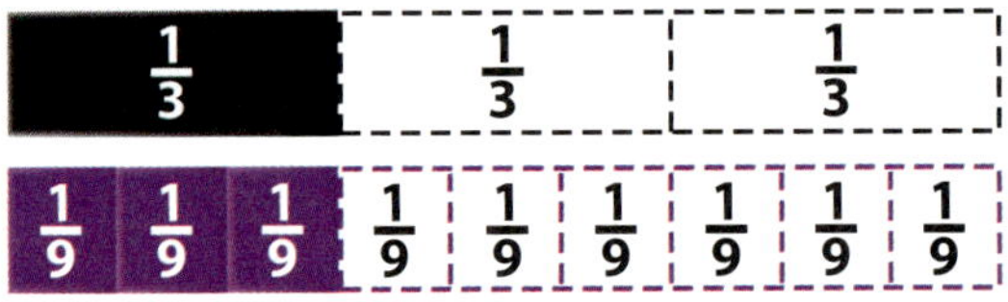

Multiplying the numerator and denominator each by 3 gives $\frac{3}{9}$.

$$\frac{1}{3} \times \frac{3}{3} = \frac{1 \times 3}{3 \times 3} = \frac{3}{9}$$

Recall that $\frac{3}{3}$ is an equivalent form of 1. To find equivalent fractions, you can multiply a fraction by an equivalent form of 1, such as $\frac{2}{2}$, $\frac{3}{3}$, or $\frac{4}{4}$.

EXAMPLE Find Equivalent Fractions by Multiplying

1 **Find two fractions that are equivalent to $\frac{1}{4}$.**

Multiply $\frac{1}{4}$ by equivalent forms of one, such as $\frac{2}{2}$ and $\frac{3}{3}$.

Multiply $\frac{1}{4}$ by $\frac{2}{2}$.

$$\frac{1}{4} \times \frac{2}{2} = \frac{1 \times 2}{4 \times 2} = \frac{2}{8}$$

Multiply $\frac{1}{4}$ by $\frac{3}{3}$.

$$\frac{1}{4} \times \frac{3}{3} = \frac{1 \times 3}{4 \times 3} = \frac{3}{12}$$

So, $\frac{2}{8}$ and $\frac{3}{12}$ are both equivalent to $\frac{1}{4}$.

Real-World EXAMPLE

2 SCIENCE Ethan measured the length of an insect to be $\frac{7}{8}$ inch. Find two equivalent measurements for the length of the insect, in inches.

Multiply $\frac{7}{8}$ by equivalent forms of one, such as $\frac{2}{2}$ and $\frac{3}{3}$.

Multiply $\frac{7}{8}$ by $\frac{2}{2}$.

$$\frac{7}{8} \times \frac{2}{2} = \frac{7 \times 2}{8 \times 2} = \frac{14}{16}$$

Multiply $\frac{7}{8}$ by $\frac{3}{3}$.

$$\frac{7}{8} \times \frac{3}{3} = \frac{7 \times 3}{8 \times 3} = \frac{21}{24}$$

So, the insect's length is equivalent to $\frac{14}{16}$ inch and $\frac{21}{24}$ inch.

> **Remember**
> There are many different fractions that are equivalent to a given fraction.

EXAMPLE Find a Missing Number

3 ALGEBRA Find the number for ■ that makes the fractions in $\frac{2}{7} = \frac{■}{21}$ equivalent.

$\frac{2}{7} = \frac{2 \times ?}{7 \times ?} = \frac{■}{21}$ THINK What number times 7 equals 21?

$\frac{2}{7} = \frac{2 \times 3}{7 \times 3} = \frac{6}{21}$ $7 \times 3 = 21$, so multiply the numerator by 3.

The missing number is 6. So, $\frac{2}{7} = \frac{6}{21}$.

CHECK What You Know

Find two fractions that are equivalent to each fraction. Check your answer using fraction tiles or number lines. See Examples 1, 2 (pp. 382–383)

1. $\frac{2}{5}$
2. $\frac{3}{4}$
3. $\frac{6}{10}$
4. $\frac{2}{8}$
5. $\frac{1}{3}$
6. $\frac{5}{6}$

Algebra Find the number for ■ that makes the fractions equivalent. See Example 3 (p. 383)

7. $\frac{1}{2} = \frac{■}{4}$
8. $\frac{2}{5} = \frac{10}{■}$
9. $\frac{4}{18} = \frac{12}{■}$

10. **Measurement** How many sixteenths of an inch are equal to $\frac{5}{8}$ inch?

11. **Talk About It** Explain how to find an equivalent fraction for $\frac{4}{9}$.

Practice and Problem Solving

EXTRA PRACTICE See page R24.

Find two fractions that are equivalent to each fraction. Check your answer using fraction tiles or number lines. See Examples 1, 2 (pp. 382–383)

12. $\frac{2}{3}$ **13.** $\frac{1}{2}$ **14.** $\frac{2}{6}$ **15.** $\frac{1}{5}$

16. $\frac{2}{12}$ **17.** $\frac{3}{6}$ **18.** $\frac{3}{5}$ **19.** $\frac{6}{8}$

20. $\frac{4}{16}$ **21.** $\frac{2}{7}$ **22.** $\frac{5}{10}$ **23.** $\frac{6}{14}$

Algebra **Find the number for ■ that makes the fractions equivalent.** See Example 3 (p. 383)

24. $\frac{1}{3} = \frac{■}{9}$ **25.** $\frac{8}{16} = \frac{16}{■}$ **26.** $\frac{6}{9} = \frac{18}{■}$ **27.** $\frac{3}{5} = \frac{9}{■}$

28. Fatima read $\frac{2}{5}$ of a book. Gary read $\frac{4}{10}$ of the same book. Did Gary read more than, less than, or the same amount as Fatima?

29. Measurement Mr. Bixler ran $\frac{5}{6}$ mile. How many twelfths and how many eighteenths of a mile are equal to $\frac{5}{6}$ mile?

30. Rodolfo ate $\frac{1}{4}$ of a cantaloupe. Aida ate the same amount from another cantaloupe, cut into eighths. How many pieces did Aida eat?

31. In 1 minute, 10 people can slide down a water slide. Complete the following. Explain what the equivalent fractions mean.

$\frac{1}{10} = \frac{5}{■}$ $\frac{1}{10} = \frac{■}{300}$

H.O.T. Problems

32. OPEN ENDED Using fraction tiles or a number line, show 3 fractions that are equivalent to each other.

33. FIND THE ERROR Jeremy and Antwon are finding an equivalent fraction for $\frac{3}{7}$. Who is correct? Explain.

Jeremy

$$\frac{3}{7} = \frac{(3+2)}{(7+2)} = \frac{5}{9}$$

Antwon

$$\frac{3}{7} + \frac{(3 \times 2)}{(7 \times 2)} = \frac{6}{14}$$

34. WRITING IN MATH Write about a real-world situation that can be represented by $\frac{3}{4}$. Then write an equivalent fraction and describe the meaning of the equivalent fraction.

Game Time

Match Up

Equivalent Fractions

Get Ready!

Players: 2 players

You will need: 32 index cards

Get Set!

Label each index card with one fraction as shown.

$\frac{1}{2}$	$\frac{1}{3}$	$\frac{2}{3}$	$\frac{1}{4}$	$\frac{2}{4}$	$\frac{3}{4}$	$\frac{2}{5}$	$\frac{3}{5}$
$\frac{4}{5}$	$\frac{1}{6}$	$\frac{5}{6}$	$\frac{2}{7}$	$\frac{1}{8}$	$\frac{2}{8}$	$\frac{3}{8}$	$\frac{2}{9}$
$\frac{6}{9}$	$\frac{4}{10}$	$\frac{5}{10}$	$\frac{8}{10}$	$\frac{2}{12}$	$\frac{4}{12}$	$\frac{2}{16}$	$\frac{4}{16}$
$\frac{4}{18}$	$\frac{6}{18}$	$\frac{15}{18}$	$\frac{12}{20}$	$\frac{15}{20}$	$\frac{6}{21}$	$\frac{3}{24}$	$\frac{9}{24}$

Go!

- Shuffle the cards. Then one player deals 5 cards to each player. The remaining cards are placed in a pile facedown on the table.
- Players place any pairs of cards that are equivalent fractions on the table. If 3 cards are equivalent, the player must choose a pair.
- Player 1 chooses a card from the pile and tries to form an equivalent fraction pair. He or she then discards any other card facedown on a discard pile of cards.
- Player 2 takes a turn choosing a card, forming pairs of equivalent fractions, and placing a card facedown on the discard pile.
- Continue playing until there are no more cards in the pile or until neither player can make an equivalent fraction pair. The player with the most pairs of equivalent fractions wins.

9-4 Simplest Form

GET READY to Learn

A praying mantis is 12 centimeters long, and a walking stick is 22 centimeters long. So, a praying mantis is $\frac{12}{22}$ the length of a stick insect. Is this the simplest way to write this fraction?

MAIN IDEA

I will write a fraction in simplest form.

New Vocabulary

simplest form

Math Online

macmillanmh.com

- Extra Examples
- Personal Tutor
- Self-Check Quiz

A fraction is written in **simplest form** when the GCF of the numerator and the denominator is 1. The simplest form of a fraction is one of its many equivalent fractions.

Real-World EXAMPLE — Simplest Form

1 **MEASUREMENT** **Refer to the information above. What fraction of a walking stick's length is the length of a praying mantis? Write the fraction in simplest form.**

Step 1 Find the GCF of the numerator and the denominator.

factors of 12: 1, **2**, 3, 4, 6, 12
factors of 22: 1, **2**, 11, 22 — The GCF of 12 and 22 is 2.

Step 2 Divide both the numerator and the denominator by the GCF. Dividing both the numerator and the denominator by the same number is equivalent to dividing by one. The appearance of the fraction changes, not its value.

$\frac{12}{22} = \frac{12 \div 2}{22 \div 2} = \frac{6}{11}$ — The GCF of 6 and 11 is 1.

So, a praying mantis' length is $\frac{6}{11}$ the length of a walking stick.

You can see from the models at the right that $\frac{12}{22} = \frac{6}{11}$.

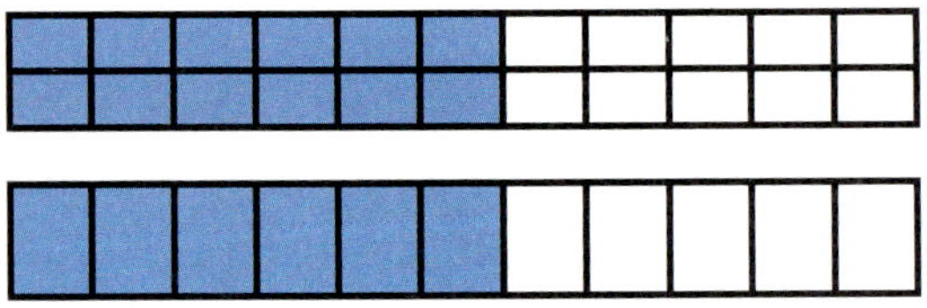

$\frac{12}{22}$

$\frac{6}{11}$

Remember

The divisibility rules are useful for finding common factors.

EXAMPLE **Simplest Form**

2 Write $\frac{18}{30}$ in simplest form.

One Way: Divide by Common Factors

$\frac{18}{30} = \frac{18 \div 2}{30 \div 2} = \frac{9}{15}$ Divide 18 and 30 by the common factor 2.

$\frac{9}{15} = \frac{9 \div 3}{15 \div 3} = \frac{3}{5}$ Divide 9 and 15 by the common factor 3.

Since 3 and 5 have no common factors other than 1, stop dividing.

Another Way: Divide by the GCF

factors of 18: 1, 2, 3, 6, 9, 18

factors of 30: 1, 2, 3, 5, 6, 10, 15, 30

The GCF of 18 and 30 is 6.

$\frac{18}{30} = \frac{18 \div 6}{30 \div 6} = \frac{3}{5}$ Divide by the GCF 6.

Using either method, $\frac{18}{30}$ written in simplest form is $\frac{3}{5}$.

Check

You can see from the models at the right that $\frac{18}{30} = \frac{3}{5}$. ✓

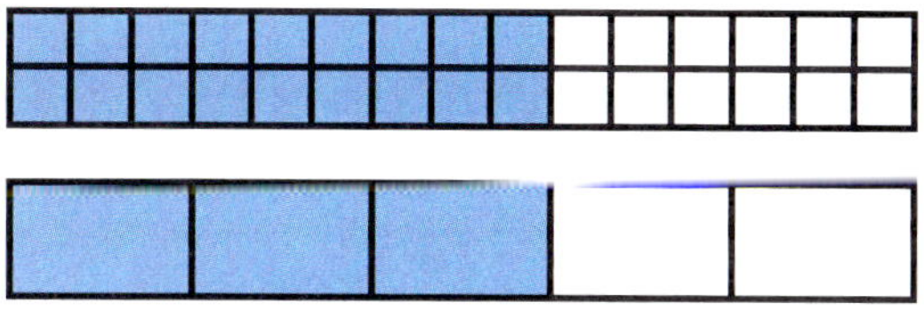

$\frac{18}{30}$

$\frac{3}{5}$

CHECK What You Know

Write each fraction in simplest form. If the fraction is already in simplest form, write *simplified*. See Examples 1, 2 (pp. 386–387)

1. $\frac{4}{6}$ **2.** $\frac{2}{12}$ **3.** $\frac{8}{24}$ **4.** $\frac{8}{9}$

5. $\frac{9}{18}$ **6.** $\frac{4}{14}$ **7.** $\frac{15}{20}$ **8.** $\frac{21}{35}$

9. Kara buys 24 bagels. Ten are whole wheat. What fraction of the bagels are whole wheat, in simplest form?

10. **Talk About It** Use at least 2 sentences to explain how to find the simplest form of any fraction.

Practice and Problem Solving

EXTRA PRACTICE See page R24.

Write each fraction in simplest form. If the fraction is already in simplest form, write *simplified*. See Examples 1, 2 (pp. 386–387)

11. $\frac{6}{8}$ **12.** $\frac{6}{10}$ **13.** $\frac{3}{18}$ **14.** $\frac{2}{15}$

15. $\frac{4}{16}$ **16.** $\frac{12}{24}$ **17.** $\frac{6}{25}$ **18.** $\frac{21}{30}$

19. $\frac{12}{40}$ **20.** $\frac{4}{11}$ **21.** $\frac{8}{28}$ **22.** $\frac{9}{24}$

23. $\frac{3}{36}$ **24.** $\frac{25}{30}$ **25.** $\frac{18}{45}$ **26.** $\frac{36}{48}$

27. A basket of fruit has 10 oranges, 12 apples, and 18 peaches. Express in simplest form the fraction of fruit that are oranges.

28. **Measurement** Andeana is 4 feet tall. Her brother Berto is 38 inches tall. What fractional part of Andeana's height is Berto's height?

Data File

The Bunker Hill Monument in Charlestown, Massachusetts, is at the location of the first major battle of the American Revolution.

- The current monument is 221 feet tall. The original monument at the site was a little more than 17 feet tall.
- There are 294 steps to the top look-out window.

Write each of the following as a fraction in simplest form.

29. You have climbed 147 out of 294 steps.

30. The original monument is $\frac{17}{221}$ as tall as the current Bunker Hill Monument.

H.O.T. Problems

31. **OPEN ENDED** Write a real-world problem that uses $\frac{14}{18}$ in the problem. Write the fraction in simplest form.

32. **WHICH ONE DOESN'T BELONG?** Identify the fraction that does not belong with the other three. Explain your reasoning.

$\frac{3}{12}$ $\frac{4}{16}$ $\frac{5}{25}$ $\frac{6}{24}$

33. **WRITING IN MATH** Explain how you would write $\frac{24}{36}$ in simplest form.

TEST Practice

34. Gil's aunt cut his birthday cake into 32 equal pieces, as shown below. Eighteen pieces were eaten at his birthday party. What fraction of the cake was left? **(Lesson 9-4)**

A $\frac{7}{16}$

B $\frac{9}{16}$

C $\frac{7}{12}$

D $\frac{9}{14}$

35. The fractions $\frac{2}{8}$, $\frac{3}{12}$, $\frac{4}{16}$, and $\frac{5}{20}$ are each equivalent to $\frac{1}{4}$. What is the relationship between the numerator and denominator in each fraction that is equivalent to $\frac{1}{4}$? **(Lesson 9-3)**

F The numerator is 4 times the denominator.

G The denominator is 4 times the numerator.

H The numerator is 4 more than the denominator.

J The denominator is 4 more than the numerator.

Spiral Review

Write two fractions that are equivalent to each fraction. **(Lesson 9-3)**

36. $\frac{4}{7}$ **37.** $\frac{2}{9}$ **38.** $\frac{4}{8}$ **39.** $\frac{1}{6}$

40. A tangerine has about 37 Calories. Is 37 *prime* or *composite*? **(Lesson 9-2)**

41. Thirty-six fourth graders, 48 fifth graders, and 24 sixth graders will attend a play. An equal number of students must sit in each row, and only students from the same grade can sit in a row. What is the greatest number of fifth graders that can sit in each row? **(Lesson 9-1)**

Write each mixed number as an improper fraction. Check using models. **(Lesson 8-4)**

42. $1\frac{2}{5}$ **43.** $3\frac{1}{8}$ **44.** $5\frac{2}{3}$

45. The table shows the distances that Terrell threw a flying disk. Find the median and mode of the data. **(Lesson 7-1)**

Throw	Distance (ft)
1	30
2	26
3	26
4	37

46. Swimming lessons cost \$62 per swimmer. A total of \$806 was collected for swimming lessons. How many people took swimming lessons? **(Lesson 4-4)**

CHAPTER 9

Mid-Chapter Check

Lessons 9-1 through 9-4

Find the common factors of each set of numbers. (Lesson 9-1)

1. 5, 15　　**2.** 12, 30

3. 24, 32, 40　　**4.** 10, 22, 30

5. MULTIPLE CHOICE Which group shows all the numbers that are common factors of 24 and 40? (Lesson 9-1)

A 1, 2, 4

B 1, 2, 4, 6

C 1, 2, 4, 8

D 1, 2, 4, 6, 8, 12

Find the GCF of each set of numbers. (Lesson 9-1)

6. 9, 21　　**7.** 12, 26

8. 20, 30, 40　　**9.** 8, 24, 32

Tell whether each number is *prime* or *composite*. (Lesson 9-2)

10. 20　　**11.** 36

12. 19　　**13.** 28

14. MULTIPLE CHOICE Which model does NOT represent a composite number? (Lesson 9-2)

F 

G 

H 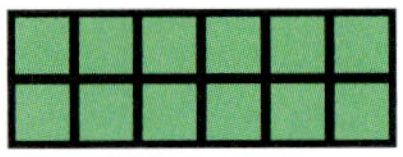

J 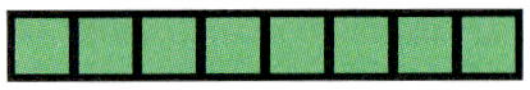

Find two fractions that are equivalent to each fraction. (Lesson 9-3)

15. $\frac{2}{7}$　　**16.** $\frac{1}{5}$　　**17.** $\frac{4}{10}$　　**18.** $\frac{3}{8}$

19. Algebra What number makes $\frac{4}{9} = \frac{16}{\blacksquare}$ a true statement? (Lesson 9-3)

20. MULTIPLE CHOICE Devin recorded the shirt color of the 30 students who rode his bus on Monday. The results are shown below.

Shirt Color	Number of Students
Blue	12
White	9
Red	5
Green	3
Other	1

Which fraction of shirts were red? (Lesson 9-4)

A $\frac{1}{3}$　　**B** $\frac{1}{4}$　　**C** $\frac{1}{5}$　　**D** $\frac{1}{6}$

Write each fraction in simplest form. If the fraction is already in simplest form, write *simplified*. (Lesson 9-4)

21. $\frac{8}{24}$　　**22.** $\frac{6}{14}$

23. $\frac{9}{20}$　　**24.** $\frac{25}{30}$

25. WRITING IN MATH Explain how you would find two fractions that are equivalent to $\frac{6}{10}$. (Lesson 9-3)

9-5 Decimals and Fractions

MAIN IDEA

I will relate decimals to fractions.

Math Online

macmillanmh.com

- Extra Examples
- Personal Tutor
- Self-Check Quiz

GET READY to Learn

A cashier weighs two peaches. The scale reads 0.75 pound. What fraction of a pound do the peaches weigh?

You can use models to write any decimal that names tenths, hundredths, or thousandths as a fraction. Use the place value of the right most digit in the decimal to name the denominator of the fraction.

Real-World EXAMPLE

Write a Decimal as a Fraction

1 **FOOD** **Refer to the information above. Write the weight of the peaches as a fraction in simplest form.**

Step 1 Shade a model of 0.75.

THINK 0.75 is 75 hundredths.

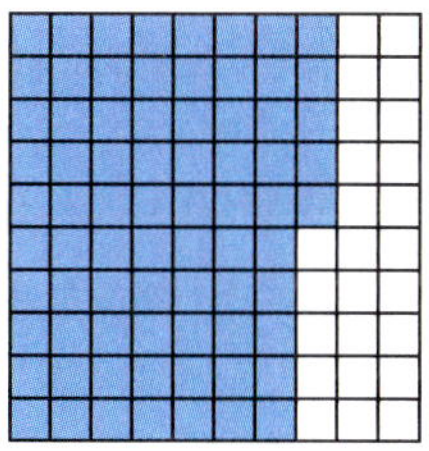

Step 2 Write a fraction with 100 as the denominator.

$$0.75 = \frac{75}{100}$$

Step 3 If necessary, simplify the fraction.

$$\frac{75}{100} = \frac{75 \div 25}{100 \div 25} \quad \text{Divide by the GCF, 25.}$$

$$= \frac{3}{4} \quad \text{Simplify.}$$

So, the peaches weigh $\frac{3}{4}$ pound.

Remember

Use the place value of the right most digit in the decimal as the denominator.

EXAMPLE Write a Decimal as a Fraction

2 **Write 0.8 as a fraction in simplest form.**

Step 1 Shade a model of 0.8.

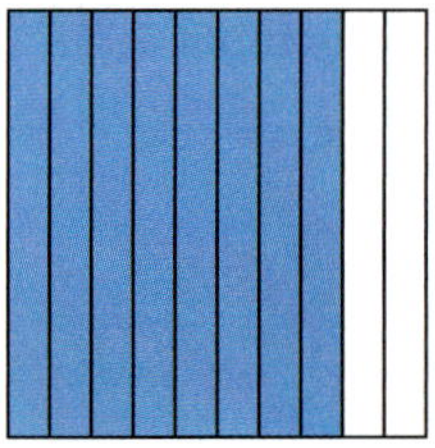

Step 2 Write a fraction with 10 as the denominator.

$0.8 = \frac{8}{10}$

Step 3 If necessary, simplify the fraction.

$\frac{8}{10} = \frac{8 \div 2}{10 \div 2}$ Divide by the GCF, 2.

$= \frac{4}{5}$ Simplify.

EXAMPLE Write a Decimal as a Fraction

3 **Write 0.009 as a fraction in simplest form.**

Shade a model of 0.009.

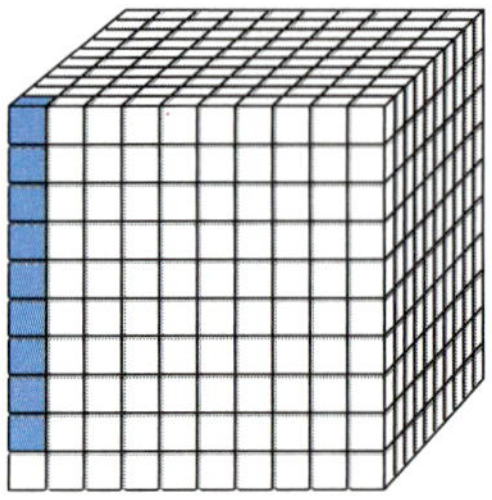

Write a fraction with 1,000 as the denominator.

$0.009 = \frac{9}{1,000}$ $\frac{9}{1,000}$ is in simplest form.

CHECK What You Know

Write each decimal or decimal model as a fraction in simplest form. See Examples 1–3 (pp. 391–392)

1. 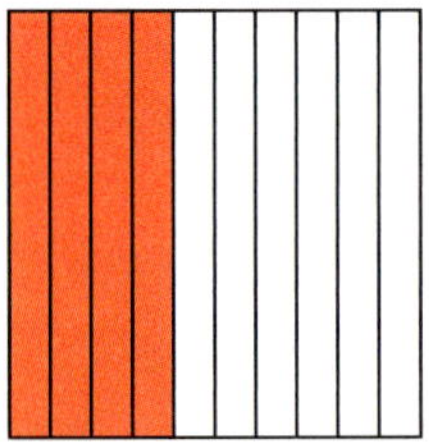

2. 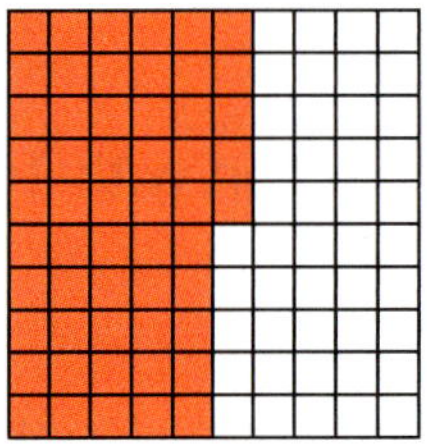

3. 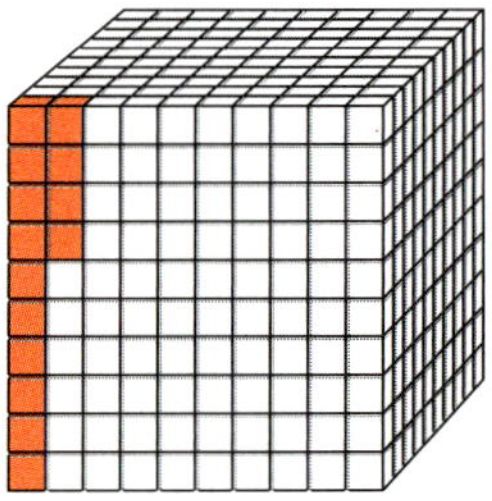

4. 0.6

5. 0.17

6. 0.125

7. It rained 0.68 inch last night. What fraction of an inch did it rain? Write in simplest form.

8. Talk About It How would you write a decimal as a fraction? Provide an example.

Practice and Problem Solving

EXTRA PRACTICE See page R25.

Write each decimal or decimal model as a fraction in simplest form.

See Examples 1–3 (pp. 391–392)

9. 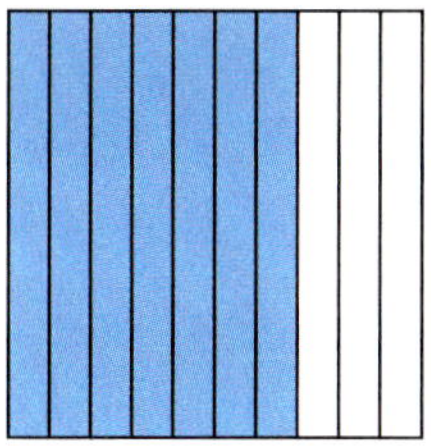

10. 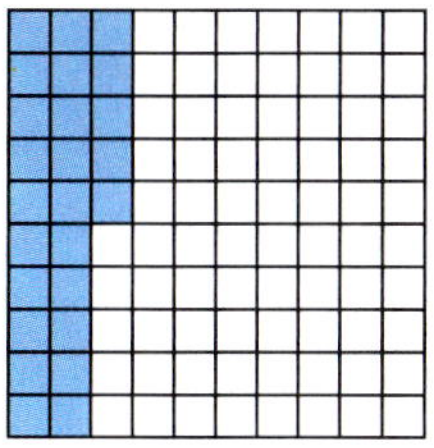

11. 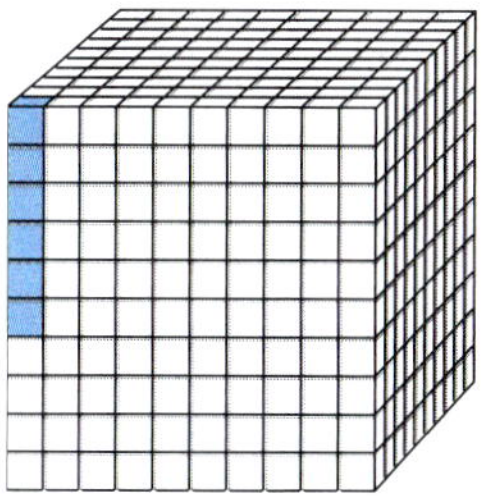

12. 0.9 **13.** 0.2 **14.** 0.5 **15.** 0.1

16. 0.65 **17.** 0.87 **18.** 0.45 **19.** 0.06

20. 0.875 **21.** 0.255 **22.** 0.045 **23.** 0.008

24. A three-toed sloth can travel at a rate of 0.07 mile per hour. Write 0.07 as a fraction in simplest form.

25. What fraction of a dollar is a penny, a nickel, a dime, a quarter, and a half dollar? Write each in simplest form.

Real-World PROBLEM SOLVING

Science The *radius* of a planet is the distance from the planet's center to its surface. The table compares the radius of three planets in the solar system to the radius of Earth.

Comparing a Planet's Radius with Earth's

Planet	Radius (in Earth radii)
Mercury	0.38 × Earth
Venus	0.95 × Earth
Earth	1 × Earth
Mars	0.53 × Earth

What fraction times Earth's radius is the radius of each planet? Write in simplest form.

26. Mercury

27. Venus

28. Mars

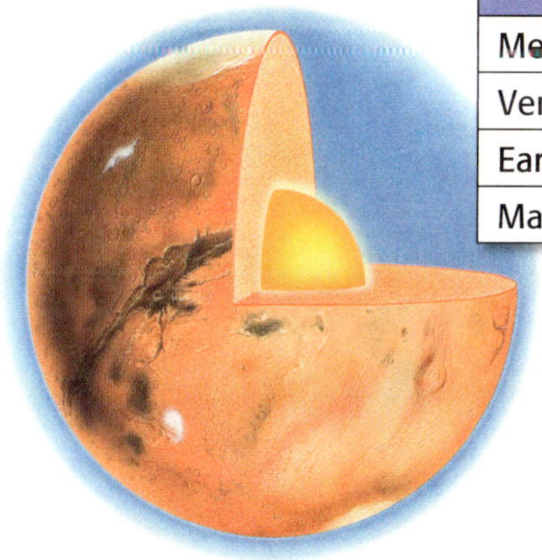

H.O.T. Problems

29. **OPEN ENDED** Write a real-world problem that relates a decimal to a fraction between $\frac{30}{100}$ and $\frac{40}{100}$.

30. **WRITING IN MATH** Explain why 0.08 is not equal to $\frac{8}{10}$.

9-6 Problem-Solving Strategy

MAIN IDEA I will solve problems by looking for a pattern.

Shawna is training to run in a half-marathon. A half-marathon is about 13 miles. On her first day of training, she ran 1.25 miles. Then she increased her distance each day according to a pattern. Here are the number of miles Shawna ran the first five days of training.

1.25, 1.85, 2.45, 3.05, 3.65

Based on her pattern, how many miles will Shawna run on the sixth day?

Understand

What facts do you know?

- We know how many miles Shawna ran each day for five days.
- She increased the distance she ran each day according to a pattern.

What do you need to find?

- The number of miles Shawna will run on the sixth day.

Plan

One way to solve the problem is by looking for a pattern among the number of miles she ran each day for five days. Then extend the pattern to find the number of miles she will run on the sixth day.

Solve

Use your plan to solve the problem.

Find the amounts by which Shawna increased her distances.

1.25 → 1.85 → 2.45 → 3.05 → 3.65 → ■

(+ 0.6, + 0.6, + 0.6, + 0.6, + 0.6)

Shawna increases her distance by 0.6 mile each day. Add 0.6 to 3.65 to find the number of miles Shawna will run on the sixth day.

$$3.65 + 0.6 = 4.25$$

So, on the sixth day, she will run 4.25 miles.

Check

Look back. $4.25 - 0.6 = 3.65$. So, the answer is correct. ✓

ANALYZE the Strategy

Refer to the problem on the previous page.

1. How many miles will Shawna run on day seven if she wants to double her normal increase?

2. Explain why Shawna cannot continue her pattern forever.

3. Explain when to use the *look for a pattern* strategy to solve a problem.

4. Can you always use the *look for a pattern* strategy when solving a problem?

PRACTICE the Strategy

EXTRA PRACTICE See page R25.

Solve. Use the *look for a pattern* strategy.

5. Draw the next two figures in the pattern.

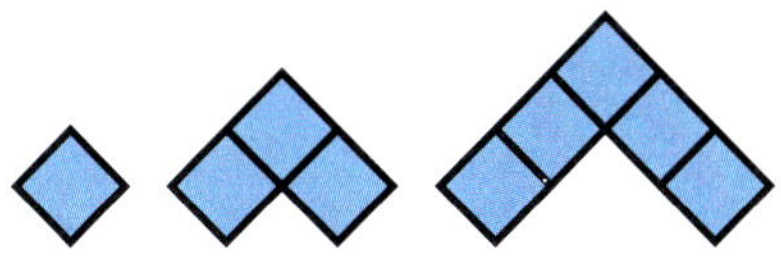

6. Stefano is buying a few pencils. The table shows the price of different numbers of pencils.

Number of Pencils	Price
10	$2.00
15	$3.00
20	$4.00
25	$5.00
30	$6.00

What is the relationship between the number of pencils and price?

7. **Measurement** Cheryl is filling a pool. She measures the depth in feet every 5 minutes. Her measurements are 2.5, 3.6, 4.7, and 5.8. If this pattern continues, how deep will the water be the next time she measures?

For Exercises 8–10, use the following information.

Gavin rode his bike for a longer distance each day while training. Here is his record of the number of miles he rode.

Mon	Tues	Wed	Thurs	Fri
3.5 mi	4.2 mi	5.0 mi	■	6.9 mi

8. Based on Gavin's pattern, how long did he ride on Thursday?

9. **Algebra** If the pattern continues, how far will Gavin ride on Saturday?

10. Explain how to find the number of miles Gavin will ride on Sunday, if the pattern continues.

11. The Fibonacci sequence is a famous pattern of numbers. The first seven numbers in the Fibonacci sequence are 1, 1, 2, 3, 5, 8, and 13. Find the next three numbers. Explain the pattern.

12. **WRITING IN MATH** Write a real-world problem that uses the *look for a pattern* strategy. Use the pattern below.

2.45, 2.8, 3.15, 3.5, . . .

9-7 Multiples

MAIN IDEA

I will identify common multiples of a set of whole numbers.

New Vocabulary

multiple

common multiple

least common multiple (LCM)

Math Online

macmillanmh.com

- Extra Examples
- Personal Tutor
- Self-Check Quiz

GET READY to Learn

Hands-On Mini Activity

A **multiple** of a number is the product of the number and any whole number. The first few multiples of 4 are 4, 8, 12, and 16.

1. Use a hundreds chart to place a colored cube on the multiples of 4. Part of a hundreds chart is shown.

×	1	2	3	4	5	6	7	8	9	10
1	1	2	3	4	5	6	7	8	9	10
2	2	4	6	8	10	12	14	16	18	20
3	3	6	9	12	15	18	21	24	27	30
4	4	8	12	16	20	24	28	32	36	40

2. On the same chart, place a different colored cube on the multiples of 6.

3. List all the numbers that have two cubes.

4. What is the least number that has two cubes?

In the Mini Activity, you found common multiples of 4 and 6. A whole number that is a multiple of two or more whole numbers is a **common multiple**.

EXAMPLE Find Common Multiples

1 **List multiples to find the first two common multiples of 8 and 12.**

multiples of 8: 8, 16, **24**, 32, 40, **48**, ... $8 \times 1, 8 \times 2, 8 \times 3, 8 \times 4, 8 \times 5, 8 \times 6 \ldots$

multiples of 12: 12, **24**, 36, **48**, 60, ... $12 \times 1, 12 \times 2, 12 \times 3, 12 \times 4, 12 \times 5, 12 \times 6, \ldots$

The first two common multiples of 8 and 12 are 24 and 48.

The **least common multiple (LCM)** is the least multiple, other than 0, common to sets of multiples. In the Mini Activity, the LCM of 4 and 6 is 12.

> **Remember**
>
> You can always find a common multiple by finding the product of the numbers. This does not always give the LCM. In Example 2, $2 \times 3 \times 4 = 24$ which is a multiple of all three numbers. But the LCM of 2, 3, and 4 is 12.

Real-World EXAMPLE — Find and Use the LCM

2 **FOOD Ben's Burgers gives away a free order of fries every 2 days, a free milkshake every 3 days, and a free hamburger every 4 days. If they gave away all three items today, in how many days will they give away all three items again?**

To solve, find the LCM of 2, 3 and 4.

multiples of 2: 2, 4, 6, 8, 10, **12** … $2 \times 1, 2 \times 2, 2 \times 3, 2 \times 4, \ldots$

multiples of 3: 3, 6, 9, **12**, 15, 18… $3 \times 1, 3 \times 2, 3 \times 3, 3 \times 4, \ldots$

multiples of 4: 4, 8, **12**, 16, 20… $4 \times 1, 4 \times 2, 4 \times 3, 4 \times 4, \ldots$

Notice that 12 is the least common multiple of 2, 3, and 4. So, Ben's Burgers will give away all three items again in 12 days.

Draw a number line to check. Use F for fries, M for milkshake, and H for hamburger. You can see that the first day that all three items appear again, after today, is day 12. So, the answer is correct.

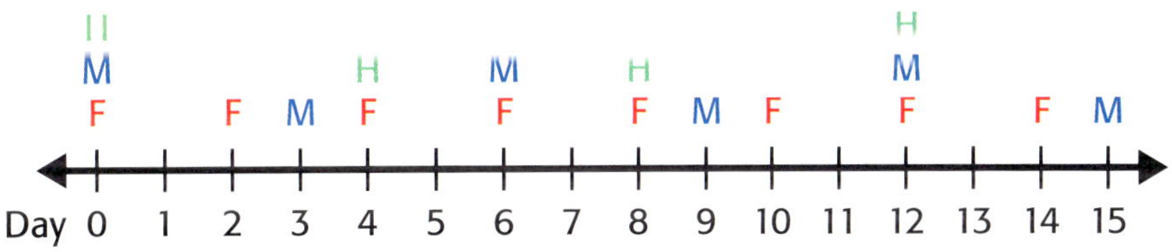

CHECK What You Know

List multiples to find the first two common multiples of each set of numbers. See Example 1 (p. 396)

1. 2 and 6
2. 4 and 10
3. 5, 6, and 10
4. 3, 4, and 6

Find the LCM of each set of numbers. Make a table or a number line.
See Example 2 (p. 397)

5. 3 and 4
6. 2 and 7
7. 4, 5, and 10
8. 3, 6, and 7

9. Inez waters her plants every two days. She trims them every 15 days. She did both today. When will she do both again?

10. Talk About It When is the LCM of two numbers one of the numbers? Give an example.

Practice and Problem Solving

EXTRA PRACTICE See page R25.

List multiples to find the first two common multiples of each set of numbers. See Example 1 (p. 396)

11. 2 and 4

12. 8 and 12

13. 3 and 12

14. 4 and 8

15. 2, 5, and 10

16. 3, 4, and 8

17. 2, 3, and 9

18. 6, 10, and 15

Find the LCM of each set of numbers. Make a table or a number line.
See Example 2 (p. 397)

19. 5 and 6

20. 3 and 5

21. 6 and 9

22. 12 and 18

23. 6, 12, and 15

24. 5, 10, and 15

25. 3, 9, and 15

26. 9, 12, and 18

27. Macy is painting a design that contains two repeating patterns. One pattern repeats every 8 inches. The other pattern repeats every 12 inches. In how many inches will the two patterns begin at the same place?

28. The science department buys the following equipment. They bought all three items this year. In how many years will they again have to buy all three items?

Item	Time Bought
Microscopes	every 5 years
Safety goggles	every 4 years
Test tubes	every 2 years

Real-World PROBLEM SOLVING

Music A trumpet player plays a note on the fourth beat and every 4 beats after that. A saxophone player plays a note on the eighth beat and every 8 beats after that.

29. On which beat will the musicians play a note together?

30. Suppose a clarinet player joins them. He plays a note on the sixth beat and every 6 beats after that. On which beat will all three musicians play a note together?

H.O.T. Problems

31. **OPEN ENDED** Write a real-world problem that involves two numbers between 9 and 21. Find the LCM of the numbers and describe what it means in the problem.

32. **FIND THE ERROR** Carrie and Bryant are finding the least common multiple of 18 and 24. Who is correct? Explain.

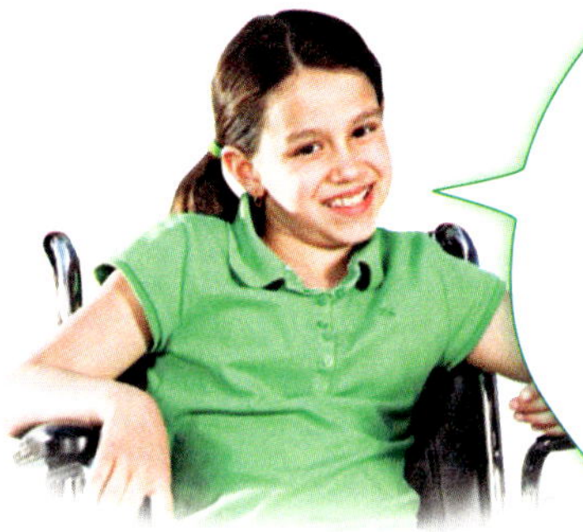

Carrie

$$\begin{array}{r} 18 \\ \times\ 24 \\ \hline 72 \\ 360 \\ \hline 432 \end{array}$$

The LCM is 432.

Bryant

multiples of 18:
18, 36, 54 0, ...
multiples of 24:
24, 48, 72, 96, ...
The LCM is 72.

33. **CHALLENGE** Consider the numbers from 2 to 10. For which two numbers is the LCM the greatest? Explain.

34. **WRITING IN MATH** How is the GCF of 36 and 45 different from their LCM?

TEST Practice

35. A tree grew 0.85 inch in the first year. What fraction of an inch did it grow in the first year? (Lesson 9-5)

A $\frac{4}{5}$ **C** $\frac{21}{25}$

B $\frac{17}{20}$ **D** $\frac{17}{50}$

36. Look for the pattern in the sequence of numbers below. Each sequence is an example of which kind of numbers? (Lesson 9-7)

3, 6, 12, 24, 48
5, 10, 20, 40, 80
8, 16, 32, 64, 128

F even numbers **H** multiples

G odd numbers **J** prime numbers

Spiral Review

37. The table shows the heights of different sizes of bleachers. If the pattern continues, what would be the height of bleachers that have 7 rows? (Lesson 9-6)

Number of Rows	Height of Bleachers (ft)
1	2
2	4
3	6

Write each decimal as a fraction in simplest form. (Lesson 9-5)

38. 0.2

39. 0.12

40. 0.08

9-8 Problem-Solving Investigation

MAIN IDEA I will choose the best strategy to solve a problem.

P.S.I. TEAM +

MYKAELA: My science teacher is giving goldfish to some of my classmates to take care of during the summer. He gave some of them to Gisela. Then he gave twice as many to Liseta. He gave twice as many to Clara as he gave to Liseta. He gave out all 28 goldfish.

YOUR MISSION: How many goldfish did each girl take home?

Understand

There are 28 goldfish. He gave some to Gisela. He gave twice as many to Liseta as to Gisela. He gave twice as many to Clara as to Liseta. You need to determine how many goldfish each girl took home.

Plan

You can use the *guess and check* strategy to find how many goldfish each girl took home.

Solve

Make a guess as to how many goldfish the teacher gave Gisela. See if it is correct. Then adjust the guess, if necessary.

Number of Goldfish

Gisela	Liseta	Clara	Total	
5	$2 \times 5 = 10$	$2 \times 10 = 20$	35	$35 > 28$; too many
3	$2 \times 3 = 6$	$2 \times 6 = 12$	21	$21 < 28$; too few
4	$2 \times 4 = 8$	$2 \times 8 = 16$	28	$28 = 28$; correct

So, the teacher gave 4 goldfish to Gisela, 8 goldfish to Liseta, and 16 goldfish to Clara.

Check

Look back. $4 + 8 + 16 = 28$. So, the answer is correct. ✓

Mixed Problem Solving

EXTRA PRACTICE
See page R26.

Use any strategy shown below to solve each problem.

PROBLEM-SOLVING STRATEGIES
- Guess and check.
- Look for a pattern.
- Solve a simpler problem.

1. Lorraine and Yori have 12 plants between them. Yori has 4 more than Lorraine. How many does each girl have?

2. **Algebra** When Cesar's Pizza Parlor makes a pizza, they use the following amount of cheese on each pizza:

Number of Pizzas	Amount of Cheese (ounces)
1	4
2	8
3	12
5	20
7	■
8	■

Complete the table and find how much cheese Cesar's uses to make 8 pizzas.

3. Annette put \$5 in her bank account each week for 14 weeks. Isabel put \$7 in her bank account each week for 11 weeks. Who saved more money? How much more?

4. During the World Series, one pitcher used a pattern when he pitched. The pattern was two fastballs followed by two sliders followed by a change-up. If the pattern continues, what kind of pitch will the eleventh pitch be?

5. Mr. Whitmore bought tickets for a movie. Adult tickets cost \$5 each and children's tickets cost \$3 each. He spent a total of \$22 for the tickets. How many adult tickets and how many children's tickets did he buy?

6. Liu has \$53 in his bank account. Each week for 5 weeks, he adds \$2.50 to the account. How much does he now have in his bank account?

7. Maggie and her younger brother, Ty, went to lunch. Ty had a sandwich and soft drink. Maggie had a hamburger and milkshake. How much more did Maggie's lunch cost than Ty's?

Menu			
Item	Cost	Item	Cost
Sandwich	\$2.25	Milkshake	\$3.00
Hamburger	\$4.50	Soft drink	\$0.75

8. A total of 48 students joined the math team. There were 12 more girls than boys who joined. How many boys and how many girls joined the math team?

9. Oscar makes leather belts. If he continues his pattern below, what will be the design of the seventeenth link in the belt?

10. WRITING IN MATH Explain how you use the *guess and check* strategy.

Explore

Technology Activity for 9-9

Compare Fractions

MAIN IDEA

I will use technology to compare fractions.

ACTIVITY

1 **Jeffrey studied for $\frac{3}{4}$ hour and Estella studied for $\frac{5}{6}$ hour. Who studied longer?**

You can use the Fractions option from the Math Tool Chest™.

- Choose Fractions. Click on Level 2.
- Click on Math Type. Select the 2 Sections option.
- At the bottom of the first section, stamp out three of the $\frac{1}{4}$ stamps in a horizontal line to represent $\frac{3}{4}$.
- Directly under the $\frac{1}{4}$ stamps and lined up with the left edge, place five of the $\frac{1}{6}$ stamps. This represents $\frac{5}{6}$.

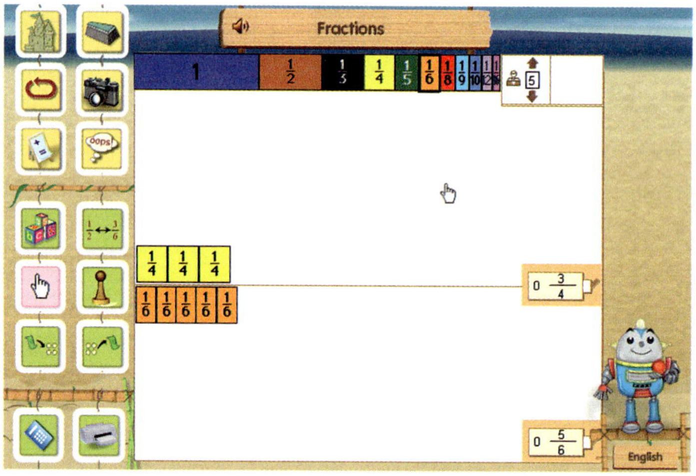

The model shows that $\frac{5}{6} > \frac{3}{4}$. So, Estella studied longer.

CHECK What You Know

Use the Fraction Option from Math Tools Chest™ to compare fractions. Then name the fraction that is greater.

1. $\frac{2}{3}$ and $\frac{3}{4}$ **2.** $\frac{2}{5}$ and $\frac{1}{4}$ **3.** $\frac{5}{8}$ and $\frac{7}{9}$ **4.** $\frac{11}{12}$ and $\frac{9}{10}$

5. $\frac{7}{8}$ and $\frac{5}{6}$ **6.** $\frac{2}{9}$ and $\frac{3}{10}$ **7.** $\frac{7}{12}$ and $\frac{1}{2}$ **8.** $\frac{3}{12}$ and $\frac{3}{8}$

Tech Link

ACTIVITY

2 **Terrence, Yasmin, and Delsin were kicking soccer balls into a net. Terrence made $\frac{6}{10}$ of his shots, Yasmin made $\frac{3}{8}$ of her shots, and Delsin made $\frac{7}{9}$ of his shots. Compare the fractions and arrange them in order from least to greatest.**

Follow the same steps as in Activity 1, with the following exceptions.

- Select the 3 Sections option from Mat Type.
- Align the stamps with the left most edge of the screen to ensure accuracy when comparing fractions.

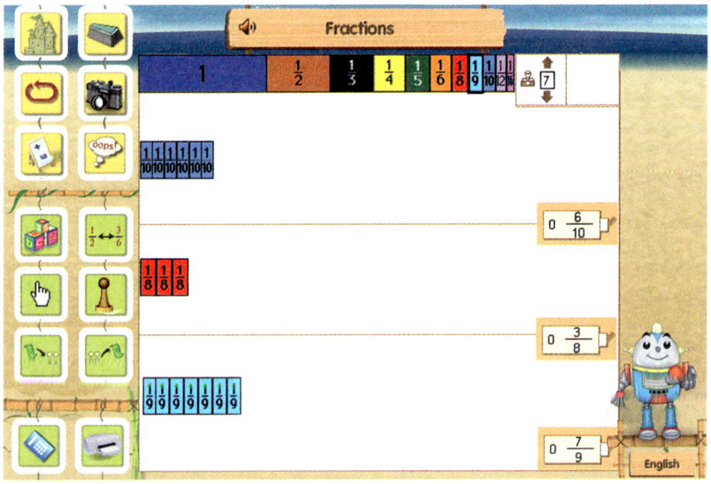

The model shows that $\frac{3}{8} < \frac{6}{10} < \frac{7}{9}$.

CHECK What You Know

Use Math Tool Chest™ to order the fractions from least to greatest.

9. $\frac{2}{5}, \frac{3}{16},$ and $\frac{3}{4}$

10. $\frac{8}{9}, \frac{3}{4},$ and $\frac{1}{2}$

11. $\frac{4}{12}, \frac{2}{5},$ and $\frac{4}{5}$

Solve. Use Math Tool Chest™.

12. Francisca lives $\frac{7}{10}$ mile from the park and Sereeta lives $\frac{3}{4}$ mile from the park. Who lives closer to the park?

13. Keith and Ines are sharing a pizza. Keith ate $\frac{5}{12}$ of the pizza and Ines ate $\frac{1}{3}$ of the pizza. Who ate more pizza?

9-9 Compare Fractions

GET READY to Learn

A class survey showed that $\frac{5}{8}$ of the class favored apple pie, $\frac{1}{4}$ favored peach pie, and $\frac{1}{8}$ of class liked pumpkin pie. Which type of pie was favored most?

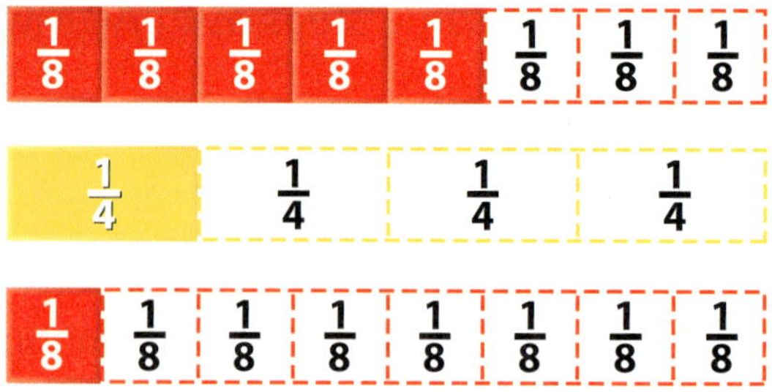

You can use models to compare fractions. If fractions have the same denominators, compare the numerators. If the fractions have different denominators, first write equivalent fractions with a common denominator. A **common denominator** of two or more fractions is a number that is a multiple of the denominators of the fractions.

Use the **least common denominator (LCD)**, or the least common multiple of the denominators, to compare fractions.

MAIN IDEA

I will compare fractions using common denominators.

New Vocabulary

common denominator

least common denominator (LCD)

Math Online

macmillanmh.com

- Extra Examples
- Personal Tutor
- Self-Check Quiz
- Concepts in Motion

EXAMPLE Compare Fractions

1 **Compare $\frac{3}{5}$ and $\frac{1}{2}$ using models and the least common denominator.**

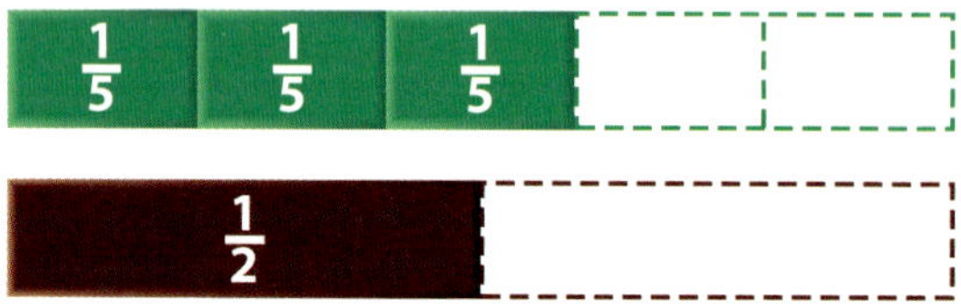

The models show that $\frac{3}{5} > \frac{1}{2}$.

Step 1 Find the LCM of the denominators. The LCM of 5 and 2 is 10.

Step 2 Find equivalent fractions with a denominator of 10.

$\frac{3}{5} = \frac{6}{10}$ THINK $5 \times 2 = 10$, $3 \times 2 = 6$

$\frac{1}{2} = \frac{5}{10}$ THINK $2 \times 5 = 10$, $1 \times 5 = 5$

Step 3 Compare the numerators. Since $6 > 5$, then $\frac{6}{10} > \frac{5}{10}$. So, $\frac{3}{5} > \frac{1}{2}$.

Remember

You can also find a set of equivalent fractions for $\frac{5}{6}$ and $\frac{7}{9}$ to find the LCD.

$\frac{5}{6}, \frac{10}{12}, \frac{15}{18}, \frac{20}{24}, \ldots$

$\frac{7}{9}, \frac{14}{18}, \frac{21}{27}, \ldots$

In Example 1, the LCD of $\frac{3}{5}$ and $\frac{1}{2}$ is 10, which can also be found by multiplying 5 and 2. You can always multiply the denominators of two fractions to find a common denominator. This method does not always give the LCD.

EXAMPLE Compare Fractions Using the LCD

2 **Compare $\frac{5}{6}$ and $\frac{7}{9}$ using the least common denominator.**

Step 1 Find the LCM of the denominators. The LCM of 6 and 9 is 18. Note that multiplying 6 by 9 gives a common denominator of 54, which is not the LCD, 18.

Step 2 Find an equivalent fraction with a denominator of 18 for each fraction.

$\frac{5}{6} = \frac{15}{18}$ THINK $6 \times 3 = 18, 5 \times 3 = 15$

$\frac{7}{9} = \frac{14}{18}$ THINK $9 \times 2 = 18, 7 \times 2 = 14$

Step 3 Compare the numerators. Since $15 > 14$, then $\frac{15}{18} > \frac{14}{18}$. So, $\frac{5}{6} > \frac{7}{9}$.

Real-World EXAMPLE

3 **SPORTS** **Trevor made 2 out of 3 field goals and Tyler made 5 out of 6. Who made a greater fraction of field goals?**

The models show $\frac{5}{6} > \frac{2}{3}$.

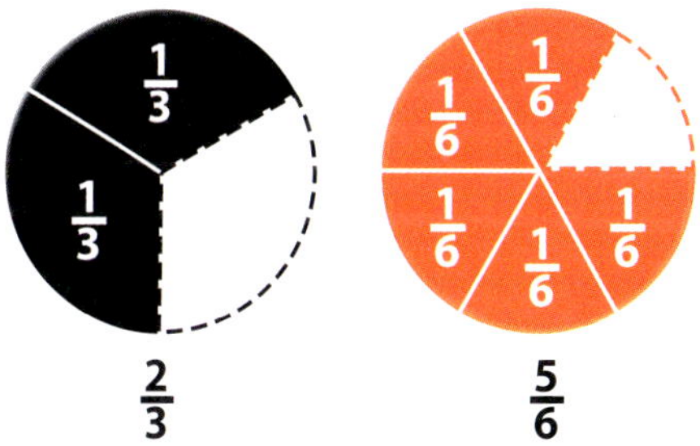

Step 1 Find the LCM of the denominators. The LCM of 3 and 6 is 6.

Step 2 Find an equivalent fraction with a denominator of 6 for each fraction.

$\frac{2}{3} = \frac{4}{6}$ THINK $3 \times 2 = 6, 2 \times 2 = 4$

$\frac{5}{6} = \frac{5}{6}$ THINK $6 \times 1 = 6, 5 \times 1 = 5$

Step 3 Compare the numerators. Since $5 > 4$, then $\frac{5}{6} > \frac{4}{6}$. So, $\frac{5}{6} > \frac{2}{3}$. Tyler made a greater fraction of field goals.

CHECK What You Know

Compare each pair of fractions using models or the LCD.
See Examples 1–3 (pp. 404–405)

1. $\frac{1}{5}$ and $\frac{1}{3}$ **2.** $\frac{1}{2}$ and $\frac{1}{6}$ **3.** $\frac{3}{4}$ and $\frac{7}{8}$ **4.** $\frac{2}{3}$ and $\frac{7}{10}$

Algebra **Replace each ● with <, >, or = to make a true statement.** See Examples 1–3 (pp. 404–405)

5. $\frac{1}{3}$ ● $\frac{5}{9}$ **6.** $\frac{2}{3}$ ● $\frac{7}{12}$ **7.** $\frac{1}{4}$ ● $\frac{1}{6}$ **8.** $\frac{2}{5}$ ● $\frac{6}{15}$

9. A recipe calls for $\frac{5}{8}$ cup of brown sugar and $\frac{2}{3}$ cup of flour. Which ingredient is greater?

10. Talk About It Explain how the LCM and the LCD are alike. How are they different?

Practice and Problem Solving

EXTRA PRACTICE See page R26.

Compare each pair of fractions using models or the LCD.
See Examples 1–3 (pp. 404–405)

11. $\frac{2}{3}$ and $\frac{3}{4}$ **12.** $\frac{1}{5}$ and $\frac{3}{15}$ **13.** $\frac{1}{6}$ and $\frac{1}{3}$ **14.** $\frac{2}{5}$ and $\frac{3}{4}$

15. $\frac{4}{5}$ and $\frac{5}{6}$ **16.** $\frac{7}{8}$ and $\frac{2}{3}$ **17.** $\frac{3}{10}$ and $\frac{1}{12}$ **18.** $\frac{5}{6}$ and $\frac{4}{9}$

Algebra **Replace each ● with <, >, or = to make a true statement.** See Examples 1–3 (pp. 404–405)

19. $\frac{2}{5}$ ● $\frac{3}{10}$ **20.** $\frac{3}{4}$ ● $\frac{3}{7}$ **21.** $\frac{1}{5}$ ● $\frac{1}{4}$ **22.** $\frac{1}{2}$ ● $\frac{6}{12}$

23. $\frac{2}{6}$ ● $\frac{3}{7}$ **24.** $\frac{11}{12}$ ● $\frac{5}{8}$ **25.** $\frac{3}{8}$ ● $\frac{5}{6}$ **26.** $\frac{15}{16}$ ● $\frac{3}{8}$

27. A trail mix has $\frac{1}{2}$ cup of raisins, $\frac{1}{4}$ cup of almonds, and $\frac{2}{3}$ cup of peanuts. Which ingredient is greater?

28. A class survey showed that $\frac{7}{15}$ of the class liked soccer, $\frac{3}{10}$ liked tennis, and $\frac{2}{5}$ liked basketball. Which sport was liked the least?

29. The amounts of water four runners drank are shown at the right. Who drank the most?

30. The fifth graders were given sandwiches for lunch during their field trip. Nathan ate $\frac{5}{6}$ of his sandwich, Leroy ate $\frac{7}{8}$ of his sandwich, and Sofia ate $\frac{5}{8}$ of her sandwich. Who had the least amount of sandwich left to eat?

Runner	Amount (bottle)
Evita	$\frac{3}{5}$
Jack	$\frac{5}{8}$
Keisha	$\frac{3}{4}$
Sirjo	$\frac{5}{10}$

H.O.T. Problems

31. OPEN ENDED Replace ■ with a number to make $\frac{■}{24} > \frac{1}{4}$ a true statement.

32. NUMBER SENSE Suppose two fractions have the same numerator and different denominators. How can you decide which fraction is greater without finding the LCD?

33. WRITING IN MATH Write a real-world problem that can be solved by comparing two fractions with different denominators. Then solve. Support your answer with a model.

TEST Practice

34. The table shows the cost of renting a bicycle. If the pattern continues, how much will it cost to rent a bicycle for 6 hours? (Lesson 9-7)

Number of Hours	Cost ($)
2	12
3	18
4	24
5	30

A $6

B $32

C $36

D $42

35. Eighteen out of 24 of Emil's CDs are country music. Five out of 8 of Imani's CDs are country music. Which is a true statement? (Lesson 9-9)

F Both of their CD collections are half country music.

G Both of their CD collections are less than half country music.

H Emil's collection is closer to half country than Imani's collection.

J Imani's collection is closer to half country than Emil's collection.

Spiral Review

36. Find the missing number in the pattern 1, 2, 4, 7, ■, 16, ... (Lesson 9-8)

Find the first two common multiples of each pair of numbers. (Lesson 9-7)

37. 4 and 6

38. 3, 9

39. 2, 5

40. 8, 20

41. The table shows the number of games won and lost by the girls' basketball team. What fraction of the games did the team win? Write the fraction in simplest form. (Lesson 9-4)

Number of Wins	Number of Losses
12	4

Problem Solving in Social Studies

SWEET DREAMS

Dreamcatchers were first made by the Chippewa people, who hung them over the beds of children to trap bad dreams. The Chippewa are one of the largest Native American groups in North America. In 1990, around 106,000 Chippewa were living throughout their original territories.

Each dreamcatcher is made with many beads and feathers. A simple dreamcatcher has 28 pony beads and is made with 7 yards of string. Today, Native Americans continue to make dreamcatchers on more than 300 reservations.

Did You Know?

The Chippewa people have signed 51 treaties with the United States government, the most of any Native American tribe.

Real-World Math

Use the information on page 408 to solve each problem.

1. In a simple dreamcatcher, how many beads do you use for each yard of string?

2. For each dreamcatcher you made, you used 12 beads. If you had 144 beads, how many dreamcatchers did you make?

3. Each time you add a feather to a dreamcatcher, you add 3 turquoise beads. Use a function table to find out how many beads you will need if you have 2, 5, 8, or 13 feathers in your dreamcatcher.

4. Find the rule for the function table you created in Exercise 3.

5. You are making dreamcatchers that require 6 beads for every 1 feather. Let f represent the number of feathers. Then write a function rule that relates the total number of beads to the number of feathers.

6. Use the function rule from Exercise 5 to find the number of beads you would use if you made a dreamcatcher with 17 feathers.

7. Suppose you use 12 feathers and a certain amount of beads to make a dreamcatcher. If you had 48 feathers and beads, how many beads did you use?

CHAPTER 9

Study Guide and Review

Math Online macmillanmh.com
- STUDY TO GO
- Vocabulary Review

FOLDABLES® Study Organizer GET READY to Study

Be sure the following Big Ideas are written in your Foldable.

Key Concepts

Prime and Composite Numbers

- A prime number has exactly two factors, 1 and itself. A composite number has more than two factors. (p. 376)

prime numbers: 2, 3, 11, 29
composite numbers: 4, 8, 12, 20

Equivalent Fractions and Fractions in Simplest Form

- Fractions that have the same value are **equivalent fractions**. (p. 382)

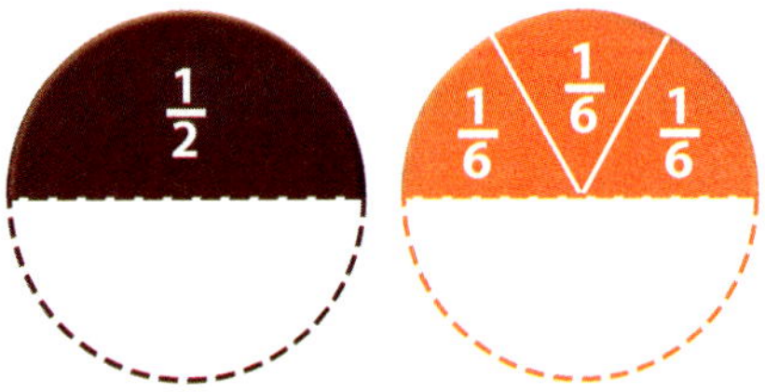

$\frac{1}{2} = \frac{3}{6}$

- A fraction is in **simplest form** when the GCF of the numerator and denominator is 1. (p. 386)

Compare Fractions

- To compare fractions with different denominators, rename the fractions using common denominators.

Key Vocabulary

common factor (p. 373)
composite number (p. 376)
equivalent fractions (p. 382)
prime number (p. 376)
simplest form (p. 386)

Vocabulary Check

Complete. Use a word from the Key Vocabulary list.

1. A whole number greater than 1 that has exactly two factors, 1 and itself, is called a(n) __?__.

2. $\frac{3}{5}$ and $\frac{6}{10}$ are called __?__.

3. A whole number that has more than two factors is called a(n) __?__.

4. A fraction is written in __?__ when the numerator and denominator have no common factor greater than 1.

5. A whole number that is a factor of two or more numbers is called a(n) __?__.

6. The fraction $\frac{5}{12}$ is written in __?__.

Lesson-by-Lesson Review

9-1 Common Factors (pp. 373–375)

Example 1
Find the greatest common factor of 6 and 21.

First, list the factors of 6 and 21.

factors of 6: **1**, 2, **3**, 6

factors of 21: **1**, **3**, 7, 21

The common factors are 1 and 3. The greatest of these is 3. So, the greatest common factor of 6 and 21 is 3.

Find the common factors of each set of numbers.

7. 6, 8
8. 9, 21, and 24

Find the GCF of each set of numbers.

9. 12, 30
10. 18, 45

11. Twelve pens and 16 pencils will be placed in bags with an equal number of each item. What is the most number of bags that can be made?

9-2 Prime and Composite Numbers (pp. 378–381)

Example 2
Tell whether 51 is *prime* or *composite*.

$51 = 1 \times 51 \qquad 51 = 3 \times 17$

factors of 51: 1, 3, 17, 51

Since 51 has more than two factors, it is a composite number.

Tell whether each number is *prime* or *composite*.

12. 23
13. 48
14. 34

15. A goliath birdeater is a spider that can grow up to 28 centimeters. Find the prime factorization of 28.

9-3 Equivalent Fractions (pp. 382–384)

Example 3
Find two fractions that are equivalent to $\frac{2}{9}$.

Multiply $\frac{2}{9}$ by $\frac{2}{2}$. $\frac{2}{9} = \frac{2 \times 2}{9 \times 2} = \frac{4}{18}$

Multiply $\frac{2}{9}$ by $\frac{3}{3}$. $\frac{2}{9} = \frac{2 \times 3}{9 \times 3} = \frac{6}{27}$

So, $\frac{2}{9} = \frac{4}{18}$ and $\frac{2}{9} = \frac{6}{27}$.

Find two fractions that are equivalent to each fraction.

16. $\frac{1}{6}$
17. $\frac{4}{5}$
18. $\frac{2}{7}$

19. Lucinda cut her birthday cake into 16 slices. If Lucinda and her friends ate $\frac{1}{4}$ of the cake, how many pieces of cake did they eat? Support your answer with a model.

Study Guide and Review

9-4 Simplest Form (pp. 386–389)

Example 4

Write $\frac{4}{20}$ in simplest form.

factors of 4: 1, 2, **4**

factors of 20: 1, 2, **4**, 5, 10, 20

The GCF of 4 and 20 is 4.

$\frac{4}{20} = \frac{4 \div 4}{20 \div 4} = \frac{1}{5}$ Divide the numerator and denominator by 4.

So, $\frac{4}{20}$ in simplest form is $\frac{1}{5}$.

Write each fraction in simplest form. If the fraction is already in simplest form, write *simplified*.

20. $\frac{2}{10}$ **21.** $\frac{4}{18}$

22. $\frac{6}{21}$ **23.** $\frac{8}{24}$

24. $\frac{12}{25}$ **25.** $\frac{20}{32}$

26. What fraction is represented by the model shown below? Write the fraction in simplest form.

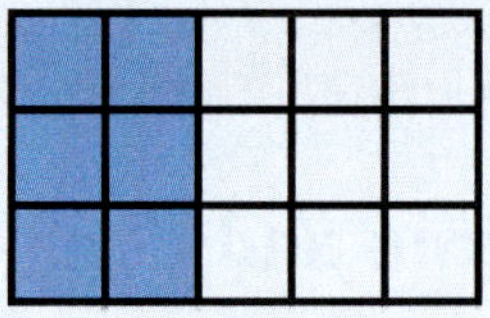

9-5 Decimals and Fractions (pp. 391–393)

Example 5

Write 0.45 as a fraction in simplest form.

Step 1
Write a fraction with 100 as the denominator.

$0.45 = \frac{45}{100}$

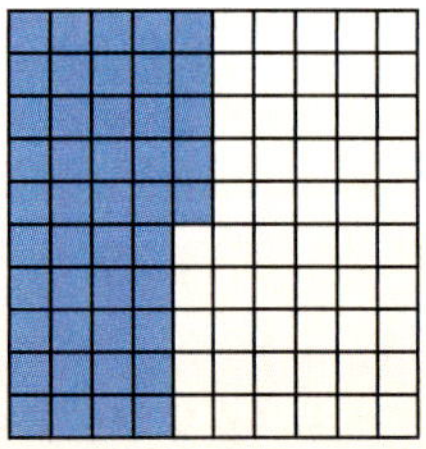

0.45 is 45 hundredths.

Step 2
Simplify the fraction.

$\frac{45}{100} = \frac{45 \div 5}{100 \div 5}$ Divide by the GCF, 5.

$= \frac{9}{20}$ Simplify.

So, $0.45 = \frac{9}{20}$.

Write each decimal as a fraction in simplest form.

27. 0.9 **28.** 0.4

29. 0.13 **30.** 0.88

31. 0.28 **32.** 0.06

33. A model train is 0.025 the length of an actual train. What fraction of the actual train length is the model? Write the fraction in simplest form.

34. A small black-legged tick is 0.125 inch long. What fraction of an inch is the black-legged tick? Write the fraction in simplest form.

9-6 Problem-Solving Strategy: Look for a Pattern (pp. 394–395)

Example 6

This stairway is made of cubes. How many cubes would be needed to make it 7 steps high?

Understand You know how many cubes are 1, 2, and 3 steps.

Plan Look for a pattern.

Solve 2 steps: $2 + 1$, or 3
3 steps: $3 + (2 + 1)$, or 6
4 steps: $4 + (3 + 2 + 1)$, or 10
7 steps: $7 + (6 + 5 + 4 + 3 + 2 + 1)$, or 28

Check Draw a picture and count the cubes. There are 28 cubes, so the answer is correct ✓

35. Find the next three numbers.
3, 7, 12, 18, 25,...

36. Bena makes bracelets. She uses red, white, and gray beads. If she continues her pattern, what color is the 15th bead?

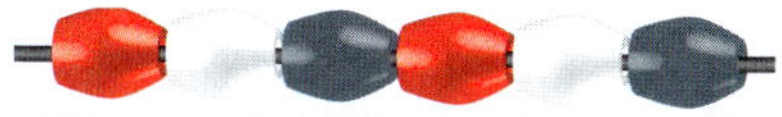

37. Draw the next two figures in the pattern.

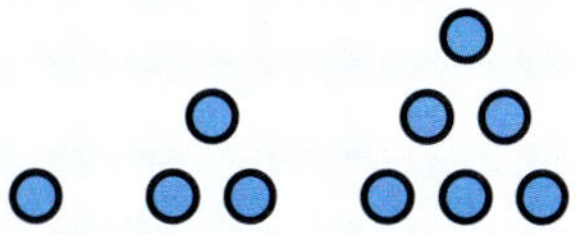

38. Jackson wrote the following fractions on the board.

$\frac{1}{2}, \frac{2}{5}, \frac{3}{8}, \frac{4}{11}, \frac{5}{14}$

If he continues writing fractions according to the pattern, what will be the next three fractions?

9-7 Multiples (pp. 396–399)

Example 7
Find the LCM of 12 and 16.

List multiples of each number to find the least common multiple.

multiples of 12: 12, 24, 36, **48**, 60 ...

multiples of 16: 16, 32, **48**, 64, 80...

The LCM of 12 and 16 is 48.

Find the LCM of each set of numbers. Make a table or a graph.

39. 5 and 9

40. 4, 7, and 14

41. Every 7 days, a video store gives free popcorn with movie rentals. Every 5 days, they offer a free movie. If they gave away popcorn and a movie today, when will they give away both again?

9-8 Problem-Solving Investigation: Choose a Strategy (pp. 400–401)

Example 8

Pilar has \$69 to spend on presents. CDs cost \$13, and DVDs cost \$15. How many CDs and DVDs can she buy?

Understand You know how much money Pilar has. You know how much CDs and DVDs cost.

Plan Use can guess and check to find how many CDs and DVDs Pilar can buy.

Solve Pilar can buy 3 CDs and 2 DVDs with \$69.

Check Look back.
\$13 + \$13 + \$13 + \$15 + \$15 = \$69
So, Pilar is correct. ✓

Solve. Use any strategy.

42. Charlotte has two hamster cages. When she cleans them, she uses $\frac{3}{8}$ bag of hamster bedding for one cage and $\frac{1}{4}$ bag for the other cage. Does she need 1 bag or 2 bags when she cleans the cages?

43. Hot dogs are sold in packages of 10. Hot dog buns are sold in packages of 8. What are the fewest packages of hot dogs and packages of buns needed so the number of hot dogs matches the number of buns?

44. The table shows the number of tickets sold for the school play. If adult tickets were \$3.50 and student tickets were \$2, what were the total sales?

Ticket	Number Sold
Adult	126
Student	205

9-9 Compare Fractions (pp. 402–405)

Example 9

Replace ● with <, >, or = to make $\frac{2}{5}$ ● $\frac{3}{4}$ a true statement.

The LCM of 5 and 4 is 20. So, 20 is the LCD of $\frac{2}{5}$ and $\frac{3}{4}$.

$\frac{2}{5} = \frac{8}{20}$ THINK $5 \times 4 = 20, 2 \times 4 = 8$

$\frac{3}{4} = \frac{15}{20}$ THINK $4 \times 5 = 20, 3 \times 5 = 15$

Since $8 < 15$, $\frac{8}{20} < \frac{15}{20}$. So, $\frac{2}{5} < \frac{3}{4}$.

Replace each ● with <, >, or = to make a true statement.

45. $\frac{1}{4}$ ● $\frac{6}{8}$

46. $\frac{2}{3}$ ● $\frac{3}{5}$

47. $\frac{2}{3}$ ● $\frac{7}{12}$

48. $\frac{5}{8}$ ● $\frac{7}{12}$

49. Christine worked on social studies homework $\frac{3}{4}$ of an hour. She worked on math for $\frac{5}{6}$ of an hour. On which subject did she spend more time?

CHAPTER 9

Chapter Test

Math Online macmillanmh.com

• Chapter Test

Find the common factors of each set of numbers.

1. 15, 45

2. 24, 32, and 40

Find the GCF of each set of numbers.

3. 8, 28

4. 21, 24, and 27

5. MULTIPLE CHOICE Which is a prime factor of the composite number 24?

A 3

B 4

C 5

D 12

6. The table shows the countries with the most wins for the Tour De France cycling race. Tell whether each number in the table is *prime* or *composite*.

Country	Number of Wins
Belgium	18
France	36
Netherlands	2
Spain	8
United States	7

7. Which fractions below are equivalent?

$\frac{4}{5}$ $\frac{6}{10}$ $\frac{24}{30}$ $\frac{2}{5}$ $\frac{16}{25}$

Write each fraction in simplest form. If the fraction is already in simplest form, write *simplified*.

8. $\frac{9}{18}$

9. $\frac{15}{16}$

10. $\frac{28}{32}$

11. $\frac{6}{27}$

12. The table shows when customers at Maltey's Burgers receive items free with the purchase of a burger deal.

Free Item	When
Milkshake	every 4 days
Tater tots	every 10 days

If they gave away both items today, in how many days will a customer be able to get both a milkshake and tater tots free again?

Write each decimal as a fraction in simplest form.

13. 0.7

14. 0.24

15. 0.875

16. 0.02

17. What is the least common multiple of 12 and 20?

18. Measurement Grasshoppers can jump 40 times the length of their body. If one foot equals 12 inches, how many feet could a 3-inch grasshopper jump?

19. MULTIPLE CHOICE Amber went to the library after school 3 of the 5 school days this week. Which fraction is less than $\frac{3}{5}$?

F $\frac{1}{2}$

G $\frac{3}{4}$

H $\frac{4}{5}$

J $\frac{5}{6}$

20. WRITING IN MATH Explain the steps you would take to make the following a true statement.

$\frac{3}{10} \bullet \frac{9}{20}$

9 Test Practice

Cumulative, Chapters 1–9

Math Online macmillanmh.com

• Test Practice

PART 1 **Multiple Choice**

Read each question. Then fill in the correct answer on the answer sheet provided by your teacher or on a sheet of paper.

1. Sancho picked up a handful of coins from a jar without looking. He got 7 pennies, 5 nickels, 3 dimes, and 2 quarters. What fraction of the coins that he picked were nickels?

A $\frac{2}{17}$

B $\frac{3}{17}$

C $\frac{5}{17}$

D $\frac{7}{17}$

2. Paige cut a cake into 20 pieces. If 14 pieces have been eaten, what fraction of the cake remains?

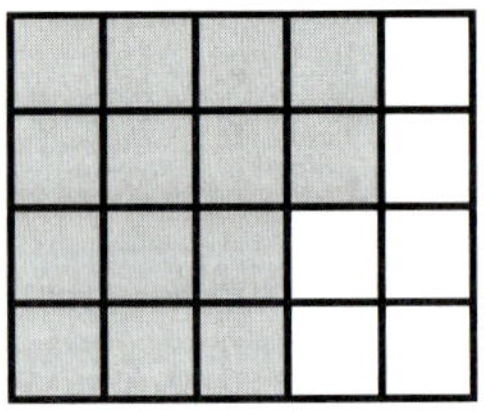

F $\frac{1}{10}$

G $\frac{1}{5}$

H $\frac{3}{10}$

J $\frac{2}{5}$

3. Natalie has washed the dishes 8 out of the last 12 nights. Which fraction shows the portion of time spent washing dishes?

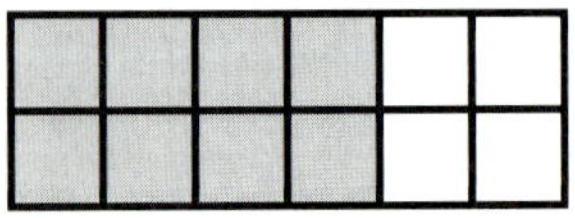

A $\frac{1}{3}$

B $\frac{1}{2}$

C $\frac{2}{3}$

D $\frac{5}{6}$

4. Emilia used 4 of her 8 stamps to mail letters. Which fraction is less than $\frac{4}{8}$?

F $\frac{5}{8}$

G $\frac{3}{4}$

H $\frac{1}{2}$

J $\frac{3}{7}$

5. Which is a prime factor of the composite number 32?

A 2

B 3

C 4

D 5

6. The table shows the number of bills of each value that Bree received for her birthday. In all, what fraction of the number of bills that Bree received for her birthday were \$10 or \$20 bills?

Birthday Money	
Value of Bill	**Number of bills**
\$5	5
\$10	3
\$20	2
\$50	1

F $\frac{5}{22}$

G $\frac{3}{11}$

H $\frac{5}{11}$

J $\frac{8}{11}$

7. Clarence bought a 3-pound can of mixed nuts for a party. One-fourth of the can is made up of walnuts, and two-fifths of the can is made up of peanuts. Which of the following shows the correct relationship between $\frac{1}{4}$ and $\frac{2}{5}$?

A $\frac{1}{4} = \frac{2}{5}$

B $\frac{1}{4} > \frac{2}{5}$

C $\frac{1}{4} < \frac{2}{5}$

D $\frac{1}{5} < \frac{3}{10}$

Preparing for Standardized Tests

For test-taking strategies and practice, see pages R42–R55.

8. An assembly hall was set up with 20 rows of chairs. Each row had 16 chairs. In addition, there were 15 chairs on stage. Which expression can be used to find how many chairs there were in all?

F $(20 \times 16) + 15$

G $(20 + 16) + 15$

H $(20 \times 15) + 16$

J $(20 + 15) \times 16$

9. Which group shows the prime factorization of the number 252?

A $2 \times 3 \times 3 \times 7$

B $2 \times 2 \times 2 \times 3 \times 5$

C $2 \times 2 \times 3 \times 3 \times 7$

D $2 \times 2 \times 2 \times 3 \times 3 \times 7$

10. A florist sells vases of roses for $35 each. If the florist sold 62 vases last weekend, how much money did she collect?

F $1,855

G $1,930

H $2,170

J $2,310

PART 2 Short Response

Record your answers on the answer sheet provided by your teacher or on a sheet of paper.

11. List all of the factors of 68.

12. A pizza was divided into eighths. You ate $\frac{3}{4}$ of the pizza. How many slices did you eat?

PART 3 Extended Response

Record your answers on the answer sheet provided by your teacher or on a sheet of paper. Show your work.

13. Explain the difference between a prime number and a composite number. Be sure to include examples of each.

14. Determine if $\frac{1}{3}$ and $\frac{3}{9}$ are equivalent fractions by using a drawing.

NEED EXTRA HELP?														
If You Missed Question...	1	2	3	4	5	6	7	8	9	10	11	12	13	14
Go to Lesson...	9-4	9-4	9-4	9-9	9-2	9-9	9-9	6-6	9-2	9-4	9-1	9-3	9-2	9-3

CHAPTER 10 Add and Subtract Fractions

BIG Idea What are like fractions?

Fractions that have the same denominator are **like fractions**.

$\frac{1}{8}$ $\frac{3}{8}$ $2\frac{5}{8}$ $5\frac{7}{8}$

You can add and subtract like fractions.

Example The average height of an African penguin is $26\frac{1}{2}$ inches. The average height of an Emperor penguin is $36\frac{1}{2}$ inches. You can subtract $26\frac{1}{2}$ from $36\frac{1}{2}$ to find the difference in height between the two penguins.

What will I learn in this chapter?

- Add and subtract like and unlike fractions.
- Estimate sums and differences of mixed numbers.
- Add and subtract mixed numbers.
- Solve problems by determining reasonable answers.

Key Vocabulary

like fractions

unlike fractions

Math Online Student Study Tools at macmillanmh.com

FOLDABLES®
Study Organizer

Make this Foldable to organize information about like and unlike fractions. Begin with a sheet of $8\frac{1}{2}'' \times 11''$ paper, four index cards, and glue.

1. **Fold** the paper in half widthwise.

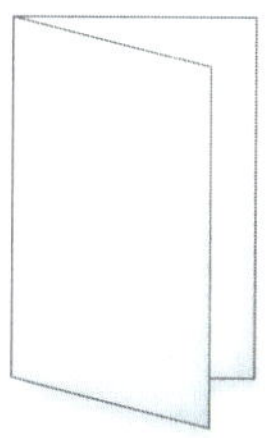

2. **Open** and fold along the length about $2\frac{1}{2}''$ from the bottom.

3. **Glue** the edges on either side to form two pockets.

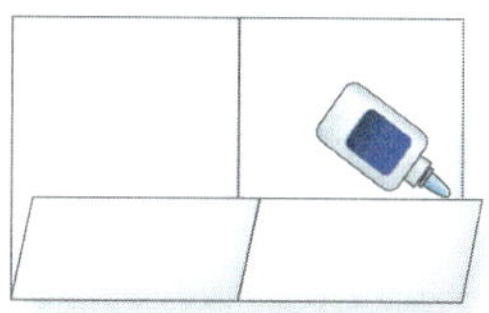

4. **Label** the pockets *Like Fractions* and *Unlike Fractions*. Place two index cards in each pocket.

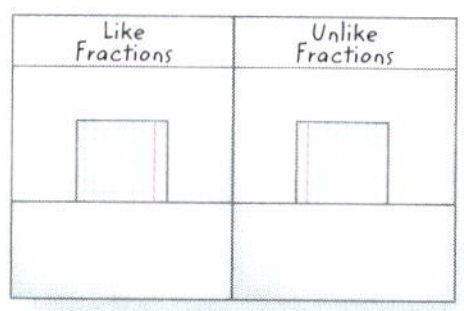

ARE YOU READY for Chapter 10?

You have two ways to check prerequisite skills for this chapter.

Option 2

Math Online Take the Chapter Readiness Quiz at macmillanmh.com.

Option 1

Complete the Quick Check below.

QUICK Check

Write each fraction in simplest form.
(Lesson 9-4)

1. $\frac{4}{8}$ **2.** $\frac{4}{12}$ **3.** $\frac{15}{20}$ **4.** $\frac{4}{24}$

5. Monica made 4 out of 16 free throws. Write the fraction of free throws she made in simplest form.

Write each improper fraction as a mixed number.
(Lesson 8-2)

6. $\frac{10}{7}$ **7.** $\frac{3}{2}$ **8.** $\frac{14}{6}$ **9.** $\frac{22}{4}$

10. A recipe for potato casserole calls for $\frac{7}{4}$ cups of cheese. Write the fraction as a mixed number.

Estimate each sum or difference by rounding. Show your work. (Lesson 2-1)

11. 10.5 − 7.1 **12.** 6.2 + 4.7 **13.** 5.2 + 2.1 **14.** 12.7 − 6.6

15. Sierra bought the two items shown at the right. About how much did she spend? Round to the nearest dollar.

16. Two classes are recycling. One class earns $17.69, and the other earns $31.15. About how much more did the second class earn? Round to the nearest dollar.

Explore

Math Activity for 10-1
Add Like Fractions

MAIN IDEA

I will use models to add fractions with like denominators.

New Vocabulary

like fractions

Math Online

macmillanmh.com

• Concepts in Motion

You can use fraction tiles to add fractions with the same denominator. Fractions with the same denominator are called **like fractions**. For example, $\frac{3}{5}$ and $\frac{1}{5}$ are like fractions because they both have a denominator of 5.

ACTIVITY

1 **Lauren sliced an apple to eat as a snack. She ate $\frac{3}{5}$ of the apple and gave $\frac{1}{5}$ of the apple to her sister. How much of the apple did they eat?**

Step 1 **Model $\frac{3}{5}$.**

Use three $\frac{1}{5}$-fraction tiles to show $\frac{3}{5}$.

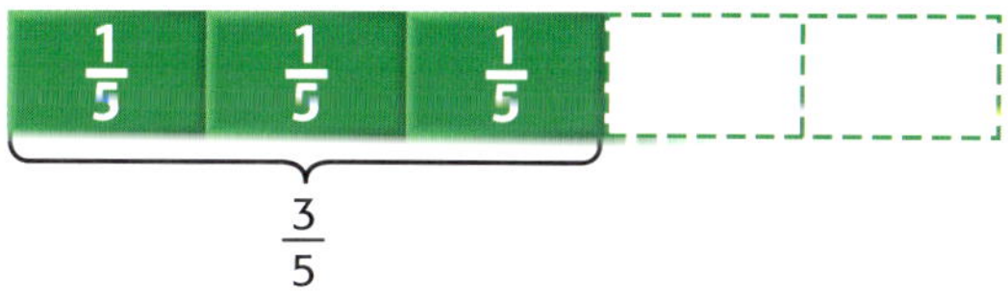

Step 2 **Model $\frac{1}{5}$.**

Add one $\frac{1}{5}$-fraction tile to show $\frac{1}{5}$.

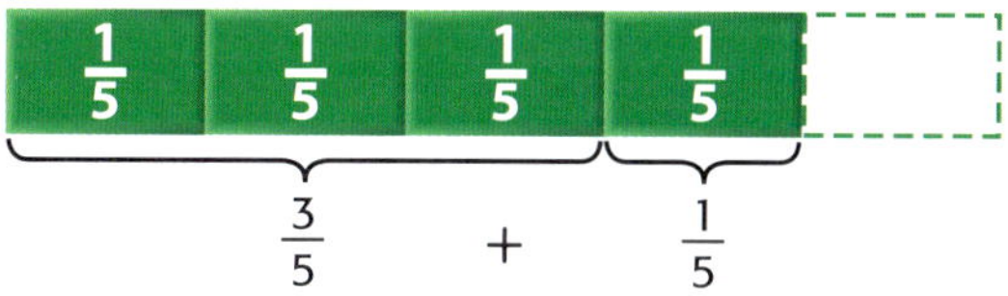

Step 3 **Add.**

Count the total number of $\frac{1}{5}$-fraction tiles.

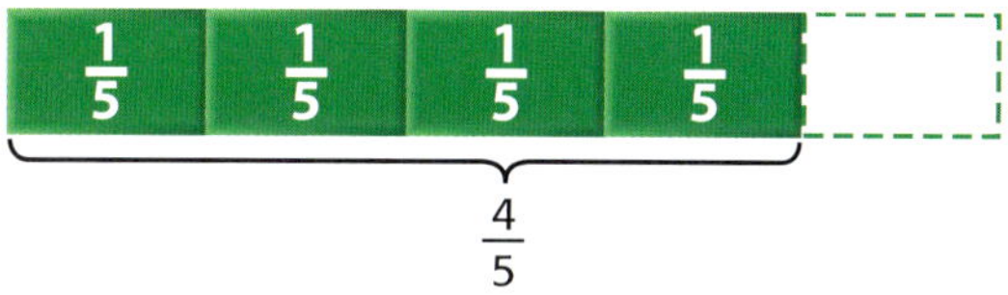

Since $\frac{3}{5} + \frac{1}{5} = \frac{4}{5}$, you can say that Lauren and her sister ate $\frac{4}{5}$ or *four fifths* of the apple.

ACTIVITY

Hands-On Activity

2 **Theo asked his class what type of pet they like the best. Of the class, $\frac{3}{10}$ said they like dogs, and $\frac{4}{10}$ said they like cats. What fraction of the class likes dogs or cats?**

Step 1 **Model $\frac{3}{10}$.**

Use three $\frac{1}{10}$-fraction tiles to show $\frac{3}{10}$.

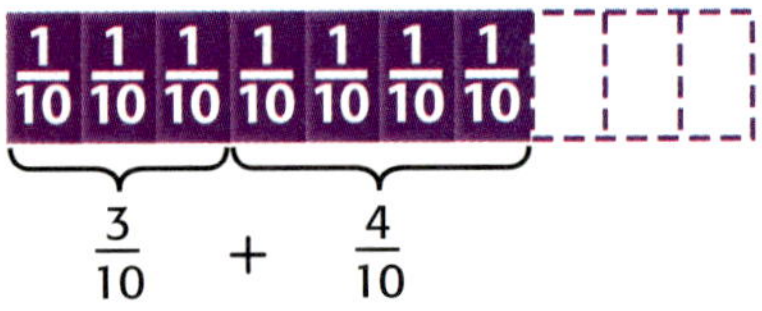

Step 2 **Model $\frac{4}{10}$.**

Use four $\frac{1}{10}$-fraction tiles to show $\frac{4}{10}$.

Step 3 **Add.**

Count the total number of $\frac{1}{10}$-fraction tiles.

$\frac{3}{10} + \frac{4}{10} = \frac{7}{10}$. So, $\frac{7}{10}$ or *seven tenths* of the class likes dogs or cats.

Think About It

1. Describe how you would model $\frac{1}{8} + \frac{6}{8}$.
2. Explain how to find $\frac{1}{8} + \frac{6}{8}$. Then find and write the sum in words.

CHECK What You Know

Model each sum using fraction tiles. Then find the sum and write it in words.

3.

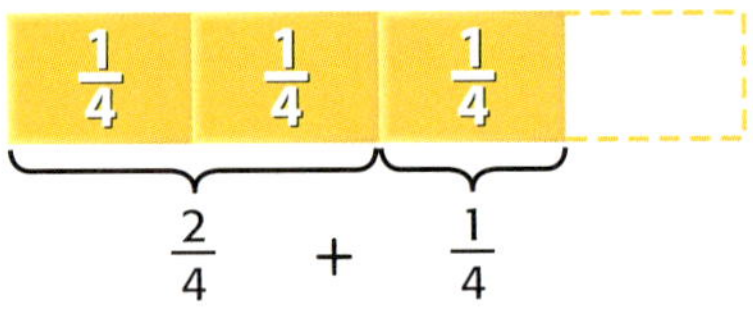

4.

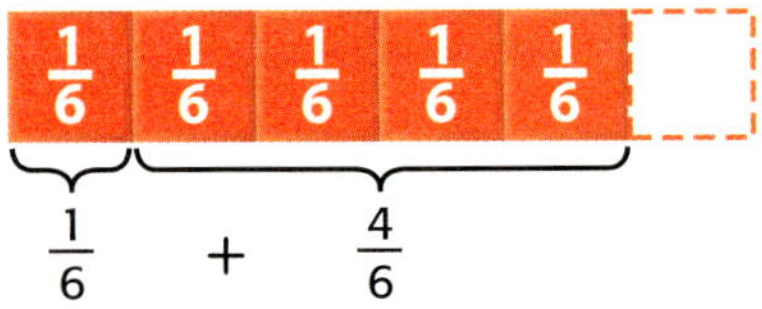

5. $\frac{3}{8} + \frac{4}{8}$

6. $\frac{5}{10} + \frac{4}{10}$

Find each sum. Use fraction tiles if needed.

7. $\frac{1}{3} + \frac{1}{3}$

8. $\frac{2}{8} + \frac{5}{8}$

9. $\frac{5}{12} + \frac{6}{12}$

10. **WRITING IN MATH** Look at the numerators and denominators in each exercise. Do you notice a pattern? Explain how you could find the sum of $\frac{1}{5} + \frac{1}{5}$ without using fraction tiles.

10-1 Add Like Fractions

MAIN IDEA

I will add fractions with like denominators.

Math Online

macmillanmh.com
- Extra Examples
- Personal Tutor
- Self-Check Quiz

GET READY to Learn

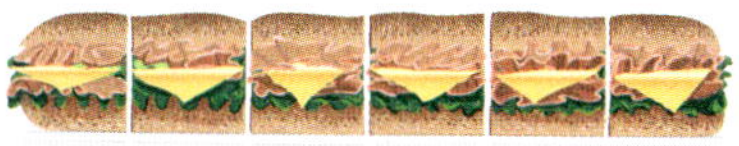

At the county fair, Lorena and her father decided to share a foot-long sub sandwich. Lorena ate $\frac{2}{6}$ of the sandwich, and her father ate $\frac{3}{6}$ of the sandwich. How much of the sandwich did they eat?

To find how much of the sub sandwich Lorena and her father ate, you can add the like fractions. When you add like fractions, the denominator names the units.

EXAMPLE Add Like Fractions

1 **Find $\frac{2}{6} + \frac{3}{6}$. Use models to check.**

$\frac{2}{6} + \frac{3}{6} = \frac{2+3}{6}$

$= \frac{5}{6}$ Add.

So, $\frac{2}{6} + \frac{3}{6} = \frac{5}{6}$.

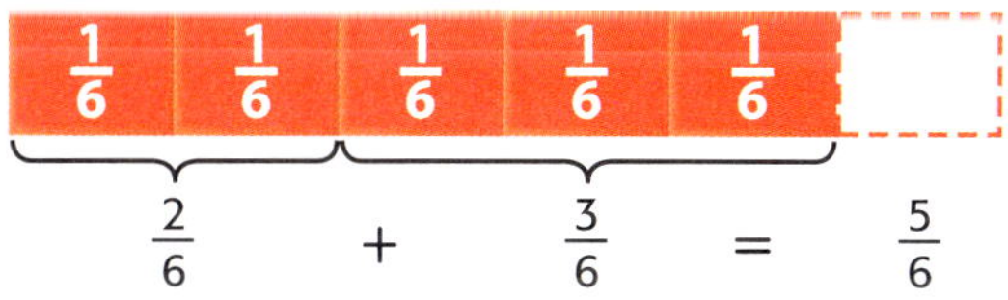

Add Like Fractions

Key Concept

Words To add fractions with the same denominator, add the numerators and use the same denominator.

Examples

Numbers

$\frac{1}{4} + \frac{2}{4} = \frac{1+2}{4}$

$= \frac{3}{4}$

Model

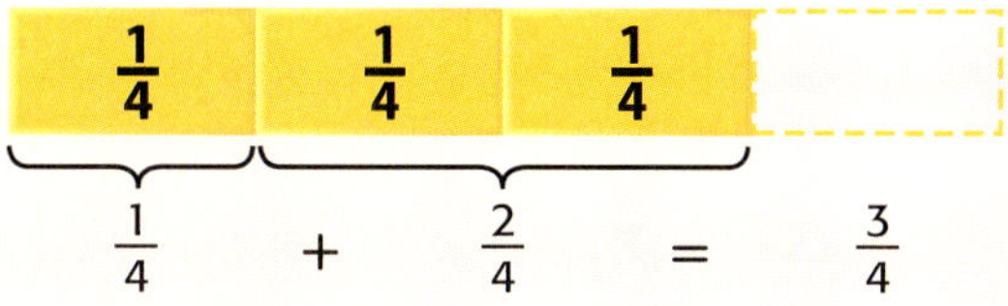

Words

One fourth plus two fourths equals three fourths.

Real-World EXAMPLE — Add Like Fractions

2 **READING The table shows how much of a book Cleveland read each day. What fraction of the book did Cleveland read on Monday and Wednesday?**

Day	Fraction
Monday	$\frac{1}{10}$
Tuesday	$\frac{4}{10}$
Wednesday	$\frac{3}{10}$
Thursday	$\frac{2}{10}$

Add $\frac{1}{10}$ and $\frac{3}{10}$.

$\frac{1}{10} + \frac{3}{10} = \frac{1+3}{10}$ — Add the numerators.

$= \frac{4}{10}$ — Simplify.

$= \frac{4 \div 2}{10 \div 2}$ — Divide the numerator and denominator by the GCF, 2.

$= \frac{2}{5}$ — Simplify. Check by drawing a picture.

So, Cleveland read $\frac{2}{5}$ of the book on Monday and Wednesday.

EXAMPLE — Add Like Fractions

3 **Find $\frac{2}{5} + \frac{4}{5}$. Use models to check.**

$\frac{2}{5} + \frac{4}{5} = \frac{2+4}{5}$ — Add the numerators.

$= \frac{6}{5}$ — Simplify.

$= 1\frac{1}{5}$ — Write as a mixed number.

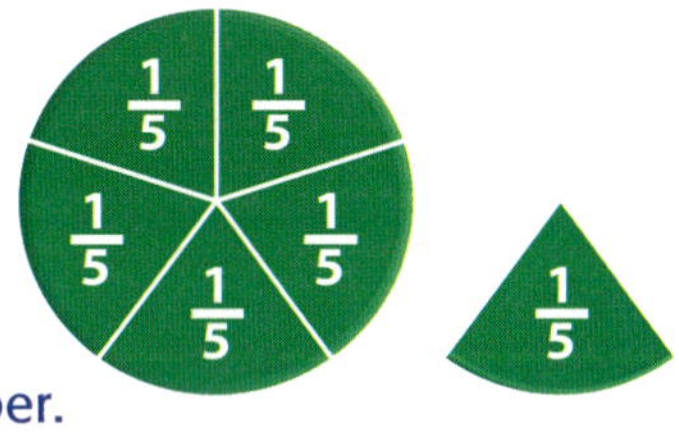

So, $\frac{2}{5} + \frac{4}{5} = 1\frac{1}{5}$.

Remember

To review writing an improper fraction as a mixed number, see Lesson 8-2 on pages 338–342.

CHECK What You Know

Add. Write each sum in simplest form. Use models to check.

See Examples 1–3 (pp. 423–424)

1. $\frac{1}{7} + \frac{3}{7}$

2. $\frac{2}{9} + \frac{3}{9}$

3. $\frac{1}{4} + \frac{1}{4}$

4. $\frac{1}{6} + \frac{1}{6}$

5. $\frac{5}{8} + \frac{3}{8}$

6. $\frac{2}{9} + \frac{8}{9}$

7. Tia painted $\frac{5}{12}$ of a fence. Rey painted $\frac{4}{12}$ of the fence. How much of the fence did they paint?

8. Talk About It — Write two sentences to explain how you solved Exercise 7.

Practice and Problem Solving

EXTRA PRACTICE
See page R26.

Add. Write each sum in simplest form. Use models to check. See Examples 1–3 (pp. 423–424)

9. $\frac{4}{7} + \frac{2}{7}$

10. $\frac{2}{10} + \frac{5}{10}$

11. $\frac{2}{6} + \frac{2}{6}$

12. $\frac{3}{8} + \frac{1}{8}$

13. $\frac{3}{4} + \frac{1}{4}$

14. $\frac{4}{9} + \frac{5}{9}$

15. $\frac{3}{5} + \frac{4}{5}$

16. $\frac{2}{3} + \frac{2}{3}$

17. What is the sum of *two fifths and one fifth*? Write your answer in words.

18. What is the sum of *six ninths and three ninths*? Write your answer in words.

19. Mia walked $\frac{9}{10}$ of a mile to the park. She walked the same distance home. How much did she walk altogether?

20. It rained $\frac{2}{8}$ of an inch in one hour. It rained twice as much in the next hour. Find the total amount of rain.

For Exercises 21 and 22, refer to the table.

Type of Parade Float	Number
Sports Team	6
Radio Station	5
High School	3
Dance Group	4

21. What fraction of the floats were from either a dance group or a radio station?

22. What fraction of the floats were *not* from a sports team?

Algebra **Find the value of x that makes a true sentence.**

23. $\frac{3}{8} + \frac{x}{8} = \frac{7}{8}$

24. $\frac{x}{9} + \frac{5}{9} = \frac{7}{9}$

25. $\frac{5}{12} + \frac{x}{12} = 1$

Data File

The recipe for North Carolina pulled pork sauce is shown.

26. If you double the recipe, how much white vinegar will you need?

27. Mr. Gellar triples the recipe. For what ingredient will he need $1\frac{1}{2}$ tsp?

Recipe for North Carolina Pulled Pork

- $\frac{2}{3}$ c white vinegar
- 1 c cider vinegar
- 1 T sugar
- 1 T cayenne pepper
- 1 T Hot sauce
- $\frac{3}{4}$ tsp salt
- $\frac{1}{2}$ tsp black pepper

H.O.T. Problems

28. **OPEN ENDED** Select two fractions whose sum is $\frac{3}{4}$ and whose denominators are the same, but not 4. Justify your selection.

29. **WRITING IN MATH** Write a real-world problem that can be solved by adding like fractions. Then solve.

Explore

Math Activity for 10-2

Subtract Like Fractions

MAIN IDEA

I will use models to subtract fractions with like denominators.

You can use fraction tiles to subtract fractions with like denominators.

ACTIVITY

1 **Miguel has a bag of marbles. Of the marbles, $\frac{5}{8}$ are blue, and $\frac{2}{8}$ are red. How many more blue marbles than red marbles are in the bag?**

Step 1 **Model $\frac{5}{8}$.**

Use five $\frac{1}{8}$-fraction tiles to show $\frac{5}{8}$.

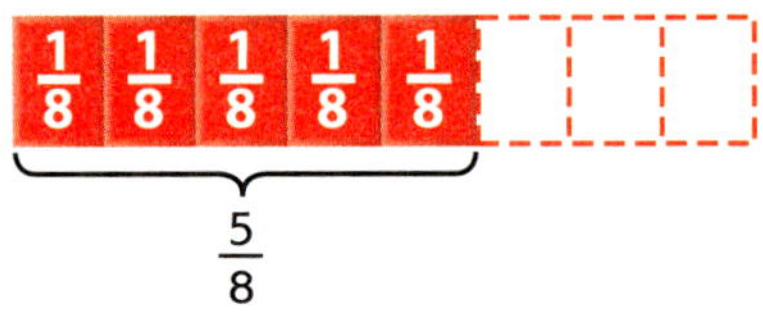

Step 2 **Subtract $\frac{2}{8}$.**

Remove two $\frac{1}{8}$-fraction tiles to show the subtraction of $\frac{2}{8}$.

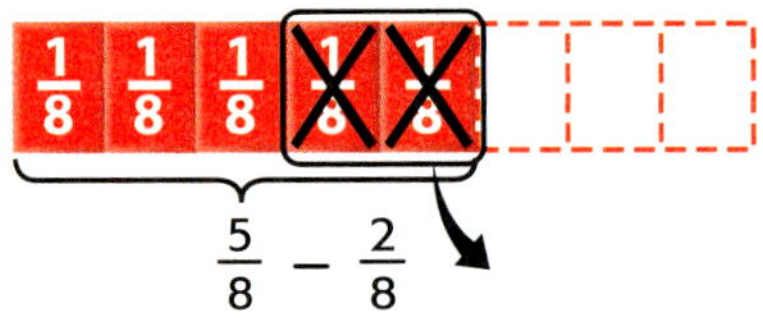

Step 3 Count the total number of $\frac{1}{8}$-fraction tiles that are left.

$\frac{5}{8} - \frac{2}{8} = \frac{3}{8}$. So, there are $\frac{3}{8}$ or *three eighths* more blue marbles.

ACTIVITY

2 **Abbi bought $\frac{9}{10}$ pound of Swiss cheese and $\frac{6}{10}$ pound of cheddar cheese. How much more Swiss cheese did she buy?**

Step 1 **Model $\frac{9}{10}$.**

Use nine $\frac{1}{10}$-fraction tiles to show $\frac{9}{10}$.

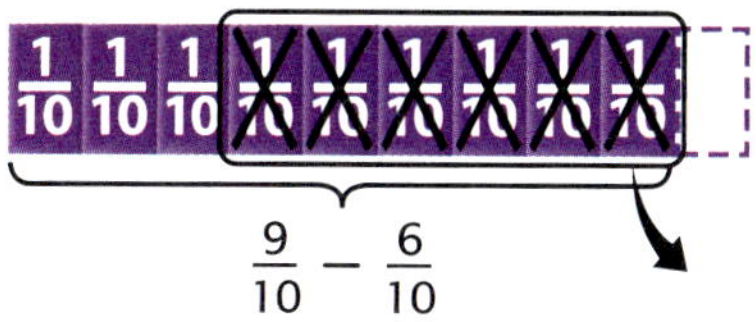

Step 2 **Subtract $\frac{6}{10}$.**

Remove six $\frac{1}{10}$-fraction tiles.

Step 3 Count the total number of $\frac{1}{10}$-fraction tiles that are left.

$\frac{9}{10} - \frac{6}{10} = \frac{3}{10}$. So, Abbi bought $\frac{3}{10}$ or *three tenths* pound more Swiss cheese.

Think About It

1. Describe how you would model $\frac{4}{5} - \frac{3}{5}$.
2. Describe how you would find the difference $\frac{4}{5} - \frac{3}{5}$. Then find the difference.

CHECK What You Know

Model each difference using fraction tiles. Then find the difference and write in words.

3. 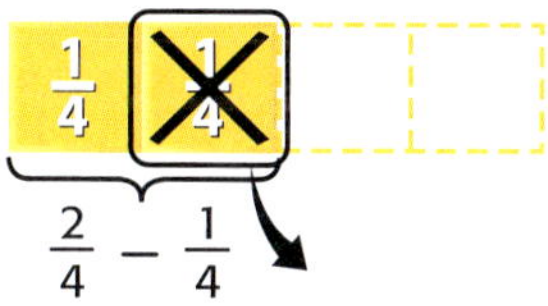

4. 

Find each difference. Use fraction tiles if needed.

5. $\frac{6}{7} - \frac{4}{7}$
6. $\frac{2}{3} - \frac{1}{3}$
7. $\frac{4}{6} - \frac{3}{6}$
8. $\frac{5}{9} - \frac{3}{9}$
9. $\frac{7}{10} - \frac{4}{10}$
10. $\frac{11}{12} - \frac{6}{12}$
11. **WRITING IN MATH** Look at the numerators and denominators in each exercise. Explain how you could find $\frac{9}{12} - \frac{4}{12}$ without using fraction tiles.

10-2 Subtract Like Fractions

MAIN IDEA

I will subtract fractions with like denominators.

Math Online

macmillanmh.com

- Extra Examples
- Personal Tutor
- Self-Check Quiz

GET READY to Learn

Frankie is walking on a nature trail that is $\frac{7}{8}$-mile long. He has already walked $\frac{4}{8}$ mile. How much farther does Frankie have to walk?

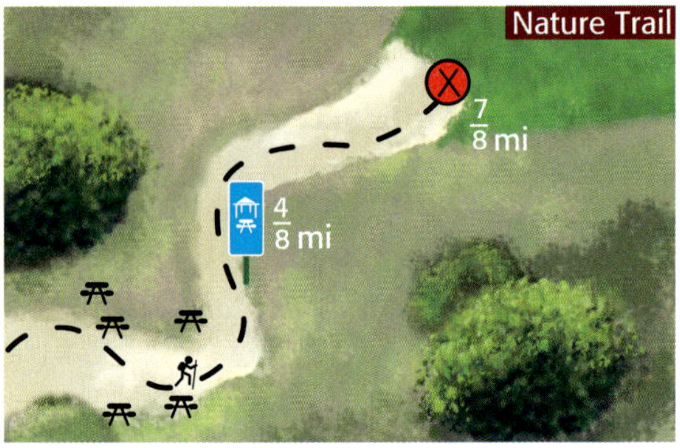

To find how much farther, subtract $\frac{4}{8}$ from $\frac{7}{8}$.

EXAMPLE Subtract Like Fractions

1 **Find $\frac{7}{8} - \frac{4}{8}$. Use models to check.**

$\frac{7}{8} - \frac{4}{8} = \frac{7-4}{8}$

$= \frac{3}{8}$ Subtract.

So, $\frac{7}{8} - \frac{4}{8} = \frac{3}{8}$.

Subtracting like fractions is similar to adding like fractions.

Subtract Like Fractions — Key Concept

Words To subtract fractions with the same denominator, subtract the numerators and use the same denominator.

Examples

Numbers

$\frac{4}{5} - \frac{2}{5} = \frac{4-2}{5}$

$= \frac{2}{5}$

Model

Words

Four fifths minus two fifths equals two fifths.

Real-World EXAMPLES Subtract Like Fractions

WEATHER The table shows the amount of rainfall several cities received in a recent month.

RAINFALL

City	Rainfall (in.)
Spring Valley	$\frac{1}{10}$
Clarksburg	$\frac{6}{10}$
Centerville	$\frac{9}{10}$
Brushton	$\frac{3}{10}$

2 How much more rain did Centerville receive than Brushton? Write in simplest form. Use models to check.

Subtract the amount of rain that fell in Brushton from the amount of rain that fell in Centerville.

$$\frac{9}{10} - \frac{3}{10} = \frac{9-3}{10}$$ Subtract the numerators.

$$= \frac{6}{10}$$ Simplify.

$$= \frac{6 \div 2}{10 \div 2}$$ Divide by the GCF, 2.

$$= \frac{3}{5}$$ Simplify.

Remember

Divide both the numerator and denominator by the greatest common factor.

Use models to check.

$\frac{9}{10} - \frac{3}{10}$

So, $\frac{3}{5}$ inch more rain fell in Centerville than in Brushton.

3 How many fewer inches of rain did Spring Valley receive than Clarksburg? Write in simplest form. Use models to check.

Subtract the amount of rain that fell in Spring Valley from the amount of rain that fell in Clarksburg.

$$\frac{6}{10} - \frac{1}{10} = \frac{6-1}{10}$$ Subtract the numerators.

$$= \frac{5}{10}$$ Simplify.

$$= \frac{5 \div 5}{10 \div 5}$$ Divide by the GCF, 5.

$$= \frac{1}{2}$$ Simplify.

Use models to check.

$\frac{6}{10} - \frac{1}{10}$

So, it rained $\frac{1}{2}$ inch less in Spring Valley than in Clarksburg.

CHECK What You Know

Subtract. Write each difference in simplest form. Use models to check. See Examples 1–3 (pp. 428–429)

1. $\frac{5}{7} - \frac{3}{7}$ **2.** $\frac{3}{5} - \frac{2}{5}$ **3.** $\frac{6}{9} - \frac{3}{9}$ **4.** $\frac{5}{6} - \frac{3}{6}$

5. Ciro spent $\frac{5}{6}$ hour drawing and $\frac{2}{6}$ hour reading. How much more time did he spend drawing than reading?

6. Talk About It Explain how you solved Exercise 5 using words.

Practice and Problem Solving

EXTRA PRACTICE See page R27.

Subtract. Write each difference in simplest form. Use models to check. See Examples 1–3 (pp. 428–429)

7. $\frac{2}{3} - \frac{1}{3}$ **8.** $\frac{3}{5} - \frac{1}{5}$ **9.** $\frac{6}{7} - \frac{5}{7}$ **10.** $\frac{3}{6} - \frac{1}{6}$

11. $\frac{5}{9} - \frac{2}{9}$ **12.** $\frac{6}{8} - \frac{4}{8}$ **13.** $\frac{3}{4} - \frac{1}{4}$ **14.** $\frac{9}{12} - \frac{3}{12}$

15. Find the difference between *seven ninths and four ninths.* Write your answer in words.

16. What is the difference between *six sevenths and five sevenths?* Write your answer in words.

17. Measurement Roshanda bought $\frac{5}{8}$ pound of ham and $\frac{7}{8}$ pound of roast beef. How much more roast beef than ham did she buy?

18. A bucket was $\frac{7}{10}$ full with water. After Vick washed the car, the bucket was only $\frac{3}{10}$ full. What part did Vick use to wash the car?

For Exercises 19 and 20, use the results of a survey of 28 students and their favorite tourist attractions.

19. What fraction of students prefer Mt. Rushmore over the Grand Canyon?

20. Suppose 4 students change their minds and choose the Statue of Liberty instead of the Grand Canyon. What part of the class now prefers Mt. Rushmore over the Statue of Liberty?

Favorite Tourist Attactions

Place	Number of Students
Mt. Rushmore	14
Grand Canyon	8
Statue of Liberty	6

Algebra Find the value of *x* that makes a true sentence.

21. $\frac{6}{9} - \frac{x}{9} = \frac{1}{9}$ **22.** $\frac{x}{8} - \frac{3}{8} = \frac{1}{8}$ **23.** $\frac{8}{12} - \frac{x}{12} = \frac{1}{4}$

H.O.T. Problems

24. **OPEN ENDED** Choose two like fractions whose difference is $\frac{1}{6}$ and whose denominators are not 6.

CHALLENGE **Compare. Write >, <, or = to make a true sentence.**

25. $\frac{5}{6} - \frac{1}{6} \bullet \frac{3}{6} - \frac{2}{6}$

26. $\frac{8}{8} - \frac{8}{8} \bullet \frac{2}{9} - \frac{2}{9}$

27. $\frac{3}{4} - \frac{2}{4} \bullet \frac{5}{5} - \frac{1}{5}$

28. **WRITING IN MATH** Write a problem about a real-world situation in which you would find $\frac{3}{4} - \frac{1}{4}$. Then solve.

TEST Practice

29. **Measurement** Paul is making dinner. He uses $\frac{1}{4}$ cup of cheese for a salad and $\frac{2}{4}$ cup of cheese for a casserole. How many cups of cheese does Paul use altogether? (Lesson 10-1)

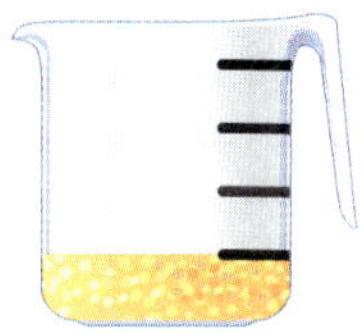
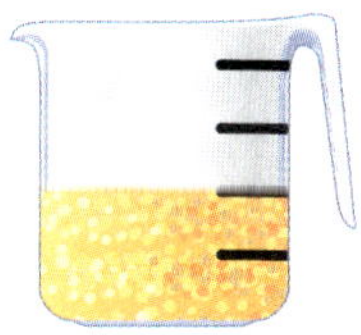

A $\frac{1}{8}$ c

B $\frac{1}{4}$ c

C $\frac{3}{8}$ c

D $\frac{3}{4}$ c

30. The pictures below show how much sausage and pepperoni pizza was left over at the end of one day.

Sausage

Pepperoni

Which fraction represents how much more sausage pizza was left over than pepperoni pizza? (Lesson 10-2)

F $\frac{3}{16}$

G $\frac{3}{8}$

H $\frac{11}{16}$

J $\frac{11}{8}$

Spiral Review

Add. Write each sum using words in simplest form. (Lesson 10-1)

31. $\frac{7}{11} + \frac{2}{11}$

32. $\frac{2}{13} + \frac{5}{13}$

33. $\frac{5}{14} + \frac{2}{14}$

34. $\frac{8}{15} + \frac{4}{15}$

35. **Measurement** A recipe for trail mix calls for $\frac{2}{3}$ cup of marshmallows, $\frac{7}{8}$ cup of pretzels, and $\frac{3}{4}$ cup of raisins. Which ingredient is the greatest amount? Which ingredient is the least amount? (Lesson 9-9)

Write each improper fraction as a mixed number. (Lesson 8-2)

36. $\frac{45}{6}$

37. $\frac{68}{8}$

38. $\frac{62}{12}$

39. $\frac{80}{15}$

Explore

Math Activity for 10-3

Add Unlike Fractions

MAIN IDEA

I will use models to add unlike fractions.

In Lesson 10-1, you learned that like fractions are fractions with the same denominator. Fractions with different denominators are called *unlike fractions.*

Like Fractions	**Unlike Fractions**
$\frac{3}{8}, \frac{4}{8}$	$\frac{1}{2}, \frac{5}{6}$

You can add fractions that have different denominators using fraction tiles.

ACTIVITY

1 **To finish building a birdhouse, Jordan uses two boards. One is $\frac{1}{2}$ foot long and the other is $\frac{1}{3}$ foot long. What is the total length of the boards?**

Step 1 Model each fraction using fraction tiles and place them side by side.

Step 2 Find fraction tiles that will match the length of the combined fractions above. Line them up below the model.

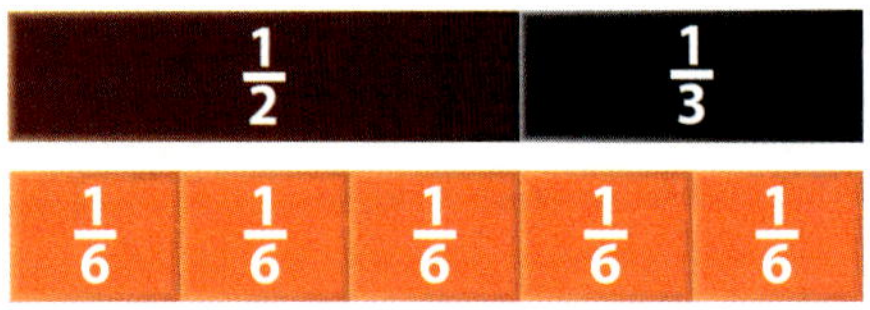

Step 3 Add. There are five of the $\frac{1}{6}$-fraction tiles in all. So, $\frac{1}{2} + \frac{1}{3} = \frac{5}{6}$.

The total length of the boards is $\frac{5}{6}$ foot.

ACTIVITY

Hands-On Activity

2 **Muna bought $\frac{3}{4}$ pound of grapes and $\frac{5}{8}$ pound of cherries. What is the combined weight of the fruit?**

Step 1 Model each fraction using fraction tiles.

Step 2 Find fraction tiles that will match the length of the combined fractions above. Line them up below the model.

Step 3 Add. There are eleven of the $\frac{1}{8}$-fraction tiles.
So, $\frac{3}{4} + \frac{5}{8} = \frac{11}{8}$ or $1\frac{3}{8}$.

The combined weight of the fruit is $1\frac{3}{8}$ pounds.

Think About It

1. How can finding the multiples of 4 and 12 help you find $\frac{3}{4} + \frac{7}{12}$?

2. Describe how you could use fraction tiles to find the sum of $\frac{2}{5}$ and $\frac{1}{10}$.

CHECK What You Know

Find the sum using fraction tiles.

3. $\frac{2}{3} + \frac{1}{6}$ **4.** $\frac{3}{4} + \frac{1}{3}$ **5.** $\frac{3}{8} + \frac{1}{4}$ **6.** $\frac{1}{2} + \frac{5}{6}$

7. $\frac{3}{10} + \frac{1}{5}$ **8.** $\frac{5}{8} + \frac{1}{4}$ **9.** $\frac{1}{2} + \frac{1}{4}$ **10.** $\frac{3}{4} + \frac{2}{3}$

11. **WRITING IN MATH** Write a real-world problem that can be solved by adding unlike fractions.

10-3 Add Unlike Fractions

GET READY to Learn

Gene spent $\frac{1}{3}$ hour writing an article for the school paper, and $\frac{1}{4}$ hour proofreading it. How long did Gene spend writing and proofreading his article?

MAIN IDEA

I will add fractions with unlike denominators.

New Vocabulary

unlike fractions

Math Online

macmillanmh.com

- Extra Examples
- Personal Tutor
- Self-Check Quiz

Before you can add two **unlike fractions**, one or both of the fractions must be renamed so that they have a common denominator.

Adding Unlike Fractions

Key Concept

To add unlike fractions, perform the following steps:

- Rename the fractions using the least common denominator (LCD).
- Add as with like fractions.
- If necessary, simplify the sum.

EXAMPLE Add Unlike Fractions

1 **Refer to the information above. Find $\frac{1}{3}$ hour + $\frac{1}{4}$ hour.**

The least common denominator of $\frac{1}{3}$ and $\frac{1}{4}$ is 12.

Step 1 Write the problem.		**Step 2** Rename using the LCD.		**Step 3** Add the like fractions.
$\frac{1}{3}$	→	$\frac{1 \times 4}{3 \times 4} = \frac{4}{12}$	→	$\frac{4}{12}$
$+\frac{1}{4}$	→	$\frac{1 \times 3}{4 \times 3} = \frac{3}{12}$	→	$+\frac{3}{12}$
				$\frac{7}{12}$

So, Gene spent $\frac{7}{12}$ hour writing and proofreading his article.

Real-World EXAMPLE

2 **MUSIC** **Catalina spent $\frac{1}{6}$ of her free time reading and $\frac{5}{12}$ of her free time practicing her flute. What fraction of her free time did she spend reading and practicing her flute?**

Add $\frac{1}{6}$ and $\frac{5}{12}$.

The least common denominator of $\frac{1}{6}$ and $\frac{5}{12}$ is 12.

Step 1	Step 2	Step 3
Write the problem.	Rename using the LCD.	Add the like fractions.
$\frac{1}{6}$ →	$\frac{1 \times 2}{6 \times 2} = \frac{2}{12}$ →	$\frac{2}{12}$
$+\frac{5}{12}$ →	$\frac{5 \times 1}{12 \times 1} = \frac{5}{12}$ →	$+\frac{5}{12}$
		$\frac{7}{12}$

So, Catalina spent $\frac{7}{12}$ of her free time reading and practicing her flute.

Remember

You can rename unlike fractions as like fractions by using the LCD.

CHECK What You Know

Add. Write in simplest form. See Examples 1, 2 (p. 434–435)

1. $\frac{3}{4} + \frac{1}{8}$

2. $\frac{2}{3} + \frac{1}{9}$

3. $\frac{2}{5} + \frac{1}{2}$

4. $\frac{5}{7} + \frac{2}{14}$

5. $\frac{2}{5} + \frac{3}{10}$

6. $\frac{1}{2} + \frac{3}{7}$

7. $\frac{5}{6} + \frac{3}{4}$

8. $\frac{2}{5} + \frac{7}{10}$

9. $\frac{4}{9} + \frac{2}{3}$

10. $\frac{5}{12} + \frac{1}{4}$

11. $\frac{4}{7} + \frac{1}{2}$

12. $\frac{5}{8} + \frac{2}{3}$

13. A farmer harvested $\frac{3}{8}$ of a pecan crop on Friday and $\frac{1}{3}$ of the crop on Saturday. What fraction of the pecan crop was harvested in the two days?

14. **Talk About It** Describe the steps for adding the fractions $\frac{5}{12}$ and $\frac{5}{6}$. What is the solution?

Practice and Problem Solving

EXTRA PRACTICE See page R27.

Add. Write in simplest form. See Examples 1,2 (pp. 434–435)

15. $\frac{2}{3} + \frac{1}{6}$ **16.** $\frac{1}{2} + \frac{1}{4}$ **17.** $\frac{1}{6} + \frac{7}{12}$ **18.** $\frac{5}{8} + \frac{1}{16}$

19. $\frac{1}{3} + \frac{1}{4}$ **20.** $\frac{1}{2} + \frac{4}{5}$ **21.** $\frac{3}{5} + \frac{3}{10}$ **22.** $\frac{3}{5} + \frac{3}{6}$

23. $\frac{2}{16} + \frac{3}{4}$ **24.** $\frac{7}{8} + \frac{1}{2}$ **25.** $\frac{3}{4} + \frac{7}{20}$ **26.** $\frac{1}{4} + \frac{3}{8}$

27. Angel has two chores after school. She rakes leaves for $\frac{3}{4}$ hour and spends $\frac{1}{2}$ hour washing the car. How long does Angel spend on her chores?

28. **Measurement** One craft project requires $\frac{3}{8}$ yard of ribbon, and another requires $\frac{1}{4}$ yard of ribbon. How much ribbon is needed for both projects?

29. Leon walked $\frac{5}{6}$ mile to the store and $\frac{1}{3}$ mile more to the theater. How far did he walk in all?

30. Tashia ate $\frac{1}{3}$ of the pizza and Jay ate $\frac{3}{7}$ of the pizza. What fraction of the pizza did they eat?

H.O.T. Problems

31. **OPEN ENDED** Write an addition problem involving two unlike fractions. One fraction should have a denominator of 12 and the other fraction should have a denominator of 9. Then, find the sum.

32. **FIND THE ERROR** Kate and Josh are finding the sum of $\frac{3}{4}$ and $\frac{9}{10}$. Who is correct? Explain your reasoning.

33. **WRITING IN MATH** Write a real-world problem that can be solved by adding two fractions. Then solve the problem.

Explore

Math Activity for 10-4
Subtract Unlike Fractions

MAIN IDEA

I will use models to subtract unlike fractions.

You can use fraction tiles to subtract fractions with unlike denominators.

ACTIVITY

1 Akio lives $\frac{3}{4}$ mile from school. Bianca lives $\frac{1}{6}$ mile from school. How much farther from school does Akio live than Bianca?

Step 1 Model each fraction using fraction tiles. Place the $\frac{1}{6}$-tiles underneath the $\frac{1}{4}$-tiles.

Step 2 Find which fraction will fill in the area of the dotted box.

Two of the $\frac{1}{3}$-tiles are too large to fit. Try a different fraction tile.

✓ Seven of the $\frac{1}{12}$-tiles fit.

Step 3 Since $\frac{7}{12}$ fills in the area of the dotted box, $\frac{3}{4} - \frac{1}{6} = \frac{7}{12}$.

So, Akio lives $\frac{7}{12}$ mile farther from school than Bianca.

ACTIVITY

Hands-On Activity

2 **Lisa and Kofi each bought a small tub of popcorn. Lisa ate $\frac{4}{5}$ of her popcorn and Kofi ate $\frac{3}{10}$ of her popcorn. What fraction more did Lisa eat than Kofi?**

Step 1 Model each fraction using fraction tiles. Place the $\frac{1}{10}$-fraction tiles underneath the $\frac{1}{5}$-fraction tiles.

Step 2 Find which fraction will fill in the area of the dotted box.

The $\frac{1}{2}$-fraction tile fits. ✓

Step 3 Since $\frac{1}{2}$ fills in the area of the dotted box, $\frac{4}{5} - \frac{3}{10} = \frac{1}{2}$.

So, Lisa ate $\frac{1}{2}$ tub more popcorn than Kofi.

Think About It

1. Would any of the other fraction tiles fit inside the dotted box for Activity 2?

2. Describe how you would use fraction tiles to find $\frac{1}{2} - \frac{1}{3}$.

CHECK What You Know

Find each difference using fraction tiles.

3. $\frac{2}{3} - \frac{1}{6} =$ 4. $\frac{5}{6} - \frac{1}{4} =$ 5. $\frac{5}{8} - \frac{1}{4} =$ 6. $\frac{4}{5} - \frac{1}{2} =$

7. **WRITING IN MATH** Write a real-world problem that can be solved by subtracting unlike fractions.

10-4 Subtract Unlike Fractions

MAIN IDEA

I will subtract fractions with unlike denominators.

Math Online

macmillanmh.com

- Extra Examples
- Personal Tutor
- Self-Check Quiz

GET READY to Learn

A female Cuban tree frog can be up to $\frac{5}{12}$ foot long. A male Cuban tree frog can be up to $\frac{1}{4}$ foot long. How much longer is the female Cuban tree frog than the male?

Subtracting unlike fractions is similar to adding unlike fractions.

Subtract Unlike Fractions — Key Concept

To subtract unlike fractions, perform the following steps:

- Rename the fractions using the LCD.
- Subtract as with like fractions.
- If necessary, simplify the answer.

EXAMPLE Subtract Unlike Fractions

1 **FROGS How much longer is the female Cuban tree frog than the male Cuban tree frog?**

Find $\frac{5}{12} - \frac{1}{4}$.

The least common denominator of $\frac{5}{12}$ and $\frac{1}{4}$ is 12.

Step 1		**Step 2**		**Step 3**
Write the problem.		Rename using the LCD.		Subtract the like fractions.
$\frac{5}{12}$	→	$\frac{5 \times 1}{12 \times 1} = \frac{5}{12}$	→	$\frac{5}{12}$
$-\frac{1}{4}$	→	$\frac{1 \times 3}{4 \times 3} = \frac{3}{12}$	→	$-\frac{3}{12}$
				$\frac{2}{12} = \frac{1}{6}$ Simplify.

A female Cuban tree frog is $\frac{1}{6}$ foot longer than the male.

Real-World EXAMPLE — Subtract Unlike Fractions

2 **HOMEWORK** **Jessie finished $\frac{1}{2}$ of her homework. Lakshani finished $\frac{4}{5}$ of her homework. What fraction more of her homework did Lakshani finish than Jessie?**

Subtract $\frac{4}{5} - \frac{1}{2}$.

The least common denominator of $\frac{4}{5}$ and $\frac{1}{2}$ is 10.

Step 1		**Step 2**		**Step 3**
Write the problem.		Rename using the LCD.		Add the like fractions.
$\frac{4}{5}$	→	$\frac{4 \times 2}{5 \times 2} = \frac{8}{10}$	→	$\frac{8}{10}$
$-\frac{1}{2}$	→	$\frac{1 \times 5}{2 \times 5} = \frac{5}{10}$	→	$-\frac{5}{10}$
				$\frac{3}{10}$

Lakshani finished $\frac{3}{10}$ more of her homework than Jessie.

CHECK What You Know

Subtract. Write in simplest form. See Examples 1, 2 (pp. 439–440)

1. $\frac{3}{8} - \frac{1}{4} =$
2. $\frac{5}{6} - \frac{1}{2} =$
3. $\frac{2}{5} - \frac{1}{4} =$
4. $\frac{4}{5} - \frac{1}{6} =$
5. $\frac{7}{8} - \frac{1}{2} =$
6. $\frac{7}{12} - \frac{1}{3} =$
7. $\frac{5}{6} - \frac{1}{3} =$
8. $\frac{2}{3} - \frac{3}{10} =$
9. **Measurement** Danielle poured $\frac{3}{4}$ gallon of water from the full bucket shown at the right. How much water is left in the bucket?

$\frac{7}{8}$ gallon

10. **Talk About It** Describe the steps you can use to find $\frac{3}{4} - \frac{1}{12}$.

Practice and Problem Solving

EXTRA PRACTICE
See page R27.

Subtract. Write in simplest form. See Examples 1,2 (pp. 439–440)

11. $\frac{5}{8} - \frac{1}{2}$

12. $\frac{2}{5} - \frac{1}{10}$

13. $\frac{1}{2} - \frac{1}{4}$

14. $\frac{4}{5} - \frac{2}{15}$

15. $\frac{5}{12} - \frac{1}{6}$

16. $\frac{7}{10} - \frac{1}{4}$

17. $\frac{5}{6} - \frac{3}{4}$

18. $\frac{2}{3} - \frac{3}{5}$

19. $\frac{7}{8} - \frac{1}{4}$

20. $\frac{7}{10} - \frac{1}{2}$

21. $\frac{5}{8} - \frac{1}{6}$

22. $\frac{7}{12} - \frac{1}{3}$

23. Denelle rides her bicycle $\frac{2}{3}$ mile to school. On Friday, she took a shortcut so that the ride to school was $\frac{1}{9}$ mile shorter. How long was Denelle's bicycle ride on Friday?

24. **Measurement** The average snowfall in April and October for Springfield is shown in the table at the right. How much more snow falls on average in April than in October?

Average Snowfall for Springfield	
Month	**Snowfall (in.)**
April	$\frac{4}{5}$
October	$\frac{3}{10}$

25. Wyatt is hiking a trail that is $\frac{11}{12}$ mile long. After hiking $\frac{1}{4}$ mile, he stops for water. How much farther must he hike to finish the trail?

26. Lavell has $\frac{7}{10}$ of his homework finished. Jaclyn has $\frac{4}{9}$ of her homework finished. How much more of his homework does Lavell have finished than Jaclyn?

27. A mosaic design is $\frac{7}{15}$ red, $\frac{1}{5}$ blue, and $\frac{1}{3}$ yellow. What fraction more of the mosaic is blue and yellow than red?

H.O.T. Problems

28. **OPEN ENDED** Write a subtraction problem involving fractions with the denominators 8 and 24. Then find the difference. Include the steps you used.

29. **CHALLENGE** Evaluate $x - y$ if $x = \frac{5}{6}$ and $y = \frac{7}{10}$.

30. **WRITING IN MATH** Describe the difference between subtracting fractions with like denominators and subtracting fractions with unlike denominators.

10-5 Problem-Solving Skill

MAIN IDEA I will solve problems by determining reasonable answers.

Leandra feeds her pet rabbit Bounce the same amount of food each day. Bounce eats three times a day. *About* how much food does Leandra feed Bounce in a week?

Time	Food (cups)
Morning	$\frac{3}{4}$
Afternoon	$\frac{3}{4}$
Evening	$\frac{1}{4}$

Understand

What facts do you know?

- Leandra feeds the rabbit the same amount every day.

What do you need to find?

- About how much food she feeds her rabbit each week.

Plan

You can use estimation to find a reasonable answer.

Solve

Round each amount of food to the nearest whole number.

Morning	Afternoon	Evening
$\frac{3}{4} \rightarrow 1$	$\frac{3}{4} \rightarrow 1$	$\frac{1}{4} \rightarrow 0$

In one day, she feeds Bounce about $1 + 1 + 0$ or 2 cups of food.

Multiply by the number of days in a week.

days in 1 week → 7; cups of food each day → 2

$7 \times 2 = 14$ ← cups of food in 7 days or 1 week

Leandra feeds Bounce about 14 cups of food in a week.

Check

Look back. Since there are 7 days in a week, multiply each amount by 7.

$(7 \times 1) + (7 \times 1) + (7 \times 0) = 14$

So, the answer is reasonable.

ANALYZE the Strategy

Refer to the problem on the previous page.

1. Explain why estimation is often the best way to find reasonable answers.

2. What other methods of computation could you use to solve the problem? Explain.

3. Find how much more food Leandra feeds her rabbit in the morning than in the evening.

4. What method of computation did you use to solve Exercise 3? Explain your reasoning.

PRACTICE the Strategy

EXTRA PRACTICE See page R28.

Solve. Determine which answer is reasonable.

5. Thirty students from the Netherlands set up a record 1,500,000 dominoes. Of these, 1,138,101 were toppled by one push. Which is a more reasonable estimate for how many dominoes remained standing after that push: 350,000 or 400,000?

6. Use the graph below. Is 20 inches, 23 inches, or 215 inches a reasonable total amount of rain that fell in May, June, and July?

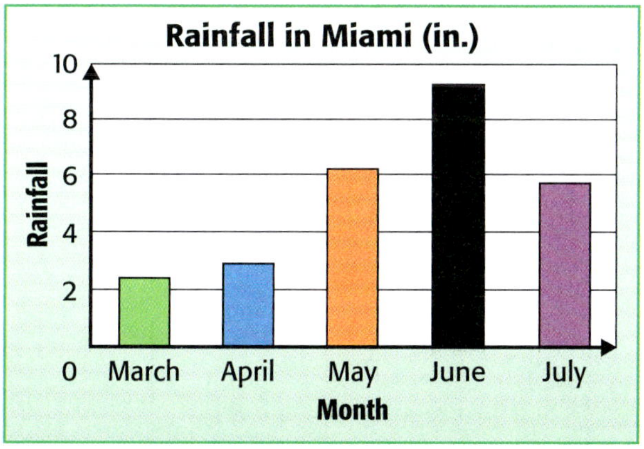

7. A puzzle book costs \$4.25. A novel costs \$9.70 more than the puzzle book. Which is a more reasonable estimate for the total cost of both items: \$14, \$16, or \$18?

8. Use the table to determine whether 245 pounds, 260 pounds, or 263 pounds is a reasonable estimate for how much more the ostrich weighs than the flamingo. Explain.

Bird	Weight (lb)
Flamingo	$9\frac{1}{10}$
Ostrich	$253\frac{1}{2}$

9. **Measurement** A grocer sells 12 pounds of apples. Of those, $5\frac{3}{4}$ pounds are green and $3\frac{1}{4}$ pounds are golden. The rest are red. Which is a more reasonable estimate for how many pounds of red apples the grocer sold: 3 pounds or 5 pounds? Explain.

10. **WRITING IN MATH** Write an addition or subtraction problem involving fractions with like denominators. Ask a classmate to determine a reasonable answer for the problem.

10-6 Estimate Sums and Differences

MAIN IDEA

I will estimate sums and differences of mixed numbers.

Math Online

macmillanmh.com

- Extra Examples
- Personal Tutor
- Self-Check Quiz

GET READY to Learn

Lucita and Alexis waited in line for the bumper cars for $7\frac{1}{6}$ minutes. Then they waited in line for the Ferris wheel for $4\frac{5}{6}$ minutes. About how long did they wait for the bumper cars and the Ferris wheel altogether?

To estimate the sum of $7\frac{1}{6}$ and $4\frac{5}{6}$, round each mixed number to the nearest whole number. Then add.

EXAMPLE Estimate Sums

1 **Estimate $7\frac{1}{6} + 4\frac{5}{6}$ to answer the problem above.**

THINK: $\frac{1}{6}$ is less than $\frac{1}{2}$. So, round $7\frac{1}{6}$ down to 7.

$7\frac{1}{6} + 4\frac{5}{6}$

THINK: $\frac{5}{6}$ is greater than $\frac{1}{2}$. So, $4\frac{5}{6}$ rounds up to 5.

Estimate $7 + 5 = 12$

So, Lucita and Alexis waited about 12 minutes altogether.

EXAMPLE Estimate Differences

2 **Estimate $3\frac{5}{8} - 1\frac{1}{8}$.**

THINK: $\frac{5}{8} > \frac{1}{2}$. Round $3\frac{5}{8}$ up to 4.

$3\frac{5}{8} - 1\frac{1}{8}$

THINK: $\frac{1}{8} < \frac{1}{2}$. Round $1\frac{1}{8}$ down to 1.

Estimate $4 - 1 = 3$

So, $3\frac{5}{8} - 1\frac{1}{8}$ is about 3.

Real-World EXAMPLE

3 **SWIMMING The table shows how many hours Alfie swam in two weeks. About how many hours did he swim altogether?**

Day	Length (hours)
Week 1	$4\frac{1}{3}$
Week 2	$2\frac{5}{6}$

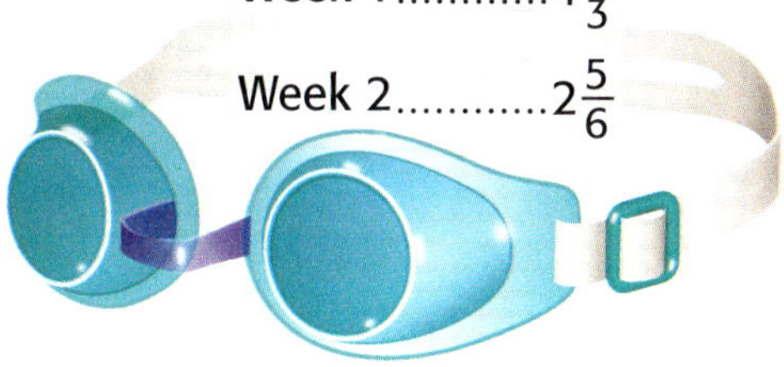

Round each mixed number to the nearest whole number. Then add.

THINK: $\frac{1}{3} < \frac{1}{2}$. Round down.

$$4\frac{1}{3} + 2\frac{5}{6}$$

THINK: $\frac{5}{6} > \frac{1}{2}$. Round up.

Estimate $4 + 3 = 7$

So, Alfie swam for about 7 hours.

Real-World EXAMPLE

4 **MEASUREMENT A fish tank can hold $10\frac{2}{5}$ gallons of water. Suppose the tank has $6\frac{1}{10}$ gallons of water. About how much more water is needed to fill the tank?**

Round $10\frac{2}{5}$ to 10 and $6\frac{1}{10}$ to 6.

Estimate $10 - 6 = 4$

So, about 4 more gallons are needed to fill the tank.

CHECK What You Know

Estimate by rounding each mixed number to the nearest whole number. See Examples 1–4 (pp. 444–445)

1. $2\frac{1}{8} + 3\frac{5}{8}$

2. $3\frac{3}{5} + 1\frac{1}{5}$

3. $5\frac{2}{9} - 3\frac{2}{3}$

4. $7\frac{4}{6} - 4\frac{3}{12}$

5. Liam spent $1\frac{3}{4}$ hours playing board games and $2\frac{1}{4}$ hours watching a movie. About how much time did Liam spend on these two activities?

6. Talk About It Write at least two sentences to explain how you would estimate $8\frac{4}{7} - 4\frac{2}{7}$.

Practice and Problem Solving

EXTRA PRACTICE See page R28.

Estimate. See Examples 1–4 (pp. 444–445)

7. $9\frac{1}{7} - 5\frac{6}{7}$ **8.** $6\frac{7}{10} - 1\frac{2}{10}$ **9.** $5\frac{3}{9} + 3\frac{7}{9}$ **10.** $8\frac{11}{12} + 4\frac{4}{12}$

11. $10\frac{2}{7} + 7\frac{5}{7}$ **12.** $12\frac{5}{10} + 9\frac{6}{10}$ **13.** $15\frac{6}{14} - 3\frac{4}{7}$ **14.** $13\frac{4}{11} - 4\frac{1}{4}$

15. $7\frac{7}{9} - \frac{15}{18}$ **16.** $8\frac{9}{15} - \frac{4}{5}$ **17.** $19\frac{3}{7} + \frac{13}{14}$ **18.** $\frac{9}{16} + 16\frac{5}{8}$

19. Polly has played soccer for $3\frac{5}{6}$ years. Gen has played soccer for $6\frac{1}{12}$ years. Estimate how many more years Gen has played soccer than Polly.

20. To clean a large painting, you need $3\frac{1}{4}$ ounces of cleaner. A small painting requires only $2\frac{3}{4}$ ounces. You have 8 ounces of cleaner. About how many ounces of cleaner will you have left if you clean a large and a small painting?

Measurement **For Exercises 21 and 22, use the picture shown.**

21. About how much taller is the birdhouse than the tree house?

22. Find the height difference between the birdhouse and the tree house. Is it greater than or less than the difference in height between the swing set and the tree house? Use estimation.

Algebra **Estimate the value of each expression if $n = 2\frac{7}{8}$.**

23. $n + 2\frac{5}{8}$ **24.** $n - \frac{6}{8}$ **25.** $15 - n$ **26.** $n + 18$

H.O.T. Problems

27. OPEN ENDED Select two mixed numbers whose estimated difference is 1. Justify your selection.

CHALLENGE **Without calculating, replace ● with < or > to make a true sentence. Explain your reasoning.**

28. $3\frac{7}{8} + 4\frac{1}{8}$ ● 9 **29.** $6\frac{7}{9} - 5\frac{3}{9}$ ● 1 **30.** 3 ● $4\frac{8}{10} - 3\frac{1}{10}$

31. **WRITING IN ▸MATH** Describe a real-world situation where it makes sense to round two numbers up even though one number could be rounded down.

CHAPTER 10 Mid-Chapter Check

Lessons 10-1 through 10-6

Add. Write each sum in simplest form. (Lesson 10-1)

1. $\frac{4}{11} + \frac{5}{11}$

2. $\frac{9}{13} + \frac{3}{13}$

3. MULTIPLE CHOICE A family bought two pizzas and ate only part of each pizza. The pictures show how much of the pizzas were left. How much of one whole pizza was left over? (Lesson 10-1)

A $\frac{7}{8}$

B $\frac{5}{8}$

C $\frac{1}{5}$

D $\frac{1}{8}$

Subtract. Write each difference in simplest form. (Lesson 10-2)

4. $\frac{6}{7} - \frac{4}{7}$

5. $\frac{7}{11} - \frac{6}{11}$

Add. Write in simplest form. (Lesson 10-3)

6. $\frac{2}{3} + \frac{1}{6}$

7. $\frac{2}{7} + \frac{1}{2}$

8. Sasha ran $\frac{2}{4}$ mile on Monday and $\frac{5}{12}$ mile on Tuesday. What is the total distance Sasha ran?

Subtract. Write in simplest form. (Lesson 10-4)

9. $\frac{6}{7} - \frac{1}{3}$

10. $\frac{2}{3} - \frac{1}{2}$

Algebra Find the value of *x* that makes a true sentence. (Lesson 10-4)

11. $\frac{x}{12} - \frac{5}{12} = \frac{1}{12}$

12. $\frac{3}{16} + \frac{x}{4} = \frac{7}{16}$

13. An $156.99 electric scooter has been discounted by $19.99. Which is a more reasonable estimate for the discounted price: $130, $137, or $140? Explain. (Lesson 10-5)

14. Measurement Mr. Nair bought $3\frac{1}{4}$ pounds of oranges. He bought $\frac{3}{4}$ pound more of bananas than oranges. *About* how many pounds of oranges and bananas did he buy? (Lesson 10-6)

Estimate by rounding each mixed number to the nearest whole number. (Lesson 10-6)

15. $11\frac{1}{6} - 2\frac{5}{6}$

16. $9\frac{7}{10} + 3\frac{6}{10}$

17. $7\frac{2}{7} + 6\frac{5}{7}$

18. $14\frac{3}{16} - 11\frac{9}{16}$

19. MULTIPLE CHOICE Mrs. Orta used $5\frac{3}{4}$ gallons of blue paint and $2\frac{1}{4}$ gallons of yellow paint. About how many gallons of paint did she use? (Lesson 10-6)

F 2 gal

G 4 gal

H 6 gal

J 8 gal

20. WRITING IN MATH Write an addition problem using words for the following model. Then find the sum. (Lesson 10-1)

10-7 Add Mixed Numbers

MAIN IDEA

I will add mixed numbers.

Math Online

macmillanmh.com

- Extra Examples
- Personal Tutor
- Self-Check Quiz

GET READY to Learn

One day Emma gathered $2\frac{1}{4}$ dozen eggs. The next day, she gathered $1\frac{1}{4}$ dozen eggs. How many dozen eggs did she gather in all?

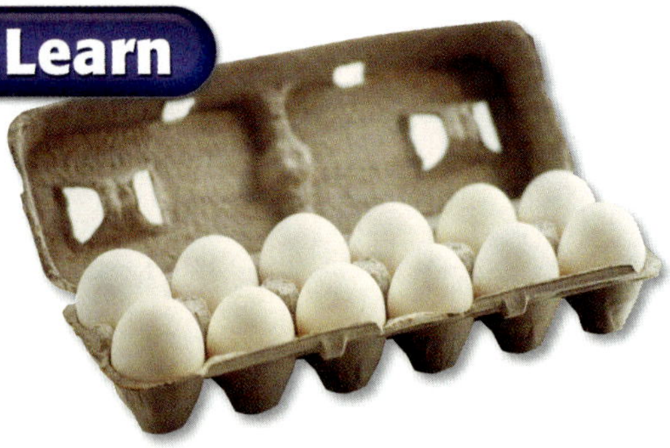

You can find an exact answer by adding the mixed numbers.

Real-World EXAMPLE — Add Mixed Numbers

1 FOOD Refer to the information above. How many dozen eggs did Emma gather?

Find $2\frac{1}{4} + 1\frac{1}{4}$. **Estimate** $2 + 1 = 3$

Step 1 Add the fractions.

$$\begin{array}{r} 2\frac{1}{4} \\ +\ 1\frac{1}{4} \\ \hline \frac{2}{4} \end{array}$$

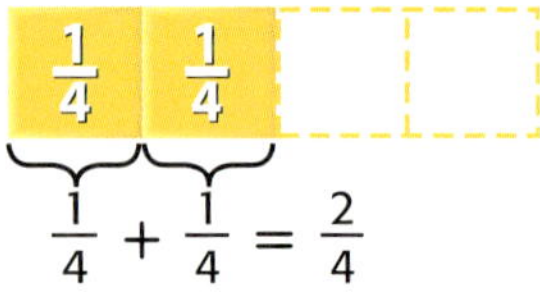

Step 2 Add the whole numbers.

$$\begin{array}{r} 2\frac{1}{4} \\ +\ 1\frac{1}{4} \\ \hline 3\frac{2}{4} \end{array}$$

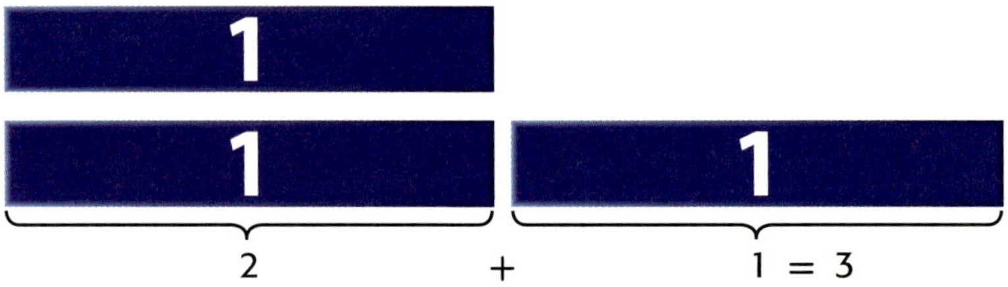

Step 3 Simplify.

$3\frac{2}{4} = 3\frac{1}{2}$ Divide the numerator and denominator by the GCF, 2.

Check for Reasonableness $3\frac{1}{2} \approx 3$ ✓

So, Emma gathered $3\frac{1}{2}$ dozen eggs.

Real-World EXAMPLE

2 **REPTILES** **The diagram shows the length of a sea turtle. What is the total length of the sea turtle?**

Find $\frac{7}{8} + 3\frac{1}{4} + 1\frac{1}{8}$.

Remember

Estimate first. Then compare your answer with the estimate.

Step 1 Write the problem.

$$\begin{array}{r} \frac{7}{8} \\ 3\frac{1}{4} \\ +1\frac{1}{8} \\ \hline \end{array}$$

Step 2 Rename the fractions using the LCD.

$$\begin{array}{rcl} \frac{7}{8} & = & \frac{7}{8} \\ 3\frac{1 \times 2}{4 \times 2} & = & 3\frac{2}{8} \\ +1\frac{1}{8} & = & 1\frac{1}{8} \\ \hline \end{array}$$

Step 3 Add the fractions and whole numbers.

$$\begin{array}{r} \frac{7}{8} \\ 3\frac{2}{8} \\ +\ 1\frac{1}{8} \\ \hline 4\frac{10}{8} \end{array}$$

Step 4 Simplify.

$4\frac{10}{8} = 4 + 1\frac{2}{8} = 5\frac{2}{8} = 5\frac{1}{4}$

The total length of the sea turtle is $5\frac{1}{4}$ feet.

Add Mixed Numbers

Key Concepts

- Rename the fraction using the LCD.
- Add the fractions and then the whole numbers.
- Simplify if needed.

CHECK What You Know

Add. Write each sum in simplest form. See Examples 1, 2 (pp. 448–449)

1. $3\frac{3}{8} + 2\frac{4}{8}$

2. $4\frac{4}{6} + 2\frac{1}{6}$

3. $5\frac{1}{10} + 5\frac{3}{10}$

4. $3\frac{4}{9} + 4\frac{2}{3}$

5. $6\frac{3}{4} + 3\frac{1}{8}$

6. $4\frac{3}{7} + 7\frac{1}{2}$

7. Yushua worked $5\frac{1}{2}$ hours on Monday, $7\frac{1}{2}$ hours on Tuesday, and $6\frac{1}{2}$ hours on Wednesday. How many hours did he work in all?

8. Talk About It Explain how to simplify $3\frac{6}{4}$.

Practice and Problem Solving

EXTRA PRACTICE See page R28.

Add. Write each sum in simplest form. See Examples 1, 2 (pp. 448–449)

9. $4\frac{3}{5} + 3\frac{1}{5}$

10. $7\frac{4}{11} + 2\frac{6}{11}$

11. $5\frac{1}{12} + 6\frac{3}{12}$

12. $8\frac{4}{15} + 3\frac{2}{15}$

13. $6\frac{1}{9} + 2\frac{1}{3}$

14. $5\frac{3}{9} + 6\frac{1}{2}$

15. $9\frac{9}{10} + 7\frac{3}{5}$

16. $14\frac{19}{20} + 8\frac{1}{4}$

17. Find *five and two eighths plus three and six eighths*. Write in words.

18. Find *ten and three sevenths plus eighteen and two sevenths*. Write in words.

19. Measurement Zita made $1\frac{5}{8}$ quarts of punch. Then she made $1\frac{7}{8}$ more quarts. How much punch did she make in all?

20. A flower is $9\frac{3}{4}$ inches tall. In one week, it grew $1\frac{1}{8}$ inches. How tall is the flower at the end of the week?

21. Pati made fruit salad using the recipe. How many cups of fruit are needed?

Recipe for

Fruit Salad

$3\frac{2}{4}$ c	Apple
$1\frac{1}{4}$ c	Grapefruit
$1\frac{3}{4}$ c	Orange
$2\frac{1}{4}$ c	Pear

22. Measurement Connor is filling a 15-gallon wading pool. On his first trip, he carried $3\frac{1}{12}$ gallons of water. He carried $3\frac{5}{6}$ gallons on his second trip and $3\frac{1}{2}$ gallons on his third trip. Suppose he carries 5 gallons on his next trip. Will the pool be filled? Explain.

H.O.T. Problems

23. OPEN ENDED Write a real-world problem involving the addition of two mixed numbers whose sum is $5\frac{1}{4}$. Then solve the problem.

24. FIND THE ERROR Urbano and Brandy are finding $4\frac{1}{5} + 2\frac{3}{5}$. Who is correct? Explain your reasoning.

Urbano
$4\frac{1}{5} + 2\frac{3}{5} = 6\frac{4}{5}$

Brandy
$4\frac{1}{5} + 2\frac{3}{5} = 6\frac{4}{10}$

25. WRITING IN MATH Is the sum of two mixed numbers *always*, *sometimes*, or *never* a mixed number? Use an example to explain.

TEST Practice

26. Marie bought $4\frac{1}{2}$ pints of ice cream for her birthday party. Her mother also bought $2\frac{1}{4}$ pints of ice cream for the party. How many pints of ice cream did Marie have for her birthday party? **(Lesson 10-5)**

A $2\frac{1}{4}$ pt

B $2\frac{3}{4}$ pt

C $6\frac{3}{8}$ pt

D $6\frac{3}{4}$ pt

27. The length and the width of Samson's swimming pool is shown.

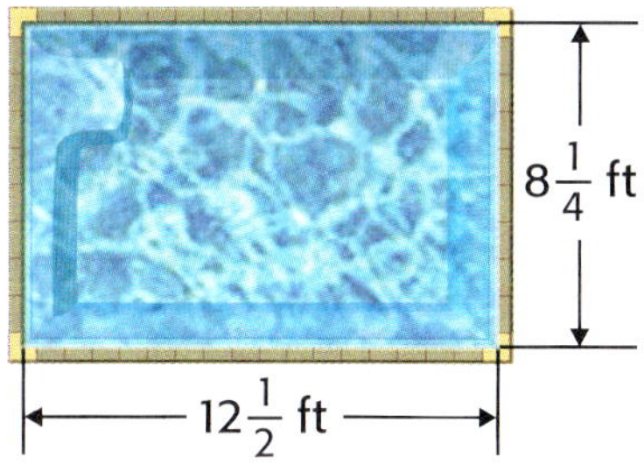

About how much longer is the length of the pool than the width of the pool? **(Lesson 10-4)**

F 3 ft

G 5 ft

H 20 ft

J 21 ft

Spiral Review

28. Nestor and Tanya rode two different rides at the fair. Nestor rode the Roller Express. The ride lasted about $1\frac{1}{3}$ minutes. Tanya rode the Rattler, which lasted about $2\frac{2}{3}$ minutes. About how much longer did the Rattler last than the Roller Express? **(Lesson 10-6)**

29. **Measurement** The distance around Saturn is 235,298 miles. The distance around Jupiter is 279,118 miles. Is 45,000 miles or 55,000 miles a more reasonable estimate for the difference between the distance around Jupiter and the distance around Saturn? Explain. **(Lesson 10-5)**

Write each decimal as a fraction in simplest form. (Lesson 9-5)

30. 0.8 **31.** 0.9 **32.** 0.29 **33.** 0.11

Write each mixed number as an improper fraction. (Lesson 8-4)

34. $3\frac{5}{6}$ **35.** $6\frac{1}{4}$ **36.** $4\frac{1}{3}$ **37.** $5\frac{2}{5}$

38. Ginny's basketball team scored 44 points in one game. If Ginny scored 16 points, how many points did the rest of team score? Write and solve an addition equation. **(Lesson 6-2)**

Divide. (Lesson 4-3)

39. $48 \div 5$ **40.** $48 \div 3$ **41.** $172 \div 4$ **42.** $264 \div 6$

10-8 Subtract Mixed Numbers

MAIN IDEA

I will subtract mixed numbers.

Math Online

macmillanmh.com

- Extra Examples
- Personal Tutor
- Self-Check Quiz

GET READY to Learn

Payat has a $2\frac{3}{4}$ cup package of cheese. He uses $1\frac{1}{4}$ cups to make a pizza. How much cheese is left?

You can find an exact answer by subtracting $1\frac{1}{4}$ from $2\frac{3}{4}$.

Real-World EXAMPLE — Subtract Mixed Numbers

1 **FOOD** **Refer to the information above. How many cups of cheese are left? Check by using fraction tiles.**

Find $2\frac{3}{4} - 1\frac{1}{4}$. **Estimate** $3 - 1 = 2$

Step 1 Subtract the fractions.

$$\begin{array}{r} 2\frac{3}{4} \\ -\ 1\frac{1}{4} \\ \hline \frac{2}{4} \end{array}$$

Step 2 Subtract the whole numbers.

$$\begin{array}{r} 2\frac{3}{4} \\ -\ 1\frac{1}{4} \\ \hline 1\frac{2}{4} \end{array}$$

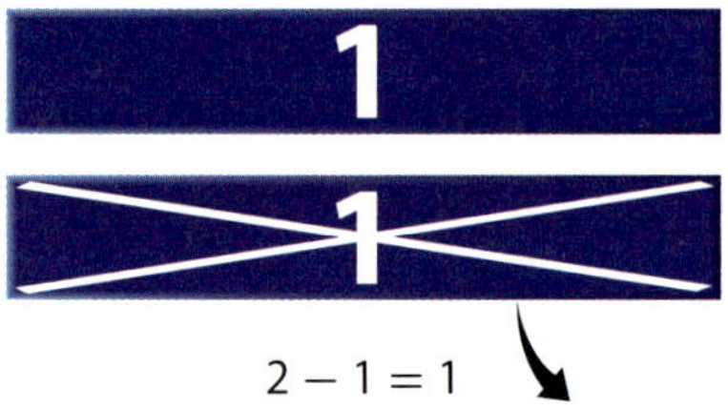

Step 3 Simplify $1\frac{2}{4}$.

$1\frac{2}{4} = 1\frac{1}{2}$ Divide the numerator and denominator by the GCF, 2.

Check for reasonableness $1\frac{1}{2} \approx 2$ ✓

So, $1\frac{1}{2}$ cups of cheese were left.

Real-World EXAMPLE — Subtract Mixed Numbers

2 **FISH** **A Pigfish and a Shiner are shown below. How much longer is the Pigfish than the Shiner?**

Find $6\frac{11}{16} - 2\frac{5}{8}$ **Estimate** $7 - 3 = 4$

Step 1	Step 2	Step 3
Write the problem.	Rename the fractions using the LCD.	Subtract the fractions and mixed numbers.
$\begin{array}{r} 6\frac{11}{16} \\ -\ 2\frac{5}{8} \\ \hline \end{array}$ →	$\begin{array}{rl} 6\frac{11}{16} & = 6\frac{11}{16} \\ -\ 2\frac{5 \times 2}{8 \times 2} & = 2\frac{10}{16} \\ \hline \end{array}$ →	$\begin{array}{r} 6\frac{11}{16} \\ -\ 2\frac{10}{16} \\ \hline 4\frac{1}{16} \end{array}$

So, the Pigfish is $4\frac{1}{16}$ inches longer than the Shiner.

Remember

Always check for reasonableness.

$4\frac{1}{16} \approx 4$ ✓

Subtract Mixed Numbers — Key Concept

- If needed, rename the fractions using the LCD.
- Subtract the fractions.
- Then subtract the whole numbers.
- Simplify if needed.

CHECK What You Know

Subtract. Write each difference in simplest form. See Examples 1, 2 (pp. 452–453)

1. $4\frac{2}{3} - 2\frac{1}{3}$

2. $5\frac{4}{5} - 3\frac{2}{5}$

3. $6\frac{5}{6} - 5\frac{2}{6}$

4. $7\frac{7}{8} - 4\frac{1}{2}$

5. $12\frac{7}{10} - 7\frac{2}{5}$

6. $15\frac{11}{12} - 4\frac{1}{3}$

7. Bella is $10\frac{5}{12}$ years old. Franco is $12\frac{7}{12}$ years old. What is the difference in their ages?

8. Talk About It — Describe the steps you would take to find $3\frac{5}{8} - 2\frac{3}{8}$.

Practice and Problem Solving

EXTRA PRACTICE See page R29.

Subtract. Write each difference in simplest form. See Examples 1, 2 (pp. 452–453)

9. $5\frac{3}{4} - 2\frac{2}{4}$ **10.** $6\frac{5}{7} - 3\frac{3}{7}$ **11.** $7\frac{8}{9} - 5\frac{3}{9}$ **12.** $8\frac{3}{8} - 2\frac{2}{8}$

13. $13\frac{9}{10} - 4\frac{4}{10}$ **14.** $12\frac{5}{6} - 7\frac{2}{6}$ **15.** $11\frac{11}{12} - 2\frac{1}{6}$ **16.** $14\frac{9}{14} - 5\frac{2}{7}$

17. $18\frac{11}{15} - 9\frac{2}{5}$ **18.** $17\frac{15}{16} - 9\frac{3}{4}$ **19.** $35\frac{7}{8} - 18\frac{5}{12}$ **20.** $44\frac{6}{7} - 21\frac{3}{4}$

21. Find *ten and seven tenths minus three and four tenths*. Write in words.

22. Find *twelve and five ninths minus five and two ninths*. Write in words.

23. **Measurement** The length of Mr. Cho's garden is $8\frac{5}{6}$ feet. Find the width of Mr. Cho's garden if it is $3\frac{1}{6}$ feet less than the length.

24. Mrs. Gabel bought $7\frac{5}{6}$ gallons of punch for the class party. The students drank $4\frac{3}{6}$ gallons of punch. How much punch was left at the end of the party?

25. Warner lives $9\frac{2}{3}$ blocks away from school. Shelly lives $12\frac{7}{8}$ blocks away from school. How many more blocks does Shelly live away from school than Warner?

26. A snack mix recipe calls for $5\frac{3}{4}$ cups of cereal and $3\frac{5}{12}$ cups less raisins. How many cups of raisins are needed?

H.O.T. Problems

27. OPEN ENDED Write a real-world problem involving the subtraction of two mixed numbers whose difference is less than $2\frac{1}{2}$. Then solve.

CHALLENGE Find the value of each variable that makes a true sentence.

28. $n + 2\frac{1}{2} = 6\frac{3}{10}$ **29.** $k + 3\frac{2}{8} = 7\frac{5}{8}$ **30.** $4\frac{1}{6} + t = 13\frac{5}{6}$

31. WHICH ONE DOESN'T BELONG? Identify the expression that does not belong with the other three. Explain your reasoning.

$5\frac{7}{10} - 3\frac{2}{10}$ $11\frac{6}{8} - 9\frac{2}{8}$ $8\frac{5}{6} - 6\frac{2}{6}$ $7\frac{3}{4} - 5\frac{2}{4}$

32. WRITING IN MATH Write a real-word problem involving subtraction of mixed numbers with unlike denominators. Then solve. Use fraction tiles to justify your solution.

Game Time

Fraction Subtraction

Subtract Mixed Numbers

Get Ready!

Players: 2 players

You will need: 12 index cards

$2\frac{1}{2} - 1\frac{1}{2}$	$5\frac{3}{4} - 4\frac{3}{4}$	$6\frac{2}{3} - 3\frac{1}{3}$
$3\frac{9}{10} - \frac{2}{5}$	$4\frac{7}{8} - 2\frac{1}{8}$	$13\frac{3}{4} - 10\frac{5}{12}$
$5\frac{15}{16} - 3\frac{3}{16}$	$10\frac{5}{6} - 7\frac{1}{3}$	$10\frac{4}{5} - 8\frac{3}{5}$
$8\frac{3}{5} - 6\frac{2}{5}$	$8\frac{6}{7} - 3\frac{2}{7}$	$7\frac{5}{7} - 2\frac{1}{7}$

Get Set!

Copy one problem shown on each index card.

Go!

- Shuffle the cards. Then spread out the cards face down on the table.
- Player 1 turns over any two cards.
- If the answers to the problems are equivalent, Player 1 keeps the cards and receives one point. Player 1 continues his or her turn.
- If the solutions are *not* equivalent, the cards are turned over and Player 2 takes a turn.
- Play continues until all matches are made. The player with most points wins.

10-9 Problem-Solving Investigation

MAIN IDEA I will choose the best strategy to solve a problem.

P.S.I. TEAM +

JACOBO: I have a bolt of material that has $6\frac{1}{4}$ yards of material on it. I have used $1\frac{3}{8}$ yards to make a large pillow. Do I have enough material to make four more pillows just like the first one?

YOUR MISSION: Find out whether Jacobo has enough material for four more pillows.

Understand	You know the bolt has $6\frac{1}{4}$ yards on it and $1\frac{3}{8}$ yards were used. You need to see if he can make four more pillows.
Plan	Use the *act it out* strategy to measure the material.
Solve	Start by marking the floor to show a length of $6\frac{1}{4}$ yards. Then mark off the amount used to make the first pillow. Then continue to mark 4 more pillows. 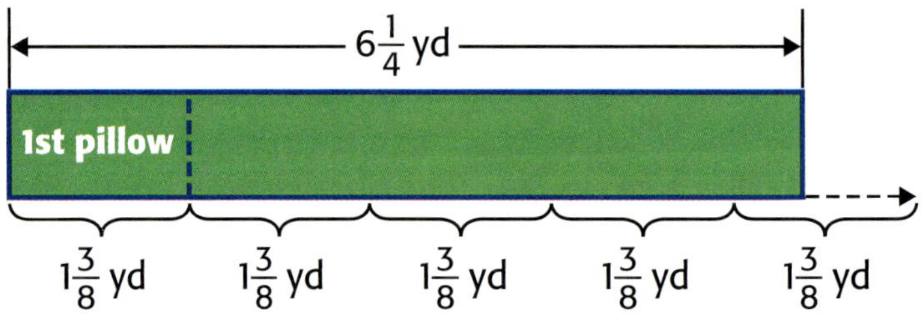 There is not enough material to make 4 more pillows.
Check	Look back. You can estimate. Round $1\frac{3}{8}$ to $1\frac{1}{2}$. $1\frac{1}{2} + 1\frac{1}{2} + 1\frac{1}{2} + 1\frac{1}{2} + 1\frac{1}{2} = 7\frac{1}{2}$ Since $7\frac{1}{2} > 6\frac{1}{4}$, the answer is correct.

Mixed Problem Solving

EXTRA PRACTICE See page R29.

Use any strategy shown below to solve each problem.

PROBLEM-SOLVING STRATEGIES

- Act it out.
- Make a graph.
- Look for a pattern.
- Use logical reasoning.

1. Alyssa needs $7\frac{5}{8}$ inches of ribbon for one project and $4\frac{7}{8}$ inches of ribbon for another project. If she has 12 inches of ribbon, will she have enough to complete both projects? Explain.

2. Berto surveyed his classmates about their favorite type of movie. He used C for comedy, A for Action, and S for scary How many more people favored comedies than action movies?

FAVORITE MOVIES

S	C	A	C	C
A	C	S	A	A
C	A	C	C	S
A	C	S	A	C
C	S	A	C	C

3. **Measurement** A high jumper starts the bar at 48 inches and raises the bar $\frac{1}{2}$ inch after each jump. How high will the bar be on the seventh jump?

4. Max, Aleta, Digna, and Tom won the first four prizes in the spelling bee. Max placed second. Aleta did not place third. Tom placed fourth. What did Digna place?

5. Shanté has eight coins in her pocket that total $1.32. What are the eight coins that she has in her pocket?

6. Gift boxes come in five different sizes. The length of the gift boxes decreases by $2\frac{1}{2}$ inches. For each $2\frac{1}{2}$-inch decrease, the price decreases by $0.75. The length of the largest box is 22 inches and costs $3.75. Find the length and cost of the smallest box.

7. What is the next figure in the pattern?

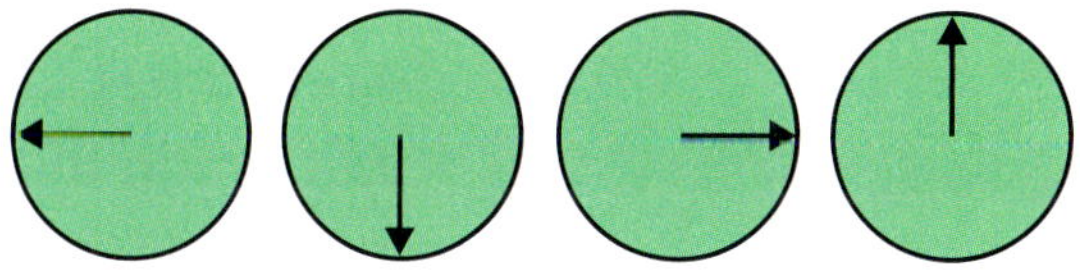

8. **Measurement** Josiah has a piece of wood that measures $9\frac{3}{8}$ feet. He wants to make 5 shelves. If each shelf is $1\frac{3}{4}$ feet long, does he have enough to make 5 shelves?

9. Franklin leaves home at 10:00 A.M. He rides his bike an average of 14 miles each hour. By 2:00 P.M., how many miles will Franklin have biked?

10. The number of siblings each student in Ms. Kennedy's class has is shown below. How many more students have two or more siblings than students who have only one sibling?

Number of Siblings					
2	1	4	2	1	0
3	2	1	1	2	3
1	1	2	0	3	1

11. **WRITING IN MATH** Refer to Exercise 4. Which strategy did you use to solve this problem? Why?

10-10 Subtraction with Renaming

MAIN IDEA

I will subtract mixed numbers.

Math Online

macmillanmh.com

- Extra Examples
- Personal Tutor
- Self-Check Quiz

GET READY to Learn

The black-tailed jackrabbit and the swamp rabbit are two mammals common to the Southern United States. A black-tailed jackrabbit weighs about $2\frac{1}{3}$ pounds. A swamp rabbit weighs about $1\frac{2}{3}$ pounds.

Sometimes the fraction in the first mixed number is less than the fraction in the second mixed number. In this case, the first mixed number needs to be renamed.

Real-World EXAMPLE — Rename Mixed Numbers to Subtract

1 ANIMALS How much more does the black-tailed jackrabbit weigh than the swamp rabbit?

You need to find $2\frac{1}{3} - 1\frac{2}{3}$.

Since $\frac{1}{3}$ is less than $\frac{2}{3}$, rename $2\frac{1}{3}$ before subtracting.

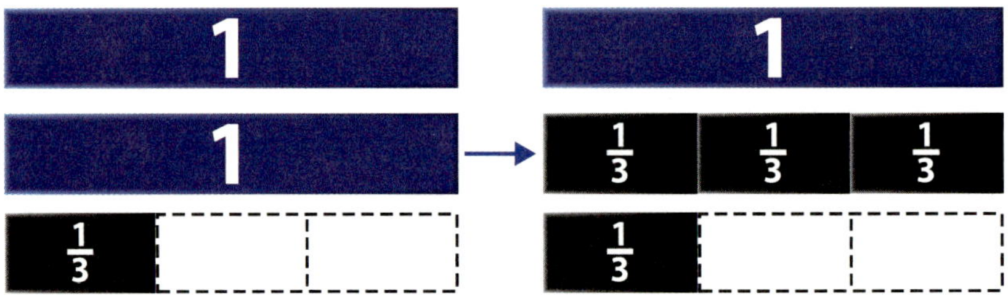

$$2\frac{1}{3} = 1 + \frac{3}{3} + \frac{1}{3} \text{ or } 1\frac{4}{3}$$

$$\begin{array}{rcr} 2\frac{1}{3} & \rightarrow & 1\frac{4}{3} \\ -\,1\frac{2}{3} & \rightarrow & -\,1\frac{2}{3} \\ \hline & & \frac{2}{3} \end{array}$$

Rename $2\frac{1}{3}$ as $1\frac{4}{3}$.

Subtract the fractions and then the whole numbers.

So, a black-tailed jackrabbit weighs about $\frac{2}{3}$ pound more than a swamp rabbit.

EXAMPLE Rename Mixed Numbers to Subtract

2 **Find $4\frac{1}{4} - 2\frac{5}{8}$.**

Rename $4\frac{1}{4}$ as $4\frac{2}{8}$ to make like fractions.

Since $\frac{2}{8}$ is less than $\frac{5}{8}$, rename $4\frac{2}{8}$ before subtracting.

THINK $4\frac{2}{8} = 3 + 1 + \frac{2}{8}$

$= 3 + \frac{8}{8} + \frac{2}{8}$ or $3\frac{10}{8}$ Rename 1 as $\frac{8}{8}$.

$$\begin{array}{rcr} 4\frac{2}{8} & \rightarrow & 3\frac{10}{8} \\ -\ 2\frac{5}{8} & \rightarrow & -\ 2\frac{5}{8} \\ \hline & & 1\frac{5}{8} \end{array}$$

Rename $4\frac{2}{8}$ as $3\frac{10}{8}$.

Subtract the fractions and then the whole numbers.

So, $4\frac{2}{8} - 2\frac{5}{8} = 1\frac{5}{8}$. Check your answer by drawing a picture.

Remember

You can always check by using fraction tiles or drawing a picture.

Real-World EXAMPLE Rename Mixed Numbers to Subtract

3 **Measurement** **Sally is making a flag. She has 2 yards of fabric. The sewing pattern calls for $1\frac{1}{4}$ yards. How much fabric will be left?**

Rename 2 as a mixed number before subtracting.

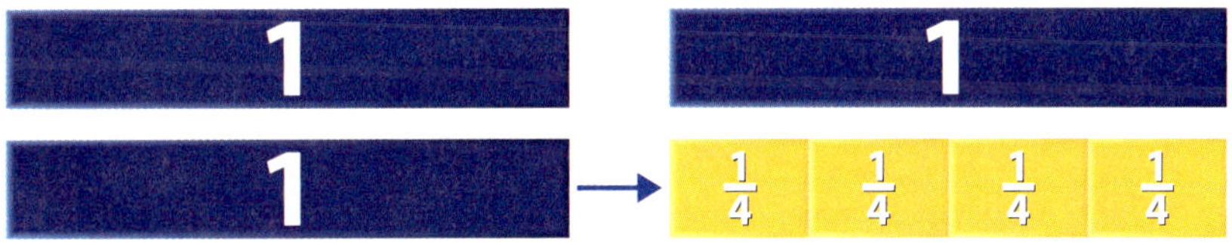

$2 = 1 + \frac{1}{4}$ or $1\frac{4}{4}$

$$\begin{array}{rcr} 2 & \rightarrow & 1\frac{4}{4} \\ -\ 1\frac{1}{4} & \rightarrow & -\ 1\frac{1}{4} \\ \hline & & \frac{3}{4} \end{array}$$

Rename 2 as $1\frac{4}{4}$.

Subtract the fractions and then the whole numbers.

So, Sally will have $\frac{3}{4}$ yard of fabric left.

CHECK What You Know

Subtract. Write each difference in simplest form. See Examples 1–3 (pp. 458–459)

1. $3\frac{1}{6} - 1\frac{1}{3}$

2. $5\frac{2}{5} - 3\frac{4}{5}$

3. $6\frac{2}{9} - 2\frac{8}{9}$

4. **Measurement** Arlo had 5 gallons of paint. He used $2\frac{10}{16}$ gallons. How much paint does he have left?

5. **Talk About It** Describe the steps you would use to solve $3\frac{2}{7} - 1\frac{4}{7}$. Then solve.

Practice and Problem Solving

EXTRA PRACTICE See page R29.

Subtract. Write each difference in simplest form. See Examples 1–3 (pp. 458–459)

6. $4\frac{3}{8} - 1\frac{5}{8}$

7. $5\frac{1}{4} - 4\frac{1}{2}$

8. $7\frac{2}{7} - 6\frac{4}{7}$

9. $9\frac{3}{10} - 5\frac{7}{10}$

10. $10\frac{1}{3} - 3\frac{6}{9}$

11. $13 - 4\frac{1}{3}$

12. $12 - 5\frac{1}{6}$

13. $18 - 9\frac{2}{8}$

14. $17 - 7\frac{3}{12}$

15. Find *ten and one fourth minus three and two fourths*. Write in words.

16. Find *nine minus four and six tenths*. Write in words.

17. Sherman's backpack weighs $6\frac{1}{4}$ pounds. Brie's backpack weighs $5\frac{3}{4}$ pounds. How much heavier is Sherman's backpack than Brie's backpack?

18. Rosa jogged $10\frac{3}{16}$ miles in one week. The next week she jogged $8\frac{7}{16}$ miles. How many more miles did she jog the first week?

Real-World PROBLEM SOLVING

Science The table shows the average lengths of common United States insects.

19. Find the difference in length between a walking stick and a bumble bee.

20. Is the difference in length between a monarch butterfly and a bumble bee greater or less than the difference in length between a walking stick and grasshopper? Explain your reasoning.

Insect	Length (in.)
Monarch Butterfly	$3\frac{4}{8}$
Walking Stick	4
Grasshopper	$1\frac{6}{8}$
Bumble Bee	$\frac{5}{8}$

Source: Natural Wildlife Federation

H.O.T. Problems

21. **OPEN ENDED** Write a subtraction problem in which you have to rename a fraction and whose solution is between 3 and 4.

22. **FIND THE ERROR** Rachel and Brandon are finding $3\frac{1}{5} - 2\frac{3}{5}$. Who is correct? Explain.

Rachel
$3\frac{1}{5} - 2\frac{3}{5} = \frac{3}{5}$

Brandon
$3\frac{1}{5} - 2\frac{3}{5} = 1\frac{2}{5}$

23. **WRITING IN MATH** Write a real-world problem involving subtraction in which you have to rename a fraction.

TEST Practice

24. Ross has 6 yards of material. He uses $2\frac{1}{3}$ yards. How many yards of material does he have left? (Lesson 10-8)

A $2\frac{2}{3}$ yd **C** $3\frac{2}{3}$ yd

B $3\frac{1}{3}$ yd **D** $8\frac{1}{3}$ yd

25. Careta swam $7\frac{5}{8}$ miles. Joey swam $5\frac{1}{8}$ miles. How many more miles did Careta swim than Joey? (Lesson 10-8)

F $13\frac{3}{4}$ mi **H** $2\frac{1}{2}$ mi

G $2\frac{6}{8}$ mi **J** $2\frac{1}{4}$ mi

Spiral Review

26. Kendra buys a sandwich for $2.79, a carton of milk for $0.65, and a bag of pretzels for $0.99. How much more can she spend without going over $6? (Lesson 10-9)

Subtract. Write each difference in simplest form. (Lesson 10-8)

27. $5\frac{3}{10} - 2\frac{2}{10}$ 28. $6\frac{9}{11} - 5\frac{2}{11}$ 29. $14\frac{7}{9} - 12\frac{1}{9}$ 30. $15\frac{6}{8} - 12\frac{1}{4}$

31. Kira and Justin are sharing a pizza. Kira eats $\frac{2}{6}$ of the pizza, and Justin eats $\frac{1}{6}$ of the pizza. What part of the pizza did they eat in all? Support your answer with a model. (Lesson 10-1)

Problem Solving in Science

Making Mixtures

Mixtures are all around you. Rocks, air, and ocean water are all mixtures. So are paints, clay, and chalk. The substances in mixtures are combined physically, not chemically. Although some substances seem to dissolve in others, each substance in a mixture keeps its own physical properties. This means that the substances in mixtures can be physically separated.

You can make some fun mixtures by using specific amounts of substances. For example, to make one type of invisible ink, you use $\frac{1}{2}$ as much baking soda as water. If you use $\frac{1}{2}$ of a cup of water, you use $\frac{1}{4}$ of a cup of baking soda. You can use other recipes to make mixtures such as sculpting clay and bubble-blowing liquid.

Real-World Math

Use the information on page 463 to solve each problem.

1. How much water do you need to make a batch of clay?
2. How much more salt than cornstarch do you need to make a batch of clay?
3. What amount of solid ingredients do you need to make a batch of clay?
4. How much liquid do you need to make bubble-blowing liquid? (*Hint:* Glycerin is a liquid.)
5. If you make three batches of clay, how much food coloring will you need?
6. If you make two batches of bubble-blowing liquid, how much water will you need?
7. If you make two batches of bubble-blowing liquid, how much soap will you need?
8. How many teaspoons of oil and food coloring do you need to make one batch of clay?

Did You Know?

Hundreds of different colors of paint can be made by mixing different amounts of just three colors: yellow, magenta, and cyan.

Clay

$2\frac{1}{3}$ cups of salt

$\frac{3}{4}$ cup of cold water

$1\frac{2}{3}$ cups cornstarch

$\frac{1}{2}$ cup boiling water

$1\frac{2}{3}$ teaspoons of oil

$\frac{2}{3}$ teaspoon food coloring

Bubble-Blowing Liquid

$4\frac{1}{4}$ cups of water

$\frac{1}{4}$ cup glycerin

$1\frac{3}{4}$ ounces grated soap

CHAPTER 10

Study Guide and Review

Math Online macmillanmh.com
• STUDY TO GO
• Vocabulary Review

FOLDABLES® Study Organizer

GET READY to Study

Be sure the following Big Ideas are written in your Foldable.

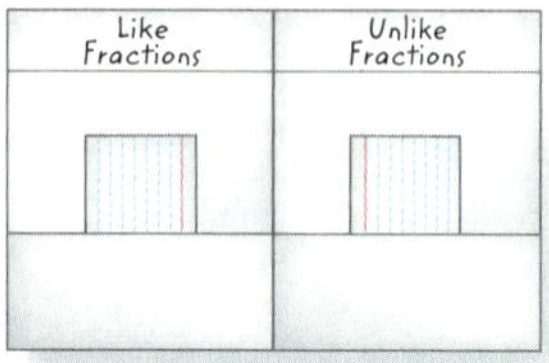

Key Concepts

Add and Subtract Like Fractions

(pp. 423, 424)

- Add or subtract the numerators. Use the same denominator.

$$\begin{array}{r} \frac{1}{4} \\ + \frac{2}{4} \\ \hline \frac{3}{4} \end{array} \qquad \begin{array}{r} \frac{5}{8} \\ - \frac{2}{8} \\ \hline \frac{3}{8} \end{array}$$

Add and Subtract Unlike Fractions

(pp. 434, 437)

- Rename the fraction using the LCD. Then add or subtract as with **like fractions**.

Estimation (p. 444)

- Estimate sums and differences of mixed numbers by rounding to the nearest whole number.

Add and Subtract **Mixed Fractions**

(pp. 448, 452)

- Add or subtract the fractions. Then add or subtract the whole numbers.

Key Vocabulary

like fractions (p. 421)
unlike fractions (p. 432)

Vocabulary Check

Choose the correct word or number that completes each sentence.

1. A number formed by a whole number and a fraction is a (mixed number, like fraction).
2. When the greatest common factor (GCF) of the numerator and denominator is 1, a fraction is written in (improper form, simplest form).
3. Fractions with the same (numerator, denominator) are called like fractions.
4. Fractions with different (numerators, denominators) are called unlike fractions.
5. When you add fractions with like denominators, you add the (numerators, denominators).
6. An improper fraction is a fraction that has a numerator that is (greater than, less than) or equal to its denominator.

Lesson-by-Lesson Review

10-1 Add Like Fractions (pp. 423–425)

Example 1

Find $\frac{4}{10} + \frac{4}{10}$. Estimate $\frac{1}{2} + \frac{1}{2} = 1$

$\frac{4}{10} + \frac{4}{10} = \frac{4+4}{10}$ Add the numerators.

$= \frac{8}{10}$ Simplify.

$= \frac{8 \div 2}{10 \div 2}$ Divide by the GCF, 2.

$= \frac{4}{5}$ Simplify.

Add. Write each sum in simplest form. Check your answer by using models.

7. $\frac{3}{9} + \frac{6}{9}$ **8.** $\frac{1}{6} + \frac{4}{6}$

9. What fraction of flowers in the table are either pansies or tulips?

Flower	Number
Mums	3
Pansies	7
Tulips	8

10-2 Subtract Like Fractions (pp. 428–431)

Example 2

Find $\frac{11}{12} - \frac{5}{12}$. Estimate $1 - \frac{1}{2} = \frac{1}{2}$

$\frac{11}{12} - \frac{5}{12} = \frac{11-5}{12}$ Subtract the numerators.

$= \frac{6}{12}$ Simplify.

$= \frac{6 \div 6}{12 \div 6}$ Divide by the GCF, 6.

$= \frac{1}{2}$ Simplify.

Subtract. Write each difference in simplest form. Check your answer by using models.

10. $\frac{2}{9} - \frac{1}{9}$ **11.** $\frac{11}{14} - \frac{4}{14}$

12. A class is surveyed to find out their favorite color. Of the class, $\frac{7}{24}$ prefers red, $\frac{4}{24}$ prefers green, and $\frac{13}{24}$ prefers blue. What fraction of the class prefers blue over red?

10-3 Add Unlike Fractions (pp. 434–436)

Example 3

Find $\frac{2}{3} + \frac{1}{2}$.

$\frac{2 \times 2}{3 \times 2} = \frac{4}{6}$ Rename the fractions using the LCD.

$+\frac{1 \times 3}{2 \times 3} = \frac{3}{6}$ Add as with like fractions.

$= \frac{7}{6} = 1\frac{1}{6}$ Simplify.

Add. Write each sum in simplest form.

13. $\frac{1}{4} + \frac{3}{8}$ **14.** $\frac{1}{2} + \frac{2}{7}$

15. On Monday, Matt ran $\frac{4}{9}$ mile. On Tuesday, he ran $\frac{1}{3}$ mile. How far did he run in all?

CHAPTER 10

Study Guide and Review

10-4 Subtract Unlike Fractions (pp. 439–441)

Example 4

Find $\frac{4}{5} - \frac{1}{4}$.

$$\frac{4 \times 4}{5 \times 4} = \frac{16}{20}$$ Rename the fractions using the LCD.

$$-\frac{1 \times 5}{4 \times 5} = \frac{5}{20}$$ Add as with like fractions.

$$= \frac{11}{20}$$

Subtract. Write each difference in simplest form.

16. $\frac{4}{6} - \frac{1}{2}$

17. $\frac{11}{12} - \frac{2}{3}$

18. Jada cleaned $\frac{7}{9}$ of her room. Trent cleaned $\frac{1}{2}$ of his room. How much more of her room did Jada clean?

10-5 Problem-Solving Skill: Determine Reasonable Answers (pp. 442–443)

Example 5

Ted Hoz has the world's largest collection of golf balls. He has 74,849 golf balls. He estimates that he has room for 95,000 golf balls. Is 20,000 or 25,000 a more reasonable estimate for how many more golf balls he can collect?

Estimate 95,000–74,849.

Step 1 Round 74,849 to the nearest thousand.

74,849 → 75,000

Step 2 Subtract.

$$\begin{array}{r} 95{,}000 \\ -\ 75{,}000 \\ \hline 20{,}000 \end{array}$$

So, Ted Hoz can collect about 20,000 more golf balls.

Solve. Determine which answer is reasonable. Explain your answer.

19. A footbag is a small bean bag controlled by the feet. The table shows how many times the male and female world record holders kicked a footbag.

Record Holder	Number of Times Kicking Footbag
Constance Constable	24,713
Ted Martin	63,326

Which is a more reasonable estimate for how many more times Ted Martin kicked the footbag than Constance Constable: 38,000 or 45,000?

20. Measurement Susan is $5\frac{5}{6}$ feet tall and her brother Nick is $4\frac{1}{6}$ feet tall. Which is a more reasonable estimate for how much taller Susan is than her brother: $1\frac{1}{2}$ feet, 2 feet, or 3 feet?

10-6 Estimate Sums and Differences (pp. 444–446)

Example 6

Estimate $8\frac{7}{9} - 5\frac{1}{9}$.

$$8\frac{7}{9} - 5\frac{1}{9}$$

$$\downarrow \quad \downarrow$$

Estimate $9 - 5 = 4$

So, $8\frac{7}{9} - 5\frac{1}{9}$ is about 4.

Estimate by rounding the mixed number to a whole number.

21. $4\frac{1}{3} + 3\frac{5}{6}$

22. $8\frac{2}{3} - 3\frac{7}{9}$

23. $14\frac{5}{12} - 8\frac{7}{12}$

24. $12\frac{8}{15} + 9\frac{4}{15}$

25. Darnell is $13\frac{3}{4}$ years old. His younger sister is $9\frac{1}{4}$ years old. About how many years older is Darnell?

10-7 Add Mixed Numbers (pp. 448–451)

Example 7

Find $5\frac{3}{6} + 2\frac{2}{6}$.

Step 1 Add the fractions.

$$\begin{array}{r} 5\frac{3}{6} \\ +\ 2\frac{2}{6} \\ \hline \frac{5}{6} \end{array}$$

Step 2 Add the whole numbers.

$$\begin{array}{r} 5\frac{3}{6} \\ +\ 2\frac{2}{6} \\ \hline 7\frac{5}{6} \end{array}$$

Add. Write each sum in simplest form.

26. $1\frac{1}{5} + 2\frac{3}{5}$

27. $2\frac{3}{9} + 6\frac{1}{3}$

28. $3\frac{3}{10} + 7\frac{7}{10}$

29. $8\frac{7}{12} + 7\frac{2}{3}$

30. Vera and Sonia went canoeing. They traveled $5\frac{3}{8}$ miles in the morning and $4\frac{1}{8}$ miles in the afternoon. How many miles did they canoe altogether?

10-8 Subtract Mixed Numbers (pp. 452–454)

Example 8

Find $4\frac{5}{6} - 3\frac{2}{6}$.

Step 1 Subtract the fractions.

$$\begin{array}{r} 4\frac{5}{6} \\ -\ 3\frac{2}{6} \\ \hline \frac{3}{6} \end{array}$$

Step 2 Subtract the whole numbers.

$$\begin{array}{r} 4\frac{5}{6} \\ -\ 3\frac{2}{6} \\ \hline 1\frac{3}{6} = 1\frac{1}{2} \end{array}$$

Subtract. Write each difference in simplest form.

31. $3\frac{4}{5} - 1\frac{3}{5}$

32. $5\frac{8}{9} - 3\frac{5}{9}$

33. $14\frac{11}{12} - 8\frac{7}{12}$

34. $19\frac{14}{15} - 12\frac{1}{5}$

35. In one week, the fifth grade class recycled $9\frac{2}{3}$ pounds of glass, and $12\frac{3}{4}$ pounds of newspaper. How many more pounds of newspaper than glass did the class recycle?

10-9 Problem-Solving Investigation: Choose a Strategy (pp. 456–457)

Example 9

After one month, Migina had saved \$25. After 2 months, she had saved \$40. After 3 months, she had saved \$55. Suppose she continues saving at this rate. How long will it take Migina to save enough money to buy a satellite radio that costs \$90?

To solve the problem, you can use the *look for a pattern* strategy.

\$25 \$40 \$55 \$70 \$85 \$100

+15 +15 +15 +15 +15

She will have saved enough money in 6 months.

Solve.

36. **Measurement** Frank is building steps for a porch. He has $12\frac{5}{6}$ feet of wood. He needs to build 4 steps. If each step uses $3\frac{1}{3}$ feet of wood, does he have enough to make 4 steps? Explain.

37. Mrs. Orta is making candles for the school craft show. The supplies needed to make a dozen candles cost \$5.25. How much profit will Mrs. Orta make if she sells all the candles for \$4.25 each?

10-10 Subtraction with Renaming (pp. 458–461)

Example 10

Find $7\frac{1}{5} - 2\frac{4}{5}$. Estimate $7 - 3 = 4$

Since $\frac{1}{5}$ is less than $\frac{4}{5}$, rename $7\frac{1}{5}$.

THINK $7\frac{1}{5} = 6 + \frac{5}{5} + \frac{1}{5} = 6\frac{6}{5}$

$7\frac{1}{5} \rightarrow 6\frac{6}{5}$ Rename $7\frac{1}{5}$ as $6\frac{6}{5}$.

$-2\frac{4}{5} \rightarrow -2\frac{4}{5}$ Subtract.

$4\frac{2}{5}$

So, $7\frac{1}{5} - 2\frac{4}{5} = 4\frac{2}{5}$.

Subtract. Write each difference in simplest form. Check your answer by using models.

38. $5\frac{1}{8} - 2\frac{6}{8}$

39. $8\frac{3}{7} - 3\frac{6}{7}$

40. $9\frac{4}{9} - 8\frac{7}{9}$

41. $15\frac{6}{10} - 8\frac{4}{5}$

42. Jin lives 10 miles from the beach. Her friend lives $6\frac{1}{3}$ miles from the beach. How much farther does Jin live from the beach than her friend?

Chapter 10 Chapter Test

Math Online macmillanmh.com

• Chapter Test

Add or subtract. Write each sum or difference in simplest form.

1. $\frac{9}{11} + \frac{1}{11}$

2. $\frac{9}{13} - \frac{7}{13}$

3. $\frac{4}{7} - \frac{1}{3}$

4. $\frac{4}{15} + \frac{3}{5}$

5. MULTIPLE CHOICE Zacharias has $\frac{2}{3}$ cup of pasta. He uses $\frac{1}{3}$ cup for a salad as shown in the measuring cups below.

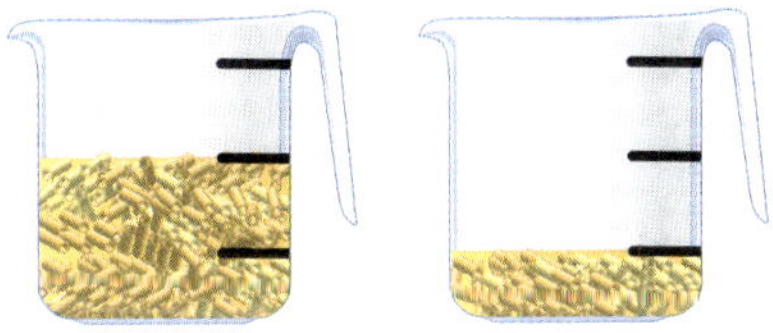

How much pasta does he have left?

A 1 c

B $\frac{1}{2}$ c

C $\frac{1}{3}$ c

D 0 c

6. Measurement On a recent trip around Kentucky, Mr. Chavez drove 83 miles from Newport to Lexington and then 77 miles from Lexington to Louisville. Which is a reasonable estimate for the total number of miles he drove: 100 miles, 160 miles, or 180 miles?

7. A sea otter remained underwater for $\frac{6}{8}$ minute. Then it came back to the surface for air. It dove a second time and stayed underwater for $\frac{3}{4}$ minute. About how long was the sea otter underwater altogether?

Estimate by rounding the mixed number to a whole number.

8. $6\frac{1}{5} - 4\frac{3}{5}$

9. $9\frac{4}{5} + 1\frac{3}{10}$

10. $8\frac{3}{11} + 3\frac{6}{11}$

11. $12\frac{8}{15} - 7\frac{1}{3}$

Add or subtract. Write each sum or difference in simplest form.

12. $9\frac{4}{6} - 5\frac{1}{2}$

13. $3\frac{1}{9} + 7\frac{6}{9}$

14. $14\frac{9}{12} - 8\frac{1}{4}$

15. $9\frac{5}{16} + 11\frac{7}{16}$

16. MULTIPLE CHOICE On Saturday, Phoebe biked $5\frac{2}{10}$ miles. Then she biked $6\frac{6}{10}$ miles on Sunday. How many miles did she bike altogether?

F $12\frac{8}{10}$ mi

G $11\frac{4}{5}$ mi

H $11\frac{8}{20}$ mi

J $1\frac{2}{5}$ mi

17. Algebra What is the next figure in the pattern?

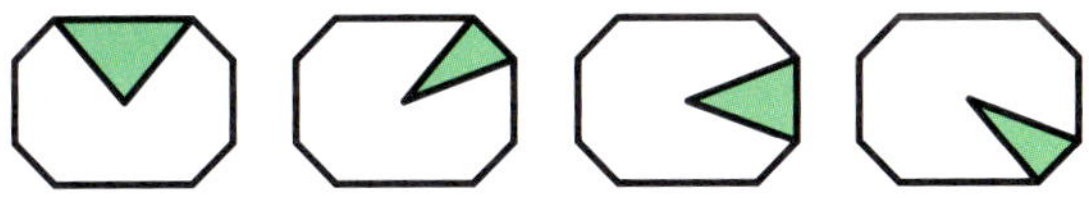

Subtract. Write each difference in simplest form.

18. $16\frac{1}{10} - 7\frac{3}{10}$

19. $20\frac{1}{3} - 5\frac{5}{6}$

20. WRITING IN MATH Explain how you would find $4 - 3\frac{5}{6}$. Justify your steps by using a model.

CHAPTER 10

Test Practice

Cumulative, Chapters 1–10

Math Online macmillanmh.com

- **Test Practice**

PART 1 Multiple Choice

Read each question. Then fill in the correct answer on the answer sheet provided by your teacher or on a sheet of paper.

1. Hakeem ate $\frac{1}{4}$ of a pie. His two brothers each ate $\frac{1}{8}$ of the pie. How much of the pie did Hakeem and his brothers eat altogether?

A $\frac{1}{3}$

B $\frac{2}{8}$

C $\frac{1}{2}$

D $\frac{5}{8}$

2. Last school week, it rained 2 out of 5 days. Which fraction is greater than $\frac{2}{5}$?

F $\frac{1}{2}$ **H** $\frac{1}{4}$

G $\frac{1}{3}$ **J** $\frac{3}{16}$

3. Javier made a pan of brownies to share with his classmates. The pan was divided evenly into 30 brownies. Javier gave away 20 brownies. What fraction of the brownies did he have left?

A $\frac{1}{4}$ **C** $\frac{2}{3}$

B $\frac{1}{3}$ **D** $\frac{3}{4}$

4. The graph shows some areas around Anica's home town.

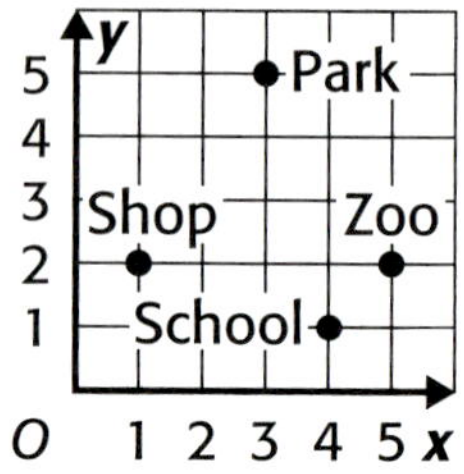

Which ordered pair best represents the point on the graph labeled "School"?

F (1, 2) **H** (5, 2)

G (4, 1) **J** (1, 4)

5. Enrique and Sydney are making oatmeal raisin cookies. Enrique's recipe calls for $\frac{1}{2}$ cup of raisins per dozen, and Sydney's recipe calls for $\frac{5}{8}$ cup of raisins per dozen. How many raisins do they need in all?

A 1

B $1\frac{1}{8}$

C $1\frac{1}{2}$

D 2

6. Malak's family bought a bag of apples at a farmer's market. If they ate $\frac{7}{12}$ of the apples, what fraction of the apples remained?

F $\frac{1}{3}$ **H** $\frac{1}{2}$

G $\frac{5}{12}$ **J** $\frac{2}{3}$

Preparing for Standardized Tests

For test-taking strategies and practice, see pages R42–R55.

7. Agustin has completed $\frac{5}{12}$ of his project, and Evelina has completed $\frac{2}{6}$ of her project. How much more of the project does Agustin have finished than Evelina?

A $\frac{1}{12}$ **C** $\frac{3}{4}$

B $\frac{2}{6}$ **D** $\frac{11}{12}$

8. Myron gives his cat $\frac{2}{5}$ cup of dry food in the morning and $\frac{1}{5}$ cup of dry food in the afternoon, as shown below. How much dry food does he give his cat each day?

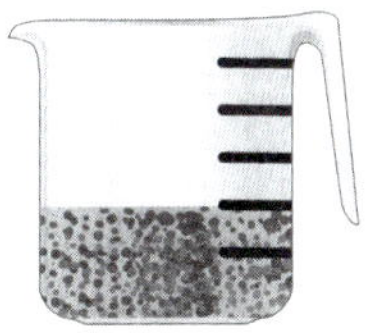
Morning

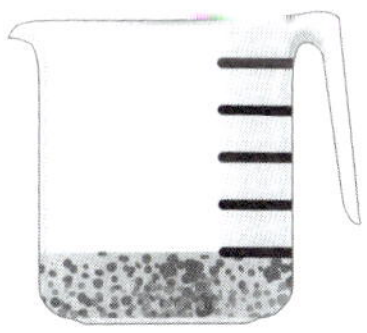
Afternoon

F $\frac{2}{5}$ cup **H** $\frac{4}{5}$ cup

G $\frac{3}{5}$ cup **J** 1 cup

9. Which fraction is greater than $\frac{3}{4}$?

A $\frac{1}{2}$ **C** $\frac{1}{3}$

B $\frac{6}{7}$ **D** $\frac{3}{8}$

PART 2 Short Response

Record your answers on the sheet provided by your teacher or on a sheet of paper.

10. Explain how to find the *x*-coordinate of point *P* shown below.

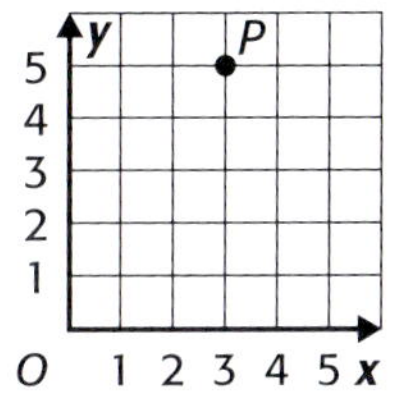

11. Malcom delivered $\frac{1}{3}$ of the newspapers. Angela delivered $\frac{2}{3}$ of the newspapers. Are there any newspapers that still need to be delivered? Explain.

PART 3 Extended Response

Record your answers on the answer sheet provided by your teacher or on a sheet of paper. Show your work.

12. Compare $\frac{2}{3}$ and $\frac{1}{8}$ using a drawing.

13. Explain how to find $5\frac{1}{8} + 6\frac{2}{4}$.

NEED EXTRA HELP?													
If You Missed Question...	1	2	3	4	5	6	7	8	9	10	11	12	13
Go to Lesson...	10–3	9–9	10–2	6–4	10–7	10–2	10–8	10–1	9–9	6–4	10–3	9–9	10–7

CHAPTER 11 Use Measures in the Customary System

BIG Idea How do you convert among customary units?

You can use multiplication or division to convert among customary units.

Example The Manhattan Bridge in New York City connects Manhattan to Brooklyn. The bridge is 1,470 feet long. This is 1,470 ÷ 3, or 490 yards.

What will I learn in this chapter?

- Choose appropriate customary units for measuring length.
- Convert customary units of length, weight, and capacity.
- Convert units of time.
- Solve problems involving elapsed time.
- Solve problems by using the *draw a diagram* strategy.

Key Vocabulary

length
customary units
weight
capacity
elapsed time

Math Online **Student Study Tools at macmillanmh.com**

FOLDABLES® Study Organizer

Make this Foldable to help you organize information about the customary system. Begin with a sheet of $8\frac{1}{2}''$ by $11''$ paper.

1. **Fold** the short sides toward the middle.

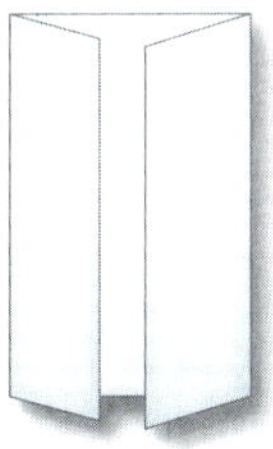

2. **Fold** the top to the bottom.

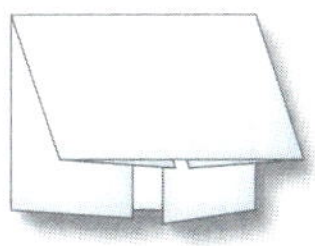

3. **Open.** Cut along the second fold to make four tabs.

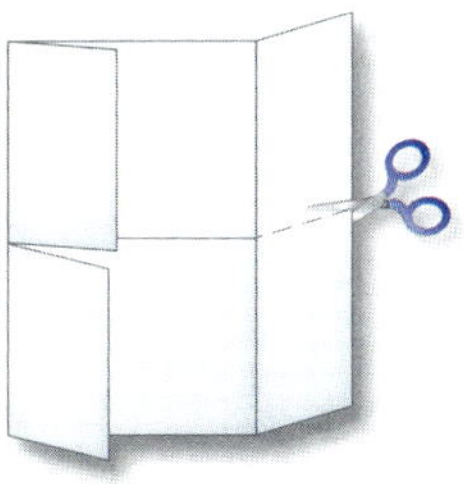

4. **Label** each of the tabs as shown.

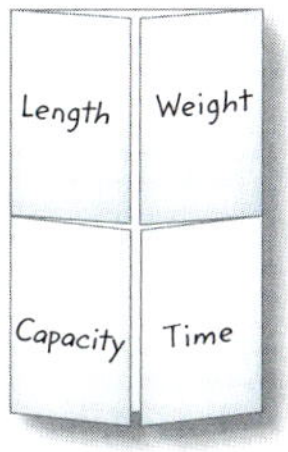

ARE YOU READY for Chapter 11?

You have two ways to check prerequisite skills for this chapter.

Option 2

Math Online Take the Chapter Readiness Quiz at macmillanmh.com.

Option 1

Complete the Quick Check below.

QUICK Check

Multiply. (Lesson 3-6)

1. 14×3

2. 36×5

3. 760×2

4. 15×12

5. 16×14

6. 280×4

7. A musical was sold out for three straight shows. If 825 tickets were sold at each performance, how many tickets were sold in all?

Divide. Write any remainders as fractions in simplest form. (Lessons 4-4 and 8-1)

8. $45 \div 3$

9. $112 \div 16$

10. $39 \div 4$

11. $52 \div 12$

12. $950 \div 20$

13. $220 \div 8$

14. A box has 144 ounces of grapes. How many 16-ounce packages of grapes can be made?

Find how much time has passed. (Prior Grade)

15.

8:10 A.M.

8:30 A.M.

16.

7:35 P.M.

7:50 P.M.

17. 6:05 A.M. to 6:45 A.M.

18. 12:25 A.M. to 12:50 A.M.

19. April walked her dog from 11:05 A.M. to 11:25 A.M. For how many minutes did she walk her dog?

Explore

Measurement Activity for 11-1

Measure with a Ruler

Length is the measurement of distance between two points. You can use a ruler like the one at the right to measure the length of objects to the nearest half inch or quarter inch.

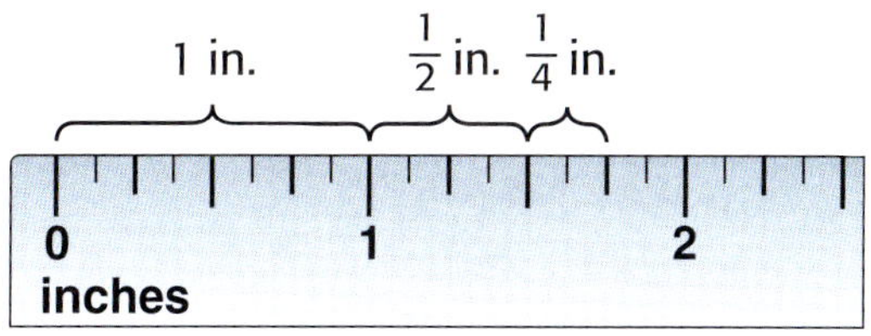

MAIN IDEA

I will measure length to the nearest half inch and quarter inch.

You Will Need

a ruler

Math Online

macmillanmh.com

• Concepts in Motion

ACTIVITY

1 Find the length of the button to the nearest half inch and quarter inch.

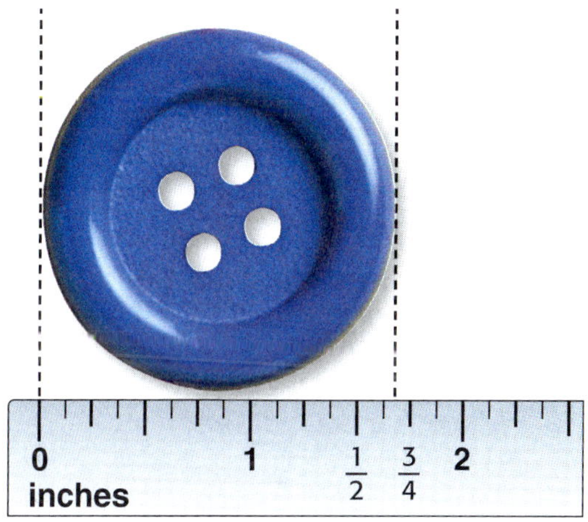

Step 1 Place the ruler against one edge of the object. Line up the zero on the ruler with the end of the object.

Step 2 Find the half inch mark that is closest to the other end. Repeat for the quarter inch mark.

To the nearest half inch, the button is $1\frac{1}{2}$ inches long. To the nearest quarter inch, it is $1\frac{3}{4}$ inches long.

Think About It

1. Explain how you can tell the difference between the half inch and quarter inch marks when measuring an object with a ruler.
2. Will you ever have the same answer when measuring to the nearest half inch and measuring to the nearest quarter inch? Explain your reasoning.

CHECK What You Know

Measure the length of each of the following to the nearest half inch and quarter inch.

3. 

4. 

5. 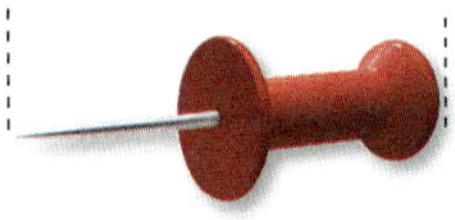

6. 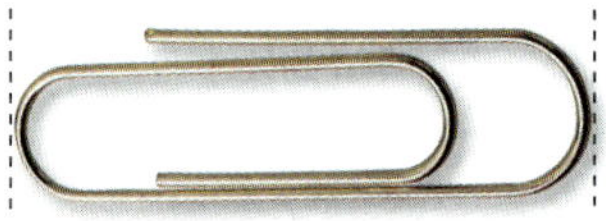

Inches **are used to measure small objects. You can measure the length of larger objects using *feet* or *yards*. *Miles* are used to measure very great lengths. Select an appropriate unit to measure each of the following.**

7. distance from your home to school

8. length of your classroom

9. width of a cell phone

10. height of a classmate

11. Copy the table below. Then complete the table using ten objects found in your classroom. The first one is done for you.

Object	Unit of Measure	Estimate	Actual Length
Height of classroom door	feet	6 feet	8 feet

Name an object that you would measure using each unit.

12. inch

13. yard

14. foot

15. mile

16. Draw a line that is between 4 and 5 inches long. Measure the length to the nearest quarter inch.

17. Draw a line that is $2\frac{1}{2}$ inches long when measured to the nearest half inch and nearest quarter inch.

18. WRITING IN MATH Suppose you know that a line is 3 inches long when measured to the nearest inch. What do you know about the actual length of the line?

11-1 Units of Length

GET READY to Learn

For many of the thrill rides at amusement parks, riders must be at least 48 inches tall.

MAIN IDEA

I will choose an appropriate customary unit for measuring length and convert customary units of length.

New Vocabulary

- length
- customary units
- foot
- inch
- yard
- mile
- convert

Math Online

macmillanmh.com

- Extra Examples
- Personal Tutor
- Self-Check Quiz

The units of **length** most often used in the United States are the inch, foot, yard, and mile. These units are called **customary units**.

Customary Units of Length

Key Concepts

1 **foot** (ft) = 12 **inches** (in.)
1 **yard** (yd) = 3 ft or 36 in.
1 **mile** (mi) = 5,280 ft or 1,760 yd

When you **convert** measurements, you change from one unit to another. To convert a larger unit to a smaller unit, *multiply*.

Real-World EXAMPLE — Convert Larger Units to Smaller Units

1 **RIDES Refer to the information above. Cheng is 4 feet tall. Is he tall enough to ride a thrill ride at an amusement park?**

4 ft = ■ in. Larger units (feet) are being converted to smaller units (inches).

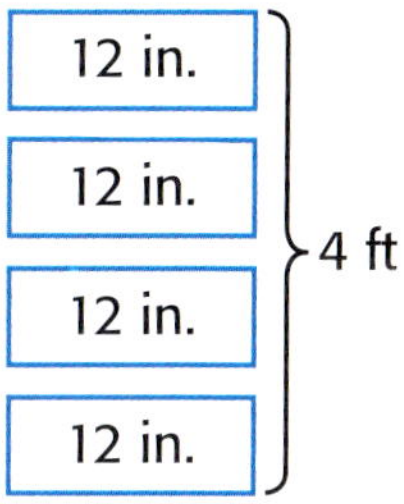

Since 1 foot = 12 inches, multiply 4 by 12.

$4 \times 12 = 48$

So, 4 ft = 48 in. Since 4 feet equals 48 inches, Cheng is tall enough to ride the thrill rides.

To convert a smaller unit to a larger unit, *divide*.

Real-World EXAMPLE Convert Smaller Units to Larger Units

2 **SPORTS A basketball court is 84 feet long. How many yards long is it?**

84 ft = ■ yd   Smaller units (feet) are being converted to larger units (yards).

Since 3 feet = 1 yard, divide 84 by 3.

84 ÷ 3 = 28
So, 84 ft = 28 yd. The basketball court is 28 yards long.

Vocabulary Link
Customary
Everyday Use commonly practiced, used, or observed
Math Use system of measurement

Units of length in the customary system can also be expressed using different units of measure or as fractions.

EXAMPLE Parts of Units

3 **Convert 42 inches to feet.**

One Way: **Use feet and inches.**

Since you are changing a smaller unit to a larger unit, divide.

42 ÷ 12 = 3 R6   12 in. = 1 ft

The remainder 6 means there are 6 inches left over.

42 in. = 3 ft 6 in.

Another Way: **Use fractions.**

42 ÷ 12 = 3 R6   3 R6 means 42 inches = 3 feet 6 inches.

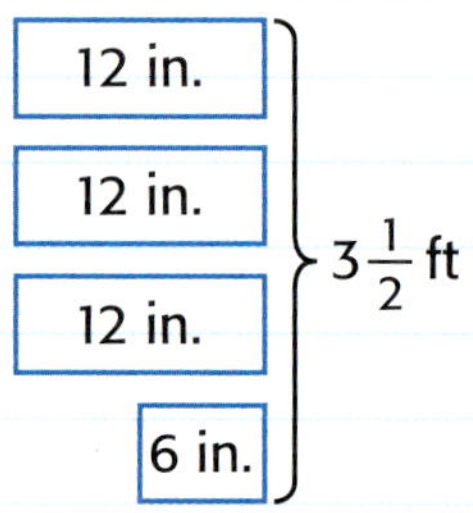

The remainder 6 means there are 6 inches out of a foot left over.

The fraction of a foot is $\frac{6}{12}$ or $\frac{1}{2}$.

42 in. = $3\frac{1}{2}$ ft

So, 42 inches is equal to 3 feet 6 inches or $3\frac{1}{2}$ feet.

Remember
All measurements are approximations. However, if you use smaller units, you will get a more *precise* measure, or a measure that is closer to the exact measure.

CHECK What You Know

Complete. See Examples 1–3 (pp. 477–478)

1. 60 in. = ■ ft

2. 5,280 ft = ■ mi

3. 9 ft = ■ in.

4. 6 yd = ■ in.

5. 22 ft = ■ yd ■ ft

6. 40 in. = ■ ft

7. Carlos is 63 inches tall. What is his height in feet?

8. **Talk About It** Explain how to convert units from feet to inches.

Practice and Problem Solving

EXTRA PRACTICE See page R29.

Complete. See Examples 1–3 (pp. 477–478)

9. 19 yd = ■ in.

10. 26,400 ft = ■ mi

11. 5 mi = ■ yd

12. 105 in. = ■ yd ■ in.

13. 15 ft 8 in. = ■ in.

14. 150 in. = ■ yd

15. **Measurement** A bull had horns that measured 98 inches across. What is this length in feet and inches? in feet?

16. Ty has two pieces of wood. Which piece of wood is longer?

Piece	Length
1	1 yd 9 in.
2	44 in.

17. The *U.S.S. Harry Truman* is an aircraft carrier that is 1,092 feet long. Find the length in yards.

18. Dana ran $\frac{1}{4}$ mile. Trish ran 445 yards. Who ran the greater distance? Explain.

Choose an appropriate unit to measure each of the following.

19. length of a cellular phone

20. length of a kitchen

21. width of a television

22. length of community swimming pool

23. distance between two cities

24. height of soccer goal posts

Real-World PROBLEM SOLVING

Social Studies Around 3000 B.C., the Egyptians developed units of length based on parts of the body.

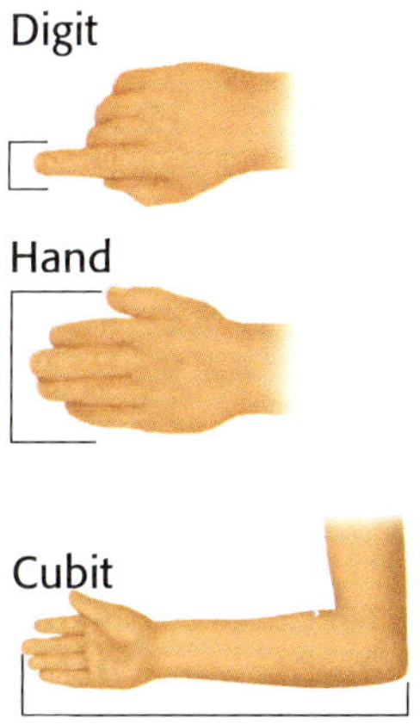

Choose the appropriate measure to find each distance.

25. width of your desk

26. width of a sheet of paper

27. your height

28. width of the classroom

H.O.T. Problems

29. **OPEN ENDED** Estimate the width of a window in your school. Then measure the width in feet and inches.

30. **CHALLENGE** There are 320 *rods* in a mile. Find the length of a *rod* in feet.

31. **WRITING IN MATH** Write a real-world problem that can be solved by converting yards to feet. Then solve.

TEST Practice

32. Which relationship between units of length is correct? (Lesson 11-1)

   A One foot is $\frac{1}{12}$ of one yard.

   B One yard is $\frac{1}{4}$ of one mile.

   C One foot is $\frac{1}{3}$ of one yard.

   D One inch is $\frac{1}{3}$ of one foot.

33. The picture shows the height of a statue. What is the height of the statue in inches? (Lesson 11-1)

   F 13 inches
   G 22 inches
   H 36 inches
   J 40 inches

Spiral Review

34. A full bag contains $7\frac{2}{4}$ cups of flour. There are $1\frac{3}{4}$ cups left in a bag. How many cups have been used? (Lesson 10-8)

35. The softball team has ten players. Suppose each player shakes hands with every other player. How many handshakes take place? (Lesson 10-7)

Add or subtract. (Lessons 10-1 and 10-2)

36. $\frac{3}{5} - \frac{1}{5}$

37. $\frac{1}{10} + \frac{3}{10}$

38. $\frac{2}{9} + \frac{8}{9}$

39. $\frac{7}{9} - \frac{4}{9}$

40. The model at the right shows 0.004. Write 0.004 as a fraction in simplest form. (Lesson 9-5)

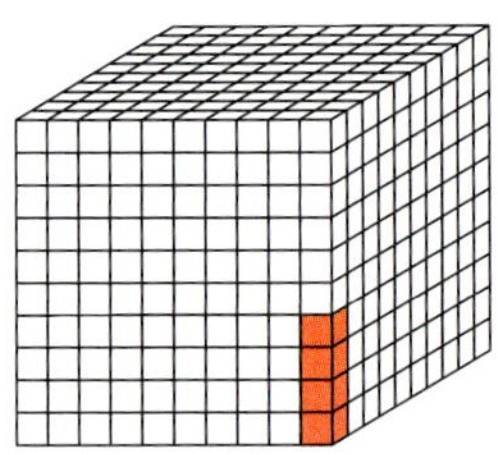

41. Four friends share three brownies equally. How many brownies does each friend get? (Lesson 8-1)

Game Time

Mystery Measurements

Using Customary Measures

Get Ready!

Players: 2

You will need: 2 yardsticks, 12 index cards

Get Set!

- Working alone, each player secretly measures the length or width of six objects in the classroom and records them on a piece of paper. The measures may be in inches or feet. This will serve as the answer sheet at the end of the game.
- Each player takes 12 index cards.
- For each object, the measurement is recorded on one card. A description of what was measured is recorded on another card. Make sure each measurement is different.

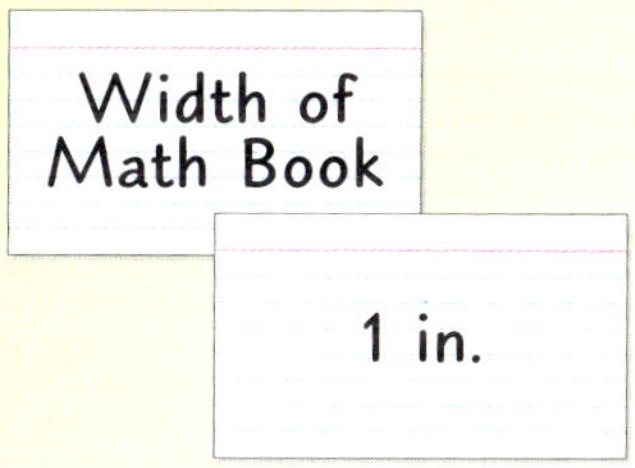

Go!

- Each player shuffles his or her cards.
- Keeping the cards facedown, players exchange cards.
- At the same time, players turn over all the cards given to them.
- Each player attempts to match each object with its measure.
- The player with more correct matches after 1 minute is the winner.

11-2 Problem-Solving Strategy

MAIN IDEA I will solve problems by drawing a diagram.

A frog and a cricket start at the same place and jump in the same direction. The table shows the distance they jump each time.

Animal	Length of Jump
frog	5 feet
cricket	3 feet

If the frog jumps 15 times and the cricket jumps 25 times, how many times will they land in the same place?

Understand

What facts do you know?

- The distance each animal jumps.

What do you need to find?

- The number of jumps each animal will make before landing in the same place.

Plan

Solve the problem by drawing a diagram.

Solve

Use your plan to solve the problem.

Draw a diagram to show how many jumps each animal makes.

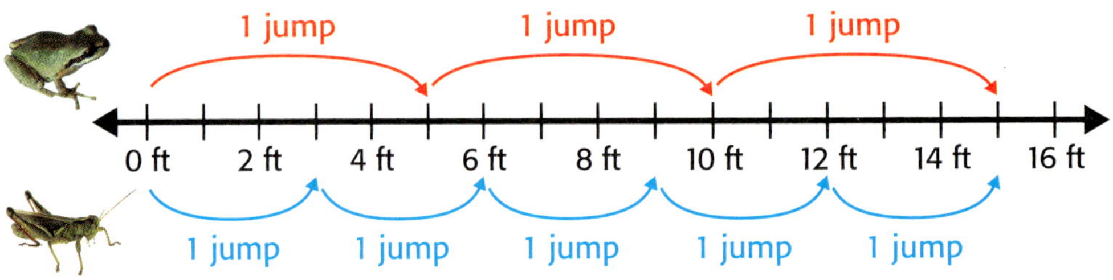

The animals meet after every 3 jumps by the frog and every 5 jumps by the cricket. The animals will land in the same place after the frog jumps three, six, nine, twelve, and fifteen times.

So, the animals will land in the same place 5 times.

Check

Look back. Divide the total number of feet jumped by the LCM of 3 and 5 to find how many times the animals are in the same place. Since $75 \div 15$ is 5, the answer is correct.

ANALYZE the Strategy

Refer to the problem on the previous page.

1. If the frog jumped 4 feet each time and the cricket jumped 3 feet each time, after how many jumps would they meet?

2. Why did it help to draw a diagram of the situation to solve the problem?

3. Can you think of a time when drawing a diagram was helpful to you?

4. Is there another strategy you could use to solve this problem?

PRACTICE the Strategy

EXTRA PRACTICE See page R30.

Solve. Use the *draw a diagram* strategy.

5. On her way home from school, Becky walked 2 blocks south to the corner store, 3 blocks east to visit a friend, and then 5 blocks north to go home. What direction is her home from the school?

6. **Measurement** Mr. Blackmon is building a fence around his garden. He wants to put fence posts every 3 feet, including each corner. How many total posts will be around the outside of the garden?

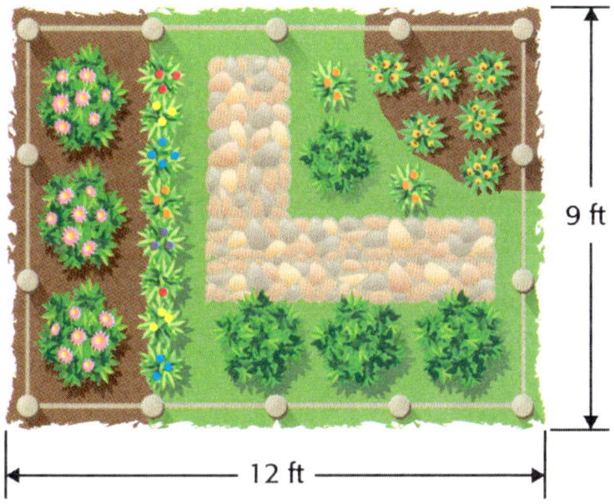

7. There are four booths in a row at the school carnival: face painting, ring toss, the dunk tank, and a cupcake walk. The dunk tank is on the far left. The ring toss is in between the face painting booth and the cupcake walk. The cupcake walk has only one neighbor. List the order of the booths from left to right.

8. For a school lunch, students must choose one entrée, one side dish, and one drink from the table shown. How many different school lunches can be purchased?

Entrée	Side dish	Drink
spaghetti	potatoes	milk
chicken	fruit cup	juice
hamburger	salad	

9. To score a touchdown, a football team needed to gain 35 yards. On their next five plays, the team gained 10 yards, lost 5 yards, lost 3 yards, gained 15 yards, and gained 10 yards. Did they score a touchdown? If not, how many more yards did they need to gain?

10. Kylie has 5 pictures to display on a shelf. She wants the picture of her family on the right end and the picture of her dog on the left end. How many ways can she arrange the pictures?

11. **WRITING IN MATH** Refer to Exercise 7. How did you use the *draw a diagram* strategy to solve this problem?

11-3 Units of Weight

GET READY to Learn

A newborn lion cub weighs about 5 pounds. How many ounces is this?

MAIN IDEA

I will convert customary units of weight.

New Vocabulary

weight
pound
ounce
ton

Math Online

macmillanmh.com

- Extra Examples
- Personal Tutor
- Self-Check Quiz

Weight is a measure of how heavy an object is. Customary units of weight are ounce, pound, and ton.

Customary Units of Weight — Key Concepts

1 **pound** (lb) = 16 **ounces** (oz)

1 **ton** (T) = 2,000 pounds

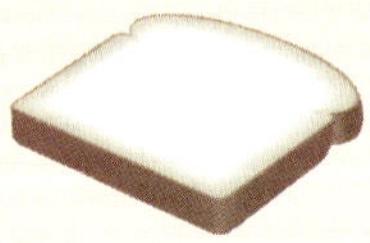

1 ounce

1 pound

1 ton

To convert a larger unit of weight to a smaller unit, *multiply*.

Real-World EXAMPLE — Convert Larger Units to Smaller Units

1 ANIMALS **Refer to the information above. How many ounces does a newborn lion cub weigh?**

5 lb = ■ oz — Larger units (pounds) are being converted to smaller units (ounces).

Since 1 pound = 16 ounces, multiply 5 by 16.

A newborn lion weighs about 5 × 16 or 80 ounces.

Real-World EXAMPLE — Parts of Units

2 **FOOD Lindsay's mother bought $1\frac{1}{2}$ pounds of hamburger. How many ounces of hamburger did she buy?**

Since $1\frac{1}{2}$ pounds means 1 pound + $\frac{1}{2}$ pound, convert each to ounces. Then add.

1 lb = 16 oz, $\frac{1}{2}$ lb = 8 oz

So, $1\frac{1}{2}$ pound = 16 + 8 or 24 ounces.

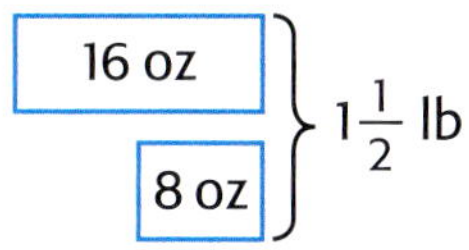

Lindsay's mother bought 24 ounces of hamburger.

To convert a smaller unit to a larger unit, *divide*.

EXAMPLE — Convert Smaller Units to Larger Units

3 **Convert 6,000 pounds to tons.**

6,000 lb = ■ T   Smaller units (pounds) are being converted to larger units (tons).

Since 2,000 pounds = 1 ton, divide 6,000 by 2,000.

6,000 ÷ 2,000 = 3

So, 6,000 pounds = 3 tons.

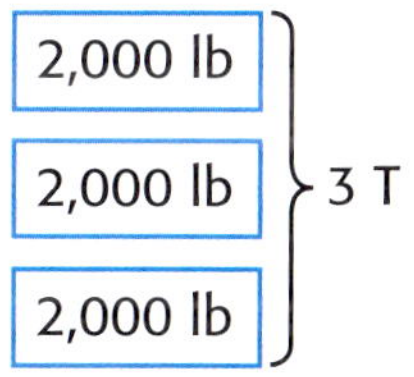

As with units of length, units of weight in the customary system can also be expressed using different units or as fractions.

EXAMPLE — Parts of Units

4 **Complete: 56 oz = ■ lb**

Since you are converting a smaller unit to a larger unit, divide.

56 ÷ 16 = 3 R8

The remainder 8 means there are 8 ounces out of a pound left over.

The fraction of a pound is $\frac{8}{16}$ or $\frac{1}{2}$.

So, 56 oz = 3 lb 8 oz or $3\frac{1}{2}$ lb.

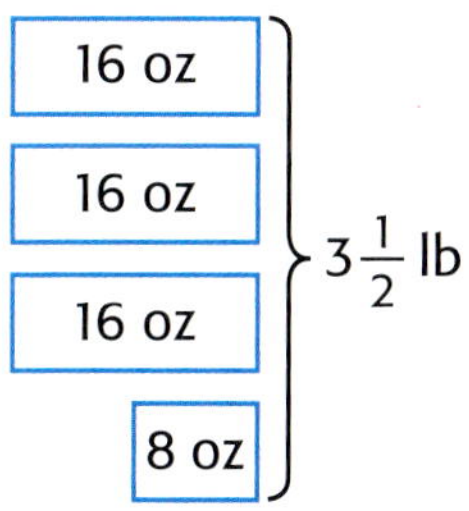

Remember

When converting measures, there will be more smaller units than larger units.

smaller units		larger units
6,000 lb	=	3 T
56 oz	=	$3\frac{1}{2}$ lb

CHECK What You Know

Complete. See Examples 1–4 (pp. 484–485)

1. 3 lb = ■ oz **2.** 32 oz = ■ lb **3.** 8,000 lb = ■ T

4. $2\frac{1}{2}$ lb = ■ oz **5.** 45 oz = ■ lb ■ oz **6.** 52 oz = ■ lb

7. A restaurant serves a 20-ounce steak. How much does the steak weigh in pounds and ounces?

8. Talk About It Explain how to convert from ounces to pounds.

Practice and Problem Solving

EXTRA PRACTICE See page R30.

Complete. See Examples 1–4 (pp. 484–485)

9. 96 oz = ■ lb **10.** 7 T = ■ lb **11.** 10,000 lb = ■ T

12. $2\frac{1}{2}$ T = ■ lb **13.** 50 oz = ■ lb ■ oz **14.** $1\frac{1}{4}$ lb = ■ oz

15. 7,000 lb = ■ T ■ lb **16.** 104 oz = ■ lb **17.** 1,500 lb = ■ T

Replace ● with <, >, or = to make a true statement. See Examples 1–4 (pp. 484–485)

18. 16 lb ● 246 oz **19.** 7,500 lb ● 4 T **20.** $\frac{1}{2}$ T ● 1,000 lb

21. 1,200 oz ● 72 lb **22.** 7 T 500 lb ● 7,300 oz **23.** 6 lb 11 oz ● 117 oz

24. Mia combines the items in the table to make potting soil. Order the items according to amount, from least to greatest.

Item	Amount
Topsoil	3 lb
Fertilizer	2 lb 9 oz
Bone meal	43 oz

25. How many $\frac{1}{4}$-pound bags of peanuts can be filled from a 5-pound bag of peanuts?

26. A puppy weighs 12 ounces. What fractional part of a pound is this?

H.O.T. Problems

27. **CHALLENGE** A baby weighs 8 pounds 10 ounces. If her weight doubles in 6 months, how much will she weigh?

28. **WRITING IN MATH** Tell which units of weight you would use to measure the following: a bag of oranges, a fork, and a submarine. Explain your reasoning.

TEST Practice

29. Ladonna is placing blocks side-by-side on a shelf, as shown below. Measure the width in inches of one block.

If the shelf is 1 foot long, what is the greatest number of blocks that Ladonna can stack on the shelf? **(Lesson 11-1)**

A 6 **C** 24

B 12 **D** 30

30. A rabbit weighs 4 pounds and 6 ounces. How many ounces does the rabbit weigh? **(Lesson 11-3)**

1 pound = 16 ounces

F 70 oz

G 64 oz

H 16 oz

J 6 oz

31. SHORT RESPONSE A cabin is 450 yards away from the lake. What is this distance in feet? **(Lesson 11-1)**

Spiral Review

32. A tennis ball is dropped from a height of 12 feet. It hits the ground and bounces up half as high as it fell. This is true for each additional bounce. What height does the ball reach on the fourth bounce? Use the *draw a diagram* strategy. **(Lesson 11-2)**

33. Measurement Vultures have been known to fly 37,000 feet above sea level. About how many miles high is this? **(Lesson 11-1)**

Estimate. (Lesson 10-6)

34. $3\frac{12}{16} + 8\frac{5}{8}$ **35.** $7\frac{5}{12} + 2\frac{7}{12}$ **36.** $8\frac{7}{10} - 6\frac{3}{10}$ **37.** $12\frac{2}{4} - 5\frac{6}{8}$

Replace each ● with <, >, or = to make a true statement. (Lesson 9-9)

38. $\frac{5}{8}$ ● $\frac{1}{2}$ **39.** $\frac{1}{3}$ ● $\frac{3}{12}$ **40.** $\frac{3}{18}$ ● $\frac{1}{6}$ **41.** $\frac{7}{10}$ ● $\frac{4}{5}$

42. Is $\frac{3}{10}$ closest to 0, $\frac{1}{2}$, or 1? Explain. **(Lesson 8-6)**

43. A CD display has 128 boxes on the bottom row. Each row has half the number of boxes as the row below. If there is one box on top, how many rows are there? **(Lesson 6-7)**

11-4 Units of Capacity

GET READY to Learn

Sondra tries to drink 9 cups of water each day. How many fluid ounces of water is 9 cups?

MAIN IDEA

I will convert customary units of capacity.

New Vocabulary

capacity
cup
fluid ounce
pint
quart
gallon

Math Online

macmillanmh.com
- Extra Examples
- Personal Tutor
- Self-Check Quiz

Capacity is the measure of how much a container can hold.

Customary Units of Capacity

Key Concepts

1 **cup** (c) = 8 **fluid ounces** (fl oz)

1 **pint** (pt) = 2 c = 16 fl oz

1 **quart** (qt) = 2 pt = 32 fl oz

1 **gallon** (gal) = 4 qt = 128 fl oz

1 fl oz | 1 cup | 1 pint | 1 quart | 1 gallon

Real-World EXAMPLE — Convert Units of Capacity

1 Refer to the information at the beginning of the lesson. How many fluid ounces of water is in 9 cups?

9 c = ■ fl oz — Larger units (cups) are being converted to smaller units (fluid ounces).

Since 1 cup = 8 fluid ounces, multiply 9 by 8.

So, 9 cups of water is equal to 9 × 8 or 72 fluid ounces.

Remember

Any substance that takes on the shape of its container, such as liquids, some solids, and air can be measured in units of capacity.

EXAMPLE Convert Units of Capacity

2 **Paco has 3 pints of juice plus 1 cup of juice. How many cups of juice does he have in all?**

First, convert 3 pints 1 cup to cups.

Since 1 pint = 2 cups, multiply 3 by 2.

$3 \times 2 = 6$

Then add the remaining 1 cup.

So, Paco has 6 + 1 or 7 cups of juice.

As with units of length and units of weight, units of capacity in the customary system can also be expressed as fractions.

EXAMPLE Parts of Units

3 **How many quarts are in 7 pints?**

7 pt = ■ qt

To convert a smaller unit to a larger unit, divide. Since 2 pints = 1 quart, divide 7 by 2.

$7 \div 2 = 3 \text{ R}1, \text{ or } 3\frac{1}{2}$

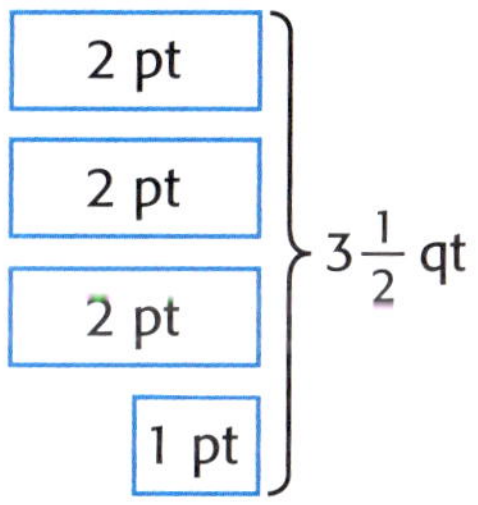

So, there are 3 quarts 1 pint or $3\frac{1}{2}$ quarts in 7 pints.

CHECK What You Know

Complete. See Examples 1–3 (pp. 488–489)

1. 3 c = ■ fl oz

2. 4 qt = ■ c

3. 18 pt = ■ qt

4. 50 gal = ■ qt

5. 16 pt 1 c = ■ c

6. 68 fl oz = ■ c

7. 5 qt = ■ gal ■ qt

8. 75 fl oz = ■ c ■ fl oz

9. The cafeteria sells lemonade in glasses that hold 12 fluid ounces. How many glasses can be filled with 3 gallons of lemonade?

10. **Talk About It** Explain how to convert from fluid ounces to pints.

Practice and Problem Solving

EXTRA PRACTICE See page R30.

Complete. See Examples 1–3 (pp. 488–489)

11. 5 c = ■ fl oz

12. 2 gal = ■ fl oz

13. 16 fl oz = ■ c

14. 25 gal = ■ qt

15. 19 c = ■ fl oz

16. 50 c = ■ pt

17. 2 gal 3 qt = ■ qt

18. 2 qt 3 c = ■ c

19. 5 c = ■ pt ■ c

20. 17 fl oz = ■ c ■ fl oz

21. 19 qt = ■ gal ■ qt

22. 18 qt = ■ gal

23. 7 c = ■ pt

24. Zach had 1 quart of milk. He used 1 pint to make pancakes and 1 cup to make scrambled eggs. How many cups of milk were left?

25. The average person drinks 1 pint of milk a day. At this rate, how many gallons will a person drink in a leap year (366 days)?

26. The table shows the amount of paint left in each jar. Which jar contains the greatest amount of paint? the least?

Jar	Amount
blue	2 pt 4 oz
purple	5 cups
green	39 fl oz

27. **Measurement** A bucket has $1\frac{1}{2}$ gallons of water. Is this amount *greater, than less than,* or *equal to* 6 quarts? Explain.

H.O.T. Problems

28. **FIND THE ERROR** Jasmine and Pablo are converting 32 cups to quarts. Who is correct? Explain.

29. **CHALLENGE** Convert the following to the greatest whole number units of capacity.

200 fl oz = ■ gal ■ qt ■ pt ■ c ■ fl oz

30. **WRITING IN MATH** Write about a real-world situation that can be solved by converting between customary units of capacity. Then solve.

CHAPTER 11 Mid-Chapter Check

Lessons 11-1 through 11-4

Complete. (Lesson 11-1)

1. 84 in. = ■ ft **2.** 2 mi = ■ ft

3. 41 in. = ■ ft ■ in. **4.** 25 ft = ■ yd

Choose an appropriate unit to measure the length of each. (Lesson 11-1)

5. height of giraffe

6. length of soccer field

7. **MULTIPLE CHOICE** Alexander is 32 inches tall. His brother Josh is 4 feet tall. What fractional part of Josh's height is Alexander's height? (Lesson 11-1)

A $\frac{1}{8}$ **C** $\frac{1}{2}$

B $\frac{1}{4}$ **D** $\frac{2}{3}$

8. Five toy remote cars are in a race. Car 2 is just ahead of Car 3. Car 3 is two places behind Car 4. Car 4 is a few seconds behind the leader, Car 1. Car 5 is in last place. Order the cars from first to last place. Use the *draw a diagram* strategy.

Complete. (Lesson 11-3)

9. $2\frac{1}{2}$ lb = ■ oz **10.** 80 oz = ■ lb

11. 35 oz = ■ lb ■ oz **12.** 7,500 lb = ■ T

13. Refer to the sign at the right. What is the weight limit in pounds? (Lesson 11-3)

14. A motorcycle weighs 500 pounds. What fractional part of a ton is this? (Lesson 11-3)

Complete. (Lesson 11-4)

15. 10 gal = ■ pt

16. 7 qt = ■ gal ■ qt

17. 28 fl oz = ■ c

18. The table below shows the bottles of cleaning products that Lucas bought. Which cleaner contains the greatest amount? the least? (Lesson 11-4)

Cleaner	Amount
Rug	62 fl oz
Bathroom	3 pt 12 fl oz
Window	2 qt

19. **MULTIPLE CHOICE** What is the total number of cups in 7 quarts? (Lesson 11-4)

1 pint = 2 cups
1 quart = 4 cups

F 6 cups

G 8 cups

H 14 cups

J 28 cups

20. **WRITING IN MATH** What is the difference between weight and capacity? Use objects to explain your answer. (Lessons 11-3 and 11-4)

11-5 Units of Time

MAIN IDEA

I will convert units of time.

Math Online

macmillanmh.com
- Extra Examples
- Personal Tutor
- Self-Check Quiz

GET READY to Learn

Joe spends 1 hour a day doing his chores. He washes dishes, takes out the trash, and walks the dog.

Units of Time

Key Concepts

1 minute (min) = 60 seconds (s)

1 hour (h) = 60 min

1 day (d) = 24 h

1 week (wk) = 7 d

1 year (y) = 52 wk = 12 months (mo)

The steps that you use to convert units of length, weight, and capacity can be used to convert units of time.

Real-World EXAMPLE — Convert Units of Time

1 MEASUREMENT Joe walked his dog for 15 minutes before he went to school. How many seconds did he walk his dog?

15 min = ■ s

To convert larger units of time to smaller units, multiply. Since 1 minute = 60 seconds, multiply 15 by 60.

$15 \times 60 = 900$

So, Joe walked his dog for 900 seconds.

Use mental math to check the answer.

10 min = 10×60 or 600 s   20 min = 20×60 or 1,200 s

Since 900 seconds is between 600 and 1,200 seconds, the answer is reasonable.

To convert smaller units of time to larger units, divide.

EXAMPLE — Use Different Units of Measure

2 Complete: 56 hours = ■ days ■ hours.

Since 24 hours = 1 day, divide 56 by 24 to find the number of days.

$56 \div 24 = 2 \text{ R}8$

2 R8 means 2 whole days and 8 hours of another day. So, 56 hours = 2 days 8 hours.

As with other units of measure, units of time can also be expressed using fractions.

EXAMPLE — Use Fractions in Measures

3 How many hours are 150 minutes?

150 min = ■ h

To convert a smaller unit to a larger unit, divide. Since 60 minutes = 1 hour, divide 150 by 60 to find the number of hours.

$150 \div 60 = 2 \text{ R}30$

2 R30 means 2 whole hours and 30 minutes of another hour. So, 150 minutes = 2 hours 30 minutes or $2\frac{1}{2}$ hours.

CHECK What You Know

Complete. See Examples 1–3 (pp. 492–493)

1. 3 h = ■ min

2. 7 d = ■ h

3. 420 s = ■ min

4. 5 h = ■ s

5. 30 mo = ■ y

6. 84 h = ■ d

7. 500 s = ■ min ■ s

8. 42 mo = ■ y ■ mo

9. Some lungfish can live up to 4 years without water by forming a cocoon around their bodies. How many months can they live without water?

10. Talk About It Would you multiply or divide to find the number of seconds in 3 minutes? Explain.

Practice and Problem Solving

EXTRA PRACTICE See page R30.

Complete. See Examples 1–3 (pp. 492–493)

11. 840 s = ■ min
12. 3 mo = ■ y
13. 8 wk = ■ d
14. 12 min = ■ s
15. 72 h = ■ d
16. 252 d = ■ wk
17. 24 h = ■ min
18. 1,095 d = ■ y
19. 270 min = ■ h
20. 156 h = ■ d
21. 36,000 s = ■ h
22. 28 mo = ■ y

23. 135 min = ■ h ■ min
24. 200 s = ■ min ■ s
25. 423 d = ■ y ■ d
26. 50 d = ■ wk ■ d
27. 1 d 2 h = ■ min
28. 8 wk 2 d = ■ d

29. **Measurement** Katija spent 40 minutes raking leaves. What fraction of an hour did she spend raking leaves?

30. Jasper recorded 1 hour and 14 minutes on a CD. The CD can hold 80 minutes of music. How many seconds of recording time are left?

31. Lamar and Jesse are running in a race. Lamar's time was 90 seconds. Jesse finished 15 seconds later. What were their times in minutes?

32. Kari and her friend were comparing their number of days off for summer break. Kari has 85 days off and her friend has 7 weeks and 2 days off. Is there a difference between the number of days off? Explain.

Data File

All United States human space flight missions are launched from the John F. Kennedy Space Center in eastern Florida. The longest space shuttle mission in United States history was the Columbia STS-80. It was launched on November 19, 1996. This mission lasted 423 hours.

33. How many days and hours did this mission last?

34. Write the number of days that this mission lasted as a mixed number in simplest form.

H.O.T. Problems

35. OPEN ENDED Write a word problem that includes a length of time that is between 4 hours and 5 hours. Then convert the time to minutes.

36. WHICH ONE DOESN'T BELONG? Identify the time that does not belong with the other three. Explain your reasoning.

2 h 104 min	2 h 114 min	3 h 54 min	234 min

37. WRITING IN MATH Explain the steps you take to convert hours to seconds.

TEST Practice

38. Mrs. Westin bought 3 gallons of apple cider for her class. What is the total number of pints in 3 gallons? **(Lesson 11-4)**

1 quart	= 2 pints
1 gallon	= 8 pints

A 8 pints
B 10 pints
C 16 pints
D 24 pints

39. Which relationship between the units of time is correct? **(Lesson 11-5)**

F One day is $\frac{1}{24}$ of one hour.

G One hour is $\frac{1}{24}$ of one day.

H One second is $\frac{1}{60}$ of one hour.

J One hour is $\frac{1}{60}$ of one second.

Spiral Review

40. Thomas is making a cake. The liquids that he uses are shown at the right. One cup is equal to 8 fluid ounces. What is the total number of cups of liquids? **(Lesson 11-4)**

Liquid	Amount (fl oz)
Milk	12
Vegetable Oil	4

Complete. (Lessons 11-3 and 11-4)

41. 28 c = ■ pt

42. 9 qt = ■ c

43. 6 lb = ■ oz

44. 7 T = ■ lb

45. Tell whether the number represented by the model is prime or composite. Explain. **(Lesson 9-2)**

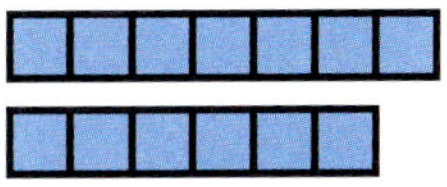

11-6 Problem-Solving Investigation

MAIN IDEA I will choose the best strategy to solve a problem.

P.S.I. TEAM +

BETHANY: They are giving away prizes at the grand opening of the CD Music Shop. At 7:00, there were two people in the line. At 7:15 when two more people arrived, there were 4 people in line. At 7:30, 4 more people arrived so there were 8 people in line. Every 15 minutes as many people as were already in line arrived.

YOUR MISSION: Find how many people were in line when the store opened at 8:00.

Understand You know how many people arrived every 15 minutes. You need to know how many people were in line when the store opened at 8:00.

Plan Make a table to show how many people are in line.

Solve

Time (A.M.)	Number Who Arrive	Number in Line
7:00	2	2
7:15	2	4
7:30	4	8
7:45	8	16
8:00	16	32

There were 32 people in line at 8:00.

Check Look back. Add the number of people who arrive.

$2 + 2 + 4 + 8 + 16 = 32$

So, the answer is correct.

Mixed Problem Solving

EXTRA PRACTICE
See page R31.

Use any strategy shown below to solve each problem.

PROBLEM-SOLVING STRATEGIES
- Look for a pattern.
- Draw a picture.
- Work backward.
- Draw a diagram.

1. The table shows the choices for ordering a sundae at the Ice Cream Shop. How many different sundaes could be made using one choice from ice cream and one choice from sauce?

Ice Cream Shop	
Ice cream	vanilla, chocolate, strawberry
Sauce	chocolate, caramel, strawberry
Toppings	sprinkles, nuts, cherries
Cones	sugar, waffle

2. Tamika left her house and rode 3 miles east and then 2 miles south to the library. From there she rode 1 mile west and 4 miles north to Jodi's house. Jodi and Tamika rode 1 mile south and 2 miles west to the park. How far north was Tamika from her house?

3. A number is divided by 6. Next the quotient is multiplied by 2. Then 4 is added to the product. If the result is 12, what is the number?

4. Alana is 4 years older than her brother Ernie. Ernie is 2 years older than their sister Amelia. Amelia is 10 years younger than their brother Mazo. If Mazo is 17 years old, how old is Alana?

5. Deidre is making a necklace by alternating long and short beads. The long beads are 0.5 inch long, and the short beads are 0.25 inch long. She starts and ends with a long bead, and the necklace is 14 inches long. How many of each size bead does she use?

6. Lake Superior is 531 feet deeper than Lake Ontario. Lake Ontario is 592 feet deeper than Lake Erie. Lake Erie is 210 feet deep. How deep is Lake Superior?

7. Annie and Max are putting roses into vases. For every 4 red roses, they put half as many white roses. If they put 18 roses in the vase altogether, how many are white?

8. **Algebra** Austin took the same amount of time each day to walk his dog last week. The table shows the time he left his house and the time he arrived home on four days. If the pattern continues, what time will he arrive home on Friday?

Day	Time Left Home	Time Arrived Back Home
Monday	4:32 P.M.	5:00 P.M.
Tuesday	6:05 P.M.	6:33 P.M.
Wednesday	7:15 P.M.	7:43 P.M.
Thursday	5:20 P.M.	5:48 P.M.
Friday	6:12 P.M.	■

9. **WRITING IN MATH** Gino has \$3.75 after spending \$4.75 on lunch and \$1.50 on bus fare. How much money did Gino have originally? Which strategy would you use to solve this problem? Explain your reasoning. Then solve.

Problem Solving in Health

Soccer Rules!

Soccer is the most popular sport in the world, although it's called football in every country except the United States. The men's World Cup has been played every four years since 1930. The women's World Cup has been played every four years since 1991. Teams from all over the world compete to win the most exciting sports tournament on Earth.

If you're serious about playing soccer, who knows—maybe you'll be on a World Cup team!

Did You Know?

In 2006, about 5 billion people watched the World Cup.

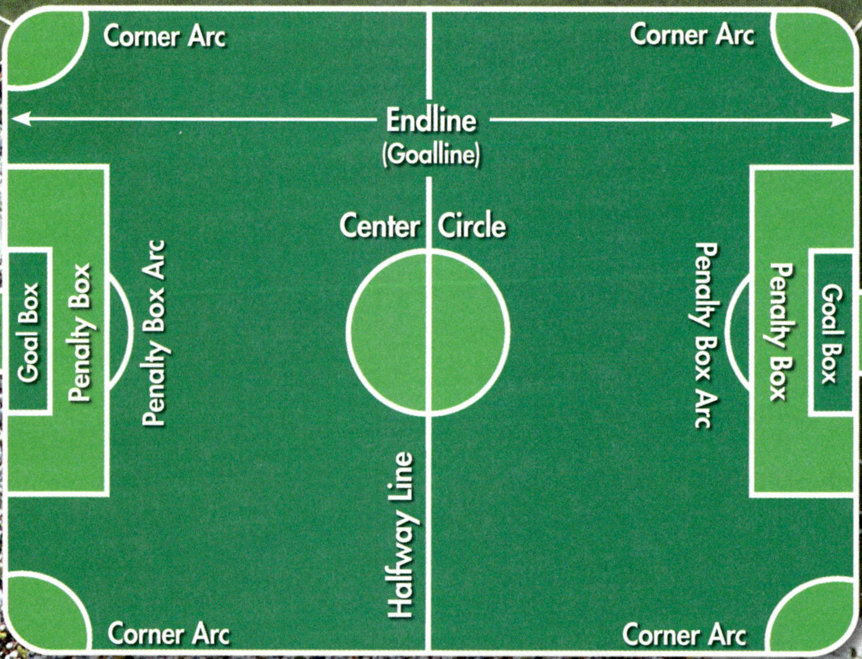

Youth Soccer Guidelines

Age (years)	Field Size (yards)	Weight of Ball (ounces)	Length of Game
14	60 x 100	15	two 45-minute halves
12	50 x 80	12	two 30-minute halves
10	40 x 70	12	two 25-minute halves
8	25 x 50	11	four 12-minute quarters
6	15 x 30	11	four 8-minute quarters

Source: U.S. Youth Soccer

Real-World Math

Use the information in the above table to solve each problem.

1. How many feet longer is the field used by 14-year-olds than the field used by 10-year-olds?

2. Suppose on one Sunday, a referee officiated three 8-year-old soccer games. How much time did the official spend refereeing, not including breaks?

3. A soccer game with 14-year-old players began at 9:30 A.M. on a Saturday. If the players rested at half-time for 15 minutes, how long was the game?

4. There are 16 players on a youth soccer team. Each player had a water bottle with $1\frac{1}{2}$ quarts of water for the game. How many gallons of water did the players have altogether?

5. A coach of a team of 10-year-olds has a bag of 6 soccer balls. What is the weight in pounds of the 6 soccer balls?

11-7 Elapsed Time

GET READY to Learn

Belinda started babysitting at 6:45 P.M. She finished at 10:55 P.M. How long did Belinda babysit?

6:45

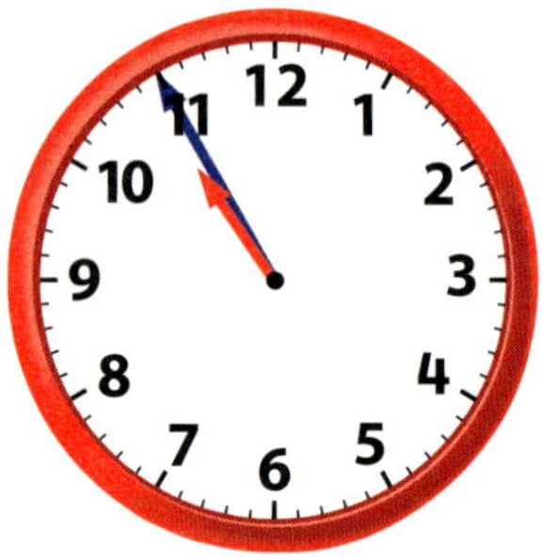

10:55

MAIN IDEA

I will add and subtract measures of time.

New Vocabulary

elapsed time

Math Online

macmillanmh.com
- Extra Examples
- Personal Tutor
- Self-Check Quiz

Elapsed time is the difference in time between the start and the end of an event.

Real-World EXAMPLE — Elapsed Time

1 **MEASUREMENT** **Refer to the information above. How long did Belinda babysit?**

Step 1 Write the times in units of hours and minutes.

Ending time:	10:55 P.M.	→	10 hours 55 minutes
Starting time:	6:45 P.M.	→	6 hours 45 minutes

Step 2 Subtract the starting time from the ending time. Make sure you subtract hours from hours and minutes from minutes.

	10 hours 55 minutes
	− 6 hours 45 minutes
Elapsed time:	4 hours 10 minutes

So, Belinda babysat 4 hours and 10 minutes.

Check

4 hours 10 minutes
+ 6 hours 45 minutes
10 hours 55 minutes

Sometimes it is necessary to rename the units before subtracting.

Real-World EXAMPLE — Rename Units of Time

2 **Ben started to do his homework at 7:30 P.M. He finished at 9:05 P.M. How long did Ben study?**

~~9~~ (8) hours ~~5~~ (60) minutes	→		8 hours 65 minutes
− 7 hours 30 minutes			− 7 hours 30 minutes
			1 hour 35 minutes

Ben studied for 1 hour 35 minutes.

Real-World EXAMPLE — From P.M. to A.M.

Remember

To find elapsed time from P.M. to A.M., remember to count through midnight.

3 **Dr. Sedaca arrived at work at 10:03 P.M. and went home at 7:27 A.M. How long was her shift?**

10:03 P.M. +	57 min	→ 11:00 P.M.	Count 1 hour and 57 minutes until 12 A.M.
11:00 P.M. +	1 h	→ 12:00 A.M.	
12:00 A.M. +	7 h 27 min	→ 7:27 A.M.	Count 7 hours and 27 minutes until 7:27 A.M.
	8 h 84 min		

8 h + 84 min = 9 h 24 min

84 min = 60 min + 24 min
= 1 h 24 min

So, Dr. Sedaca's shift was 9 hours 24 minutes long.

CHECK What You Know

Find the elapsed time. See Examples 1–3 (pp. 500–501)

1. 6:14 A.M. to 10:30 A.M.

2. 8:18 P.M. to 9:22 P.M.

3. 11:50 A.M. to 2:04 P.M.

4. 7:22 A.M. to 9:20 A.M.

5. 11:30 P.M. to 2:14 A.M.

6. 3:40 P.M. to 6:09 P.M.

7. Kevin finished walking a trail at 11:44 A.M., and Rogelio finished at 12:16 P.M. How many minutes faster was Kevin than Rogelio?

8. Quan leaves for school at 7:15 A.M. He gets back home from school at 3:45 P.M. How long is he away from his house on a school day?

9. **Measurement** An all night movie marathon begins at 9:30 P.M. The last movie ends at 5:27 A.M. How long is the movie marathon?

10. Talk About It Compare how to find the elapsed time from 8:30 A.M. to 11:30 A.M. and from 10:30 P.M. to 1:30 A.M.

Practice and Problem Solving

EXTRA PRACTICE See page R31.

Find the elapsed time. See Examples 1–3 (pp. 500–501)

11. 4:00 A.M. to 10:23 A.M.

12. 9:20 A.M. to 11:58 A.M.

13. 1:27 P.M. to 5:30 P.M.

14. 8:15 P.M. to 1:11 A.M.

15. 3:15 A.M. to 11:00 A.M.

16. 10:58 A.M. to 5:29 P.M.

17. 9:15 A.M. to 3:20 P.M.

18. 10:30 P.M. to 7:15 A.M.

19. Tyson starts talking on the phone at 6:29 P.M. He finishes 55 minutes later. At what time did he finish talking on the phone?

20. Sed left his house at 4:58 P.M. to be at band practice at 5:45 P.M. How much time does he have to get to practice?

21. Alejandra was selling cookies at a bake sale. She started at 8:13 A.M. and finished at 5:47 P.M. How long did Alejandra sell cookies?

22. Baltimore, Maryland, is two hours ahead of Cheyenne, Wyoming. Griselda left at 3:42 P.M. She arrived in Cheyenne at 9:58 P.M. How long was her flight?

23. Part of a bus schedule is shown below. Which trip from Springdale to Cheswick takes the most time?

Bus Schedule				
Leave Springdale	6:52 A.M.	7:45 A.M.	8:43 A.M.	9:58 A.M.
Arrive in Cheswick	7:16 A.M.	8:20 A.M.	9:13 A.M.	10:23 A.M.

H.O.T. Problems

24. OPEN ENDED Write a beginning time and an ending time so that the elapsed time is 2 hours 16 minutes.

25. FIND THE ERROR Megan and Anita are finding the elapsed time from 2:30 P.M. to 5:46 P.M. Who is correct? Explain.

Megan

$$\begin{array}{r} 5\text{ h }46\text{ min} \\ +\ 2\text{ h }30\text{ min} \\ \hline 8\text{ h }16\text{ min} \end{array}$$

Anita

$$\begin{array}{r} 5\text{ h }46\text{ min} \\ -\ 2\text{ h }30\text{ min} \\ \hline 3\text{ h }16\text{ min} \end{array}$$

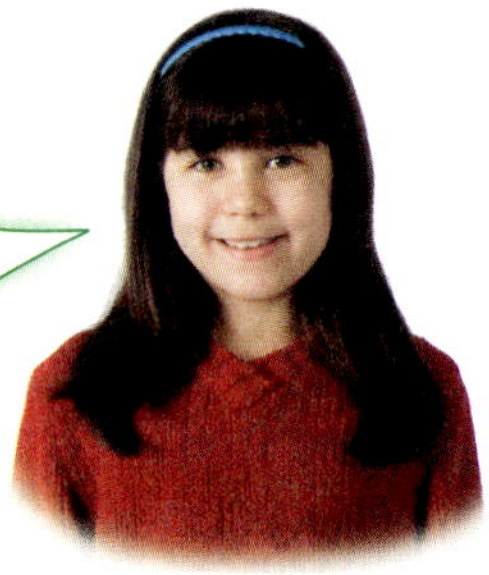

26. WRITING IN ▸MATH Write a story that takes place all in one day, using the times 6:45 A.M., 1:07 P.M., and 8:39 P.M. Include the elapsed times in your story.

TEST Practice

27. The Williams family spent 4 hours at a theme park. What fractional part of a day is 4 hours? (Lesson 11-5)

A $\frac{1}{12}$

B $\frac{1}{6}$

C $\frac{1}{4}$

D $\frac{1}{3}$

28. Jordan went to the pool from 11:20 A.M. to 3:45 P.M., as shown on the clocks below.

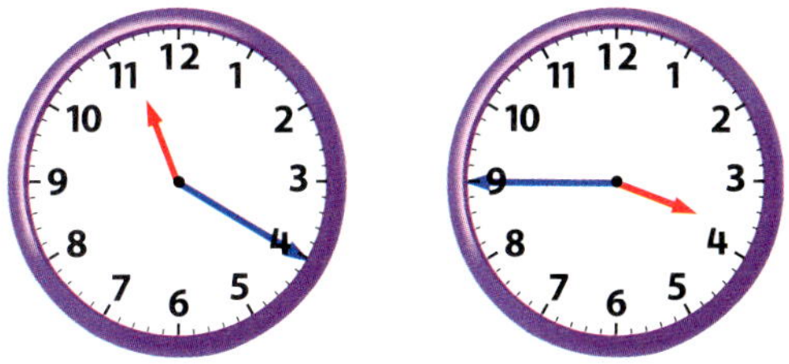

How many hours and minutes was Jordan at the pool? (Lesson 11-7)

F 4 h 5 min **H** 4 h 20 min

G 4 h 15 min **J** 4 h 25 min

Spiral Review

29. Mrs. Spring needs to buy 2 dozen muffins for a family brunch. According to the sign, how much will she save by buying the muffins by the dozen instead of individually? (Lesson 11-6)

Complete. (Lesson 11-5)

30. 360 s = ▪ min **31.** 7 wk = ▪ d

32. 12 h = ▪ min **33.** 135 min = ▪ h ▪ min

34. Emily has a 4-foot long board to make some shelves for her desk. Her father cuts two shelves, each 19 inches long, from the board. How long is the piece of the board that is left? (Lesson 11-1)

Add. Write each sum in simplest form. Check your answer by drawing a picture. (Lesson 10-1)

35. $\frac{1}{3} + \frac{1}{3}$ **36.** $\frac{2}{5} + \frac{1}{5}$

37. $\frac{5}{16} + \frac{7}{16}$ **38.** $\frac{9}{10} + \frac{3}{10}$

Write each improper fraction as a mixed number. (Lesson 8-2)

39. $\frac{9}{2}$ **40.** $\frac{13}{4}$ **41.** $\frac{20}{3}$ **42.** $\frac{27}{5}$

CHAPTER 11

Study Guide and Review

Math Online macmillanmh.com
- STUDY TO GO
- Vocabulary Review

FOLDABLES® Study Organizer GET READY to Study

Be sure the following Big Ideas are written in your Foldable.

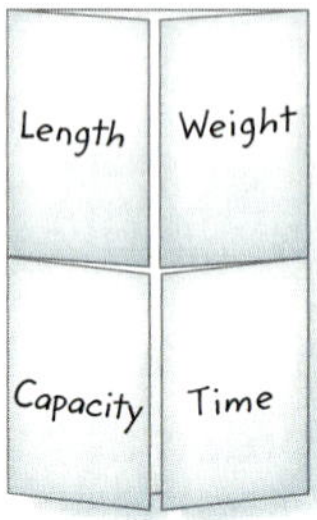

Key Concepts

Customary Units of Length (p. 477)

1 foot (ft) = 12 inches (in.)

1 yard (yd) = 3 ft or 36 in.

1 mile (mi) = 5,280 ft or 1,760 yd

Customary Units of Weight (p. 484)

1 pound (lb) = 16 ounces (oz)

1 ton (T) = 2,000 pounds

Customary Units of Capacity (p. 488)

1 cup (c) = 8 fluid ounces (fl oz)

1 pint (pt) = 2 c = 16 fl oz

1 quart (qt) = 2 pt = 32 fl oz

1 gallon (gal) = 4 qt = 128 fl oz

Units of Time (p. 492)

1 minute (min) = 60 seconds (s)

1 hour (h) = 60 min

1 day (d) = 24 h

1 week (wk) = 7 d

1 year (y) = 52 wk = 12 months (mo)

Key Vocabulary

capacity (p. 488)
customary units (p. 477)
elapsed time (p. 500)
length (p. 475)
weight (p. 484)

Vocabulary Check

State whether each sentence is *true* or *false*. If *false*, replace the underlined word or number to make a true sentence.

1. Capacity is the amount that a container can hold.
2. The inch, foot, yard, and mile are called metric units.
3. Three feet equals 1 yard.
4. One gallon equals 4 pints.
5. Fluid ounce is a customary measure of weight.
6. To convert from feet to inches, divide by 12.
7. A reasonable estimate for the height of an oak tree is 30 feet.
8. Elapsed time is the amount of time that passes between two events.
9. To change 3 days to hours, multiply 3 by 60.

Lesson-by-Lesson Review

11-1 Units of Length (pp. 477–480)

Example 1
Convert 54 inches to feet.

To change a smaller unit to a larger unit, divide.

Since 12 in. = 1 ft, divide 54 by 12.

54 ÷ 12 = 4 R6

4 R6 means 4 feet and 6 inches of another foot.

So, 54 inches = 4 feet 6 inches or

$4\frac{1}{2}$ feet.

Complete.

10. 8 ft = ■ in.

11. 7 yd = ■ ft

12. 32 in. = ■ ft ■ in.

13. 7,920 ft = ■ mi

14. Which unit of length would you use to measure the distance between two fire stations?

15. The bill of an Australian pelican can be as long as 18 inches. Write this measure in feet and inches.

11-2 Problem-Solving Strategy: Draw a Diagram (pp. 482–483)

Example 2
Mrs. Juarez left her house and drove 5 miles north to the bank, 6 miles west to the post office, 3 miles south to the store, 2 miles east to the cleaners, and 2 miles south to the school. How many miles is she from her house?

Solve by drawing a diagram.

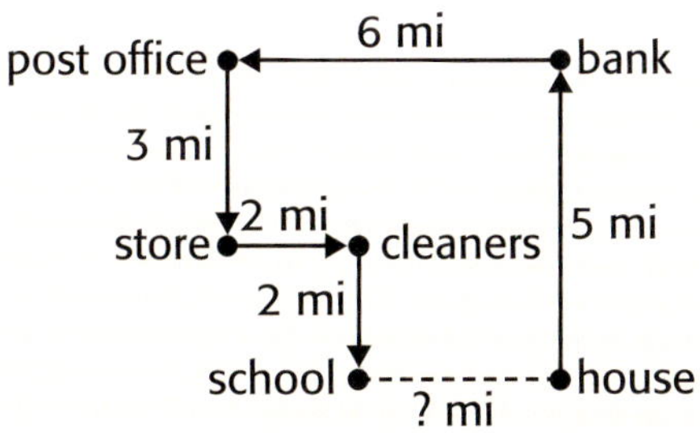

Mrs. Juarez is 4 miles from her house.

16. Mr. Muhammad rented a 5-gallon smoothie machine for a carnival. The smoothies will be sold in two sizes: 12 fluid ounces and 20 fluid ounces. Find two different combinations of both drink sizes that equal 5 gallons.

17. At a bakery, a tray of cookies is taken out of the oven every 10 minutes, and a pan of brownies is taken out every 25 minutes. At 1:00 P.M., both are taken out of the oven. How many trays of cookies will be taken out before both are taken out of the oven at the same time? What time will it be?

Study Guide and Review

11-3 Units of Weight (pp. 484–487)

Example 3
In two weeks, Teresa feeds her cat 56 ounces of cat food. How many pounds of cat food does she feed her cat?

To change a smaller unit to a larger unit, divide. Since 16 oz = 1 lb, divide 56 by 16.

$56 \div 16 = 3$ R8

3 R8 means 3 pounds and 8 ounces of another pound.

So, 56 ounces = 3 pounds 8 ounces or $3\frac{1}{2}$ pounds.
Teresa feeds her cat $3\frac{1}{2}$ pounds of cat food.

Complete.

18. 112 oz = ■ lb

19. 12,000 lb = ■ T

20. 36 oz = ■ lb ■ oz

21. 7,000 lb = ■ T

22. A 1-pound package of butter has four sticks. How many ounces does each stick weigh?

11-4 Units of Capacity (pp. 488–490)

Example 4
How many pints are in 3 gallons?

3 gal = ■ pt

To convert a larger unit to a smaller unit, multiply. Since 1 gal = 8 pt, multiply 3 by 8.

$3 \times 8 = 24$

So, there are 24 pints in 3 gallons.

Complete.

23. 14 qt = ■ pt

24. 5 c = ■ fl oz

25. 90 fl oz = ■ c ■ fl oz

26. 19 qt = ■ gal

27. A container has 24 fluid ounces of hot chocolate. Is 24 fluid ounces *greater than*, *less than*, or *equal to* $1\frac{1}{2}$ pints? Explain.

11-5 Units of Time (pp. 492–495)

Example 5
Complete: 200 minutes = ■ hours.

To change from a smaller unit to a larger unit, divide. Since 1 min = 60 s, divide 200 by 60.

200 ÷ 60 = 3 R20

3 R20 means 3 whole hours and 20 minutes of another hour. So,

200 minutes = 3 hours 20 minutes or $3\frac{1}{3}$ hours.

Complete.

28. 5 h = ■ min

29. 420 s = ■ min

30. 2 wk = ■ d

31. 580 min = ■ h ■ min

32. Laura practices the piano 30 minutes every day. How many hours a week is this?

11-6 Problem-Solving Investigation: Choose a Strategy (pp. 496–497)

Example 6
An electronics store is having a grand opening in which every 15th customer receives a free CD and every 25th customer receives a free DVD. Which customer will be first one to receive a CD and a DVD?

Make a table to solve.

Multiples of 15	15	30	45	60	75
Multiples of 25	25	50	75	100	125

So, the 75th customer receives a CD and a DVD.

33. A forest fire covered 51 square miles by Friday. This is 3 less than 3 times the number of square miles it covered on Wednesday. How many square miles did it cover on Wednesday?

34. A new train glides along a magnetic field. The train takes 5 hours to travel 1,200 miles. How far can it travel in 2 hours?

35. The Eagles won 13 games and lost 5 games. The Gators won 12 games and lost 4 games. Which team won a greater fraction of their games?

11-7 Elapsed Time (pp. 500–503)

Example 7

Delmar started washing his bike at 4:16 P.M. He finished at 4:57 P.M. How long did it take Delmar to wash his bike?

Step 1 Write the times in units of hours and minutes.

End: 4:57 P.M. → 4 h 57 min

Start: 4:16 P.M. → 4 h 16 min

Step 2 Subtract the time starting from the ending time.

	4 hours 57 minutes
	– 4 hours 16 minutes
Elapsed time:	0 hours 41 minutes

So, Delmar spent 41 minutes washing his bike.

Example 8

Find the elapsed time from 2:20 P.M. to 9:15 P.M.

Step 1 Write the times in units of hours and minutes.

End: 9:15 P.M. → 9 h 15 min

Start: 2:20 P.M. → 2 h 20 min

Step 2 Subtract the starting time from the ending time.

9 h 15 min	→	8 h 75 min
– 2 h 20 min		– 2 h 20 min
		6 h 55 min

The elapsed time is 6 hours 55 minutes.

Find each elapsed time.

36. 4:15 P.M. to 5:40 P.M.

37. 4:45 A.M. to 8:05 A.M.

38. 12:17 A.M. to 1:57 A.M.

39. 8:34 P.M. to 3:08 A.M.

40. 3:16 P.M. to 9:26 A.M.

41. A turkey is put into the oven at 11:25 A.M. The turkey was done at 4:10 P.M. How long did it take the turkey to cook?

42. Erica arrived at school at 8:15 A.M. She left the house at 7:48 A.M. How long did it take Erica to get to school?

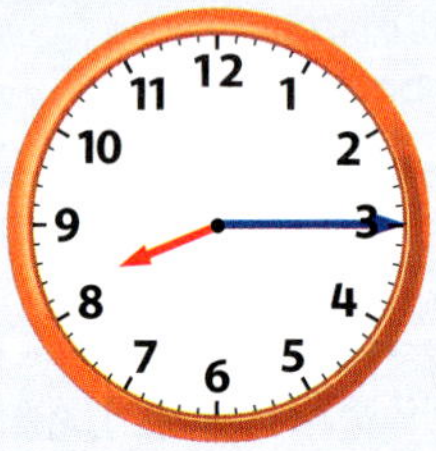

43. Mr. Torre makes some bread for dinner using his bread machine. If he starts his bread at 2:45 P.M. and it is done at 5:30 P.M., how long did it take to make the bread?

Chapter 11

Chapter Test

Math Online macmillanmh.com
• Chapter Test

Complete.

1. 132 in. = ■ ft
2. 4 mi = ■ yd
3. 64 in. = ■ ft
4. 500 ft = ■ yd ■ ft
5. Mariah is filling a wading pool with water. Every two minutes, the water level increases by $1\frac{1}{2}$ inches. If the pool is 9 inches deep, how long will it take to fill the pool to its capacity?

Complete.

6. 96 oz = ■ lb
7. 60 oz = ■ lb ■ oz
8. 1,500 lb = ■ T
9. 22 qt = ■ gal ■ qt
10. **MULTIPLE CHOICE** A recipe for punch is shown below.

Ingredient	Amount
fruit juice	1 gal
lemon-lime soda	3 qt

Suppose you want to double the recipe. How many gallons of punch will the recipe make?

A $1\frac{3}{4}$ gal
B 3 gal
C $3\frac{1}{2}$ gal
D 14 qt

11. Mr. Roland fences in a 20-foot by 25-foot section of his yard for his dog. He puts fence posts every 5 feet and at the corners. How many posts are there?
12. Manny bought $2\frac{1}{2}$ pounds of coleslaw and 42 ounces of potato salad. Which food item weighed more?

Complete.

13. 12 wk = ■ d
14. 585 min = ■ h
15. 84 h = ■ d ■ h
16. Michelle leaves for school at 7:50 A.M. She gets home at 4:10 P.M. How long is Michelle gone from home?

Find each elapsed time.

17. 7:39 A.M. to 11:50 A.M.
18. 10:30 P.M. to 5:08 A.M.
19. **MULTIPLE CHOICE** Elijah leaves his house in the morning at the time shown on the clock.

He walks for 15 minutes to his friend's house. They play two video games for 25 minutes each game. Then they go outside. At what time do they go outside?

F 10:10 A.M.
G 10:25 A.M.
H 10:30 A.M.
J 10:35 A.M.

20. **WRITING IN ▸MATH** When you are finding the elapsed time between two events, why is it important to note whether the times are A.M. or P.M.?

Chapter 11 Test Practice

Cumulative, Chapters 1–11

Math Online macmillanmh.com

• Test Practice

PART 1 Multiple Choice

Read each question. Then fill in the correct answer on the answer sheet provided by your teacher or on a sheet of paper.

1. Use a ruler to measure the line segment along the route from the lake to the archery field to the nearest inch. What is the actual distance in yards?

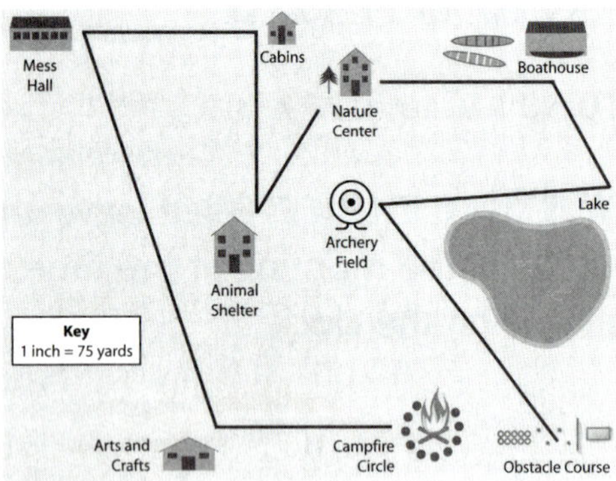

A 2 yd

B 6 yd

C 75 yd

D 150 yd

2. Refer to the map in Exercise 1. Use a ruler to measure the line segments along the route from the campfire circle to the cabins to the nearest $\frac{1}{4}$ inch. What is the total distance in yards?

F 100 yd

G 225 yd

H 300 yd

J 400 yd

3. The fractions $\frac{2}{6}$, $\frac{3}{9}$, $\frac{4}{12}$, $\frac{5}{15}$, and $\frac{6}{18}$ are each equivalent to $\frac{1}{3}$. What is the relationship between the numerator and denominator in each fraction that is equivalent to $\frac{1}{3}$?

A The denominator is three more than the numerator.

B The numerator is three more than the denominator.

C The denominator is three times the numerator.

D The numerator is three times the denominator.

4. Which group shows all the numbers that are common factors of 24 and 36?

F 1, 2, 4, 6, 12

G 1, 2, 3, 4, 6, 12

H 1, 2, 3, 4, 6, 8, 12

J 1, 2, 3, 4, 6, 8, 9, 12

5. Harada wants to watch a television special. The program starts at 8:00 P.M. and is 105 minutes long. What time will the television special end?

A 9:00 P.M.

B 9:15 P.M.

C 9:30 P.M.

D 9:45 P.M.

Preparing for Standardized Tests
For test-taking strategies and practice, see pages R42–R55.

6. Tori needs a string that is 2 inches long for a bracelet. Use the ruler on the Mathematics Chart to measure the line segment under each string. Which string is 2 inches long?

F

G

H

J

7. A new action movie is 134 minutes long. What is this time in hours and minutes?

A 1 hour 14 minutes

B 1 hour 34 minutes

C 2 hours 14 minutes

D 2 hours 34 minutes

8. Five friends share three sandwiches equally. How much does each friend get?

F $\frac{3}{5}$ sandwich

G $1\frac{1}{3}$ sandwich

H $1\frac{3}{5}$ sandwich

J $1\frac{2}{3}$ sandwich

PART 2 Short Response

Record your answers on the sheet provided by your teacher or on a sheet of paper.

9. Mykia weighed 7 pounds 5 ounces when she was born. How many ounces did she weigh when she was born?

10. Name two unlike fractions that have a sum of $3\frac{5}{6}$.

11. Write any four digit number that has a 3 in the hundreds place and a 7 in the tens place.

PART 3 Extended Response

Record your answers on the answer sheet provided by your teacher or on a sheet of paper. Show your work.

12. For each item below, choose an appropriate unit. Choose from inches, feet, yards, or miles. Explain your choice.

- the length of a football field
- the distance around Earth
- the length of a toothbrush
- the height of a rollercoaster

NEED EXTRA HELP?												
If You Missed Question...	1	2	3	4	5	6	7	8	9	10	11	12
Go to Lesson...	11-1	11-1	9-3	9-1	11-5	11-1	11-5	8-1	11-3	10-3	1-1	11-1

CHAPTER 12

Use Measures in the Metric System

BIG Idea What is the metric system?

The **metric system** is a decimal system of measurement.

Example Speed skating at the Olympic Games consists of the events listed in the table.

Speed Skating Events	
• 500 meter	• 1,500 meter
• 1,000 meter	• 5,000 meter

In the metric system, a meter is a unit of length.

What will I learn in this chapter?

- Choose appropriate metric units for measuring length.
- Convert metric units of length, mass, and capacity.
- Use integers to represent real-world situations.
- Solve problems involving changes in temperature.
- Solve problems by determining reasonable answers.

Key Vocabulary

metric system
mass
negative number
positive number
integer

Math Online **Student Study Tools at macmillanmh.com**

FOLDABLES® Study Organizer

Make this Foldable to help you organize information about the metric system. Begin with a sheet of 11″ by 17″ paper.

1. **Fold** the short sides toward the middle.

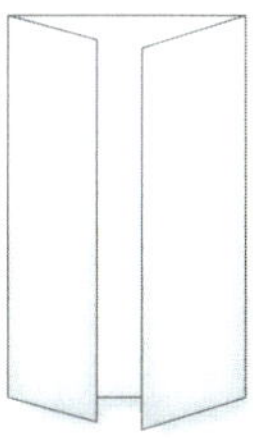

2. **Fold** the top to the bottom.

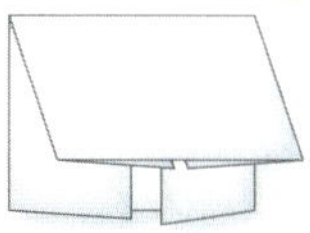

3. **Open.** Cut along the second fold to make four tabs.

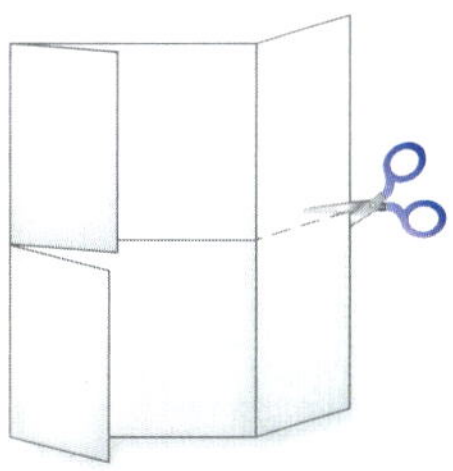

4. **Label** each tab as shown.

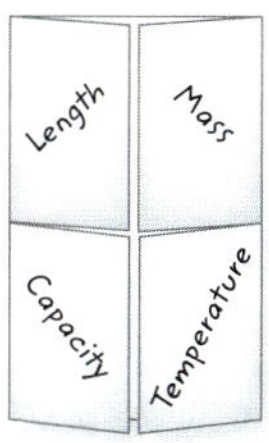

ARE YOU READY for Chapter 12?

You have two ways to check prerequisite skills for this chapter.

Option 2

Math Online Take the Chapter Readiness Quiz at macmillanmh.com.

Option 1

Complete the Quick Check below.

QUICK Check

Multiply. **(Lessons 3-1 and 3-8)**

1. 6 × 1,000 **2.** 15 × 100 **3.** 180 × 10

4. 947 × 100 **5.** 36 × 10 **6.** 24 × 1,000

7. A bean bag chair costs $16. How much do one hundred bean bag chairs cost?

Divide. **(Lessons 4-1 and 4-7)**

8. 150 ÷ 10 **9.** 500 ÷ 100 **10.** 140 ÷ 10

11. 64,000 ÷ 1,000 **12.** 7,900 ÷ 100 **13.** 3,120 ÷ 10

14. Roz has $480 to spend on her 10-day trip. If she wants to spend the same amount daily, how much can she spend each day?

Write the temperature shown on each thermometer. **(Prior Grade)**

15.

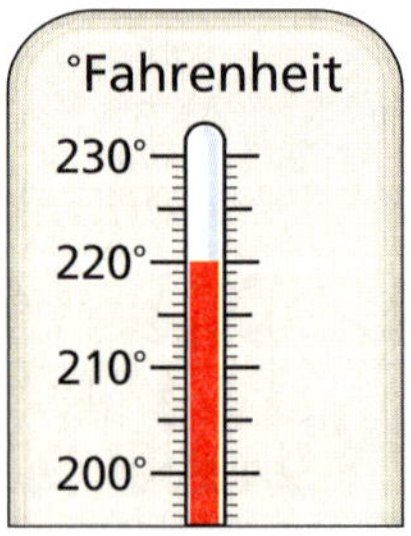

16.

17.

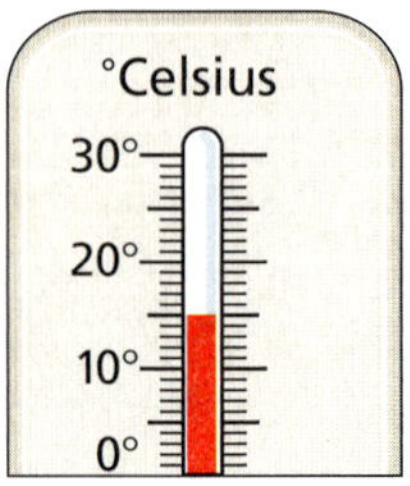

18.

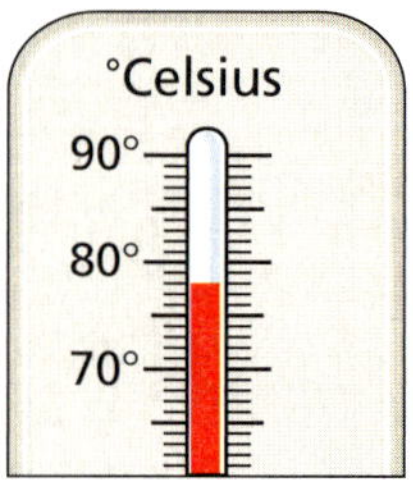

Explore

Measurement Activity for 12-1
Metric Rulers

MAIN IDEA

I will measure length to the nearest millimeter.

You Will Need

a ruler

Math Online

macmillanmh.com

• Concepts in Motion

In the customary system, you measure length using inches, feet, or yards. In the metric system, you use meters, centimeters, or millimeters.

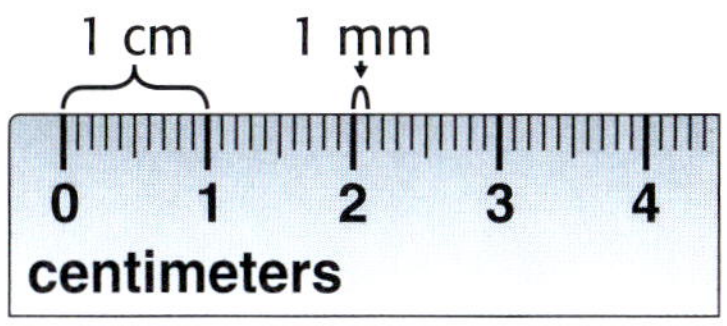

Use a ruler like the one above to measure objects to the nearest centimeter or to the nearest millimeter.

ACTIVITY

1 Find the length of the piece of chalk to the nearest centimeter.

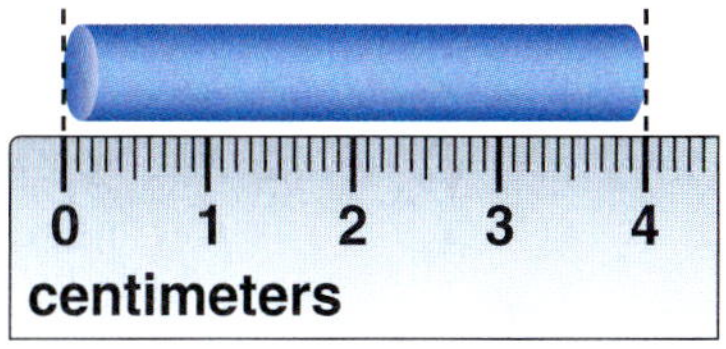

Step 1 Place the ruler against the piece of chalk. Line up the zero on the ruler with the end of the piece of chalk.

Step 2 Find the centimeter mark that is closest to the other end.

To the nearest centimeter, the length of the piece of chalk is 4 centimeters long.

ACTIVITY

2 Find the length of the toy car to the nearest millimeter.

To the nearest millimeter, the toy car is 82 millimeters long.

Think About It

1. Is it easier to measure objects to the nearest centimeter or to the nearest millimeter? Explain.

2. Will you get a more exact measurement if you measure an object to the nearest centimeter or to the nearest millimeter? Explain your reasoning.

CHECK What You Know

Use a metric ruler to find the length of each object to the nearest centimeter and to the nearest millimeter.

3. 

4. 

5. 

***Millimeters* and *centimeters* are used to measure small objects. You can measure the length of larger objects using *meters*. One meter is a little longer than one yard. Select an appropriate unit to measure the length of each object.**

6. width of your textbook
7. height of a classmate
8. length of classroom
9. length of an ant

10. Copy the table below. Then complete the table using ten objects found in your classroom. The first one is done for you.

Object	Unit of Measure	Estimate	Actual Length
Pencil	centimeter	15 centimeters	17 centimeters

Name an object that you would measure using each unit.

11. millimeter
12. centimeter
13. meter

14. **OPEN ENDED** Draw a line that is between 5 and 6 centimeters long. Then measure the length of the line to the nearest millimeter.

15. **WRITING IN ▸MATH** Would you measure the length of a bicycle in centimeters or millimeters? Explain your reasoning.

12-1 Units of Length

MAIN IDEA

I will choose an appropriate metric unit for measuring length and convert metric units of length.

New Vocabulary

metric system
centimeter
millimeter
meter
kilometer

Math Online

macmillanmh.com

- Extra Examples
- Personal Tutor
- Self-Check Quiz

GET READY to Learn

The tree shown at the right is estimated to be 150 years old and 45 meters or 150 feet tall. The tallest tree in the world is over 370 feet tall.

The **metric system** is a decimal system of measurement. The common units of length in the metric system are millimeter, centimeter, meter, and kilometer.

Metric Units of Length

Key Concepts

1 **centimeter** (cm) = 10 **millimeters** (mm)

1 **meter** (m) = 100 cm or 1,000 mm

1 **kilometer** (km) = 1,000 m

1 millimeter thickness of a dime

1 centimeter width of pinky finger

1 meter height of a doorknob

1 kilometer 6 city blocks

Real-World EXAMPLE — Select an Appropriate Unit

1 **SCIENCE Which unit would you use to measure the length of a river: *millimeter*, *centimeter*, *meter*, or *kilometer*?**

The length of a river is much greater than the height of a doorknob. So, *kilometer* is an appropriate unit of measure.

> **Remember**
>
> To convert a larger unit to a smaller unit, *multiply*.
>
> To convert a smaller unit to a larger unit, *divide*.

In the chart below, each place value is 10 times the place value to its right. To convert metric units, multiply or divide by a multiple of 10, such as 10, 100, or 1,000.

Thousands	Hundreds	Tens	Ones	Tenths	Hundredths	Thousandths
		4	5.			
kilo	hecto	deca	meter	deci	centi	milli

1,000 (kilo to meter) 100 (meter to centi) 10 (centi to milli)

Real-World EXAMPLE — Convert Larger Units to Smaller Units

2 **ART Cynthia cut a piece of ribbon that is 5 meters long. How many centimeters long is the ribbon?**

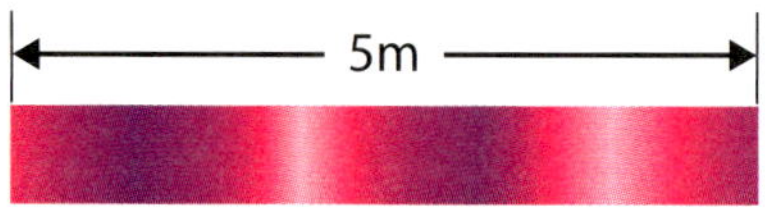

You need to convert 5 meters to centimeters.

5 m = ■ cm — A larger unit (m) is being converted to a smaller unit (cm), so you will multiply.

$5 \times 100 = 500$ — Since 1 m = 100 cm, multiply 5 by 100.

So, 5 m = 500 cm.

The piece of ribbon is 500 centimeters long.

> **Remember**
>
> To multiply by 10, 100, or 1,000, use basic facts and count the number of zeros in the factors.

Real-World EXAMPLE

Convert Smaller Units to Larger Units

3 **GAMES Roshonda has 50 dominoes. Each domino is 4 centimeters long. She lines them up end to end as shown. How many meters long is the line of dominoes?**

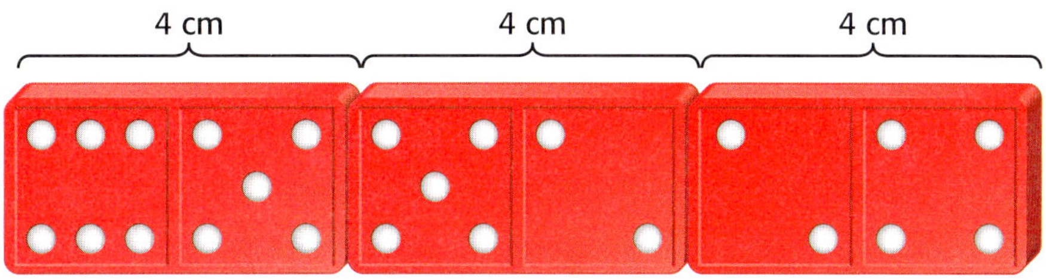

Step 1 Find the length in centimeters.

number of dominoes		length of each domino		total length
50	×	4 cm	=	200 cm

Step 2 Convert 200 centimeters to meters.

200 cm = ■ m — A smaller unit (cm) is being converted to a larger unit (m), so divide.

200 ÷ 100 = 2 — Since 100 cm = 1 m, divide 200 by 100.

So, 200 cm = 2 m.

The line of 50 dominoes is 2 meters long.

Remember

To divide by 10, 100, or 1,000, cross out the same number of zeros in both the dividend and divisor.

CHECK What You Know

Select an appropriate unit to measure each length. Write *millimeter*, *centimeter*, *meter*, or *kilometer*. See Example 1 (p. 518)

1. soccer field

2. necklace

3. distance between two cities

Complete. See Examples 2, 3 (pp. 518–519)

4. 5 m = ■ cm

5. 9 km = ■ m

6. 700 cm = ■ m

7. 20 mm = ■ cm

8. 6,000 m = ■ km

9. 45 cm = ■ mm

10. Which is the most reasonable estimate for the depth of a pond: 6 millimeters, 6 centimeters, or 6 meters? Explain.

11. Talk About It — Find three items in your classroom: one that is about 3 meters long, one that is about 3 centimeters long, and one that is about 3 millimeters long. Check by measuring each item.

Practice and Problem Solving

EXTRA PRACTICE
See page R31.

Select an appropriate unit to measure each length. Write *millimeter*, *centimeter*, *meter*, or *kilometer*. See Example 1 (p. 518)

12. height of oak tree **13.** cell phone **14.** water slide

15. ladybug **16.** train route **17.** book

Complete. See Examples 2, 3 (pp. 518–519)

18. 2 m = ■ mm **19.** 73,000 m = ■ km **20.** 3 cm = ■ mm

21. 170 mm = ■ cm **22.** 15 km = ■ m **23.** 8,000 mm = ■ m

24. 9 m = ■ cm **25.** 300 cm = ■ m **26.** 6 cm = ■ mm

27. A spider is 6 millimeters long. What fractional part of 1 centimeter is 6 millimeters?

28. Which is the most reasonable estimate for the length of a piano: 170 millimeters, 170 centimeters, or 170 meters? Explain.

29. Two lizards are shown below. How many millimeters longer is the larger lizard than the smaller lizard?

30. Measure the distance across the sunflower shown. What is this measurement to the nearest centimeter? How many centimeters smaller than 1 meter is the width of the sunflower?

31. A hiking trail is 1 kilometer long. Ronan just passed the 250-meter marker. What fractional part of the trail does he still have to hike?

32. The table shows the lengths of Julian's backpack and notebook binder. How much longer is the backpack than the binder?

Object	Length
Backpack	60 cm
Notebook binder	430 mm

Real-World PROBLEM SOLVING

Science The largest active volcano in the world is Mauna Loa in Hawaii.

- Its crater is 180 meters deep.
- Its dome is 120 kilometers long and 50 kilometers wide.
- Its summit is 17 kilometers above its base.

33. What is the depth of the crater in centimeters?

34. How many centimeters above the base is the summit?

35. How many meters greater is the length of the dome than the width?

H.O.T. Problems

36. **OPEN ENDED** Estimate the length of three objects in your classroom. Then measure and compare the measurements to your estimates. Tell what metric units you used.

37. **REASONING** Explain how you decide which metric unit to use when measuring the length of an object. Provide examples to explain your reasoning.

38. **WHICH ONE DOESN'T BELONG?** Identify the measure that does not belong with the other three. Explain your reasoning.

3,500 km	35 m	350 cm	3,500 mm

39. **CHALLENGE** Explain how to find 30 cm + 1 m + 4,000 mm. Then solve.

40. **WRITING IN MATH** Compare and contrast converting customary units of length and converting metric units of length. Which type of conversion is easier? Explain.

12-2 Problem-Solving Skill

MAIN IDEA I will solve problems by determining reasonable answers.

Juanita is trimming hedges. They are 37 meters from an electrical outlet. Her extension cord is 3,500 centimeters long. Juanita estimates that the extension cord is long enough to reach the hedges. Is she correct? If not, how much longer does an extension cord need to be to reach the hedges?

Understand	**What facts do you know?** • The distance from the hedges to the electrical outlet. • The length of the extension cord in centimeters. **What do you need to find?** • Does Juanita have a long enough extension cord?
Plan	Convert 3,500 centimeters to meters. Then compare.
Solve	First, convert 3,500 centimeters to meters. 3,500 centimeters = ■ meters $3,500 \div 100 = 35$ So, 3,500 centimeters = 35 meters. Since $35 < 37$ meters, Juanita's extension cord will not be long enough to reach the hedges. To find how much longer the extension cord needs to be, subtract. $37 - 35 = 2$ So, Juanita will need an extension cord that is 2 meters or 200 centimeters longer to reach the hedges.
Check	Look back. Since $3,700 > 3,500$ and $3,700 - 3,500 = 200$. The answer is reasonable. ✓

ANALYZE the Skill

Refer to the problem on the previous page.

1. Would Juanita be able to reach the hedges using one extension cord that is 4,000 centimeters long? Explain.

2. Juanita wants to trim a tree that is 75 meters from the outlet. How many 3,500-centimeter extension cords will she need?

3. Describe another method you could use to check if an estimate is reasonable.

4. Explain why it is always a good idea to check if your answers are reasonable.

PRACTICE the Skill

EXTRA PRACTICE
See page R32.

Solve. Determine reasonable answers.

5. Estella needs 4 pints of vegetable broth to make soup. She has only a 1-cup measuring cup. Will Estella need 4 cups, 8 cups, or 16 cups of broth? Explain.

6. Dylan is making bookmarks. It takes him 15 minutes to make one bookmark. Dylan estimates that he can make 14 bookmarks in 3 hours. Is he correct? If not, how many bookmarks can he make in 3 hours?

7. For a small art project, Mr. Adams estimates that each student will need the amount of clay shown below. Does this seem reasonable? Explain.

8. To make one cup of hot chocolate you need 8 ounces of water. Elsu's mother is making 12 cups of hot chocolate. Will she need 2 quarts, 3 quarts, or 4 quarts of water? Explain.

9. Ahmik buys a carpet that is 7,300 centimeters long in order to cover the hallway shown below. Is the carpet long enough to cover the hallway? If not, how much of the hallway will not be covered by the carpet?

10. Tonya needs to buy a cable that is at least 12 yards long. At the store, all of the cables are marked in feet. Tonya estimates that a 40-foot cable will be long enough. Is her estimate reasonable? Explain.

11. Tommy estimates that his skateboard is about 90 millimeters long. Is this a reasonable estimate? Explain.

12. **WRITING IN MATH** Write a real-world problem that has an unreasonable answer. Explain why the answer is unreasonable.

12-3 Units of Mass

GET READY to Learn

The goliath beetle is the heaviest insect in the world. At 100 grams, it has about the same *mass* as a can of sardines.

MAIN IDEA

I will convert metric units of mass.

New Vocabulary

- mass
- gram
- milligram
- kilogram

Math Online

macmillanmh.com

- Extra Examples
- Personal Tutor
- Self-Check Quiz

Mass is a measure of the amount of matter in an object. Metric units of mass are milligram, gram, and kilogram.

Metric Units of Mass

Key Concepts

1 **gram** (g) = 1,000 **milligrams** (mg)

1 **kilogram** (kg) = 1,000 g

1 milligram
a bread crumb

1 gram
a slice of bread

1 kilogram
a loaf of bread

Real-World EXAMPLE — Convert Larger Units to Smaller Units

1 **SCIENCE In 1876, pieces of a meteorite were found in Tennessee. The largest single piece of meteorite had a mass of 136 kilograms. What was the mass of this piece in grams?**

136 kg = ■ g — A kilogram is a larger unit than a gram.

136 × 1,000 = 136,000 — 1 kg = 1,000 g, so multiply 136 by 1,000.

So, 136 kg = 136,000 g.

The mass of the meteorite was 136,000 grams.

Remember

Mass and weight are different measures. If you were flying in the space shuttle, you would have the same mass as on Earth, but a different weight.

Real-World EXAMPLE — Convert Smaller Units to Larger Units

2 FOOD Mr. Benavides bakes muffins that have a mass of about 2,000 milligrams. What is the mass in grams?

2,000 mg = ■ g — A milligram is smaller than a gram.

$2{,}000 \div 1{,}000 = 2$ — 1,000 mg = 1 g, so divide 2,000 by 1,000.

So, 2,000 mg = 2 g.

Each muffin has a mass of 2 grams.

Real-World EXAMPLE — Compare Mass

3 MAIL Luke is shipping a box that has a mass of 4,300 grams. If the mass of the box is greater than 5 kilograms, shipping will cost extra. Will shipping cost extra? Explain.

5 kg = ■ g — Convert a larger unit to a smaller unit.

$5 \times 1{,}000 = 5{,}000$ — 1 kg = 1,000 g, so multiply 5 by 1,000.

So, 5 kg = 5,000 g.

The mass of the box is 4.3 kilograms. Since 4,300 grams $<$ 5,000 grams, shipping will not cost extra.

CHECK What You Know

Complete. See Examples 1, 2 (pp. 524–525)

1. 5,000 mg = ■ g
2. 9 g = ■ mg
3. 230 mg = ■ g
4. 8,000 g = ■ mg
5. 4 kg = ■ g
6. 5,000 g = ■ kg

Replace ● with $<$, $>$, or = to make a true statement. See Example 3 (p. 525)

7. 2,300 mg ● 2 g
8. 3 kg ● 3,000 g
9. 75 g ● 800 mg
10. One highlighter has a mass of 11 grams. Another highlighter has a mass of 108 milligrams. Which highlighter has the greater mass?

11. **Talk About It** Which is a more reasonable estimate for the mass of a baseball: 140 milligrams, 140 grams, or 140 kilograms? Explain.

Practice and Problem Solving

EXTRA PRACTICE See page R32.

Complete. See Examples 1, 2 (pp. 524–525)

12. 2 g = ■ mg **13.** 6 kg = ■ g **14.** 3,000 g = ■ kg

15. 1,000 mg = ■ g **16.** 4,000 g = ■ kg **17.** 7 g = ■ mg

Replace ● with <, >, or = to make a true statement. See Example 3 (p. 525)

18. 1.9 kg ● 1,900 g **19.** 3,500 mg ● 0.35 g **20.** 814 g ● 8.14 kg

21. 0.7 g ● 700 mg **22.** 690 g ● 6,900 mg **23.** 2.2 g ● 22,000 mg

For Exercises 24–26, use the table at the right.

Macaws	
Species	**Mass (grams)**
Blue and Gold	800
Green-winged	900
Red-footed	525
Yellow-collared	250

24. Which macaw has a mass closest to 1 kilogram?

25. How many yellow-colored macaws would have a combined mass of 1 kilogram?

26. Is the combined mass of two red-footed macaws and three blue and gold macaws closer to 3 kilograms or 4 kilograms? Explain.

27. One computer has a mass of 0.8 kilogram and another has a mass of 800 grams. Compare the masses of the computers.

H.O.T. Problems

28. **OPEN ENDED** Estimate how many paper clips have a mass of 10 grams. Then use a balance to check your estimate.

29. **FIND THE ERROR** Terrez and Ella are converting 3,000 grams to kilograms. Who is correct? Explain.

Ella
3,000 g ÷ 100 = 30 kg

Terrez
3,000 g ÷ 1,000 = 3 kg

30. **WRITING IN ►MATH** Explain which units of mass you would use to measure the following: a grain of salt, a bowl of cereal, a football player, and a tube of toothpaste.

12-4 Units of Capacity

GET READY to Learn

The pitcher of orange juice at the right holds 1 liter. This is a little more than a quart.

MAIN IDEA

I will convert metric units of capacity.

New Vocabulary

liter
milliliter

Math Online

macmillanmh.com

- Extra Examples
- Personal Tutor
- Self-Check Quiz

In the metric system, the common units of capacity are liter and milliliter.

Metric Units of Capacity — Key Concept

1 **liter** (L) = 1,000 **milliliters** (mL)

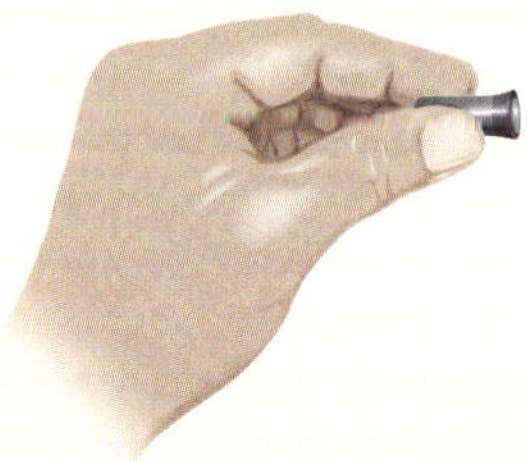

1 milliliter
amount of liquid in an eyedropper

1 liter
a medium-sized sports drink

Convert units of capacity just as you convert units of length.

Real-World EXAMPLE — Convert Larger Units to Smaller Units

1 WATER A faucet that is constantly dripping wastes about 90 liters of water every week. How many milliliters of water is this?

90 L = ■ mL — A liter is larger than a milliliter, so multiply.

90 × 1,000 = 90,000 — 1 L = 1,000 mL, so multiply 90 by 1,000.

90 L = 90,000 mL — So, 90,000 milliliters of water are wasted.

Remember

In everyday life, customary units of capacity such as gallons and pints are often compared to the metric units liters and milliliters.

Real-World EXAMPLES Convert Units of Capacity

2 JUICE A container of orange juice holds 580 milliliters. How many liters is 580 milliliters?

Estimate 580 mL < 1,000 mL, so the number of liters is less than 1.

580 mL = ■ L — 580 mL is what part of 1,000 mL?

580 mL = $\frac{580}{1,000}$ L or 0.58 L — Write $\frac{580}{1,000}$ as a decimal.

So, 580 mL = 0.58 L. — 0.58 liter is less than a whole liter. So, the answer is reasonable.

3 ALGEBRA The table shows the number of water bottles sold on a recent day. Were more than 100,000 milliliters sold?

Bottle	Number Sold
1-liter	55
2-liter	30

First, find the total number of liters sold.

$(1 \times 55) + (2 \times 30) = 55 + 60$ Multiply.

$= 115$ L Add.

Next, convert 115 liters to milliliters.

$115 \times 1,000 = 115,000$ — 1 L = 1,000 mL, so multiply 115 by 1,000.

So, 115 L = 115,000 mL.

Since 115,000 > 100,000, more than 100,000 milliliters of water were sold.

CHECK What You Know

Complete. See Examples 1, 2 (pp. 527–528)

1. 6 L = ■ mL
2. 7,000 mL = ■ L
3. 4 L = ■ mL
4. 325 mL = ■ L
5. 42 mL = ■ L
6. 1.5 L = ■ mL

Replace each ● with <, >, or = to make a true statement. See Example 3 (p. 528)

7. 1.7 L ● 1,000 mL
8. 390 mL ● 0.39 L

9. A detergent bottle holds 700 milliliters. Find the capacity in liters.
10. **Talk About It** Which unit would you use to measure the capacity of a glass of milk? Explain.

Practice and Problem Solving

EXTRA PRACTICE
See page R32.

Complete. See Examples 1, 2 (pp. 527–528)

11. 70 L = ■ mL
12. 4 L = ■ mL
13. 3,000 mL = ■ L
14. 230 mL = ■ L
15. 6 L = ■ mL
16. 10 mL = ■ L
17. 5,000 mL = ■ L
18. 0.5 L = ■ mL
19. 1.5 L = ■ mL

Replace each ● with <, >, or = to make a true statement. See Example 3 (p. 528)

20. 82.5 L ● 825 mL
21. 0.07 L ● 70 mL
22. 834 mL ● 8.34 L

23. To prepare for his camping trip, Emanuel filled his canteen with water. Is 15,000 milliliters or 1,500 milliliters a more reasonable estimate for the amount of water in the canteen? Explain.

24. One serving of punch is 250 milliliters. Will ten servings fit in a 2-liter bowl? Explain.

25. Yesterday, Audrey drank the liquids shown. How many liters of liquids did she drink in all?

26. The Nail Shop purchases nail polish in 13-milliliter bottles. Find the total capacity of 1,000 bottles in liters.

Liquid	Amount
Juice	210 mL
Milk	480 mL
Water	1.2 L

H.O.T. Problems

27. **OPEN ENDED** Name three things that have a capacity greater than 10 liters.

28. **FIND THE ERROR** Joseph and Kendra are converting 14 milliliters to liters. Who is correct? Explain.

Kendra
$14 \div 1{,}000 = \frac{14}{1{,}000}$
14 mL = 0.014 L

Joseph
$14 \times 1{,}000 = 1{,}400$
14 mL = 1,400 L

29. WRITING IN ►MATH Write a real-world problem that can be solved by converting milliliters to liters. Then solve.

TEST Practice

30. How many milligrams are equivalent to 900 grams? **(Lesson 12-3)**

A 0.9 mg

B 9 mg

C 90 mg

D Not here

31. Claudio's fish tank has 3 liters of water in it. How many milliliters of water are in the fish tank? **(Lesson 12-4)**

F 30 mL

G 300 mL

H 3,000 mL

J 30,000 mL

Spiral Review

Complete. **(Lessons 12-1 and 12-3)**

32. 12 km = ■ m

33. 400 cm = ■ m

34. 8,000 cm = ■ mm

35. 34 g = ■ mg

36. 9 kg = ■ g

37. 2,000 mg = ■ g

38. Mara wants to put 90 CDs on the shelf shown below. Each CD is 1 centimeter wide. Is it reasonable for her to expect to fit all the CDs on the shelf? Explain. **(Lesson 12-2)**

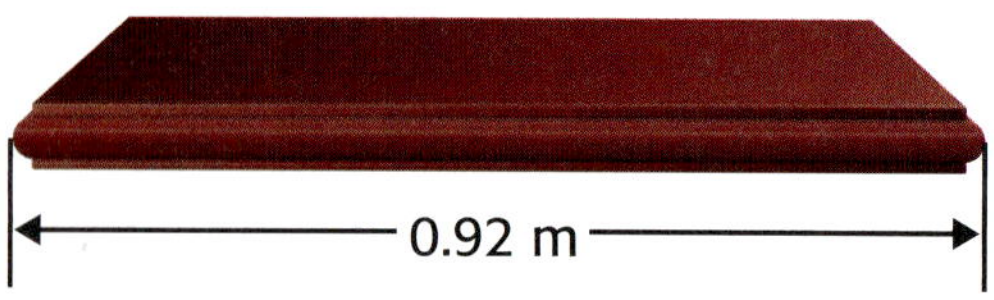

Find each elapsed time. **(Lesson 11-7)**

39. 3:10 A.M. to 5:20 A.M.

40. 1:08 P.M. to 7:39 P.M.

41. 10:30 A.M. to 2:14 P.M.

Subtract. **(Lessons 10-8 and 10-10)**

42. $8\frac{5}{6} - 6\frac{2}{6}$

43. $10\frac{2}{5} - 3\frac{1}{5}$

44. $8\frac{3}{12} - 5\frac{1}{12}$

45. $3\frac{1}{4} - 1\frac{3}{4}$

46. $6\frac{1}{5} - 1\frac{3}{5}$

47. $7\frac{4}{8} - 4\frac{5}{8}$

48. The model represents 0.014. Write 0.014 as a fraction in simplest form. **(Lesson 9-5)**

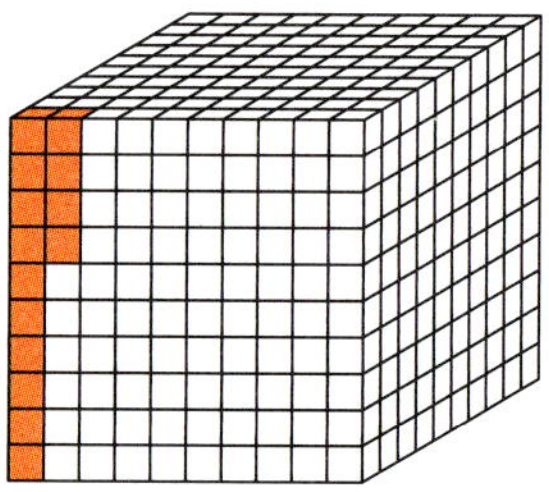

49. Mrs. Rexroad's cell phone bill for one month was $48.70. The next month it was $56.04. Estimate the total cost of the two bills using compatible numbers. **(Lesson 2-2)**

Game Time

Metric Pairs!

Identifying Equivalent Metric Units

Get Ready!

Players: 2

You will need: 20 index cards

1 km	1,000 m
10 cm	100 mm
10 m	0.01 km
100 cm	1,000 mm
10 g	10,000 mg
10,000 g	10 kg
1,000 mg	1 g
1 L	1,000 mL
0.1 L	100 mL
10 mL	0.01 L

Get Set!

Write each measure shown at the right on a separate index card.

Go!

- Shuffle the index cards.
- Place the cards facedown in five rows and four columns.
- The first player chooses two cards. If the measurements are equal, the player keeps the cards and chooses two more. If the measurements are not equal, the cards are placed back facedown.
- The next player takes a turn choosing two cards.
- The game continues until all of the cards have been paired up correctly.
- The player with more pairs wins.

CHAPTER 12

Mid-Chapter Check

Lessons 12-1 through 12-4

Choose an appropriate unit to measure each length. Write *millimeter, centimeter, meter,* or *kilometer*. (Lesson 12-1)

1. pencil

2. house

3. distance from Earth to the moon

4. Measure the length and width of the rectangle to the nearest millimeter. (Lesson 12-1)

5. **MULTIPLE CHOICE** Choose the most reasonable measurement for the height of a classroom door. (Lesson 12-1)

A 20 cm

B 20 m

C 200 mm

D 200 cm

Complete. (Lesson 12-1)

6. 4 m = ■ cm

7. 750 mm = ■ cm

8. 1,000 m = ■ km

9. 63 cm = ■ mm

10. Which of the following is a reasonable estimate for the height of a fifth grade student: 75 cm, 125 cm, or 175 cm? Explain. (Lesson 12-2)

11. The table shows the average brain mass of a human and of an African elephant. How many grams greater is the mass of an African elephant brain than the mass of a human brain? (Lesson 12-3)

Brain	Average Mass (kg)
African elephant	5.4
Human	1.4

Complete. (Lesson 12-3)

12. 7 kg = ■ g

13. 10,000 g = ■ kg

14. 2,000 mg = ■ g

15. Tamara has a bag of dog food that weighs 4 kilograms. How many grams are in the bag? (Lesson 12-3)

16. **MULTIPLE CHOICE** Which unit is $\frac{1}{1,000}$ of a kilogram? (Lesson 12-3)

F milligram

G gram

H centigram

J Not Here

Complete. (Lesson 12-4)

17. 6 L = ■ mL

18. 280 mL = ■ L

19. 3,000 mL = ■ L

20. WRITING IN MATH Which metric unit would you use to measure the capacity of a bathtub? Explain. (Lesson 12-4)

12-5 Integers and Graphing on Number Lines

GET READY to Learn

The top of an underwater mountain is about 2 kilometers above sea level. The base of the mountain is 6 kilometers below sea level. You can represent the distance *2 km above sea level* as +2 or 2, and the distance *6 km below sea level* as −6.

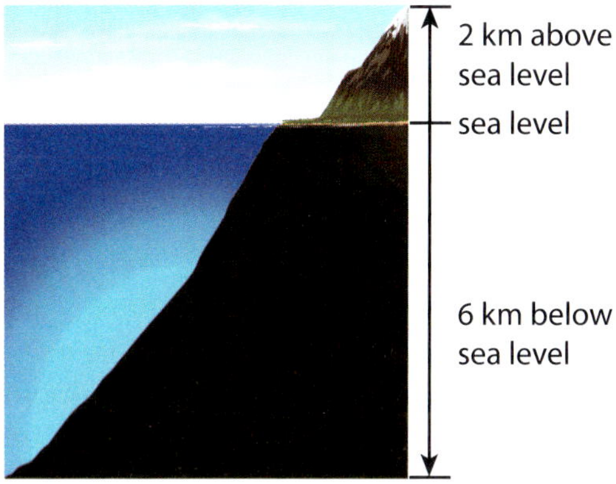

MAIN IDEA

I will use integers to represent real-life situations and graph them on a number line.

New Vocabulary

positive number
negative number
integer
negative integers
positive integers
opposite integers

Math Online

macmillanmh.com

- Extra Examples
- Personal Tutor
- Self-Check Quiz

The number 2 is a **positive number**, or a number greater than 0. The number −6 is a **negative number**, or a number less than 0. Numbers like 2 and −6 are called **integers**.

Negative integers are integers less than zero. They are written with a − sign.

Positive integers are integers greater than zero. They can be written with or without a + sign.

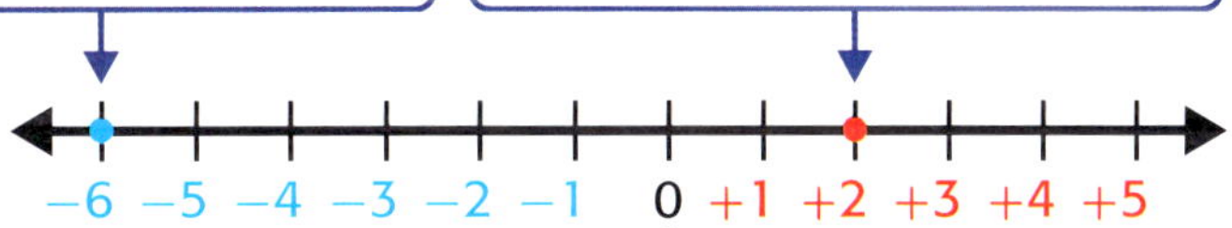

Zero is neither negative nor positive.

Real-World EXAMPLE — Number Line

1 **TEMPERATURE** **Yesterday, the temperature was 4 degrees below zero. Today, it is 4 degrees above zero. Use integers to represent these situations. Then graph the integers on a number line.**

4° below: −4 4° above: +4 or 4

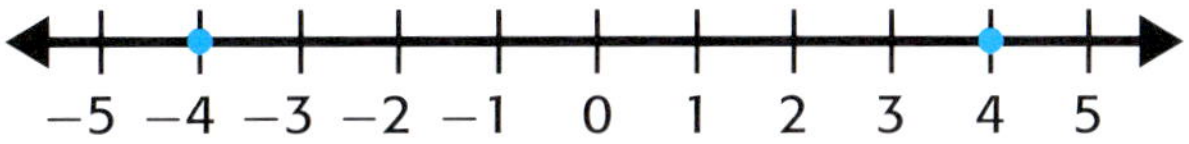

Opposite integers are integers that are the same distance from 0 on the number line, but on opposite sides of 0. The integers −4 and 4 are opposite integers.

- The opposite of 4 is −4.
- The opposite of −4 is 4.

Real-World EXAMPLES Opposites

2 **TEMPERATURE** **One winter day, the temperature in Rapid City, South Dakota, was 5° below zero. Write an integer to represent this situation. Then write its opposite.**

5° below zero: −5
The opposite of −5 is +5 or 5.

So, −5 represents this situation. The integer +5 or 5 is its opposite.

3 **MONEY** **Demont deposited $75 into his bank account. Write an integer to represent this situation. Then write its opposite.**

deposited $75: +75 or 75

The opposite of 75 is −75. It represents withdrawing $75 from the account.

CHECK What You Know

Write an integer to represent each situation. Then graph the integer on a number line. See Example 1 (p. 533)

1. lost $2

2. 20 degrees above 0

3. 5 points deducted from a grade

4. 6 yards gained in football

Write an integer to represent each situation. Then write its opposite. See Examples 2, 3 (p. 534)

5. Meagan spent $35.

6. Geraldo gained 9 yards on the play.

7. The temperature is 14° below zero.

8. Mai earned $28 babysitting.

9. Death Valley National Park in California is 282 feet below sea level. Write an integer to represent this situation.

10. Talk About It Explain how to find the opposite of an integer using a number line.

Practice and Problem Solving

EXTRA PRACTICE See page R33.

Write an integer to represent each situation. Then graph the integer on a number line. See Example 1 (pp. 533–534)

11. spent \$3

12. profit of \$8

13. 40° above zero

14. loss of 15 yards in football

15. 25 feet below sea level

16. 200 feet above ground

For Exercises 17–22, write an integer to represent each situation. Then write its opposite. See Examples 2, 3 (p. 534)

17. Sandi had to backtrack 32 meters.

18. The lake was 42 feet deep.

19. The temperature was 11° below zero.

20. The cliff was 140 feet above sea level.

21. A Ferris wheel goes up 212 feet.

22. The elevation of Daytona Beach is 7 feet above sea level.

Real-World PROBLEM SOLVING

Science The table shows the deepest dives of birds.

Bird	Deepest Dive (m)
Flying: thick-billed murre	210
Non-flying: Emperor penguin	534

23. Represent the dive of each bird using an integer.

24. Which bird is able to dive deeper? Explain how you know.

H.O.T. Problems

25. **OPEN ENDED** Write an integer to represent an outside temperature today. Then write the opposite.

26. **WHICH ONE DOESN'T BELONG?** Identify the situation that does not belong with the other three. Explain your reasoning.

17 feet below sea level	17 degrees	spending \$17.00	17 points subtracted from a perfect score

27. **WRITING IN MATH** Write about a real-world situation that can be described using the integers −18 and 10.

Explore

Technology Activity for 12-6
Units of Temperature

Tech Link

MAIN IDEA

I will use technology to make and explain line graphs.

Mrs. Rodriguez did a science experiment for her class that measured how fast a cup of hot water cooled. She measured its temperature every two minutes. The line graph shows her data.

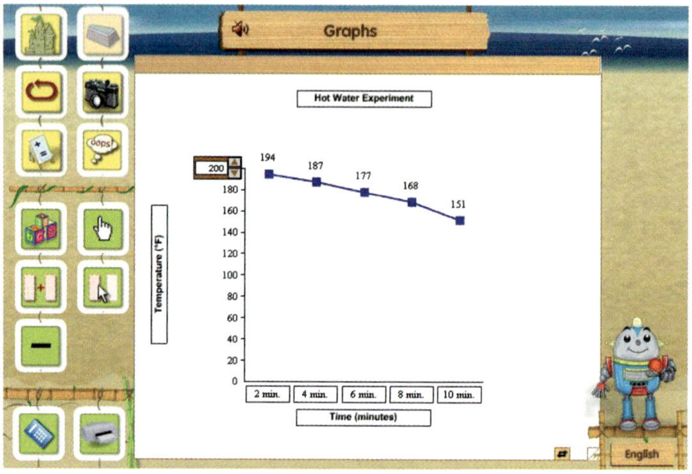

In the following Activity, you will make a similar line graph.

ACTIVITY Graphing Temperature Change

Step 1 Pour 1 cup of cold water into a glass.

Step 2 Measure the temperature of the water every two minutes for ten minutes.

Step 3 Use the Graph feature from the Math Tool Chest™ to make a line graph of the data.

Think About It

1. Compare and contrast your graph with the graph above.
2. After 10 minutes, what was the change in temperature of your water?
3. Predict what the temperature will be if 5 more minutes pass.
4. Room temperature is about 65°F. Predict how long it will be until the temperature of the water reaches room temperature. Check your prediction by continuing to measure the temperature of the water every five minutes.

12-6 Units of Temperature

GET READY to Learn

Animals that are cold-blooded take on the temperature of their surroundings. So, if the outside temperature is 70°F, the body temperature of a snake will also be 70°F.

MAIN IDEA

I will choose appropriate temperatures in degrees Fahrenheit and Celsius.

New Vocabulary

degrees
Celsius (°C)
Fahrenheit (°F)

Math Online
macmillanmh.com
- Extra Examples
- Personal Tutor
- Self-Check Quiz

Degrees are the units of measurement used to describe temperature. Temperature can be measured in degrees **Celsius (°C)** and in degrees **Fahrenheit (°F)**.

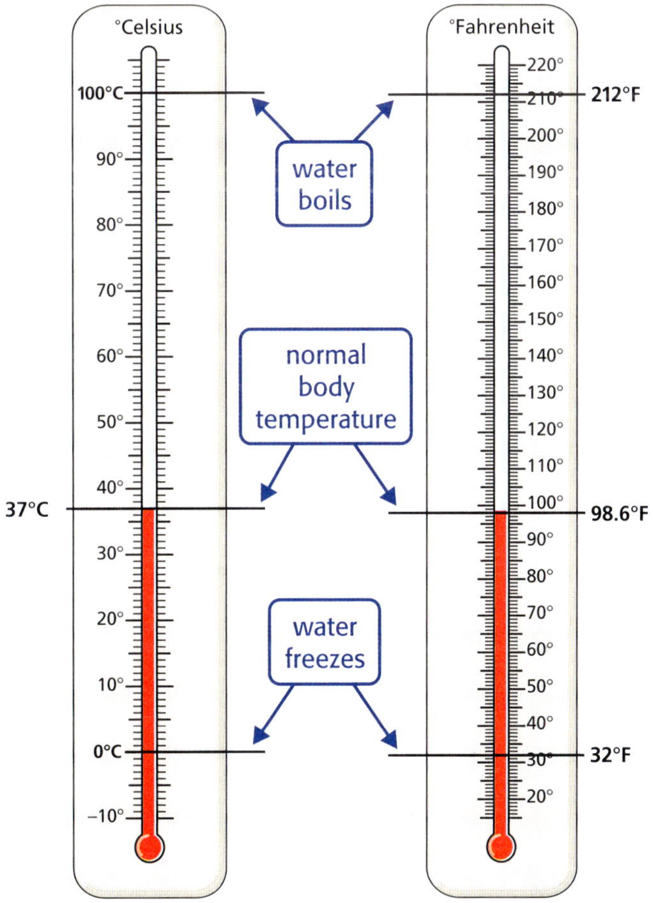

Remember

Some thermometers have both °F and °C. If you know the temperature in one scale, you can read across to tell the temperature in the other scale.

Real-World EXAMPLES Choose Reasonable Temperatures

1 **WEATHER Which shows a more reasonable temperature for a snowy day?**

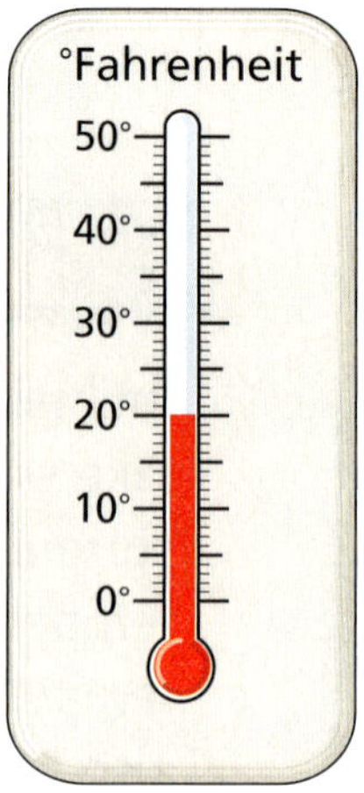

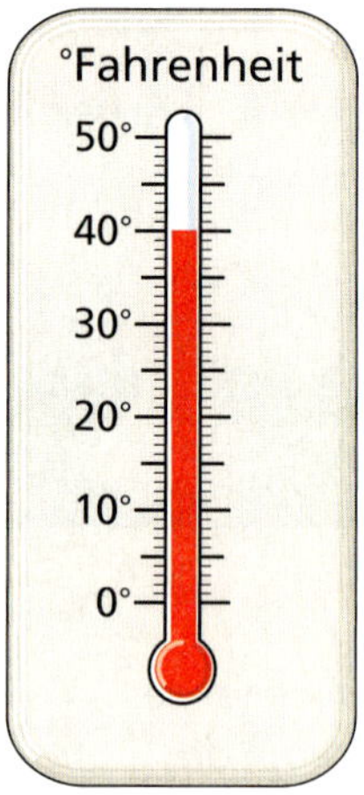

The freezing point of water is 32°F. 20°F is below the freezing point of water. 40°F is too warm for snow. So, the more reasonable temperature is 20°F.

2 **Which is a more reasonable temperature for warm water: 23°C or 43°C? Use the thermometers on page 537 to help you decide.**

23°C is cooler than body temperature. Water that is 23°C would feel cool to the touch. So, the more reasonable estimate is 43°C.

You can find changes in temperature by using subtraction.

EXAMPLE Subtract Temperature

3 **TEMPERATURE The temperature this afternoon was 48°F. By evening, the temperature was 30°F. Find the change in temperature. Use an integer to represent the change.**

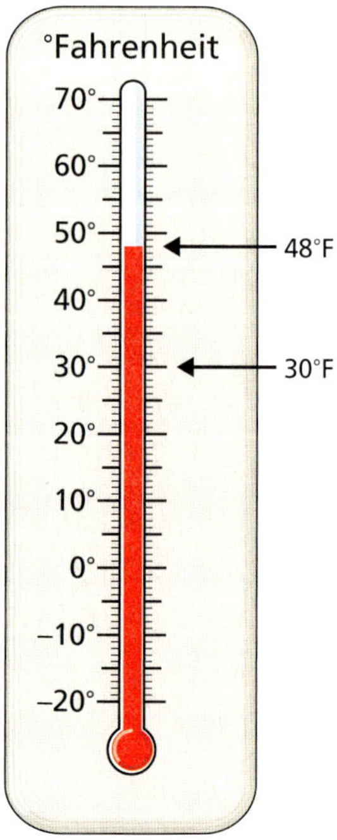

change in temperature

= higher temperature – lower temperature

$= 48^\circ - 30^\circ$ Substitute the temperatures.

$= 18^\circ$ Subtract.

The temperature decreased 18 degrees.

The change can be represented by the integer –18.

CHECK What You Know

Choose the more reasonable temperature for each situation. Use the thermometers on page 537. See Examples 1, 2 (p. 538)

1. a cold day: 5°C or 32°C

2. hot water: 65°F or 190°F

3. a snow cone: 30°C or 30°F

4. warm bowl of soup: 82°C or 82°F

5. The thermometer at the right shows the temperature outside. Could it snow today? Explain.

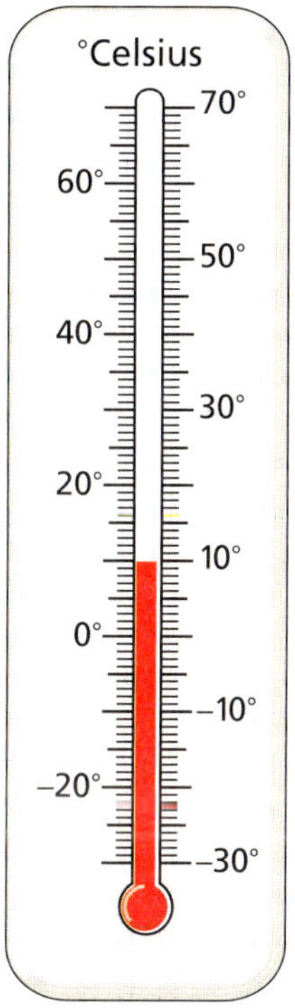

Find each change in temperature. Use an integer to represent the change. See Example 3 (p. 538)

6. 0°C to 12°C

7. 65°F to 59°F

8. Yesterday, the temperature of the water in a swimming pool was 82°F. Today, the temperature of the water is 78°F. Describe the change in temperature with an integer.

9. Talk About It Describe how you can estimate the temperature in degrees Celsius when you know the temperature in degrees Fahrenheit. Give an example.

Practice and Problem Solving

EXTRA PRACTICE See page R33.

Choose the more reasonable temperature for each situation. Use the thermometers on page 537. See Examples 1, 2 (p. 538)

10. person with a fever: 38°C or 98°C

11. glass of lemonade: 46°F or 10°F

12. bicycling: 130°F or 75°F

13. swimming: 30°C or 10°C

14. a summer day: 82°C or 82°F

15. boiling water: 100°F or 100°C

16. frozen yogurt: 20°F or 20°C

17. melting ice: 1°C or 1°F

Find each change in temperature. Use an integer to represent the change. See Example 3 (p. 538)

18. 55°F to 65°F

19. 16°C to 0°C

20. 36°C to 12°C

21. 8°C to 11°C

22. 94°F to 61°F

23. 49°F to 77°F

For Exercises 24–26, use the table at the right. It shows the high and low temperatures for several cities for a certain day in January.

City	High Temperature (°F)	Low Temperature (°F)
Boston	37	22
Detroit	31	18
Omaha	32	12
Pittsburgh	35	20
Seattle	43	36

24. Which city had the greatest temperature change? What was the temperature change?

25. Which city had the least temperature change? What was the temperature change?

26. On the same day, Denver's high temperature was 43°F and low temperature was 15°F. Does this change your answer to Exercise 24 or 25? If so, how?

27. Normal body temperature for a human is 98.6°F. Lilly's little brother had a temperature of 101.3°F. How much greater is his temperature than normal body temperature?

28. The body temperature of a snake is the same as its environment. Suppose it was 25°C outside, and the temperature is now 21.5°C. How much did the snake's body temperature decrease?

Estimate each temperature in degrees Celsius or degrees Fahrenheit. Use the thermometers on page 537.

29. 1°C is about ■ °F

30. 212°F is about ■ °C

31. 68°F is about ■ °C

32. 30°F is about ■ °C

33. 15°C is about ■ °F

34. 44°F is about ■ °C

35. The preferred temperature for the inside of a refrigerator is about 35°F. Estimate this temperature in degrees Celsius.

36. If you wanted to go to a water park, describe a good outside temperature in degrees Celsius.

Data File

In New Orleans, Louisiana, it is not uncommon for summer days to reach 100°F. The average temperature in August is 83°F. The temperature at night may drop to 74°F.

Estimate each temperature in degrees Celsius.

37. 83°F

38. 74°F

Use an integer to represent each change in temperature.

39. 83°F to 100°F

40. 83°F to 74°F

H.O.T. Problems

41. OPEN ENDED Describe two real-world situations in which the temperatures 21°C and 210°F would be appropriate.

42. CHALLENGE Cora was in a place where the temperature was about 10°C. When she walked to a different place, the temperature was about 26°C. Describe a situation in which these temperatures are reasonable.

43. WRITING IN ► MATH Write a problem that requires you to find the change in temperature. Then exchange problems with a classmate and solve.

TEST Practice

44. Which situation is best represented by the integer graphed below? (Lesson 12-5)

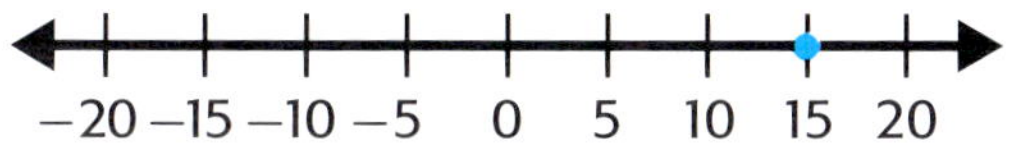

A 15° below zero

B giving away $15

C 15 feet above sea level

D 15 meters deep

45. The temperature at 10:15 A.M. in Chicago was 57°F. By 3:45 P.M., the temperature was 78°F. How many degrees Fahrenheit did the temperature rise? (Lesson 12-6)

F 5°F

G 21°F

H 23°F

J 30°F

Spiral Review

Write an integer to represent each situation. Then write its opposite. (Lesson 12-5)

46. An altitude is 139 feet below sea level.

47. A baby gained 12 ounces.

48. The temperature is 58° above zero.

49. Hai spent $4.

Complete. (Lesson 12-4)

50. 2 L = ■ mL

51. 5,000 mL = ■ L

52. 750 mL = ■ L

53. One can of soup is 12 fluid ounces and makes two servings. If 8 fluid ounces of water are added, what is the capacity of one serving? (Lesson 11-4)

Problem Solving in Social Studies

The Wright Measurements

The Wright brothers were self-trained engineers from Ohio who designed, built, and piloted the first engine-powered airplane. On December 17, 1903, the Wright brothers completed the world's first successful controlled flight. They later named the flyer the *Kitty Hawk*, after the location in North Carolina near where they made this historic flight.

The temperature at Kitty Hawk on this day was 34°F, but because of the wind chill factor, the temperature felt like 8°F. These might not have been the most comfortable weather conditions, but the winds definitely helped the Wright Brothers' flyer to stay in the air!

On that cold December day, the Wright brothers made four flights in their flyer. On the first flight, which was piloted by Orville Wright, the flyer traveled 39 meters in 12 seconds. On the fourth flight, Wilbur flew 279 meters in 59 seconds.

Wright Brothers' 1903 Flyer Data	
Wingspan	12.3 m
Length	6.4 m
Height	2.8 m
Wing Droop	25.4 cm
Mass	229 kg
Speed	17 km/h

Orville and Wilbur Wright

Did You Know?

Before their experiments with airplanes, the Wright brothers were successful bicycle manufacturers.

Real-World Math

Use the information and the table on page 542 to solve each problem.

1. What was the wingspan of the *Kitty Hawk* flyer in centimeters?
2. What was the mass of the flyer in grams?
3. What was the wing droop of the flyer in millimeters?
4. What was the air speed of the flyer in meters per hour?
5. How many more meters did Wilbur fly on the fourth flight than Orville flew on the first flight?
6. What was the difference between the wingspan and the length of the flyer?
7. If Orville Wright's mass was 81 kilograms at the time of the flight, what was the combined mass of the flyer and Orville Wright?

12-7 Problem-Solving Investigation

MAIN IDEA I will choose the best strategy to solve a problem.

P.S.I. TEAM +

ARIANA: I checked the temperature this morning, and according to the thermometer, it was −3°F. This afternoon, the temperature was 7°F. I know it got warmer outside, but by how much?

YOUR MISSION: Find the change in temperature.

Understand

The morning temperature was −3°F. The afternoon temperature was 7°F. You need to find how many degrees the temperature increased.

Plan

You can use a model such as a number line to find the change in temperature. Graph the morning and afternoon temperatures on the number line and find the distance between them.

Solve

Draw a number line that includes −3 and 7.

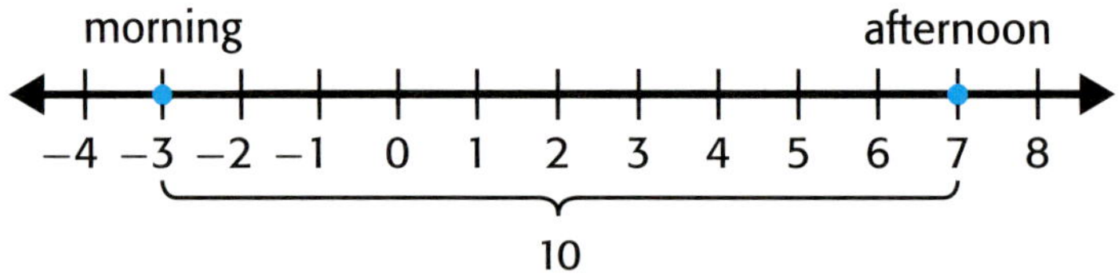

Since the distance between −3 and 7 is 10, the temperature rose 10° from the morning to the afternoon.

Check

The increase in temperature from −3°F to 0°F is 3 degrees. The increase in temperature from 0°F to 7°F is 7 degrees. Since $3 + 7 = 10$, the answer is reasonable.

Mixed Problem Solving

EXTRA PRACTICE
See page R34.

Use any strategy shown below to solve each problem.

PROBLEM-SOLVING STRATEGIES
- Work backward.
- Look for a pattern.
- Use a model.
- Solve a simpler problem.

1. **Measurement** Charlene is putting up a border along both sides of a path. Between each stake, she will use 0.61 meter of rope. She will need 48 stakes for each side of the path. There is a stake at the beginning and at the end of the path. Which is the best estimate for the number of centimeters of rope she will need; 280 cm, 2,800 cm, or 28,000 cm? Explain.

2. Gabriella is cutting out stars. First she cuts a 5-centimeter star. Then she cuts a 4.5-centimeter star, followed by a 4-centimeter star. The last star she cuts is a 2-centimeter star. If she followed the pattern, how many stars did she make?

3. Two students make 14 party bags in 20 minutes. How many party bags can 4 students make at the same rate in 40 minutes?

4. **Measurement** It takes Jasmine 40 minutes to paint a bookshelf with one coat of paint. After each coat, she waits 50 minutes for the paint to dry. How long will it take Jasmine to apply three coats of paint to the bookshelf?

5. The greatest temperature change on Earth in a 24-hour period was in Loma, Montana, on January 15, 1972. The temperature rose from −54°F to 49°F. How much did the temperature increase?

6. Brady planted vegetables in his garden. The table shows the height of a plant during a 2-week period. If the plant grows at the same rate, estimate its height on June 15th.

Vegetable Heights

Date	Height (cm)
May 18	48.5
May 25	54.9
June 1	61.3

7. **Algebra** Describe the pattern below. Then find the next three numbers in the pattern.

   2, 4, 7, 11, 16, 22, ■, ■, ■ . . .

8. **Algebra** A number is divided by 3. Next, the quotient is multiplied by 5. Then 5 is added to the product. If the result is 25, what is the number?

9. **WRITING IN MATH** The temperature in Calgary rose from −17°C to 13°C in four hours on January 11, 1983. Explain how to use a number line to find the change in temperature.

CHAPTER 12

Study Guide and Review

Math Online macmillanmh.com
- STUDY TO GO
- Vocabulary Review

FOLDABLES® Study Organizer GET READY to Study

Be sure the following Big Ideas are written in your Foldable.

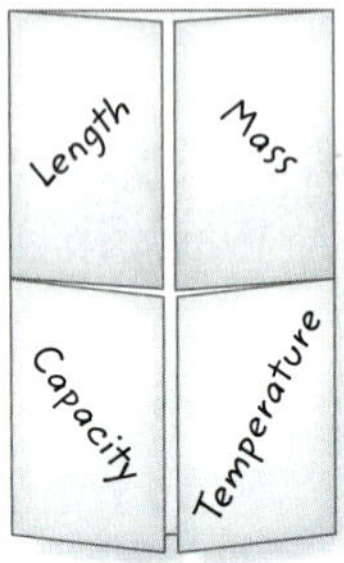

Key Concepts

Metric Units of Length (p. 517)

- 1 centimeter (cm) = 10 millimeters (mm)
- 1 meter (m) = 100 cm or 1,000 mm
- 1 kilometer (km) = 1,000 m

Metric Units of Mass (p. 524)

- 1 gram (g) = 1,000 milligrams (mg)
- 1 kilogram (kg) = 1,000 g

Metric Units of Capacity (p. 527)

- 1 liter (L) = 1,000 mL

Integers (p. 533)

- **Negative numbers** are less than 0.
- **Positive numbers** are greater than 0.
- **Integers** are negative and positive whole numbers and zero.

Units of Temperature (p. 537)

- Temperature can be measured in degrees **Fahrenheit** (°F) or degrees **Celsius** (°C).

Key Vocabulary

integer (p. 533)
mass (p. 524)
metric system (p. 517)
negative number (p. 533)
positive number (p. 533)

Vocabulary Check

Choose the correct word or number that completes each sentence.

1. One (liter, kiloliter) equals 1,000 milliliters.
2. A (centimeter, kilometer) is one hundredth of a meter.
3. One thousand grams equals 1 (milligram, kilogram).
4. Gram is a metric measure of (mass, length).
5. Temperature is measured in (grams, degrees).
6. A good outside temperature for water sports is 30 degrees (Celsius, Fahrenheit).
7. A reasonable estimate for the capacity of a soup can is (360, 36) milliliters.
8. To change meters to millimeters, multiply by (1,000, 100).

Lesson-by-Lesson Review

12-1 Units of Length (pp. 517–521)

Example 1

Complete: 7 m = ■ cm.

$7 \times 100 = 700$ 1 m = 100 cm

So, 7 meters = 700 centimeters.

Example 2

Complete: 6,000 m = ■ km.

$6{,}000 \div 1{,}000 = 6$ 1,000 m = 1 km

So, 6,000 meters = 6 kilometers.

Complete.

9. 4,000 m = ■ km

10. 5 m = ■ mm

11. 30 mm = ■ cm

12. 12 cm = ■ mm

13. A giant squid that was found in the 1800s had a body 6 meters long and a tentacle 11 meters long. How many centimeters longer was the tentacle than the body?

12-2 Problem-Solving Skill: Determine Reasonable Answers (pp. 522–523)

Example 3

A marathon race is about 42 kilometers long. The length of the average person's stride is 1 meter. Is it reasonable to say that a person takes about 4,200 strides in a marathon race?

$42 \times 1{,}000 = 42{,}000$ 1 km = 1,000 m

A marathon is about 42,000 meters long.

Since a person runs about 1 meter for each stride, the average person takes about 42,000 strides in a marathon race. So, 4,200 strides is not a reasonable estimate.

Solve. Determine reasonable answers.

14. A cube of small self-stick notes is 5.2 centimeters long. Will it fit in a square container that is 50 millimeters long? Explain.

15. A doorway is 0.95 meter wide, and a desk is 120 centimeters wide. Will the desk fit through the doorway without having to tilt it? Explain.

16. Leroy estimates that his kite flew 2,000 centimeters high. Does this seem reasonable? Explain.

12-3 Units of Mass (pp. 524–526)

Example 4
A bag of flour has a mass of 2,000 grams. What is the mass of the bag of flour in kilograms?

To convert a smaller unit to a larger unit, divide.

2,000 ÷ 1,000 = 2   1,000 g = 1 kg

So, 2,000 grams equals 2 kilograms.

The mass of the bag of flour is 2 kg.

Complete.

17. 8 kg = ■ g

18. 24,000 g = ■ kg

19. 9 g = ■ mg

20. 165 mg = ■ g

21. 75 kg = ■ g

22. Mrs. Mathews bought the cheese shown in the table. How many grams of cheese did she buy altogether?

Cheese	Amount
American	8,000 mg
Swiss	7,000 mg

12-4 Units of Capacity (pp. 527–530)

Example 5
Mr. Rueben bought 15 liters of orange juice for a class party. How many milliliters of orange juice did he buy?

To convert a larger unit to a smaller unit, multiply.

15 × 1,000 = 15,000   1 L = 1,000 mL

15 liters = 15,000 milliliters

So, Mr. Rueben bought 15,000 milliliters of orange juice.

Complete.

23. 3 L = ■ mL

24. 6,000 mL = ■ L

25. 4,000 mL = ■ L

26. 250 mL = ■ L

27. 1 L = ■ mL

28. A 2-liter bottle of fruit juice is used to fill 3 glasses. Each glass holds 300 milliliters. How many milliliters are left in the bottle?

12-5 Integers and Graphing on Number Lines (pp. 533–535)

Example 6

A swimmer dove 6 feet below the surface of the water. Write an integer to represent this situation. Then graph the integer on a number line.

6 feet below: −6

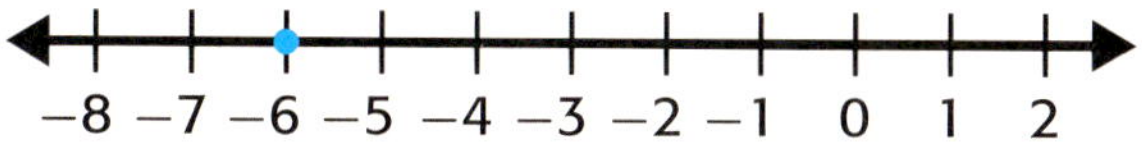

Example 7

A plant grew to a height of 8 inches. Write an integer to represent this situation. Then write its opposite.

grew 8 inches: +8 or 8

The opposite of 8 is −8.

Write an integer to represent each situation. Then graph the integer on a number line.

29. a golf score of 3 under par

30. stock value up $1

Write an integer to represent each situation. Then write its opposite.

31. gaining 12 points

32. 10 miles below the surface

33. An airport control tower is 18 meters above the ground. The subway is 6 meters below the ground. Write two integers to represent these situations.

12-6 Units of Temperature (pp. 537–541)

Example 8

Which is the more reasonable temperature for a chilly room: 60°C or 60°F?

- 60°C is warmer than body temperature.
- 60°F is cooler than body temperature.

The more reasonable temperature is 60°F.

Example 9

The temperature changed from 77°F to 70°F in one day. Use an integer to represent the change in temperature.

77° − 70° = 7° decrease in temperature

The change in temperature is −7.

Choose the more reasonable temperature for each situation.

34. hot sandwich: 40°F or 160°F

35. inside a refrigerator: 5°C or 50°C

Find each change in temperature. Use an integer to represent the change.

36. 29°C to 31°C **37.** 14°F to 0°F

38. The temperature at 6:30 P.M. was 43°F. By 10:00 P.M. it was 28°F. Find the change in temperature. Use an integer to represent the change.

12-7 Problem-Solving Investigation: Choose a Strategy (pp. 544–545)

Example 10

Selena has $80. She wants to buy 2 shirts, a pair of jeans, and a belt. The belt costs $8. Each shirt costs twice this amount. Together, both shirts cost $10 less than the jeans. Does Selena have enough money to buy all the items?

To solve the problem, you can use the *work backward* strategy.

One shirt costs twice what the belt costs. So, multiply the cost of the belt by 2.

$\$8 \times 2 = \$16$

Since she bought 2 shirts, multiply the cost of one shirt by 2.

$2 \times \$16$ or $\$32$

The cost of the jeans is $10 more than the cost of both shirts. So, add 10 to the cost of the 2 shirts.

$\$32 + \$10 = \$42$

Next, find the total cost of all the items.

belt + 2 shirts + jeans = total cost

$$\$8 + \$32 + \$42 = \$82$$

Since $\$82 > \$80$, Selena does not have enough money to buy all the items.

Use any strategy to solve each problem.

39. Dominique made party invitations on her computer. She gave out half of the invitations, while her friend gave out 11. There are 5 more invitations that need to be delivered. How many invitations did Dominique make?

40. An antique desk is 1.5 meters wide. Will it fit in a space that is 2,000 centimeters wide? Explain.

41. **Algebra** Describe the change in temperature from 1:00 to 3:00.

Time	Temperature (°F)
1:00 P.M.	59
3:00 P.M.	65

42. On Day 1, Troy swam 350 meters. On Day 2, he swam 500 meters, and on Day 3 he swam 650 meters. If he continues this pattern, how many meters will he have swum in 5 days?

43. Andrew and 2 friends can blow up 15 balloons in 10 minutes. How many balloons can Andrew and 5 friends blow up at the same rate in 20 minutes?

CHAPTER 12

Chapter Test

Math Online macmillanmh.com

• Chapter Test

Complete.

1. 150 mm = ■ cm **2.** 4 km = ■ m

3. 3,000 m = ■ km **4.** 8 m = ■ cm

5. **MULTIPLE CHOICE** Lance needs to draw line segment *PL* to complete the figure. Use a metric ruler to measure the distance from point *P* to point *L*.

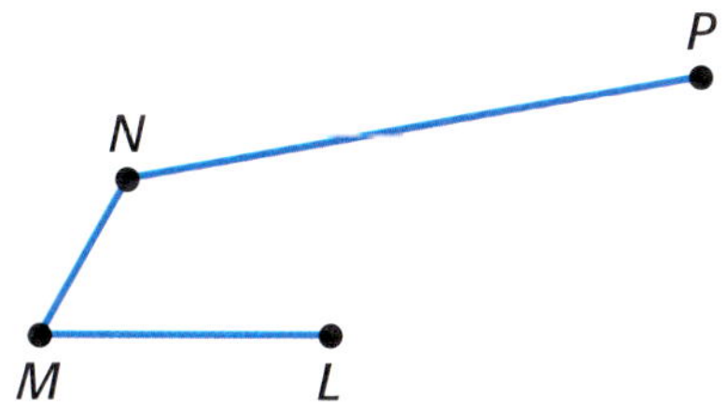

To the nearest centimeter, what is the length of line segment *PL*?

A 2 cm **C** 4 cm

B 3 cm **D** 5 cm

6. Is 20 kilometers a reasonable estimate for the length of an Olympic-sized swimming pool? Explain.

Complete.

7. 21,000 g = ■ kg **8.** 390 mg = ■ g

9. 4,000 mL = ■ L **10.** 74 L = ■ mL

11. A loaf of bread has 20 slices. Each slice has a mass of 24 grams. Find the mass of the loaf in kilograms.

12. A nickel has a mass of 5 grams. Find the total mass of the roll of nickels shown in grams.

Find each change in temperature. Use an integer to represent the change.

13. 20°C to 11°C **14.** 43°F to 58°F

15. 35°C to 48°C **16.** 92°F to 74°F

17. **MULTIPLE CHOICE** Which is the best estimate for the capacity of a trash can?

F 2 mL **H** 2 L

G 20 mL **J** 20 L

Write an integer to represent each situation. Then write its opposite.

18. 11° below zero

19. a hole 3 feet deep

20. 5 points added to a grade

21. **Algebra** Write a real-world situation that can be represented by the integer graphed.

Choose the more reasonable temperature for each situation.

22. hot tea: 300°F or 200°F

23. cold water: 5°C or 25°C

24. Jayden has a tropical fish tank. Is 40° Fahrenheit or 75° Fahrenheit a more reasonable temperature for the water in the tank? Explain.

25. **WRITING IN MATH** Explain how you can use integers to represent changes in temperature.

CHAPTER 12

Test Practice

Cumulative, Chapters 1–12

Math Online macmillanmh.com

- Test Practice

PART 1 Multiple Choice

Read each question. Then fill in the correct answer on the answer sheet provided by your teacher or on a sheet of paper.

1. A bag of dog food has a mass of 96 kilograms. The food is divided equally into 2 containers. How many grams of dog food are in each container?

A 48,000 grams

B 4,800 grams

C 480 grams

D Not Here

---

2. Xavier used the lemon juice shown to make lemonade. What fraction of a liter did he use?

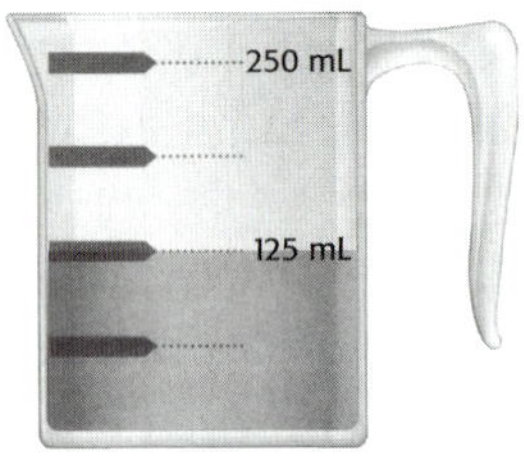

F $\frac{1}{4}$

G $\frac{1}{8}$

H $\frac{1}{12}$

J $\frac{1}{16}$

---

3. Eduardo says that the next term in the sequence below is 35. Which shows that his solution is not reasonable?

55, 47, 39, 31, ...

A The terms are increasing.

B The terms are decreasing.

C The terms are multiples of 5.

D The terms are odd numbers.

4. An advertisement is shown below. Which word problem matches this advertisement?

F The regular price is \$25. The television is on sale for 24.5% off. What is the sale price?

G The regular price is \$245. The television is on sale for 25% off. What is the sale price?

H The sale price is \$245 at 25% off. What is the regular price of a television?

J The regular price is \$245. If you buy two televisions, the second one is priced at 25% off the regular price. What is the total cost of two televisions?

---

5. Dion and his brother bought a bag of roasted nuts at the fair. If they ate $\frac{5}{6}$ of the roasted nuts, what fraction of the nuts remained?

A $\frac{1}{2}$

B $\frac{1}{4}$

C $\frac{1}{5}$

D $\frac{1}{6}$

Preparing for Standardized Tests
For test-taking strategies and practice, see pages R42–R55.

6. Hunter has four old stamps. Stamp A is worth \$3. Stamp B is worth 4 times the value of stamp A. Stamp C is worth 5 times the value of Stamp A. The stamps are worth \$45 altogether. What is the value of stamp D?

F \$12 **H** \$18

G \$15 **J** \$27

7. What fraction of their games did the soccer team win?

Soccer Team's Games	
Played	Won
20	15

A $\frac{1}{5}$ **C** $\frac{3}{4}$

B $\frac{1}{4}$ **D** $\frac{4}{5}$

8. Larry ran a 5-kilometer race. When he was halfway to the finish line, how many meters did he have left to run?

F 5,000 meters

G 2,500 meters

H 500 meters

J 250 meters

PART 2 Short Response

Record your answers on the answer sheet provided by your teacher or on a sheet of paper.

9. The table shows the number of cars washed during the 3 days of a fundraiser car wash. Estimate how many cars were washed in all. Is your estimate greater or less than the exact number?

Day	Cars Washed
Friday	62
Saturday	83
Sunday	78

PART 3 Extended Response

Record your answers on the answer sheet provided by your teacher or on a sheet of paper.

10. Write an example where the temperature drops 10°F and an example where the temperature rises 10°F.

11. A fence is placed around a playground in the shape of a rectangle. The length of the fence is 32 meters. The width of the fence is 1,200 centimeters. How much fence is needed for the playground? Explain.

NEED EXTRA HELP?											
If You Missed Question...	1	2	3	4	5	6	7	8	9	10	11
Go to Lesson...	12-3	12-4	6-6	5-3	10-4	6-2	9-3	12-1	2-4	12-6	12-1

CHAPTER 13

Identify, Compare, and Classify Geometric Figures

BIG Idea What is geometry?

Geometry is the study of lines and shapes.

Example Every year, a sandcastle building competition is held along the Outer Banks of North Carolina. Sandcastles are composed of many geometric figures. Geometric figures include triangles, squares, and rectangles.

What will I learn in this chapter?

- Identify and label basic geometric terms.
- Identify characteristics of triangles and quadrilaterals.
- Sketch translations, rotations, and reflections on a coordinate grid.
- Identify transformations.
- Solve problems by using *logical reasoning*.

Key Vocabulary

parallel lines
perpendicular lines
translation
reflection
rotation

Math Online **Student Study Tools at macmillanmh.com**

FOLDABLES® Study Organizer

Make this Foldable to help you organize information about geometric figures. Begin with a sheet of $8\frac{1}{2}'' \times 11''$ paper.

1. **Fold** lengthwise to the holes.

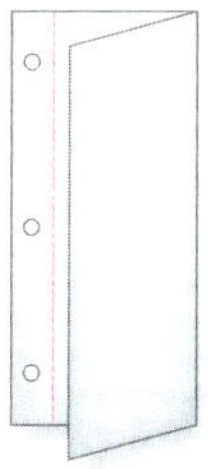

2. **Cut** along the top line. Then make equal cuts to form 10 tabs.

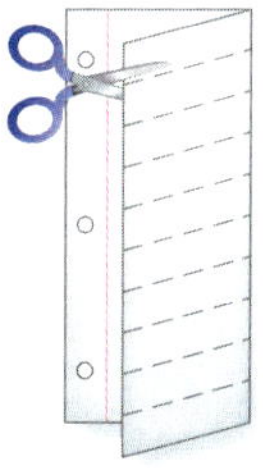

3. **Label** each tab as shown.

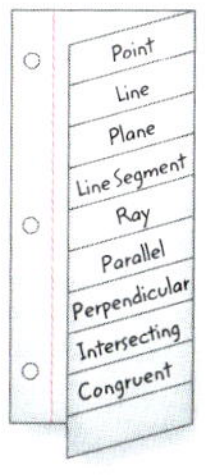

ARE YOU READY for Chapter 13?

You have two ways to check prerequisite skills for this chapter.

Option 2

Math Online Take the Chapter Readiness Quiz at macmillanmh.com.

Option 1

Complete the Quick Check below.

QUICK Check

Describe the number of sides and the number of angles in each figure. **(Prior Grade)**

1. 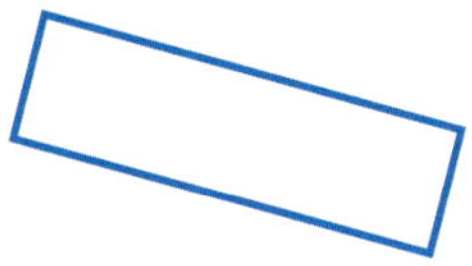

2. 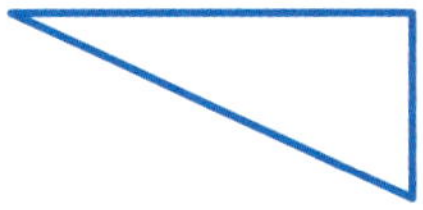

3. 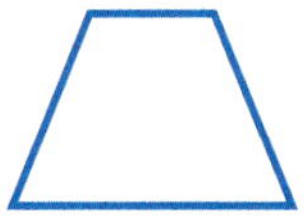

Use the figure below for Exercises 4 and 5. **(Prior Grade)**

4. Which side appears to have the same length as side *AB*?

5. At which point do sides *BC* and *DC* meet?

6. Anthony is drawing a triangle that has two sides that are equal. Draw a sketch of this triangle.

Graph each point on a coordinate grid. **(Lesson 6-5)**

7. $J(1, 7)$

8. $K(6, 0)$

9. $L(5, 6)$

10. $M(3, 3)$

13-1 Geometry Vocabulary

MAIN IDEA

I will identify and label basic geometric terms.

New Vocabulary

- **point**
- **line**
- **ray**
- **line segment**
- **plane**
- **intersecting lines**
- **perpendicular lines**
- **parallel lines**
- **congruent line segments**

Math Online

macmillanmh.com

- Extra Examples
- Personal Tutor
- Self-Check Quiz

GET READY to Learn

The butterfly kite at the right is made up of different geometric figures. Can you identify a point and a line segment on the kite?

The table shows basic geometric figures.

Geometric Figures — Key Concepts

Definition	Model
A **point** is an exact location in space, represented by a dot.	 **Words** point *A*
A **line** is a set of points that form a straight path that goes in opposite directions without ending.	 **Words** line *CD* or line *DC* **Symbols** $\overleftrightarrow{CD}$ or $\overleftrightarrow{DC}$
A **ray** is a line that has an endpoint and goes on forever in one direction.	 **Words** ray *ST* **Symbols** $\overrightarrow{ST}$
A **line segment** is part of a line between two endpoints.	 **Words** line segment *GH* or line segment *HG* **Symbols** $\overline{GH}$ or $\overline{HG}$
A **plane** is a flat surface that goes on forever in all directions.	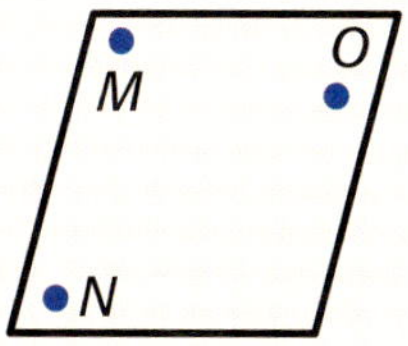 **Words** plane *MNO*

EXAMPLE Identify a Figure

1 Identify the figure at the right. Then name it using symbols.

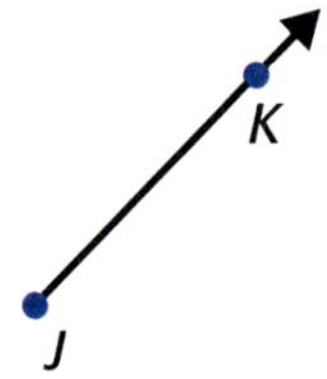

The figure has one endpoint. The arrow indicates that it goes on forever in one direction. So, it is a ray.

symbol: $\overrightarrow{JK}$

> **Remember**
> The endpoint is named first in a ray. The ray in Example 1 cannot be named $\overrightarrow{KJ}$.

Two lines in a plane can be related in three ways. They can be intersecting, perpendicular, or parallel.

Pairs of Lines — Key Concepts

Definition	Model
Intersecting lines are lines that meet or cross at a point.	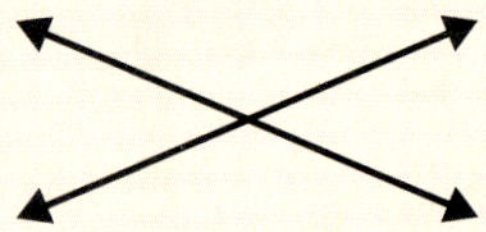
Perpendicular lines are lines that meet or cross each other to make a square corner.	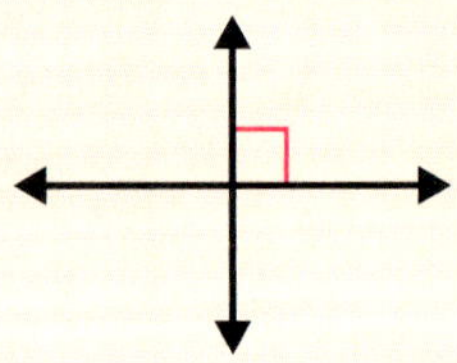
Parallel lines are lines that are the same distance apart and do not intersect.	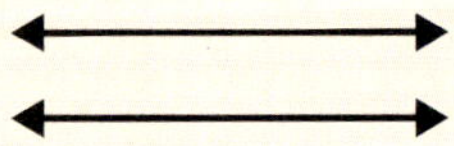

> **Vocabulary Link**
> **Perpendicular**
> **Everyday Use** vertical or meeting at a corner

EXAMPLE Describe a Pair of Lines

2 Describe the lines at the right as *intersecting, perpendicular,* or *parallel.* Choose the most specific term.

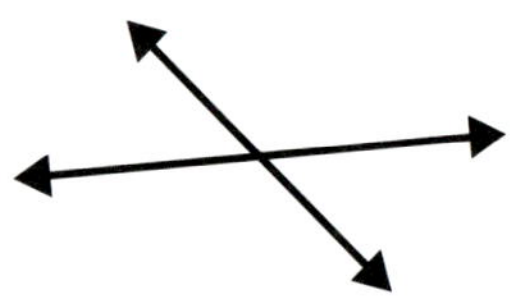

The lines cross at one point, so they are intersecting. Since they do not form a square corner, they are not perpendicular lines.

Congruent Segments

Key Concept

Line segments that have the same length are called **congruent line segments**.

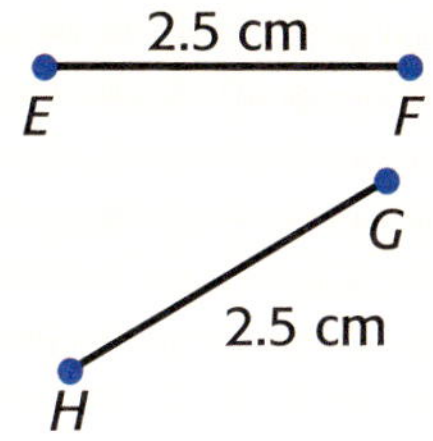

Words $\overline{EF}$ is congruent to $\overline{HG}$.

Symbols $\overline{EF} \cong \overline{HG}$

EXAMPLE Identify Congruent Line Segments

3 **MEASUREMENT Determine whether the line segments at the right are congruent.**

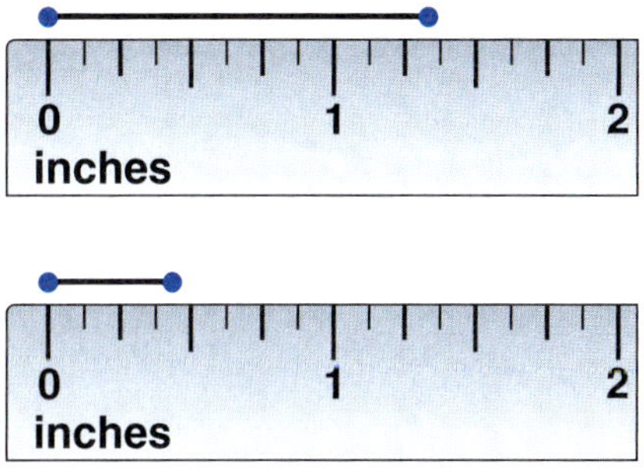

The segments do not have the same length. So, they are not congruent.

CHECK What You Know

Identify each figure. Then name it using symbols. See Example 1 (p. 558)

1.

2.

3. • *T*

Describe each pair of lines as *intersecting*, *perpendicular*, or *parallel*. Choose the most specific term. See Example 2 (p. 558)

4.

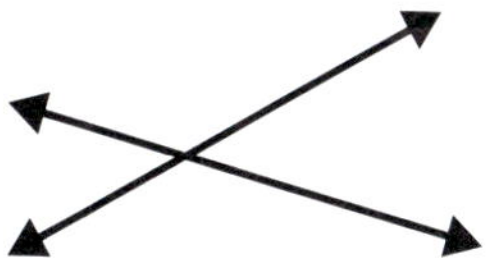

5.

Measure each segment. Then determine whether each pair of line segments are congruent. Write *yes* or *no*. See Example 3 (p. 559)

6.

7.

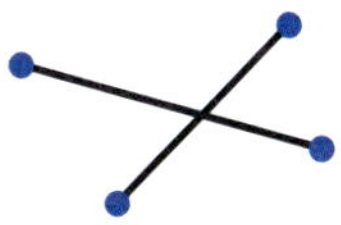

8. What type of lines are the double yellow lines on the road at the right? Explain.

9. Talk About It Describe the difference between a ray and a line.

Practice and Problem Solving

EXTRA PRACTICE See page R34.

Identify each figure. Then name it using symbols. See Example 1 (p. 558)

10. 

11. 

12. 

13. 

14. 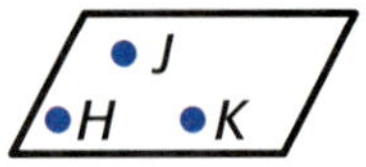

15. 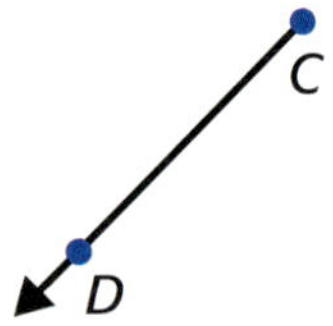

Describe each pair of lines as *intersecting, perpendicular,* or *parallel.* Choose the most specific term. See Example 2 (p. 558)

16. 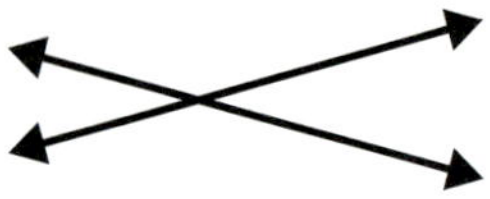

17. 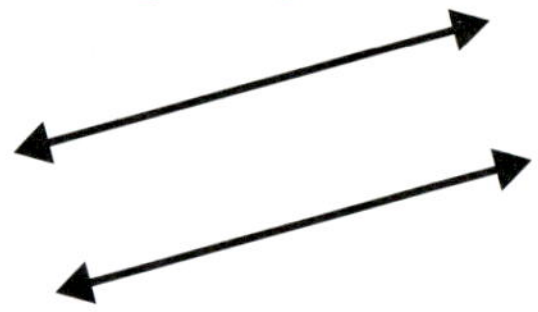

18. 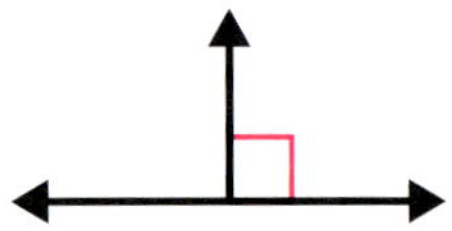

Measure each line segment. Then determine whether each pair of line segments are congruent. Write *yes* or *no*. See Example 3 (p. 559)

19. 

20. 

21. 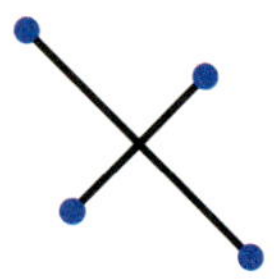

22. Name the letters shown at the right that appear to contain parallel line segments.

A	D	E
H	K	L
F	P	T

23. Describe an object in your room that contains parallel lines. Then describe an object that contains lines that are perpendicular.

24. In gymnastics, the floor exercises are done on a mat that is 40 feet long and 40 feet wide. Is the mat an example of a point, a line, a line segment, or part of a plane? Explain.

H.O.T. Problems

25. OPEN ENDED Name three objects in your classroom that are a part of a plane.

26. CHALLENGE Are the lines at the right *intersecting*, *parallel*, or *neither*? Explain your reasoning.

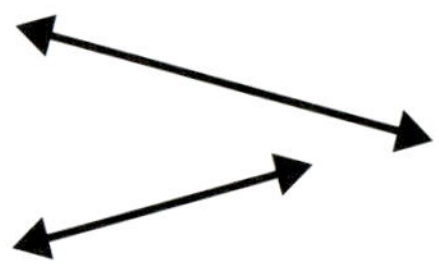

27. WRITING IN MATH Compare perpendicular lines and parallel lines.

Geometry Concentration

Identifying Geometry Attributes

Get Ready!

Players: 2 or more

You will need: 20 index cards

Get Set!

Make ten index cards like the ones shown at the right. Then make two sets of each of the following symbols:

P, $\overrightarrow{PR}$, $\overleftrightarrow{PR}$, $\overline{PR}$, plane MNO

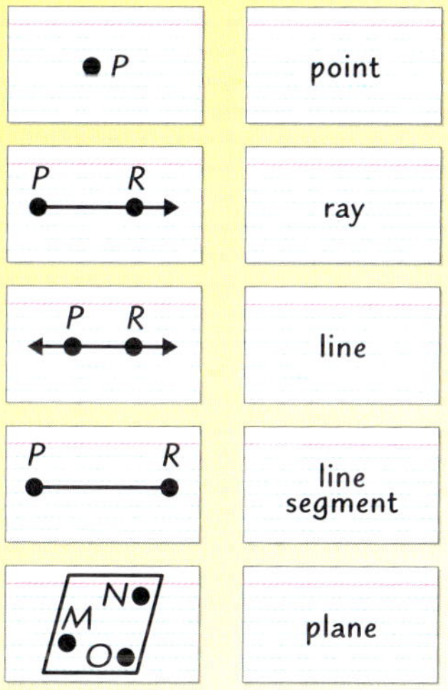

Go!

- Shuffle all the index cards.
- Place the cards facedown.
- Player 1 turns over two cards. The player tries to match a geometric symbol with the correct term or drawing for the symbol.
- If the cards match, Player 1 keeps the cards and turns over two more. If no match is made, turn the cards facedown again.
- Player 2 then takes a turn choosing two cards.
- The game continues until all of the cards have been paired up.
- The player with the most pairs wins.

13-2 Problem-Solving Strategy

MAIN IDEA I will solve problems by using logical reasoning.

Maggie, Sam, Aisha, and Nicolás each have a different colored notebook: blue, red, purple, and green. Use the clues to determine which person has each notebook.

1. Sam and the girl with the green notebook are in the same class.
2. A girl has the purple notebook.
3. Nicolás and the person with the red notebook eat lunch together.
4. Maggie is not in the same class as Sam.

Understand

What facts do you know?

- The four clues that are listed above.

What do you need to find?

- Which person has each notebook.

Plan

You can use logical reasoning to find which person has each notebook. Make a table to help organize the information.

Solve

Place an "X" in each box that cannot be true.

	Blue	Red	Purple	Green
Maggie	X	X	yes	X
Sam	X	yes	X	X
Aisha	X	X	X	yes
Nicolás	yes	X	X	X

- Clue 3 shows that Nicolás does not have the red notebook.
- Clues 1 and 2 show that girls have the green and purple notebooks and the boys have the blue and red notebooks.
- Clue 4 shows that Maggie is not in the same class as Sam, so she does not have the green notebook.

So, Maggie has a purple notebook, Sam has a red notebook, Aisha has a green notebook, and Nicolás has a blue notebook.

Check

Look back. Since all of the answers match the clues, the solution is reasonable.

ANALYZE the Strategy

Refer to the problem on the previous page.

1. If you did not know that a girl had the purple notebook, would it be possible to determine who had each notebook? Explain your reasoning.

2. Suppose Aisha is not in the same class as Sam. Who has which notebook?

3. The area of a garden is 16 square feet. If the length and width are whole numbers, is the garden definitely a square? Explain.

4. Explain when to use the *logical reasoning* strategy to solve a problem.

PRACTICE the Strategy

EXTRA PRACTICE See page R34.

Solve the problem. Use *logical reasoning*.

5. Main Street and Park Street do not meet. They are always the same distance apart. Central Avenue crosses both streets to form square corners. Central Avenue and Fletcher Avenue also do not meet. Which streets are perpendicular?

6. **Algebra** If the pattern below continues, how many pennies will be in the fifth figure?

Figure 1 **Figure 2** **Figure 3**

7. Charlotte, Ramon, and Nora have different professions: scientist, athlete, and teacher. Charlotte does not like sports. Ramon is not a teacher nor an athlete. Nora likes to run. Who is the teacher?

8. Three dogs are sitting in a line. Rocky is not last. Coco is in front of the tallest dog. Marley is sitting behind Rocky. List the dogs in order from first to last.

9. Ethan has $1.25 in change. He has twice as many dimes as pennies, and the number of nickels is one less than the number of pennies. How many dimes, nickels, and pennies does he have?

10. There are 4 more girls in Mrs. Pitt's class than Mr. Brown's class. Five girls moved from Mrs. Pitt's class to Mr. Brown's class. Now there are twice as many girls in Mr. Brown's class as there are in Mrs. Pitt's. How many girls were in Mr. Brown's class to begin with?

11. **Geometry** Set up 12 toothpicks as shown below. Move three toothpicks so that you form four squares.

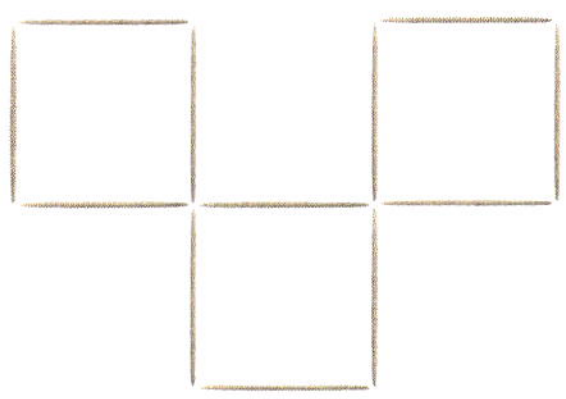

12. **WRITING IN MATH** How did you use logical reasoning to determine that Nora is not the teacher in Exercise 7?

Explore

Geometry Activity for 13-3
Identify Angles

MAIN IDEA

I will use turns on circles to identify angles.

New Vocabulary

angle
vertex
degree
right angle
acute angle
obtuse angle

You Will Need

protractor

Math Online

macmillanmh.com
- Concepts in Motion

An **angle** is formed by two rays with a common endpoint. The point where the two rays meet is called a **vertex**. The plural form of vertex is *vertices.*

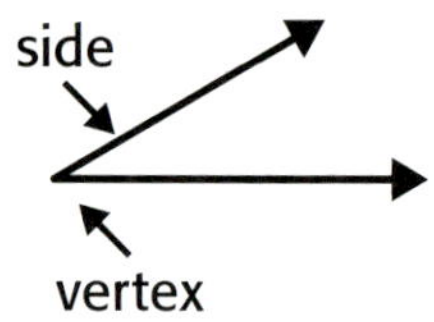

The unit used to measure an angle is called a **degree** (°). A circle contains 360°. So, a full turn on a circle is 360°.

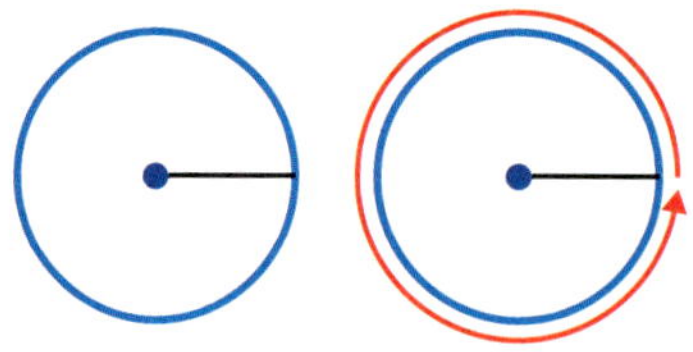

1 full turn = 360°

$1^\circ = \frac{1}{360}$ of a turn

When a turn on a circle is less than full, the angle formed is less than 360°.

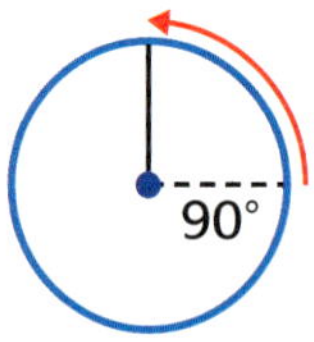

1 quarter turn

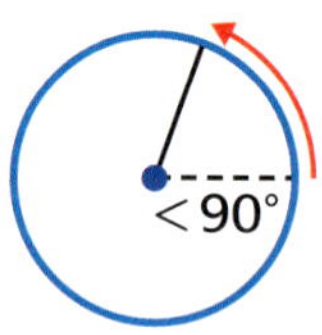

less than 1 quarter turn

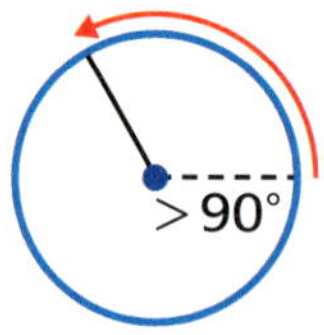

more than 1 quarter turn

Angles can be identified according to whether they measure 90°, less than 90°, or greater than 90°.

Angles
Key Concepts

Right Angle

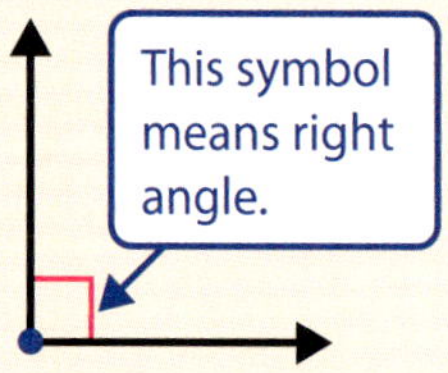

A **right angle** measures 90°.

Acute Angle

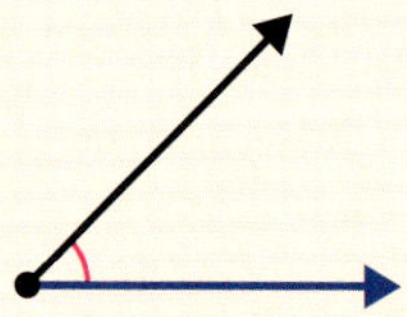

An **acute angle** measures between 0° and 90°.

Obtuse Angle

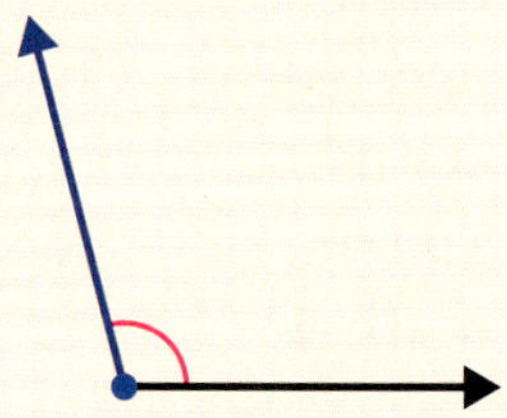

An **obtuse angle** measures between 90° and 180°.

It is easy to identify acute and obtuse angles because they are less than or greater than 90°. You can use a protractor.

ACTIVITY

1 Identify the angle as *acute*, *right*, or *obtuse*.

The angle appears to be a right angle. Use a protractor to measure the angle.

So, the measure of the angle is 90°. It is a right angle.

Step 3: Read the measure on the protractor where the other ray crosses the protractor.

Step 2: Make sure one ray of the angle passes through zero on the protractor.

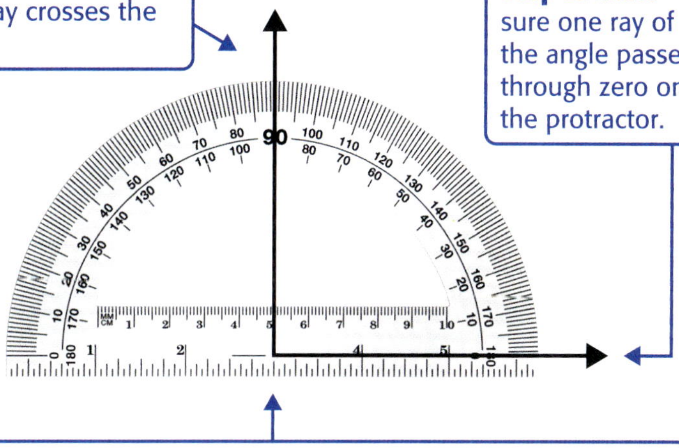

Step 1: Align the center of the protractor with the vertex of the angle.

CHECK What You Know

Use a protractor to identify each angle as *acute*, *right*, or *obtuse*.

1. 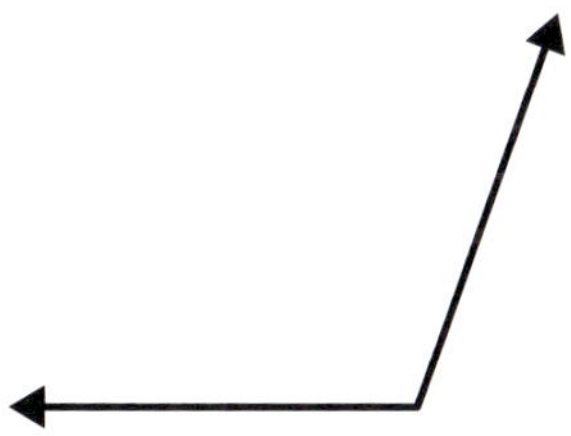

2. 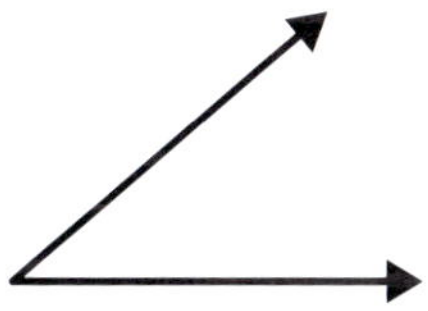

3. 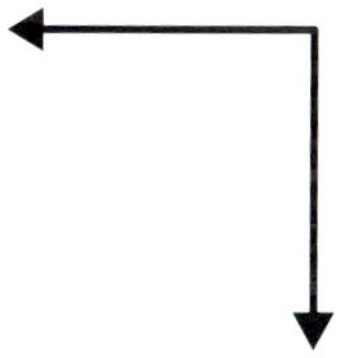

4. 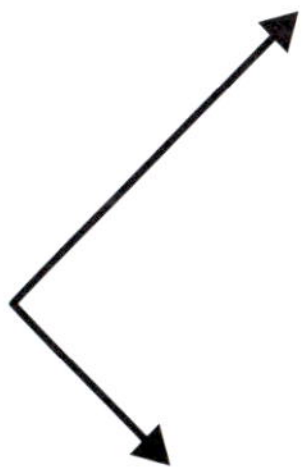

5. 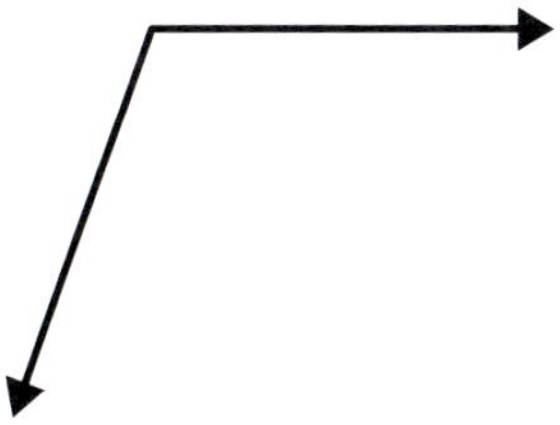

6. 

7. **OPEN ENDED** Draw an obtuse angle.

8. **WRITING IN MATH** Write a definition for perpendicular lines that includes the words *right angle*.

13-3 Triangles

GET READY to Learn

There is a large pyramid standing in front of the Louvre (loo-vrah) museum in Paris, France. The sides of the pyramid are shaped like triangles.

MAIN IDEA

I will identify characteristics of triangles.

New Vocabulary

- **isosceles triangle**
- **equilateral triangle**
- **scalene triangle**
- **acute triangle**
- **right triangle**
- **obtuse triangle**

Math Online

macmillanmh.com

- Extra Examples
- Personal Tutor
- Self-Check Quiz

You can classify triangles by the lengths of their sides.

Classify Triangles by Angles

Key Concepts

Isosceles Triangle

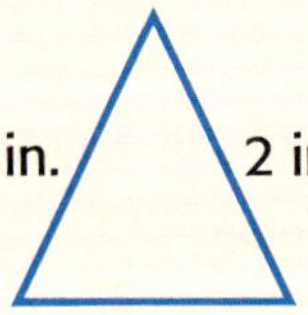

at least two sides congruent

Equilateral Triangle

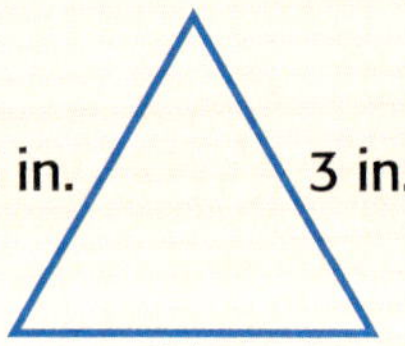

all sides congruent

Scalene Triangle

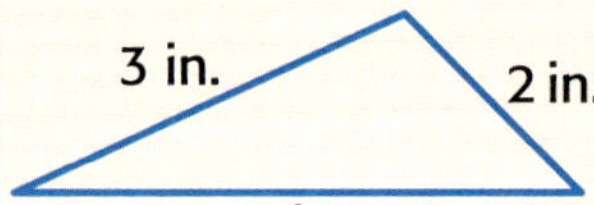

no sides congruent

Real-World EXAMPLE Identify Sides

1 **MEASUREMENT Measure each side of the triangle. Then find the number of congruent sides. State whether any of the sides appear to be perpendicular. Write *yes* or *no*.**

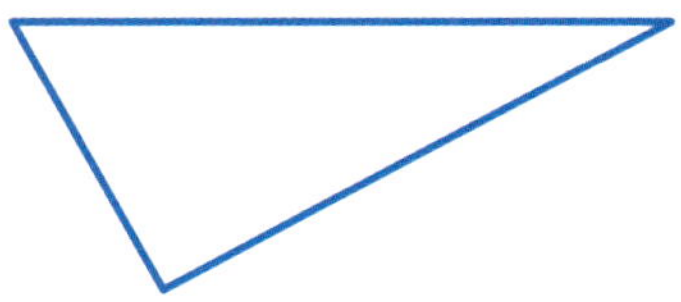

None of the sides of the triangle have the same length. So, no sides are congruent.

Yes; two sides of the triangle appear to be perpendicular.

Remember
A right angle is formed by perpendicular lines.

Hands-On Mini Activity

Step 1 Draw and cut out three different triangles that each have one right angle. Draw and cut out three different triangles that do not have any right angles.

Right Triangles **Not Right Triangles**

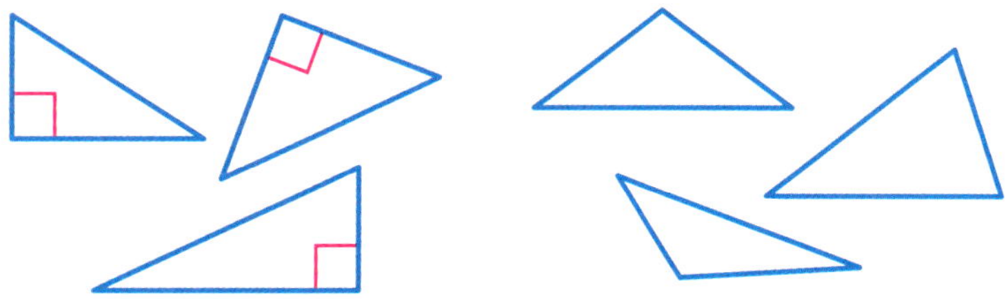

Step 2 Draw and cut out three different triangles that each have one obtuse angle.

Step 3 Draw and cut out three different triangles that do not have either a right angle or an obtuse angle.

Step 4 Separate your triangles into three different groups, based on the measures of the angles.

In the Hands-On Mini Activity, you classified triangles by the measures of their angles.

Classify Triangles by Angles — Key Concepts

Acute Triangle	Right Triangle	Obtuse Triangle
	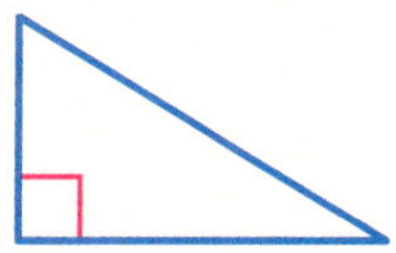	
3 acute angles	1 right angle, 2 acute angles	1 obtuse angle, 2 acute angles

Real-World EXAMPLE — Identify Angles

2 **GEOMETRY Triangles form the sides of the Khafre Pyramid in Egypt. Identify the kinds of angles in the triangle.**

All three angles are acute.

CHECK What You Know

Measure the sides of each triangle. Then find the number of congruent sides. State whether any of the sides appear to be perpendicular. Write *yes* or *no*. See Example 1 (p. 566)

1. 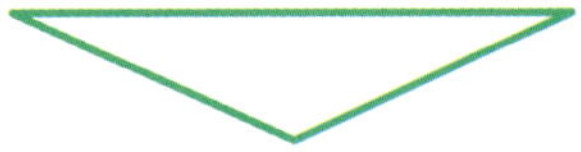

2. 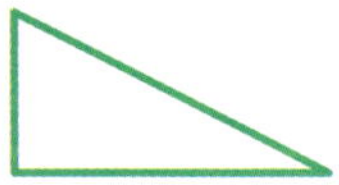

Identify the kinds of angles in each triangle. See Example 2 (p. 567)

3. 

4. 

5. A triangle is formed by the racked pool balls shown in the photograph. Find the number of congruent sides in the triangle.

6. Talk About It Write a description of an isosceles right triangle.

Practice and Problem Solving

EXTRA PRACTICE See page R35.

Measure the sides of each triangle. Then find the number of congruent sides. State whether any of the sides appear to be perpendicular. Write *yes* or *no*. See Example 1 (p. 566)

7. 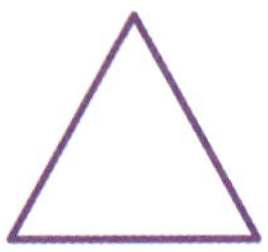

8. 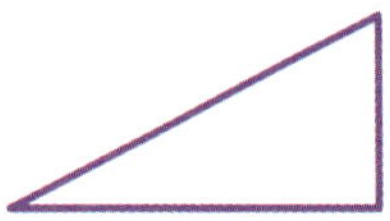

9. 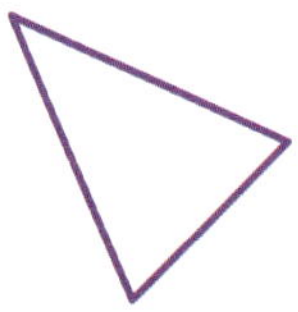

10. 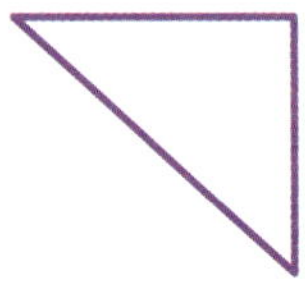

Identify the kinds of angles in each triangle. See Example 2 (p. 567)

11. 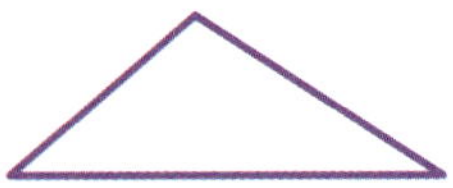

12. 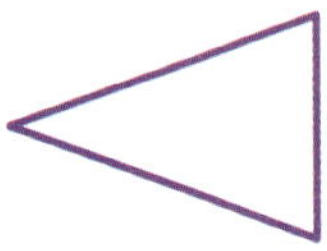

13. 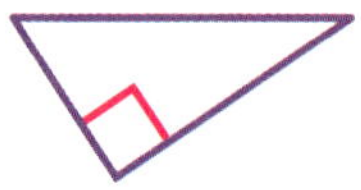

14. 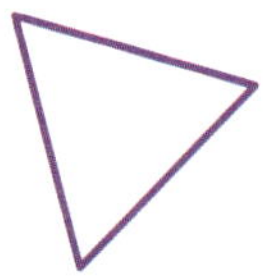

15. the triangles in the bridge

16. half of a square sandwich

17. Look at the triangle on the top of the White House on a twenty dollar bill. Describe the sides and angles of the triangle.

18. The sum of the measures of the angles of a triangle is 180°. In a right triangle, what is the sum of the measures of the two acute angles?

Real-World PROBLEM SOLVING

Art The image shown at the right contains many triangles.

19. Describe the different types of triangles found in the image.

20. Look at the purple triangle. State whether any sides appear to be perpendicular. Then identify the triangle.

H.O.T. Problems

21. **OPEN ENDED** Draw a triangle that has all acute angles and two congruent sides. Then classify the triangle by its side lengths and by its angle measures.

22. **WHICH ONE DOESN'T BELONG?** Identify the triangle that does not belong with the other three. Explain your reasoning.

23. **CHALLENGE** Emma, Gabriel, Jorge, and Makayla each have a different triangle. Use the clues below to describe each person's triangle as isosceles, equilateral, or scalene and as acute, right, or obtuse. Explain your process.
    - Gabriel and Jorge each have a 90° angle in their triangles.
    - Gabriel's triangle does not have any congruent sides.
    - One of Emma's angles measures greater than 90°.
    - Each side of Makayla's triangle and two sides of Emma's and Jorge's triangles are four centimeters long.

24. **WRITING IN ▶MATH** A triangle has two sides that are perpendicular. Could the triangle be isosceles, equilateral, or scalene? Explain.

13-4 Quadrilaterals

MAIN IDEA

I will identify characteristics of quadrilaterals.

New Vocabulary

quadrilateral
rectangle
square
parallelogram
rhombus
trapezoid

Math Online

macmillanmh.com
- Extra Examples
- Personal Tutor
- Self-Check Quiz

GET READY to Learn

The image shown at the right includes squares and rectangles. These are two different types of *quadrilaterals*.

A **quadrilateral** is a polygon with four sides and four angles.

Hands-On Mini Activity

Draw and cut out three different parallelograms like the ones shown. Then draw and cut out three different quadrilaterals that are *not* parallelograms.

Parallelograms **Not Parallelograms**

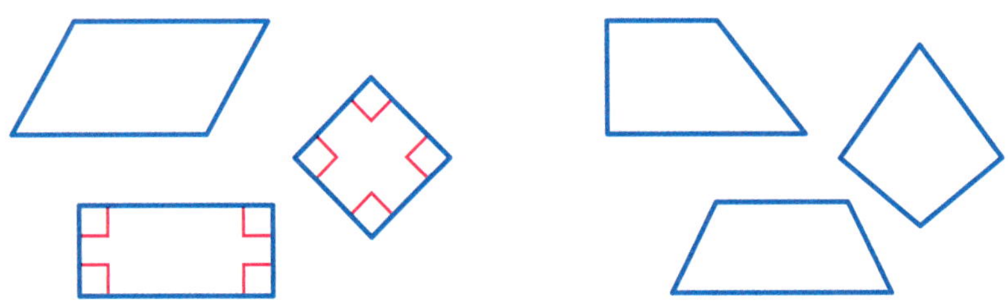

a. What attribute do all the parallelograms have that the other quadrilaterals do not?

b. Use the figures above and your figures to write a definition for *parallelogram*.

You can classify quadrilaterals using one or more of the attributes listed below.

- congruent sides
- parallel sides
- perpendicular sides

Classifying Quadrilaterals

Key Concepts

Quadrilateral	Example	Attributes
Rectangle	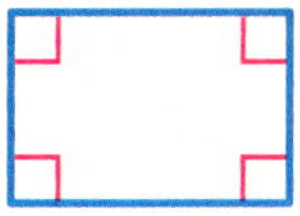	• Opposite sides congruent • All angles are right angles • Opposite sides parallel
Square	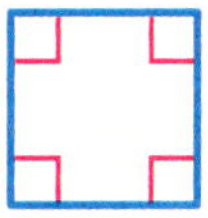	• All sides congruent • All angles are right angles • Opposite sides parallel
Parallelogram	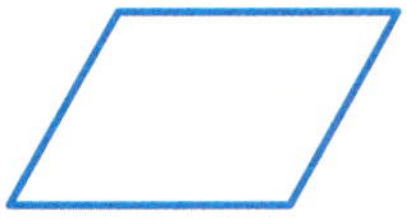	• Opposite sides congruent • Opposite sides parallel
Rhombus	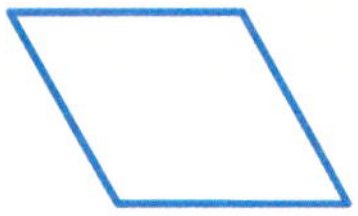	• All sides congruent • Opposite sides parallel
Trapezoid	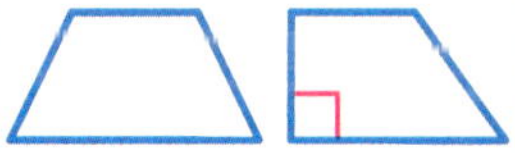	• Exactly one pair of opposite sides parallel

Remember

The square corners on the angles indicate which angles are right angles.

EXAMPLES Describe Sides and Angles

1 Describe the congruent sides in the quadrilateral shown at the right. Then state whether any sides appear to be parallel or perpendicular.

Opposite sides are congruent and parallel. Adjacent sides are perpendicular.

Vocabulary Link

Prefixes

The prefix *quad-* means four. A **quadruped** is an animal that has four feet.

2 The design below is made up of repeating quadrilaterals. Find the number of acute and obtuse angles in each quadrilateral.

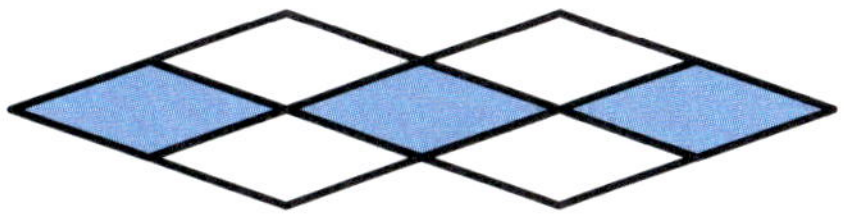

Each quadrilateral has two acute angles and two obtuse angles.

CHECK What You Know

Describe the sides that appear to be congruent in each quadrilateral. Then state whether any sides appear to be parallel or perpendicular.
See Example 1 (p. 571)

1. 

2. 

Find the number of acute angles in each quadrilateral. See Example 2 (p. 571)

3. 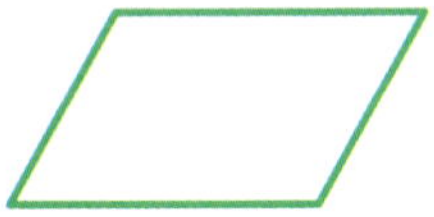

4. 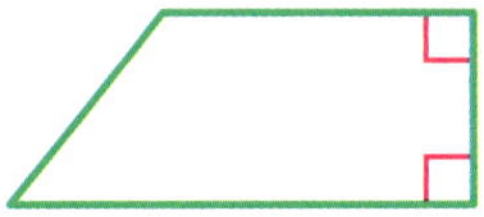

5. 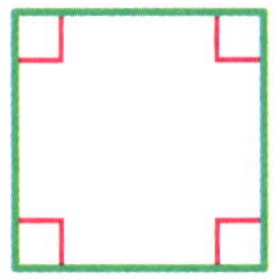

6. Many aircraft display the shape of the American flag as shown below to indicate motion. Find the number of obtuse angles in each figure.

7. Talk About It: Tell the difference between a rhombus and a trapezoid.

Practice and Problem Solving

EXTRA PRACTICE See page R35.

Describe the sides that appear to be congruent in each quadrilateral. Then state whether any sides appear to be parallel or perpendicular.
See Example 1 (p. 571)

8. 

9. 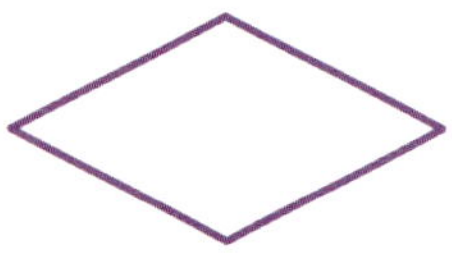

10. 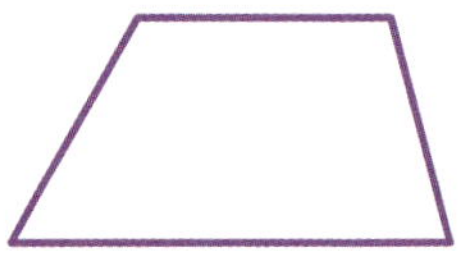

11. 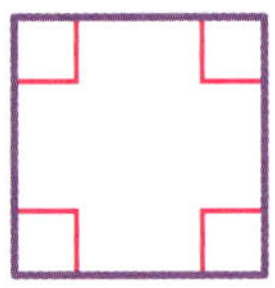

Find the number of acute angles in each quadrilateral.
See Example 2 (p. 571)

12. 

13. 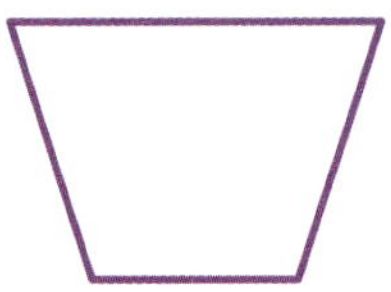

14. 

15. 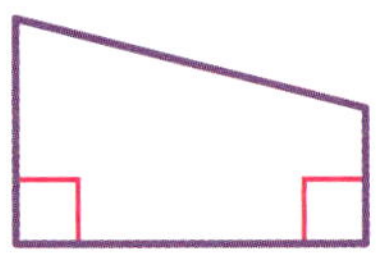

Determine whether each statement is *true* or *false*. Explain.

16. All squares are parallelograms.

17. Some rhombi are squares.

18. All rectangles are squares.

19. Some rectangles are parallelograms.

Real-World PROBLEM SOLVING

Art **For Exercises 20 and 21, use the photo of the New York Knicks basketball court.**

20. What kind of quadrilateral does the basketball court resemble most?

21. Describe two more quadrilaterals that are shown in the photo.

22. Traci has a piece of wood that is 1 inch wide and 1 foot long. She cuts the wood into four 3-inch strips. What type of quadrilateral can the strips be classified as?

Name the quadrilaterals that have the given attributes.

23. two pairs of parallel sides

24. all adjacent sides are perpendicular

25. exactly one pair of parallel sides

26. four congruent sides

H.O.T. Problems

27. OPEN ENDED Draw a parallelogram that is not a square, rhombus, or rectangle.

28. FIND THE ERROR Aliane and Levon are discussing the relationship between quadrilaterals. Who is correct? Explain your reasoning.

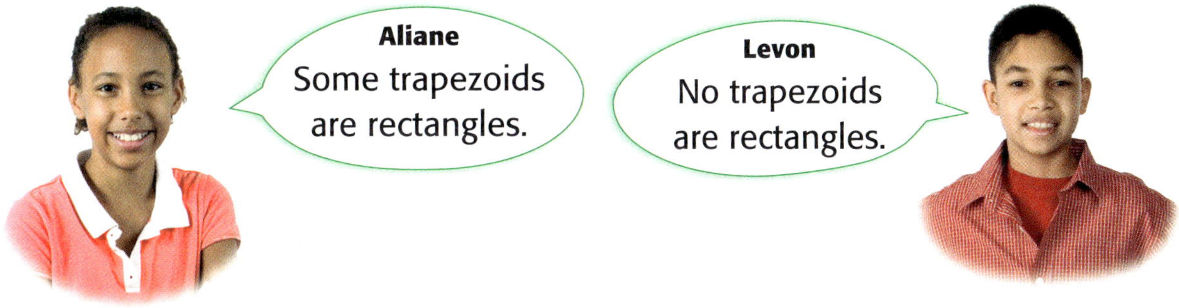

29. WRITING IN MATH Write a real-world problem that involves quadrilaterals. Solve and explain your reasoning.

TEST Practice

30. Which statement about the figures shown below is true? (Lessons 13-3 and 13-4)

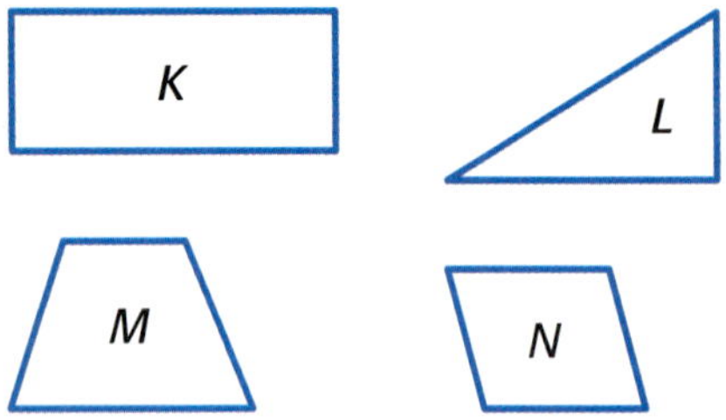

A Figures *K* and *L* are congruent.

B Figures *L* and *N* have all acute angles.

C Figures *M* and *N* each have at least two obtuse angles.

D Figures *M* and *N* are congruent.

31. Which is NOT a true statement? (Lesson 13-4)

F All parallelograms have opposite sides parallel.

G Squares have four congruent angles and sides.

H All trapezoids have exactly one pair of parallel sides.

J Parallelograms have exactly one pair of parallel sides.

Spiral Review

Identify the kinds of angles in each triangle. (Lesson 13-3)

32.

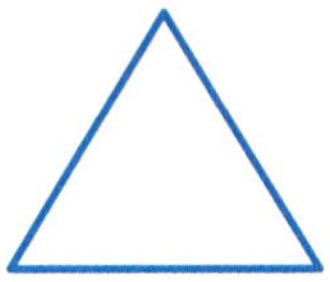

33.

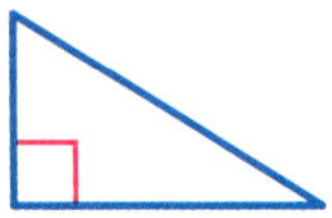

34.

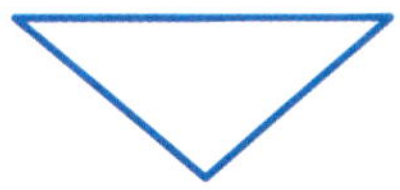

35. Can a triangle be both right and obtuse? Explain your reasoning. (Lesson 13-2)

Complete. (Lesson 12-4)

36. 3 L = ■ mL

37. 900 mL = ■ L

38. 7,000 mL = ■ L

39. **Algebra** A bag contained 16 balloons. Rama's mom used 9 balloons to decorate her bedroom. Which of the following equations can be used to find the number of balloons left in the bag: $y = 16 + 9$, $y = 16 - 9$, or $y = 16 \times 9$? Then find the number of balloons. (Lesson 6-1)

40. **Algebra** Some bamboo plants can grow 3 feet in one day. Write an expression to show the number of feet a bamboo plant can grow in x days. (Lesson 5-3)

CHAPTER 13

Mid-Chapter Check

Lessons 13-1 through 13-4

Identify each figure. Then name it using symbols. (Lesson 13-1)

1. 

2. 

Describe each pair of lines as *intersecting, perpendicular*, or *parallel*. (Lesson 13-1)

3. 

4. 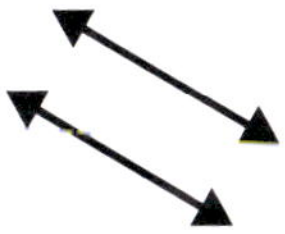

5. On Monday, Gavin bought some apples. He bought twice as many on Tuesday as he did on Monday. On Wednesday, he bought 5 more than he did on Monday. He bought a total of 21 apples. How many apples did he buy on Tuesday? (Lesson 13-2)

6. The sum of the measures of the angles in the figure below is 540°.

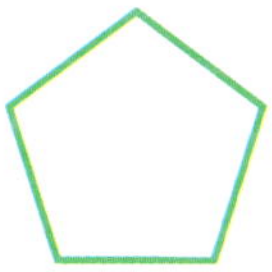

If all the angles have equal measure, what is the measure of each angle? (Lesson 13-2)

Measure the sides of each triangle. Then find the number of congruent sides. State whether any of the sides appear to be perpendicular. Write *yes* or *no*. (Lesson 13-3)

7. 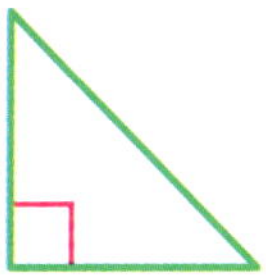

8. 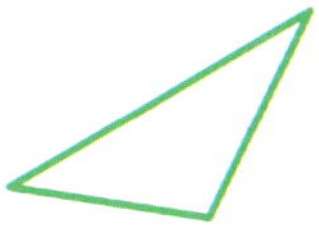

Identify the kinds of angles in each triangle. (Lesson 13-3)

9. 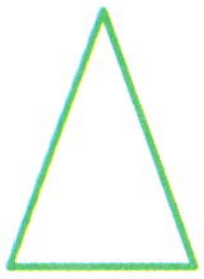

10. 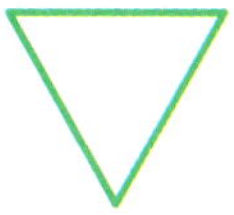

11. **MULTIPLE CHOICE** Which shape could never have parallel sides? (Lessons 13-3 and 13-4)

A rectangle **C** trapezoid

B rhombus **D** triangle

Find the number of acute angles in each quadrilateral. (Lesson 13-4)

12. 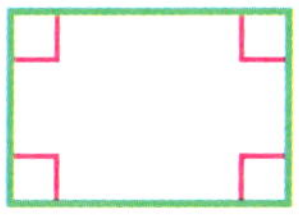

13. 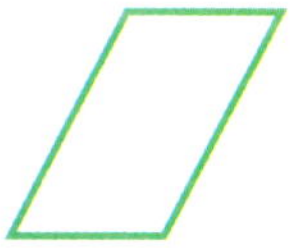

14. **MULTIPLE CHOICE** Which statement about the trapezoid shown at the right is true? (Lesson 13-4)

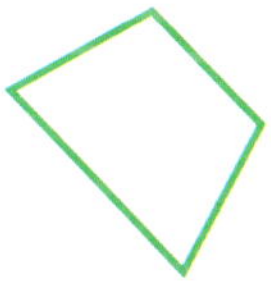

F The trapezoid has two right angles.

G The trapezoid has two acute angles.

H The trapezoid has two pairs of parallel sides.

J The trapezoid has three obtuse angles.

15. **WRITING IN MATH** Is every parallelogram a quadrilateral? Explain. (Lesson 13-4)

13-5 Problem-Solving Investigation

MAIN IDEA I will choose the best strategy to solve a problem.

P.S.I. TEAM +

EMILIO: To make a quilt pattern, I pieced together triangles to make squares of different sizes. The first square has 2 triangles, the second square has 8 triangles, and the third square has 18 triangles. The quilt will have squares of five different sizes.

YOUR MISSION: Find how many triangles are in the fifth square.

Understand	You know how many triangles are in the first, second, and third squares. You need to find how many triangles are in the fifth square.
Plan	Look for a pattern to find the number of triangles.
Solve	Each square has twice as many triangles as small squares. First square 2×1 or 2 triangles Second square 2×4 or 8 triangles Third square 2×9 or 18 triangles Continuing the pattern, the fourth square has 2×16 or 32 triangles. The fifth square has 2×25 or 50 triangles.
Check	Draw the fifth square and count the number of triangles. Since there are 50 triangles in the fifth square, the answer is correct. ✓

Mixed Problem Solving

EXTRA PRACTICE
See page R35.

Use any strategy shown below to solve each problem.

PROBLEM-SOLVING STRATEGIES
- Draw a diagram.
- Look for a pattern.
- Use logical reasoning.

1. Mr. Toshi's fifth grade class sold containers of popcorn and peanuts. If each day they sold 25 less containers of peanuts than popcorn, how many containers of popcorn and peanuts did they sell in all?

	Day 1	Day 2	Day 3	Day 4
Popcorn	225	200	150	300
Peanuts	■	■	■	■

2. **Algebra** Find the fifteenth term in the pattern shown below.

   5, 4, 7, 6, 9, 8, 11, ...

3. Selma is taller than Motega and shorter than Cheye. If Cheye is shorter than Dominic, who is the shortest person?

4. There are 8 girls for every 7 boys on a field trip. If there are 56 girls on the trip, how many students are on the trip?

5. **Measurement** When Cheryl goes mountain climbing, she rests 5 minutes for every 15 minutes that she climbs. If Cheryl climbs for 2 hours, how many minutes does she rest?

6. The fraction $\frac{a}{b}$ is equivalent to $\frac{5}{20}$, and $b - a = 3$. Find the values of a and b.

7. A family has four cats. Fluffy is 8 years old and is 4 years younger than Tiger. Tiger is 2 years older than Max, and Max is 3 years older than Patches. List the cats from oldest to youngest.

8. The number of fifth grade students who helped clean the park this year was 5 less than twice as many as last year. If 39 fifth graders helped clean up the park this year, how many cleaned the park last year?

9. Five friends go to a batting cage. Andrea bats after Daniel and before Jessica. Juwan bats after Andrea and before Jessica and Filipe. Jessica always bats immediately after Juwan. Who bats last?

10. Madeline has 2 times the number of games as Paulo. Paulo has 4 more games than Tyler. If Tyler has 9 games, how many games are there between the 3 friends?

11. **Algebra** The first three *triangular numbers* are shown below. How many dots will be in the sixth triangular number?

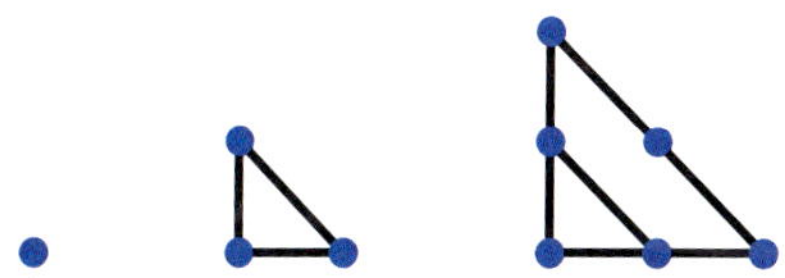

1 3 6

12. WRITING IN MATH In addition to logical reasoning, what is another strategy that you could use to solve Exercise 11?

13-6 Translations and Graphs

MAIN IDEA

I will sketch translations on a coordinate grid.

New Vocabulary

transformation
image
translation

Math Online

macmillanmh.com

- Extra Examples
- Personal Tutor
- Self-Check Quiz

GET READY to Learn

Helena slid her desk from one side of her room to the other. This movement is an example of a translation.

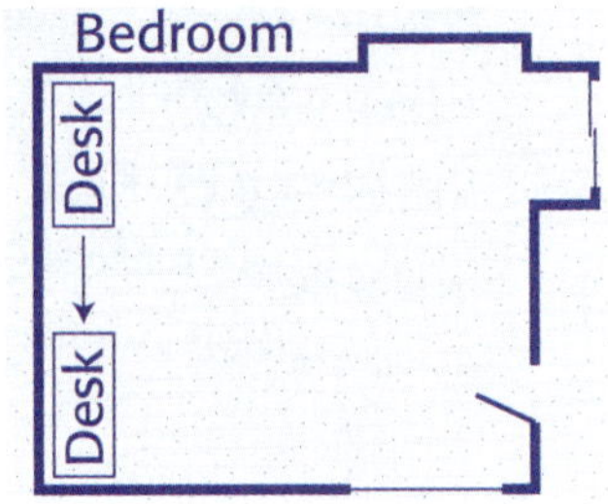

A **transformation** is a movement of a geometric figure. The resulting figure is called the **image**. One type of transformation is a translation.

Translation

Key Concept

Sliding a figure without turning it is called a **translation**. A translation does not change the size or shape of a figure.

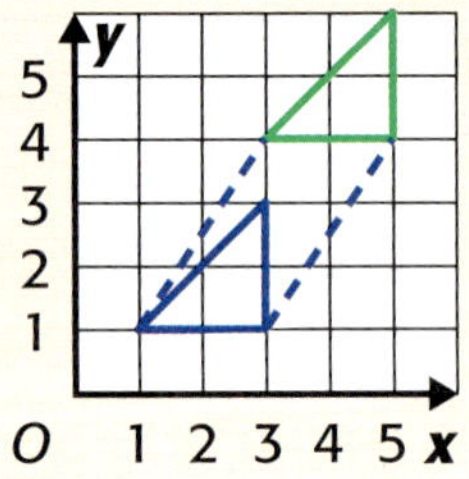

To translate a figure, move all of the vertices the same distance and in the same direction.

Hands-On Mini Activity

A triangle has vertices at *A*(3, 6), *B*(4, 9), and *C*(7, 6). Draw a coordinate grid on graph paper. Copy the triangle.

a. With a different colored pencil, graph points *A*, *B*, and *C* after they are moved down 4 units.

b. Connect the points.

c. What are the vertices of the image?

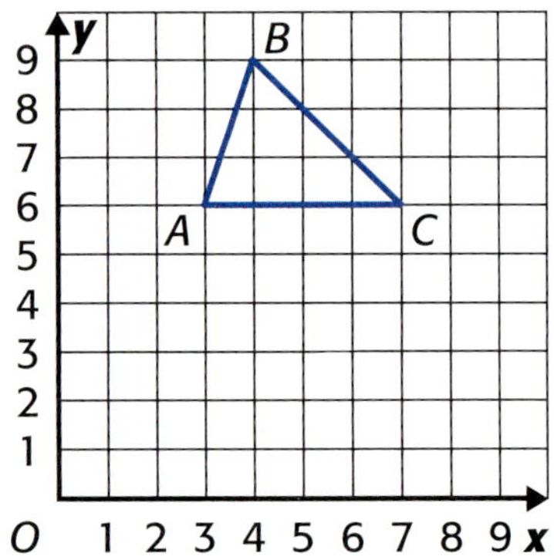

Real-World Math

Use the image above of the design on a Pompeii building to solve each problem.

1. Identify all of the geometric figures in the design.
2. Where do you see acute angles in the design?
3. Where do you see obtuse angles in the design?
4. Are there any right angles in the design? If so, where?
5. Where in the design do you see parallel lines?
6. Where in the design do you see perpendicular lines?
7. What can you tell about the triangles in the design?
8. Identify any transformations that could have been used to create the design.

CHAPTER 13

Study Guide and Review

Math Online macmillanmh.com
- STUDY TO GO
- Vocabulary Review

FOLDABLES® Study Organizer GET READY to Study

Be sure the following Big Ideas are written in your Foldable.

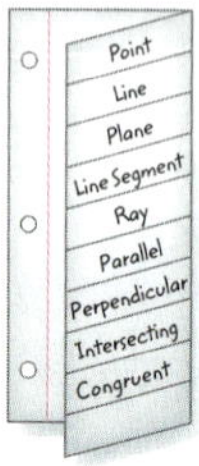

Key Concepts

Triangles

- Triangles can be classified by the lengths of their sides. (p. 566)

Triangle	Description
Isosceles	at least 2 sides congruent
Equilateral	all sides congruent
Scalene	no sides congruent

- Triangles can be classified by the measures of their angles. (p. 567)

Triangle	Description
Acute	3 acute angles
Right	1 right angle, 2 acute angles
Obtuse	1 obtuse angle, 2 acute angles

Quadrilaterals (p. 571)

- A parallelogram has both pairs of opposite sides parallel and congruent.
- Rectangles, rhombi, and squares are parallelograms.
- A trapezoid has exactly one pair of opposite sides parallel.

Transformations

- A **translation** is a slide. (p. 578)
- A **reflection** is a flip. (p. 582)
- A **rotation** is a turn. (p. 586)

Key Vocabulary

parallel lines (p. 558)
perpendicular lines (p. 558)
reflection (p. 582)
rotation (p. 586)
translation (p. 578)

Vocabulary Check

State whether each sentence is true or false. If false, replace the underlined word or number to make a true sentence.

1. In a rotation, a figure is moved without being turned or flipped.
2. Intersecting lines are lines that cross each other at right angles.
3. Parallel lines always intersect.
4. A rectangle has opposite sides congruent and parallel.
5. A ray is a line that has one endpoint and goes on forever in one direction.
6. Flipping a figure over a line to create a mirror image of the figure is called a reflection.
7. A translation changes the size of the figure.

Lesson-by-Lesson Review

13-1 Geometry Vocabulary (pp. 557–560)

Example 1

Identify the figure. Then name it using symbols.

The figure is a line segment. In symbols, this is written as $\overline{LM}$ or $\overline{ML}$.

Example 2

Describe the pair of lines as *intersecting*, *perpendicular*, or *parallel*.

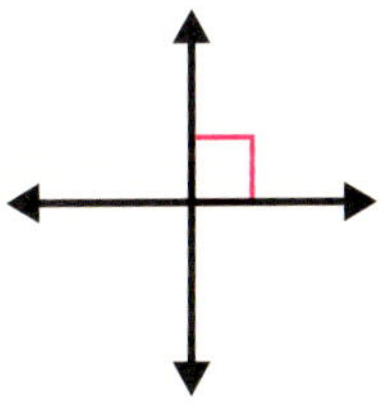

The lines intersect to form right angles. They are intersecting perpendicular lines.

Identify each figure. Then name it using symbols.

8.

9.

Describe each pair of lines as *intersecting, perpendicular*, or *parallel*.

10.

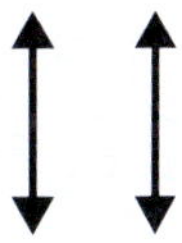

11.

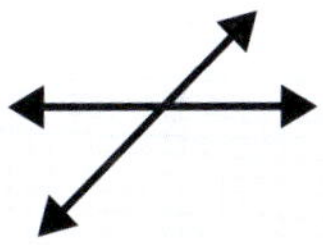

12. Draw a ray that can be used to show the direction north on a map.

13-2 Problem-Solving Strategy: Use Logical Reasoning (pp. 562–563)

Example 3

Angie, Carlo, and Camille each play a different sport: basketball, soccer, or football. Angie does not like soccer. Carlo's favorite sport is not played with a round ball. Who plays each sport?

Make a table to organize the information.

	Basketball	Soccer	Football
Angie	yes	X	X
Carlo	X	X	yes
Camille	X	yes	X

Angie likes basketball, Carlo likes football, and Camille likes soccer.

Solve. Use the *use logical reasoning* strategy.

13. Two walls intersect. Is the intersection an example of a point, line, ray, or line segment?

14. Steve is taller than Lorena. Riley is shorter than Steve. Lorena is not the shortest. List the people from shortest to tallest.

15. Five dogs are getting groomed. Duke is groomed after Daisy and before Spike. Sadie is groomed after Duke and before Spike and Rusty. Spike is groomed immediately after Sadie. Which dog is groomed last?

Study Guide and Review

13-3 Triangles (pp. 566–569)

Example 4

Measure each side of the triangle. Then find the number of congruent sides. State whether any of the sides appear to be perpendicular.

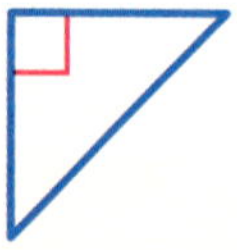

Two sides of the triangle are congruent. Two sides are perpendicular.

Example 5

Identify the kinds of angles in the triangle above.

Two angles are acute. One angle is right.

Measure the sides of each triangle. Then find the number of congruent sides. State whether any of the sides appear to be perpendicular. Write *yes* or *no*.

16. 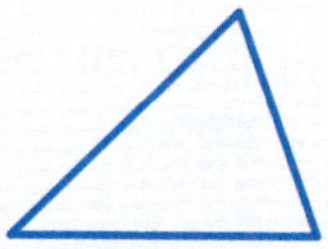

17. 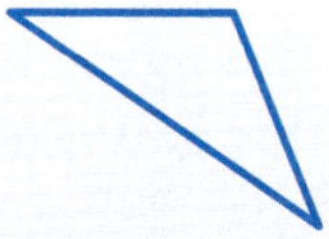

18. Find the number of congruent sides in the triangular sign.

13-4 Quadrilaterals (pp. 560–574)

Example 6

Describe the congruent sides in the quadrilateral. Then state whether any sides appear to be parallel or perpendicular.

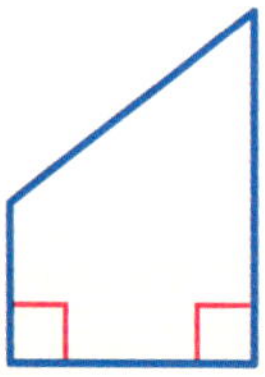

No sides are congruent. Two sides appear to be parallel. Two pairs of adjacent sides appear to be perpendicular.

Example 7

Refer to the figure in Example 6. Find the number of acute angles.

The figure has 1 acute angle.

Describe the sides that appear congruent in each quadrilateral. Then state whether any sides appear to be parallel or perpendicular.

19. 

20. 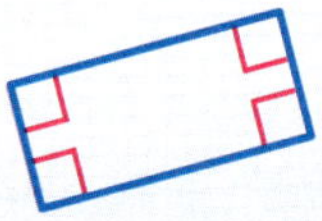

Find the number of acute angles in each quadrilateral.

21. 

22. 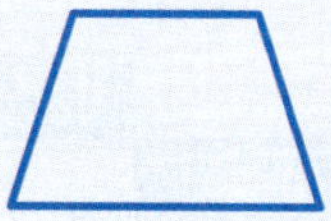

23. Miss Cruz is cutting out a quadrilateral. It has four congruent sides and no right angles. What figure is it?

13-5 Problem-Solving Investigation: Choose a Strategy (pp. 576–577)

Example 8
Algebra Find the eighth number in the pattern below.

18, 19, 15, 16, 12, 13,...

Find the pattern in the list of numbers.

18, 19, 15, 16, 12, 13,...
+1 −4 +1 −4 +1

The pattern is to add 1, and then subtract 4.

So, the seventh number in the pattern is 13 − 4 or 9. The eighth number is 9 + 1 or 10.

Solve.

24. Holly is 6 years younger than her sister. Their mother is 44 years old, and her age is twice the sum of her two children's ages. How old is Holly?

25. How many 2-inch squares fit inside a rectangle 6 inches by 8 inches?

26. Caden uses one pencil the first week of drawing class, and twice as many pencils each week as he did the week before. How many pencils does he use the fifth week?

13-6 Translations and Graphs (pp. 578–581)

Example 9
A triangle has vertices *A*(2, 2), *B*(1, 4), and *C*(5, 2). Graph the triangle. Then graph its translation image 1 unit right and 5 units up. Write the ordered pairs for the vertices of the image.

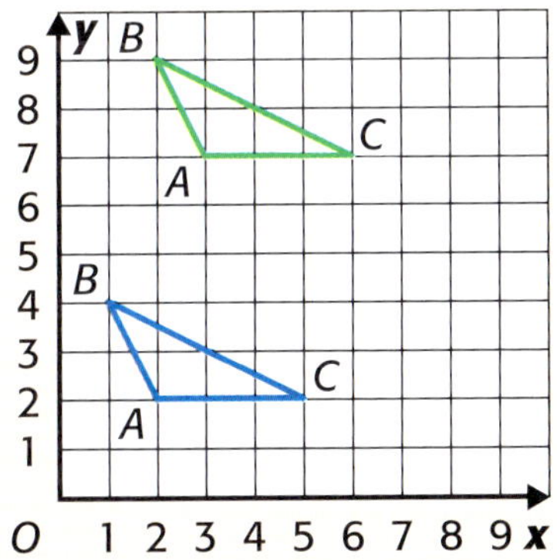

The new vertices are *A*(3, 7), *B*(2, 9), and *C*(6, 7).

Graph each figure and the translation image described. Write the ordered pairs for the vertices of the image.

27. quadrilateral with vertices *F*(2, 9), *G*(7, 9), *H*(8, 7), *J*(5, 7); translated 6 units down

28. triangle with vertices *T*(7, 3), *U*(9, 8), *V*(9, 4); translated 3 units left, 1 unit up

29. A triangular stool has legs at (5, 3), (9, 3), and (7, 6). It is moved 5 units to the right. What are the new coordinates?

13-7 Reflections and Graphs (pp. 582–585)

Example 10

Graph the figure after a reflection across the line. Then write the ordered pairs for the vertices of the image.

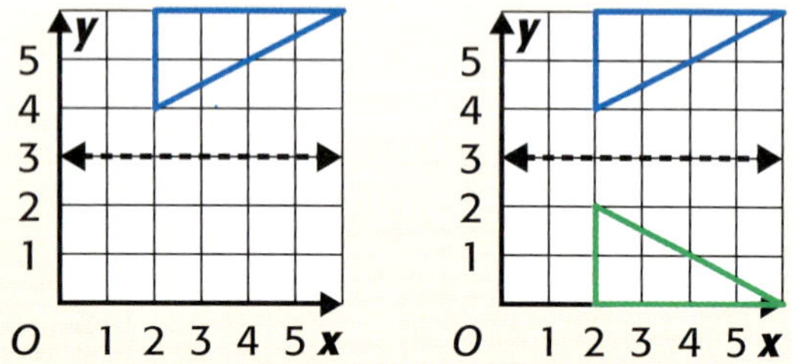

The ordered pairs for the new vertices are (2, 0), (2, 2), and (6, 0).

Graph each figure after a reflection across the line. Then write the ordered pairs for the vertices of the image.

30.

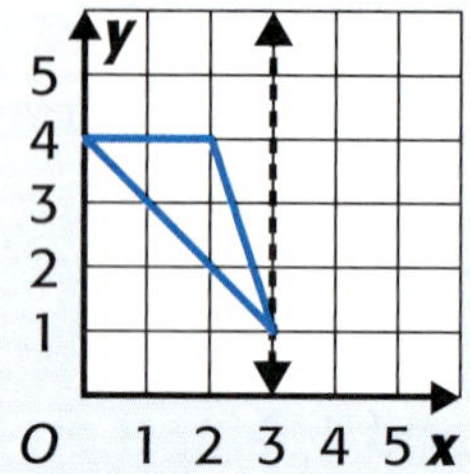

31.

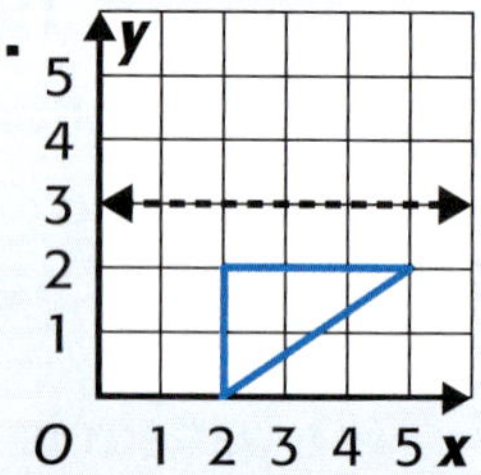

13-8 Rotations and Graphs (pp. 586–590)

Example 11

Graph the rotation of the triangle clockwise about point *W*. Write the ordered pairs for the new vertices.

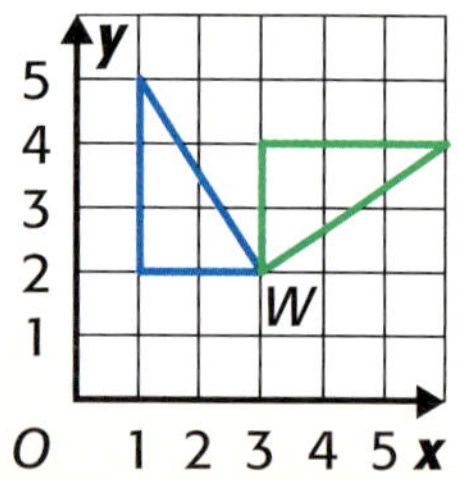

The ordered pairs for the new vertices are (3, 2), (3, 4), and (6, 4).

Graph each figure and the rotation described. Write the ordered pairs for the new vertices.

32. triangle with vertices $C(2, 6)$, $D(5, 4)$, $E(3, 2)$; rotated 90° counterclockwise about C

33. triangle with vertices $M(2, 8)$, $N(5, 6)$, $P(4, 4)$; rotated 180° clockwise about N

13-9 Identify Transformations (pp. 591–593)

Example 12

Determine whether the transformation is a *translation*, *reflection*, or *rotation*.

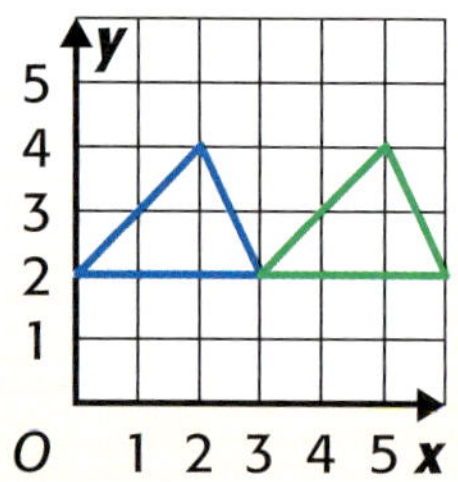

The triangle slid 3 units right. This is a translation.

Determine whether each transformation is a *translation*, *reflection*, or *rotation*.

34.

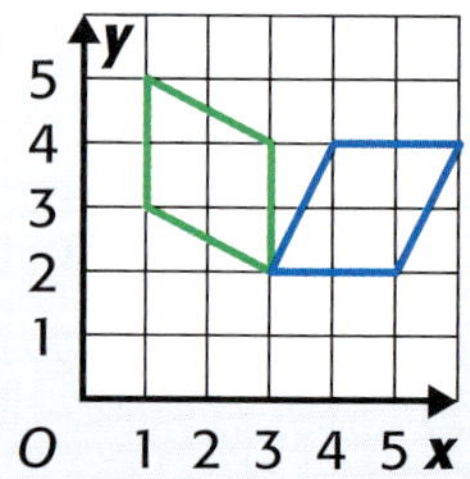

35.

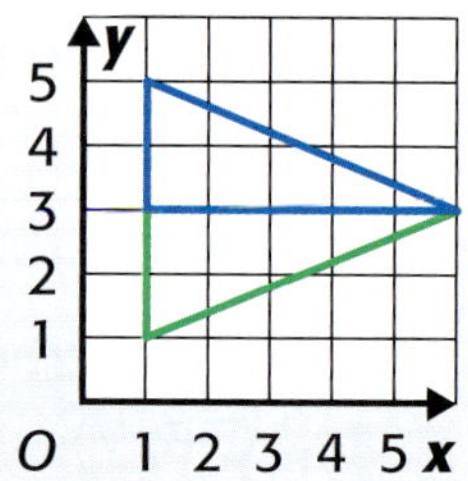

Preparing for Standardized Tests
For test-taking strategies and practice, see pages R42–R55.

7. Mr. Cortez determined that the cost of renting a popcorn machine for 9 hours was $82. Which shows that his solution is NOT reasonable?

Number of Hours	Cost ($)
1	32
3	47
5	62
7	77

A The terms are decreasing.

B The terms are multiples of 11.

C The terms are increasing by 15.

D The terms are multiples of 15.

8. An isosceles triangle is shown. Which statement about the triangle is true?

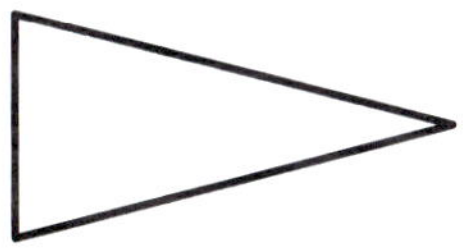

F None of the sides are congruent.

G All the angles are right angles.

H The triangle has only 2 sides that are congruent.

J Two of the sides are perpendicular.

9. What fraction is equivalent to 0.32?

A $\frac{32}{1000}$

B $\frac{32}{100}$

C $\frac{32}{10}$

D $3\frac{2}{10}$

PART 2 Short Response

Record your answers on the answer sheet provided by your teacher or on a sheet of paper.

10. Julie practiced the piano one afternoon, as shown. Find the number of minutes she practiced the piano.

Start **Finish**

11. What type of angle will the hands of a clock show at 1:15?

PART 3 Extended Response

Record your answers on the answer sheet provided by your teacher or on a sheet of paper. Show your work.

12. Use a Venn diagram to compare characteristics of perpendicular lines and intersecting lines.

13. Describe two ways to represent $1.76 using dollars and coins. You may NOT use more than 6 coins.

NEED EXTRA HELP?													
If You Missed Question...	1	2	3	4	5	6	7	8	9	10	11	12	13
Go to Lesson...	13-4	13-1	13-9	13-9	13-3	8-2	6-6	13-3	1-4	11-7	13-3	13-1	1-8

CHAPTER 14

Measure Perimeter, Area, and Volume

BIG Idea What are perimeter and area?

Perimeter is the distance around a closed figure. **Area** is the number of square units needed to cover a surface.

Example A Kentucky farm has 6 acres of woods with horseback riding trails. The perimeter is the distance around the woods. The area is the total surface of the woods, 6 acres.

What will I learn in this chapter?

- Find perimeters of polygons.
- Find and estimate the areas of figures by counting squares and using formulas.
- Identify characteristics of three-dimensional figures.
- Select and use appropriate units and formulas to measure length, perimeter, area, and volume.
- Solve problems by using the *make a model* strategy.

Key Vocabulary

area
perimeter
polygon
prism
three-dimensional figure

Math Online Student Study Tools at macmillanmh.com

FOLDABLES® Study Organizer

Make this Foldable to help you organize information about perimeter, area, and volume. Begin with a sheet of 11″ × 17″ paper and six index cards.

1. **Fold** the paper lengthwise about 3″ from the bottom.

2. **Fold** in thirds. Open and staple the edges on either side to form three pockets.

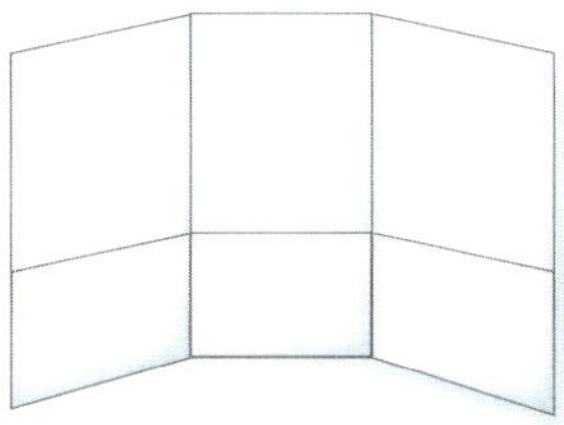

3. **Label** each pocket as shown. Place two index cards in each pocket.

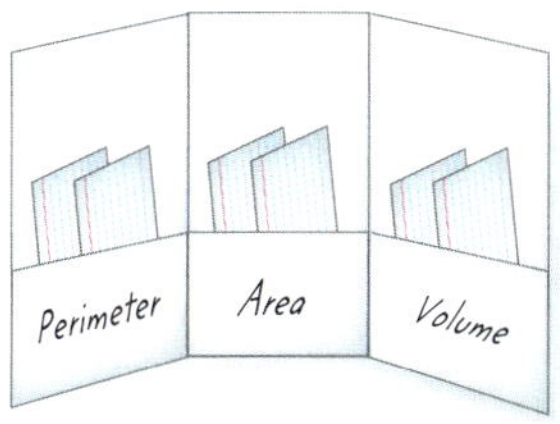

ARE YOU READY for Chapter 14?

You have two ways to check prerequisite skills for this chapter.

Option 2

Math Online Take the Chapter Readiness Quiz at macmillanmh.com.

Option 1

Complete the Quick Check below.

QUICK Check

Add. (Lessons 2-4, 2-6, and 10-7)

1. $15 + 20 + 25 + 7$

2. $9\frac{1}{2} + 11 + 14\frac{1}{2}$

3. $8\frac{1}{4} + 12 + 12$

4. $5 + 13 + 19$

5. $16.3 + 16.3 + 16.3$

6. $4 + 9.1 + 3.2 + 8$

7. The amount of money that Tyrese spent shopping is shown in the table. Find the total amount that he spent.

Item	Amount ($)
CD	14.99
T-shirt	26.30
Snack	5.20

Multiply. (Lessons 3-4 and 3-6)

8. 10×26

9. 12×14

10. 75×2

11. 25×48

12. 25×6

13. 5×32

14. 132×13

15. 45×45

16. Mrs. Ohlin sold 3 handmade bookshelves for $160 each. How much money did she earn in all?

Multiply. (Lessons 3-4 and 3-6)

17. $12 \times 3 \times 5$

18. $8 \times 6 \times 4$

19. $14 \times 10 \times 3$

20. $15 \times 9 \times 6$

21. $13 \times 9 \times 11$

22. $12 \times 7 \times 14$

Explore

Measurement Activity for 14-1
Perimeters of Rectangles

MAIN IDEA

I will use models to find the perimeters of rectangles.

New Vocabulary

perimeter

The **perimeter** of a figure is the distance around the figure. Perimeter is a measure of length. The perimeter of the rectangle at the right is 6 + 4 + 6 + 4 or 20 centimeters.

ACTIVITY Copy and complete the table.

Rectangle	Length (ℓ)	Width (w)	2ℓ	$2w$	Perimeter (P)
	2	1	4	2	$2 + 1 + 2 + 1 = 6$

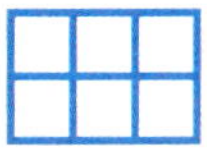					

CHECK What You Know

1. **WRITING IN ▸MATH** Refer to the table above. How are ℓ and w related to the perimeter of the rectangles? Then use P, ℓ, and w to write an equation for the perimeter of a rectangle.

2. Use the formula you wrote in Exercise 1 to find the perimeter of the rectangle. Select and use appropriate units.

3. In Exercise 2, only two sides of the rectangle are labeled. Explain why this is enough information to find the perimeter.

4. Find $2\ell + 2w$ for the rectangle in Exercise 2. Then write an equation to describe the relationship between P, ℓ, and w.

14-1 Perimeters of Polygons

MAIN IDEA

I will find perimeters of polygons.

New Vocabulary

polygon

Math Online

macmillanmh.com

- Extra Examples
- Personal Tutor
- Self-Check Quiz

GET READY to Learn

A city park is building a fence around a dog run. They need to know the *perimeter*, or distance around the run, to determine how much fencing they will need.

A **polygon** is a closed figure made up of line segments that do not cross each other.

Polygons **Not Polygons**

The perimeter of a polygon is measured in units of length, such as inches, feet, meters, or yards.

EXAMPLE **Find the Perimeter by Adding Side Lengths**

1 **Find the perimeter of the figure below.**

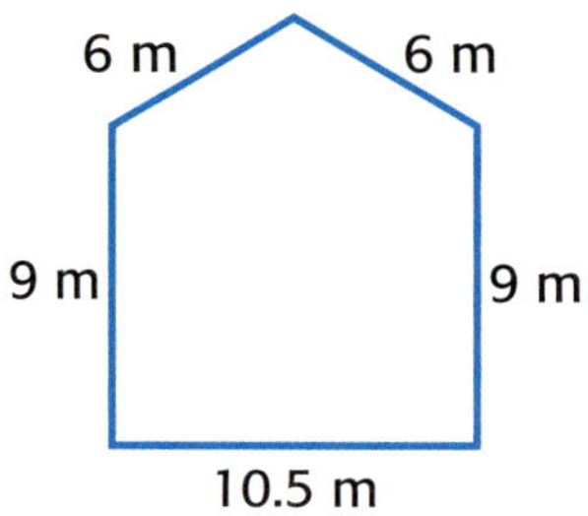

Estimate $10 + 10 + 10 + 10 + 10 = 50$ m

$P = 6 + 6 + 9 + 10.5 + 9$ Add the length of each side.

$= 40.5$

The perimeter is 40.5 meters. This is close to the estimate, so the answer is reasonable.

Remember

A square has all sides congruent. All angles are right angles.

A rectangle has both pairs of opposite sides parallel and congruent. All angles are right angles.

Hands-On Mini Activity

Copy and complete the table.

Square	1	2	3	4
Side Length (*s*)	1			
Perimeter (*P*)	4			

Describe the relationship between the perimeter of a square and side length. Then write an equation using P and s.

Perimeter of a Square

Key Concept

Words The perimeter P of a square is 4 times the side length s.

Symbols $P = s + s + s + s$ or $4s$

Model

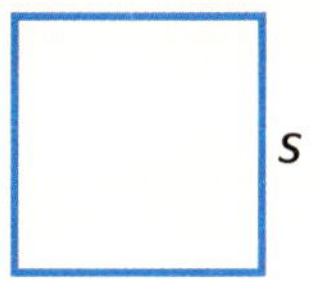

Real-World EXAMPLE — Perimeter of a Square

2 **ART** **Hai and his uncle tiled the kitchen floor using square tiles like the one shown at the right. What is the perimeter of the tile?**

2 ft

$P = 4s$ Perimeter of a square

$P = 4(2)$ Replace s with 2.

$P = 8$ Multiply.

The perimeter of the tile is 8 feet.

Remember

You can always find the perimeter of a rectangle or square by adding the lengths of the four sides.

Perimeter of a Rectangle

Key Concept

Words The perimeter P of a rectangle is two times the length ℓ plus two times the width w.

Symbols $P = \ell + \ell + w + w$ or $2\ell + 2w$

Model

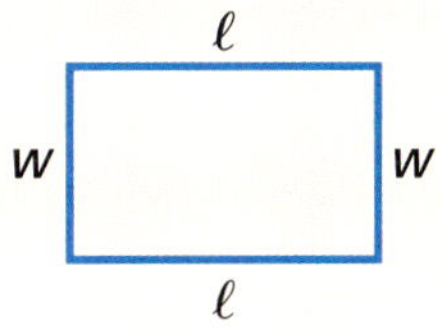

Real-World EXAMPLE — Perimeter of a Rectangle

3 CRAFTS Christa is sewing a lace border around the edges of her scrapbook. How many inches of lace will Christa need?

Find the perimeter of the scrapbook.

$P = 2\ell + 2w$	Perimeter of a rectangle
$P = 2(7) + 2(9)$	$\ell = 7$ and $w = 9$
$P = 14 + 18$	Multiply.
$P = 32$	Add.

So, Christa will need 32 inches of lace.

CHECK What You Know

Find the perimeter of each figure. See Example 1 (p. 608)

1. 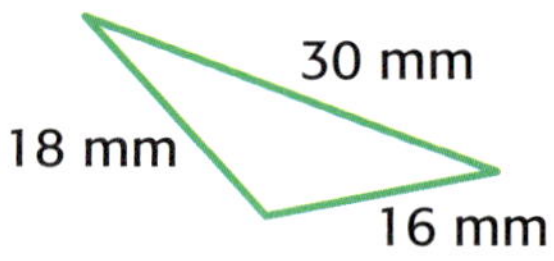

2. 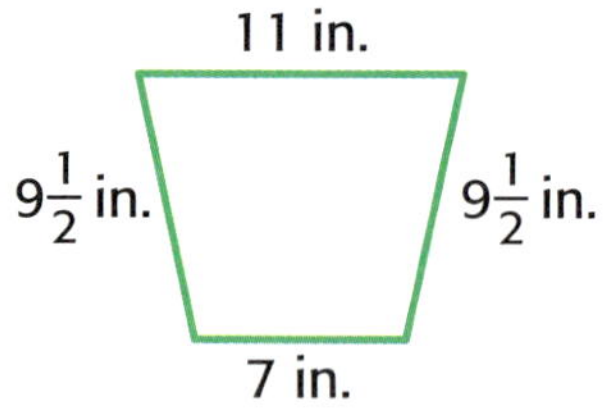

Find the perimeter of each square or rectangle.
See Examples 2, 3 (pp. 609–610)

3. 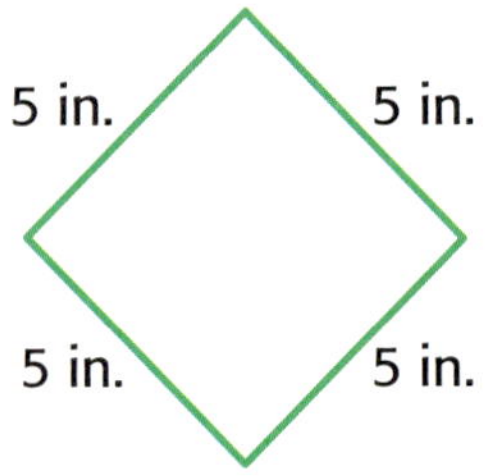

4. 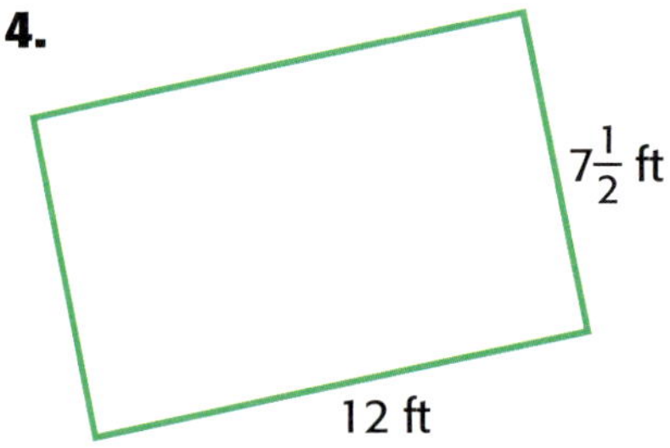

5. 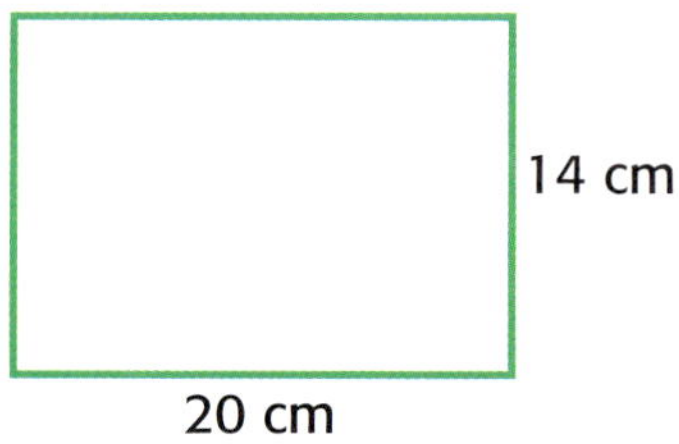

6. A rectangular playground is 32 feet long and 14 feet wide. How many feet of edging are needed to enclose the playground?

7. **Talk About It** Describe two ways to find the perimeter of a rectangle.

Practice and Problem Solving

EXTRA PRACTICE See page R37.

Find the perimeter of each figure. See Example 1 (p. 608)

8.

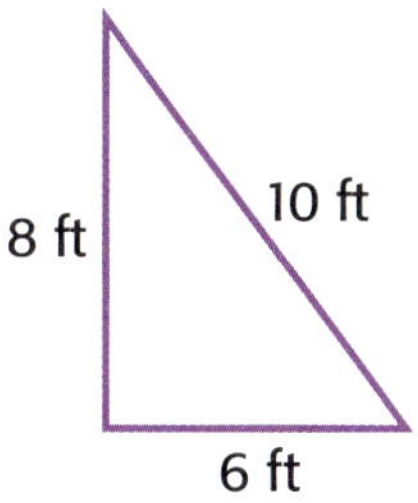

9.

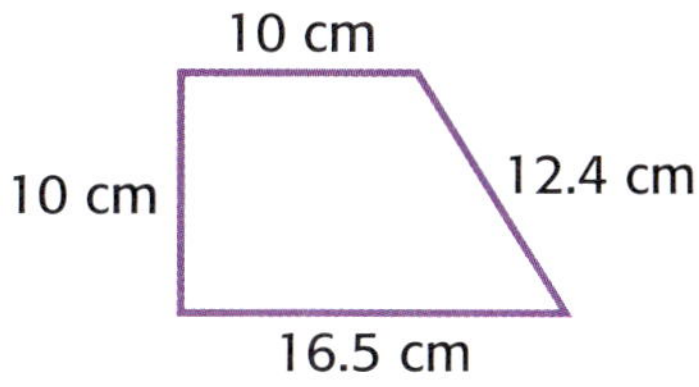

10.

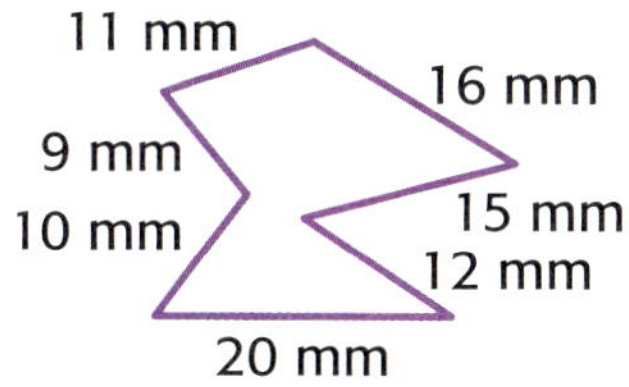

Find the perimeter of each square or rectangle. See Examples 2, 3 (pp. 609–610)

11.

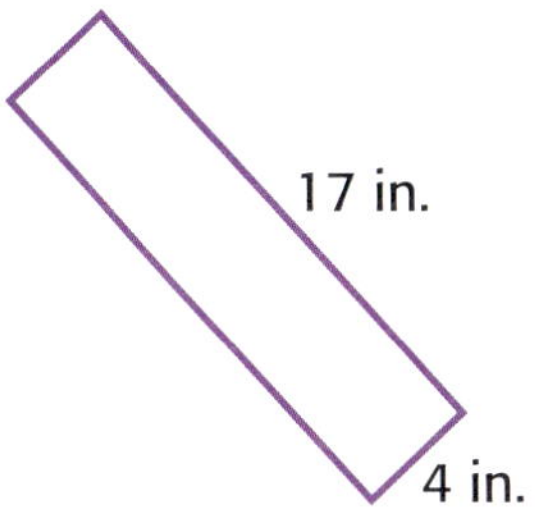

12.

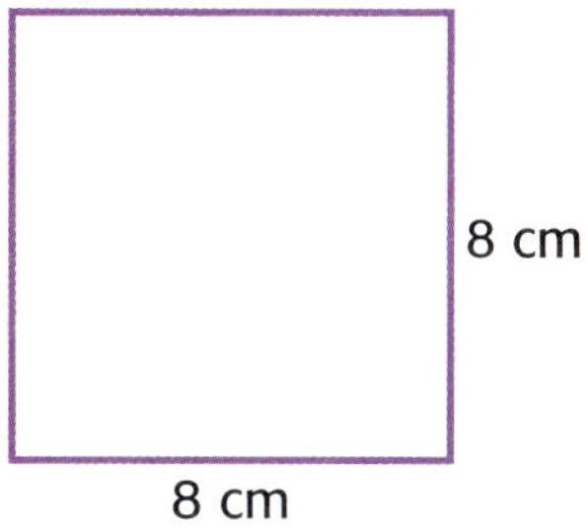

13.

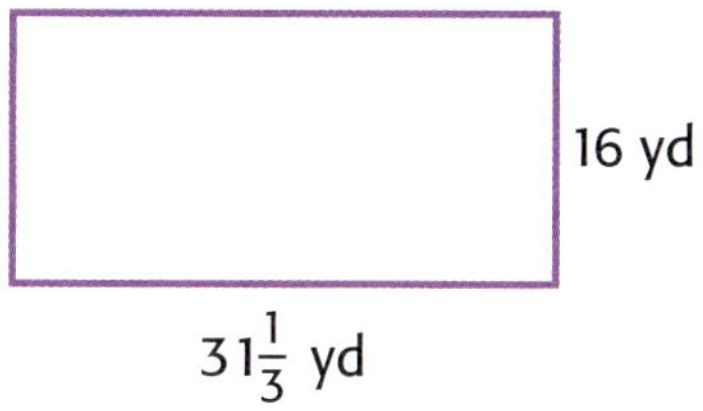

14.

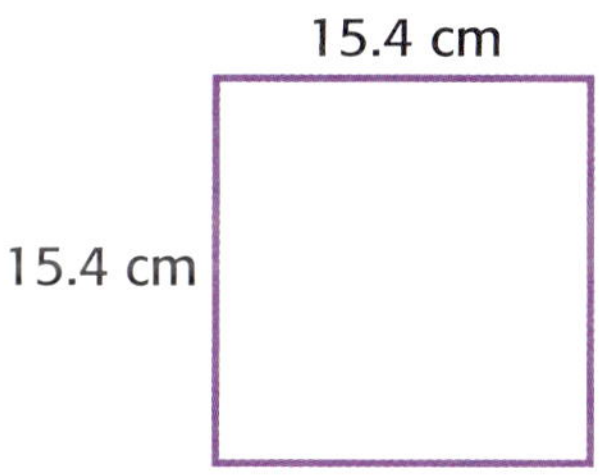

15.

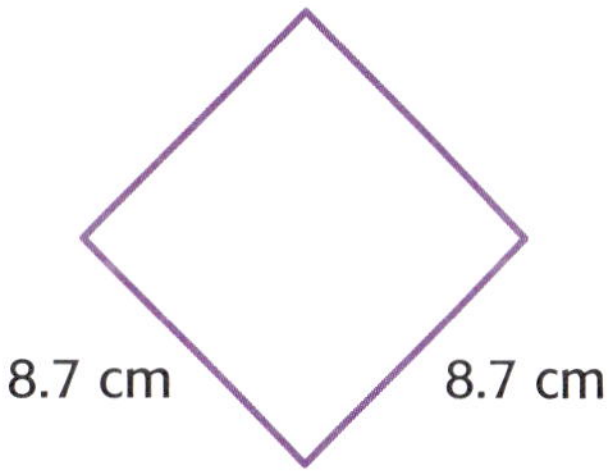

16.

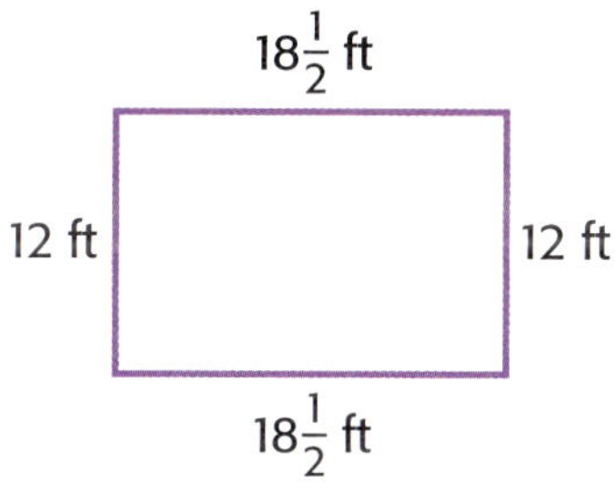

17. An octagon-shaped table has two sides measuring 4 feet and the other sides each measuring 1 foot each. What is the perimeter of the table?

18. A billiards table is twice as long as it is wide. If the perimeter of a billiards table is 24 feet, what is the length and width of the table?

19. Use a centimeter ruler to measure the side lengths rectangle shown at the right. Select and use appropriate units to find the perimetter of the rectangle.

H.O.T. Problems

20. **OPEN ENDED** Use a ruler to draw two different rectangles that have the same perimeter.

21. **WRITING IN MATH** Write a real-world problem that can be solved by finding the perimeter. Then solve the problem.

14-2 Areas

MAIN IDEA

I will find and estimate the areas of figures by counting squares.

New Vocabulary

area

Math Online

macmillanmh.com

- Extra Examples
- Personal Tutor
- Self-Check Quiz

GET READY to Learn

A checkerboard is made up of sixty-four 1-inch squares. You can describe the board by saying that it has an *area* of 64 square inches.

Area is the number of square units that cover the surface of a closed figure.

If the figure is not a square or a rectangle, count the number of whole squares and the number of half squares.

EXAMPLE Estimate Areas

1 Find the area of the figure at the right.

Step 1 Count the number of whole squares in the figure.

9 whole squares = 9 square units

Step 2 Count the number of half squares in the figure.

5 half squares = $2\frac{1}{2}$ square units

Step 3 Add the number of whole and half squares.

9 square units + $2\frac{1}{2}$ square units = $11\frac{1}{2}$ square units

So, the area of the figure is $11\frac{1}{2}$ square units.

> **Remember**
> Some common units of area are *square inch, square foot, square yard, square mile, square centimeter,* and *square meter.*

When you cannot count square units or half square units exactly, you can estimate the area.

Real-World EXAMPLES Estimate Areas

2 **TREE HOUSES The diagram shows the floor plan for a tree house. One square on the grid represents 1 square foot. About how many square feet is the area of the floor?**

Step 1 Count the number of whole squares in the diagram.

38 whole squares = 38 square feet

Step 2 Count the partial squares circled in the diagram.

10 partial squares is about 5 square feet

Step 3 Add the number of whole and partial squares.

$38 + 5 = 43$ square feet

The tree house floor has an area of about 43 square feet.

3 **LANDSCAPING A landscape architect designed the pond at the right. Each square represents 1 square meter. Estimate the area of the pond.**

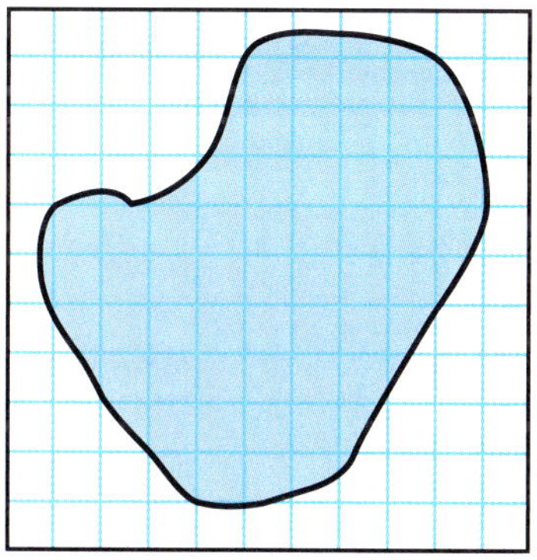

Step 1 Count the number of whole squares. There are 44 whole squares which is 44 square meters.

Step 2 Count the partial squares.

26 partial squares is about 13 square meters.

Step 3 Add the whole squares and partial squares.

$44 + 13 = 57$ square meters

The area of the pond is about 57 square meters.

> **Remember**
> The area of the figure on the previous page is exact. The areas of the figures in Examples 2 and 3 are estimates.

CHECK What You Know

Estimate the area of each figure. Each square represents 1 square centimeter. See Examples 1-3 (pp. 612–613)

1.

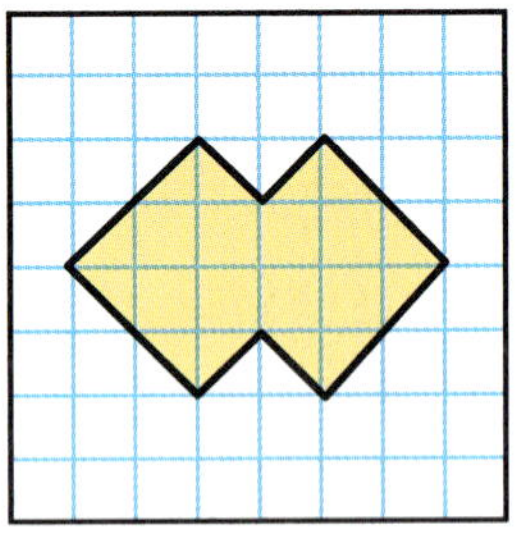

2.

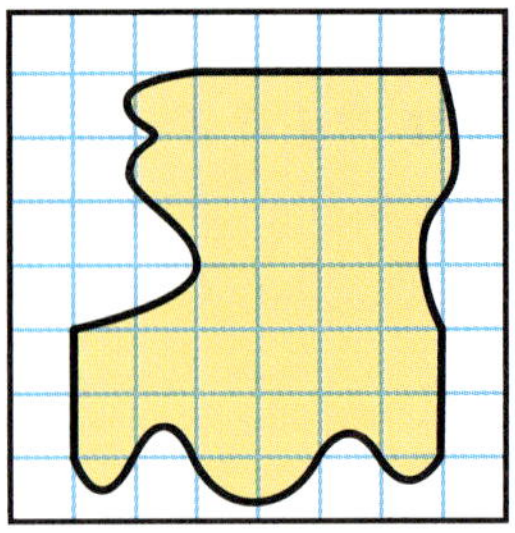

3.

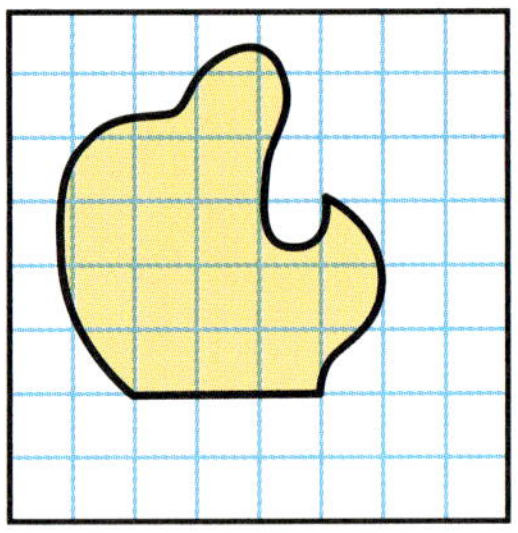

4. A cake decorator is drawing a heart on a cake. Each square represents 1 square inch. Estimate the area of the heart.

5. **Talk About It** Describe one way to estimate the area of an irregular figure that is drawn on grid paper.

Practice and Problem Solving

EXTRA PRACTICE See page R37.

Estimate the area of each figure. Each square represents 1 square centimeter. See Examples 1-3 (pp. 612–613)

6.

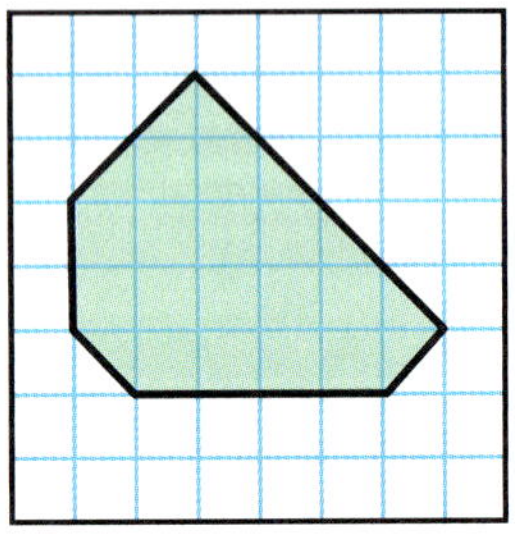

7.

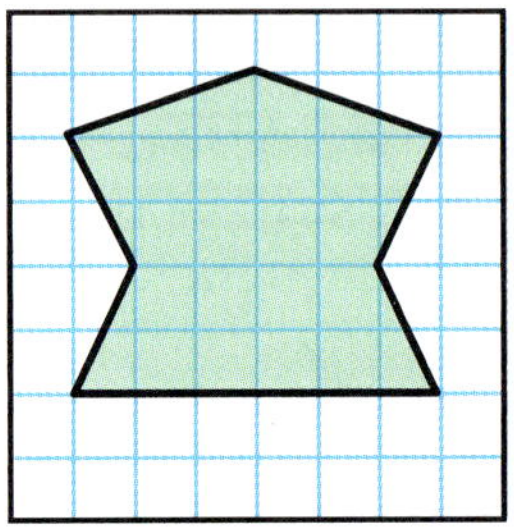

8.

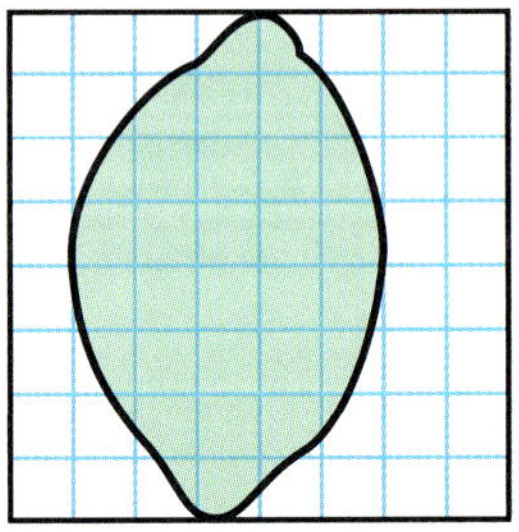

9.

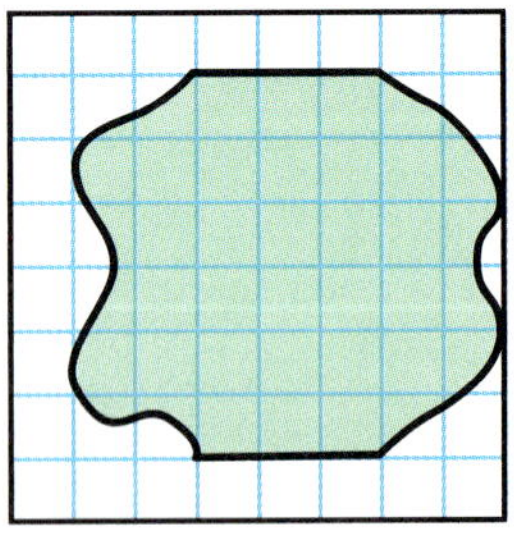

10.

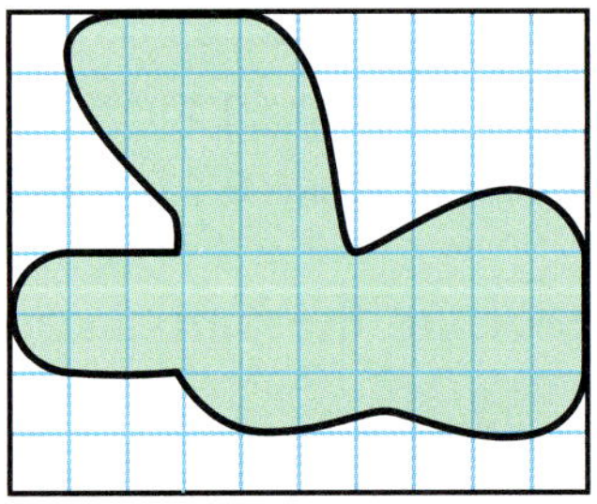

11.

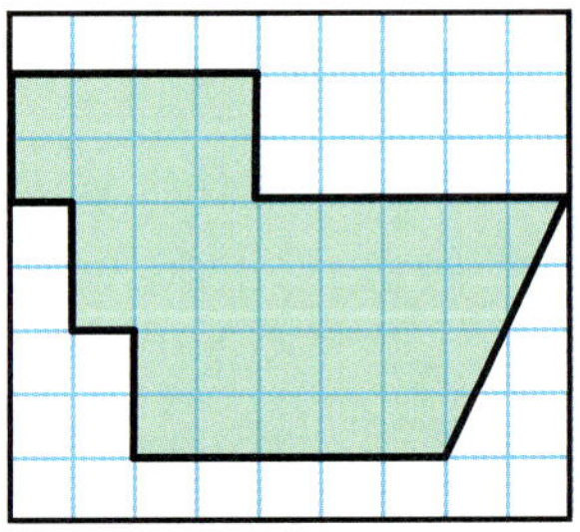

12. Isaiah made a sign for his yard sale shown at the right. If each square represents 1 square inch, estimate the area of the sign.

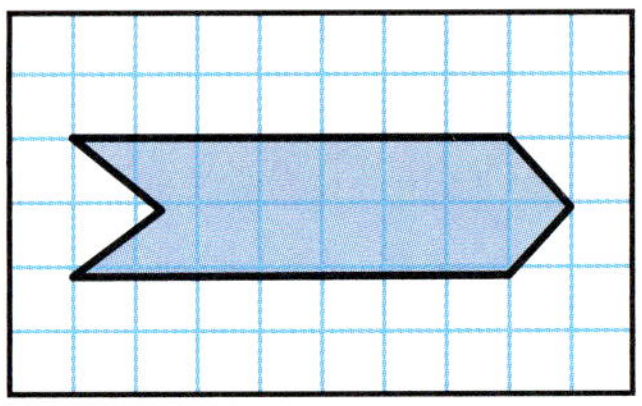

13. The flower patch at the right is on Cindy's backpack. One square represents 1 square centimeter. Estimate the total area of the patch.

H.O.T. Problems

14. **OPEN ENDED** Draw a figure on grid paper with an approximate area of 38 square units.

15. **WRITING IN MATH** Describe some real-life examples of when it would be useful to know how to estimate the area of figures.

TEST Practice

16. The student council is making a sign 8 feet long and 3 feet wide. They want to glue a colorful border around the four edges of the sign. How many feet of border will be needed? (Lesson 14-1)

   A 24 ft
   B 22 ft
   C 19 ft
   D 14 ft

17. Which is the best estimate for the area of the figure? (Lesson 14-2)

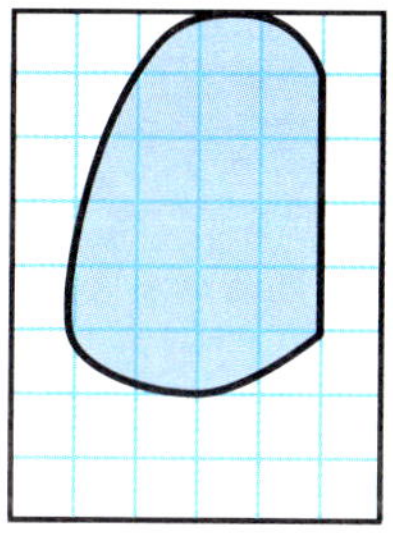

   F 12 square units
   G 15 square units
   H 18 square units
   J 24 square units

Spiral Review

Find the perimeter of each figure. (Lesson 14-1)

18.

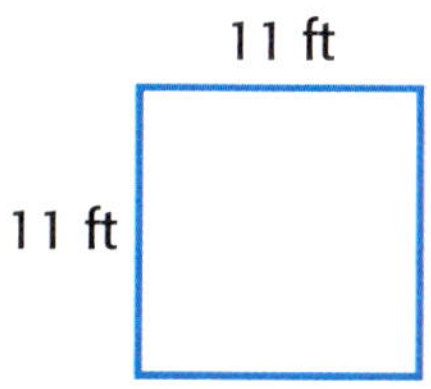

19.

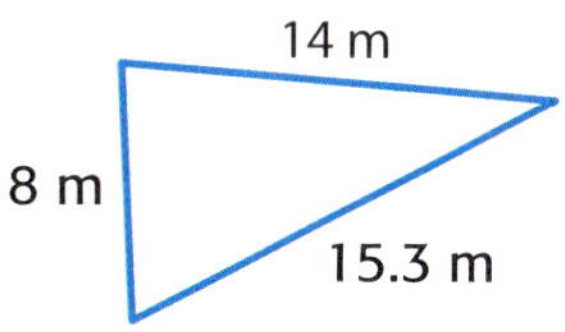

20.

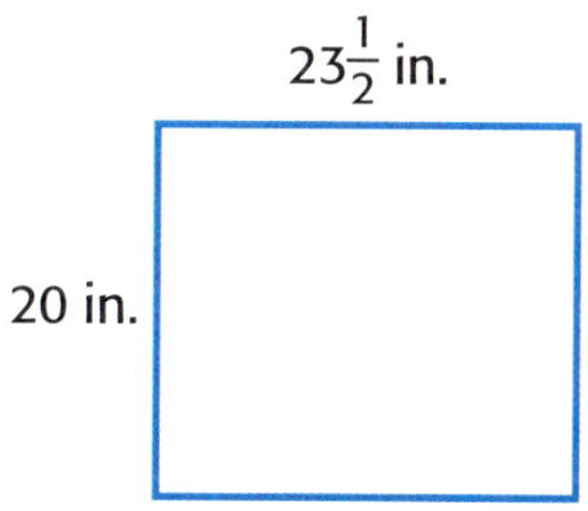

21. Triangle *ABC* has vertices at *A*(1, 1), *B*(4, 1), and *C*(3, 5). After a transformation, the vertices are at *A*(4, 1), *B*(7, 1), and *C*(6, 5). Determine whether the transformation is a translation, reflection, or rotation. (Lesson 13-9)

22. The temperature was 54°F at 3:00. Three hours later, the temperature was 48°F. Use an integer to represent the change. (Lesson 12-6)

14-3 Areas of Rectangles and Squares

MAIN IDEA

I will find the areas of rectangles.

Math Online

macmillanmh.com

- Extra Examples
- Personal Tutor
- Self-Check Quiz

GET READY to Learn

The largest flying American Flag is located in Gaston, North Carolina. The flag is 114 feet long and 65 feet wide. What is the area of the flag?

Hands-On Mini Activity

Copy and complete the table below. Use centimeter cubes to create and measure the rectangles shown.

Rectangle	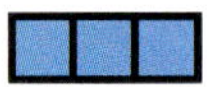	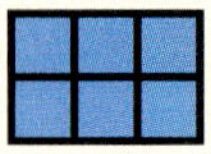	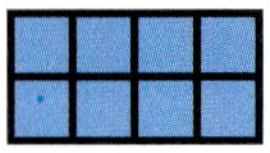	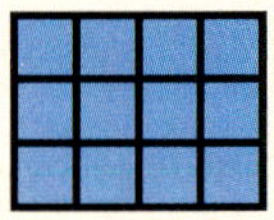
Length (ℓ)	3			
Width (w)	1			
Area (A)	3			

a. Study the pattern in the table. How are the length and width of the rectangles related to the areas?

b. Use A, ℓ, and w to write a formula for the area of a rectangle.

Area of a Rectangle — Key Concept

Words The area A of a rectangle equals length ℓ times the width w.

Symbols $A = \ell w$

Model

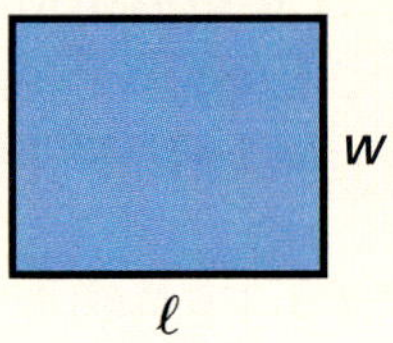

Remember

Different shapes have different formulas for area.

Real-World EXAMPLE — Area of a Rectangle

1 FLAGS Refer to the information at the beginning of the lesson. Find the area of the flag that is described.

The rectangle at the right represents the flag. The flag is 114 feet long and 65 feet wide.

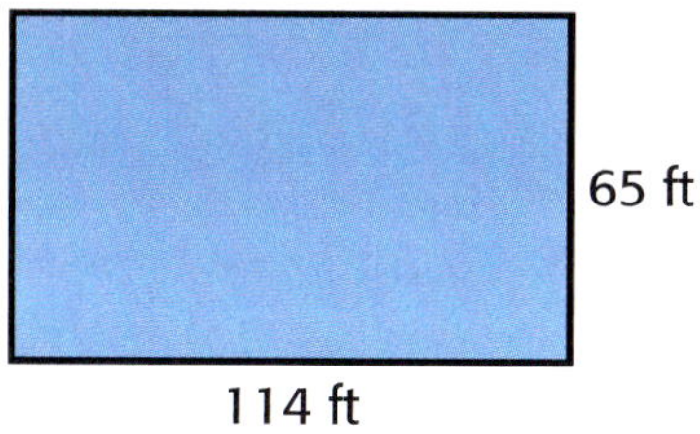

$A = \ell w$	Formula for area of a rectangle
$A = 114 \times 65$	Replace ℓ with 114 and w with 65.
$A = 7{,}410$	Multiply.

The area of the flag is 7,410 square feet.

Recall that a square is a rectangle with four congruent sides. Each side length is represented by s. So, you can replace ℓ and w in the formula $A = \ell w$ with s.

Remember

The expression s^2 is read *s squared* because its model forms a square with side *s*.

Area of a Square — Key Concept

Words The area A of a square equals the square of the side length s.

Symbols $A = s \times s$ or $A = s^2$

Model

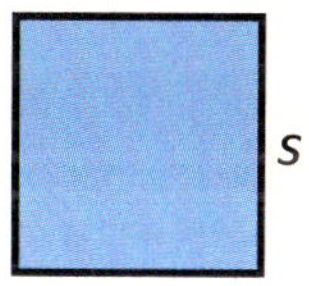

Real-World EXAMPLE — Area of a Square

2 SPORTS A baseball diamond is actually a square. Find the area of the baseball diamond at the right.

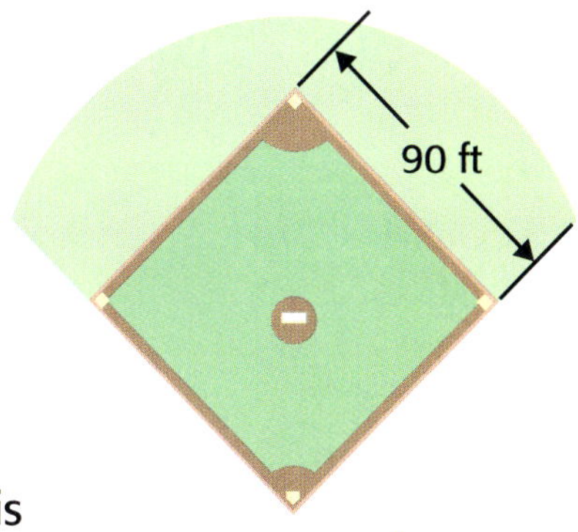

$A = s^2$	Formula for area of a square
$A = 90 \times 90$	Replace s with 90.
$A = 8{,}100$	Simplify.

The area of the baseball diamond is 8,100 square feet.

CHECK What You Know

Find the area of each rectangle or square. See Examples 1, 2 (p. 617)

1.

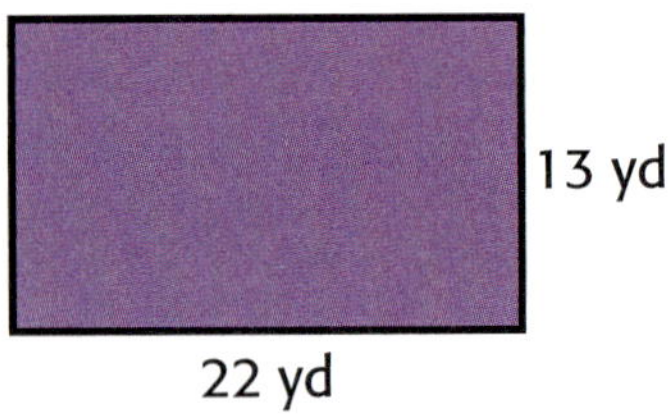

2.

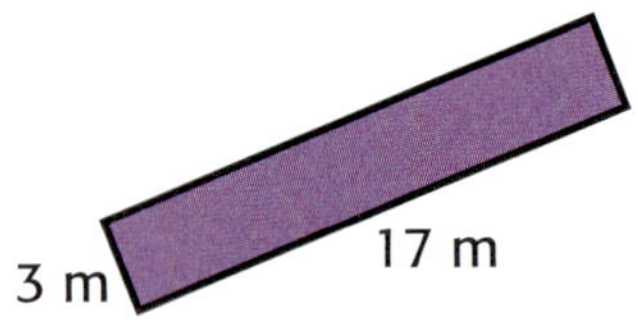

3.

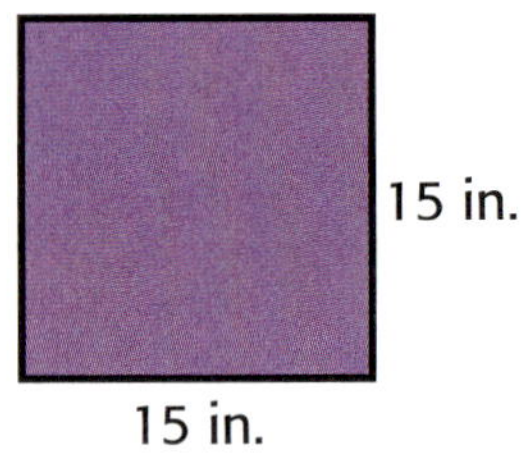

4. $\ell = 9$ km, $w = 1$ km

5. $\ell = 8$ cm, $w = 6$ cm

6. The Parthenon of ancient Greece had the rectangular floor plan shown at the right. How much area does the building cover?

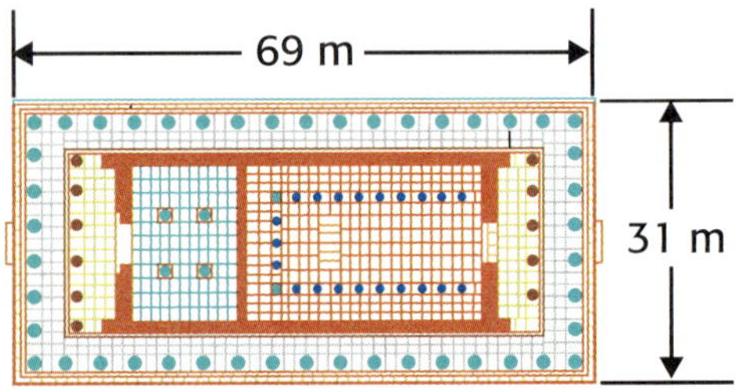

7. Talk About It Write the formulas for the area of a rectangle and a square. Explain what each variable represents.

Practice and Problem Solving

EXTRA PRACTICE See page R38.

Find the area of each rectangle or square. See Examples 1, 2 (p. 617)

8.

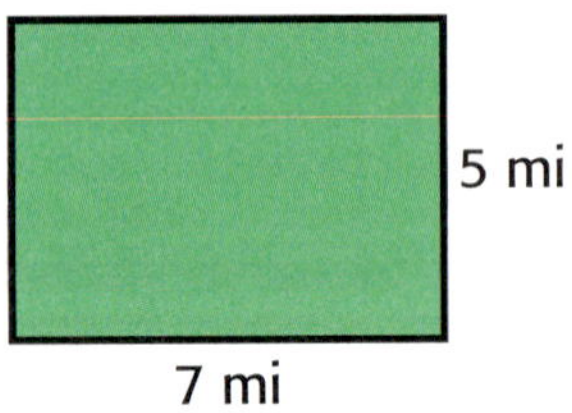

9.

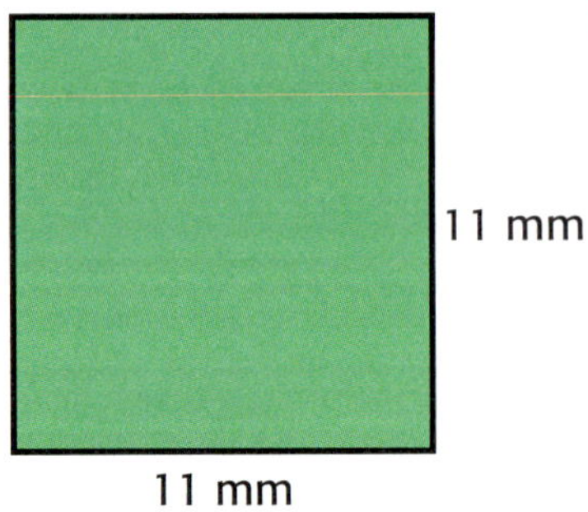

10.

11.

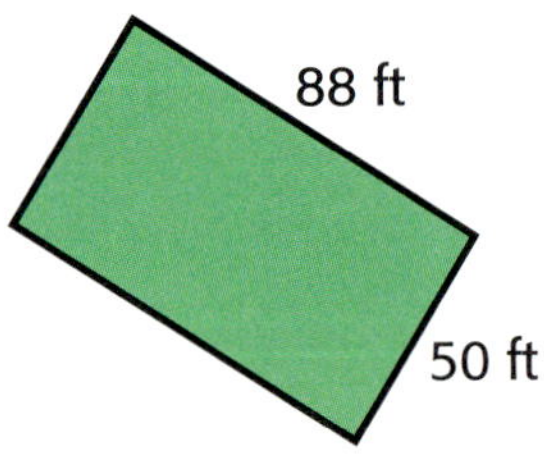

12.

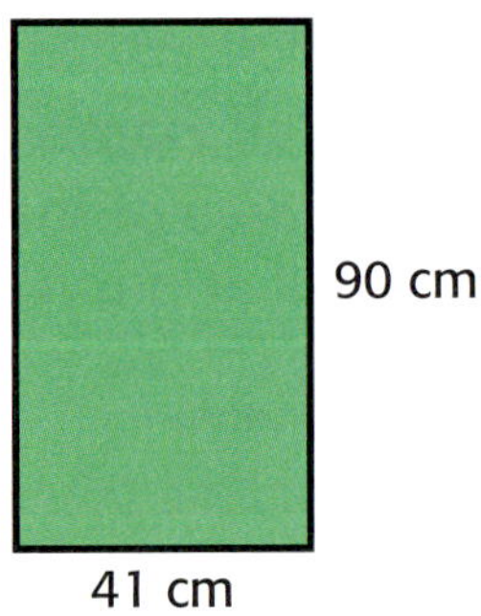

13.

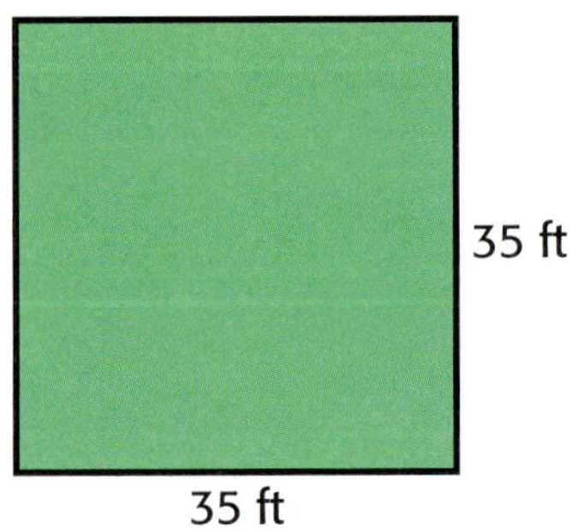

14. $\ell = 18$ m
$w = 5$ m

15. $\ell = 24$ m
$w = 37$ m

16. $\ell = 12$ cm
$w = 10$ cm

17. Use a centimeter ruler to draw two different rectangles and one square that each have an area of 16 square centimeters.

18. Use a centimeter ruler to measure the side lengths of the figures shown. Select and use appropriate formulas and units to find the area.

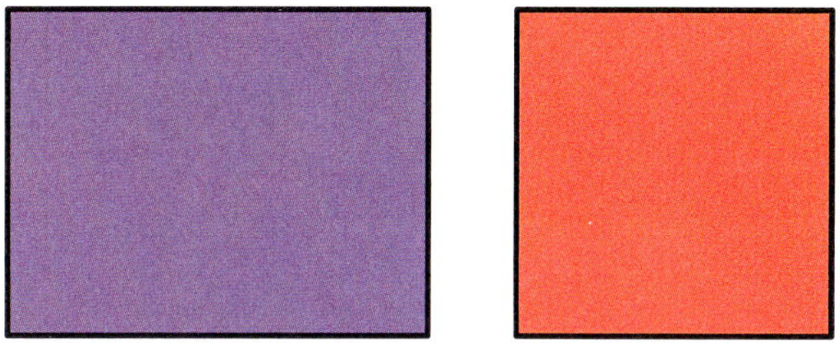

19. A square has an area of 196 square inches. What is the side length?

20. The four boxes whose bases are described in the table are being used as props for the school's spring play. They can not take up more than 90 square feet of area on the stage. Can all the boxes be used? Explain.

Box	Length (ft)	Width (ft)
1	4	3
2	5	4
3	6	2
4	2	8

21. A soccer field has to be 100 to 130 yards long and 50 to 100 yards wide. Find the least and greatest areas for the soccer field.

22. The door of a new building measures 7 feet by 3 feet. It is to be covered with 12-inch square metal tiles that cost $15 each. How much will it cost to cover the door? Explain.

Data File

All of the license plates in the United States may have a different design, but they all come in one standard size.

License Plate Size	
Customary Units	Metric Units
12 in. × 6 in.	300 mm × 150 mm

Find the area of the license plate using each type of unit.

23. square inches

24. square millimeters

25. square centimeters

H.O.T. Problems

26. **OPEN ENDED** Give the dimensions of a rectangle whose area is between 100 and 200 square centimeters. Find the area.

27. **CHALLENGE** Suppose you double the length and the width of a rectangle. Would the area also double? Explain.

28. **WRITING IN MATH** Write about a real-life situation that can be solved by finding the area of a rectangle. Then solve.

Extend

Math Activity for 14-3

Areas of Parallelograms

You can create a parallelogram from a rectangle. The area of the parallelogram will be the same as the area of the rectangle.

MAIN IDEA

I will use models to find the area of parallelograms.

You Will Need

graph paper

ACTIVITY 1

Step 1 Cut out a rectangle using grid paper like the one shown below. The area is 8 square units.

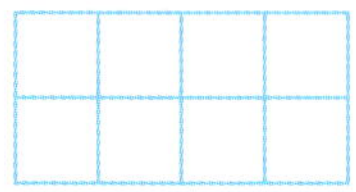

Step 2 Cut a triangle from one side of the rectangle and move it to the other side to form a parallelogram.

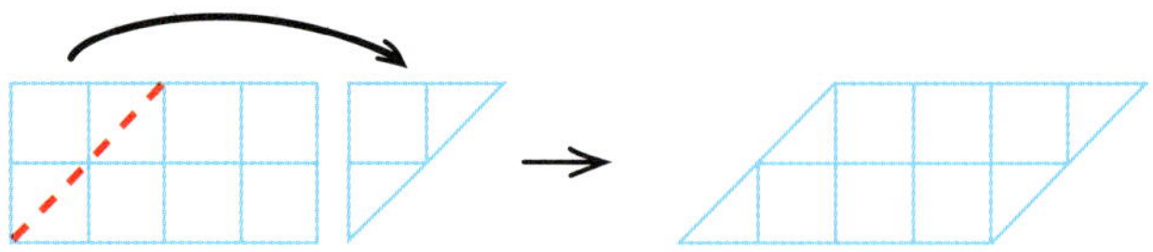

The area is still 8 square units.

ACTIVITY 2

Step 1 Cut out a rectangle using graph paper like the one shown below. The area is 12 square units.

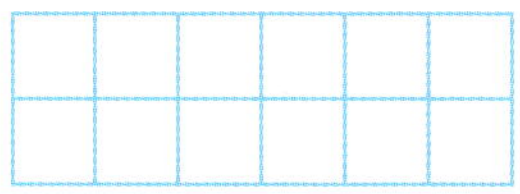

Step 2 Cut a triangle from one side of the rectangle and move it to the other side to form a parallelogram.

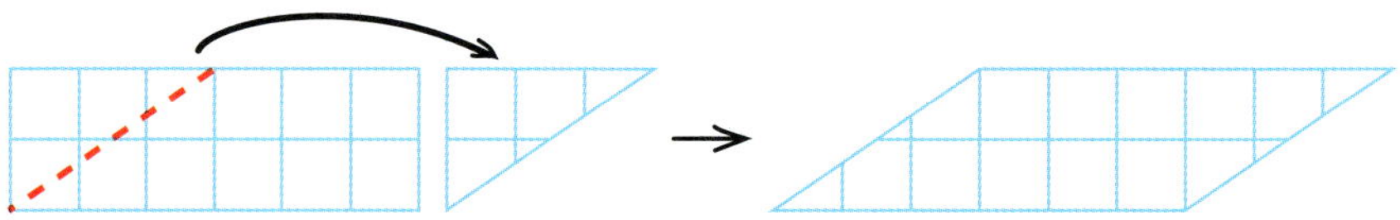

The area is still 12 square units.

ACTIVITY

Hands-On Activity

3 Find the area of the parallelogram to the right by using a model.

Step 1 Draw the parallelogram on grid paper.

Step 2 Fold and cut along the dotted line.

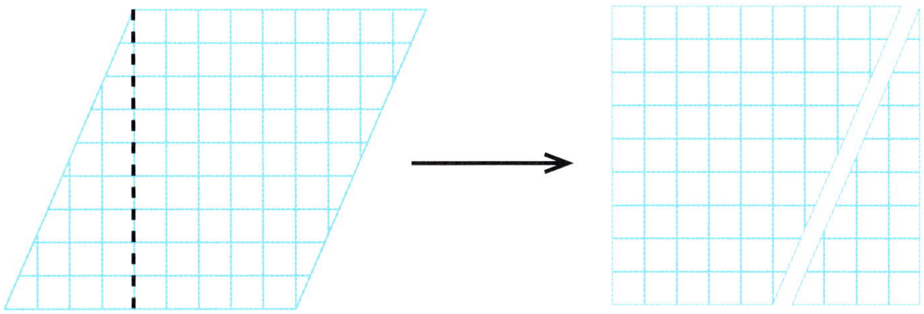

Step 3 Move the triangle to the right to make a square.

Step 4 Count up the number of units in the square or use the formula $A = \ell w$.

$A = 81$ square units

Think About It

1. Explain how to use a model to find the area of a parallelogram.

CHECK What You Know

Use a model to find the area of each parallelogram.

2. 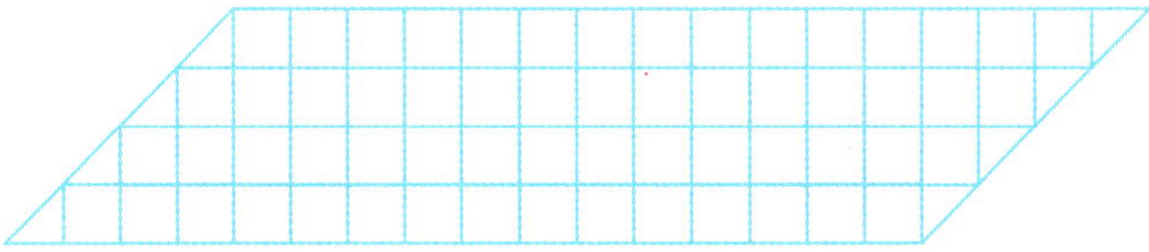

3. 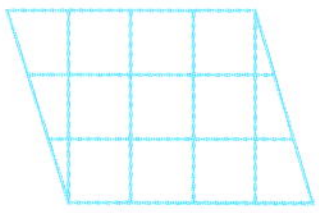

4. 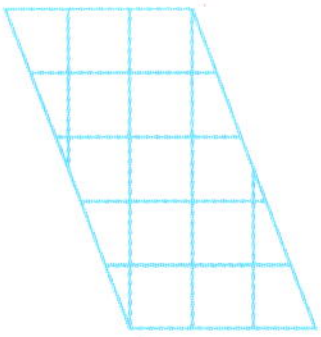

5. 

6. **WRITING IN ▶MATH** The formula for finding the area of a rectangle is $A = \ell w$. Can the same formula be used to find the area of a parallelogram?

Game Time

What's the Area?

Measuring Areas

Get Ready!

Players: 2 to 4

You will need: 18 cards with sketches of different sized rectangles, centimeter ruler, paper, pencils

Get Set!

Shuffle and turn the cards facedown in a pile. Give paper and pencil to each player.

Go!

- Turn the first card face up.
- Each player estimates the area of the figure in square centimeters and records that number.
- Players work together to measure the figure and calculate the area. Select and use appropriate units and formulas.
- Each player compares the actual area to their estimate. The player with the closest estimate earns 1 point.
- Continue playing until all the cards are used. The player with the most points wins.

CHAPTER 14

Mid-Chapter Check

Lessons 14-1 through 14-3

Find the perimeter of each square or rectangle. (Lesson 14-1)

1. 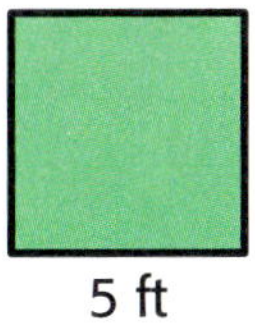

2. 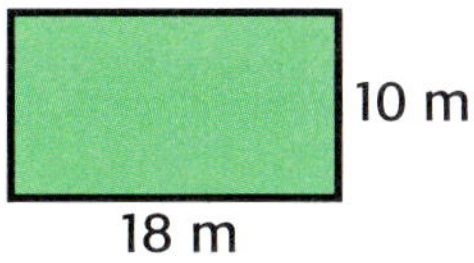

3. **MULTIPLE CHOICE** Chelsea wants to plant flowers around her triangle-shaped garden. The sides of the garden measure 2 yards, 3 yards 2 feet, and 8 feet. What is the perimeter of the garden in feet? (Lesson 14-1)

   A 15 ft

   B 25 ft

   C 41 ft

   D 47 ft

4. A horse stall is a square with a side length of 12 feet. What is the perimeter of the stall? (Lesson 14-1)

5. A doghouse is a rectangle that measures $2\frac{1}{3}$ feet by 3 feet. What is the perimeter of the doghouse? (Lesson 14-1)

Estimate the area of each figure. Each square represents 1 square foot. (Lesson 14-2)

6. 

7. 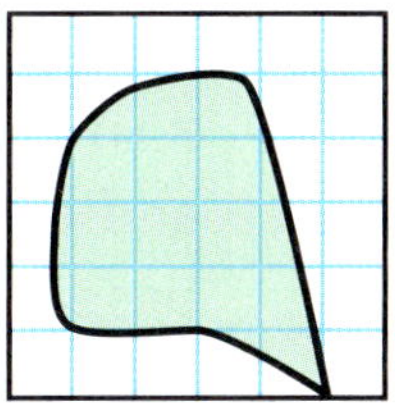

8. Estimate the area of the stop sign below. (Lesson 14-2)

Find the area of each rectangle or square. (Lesson 14-3)

9. 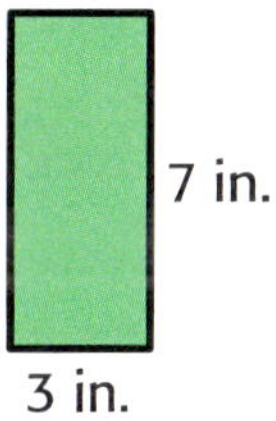

10. 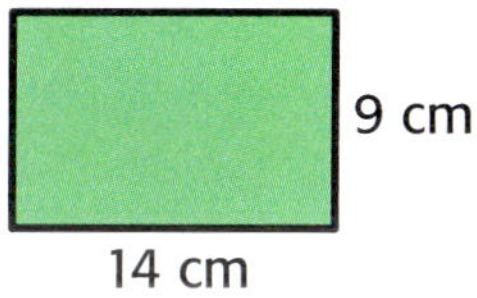

11. 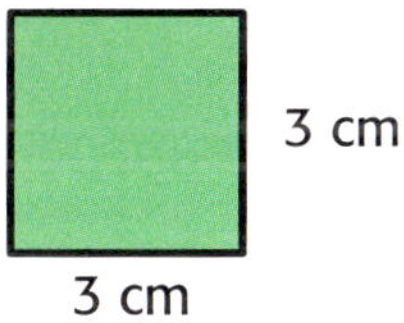

12. 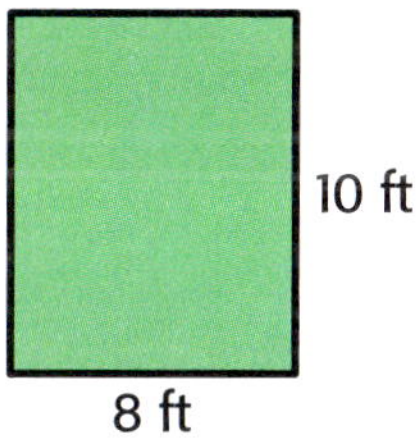

13. **MULTIPLE CHOICE** A square has a length of 20 inches. What is the area? (Lesson 14-3)

    F 40 square inches

    G 80 square inches

    H 200 square inches

    J 400 square inches

14. **WRITING IN MATH** Describe how to estimate the area of the figure in Exercise 7. (Lessons 14-1 and 14-3)

14-4 Three-Dimensional Figures

GET READY to Learn

The building at the right is made up of shapes called *rectangular prisms*.

MAIN IDEA

I will identify characteristics of three-dimensional figures.

New Vocabulary

- three-dimensional figure
- polyhedron
- prism
- base
- face
- edge
- vertex
- rectangular prism
- triangular prism
- cylinder
- cone

Math Online

macmillanmh.com

- Extra Examples
- Personal Tutor
- Self-Check Quiz

A two-dimensional figure is a plane figure that has length and width. A **three-dimensional figure** has length, width, and height. A three-dimensional figure with faces that are polygons is called a **polyhedron**. A **prism** is a polyhedron with two parallel congruent faces, called **bases**.

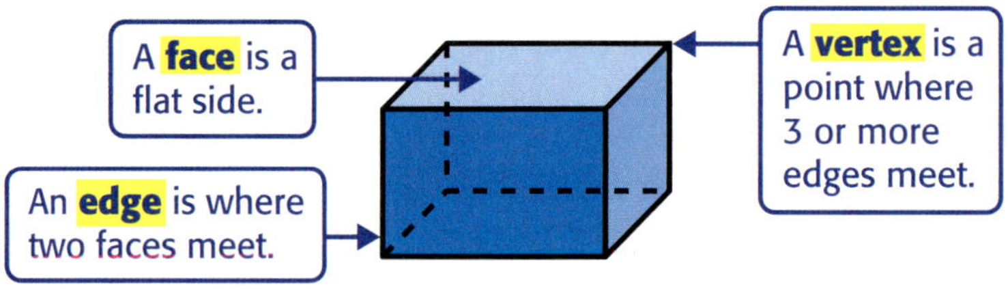

Three-dimensional Figures

Key Concepts

Figure	Example	Characteristics
rectangular prism	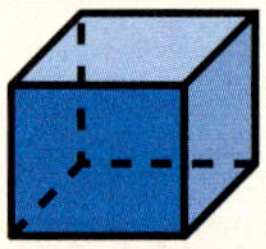	a prism with six rectangular faces including two rectangular bases
triangular prism	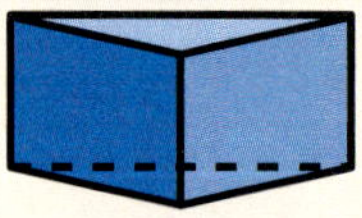	a prism that has triangular bases
cylinder		a solid with two parallel congruent circular bases; a curved surface connects the bases
cone		a solid that has a circular base and one curved surface from the base to a vertex

Remember

Bases, faces, edges, and vertices are all parts of three-dimensional figures.

EXAMPLE Characteristics of Solids

1 **Describe parts of the figure that are parallel and congruent. Then identify the figure.**

faces This figure has 5 faces. The triangular bases are parallel and congruent. The rectangular faces appear to be congruent.

edges There are 9 edges. The edges that form the vertical sides of the rectangles are parallel and congruent.

vertices This figure has 6 vertices.

So, the figure is a triangular prism.

Real-World EXAMPLE Characteristics of Solids

2 **SPORTS** **Describe parts of the tennis ball container that are perpendicular and congruent. Then identify the shape of the container.**

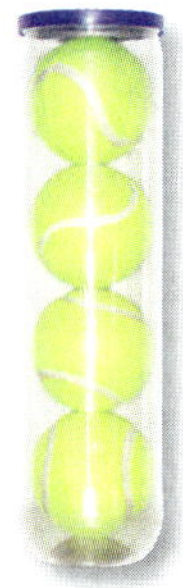

faces The circular bases are congruent. They are perpendicular to the curved surface of the container.

edges The container has no edges.
So the container is a cylinder.

CHECK What You Know

1. Describe parts of the figure that are parallel and congruent. Then identify the figure. See Examples 1, 2 (p. 625)

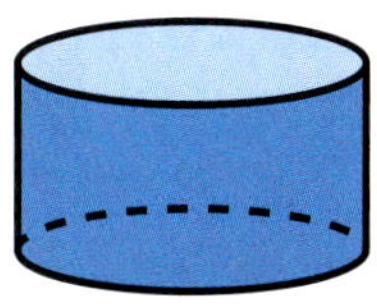

2. Describe parts of the hamster cage that are perpendicular and congruent. Then identify the shape of the cage.

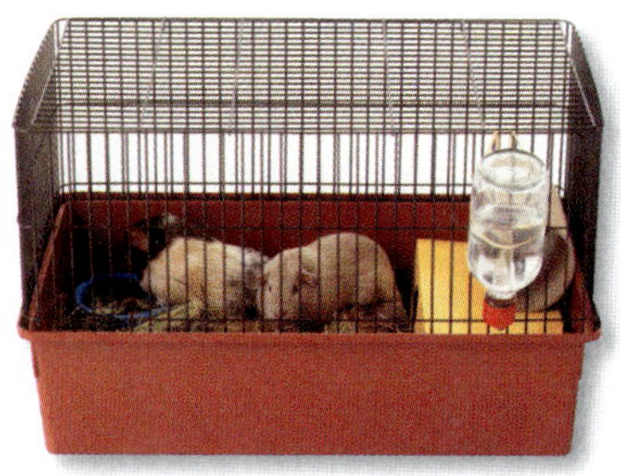

3. **Talk About It** Describe the differences between a cylinder and a rectangular prism.

Practice and Problem Solving

EXTRA PRACTICE
See page R39.

Describe parts of each figure that are parallel and congruent. Then identify the figure. See Examples 1, 2 (p. 625)

4. 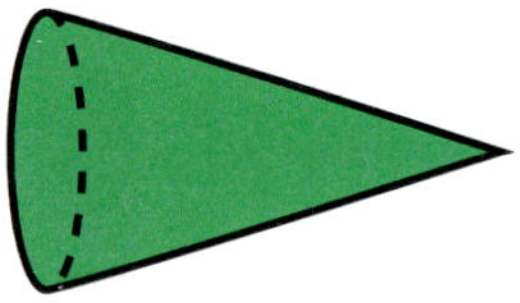

5. 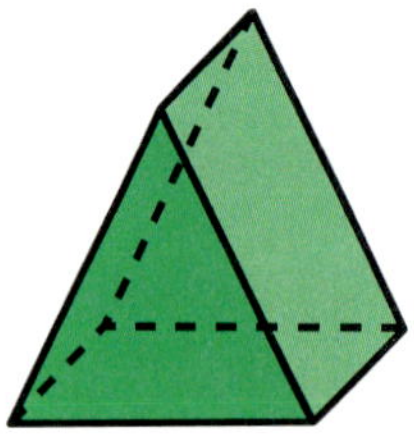

6. 

7. 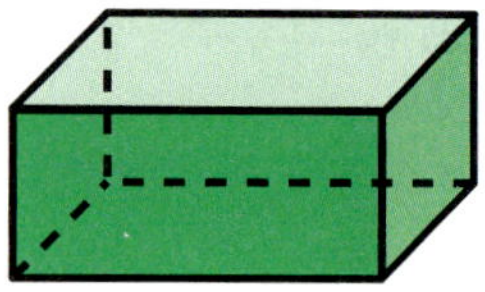

Describe parts of each figure that are perpendicular and congruent. Then identify the figure. See Examples 1, 2 (p. 625)

8. 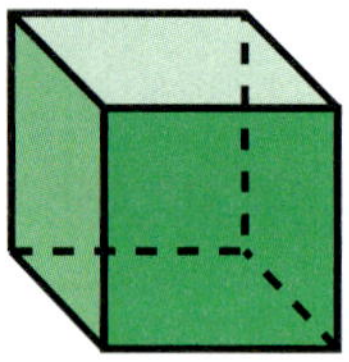

9. 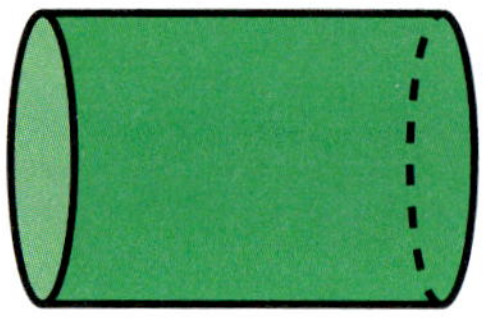

10. 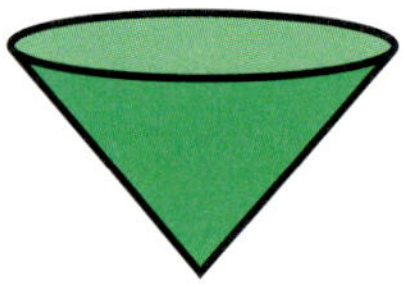

11. 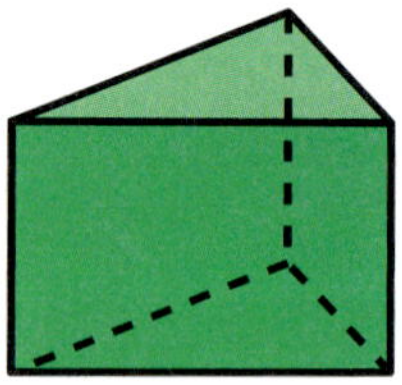

12. What kind of figure is the tomato soup can at the right?

13. Describe the number of vertices and edges in a closed book. Identify the shape of the book.

14. Vera's closet is in the shape of a rectangular prism. Describe the pairs of parallel planes that make up her closet.

H.O.T. Problems

15. **WHICH ONE DOESN'T BELONG?** Which figure does not belong with the other three? Explain your reasoning.

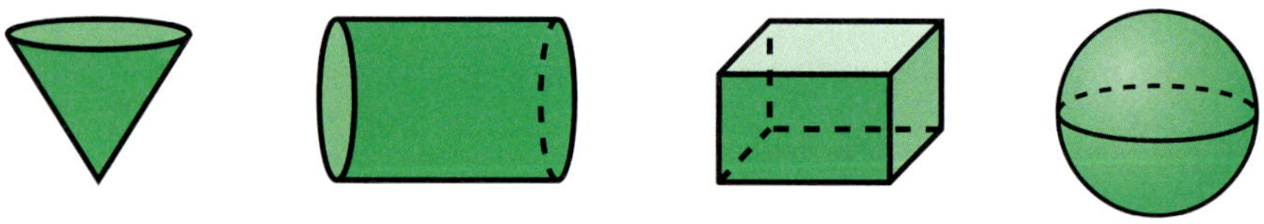

16. **CHALLENGE** Suppose the figure is folded on the dashed lines. What three-dimensional figure is formed?

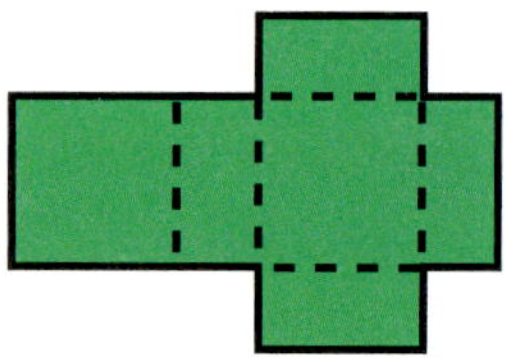

17. **WRITING IN MATH** Describe the similarities and differences of a rectangular prism and a triangular prism.

TEST Practice

18. A rectangular fish tank is shown below.

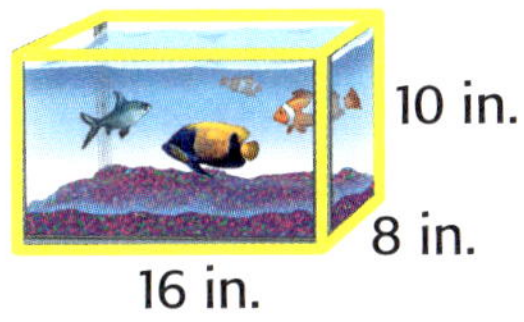

What is the area of the bottom of the fish tank? **(Lesson 14-3)**

A 24 square inches

B 56 square inches

C 80 square inches

D 128 square inches

19. Look at the figure below.

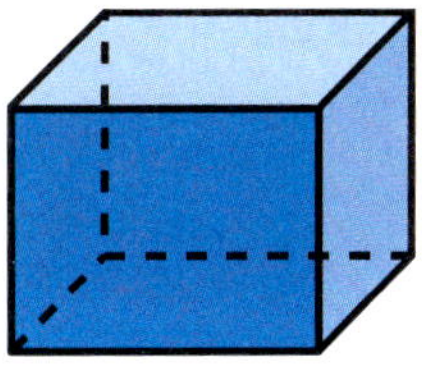

Which statement is true? **(Lesson 14-4)**

F The figure has a triangular base.

G The figure has exactly 3 pairs of parallel faces.

H The figure has exactly 2 pairs of parallel faces.

J The figure has no perpendicular sides.

Spiral Review

Find the area of each rectangle or square. (Lesson 14-3)

20.

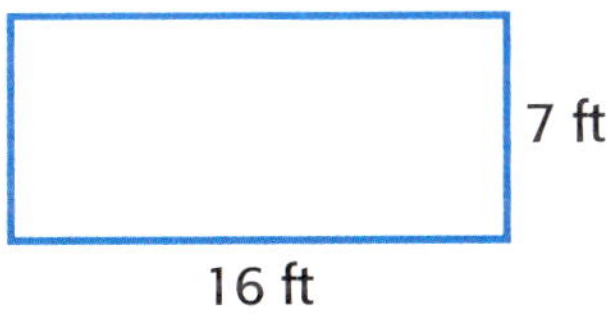

21.

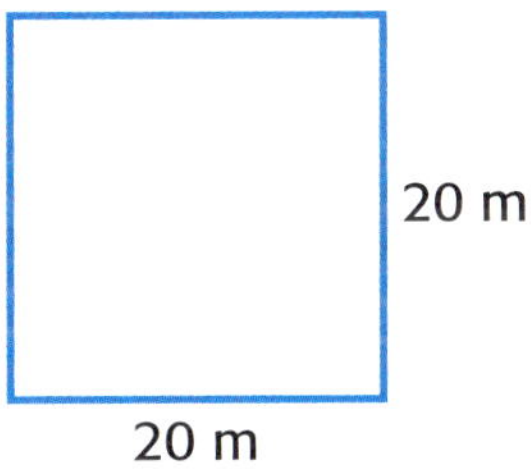

22.

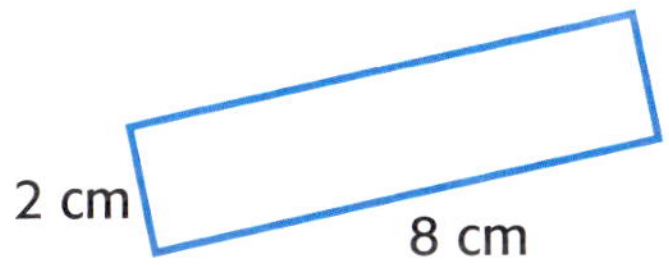

23. Estimate the area of the figure at the right. Each square represents 1 square centimeter. **(Lesson 14-2)**

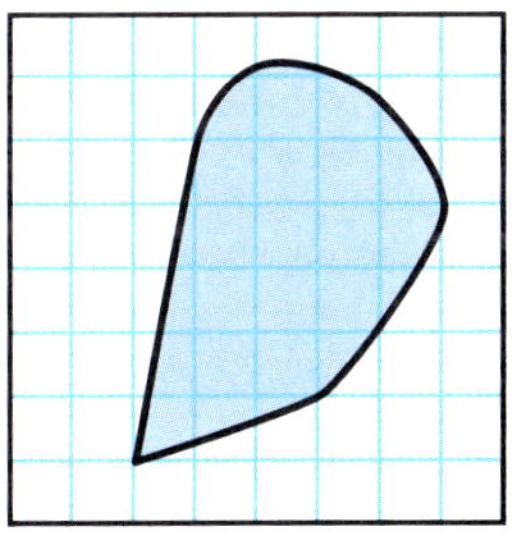

24. What is the perimeter of a rectangular building measuring 42 feet by 30 feet? **(Lesson 14-1)**

Graph each figure and the translation described. Write the ordered pairs for the new vertices. (Lessons 13-6 and 13-8)

25. triangle *XYZ* with vertices *X*(1, 5), *Y*(5, 8), *Z*(7, 6); translated 4 units down

26. triangle *ABC* with vertices *A*(3, 0), *B*(3, 3), *C*(5, 0); translated up 1 unit and to the right 3 units.

Complete. (Lesson 12-4)

27. 40 L = ■ mL

28. 2 L = ■ mL

29. 16,000 mL = ■ L

14-5 Problem-Solving Strategy

MAIN IDEA I will solve problems by making a model.

Nick is helping his younger sister put away her alphabet blocks. She has already put away one layer of blocks. To fill up one layer it takes nine blocks. If the box is filled with six layers of blocks, how many blocks would be in the box?

Understand

What facts do you know?

- The number of blocks in one layer of a box.
- The number of layers in the box.

What do you need to find?

- The number of blocks in the box when there are six layers.

Plan

Solve the problem by making a model.

Solve

Use your plan to solve the problem.

Make a model of one layer of the box by arranging 9 cubes in a 3×3 array.

Continue stacking the cubes until there are six layers.

There are a total of 54 cubes. So, the box would have 54 blocks.

Check

Look back. Use logical reasoning and multiplication. There are 6 layers and each layer has 9 cubes. So, the total number of cubes is 6×9 or 54. The answer is correct. ✓

ANALYZE the Strategy

Refer to the problem on the previous page.

1. How many blocks would the box contain if it had only five layers of blocks?

2. If you stacked two boxes of the original size on top of each other, what would be the total number of blocks in the boxes?

3. What are the advantages of the *make a model* strategy?

4. List some objects that you could use to make a model.

PRACTICE the Strategy

EXTRA PRACTICE
See page R38.

Solve. Use the *make a model* strategy.

5. **Measurement** On an assembly line that is 150 feet long, there is a work station every 15 feet. The first station is at the beginning of the line. How many work stations are there?

6. A store is stacking cans of food into a pyramid-shaped display. The bottom layer has 9 cans. There are 5 layers. If there are two less cans in each layer, how many cans are in the display?

7. **Measurement** The distance around the center ring at the circus is 80 feet. A clown stands every 10 feet along the circle. How many clowns are there?

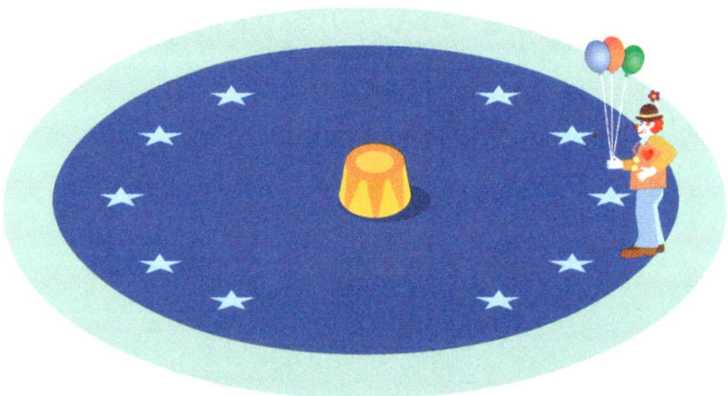

8. **Measurement** Martino wants to arrange 18 square tiles into a rectangular shape with the least perimeter possible. How many tiles will be in each row?

9. In the figure below, there are 22 marbles in Box A. To go from Box A to Box B, four marbles can pass through the triangular machine at a time. Five marbles can pass through the square machine at a time. Describe how to move all the marbles from Box A to Box B in the fewest moves possible.

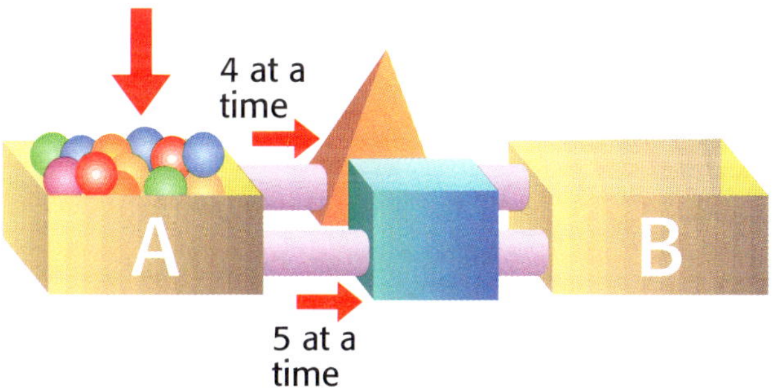

10. Drake lined up 15 pennies on his desk. He replaced every third penny with a nickel. Then he replaced every fourth coin with a dime. Finally, he replaced every fifth coin with a quarter. What is the value of the remaining 15 coins on his desk? Explain.

11. **WRITING IN MATH** Describe when you would use the *make a model* strategy.

Explore

Measurement Activity for 14-6

Volumes of Prisms

MAIN IDEA

I will use models to find the volumes of prisms.

You can use centimeter cubes to build rectangular prisms like the ones shown at the right.

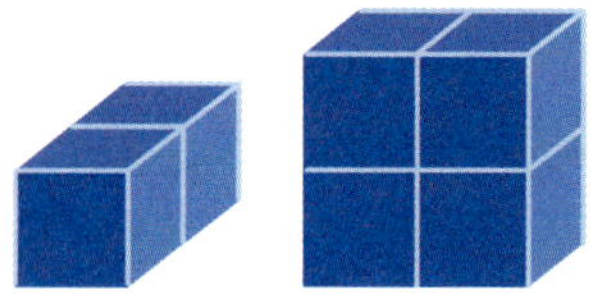

ACTIVITY

Step 1 Use centimeter cubes to build four different rectangular prisms.

Step 2 For each prism, record the dimensions and the number of cubes used in a table like the one below.

Prism	Length (ℓ)	Width (w)	Height (h)	Area of Base (B)	Number of Cubes
A					
B					
C					
D					

Since volume can be measured using cubes, volume is measured in cubic units.

CHECK What You Know

1. Describe the relationship between the dimensions of the prism and number of cubes.

2. Use ℓ, w, and h to write a formula for the volume V of a rectangular prism.

3. Use the formula you wrote in Exercise 2 to find the volume of the prism at the right in appropriate units. Verify your solution by counting the number of cubes.

14-6 Volumes of Prisms

MAIN IDEA

I will find the volumes of rectangular prisms.

New Vocabulary

volume

Math Online

macmillanmh.com

- Extra Examples
- Personal Tutor
- Self-Check Quiz

GET READY to Learn

Armando makes sand paintings by filling clear plastic cases with colored sand. The amount of sand he uses depends on the amount of space in the cases.

Volume is the amount of space that a three-dimensional figure contains. Volume is measured in cubic units. A cubic unit has length, width, and height.

1 cubic unit

2 cubic units

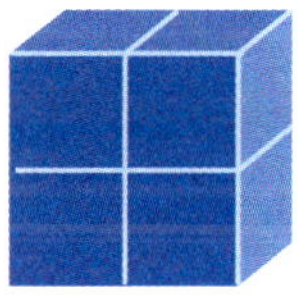
4 cubic units

Some common units of volume are *cubic inch*, *cubic foot*, *cubic yard*, *cubic centimeter*, and *cubic meter*.

You can find the volume of a rectangular prism by using models or a formula.

Volume of a Rectangular Prism — Key Concept

Words The volume V of a rectangular prism is length ℓ times width w times height h.

Symbols $V = \ell wh$

Model

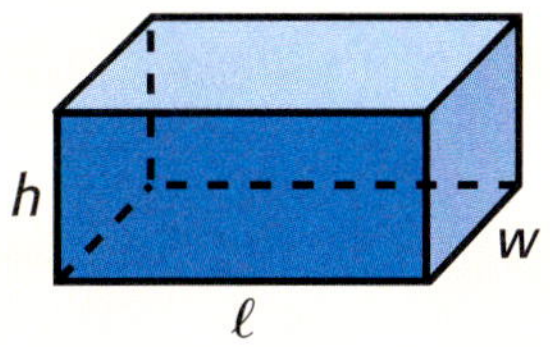

Real-World EXAMPLE Volume of a Prism

Remember

A cube with 1 unit on an edge is a standard unit for measuring volume. When cubes are placed in a prism to determine volume, there are no gaps or overlaps between the cubes.

1 **GAMES** **What is the volume of a video game system that is 6 inches long, 4 inches wide, and 4 inches tall?**

One Way: Use a Model

Count the number of 1-inch cubes that will fill the bottom of the rectangular prism. The prism is 6 cubes long and 4 cubes wide. There are 24 cubes on the bottom.

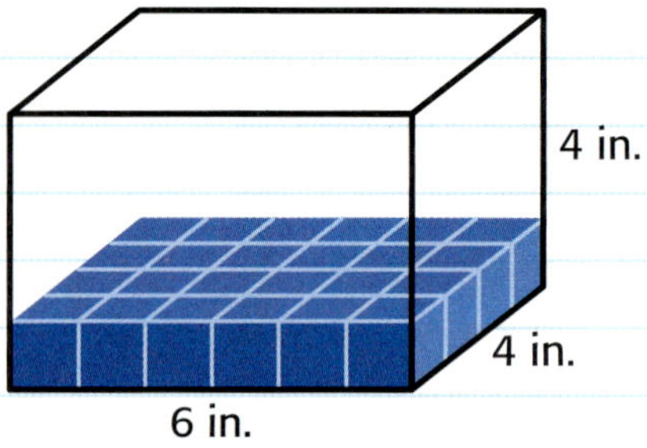

There are 4 layers of cubes. So, there are 4 × 24 or 96 cubes.

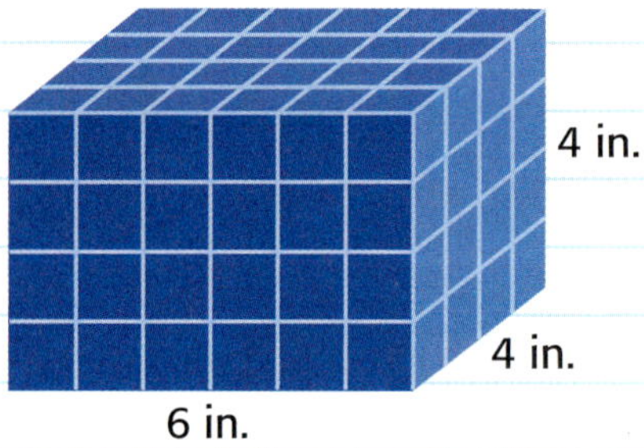

Another Way: Select and Use a Formula

$V = \ell wh$	Formula for the volume of a rectangular prism
$V = 6 \times 4 \times 4$	$\ell = 6, w = 4, h = 4$
$V = 96$	Multiply.

The volume of the video game system is 96 cubic inches.

EXAMPLE Volume of a Prism

2 **Find the volume of the prism.**

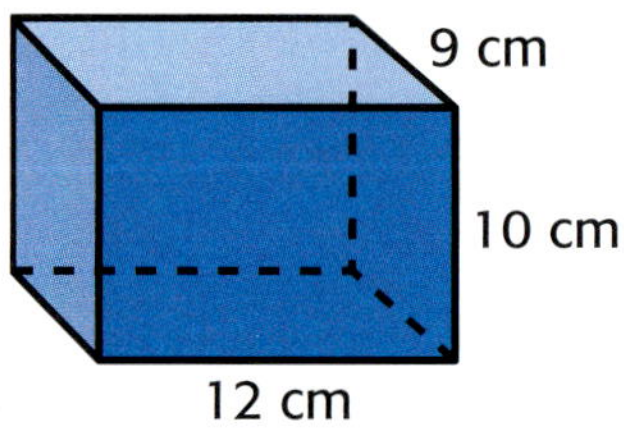

$V = \ell wh$ Formula for the volume

Estimate $10 \times 10 \times 10 = 1,000$

$V = 12 \times 9 \times 10$ $\ell = 12, w = 9, h = 10$

$V = 1,080$ Multiply.

The volume of the prism is 1,080 cubic centimeters. This is close to the estimate, 1,000. So, the answer is reasonable.

CHECK What You Know

Find the volume of each prism. See Examples 1, 2 (p. 632)

1.

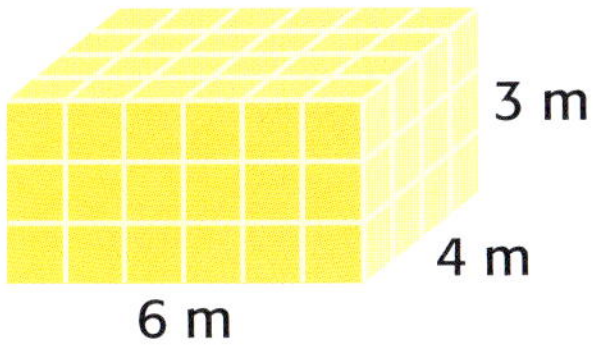

2.

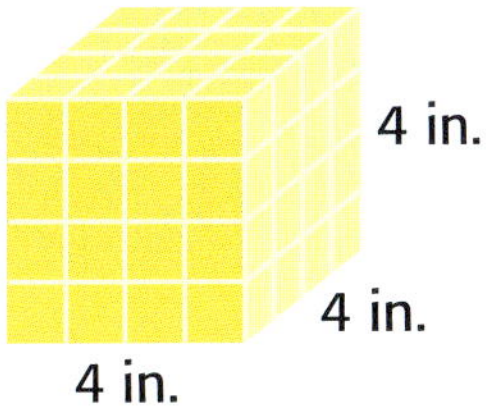

3.

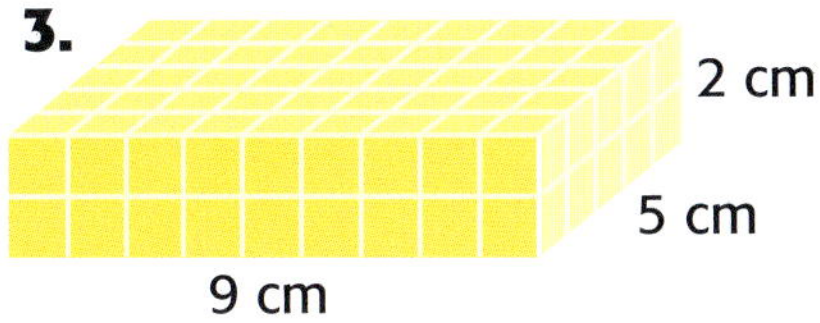

4. $\ell = 21$ cm, $w = 8$ cm, $h = 4$ cm

5. $\ell = 19$ ft, $w = 9$ ft, $h = 16$ ft

6. Find the cubic feet of air in a room that is 13 feet long, 10 feet high, and 11 feet wide.

7. **Talk About It** Describe which units would be appropriate to measure the volume of a jewelry box. What other units might be reasonable to use? Would it be reasonable to use the same units to measure the volume of a garage? Explain.

Practice and Problem Solving

EXTRA PRACTICE See page R39.

Find the volume of each prism. See Examples 1, 2 (p. 632)

8.

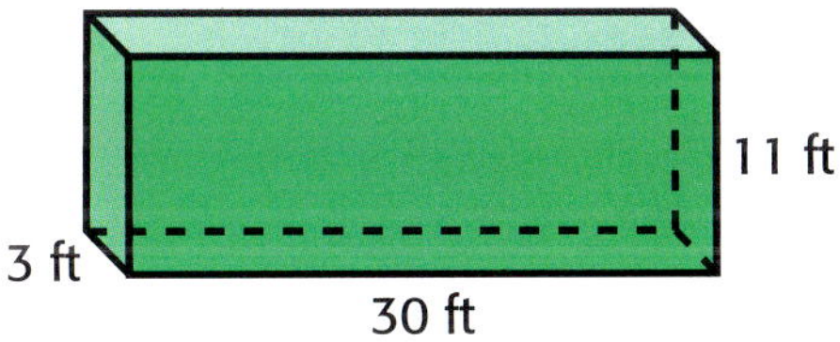

9.

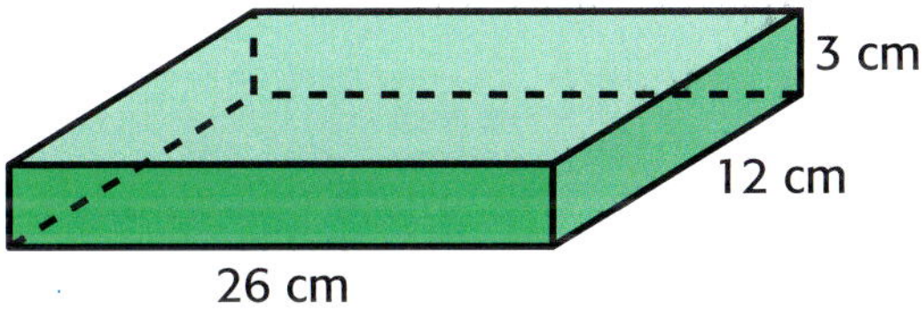

10.

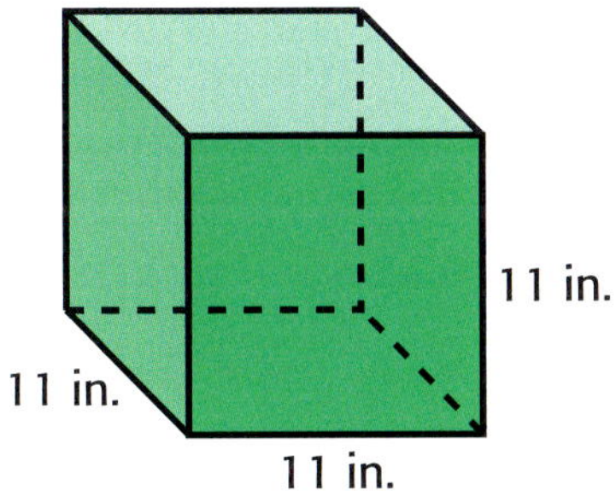

11.

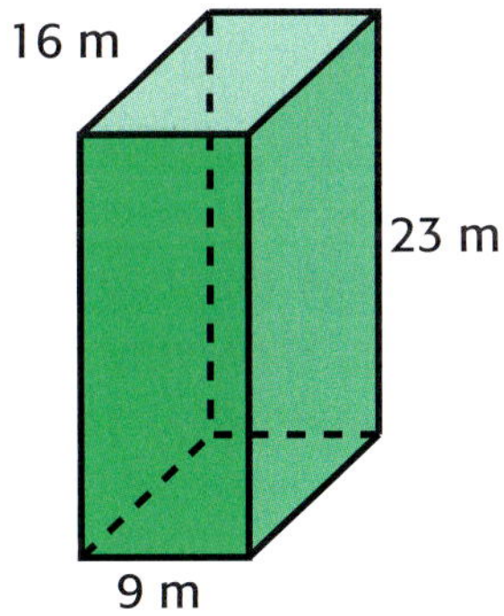

12.

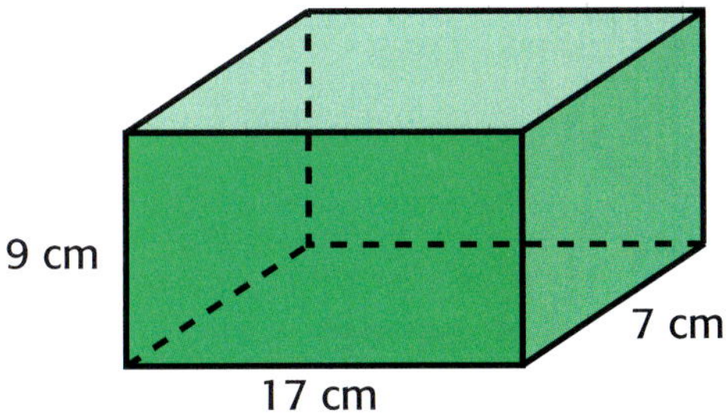

13.

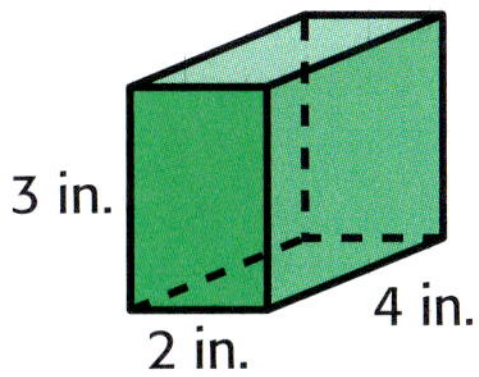

Find the volume of each prism. See Examples 1, 2 (p. 632)

14. $\ell = 5$ yd, $w = 16$ yd, $h = 6$ yd

15. $\ell = 2$ m, $w = 8$ m, $h = 10$ m

16. $\ell = 13$ in., $w = 3$ in., $h = 2$ in.

17. $\ell = 13$ cm, $w = 8$ cm, $h = 10$ cm

18. Find the volume of a bank vault that is 14 feet by 20 feet by 19 feet.

19. Which size container has the greater volume? Explain.

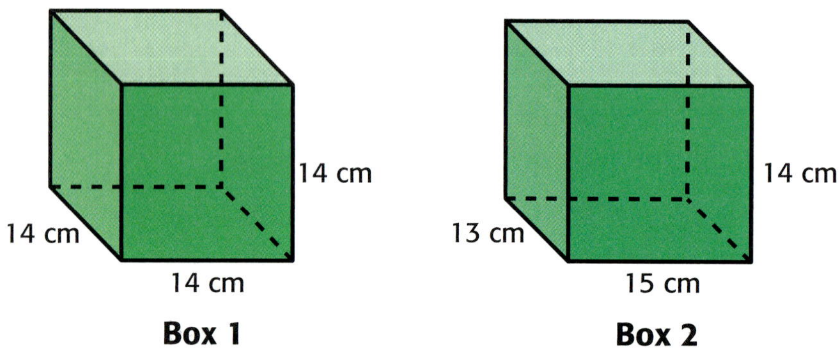

20. Sherita needs 1,400 cubic meters of storage space for her furniture. The space available at a storage company has a length of 11 meters, width of 10 meters, and height of 12 meters. Is the space large enough for Sherita's furniture? Explain.

H.O.T. Problems

21. **OPEN ENDED** Estimate the volume of a shoe box. Then measure the box. Check your estimate by finding the actual volume.

22. **NUMBER SENSE** Describe the dimensions of two different prisms that have a volume of 2,400 cubic centimeters.

23. **CHALLENGE** A store sells lunch boxes that measure 11 inches by 7 inches by 4 inches. How many lunch boxes will fit in a box that measures 22 inches by 15 inches by 8 inches? Explain.

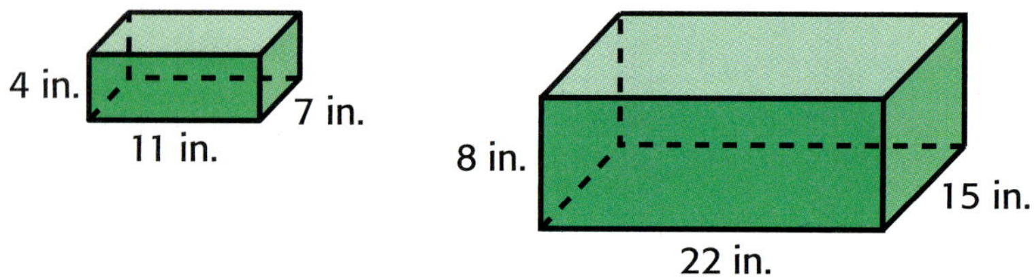

24. **WRITING IN ▶MATH** Write about a real-life situation that can be solved by finding the volume of a prism. Then solve.

TEST Practice

25. Popcorn tins are stacked in a display so that there are 12 tins in the bottom row. There are 10 tins in the next row, and 8 tins in the row above that. There are five rows of tins. If the pattern continues, how many popcorn tins are there in all? (Lesson 14-5)

A 22

B 30

C 40

D 42

26. **SHORT RESPONSE** Find the volume in cubic inches of a rectangular prism with length 8 inches, width 5 inches, and height 11 inches. (Lesson 14-6)

27. Which of these rectangular prisms has a volume of 20 cubic units? (Lesson 14-6)

F

G

H

J

Spiral Review

28. Estimate the volume of one of your textbooks in cubic centimeters. Explain how you could make a model to test your estimate. (Lesson 14-5)

29. What kind of three-dimensional shape is shown below? (Lesson 14-4)

30. Estimate the area of the figure shown below. (Lesson 14-2)

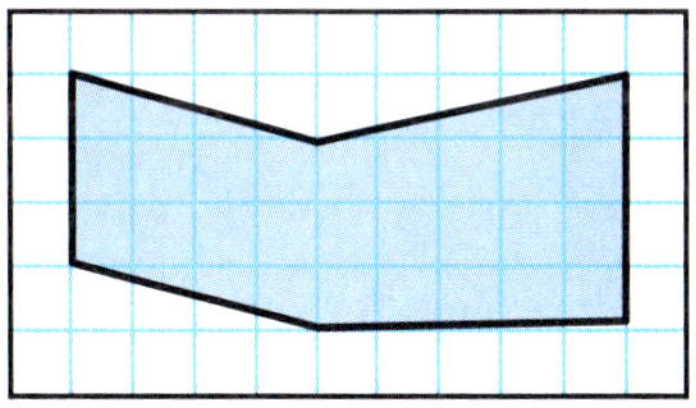

Identify whether each group of objects represents a prime number or a composite number. (Lesson 9-2)

31.

32.

Problem Solving in Science

Birdseye View

You probably eat packaged frozen food every day. Frozen food might seem like a simple concept, but there's more to it than just putting a container of food in the freezer.

Clarence Birdseye is sometimes called "the father of frozen food" because he was the first to develop a practical way to preserve food by flash freezing.

Birdseye experimented with freezing fruits and vegetables, as well as fish and meat. His method of freezing food preserved the food's taste, texture, and appearance. He also was the first to package food in waxed cardboard packages that could be sold directly to consumers.

Did You Know?

148 patents were issued that related to Clarence Birdseye's flash-freezing method, his type of packaging, and the packaging materials he used.

Dimensions of Frozen Food Packages in Inches

Item	Length	Width	Height
Pizza	12	12	2
Vegetables	5	6	2
Frozen Dinner	11	8	2
Fish Sticks	9	5	3
Hamburger Patties	9	10	4

Real-World Math

Use the information above to solve each problem.

1. What is the volume of a frozen pizza package?
2. How much more space does a package of fish sticks occupy than a package of vegetables?
3. Is 175 cubic inches a reasonable estimate for the volume of a frozen dinner package? Explain.
4. A freezer has 2,600 cubic inches of available space. After seven packages of hamburger patties are placed inside, how much available freezer space is left?
5. A larger package of frozen vegetables has the same length and width but twice the height. What is the volume of this package?
6. Use an inch ruler to measure the length, width, and height of an actual frozen food package to the nearest whole unit. Then find the volume of the package.
7. **WRITING IN MATH** Explain the differences between area and volume and the units used to represent them.

Explore

Math Activity for 14-7

Surface Area of Prisms

MAIN IDEA

I will use models to find the surface area of rectangular prisms.

You Will Need

graph paper
scissors

New Vocabulary

net

To find the *surface area* of a rectangular prism, you add the areas of all the faces of the prism.

All six faces can be seen by using a *net*. A **net** is a two dimensional pattern of a three dimensional figure.

ACTIVITY

1 Create a net to find the surface area of the prism.

Step 1 Draw and cut out the net below.

Step 2 Fold along the dotted lines.
Tape the edges together to form a prism.

Step 3 Find the area of each of the six faces of the prism.

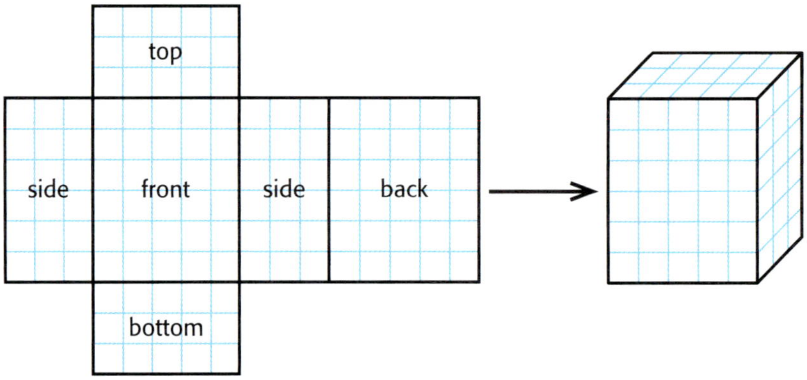

Face	front and back	top and bottom	two sides
Model	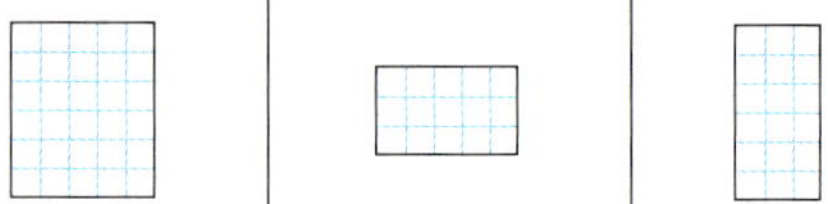		
Area (cm^2)	30	15	18

Step 4 Find the sum of the areas.

$A = 30 + 30 + 18 + 18 + 15 + 15$

$A = 126\ cm^2$ Surface area has square units because it measures area.

ACTIVITY

Hands-On Activity

2 **Find the surface area of the rectangular prism.**

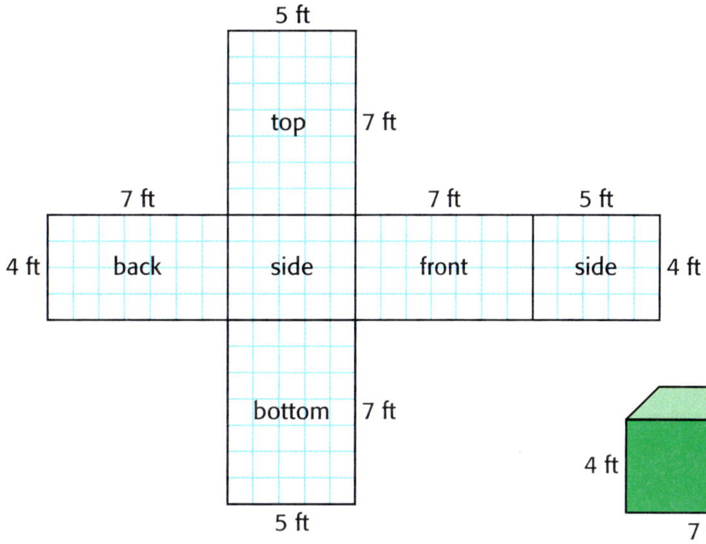

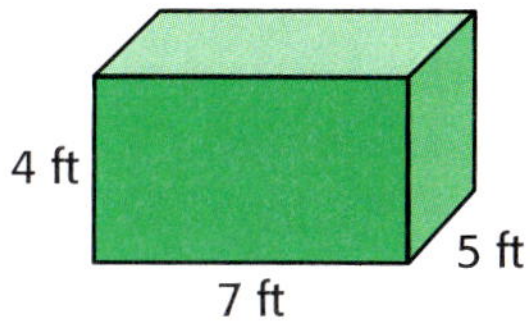

Find the area of each face. Then add.

Face	**front and back**	**top and bottom**	**two sides**
Model	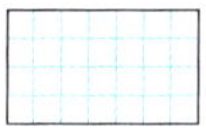	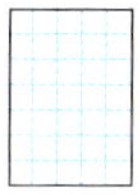	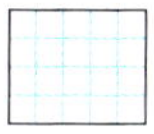
Area (cm^2)	28	35	20

$A = 28 + 28 + 35 + 35 + 20 + 20$ or 166 square feet

Think About It

1. Explain how to find the surface area of a prism by using a net.

CHECK What You Know

Make a net to find the surface area of each rectangular prism.

2.

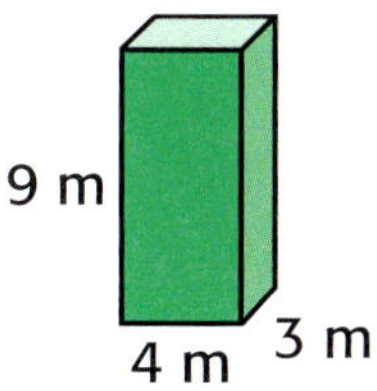

3.

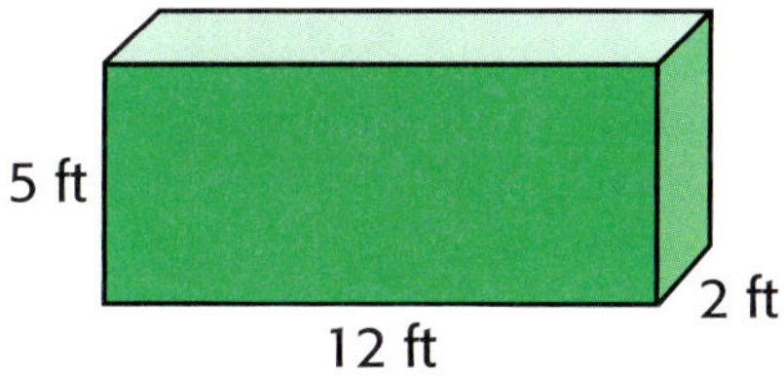

4. WRITING IN ►MATH Will the top side of a rectangular prism always have the same area as the bottom side? Explain.

14-7 Surface Areas of Prisms

MAIN IDEA

I will find the surface areas of rectangular prisms.

New Vocabulary

surface area

Math Online

macmillanmh.com

- Extra Examples
- Personal Tutor
- Self-Check Quiz

GET READY to Learn

Wrapping paper is used to cover the surface area of a box.

The sum of the areas of all the faces of a prism is called the **surface area** of the prism.

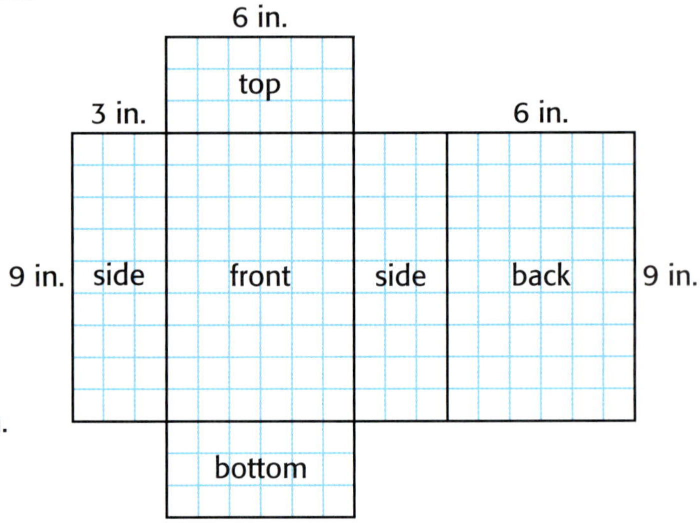

To find the surface area, you could add the areas of all six faces.

In the diagram above each face has a congruent opposite face. The front is congruent to the back, the top is congruent to the bottom, and the two sides are congruent.

So, the following formula can also be used to find surface area.

Surface Area of a Rectangular Prism

Key Concept

Words The surface area S of a rectangular prism with length ℓ, width w, and height h is the sum of the areas of the faces.

Symbols $S = 2\ell w + 2\ell h + 2wh$

Model

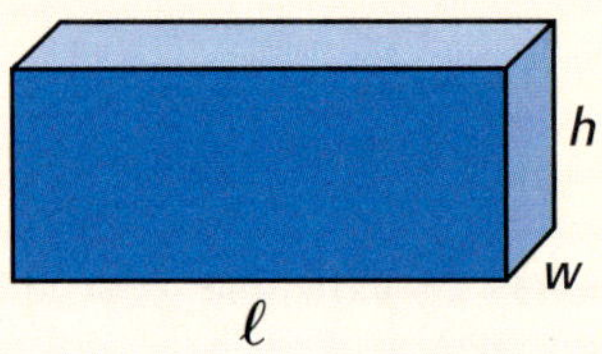

Real-World EXAMPLE — Find the Surface Area

1 **GIFTS Find the surface area for the amount of wrapping paper needed to cover the gift on page 640.**

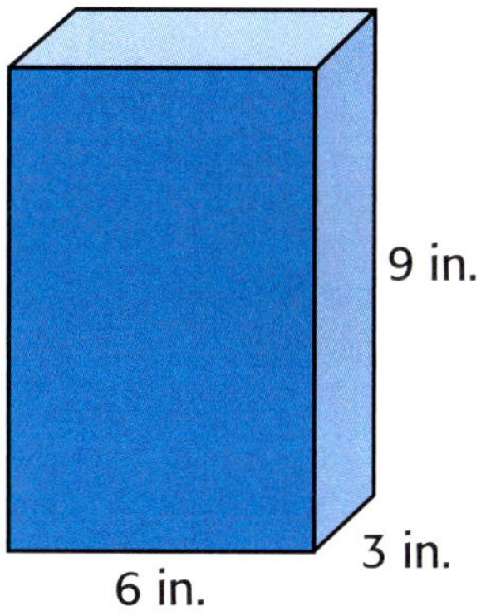

Find the area of each face.

top and bottom:
$2(\ell w) = 2(6 \times 3)$ or 36

front and back:
$2(\ell h) = 2(6 \times 9)$ or 108

two sides:
$2(wh) = 2(3 \times 9)$ or 54

Add to find the surface area.

The surface area is 36 + 108 + 54 or 198 square inches.

Remember

The top face has the same area as the bottom face. The front face has the same area as the back face. Both side faces have the same area.

Real-World EXAMPLE — Find the Surface Area

2 **CAMERAS Digital cameras are made small enough to fit in a pocket. This camera is shaped like a rectangular prism. Find the surface area of the camera.**

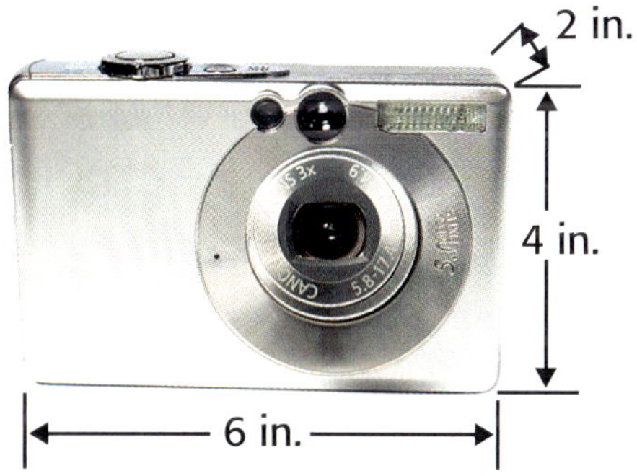

Find the area of each face.

top and bottom: $2(\ell w) = 2(6 \times 2)$ or 24

front and back: $2(\ell h) = 2(6 \times 4)$ or 48

two sides: $2(wh) = 2(2 \times 4)$ or 16

Add to find the surface area.

The surface area is 24 + 48 + 16 or 88 square inches.

CHECK What You Know

Find the surface area of each rectangular prism. See Example 1 (p. 641)

1.

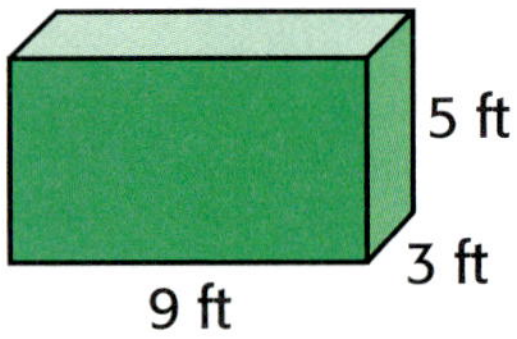

2.

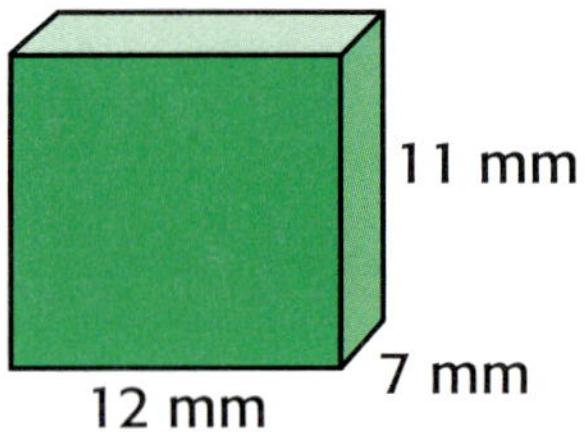

3.

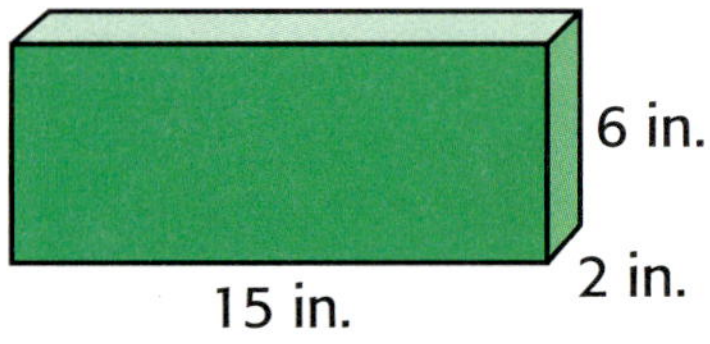

4. A box of animal crackers is shaped like a rectangular prism. What is the surface area of the box of crackers?

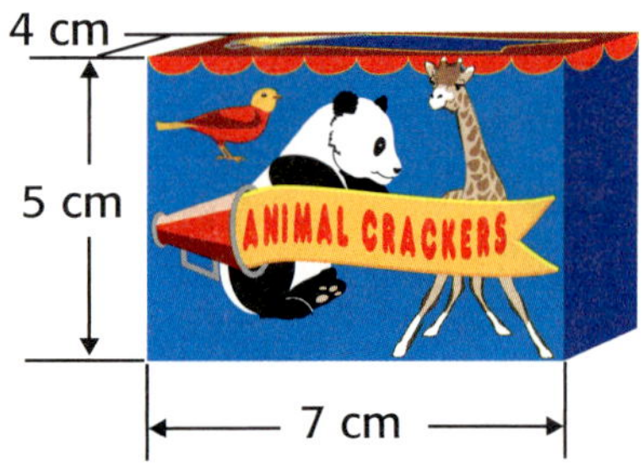

5. Talk About It The formula for the surface area of a rectangular prism is $S = 2\ell w + 2\ell h + 2wh$. Explain why there are three 2s in the formula.

Practice and Problem Solving

EXTRA PRACTICE See page R39

Find the surface area of each rectangular prism. See Example 1 (p. 641)

6.

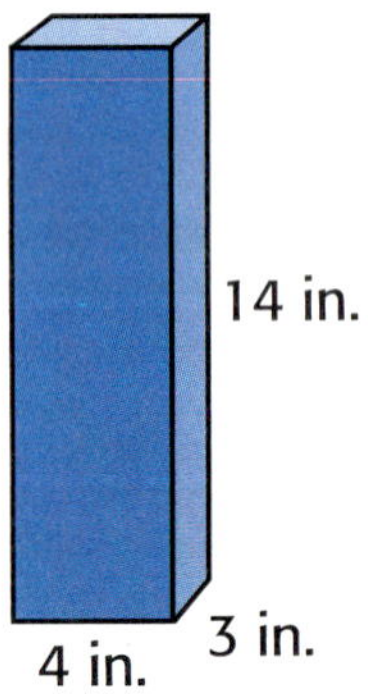

7.

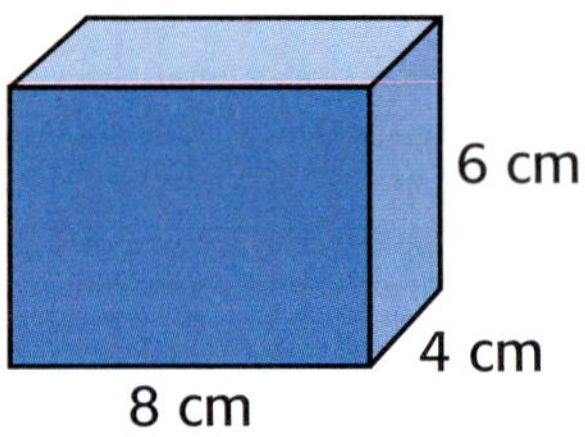

8.

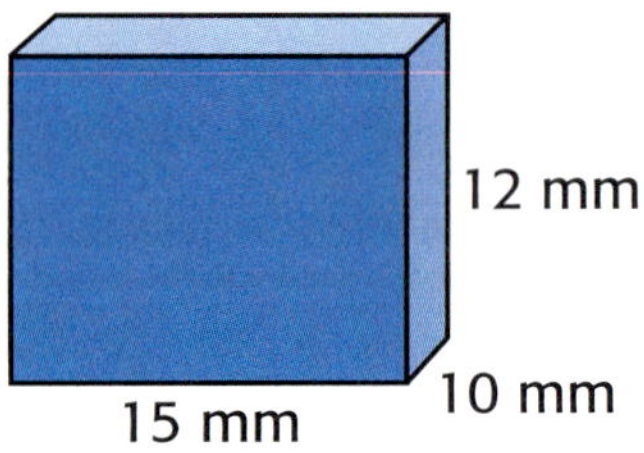

9.

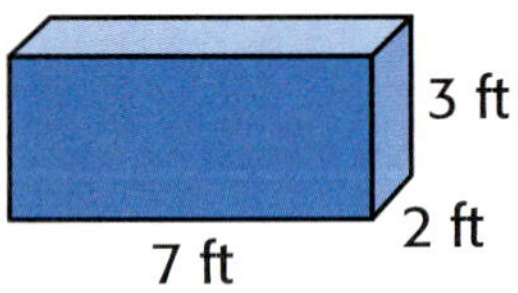

10.

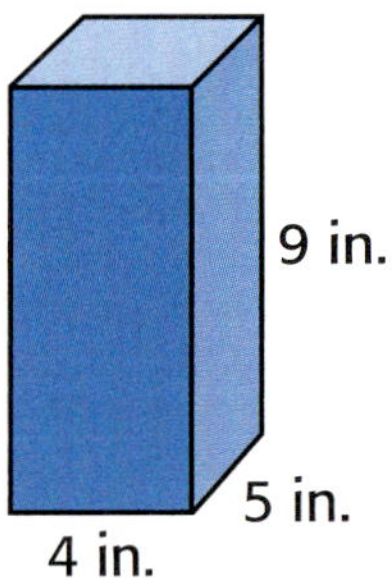

11.

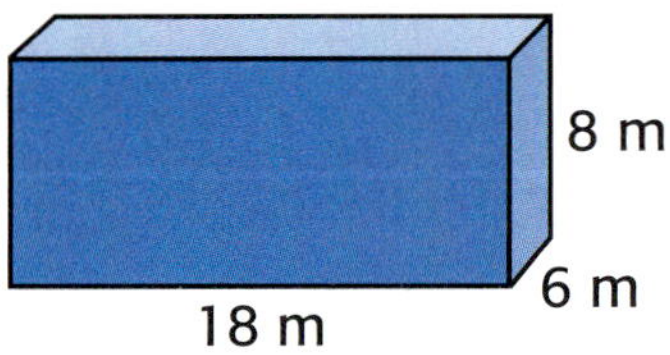

12. Alyssa owns a toolbox that is 16 inches by 22 inches by 5 inches. What is the surface area of the toolbox?

13. Michelle put her sister's birthday present in a box with a length of 13 mm, a width of 4 mm, and a height of 8 mm. How many square millimeters of wrapping paper will Michelle need to completely cover the box?

14. A package of three golf balls comes in the box shown. What is the surface area of the box?

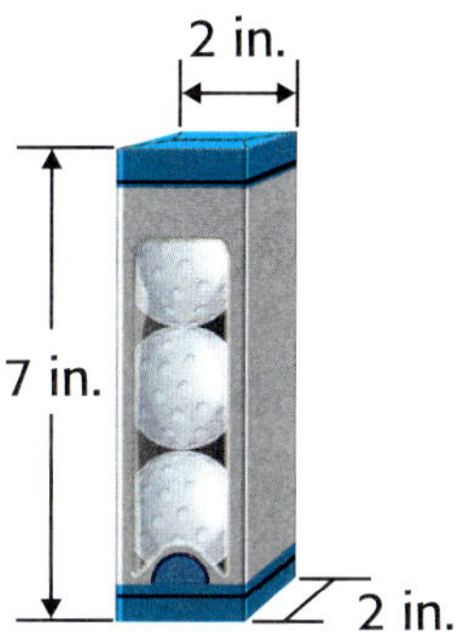

H.O.T. Problems

15. **OPEN ENDED** What is the possible length, width, and height of a rectangular prism with the surface area of 110 square centimeters?

CHALLENGE For Exercises 16 and 17, use the rectangular prism shown.

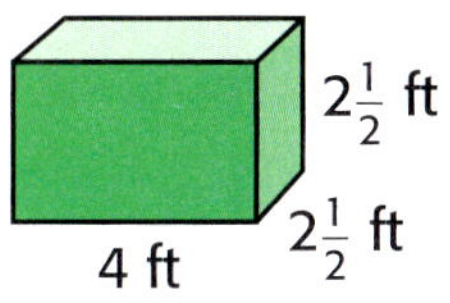

16. How many rectangles and how many squares would the net of the prism make?

17. Find the surface area of the rectangular prism.

18. **WRITING IN MATH** Write a real-world problem about a time when you would need to find the surface area of a rectangular prism.

TEST Practice

19. A shoebox has a length of 10 inches, a width of 5 inches, and a height of 6 inches. What is the surface area of the shoebox? (Lesson 14-7)

A 220 in^2 **C** 325 in^2

B 280 in^2 **D** 340 in^2

20. **SHORT RESPONSE** If the surface area of the top of a rectangular prism is 16 square centimeters, what is the surface area of the bottom? (Lesson 14-7)

Spiral Review

21. Find the volume of a cube that has a length, width, and height of 7 inches. (Lesson 14-6)

22. Identify the kinds of angles in the triangle shown at the right. (Lesson 13-3)

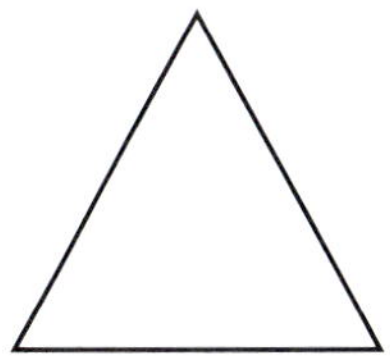

14-8 Select Appropriate Measurement Formulas

MAIN IDEA

I will select and use appropriate units and formulas to measure length, perimeter, area, and volume.

Math Online

macmillanmh.com

- Extra Examples
- Personal Tutor
- Self-Check Quiz

GET READY to Learn

The 2007 Women's World Cup was played in China. The field at Chengdu Stadium is 109 meters long by 75 meters wide.

You have learned to find the perimeter, area, and volume of figures. It is important to be able to choose the appropriate measurement for a given situation.

Measurement Formulas — Key Concept

Measure	Used to Find	Model	Formula
Perimeter	distance around a figure	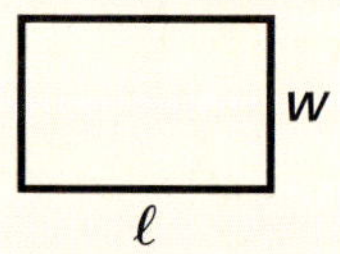	$P = 2\ell + 2w$
Area	space covered by a figure	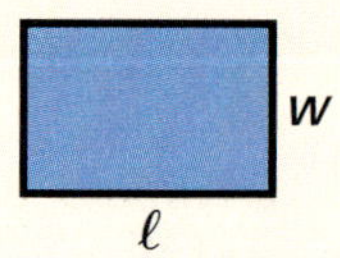	$A = \ell w$
Volume	space enclosed by a figure	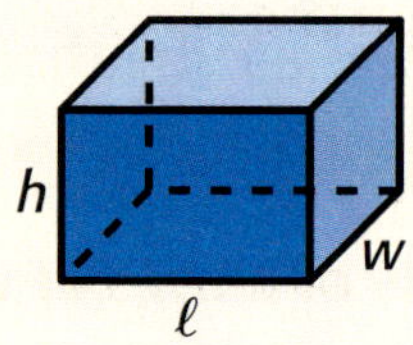	$V = \ell wh$

Remember

Perimeter is given in units, area is given in square units, and volume is given in cubic units.

Real-World EXAMPLES — Determine the Appropriate Measurement

1 **SOCCER A grounds crew will be cutting the grass on the field at Chengdu stadium. Determine whether they will be cutting the perimeter, area, or volume of the grass. Then solve.**

The field is a rectangle that is 109 meters long and 75 meters wide.

They need to find the area to determine the size of the surface that needs to be cut.

$A = \ell w$	Formula for area of a rectangle
$A = 109 \times 75$	$\ell = 109$ and $w = 75$
$A = 8{,}175$	Multiply.

The area of the field is 8,175 square meters.

2 **SWIMMING Mr. Clive needs to install a rubber strip around the edge of the swimming pool shown below. Determine whether he should find the perimeter, area, or volume of the swimming pool. Then solve.**

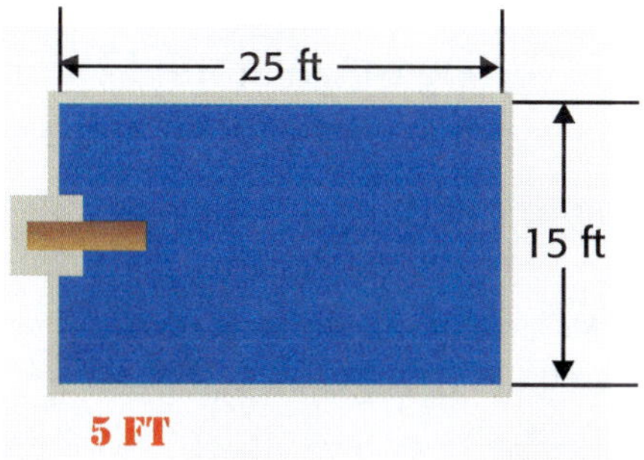

Mr. Clive needs to know the distance around the pool. So, he needs to find the perimeter.

$P = 2\ell + 2w$	Formula for perimeter of a rectangle
$P = 2(25) + 2(15)$	$\ell = 25$ and $w = 15$
$P = 80$	Simplify.

The distance around the pool is 80 feet.

Real-World EXAMPLE

Determine the Appropriate Measurement

3 **DESIGN An architect needs to calculate how much cement to use for a decorative column. The figure represents the column. Determine whether she should find the perimeter, area, or volume of the column. Then solve.**

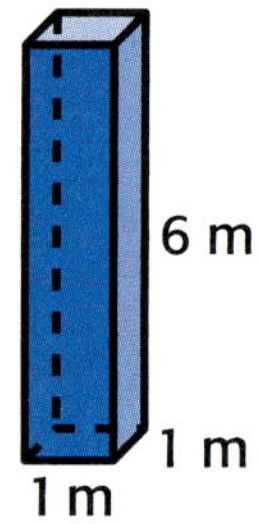

The architect needs to know how much space the column encloses. So, she needs to find the volume.

$V = \ell wh$	Formula for volume of a rectangular prism
$V = 1 \times 1 \times 6$	$\ell = 1$, $w = 1$, and $h = 6$
$V = 6$	Simplify.

So, 6 cubic meters of cement are needed.

CHECK What You Know

Determine whether you need to find the perimeter, area, or volume. Then solve. See Examples 1–3 (pp. 644–645)

1. Carmella is making a rectangular flower garden in her backyard. The space she wants to use is 4 meters in length and 2 meters wide. How much space will she have in her garden?

2. Mrs. Hernandez is sewing fringe around curtains that are used in a school play. There are four rectangular panels, each 3 feet wide and $5\frac{1}{2}$ feet long. How much fringe does she need to buy?

3. How much water is needed to fill a pool that is 50 meters long, 25 meters wide, and 3 meters deep?

4. Which units would be most appropriate to measure the volume of a cake pan: cubic inches, cubic feet, or cubic yards? Explain.

5. A basketball court that is 50 feet wide and 84 feet long needs to be refinished. The cost for refinishing is $6.00 per square foot. What will be the total cost?

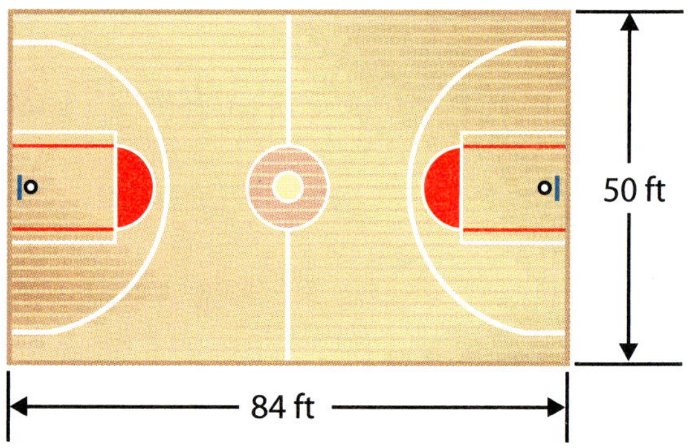

6. Talk About It Explain how you determine whether to use the formula for perimeter, area, or volume for a given situation.

Practice and Problem Solving

EXTRA PRACTICE
See page R39.

Determine whether you need to find the perimeter, area, or volume. Then solve. See Examples 1–3 (pp. 644–645)

7. A path is 3 feet wide and 14 feet long. How much gravel will Mr. James need if he wants to add 2 inches of gravel over the entire path?

8. A room is 8 meters by 16 meters. How much carpet is needed?

Refer to the pool shown at the right for Exercises 9 and 10.

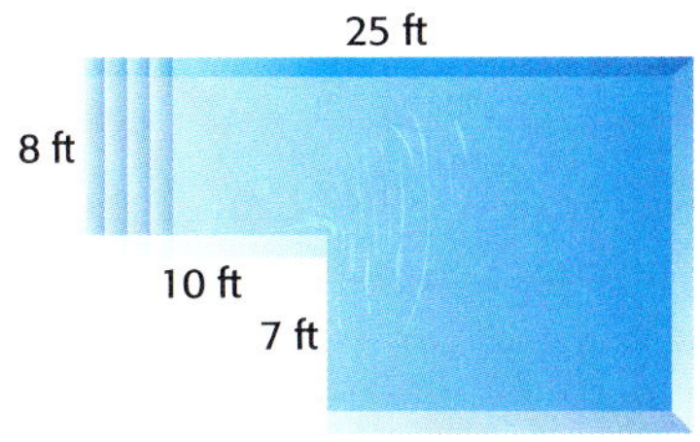

9. Decorative tiles 6 inches long are to be placed around the edges of the pool. How many tiles will be needed?

10. What size tarp would be needed to cover the pool?

Real-World PROBLEM SOLVING

Measurement In a fish tank, 30 square centimeters of water surface are needed for each centimeter of fish length. So, two fish that are 6 centimeters long need 360 square centimeters of water.

Tank	Size (cm)
A	$\ell = 24, w = 12, h = 12$
B	$\ell = 45, w = 25, h = 25$
C	$\ell = 60, w = 30, h = 38$

11. An angelfish is 12 centimeters long. How many angelfish could be placed in Tank B?

12. A fancy guppy is 5 centimeters long. Which tank could hold 2 angelfish and 4 fancy guppies?

H.O.T. Problems

13. FIND THE ERROR Martin and Ryan are finding the volume of a prism with length 3 meters, height 8 meters, and width 17 meters. Who is correct? Explain your reasoning.

Martin

$V = 2(3) + 2(8)$
$= 22$ cubic meters

Ryan

$V = 3 \times 8 \times 17$
$= 408$ cubic meters

14. WRITING IN ▶MATH Describe the steps you would take to find the area of your bedroom floor.

14-9 Problem-Solving Investigation

MAIN IDEA I will choose the best strategy to solve a problem.

P.S.I. TEAM +

JACINDA: I am helping my mom cover the swing set area with mulch. The base of the swing set is rectangular in shape and measures 4 meters by 2 meters. The area we want to cover extends 1 meter in each direction from the edge of the swing set.

YOUR MISSION: Find the area of the space covered with mulch.

Understand	You know the dimensions of the swing set. You need to find the area of the space covered with mulch.
Plan	Solve the problem by drawing a diagram.
Solve	Draw a diagram of the area to be covered with mulch. Find the length. 4 m + 1 m + 1 m, or 6 m Find the width. 2 m + 1 m + 1 m, or 4 m $A = \ell w$ Formula for area of a rectangle. $A = 6 \times 4$ Replace ℓ with 6 and w with 4. $A = 24$ Multiply. The area of the space to be covered is 24 square meters.
Check	Look back. Reread the problem to see if the diagram matches the information given. ✓

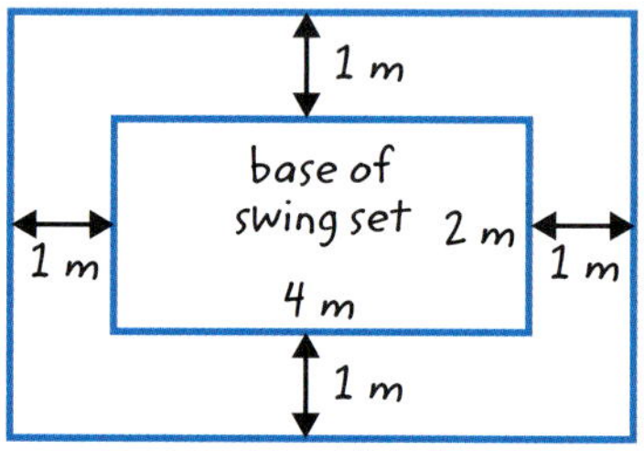

Mixed Problem Solving

EXTRA PRACTICE
See page R40.

Use any strategy shown below to solve each problem.

PROBLEM-SOLVING STRATEGIES

- Guess and check.
- Look for a pattern.
- Make a table.
- Draw a diagram.

1. **Geometry** Mariana stacked 8 cubes on top of each other to make a tower 8 cubes high. How many of the cubes' faces can Mariana see?

2. **Measurement** A hexagon that has each side equal to 1 inch has a perimeter of 6 inches.

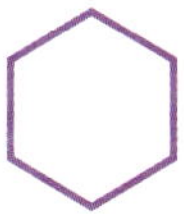

perimeter = 6 in.

Two hexagons placed side by side have a perimeter of 10 inches. Three hexagons have a perimeter of 14 inches.

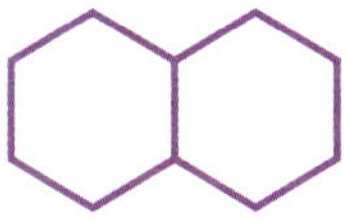

perimeter = 10 in.

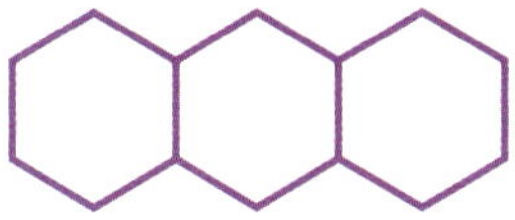

perimeter = 14 in.

What would be the perimeter of five hexagons placed side by side?

3. Five friends are standing in a circle and playing a game where they toss a ball of yarn to one another. If each person tosses the yarn to each other only once, how many lines of yarn will be between them?

4. Pedro has \$42 in his pocket. He has only \$5 and \$1 bills. He has a total of 14 bills. What combination of bills does he have?

5. **Algebra** The table below shows the number of minutes Danielle spent practicing the trumpet over the last 7 days. If she continues this pattern of practicing, in how many days will she have practiced 555 minutes?

Day	Time (min)
1	20
2	20
3	35
4	20
5	20
6	35
7	20

For Exercises 6 and 7, use the following information.

Marita wants to make a rectangle with a perimeter of 20 inches.

6. How many rectangles can Marita make if she only uses whole numbers for the side lengths? List the dimensions.

7. Which rectangle has the greatest area?

8. **WRITING IN MATH** One wall of a building is 80 feet long and 16 feet high. A one-gallon can of paint covers up to 450 square feet. If each can of paint costs \$22.50, find the total cost of paint for the wall. Explain the steps you used to solve the problem.

CHAPTER 14

Study Guide and Review

Math Online macmillanmh.com
- STUDY TO GO
- Vocabulary Review

FOLDABLES® Study Organizer GET READY to Study

Be sure the following Big Ideas are written in your Foldable.

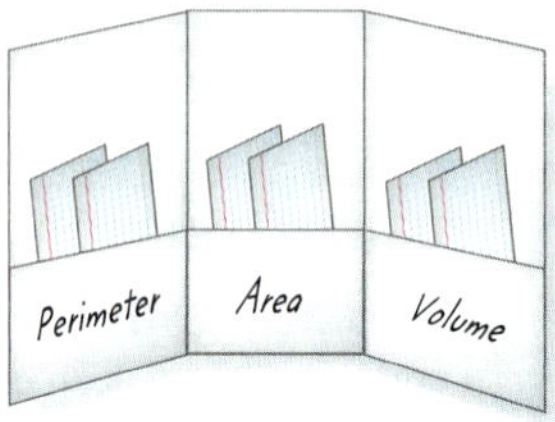

Key Concepts

Perimeters of Polygons

- The perimeter P of a square is 4 times the side length s. (p. 609)

$$P = s + s + s + s \quad \text{or} \quad 4s$$

- The perimeter P of a rectangle is two times the length ℓ plus two times the width w. (p. 609)

$$P = \ell + \ell + w + w \quad \text{or} \quad 2\ell + 2w$$

Areas of Rectangles

- The area A of a rectangle is the length ℓ times the width w. (p. 616)

$$A = \ell w$$

- The area A of a square is the square of the side length s. (p. 617)

$$A = s^2 \quad \text{or} \quad s \times s$$

Surface Areas of Rectangular Prisms

- The surface area S of a rectangular prism is the sum of the areas of the faces. (p. 640)

$$S = 2\ell w + 2\ell h + 2wh$$

Volumes of Prisms

- The volume V of a rectangular prism is length ℓ times width w times height h. (p. 631)

$$V = \ell wh$$

Key Vocabulary

area (p. 612)
cone (p. 624)
cylinder (p. 624)
perimeter (p. 607)
polygon (p. 608)
prism (p. 624)
rectangular prism (p. 624)
surface area (p. 640)
triangular prism (p. 624)
volume (p. 631)

Vocabulary Check

State whether each sentence is *true* or *false*. If false, replace the underlined word or number to make a true sentence.

1. The perimeter of a rectangle is the length times the width.
2. A rectangular prism with all sides 4 centimeters long has a volume of 64 cubic centimeters.
3. The area of a square with a side length of 8 inches is 32 square inches.
4. A three-dimensional figure with faces that are polygons is called a polyhedron.
5. A cylinder has two parallel congruent circular bases.

Lesson-by-Lesson Review

14-1 Perimeters of Polygons (pp. 608–611)

Example 1

Find the perimeter of the rectangle.

$P = 2\ell + 2w$ — Perimeter of rectangle

$P = 2(16) + 2(9)$ — $\ell = 16$, $w = 9$

$P = 50$ in. — Simplfiy.

The perimeter is 50 inches.

Find the perimeter of each figure.

6.

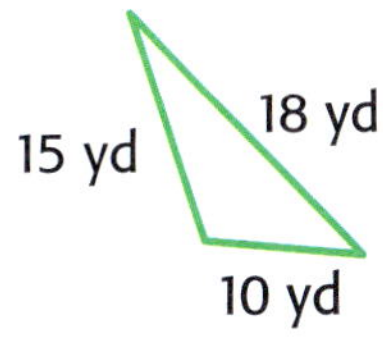

7.

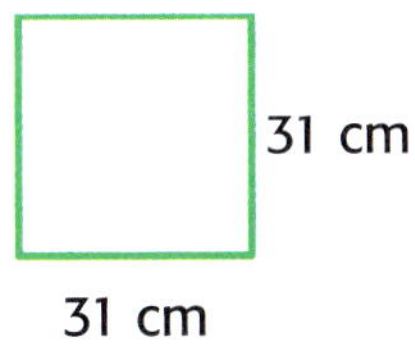

8. A garden in the shape of a square is 15 feet on each side. What is the perimeter?

14-2 Areas (pp. 612–615)

Example 2

Estimate the area of the figure. Each square represents 1 square inch.

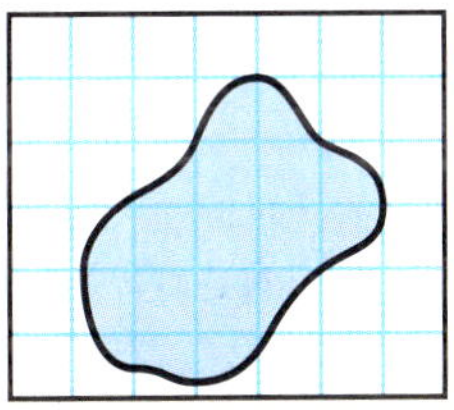

7 whole squares = 7 square inches

11 partial squares is about $5\frac{1}{2}$ square inches

The area is about $7 + 5\frac{1}{2} = 12\frac{1}{2}$ square centimeters.

Estimate the area of each figure. Each square represents 1 square centimeter.

9.

10.

14-3 Areas of Rectangles and Squares (pp. 616–619)

Example 3

Find the area of the rectangle.

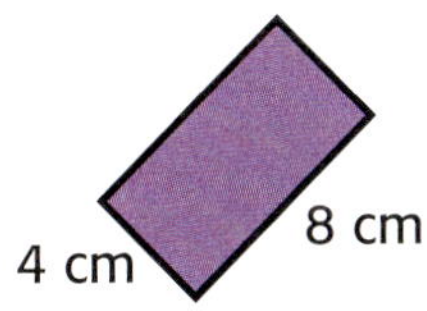

$A = \ell w$

$A = 8 \times 4$ — $\ell = 8$, $w = 4$

$A = 32$ square centimeters

Find the area of each rectangle or square.

11.

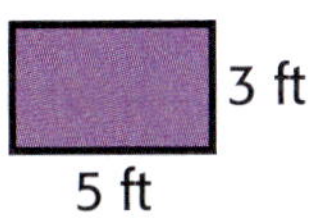

12.

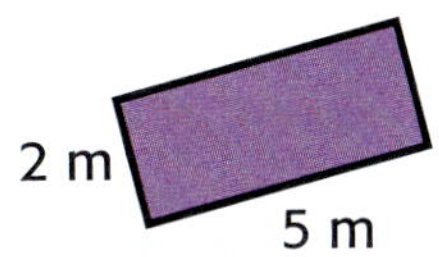

13. A new building measures 42 feet by 30 feet. How much land does it cover?

14-4 Three-Dimensional Figures (pp. 624–627)

Example 4

Describe parts of the figure that are parallel, perpendicular and congruent. Then identify the figure.

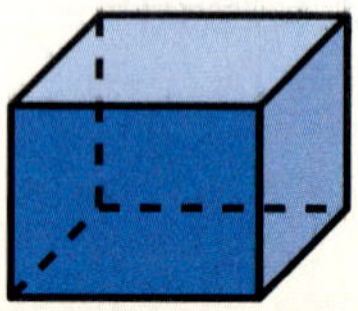

Opposite faces are parallel and congruent. Adjacent faces form right angles, so they are perpendicular.

The figure is a rectangular prism.

Describe parts of each figure that are parallel, perpendicular, and congruent. Then identify the figure.

14. 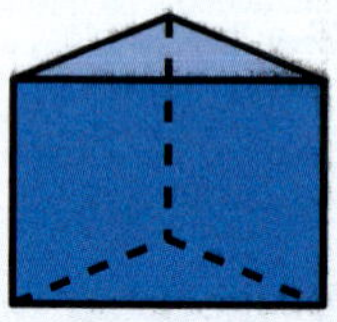

15. 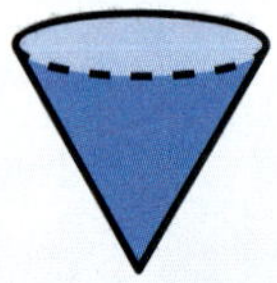

16. Describe parts of the vase that are parallel and congruent. Then identify the shape of the vase.

14-5 Problem-Solving Strategy: Make a Model (pp. 628–629)

Example 5

How many centimeter cubes will fit in the container at the right?

You can use cubes to model the situation.

First, arrange 2 rows of 5 cubes.

Next, add three more layers of cubes.

The total number of cubes used is 40. So, 40 centimeter cubes will fit in the container.

Solve by making a model.

17. A box is filled with 48 cubes that measure 1 inch on each side. The cubes completely fill the box. What are possible dimensions of the box?

18. Haley is making a bracelet by placing beads and charms on a 6-inch chain. She places a charm at 1 inch from each end, and at every $\frac{1}{2}$ inch in between. How many charms does she use?

19. Destiny has 24 feet of fencing material to make a pet enclosure. Describe three different rectangular areas that can be enclosed by the fencing.

14-6 Volumes of Prisms (pp. 631–635)

Example 6

Find the volume of the prism.

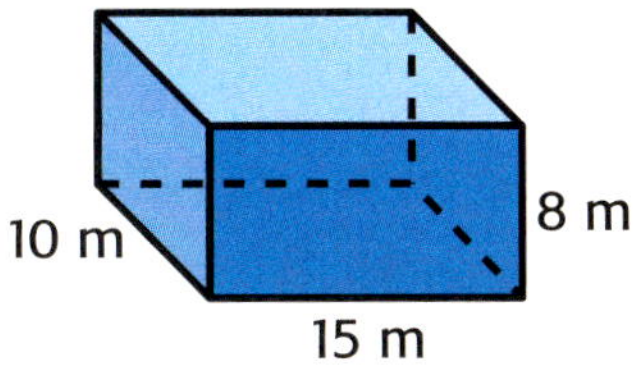

$V = \ell wh$ Volume of a prism

$V = 15 \times 10 \times 8$ $\ell = 15, w = 10, h = 8$

$V = 1{,}200$ Multiply.

The volume of the prism is 1,200 cubic meters.

Find the volume of each prism.

20. 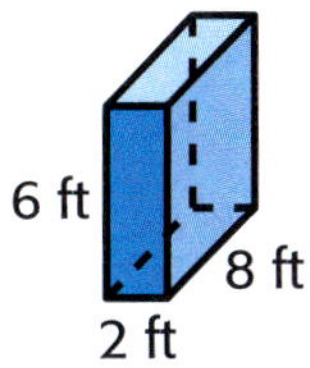

21. 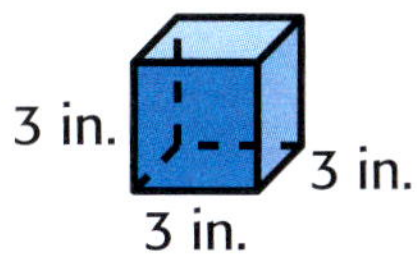

22. 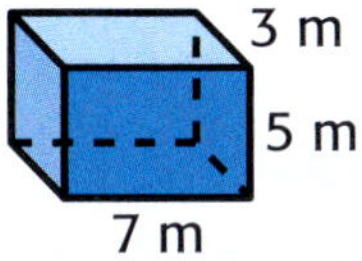

23. 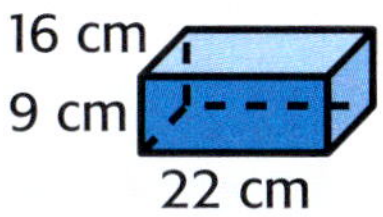

24. Victoro keeps his pet rabbit in a cage that is shaped like a rectangular prism. The cage measures 2 feet by 3 feet by 2 feet. What is the volume of the cage?

14-7 Surface Area of Prisms (pp. 640-643)

Example 7

Find the surface area of the rectangular prism.

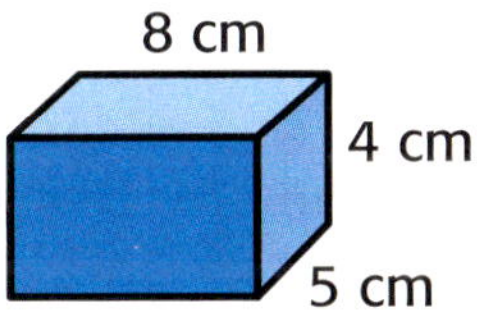

$S = 2\ell w + 2\ell h + 2wh$

top and bottom: $2(\ell w) = 2(8 \times 5)$ or 80

front and back: $2(\ell h) = 2(8 \times 4)$ or 64

two sides: $2(wh) = 2(5 \times 4)$ or 40

The surface area is 80 + 64 + 40 or 184 square centimeters.

Find the surface area of each rectangular prism.

25. 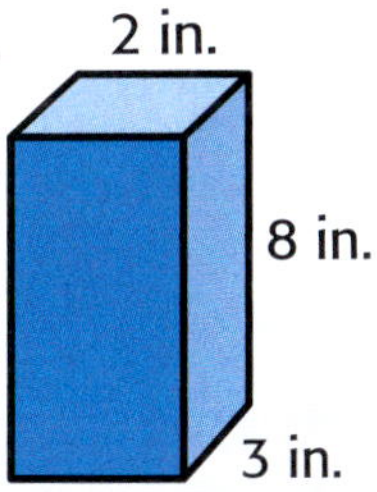

26. 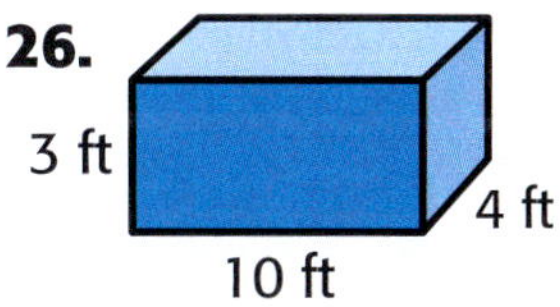

27. A DVD player measures 17 inches by 15 inches by 3 inches. What is the minimum surface area of a box to hold the DVD player?

14-8 Select Appropriate Measurement Formulas (pp. 644–647)

Example 8

The park shown below is to be covered with new sod. How much sod is needed? Determine whether you need to find the perimeter, area, or volume. Then solve.

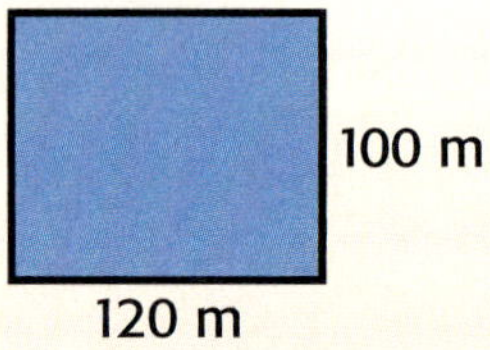

The sod is to cover the entire surface of the park, so the area needs to be found.

$A = \ell w$	Area of a rectangle
$A = 120 \times 100$	$\ell = 120, w = 100$
$A = 12{,}000$	Multiply.

The area that needs to be covered with sod is 12,000 square meters.

Determine whether you need to find the perimeter, area, or volume. Then solve.

28. Ray is sweeping a rectangular floor that is 12 feet long and 9 feet wide. How much does he have to sweep?

29. A gym mat measures 8 feet by 4 feet. The edges of the mat need to be repaired. What is the total length of the edges?

30. Planters that are 16 inches long, 7 inches wide, and 5 inches high are to be placed around a restaurant patio. How much soil is needed to fill 8 planters?

14-9 Problem-Solving Investigation: Choose a Strategy (pp. 648–649)

Example 9

What two whole numbers have a sum of 12 and a product of 32?

One way to solve the problem is to use the guess and check strategy.

Guess: 3 and 9
Check: $3 + 9 = 12, 3 \times 9 = 27 \neq 32$

Guess: 4 and 8
Check: $4 + 8 = 12, 4 \times 8 = 32$ ✓

The whole numbers are 4 and 8.

Use any strategy to solve.

31. Barrett has 18 sports cards. He collects football and baseball cards. He has twice as many baseball cards. How many of each kind does he have?

32. Leon has \$5 to buy a bottle of water that costs \$1.49, a granola bar for \$1.09, and a newspaper for \$2.25. Does he have enough money? Explain.

CHAPTER 14

Chapter Test

Math Online macmillanmh.com

• Chapter Test

Find the perimeter of each rectangle or square.

1.

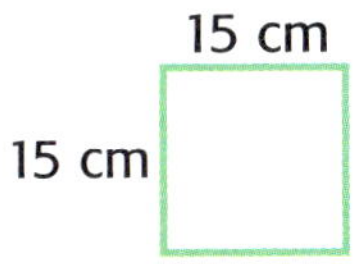

2.

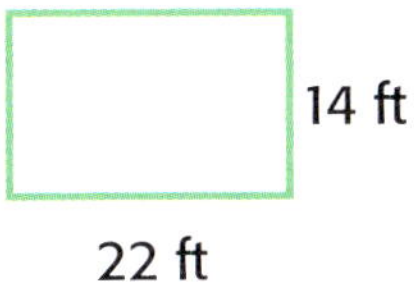

3. **MULTIPLE CHOICE** A rectangular picture frame is 10 inches by 12 inches. Jodie wants to add a lace border around the frame. Which length would fit around the frame with the least amount left?

A 1 foot **C** 4 feet

B 2 feet **D** 5 feet

Find the area of each rectangle or square.

4.

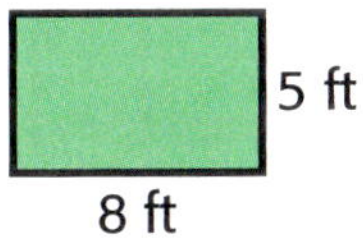

5.

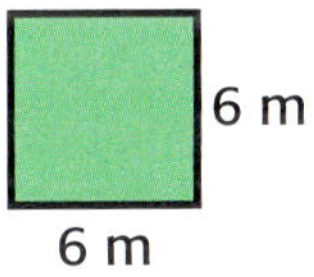

6. Estimate the area of the figure. Each square represents 1 square centimeter.

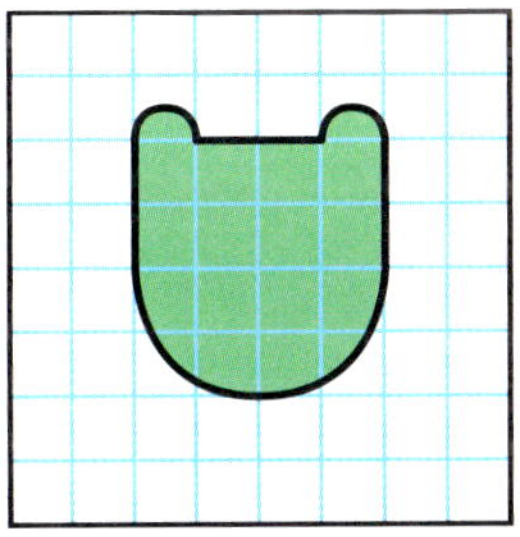

7. If you place one cube on a table, you can see 5 faces of the cube. If you place a second cube on top of the first, you can see 9 faces. How many faces can you see in a stack of 6 cubes?

8. A backyard is in the shape of a right triangle. The sides measure 30 feet, 40 feet, and 50 feet. How much fencing is needed to enclose the entire backyard?

9. **MULTIPLE CHOICE** Which figure below has 3 more edges than faces?

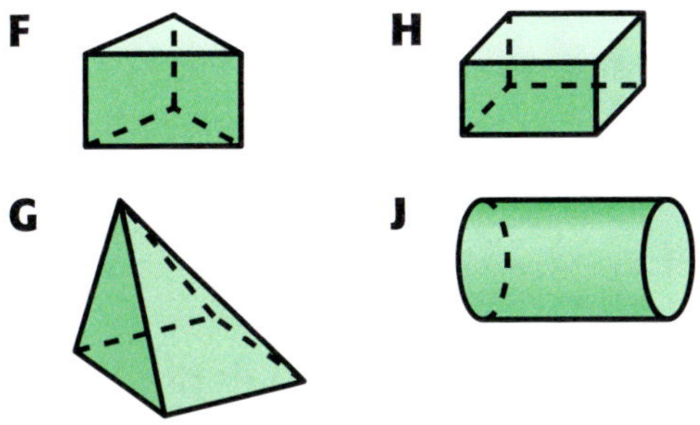

Find the volume of each prism.

10.

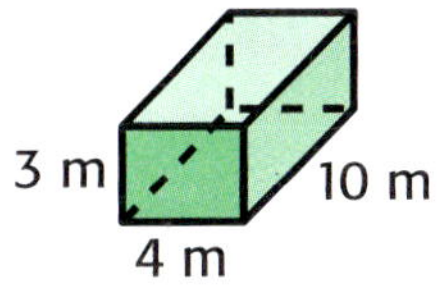

11.

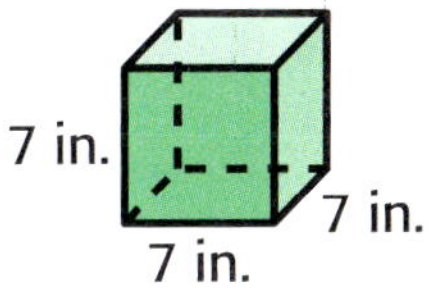

A pool is 50 meters long, 20 meters wide, and 3 meters deep. For each problem, determine whether you need to find the perimeter, area, or volume. Then solve.

12. The bottom of the pool needs to be painted. How much paint is needed?

13. How many lifeguards are needed if they are posted every 35 meters?

14. Find the surface area of the rectangular prism.

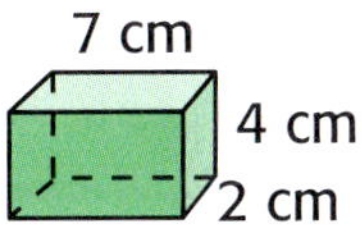

15. **WRITING IN MATH** Describe the difference between finding the area of a rectangle and finding the volume of a rectangular prism.

CHAPTER 14

Test Practice

Cumulative, Chapters 1–14

Math Online macmillanmh.com

• Test Practice

PART 1 Multiple Choice

Read each question. Then fill in the correct answer on the answer sheet provided by the teacher or on a sheet of paper.

1. A square has a perimeter of 36 meters. What is the area of the square?

A 81 m^2

B 72 m^2

C 9 m^2

D 6 m^2

2. Which of the following would you use to find the volume of the figure shown?

F $V = \ell \times w$

G $V = 2\ell + 2w$

H $V = \ell \times w \times h$

J $V = 2\ell \times 2w \times 2h$

3. How many faces, edges, and vertices does the figure have?

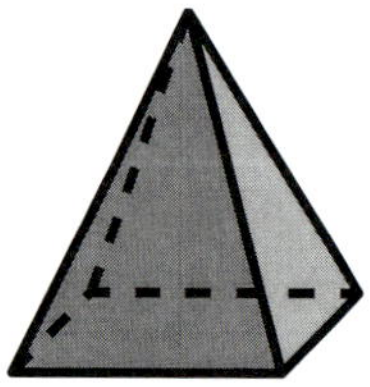

A 5 faces, 8 edges, 5 vertices

B 5 faces, 6 edges, 8 vertices

C 5 faces, 8 edges, 6 vertices

D 6 faces, 10 edges, 6 vertices

4. Bansi needs 48 ounces of buttermilk for a recipe. How many cups of buttermilk does she need?

F 4 c

G 5 c

H 6 c

J 7 c

5. Which transformation is represented in the diagram?

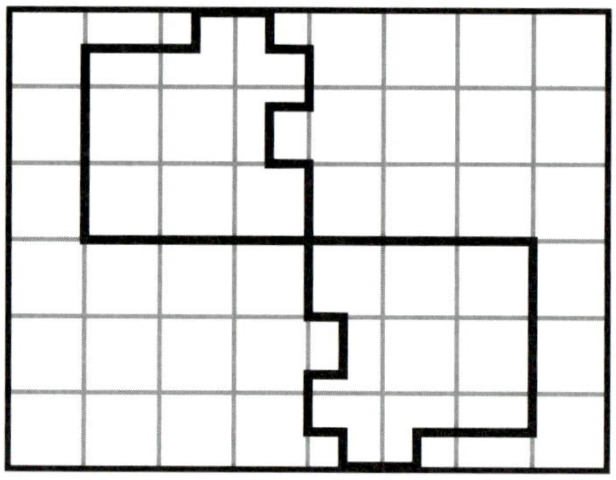

A Reflection

B Translation

C Rotation

D Not here

6. Look at the pattern of numbers shown below.

7, ___, 17, 22, 27, 32

Which expression could be used to find the missing number in the pattern?

F $(27 - 18) + 3$

G $(7 + 12) - 5$

H $(17 - 12) + 5$

J $(28 - 23) + 3$

Preparing for Standardized Tests
For test-taking strategies and practice, see pages R42–R55.

7. Which statement about the figures shown below is true?

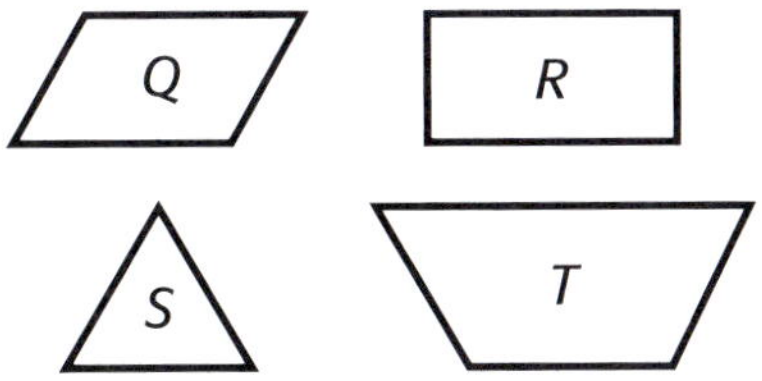

A Figures *Q* and *R* are congruent.

B Figures *S* and *T* are squares.

C Figures *S* and *R* have the same number of sides.

D Figures *Q* and *T* each have at least two acute angles.

---

8. The drawing below represents a parking lot at a pet store.

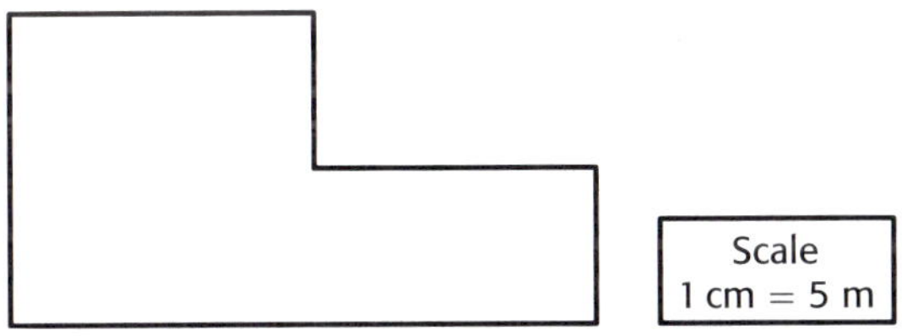

Use the ruler on the Mathematics Chart to measure the dimensions of the parking lot to the nearest tenth of centimeter. Which is the closest to the perimeter of the parking lot in meters?

F 125 m　　**H** 75 m

G 100 m　　**J** 18 m

PART 2 Short Response

Record your answers on the answer sheet provided by your teacher or on a sheet of paper.

9. A rectangular driveway measures 16 feet by 12 feet. What is the area of the driveway in square feet?

---

10. Find the number of millimeters that are equivalent to 50 centimeters.

PART 3 Extended Response

Record your answers on the answer sheet provided by your teacher or on a sheet of paper.

11. Derrick is painting a toy chest that is 14 inches tall, 9 inches wide, and 11 inches long. Draw a diagram of Derrick's toy chest. Then, find the surface area and volume of the chest.

---

12. It takes 3 feet of wood to make 1 birdhouse. If you have 23 feet of wood, can you make 8 birdhouses? Explain.

NEED EXTRA HELP?												
If You Missed Question...	1	2	3	4	5	6	7	8	9	10	11	12
Go to Lesson...	14-3	14-6	14-4	12-4	13-9	6-6	13-1	14-1	14-3	12-1	14-6	4-6

CHAPTER 15 Use Probability to Make Predictions

BIG Idea What is probability?

Probability is the chance that a given event will happen.

Example In his pocket, Jeremy has the three state quarters shown below. If he takes a quarter from his pocket without looking, what is the probability that it is the New Jersey quarter?

The probability is **1 out of 3**, or $\frac{1}{3}$, that it will be the New Jersey quarter.

What will I learn in this chapter?

- Determine the likelihood of an event.
- Use fractions to describe the results of an experiment.
- Use experimental results to make a prediction.
- List outcomes of a probability experiment.
- Solve problems by *making an organized list*.

Key Vocabulary

probability
outcome
probability experiment
tree diagram

Math Online **Student Study Tools at macmillanmh.com**

FOLDABLES® **Study Organizer**

Make this Foldable to help you organize information about probability. Begin with a sheet of 11″ × 17″ paper.

1. **Fold** the short sides toward the middle.

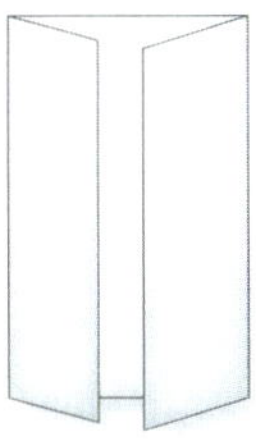

2. **Fold** the top to the bottom.

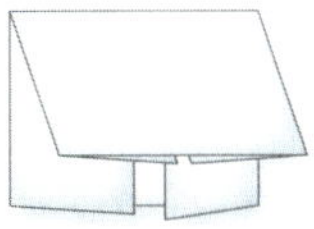

3. **Open.** Cut as shown to make four tabs.

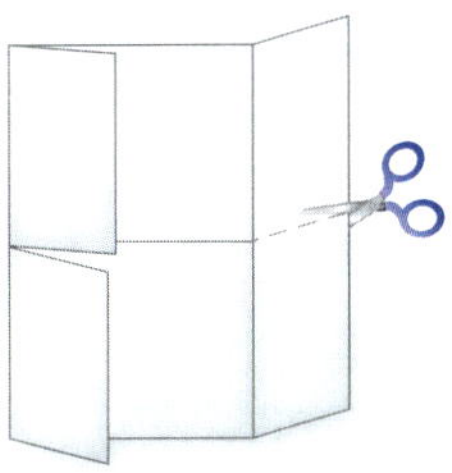

4. **Label** each tab as shown.

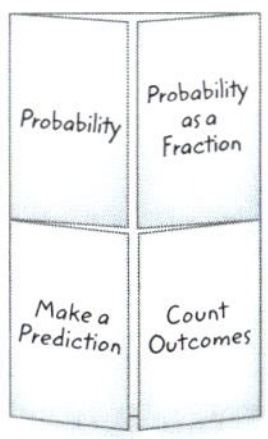

ARE YOU READY for Chapter 15?

You have two ways to check prerequisite skills for this chapter.

Option 2

Math Online Take the Chapter Readiness Quiz at macmillanmh.com.

Option 1

Complete the Quick Check below.

QUICK Check

Choose from *certain, impossible, likely,* or *unlikely* to describe each probability. (Prior Grade)

1. If you choose a letter from the word EAR, it will be a vowel.

2. If you spin the spinner at the right, the number will be 8.

3. If you spin the spinner at the right, the number will be 5.

4. If you choose a letter from the word MATHEMATICS, it will be Q.

5. If you toss a coin, it will come up either heads or tails.

Write each fraction in simplest form. (Lesson 9-4)

6. $\frac{10}{12}$ **7.** $\frac{4}{8}$ **8.** $\frac{5}{15}$ **9.** $\frac{14}{21}$

10. $\frac{6}{10}$ **11.** $\frac{9}{24}$ **12.** $\frac{12}{16}$ **13.** $\frac{28}{36}$

14. Paloma goes to school 20 out of the 30 days in April. Write the number of days out of the month that she goes to school as a fraction in simplest form. (Lesson 9-4)

15. Daryl is meeting his friends on either Saturday or Sunday. They are either going to lunch or going to see a movie. Describe two different situations that could happen. (Prior Grade)

16. Manning is choosing a sandwich and a beverage from the table at the right. Describe three different choices. (Prior Grade)

Sandwich	Beverage
Cheese	Iced tea
Tuna	Lemonade
Turkey	

15-1 Probability

MAIN IDEA

I will determine the likelihood of an event.

New Vocabulary

probability
certain
impossible
equally likely
outcome
probability experiment

Math Online

macmillanmh.com

- Extra Examples
- Personal Tutor
- Self-Check Quiz

GET READY to Learn

One cube is drawn from each bag without looking. Write *certain*, *impossible*, or *equally likely* to make each a true sentence.

Bag 1

It is ___?___ that a black cube will be drawn.

Bag 2

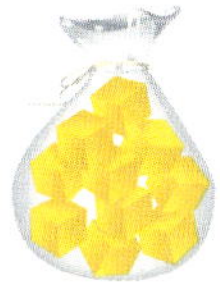

It is ___?___ that a yellow cube will be drawn.

Bag 3

It is ___?___ that a yellow cube will be drawn.

Probability is the chance that an event will happen.

Probability		
Description	**Meaning**	**Example**
Certain	The event will definitely happen.	Drawing a yellow cube from Bag 2.
Impossible	There is no chance the event will happen.	Drawing a yellow cube from Bag 3.
Equally likely	There is an equal chance the event will happen.	Drawing a black cube from Bag 1.

An **outcome** is a possible result in a **probability experiment**. So, when drawing a cube from Bag 1 above, the possible outcomes are a black cube and a green cube.

EXAMPLE List Outcomes

1 **Cole spins the spinner at the right. List the possible outcomes.**

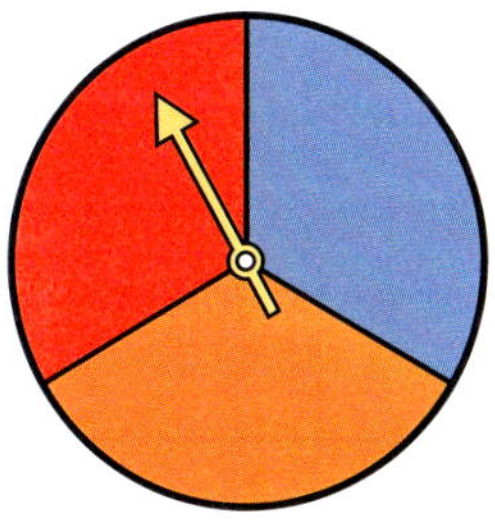

The spinner could land on the red space, the blue space, or the orange space.

outcomes: red, blue, orange

If the probability that an event will occur is *more* than equally likely, use the phrase *likely*. If the probability is *less* than equally likely, use the phrase *unlikely* to describe it.

Remember

At random or *randomly* means choosing a marble without looking. Each marble is equally likely to be chosen.

EXAMPLE Describe Probability

2 One marble is chosen at random. Describe the probability of choosing a green marble. Write *certain*, *impossible*, *likely*, *unlikely*, or *equally likely*.

event: choosing a green marble

outcomes: red, blue, green, yellow

There is only 1 green marble, compared to 9 other marbles. So, the probability of choosing a green marble is *unlikely*.

CHECK What You Know

List the possible outcomes in each probability experiment. See Example 1 (p. 661)

1. spinning the spinner

2. tossing a quarter

3. choosing a card at random

One disc is randomly drawn from the bag. Describe the probability of drawing each disc. Write *certain, impossible, likely, unlikely,* or *equally likely*. See Example 2 (p. 662)

4. blue

5. red

6. green

7. blue, red, or yellow

8. How many possible outcomes are there for choosing a letter in the word CERTAIN?

9. Talk About It Describe outcomes that are likely and unlikely to occur when a number cube labeled 1 to 6 is tossed. Explain.

Practice and Problem Solving

EXTRA PRACTICE See page R40.

List the possible outcomes in each probability experiment. See Example 1 (p. 661)

10. choosing one coin at random

11. randomly choosing one can of soup

12. choosing one cube without looking

13. spinning the spinner

14. randomly choosing one letter from the word EVENT

One card is drawn without looking. Describe the probability of drawing each card. Write *certain, impossible, likely, unlikely,* or *equally likely*. See Example 2 (p. 662)

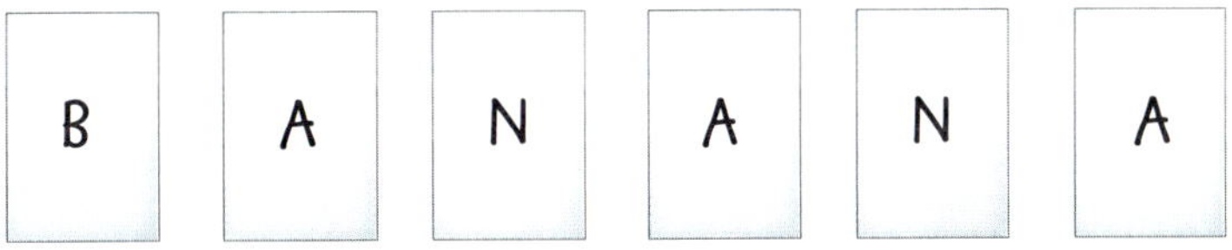

15. B

16. A

Suppose you spin the spinner at the right. Describe the probability of landing on each color. Write *certain, impossible, likely, unlikely,* or *equally likely*. See Example 2 (p. 662)

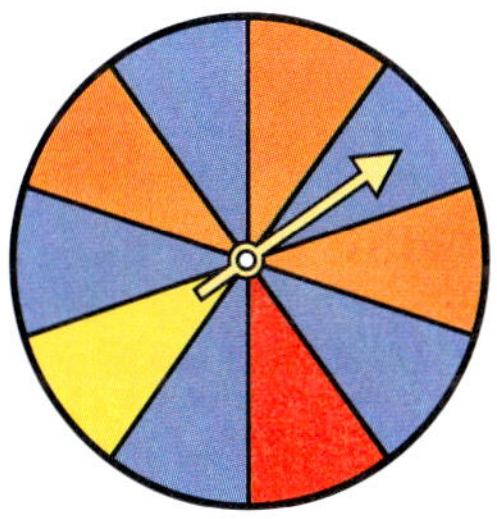

17. orange rather than red

18. green

19. orange rather than blue

20. *not* purple

H.O.T. Problems

21. CHALLENGE Describe a group of 10 cubes that have the following characteristics.

- There are 4 different colors.
- When a cube is drawn, one color is more likely to be drawn than any other.
- Exactly two of the remaining colors are equally likely to be drawn.

22. WRITING IN MATH Write a real-world problem that can be solved by describing its probability. Then solve the problem.

WILD ABOUT WILDFLOWER HABITATS

Many people like to grow flowers in their yards. The National Wildlife Federation encourages people to grow wildflowers and also to include plants that provide protective cover and food for another type of wildlife—animals!

A wildlife habitat for animals needs to have four essential ingredients: food, water, protective cover, and places for animals to raise their young. If you can provide these elements, you can enjoy a wildlife habitat in your own backyard!

Real-World Math

Use the table below to solve each problem.

1. Suppose you pick one seed at random from the packet of wildflower habitat mix. Is the probability of picking a grain *greater than* or *less than* picking a grass?

2. If you pick one seed at random from the packet of wildflower habitat mix, is the probability of picking a clover *likely* or *unlikely*?

3. If there are 700 seeds in the wildflower habitat mix, how many would be annual flowers?

4. Suppose you pick one seed at random from the packet of wildflower habitat mix. What is the probability that you would pick a flower seed? Write your answer as a fraction.

5. Describe your answer for Exercise 4 as *certain, impossible,* or *equally likely.*

6. **WRITING IN MATH** Explain how the fraction of seeds in the wildlife habitat mix will result in a well-balanced wildlife habitat.

WILDFLOWER HABITAT MIX

Grasses	$\frac{7}{20}$
Clovers	$\frac{1}{20}$
Grains	$\frac{1}{10}$
Annual flowers	$\frac{1}{4}$
Perennial flowers	$\frac{1}{4}$

Did You Know?

A lawn costs about $700 per acre each year. A wildflower meadow costs about $30 per acre each year.

Explore

Probability Activity for 15-2
Make a Prediction

MAIN IDEA

I will use probability to make a prediction.

You Will Need

centimeter cubes

bag

ACTIVITY

Step 1 Place 5 blue cubes, 3 yellow cubes, and 2 red cubes in a bag.

What fraction of the cubes is blue? yellow? red? Write each fraction in a table like the one below.

Outcome	Fraction	Prediction	Tally	Number
Blue	$\frac{1}{2}$			
Yellow	$\frac{3}{10}$			
Red	$\frac{1}{5}$			

Step 2 Suppose you draw a cube and then return it to the bag. If you do this 40 times, predict the number of times a blue, a yellow, and a red cube will be drawn. Record your predictions in the table.

Step 3 Without looking, draw a cube from the bag. Record the color in the Tally column of your table.

Step 4 Replace the cube and repeat Step 3 for a total of 40 times. Add the tally marks and record the numbers in the table.

Hands-On Activity

Think About It

1. Explain how you predicted the number of blue, yellow, and red cubes that would be drawn.

2. Compare your predictions in Step 2 with the actual number of cubes that were drawn. Describe any differences.

3. In your experiment, what fraction of the cubes drawn is blue? yellow? red? How do these compare to the actual fractions? Explain any differences.

4. Suppose this experiment was performed an additional 20 times for a total of 60 times. Based on the experimental results, predict the number of times you would draw a red cube.

CHECK What You Know

5. Perform this experiment an additional 20 times for a total of 60 times. Copy and complete the table below with your predictions and results.

Outcome	Fraction	Prediction	Tally	Number
Blue	$\frac{1}{2}$			
Yellow	$\frac{3}{10}$			
Red	$\frac{1}{5}$			

A bag has 6 marbles. One marble is drawn and replaced 30 times. The results are shown in the table.

Color	Number of Times Drawn
Red	25
White	5

6. Predict the number of red marbles in the bag. Explain.

7. Based on the experiment, describe the likelihood that there is a blue marble in the bag. Explain.

8. Predict the number of white marbles in the bag. Explain.

9. **WRITING IN ▶MATH** The same experiment was performed with a bag containing 18 marbles and the same results were achieved. Predict the number of red marbles in the bag. Explain.

15-2 Probability as a Fraction

MAIN IDEA

I will use fractions to describe probability.

New Vocabulary

favorable outcome

Math Online

macmillanmh.com

- Extra Examples
- Personal Tutor
- Self-Check Quiz

GET READY to Learn

When the spinner shown is spun, what is the probability that it will land on G?

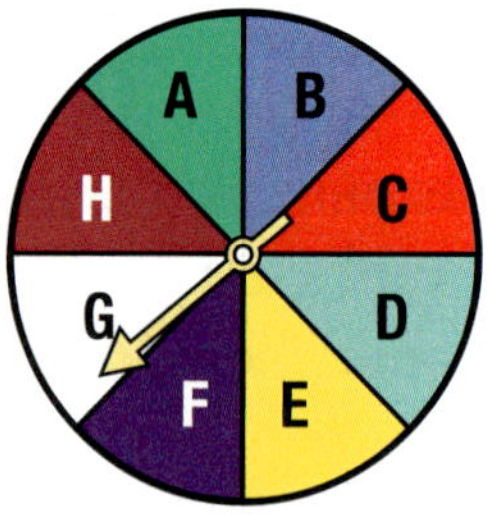

The probability that the spinner above will land on G can be described using a fraction.

$$P(\text{G}) = \frac{1}{8} \quad \begin{matrix} \leftarrow \text{number of ways to land on G} \\ \leftarrow \text{number of possible outcomes} \end{matrix}$$

Since you are finding the probability of landing on G, the outcome of landing on G is called a **favorable outcome**.

Probability — Key Concept

Words The probability of an event is a fraction that compares the number of favorable outcomes to the number of possible outcomes.

Symbols $P(\text{event}) = \dfrac{\text{number of favorable outcomes}}{\text{number of possible outcomes}}$

The probability of an event can be described by a number from 0 to 1.

- An event that is *impossible* has a probability of 0.
- An event that is *certain* to happen has a probability of 1.

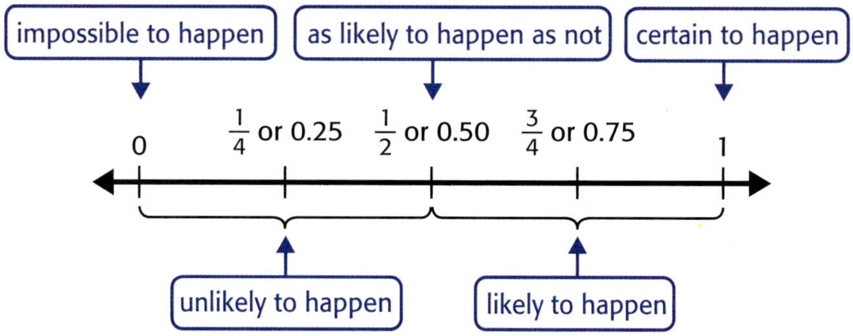

EXAMPLE Use Fractions to Describe Probability

1 One marble is randomly chosen from the bag. Find the probability that a blue marble is chosen.

Use a fraction to describe the probability that a blue marble is chosen.

$$P(\text{event}) = \frac{\text{number of favorable outcomes}}{\text{number of possible outcomes}}$$

$$P(\text{blue}) = \frac{4}{12} \quad \begin{array}{l}\leftarrow \text{number of blue marbles} \\ \leftarrow \text{total number of marbles}\end{array}$$

$$P(\text{blue}) = \frac{1}{3} \quad \text{Simplify.}$$

So, the probability of choosing a blue marble is $\frac{1}{3}$.

Remember

P(blue) means the probability of choosing blue.

Real-World EXAMPLE

2 BALLOONS Latanya has a bag of different colored balloons, as shown in the table. If she takes one balloon without looking, what is the probability that she gets a pink or white balloon?

Color	Number of Balloons
Pink	6
White	8
Orange	3
Green	4

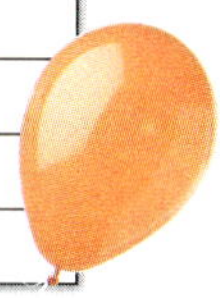

There are 6 + 8 + 3 + 4 or 21 balloons in all. There are 6 + 8 or 14 balloons that are either pink or white.

$$P(\text{event}) = \frac{\text{number of favorable outcomes}}{\text{number of possible outcomes}}$$

$$P(\text{pink or white}) = \frac{6+8}{6+8+3+4} \quad \begin{array}{l}\leftarrow \text{pink or white balloons} \\ \leftarrow \text{total number of balloons}\end{array}$$

$$= \frac{14}{21} \quad \text{Add.}$$

$$= \frac{2}{3} \quad \text{Simplify.}$$

So, the probability that Latanya gets a pink or white balloon is $\frac{2}{3}$.

CHECK What You Know

The spinner is spun once. Find the probability of each event. Write as a fraction in simplest form. See Examples 1, 2 (p. 669)

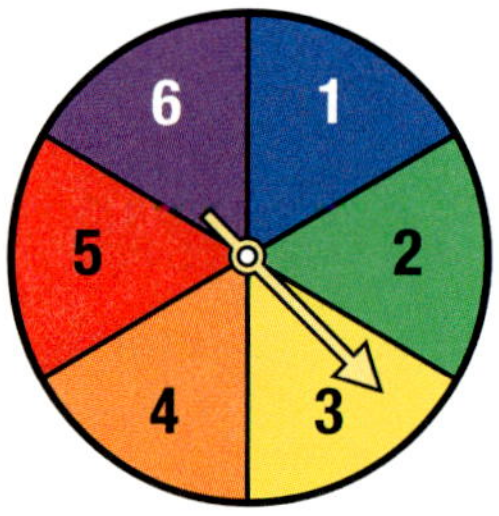

1. $P(4)$

2. P(odd number)

3. P(number less than 6)

4. P(1 or 6)

5. $P(9)$

6. P(positive number)

7. There are 9 kittens in a large basket. Three are gray, two are white, and four are striped. Miss Perez reaches in and randomly picks up one of the kittens. What is the probability that she picks up a striped kitten?

8. Talk About It Use an example to describe the difference between a favorable outcome and an outcome that is not favorable.

Practice and Problem Solving

EXTRA PRACTICE See page R40.

A number cube labeled 1 through 6 is rolled. Find the probability of each event. Write as a fraction in simplest form. See Examples 1, 2 (p. 669)

9. $P(6)$

10. P(even number)

11. P(a number less than 5)

12. P(a negative number)

13. P(a number less than 13)

14. P(a prime number)

One block is drawn from the blocks shown. Find the probability of each event. Write as a fraction in simplest form.
See Examples 1, 2 (p. 669)

15. P(red)

16. P(blue)

17. P(*not* yellow)

18. P(yellow, red, or blue)

19. P(white)

20. P(red or yellow)

21. A letter is chosen at random from the word FRACTION. What is the probability that the letter chosen is a consonant?

22. An amusement park has a ride with 20 cars numbered 1 through 20. Leroy chooses a car at random. What is the probability that he chooses an even-numbered car?

23. Dawn has 16 pennies, 19 nickels, and 15 dimes in a piggy bank. If she turns the bank over and a coin falls out, what is the probability that it will be a dime?

24. A band has a drummer, 2 guitar players, a keyboard player, and a lead singer. One of their names is randomly chosen. What is the probability that it is the name of the drummer or lead singer?

25. Darius has a magnetic construction set that has plastic pieces in different geometric shapes, as shown in the table. If he chooses one piece from the box without looking, what is the probability that he chooses a square or pentagon?

Shape	Number of Pieces
Triangle	26
Square	16
Rhombus	16
Pentagon	12

Real-World PROBLEM SOLVING

Science When one pea plant fertilizes another pea plant, a seed forms that can grow into an offspring plant. Each pea plant has two genes, one from each parent. Whether the plant grows to be tall or short depends on which pair of genes the plant has.

- If the plant has the genes TT, then it will be tall.
- If the plant has the genes Tt, then it will be tall.
- If the plant has the genes tt, then it will be short.

The table shows the possible outcomes for the offspring of two plants that each have Tt genes. Each of the four outcomes is equally likely.

Pea Plant 1

Genes	T	t
T	TT tall	Tt tall
t	Tt tall	tt short

Pea Plant 2

Find each probability.

26. The offspring will have the genes TT.

27. The offspring will be tall.

28. The offspring will have the genes Tt.

H.O.T. Problems

29. **OPEN ENDED** Create a spinner so that the probability of landing on red is less than the probability of landing on any other single color. Use red and at least two other colors. State the probability of each color using a fraction.

30. **CHALLENGE** Suppose a 6-sided number cube is rolled. Describe two different events that have a probability of $\frac{1}{3}$.

31. **WRITING IN MATH** Write a real-world problem that can be solved by finding the probability. Then solve the problem.

TEST Practice

32. One cube is drawn at random from the bag. Which is a true statement? (Lesson 15–1)

A Drawing a red cube is impossible.

B Drawing an orange cube is certain.

C Drawing a red cube is unlikely.

D Drawing an orange cube is equally likely.

33. Ronada has a bag of coins, as shown in the table.

Coin	Number of Coins
Penny	10
Nickel	8
Dime	6
Quarter	3

If she takes one coin without looking, what is the probability that she will pick a dime or quarter? (Lesson 15-2)

F $\frac{1}{4}$ **H** $\frac{1}{2}$

G $\frac{1}{3}$ **J** $\frac{3}{4}$

Spiral Review

Suppose you spin the spinner at the right. Describe the probability of landing on each letter. Write *certain*, *impossible*, *likely*, *unlikely*, or *equally likely*. (Lesson 15–1)

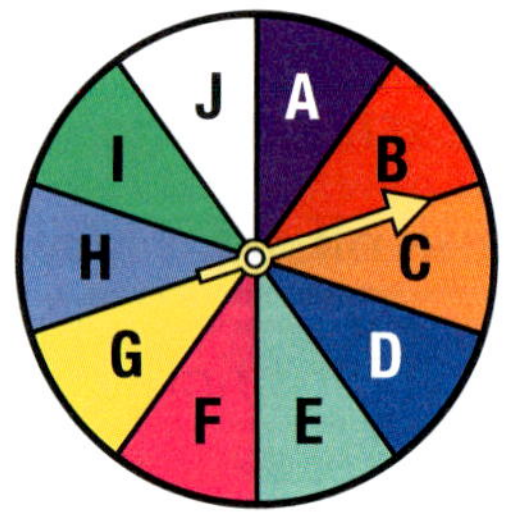

34. F **35.** M

36. a consonant **37.** *not* Z

Determine whether you need to find the perimeter, area, or volume. Then solve. (Lesson 14-8)

38. **Measurement** A wall 12 feet long and 8 feet high is being painted with chalkboard paint. How much space is to be painted?

39. **Measurement** Elijah is making a rectangular wooden picture frame that is $5\frac{1}{2}$ inches wide and 7 inches long. What length of wood does he need?

Find the area of each rectangle. (Lesson 14–3)

40. $\ell = 16$ cm, $w = 13$ cm **41.** $\ell = 12$ m, $w = 8$ m

42. $\ell = 18$ yd, $w = 16$ yd **43.** $\ell = 15$ ft, $w = 19$ ft

Extend

Technology Activity for 15-2

Probability Experiment

Tech Link

MAIN IDEA

I will use technology to describe probability as a fraction.

Juana and Chad are playing a game that uses a spinner. The spinner is divided into 4 equal sections. Each section is a different color. If they spin the spinner 40 times, predict how many times the outcome would be green.

You can use the Math Tool Chest™ to conduct an experiment.

- Choose Spinner.
- Increase the number of trials to 40.
- Set speed to spin slow and click go.
- Click on the Link button in the bottom right-hand corner.
- Select table.

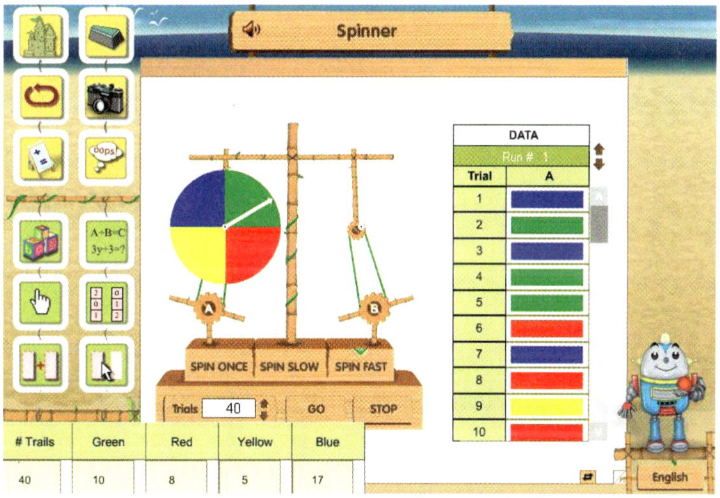

In this experiment, green was the outcome 10 times.

CHECK What You Know

1. How many times out of 40 spins would you have expected the outcome to be green? Explain.

2. If you were to spin the spinner 100 times, how many outcomes would you predict to be green? 1,000 times?

3. If you were to spin the spinner 100 times, what would you predict to be the probability for green, yellow, or blue?

4. **WRITING IN ▸MATH** Write your own real-world probability problem. Use the spinner from Math Tool Chest.™

15-3 Problem-Solving Strategy

MAIN IDEA I will solve problems by making an organized list.

Edgar saw the following items at a store: a batting glove for \$8.95, inline skates for \$39.75, weights for \$5.50 each, and a can of tennis balls for \$2.75. Which items can Edgar buy and spend about \$15?

Understand

What facts do you know?

- The cost of the items and that Edgar has \$15 to spend.

What do you need to find?

- You need to find which items Edgar can buy and spend about \$15.

Plan

One way to solve the problem is by making an organized list.

Solve

Since the inline skates cost more than \$15, eliminate the inline skates as an option. Round the other costs to the nearest dollar.

Batting glove: \$8.95 $\approx$ \$9
Weights: \$5.50 $\approx$ \$6
Can of tennis balls: \$2.75 $\approx$ \$3

Start with the batting glove:
- 1 glove + 1 weight $\approx$ \$9 + \$6, or \$15
- 1 glove + 2 cans of tennis balls $\approx$ \$9 + \$6, or \$15

List other combinations that contain the weights:
- 2 weights + 1 can of tennis balls $\approx$ \$12 + \$3, or \$15
- 1 weight + 3 cans of tennis balls $\approx$ \$6 + \$9, or \$15

List any remaining combination that contain the tennis balls:
- 5 cans of tennis balls $\approx$ \$15

Check

Check the list to be sure that all of the possible combinations of sporting good items that total no more than \$15 are included. ✓

ANALYZE the Strategy

Refer to the problem on the previous page.

1. Which items can Edgar buy and spend between \$20 and \$25?
2. What is the least amount of money Edgar would need if he wanted to buy the inline skates and one other item?
3. What strategy is similar to *making an organized list*?
4. Describe how making an organized list is helpful in solving a problem.

PRACTICE the Strategy

EXTRA PRACTICE See page R41.

Solve by *making an organized list*.

5. How many different products are possible using the digits 1, 3, 5, and 7?

$$\begin{array}{r} \square.\square \\ \times\ \square.\square \\ \hline \end{array}$$

6. Lawrence has \$0.20 in his pocket. How many different possibilities of coins could he have? List the possibilities.
7. Laura hit the dartboard shown below with 3 darts. How many total scores are possible?

8. Awenita is selecting 2 charms for her charm bracelet. She has 4 charms to choose from. How many different arrangements of 2 charms can she choose? Describe the possibilities.
9. A red marble, a blue marble, a green marble, and a yellow marble are placed in a brown paper bag. Suppose if you take one marble out of the bag at a time. How many different orders can all four marbles be removed from the bag? List all possibilities.
10. Sean has the three cards shown below. How many different ways can he arrange the three letters? List them.

11. The following four numbers are used for employee identification at a small company: 1, 2, 3, and 4. How many different employee identification numbers can be made if 1 is always the first number?
12. **WRITING IN MATH** Mrs. Glover has four pictures to display in a row on her desk. Explain how to use the *make an organized list* strategy to find the different ways she can display the pictures.

Mid-Chapter Check

CHAPTER 15

Lessons 15-1 through 15-3

List the possible outcomes in each probability experiment. (Lesson 15-1)

1. choosing one card without looking

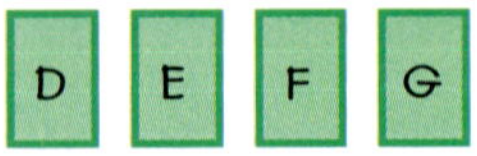

2. spinning the spinner

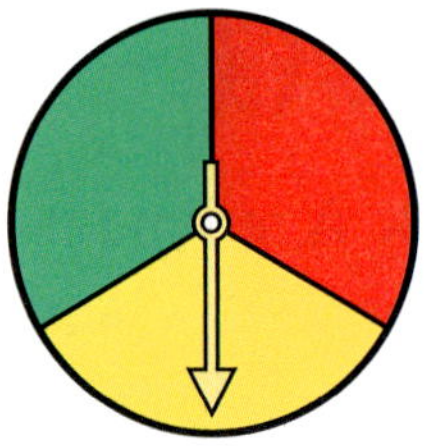

One marble is randomly drawn from the bag. Describe the probability of drawing each marble. Write *certain, impossible, likely, unlikely,* or *equally likely*. (Lesson 15-1)

3. blue

4. purple

5. red, blue, green, or yellow

6. yellow or green

7. **MULTIPLE CHOICE** Desiree has 4 red pens, 6 blue pens, and 2 purple pens in her desk drawer. If she takes 1 pen from her drawer without looking, what is the probability that it will be a blue pen? (Lesson 15-2)

A $\frac{2}{5}$ **C** $\frac{6}{11}$

B $\frac{1}{2}$ **D** $\frac{3}{4}$

One cube is drawn from the bag. Find the probability of each event. Write as a fraction in simplest form. (Lesson 15-2)

8. P(green) **9.** P(blue)

10. P(green or black) **11.** P(*not* black)

12. **MULTIPLE CHOICE** The table shows the results of 20 spins on a spinner. Based on these results, what is the probability that the spinner will land on green? (Lesson 15-2)

Color	Number of Spins
Red	7
Orange	2
Green	8
Blue	3

F $\frac{4}{5}$ **H** $\frac{1}{4}$

G $\frac{2}{5}$ **J** $\frac{1}{9}$

13. A quarter and a nickel are tossed. How many different outcomes are possible? Make a list. (Lesson 15-3)

14. Pete's Pizza offers thin or thick crust and pepperoni, sausage, mushroom, onion, and green peppers as toppings. How many different 1-topping pizzas are possible? Make a list. (Lesson 15-3)

15. **WRITING IN MATH** Explain why one event may be more likely to occur than another event in an experiment.

15-4 Counting Outcomes

MAIN IDEA

I will list outcomes of a probability experiment.

New Vocabulary

tree diagram

Math Online

macmillanmh.com

- Extra Examples
- Personal Tutor
- Self-Check Quiz

GET READY to Learn

The stone shown is made from topaz. Topaz stones come in different colors, such as blue, pink, or clear. They can have different cuts such as a regular cut or a star cut.

You can use a tree diagram to show all possible color-cut combinations of topaz. A **tree diagram** is a diagram that shows all possible outcomes of an event.

Real-World EXAMPLE — Use Tree Diagrams to List Outcomes

1 **GEMSTONES** **Refer to the information above. Make a tree diagram to show all possible color-cut combinations of the topaz described.**

The colors are blue, pink, and clear. List the colors. The cuts are a regular cut and a star cut. For each color, list the cuts.

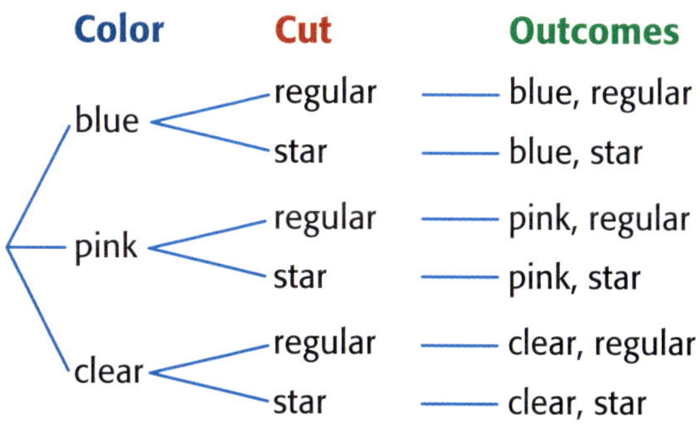

There are six possible combinations. These are listed as outcomes on the tree diagram.

Remember

Outcomes are written at branch ends.

EXAMPLE Find Probability

2 **Suppose you toss a penny, a nickel, and a dime. What is the probability of getting 3 heads?**

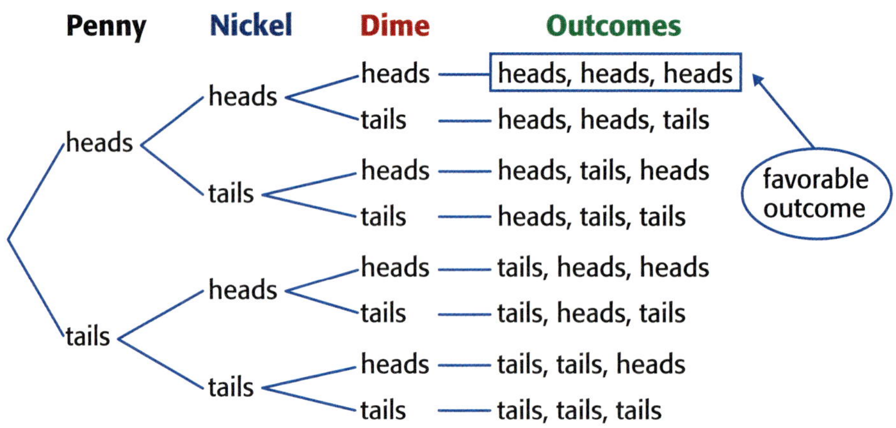

$$P(\text{3 heads}) = \frac{\text{number of favorable outcomes}}{\text{number of possible outcomes}}$$

$$= \frac{1}{8}$$ ← number of favorable outcomes / ← total number of outcomes

CHECK What You Know

A coin is tossed twice. See Examples 1, 2 (pp. 677–678)

1. Make a tree diagram to show all possible outcomes.

2. What is the probability of tossing two tails?

3. What is the probability of tossing one tail and one head?

The spinner is spun and two coins are tossed. See Examples 1, 2 (pp. 677–678)

4. Make a tree diagram to show all possible outcomes. Tell how many outcomes are possible.

5. What is the probability of landing on 2 and tossing two tails?

6. How many outcomes involve landing on 3 and tossing a head and a tail (in any order)? What is the probability of landing on 3 and tossing both a head and a tail?

7. Trent randomly chooses a belt and a pair of pants from his closet. What is the probability of choosing a black belt and black pants?

Belt	Pants
brown	tan
black	black
	blue

8. **Talk About It** Describe the steps you take to make a tree diagram when there are two probability experiments involved.

Practice and Problem Solving

EXTRA PRACTICE
See page R41.

A 4-sided die, called a tetrahedron, numbered 1 through 4 is tossed and a coin is tossed. See Examples 1, 2 (pp. 677–678)

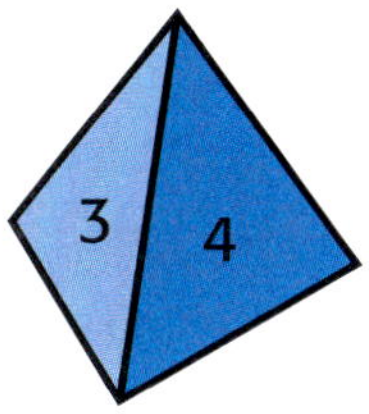

9. Make a tree diagram to show all possible outcomes. Tell how many outcomes are possible.

10. What is the probability of tossing an odd number and a tail?

The two spinners at the right are spun.
See Examples 1, 2 (pp. 677–678)

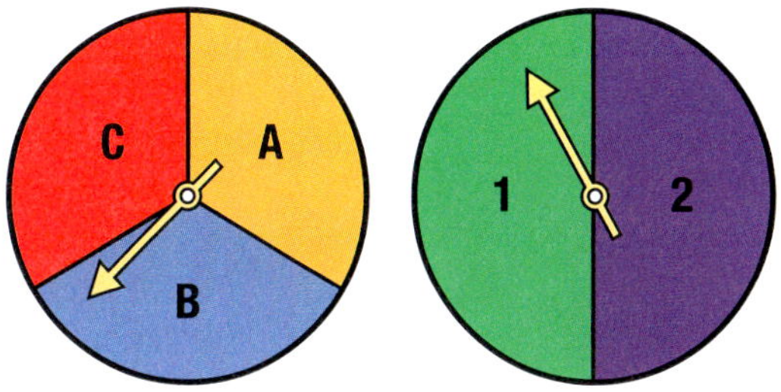

11. Make a tree diagram to show all possible outcomes. How many outcomes are possible?

12. What is the probability of spinning an A and a 1?

13. What is the probability of spinning *not* C?

Use the table at the right. A customer randomly chooses a type of bread, one meat, and one vegetable for a sandwich. See Examples 1, 2 (pp. 677–678)

Bread	Meat	Vegetable
white	turkey	lettuce
wheat	ham	tomato
	beef	

14. Make a tree diagram to show all possible outcomes. How many outcomes are possible?

15. How many sandwiches include wheat bread and turkey?

16. What is the probability that the sandwich has ham and tomato?

17. A store has 6 different shades of blue paint. The paint can be either oil or latex. The shine can be gloss, semi-gloss, or flat. How many combinations include blue latex paint?

Data File

Fishing is a popular sport in Michigan. There are over 11,000 inland lakes and 3,126 miles of Great Lakes shoreline. The table shows some different fishing possibilities that people could choose when visiting a Michigan lake.

Michigan Fishing		
Lake	**Location**	**Type of Fish**
Hubbard	boat	bass
Jewell	shoreline	perch
Green		bluegill

18. Make a tree diagram to show all different fishing possibilities.

19. How many different ways to fish are possible?

H.O.T. Problems

20. OPEN ENDED Suppose two number cubes are rolled. Describe one possible event. What is the probability of the event occurring?

21. FIND THE ERROR Jack and Makayla are finding the probability of tossing heads twice when a dime is tossed twice. Who is correct? Explain your reasoning.

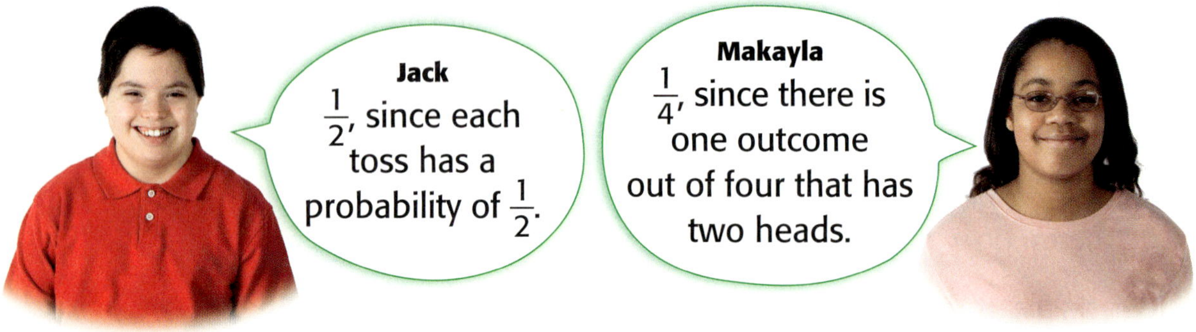

22. WRITING IN ▶MATH Describe how the number of possible outcomes changes if a spinner is spun twice rather than once.

TEST Practice

23. The eye color of an Abyssinian cat can be green, blue, gold, or hazel. Their fur color can be brown or black. How many different eye and fur color combinations are possible? (Lessons 15-3 and 15-4)

A 4

B 6

C 8

D 10

24. The spinners are spun once. What is the probability of spinning a 5 and a B? (Lesson 15-4)

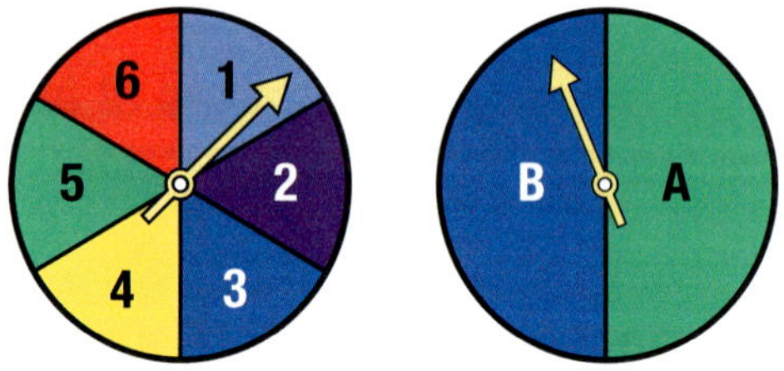

F $\frac{1}{12}$

G $\frac{1}{6}$

H $\frac{1}{5}$

J $\frac{2}{7}$

Spiral Review

25. How many different 3-letter arrangements can be made from the letters in Ben's first name? Make a list. (Lesson 15-3)

A spinner with eight equal sections numbered 1–8 is spun once. Find the probability of each event. Write as a fraction in simplest form. (Lesson 15-2)

26. *P*(6)

27. *P*(10)

28. *P*(7 or 8)

Game Time

Bean Game

Counting Outcomes

Get Ready!

Players: 2, 3, or 4

You will need: 6 dry beans
bowl
marker

Get Set!

Color one side of each bean with the marker.

Go!

The first player places the beans in the bowl, gently tosses the beans into the air, and catches them in the bowl. Points are scored as follows.

- If all of the beans land with the unmarked sides up, score 6 points.
- If all of the beans land with the marked sides up, score 4 points.
- If exactly one bean lands with the marked or unmarked side up, score 2 points.
- If three beans are marked and three beans are unmarked, score 1 point.

If a toss scores points, the player takes another turn. If a toss does not score any points, it is the next player's turn.

The winner is the player with the most points after a given number of rounds.

15-5 Problem-Solving Investigation

MAIN IDEA I will choose the best strategy to solve a problem.

P.S.I. TEAM +

DREW: I am making a flag to represent our class at the school assembly. The flag must have three solid-colored horizontal stripes (one red, one blue, and one yellow) with a gray star in the center of the middle stripe.

YOUR MISSION: Find how many different flags Drew can make.

Understand

You know that the flag will have a red, blue, and yellow stripe and that a star will be in the center of the middle stripe. You need to find how many different flags Drew can make with three stripes and one star.

Plan

You can use the *make a picture* strategy.

Solve

Continue drawing flags until no more flags can be made.

After drawing the flags, you find that 6 different flags can be made with 3 horizontal stripes with a star in the center of the middle stripe.

Check

Look back. Make a list of all the possible flags.

RBY, RYB, YBR, YRB, BYR, BRY

Since there are 6 items in the list and 6 different flags, the answer is correct. ✓

Mixed Problem Solving

EXTRA PRACTICE See page R40.

Use any strategy shown below to solve each problem.

PROBLEM-SOLVING STRATEGIES
- Make an organized list.
- Draw a picture.
- Solve a simpler problem.

1. Vince is ordering lunch from Taco Express. The choices are shown in the table below.

Tacos	Filling	Salsa
soft	beef	mild
hard	chicken	medium
	pork	hot
	vegetables	

How many different possibilities are there if Vince orders a taco with one filling and one type of salsa?

2. **Geometry** A window design is made from a rectangle divided by two diagonals. How many sections are there? What are their shapes?

3. Isabel is playing a game with the set of cards shown below. She takes one card from this set without looking. What is the probability that the card will have either a triangle or circle on it?

4. Monya has three different shirts and two pairs of pants. She wants to make different outfits, each with one pair of pants and one shirt. How many different outfits can she make?

5. **Geometry** A student divides a triangle into sections by drawing a line from each vertex to the center of the opposite side. How many sections are there, and what are their shapes?

6. **Measurement** Three students can make 9 posters in 45 minutes. How many posters can 6 students make at the same rate in 90 minutes?

7. Logan is buying a digital music player. The choices are shown below.

Color	Capabilities
black	music
blue	music and photos
pink	music, photos, and movies
silver	
white	

How many different possibilities of color and capabilities are there?

8. **WRITING IN MATH** Jeff said that since $3 + 3 = 6$, there are 6 different possibilities of cereal and juice for breakfast. Tell what mistake he made. Explain how to correct it.

Cereal	Juice
oatmeal	orange
corn flakes	apple
wheat squares	pineapple

Chapter 15 Study Guide and Review

Math Online macmillanmh.com
- STUDY TO GO
- Vocabulary Review

FOLDABLES® Study Organizer GET READY to Study

Be sure the following Big Ideas are written in your Foldable.

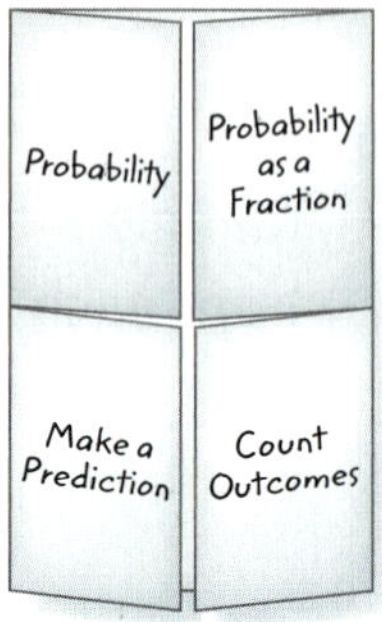

Key Concepts

Probability

- **Probability** is the chance that an event will happen. (p. 661)

Probability	Meaning
Certain	The event will definitely happen.
Impossible	There is no chance the event will happen.
Equally likely	There is an equal chance the event will happen.

- An **outcome** is a possible result in a **probability experiment.** (p. 661)

Describe Probability using Fractions

- The probability of an event can be described using a fraction. (p. 668)

$$P(\text{event}) = \frac{\text{number of favorable outcomes}}{\text{number of possible outcomes}}$$

- An event that is impossible has a probability of 0.
- An event that is certain to happen has a probability of 1.

Key Vocabulary

certain (p. 661)
impossible (p. 661)
outcome (p. 661)
probability (p. 661)
probability experiment (p. 661)
tree diagram (p. 677)

Vocabulary Check

Complete. Use a word from this Key Vocabulary list.

1. An event that will definitely happen is ___?___ to happen.
2. When a coin is tossed, the two ___?___ are heads and tails.
3. ___?___ is the chance that an event will occur.
4. An outcome is a possible result in a(n) ___?___.
5. A(n) ___?___ shows all possible outcomes of an experiment.
6. An event that can never happen can be described as ___?___ to occur.

Lesson-by-Lesson Review

15-1 Probability (pp. 661–663)

Example 1
Describe the probability of the spinner landing on 1.

The chance of landing on 1 is equally likely.

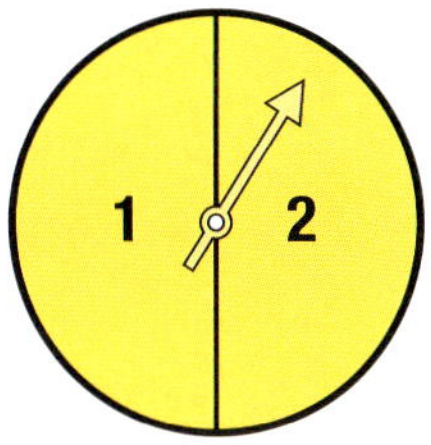

One letter is randomly chosen from the word OUTCOME. Describe the probability of choosing each letter. Write *certain*, *impossible*, *likely*, *unlikely*, or *equally likely*.

7. T **8.** E **9.** A

15-2 Probability as a Fraction (pp. 668–672)

Example 2
One marble is randomly chosen from the bag. Find the probability that a green marble is chosen.

$P(\text{event}) = \dfrac{\text{number of favorable outcomes}}{\text{number of possible outcomes}}$

$P(\text{green}) = \dfrac{2}{7}$

So, the probability that a green marble is chosen is $\frac{2}{7}$.

The spinner is spun once. Find the probability of each event. Write as a fraction in simplest form.

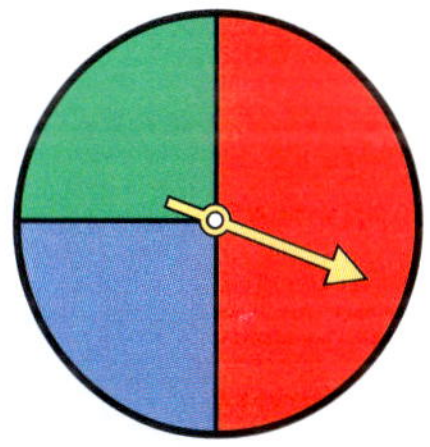

10. P(blue) **11.** P(red)

12. P(green, red, or blue)

15-3 Problem-Solving Strategy: Make an Organized List (pp. 674–675)

Example 3
How many different sums are possible using the digits 1, 2, and 3?

■■ + ■

12 + 3 = 15	13 + 2 = 15
21 + 3 = 24	23 + 1 = 24
31 + 2 = 33	32 + 1 = 33

There are 3 possible sums.

Solve by *making an organized list*.

13. There are 2 movies that Bailey wants to see. Each movie is showing at 5 different times. How many choices does she have?

Study Guide and Review

15-4 Counting Outcomes (pp. 677–680)

Example 4

A coin is tossed and the spinner is spun. What is the probability that the outcome is tails and red?

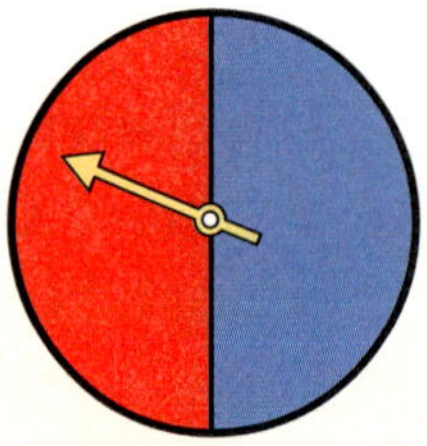

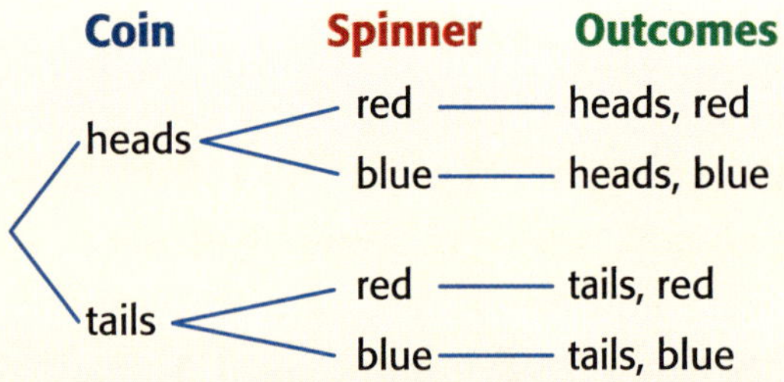

There are four possible outcomes. One outcome is tails and red. So, the probability of that outcome is $\frac{1}{4}$.

A number cube labeled 1 to 6 is rolled and a coin is tossed.

14. Make a tree diagram to show all possible outcomes. Tell how many outcomes are possible.

15. What is the probability of rolling the number 2 and tossing heads?

16. What is the probability of rolling an even number and tossing tails?

17. A store has roses, tulips, and carnations. They each come in red and yellow. How many outcomes are possible?

15-5 Problem-Solving Investigation: Choose a Strategy

(pp. 682–683)

Example 5

Miranda has a black purse and a tan purse. She has a black hat and a red hat. How many different purse-hat possibilities are there?

Make a list of the different possibilities.

black purse and black hat
black purse and red hat
tan purse and black hat
tan purse and red hat

So, there are 4 different purse-hat possibilities.

18. For lunch, Mazo can choose a soup or salad, a hamburger or grilled cheese, and a fruit cup or yogurt. How many different lunch possibilities are there?

19. A student divides a hexagon into sections by drawing three diagonals from one vertex. How many sections are there? What are their shapes?

CHAPTER 15 Chapter Test

1. Marissa spins the spinner. List the possible outcomes.

One block is randomly drawn from the bag. Describe the probability of drawing each marble. Write *certain*, *impossible*, *likely*, *unlikely*, or *equally likely*.

2. red
3. green
4. yellow
5. not green

6. **MULTIPLE CHOICE** Each letter in the word HOMEWORK is written on a separate note card. If one card is picked without looking, what is the probability that it will have a vowel on it?

   A $\frac{1}{4}$

   B $\frac{3}{8}$

   C $\frac{1}{2}$

   D $\frac{3}{4}$

7. **Geometry** Mrs. Hong has two sets of math shapes. One set has a square and a triangle. The other set has a circle, a rectangle, and a pentagon. If she chooses one shape from each set, how many possibilities are there?

8. **MULTIPLE CHOICE** Jana tossed a coin and a number cube marked 1 to 6. What is the probability that the results were tails and 3?

   F $\frac{1}{4}$ **H** $\frac{1}{8}$

   G $\frac{1}{6}$ **J** $\frac{1}{12}$

Marlon grabs a pair of shoes and a pair of socks without looking. He has black, brown, and red shoes. He has four pairs of socks: white, blue, yellow, and red.

9. Make a tree diagram to show the possible outcomes. Tell how many outcomes are possible.

10. What is the probability that the shoes and socks are both red?

11. What is the probability that the socks are *not* white?

The spinner is spun once. Find the probability of each event. Write as a fraction in simplest form.

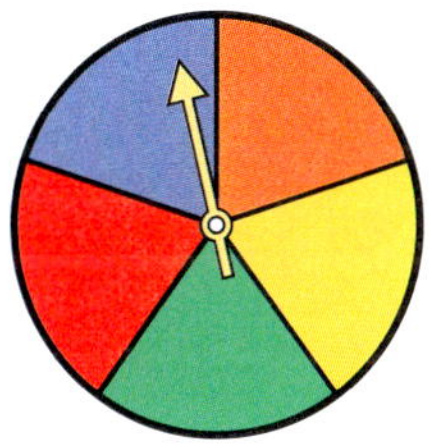

12. P(red)
13. P(blue or yellow)
14. P(black)
15. P(*not* purple)

16. **WRITING IN MATH** Gabe is downloading 3 songs from a group of 5 songs. Explain how to find the different possibilities for downloading the 3 songs.

CHAPTER 15

Test Practice

Cumulative, Chapters 1–15

Math Online macmillanmh.com

• Test Practice

PART 1 Multiple Choice

Read each question. Then fill in the correct answer on the answer sheet provided by your teacher or on a sheet of paper.

1. The table shows the tips that Stella earned each week. Based on these results, what is the probability that Stella will earn more than $100 in tips next week?

Week	Tips Earned ($)
1	94
2	132
3	115
4	104

A $\frac{1}{4}$ **C** $\frac{1}{2}$

B $\frac{1}{3}$ **D** $\frac{3}{4}$

2. If each digit 1, 3, and 5 is used only once, which group shows all the possibilities of 3-digit numbers?

F 135, 315, 531

G 315, 135, 513, 531

H 135, 315, 531, 153, 513

J 315, 351, 135, 153, 513, 531

3. The table shows the choices for frozen yogurt sundaes. From how many different combinations of 1 type of yogurt and 1 type of topping can a customer choose?

Yogurt	Topping
Strawberry	Nuts
Vanilla	Granola
Lemon	Strawberry
	Pineapple

A 12 **C** 7

B 9 **D** 6

4. Eleven cards spell the word MATHEMATICS when put together. If one card is chosen without looking, what is the probability that it will have the letter M on it?

F $\frac{1}{11}$ **H** $\frac{4}{11}$

G $\frac{2}{11}$ **J** $\frac{9}{11}$

5. A fifth grade class voted for the class mascot. Based on these results, which is the most reasonable prediction of the number of votes a bear would receive if 50 students voted?

Mascot	Number of Students
Bear	7
Falcon	4
Panther	11
Ram	3

A 22 **C** 8

B 14 **D** 6

6. Look for the pattern in the sequence of numbers below.

5, 10, 7, 14, 11, 22, 19, ...

Which rule describes this pattern best?

F Add 5, subtract 3.

G Multiply by 2, subtract 3.

H Add 5, multiply by 2.

J Multiply by 2, add 3.

Preparing for Standardized Tests

For test-taking strategies and practice, see pages R42–R55.

7. Teams are formed for a game so they each have 1 boy and 1 girl. There are 5 girls and 5 boys. How many different combinations are possible?

   A 5
   B 10
   C 25
   D 50

8. The table shows the grades Jake earned on 13 tests. Based on these results, what is the probability that Jake will earn a B on his next spelling test?

Spelling Tests	
Grade	**Number**
A	10
B	2
C	1

   F $\frac{1}{13}$
   G $\frac{2}{13}$
   H $\frac{3}{13}$
   J $\frac{10}{13}$

9. Five horses were in a race. They wore different colored blankets. Use the clues below to name a possible order of the horses from first to last.

Blanket	Finish
Red	First
Orange	Between blue and yellow
Green	Fifth

   A green, yellow, orange, blue, red
   B red, green, yellow, blue, orange
   C blue, red, orange, yellow, green
   D red, blue, orange, yellow, green

PART 2 Short Response

Record your answers on the answer sheet provided by your teacher or on a sheet of paper.

10. The temperature outside at 6:45 A.M. was 56°F. By noon, the temperature was 62°F. Write an integer to represent this situation.

11. Name one object that would be measured using milligrams, one that would be measured using grams, and one that would be measured with kilograms.

PART 3 Extended Response

Record your answers on the answer sheet provided by your teacher or on a sheet of paper.

12. Write a real-world problem that can be solved using the equation $24 = 3p$.

13. Which shape would have a larger perimeter, an equilateral triangle with sides that are each 14 inches, or a square with sides that are each 1 foot? Explain.

NEED EXTRA HELP?													
If You Missed Question...	1	2	3	4	5	6	7	8	9	10	11	12	13
Go to Lesson...	15-2	15-4	15-4	15-2	15-2	9-6	15-4	15-2	15-3	12-5	12-3	6-2	13-3

Looking Ahead

Let's Look Ahead!

Multiplying Decimals

MAIN IDEA

What You'll Learn

I will multiply a decimal by a whole number and by another decimal.

Materials:

grid paper
colored pencils
scissors

Math Online

macmillanmh.com

- Extra Examples
- Personal Tutor
- Self-Check Quiz

Hands-On Mini Lab

Recall that a 10-by-10 grid represents the number one.

ACTIVITY

1 Model 0.7 × 0.3 using decimal models.

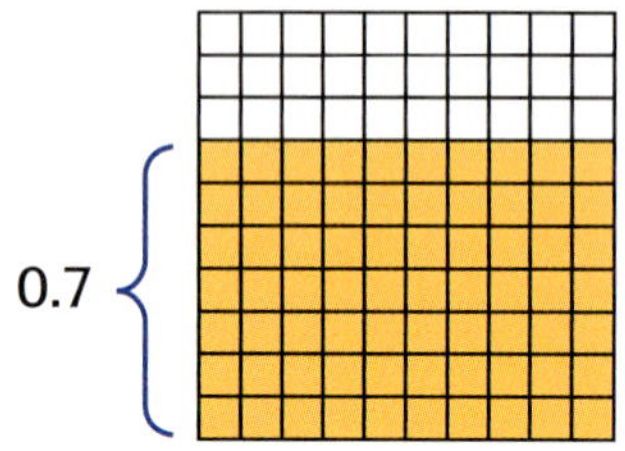

Shade seven rows of the model yellow to represent the first factor, 0.7.

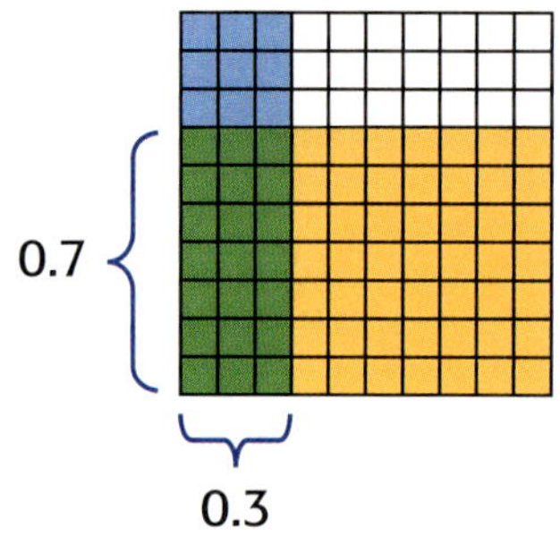

Shade three columns of the model blue to represent the second factor, 0.3. The green region has been shaded twice. It represents the product.

There are 21 hundredths in the region where the colors overlap. So, 0.7 × 0.3 = 0.21.

Draw decimal models to show each product.

a. 3 × 0.2 **b.** 2 × 0.5 **c.** 0.4 × 0.8 **d.** 0.6 × 0.4

2 Model 0.4 × 2 using decimal models.

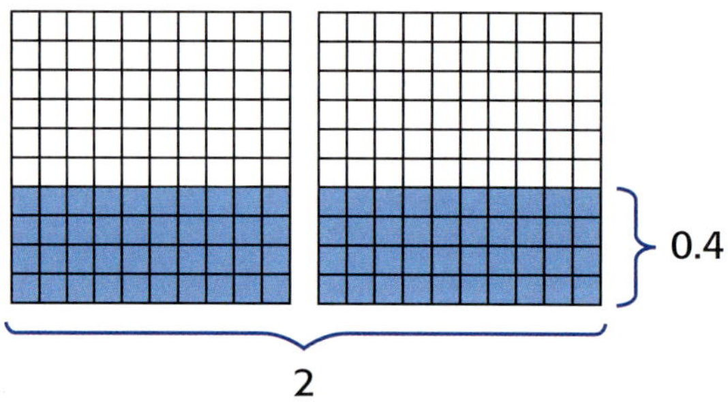

Shade four rows of each decimal model to represent 0.4.

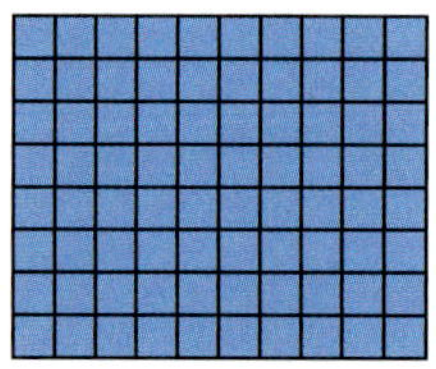

Cut off the shaded rows and rearrange them to form as many 10-by-10 grids as possible. The product is eight tenths.

So, 0.4 × 2 = 0.8.

EXAMPLES Multiply Decimals by a Whole Number

1 **Find 7 × 0.96.**

One Way: **Use estimation.**

Round 0.96 to 1. $7 \times 0.96 \longrightarrow 7 \times 1$ or 7

$$\begin{array}{r} \scriptstyle 4 \\ 0.96 \\ \times \quad 7 \\ \hline 6.72 \end{array}$$

Since the estimate is 7, place the decimal point after the 6.

Another Way: **Count decimal places.**

$$\begin{array}{r} \scriptstyle 4 \\ 0.96 \\ \times \quad 7 \\ \hline 6.72 \end{array}$$

There are two places to the right of the decimal point.

Count two decimals places from right to left.

2 **Measurement** **Find the area of a board that is 4 feet by 3.62 feet.**

Estimate $4 \times 3.62 \longrightarrow 4 \times 4$ or 16

$$\begin{array}{r} \scriptstyle 2 \\ 3.62 \\ \times \quad 4 \\ \hline 14.48 \end{array}$$

3.62 ← There are two places to the right of the decimal point.

14.48 ← Count two decimals places from right to left.

The area of the bulletin board is 14.48 feet.

EXAMPLE Multiply Decimals

3 **Find 5.2 × 3.4.** **Estimate** $5.2 \times 3.4 \longrightarrow 5 \times 3$ or 15

$$\begin{array}{r} 5.2 \\ \times\ 3.4 \\ \hline 208 \\ +156 \\ \hline 17.68 \end{array}$$

5.2 ← one decimal place

× 3.4 ← one decimal place

17.68 ← two decimal places

The product is 17.68.

Check for Reasonableness Compare 17.68 to the estimate.

$17.68 \approx 15$ ✓

CHECK What You Know

Multiply. See Examples 1–3, p. LA3

1. 6 × 0.5 **2.** 4 × 2.6 **3.** 7 × 0.89

4. 3 × 2.49 **5.** 52 × 2.1 **6.** 3.4 × 2.7

7. 5.4 × 0.9 **8.** 8.2 × 5.8 **9.** 5.7 × 0.6

10. A recipe for a cake calls for 3.5 cups of sugar. How many cups of sugar are needed for 4 cakes?

11. Talk About It Is the product of 2.8 and 1.5 greater than 6 or less than 6? How do you know?

Practice and Problem Solving

Multiply. See Examples 1–3, p. LA3

12. 2 × 1.3 **13.** 3 × 0.5 **14.** 1.8 × 9

15. 2.4 × 8 **16.** 4 × 0.02 **17.** 0.66 × 5

18. 0.7 × 0.4 **19.** 1.5 × 2.7 **20.** 0.4 × 3.7

21. 0.8 × 7.3 **22.** 2.4 × 3.8 **23.** 6.2 × 0.3

Algebra **Evaluate each expression if $x = 3$, $y = 0.2$, and $z = 4.5$.**

24. xy **25.** $7.3y$ **27.** xyz

28. $(7 \times 2) \times y$ **29.** xz **30.** $(9 - x) \times y$

31. Miguel is trying to eat less than 750 Calories at dinner. A 4-serving, thin crust cheese pizza has 272.8 Calories per serving. A dinner salad has 150 Calories. Will Miguel be able to eat the salad and two pieces of pizza for under 750 Calories? Explain.

Real-World PROBLEM SOLVING

Science **A panda spends about 0.5 of the day eating. They can eat up to 33 pounds of bamboo in a single day.**

32. How long will the panda spend eating in 7 days?

33. How many pounds of bamboo will a panda eat in 30 days?

Measurement **Find the area of each rectangle.**

34.

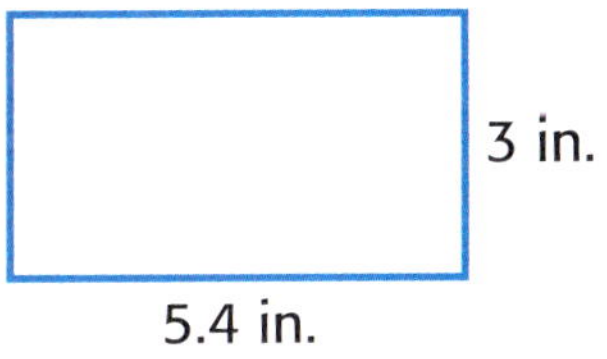

35.

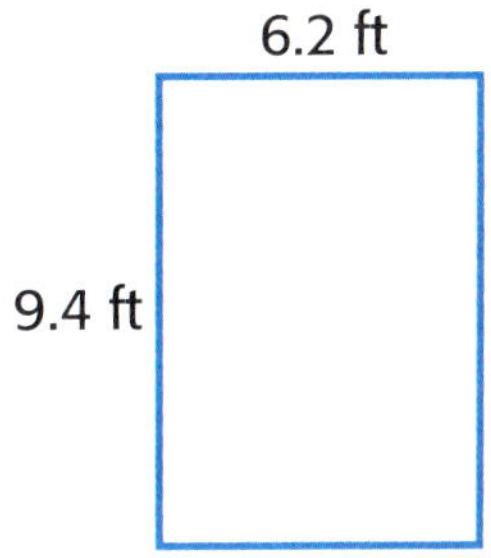

H.O.T. Problems

36. **OPEN ENDED** Write a multiplication problem in which the product has two decimal places.

37. **FIND THE ERROR** Armando and Kellis are finding the product of 0.52 and 21. Who is correct? Explain.

Armando	Kellis
$\begin{array}{r} 0.52 \\ \times\ 21 \\ \hline 1{,}092 \end{array}$	$\begin{array}{r} 21 \\ \times\ 0.52 \\ \hline 10.92 \end{array}$

38. **NUMBER SENSE** Place the decimal point in the answer to make it correct. Explain your reasoning.
$4.98 \times 8.32 = 414336$

39. **WRITING IN MATH** Write a real-world problem that can be solved using multiplication. One factor should be a decimal.

Multiplying Fractions

GET READY to Learn

Michael planted a vegetable garden. Two-thirds of the vegetables that he planted were green. Two-fifths of the green vegetables were peppers. The expression $\frac{2}{3} \times \frac{2}{5}$ represents the fraction of all the vegetables that Michael planted that were green peppers.

MAIN IDEA

I will multiply fractions.

Math Online

macmillanmh.com

- Extra Examples
- Personal Tutor
- Self-Check Quiz

EXAMPLE Multiply Fractions

1 Find $\frac{2}{3} \times \frac{2}{5}$ using a model. Write in simplest form.

To find $\frac{2}{3} \times \frac{2}{5}$, find $\frac{2}{5}$ of $\frac{2}{3}$.

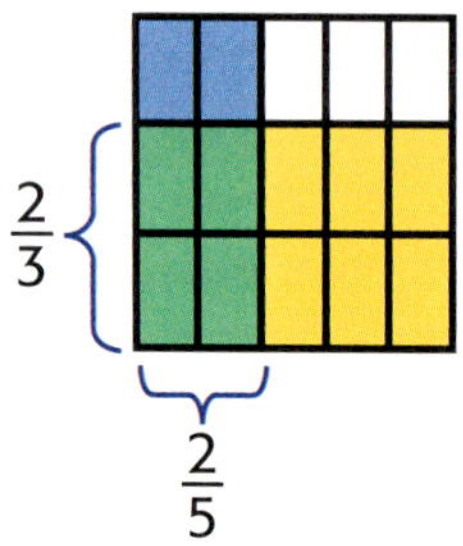

Shade $\frac{2}{3}$ of the square yellow.

Shade $\frac{2}{5}$ of the square blue.

The green region has been shaded twice. It represents the product.

Four out of 15 parts are shaded green. So, $\frac{2}{3} \times \frac{2}{5} = \frac{4}{15}$.

Multiplying Fractions — Key Concept

Words To multiply fractions, multiply the numerators and multiply the denominators.

Numbers $\frac{3}{5} \times \frac{1}{2} = \frac{3 \times 1}{5 \times 2}$

Algebra $\frac{a}{b} \times \frac{c}{d} = \frac{a \times c}{b \times d}$, where b and d are not 0.

You can simplify the fractions before or after you multiply them.

EXAMPLE Multiply Fractions

2 **Find $\frac{3}{4} \times \frac{5}{9}$.**

One Way: Simplify after multiplying.

$$\frac{3}{4} \times \frac{5}{9} = \frac{3 \times 5}{4 \times 9}$$

$$= \frac{15}{36} = \frac{5}{12}$$ (÷ 3 top and bottom) Simplify.

Another Way: Simplify before multiplying.

The numerator and denominator have a common factor, 3.

$$\frac{3}{4} \times \frac{5}{9} = \frac{\overset{1}{\cancel{3}} \times 5}{4 \times \underset{3}{\cancel{9}}}$$

Divide both the numerator and the denominator by 3.

$$= \frac{5}{12}$$ Simplify.

Real-World EXAMPLE

3 **FOOD The student council voted for the kind of food served at their school's year-end celebration. There are 10 council members, and $\frac{4}{8}$ of them voted for pizza. How many students voted for pizza?**

$$\frac{4}{8} \times 10 = \frac{4 \times 10}{8 \times 1}$$ Rewrite 10 as $\frac{10}{1}$.

$$= \frac{40}{8} = \frac{5}{1}$$ (÷ 8 top and bottom) Simplify.

$$\frac{5}{1} = 5$$

So, 5 of the students voted for pizza.

CHECK What You Know

Multiply. Write in simplest form. (See Examples 1–3, pp. LA6–LA7)

1. $\frac{1}{7} \times \frac{1}{2}$ **2.** $\frac{4}{5} \times \frac{3}{4}$ **3.** $\frac{5}{6} \times \frac{3}{4}$

4. $\frac{3}{10} \times \frac{5}{6}$ **5.** $\frac{3}{4} \times \frac{2}{7}$ **6.** $\frac{3}{5} \times \frac{5}{6}$

7. $\frac{3}{4} \times \frac{5}{12}$ **8.** $\frac{2}{9} \times \frac{1}{3}$ **9.** $\frac{6}{7} \times \frac{3}{4}$

10. Melody is putting together a puzzle that has 50 pieces. She has $\frac{7}{10}$ of the puzzle complete. How many pieces does Melody have in place?

11. Adults should sleep $\frac{1}{3}$ of the day. How many hours of the day should adults sleep?

12. Talk About It Will the product of $\frac{2}{9} \times \frac{1}{3}$ be the same as the product of $\frac{2}{9} \times \frac{2}{6}$? Explain.

Practice and Problem Solving

Multiply. Write in simplest form. (See Examples 1–3, pp. LA6–LA7)

13. $\frac{2}{3} \times \frac{1}{4}$ **14.** $\frac{5}{6} \times \frac{2}{3}$ **15.** $\frac{3}{4} \times \frac{2}{5}$

16. $\frac{1}{3} \times \frac{2}{5}$ **17.** $\frac{3}{5} \times \frac{5}{7}$ **18.** $\frac{4}{9} \times \frac{3}{8}$

19. $\frac{3}{4} \times \frac{5}{8}$ **20.** $\frac{1}{8} \times \frac{3}{4}$ **21.** $\frac{1}{2} \times \frac{4}{9}$

22. Carrie ate $\frac{1}{5}$ of the oranges that her mother brought home from the grocery store. If there were 10 oranges, how many oranges did Carrie eat?

Algebra **Evaluate each expression if $a = \frac{3}{4}$, $b = \frac{2}{3}$, and $c = \frac{1}{6}$.**

23. ab

24. cb

25. ac

26. $\frac{3}{5}a$

27. $\frac{5}{6}a$

28. abc

29. Lydia is 63 inches tall. Her baby brother is $\frac{1}{3}$ of her height.

How many inches tall is Lydia's baby brother?

30. Collin and his family are going on vacation for 6 days. They plan on spending $\frac{2}{3}$ of the days at the beach.

How many days will Collin and his family spend at the beach?

H.O.T. Problems

31. **OPEN ENDED** How can you determine if the product of $\frac{1}{2} \times \frac{4}{9}$ will be larger or smaller than $\frac{1}{2}$?

REASONING **State whether each statement is true or false. If the statement is false, provide a counterexample.**

32. The product of a whole number and a fraction is always a whole number.

33. The product of two fractions that are each between 0 and 1 is also between 0 and 1.

34. **NUMBER SENSE** If you toss a coin 20 times is it possible to land on heads $10\frac{1}{2}$ times?

35. **WRITING IN MATH** When multiplying $\frac{5}{6} \times \frac{3}{4}$, can you simplify before you multiply?

Ratios

Looking Ahead 3

MAIN IDEA

What You'll Learn
Express ratios and rates in fraction form.

New Vocabulary

ratio
equivalent ratios

Math Online

macmillanmh.com

- Extra Examples
- Personal Tutor
- Self-Check Quiz

GET READY to Learn

CLOTHES The table shows how many shirts of each color are on a shelf.

Shirts	
Color	**Number**
Black	6
Yellow	10
Blue	5
Red	4
Green	7

1. Write a sentence that compares the number of green shirts to the number of red shirts. Use the word *less* in your sentence.
2. Write a sentence that compares the number of blue shirts to the number of yellow shirts. Use the word *half* in your sentence.
3. Write a sentence comparing the number of black shirts to the total number of shirts. Use a fraction in your sentence.

There are many ways to compare numbers. A **ratio** is a comparison of two numbers by division. A ratio of 7 green shirts to 10 yellow shirts can be written in three ways.

Ratio	Using *to*	Using:	Using a *Fraction*
green shirts to yellow shirts	7 to 10	7:10	$\frac{7}{10}$

Real-World EXAMPLE — **Write a Ratio in Simplest Form**

1 VEGETABLES Write the ratio that compares the number of carrots to the pieces of broccoli.

carrots → 4, broccoli → 6

$$\frac{4}{6} = \frac{2}{3}$$

The ratio of carrots to broccoli is $\frac{2}{3}$, 2 to 3, or 2:3. $\frac{4}{6}$ and $\frac{2}{3}$ are said to be **equivalent ratios** since $\frac{4}{6} = \frac{2}{3}$.

EXAMPLE Use Ratios to Compare Parts to a Whole

2 **FLOWERS** **Write the ratio that compares the number of red flowers to the total number of flowers.**

red flowers → $\frac{4}{12} = \frac{1}{3}$
total flowers →

The ratio of red flowers to the total number of flowers is $\frac{1}{3}$, 1 to 3, or 1:3. For every one red flower, there are three total flowers.

EXAMPLE Use Ratio Tables

3 **FOOD** **To make 5 peach pies, you need 2 pounds of peaches. How many pounds of peaches do you need to make 20 pies?**

Set up a ratio table.

Number of Pies	5		20
Pounds of Peaches	2		

Label the rows with the two quantities being compared. Then fill in what is given.

Multiply to find the desired quantity.

Number of Pies	5	× 4	20
Pounds of Peaches	2	× 4	8

Multiply each quantity by 4.

So, use 8 pounds of peaches to make 20 pies.

CHECK What You Know

Write each ratio as a fraction in simplest form. (See Examples 1–3 pp. LA10–LA11)

1. 6 dogs to 8 cats

2. 15 pens to 45 pencils

3. 10 mosquitoes out of 30 insects

4. 4 pretzels out of 24 snacks

5. 14 dimes to 24 nickels

6. 15 rubies to 25 emeralds

7. Talk About It Example 1 gave a part to part ratio, and Example 2 gave a part to whole ratio. Explain the difference between a ratio comparing part to part and a ratio comparing part to whole.

Practice and Problem Solving

Write each ratio as a fraction in simplest form. (See Examples 1–3 pp. LA10–LA11)

8. 15 elm trees to 10 pine trees

9. 8 circles to 22 squares

10. 6 iguanas out of 21 lizards

11. 4 cell phones out of 18 phones

12. 10 girls out of 24 students

13. 32 apples out of 72 pieces of fruit

Write an equivalent ratio to each ratio given.

14. 2:3

15. 4 to 7

16. $\frac{5}{9}$

17. 5:6

18. 3 to 11

19. $\frac{3}{8}$

20. Draw a picture showing 4 pencils and a number of pens in which the ratio of pencils to pens is 2:3.

21. In a certain store, the ratio of high definition televisions sold to regular televisions is 1 to 4. Explain the meaning of this ratio.

22. Find the ratio of the number of vowels in the word *Mississippi* to the number of consonants. Write as a fraction in simplest form.

Real-World PROBLEM SOLVING

Social Studies There are 23 states in the United States that border an ocean. Only 5 of those states border the Pacific Ocean.

23. Write a ratio for the number of states bordering the Pacific Ocean to the number of states bordering any ocean.

24. Write a ratio for the number of states that border an ocean to the number of states in the United States.

25. It is school policy that for field trips there is 1 adult to go along with every 8 students. How many adults will go on a field trip with 48 students?

Number of Adults	1	× ?	■
Number of Students	8	× ?	48

26. At a school cafeteria, 3 out of every 5 students order a hamburger. If 60 students are eating in the cafeteria, how many students order a hamburger?

Number of Hamburgers	3	× ?	■
Number of Students	5	× ?	60

For Exercises 27 and 28, use the graphic at the right. Write each ratio in simplest form.

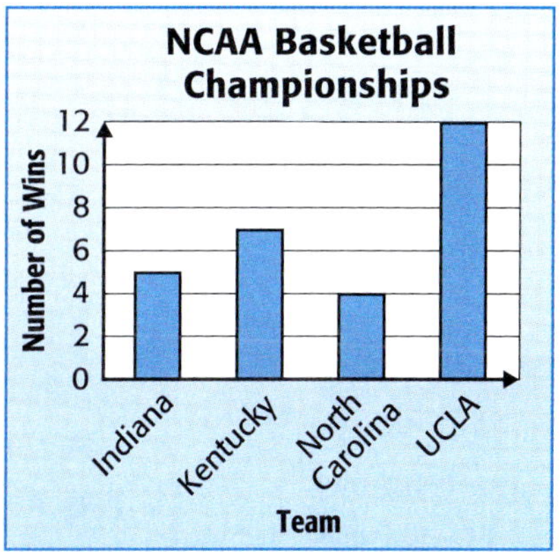

27. What ratio compares the number of wins for Indiana to the number of wins for Kentucky?

28. What ratio compares the number of wins for North Carolina to the number of wins for UCLA?

H.O.T. Problems

29. **NUMBER SENSE** Write the ratio 6 robins out of 15 birds in three different ways.

30. **CRITICAL THINKING** If 12 out of 40 students received above a 95% on the test, what ratio of students received a 95% or below?

31. **FIND THE ERROR** There are 6 red, 5 blue, 9 green, and 4 yellow marbles in a bag. Ivan and Martha are each writing a part to whole ratio for the number of blue marbles. Who is correct? Explain.

Ivan	Martha
$\frac{\text{blue}}{\text{red}} = \frac{5}{6}$	$\frac{\text{blue}}{\text{total marbles}} = \frac{5}{24}$

32. **WRITING IN MATH** The ratio of quarters to pennies in a piggy bank is 1 to 3. Explain how to write an equivalent ratio showing the number of pennies in the bank if there are 7 quarters.

Looking Ahead 4

Rates

MAIN IDEA

I will express rates in fraction form.

New Vocabulary

rate

unit rate

Math Online

macmillanmh.com

- Extra Examples
- Personal Tutor
- Self-Check Quiz

GET READY to Learn

One of the most famous marathons in the world is the Boston Marathon. The push rim wheel chair race at the marathon is about 26 miles. Some athletes must have a qualifying time of 2 hours in order to race.

26 miles in 2 hours $= \frac{26 \text{ mi}}{2 \text{ h}} = \frac{13 \text{ mi}}{1 \text{ h}}$

The average rate, of the athlete must be 13 miles per hour.

A ratio that compares two quantities with different kinds of units is called a **rate**. The example above compares miles and hours.

When a rate is simplified so that it has a denominator of 1 unit, it is called a **unit rate**. The table shows common unit rates.

Ratio	Unit Rate	Name
$\frac{\text{number of miles}}{\text{1 hour}}$	miles per hour	speed
$\frac{\text{number of miles}}{\text{1 gallon}}$	miles per gallon	gas mileage
$\frac{\text{number of dollars}}{\text{1hour}}$	dollars per hour	hourly wage

EXAMPLE Find Unit Rates

1 Write 300 feet in 30 seconds as a unit rate in feet per second.

$= \frac{300 \text{ ft}}{30 \text{ s}}$ Write the rate as a fraction.

$= \frac{300 \text{ ft} \div 30}{30 \text{ s} \div 30}$ Divide the numerator and the denominator by 30.

$= \frac{10 \text{ ft}}{1 \text{ s}}$ Simplify.

So, the unit rate is 10 feet per second.

Real-World EXAMPLE

2 **A family of four attend a baseball game and want to eat hot dogs. Find the unit rate if it costs $12 for 4 hot dogs.**

$$\$12 \text{ for 4 hot dogs} = \frac{\$12}{4 \text{ hot dogs}}$$ Write the rate as a fraction.

$$= \frac{\$12 \div 4}{4 \div 4}$$ Divide the numerator and the denominator by 4.

$$= \frac{\$3}{1 \text{ hot dog}}$$ Simplify.

So, the unit rate is $3 per hot dog.

In Example 2, you found a special kind of unit rate, called the *unit price.* This is the price per unit and is useful when you want to compare the cost of an item that comes in different sizes.

EXAMPLE Choose the Best Buy Using Estimation

3 **The costs of different sized bags of sand used to fill a sandbox are shown. Which bag costs the least per pound?**

Size	Price
3 lb	$12.05
4 lb	$19.99
8 lb	$40.25

Find the unit price, or the cost per pound, of each bag. Divide the price by the number of pounds.

Estimated cost

3-pound bag	$\$12 \div 3$ pounds $= \$4$ per pound
4-pound bag	$\$20 \div 4$ pounds $= \$5$ per pound
8-pound bag	$\$40 \div 8$ pounds $= \$5$ per pound

The 3-pound bag costs the least per pound.

CHECK What You Know

Find each unit rate. (See Examples 1–3, pp. LA14–LA15)

1. $36 for 12 gallons

2. 1,500 words in 25 minutes

3. 55 pounds for $11

4. 28 cans of juice for $7

5. A person jumps rope 36 times in 18 seconds. What is the unit rate?

6. Which has the better unit price: a 6-pack of soda for $3 or a 12-pack for $4?

7. WRITING IN MATH Ethan can buy 4 DVDs for $72.12 at DVD World or 9 DVDs for $153.25 at Movie Town. Estimate to find which has the better unit price. Explain.

Practice and Problem Solving

Find each unit rate. (See Examples 1–3, pp. LA14–LA15)

8. \$45 for 5 pounds

9. \$96 for 8 ounces

10. 150 people for 5 classes

11. 420 miles in 6 hours

12. 210 visitors in 35 days

13. 510 Calories in 3 servings

14. 40 meters in 4 seconds

15. 84 miles in 14 gallons

16. 70 yards in 7 minutes

17. \$45 in 5 hours

Use estimation to choose the better value.

18. \$47.99 for a 16-ounce bag or \$23.60 for a 12-ounce bag

19. vitamins sold in bottles of 24 for \$3.69, 50 for \$5.49, 100 for \$10.29, or 180 for \$11.99

Use the table at the right for Exercises 20 and 21.

Container	Serving Size (oz)	Price
A	18	\$5.80
B	16	\$4.34
C	12	\$3.72
D	10	\$2.30

20. Estimate the cost of each container to the nearest dollar amount. Which container has the best value?

21. Which two containers have about the same unit price?

22. A fountain pumps 60,000 gallons of water every 15 minutes. What is the unit rate?

23. Find the unit rate if 40 tickets are sold in 8 minutes.

24. Rebecca blinks her eyes 60 times in 5 minutes. At this rate, how many times does she blink in one minute?

25. Luke can type 300 words in 5 minutes. At this rate, how many words can he type in one minute?

Use the table at the right for Exercises 26–27.

Job	Total Paid	Days Per Week
Server	\$160	4
Valet	\$168	3
Cashier	\$144	2
Librarian	\$256	4

26. Lannie is looking for a job that pays at least 64 dollars a day. However, she must work at least 3 days a week. Use the table to determine which job fits Lannie's needs the best. Explain.

27. Which job pays the most money per day?

Real-World PROBLEM SOLVING

SHARKS The Shortfin Mako uses its incredible speed to track down fish like the tuna or the sword fish. The Mako is the fastest shark in the ocean. It can travel as far as 60 miles in only 3 hours.

28. How many miles can the Mako shark travel in one hour?

29. How long would it take the Mako shark to travel 80 miles if were traveling at top speed?

H.O.T. Problems

30. **NUMBER SENSE** In which situation will the rate $\frac{x \text{ ft}}{y \text{ min}}$ increase? Explain your reasoning.

a. x increases, y is unchanged
b. x is unchanged, y increases

31. **CHALLENGE** A rate is always a ratio, but a ratio is not always a rate. Write a sentence or two to explain this statement, and give an example of when a ratio is not a rate.

32. **WHICH ONE DOESN'T BELONG?** Identify the measurement that is different from the other three. Explain your reasoning.

8 ft per s	25 mi
6 cans per pack	$16 per lb

33. **CHALLENGE** The stationery store sold 6 boxes of colored notebook paper in 15 minutes. At this rate, how many boxes will they sell per hour?

34. **WRITING IN MATH** Write a sentence describing how unit price can help you spend less money at the grocery store.

Order of Operations

MAIN IDEA

I will use the order of operations to find the value of expressions.

New Vocabulary

order of operations

Math Online

macmillanmh.com

- Extra Examples
- Personal Tutor
- Self-Check Quiz

GET READY to Learn

CHORES **The table shows the number of minutes Erica spends doing each activity after school.**

Activity	Time Spent (min)
walking the dog	25
watering plants	10

1. How many total minutes are spent if Erica walks the dog for five days after school?

2. How many total minutes are spent if Erica walks the dog and waters plants for four days after school?

3. What two operations did you use in Exercise 2? Explain how to find the answer to Exercise 2 using these operations.

A numerical expression like $25 \times 4 + 10 \times 4$ is a combination of numbers and operations. The **order of operations** tells you which operation to perform to evaluate the expression.

Order of Operations — Key Concept

1. Do the operations in the parentheses first.

2. Multiply and divide in order from left to right.

3. Add and subtract in order from left to right.

EXAMPLES Use Order of Operations

1 **Find $25 \times 4 + 10 \times 4$.**

$25 \times 4 + 10 \times 4$ — Write the expression.

$100 + 40$ — Since there are no parentheses, multiply 25 by 4 and 10 by 4.

140 — Add 100 and 40.

2 **Find $7 \times (9 - 3)$.**

$7 \times (9 - 3)$ — Write the expression.

7×6 — Find 9 – 3 first because it is in parentheses.

42 — Multiply 7 and 6.

Real-World EXAMPLE

Write and Find the Value of Expressions

3 **CHORES Refer to the lesson opener. Write an expression to find the total number of minutes Erica spends walking the dog and watering plants for three days after school. Then find the value of the expression.**

First, write the expression.

Words	number of minutes spent walking the dog for three days.	+	number of minutes spent watering plants for three days.
Expression	25×3	+	10×3

$25 \times 3 + 10 \times 3 = 75 + 30$ First, multiply 25 by 3 and 10 by 3.

$= 105$ Add.

So, Erica spends a total of 105 minutes walking the dog and watering the plants for three days after school.

CHECK What You Know

Find the value of each expression. See Examples 1, 2 (p. LA18)

1. $8 + 3 \times 2$

2. $5 + 4 \times 6$

3. $10 \div 2 + 1$

4. $13 + 16 \div 4$

5. $4 \times 3 + 3 \times 9$

6. $6 \times 5 + 2 \times 2$

7. $8 + (7 \times 3)$

8. $20 - (3 \times 5)$

9. $(4 + 2) \times 8$

10. $9 \times (3 + 4)$

11. $18 \div (3 + 3)$

12. $1 + (15 \div 3)$

13. Makayla and Samson are entered in a two-person relay race. Makayla will run 2 miles and Samson will bicycle 4 miles. Makayla can run one mile in 9 minutes and Samson can bicycle one mile in 4 minutes. Write an expression to find the total time to finish the race. Then find the value of the expression See Example 3 (p. LA19)

14. A store sells DVDs for \$18 each and CDs for \$12 each. Write an expression to find the total cost of four DVDs and four CDs. Then find the value of the expression.
See Example 3 (p. LA19)

15. **Talk About It** What operation would you perform first in evaluating the expression $8 - (3 \times 4) + 5$? Explain.

Practice and Problem Solving

Find the value of each expression. See Examples 1, 2 (p. LA18)

16. $7 + 5 \times 4$

17. $3 + 3 \times 3$

18. $14 + 2 \times 6$

19. $8 + 5 \times 7$

20. $25 \div 5 + 3$

21. $12 \div 4 - 1$

22. $28 \div 4 + 3$

23. $18 \div 9 + 11$

24. $5 \times 7 + 3 \times 4$

25. $8 \times 4 + 3 \times 7$

26. $9 \times 3 + 3 \times 2$

27. $6 \times 3 + 2 \times 8$

28. $3 + (6 \times 3)$

29. $17 - (2 \times 3)$

30. $(7 + 3) \times 4$

31. $9 \times (12 \div 4)$

32. $25\ (3 + 2)$

33. $4 + (16 \div 8)$

34. On Monday, Mrs. Hinderer drove at an average speed of 50 miles per hour. On Tuesday, she drove at an average speed of 55 miles per hour. Write an expression to find the total number of miles she drove if she drove for 4 hours on Monday and 2 hours on Tuesday. Then find the value of the expression. See Example 3 (p. LA19)

35. One apple contains 70 Calories and one pear contains 100 Calories. Write an expression to find the total number of Calories that are in 3 apples and 2 pears. Then find the value of the expression. See Example 3 (p. LA19)

70 calories

100 calories

36. Philip earns \$12 an hour for mowing lawns and \$9 an hour for raking leaves. Write an expression to find the total amount Philip would earn mowing and raking for 5 hours each. Then find the value of the expression. See Example 3 (p. LA19)

37. The table gives the price of each type of admission to the Museum of Natural History. Seven eleven-year olds and three adults will buy tickets for admission. Write an expression to find the total admission cost. Then find the value of the expression.

Museum of Natural History Admission Prices

Type of Admission	Price (\$)
Under 2 years	Free
2–12 years	3
over 12 years	6

Real-World PROBLEM SOLVING

Science A housecat spends about 16 hours a day asleep. It also spends about 4 hours grooming.

38. In 3 days, how long will a cat spend sleeping? grooming?

39. How much total time does a housecat spend sleeping and grooming in 7 days?

40. Write an expression to find the total time a housecat spends sleeping and grooming in 30 days.

H.O.T. Problems

41. OPEN ENDED Write a numerical expression involving parentheses for which you would use the order of operations to find its value. Then find the value of the expression.

42. FIND THE ERROR Marty and Shenequa are finding the value of the expression $7 + (21 \div 7) - 4$. Who is correct? Explain.

Marty	Shenequa
$7 + (21 \div 7) - 4$	$7 + (21 \div 7) - 4$
$= 7 + 3 - 4$	$= 28 \div 7 - 4$
$= 10 - 4$	$= 4 - 4$
$= 6$	$= 0$

CHALLENGE For Exercises 43–46, use the order of operations to find the value of each expression.

43. $5 + (6 \times 2) - 3 + (4 \times 4)$

44. $30 - (3 \times 6) + (12 \div 4) - 2$

45. $24 \div (7 + 1) \times 2 + 11$

46. $9 + (49 \div 7) - 1 + (5 \times 3)$

47. WRITING IN ► MATH Write a real-world problem that can be solved by first writing a numerical expression and then by using the order of operations. Then solve.

Looking Ahead 6

Algebraic Expressions

MAIN IDEA

I will use the order of operations to evaluate algebraic expressions.

Math Online

macmillanmh.com

- Extra Examples
- Personal Tutor
- Self-Check Quiz

GET READY to Learn

Tom is counting his money. His piggybank is full of quarters and dimes. He has four additional quarters.

1. Let x represent the number of quarters that are in Tom's piggybank. Write an expression to represent the total number of quarters that Tom has.

2. Let y represent the number of dimes in Tom's piggybank. Write an expression to represent the total number of coins that Tom has.

3. If there are 37 quarters in Tom's piggybank and 15 dimes, how many total coins does he have?

In Chapter 5, you learned to evaluate simple algebraic expressions such as $x + 4$, $5x$, and $x - 9$. You can also use the order of operations to evaluate algebraic expressions when more than one operation is involved.

EXAMPLES Evaluate Algebraic Expressions

1 Evaluate the expression $x + 2y$ if $x = 5$ and $y = 7$.

$x + y = 5 + 2(7)$	Replace x with 5 and y with 7.
$= 5 + 14$	Multiply 2 and 7.
$= 19$	Add 5 and 14.

2 Evaluate the expression $3a - b$ if $a = 9$ and $b = 4$.

$3a - b = 3(9) - 4$	Replace a with 9 and b with 4.
$= 27 - 4$	Multiply 3 and 9.
$= 23$	Subtract 4 from 27.

3 Evaluate the expression $6w + 7(z - 2)$ if $w = 8$ and $z = 11$.

$6w + 7(z - 2) = 6(8) + 7(11 - 2)$	$w = 8$ and $z = 11$
$= 6(8) + 7(9)$	Subtract 2 from 11.
$= 48 + 63$	Multiply 6 by 8 and 7 by 9.
$= 111$	Add 48 and 63.

Real-World EXAMPLE

4 AMUSEMENT PARKS An amusement park has an admission cost of \$25. Paulo has a gift certificate for two free admissions. The expression $25(n - 2)$ represents the total admission cost in dollars for n friends to go to the park. Find the total cost of admission if $n = 6$.

$25(n - 2) = 25(6 - 2)$	Replace n with 6.
$= 25(4)$	Find $6 - 2$.
$= 100$	Multiply 25 by 4.

So, the total cost of admission for six friends is \$100.

CHECK What You Know

Evaluate each expression if $m = 7$ and $n = 3$. (See Examples 1-3, p. LA22)

1. $m + 3n$
2. $4m + n$
3. $5m + 2n$
4. $2m + 7n$
5. $m - n$
6. $6m - 2n$
7. $m - 2n$
8. $3m - n$
9. $4m + 3(n - 1)$
10. $3m + 2(n + 4)$
11. $m + 5(n + 2)$
12. $2m + 3(n - 3)$
13. The cost of a large pizza at Papa Pepperoni's is \$9. Meghan has a coupon for a total of \$3 off any order. The expression $9p - 3$ represents the total cost in dollars for p large pizzas with Meghan's coupon. Find the total cost if $p = 4$. (See Example 4, p. LA23)

14. Tyler has k baseball cards. His friend Antwon has five more baseball cards. Tyler's brother Keith has twice as many baseball cards as Antwon. The expression $2(k + 5)$ represents the number of baseball cards that Keith has. Find how many baseball cards Keith has if $k = 17$. (See Example 4, p. LA23)
15. Talk About It When evaluating the expression $5h + 4(h + 3)$ for $h = 7$, which operation would you perform first? Explain.

Practice and Problem Solving

Evaluate each expression if $c = 8$ and $d = 2$. (See Examples 1-3, p. LA22)

16. $c + 5d$ **17.** $2c + d$ **18.** $3c + 4d$

19. $6c + 7d$ **20.** $c - d$ **21.** $5c - 3d$

22. $c - 2d$ **23.** $4c - d$ **24.** $3(c + 2d)$

25. $3(3c + d)$ **26.** $2(c - d)$ **27.** $4(3c - d)$

28. $2(2c + 3d)$ **29.** $2(3c + 4d)$ **30.** $2c + 5(d - 1)$

31. $4c + 2(d + 7)$ **32.** $c + 3(d + 2)$ **33.** $4c + 6(d + 1)$

34. **Measurement** The perimeter of a rectangle is given by the expression $2\ell + 2w$. Find the perimeter of a rectangle if $\ell = 13$ centimeters and $w = 9$ centimeters. (See Example 4, p. LA23)

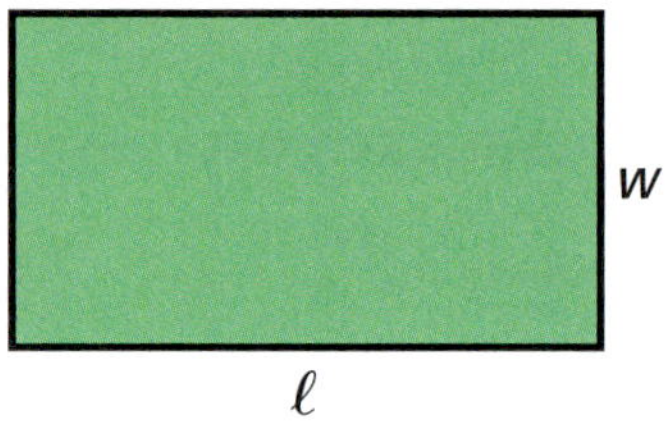

35. Mrs. Hamilton's class is selling magazine subscriptions. The subscription costs are shown in the table. The expression $30a + 18b$ gives the total amount earned from selling a 12-month subscriptions and b 6-month subscriptions. Find the total amount earned if $a = 4$ and $b = 3$. (See Example 4, p. LA23)

Costs of Magazine Subscriptions

Type of Subscription	Cost per Month ($)
12 months	30
6 months	18

36. Movie tickets at Studio 19 cost $8 each. Celeste and five of her friends will buy tickets. The cost of a large popcorn is $3 each. The expression $6 \times 8 + 3m$ gives the total cost for the six friends to see a movie if m of the friends also buy a large popcorn. Find the total cost if $m = 4$. (See Example 4, p. LA23)

37. At a pet store, goldfish cost $2 each and hamsters cost $9 each. The expression $2g + 9h$ gives the total cost of g goldfish and h hamsters. Find the total cost if $g = 8$ and $h = 2$. (See Example 4, p. LA23)

Real-World PROBLEM SOLVING

Science An airplane is flying at an average speed of 500 miles per hour. A car below is traveling at an average speed of 60 miles per hour. The expression $500h$ gives the total distance in miles that the airplane will travel in h hours. The expression $60h$ gives the total distance in miles that the car will travel h hours.

38. How many total miles will the airplane travel in 4 hours? The car?

39. The expression $500h - 60h$ gives the difference in the number of miles that the airplane and car have traveled after h hours. How many miles farther will the airplane travel in 6 hours than the car?

40. **Measurement** The expression $\frac{1}{2}bh$ gives the area of a triangle, where b is the length of the base of the triangle and h is the height of the triangle. Find the area of a triangle if $b = 12$ inches and $h = 10$ inches.

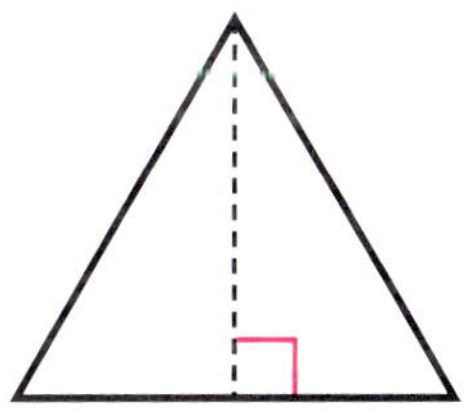

H.O.T. Problems

41. **OPEN ENDED** Write an algebraic expression for which $x = 5$ and $y = 8$. Then evaluate your expression.

CHALLENGE For Exercises 42–45, use the order of operations to evaluate each expression if $a = 6$, $b = 3$, and $c = 9$.

42. $4a + 2(b + 7) - 3c$

43. $a \times b + 36 \div 2c$

44. $3c \div b + 5a \div b$

45. $6a + 3b \div c + a$

46. **WRITING IN MATH** You and a friend are each evaluating the expression $2(n - 1) + n$ if $n = 3$. Your friend says the answer is $2 \times 3 - 1 + 3$, or 8. Write one or two sentences explaining their error. Then find the correct answer.

Problem-Solving Projects

Problem-Solving Projects

PROJECT 1

Go the Distance

The first Olympic Games with a recorded winner was in Greece in 776 BCE. In the beginning, there was only one event, a sprint. The winner received a wreath of olive branches to place on his head because olive trees were thought to be sacred.

Getting Started

Day 1 The Long Jump Challenge

- Many Olympic long jumpers are able to jump over 20 feet. Estimate how far you think you can jump. Suppose the lengths of all of the jumps of everyone in your class were added together. About how long do you think this would be?
- Go outside or in your gymnasium and set up a long jump site. Everyone should jump once. Record the exact measures.
- Add the distances to find the total length of jumps for the class. Then compare the actual amount to the estimate. Who had the closest estimate?

Day 2 On Your Mark, Get Set, GO!

- One Olympic event is the 100-meter dash. Today you will run the 50-yard dash. Go outside and mark off an area that is 50 yards long.
- Find a partner. Time each other running the 50-yard dash. Record your times.
- Find the median and mode of the times for everyone in your class.

Day 3 Sponge Relay

- Another Olympic event is the 4-by-400 meter relay. Today you will run a relay. Work in teams that have the same number of members. Each team has an equal-size empty container. Each team races to fill their container to the appropriate line by dunking the sponge into a large bucket, running to the empty container, and wringing the water into it. Record the times for each team to fill their container. Compare the times. Order the times from least to greatest.

Day 4 Frisbee Frenzy

The Olympic event, the discus, focuses on distance. Today you will throw a frisbee but will focus on accuracy.

- Set up a Frisbee toss outside. Make a bull's-eye target like the one shown. The outer section is $\frac{1}{4}$, or 0.25, of a point. The middle section is $\frac{1}{2}$, or 0.5, of a point. The center circle or bull's-eye is worth 1 point. Each person gets three tosses.

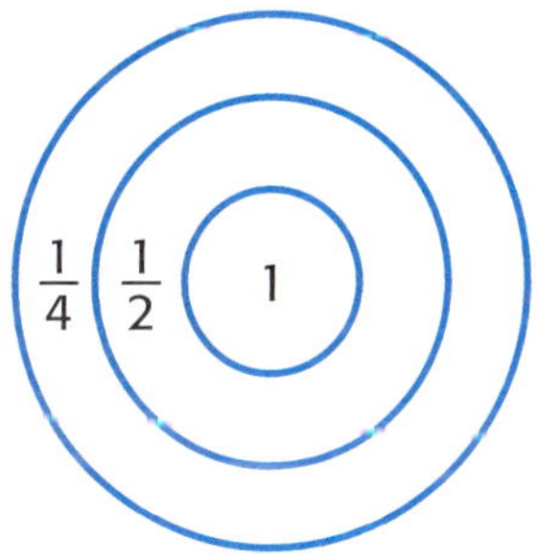

- After your three tosses, add up your total points. Find the median and mode of total points for everyone in your class.

Day 5 Now You Are the Olympic Judge!

- Now it is time to take what you have learned and teach other classes. You may need to make a few adjustments for the younger grades.
- Divide your class into four groups of equal size. Each group is in charge of one of the activities.

Wrap-Up

- How did you use math in this project?
- Describe how you used measurement in the above events.
- Explain why exact measurements and not estimates are need for Olympic events.

PROJECT 2

Arranging Space

Do you know an interior designer? Some people go to college to learn how to arrange rooms in an appealing and practical fashion. Practice your design skills by rearranging your classroom and by creating a design of your own dream home.

Getting Started

Day 1 Measure and Map It

- Measure to find the perimeter and area of your classroom to the nearest yard. Then convert your measurements to feet.
- Measure the furniture and study its placement in the classroom. Could it be set up in a different way?
- Use graph paper to create a drawing of a rearrangement of the classroom furniture. Be sure to label everything.

Day 2 Persuading the Client

- Create a persuasive speech to explain to the class why your design should be used to rearrange the classroom. Tell why you decided to place objects where you did. Think about how your design might make it easier for the teacher to teach and your classmates to learn.
- Deliver your speech and share your design with the class.

Projects

Day 3 The Winning Model

- Walk around the room and look at all of the designs. Consider the speeches that were presented yesterday. Vote for the one that you think will work the best for your classroom.
- Discuss the probability of certain designs being selected.
- Record the votes of everyone in the class. Then rearrange the classroom to match the winning design.

Day 4 Dream Design

You will create a model of a dream house.

- Work with a group to glue smaller boxes inside of a larger box to create walls in your group's dream home.
- Find the perimeter and area of each room in your group's dream home.
- Cut out pictures of furniture, swimming pools, and other features you want in your group's dream home from magazines and catalogs and place them in the correct rooms in the box.

Day 5 Show it Off

- Use the Internet to find information and floor plans from real homes in your area.
- With your group, create a brochure highlighting all the amazing features your dream home has to offer. Make sure to include the home's dimensions.
- Have a "Tour of Homes" and invite other classes to visit.

Wrap-Up

- How did you use math to design your dream home?
- Explain why you needed exact measurements when designing your dream classrooms.
- Which type of graph would you use to display the number of votes for the best design? Explain why. Then make the graph.

PROJECT 3

Mail Mania

One way people communicate with each other is through mail. Sending mail across the country today is easy. You just apply the proper postage and drop it off at the post office or in a mailbox.

Getting Started

Day 1 The Old Pony Express

- In 1860, there were no mail trucks or planes. But there was the Pony Express. The Pony Express was a team of horses and riders that carried mail from St. Joseph, Missouri, to Sacramento, California. Look at a United States map. Use the scale to find this approximate distance in miles. How long might it have taken them?
- If there was a Pony Express station every 20 miles along the route, how many stations were there in all?
- Write a journal entry as if you were a Pony Express rider back in 1860.

Day 2 Coordinate Your School

- Each day, many mail carriers walk their mail routes. Why do you think it is important to have specific routes?
- Draw a mail route for your school. Using grid paper, draw a coordinate grid labeled 0 to 20. Mark and label the coordinates of the classrooms you want on your mail route.

Day 3 Weighing In

- The price of sending packages through the United States Postal Service depends on the type of package, its weight, and how far it will be sent. Pick a city in the United States to send a 3-pound package. Use the Internet or another source to find the cost.
- Your teacher has set out different packages that need to be mailed. Based on what you have learned above, weigh each package, and calculate the cost of sending it to the city you selected.

Day 4 Overseas Friends

- If you were to send a package from your local post office to a friend overseas, it might travel in many ways. It might be sent in a truck, a plane, or via a mail carrier. Pick one city overseas in which you would like to send a 3-pound package. Track how many miles your package would have to travel from your school to that city. Then find the cost of sending the package.
- Suppose someone is sending you a 3-pound package from the same city you chose. Research the currency that is used in that country to find out how much it will cost to send the package.

Day 5 A Trip to the Post Office

- Using the Internet, find the cost of a stamp for the following years: 1950, 1960, 1970, 1980, 1990, and 2000. Make a table to display the data.
- What is the difference between the cost of a stamp from 1950 to 1960? 1960 to 1970? 1970 to 1980? 1980 to 1990? 1990 to 2000?
- Which years had the greatest increase in price? Which years had the least increase in price?

Wrap-Up

- Almost every year, the price of sending mail increases. Why do you think this happens?
- Why do you think it costs more to send mail overseas?
- Which type of graph would you use to best display the cost of a stamp from 1950 to 2000? Explain your reasoning.

PROJECT 4

It's How Big?

This pie holds the Guinness World Record for the largest pumpkin pie. It was baked in October of 2005 in New Bremen, Ohio. How much do you think it weighs? How many people do you think it would serve?

Getting Started

Day 1 Find out the Favorite

- As a class, create a survey about favorite types of pie.
- Have the entire class take the survey and determine the results.
- Survey other students in the school to find their favorite type of pie.

Day 2 Chart the Results

- Record the data received from your surveys in a frequency table.
- Work in small groups to create bar graphs, pictographs, and line plots on poster board.

Day 3 Make the World's Largest Pie

- Look at the picture of the world record pie. Draw a large pie resembling the world's largest pumpkin pie on construction paper.
- Work in groups to convert a recipe for a normal sized pumpkin pie into this large sized pie. Determine the amount of ingredients needed for the largest pie. Then find the cost of making the largest pie using a calculator.
- Record all the information and display your pie for the school.

Day 4 Tell Everyone!

- Pretend that your class broke the record for the world's largest pie and write a newspaper article about it. Make sure to include all the information that was recorded about the pie yesterday.

Day 5 Magnificent Mud

- In small groups, use the Internet or cookbooks to find a recipe for "mud pie."
- Make the pie using the recipe.
- As a class, set up a taste test for teachers. Survey the teachers about the taste test.
- Record and display the taste test results in a bar graph.
- Discuss the results of the taste test.

Wrap-Up

- Explain why it was important to display the data about favorite types of pies.
- Explain which type of graph best displays this data.
- You used a calculator to find the cost of making the largest pie. Explain the benefits of using a calculator to find total costs.
- Explain how you use math to make your mud pie.

Student Handbook

Built-In Workbook

Reference

How to Use the Student Handbook

The Student Handbook is the additional skill and reference material found at the end of books. The Student Handbook can help answer these questions.

What If I Need More Practice?

You, or your teacher, may decide that working through some additional problems would be helpful. The **Extra Practice** section provides these problems for each lesson so you have ample opportunity to practice new skills.

What If I Need to Prepare for a Standardized Test?

The **Preparing for Standardized Tests** section provides worked-out examples and practice problems for multiple-choice, short-response, and extended response questions.

What if I Want to Learn Additional Concepts and Skills?

Use the Concepts and Skills Bank section to either refresh your memory about topics you have learned in other math classes or learn new math concepts and skills.

What If I Forgot a Vocabulary Word?

The **English-Spanish Glossary** provides a list of important, or difficult, words used throughout the textbook. It provides a definition in English and Spanish as well as the page number(s) where the word can be found.

What If I Need to Find Something Quickly?

The **Index** alphabetically lists the subjects covered throughout the entire textbook and the pages on which each subject can be found.

What If I Forget Measurement Conversions, Multiplication Facts, or Formulas?

Inside the back cover of your math book is a list of measurement conversions and formulas that are used in the book. You will also find a multiplication table inside the back cover.

Extra Practice

Lesson 1-1

Pages 17–19

Name the place value of the underlined digit. Then write the number it represents.

1. 51,424
2. 324,856
3. 80,885,004
4. 65,080,050,000
5. 413,800,560,399
6. 79,707,010

Write each number in standard form.

7. 7 million, 760 thousand, 400
8. six billion, four hundred five million, three hundred

Write in expanded form. Then read and write in word form.

9. 850,120
10. 30,335,012
11. 61,850,002,050

Lesson 1-2

Pages 20–23

Replace each ● with <, >, or = to make a true sentence.

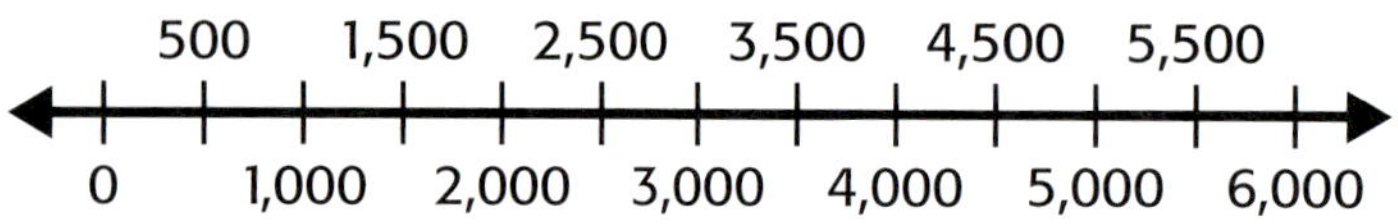

1. 600 ● 1,100
2. 775 ● 875
3. 1433 ● 1973
4. 5,551 ● 5,545
5. 775 ● 775
6. 205 ● 3,205

Replace each ● with <, >, or = to make a true sentence.

7. 890 ● 4,080
8. 10,600 ● 340
9. 7,500 ● 7,000
10. 105,706 ● 90,805
11. 12 ● 1,200
12. 7,900 ● 9,700

Lesson 1-3

Pages 24–25

Use the four-step plan to solve each problem.

1. A sprinter set three Olympic records. Her times were 2:02 minutes, 53.7 seconds, and 26.5 seconds. She competed in the 400-meter dash, the 800-meter run, and the 200-meter dash. What were her times for each event? Explain how you know.
2. Fernando gets out of school at 4:00 P.M. He goes to bed at 9:00 P.M. How much time does he have left if he spends 2 hours at football practice, 1 hour and 30 minutes on his homework, and 50 minutes eating?
3. Your mother agrees to triple whatever you put into a savings account at the bank. If you have deposited $25 each year for the last 3 years, how much money has been deposited?

Lesson 1-4

Pages 28–30

Use a model to write each fraction as a decimal.

1. $\frac{1}{2}$
2. $\frac{8}{10}$
3. $\frac{94}{100}$
4. $\frac{34}{100}$
5. $\frac{187}{1,000}$
6. $\frac{333}{1,000}$
7. $\frac{7}{100}$
8. $\frac{17}{1,000}$
9. $\frac{500}{1,000}$
10. $\frac{775}{1,000}$
11. $\frac{663}{1,000}$
12. $\frac{250}{1,000}$
13. The average snowfall in Amarillo, Texas is 15.4 inches. Write this decimal as a fraction.
14. In a survey, $\frac{56}{100}$ of the students preferred hamburgers to hot dogs. Write this fraction as a decimal.

Lesson 1-5

Pages 32–35

Name the place value of each underlined digit. Then write the number it represents.

1. $42.2\underline{3}$
2. $7.\underline{3}5$
3. $1.09\underline{6}$
4. $36.\underline{9}37$

Write each number in standard form.

5. 16 and 7 tenths
6. thirty-three and two hundredths
7. $11 + 2 + 0.4 + 0.06 + 0.005$
8. $9 + 0.09 + 0.001$

Write each number in expanded form. Then read and write in word form.

9. 6.78
10. 0.775
11. 50.05
12. 84.993

Lesson 1-6

Pages 36–39

Replace each ● with $<$, $>$, or $=$ to make a true sentence.

1. 2.2 ● 2.8
2. 0.55 ● 0.66
3. 0.27 ● 0.277
4. 9.456 ● 9.45
5. 11.74 ● 10.25
6. 4.55 ● 4.54
7. 0.09 ● 0.090
8. 75.75 ● 75.70
9. 5.8 ● 8.5
10. 25.5 ● 25.00
11. 0.01 ● 0.010
12. 82.02 ● 82.20
13. Roy can run the 100 meter dash in 11.04 seconds. Malik can run the same distance in 11.40 seconds. Who is faster, Roy or Malik?

Lesson 1-7

Pages 42–46

Order each set of numbers from least to greatest.

1. 55, 42, 43, 29
2. 109, 167, 87, 99
3. 2,984, 2,893, 4,367, 2,335, 4,387
4. 3.8, 5.9, 2.7, 1.9, 5.6
5. 59,033, 52,456, 59,999, 51,092
6. 63.09, 61.99, 68.47, 63.10
7. 44.4, 4.44, 0.444, 444, 0.044
8. 7.27, 7.79, 0.772, 77.5, 76.903
9. 7.5, 5.7, 7.55, 5.77
10. 9, 8.9, 8.96, 9.01, 9.001
11. Clara's cat weighs 9.72 pounds. Lucia's cat weighs 9.8 pounds. Write a sentence comparing the cats' weights.

Lesson 1-8

Pages 48–49

Solve. Use the *guess and check* strategy.

1. Hunter saw 16 wheels on a total of 5 cars and motorcycles at the store. How many cars and motorcycles are there at the store?

2. The sum of two numbers is 17. Their product is 72. What are the two numbers?

3. Shirley bought two hot dogs from a street vendor and received $2.50 back in change. The vendor gave her the change in quarters and nickels. If she received 14 coins, how many of each coin did she get?

4. A total of 23 students and teachers from Western Middle School went to the zoo. Student admission price was $3 for each student. Each teacher had to pay $4 for admission. The total cost was $71. How many students went to the zoo?

Lesson 2-1

Pages 61–63

Round each number to the underlined place.

1. $\underline{1}6$
2. $8\underline{2}3$
3. $2{,}\underline{5}99$
4. $\underline{4}{,}999$
5. $\underline{1}7{,}347$
6. $409{,}1\underline{6}8$
7. $5{,}\underline{5}55$
8. $3\underline{3}3{,}225$

Round each decimal to the place indicated.

9. 7.8; ones
10. 2.34; tenths
11. 0.928; hundredths
12. 56.10; ones
13. 4.298; tenths
14. 22.399; hundredths
15. 5.345; ones
16. 0.687; tenths
17. The thickness of a United States penny is 1.27 millimeter. Round this number to the nearest tenth.

Lesson 2-2

Pages 64–67

Estimate each sum or difference. Use rounding or compatible numbers. Show your work.

1. 44 − 21

2. 1,833 + 3,109

3. 472 − 268

4. 6.9 + 3.5

5. 299.5 + 700.3

6. 8,723 − 3,114

7. Shanti has 472 baseball cards. Her brother has 835 baseball cards. About how many baseball cards do they have altogether? Show your work.

Lesson 2-3

Pages 68–69

Solve. Use the *work backward* strategy.

1. The local girl scout troop is selling cookies for a fundraiser. They sold all 30 of the boxes that cost $3 and the rest of the boxes they sold were $2 each. If they made $170, how many boxes of cookies did they sell?

2. Calvin's mother gave him $3.35 in change that was left over after she bought groceries. The grocery receipt was for $32.23. How much money did Calvin's mother have before she went grocery shopping?

3. Lola went to Chicago with friends. She wanted to be home no later than 9:00 P.M. on Sunday. It will take Lola 7 hours to ride the train home or 6 hours if she takes the bus. What time will she need to leave Chicago if she rides the bus home?

Lesson 2-4

Pages 70–72

Add or subtract.

1. 45 + 18

2. 620 − 430

3. 4,320 + 6,109

4. 560 − 350

5. 17,700 + 13,356

6. 4,350 + 360

7. 934 − 275

8. 20,020 − 12,987

9. Corey bought a pair of shoes for $49, a shirt for $28, and jeans for $55. How much did he spend on his new clothes?

Lesson 2-5

Pages 74–75

For each problem, determine whether you need an estimate or an exact answer. Then solve.

1. A giant submarine sandwich can feed 13 students. Mr. Smith's science class is having a party for perfect attendance, and they want to order enough food to feed 37 students. How many subs will they need to order?

2. Four friends are sharing 3 pizzas. Each pizza costs $12.96. How much will each person need to pay?

3. A school spends $132 on art supplies for each student. There are 186 students in the school, and the school's art budget is $27,000. Does the school have enough money in the budget to cover the students' supplies?

Lesson 2-6

Pages 80–82

Add or subtract.

1. $\begin{array}{r} 2.4 \\ +\ 4.7 \\ \hline \end{array}$ **2.** $\begin{array}{r} 7.6 \\ +\ 2.56 \\ \hline \end{array}$ **3.** $\begin{array}{r} 0.78 \\ -\ 0.04 \\ \hline \end{array}$ **4.** $\begin{array}{r} 8 \\ -\ 3.5 \\ \hline \end{array}$

5. 5.14 + 3.66 **6.** 0.6 − 0.11

7. Brody, Elvio, Jamil and Tito were on the relay team for track and field. The table lists their times. What was the team's total time?

Name	Time (in seconds)
Brody	58.6
Elvio	57.93
Jamil	59.2
Tito	56.8

Lesson 2-7

Pages 84–87

Identify the addition property used to rewrite each problem.

1. 10 + 5 = 5 + 10 **2.** (22 + 50) + 25 = 22 + (50 + 25)

3. 9 + 23 + 75 = 9 + 75 + 23 **4.** 45 + 0 + 5 = 45 + 5

Use properties of addition to find each sum mentally. Show your steps and identify the properties that you used.

5. 5 + 30 + 11 **6.** 22 + 54 + 6 **7.** 3.5 + 7.6 + 19.5

8. 10.6 + 74 + 2 **9.** 49 + 27 **10.** 50.4 + 13.6 + 4.5

Find the value that makes each sentence true.

11. 21 + (45 + 7) = 7 + (21 + ■) **12.** 13.3 + 2.6 + 6 = ■ + 21

13. 52 + 0 = ■ **14.** 17 + 32 + 3 = 17 + ■ + 32

Lesson 2-8

Pages 88–91

Add or subtract mentally. Use compensation.

1. 43 + 21	**2.** 57 + 35	**3.** 79 − 31
4. 88 − 29	**5.** 25 − 15	**6.** 205 + 675
7. 4.3 − 3.2	**8.** 95 − 77	**9.** 29.4 + 22.6
10. 74.2 − 41.2	**11.** 59.4 + 38.6	**12.** 60.5 − 20.3
13. 398 + 492	**13.** 62.6 − 41.9	**14.** 492 − 398

15. In a fish tank, one angelfish measures 5.7 inches and another one measures 4.9 inches. What is the total length of both angelfish?

Lesson 3-1

Pages 103–105

Find each product mentally.

1. 4 × 30	**2.** 70 × 3	**3.** 22 × 10
4. 50 × 40	**5.** 300 × 5	**6.** 620 × 10
7. 30 × 400	**8.** 800 × 700	**9.** 1,000 × 40
10. 4,000 × 5	**11.** 300 × 70	**12.** 25 × 500
13. 25 × 20	**14.** 600 × 600	**15.** 3,000 × 20

16. Celeste is making bracelets for her friends. Each bracelet uses 50 beads. If she wants to make 20 bracelets, how many beads does she need?

Lesson 3-2

Pages 108–111

Rewrite each expression using the Distributive Property. Then evaluate.

1. 5 × (8 + 2)	**2.** 3 × (20 + 7)	**3.** 8 × (40 + 2)
4. 4 × (7 + 7)	**5.** 6 × (5 + 9)	**6.** 2 × (90 + 40)

Find each product mentally using the Distributive Property. Show the steps that you used.

7. 3 × 12	**8.** 5 × 48	**9.** 7 × 23	**10.** 2 × 76
11. 33 × 6	**12.** 94 × 5	**13.** 2 × 43	**14.** 55 × 6

15. Arnaldo is packing 8 red model cars and 5 blue model cars into each box. If he needs to pack 25 boxes, how many model cars will he need? Use the Distributive Property. Show your steps.

16. Maurice is a sports cards dealer. On Tuesday, he sold 13 cards that cost $15 each. He also sold 10 cards that cost $8 each. How much money did Maurice make on Tuesday?

Extra Practice

Lesson 3-3

Pages 112–115

Estimate by rounding. Show your work.

1. 38×5

2. 52×7

3. 49×79

4. 102×38

5. 320×73

6. 320×17

7. 79×59

8. 520×437

9. 289×132

Estimate by using compatible numbers. Show your work.

10. 85×221 **11.** 118×94 **12.** 327×75

13. Thi's class is ordering books for the reading club. Each book costs $7.55. If there are 12 people in the reading club, about how much will the books cost? Show how you estimated.

Lesson 3-4

Pages 116–118

Multiply.

1. 32×8

2. 47×6

3. 257×5

4. 442×2

5. 321×4 **6.** 63×5 **7.** 7×321 **8.** 94×2

9. Willy wants to buy diet soda for 6 people. The sodas cost $1.39 each and he has $10. Will he have enough money? How much will be left over?

Lesson 3-5

Pages 120–121

Solve. Use the *draw a picture* strategy.

1. Denitra is making bracelets from a piece of string that is 50 inches long. After she cuts eight equal size pieces, she has 2 inches left. How long was each piece?

2. Mr. Morris is hanging a light from a ceiling. The height from the ceiling to the floor is 12 feet. If the fixture is 2 feet 4 inches from the ceiling, how far is the fixture to the floor?

4. A bike trail has markers at every other mile beginning with mile one. There is also one at the end of the trail. The trail is 16.3 miles long. How many markers are there?

Lesson 3-6

Pages 122–124

Multiply.

1. $\begin{array}{r} 45 \\ \times\ 41 \\ \hline \end{array}$

2. $\begin{array}{r} 62 \\ \times\ 68 \\ \hline \end{array}$

3. $\begin{array}{r} 17 \\ \times\ 59 \\ \hline \end{array}$

4. $\begin{array}{r} 172 \\ \times\ 48 \\ \hline \end{array}$

5. 17×13

6. 56×72

7. 473×59

8. 182×35

9. Kate swims 18 laps every day in the school's pool. The length of the pool is 50 meters. How many meters will she swim in 28 days?

Lesson 3-7

Pages 126–129

Identify the multiplication property used to rewrite each problem.

1. $13 \times 4 = 4 \times 13$

2. $46 = 1 \times 46$

3. $7 \times 15 \times 42 = 7 \times 42 \times 15$

4. $5 \times (8 \times 10) = (5 \times 8) \times 10$

Use properties of multiplication to find each product mentally. Show your steps and identify the properties that you used.

5. $10 \times 4 \times 7$

6. $15 \times (4 \times 5)$

7. $100 \times 32 \times 3$

8. $4 \times (5 \times 18)$

9. $2 \times 24 \times 5$

10. $25 \times (4 \times 17)$

11. Colby delivers papers every weekday. It takes him 80 minutes each day. If he works 5 days a week for 4 weeks, how many total minutes will it take him to deliver the papers?

Lesson 3-8

Pages 132–135

Estimate by rounding.

1. $2.30 × 8

2. $5.87 × 4

3. $38.09 × 6

4. $19.95 × 3

5. 3,272 × 9

6. 485 × 724

7. Lauren bought 3.2 pounds of lunch meat. It costs $4 per pound. About how much did Lauren pay for the lunch meat?

8. Rodrigo is buying DVDs. He buys two DVDs that cost $19.98 each and three that cost $22.50 each. Estimate the total cost of the DVDs.

Lesson 3-9

Pages 136–137

Solve each problem. If there is extra information, identify it. If there is not enough information, tell what information is needed.

1. Hayden purchases a new bicycle for $149. The color of the bicycle is blue with red stripes. He needs to make 12 monthly payments of $9 to pay off the balance on the bike. How much was the down payment?

2. Shawnel and Cynthiana are participating in a magazine sale. Each magazine subscription costs $2 per week. How many more magazine subscriptions did Cynthiana sell than Shawnel?

Person	Subscriptions
Shawnel	38
Cynthiana	77

3. An arts and crafts store sells three sizes of candles. The prices for the candles are $1.50 for the small size, $2.50 for the medium size, and $5.00 for the large size. The store averages $335 in candle sales each week. How many large candles do they sell on average per week?

Lesson 4-1

Pages 149–151

Divide mentally.

1. 400 ÷ 4 **2.** 600 ÷ 3 **3.** 270 ÷ 10 **4.** 160 ÷ 8

5. 5,400 ÷ 6 **6.** 800 ÷ 8 **7.** 2,700 ÷ 9 **8.** 16,000 ÷ 8,000

9. 28,000 ÷ 2 **10.** 45,000 ÷ 5 **11.** 90,000 ÷ 300 **12.** 42,000 ÷ 6

13. Griffen made $350 doing yard work. If he makes $10 per hour, how many hours did he work?

Lesson 4-2

Pages 152–155

Estimate by using compatible numbers. Show your work.

1. 277 ÷ 3 **2.** 778 ÷ 21 **3.** 990 ÷ 333

4. 721 ÷ 34 **5.** 110 ÷ 9 **6.** 320 ÷ 37

7. 499 ÷ 23 **8.** 655 ÷ 222 **9.** 5,322 ÷ 63

10. 8,672 ÷ 218 **11.** 4,776 ÷ 239 **12.** 21,356 ÷ 3,200

13. Mr. Jerome can drive 320 miles on one tank of gas. If his gas tank holds 11 gallons of gasoline, about how many miles can he drive on one gallon? Show how you estimated.

Lesson 4-3

Pages 158–161

Divide.

1. 76 ÷ 4
2. 235 ÷ 5
3. 244 ÷ 8
4. 333 ÷ 2
5. 222 ÷ 3
6. 632 ÷ 4
7. 933 ÷ 3
8. 420 ÷ 4
9. 302 ÷ 4
10. 622 ÷ 3
11. 721 ÷ 7
12. 432 ÷ 6
13. Trey used a total of 13,335 Calories for the week. On average, how many Calories a day did he use?
14. If Trey eats 3 meals a day, how many Calories per meal can he have?

Lesson 4-4

Pages 162–164

Divide.

1. 73 ÷ 11
2. 81 ÷ 30
3. 43 ÷ 13
4. 82 ÷ 44
5. 443 ÷ 66
6. 211 ÷ 17
7. 525 ÷ 75
8. 321 ÷ 11
9. 150 ÷ 30
10. 756 ÷ 50
11. 923 ÷ 71
12. 388 ÷ 24
13. Paz's class is making birdhouses for a project. They have 524 inches of wood. If each birdhouse takes 24 inches to complete, how many birdhouses can they build? What does your remainder represent?

Lesson 4-5

Pages 166–167

Solve. Use the *act it out* strategy.

1. The top three finishers in the local swimming competition were Melanie, Yasmin, and Francisca. In how many different ways can first, second, and third place be awarded?
2. Elio's mother asked him to roll the family's extra change. The table shows the coins he rolled, how many rolls he made, and the value of money in the rolls. How many total coins did Elio roll?

Coin	Number of rolls	Value of coins (in dollars)
Quarter	2	20.00
Dime	2	10.00
Nickel	3	6.00

Lesson 4-6

Pages 170–173

Solve. Tell how you interpreted the remainder.

1. Deborah decided to purchase T-shirts at an amusement park to give as souvenirs. How many T-shirts can she buy with $35?
2. It takes 5 bags of beads to make 3 necklaces. How many necklaces can be made with 36 bags of beads?
3. Mrs. Heaton cuts her pie into 7 pieces. She needs to have 83 pieces for a charity event. How many pies must she bake to have enough pieces? How many pieces will be left over?

Lesson 4-7

Pages 174–176

Estimate.

1. $5\overline{)\$8.25}$
2. $7\overline{)\$19.88}$
3. $2\overline{)\$33.50}$
4. Papina, Malik, and Silvia made a total of $63.21 at a yard sale. They divide the money evenly. About how much does each person get?

Lesson 4-8

Pages 180–181

Use any strategy to solve each problem.

1. An artist painted twice as many pieces on Tuesday as he did on Monday. He painted 36 pieces total on the two days. How many did he paint on Monday?
2. Ruth has 43 cents in coins in her pocket. If you know that one of the coins is a quarter and she has six coins in her pocket, what are the other coins?
3. Luz is saving up to buy a pair of inline skates that cost $34.98. If she saves $5.00 each week, how many weeks will it take until she can buy the skates?
4. Amiel is heading out for his daily jog. He needs to be home by 6:15 P.M. to do his homework. It takes him 15 minutes to warm up, 45 minutes to jog, and 10 minutes to cool down. What time should he leave for his jog?
5. Akiko is buying books to hold her stamp collection. Each book can hold 120 stamps. If she has 76 envelopes that contain 4 stamps each, how many books will she need?

Lesson 5-1

Pages 193–195

Evaluate each expression if $x = 4$ and $y = 7$.

1. $x + 6$
2. $3 + y$
3. $2 + x$
4. $y + 27$
5. $17 + y$
6. $x + 21$
7. $x + 29$
8. $x + y$

Write an expression for the real-world situation. Then evaluate it.

9. Sareeta is t years old. Her sister is 6 years older. If $t = 10$, how old is Sareeta's sister?

Lesson 5-2

Pages 196–197

Solve. Use the *solve a simpler problem* strategy.

1. For a play, five students can paint 5 props in 5 hours. At this rate, how many props can 7 students paint in 10 hours?
2. What is the sum of the whole numbers from 10 through 19? 20 through 29? 30 through 39? Can you predict the sum of the numbers 50 through 59?
3. Monty is cutting wood for shelves. He has 40 feet of lumber. Each shelf needs to be 5 feet long. If each cut takes 90 seconds, how long will it take Monty to make the cuts?
4. A newspaper delivery person can fit 35 newspapers into their carry bag on Monday through Saturday. On Sunday they can fit 21 papers. They deliver the newspaper to 88 customers every day. How many times do they have to load their carry bag on Wednesdays?

Lesson 5-3

Pages 198–201

Evaluate each expression if $x = 5$ and $y = 3$.

1. $3x$
2. $6y$
3. $7x$
4. $13y$

Evaluate each expression if $a = 9$ and $b = 5$.

5. $4b$
6. $11a$
7. $20b$
8. $8a$
9. $17b$
10. $31a$
11. $45b$
12. $9b$
13. Mei can walk 3 miles in one hour. Saturday she walked for t hours. Write an expression to show the distance she walked.
14. Mrs. Turner is providing fruit slices for the football team. She can get 8 slices from one orange. Write an expression to show how many slices she can get from f oranges. How many slices can Mrs. Turner get from 15 oranges?

Lesson 5-4

Pages 202–204

Write an expression for each phrase.

1. half of c **2.** 12 times w **3.** 19 more than k

4. 20 less than x **5.** twice p **6.** the sum of m and 5

Evaluate each expression if $r = 3$, $s = 5$, and $t = 9$.

7. $r \times 31$ **8.** $13t$ **9.** $4r$ **10.** $t \div 3 \times s$

11. There were t questions on a test. Eva missed 4 questions. If there were 35 questions on the test, write and evaluate an expression for the number of questions answered correctly.

Lesson 5-5

Pages 206–207

Use any strategy to solve each problem.

1. Jonas' parents give him $15 each week for school lunches. If Jonas buys one of each item every day, how much money does he have left on Friday?

Item	Price (in dollars)
pizza	1.50
drink	0.65
fruit	0.75

2. Marlo is twice as old as his sister Naomi. Four years ago he was three times as old. What are their ages now?

3. A large commercial jet seats 416 passengers. On a recent flight, there was one empty seat for every three passengers. How many passengers were on the flight?

Lesson 5-6

Pages 210–213

Copy and complete each function table for each real-world situation.

1. Cora has 11 more trains than Luis.

Input (x)	$x + 11$	Output
12		
14		
17		

2. Each package weighs 10 pounds.

Input (x)	$10x$	Output
7		
11		
15		

Lesson 5-7

Pages 218–222

Evaluate each expression.

1. $(14 \times 7) - 3$
2. $14 \times (7 - 3)$
3. $7 + (2 \times 9)$
4. $(7 + 2) \times 9$
5. $(23 + 17) \times 5$
6. $23 + (17 \times 5)$
7. Mrs. Walker is making banners for the middle school sports teams. She needs 8 yards of gold fabric and 6 yards of maroon fabric. The gold fabric costs $6 per yard and the maroon fabric costs $10 per yard. How much will she spend for the fabric?

Lesson 6-1

Pages 237–239

Solve each equation. Check your solution.

1. $x + 8 = 14$
2. $7 - y = 2$
3. $e + 15 = 29$
4. $q + 4 = 17$
5. $17 - w = 5$
6. $9 + h = 21$
7. $t - 19 = 6$
8. $29 - y = 1$

Write an equation and then solve. Check your solution.

9. Lei is thinking of a number. Elsa incorrectly guessed the number to be 25. Lei said the difference between the two numbers is 36. What was her number?
10. The school's lacrosse team has won 5 straight games. Their record is now 13 wins and 4 losses. What was their record before the winning streak?
11. Tyran owns 24 movies. He bought 11 with his own money. The other movies were gifts from others. How many did he receive as gifts?

Lesson 6-2

Pages 244–247

Solve each equation. Check your solution.

1. $6c = 24$
2. $21 = 3c$
3. $9g = 45$
4. $66 = 2p$
5. $17y = 102$
6. $93 = 31h$
7. $49 = 7k$
8. $21s = 42$

Write an equation and then solve. Check your solution.

9. Every player on a basketball team practiced for 30 hours during the two week summer camp. The team practiced for a total of 330 hours. How many players are on the basketball team?
10. A shoe store sold 84 pairs of shoes last weekend. Each clerk sold the same number of shoes. There are 7 clerks at the store. How many pairs of shoes did each sell?

Lesson 6-3

Pages 248–249

Solve. Use the *make a table* strategy.

1. Francisco is 17 years old. His grandfather is 77. How old will Francisco's grandfather be when he is exactly 4 times as old as Francisco?
2. The first week of track practice Cesar ran the 400 meter dash in 1 minute 8 seconds. The third week he ran the 400 meter dash in 1 minute 5 seconds. He continued this pattern until the end of the season. How fast could Cesar run the 400 meter dash in week 9?
3. Marsha's little brother tells her he will clean her room every day for the next two weeks if she pays him by doubling the amount of money paid from the day before. He offers to start for $0.10. How much will he make on the seventh day?
4. If Marsha agrees to his plan, did she make a good deal? Explain.

Lesson 6-4

Pages 250–252

Name the ordered pair for each point.

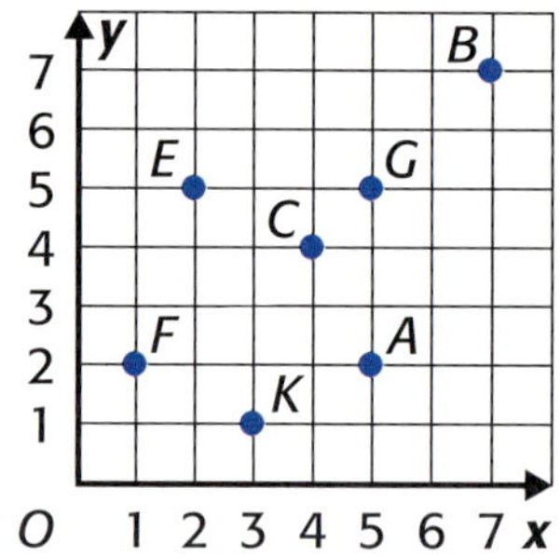

1. *B*
2. *F*
3. *E*
4. *A*
5. *K*
6. *G*
7. Suppose point *C* was moved one unit to the right and 2 units down. After the move what point will be the same as point *C*?
8. Garcia located a point that was 6 points to the right of the origin and 3 points above the origin. What was the ordered pair?

Lesson 6-5

Pages 254–257

Graph and label each point on a coordinate grid.

1. *W* (3, 4)
2. *R* (1, 8)
3. *H* (7, 3)
4. *T* (5, 5)
5. *B* (5, 2)
6. *J* (3, 6)
7. *P* (6, 8)
8. *C* (2, 4)
9. Mr. Rollins wants to plant trees. Each tree costs $25, and he must pay a delivery charge of $10. Given the function rule $25t + 10$, make a function table to find the total amount Mr. Rollins would pay if he purchased 3 trees, 4 trees, 5 trees, and 6 trees.
10. The Williams family is taking a trip. They travel for 20 miles before they begin timing the length of the trip. Given the function rule $55h + 20$, make a function table to find the distance traveled if they drove for 3 hours, 4 hours, 5 hours, and 6 hours.

Lesson 6-6

Pages 260–262

Solve using a function table or equation.

1. A vendor sells gyros. How much would it cost for a group of 6 people to each eat one gyro?

2. On average Elizabeth reads 82 pages of her book each night. If her book is 548 pages, how long will it take her to read the entire book?
3. A pet store sells goldfish for $0.30 each. Alesha bought 12 goldfish. How much did she spend at the pet store?
4. A pumpkin pie recipe calls for 2 cups of sugar. How much sugar is needed to make 4 pumpkin pies?

Lesson 6-7

Pages 266–267

Use any strategy to solve each problem.

1. Olinda, Danica, and Kimi each like different flavors of ice cream. The flavors they like are vanilla, chocolate, and strawberry. Danica does not like vanilla. Kimi does not like chocolate or vanilla. What type of ice cream does each girl like?
2. A store is selling a television at a clearance price. The clearance price of the television is listed with its original price. If the store sold 7 televisions, what was the total difference between selling them at clearance price and selling them at regular price?

3. Yasu is painting eggs for the local egg hunt. He can paint 3 eggs in 20 minutes. How many eggs can he paint in 1 hour and 40 minutes?

Lesson 7-1

Pages 279–281

Find the mean, median, and mode of each set of data.

1. points scored by a basketball team: 55, 67, 55, 96, 87
2. weight of rocks in pounds: 4, 12, 45, 17, 12
3. cups of flour: 9, 2.5, 4.25, 2.5, 1.75

Lesson 7-2

Pages 282–283

Use any strategy to solve each problem.

1. Henry bought two greeting cards. One card was $0.50 more than the other. The total cost was $7.00. How much did Henry spend for each card?
2. Waban, Josie, and Jacylyn all like different types of books. Josie does not like mysteries or biographies. Jacylyn does not like mysteries or fairytales. Which type of book does each like to read?
3. Wanda wants to drive 300 miles to visit her brother. If she can drive 25 miles on one gallon of gasoline, how many gallons of gasoline will she need to make the trip?

Lesson 7-3

Pages 284–288

Draw a line plot for each set of data. Then find the median, mode, range, and any outliers of the data shown in the line plot.

1.

Student Height in inches for Mrs. Foster's 5th grade class			
52	48	52	51
52	65	58	48
60	45	50	52
56	48	53	58
62	49	51	49

2.

Daily Low Temperatures for January				
23	17	30	20	17
14	22	31	32	22
32	20	8	31	32
33	27	15	32	30
32	28	20	40	27
33	29	18	14	15

3.

Distances of Paper Airplanes (ft)					
1	5	5	8	3	2
1	4	3	3	6	9
0	2	2	6	3	1
4	7	5	2	4	8

4.

Number of Birds Counted			
30	20	18	22
20	18	21	23
20	20	21	19
18	19	20	23

Lesson 7-4

Pages 289–292

The following are speed limits for different roads located in a city's limits:

55, 35, 25, 25, 35, 45, 40, 40, 25, 20, 25, 50, 35, 40, 25, 25

1. Make a frequency table of the data.
2. Find the median, mode, and range of the data. Identify any outliers.

Lesson 7-5

Pages 294–298

The table shows the cost of athletic shoes.

Athletic Shoe Prices (in dollars)				
75	60	60	110	60
100	90	90	85	45
90	75	65	65	55
60	85	110	60	80

1. Choose an appropriate scale and interval size for a frequency table that will represent the sales. Describe the intervals.
2. Create a frequency table using the scale and interval size you described.
3. Write a sentence or two to describe how the prices are distributed among the intervals.

Lesson 7-6

Pages 299–303

The table shows the number of each type of pie sold at a restaurant during lunch.

Pie Sales	
Flavor	**Number**
cherry pie	3
pumpkin pie	8
pecan pie	7
raspberry pie	6
apple pie	10

1. Make a bar graph of the data. Describe the scale and interval size that you used.
2. Which pie was purchased the most?
3. Which pie represents the median number sold? Explain.

For Exercises 4 and 5, use the bar graph below.

4. Based on the graph below, which state has about twice the area as Kansas? Which state is about $\frac{1}{3}$ the size of Texas?

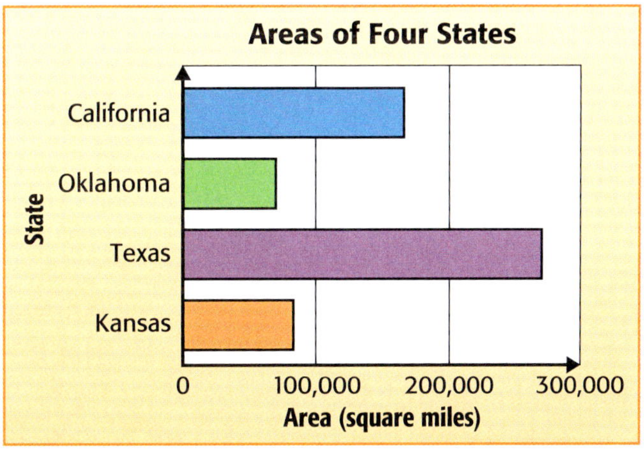

5. About how many more people live in California than Oklahoma?

Extra Practice

Lesson 7-7

Pages 306–310

The table shows the amount of growth of two sunflower plants Juanita grew for her science fair project.

Sunflower growth control plant													
Week	0	1	2	3	4	5	6	7	8	9	10	11	12
Height (inches)	0	7	14	27	40	52	68	82	90	99	100	101	101
Sunflower growth experimental plant													
Height (inches)	0	3	10	15	18	21	24	28	28	28	32	32	32

1. Make a double line graph of the data.
2. What is the scale of each axis?
3. Would your scale be different if you only had the top data to graph? Explain.
4. Write a sentence or two for each line describing the changes over time.
5. Give a possible explanation for the differences between the two lines.

Lesson 7-8

Pages 312–317

Which type of graph would you use to display the data in each table? Write *line plot, bar graph, double bar graph, line graph, double line graph*, or *pictograph*. Explain why. Then make the graph.

1.

Students' Favorite Drinks In School Cafeteria	
White Milk	157
Chocolate Milk	93
Water	45
Orange Juice	140
Apple Juice	65

2.

Neighborhood Pets	Cats	Dogs
House 1	2	0
House 2	0	3
House 3	1	2
House 4	2	2
House 5	3	0
House 6	0	1
House 7	0	0
House 8	3	1

3. You want to show your friends how easy it is to save money and what happens to that money over time. Which type of graph would be best to display the data? Explain.
4. Orlando took a survey of his classmates' favorite cafeteria food. What type of graph should he use if he wants to present the data to the principal? Explain.

Lesson 7-9

Pages 320–321

Solve by using a graph.

1. The table shows the number of books read by students during the summer. What was the most common number of books to read? How can you determine the smallest amount of books read just by looking at the graph? What kind of graph did you make?

Number of Books Read					
5	4	1	6	7	4
3	2	3	1	4	2
2	1	3	4	5	9
2	4	5	3	3	4

2. Ty wrote down the amount of time that he read on school nights. What day was the peak of his reading? What kind of graph did you make? How can you determine the peak of his reading just by looking at the graph?

Day of the Week	Sunday	Monday	Tuesday	Wednesday	Thursday
Time (hours)	2	1.5	3.5	2.5	1

Lesson 8-1

Pages 333–335

Represent each situation using a fraction. Then solve.

1. Seven gallons of water are needed to wash 9 cars. How much water was needed to wash each car?
2. Three tons of sand is put into 4 volleyball courts. How many tons of sand did each court receive?
3. One pizza is divided between 6 people. How much pizza did each person receive?
4. Twenty six bags of soil are used to fill in 6 holes. How many bags of soil does each hole use?

Lesson 8-2

Pages 338–342

Write each improper fraction as a mixed number.

1. $\frac{6}{5}$	**2.** $\frac{7}{2}$	**3.** $\frac{19}{8}$	**4.** $\frac{42}{5}$
5. $\frac{27}{7}$	**6.** $\frac{15}{4}$	**7.** $\frac{8}{7}$	**8.** $\frac{21}{8}$
9. $\frac{10}{3}$	**10.** $\frac{44}{6}$	**11.** $\frac{11}{3}$	**12.** $\frac{38}{5}$

Lesson 8-3

Pages 344–345

Solve by *using logical reasoning*.

1. In a class of 30 students, 18 say their favorite subject is math, 5 say their favorite subject is social studies, and 3 say they love both math and social studies. How many students have favorite subjects other than math or social studies?
2. In a school of 500 students, 185 students are in the band, 300 are on sports teams, and 160 participate in both activities. How many students are involved in either band or sports?
3. There were six dogs, four cats, and two snakes in a vet's office. Two people owned a cat and dog, and one person owned a dog and snake. If no one else owned multiple animals, how many people were in the office?

Lesson 8-4

Pages 346–348

Write each mixed number as an improper fraction.

1. $6\frac{1}{2}$	**2.** $4\frac{2}{3}$	**3.** $9\frac{5}{7}$	**4.** $7\frac{4}{9}$
5. $2\frac{5}{8}$	**6.** $5\frac{2}{13}$	**7.** $2\frac{3}{5}$	**8.** $4\frac{7}{8}$
9. $3\frac{7}{12}$	**10.** $1\frac{5}{6}$	**11.** $13\frac{5}{12}$	**12.** $5\frac{1}{4}$

13. Ines can make $4\frac{1}{3}$ necklaces out of one bag of beads. Write this number as an improper fraction.

Lesson 8-5

Pages 350–353

Replace each ● with < or > to make a true statement.

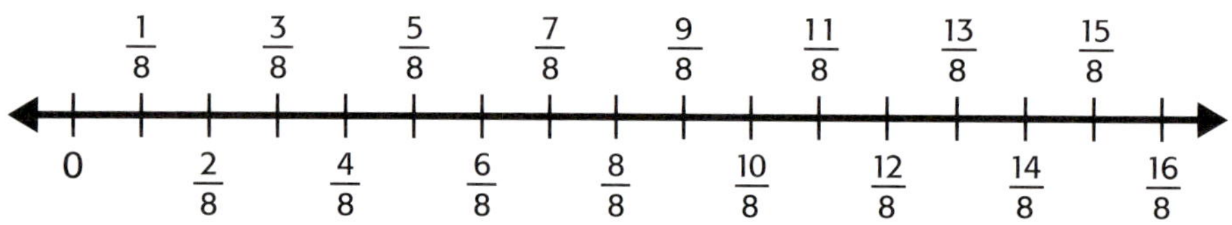

1. $\frac{5}{8}$ ● $\frac{3}{8}$ **2.** $2\frac{4}{8}$ ● $2\frac{2}{8}$ **3.** $10\frac{7}{8}$ ● $10\frac{5}{8}$

Replace each ● with < or > to make a true statement.

4. $\frac{6}{9}$ ● $\frac{4}{9}$ **5.** $\frac{9}{5}$ ● $3\frac{5}{9}$ **6.** $10\frac{3}{4}$ ● $2\frac{1}{3}$

5. $\frac{2}{3}$ ● $\frac{1}{2}$ **6.** $2\frac{5}{8}$ ● $1\frac{1}{4}$ **7.** $\frac{21}{3}$ ● $7\frac{1}{8}$

8. Ricky said he could make $\frac{4}{5}$ of the baskets he shot at practice. Omar said he could make $\frac{6}{7}$ of the baskets he shot. Who claimed to make more baskets at practice?

Lesson 8-6

Pages 356–359

State whether each fraction is closest to 0, $\frac{1}{2}$, or 1.

1. $\frac{7}{9}$

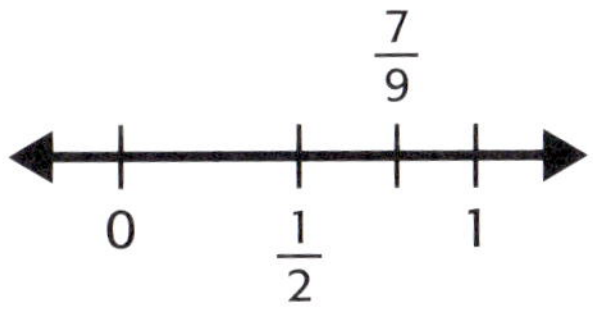

2. $\frac{1}{5}$

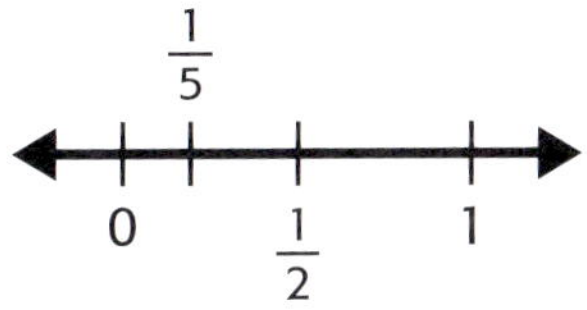

Round each fraction to 0, $\frac{1}{2}$, or 1.

3. $\frac{4}{13}$ **4.** $\frac{5}{7}$ **5.** $\frac{12}{15}$ **6.** $\frac{8}{12}$

7. $\frac{7}{11}$ **8.** $\frac{6}{10}$ **9.** $\frac{15}{17}$ **10.** $\frac{1}{16}$

11. Lewis has finished running $\frac{5}{8}$ of a mile. Has he run half a mile or almost all of a mile?

Lesson 8-7

Pages 360–361

Use any strategy to solve each problem.

1. Billiards players use the dots on the edge of the table to guide their shots. If there are 6 dots on each side of the table and 3 dots on each end, how many total dots are there around the perimeter of the billiards table?

2. What two positive integers have a sum of 17 and a product of 72?

3. A salesperson at a department store makes the following commissions. In one day, the sales person sold 8 shirts, 3 pairs of pants, and 4 pairs of shoes. How much did the salesperson make in commissions on that day?

Article of Clothing	Commission
Shirt	\$2
Pants	\$4
Shoes	\$7

Lesson 9-1

Pages 373–375

Find the common factors of each set of numbers.

1. 7, 28 **2.** 12, 40 **3.** 6, 30 **4.** 27, 45

Find the GCF of each set of numbers.

5. 6, 18 **6.** 20, 24 **7.** 44, 12 **8.** 35, 14

9. There are 36 dogs and 48 cats in a pet show. The show planner wants to put an equal number of dogs and cats in each row. What is the greatest number of cats that can be in each row?

Lesson 9-2

Pages 378–381

Tell whether each number is *prime* or *composite*.

1. 12 **2.** 23 **3.** 28 **4.** 30

5. 55 **6.** 43 **7.** 17 **8.** 62

9. Kaya wants to arrange her 12 field hockey trophies on a shelf. How many different ways can she arrange her trophies so an equal number of trophies are in each row? List the ways.

10. What is the only even prime number?

Lesson 9-3

Pages 382–384

Find two fractions that are equivalent to each fraction.

1. $\frac{6}{7}$ **2.** $\frac{3}{9}$ **3.** $\frac{8}{9}$ **4.** $\frac{3}{10}$

5. $\frac{6}{18}$ **6.** $\frac{8}{14}$ **7.** $\frac{4}{20}$ **8.** $\frac{7}{8}$

9. Khalid wants to buy $\frac{24}{32}$ of a yard of chain. How many fourths of a yard is this?

10. A craft project takes $\frac{16}{24}$ of a yard of fabric. Ito wants to buy enough for one project. The store only sells fabric in thirds. How many thirds should Ito buy?

Lesson 9-4

Pages 386–389

Write each fraction in simplest form. If the fraction is already in simplest form, write *simplified*.

1. $\frac{4}{6}$ **2.** $\frac{4}{10}$ **3.** $\frac{9}{21}$ **4.** $\frac{8}{12}$

5. $\frac{12}{32}$ **6.** $\frac{17}{35}$ **7.** $\frac{20}{45}$ **8.** $\frac{6}{42}$

9. $\frac{22}{44}$ **10.** $\frac{9}{12}$ **11.** $\frac{5}{15}$ **12.** $\frac{10}{25}$

13. Victoria has 16 white socks, 10 pink socks, 4 green socks and 6 blue socks in her drawer. Express in simplest form the fraction of socks in her drawer that are white; pink; blue.

14. Marta and Nicki were sharing a pizza. Marta wanted $\frac{1}{4}$ of the pizza and Nicki wanted $\frac{3}{8}$ of the pizza. Should they get the pizza cut into 4 or 8 pieces? How many pieces would each girl get?

Lesson 9-5

Pages 391–393

Write each decimal as a fraction in simplest form.

1. 0.5 **2.** 0.7 **3.** 0.13 **4.** 0.75

5. 0.321 **6.** 0.340 **7.** 0.08 **8.** 0.50

9. In 1911, Ty Cobbs' batting average was 0.420. Write this rate as a fraction in simplest form.

Lesson 9-6

Pages 394–395

Solve. Use the *look for a pattern* strategy.

1. Look at the pattern below.

17, 58, 99, 140

Describe the rule for determining the last 3 numbers shown in this pattern.

2. Mrs. Hintz's fifth grade class is raising money for the American Red Cross. They raise $66 the first week. The next two weeks are shown on the table. If this pattern continues, how much should the class expect to raise in the fourth week?

Week	1	2	3
Amount raised ($)	66	87	108

3. Jalen's test scores are continually improving. Here is a record of four of his first five tests. Based on the pattern, what was his third test score?

Test 1	Test 2	Test 3	Test 4	Test 5
63	69	■	81	87

Lesson 9-7

Pages 396–399

List multiples to find the first two common multiples of each pair of numbers.

1. 3 and 6 **2.** 4 and 16 **3.** 5 and 20 **4.** 7 and 14

Find the LCM of each set of numbers.

5. 4 and 5 **6.** 7 and 9 **7.** 4, 6, and 8 **8.** 7 and 15

9. The ages of Mrs. Thorne's children are 6, 8, and 12. What is the least common multiple of their ages?

Lesson 9-8

Pages 400–401

Use any strategy to solve each problem.

1. Brad, Landon, and Amanda each play different sports. Amanda does not play baseball or tennis. Landon does not play basketball or baseball. What sport does each person play?
2. A DNA strip follows this pattern: TCTTCGTCTTCGT _ _ _ What three letters finish the pattern?
3. A total of 42 students were on the quiz bowl team. There were twice as many boys as girls. How many girls were on the team?

Lesson 9-9

Pages 404–407

Compare each pair of fractions using models or the LCD.

1. $\frac{1}{2}$ and $\frac{5}{6}$
2. $\frac{3}{8}$ and $\frac{1}{12}$
3. $\frac{1}{2}$ and $\frac{3}{10}$
4. $\frac{1}{3}$ and $\frac{4}{7}$

Replace each ● with <, >, or = to make a true statement.

5. $\frac{3}{4}$ ● $\frac{2}{3}$
6. $\frac{5}{8}$ ● $\frac{10}{16}$
7. $\frac{3}{8}$ ● $\frac{1}{3}$
8. $\frac{5}{9}$ ● $\frac{7}{12}$
9. Mr. Torres assigned thirty math problems for homework. Aisha worked for $\frac{1}{3}$ of an hour, Taro worked for $\frac{2}{5}$ of an hour, and Lucas worked for $\frac{1}{2}$ of an hour. Who worked the longest on the math homework?
10. Marcela made punch for the class party. She used $\frac{2}{3}$ quart of orange juice and $\frac{3}{4}$ quart of grape juice. Did she use more orange juice or more grape juice? Explain.

Lesson 10-1

Pages 423–425

Add. Write each sum in the simplest form.

1. $\frac{3}{6} + \frac{5}{6}$
2. $\frac{7}{15} + \frac{11}{15}$
3. $\frac{2}{8} + \frac{4}{8}$
4. $\frac{2}{4} + \frac{4}{4}$
5. $\frac{7}{5} + \frac{2}{5}$
6. $\frac{7}{13} + \frac{3}{13}$
7. $\frac{2}{9} + \frac{7}{9}$
8. $\frac{11}{20} + \frac{17}{20}$
9. Mr. Chang and his daughter Ping were building shelves for her room. One day they worked $\frac{2}{3}$ of an hour, and the second day they worked twice as long. How much total time did they work on the shelves?
10. Delmar was mixing paint to use on a school project. He mixed $\frac{3}{4}$ gallon of white paint, $\frac{3}{4}$ gallon of red paint, and $\frac{2}{4}$ gallon of yellow paint. How much total paint did Delmar have?

Lesson 10-2

Pages 428–431

Subtract. Write each difference in simplest form. Check your answer by using fraction tiles or drawing a picture.

1. $\frac{3}{6} - \frac{2}{6}$
2. $\frac{12}{15} - \frac{11}{15}$
3. $\frac{7}{8} - \frac{4}{8}$
4. $\frac{3}{4} - \frac{1}{4}$
5. $\frac{7}{5} - \frac{2}{5}$
6. $\frac{7}{13} - \frac{3}{13}$
7. $\frac{9}{9} - \frac{7}{9}$
8. $\frac{19}{20} - \frac{11}{20}$
9. $\frac{15}{16} - \frac{3}{16}$
10. Ken runs $\frac{3}{8}$ of a mile. Isabel runs $\frac{5}{8}$ of a mile in the same time. How much farther does Isabel run?

Lesson 10-3

Pages 434–436

Add. Write in simplest form.

1. $\frac{5}{14} + \frac{1}{7}$
2. $\frac{1}{3} + \frac{1}{2}$
3. $\frac{2}{9} + \frac{1}{3}$
4. $\frac{1}{2} + \frac{3}{4}$
5. $\frac{1}{4} + \frac{3}{12}$
6. $\frac{9}{12} + \frac{13}{24}$
7. $\frac{8}{15} + \frac{2}{3}$
8. $\frac{5}{14} + \frac{11}{28}$
9. $\frac{7}{16} + \frac{3}{4}$
10. Ahmed ate $\frac{2}{5}$ of the cookies and Sarah ate $\frac{1}{3}$ of the cookies. What fraction of the cookies were eaten altogether?

Lesson 10-4

Pages 439–441

Subtract. Write in simplest form.

1. $\frac{13}{20} - \frac{3}{10}$
2. $\frac{5}{9} - \frac{1}{3}$
3. $\frac{5}{8} - \frac{2}{5}$
4. $\frac{3}{4} - \frac{1}{2}$
5. $\frac{7}{8} - \frac{3}{16}$
6. $\frac{2}{3} - \frac{1}{6}$
7. $\frac{9}{16} - \frac{1}{2}$
8. $\frac{5}{8} - \frac{11}{20}$
9. $\frac{9}{12} - \frac{2}{3}$
10. Terrell finished $\frac{4}{9}$ of his report on Wednesday and $\frac{1}{3}$ of his report on Thursday. What fraction of the report does Terrell have left to finish?

Lesson 10-5

Pages 442–443

Solve. Determine which answer is reasonable.

1. Teak wants to buy a new skateboard with special wheels. The skateboard costs \$38.45, the wheels cost \$8.95, and the tools needed to install them are \$10.49. Which is a more reasonable estimate for the money Teak needs to save: \$55, \$60, or \$65?
2. A shoe store had a total of 3,868 pairs of shoes in stock. A week later, 997 pairs of shoes were sold. Which is a more reasonable estimate for the number of pairs of shoes remaining in the store: 3,000 or 2,500?
3. After school, Trina spends $\frac{2}{4}$ of an hour cleaning her room, $\frac{3}{4}$ of an hour practicing the flute, and $\frac{3}{4}$ of an hour doing her homework. Which is a more reasonable estimate for the amount of time she has spent working: 1 hour, 2 hours or 3 hours?

Lesson 10-6

Pages 444–446

Estimate.

1. $3\frac{4}{9} + 7\frac{2}{9}$
2. $10\frac{3}{11} - 4\frac{2}{11}$
3. $5\frac{7}{12} + 7\frac{2}{3}$
4. $10\frac{2}{11} - 3\frac{3}{22}$
5. $7\frac{5}{6} - 4\frac{1}{6}$
6. $7\frac{7}{15} + 4\frac{6}{15}$
7. $6\frac{5}{8} - 5\frac{1}{4}$
8. $19\frac{1}{15} + 11\frac{1}{15}$
9. $4\frac{5}{7} - 1\frac{6}{7}$
10. Clarissa's first long jump attempt was $4\frac{5}{6}$ feet. Her second attempt was $5\frac{1}{2}$ feet. About how much longer was Clarissa's second attempt?

Lesson 10-7

Pages 448–451

Add. Write each sum in simplest form. Check your answer by using fraction tiles or drawing a picture.

1. $2\frac{4}{7} + 6\frac{2}{7}$
2. $8\frac{1}{3} + 2\frac{2}{9}$
3. $3\frac{7}{10} + 5\frac{4}{5}$
4. $6\frac{1}{5} + 12\frac{9}{20}$
5. $1\frac{1}{8} + 2\frac{5}{8}$
6. $7\frac{7}{17} + 6\frac{6}{17}$
7. $4\frac{1}{2} + 3\frac{2}{10}$
8. $17\frac{1}{13} + 13\frac{1}{13}$
9. $2\frac{4}{6} + 1\frac{2}{3}$
10. Mr. Woods needs $1\frac{3}{4}$ pounds of ground beef to make hamburgers and $2\frac{1}{2}$ pounds to make meatloaf. How much ground beef does Mr. Woods need altogether?

Lesson 10-8

Pages 452–454

Subtract. Write each difference in simplest form. Check your answer by using fraction tiles or drawing a picture.

1. $7\frac{9}{10} - 4\frac{7}{10}$ **2.** $10\frac{4}{7} - 2\frac{3}{7}$ **3.** $9\frac{2}{3} - 7\frac{7}{12}$

4. $16\frac{1}{3} - 12\frac{4}{27}$ **5.** $7\frac{5}{9} - 2\frac{4}{9}$ **6.** $7\frac{7}{19} - 6\frac{6}{19}$

7. The average rainfall in Abilene for the month of August is $2\frac{4}{5}$ inches. The average rainfall in Zapata is $1\frac{7}{10}$ inches. What is the difference in the average amount of rainfall between the two cities?

Lesson 10-9

Pages 456–457

Use any strategy to solve each problem.

1. A one topping pizza with eight slices costs $6. If the cost per slice remains the same, how much would a one topping pizza with fourteen slices cost?

2. What is the next figure in the pattern? → ← ↑ ↓ →

3. At the Henderson's garage sale, they are selling T-shirts for $0.80 each and bicycles for $15.50 each. If someone bought 3 T-shirts and 1 bicycle, how much did they spend at the garage sale?

Lesson 10-10

Pages 458–461

Subtract. Write each difference in simplest form. Check your answer by using fraction tiles or drawing a picture.

1. $9\frac{2}{6} - 5\frac{5}{6}$ **2.** $8\frac{4}{9} - 6\frac{7}{9}$ **3.** $5\frac{1}{5} - 1\frac{2}{5}$ **4.** $7\frac{1}{3} - 3\frac{2}{3}$

5. $13 - 10\frac{5}{8}$ **6.** $15\frac{1}{4} - 12\frac{3}{4}$ **7.** $10\frac{3}{7} - 5\frac{5}{7}$ **8.** $15 - 11\frac{7}{10}$

9. Hala's dog Max weighs $45\frac{3}{8}$ pounds. Berto's dog Teddy weighs $23\frac{5}{8}$ pounds. How much more does Max weigh than Teddy?

Lesson 11-1

Pages 477–480

Complete.

1. 4 ft = ■ in. **2.** 14 yd = ■ in. **3.** 39 ft = ■ yd

4. 132 in. = ■ ft. **5.** 24 yd 3 ft = ■ ft **6.** 8 ft 24 in. = ■ ft

7. The beluga whale grows to be about 15 feet in length. What is the length of the whale in yards? In inches?

Lesson 11-2

Pages 482–483

Solve. Use the *draw a diagram* strategy.

1. Jai is taking her dog for a walk. She leaves the house, turns left and walks three blocks. Then she turns right, walks three blocks, turns left, walks 2 more blocks, then turns left again and walks 5 blocks. How far from home is she?

2. Mr. Costa is making cookies for a party. He has two cookie sheets. One is 14 inches wide by 16 inches long and the other is 12 inches by 18 inches. If each cookie is 2 inches in diameter and he places them 1 inch apart, which cookie sheet holds more cookies?

Lesson 11-3

Pages 484–487

Complete.

1. 80 oz = ■ lb
2. 3 T = ■ lb
3. 12 lb = ■ oz
4. 3,000 lb = ■ T ■ lb
5. 23 lb 48 oz = ■ lb
6. 144 oz = ■ lb
7. Mrs. Wilson needs 240 ounces of potatoes for her school potluck dinner. How many pounds of potatoes does she need?

Lesson 11-4

Pages 488–490

Complete.

1. 6 c = ■ fl oz
2. 6 gal = ■ fl oz
3. 34 c = ■ pt
4. 8 qt = ■ gal
5. 5 qt 3 c = ■ c
6. 16 pt = ■ qt
7. 9 c = ■ pt ■ c
8. 7 gal = ■ qt
9. 22 fl oz = ■ c ■ fl oz
10. Alvar's mother brought home 24 bottles of water. Each bottle contained 20 ounces. How many quarts of water did she bring home?
11. Mr. Chen's car holds $12\frac{1}{2}$ gallons of gasoline. How many quarts is this? How many fluid ounces?

Lesson 11-5

Pages 492–495

Complete.

1. 660 s = ■ min
2. 3 wk = ■ d
3. 1,825 d = ■ y
4. 1,990 s = ■ min ■ s
5. 240 min = ■ h
6. 3,211 d = ■ wk ■ d
7. The average lifespan of a Border Collie is 13 years. The average lifespan of a Jack Russell Terrier is 163 months. On average, which breed of dog lives longer? How much longer?

Lesson 11-6

Pages 496–497

Use any strategy to solve each problem.

1. Mount Kilimanjaro, the highest mountain in Tanzania, is 5,895 meters tall. Mount Meru, which is near Kilimanjaro, is 4,566 meters tall. What is the difference in height between the two?
2. Tory's cow is 3 times heavier than Tom's. If Tory's cow weighs 840 pounds, how much does Tom's cow weigh?
3. Marla and Angelina are hiking. They can hike 6 miles in 2 hours, 9 miles in 3 hours, and 12 miles in 4 hours. How many miles can they hike in 5 hours?
4. Mr. Stevens grades a test with 20 questions. Each correct answer is worth 2 points. Each wrong answer takes one point away from the total. Lana's score is 25. Continue the table to find how many of her answers are correct.

Number Correct	20	19	18
Number Wrong	0	1	2
Total Score	40	37	34

Lesson 11-7

Pages 500–503

Find the elapsed time.

1. 7:00 A.M. to 12:15 P.M.
2. 1:30 P.M. to 8:15 A.M.
3. 4:46 P.M. to 5:39 P.M.
4. 8:04 P.M. to 6:37 A.M.
5. Bryce started babysitting at 6:45 P.M. and finished at 9:54 P.M. How long did he babysit?

Lesson 12-1

Pages 517–521

Complete.

1. 6 cm = ■ mm
2. 4,000 mm = ■ m
3. 700 cm = ■ m
4. 5 m = ■ cm
5. 14,000 mm = ■ m
6. 18 cm = ■ mm

Select an appropriate unit to measure the length of each of the following. Write *millimeter, centimeter, meter*, or *kilometer*.

7. lightpole
8. notebook
9. postage stamp
10. Mira has a cordless phone that allows her to talk up to 20 meters from the base of the phone. Can she continue to talk on the phone while going to her mail box which is 2,200 centimeters away from the base of the phone? Explain.

Extra Practice

Extra Practice

Lesson 12-2

Pages 522–523

Solve. Determine *reasonable* answers.

1. A label on a mountain bike states that the weight of the bike is 100 pounds. Is this label accurate? Explain.
2. Mrs. Cashman estimates that she uses a cup and a half of sugar in her pumpkin pie recipe. Does this seem like a reasonable amount to use? Explain.
3. Parker is at the lumber yard looking at plywood to build a toy chest. The toy chest needs 36 square feet of lumber to build it. The plywood comes in sheets of 4 feet × 8 feet. Parker reasons that 4 sheets of plywood will be just enough. Is this a reasonable assumption? Explain.
4. Shaniqua was measuring her locker to see if her books would fit. She claimed her notebooks were 21 centimeters wide and 30 centimeters long. Is she correct? Explain.

Lesson 12-3

Pages 524–526

Complete.

1. 4 g = ■ mg
2. 9 kg = ■ g
3. 12 g = ■ mg
4. 6,000 g = ■ kg
5. 2,000 mg = ■ kg
6. 1 kg = ■ g
7. Which is a more reasonable estimate for the mass of a stapler: 130 milligrams, 130 grams, or 130 kilograms?
8. A sugar company donated 50 kg of sugar to a local high school. If the sugar was divided into equal bags of 250 g, how many bags are there?

Lesson 12-4

Pages 527–530

Complete.

1. 40 L = ■ mL
2. 8,000 mL = ■ L
3. 7 L = ■ mL
4. 4,000 mL = ■ L
5. 5 L = ■ mL
6. 8 L = ■ mL
7. Which metric unit would you use to measure the capacity of a bath tub?
8. A coffee mug holds 600 milliliters. Find the capacity in liters.
9. Jenn bought 6 bottles of juice that were marked 750 mL. How many liters of juice did she buy?

Lesson 12-5

Pages 533–535

Write an integer to represent each situation. Then graph the integer on a number line.

1. spent $12 on a CD
2. 8 degrees warmer
3. The puppy gained 2 pounds
4. lost $10

Write an integer to represent each situation. Then write its opposite.

5. earned $56 mowing grass
6. scored a three point basket in basketball
7. 40 plants were dead
8. 2 inches of rain in a gauge

Lesson 12-6

Pages 537–541

Choose the more reasonable temperature for each situation.

1. skiing: 56°F or 7°C
2. frozen fish: 40°F or 0°C
3. July 4th in Florida: 18°C or 92°F
4. playing tennis: 5°C or 75°F

The table shows the highest recorded temperatures for several U.S. states.

State	Temperature (°F)	State	Temperature (°F)
Alabama	112	Florida	109
Connecticut	100	Idaho	118
Arizona	128	California	134
Arkansas	120	Texas	120
Colorado	118	Maine	105

Source: Fact Monster

5. How much greater is California's highest temperature than Maine's highest temperature?
6. How much greater is Arizona's highest temperature than Florida's highest temperature?

Extra Practice

Lesson 12-7

Pages 544–545

Use any strategy to solve each problem.

1. Tyler runs for 8 minutes then walks for 4 minutes. How many sets of this pattern will he complete if he exercises for 65 minutes?
2. Tickets for a movie cost \$3 for children and \$5 for adults. The movie took in \$126 in one showing. At that showing there were 12 children. How many adults were there?
3. The Empire State Building is 1,250 ft tall. How many inches is half of the building?
4. Gary claimed that he is older than Diane. Diane is twice as old as Marty. Marty is 3 years short of being half as old as Gary. Is Gary's claim true?

Lesson 13-1

Pages 557–560

Identify each figure. Then name it using symbols.

1. 

2. 

3. 

4. Are these two lines parallel? Explain your answer.

Lesson 13-2

Pages 562–563

Solve. Use *logical reasoning*.

1. If Tiara continues making the figures shown below, how many triangular blocks will be in the fifth figure?

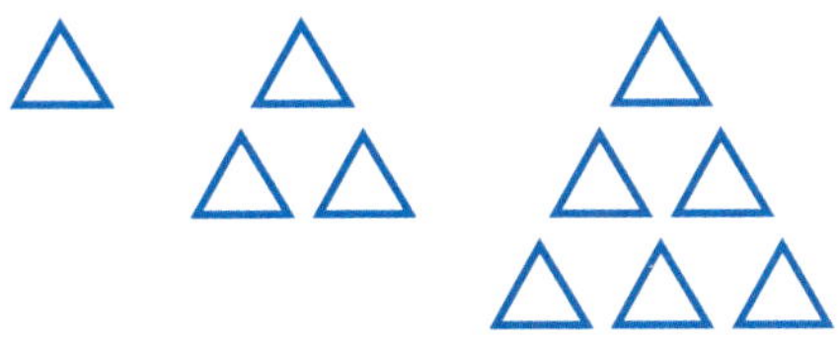

2. Sebastian made 44 more necklaces than Tina made. Together they made 196 necklaces. How many necklaces did Tina make?
3. Quinn, Andy, and Chase are friends with three different hobbies: motocross, art, and skating. Andy has no artistic skill. Chase can not draw or skate. Quinn is a tremendous painter. Who is the friend that rides motocross?
4. There are three fish bowls with five fish in each bowl. Two of the bowls have two orange fish, two bowls have two yellow fish, two bowls have two gold fish and all three have one silver fish. What are the colors of fish in each bowl?

Lesson 13-3

Pages 566–569

Measure the sides of each triangle. Then find the number of congruent sides. State whether any of the sides appear to be perpendicular. Write yes or no.

1. 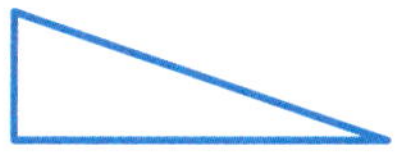

2. 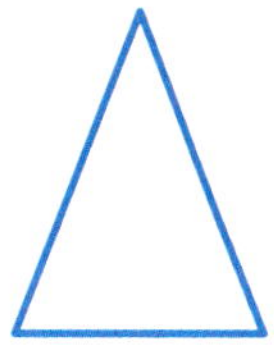

3. 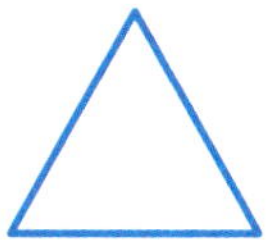

4. 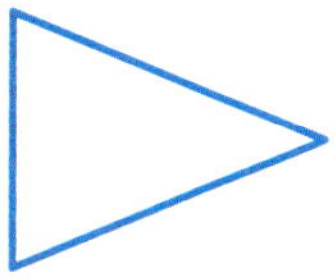

Lesson 13-4

Pages 570–574

Determine whether each statement is *true* or *false*. Explain.

1. Some rhombi are rectangles.
2. Some trapezoids are parallelograms.
3. All parallelograms are rectangles.
4. All squares are rhombi.

Lesson 13-5

Pages 576–577

Use any strategy to solve each problem.

1. Seven trains pass through a town every day. The times for the first four trains are 9:10 A.M., 9:45 A.M., 10:20 A.M., and 10:55 A.M. At what time will the last train of the day pass through the town?
2. There are 12 pieces of red candy in a jar for every 8 pieces of blue candy. If there are 60 pieces of red candy in the jar, how many total pieces of candy are in the jar?
3. Ramous' batting average is 0.050 points higher than Albert's. Albert's average is 0.180 points lower than Rashid's. List the players in order of their batting average from least to greatest.
4. The Fibonacci Sequence is a special mathematical sequence that occurs frequently in nature. The first six numbers of the sequence are 1, 1, 2, 3, 5, and 8. What is the seventh term? The tenth?

Lesson 13-6

Pages 578–581

Graph each figure and the translation described. Then write the ordered pairs for the vertices of the translation image.

1. triangle *XYZ* with vertices *X*(3, 2), *Y*(5, 4), *Z*(2, 6); translated 2 units right
2. quadrilateral *LMNO* with vertices *L*(1, 8), *M*(1, 6), *N*(5, 6), *O*(5, 8); translated 3 units up
3. triangle *KLM* with vertices *K*(2, 5), *L*(4, 7), and *M*(5, 5); translated 3 units right, 4 units down
4. triangle *ABC* with vertices *A*(3, 6), *B*(3, 9), *C*(7, 6); translated 2 units left and 3 units down

Lesson 13-7

Pages 582–585

Graph each figure after a reflection across the line. Then write the ordered pairs for the vertices of the relection image.

1.

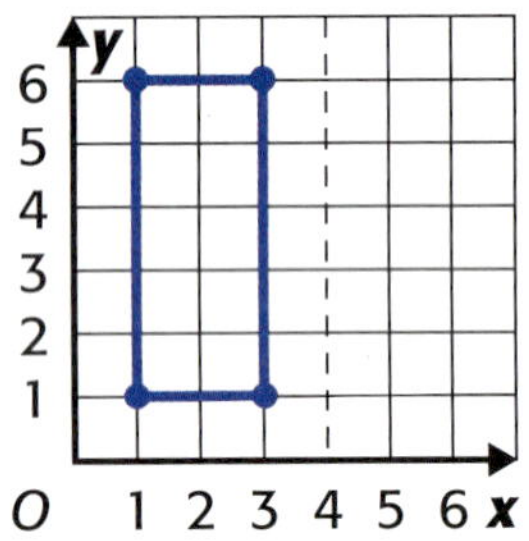

2.

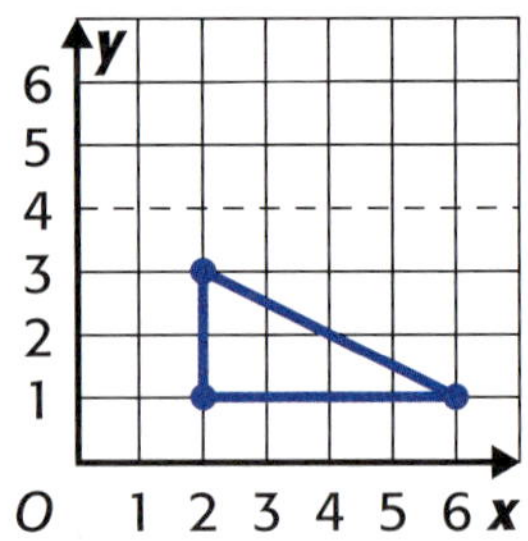

Lesson 13-8

Pages 586–590

Graph the triangle after each rotation. Then write the ordered pairs for the vertices of the rotation image.

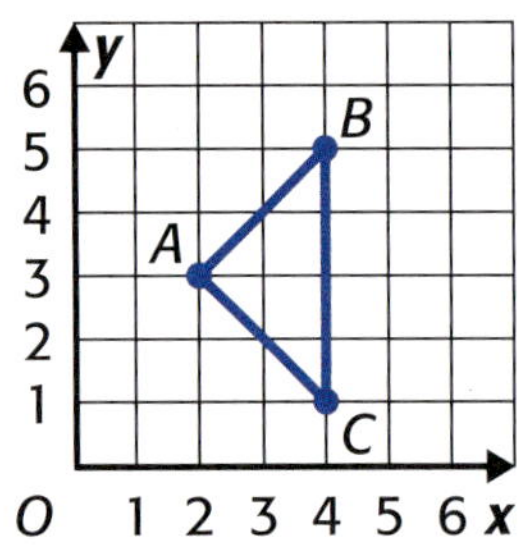

1. 90′ clockwise about point *C*
2. 90′ counterclockwise about point *B*
3. 90′ counterclockwise about point *A*

Lesson 13-9

Pages 591–593

Determine whether each transformation is a *translation*, *reflection*, or *rotation*.

1. 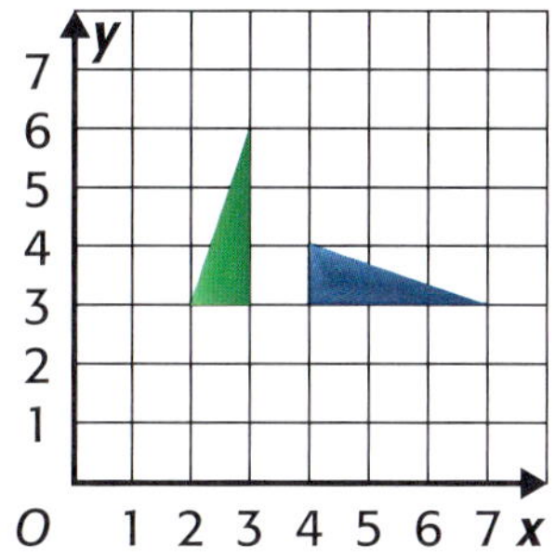

2. 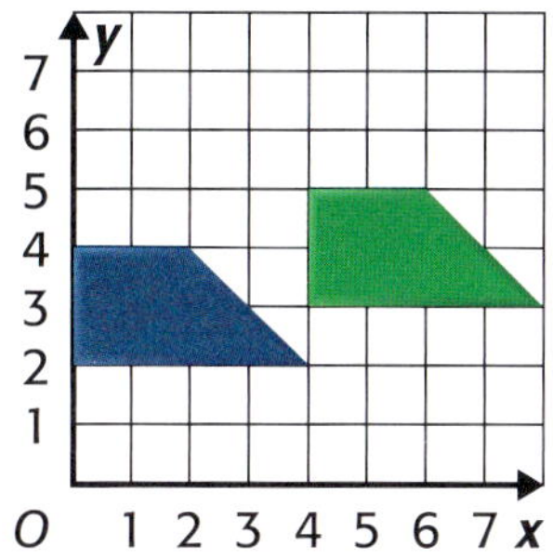

3. 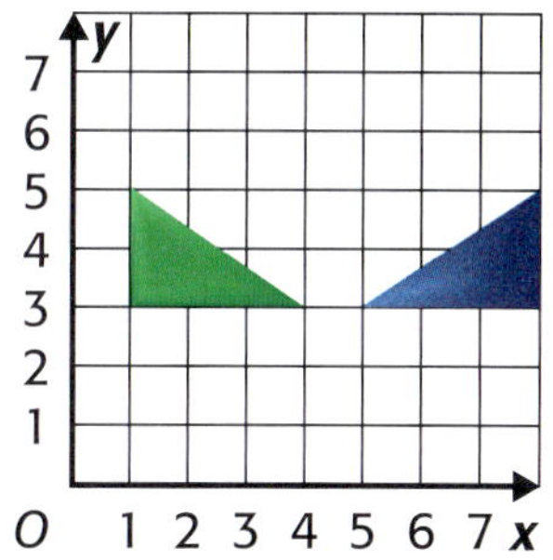

Lesson 14-1

Pages 608–611

Find the perimeter of each figure.

1. 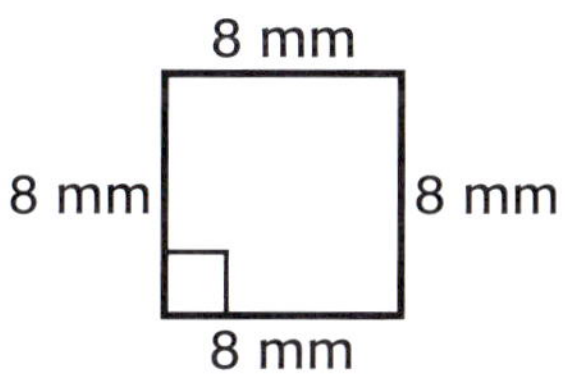

2. 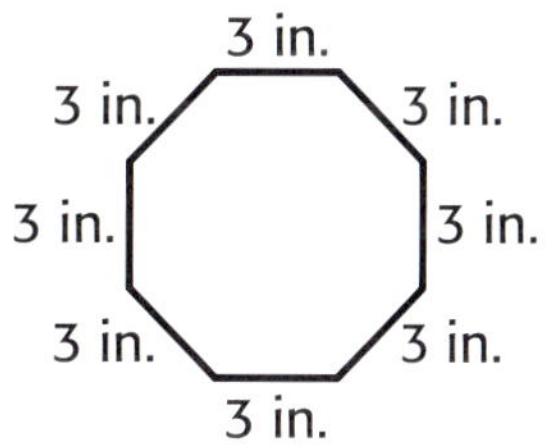

3. 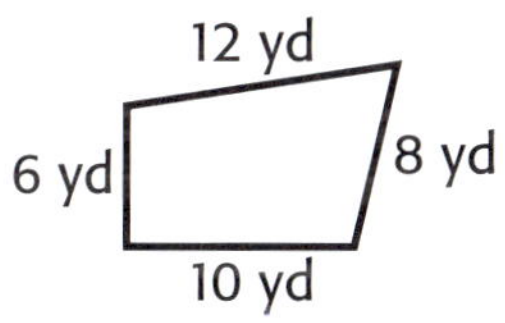

4. 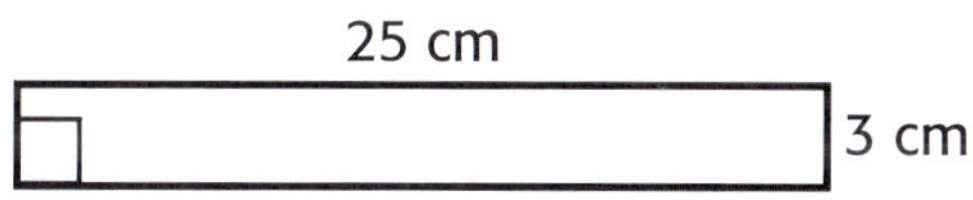

Lesson 14-2

Pages 612–615

Estimate the area of each figure. Each square represents 1 square centimeter.

1. 

2. 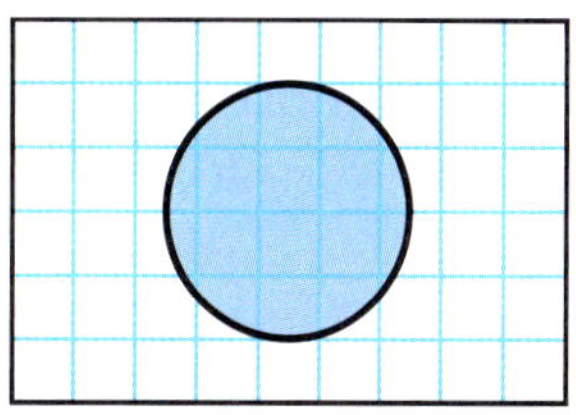

3. 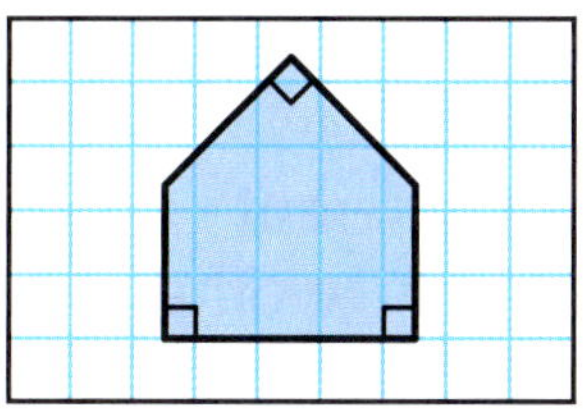

4. 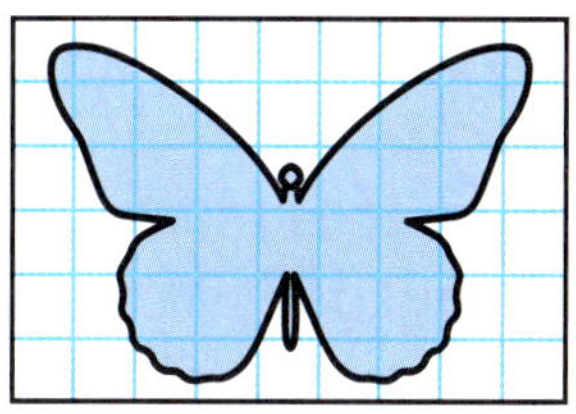

Lesson 14-3

Pages 616–619

Find the area of each rectangle.

1. 

2. 

3. $\ell = 6$ cm
$w = 12$ cm

4. $\ell = 15$ yd
$w = 10$ yd

5. $\ell = 7$ ft
$w = 21$ ft

6. Mrs. Ortega is painting three walls in a room. The walls are 8 feet high and 13 feet long. One gallon of paint will cover 350 ft^2. If she buys one gallon of paint, will she have enough? Explain.

Lesson 14-4

Pages 624–627

Describe parts of each figure that are parallel and congruent. Then identify the figure.

1. 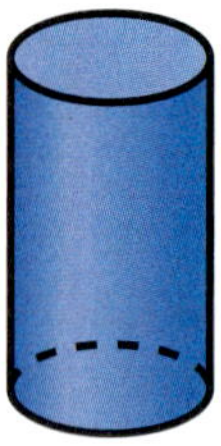

2. 

3. 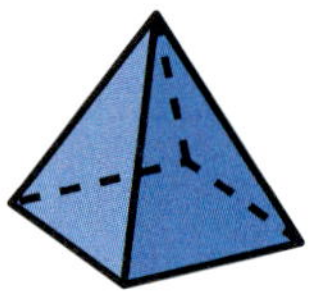

Lesson 14-5

Pages 628–629

Solve. Use the *make a model* strategy

1. Ms. Jacobson is passing out notebooks to her class of 27 students. She has four different colors of notebooks; red, green, blue, and yellow. If she passes out a red notebook to every fourth student, how many red notebooks does she pass out?

2. The students in Mr. Lincoln's gym class were asked to run around three cones placed in a line. The students must run down and back to complete one run. How many times will the students go between the cones in their attempt to complete six runs?

3. Pentominoes are tiles made by placing five squares in different designs. One way to place the squares is in a straight line. Another is to form an L. How many different designs are there?

Lesson 14-6

Pages 631–635

Find the volume of each prism.

1.

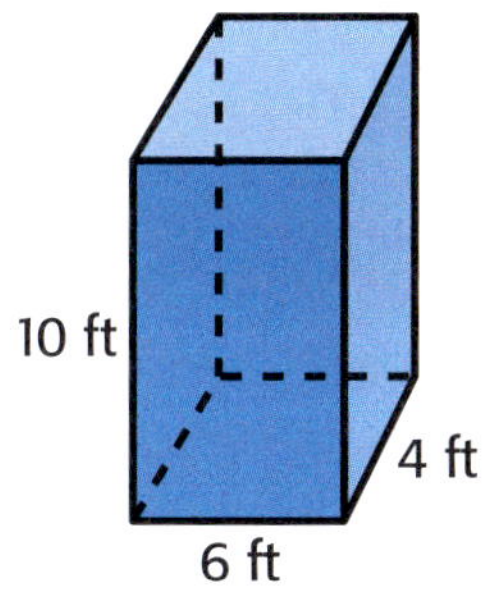

2.

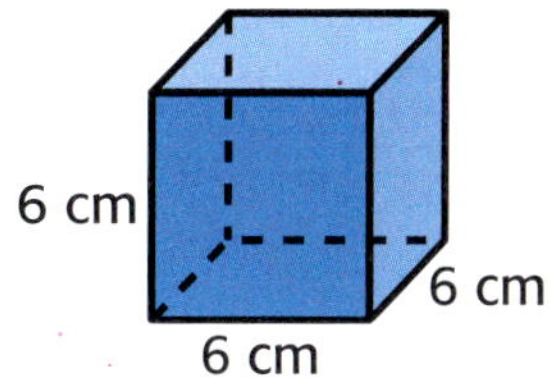

3. Prism A has dimensions of 9 yards × 6 yards × 3 yards and Prism B has dimensions of 3 yards × 2 yards × 1 yard. How much larger is the volume of Prism A than Prism B in cubic feet?

Lesson 14-7

Pages 640–643

Find the surface area of each rectangular prism.

1.

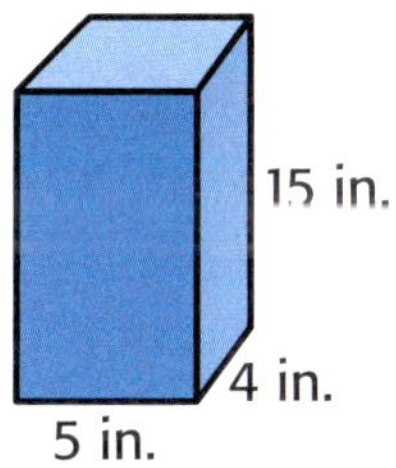

2.

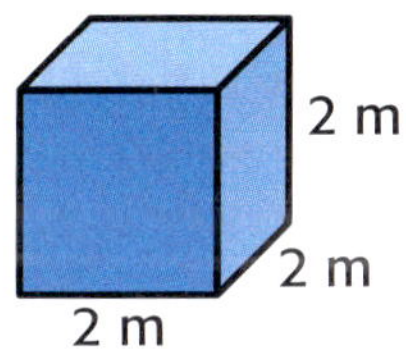

3.

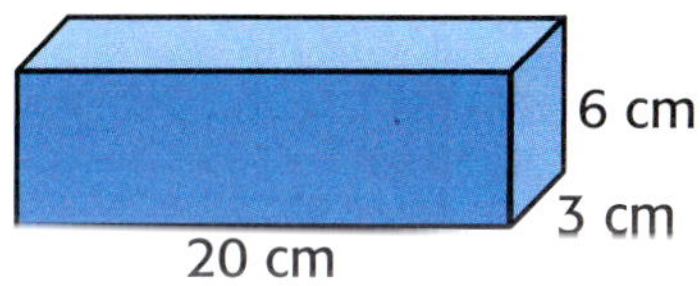

4. Natalie finds the measurements of a rectangular prism. The length is 13 feet, the width is 7 feet, and the height is 9 feet. Find the surface area.

Lesson 14-8

Pages 644–647

Determine whether you need to find the perimeter, area, or volume. Then solve.

1. The basketball team warms up by running around the gym, which is 120 feet by 86 feet. If Chet runs 6 laps, how far has he run?

2. Freda is laying mulch in her garden. The garden is 8 feet by 12 feet and the mulch should be 3 inches deep. How much mulch does she need?

3. Maya wants new carpet for her bedroom. The room is 5 yards wide and 4 yards long. The carpet she wants costs \$23.00 per square yard. How much will it cost to carpet her room?

Lesson 14-9

Pages 648–649

Use any strategy to solve each problem.

1. Tamika has 33 stuffed animals. She gave $\frac{1}{3}$ to her sister and $\frac{1}{2}$ of the rest to charity. She says she has more than 10 stuffed animals left. Is she correct? How many stuffed animals are left?
2. Mr. Ruiz is making cookies. If each batch of cookies requires 14 ounces of milk, how many quarts of milk will he need to make 8 batches?
3. The middle school soccer team had the following record for the past five years. What fraction of the games did they win?

Year	2002	2003	2004	2005	2006
Won	12	10	4	7	13
Lost	3	5	11	8	2

Lesson 15-1

Pages 661–663

List the possible outcomes in each probability experiment.

1. spinning the spinner

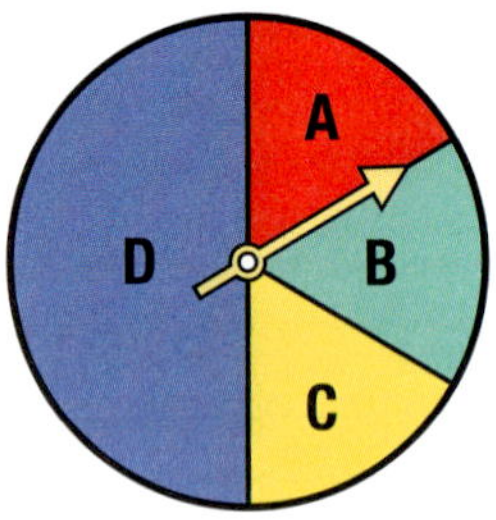

2. choosing one number out of a bowl

3. Sarah randomly chose one letter from the word BEEKEEPER. Which letter did she most likely pick? How likely is it that she chose a vowel?

Lesson 15-2

Pages 668–672

The spinner is spun once. Find the probability of each event. Write as a fraction in simplest form.

1. *P*(1)
2. *P*(2)
3. *P*(prime number)
4. *P*(odd number)

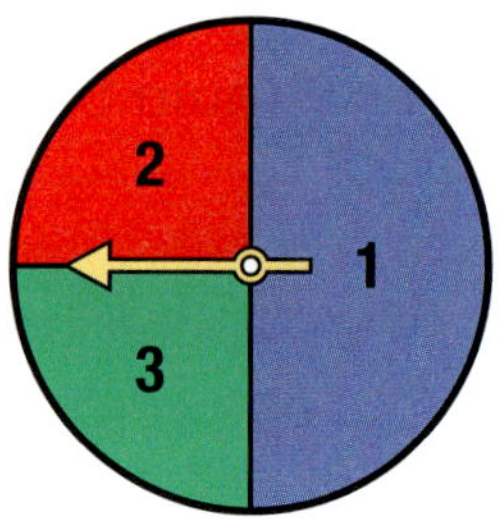

Lesson 15-3

Pages 674–675

Solve by making an organized list.

1. Two years ago, Mr. Braxton counted seven hickory trees in his yard. Last year he counted 14 trees in his yard. This spring he counted 28 hickory trees. In how many years will there be 224 hickory trees?

2. Thomas has four books colored blue, red, green, and yellow. How many different ways can he combine them on a shelf?

Lesson 15-4

Pages 677–680

Two bags each contain three different colored marbles: green, blue, and yellow. Make a tree diagram to show all possible outcomes if you choose a marble from each bag.

1. What is the probability of pulling a green marble from the first bag, then a blue marble from the second bag?

2. What is the probability of pulling a yellow marble from each bag?

3. What is the probability that you will pull the same colored marble from each bag?

Lesson 15-5

Pages 682–683

Use any strategy to solve each problem.

1. Sydney has been randomly tossing a coin. She has landed on heads 16 times and tails 8 times. Based on these results, if she tosses a coin what is the probability that she will land on tails?

2. A train engineer said that he traveled 1,458 miles in his train during a single 8 hour work day. Is his claim reasonable? Explain.

3. Mona is cutting different size pieces of fabric for a quilt. The first piece is 1 inch long, the second piece is 2 inches long, the third piece is 4 inches long, and so on. If she has 55 inches of fabric, how many pieces can she cut, and how long is each piece?

Preparing for Standardized Tests

Throughout the school year, you may be required to take several tests, and you may have many questions about them. Here are some answers to help you get ready.

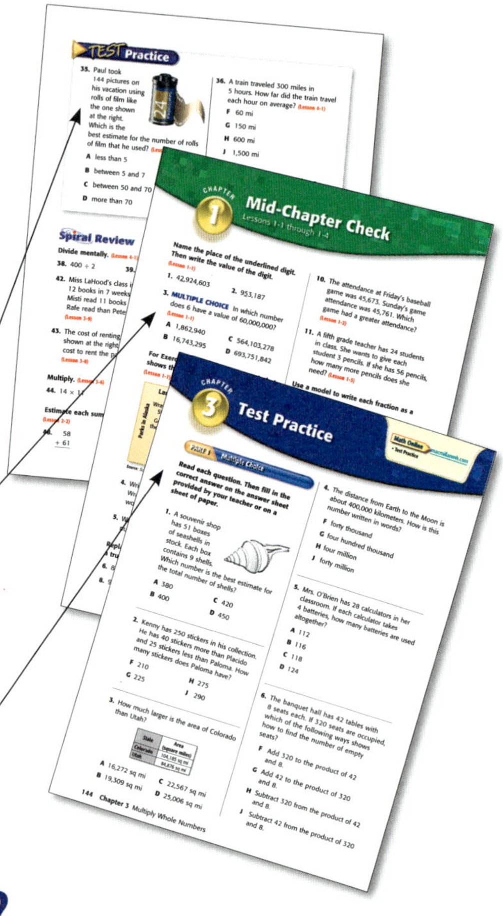

How Should I Study?

The good news is that you've been studying all along– a little bit every day. Here are some of the ways your textbook has been preparing you.

- **Every Day** The lessons had multiple-choice practice questions.
- **Every Week** The Mid-Chapter Check and Chapter Test also had several multiple-choice practice questions.
- **Every Month** The Test Practice pages at the end of each chapter had even more questions, including short-response and extended-response questions.

Are There Other Ways to Review?

Absolutely! The following pages contain even more practice for standardized tests.

Tips for SUCCESS

Before the Test

- Go to bed early the night before the test. You will think more clearly after a good night's rest.
- Become familiar with common measurement units and when they should be used.
- Think positively.

During the Test

- Read each problem carefully. Underline key words and think about different ways to solve the problem.
- Watch for key words like *not.* Also look for order words like *least, greatest, first,* and *last.*
- Answer questions you are sure about first. If you do not know the answer to a question, skip it and go back to that question later.
- Check your answer to make sure that it is reasonable.
- Make sure that the number of the question on the answer sheet matches the number of the question on which you are working in your test booklet.

Whatever you do...

- Don't try to do it all in your head. If no figure is provided, draw one.
- Don't rush. Try to work at a steady pace.
- Don't give up. Some problems may seem hard to you, but you may be able to figure out what to do if you read each question carefully or try another strategy.

Multiple-Choice Questions

Incomplete shading
(A) (B) (C) (D)

Too light shading
(A) (B) (C) (D)

Correct shading
(A) (B) (C) (D)

Multiple-choice questions are the most common type of questions on standardized tests. You are asked to choose the best answer from four possible answers.

To record a multiple-choice answer, you may be asked to shade in a bubble that is a circle or an oval. Always make sure that your shading is dark enough and completely covers the bubble.

Example

1 The table shows the price of cheese per pound at a local farmers' market.

Amount (lb)	Price
1	\$5
2	\$10
3	\$15

If the price increases at the same rate, how much would you pay for 5 pounds of cheese?

A \$35 **B** \$25 **C** \$20 **D** \$15

Read the Problem Carefully You know the price of cheese per pound in dollars. Find how much you will pay if you buy 5 pounds of cheese.

STRATEGY

Patterns Can you find a pattern to solve the problem?

Solve the Problem Look for a pattern. One pound of cheese costs \$5. Two pounds cost \$10. Three pounds cost \$15. So, for each pound of cheese, the price increases by \$5.

Extend the pattern to find the price of five pounds of cheese.

4 pounds → \$15 + \$5 or \$20

5 pounds → \$20 + \$5 or \$25

So, 5 pounds of cheese will cost \$25.

The correct choice is B.

STRATEGY

Key Words When reading a question, look for words such as *not* or *both*.

Example

2 **The shaded part of the figure below represents the fraction $\frac{2}{3}$.**

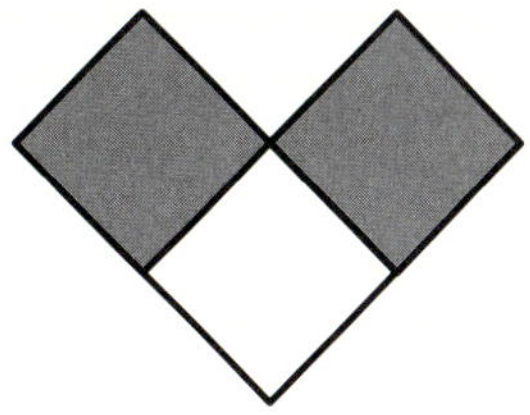

Which fraction is NOT equivalent to $\frac{2}{3}$?

F $\frac{6}{9}$ **G** $\frac{4}{6}$ **H** $\frac{2}{6}$ **J** $\frac{10}{15}$

Read the Problem Carefully You are asked to use the diagram to find which fraction is NOT equivalent to $\frac{2}{3}$.

Solve the Problem Find the fraction that is not equivalent to $\frac{2}{3}$.

$\frac{2}{3} \times \frac{3}{3} = \frac{6}{9}$ ← equivalent

$\frac{2}{3} \times \frac{2}{2} = \frac{4}{6}$ ← equivalent

$\frac{2}{3} \times \frac{1}{2} = \frac{2}{6}$ ← NOT equivalent

$\frac{2}{3} \times \frac{5}{5} = \frac{10}{15}$ ← equivalent

The correct choice is H.

Example

3 **A book has five chapters. Each chapter has 5 more pages than the previous chapter. Chapter 5 has 38 pages. How many pages were in Chapter 2?**

A 18 **B** 23 **C** 25 **D** 33

Read the Problem Carefully You are asked to find the number of pages in Chapter 2. You know how many pages were in Chapter 5.

Solve the Problem You need to find the number of pages in Chapter 2. To find the number of pages, count backward by five.

Chapter 5	38 pages	
Chapter 4	33 pages	−5
Chapter 3	28 pages	−5
Chapter 2	23 pages	−5

The correct choice is B.

STRATEGY

Work Backward Can you work backward from the total to find the unit cost?

Multiple-Choice Practice

DIRECTIONS
Read each question. Choose the best answer.

1. A car wash company charges $8 per car. If 94 cars were washed in one day, how much money would the company collect?

A $752

B $740

C $702

D $688

2. Which fractional part of the model is shaded?

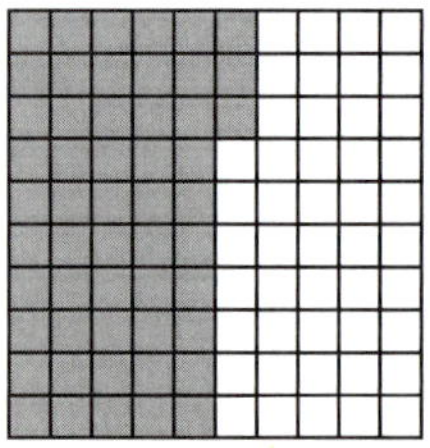

F $\frac{53}{1,000}$ **H** $\frac{53}{10}$

G $\frac{53}{100}$ **J** 53

3. Which group shows all the numbers that are common factors of 24 and 32?

A 1, 2, 4, 8

B 1, 2, 3, 4, 8

C 1, 2, 4, 6, 8

D 1, 2, 4, 8, 12

4. Brittany is having a party on a date in May that is NOT a prime number. Which of the following could be the date of her party?

F May 11 **H** May 21

G May 17 **J** May 31

5. The table shows how much money Mrs. Stoehr spends on bus fare.

Bus Fare	
Number of Weeks	Total Amount Spent ($)
4	48
5	60
6	72
7	84

What is the relationship between the number of weeks and the total amount spent?

A The total amount spent is 12 times the number of weeks.

B The number of weeks is 44 less than the total amount spent.

C The total amount spent is 55 more than the number of weeks.

D The number of weeks is 12 times the total amount spent.

6. Which figure does NOT contain any right angles?

F 

G 

H 

J 

7. Suppose the temperature outside at 5:15 P.M. was 54°F. By midnight, the temperature was 37 °F. How many degrees did the temperature drop by midnight?

A 13°F

B 17°F

C 23°F

D 27°F

8. Which pair of moons shows only a translation?

F

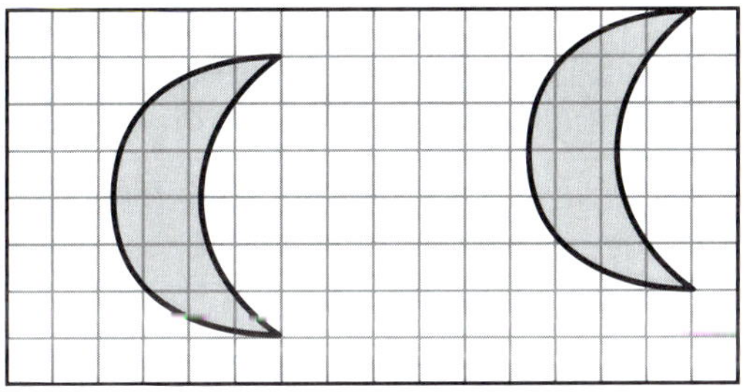

G

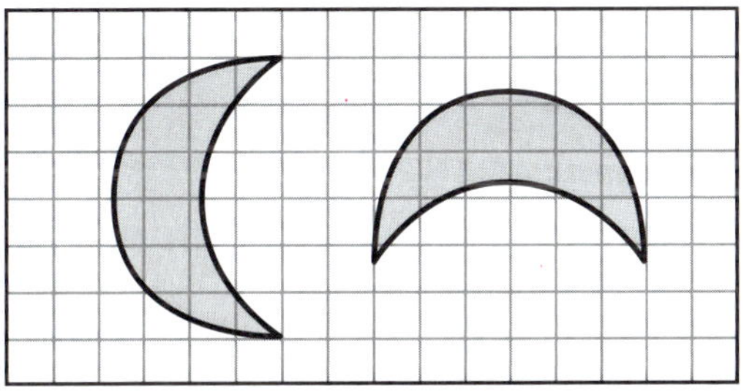

H

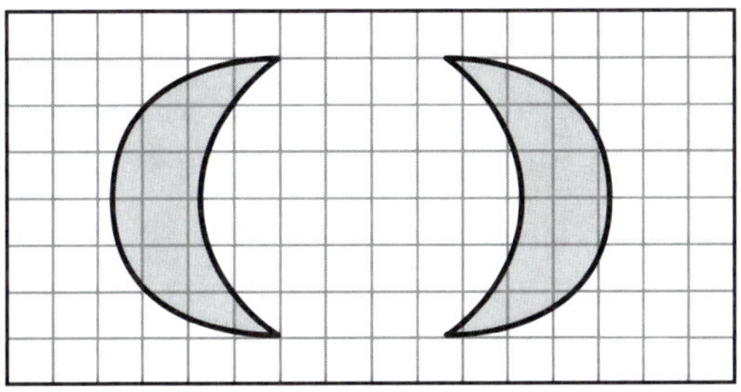

J

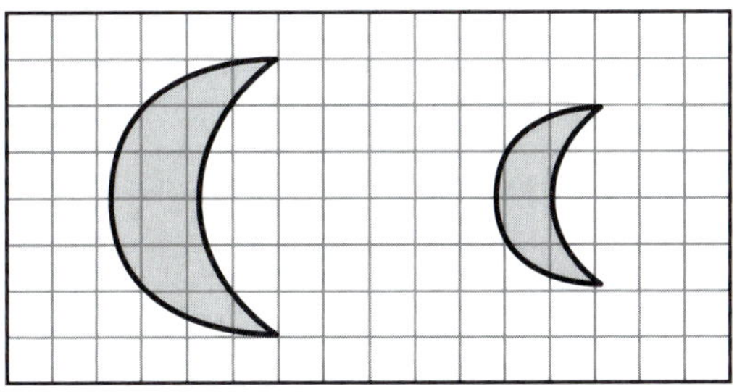

9. What fractional part of a kilogram is a gram?

A $\frac{1}{4}$

B $\frac{1}{10}$

C $\frac{1}{100}$

D $\frac{1}{1,000}$

10. Nico has 10 letter cards that spell the word *ELEMENTARY* when put together. If he picks one card without looking, what is the probability that it will have the letter *E* on it?

F $\frac{3}{10}$

G $\frac{2}{5}$

H $\frac{3}{5}$

J $\frac{7}{10}$

11. Paulo spun each spinner once.

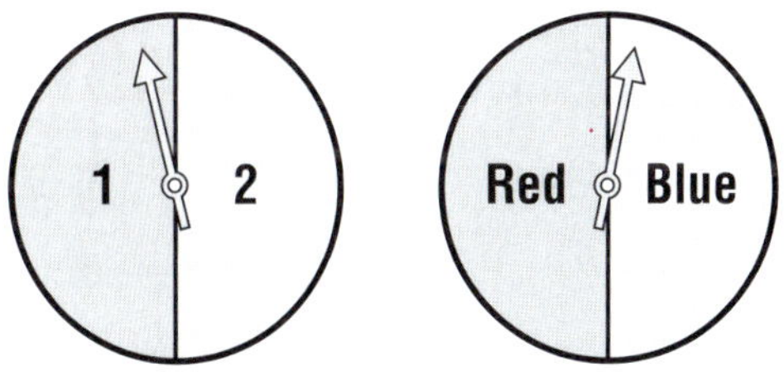

Which shows all the unique combinations of letters and numbers that are possible?

A Red, Blue, 1, 2

B Red 1, Blue 2, Red 1

C Red 1, Blue 1, Red 2, Blue 2

D Blue Red, Red Blue, 21, 12

Short-Response Questions

Short-response questions ask you to find the answer to the problem as well as any method, explanation, and/or justification you used to arrive at the solution. You are asked to solve the problem, showing your work.

The following is a sample rubric, or scoring guide, for scoring short-response questions.

Credit	Scores	Criteria
Full	2	Full Credit: The answer is correct and a full explanation is provided that shows each step in arriving at the final answer.
Partial	1	Partial Credit: There are two different ways to receive partial credit. • The answer is correct, but the explanation provided is incomplete or incorrect. • The answer is incorrect, but the explanation and method of solving the problem is correct.
None	0	No credit: Either an answer is not provided or the answer does not make sense.

Example

1 **A restaurant received a shipment of 36 cartons of eggs. Each carton had 12 eggs. How many eggs did the restaurant receive in all?**

Full Credit Solution

First, I will decide which operation to use. Since each carton has the same number of eggs, I can use repeated addition or multiplication. I will use multiplication to find 36 × 12.

The steps, calculations, and reasoning are clearly stated.

$$\begin{array}{rl} \overset{1}{36} & \text{cartons} \\ \times\ 12 & \text{eggs} \\ \hline 72 & \\ +360 & \\ \hline 432 & \text{total eggs} \end{array}$$

The correct answer is given.

The restaurant received 432 eggs in all.

Partial Credit Solution

In this sample solution, the answer is correct. However, there is no explanation for any of the calculations.

36 cartons, 12 eggs

There are 432 eggs in all.

There is no explanation of how the problem was solved.

Partial Credit Solution

In this sample solution, the answer is incorrect. However, the calculations and reasoning are correct.

Each carton has the same number of eggs, so I can use repeated addition or multiplication. I will use multiplication to find 36 × 12.

$$\begin{array}{rl} 36 & \text{cartons} \\ \times\ 12 & \text{eggs} \\ \hline 62 & \\ +\ 360 & \\ \hline 422 & \text{total eggs} \end{array}$$

The student forgot to carry the ten.

There are 422 eggs in all.

The answer is incorrect.

No Credit Solution

In this sample solution, the answer is incorrect, and there is no explanation for any calculations.

36 + 12 = 48

There are 48 eggs.

The student does not understand the problem and adds 36 and 12.

Short-Response Practice

DIRECTIONS
Solve each problem.

1. The table shows the cost of Miss Rodriguez's lunch items.

Lunch	
Item	**Cost**
Sandwich	$3.85
Salad	$0.90
Pudding	$0.63
Iced Tea	$1.10

She has a $5 bill in her pocket. How much more money does Miss Rodriguez need?

2. Buses are being used to transport students on a field trip. Each bus can hold 62 students. How many buses are needed to transport 180 students?

3. Mr. Solis is buying supplies to install a ceiling fan. The fan costs $64, the support brace costs $8, and a roll of electrical tape costs $2. All prices include sales tax. If Mr. Solis pays with a $100 bill, how much change in dollars should he receive?

4. Look for a pattern in the sequences of numbers shown below.

3, 6, 9, 12, 15, 18, …

5, 10, 15, 20, 25, …

8, 16, 24, 32, 40, 48, …

Another sequence begins with the number 4 and follows the same pattern. Which is the third number in this sequence?

5. The table shows the numerators and denominators of fractions that are equivalent to $\frac{2}{3}$. What is the denominator if the numerator is 54?

Numerator	Denominator
2	3
6	9
18	27
54	?

6. Mrs. Smith told her class she was thinking of a number. She told them that when 12 is subtracted from the number and the result is doubled, the final number is 26. What was the original number that Mrs. Smith was thinking of?

7. Sarika wants to go to a movie that starts at 9:10 P.M. The movie is 1 hour 45 minutes long. At what time will the movie end?

8. A rectangular prism made of 1-inch cubes is shown below.

What is the volume of the prism?

9. Natalie needs 24 ounces of milk for a recipe. How many cups of milk does she need?

10. What single transformation is shown below?

11. What is the perimeter of the rectangular field shown below?

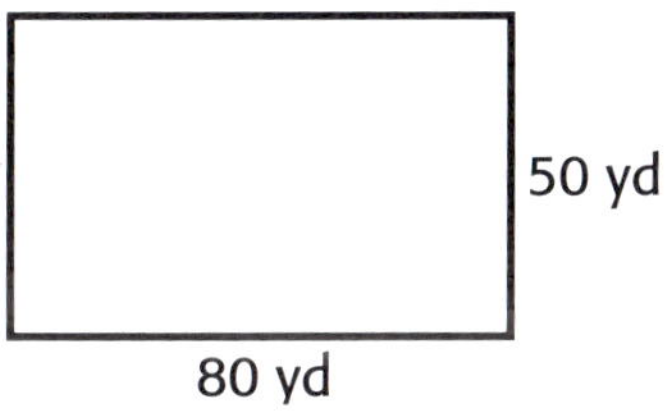

12. Shada's quiz scores are shown in the table.

Quiz	Score
1	84
2	90
3	88
4	92
5	89

On which quiz did Shada receive the median score?

13. The ages of the students in Mr. Jeffrey's reading group are 11, 12, 10, 9, 11, 13, 12, and 11. What is the mode of the ages?

14. Jenny counted the number of coins in her wallet. She had 4 pennies, 3 nickels, 6 dimes, and 2 quarters. What fraction represents the probability of picking a nickel?

15. The table shows the results of 20 spins that Kendra made with a spinner.

Spinner Results	
Color	**Number of Spins**
Blue	3
Red	8
Green	5
White	4

Based on these results, what is the probability that Kendra's spinner will land on red on her next spin?

16. Jermaine spent 32, 38, 36, 28, 40, 33, and 36 minutes working on homework. What is the range of the data?

17. The graph below represents the number of birds at a bird feeder one afternoon.

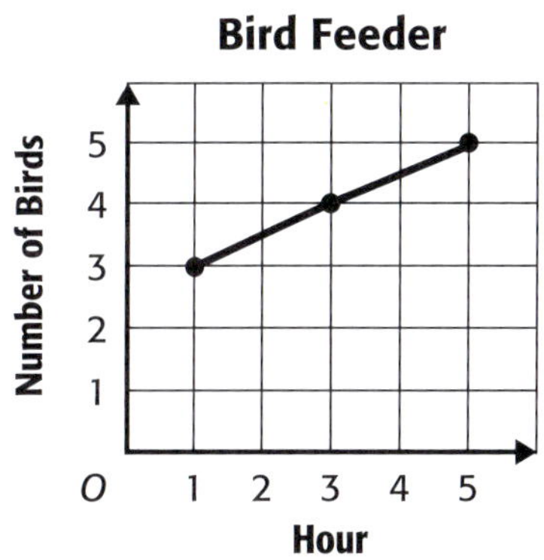

If the pattern continues, how many birds will be at the feeder at the seventh hour?

Extended-Response Questions

Most extended-response questions have multiple parts. You must answer all parts to receive full credit.

In extended-response questions, you must show all of your work in solving the problem. A rubric is used to determine if you receive full, partial, or no credit. The following is a sample rubric for scoring extended-response questions.

Credit	Scores	Criteria
Full	4	Full Credit: The answer is correct and a full explanation is given that shows each step in finding the answer.
Partial	3, 2, 1	Partial Credit: Most of the solution is correct but it may have some mistakes in the explanation or solution. The more correct the solution, the greater the score.
None	0	No credit: Either an answer is not provided or the answer does not make sense.

Make sure that when the problem says to *show your work*, you show every part of your solution. This includes figures, graphs, and any explanations for your calculations.

Example

1 **The bar graph shows the top speeds of four roller coasters. Explain how to use the bar graph to find the range of the roller coaster speeds shown.**

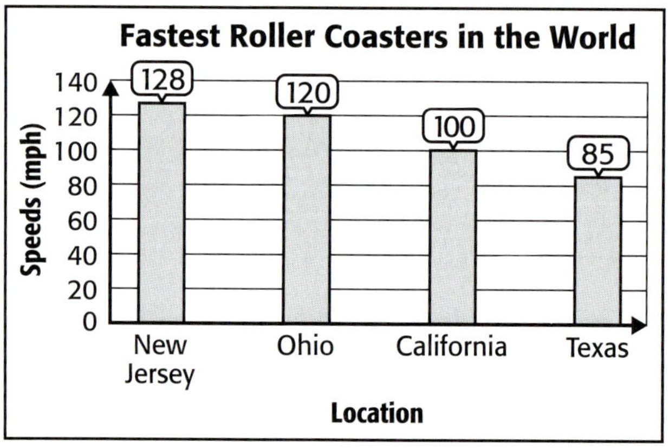

Full Credit Solution

In this sample answer, the student explains how to read the bar graph, what calculations need to be done and finds the correct solution.

The steps, calculations, and reasoning are clearly stated.

First, I will use the bar graph to find the fastest speed and slowest speed. Then I will find the difference of the two speeds.

The bar graph shows the speeds (mph) in each of the four states: New Jersey: 128, Ohio: 120, California: 100, and Texas: 85.

128 mph	fastest roller coaster
− 85 mph	slowest roller coaster
43 mph	

The range of the given speeds is 43 mph.

The correct answer is given.

Partial Credit Solution

In this sample answer, the student explains what calculations need to be done. However, there is an error in the calculations.

The steps, calculations, and reasoning are clearly stated.

First, I will use the bar graphs to find the fastest speed and slowest speed. Then I will find the difference of the two speeds.

The bar graph shows the speeds (mph) in each of the four states: New Jersey: 128, Ohio: 120, California: 100, Texas: 85

128 mph − 85 mph = 143 mph

There is an error.

$128 - 85 \neq 143$

The range of the given speeds is 143 mph.

No Credit Solution

A solution for this problem that will receive no credit may include incorrect answers and an inaccurate explanation.

I will find the range by listing all of the speeds.
New Jersey: 128, Ohio: 120, California: 110, Texas: 85

228 + 120 + 110 + 85 = 433 mph

The range is 143 mph.

Extended-Response Practice

DIRECTIONS:
Solve each problem. Show all your work.

1. Each month Carmina saves $24.80 from her paychecks. How can she estimate the amount of money she will save in 4 months?

2. The table below shows the amount of rain in a city during a 3-month period.

Amount of Rainfall	
Month	**Amount of Rain (centimeters)**
1	15.1
2	18.5
3	20.2

Estimate the total rainfall in these three months. Explain how to find the difference between your estimate and the actual total rainfall.

3. Write the instructions of how to make $4\frac{1}{5}$ into an improper fraction.

4. Shawnda needed 12 yards of fabric. How many feet of fabric did she need? What operation did you use to solve the problem?

5. Jane is sorting the numbers 2 through 20 into two groups.

Group 1: 2, 3, 5, 7, 11, 13, 17

Group 2: 4, 6, 8, 9, 12, 14, 15, 16, 18

How is she sorting them? In which groups should she place 19 and 20?

6. The dimensions of a rectangle are shown. Find the area. Show your work.

7. The figure below is made of 1-unit cubes. Describe how to find the volume of the figure.

8. Mykia's dance class started at 10:45 A.M. and ended at 12:00 P.M. How many hours and minutes was her dance class? Explain your reasoning.

9. The coordinate grid below represents a playground.

Playground

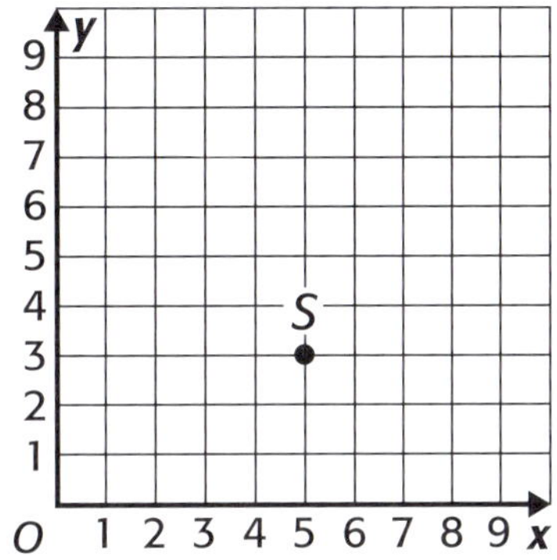

A slide is at point S on the playground. A set of swings that is not shown on the grid is 4 units up from the slide. Explain how to find the coordinates of the swings.

10. The figure below is a rectangular prism.

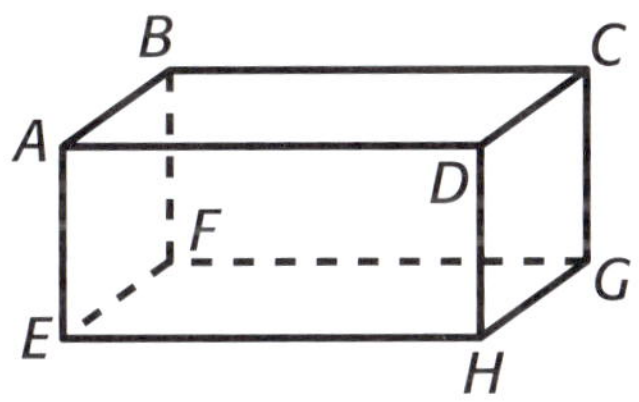

Face *ABFE* is congruent to face CDHG. Name another two faces that are congruent. Explain why they are congruent.

11. The table shows the prices at a used media store including tax. Ty has $24 to spend at the store. List two combinations of items that he can buy. Show your work.

Item	Price
CD	$4
DVD	$5
Video Game	$6

12. The table shows the results of a survey.

Class Pets	
Pet	**Number of Students**
Cat	7
Dog	8
Fish	6
Bird	2

A student made the following graph to display the data.

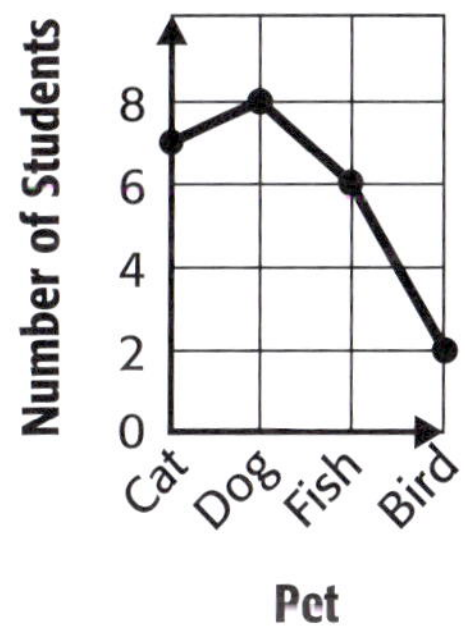

Explain why this type of a graph is not appropriate for the data shown in the table.

13. The graph shows how much time Jasmine spent on her project. How many total minutes were spent on this project? How many hours and minutes is this? Explain your reasoning.

Time Spent on Science Project

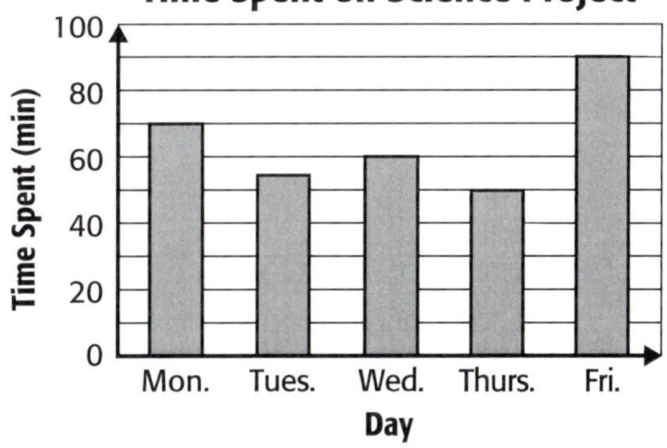

Concepts and Skills Bank

1 Percents as Fractions, and Decimals

The model to the right shows 25 squares shaded out of 100. This can be written as the fraction $\frac{25}{100}$ or $\frac{1}{4}$. It can also be written as the decimal 0.25.

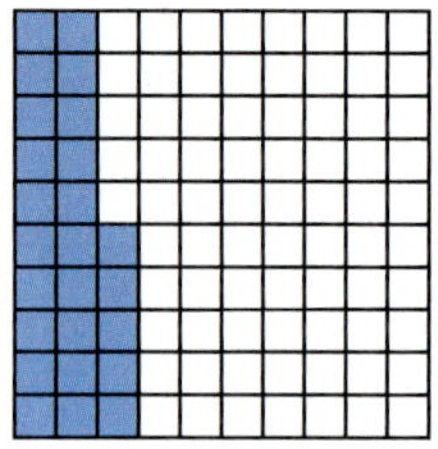

A **percent** is a ratio that compares a number to 100.
$25\% = 25$ out of 100 or $\frac{25}{100}$.

EXAMPLE Write a percent as a fraction

1 Write 75% as a fraction in simplest form.

75% means "75 out of 100."

$75\% = \frac{75}{100}$ Write as a fraction with a denominator of 100.

$= \frac{\overset{3}{\cancel{75}}}{\underset{4}{\cancel{100}}} = \frac{3}{4}$ Simplify.

EXAMPLE Write a percent as a decimal

2 Write 32% as a decimal in simplest form.

32% means "32 out of 100."

$32\% = 0.32$ Write as a decimal.

Exercises

Write each percent as a fraction in simplest form.

1. 29% **2.** 30% **3.** 60% **4.** 84%

5. 92% **6.** 8% **7.** 15% **8.** 22%

Write each percent as a decimal.

9. 4% **10.** 17% **11.** 12% **12.** 50%

13. Malak bought a box of colored paper clips. If 15% are green, what fraction of the paper clips are green?

14. Of the students in a class, 65% have more than 1 pet. Write this amount as a decimal.

2 Squared Numbers

The product of a number and itself is the **square** of that number.

A square with an area of 16 square units is shown. The number 16 is a square number because the product of 4 and itself is 16.

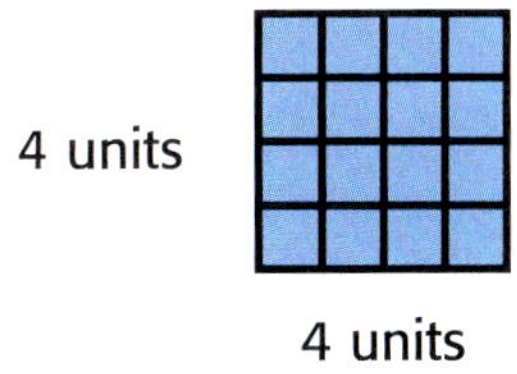

EXAMPLES

1 Find the square of 5.

$5 \times 5 = 25$. Multiply 5 by itself.

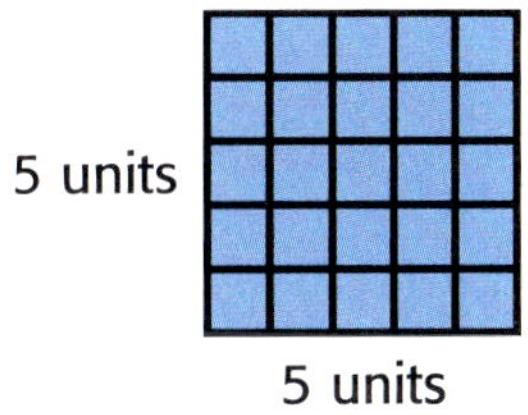

2 Use models to determine if 9 is a square number.

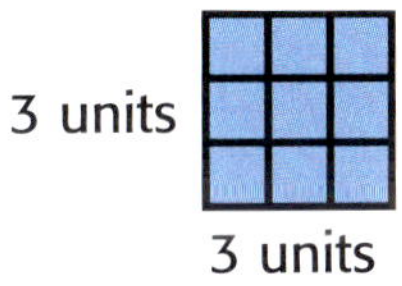

9 units can be arranged to make a square because $3 \times 3 = 9$.

Yes, 9 is a square number

Exercises

Find the square of each number.

1. 6 **2.** 10 **3.** 15 **4.** 12

5. 17 **6.** 22 **7.** 37 **8.** 50

Use models to determine if each number is a square number. Write yes or no.

9. 4 **10.** 12 **11.** 17 **12.** 36

13. 49 **14.** 50 **15.** 64 **16.** 81

17. How much greater is the area of a square that is 10 meters by 10 meters than the area of a square that is 9 meters by 9 meters?

18. A square garden has an area of 121 square feet. How much fencing is needed to place a fence around the entire garden?

3 Congruent and Similar Triangles

Congruent and Similar Triangles

Key Concepts

Words If two triangles are congruent, they have the same angle measures and side lengths.

Model

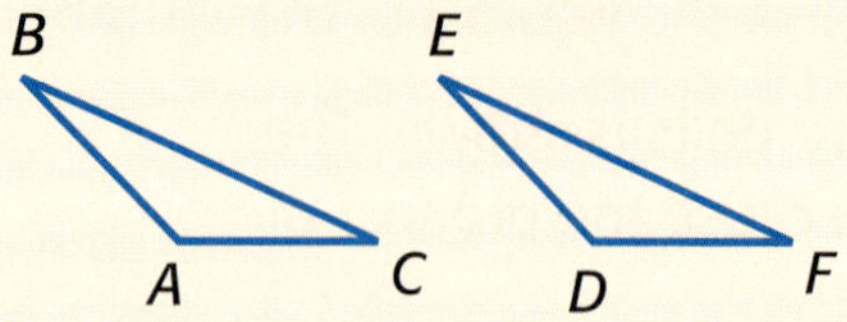

Symbols The symbol $\cong$ means congruent. $\triangle ABC \cong \triangle DEF$

Congruent sides: $\overline{AB} \cong \overline{DE}$; $\overline{AC} \cong \overline{DF}$; $\overline{BC} \cong \overline{EF}$

Congruent angles: $\angle A \cong \angle D$; $\angle B \cong \angle E$; $\angle C \cong \angle F$

Words If two triangles are similar, they have the same angle measures, but different side lengths.

Model

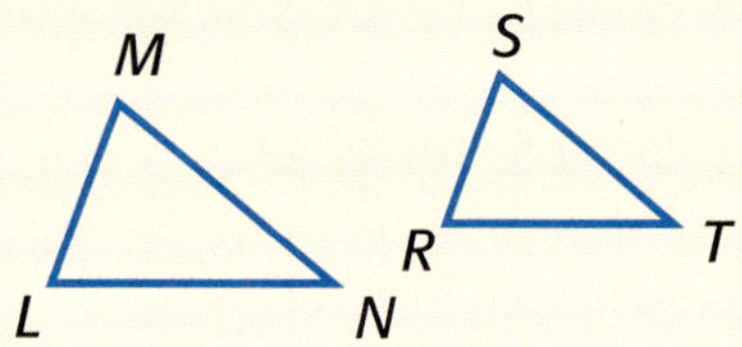

Symbols The symbol ~ means similar. $\triangle LMN \sim \triangle RST$

Congruent angles: $\angle L \cong \angle R$; $\angle M \cong \angle S$; $\angle N \cong \angle T$

note: Congruent figures are also similar.

EXAMPLE Congruent Triangles

1 IF $\triangle JKM \cong \triangle STU$ name the congruent sides and angles.

$\cong$ **sides:** $\overline{JM} \cong \overline{SU}$; $\overline{KM} \cong \overline{TU}$; $\overline{JK} \cong \overline{ST}$

$\cong$ **angles:** $\angle J \cong \angle S$; $\angle K \cong \angle T$; $\angle M \cong \angle U$

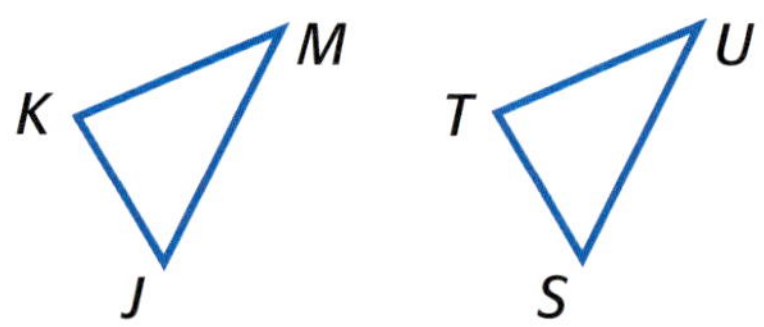

EXAMPLE Similar Triangles

2 IF $\triangle MNP \sim \triangle ABC$ name the congruent angles.

$\cong$ **angles:** $\angle P \cong \angle C$; $\angle M \cong \angle A$; $\angle N \cong \angle B$

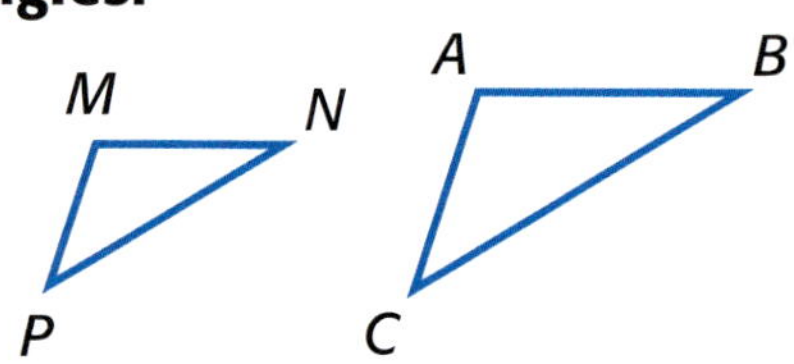

Exercises

Tell whether the triangles appear to be *congruent*, *similar*, or *neither*.

1. 

2. 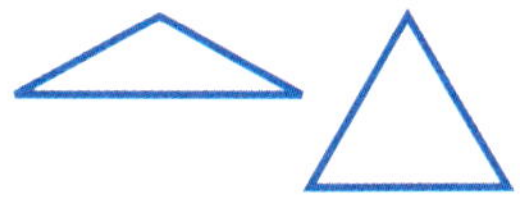

3. 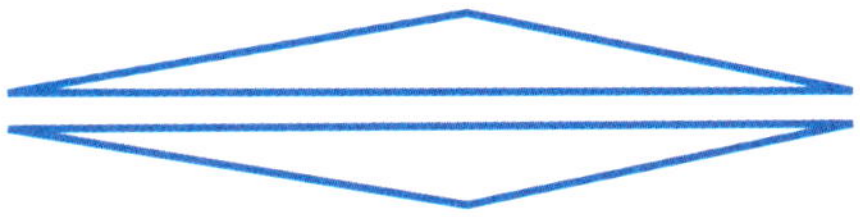

4. 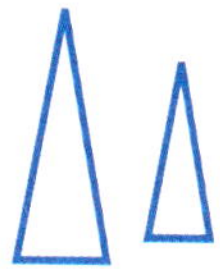

Identify the corresponding angle in the similar triangles shown.

5. $\angle A$

6. $\angle F$

7. $\angle B$

8. $\angle D$

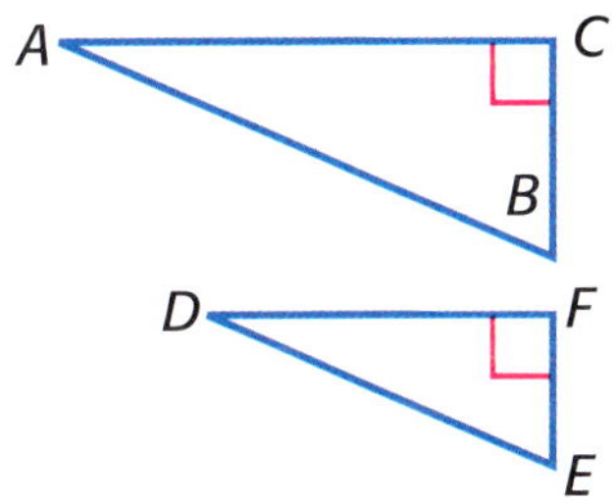

Identify the corresponding side in the congruent triangles shown.

9. $\overline{GH}$

10. $\overline{IH}$

11. $\overline{LJ}$

12. $\overline{GH}$

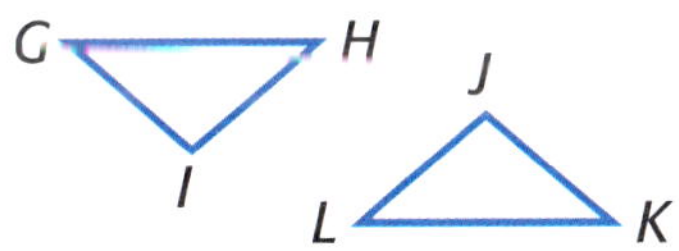

Solve.

13. Two triangles are similar. The height of one triangle is 4 times greater than the other triangle. If the smaller triangle is 33 centimeters tall, how tall is the larger triangle?

14. Mia is cutting out 12 triangles for a project. She decides to speed up the process by cutting multiple sheets of paper at once. Is Mia cutting congruent triangles or similar triangles? Explain.

15. Marcus is building a triangular frame for his garden. Before he cuts the wood for the frame, he draws the triangle shown. If one inch represents 2 feet, find the dimensions of the sides of the frame.

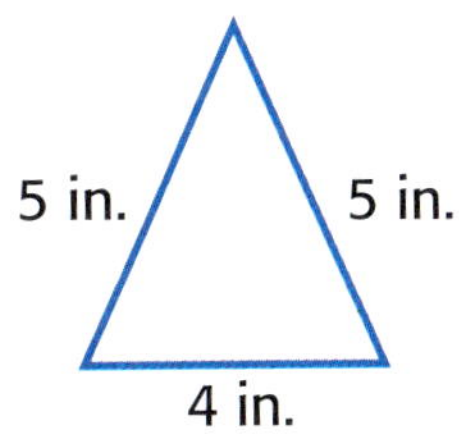

16. In Exercise 15, is Marcus' drawing similar or congruent to the frame he built? Explain.

4 Interior Angle Measures of Triangles

Sum of Angle Measures in a Triangle

Key Concept

Words

The sum of the measures of the angles in a triangle is 180°.

Model

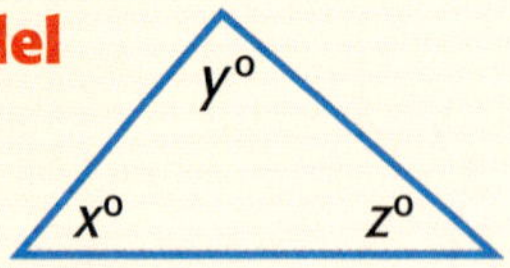

Symbols $x° + y° + z° = 180°$

EXAMPLE Find Angle Measures

1 Find the value of *x* in the triangle.

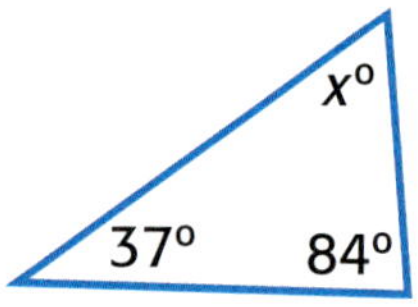

Since the sum of the angle measures in a triangle is 180°, $x + 37 + 84 = 180$.

$x + 37 + 84$	$=$	180	Write the equation.
$x + 121$	$=$	180	Add 37 and 84.
-121	$=$	-121	Subtract 121 from each side.
x	$=$	59	

So, the value of x is 59.

Exercises

Find the value of the missing angle *x*.

1.

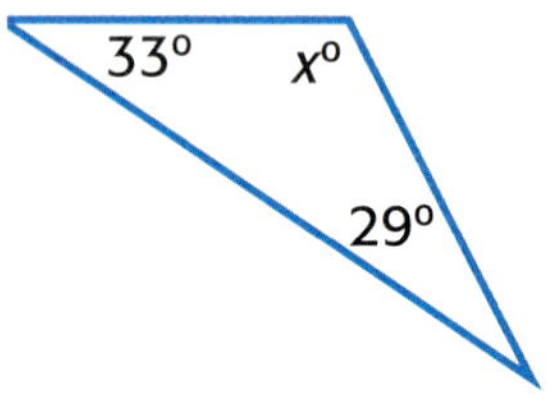

2.

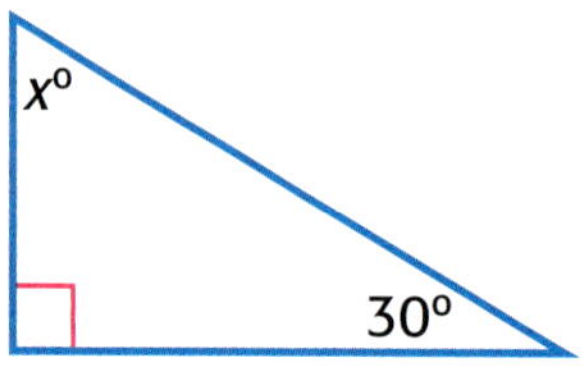

3.

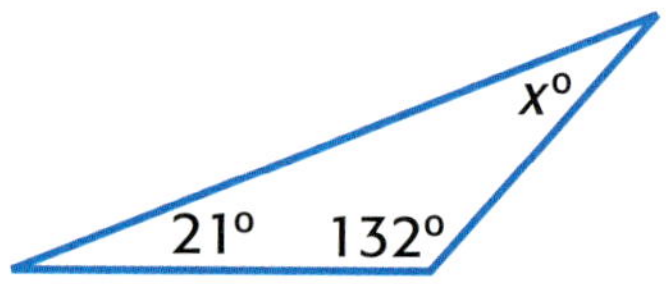

4.

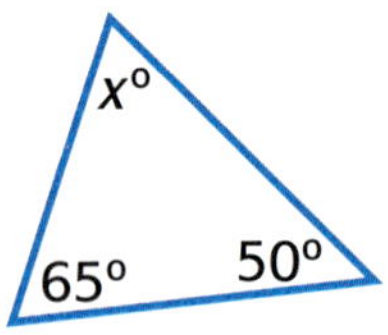

5.

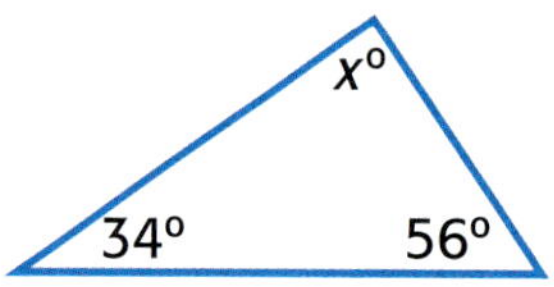

6.

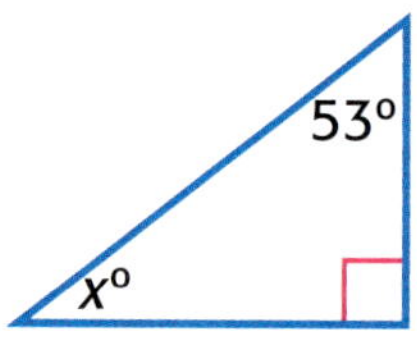

7. Lamar drew a triangle with three equal sides. What is the measure of each angle? How did you find the answer?

8. Adrian was asked to draw a triangle in which each angle is 10° greater than the next angle. If the largest angle is 70°, what is the measure of the other two angles? How can you check your solution?

5 Interior Angle Measures of Quadrilaterals

Sum of Angle Measures in a Quadrilateral — Key Concept

Words

The sum of the measures of the angles in a quadrilateral is 360°

Model 360°

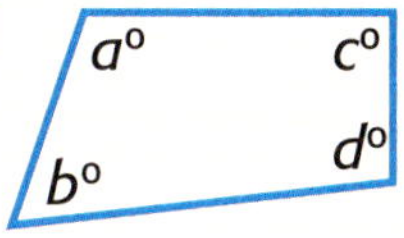

Symbols $a° + b° + c° + d° =$

EXAMPLE Find Angle Measures

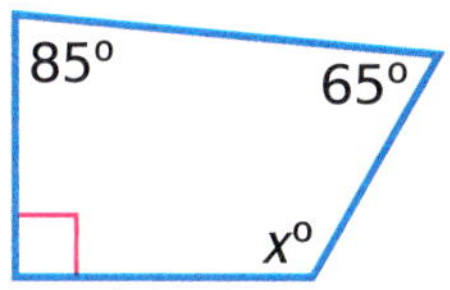

1 Find the value of *x* in the quadrilateral.

The sum of the angle measures in a quadrilateral is 360°.

$$\begin{aligned} x + 65 + 85 + 90 &= 360 \\ x + 240 &= 360 && \text{Add 65, 85, and 90.} \\ -240 &= -240 && \text{Subtract 240 from each side.} \\ \hline x &= 120 \end{aligned}$$

So, the value of x is 120.

Exercises

Algebra Find the value of *x* in each quadrilateral.

1.

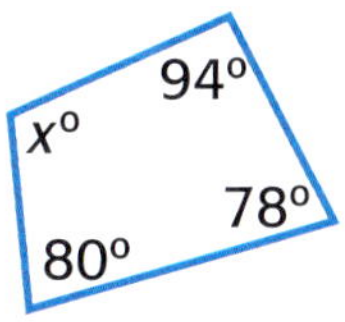

2.

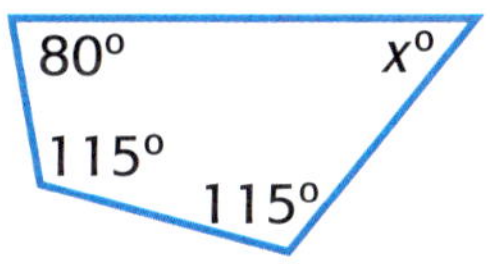

3.

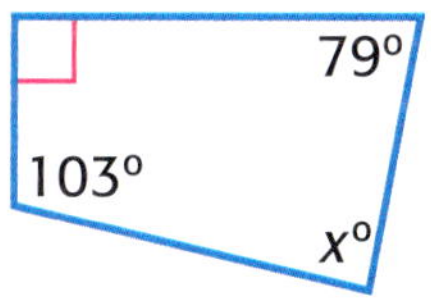

4.

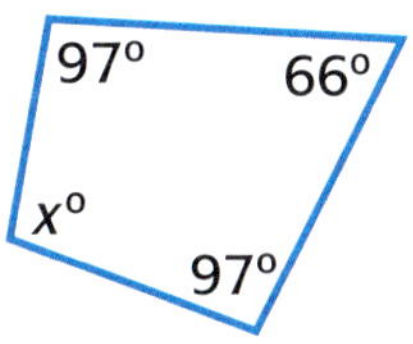

5.

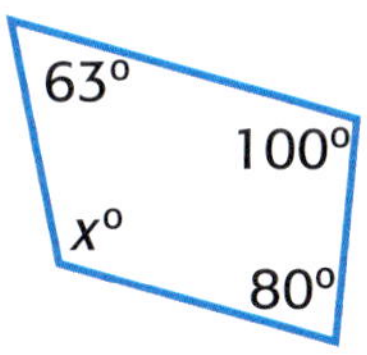

6.

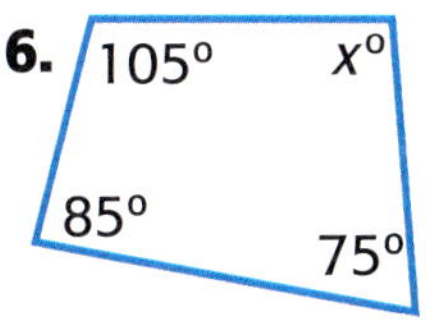

7. Jacob was asked to draw a quadrilateral in which each angle is 10° greater than the next angle. If the smallest angle is 75°, what is the measure of the other three angles? How can you check your solution?

Concepts and Skills

6 Two-Dimensional Figures

A two-dimensional figure is a closed figure with length and width. Two-dimensional figures are also known as plane figures.

A **polygon** is a simple closed figure formed by three or more sides. The number of sides determines the name of the polygon.

A circle is not a polygon because it is a curve.

Polygons — Key Concept

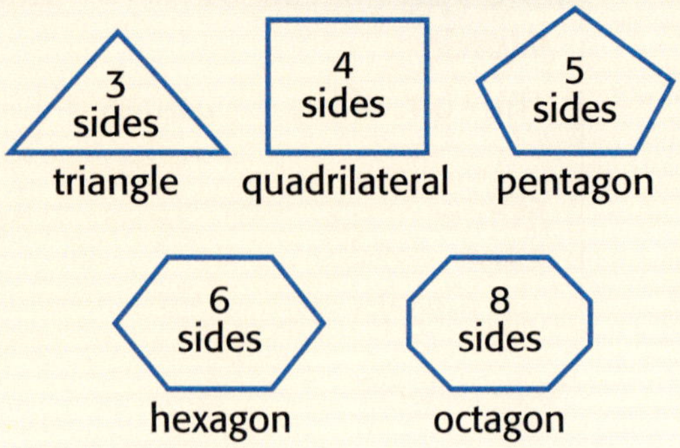

Polygons	Not Polygons
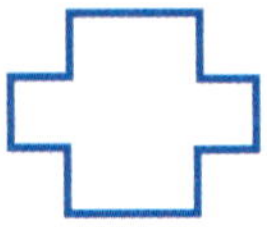 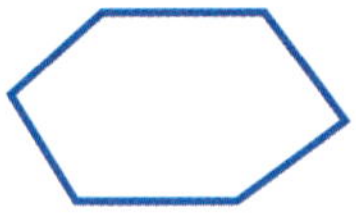 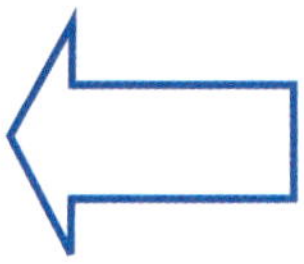	 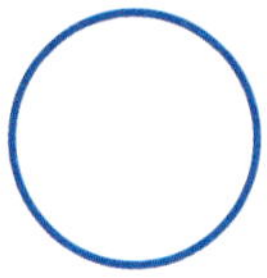 

EXAMPLES

Tell whether each shape is a polygon. If it is a polygon, identify the polygon.

1. 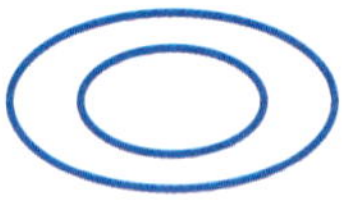

No. It has curves.

2. 

Yes. It is a closed figure with 6 sides. It is a hexagon.

Exercises

Tell whether each shape is a polygon. If it is a polygon, identify the polygon.

1. 

2. 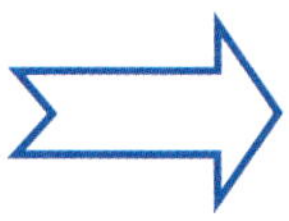

3. 

Identify the type polygon for each sign.

4. 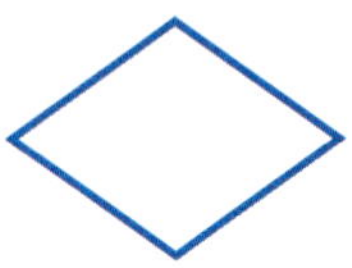

5. 

6. 

7 Mean

The **mean** is a type of average. To find the mean of a set of data, you can add the data, then divide by the total number of data.

EXAMPLE **Find the Mean**

1 **Find the mean of the following test scores: 75, 77, 89, 95, 66, 81, 54, 99**

$75 + 77 + 89 + 95 + 66 + 81 + 54 + 99 = 636$ Add the data.

$= \frac{636}{8}$ Divide by the number of test scores.

$= 79.5$

So, the mean is 79.5.

Exercises

Find the mean.

1. Number of DVDs: 21, 23, 25, 27, 19
2. Test scores: 99, 87, 81, 95, 94, 84, 67
3. Number of pets: 2, 3, 7, 4, 5, 8, 6
4. Points scored: 11, 17, 34, 57, 14, 49, 35
5. Coins collected: 105, 112, 155, 142, 164, 187, 123
6. Yards gained: 751.1, 857.1, 801.4, 610.1
7. Miles traveled: 21.5, 25.9, 34.1, 24.7, 22.6
8. Students from Mrs. Whittier's class went on a field trip to collect different kinds of leaves for their science project. Use the chart to determine the mean number of leaves collected.

Student	Number of leaves
Manny	17
Tanya	4
Jai	7
Randy	11
Kelly	21

9. Trisha went to the mall and walked by several jewelry displays. There were 30 pairs of earrings in the first display. There were 40 necklaces in the next display. The third display had 25 rings. The final display had 50 bracelets. Find the mean number of jewelry in the displays.

Concepts and Skills

8 Stem-and-Leaf Plots

A **stem-and-leaf plot** is a way to organize and distribute data.

- The leaf is the last digit of the number.
- The other digits to the left of the leaf form the stem.

For the numbers 21, 24, 35, and 38, 2 and 3 are the stems. The numbers 1, 4, 5 and 8 are the leaves.

Stem	Leaf
2	1 4
3	5 8

EXAMPLE

1 SPORTS Make a stem-and-leaf plot of the basketball scores below.

68, 52, 85, 64, 59, 51, 62, 66

51, 52, 59, 62, 64, 66, 68, 85 — Write the data from least to greatest.

51, 52, 59
62, 64, 66, 68
85 — Group the numbers with the same first digit.

Separate each stem from each leaf.

Stem	Leaf
5	1 2 9
6	2 4 6 8
7	
8	5

Exercises

Make a stem-and-leaf plot for each set of numbers.

1. 83, 86, 99, 43, 75, 91

2. 33, 31, 62, 20, 32, 25

Write the set of numbers from least to greatest used to form each stem-and-leaf plot.

3.

Stem	Leaf
0	4 5 8
1	3 4 7
2	6

4.

Stem	Leaf
4	1
5	1 2 6 8

5. Sarah wants to use a stem-and-leaf plot to organize her test scores. List the digits that will make up the stem portions of the plot for the scores 80, 92, 88, 85, 76, 94, 98.

Photo Credits

Unless otherwise credited, all United States coin images from the United States Mint.

iv Doug Martin; **v** (bc)Dinah Zike, (rest)Doug Martin; **vi-vii** Tancrediphoto.com/Getty Images; **viii-ix** Kerrick James/Getty Images; **x-xi** Miles Ertman/Masterfile; **xii-xiii** George H. H. Huey/CORBIS; **xiv-xv** Taxi/Getty Images; **xvi-xvii** Robert Landau/CORBIS; **xviii-xix** Richard Cummins/CORBIS; **xx-xxi** Eduardo Garcia/Photographer's Choice/Getty Images; **xxiii** Darrell Gulin/The Image Bank/Getty Images; **xxv** Purestock/PunchStock; **xxvi** Tim Fuller; **xxvii** Eclipse Studios; **OK0-OK1** Eastcott Momatiuk/Getty Images; **OK26** (tr cl)Getty Images, (bl)Jupiterimages/Comstock Images/Alamy; **OK32** Jeremy Woodhouse/Getty Images; **1** Sandra Baker/Alamy; **2** Kenneth Murray/Photo Researchers; **3** Peter Griffith/Masterfile; **4** Alan Schein/Alamy; **5** Neal and Molly Jansen/Alamy; **6** Keith Srakocic/AP Images; **7** John Anderson/Alamy; **8** Bettman/CORBIS; **9** Andre Jenny/Alamy; **10** Dennis MacDonald/Alamy; **11** Jim Nicholson/Alamy; **12** Patrick Mallette/Alamy; **13** Photography courtesy of the North Carolina Museum of Art; **14-15** Richard Broadwell/Alamy; **17-19** CORBIS; **22** Darrell Gulin/Getty Images; **24** Ed-imaging; **28** A & L Sinibaldi/Stone/Getty Images; **30** Ed-Imaging; **32** Al Bello/Getty Images; **34** Dennis Flaherty/Getty Images; **36** Ed-Imaging; **38** The Art Archive/CORBIS; **40-41** Melba Photo Agency/Punchstock; **44** Stephen Simpson/Getty Images; **45** (tr)Joseph T. Collins/Photo Researchers, (others)Ed-Imaging; **46** David Andrews/Tennessee Aquarium; **47** Ed-Imaging; **48** George Holton/Photo Researchers; **58-59** Getty Images; **61** A. Fifis/AP Images; **66** Ed-Imaging; **68** Flip De Nooyer/Foto Natura/Minden Pictures; **70** Deborah Feingold/CORBIS; **74** Ed-Imaging; **76** Alan Jakubek/CORBIS; **76-77** Janusz Wrobel/Alamy; **78** Ed-Imaging; **80** Barry Gregg/CORBIS; **81** Bernard Annebicque/CORBIS; **82** John Lamb/Stone/Getty Images; **83** Ed-Imaging; **84** Richard Hutchings/CORBIS; **90** (tr)Christian Darkin/Photo Researchers, (others)Ed-Imaging; **91** Jeff Vanuga/CORBIS; **100-101** Antony Nagelmann/Getty Images; **103** Courtesy Schlitterbahn Waterpark Resort; **105** W. Treat Davidson/Photo Researchers; **108** Bob Krist/CORBIS; **109** Jim Zipp/Photo Researchers; **110** Ed-Imaging; **112** Norbert Rosing/National Geographic Image Collection; **115** Ed-imaging; **116** Elyse Lewin/Getty Images; **117** Rich Reid/National Geographic/Getty Images; **120** Doug Menuez/Getty Images; **122** Creatas/PunchStock; **123** Bloomimage/CORBIS; **125-126** Ed-Imaging; **127** C Squared Studios/Getty Images; **130-131** Anthony Johnson/Getty Images; **131** D. Hurst/Alamy; **132** Catapult/Getty Images; **136** Ed-Imaging; **146-147** Tom Brakefield/Digital Vision/Getty Images; **149** Altrendo Nature/Altrendo/Getty Images; **150** Gary Neil Corbett/SuperStock; **151** Ed-Imaging; **152** Yellow Dog Productions/The Image Bank/Getty Images; **158** Cedar Fair Entertainment Company; **164** (tr)Elliot Elliot/Johner Images/Getty Images, (others)Ed-Imaging; **166 168 169** Ed-Imaging; **170** Greg Pease/Stone/Getty Images; **172** Douglas Johns Studio/StockFood; **174** Thinkstock/CORBIS; **175** CORBIS; **176** Nick Koudis/Getty Images; **178-179** Everett C. Johnson/eStock Photo; **179** CORBIS; **180** Ed-Imaging; **190-191** Richard Cummins/CORBIS; **195** Raymond Gehman/CORBIS; **196** Michael Rosenfeld/Getty Images; **202** Doug Pensinger/Time Life Pictures/Getty Images; **206** Ed-Imaging; **210** Millard H. Sharp/Photo Researchers; **212** Ed-Imaging; **216-217** Jeff Rotman/Getty Images; **221** Don Farrall/Getty Images; **232-233** Theo Allofs/zefa/CORBIS; **239** (bl)Image Source/SuperStock, (br)George Doyle/Getty Images; **245** (l)CORBIS, (r)C Squared Studios/Getty Images; **246** Bob Wickley/SuperStock; **247** Ryan McVay/Getty Images; **248** Ed-Imaging; **256** Patricio Robles Gil/Sierra Madre/Minden Pictures; **258** CORBIS; **258-259** SIME s.a.s/eStock Photo; **260** Tom Stewart/CORBIS; **261** Brand X Pictures/PunchStock; **262 263 266** Ed-Imaging; **276-277** Taxi/Getty Images; **282** Ed-Imaging; **285** Purestock/Getty Images; **286** Eric Meola/The Image Bank/Getty Images; **287** Ryan McVay/Getty Images; **288** Eric Meola/The Image Bank/Getty Images; **292** Jean-Paul Ferrero/Minden Pictures; **296** Mark Raycroft/Minden Pictures; **297** John Strohsacker/WireImage/Getty Images; **298** Friso Gentsch/epa/CORBIS; **299** Margarette Mead/The Image Bank/Getty Images; **301** DLILLC/CORBIS; **303** Ed-Imaging; **304-305** Tim Cuff/Alamy; **311** Ed-Imaging; **312** Jose Fuste Raga/CORBIS; **317** Ed-Imaging; **320** ThinkStock LLC/Index Stock Imagery; **330-331** Janis Christie/Photodisc Green/Getty Images; **341** (tr)Gerry Ellis/Science Faction/Getty Images, (others) Ed-Imaging; **343** Ed-Imaging; **344** Ariel Skelley/CORBIS; **345** Photodisc/PunchStock; **346** Juniors Bildarchiv/Alamy; **347** David Steele/Gallo Images/Getty Images; **348** Image courtesy Burpee Museum of natural History Rockford, IL; **349** CMCD/Getty Images; **350** Eising/Getty Images; **353** Ed-Imaging; **354-355** Getty Images; **356** age fotostock/SuperStock; **360** Ed-Imaging; **370-371** Arnaldo Pomodoro, Disk in the Form of a Desert Rose, Frederik Meijer Gardens & Sculpture Park cast 1999-2000. Gift of Fred and Lena Meijer. Photo by William J. Hebert; **373** Laura Doss/Brand X/CORBIS; **375** Dr. Nick Kurzenko/Photo Researchers; **384** Ed-Imaging; **386** Gail Shumway/Taxi/Getty Images; **388** Scenics of America/PhotoLink/Getty Images; **393** Dorling Kindersley/Getty Images; **394** David Madison/Getty Images; **398** Wilfried Krecichwost/Getty Images; **399** (l)Paul Burns/Getty Images, (r)Ed-Imaging; **400** Ed-Imaging; **407** Ryan McVay/Getty Images; **408-409** Franck Jeannin/Alamy; **409** (inset r)Oleg Moiseyenk/Alamy, (inset b)Getty Images; **418-419** Gallo Images/CORBIS; **425** Ingram Publishing/Alamy; **430** Geostock/Getty Images; **434** Laurence Mouton/Photoalto/PictureQuest/Jupiterimages; **436** (l)Stockdisc/Getty Images, (r)image100 Ltd; **439** Samuel R. Maglione/Photo Researchers, Inc.; **442** Bob Daemmrich/

Photo Credits

PhotoEdit; **444** Cosmo Condina/Stone/Getty Images; **448** Lew Robertson/FoodPix/Jupiterimages; **449** Norgert Wu/Minden Pictures; **450** Ed-Imaging; **451** Purestock/Getty Images; **452** ImageShop/CORBIS; **453** (l)age fotostock/SuperStock; (r)Dan Johnson; **455 456** Ed-Imaging; **458** Darrell Gulin/CORBIS; **460** Pete Turner/The Image Bank/Getty Images; **461** (l)Ed-Imaging, (r)Ben Blackenburg/CORBIS; **462-463** Getty Images; **463** (t)Getty Images, (b)Philip James Corwin/CORBIS; **472-473** Robert Glusic/Getty Images; **475** C Squared Studios/Getty Images; **476** (tl)C Squared Studios/Getty Images, (tr)G.K. Vikki Hart/Getty Images, (bl)Photodisc/Getty Images, (br)C Squared Studios/Getty Images; **477** Randy Faris/CORBIS; **481** Ed-Imaging; **482** (tr)National Geographic/Getty Images, (c)Photodisc/Getty Images; (b)Darlyne A Murawski/National Geographic/Getty Images; **484** Anup Shah/Getty Images; **488** Jose Luis Pelaez/Iconica/Getty Images; **490** Ed-Imaging; **492** Marc Debnam/Digital Vision/Getty Images; **494** Dennis MacDonald/Alamy; **496** Ed-Imaging; **498-499** EuroStyle Graphics/Alamy; **502** Ed-Imaging; **512-513** Tim De Waele/Isosport/CORBIS; **515** Dorling Kindersley/Dorling Kindersley/Getty Images; **516** (c)Photos.com/Jupiterimages; (r)Jonathan Kitchen/Getty Images; **517** Laurence Parent Photography/Laurence Parent Photography, Inc.; **520** Chris Cheadle/Photographer's Choice/Getty Images; **521** NASA/Photo Researchers; **522** C Borland/PhotoLink/Getty Images; **524** Piotr Naskrecki/Minden Pictures; **525** CORBIS; 526 (tr)IT Stock/PunchStock, (bl)Stockbyte/Getty Images, (br)Ed-Imaging; **527** (tr) Foodcollection/Foodcollection/Getty Images; **528** Veronique Rolland/Stone/Getty Images; **529** Ed-Imaging; **535** Daniel J Cox/The Image Bank/Getty Images; **537** Joe McDonald/Visuals Unlimited/Getty Images; **540** Ilene MacDonald/Alamy; **542-543** (plane)Museum of Flight/CORBIS, (sky)PhotoLink/Getty Images; **543** (inset)CORBIS; **544** Ed-Imaging; **548** Michael Scott/The McGraw-Hill Companies, Inc.; **554-555** Eduardo Garcia/Photographer's Choice/Getty Images; **557** Courtesy New Tech Kites; **559** Photodisc/Getty Images; **561** Ed-Imaging; **562** MTR Photography; **566** Andrew Ward/Life File/Getty Images; **567** Kazuyoshi Nomachi/CORBIS; **568** Matthias Kulka/zefa/CORBIS, (bl)Colin Mead Enterprises/Getty Images, (br)Ryman Cabannes/photocuisine/CORBIS; **569** (tr)Michael Houghton/StudiOhio, (br)Purestock/Getty Images; **570** Purestock/Getty Images; **573** (tr)Gail Mooney/CORBIS, (others)Ed-Imaging; **576** Blend Images/SuperStock; **585** Ed-Imaging; **586** image100/CORBIS; **589** (l)Siede Preis/Getty Images, (c)Getty Images, (r)Creatas/PunchStock; **591** Jon Arnold Images/Alamy; **592** MTR Photography; **593** Lew Robertson/CORBIS; **594-595** Robert Harding Picture Library/Alamy; **595** Martin Moos/Lonely Planet Images; **598** David Frazier/CORBIS; **604-605** Darrell Gulin/The Image Bank/Getty Images; **608** Photoalto/Photolibrary; **609** Jules Frazier/Getty Images; **610** Andrea Rugg/Beateworks/CORBIS; **612** Siede Preis/Getty Images; **616** United Veterans of America; **619** ASSOCIATED PRESS; **621** Roberto Benzi/age footstock; **622** Ed-Imaging; **624** pixie/Emporis; **625** (c)Image Source Pink/Getty Images, (b)Paul Bricknell/Dorling Kindersley/Getty Images; **626** Ken Karp/The McGraw-Hill Companies; **631** The McGraw-Hill Companies; **635** (l to r, t to b) C Squared Studios/Getty Images, Digital Vision/Getty Images; **636-637** Elisabeth Coelfen/Alamy; **641** Judith Collins/Alamy; **644** Getty Images; **647** (tr) Purestock/Getty Images, (others)Ed-Imaging; **648** Ned Frisk/CORBIS; **658-659** Digital Vision/Getty Images; **664-665** Ace Stock Limited/Alamy; **666** Ed-Imaging; **669** Photodisc/Getty Images; **674** (l)Ryan McVay/Getty Images, (c)Getty Images, (r)CORBIS; **677** Nona Darryl Whittington/Darmar Enterprises; **679** Little Blue Wolf Productions/CORBIS; **680-681** Ed-Imaging; **682** George Doyle/Stockdisc Classic/Getty Images; **683** Masterfile; **LA0** Mark Steinmetz; **LA1** Amos Morgan/Getty Images; **LA3** PunchStock; **LA4** Ingram Publishing/Alamy Images; **LA5** Purestock/PunchStock; **LA6** imagebroker/Alamy; **LA8** Stockdisc/PunchStock; **LA9** Creatas/PunchStock; **LA10** (t)Stockdisc/PunchStock, (b)D. Hurst/Alamy Images; **LA11** Getty Images; **LA14** Oleg Raisky/Alamy Images; **LA17** Richard Herrmann/Getty Images; **LA18** G.K. & Vikki Hart/Getty Images; **LA21** CORBIS; **LA22** Getty Images; **LA23** C Squared Studios/Getty Images; **LA24** G.K. & Vikki Hart/Getty Images; **LA25** CORBIS/PunchStock; **P00** (tl)Getty Images, (cr)Punchstock, (bl)Bob Daemmrich/PhotoEdit; **P01** Tim Fuller; **P02** Reuters/CORBIS; **P03** Jason Reed/Reuters/CORBIS; **P04** Mika/zefa/CORBIS; **P05** Ed-Imaging; **P06** Nati Harnik/AP Images; **P07** Ed-Imaging; **P08** Jeff Pape/New Bremen Giant Pumpkin Growers; **P09** Ed-Imaging; **R00** Eclipse Studios; **R43** Tim Fuller.

McGraw-Hill would like to acknowledge the artists and agencies who contributed to illustrating this program: Cover Mick McGinty, represented by Mendola Ltd.; American Artists Rep. Inc.; Argosy; Articulate Graphics; Terri Chicko, represented by Cornell & McCarthy, LLC; Richard Carbajal, Mark Collins, Dick Gage, represented by Deborah Wolfe Limited; Epigraphics; Laserwords; Kristine Walsh, represented by Bill Smith Studio; The McGraw-Hill Companies, Inc.; Navta Associates; Precision Graphics; Quebecor World Premedia.

Glossary/Glosario

Math Online A mathematics multilingual glossary is available at www.macmillanmh.com. The glossary includes the following languages.

Arabic	Cantonese	Korean	Tagalog
Bengali	English	Russian	Urdu
Brazilian Portuguese	Haitian Creole	Spanish	Vietnamese
	Hmong		

Cómo usar el glosario en español:

1. Busca el término en inglés que desees encontrar.
2. El término en español, junto con la definición, se encuentran en la columna de la derecha.

English | Español

A

acute angle (p. 564) An *angle* with a measure between 0° and 90°.

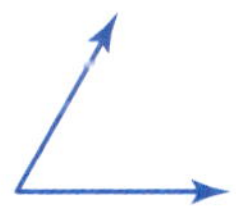

ángulo agudo *Ángulo* que mide entre 0° y 90°.

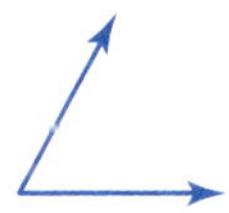

acute triangle (p. 567) A *triangle* with all three *angles* less than 90°.

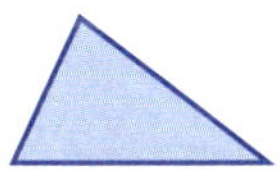

triángulo acutángulo *Triángulo* cuyos tres *ángulos* miden menos de 90°.

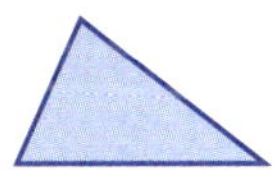

addition (p. 70) An operation on two or more *addends* that results in a *sum*.

$$9 + 3 = 12$$

sumar (suma) Operación en dos o más *sumandos* que resulta en una *suma*.

$$9 + 3 = 12$$

algebra (p. 193) A branch of mathematics that uses symbols, usually letters, to explore relationships between quantities.

álgebra Rama de las matemáticas que usa símbolos, generalmente letras para explorar relaciones entre cantidades.

algebraic expression (p. 193) A group of numbers, symbols, and variables that represent an operation or series of operations.

$3x + 5$ or $y + 5$

expresión algebraica Grupo de números, símbolos y variables que representan una operación o una serie de operaciones.

$3x + 5$ o $y + 5$

angle (p. 564) Two rays with a common endpoint.

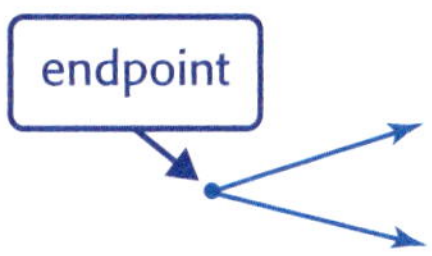

ángulo Dos rectas con un extremo común.

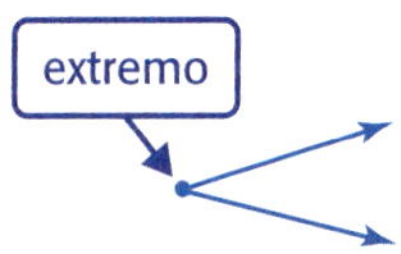

area (p. 612) The number of *square units* needed to cover the surface of a closed figure.

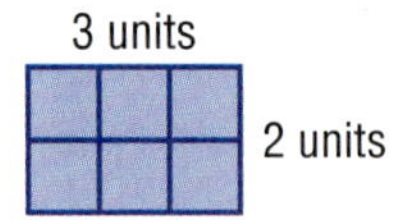

area = 6 square units

área Número de *unidades cuadradas* necesarias para cubrir la superficie de una figura cerrada.

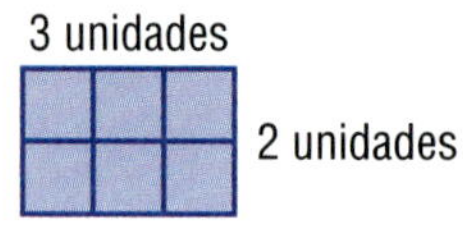

aŕea = 6 unidades cuadrados

Associative Property of Addition (p. 84) Property that states that the way in which numbers are grouped does not change the sum.

propiedad asociativa de la suma Propiedad que establece que la manera en que se agrupan los números no altera la suma.

Associative Property of Multiplication (p. 126) Property that states that the way in which factors are grouped does not change the product.

propiedad asociativa de la multiplicación Propiedad que establece que la manera en que se agrupan los factores no altera el producto.

axis (p. 250) A horizontal or vertical number line on a graph. Plural is *axes*.

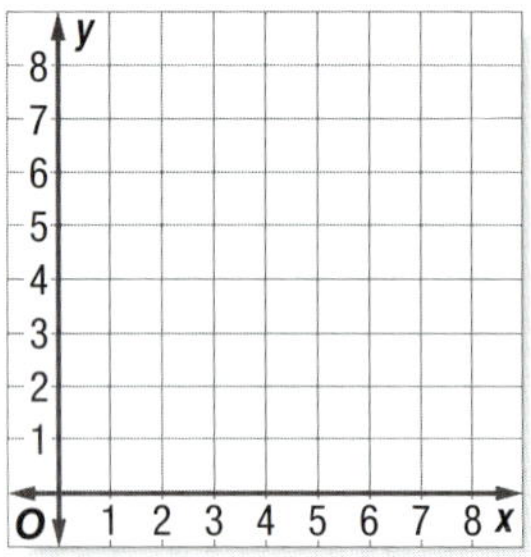

eje Recta numérica horizontal o vertical en una gráfica.

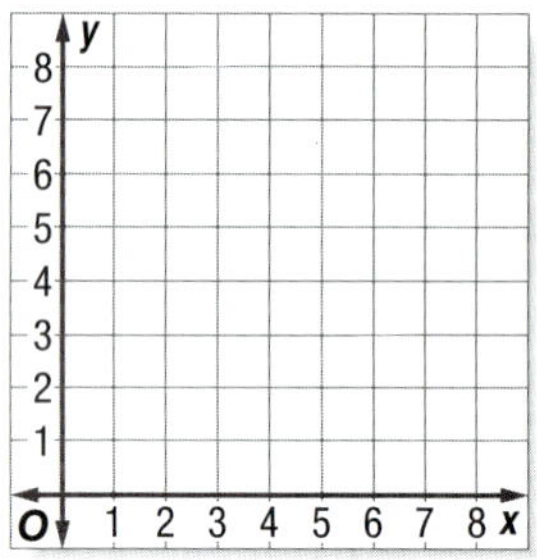

B

bar graph (p. 299) A graph that compares *data* by using bars to display the number of items in each group.

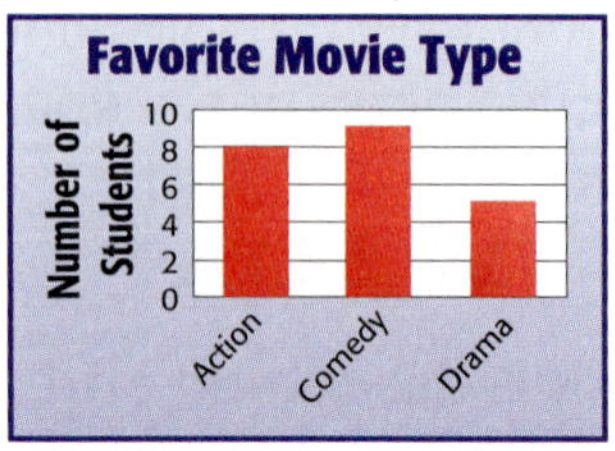

gráfica de barras Gráfica que compara *datos* usando barras para mostrar el número de artículos en cada grupo.

base (p. 624) One of two parallel congruent faces in a prism.

base Una de dos caras congruentes paralelas en un prisma.

C

capacity (p. 488) The amount a container can hold.

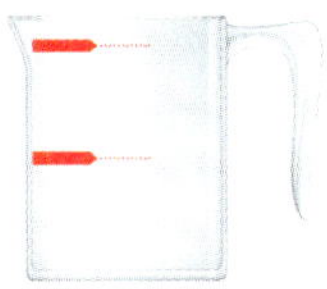

capacidad Cantidad que puede contener un envase.

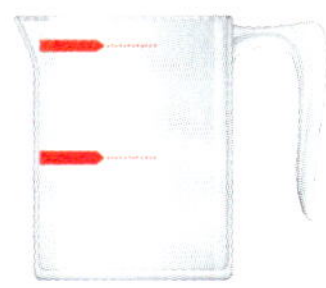

Celsius (°C) (p. 537) The unit used to measure temperature in the metric system.

Celsios (°C) Unidad que se usa para medir la temperatura en el sistema métrico.

centimeter (cm) (p. 517) A *metric unit* for measuring *length*.

100 centimeters = 1 meter

centímetro (cm) *Unidad métrica* de *longitud*.

100 centímetros = 1 metro

certain (p. 661) The probability that an event will definitely happen.

cierto La probabilidad de que ocurra un evento.

common denominator (p. 404) A number that is a multiple of the denominators of two or more fractions.

denominador común Número que es múltiplo de los denominadores de dos o más fracciones.

common factor (p. 373) A number that is a *factor* of two or more numbers.

3 is a common factor of 6 and 12.

factor común Un número *entero factor* de dos o más números.

3 es factor común de 6 y de 12.

common multiple (p. 396) A *whole number* that is a *multiple* of two or more numbers.

24 is a common multiple of 6 and 4.

múltiplo común *Número entero múltiplo* de dos o más números.

24 es un múltiplo común de 6 y 4.

Commutative Property of Addition (p. 84) Property that states that the order in which numbers are added does not change the sum.

propiedad conmutativa de la suma Propiedad que establece que el orden en que se suman los números no altera la suma.

Commutative Property of Multiplication (p. 126) Property that states that the order in which factors are multiplied does not change the product.

propiedad conmutativa de la multiplicación Propiedad que establece que el orden en que se multiplican los factores no altera el producto.

compatible numbers (p. 64) Numbers in a problem that are easy to work with mentally.

720 and 90 are compatible numbers for division because $72 \div 9 = 8$.

compensation (p. 88) Adding a number to one addend and subtracting the same number from another addend to add mentally.

composite number (p. 376) A whole number that has more than two factors.

12 has the factors 1, 2, 3, 4, 6, and 12.

cone (p. 624) A solid that has a circular base and one curved surface from the base to a vertex.

congruent line segments (p. 559) Line segments that have the same length.

convert (p. 477) To change one unit to another.

coordinate (p. 250) One of two numbers in an *ordered pair*.

The 1 is the number on the *x*-axis, the 5 is on the *y*-axis. A coordinate can be positive or negative.

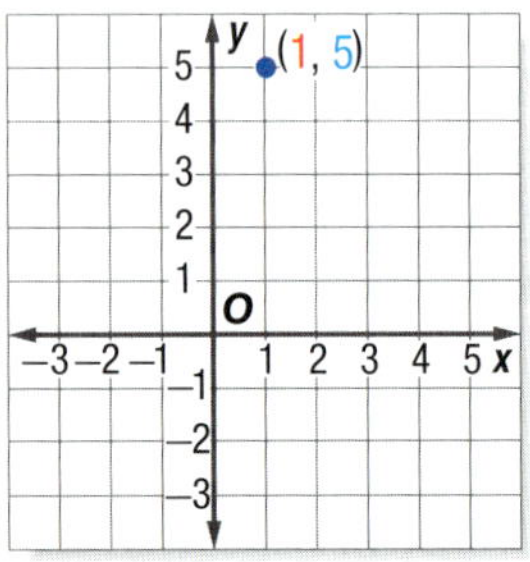

coordinate grid (p. 250) A grid that is formed when two number lines intersect at a right angle.

cube (p. 624) A rectangular *prism* with six faces that are congruent squares.

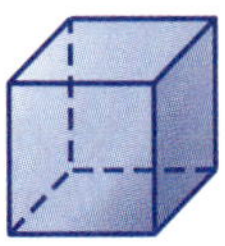

números compatibles Números en un problema con los cuales es fácil trabajar mentalmente.

720 y 90 son números compatibles en la división porque $72 \div 9 = 8$.

compensación Sumar un número a un sumando y restar el mismo número de otro sumando con el fin de sumar mentalmente.

número compuesto Número entero que tiene más de dos factores.

12 tiene a los factores 1, 2, 3, 4, 6 y 12.

cono Sólido con una base circular y una superficie curva desde la base hasta el vértice.

segmentos congruentes de recta Segmentos de recta que tienen la misma medida.

convertir Cambiar una unidad en otra.

coordenada Uno de los dos números de un *par ordenado*.

El 1 es el número en el eje *x* y el 5 está en el eje *y*. Una coordenada puede ser positiva o negativa.

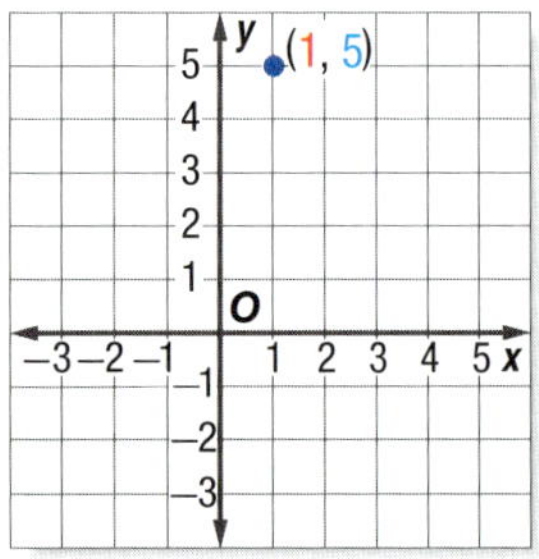

plano de coordenadas cuadriculado que se forma cuando dos rectas numéricas se intersecan a ángulos rectos.

cubo *Prisma* rectangular con seis caras que son cuadrados congruentes.

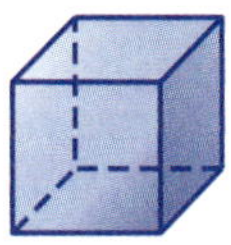

cubic unit (p. 631) A unit for measuring *volume*, such as a cubic inch or a cubic centimeter.

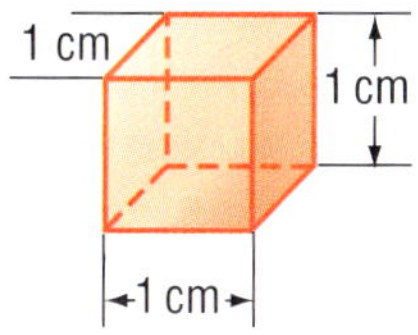

cup (p. 488) A *customary unit* of *capacity* equal to 8 fluid ounces.

customary units (p. 477) The units of measurement most often used in the United States. These include foot, pound, quart, and degrees Fahrenheit

cylinder (p. 624) A solid with two parallel congruent circular bases and a curved surface that connects the bases.

unidad cúbica Unidad de *volumen*, como una pulgada cúbica o un centímetro cúbico.

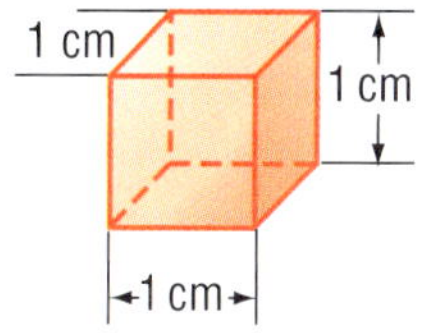

taza *Unidad inglesa* de *capacidad* igual a 8 onzas líquidas.

unidades inglesas Las unidades de medida de uso más frecuente en Estados Unidos. Incluyen el pie, la libra, el cuarto de galón y los grados Fahrenheit.

cilindro Sólido con dos bases paralelas y congruentes y una superficie curva que las conecta.

D

data (p. 279) Pieces of information that are often numerical.

decimal (p. 26) A number that has a digit in the tenths place, hundredths place, and beyond.

decimal point (p. 26) A period separating the ones and the *tenths* in a decimal number.

0.8 or $3.77

defining the variable (p. 238) Choosing a variable to represent an unknown value.

degree (°) (pp. 537, 564) **a.** A unit of measure used to describe temperature. **b.** A unit for measuring *angles*.

denominator (p. 333) The bottom number in a *fraction*. It represents the number of parts in the whole.

In $\frac{5}{6}$, 6 is the denominator.

digit (p. 17) A symbol used to write numbers. The ten digits are 0, 1, 2, 3, 4, 5, 6, 7, 8, and 9.

datos Piezas de información que con frecuencia son numéricas.

decimal Número que tiene un dígito en el lugar de las décimas, centésimas y más allá.

punto decimal Punto que separa las unidades y las *décimas* en un número decimal.

0.8 ó $3.77

definir la variable Elegir una variable para representar un valor desconocido.

grado (°) **a.** Unidad de medida que se usa para describir la temperatura. **b.** Unidad para medir ángulos.

denominador El número inferior en una *fracción*. Representa el número de partes en el todo.

En $\frac{5}{6}$, 6 es el denominador.

dígito Símbolo que se usa para escribir números. Los diez dígitos son 0, 1, 2, 3, 4, 5, 6, 7, 8 y 9.

Distributive Property (p. 108) To multiply a *sum* by a number, you can multiply each *addend* by the same number and add the *products*.

$$8 \times (9 + 5) = (8 \times 9) + (8 \times 5)$$

divide (division) (p. 149) An operation on two numbers in which the first number is split into the same number of equal groups as the second number.

12 ÷ 3 means 12 is divided into 3 equal size groups

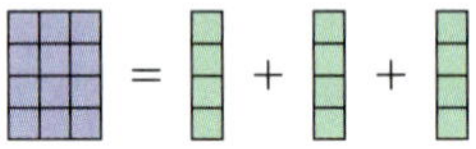

dividend (p. 149) A number that is being divided.

$3\overline{)429}$ 429 is the dividend

divisible (p. 149) Describes a number that can be divided into equal parts and has no remainder.

39 is divisible by 3 with no remainder.

divisor (p. 149) The number by which the dividend is being divided.

$3\overline{)19}$ 3 is the divisor

double bar graph (p. 300) A graph used to display two sets of data dealing with the same subject.

double line graph (p. 307) A graph used to display two different sets of data using a common scale.

propiedad distributiva Para multiplicar una *suma* por un número, puedes multiplicar cada *sumando* por el mismo número y sumar los *productos*.

$$8 \times (9 + 5) = (8 \times 9) + (8 \times 5)$$

dividir (división) Operación en dos números en que el primer número se separa en tantos grupos iguales como indica el segundo número.

12 ÷ 3 significa que 12 se divide en 3 grupos de igual tamaño.

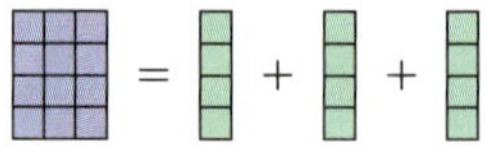

dividendo Número que se divide.

$3\overline{)429}$ 429 es el dividendo

divisible Describe un número que puede dividirse en partes iguales, sin residuo.

39 es divisible entre 3 sin residuo.

divisor Número entre el que se divide el dividendo.

$3\overline{)19}$ 3 es el divisor

gráfica de barras dobles Gráfica que se usa para mostrar dos conjuntos de datos que tienen que ver con el mismo tema.

gráfica lineal doble Gráfica que se usa para mostrar dos conjuntos diferentes de datos usando una escala común.

E

edge (p. 624) The *line segment* where two *faces* of a *3-dimensional figure* meet.

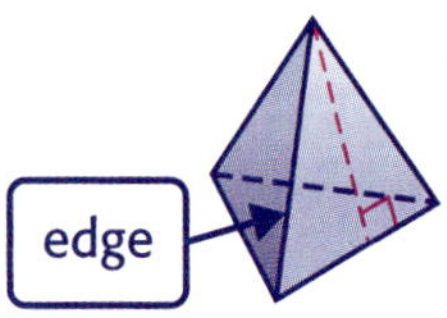

elapsed time (p. 500) The difference in time between the start and the end of an event.

arista Segmento de recta donde concurren dos caras de una *figura tridimensional*.

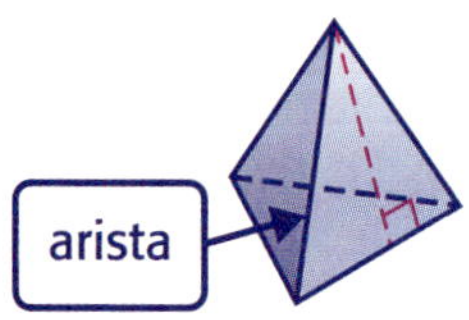

tiempo transcurrido La diferencia en tiempo entre el comienzo y el final de un evento.

equally likely (p. 661) Having the same chance of occurring.

In a coin toss you are equally likely to flip a head or a tail.

equals sign (p. 235) A symbol of equality, =.

equation (p. 235) A number sentence that contains an equal sign, showing that two expressions are equal.

equilateral triangle (p. 566) A *triangle* with three *congruent* sides.

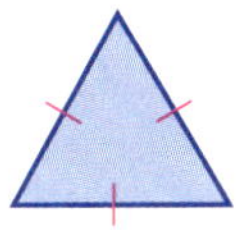

equivalent decimals (p. 37) Decimals that have the same value.

0.3 and 0.30

equivalent fractions (p. 382) *Fractions* that have the same value.

$$\frac{3}{4} = \frac{6}{8} = \frac{9}{12}$$

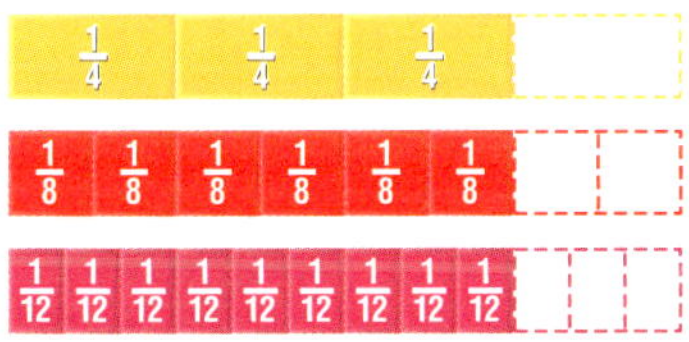

estimate (p. 64) A number close to an exact value. An estimate indicates *about* how much.

47 + 22 (round to 50 + 20)
The estimate is 70.

evaluate (p. 193) To find the *value* of an *expression* by replacing variables with numbers.

even number (p. 377) A whole number that is divisible by 2.

expanded form (p. 17) A way of writing a number as the sum of the values of its digits.

expression (p. 193) A combination of numbers, variables, and at least one operation.

equiprobable Que tienen la misma posibilidad de ocurrir.

Al lanzar una moneda, tienes la misma posibilidad de sacar cara o cruz.

signo de igualdad Símbolo de igual, =.

ecuación Expresión numérica que contiene un signo de igualdad que muestra que dos expresiones son iguales.

triángulo equilátero *Triángulo* con tres lados *congruentes*.

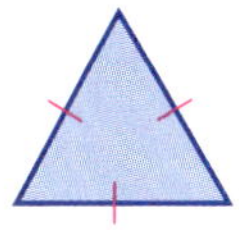

decimales equivalentes Decimales que tienen el mismo valor.

0.3 y 0.30

fracciones equivalentes *Fracciones* que representan el mismo número.

$$\frac{3}{4} = \frac{6}{8} = \frac{9}{12}$$

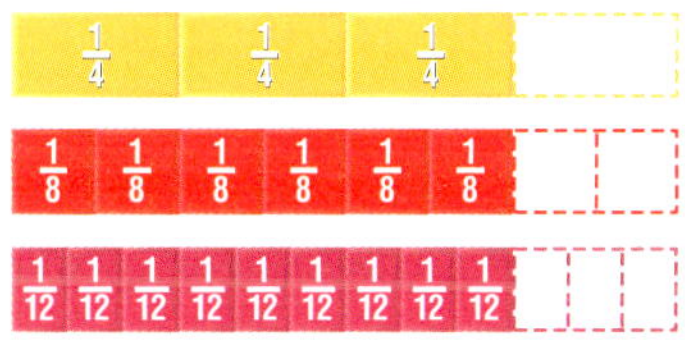

estimación Un número cercano a un valor exacto. Una estimación indica *aproximadamente* cuánto.

47 + 22 se redeondea a 50 + 20
La estimación es 70.

evaluar Calcular el *valor* de una expresión reemplazando las variables con números.

número par Número entero divisible entre 2.

forma desarrollada Una manera de escribir un número como la suma de los valores de sus dígitos.

expresión Combinación de números, variables y por lo menos una operación.

F

face (p. 624) The flat part of a 3-dimensional figure.

A square is a face of a cube.

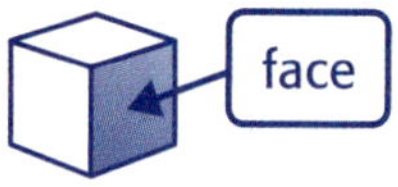

factor (p. 103) A number that is multiplied by another number.

Fahrenheit (°F) (p. 537) The unit used to measure temperature in the customary system.

favorable outcome (p. 668) Desired results in a *probability experiment.*

fluid ounce (p. 488) A *customary unit* of *capacity*.

foot (ft) (p. 477) A *customary unit* for measuring *length*. Plural is *feet*.

1 foot = 12 inches

fraction (p. 333) A number that represents part of a whole or part of a set.

$\frac{1}{2}, \frac{1}{3}, \frac{1}{4}, \frac{3}{4}$

frequency (p. 289) The number of times a result occurs or something happens in a set amount of time or collection of data.

frequency table (p. 289) A table for organizing a set of *data* that shows the number of times each result has occurred.

function (p. 210) A relationship between two variables in which one input quantity is paried with exactly one output quantity.

function rule (p. 210) An expression that describes the relationship between each input and output.

cara La parte llana de una figura tridimensional.

Un cuadrado es una cara de un cubo.

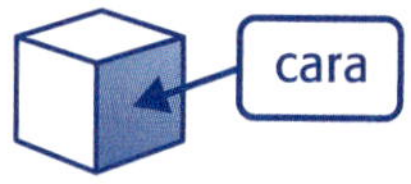

factor Número que se multiplica por otro número.

Fahrenheit Unidad que se usa para medir la temperatura en el sistema inglés.

resultados favorables Resultados deseados en un *experimento probabilístico.*

onzas líquidas *Unidad inglesa* de *capacidad.*

pie (pie) *Unidad inglesa* de *longitud.*

1 pie = 12 pulgadas

fracción Número que representa parte de un todo o parte de un conjunto.

$\frac{1}{2}, \frac{1}{3}, \frac{1}{4}, \frac{3}{4}$

frecuencia Número de veces que ocurre un resultado o sucede algo en un período de tiempo dado o en una colección de datos.

tabla de frecuencias Tabla para organizar un conjunto de *datos* que muestra el número de veces que ha ocurrido cada resultado.

función Relación entre dos variables en que una cantidad de entrada se relaciona exactamente con una cantidad de salida.

regla de funciones Expresión que describe la relación entre cada valor de entrada y cada valor de salida.

function table (p. 210) A table of ordered pairs that is based on a rule.

Rule: $8h = r$	
Input (h)	Output (r)
1	8
2	16
3	24
4	32

tabla de funciones Tabla de pares ordenados que se basa en una regla.

Regla: $8h = r$	
Entrada (h)	Salida (r)
1	8
2	16
3	24
4	32

G

gallon (gal) (p. 488) A *customary unit* for measuring *capacity* for liquids.

1 gallon = 4 quarts

galón (gal) Unidad de *medida inglesa* de *capacidad* de líquidos.

1 galón = 4 cuartos

gram (g) (p. 524) A *metric unit* for measuring *mass*.

gramo (g) Una *unidad métrica* para medir *masa*.

graph (p. 254) Place a point named by an ordered pair on a coordinate grid.

graficar Colocar un punto indicado por un par ordenado en un plano de coordenadas.

greater than > (p. 20) An inequality relationship showing that the number on the left of the symbol is greater than the number on the right.

$5 > 3$

5 is greater than 3

mayor que > Relación de desigualdad que muestra que el número a la izquierda del símbolo es mayor que el número a la derecha.

$5 > 3$

5 es mayor que 3

Greatest Common Factor (GCF) (p. 374) The greatest of the common factors of two or more numbers.

The greatest common factor of 12, 18, and 30 is 6.

máximo común divisor (MCD) El mayor de los factores comunes de dos o más números.

El máximo común divisor de 12, 18 y 30 es 6.

H

horizontal axis (p. 250) The axis in a coordinate plane that runs left and right (↔). Also known as the *x*-axis.

eje horizontal Eje en un plano de coordenadas que va de izquierda a derecha (↔). También conocido como eje *x*.

Glossary/Glosario

hundredth (p. 28) A place value position. One of one hundred equal parts.

In the number 0.57, 7 is in the hundredths place.

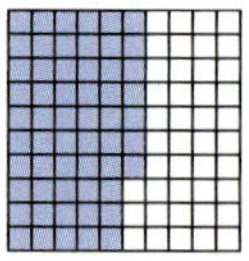

centésima Valor de posición. Una de cien partes iguales.

En el número 0.57, 7 está en el lugar de las centésimas.

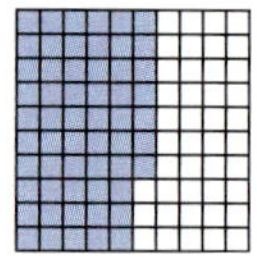

I

Identity Property of Addition (p. 84) Property that states that the sum of any number and 0 equals the number.

propiedad de identidad de la suma Propiedad que establece que la suma de cualquier número y 0 es igual al número.

Identity Property of Multiplication (p. 126) Property that states that the product of any number and 1 equals the factor.

propiedad de identidad de la multiplicación Propiedad que establece que el producto de cualquier número por 0 es igual al factor.

image (p. 578) The resulting image after a geometric figure has been transformed.

imagen La imagen que resulta después de transformar una figura geométrica.

impossible (p. 661) There is no chance an event will happen. An *outcome* or *event* is impossible if it has a *probability* of 0.

It is impossible to choose a yellow tile.

imposible Un *resultado* o un *evento* es imposible si tiene una *probabilidad* igual a 0.

Es imposible que elijas un azulejo amarillo.

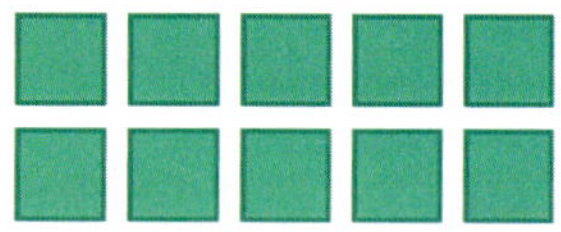

improper fraction (p. 337) A fraction with a numerator that is greater than or equal to the denominator.

$\frac{17}{3}$ or $\frac{5}{5}$

fracción impropia Fracción con un numerador mayor que o igual al denominador.

$\frac{17}{3}$ o $\frac{5}{5}$

inch (in.) (p. 477) A *customary unit* for measuring *length*. The plural is *inches*.

pulgada (pulg) *Unidad inglesa* de *longitud*.

inequality (p. 20) Two quantities that are not equal.

desigualdad Dos cantidades que no son iguales.

integer (p. 533) Whole numbers and their opposites, including zero.

…−3, −2, −1, 0, 1, 2, 3…

entero Los números enteros y sus opuestos, incluyendo el cero.

…−3, −2, −1, 0, 1, 2, 3…

intersecting lines (p. 558) *Lines* that meet or cross at a common *point*.

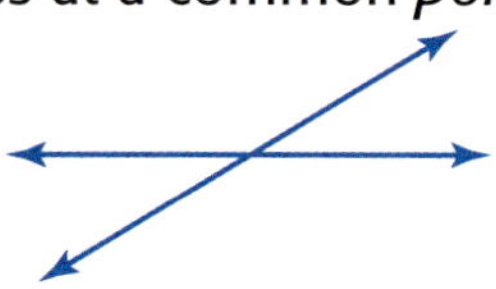

rectas secantes *Rectas* que se intersecan o se cruzan en un *punto* común.

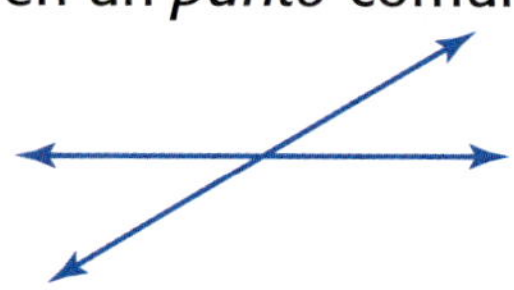

interval (p. 294) The distance between successive values on a scale.

intervalo Distancia entre dos valores sucesivos en una escala.

isosceles triangle (p. 566) A *triangle* with at least 2 *sides* of the same *length*.

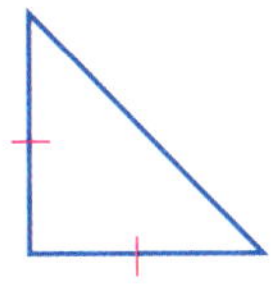

triángulo isósceles *Triángulo* que tiene por lo menos 2 *lados* del mismo largo.

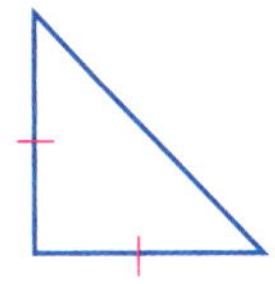

K

kilogram (kg) (p. 524) A *metric unit* for measuring *mass*.

kilogramo (kg) *Unidad métrica* de *masa*.

kilometer (km) (p. 517) A *metric unit* for measuring *length*.

kilómetro (km) *Unidad métrica* de *longitud*.

L

Least Common Denominator (LCD) (p. 404) The *least common multiple* of the *denominators* of two or more *fractions*.

$\frac{1}{12}, \frac{1}{6}, \frac{1}{8}$; LCD is 24.

mínimo común denominador (mcd) El *mínimo común múltiplo* de los *denominadores* de dos o más *fracciones*.

$\frac{1}{12}, \frac{1}{6}, \frac{1}{8}$; el mcd es 24.

Least Common Multiple (LCM) (p. 397) The smallest *whole number* greater than 0 that is a common *multiple* of each of two or more numbers.

The LCM of 2 and 3 is 6.

mínimo común múltiplo (mcm) El menor *número entero*, mayor que 0, *múltiplo* común de dos o más números.

El mcm de 2 y 3 es 6.

length (p. 475) Measurement of the distance between two points.

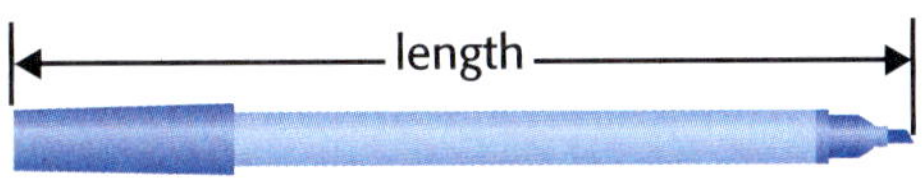

longitud Medida de la distancia entre dos puntos.

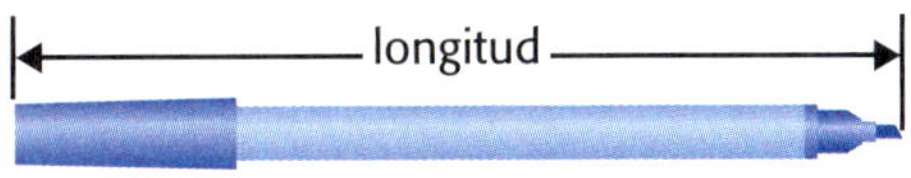

less than $<$ (p. 20) The number on the left side of the symbol is smaller than the number on the right side.

$4 < 7$

4 is smaller than 7

menor que $<$ El número a la izquierda del símbolo es más pequeño que el número a su derecha.

$4 < 7$

4 es menor que 7

like fractions (p. 421) Fractions that have the same denominator.

$\frac{1}{5}$ and $\frac{2}{5}$

fracciones semejantes Fracciones que tienen el mismo denominador.

$\frac{1}{5}$ y $\frac{2}{5}$

likely (p. 662) An event that will probably happen.

It is likely you will choose a red cube.

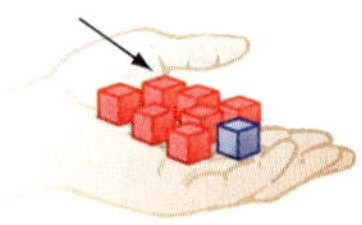

line (p. 557) A set of *points* that form a straight path that goes on forever in opposite directions.

line graph (p. 306) A graph that uses points connected by *line segments* to show changes in data over time.

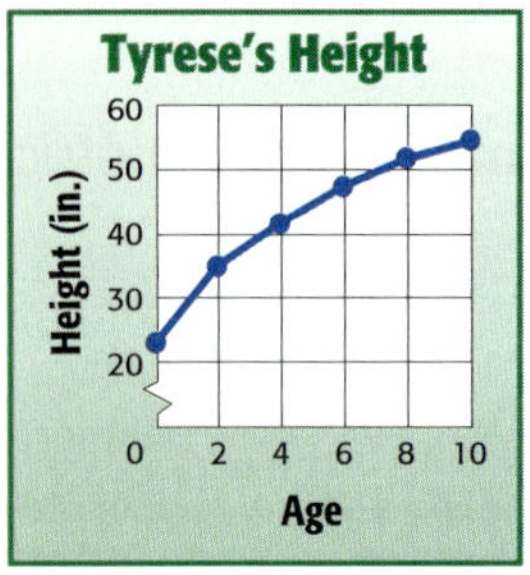

line of reflection (p. 582) The line an image is reflected over.

line plot (p. 284) A graph that uses columns of Xs above a *number line* to show the number of times values in a set of data occur.

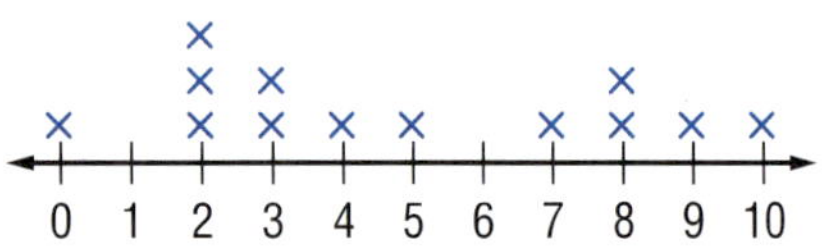

line segment (p. 557) A part of a *line* that connects two points.

liter (L) (p. 527) A *metric unit* for measuring *volume* or *capacity*.

1 liter = 1,000 milliliters

M

mass (p. 524) Measure of the amount of matter in an object.

posible Un evento que probablemente sucederá.

Es posible que elijas un cubo rojo.

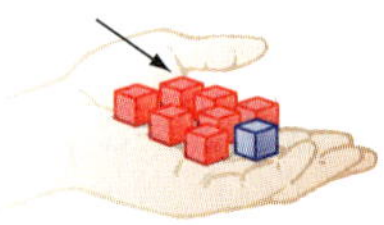

recta Conjunto de *puntos* que forman una trayectoria recta sin fin en direcciones opuestas.

gráfica lineal Gráfica que usa puntos unidos por *segmentos de recta* para mostrar cambios en los datos con el tiempo.

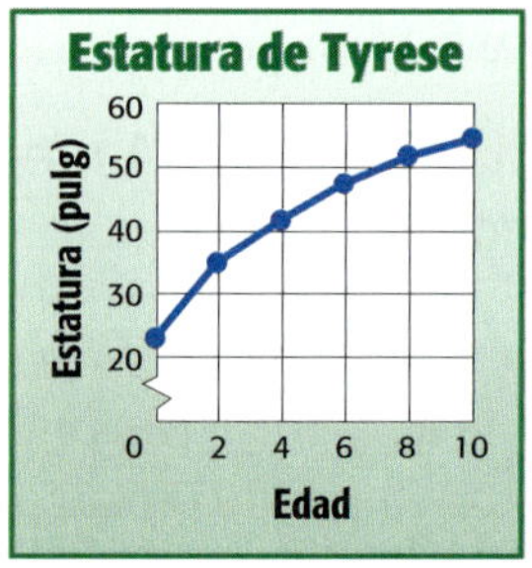

línea de reflexión Línea sobre la cual se refleja una imagen.

esquema lineal Gráfica que usa columnas de X sobre una *recta numérica* para mostrar el número de veces que en un conjunto de datos.

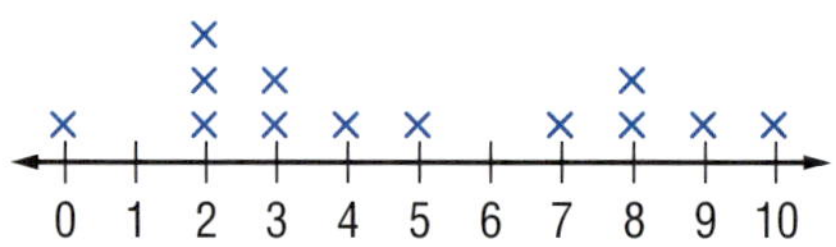

segmento de recta Parte de una *recta* que conecta dos puntos.

litro (L) *Unidad métrica* de *volumen* o *capacidad*.

1 litro = 1,000 mililitros

masa Medida de la cantidad de material en un objeto. Dos ejemplos de unidades de esta medida son la libra y el kilogramo.

mean (p. 279) The quotient found by adding the numbers in a set of data and dividing this sum by the amount of numbers in the data set.

median (p. 279) The middle number in a set of data that has been written in order from least to greatest. If the set contains an even number of numbers, the median is the number exactly halfway between the two middle numbers.

3, 4, 6, 8, 9, 9

The median is $7 = \frac{(6 + 8)}{2}$.

meter (p. 517) A *metric unit* used to measure length.

metric system (SI) (p. 517) The decimal system of measurement. Includes units such as meter, gram, liter, and degrees Celsius.

mile (mi) (p. 477) A *customary unit* of measure for length.

1 mile = 5,280 feet

milligram (mg) (p. 524) A *metric unit* used to measure *mass*.

1,000 milligrams = 1 gram

milliliter (mL) (p. 527) A *metric unit* used for measuring *capacity*.

1,000 milliliters = 1 liter

millimeter (mm) (p. 517) A *metric unit* used for measuring *length*.

1,000 millimeters = 1 meter

mode (p. 279) The number(s) that occurs most often in a set of data.

7, 4, 7, 10, 7, and 2 The mode is 7.

multiple (multiples) (p. 396) A multiple of a number is the *product* of that number and any whole number.

15 is a multiple of 5 because $3 \times 5 = 15$.

medía Cociente que se calcula sumando los números en un conjunto de datos y dividíendo esta suma entre el número de sumandos.

mediana Número central de un conjunto de datos escritos en orden de menor a mayor. Si el conjunto contiene una cantidad par de números, la mediana es el número que está exactamente a mitad de camino entre los dos números centrales.

3, 4, 6, 8, 9, 9

La mediana es $7 = \frac{(6 + 8)}{2}$.

metro *Unidad métrica* que se usa para medir la longitud.

sistema métrico (sm) Sistema de medición que se basa en potencias de 10 el cual incluye unidades como el metro, el gramo, el litro y los grados Celsius.

milla (ml) *Unidad inglesa* de longitud.

1 milla = 5,280 pies

miligramo (mg) *Unidad métrica* de *masa*.

1,000 miligramos = 1 gramo

mililitro (mL) *Unidad métrica* de *capacidad*.

1,000 mililitros = 1 litro

milímetro (mm) *Unidad métrica* de *longitud*.

1,000 milímetros = 1 metro

moda Número o números que ocurren con mayor frecuencia en un conjunto de datos.

7, 4, 7, 10, 7, y 2 La moda es 7.

múltiplo (múltiplos) Un múltiplo de un número es el *producto* de ese número por cualquier otro número entero.

15 es múltiplo de 5 porque $3 \times 5 = 15$.

multiplication (p. 103) An operation on two numbers to find their *product*. It can be thought of as repeated *addition*.

4 × 3 is another way to write the *sum* of four 3s, which is 3 + 3 + 3 + 3 or 12.

multiplicación Operación que se realiza en dos números para calcular su *producto*. También se puede interpretar como una *suma* repetida.

4 × 3 es otra forma de escribir la *suma* de cuatro veces 3, la cual es 3 + 3 + 3 + 3 o 12.

N

negative integer (p. 533) Integers less than zero. Written with a – sign.

negative number (p. 533) Numbers less than zero.

number line (p. 20) A line that represents numbers as points.

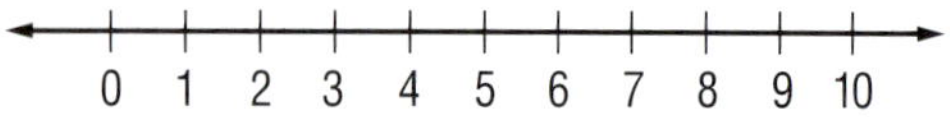

numerator (p. 333) The top number in a *fraction*; the part of the fraction that tells the number of parts you have.

numerical expression (p. 193) A combination of numbers and operations.

entero negativo Enteros menores que cero. Se escriben con un signo –.

número negativo Números menores que cero.

recta numérica Recta que representa números como puntos.

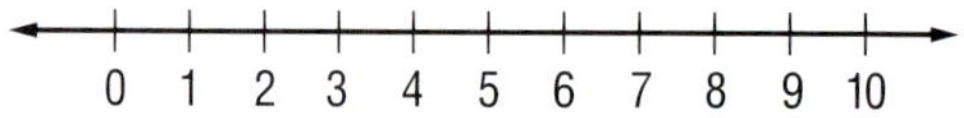

numerador Número que se escribe arriba de la barra de *fracción*; la parte de la fracción que indica el número de partes que tienes.

expresión numérica Combinación de números y operaciones.

O

obtuse angle (p. 564) An *angle* that measures between 90° and 180°.

obtuse triangle (p. 567) A *triangle* with one *obtuse angle*.

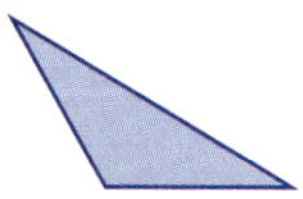

odd number (p. 377) A number that is not divisible by 2; such a number has 1, 3, 5, 7, or 9 in the ones place.

operation (p. 190) A mathematical process such as addition (+), subtraction (–), multiplication (×), division (÷), and raising to a power.

ángulo obtuso *Ángulo* que mide entre 90° y 180°.

triángulo obtusángulo *Triángulo* con un *ángulo obtuso*.

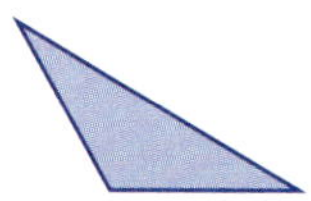

número impar Número que no es divisible entre 2, tal número tiene 1, 3, 5, 7 ó 9 en el lugar de las unidades.

operación Proceso matemático como la suma (+), la resta (–), la multiplicación (×), la división (÷) y la potenciación.

opposite integers (p. 534) Two different integers that are the same distance from 0 on a number line.

5 and −5

ordered pair (p. 250) A pair of numbers that is used to name a point on the coordinate grid.

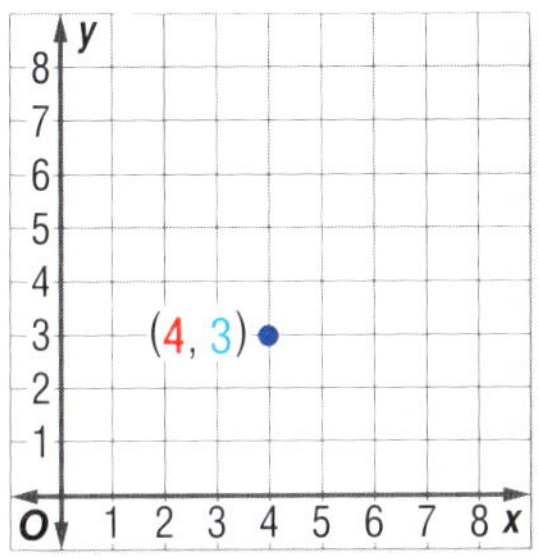

origin (p. 250) The point (0, 0) on a *coordinate grid* where the vertical axis meets the horizontal axis.

ounce (oz) (p. 484) A *customary unit* for measuring *weight* or *capacity*.

outcome (p. 661) A possible result of a probability experiment.

outlier (p. 285) A number in a set of data that is much larger or much smaller than most of the other numbers in the set.

enteros opuestos Dos enteros diferentes que equidistan de 0 en una recta numérica.

5 y −5

par ordenado Par de números que se usan para nombrar un punto en un cuadriculado de coordenadas.

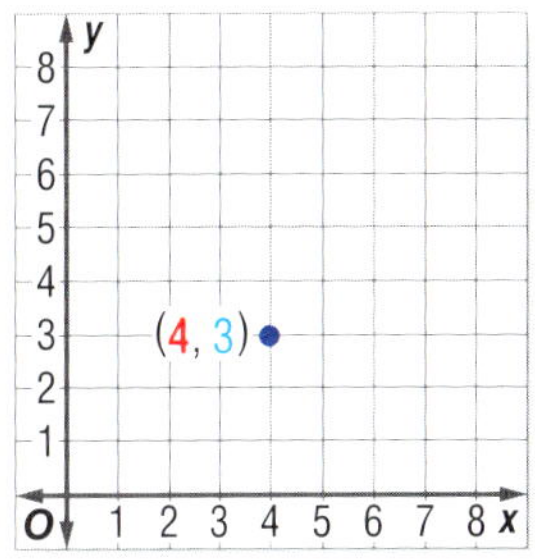

origen El punto (0, 0) en un *cuadriculado de coordenadas* donde el *eje* vertical interseca el eje horizontal.

onza (oz) *Unidad inglesa* de *peso* o *capacidad*

resultado Resultado posible de un experimento probabilístico.

valor atípico Número en un conjunto de datos que es mucho mayor o mucho menor que la mayoría de los otros números del conjunto.

Glossary/Glosario

P

parallel lines (p. 558) Lines that are the same distance apart. Parallel lines do not intersect.

parallelogram (p. 571) A quadrilateral with four sides in which each pair of opposite sides are parallel and congruent.

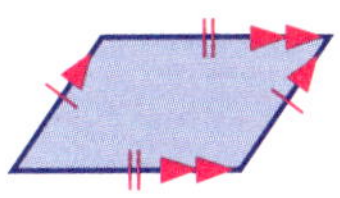

rectas paralelas Rectas separadas por la misma distancia. Las rectas paralelas no se intersecan.

paralelogramo Cuadrilátero de cuatro lados en que cada par de lados opuestos son paralelos y congruentes.

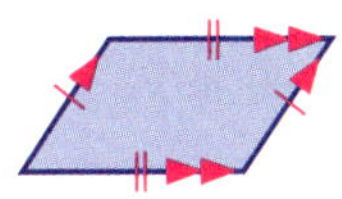

perimeter (p. 608) The *distance* around a polygon.

period (p. 17) Each group of three digits on a place-value chart.

perpendicular lines (p. 558) *Lines* that cross each other at *right angles*.

pint (pt) (p. 488) A customary *unit* for measuring *capacity*.

1 pint = 2 cups

place value (p. 17) The value given to a digit by its position in a number.

place-value chart (p. 17) A chart that shows the value of the digits in a number.

plane (p. 557) A flat surface that goes on forever in all directions.

point (p. 557) An exact location in space that is represented by a dot.

polygon (p. 608) A closed figure made up of line segments that do not cross each other.

polyhedron (p. 624) A three-dimensional figure with faces that are polygons.

positive integer (p. 533) Integers greater than zero. They can be written with or without a + sign.

positive number (p. 533) Numbers that are greater than zero.

possible outcomes (p. 677) Any of the results that could occur in an experiment.

pound (lb) (p. 484) A *customary unit* for measuring *weight* or *mass*.

1 pound = 16 ounces

perímetro *Distancia* alrededor de un polígono.

período Cada grupo de tres dígitos en una tabla de valor de posición.

rectas perpendiculares *Rectas* que se cruzan a *ángulos rectos*.

pinta (pt) *Unidad inglesa* de *capacidad.*

1 pinta = 2 tazas

valor de posición Valor dado a un dígito según su posición en el número.

tabla de valor de posición Tabla que muestra el valor de los dígitos en un número.

plano Superficie plana que se extiende infinitamente en todas direcciones.

punto Ubicación exacta en el espacio que se representa con un marca puntual.

polígono Figura cerrada compuesta por segmentos de recta que no se intersecan.

poliedro Figura tridimensional con caras en forma de polígonos.

entero positivo Enteros mayores que cero. Se pueden escribir con o sin el signo +.

número positivo Números mayores que cero.

resultados posibles Cualquiera de los resultados que puede ocurrir en un experimento.

libra (lb) *Unidad inglesa* de *peso* o *masa.*

1 libra = 16 onzas

Glossary/Glosario

prime factorization (p. 379) A way of expressing a *composite number* as a product of its *prime factors*.

prime number (p. 376) A *whole number* with exactly two *factors*, 1 and itself.

7, 13, and 19

prism (p. 624) A polyhedron with two *parallel, congruent faces,* called *bases*.

probability (p. 661) The chance that an event will happen. It can be described as a number from 0 to 1.

probability experiment (p. 661) An experiment to determine the chance that an event will happen.

product (p. 103) The answer to a multiplication problem.

proper fraction (p. 338) A fraction in which the numerator is less than the denominator.

$\frac{1}{2}$

factorización prima Una manera de escribir un *número compuesto* como un producto de sus *factores primos*.

número primo *Número entero* que tiene exactamente dos *factores*, 1 y sí mismo.

7, 13, y 19

prisma Poliedro con dos *caras paralelas* y *congruentes* llamadas *bases.*

probabilidad La posibilidad de que ocurra un evento. Se puede describir como un número de 0 a 1.

experimento probabilístico Experimento para determinar la posibilidad de que ocurra un evento.

producto Repuesta a un problema de multiplicación.

fracción propia Fracción en que el numerador es menor que el denominador.

$\frac{1}{2}$

Q

quadrilateral (p. 570) A polygon that has 4 sides and 4 angles.

square, rectangle, and parallelogram

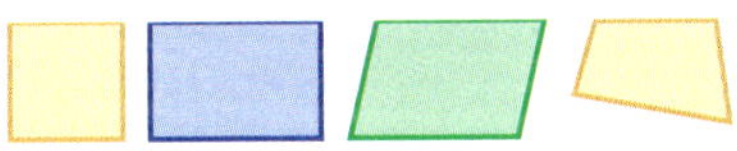

quart (qt) (p. 488) A *customary unit* for measuring *capacity*.

1 quart = 4 cups

quotient (p. 149) The result of a *division* problem.

cuadrilátero Polígono con 4 lados y 4 ángulos.

cuadrado, rectángulo y paralelogramo

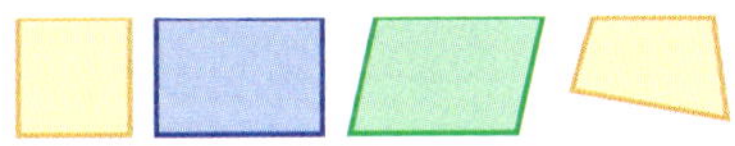

cuarto (ct) *Unidad inglesa* de *capacidad*.

1 cuarto = 4 tazas

cociente El resultado de un problema de *división*.

R

range (p. 285) The *difference* between the greatest and the least values in a set of data.

rango La *diferencia* entre el mayor y el menor de los valores en un conjunto de datos.

ray (p. 557) A line that has one endpoint and goes on forever in only one direction.

rectangle (p. 571) A *quadrilateral* with four *right angles*; opposite *sides* are equal and *parallel*.

rectangular prism (p. 624) A polyhedron with six rectangular faces.

reflection (p. 582) An figure that is flipped over a line to create a mirror image of the figure.

remainder (p. 159) The number that is left after one whole number is divided by another.

rhombus (p. 571) A *parallelogram* with four *congruent sides*.

right angle (p. 564) An *angle* with a measure of 90°.

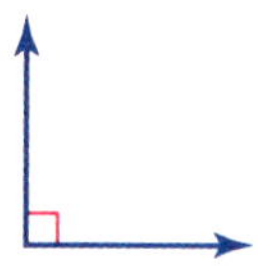

right triangle (p. 567) A *triangle* with one *right angle*.

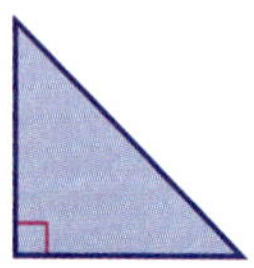

rotation (p. 586) Rotating a figure about a point.

round (p. 61) To find the approximate value of a number.

6.38 rounded to the nearest tenth is 6.4.

rayo Recta con un extremo y la cual se extiende infinitamente en una sola dirección.

rectángulo *Cuadrilátero* con cuatro *ángulo rectos*; los *lados* opuestos son iguales y *paralelos*.

prisma rectangular Poliedro con seis caras rectangulares.

reflexión Figura que se vuelca sobre una línea para crear una imagen especular de la figura.

residuo Número que queda después de dividir un número entero entre otro número entero.

rombo *Paralelogramo* con cuatro *lados congruentes*.

ángulo recto *Ángulo* que mide 90°.

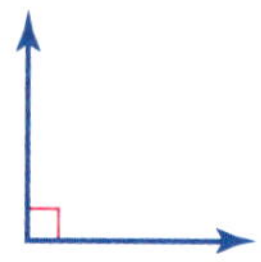

triángulo rectángulo *Triángulo* con un *ángulo recto*.

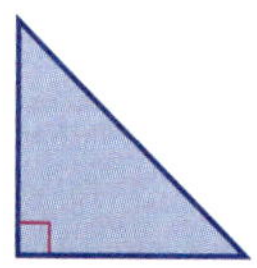

rotación Rotar una figura alrededor de un punto.

redondear Calcular el valor aproximado de un número.

6.38 redondeado a la décima más cercana es 6.4.

S

scale (p. 294) A set of numbers that includes the least and greatest values separated by equal intervals.

escala Conjunto de números que incluye los valores menor y mayor separados por intervalos iguales.

scalene triangle (p. 566) A *triangle* with no *congruent sides*.

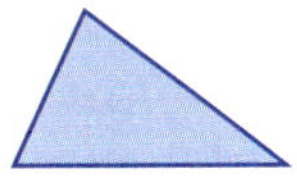

simplest form (p. 386) A fraction in which the GCF of the numerator and the denominator is 1.

solution (p. 235) The value of a variable that makes an equation true. The solution of $12 = x + 7$ is 5.

solve (p. 235) To replace a variable with a value that results in a true sentence.

square (p. 571) A rectangle with four *congruent sides*.

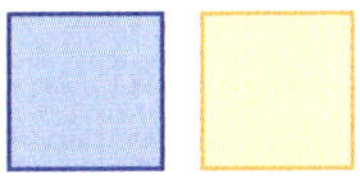

square unit (p. 612) A unit for measuring *area*, such as *square inch* or *square centimeter*.

standard form (p. 17) The usual or common way to write a number using digits.

subtraction (subtract) (p. 64) An operation on two numbers that tells how many are left (*difference*), when some or all are taken away. Subtraction is also used to compare two numbers.

$$14 - 8 = 6$$

sum (p. 64) The answer to an addition problem.

surface area (p. 640) The sum of the areas of all the faces of a prism.

triángulo escaleno *Triángulo* sin *lados congruentes*.

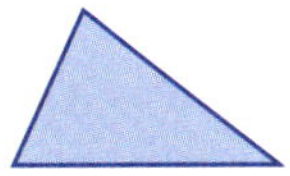

forma reducida Fracción en que el MCD del numerador y del denominador es 1.

solución Valor de una variable que hace verdadera la ecuación. La solución de $12 = x + 7$ es 5.

resolver Despejar una variable y reemplazar este valor en la variable para hacer verdadera la ecuación.

cuadrado Rectángulo con cuatro *lados congruentes*.

unidad cuadrada Unidad de *área*, como una *pulgada cuadrada* o un *centímetro cuadrado*.

forma estándar La manera usual o común de escribir un número usando dígitos.

restar (resta) Operación que se realiza en dos números y que indica cuántos quedan (*diferencia*), cuando se eliminan algunos o todos. La resta también se usa para comparar dos números.

$$14 - 8 = 6$$

suma Respuesta a un problema de suma.

área total La suma de todas las área de todas las caras de un prisma.

T

tally mark(s) (p. 289) A mark made to keep track and display data recorded from a survey.

marcas(s) de conteo Marca que se hace para llevar la cuenta y representar datos reunidos en una encuesta.

tenth (p. 33) A place value in a decimal number or one of ten equal parts or $\frac{1}{10}$.

thousandth(s) (p. 33) One of a thousand equal parts or $\frac{1}{1,000}$. Also refers to a place value in a decimal number.
In the decimal 0.789, the 9 is in the thousandth place.

three-dimensional figure (p. 624) A solid figure that has *length*, *width*, and *height*.

ton (T) (p. 484) A customary unit to measure weight. 1 ton = 2,000 pounds

transformation (p. 578) A movement of a figure that does not change the size or shape of the figure.

translation (p. 578) Sliding a figure in a straight line horizontally, vertically, or diagonally.

trapezoid (p. 571) A *quadrilateral* with exactly one pair of *parallel* sides.

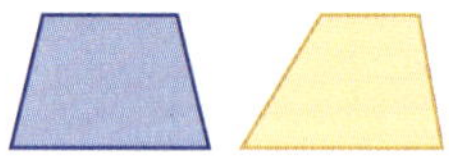

tree diagram (p. 677) A diagram that shows all the *possible outcomes* of an event.

triangle (p. 566) A *polygon* with three sides and three angles.

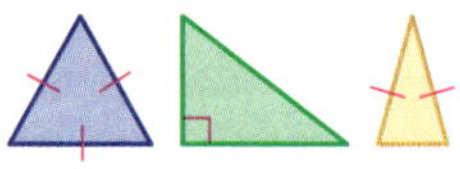

triangular prism (p. 624) A prism that has triangular bases.

U

unlike fractions (p. 432) Fractions that have different denominators.

unlikely (p. 662) An event that is improbable or will probably *not* happen.

It is unlikely you will choose a blue cube.

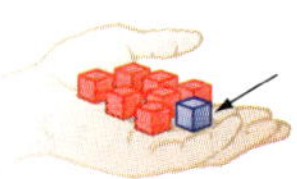

décima Valor de posición en un número decimal o una de diez partes iguales ó $\frac{1}{10}$.

milésima(s) Una de mil partes iguales ó $\frac{1}{1,000}$. También se refiere a un valor de posición en un número decimal.
En el decimal 0.789, el 9 está en el lugar de las milésimas.

figura tridimensional Figura sólida que tiene *largo, ancho* y *alto*.

tonelada (T) Unidad inglesa de peso
1 tonelada = 2,000 libras

transformación Movimiento de una figura que no cambia el tamaño o la forma de la figura.

traslación Deslizar una figura horizontal, vertical o diagonalmente en línea recta.

trapecio *Cuadrilátero* con exactamente un par de lados *paralelos*.

diagrama de árbol Diagrama que muestra todos los *resultados posibles* de un evento.

triángulo *Polígono* con tres lados y tres ángulos.

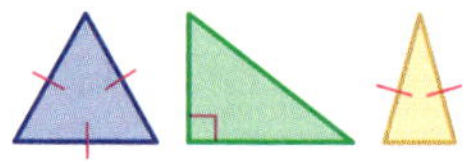

prisma triangular Prisma con bases triangulares.

fracciones no semejantes Fracciones que tienen denominadores diferentes.

improbable Evento que es improbable o que es probable que *no* suceda.

Es improbable que elijas un cubo azul.

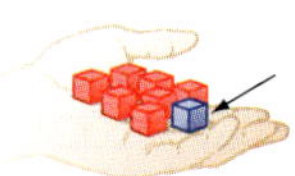

V

value (p. 17) A number amount or the worth of an object.

valor Cantidad numérica o lo que vale un objeto.

variable (p. 193) A letter or symbol used to represent an unknown quantity.

variable Letra o un símbolo que se usa para representar una cantidad desconocida.

vertex (pp. 564, 624) **a.** The *point* where two rays meet in an *angle*. **b.** The point on a three-dimensional figure where 3 or more edges meet.

vértice **a.** *Punto* donde concurren dos rayos de un *ángulo*. **b.** *Punto* en *una figura tridimensional* donde se intersecan 3 ó más aristas.

vertical axis (p. 250) A vertical number line on a graph (↕). Also known as the *y*-axis.

eje vertical Recta numérica vertical en una gráfica (↕). También conocido como eje *y*.

volume (p. 631) The amount of space that a *3-dimensional figure* contains.

volumen Cantidad de espacio que contiene una *figura tridimensional*.

W

weight (p. 484) A measurement that tells how heavy an object is.

peso Medida que indica la pesadez un cuerpo.

whole number (p. 20) The numbers 0, 1, 2, 3, 4…

número entero Los números 0, 1, 2, 3, 4…

width (p. 616) The measurement of distance from side to side telling how wide.

ancho Medida de la distancia de lado a lado y que indica amplitud.

X

***x*-axis** (p. 250) The horizontal axis (↔) in a coordinate plane.

eje *x* Eje horizontal (↔) en un plano de coordenadas.

***x*-coordinate** (p. 250) The first part of an ordered pair that indicates how far to the right or left of the *y*-axis the corresponding point is.

coordenada *x* Primera parte de un par ordenado que indica la distancia a que está el punto correspondiente a la derecha del eje *y*.

Y

yard (p. 477) A *customary unit* of *length* equal to 3 feet or 36 inches.

yarda *Unidad inglesa* de *longitud* igual a 3 pies ó 36 pulgadas.

***y*-axis** (p. 250) The vertical axis (↕) in a coordinate plane.

eje *y* El eje vertical (↕) en un plano de coordenadas.

***y*-coordinate** (p. 250) The second part of an ordered pair that indicates how far above or below the *x*-axis the corresponding point is.

coordenada *y* Segunda parte de un par ordenado que indica la distancia a que está el punto correspondiente por encima del eje *x*.

Index

A

B

C

D

Index

E

Index

F

G

H

I

K

L

M

Index

N

O

P

Q

T

Index

Measurement Conversions

Measure	Metric	Customary
Length	1 kilometer (km) = 1,000 meters (m) 1 meter = 100 centimeters (cm) 1 centimeter = 10 millimeters (mm)	1 foot (ft) = 12 inches (in.) 1 yard (yd) = 3 feet or 36 inches 1 mile (mi) = 1,760 yards or 5,280 feet
Volume and Capacity	1 liter (L) = 1,000 milliliters (mL) 1 kiloliter (kL) = 1,000 liters	1 cup (c) = 8 fluid ounces (fl oz) 1 pint (pt) = 2 cups 1 quart (qt) = 2 pints 1 gallon (gal) = 4 quarts
Weight and Mass	1 kilogram (kg) = 1,000 grams (g) 1 gram = 1,000 milligrams (mg) 1 metric ton = 1,000 kilograms	1 pound (lb) = 16 ounces (oz) 1 ton (T) = 2,000 pounds

Time	1 minute (min) = 60 seconds (s) 1 hour (h) = 60 minutes 1 day (d) = 24 hours 1 week (wk) = 7 days 1 year (yr) = 12 months (mo) 1 year = 52 weeks 1 year = 365 days 1 leap year = 366 days

Formulas

Perimeter	square	$P = 4s$
	rectangle	$P = 2\ell + 2w$ or $P = 2(\ell + w)$
Area	square	$A = s^2$
	rectangle	$A = \ell w$
	parallelogram	$A = bh$
	triangle	$A = \frac{1}{2}bh$
Surface Area	rectangular prism	$S = 2\ell w + 2\ell h + 2wh$
Volume	prism	$V = \ell wh$ or Bh